POLITICAL THEORY

For B.A. (Pass and Honours) Students of all Indian Universities and Aspirants of Various Competitive Examinations

Thirteenth Edition

Dr. EDDY ASIRVATHAM, Ph.D.
Former Professor of Political Science and Public Administration at various universities in India and U.S.A.

and

K.K. MISRA, M.A.
Former Reader, Hindu College, Delhi University, Delhi

S Chand And Company Limited

(ISO 9001 Certified Company)

S Chand And Company Limited

(ISO 9001 Certified Company)

Head Office: D-92, Sector–2, Noida – 201301, U.P. (India), Ph. 91-120-4682700

Registered Office: A-27, 2nd Floor, Mohan Co-operative Industrial Estate, New Delhi – 110 044, Phone: 011-49731800

www.**schandpublishing.com**; e-mail: **info@schandpublishing.com**

Marketing Offices:

Chennai	:	Ph: 23632120; chennai@schandpublishing.com
Guwahati	:	Ph: 2738811, 2735640; guwahati@schandpublishing.com
Hyderabad	:	Ph: 40186018; hyderabad@schandpublishing.com
Jalandhar	:	Ph: 4645630; jalandhar@schandpublishing.com
Kolkata	:	Ph: 23357458, 23353914; kolkata@schandpublishing.com
Lucknow	:	Ph: 4003633; lucknow@schandpublishing.com
Mumbai	:	Ph: 25000297; mumbai@schandpublishing.com
Patna	:	Ph: 4011400; patna@schandpublishing.com

First Edition 1936
Subsequent Editions and Reprints 1957, 79, 80, 82, 84, 88, 90, 92, 93, 95, 97, 98, 2000, 2001, 2003, 2004, 2005, 2006, 2008, 2009 (Twice), 2011, 2012, 2013, 2014, 2016, 2017, 2018 (Twice), 2019, 2021 (Twice), 2022 (Twice), 2023 (Twice)

Reprint 2025

ISBN: 978-81-219-0346-2 **Product Code:** H5POL41PLSC10ENAM0XO

PRINTED IN INDIA

By Vikas Publishing House Private Limited, Plot 20/4, Site-IV, Industrial Area Sahibabad, Ghaziabad – 201 010 and Published by S Chand And Company Limited, A-27, 2nd Floor, Mohan Co-operative Industrial Estate, New Delhi – 110 044.

PREFACE TO THE THIRTEENTH EDITION

All former editions of the book, edited and co-authored by me from time to time, were very well received by the students and teachers all over India. The courses on Political Theory have been thoroughly revised and made more comprehensive by a number of Indian universities. This edition incorporates all these new themes, such as politics as a social process; history, political theory and ideology; Liberal and Marxist views of politics; comparative dimensions of the State; the State in capitalist, socialist and developing societies; Marxist theory of the origin and function of the State; the concept of justice, liberty and equality; contemporary theories of Democracy; Marxist theories of man, freedom, alienation, State and revolution; theories of political obligation; political ideologies in the third world; behaviouralism and post-behaviouralism.

I am grateful to Messrs S. Chand & Company Ltd. for arranging an early publication of the thoroughly revised thirteenth edition of this classic work, originally penned by Dr. E Asirvatham. In my own humble way, I have tried to maintain the style, spirit and high standard of scholarship of this eminent author. It is hoped that this edition will be even more useful to both graduating students and candidates preparing for various competitive examinations.

K.K. MISHRA

80, Kadambari
Sector 9, Rohini
Delhi - 110 085

PREFACE TO THE TENTH EDITION

Dr. Eddy Asirvatham was a liberal scholar, belonging to the Idealist school of T.H. Green and Bosanquet. His work on Political Theory became a classic in Indian political literature, which was consulted by a large number of students and teachers all over India. The first edition of *Political Theory* appeared in 1936 and though it was revised on several occasions, yet its basic structure and ideological approach remained unaltered.

While editing this scholarly work, I have added new material for practically every chapter and contributed a new chapter on Political Philosophy of Laski. New matter has been added on the Nature of Politics as a Social Science, Socio-economic basis of the State, the Sphere of State Activity, Theories of Rights and Particular Rights, Sovereignty and Pluralism, Classification of State, The Role of Law, Democracy, Liberalism, Socialism, Communism, Fascism, Nationalism, Internationalism and Imperialism.

In order to limit the size of the book, those portions of the earlier edition, which were no longer relevant or useful, have been omitted. In the process of editing, about one-third of the total content of the book has been altered and written afresh. As regards the new approach adopted in the book, I may indicate it by quoting the following words of Laksi: "The idealist theory of the State, in its famous formulation by Bosanquet, remains a formulation of a conceptual State *in Posse* rather than of the States we know. The liberal and anti-idealist view, as expressed by L.T. Hobhouse, assumes, but does not prove, that, given time, reason will always be victorious in matters of social conflict. Neither Bosanquet's view, nor that of Hobhouse, fulfils the scientific canon of prediction. Broadly speaking, the Marxian theory of the State has so defined its nature and functioning as to enable us to predict with assurance the course its operations will follow. As an index to the problems of our age, it decisively, in my judgement, holds the field." (*A Grammar of Politics*, p. v).

In Delhi University, as in other Indian universities, *A Grammar of Politics* has been used for a long time as one of the standard texts. By incorporating the main themes of Laski's well-known works in the new edition, I have made this book even more useful for students who found it a little difficult to follow Laski's original work.

Without underestimating the contribution of Behaviourialist School in Political Science, I would like to agree with Dr. Asirvatham in rejecting the attitude of those behaviourialists, who "today place undue emphasis on methods, techniques and skills, almost to the exclusion of first principles and value judgments."

80 Kadambari
Street 9, Rohini
Delhi - 110 085

K.K. MISHRA

EXPLANATORY NOTE

The first figure in parenthesis in the body of the book refers to the serial number of the book listed in the bibliography and the second figure refers to the page of the book.

CONTENTS

Cahpter *Pages*

CHAPTER 1

THE NATURE, SCOPE AND METHODS OF POLITICAL SCIENCE

Political science is a science which deals with the State and government. In its classical form, Western political thought had its origin in the city-states of ancient Greece. The oriental peoples had speculated on the State and its problems even before the time of the Greeks. But they did not develop political science in its pure and systematic form. It was mixed up with a great deal of mythology and superstition. Religion and politics were so closely intertwined that no attempt was made to develop an independent science of politics. The social sciences were treated as a branch of theology. The task of separating politics from religion, superstition, and mythology first fell to the lot of the Greeks. Thus it was that the Greeks were the first people to develop political science in its pure and systematic form.

Early Hindu thought has much to say on kingship, village republics, organization of government, and the duties of rulers and subjects. All of this, however, does not produce a comprehensive political theory. Confucius of China and Kautilya of India seem to have been more concerned with the art of government than with the theory of the State.

TERMINOLOGY AND SCOPE

A difficulty which confronts us at the very outset in undertaking a study of political science concerns the precise meaning of such terms as politics, political science and comparative government. We cannot hope to go very far in understanding problems pertaining to the State unless we make clear to ourselves what these terms mean. Although political science has its roots in the Greek past, it is in its modern form a comparatively new science. Consequently, it has not yet acquired a definite terminology of its own. In France and Germany, however, it seems to have attained a greater degree of perfection than in the Anglo-Saxon countries.

1. Politics

Earlier writers on the subject simply use the term politics in describing the entire science of the State. Aristotle's celebrated treatise has for its title the simple name *Politics*. The term politics is derived from the Greek words *polis* or 'city state' and *politeia*. In the Greek view, politics embraces everything that touches the life of the State. Used in that sense it is the equivalent of political science. Writers of an earlier generation like Jellinek, Holtzendorff, and Sidgwick prefer the term politics to political science which is in current use today. Among modern writers there is distinct aversion to using the term politics in its wide sense to cover a study of the phenomena relating to the State and government. Politics, as ordinarily used today, refers either : (1) to practical politics, as meaning 'the art of controlling a party and securing the nomination and election or the appointment of particular persons to office' or (2) to the art of government, the art of directing or guiding the policy of the government towards a particular goal.

In the former sense, it includes such details as the organisation of political parties, the setting up of candidates, the winning (or losing) of elections, the favouring of the party-men by the distribution of public offices among them and the like.

From the practical point of view, politics is sometimes defined as the technique of compromise. Politics is the game of the second best. Even the staunchest of idealists have had to adjust themselves to hard facts, practical realities, and popular prejudices. Bismarck defined politics as 'the art of the possible'.

Sir Frederick Pollock, using the term politics in its broad sense, divides it into theoretical politics and practical or applied politics. Under the first head he includes :

(a) the theory of the State,
(b) the theory of government,
(c) the theory of legislation, and
(d) the theory of the State as an artificial person.

Under the second division he includes :

(a) the State (actual forms of government),
(b) the government (the working of government, administration, etc.),
(c) laws and legislation (procedure, courts, etc.), and
(d) the State personified (diplomacy, peace, war and international dealings).

Sir Ernest Benn humorously defines politics as 'the art of looking for trouble, finding it whether it exists or not, diagnosing it wrongly, and applying the wrong remedy'.

Theoretical politics deals with the basic problems of the State, without concerning itself with the activities of any particular government or the means by which the ends of any particular State are attained. Practical politics on the other hand, deals with the actual way in which governments work out the various institutions comprising political life *(28:2)*. It will no doubt be generally agreed that this is both a useful and convenient distinction but many would prefer the term political science to politics in the present context.

2. Political Science

The term political science in its current usage is much more comprehensive than the term politics. It connotes the whole range of knowledge regarding the State and embraces the theory of the State. It includes both theoretical politics and practical or applied politics. On the theoretical side, it is concerned with questions like the nature, origin, purpose and justification of the State and is known as the theory of the State or political philosophy. On the practical side, it is concerned with the structure, functions, and forms of political institutions, and is known as comparative politics or constitutional government. A succinct definition of political science is given by Paul Janet, a distinguished French writer, who says that political science is 'that part of social science which treats of the foundations of the State and the principles of government'. According to Gettell, political science is 'a historical investigation of what the State has been, an analytical study of what the State is, and a politico-ethical discussion of what the State should be *(24:4)*.' Sidgwick writes that in our study of political science, as distinguished from a study of political philosophy, we are concerned with various types, but not necessarily with the ideal type or with models. Political science looks out for resemblances and differences, for arrangement and classification, for cause and effect.

The three major branches of political science today seem to be (*i*) political science proper; (*ii*) public administration; and (*iii*) international relations. While the latter two are really branches of political science, on account of their great importance in the modern world, there is an increasing tendency to give them an almost independent status. Public administration in turn is divided into such parts as personnel administration, social administration, and administration of local self-governing units, etc. International relations likewise include theory or theories of international relations, international organization, and diplomacy. Since international relations cover the entire world, students today specialize in regional studies, such as those relating to South East Asia, West Asia etc. In studying diplomacy one studies not only the theory and practice of diplomacy but also its history.

3. Political Philosophy

Poiltical philosophy is another term which gives rise to confused thinking in studying the phenomenon of the State. To some English political thinkers, political philosophy is the major portion of political science, political philosophy being that part of philosophy which deals with the State which is a part of the universe with which philosophy proper is concerned. This view evolves from the belief that philosophy, being the unifier of all knowledge, should regard the study of the State as one of its sub-divisions. This point of view is not tenable, because the modern age of specialization calls not so much for a synthesis of all knowledge as for an analysis of it. Progress in political thinking, just as much as in other fields of thought, calls for specialization and delimitation of the various fields.

J. H. Hallowell rightly says that political philosophy is not concerned so much with political institutions as with the ideas and aspirations that are embodied in institutions. In his own words, 'It is not so much interested in how things occur as it is in what occurs and why *(31:9)*'.

The distinction between political science (Staatwissenschaft) and political theory or political philosophy (Staatslehre or Staatsphilosophie) is generally observed by Continental writers, though it is difficult to point to the exact line of demarcation. Political science, as we use the term today, is broader in scope than political philosophy and carries with it a greater precision of meaning. 'Political philosophy deals with the fundamental problems of the nature of the State, citizenship, questions of duty and right, and political ideals *(28:31)*.' 'It is in a sense prior to political science, for the fundamental assumptions of the former are a basis to the latter *(28:31)*.' Nevertheless, if political philosophy is not to become vague and imaginative, it must use the material supplied by political science. Political theory and objective political conditions act and react upon one another.

4. Theory of the State

The 'theory of the State' is in many ways preferable to the term political philosophy, although the subject-matter of both is much the same. Political philosophy tends to suggest something abstract and speculative, but the theory of the State, or political theory, is much clearer and its boundaries are better marked. It is not a study of the structure of the forms of government nor a comparison of the various forms of government. These are dealt with in that branch of political science known as comparative government. The theory of the State, likewise, is not a study of the historical development of the State or of law. Nor is it an attempt to discover the ideal State. Neither is it a study of the art of governing or of adminis tration. It no doubt pre-supposes some knowledge of all these things as a necessary pre-requisite. But it is not concerned with the structure and activities of any one State. It deals with the essentials of the State and is based upon a study of the State both as it is and as it has been.

5. Comparative Government and Legislation

An important division of political science is a comparative study of constitutions. Writers from Aristotle to Herman Finer have attempted this task in a masterly way. Constitutions are studied one by one or in comparison with each other. Under the latter heading we may study the executive, the legislature, the judiciary, and the civil service of different countries in a comparative way; and in so doing we may even evolve a theory or theories of constitutions and government. Likewise, it is possible to evolve a theory or theories of legislation from a comparative study of legislation in many lands. A study of constitutional law is assuming a greater and greater importance in present-day study of political science.

Prof. Goodnow claims that political science divides itself into three distinct parts, *viz.*

(1) the expression of the State will;

(2) the content of the State will as expressed; and

(3) the execution of the State will.

The first division includes political theory and the network of extra-legal customs and extra-legal organizations which influence the political system of a country. The second is, in effect, a synonym for law. The third deals with the ascertainment and application of the correct principles of administration.

Suffice it to say that Prof. Goodnow conceives the scope of political science rather narrowly. His description does not seem to include such questions as the nature and characteristics of the State and the relation between authority and obligation.

VALUE OF A STUDY OF POLITICAL THOUGHT

There is a disposition in some quarters today to minimize the value of a study of political theory as being an abstract and a barren subject. This underestimation comes about largely because of the habit of laughing at all theory, a habit which seems to be a feature of the matter-of-fact, mechanical, and industrialized society of today. Ivor Brown rightly says, 'Sensibly handled with a commonsense attitude to the real value of social life, it (political theory) is both a concrete and a fruitful study.'

Prof. Gettell carefully sums up the arguments for and against a study of political thought, which will be stated here as briefly as possible. It is often said that political theory has little relation to reality, that it cannot be applied in practice, that it deals with legal fictions and absolute concepts, that it is inexact, that it is incapable of giving definite answers to disputed questions and that it is sometimes disastrous to actual politics. The opponents of political theory might very well use the aphorism of Emerson that there is 'nothing new, nothing true and nothing matters'.

To counteract the above charges, certain values of a study of political theory may be enumerated. It gives precision and definiteness to the meaning of political terms. It is conducive to clarity and honesty of thought. It is an aid to the interpretation of history. A knowledge of past political thought is an invaluable help in understanding present-day politics and international relations. Constructive political progress rests upon a sound and comprehensive political theory, applicable to present-day conditions and needs. Political thought represents a high type of intellectual achievement. Finally, if governments can be shaped and improved by human ingenuity, no study is more valuable than a study of political theory. Political theory is thus intensely practical and intensely important. It is the abstract treatment of a concrete subject.

The charge that political theory is too far removed from actual conditions is not true. What is needed is accurate definition and close analysis. Wise statesmanship requires more than mere hazy and often conflicting intuitions. It requires a sound philosophy or a scheme of moral values, and that is exactly what political theory endeavours to give. Statesmanship is essentially a moral task. That some political theorists have been mere pedants is no reason for condemning political theory wholesale. By its very nature political theory cannot always give clear-cut answers. While it may not lead to unity in political discussion, it will be at least an aid to mutual respect and toleration. If it is true that where there is practice, there should be theory also, a study of political theory is invaluable to political practice.

A study of political theory is especially valuable to students in India because of the philosophical background of the people. It is not to be viewed as a mere abstract and speculative study. It is a theoretical study of a practical and concrete subject. While a mere study of political theory cannot make one a successful politician, it can give him a clarity of ideas and sanity of outlook in the practical world.

In India there is an urgent need to graft the valuable political ideas of the entire world to the ancient tree of Indian tradition and culture. In so doing we may revive and revitalize such ancient concepts as *dharma*, *ahimsa*, and *asanga*, and put a new meaning into them and provide them with new workable sanctions.

POLITICAL SCIENCE AND ITS RELATION TO ALLIED SCIENCES

Political science does not stand alone, since it is not the only science which concerns itself with man in organized society. Being one of the many sciences dealing with the relations of man to man, it has its close connections with other social sciences. Thus Paul Janet remarks that political science is 'closely connected with political economy or the science of wealth; with law, either natural or positive, which occupies itself principally with the relations of citizens to one another; with history, which furnishes the facts of which it has need; with philosophy, and especially with morals, which gives to it a part of its principles (*23:29*)'.

1. Political Science and History

Political science and history are very intimately connected. The relation between the two is well brought out in the sentence: 'history is past politics, politics present history'. As Seeley puts it: 'History without political science has no fruit. Political science without history has no root'. To quote the same writer again: 'Politics are vulgar when not liberalised by history, and history fades into mere literature when it loses sight of its relation to politics.' History provides the raw material for political science. According to Seeley, political science and history will ultimately become identical with one another. But this seems improbable, if not impossible, Though both sciences are interdependent and mutually complementary, there are some fundamental differences between them.

(a) *In Their Method of Treatment*. History, being narrative, deals with facts in their chronological order, whereas political science selects only such events as relate to political evolution. The method of political science is reflective. Using the material provided by history, it seeks to discover general laws and principles.

(b) *In Scope*. History is more comprehensive because it deals with the economic, religious, and military aspects of the social life, whereas political science is not interested in them except in so far as they throw some light on the nature of the State, and the development of political control.

(c) *In Their End.* History is much less philosophical than political science. History deals with concrete facts and political science deals with ideals and abstract types. Political science deals with the State as it ought to be; history deals with the State as it is and has been.

The conclusion, then, is that political science must make use of history only to transcend it. The historian's task is not to pass moral judgments[1], but the political scientist is bound to make such judgments. It is there that political science joins hands with ethics and parts company with economics and sociology.

Lord Bryce claims that 'political science stands midway between history and politics, between the past and the present. It has drawn its materials from the one, it has to apply them to the other.'

To give some concrete illustrations, we cannot understand the constitution which governs India today without a knowledge of all the previous efforts at constitution-making since at least 1908-1909; nor the present-day passion for *panchayat raj* without relating it to its roots in the dim past.

2. Political Science and Economics

Political science and economics are very closely related. They exert considerable influence on each other and cover a common ground to a large extent. Production and distribution of wealth are affected by the regulations of the State. All economic activity is carried on within the State on conditions laid down by the State through laws. Political movements, on the other hand, are profoundly influenced by economic causes. Our economic life is conditioned by political institutions and ideas. Some of the important questions of present-day politics are at the same time questions which vitally concern economics; *e.g.*, questions relating to tariff laws, labour legislation, national planning, and government ownership. The relation between the two sciences is so great that a century ago scientific writers regarded economics as a branch of political science, and the subject itself was described as political economy. As late as the eighteenth century, political economy was regarded as 'a branch of statesmanship'.

Although the two sciences are closely related, there are still some fundamental differences between them. Commenting upon the question, Ivor Brown remarks that economics is concerned with things, while political science is concerned with people; one deals with prices and the other with values. If economics is concerned with people, it is not with people as ends in themselves, but only in relation to the things they make,

1. In the words of Sidwick, history cannot determine the ultimate end and standard of good and bad, right and wrong, in political institutions.

sell, and use Political science also takes things into account, but this it does only in relation to human or moral values. Thus it is that political science easily becomes a normative science, while economics remains a descriptive science. As someone has humorously remarked, an economist is one who knows the price of everything, but the value of nothing.

In present-day India students of both political science and economics are vitally concerned with such matters as our various five-year plans, the socialistic pattern of society and the community development projects.

It is a welcome sign of the times that economics is becoming more and more a normative science, concerning itself not merely with the production of wealth, but also with its just distribution. At the same time it is the boast of economics that it is becoming more and more of a science than political science with the help of mathematics and statistics. It is obvious, however, that neither political science nor economics can attain exact mathematical accuracy.

3. Political Science and Sociology

What philosophy is to the mental sciences, sociology is to the social sciences. Both of them aim at a unification of the subject-matter which belongs to the several allied subjects. Thus both possess an all-embracing character. Political science is narrower than sociology and is, in a general sense, a sub division of sociology. Sociology is the fundamental social science. The field covered by sociology is so vast that present-day writers prefer to limit it to the study of certain phases of the life of society, other than for its political aspects. Prof. Giddings remarks that "to teach the theory of the state to men who have not learned the first principles of sociology, is like teaching astronomy or thermodynamics to men who have not learned the Newtonian laws of motion." *(108:37)*

Sociology in its widest significance denotes a study of society in all its manifestations, whereas political science is only a study of the State and government. Putting the same thought in other words, we may say that while sociology deals with man in all his social relations, political science deals with man in his political relations alone. This may not be true of the State in its early stages but it is emphatically true of the modern State. In its early stages, the State was more a social than a political institution. In the words of Gilchrist, 'Sociology is the science of society; political science is the science of the State, or political society. Sociology studies man as a social being, and as political organization is a special kind of social organization, political science is a more specialized science than sociology'. Or, as Kranenburg states, 'while sociology examines the formation and operation of groups as such, political theory focuses its attention on a special group, namely the State.'

Sociology deals not only with organized communities but also with unorganized communities. The concern of political science is only the former. It deals only with societies which have received the impress of political organization. Thus it is later in origin than sociology.

Sociology deals with the legal and coercive relationships of man with his fellows as well as with the evolution of customs, manners, religion, and economic life. Political science deals only with the former.

Unlike political science which treats only of the conscious activities of man, sociology treats of unconscious social activities as well.

Political science starts with the assumption that man is a political being. Sociology goes behind this assumption and seeks to explain how and why man became a political animal.

Sociology is concerned with what has happened or does happen, and not with what ought to happen. Political science, at least in one of its aspects, is concerned with what ought to be done[2].

Social conditions in India provide a rich mine of information for the political thinker. In creating a better India, the political scientist may have various ideas and ideals, but whether they are capable of being realized or not will, to a certain extent, depend upon our social institutions and social customs and *mores*. Up till recently at least the joint family system, the stronghold of caste, and various practices relating to marriage, property and inheritance had an adverse effect upon progressive ideas in politics.

4. Political Science and Ethics

Political science is the science of the political order and ethics is the science of the moral order. Both have to deal with questions of right and wrong. The relation between the two is so close that Plato considered politics a sub-division of ethics. The State, he believed, should train men in a life of virtue. The capital advance made by Aristotle upon Plato is said to be his separation of ethics and politics. But this separation turns out to be one of methodology rather than of substance. Aristotle, too, posits a close relation between ethics and politics and allows political questions to be influenced by man's highest moral judgment. The end of the State is, according to him, good life or a community of well-being. Machiavelli is the first writer of any note in the Western world sharply to separate politics from ethics. To him, religion and morality are not the masters of the State, not even safe guides, but useful servants and agents.

The idealist view is, on the whole, in favour of maintaining a close relation between ethics and political science[3]. Lord Acton goes so far as to say: 'The great question is to discover, not what governments prescribe,

2. Taking the opposite point of view, Heymans, quoted by Kranenburg, writes: "The objection that sociology can offer us nothing but bare facts, instead of ideals, and uniformities instead of values, can be answered in a single sentence: 'Not so; the ideals in fact live and act uniformly within us'."

3. According to Foy, if a thing is morally wrong, it never be politically right. This, however, is not the usual view.

but what they ought to prescribe.' Another writer holds that to separate ethics and politics is disastrous to both. Politics divorced from ethics rests on a foundation of shifting sand; ethics divorced from politics is narrow and abstract; it leads to the commercialization and vulgarization of values. Ivor Brown maintains that the difference between politics and ethics is one of quantity, not of quality; for 'politics is but ethics writ large'. He goes on to say: 'Ethical theory is incomplete without political theory, because man is an associated creature and cannot live fully in isolation; political theory is idle without ethical theory, because its study and its result depend fundamentally on our scheme of moral values, our conceptions of right and wrong.'

A lasting contribution of Mahatma Gandhi to politics is his insistence upon the spiritualization of politics, *i.e.*, the application of such spiritual and moral principles as truth, love, non-violence, non-attachment, and self-suffering to man's social life.

The ultimate justification of the State is determined by the moral end or purpose which the State serves. Thus the ideals of both ethics and political science must be in agreement. Yet the bulk of the material with which the two sciences deal is distinct. Catlin contends that from ethics the statesman may learn which courses among several are desirable and from political science he may learn which among several may be feasible.

6. Political Science and Psychology

Psychology, as we know it today, is a comparatively new science and its advocates are trying to apply psychological methods to every part of man's individual and social life. E. Barker aptly remarks: 'The application of the psychological clue to the riddles of human activity has indeed become the fashion of the day. If our fathers thought biologically, we think psychologically.' There can be little doubt that the psychological approach to politics upon which much insistence is placed these days is very valuable. It may be that politics has been too long under the sway of philosophy and has not given enough attention to the facts of human behaviour. We need 'to reinvigorate our minds from the wells of direct observation.' We cannot go very far in our study of political science without understanding the way in which human beings behave as individuals and as members of society when subjected to various kinds of stimuli. We need to study such factors as habit and instinct, imitation and suggestion, if we are to understand human behaviour aright. 'Government to be stable and really popular must reflect and express the mental ideas and moral sentiments of those who are subject to its authority; in short, it must be in harmony with what Le Bon calls the "mental constitution of the race *(22:38)*".'

At the same time it is necessary to remember that it is easy to exaggerate the importance of psychology to political science. E. Barker clearly brings out the limitations of the psychological method as follows:

(1) The psychologist does not and cannot deal in terms of value. Values

belong to the moralist. Psychology deals with things as they are; ethics with things as they ought to be. Therefore, political theory should look to ethics rather than to psychology for constructive help.

(2) Psychology seeks to explain civilized life in terms of savage instinct —the higher by the lower. This does not seem to be the correct evolutionary method. The right procedure would be to explain the lower by the higher. Man explains the monkey, and not monkey the man. It is illogical to explain civilized life by the conditions of life in pre-historic times. Reason is nonetheless reason when it is not conscious inference. Habit and instinct, suggesttion and imitation exist, but they exist in connection with intelligence. Because a thing is primitive, it does not mean that it is final.

In spite of these limitations, a study of psychology, particularly of social psychology, is of inestimable value to the student of political science. It shows him clearly that men in general are not moved as much by ideas and ideals, by theories and the logic of facts as by their preconceived notions, and dispositions, and their fears and prejudices. Man is more sub-rational and irrational than rational. L. Lipson argues that "while political science must embrace a theory of what the state ought to be, the latter (ethics) must respect the limits of the possible".

6. Political Science and Law

The State is both a social phenomenon and a legal institution and any attempt to explain the State in its entirety must include both these points of view. From the legal standpoint, the State is a person in the sense that it is subject of rights and duties. It can sue and be sued in a law court. Or, to put it in the form of a definition, it is 'a corporation composed of men domiciled upon a particular territory and endowed with original ruling power *(19)*'.

Jurisprudence may be defined as the science of law. Although, strictly speaking, a sub-division of political science, it is, owing to the vastness of its scope and its technical nature, studied as a separate branch of study.

Constitutional law defines the organs of the State, their relations to one another, and the relations of the State to the individual. International law regulates the relations of states to one another.

Stoicism and Roman jurisprudence have made much contribution to the development of Western law. Hallowell observes that the universal brotherhood of man and the universal law of reason are the principal contributions of Stoicism to Western civilization.

It is no accident that lawyers in India have made a great contribution to the development of political institutions and the freedom movement in India. A study of law in some of its phases is indispensable to a student of constitutions and public administration. The function of legislators is primarily one of law-making; and that calls for more than a nodding acquaintance with the intricacies of law. Such concepts as fundamental rights and directive principles of state policy impinge as much on law as on ethics and politics.

7. Political Science and Geography

Man is, to a considerable extent, influenced by his physical environment and the geographical conditions under which he lives. It is easy to exaggerate the influence of the climate, topography, and physical features of a country upon the character, institutions and accomplishments of a people. While these external factors play an important part in man's life, it is necessary to remember that civilized man is not a passive tool of Nature. Like the lower animals, he does not blindly allow himself to be adapted to nature. By the use of intelligence and forethought he adapts nature to his purposes.

After making due allowance for exaggeration, it remains undoubtedly true that geographical conditions have influenced in considerable measure the determination of national policies and to some extent the character of political institutions (*23:42-66*). At the same time we are safe in saying that geography is a much less important factor in moulding social and political institutions today than it was in earlier times.

An emerging science known as 'Geopolitics' is of a great value today, even though it was prostituted to low ends by certain German scholars. It was made to do service to Nazi aggression. Rightly understood, it means that mountains, great rivers, and oceans have more to do with theories of State action, international relations, and the like than beautiful theories of the State written from an armchair. A good illustration of the importance of 'Geopolitics' is the way in which Canada and the U.S.A. have harnessed the waters of St. Lawrence for the material benefit of both. As a result of it, ocean-going steamers can now go right up to Chicago, more than 1400 kilometers away from the Atlantic sea border. The Atlantic and Pacific Oceans and the Himalayas are not the insuperable barriers which they were once thought to be.

IS POLITICAL SCIENCE A SCIENCE?

It is admitted by all writers that political science is an inexact science. It does not aim at absolute truth. It aims at relative truth. Consequently there is bound to be difference of opinion with regard to almost all political questions. What is sound politically today may not be sound a hundred years hence. Therefore, no theory of the State can be considered as ultimate truth.

Because of these limitations some thinkers even refuse to give the name 'science' to a study of political theory. For example, F. W. Maitland writes: "When I see a good set of examination questions headed by the words 'political science' I regret not the questions but the title." (Collected Papers, Vol. III, p. 302). It is true that political science is not exact like mathematics, physics or chemistry. Two plus two makes four everywhere in the world except in a lunatic asylum. Two parts of hydrogen and one part of oxygen produce water whenever they chemically combine. These are universal and unvarying laws. But such laws we do not find in studying social sciences owing to the variability of human behaviour. It is difficult, if not impossible, to draw precise conclusions from political phenomena or to make exact forecast about the future. Still, by a close and prolonged observation of political phenomena we can arrive at general laws and principles which can be of real help to us in solving the practical problems of government.

We cannot experiment with human society or the political order in the way in which a scientist can experiment with physical or chemical substances. President Lowell considered politics 'an observational and not an experimental science'. We cannot at will introduce democracy in one state and aristocracy in another in order to study the effects of these respective forms of government. Physical phenomena and social phenomena differ fundamentally. Nevertheless, every law passed is an experiment, and a careful student can arrive at general conclusions based on particular phenomena. A study of political theory, thus, does not enable us to reach conclusions with mathematical precision. However, it can help us to discover probable truths, and 'probability,' as Samuel Butler remarks, 'is the guide of life'. Lord Bryce considered politics to be a science in the sense meteorology is considered a science. Sir Frederick Pollock maintained that "there is a political science in the same sense that there is a science of morals." (*History of the Science of Politics*, p. 2). Garner, too, considered politics a science but "still probably the most incomplete and undeveloped of all the social sciences." (23; 1951 Indian ed: p. 13). Prediction in physics may be certain; in politics it can at best be no more than probable (7).'

METHODS OF POLITICAL SCIENCE

A great many modern thinkers have given their thought and attention to the methods by which political phenomena can be collected and classified, with a view to reaching practical results. According to Augustus Comte, the principal methods are *observation, experiment*, and *comparison*. Bluntschli holds that the true methods are philosophical and historical. To a great many present-day thinkers, inductive and pragmatic methods are more certain to lead to positive results in political science than deductive and dogmatic methods.

The methods which are generally favoured by them are :—

(1) the experimental method,
(2) the historical method,
(3) the comparative method,
(4) the method of observation, and
(5) the philosophical method.

The first four of these methods have a great deal of similarity and so can easily be bracketed together. The fifth method belongs to a category of its own. A combination of these two types of methods alone can lead to valuable results. The inductive and deductive methods are complementary to one another.

1. The Experimental Method

As seen already, there is little opportunity for conscious experimentation in a field in which human beings constitute the subject. Human motives and human values cannot be weighed and tabulated like a chemical substance. Nevertheless, all laws, policies, and political systems are instituted within a necessary framework of experiment, and by studying such experiments the political scientist is able to reach positive conclusions. It is his task to take note of the political events and innovations that constantly go on about him and to make deductions from them. Governments are ever trying experiments on the community. History is experimentation on a vast scale.

In the modern world, we do not rely on unconscious experimentation. We make conscious political experiments, in the light of past experience, when and where circumstances permit. Witness, for example, the grant of responsible self-government to Canada based on the Durham Report of 1839 and the transfer of complete power to India by constitutional methods. Thus there is a definite and distinct place for the experimental method in political science.

Since the termination of World War II several areas in Asia and Africa have received their independence and practically all of them operate today under more or less democratic constitutions. The careful student of political science will find a great deal of valuable source material in the constitutions and governments of newly freed countries extending from Indo-China and Indonesia in South-East Asia to Ghana, Guinea, and Cameroons in Africa.

2. The Historical Method

The historical method may be regarded as a form of the experimental method. A proper study of history is an invaluable aid to the student of political science. It is a corrective to hasty and one-sided conclusions in politics. The value of studying the origin, growth and development of political institutions is the fact that from such a study we can draw conclusions for future guidance. History not only explains the past; it contains the key for interpreting the future.

The historical method is mainly inductive in character. It is based on observation and the study of historical facts. Its chief limitation is that it cannot, and does not, deal in values. Hence it has to be supplemented by the philosophical or ethical method which involves ultimate ends and values. Yet indirectly the historical method does enable us to judge the goodness or badness of actions.

In using the historical method, there are certain precautions that the student will do well to take.

(a) He should guard against superficial resemblances and parallels.

(b) He should not let the present and the future be determined solely by the past. The historical method should not become a synonym for hidebound conservatism. Because a thing has been thus and so in the past, it does not follow that it should be thus and so in the present.

(c) He should avoid the temptation to make history support his preconceived notions. He should be altogether objective or scientific in his outlook.

(d) He should remember that the oft-quoted saying that history repeats itself is only a half-truth. The other half-truth is that history never repeats itself. Historical conditions never exactly reproduce themselves. 'One cannot step twice into the same river (7).'

In recent years Sir Arnold Toynbee has given the world a masterly analysis of world civilizations. He has attempted to show how civilizations rise and fall. A careful student of political science is bound to derive much value from a study of his writings. One of his generalizations is that civilizations are not murdered, but commit suicide. Another generalization is that history is to be interpreted in terms of challenge and response.

3. The Comparative Method

The comparative method supplements the historical method. It goes back to the time of Aristotle and has been used effectively in recent times by De Tocqueville, Bryce, and others. A study of history is useless if we cannot make valid comparisons. The ocmparative method helps us to relate events, to establish causes and effects, and to arrive at general principles. It gathers together the multiplicity of phenomena, arranges them in order, and selects the elements common to them.

If this method is to be usefully employed, we must take into account not only resemblances but also differences. We are not to be in a hurry to come to conclusions. The phenomena from which the common elements are to be selected must be too different in character. Comparisons must not be pushed too far and analogies must not be far-fetched. Generalizations of a vague and broad character should be avoided. It is profitable on the whole to confine our investigations to the States which have sprung from a common historical background and which are relatively near in point of time.

A particular form of the comparative method is the analogical method. It is very useful in political science, provided analogy is not pushed to the limit of identity. To establish an analogy between two things is not to establish their identity. Analogy is not proof. It can give us probability, but not certainty.

Herbert Spencer is guilty of pushing analogy to an absurd conclusion: His conception of the organic theory of society is mechanical and even ludicrous when, for example, he compared the up and down lines of a railway to the arteries and veins of a physical organism.

4. The Method of Observation

Like the foregoing, the method of observation is an inductive one. President Lowell declares that "politics is an observational and not an experimental science", and that the method of observation is the true method of investigation. A library, he says, is a laboratory of political science only in a limited sense; books for the most part being no more original sources for the "physiology of politics" than they are for geology or astronomy. "The main laboratory for the actual working of political institutions", he adds, "is not a library but the outside world of political life", and there the phenomena must be sought and observed at first hand.[4] The method of observation was followed by Lord Bryce to a very great extent. It rests upon an observation of the actual working of political institutions at close range. Before undertaking his monumental works, *The American Commonwealth* and *Modern Democracies,* Lord Bryce visited the countries concerned and based his conclusions upon personal conversations with public men and the observation of governments at work. A method like this, based as it is on direct observation and reflection, has much to commend it. It is practical and concrete and has a refreshing sense of reality about it. It is in living touch with facts and is free from the charge of being abstract and doctrinaire. Nonetheless, it is a method which has to be used with caution. When the facts are very many and often conflicting, only a man with a trained eye and mature judgment can arrive at sound conclusions. One must have the ability to sift evidence and rightly interpret one's data. There is a danger of seeing the things that one wants to see and leaving out those things of which one chooses to be oblivious. Likewise, there is a danger of missing the wood for the trees. The first desideratum is no doubt to get at facts. But facts are of little use in and by themselves. A penetrating and understanding mind is needed to interpret them aright and to make them real and living.

To give just one illustration of the value of the method of observation, one can profitably study the operation of military dictatorships in many modern countries and come out with some useful generalizations.

5. The Philosophical Method

Unlike the foregoing methods, the philosophical method is of a deductive or *a priori* kind. Its chief exponents are Rousseau, Mill and Sidgwick. On philosophical and ethical grounds, it first determines the nature and end or purpose of the State and then casts about for the best forms of political institutions for the realization of this end. It begins with abstract concepts, then attempts to harmonize them with the actual facts of history. The chief danger of this method is that it may easily become imaginative and visionary, as seen in More's *Utopia* and, to some extent, in Plato's *Republic.* It may not have any basis whatever in historical facts and may thus sink

4. "The Physiology of Politics". *American Political Science Review,* Vol. IV, p. 82.

into empty ideology, Attempts to construct an ideal type of State have engaged the attention of thinkers from the days of Greek philosophy, through the scholasticism of the Middle Ages, down to the present day.

Conclusion. Leslie Lipson says that Plato, Aristotle and Machiavelli represent three points of view in politics. Plato projects his imagination into the future and, on the basis of what he saw in Sparta and Athens, portrays a picture of an ideal State. For this reason his method is called idealistic. Aristotle is more scientific and realistic. He relies upon the wisdom of experience and bases his conclusions upon a close analysis of what he saw around him. For this reason his method is called scientific and realistic. Machiavelli, on the other hand, is brutally realistic. "His preoccupation", says Lipson, is "with the techniques that will lead to the desired goal". Questions of right and wrong do not much enter his calculations.

The careful student would seek to combine the historical and philosophical methods. He would test and correct his deductive principles by the actual facts of human experience and interpret the facts of life in the light of abstract or *a priori* principles. While his feet stand four square on solid facts, his head would soar high into the skies. He would seek to bring about a happy blend of realism and idealism. He would have no use for that type of realism which does not look much beyond one's own nose, nor for that type of idealism which loses itself in the clouds. He would follow the footsteps of men like Aristotle and Marx who combine in their writings the historical and philosophical methods.

In the light of this conclusion, it is somewhat disconcerting to find that many American writers today place undue emphasis on methods, techniques and skills, almost to the exclusion of first principles and value judgments. In Great Britain, on the other hand, as Dr. Macpherson points out, there is much "less emphasis on purely empirical research and more inclination to examine political institutions and processes from the point of view of purpose—the purpose they serve and the purpose they ought to serve".[5] Political scientists in Britain are not much worried about new techniques. There is in that country "an appreciation of value judgments and a perceptible mistrust of purely empirical research".

Even in the United States there are writers like Prof. J. H. Hallowell who rightly observe: "The social sciences are not so much in need of new research techniques as some suppose, but of convictions based upon rational principles." *(13:2)*.

Politics as a Social Science

Politics is an ancient art, perhaps as old as the State itself, but its development as a social science is comparatively of recent origin. However, the true character of politics as a science has not yet been decided conclusively. Politics, according to Marx, is nothing but concentrated economics. Political science, therefore, is an ideological superstructure built on economic or material foundations.

5. ***American Political Science Review,*** **Vol. XLVIII, June 1954, p. 436.**

Liberals, however, do not accept this view. They either emphasise the primacy of politics over economics or assert the mutual interdependence of the two social sciences. "Nevertheless," says Sabine, "the idea of economic causation was probably the most fertile suggestion added to social studies in the nineteenth century."

Theories of politics do not refer to an external reality but are created as an essential element of the socio-economic system in which politics itself has its being. Reflection upon the goals of political behaviour and analysis of the means of achieving them constitute an intrinsic part of the entire process. Political theory evolves along with the rise and decline of specific political systems, which, one is tempted to say, it in some degree controls. Political theory, in one sense, has always been a part of contemporary philosophy and science and an application to politics of the relevant intellectual and critical apparatus which society has evolved in a given age. In addition, it is also a reflection upon the ethical norms, legal postulates, religious precepts, governmental organisation and economic institutions of any established community of human beings in a particular epoch.

Scope of Political Analysis

A theory of the State is also a theory of society and of the distribution of power in that society. Political science should start its analysis by identifying *three* types of social orders—feudal, capitalist and socialist—which, have characterised most of the medieval and modern history of the human race.

In order to understand a political system, it is necessary to learn about the major economic and social characteristics of the society in which that political system operates. This will enable us to appreciate the pattern of economic and political power, which is to be found in that society.

On the basis of the above analysis, a political scientist can proceed towards the description of the main institutions of the political system and the social composition of the ruling class or the governing elite in that political system.

This can lead to the clarification and discussion of the purpose and role of governments in the context of the prevailing ideology of the ruling class such as feudalism, capitalism or socialism. It may elucidate the part played by the bureaucracy, the military establishment and the judicial hierarchy in consolidating a specific pattern of class power in a given political system.

Contemporary political science also examines the role of the State in the conflict and competition between different social groups such as the bourgeoisie and feudal lords in medieval society or the proletariat and the capitalists in modern social history.

In addition, contemporary political science discusses what political sociologists describe as the agencies of legitimation such as the political parties, the mass media of communication and the organisation of education.

Finally, political theory makes an attempt to predict some of the directions in which the political systems of today—pre-industrial, advanced capitalistic or planned socialistic—are moving. Political theory can no longer maintain an exclusively Anglo-Saxon or European bias but must make an earnest effort to explain political developments on a global scale including the politics of economically underdeveloped areas of Asia, Africa and Latin America and the politics of socialist nations, old and new, which are experiencing an unprecedented rate of economic growth.

Correct Approach to the Study of Politics

Society is a complex whole which we can study, by using the scientific method, from different points of view—legal, sociological, economic or political. We have no right to regard as absolute the aspects of social reality obtained in this manner and to separate them in isolated compartments. We are not justified in considering any one sphere of social reality such as the *political* as absolute in the sense of treating it as an independent process of development.

Nevertheless, some schools of social science treat politics as a self-contained, independent domain of study, torn away from the other spheres of social life. They rely on *juristic* and *normative* methods consisting in a formal analysis of constitutional rules guiding the working of State organs and reflection of certain political ideals to be realized in future.

The *correct* approach to the study requires that the investigation of political phenomena is intimately related to the investigation of the other social phenomena. Politics, therefore, may be considered as a social science, which studies in a systematic way the phenomena connected with the State, law, government, revolution, economy and culture as a part of the general social development. The social development as conceived here is from a definite point of view as suggested by Laski in his characteristic phrase—"property relations determined by the modes of production in a given society."

While emphasizing the relevance of a sociological analysis in the study of politics, one must avoid the 'sociologism' of writers like Pareto, Durkheim and Stammler, who reduce the question of the social basis to a psychological principle or an ethical norm. Political sociologists, who do not recognise the materialistic basis of social institutions, may characterise a socialist political system as oligarchical and a capitalistic political order as fully democratic on the basis of a superficial and one-sided study of political structures.

Though the importance of economic and sociological analysis in politics is obvious, yet political institutions, being manifestations of the ideological superstructure, have a certain capacity for autonomous development. The behaviourist school in political science has emphasised the study of political behaviour and political systems concerning itself with an empirical analysis of political processes.

CHAPTER 2

POLITICS AS A SOCIAL PROCESS

Politics as Political Activity

Till today, the meaning of the term politics remains ambiguous. It means differently to different people. Sometimes, it is understood to mean an activity of a certain type directed towards the achievement of common goals shared by a class or state or community or group or party. Sometimes, it is understood to mean the body of knowledge, more or less systematic, about that activity. Some thinkers make a distinction between politics as the practical activity related to a particular dimension of the social process and political science as a specific discipline engaged in the study and theoretical investigation of the practical activity related to the political process. Political thinkers from Aristotle to Laski have used the term politics to designate both the political activity and the science that deals with that activity.

Seeing the rumble and tumble that goes on in democracies, some persons have associated politics with the functioning of democratic forces and institutions and have found it disgusting and distasteful. To the Portuguese dictator Antonio Salazar, politics represented: "all those noisy and incoherent promises, the impossible demands, the hotchpotch of unfounded ideas and impractical plans, opportunism that cares neither for truth nor justice, the inglorious chase after unmerited fame, the unleashing of uncontrollable passions, the exploitation of the lowest instincts, the distortion of facts and all that feverish and sterile fuss." (*187:12*). Politics, thus understood, may be defined as the art of governing mankind by deceiving them. This was the view of politics proclaimed by Mussolini in Italy, Hitler in Germany, General Franco in Spain and many other mini-dictators in Asia, Africa and Latin America.

In so many countries, the slogan has been raised that the general, or the leader, or the party is protecting the nation from the domination of politicians, who practise corrupt and unprincipled politics. This perverted view of politics is today upheld by a large number of people even in democratic countries and Bernard Crick observes about this: "Many people, of course, even in regimes which are clearly political, think that they are not interested in politics, and even act as if they are not; but they are probably few compared to the many who think that politics is muddled, contradictory, selfdefeatingly recurrent, unprogressive, unpatriotic, inefficient, mere compromise, or even a sham or conspiracy by which political parties seek to preserve some particular and peculiar social systems against the challenge of the inevitable future, etc. The anti-political are very right to think that politics is an achievement far more limited in time and place than politically-minded men, or men who practise this odd thing politics, normally presume." (*187:17*).

Politics is often regarded as an inherently dependent and subsidiary social activity and is rarely credited with a life and character of its own. Politics is also often confused with religion, ethics, law, history or economics. Some people equate it with one political doctrine, such as nationalism, communism, socialism, liberalism, conservatism or fascism. Though politics may contain elements of most of these things, yet it is a fundamental activity in its own right and possesses a character of its own. Bernard Crick has rightly pleaded: "Politics, to be valued as itself, not because it is 'like' or 'really is' something else more respectable or peculiar Politics is politics. The person who wishes not to be troubled by politics and to be left alone finds himself the unwitting ally of those to whom politics is a troublesome obstacle to their well-meant intentions to leave nothing alone" (*187:16*).

Aristotle was the first great political thinker who recognized the distinctive quality of politics as one of the basic human activities. He criticized Plato's scheme of ideal state on the ground that Plato in his *Republic* made the mistake of trying to reduce everything in the polis to a unity, which actually implied the abolition of 'politics'. Against this, Aristotle argued in his *Politics*: "There is a point at which a polis, by advancing in unity, will cease to be a polis: there is another point, short of that, at which it may still remain a polis, but will nonetheless come near to losing its essence, and will thus be a worse polis. It is as if you were to turn harmony into mere unison, or to reduce a theme to a single beat. The truth is that the polis is an aggregate of many members." (*176 : 51*). According to Aristotle, politics arises in organised communities, which permit the simultaneous existence of different groups, which represent conflicting traditions and divergent interests, within the same state. For Aristotle as well as for many modern liberal thinkers, politics represents at least a degree of tolerance of controversies and some understanding of the principle that government is best conducted, amid the open propagation of mutually antagonistic interests.

Common usage of the term 'politics' may lead us to believe that politics is a real force in every organised state. Bernard Crick, following Aristotle, however, argues that real politics is not possible under tyranny or even oligarchy. Tyranny represents the rule of one person in his own interest and oligarchy implies the rule of one group in its own interest. Both the tyrant and the oligarch use coercion to suppress the expression of rival interests and this means the elimination of all political controversy and debate. The democratic method of rule is "to listen to these other groups so as to conciliate them as far as possible, and to give them a legal position, a sense of security, some clear and reasonably safe means of articulation, by which these other groups can and will speak freely." (*187:18*). Politics draws all these groups into each other so that they separately and jointly can make a positive contribution towards the general business of government.

Bernard Crick, presenting the modern liberal view of politics, says: "Politics, then, can be simply defined as the activity by which differing interests within a given unit of rule are conciliated by giving them a share in power in proportion to their importance to the welfare and the survival of the whole community. And to complete the formal definition, a political system is that type of government where politics proves successful in ensuring reasonable stability and order." (*187:21*). Politics, as Aristotle rightly said, was a 'master science' not in the sense that it included or could explain all other sciences, all social activities and group interests, but in that it gave them some priority and some order in their conflicting demands on the always scarce resources of any given community. Bernard Crick further explains: "The way of establishing these priorities is by allowing the right institutions to develop by which the various 'sciences' can demonstrate their actual importance in the common task of survival. Politics is, as it were, the market place and the price mechanism of all social demands—though there is no guarantee that a just price will be struck; and there is nothing spontaneous about politics—it depends on deliberate and continuous individual activtiy." (*187:23*).

Different Approaches to Politics

According to David E. Apter, there are six different views of politics or systems of political analysis: Political Philosophy, Institutionalism, Behaviouralism, Pluralism, Structuralism and Developmentalism.

Political Philosophy is based on the application of reason to the study of human affairs. This view dominated the classical tradition of political thought and was the main trend in the study of politics for a long time. The emphasis of political philosophy was on moral principles and purposes. Plato and Aristotle are the founders of the philosophical approach to politics. As the Greeks used the precepts of philosophy to solve the problem of justice and good government under the laws, political philosophy became a guide to political action as well. Certain institutions of government came to symbolize and concretise distinct philosophical norms and ideals. To David Apter: "Political philosophy tends to be concerned with the establishment of moral purposes, the ethical basis of the political community, and a logic which establishes their priority or validity. The results comprise the field of normative political theory and the evolution of the normal basis of the state." (*172:12*).

Institutionalism is the second system of political analysis which assumes certain ethical priorities as given and attempts to realize them in the mechanisms of the government. Therefore, its emphasis is on legal and historical analysis, descriptive and comparative methods and interest group theory. The specific fields covered by the institutionalists are national, comparative and international politics and more specialized subjects like constitutions, bureaucracies, parties, legislatures etc. This view of politics suggests that political institutions realize philosophical ideals in governmental practices. For example, the representative assemblies and independent and politically neutral courts are the institutional prerequisites of democracy.

Behaviouralism is the third system of political analysis which takes the individual as political actor. Behaviouralism shifts the emphasis from political institutions to the study of how people behave in the political field and what motivates their political behaviour. It deals with their opinions, their political choices, their attitudes towards the established rules, their tendencies towards violent action, their tolerance of the views of the rival groups, and the nature and extent of citizens' participation in electoral and other political activities. To David Apter : "Behaviouralism, which focuses on both individual and aggregate, emphasises experimental methods in group situations, how decisions are made, and organisational aspects affecting action. Courses in the field include methodology, the study of public opinion and voting, how opinions form and belief-systems are established, political psychology and theories of political coalition and games." *(172:13)*.

Pluralism is the fourth system of political analysis. Incorporating the institutionalist's emphasis on democracy and representative institutions and building upon the empirical research of the behaviouralists, the pluralists deal with modes of competitive and cooperative interaction among groups and the connections between different forms of organizational behaviour. It examines the influence of group activities on the functioning of the pluralist democracy in a modern industrial society based on advanced capitalism. The primary emphasis is on the study of democratic participation, empirical methods, coalition theory, electoral systems, political parties, legislative behaviour, decentralization of functions, and democratic elitism in civil and national government. David Apter says: "Critics of pluralism believe that this approach to political analysis and the behavioural approach deny the consequences of political philosophy by taking the political world at face value, without accounting for the underlying relationships that connect them both to the larger purposes and meanings of government." *(172:9)*.

Structuralism is the fifth system of political analysis. It is a variant of both institutionalism and behaviouralism and, therefore, it concentrates on the relation between the individual and the community. Structuralism is concerned with the 'hidden agenda' behind political action and seeks to discover the economic, cultural and psychological determinants of political phenomena. Hence, its preoccupation is with class analysis, exchange theory, and functionalist and dialectical methods of determining the boundaries of political system. The structuralists, who are Marxists as well as non-Marxists, generally concentrate their attention on the behaviour of elites and classes, the phenomena of change and revolution, the connection between social status and ideologies and the factors which promote equilibrium and disequilibrium in the social and political system.

Developmentalism is the sixth system of political analysis. · Just as institutionalism represents the empirical application of political philosophy to the organized practice of politics, so developmentalism, a new 'applied' and inter-disciplinary approach to the study of politics, attempts to examine the processes of cultural modernization and economic development and change and their impact on structures and policies of various governments. Thus, developmentalism is concerned with the theories of transition from one type of political system to another, causes and effects of innovation, political regimes of the developing countries, nationalism of the new nations, decolonization and neo-colonialism. As David Apter rightly says: "The developmental changes in the world include, in addition to internal problems, power conflicts occurring between the first or democratic industrial world, the second or socialist industrial world, and the third or developing world. All analytical systems can be linked to the concept of developmentalism, its patterns of change and innovation, and the impact of the more powerful and dynamic countries on weaker, peripheral, and developing nations. But ideas about how to direct change and what its purposes are also bring us back to issues of philosophy. We have ideologically come full circle." *(172:10)*.

In terms of the foregoing six views of politics and political analysis, a continuous debate has been going on between the adherents of political philosophy and institutionalism on the one hand and the supporters of behaviouralism and structuralism on the other. One major defect of David Apter's scheme is to club the functional view and the dialectical view of politics together in one category. The functionalist view of politics professed by Talcott-Parsons, David Easton and Almond, emphasizes the equilibrium perspective of a political system. The dialectical view of politics, upheld by the Marxist school, studies political systems from the conflict perspective.

Politics as a Concept of Power

The science of politics today may be tentatively defined as a study of the structure of power in the political systems which are at various levels of cultural, economic and political development. The basic questions to be asked are: How one can describe the structure of power in the contemporary state? Who governs? How do they govern? For whom do they govern?

One answer to these questions is found in Marxist thought. Marx said that the government is nothing more than an administrative committee of the bourgeois class. The expression is forceful but generic which requires adjustment in analysing power-structure in concrete situations. In the *Eighteenth Brumaire,* Marx applied his approach in a flexible manner in analysing the character of several French regimes and his analysis could have been accepted by a liberal thinker like Tocqueville. Marx considered the analysis of the social relationships of production necessary, but not a sufficient condition for understanding the specific phenomenon of political power.

Another answer to these questions is found in the elite theory of Mosca, Pareto and Michels. They maintain that in every political system, feudal or capitalist, a ruling elite commands and the subject masses obey. The ruling elite lives at the expense of the masses, who obey and produce. Further, the 'political formula' or the ideology by which the elite establishes the legitimacy of its rule is always a byproduct of relationships originally imposed by force. First, a social class imposes itself on another through the use of force, then it legitimises it with a political doctrine around which it organises a consensus. Robert Michels shows how 'democratic' parties are really oligarchical structures.

C. Wright Mills and Ralph Miliband have developed the theory of 'Power Elite' as a substitute for the Marxian doctrine of the ruling class. They maintain that large economic enterprises in the political systems of the economically advanced countries can not only use their power to exert direct and indirect pressures on the government but also can take decisions which affect the destiny of a large number of people in the same way as those of the ministers and officials of the state. The big capitalists together with top military and political leaders constitute the power elite that rules America and other Western countries.

Robert Dahl, of course, contests both the ruling class model of Marx and the power elite model of C. Wright Mills. According to Dahl, politics in a democracy is based on competition for seeking influence. Every interest group tries to exert pressure on the government in order to realize its demands. The government, while meeting the challenges coming from different directions, tries to secure a balance between competing interests. Thus no class, elite or group is able to establish monopolistic control over the political system. Other advocates of the group theory are Bentley, Truman and Kautsky who subscribe to the pluralist model of power structure. Kautsky, however, holds that the pluralist model is not applicable to the third world countries.

Charles Merriam, Lasswell, Catlin, Kaplan and Morgenthau are the advocates of the power theory in politics. Lasswell and Kaplan observe that: "the concept of power is perhaps the most fundamental in the whole of political science : the political process is the shaping, dissolution and exercise of power. What men seek in their political negotiations is power." *(213:240)*. Power is of three types—economic, political and ideological. Politics is a *study of the interaction* of the economic, political and ideological dimensions of powers.

Wealth is the source of the economic dimension of power. In a feudal society, the ownership of land enabled the feudal lord to acquire wealth and therefore, he enjoyed economic power. In a capitalist society, ownership of factories, mines as well as other means of production is the chief source of wealth. The industrialists, merchants and bankers, possess great economic power in all capitalist countries. In a socialist society, land, factories, banks and other means of production and distribution are owned by the society as a whole. Therefore, no social class in a socialist country can amass wealth and exert economic power. In a society divided into classes, the class which owns the means of production has the power to exploit other classes, which are denied this ownership. But in a socialist society, the exploitation of one class by another is abolished.

The political dimension of power owes its genesis to the institutionalised power exerted by state apparatus. In a feudal society, the land-owning aristocracy controlled and dominated the organ of government. The feudal lords exercised political power as ministers, executive officers, law-makers and judges. As the Church was the biggest landowner in a feudal society, the priests assisted the feudal lords in running the medieval government. In a modern society, the capitalists do not control and dominate the state apparatus directly. A political elite recruited from different classes such as the aristocrats, the middle classes and intelligentsia and also the bourgeoisie runs the government on the condition that it would follow policies to promote the major interest of the capitalist class. The military top brass and bureaucratic elites may also be drawn from different classes but they, like the political elite, serve the interests of the capitalist class. In a socialist society, the revolutionary elite serves the interest of the working class and the other oppressed classes though sometimes a distortion may take place in implementing such policies due to the cult of personality or bureaucratism.

The ideological dimension of power emanates from the power exerted by religion, education, mass media, legal ideas and cultural beliefs. Religion was the main ideological prop of the feudal power. Similarly, the legal ideology, education and mass media controlled by money power are the main props of the capitalist power. Gramsci spoke of the importance of ideological power in supporting the structure of bourgeois democracy. Mao Tse-tung also realized the importance of ideological transformation for stabilizing the base of socialist power of China.

The Concept of Political System

The concept of political system came to political science from biology through anthropology and sociology. Talcott Parsons and Robert K. Merton exercised great influence on the use of the concept of system in political analysis. While the interest of Parsons was in building a general theory and an all-embracing set of categories, Merton was interested in specific phenomena and the 'middle range' theory. They influenced political scientists like Almond Powell, Coleman, Apter, Pye and others who founded the structural-functional school in political science. They ask three basic questions in their political analysis: (a) what basic functions are fulfilled in any given political system, (b) by what structures, political or nonpolitical, and (c) under what conditions?

A function may be defined as the objective consequence of a pattern of action for the system in which it occurs. Functions make for the adaptation or adjustment of a given system while dysfunctions lessen the adaptation or adjustment of the system. Structures refer to those arrangements within the system which perform functions.

Almond defines a political system as "that system of interactions to be found in all independent societies, which performs the functions of integration and adaptation (both internally and vis-a-vis other societies) by means of the employment or threat of employment, of more or less legitimate physical compulsion." As Meehan says, Almond's definition of the political system combines here "Weber's definition of the state, Easton's conception of authoritative allocation of value and Parsons' view of the function of the political sub-system in society." A political system has three characteristics:

(1) comprehensiveness as it includes all the inter-actions, inputs as well as outputs, in all the structures;
(2) interdependence as a change in one sub-set of the system produces change in all the other sub-sets; and
(3) existence of boundaries as points where other systems end and the political system begins.

A fourth characteristic inferred from Almond's thesis is that the political system has a tendency towards equilibrium, a condition of harmony, stability or balance.

As a behaviouralist Almond is more interested in processes than in institutions and these processes are to be studied in the light of seven variables. Four of these are input variables: (1) political socialisation and recruitment, (2) interest articulation, (3) interest aggregation, and (4) political communication. Three of these are output variables: (1) rule-making, (2) rule-application, and (3) rule-adjudication. The input functions are performed by the non-governmental sub-systems, by the society and the general environment while the output functions are performed by governmental structures.

Political socialisation is the process of induction into the political culture and the psychological dimension of the political system. Interest articulation and aggregation are the functions of the interest groups, political parties etc. and political communication is the function of the mass media. The capabilities of political systems are described as (1) extractive (control of resources); (2) regulative (control over groups and individuals); and (3) distributive (control over goods and services to be shared). Besides these, the system should have symbolic and responsive capabilities to meet challenges which could come (1) from within the political system—from the elites, (2) from the environment, from social groups, and (3) from other political systems.

Apart from Almond, the significant contribution to the system theory has come from David Easton. He defines the political system as the "institutions, processes and interactions through which values are authoritatively allocated in a society." The values are valued as material objects in society which are to be distributed among groups and individuals through laws, legislation, administrative decisions and adjudication by the courts.

By the environment, Easton means the social, biological and personality forces both inside and outside a particular society that affect and are affected by the political system but are analytically distinct from it. In short, the environment means the social system as a whole. By inputs, he means those events in the environment that act upon the political system and evoke some kind of response from it. There are two types of inputs—demands and supports. The demands can be specific or broad, precisely expressed or vague. The supports can be applied either to the political community or to the regime or to the government.

By conversion process, Easton means the processes, institutions and interactions by which the political system converts demands and supports into outputs. In short, the outputs are the functions of the government. The outputs are the authoritative decisions and policies through which the political system influences the environment. The changes in the nature, intensity, and volume of demands and supports brought about by the outcome of the outputs are described by Easton as the feedback. It gives rise to a new set of demands and supports.

Political Socialisation and Political Culture

The political culture of a political system consists of those values, beliefs and emotions that give meaning to politics. Within a given country, many things are accepted because cultural norms lead citizens to believe in them. Cultural norms express often inarticulate ideas and assumptions about how politics should be conducted or what political goals should be pursued. As Richard Rose points out : "Englishmen believe a monarchy is a normal form of democratic government, just as Americans expect a democracy to be a republic." Thus the political culture is a more or less harmonious mixture of the value preferences, beliefs and emotions of the citizens.

The values, beliefs and emotions of the political culture are transmitted from generation to generation through a series of socialization experiences in the family, at school and at work. The political outlooks of citizens reflect attitudes learned early in life as well as contemporary judgements on contemporary events. Socialization experiences influence the 'anti-system' outlook of the radical youth as well as the 'pro-system' behaviour of a large majority of ordinary citizens who have become conservative on account of the socialization process. Political socialization is a life-long process.

Herbert Hyman says that the study of political socialization should emphasize cognitive as well as emotional and motivational factors. He states : "Men are urged to certain ends but the political scene in which they act is perceived and given meaning. Some cognitive map accompanies their movement towards their end."

The psycho-analytical theory of socialisation emphasized only the unconscious and latent attitudes stressing the role of primary structures such as the family in the political "learning process." On the other hand, the early liberals and rationalists had emphasized the role of education in developing the 'civic spirit' of the nation. They considered the study of intellectual and social history and political theory as a necessary instrument of 'citizenship training'—their term for socialisation. Hyman has tried to balance both these interpretations of socialisation process.

Political socialisation may be manifest or latent. It is manifest when it relates to role, inputs and outputs of the political system directly. It is latent when it relates to the political processes through analogous roles etc. in the family or other such structures. Political socialisation may be specific or diffuse. It is specific in modern but diffuse in traditional or primitive systems. Similarly, the political socialization function in a modern political system is universalistic while in a traditional one, it is particularistic. In a modern system the citizen's role receives primacy over all the other particularistic roles but in a traditional system, kinship, village or caste may be given greater importance.

Finally, the political socialization function in a modern system is instrumental, while in a traditional one, it is affective. In a primitive political system, love of the polity is simple, direct and sentimental while in a modern one, it is based on rational policy preferences and strategies of influence. Depending upon the level and qualities of political socialisation, Edward Shils points out four types of political cultures:

(1) Parochial culture generally found in tribal, rural and preindustrial political systems;
(2) Subject culture generally found in totalitarian and authoritarian systems;
(3) Participatory culture found in all liberal-democratic systems; and
(4) Civic culture found in the Anglo-American political systems with vigorous voluntary group activity.

Actually, a political system may combine different types of political cultures e.g. the elite and masses or the people living in villages and those living in big cities may possess different political cultures. France and India may be cited as political systems having fragmented political cultures.

LIBERAL AND MARXIAN VIEWS OF POLITICS

Liberal View—Politics as Conciliation of Interests

The social process is a complex, multi-dimensional entity. Its four important dimensions are psychological, cultural, economic and political. Since the constituents of the social process are largely conceptual, therefore, it is elusive to comprehend its nature and also the very constituents that participate in its composition.

The first dimension of social process is *psychological*. It consists of the personality structures of the individuals living in a particular society—

their actions, reactions and interactions in accordance with their personal opinions, ideas and belief-systems. Every social system is founded on a specific view of human nature and basic motivations of the conduct of men and women in a society. The character of men living in a tribal, a feudal, a capitalist or a socialist society is not identical. Thus man's psychology, itself a slow product of the socio-economic environment, also affects the social process in general and, thereby, the political system too.

The liberal view of politics is based on the assumption that human beings are basically egoistic and are guided by the motives of self-interest in their day-to-day life. Both Machiavelli and Hobbes declared that men were primarily selfish creatures engaged in promoting their private interest whether it was acquisition of power or honour or accumulation of wealth. The liberal credentials of both of them are somewhat doubtful despite Laski's claim in his *Rise of European Liberalism* that they are basically liberal thinkers. The view of man propounded by Machiavelli and Hobbes became the foundation of all subsequent liberal thinking on politics from Locke to Bentham. It undermined the traditional views inherited from the tribal or the feudal past which asserted the moral superiority of the community over individuals.

The second dimension of the social process is *cultural*. Every historical epoch has given rise to a specific cultural milieu of its own. For example, the tribal culture is dominated by magic and the feudal culture is dominated by religion. As Max Weber points out, the post-renaissance culture of modern Europe was both secular and rational. Both secularism and rationalism are distinguishing traits of the rising liberal society in the western countries during the seventeenth, eighteenth and nineteenth centuries. The new secular and rational culture undermined the authoritarian and dogmatic temper of the old traditional culture, which it replaced, and promoted a new libertarian and individualistic spirit in the social and political behaviour of men in all liberal and liberal-democratic societies. The emphasis now was on the activities of voluntary groups and creativity of individual minds for promoting the literary, artistic, scientific, philosophical and even religious aspirations of the people. The state was expected to create the external conditions of public peace and order so that the individuals either independently or in association with the like-minded members of the civic community were perfectly free to act as they pleased in the realm of art, literature, religion, science or industry.

The third dimension of the social process is *economic*. Every historical epoch has given rise to a specific mode of production depending upon innovations in the field of technology and the changes in the technological scene bring in a corresponding reshuffling of class relations. Liberalism is the slow product of the gradual transformation of a feudal-agrarian mode of production into a capitalist-industrial mode that characterizes the economic development of all advanced capitalist countries today.

Max Weber has argued that the protestant ethics and rational-legal culture of modern Europe gave rise to capitalism, which was, according to him, the application of rational principles to economic life and management of the economy. The state was expected to keep itself aloof from the productive, commercial and financial activities of individuals as well as autonomous economic corporations. Later, the state was allowed a restricted role on the condition that it limited its activities to co-ordination only and refrained from undue intervention in the pursuit of profits by private individuals and companies or capital-labour relations except when the strong arm was needed to suppress the class-struggles of the workers.

The fourth dimension of the social process is *political*. Though liberals speak of the interpenetration of the various dimensions of social process, yet unlike the Marxists, they ascribe a considerable autonomy to the political process. The liberal thinkers from Max Weber to Bernard Crick subscribe to the liberal view of political systems which aim at co-ordination and conciliation of diverse private interests of individuals and groups that compete for survival in every modern society based on a certain minimum level of industrialization. As pointed out earlier, David Easton, a liberal writer of the behaviourist school, has suggested that politics involves the authoritative allocation of values within a society, for the society as a whole, backed by the ultimate use of a monopoly of physical force. Karl Deutsch, giving another liberal definition of politics, says that politics is "more or less incomplete control of human behaviour through voluntary habits of compliance in combination with threats of probable enforcement."

The classical liberal view as stated by Bentham, Adam Smith and James Mill emphasized the individual as the basic unit in social behaviour and the state was required to promote the greatest good of the greatest number by permitting individuals to maximize their private good under conditions of *laissez-faire*. Later, John Stuart Mill and T. H. Green modified the liberal view of politics in the sense that they developed the concept of the common good which allowed the state to regulate distribution of private incomes in the interest of social justice, without, of course, interfering with the rights of private ownership of the means of production. The contemporary liberal view is exemplified in the writings of the pluralist liberals and one of them, Robert Dahl, considers the group led by its elite as the basic political unit and, therefore, politics is the competitive activity of the rival groups and elites for influencing the decision-making process in a political system.

This implies that controversy is an important element in the liberal definition of politics. As Stephen Wasby says: "Where there is politics, it is said, there is controversy; where there are issues, there is politics. Where no controversy exists, where no issues are being debated, politics does not exist. This controversy, it should be noted, is not limited to the activities of contending political parties, but includes other groupings and individuals, whether explicitly political or not." *(256:14)*, Peter Odegard believes that conflict *per se* was not political unless it was directed at something, particularly the control of matters external to those in conflict. In addition, he felt that, if political activity is to occur, there must be common agreement among the contending groups that adherence to certain rules alone will bring them success.

While the liberal view of politics does not deny the existence of cleavage and contradictions, it does argue that these conflicts can be satisfactorily resolved through a consensus brought about by the co-ordinating and conciliating functions of the political party, legislature and government. As Stephen Wasby puts it: "Consensus is necessary for conflict to occur; agreement on a number of values usually undergirds conflict about other values. Sometimes basics are agreed on and only specifics are the subject of argument, but there are other times when even basics become the area of clash." (*256:15*).

When this happens, the liberal polity is likely to break up and perish in a revolution or anarchy. The liberal view of politics can best be summarized in the following passage from Bernard Crick's book *In Defence of Politics*: "Now it is often thought that for this 'master science' to function, there must be already in existence some shared idea of a 'common good', some 'consensus' or *consensus juris*. But this common good is itself the process of practical reconciliation of the interests of the various 'sections', aggregates or groups which compose a state; it is not some external and intangible spiritual adhesive, or some allegedly objective 'general will' or 'public interest'. These are misleading and pretentious explanations of how a community holds together; worse, they can even be justifications for the sudden destruction of some elements in the community in favour of others—there is no right to obstruct the general will, it is said. But diverse groups hold together, firstly, because they have a common interest in sheer survival, and secondly, because they practise politics—not because they agree about 'fundamentals', or some such concept too vague, too personal, or too divine ever to do the job of politics for it. The moral consensus of a free state is not something mysteriously prior to or above politics: it is the activity (the civilizing activity) of politics itself." (*187:24*).

The liberal view of politics is quite compatible with conservatism, reformist liberalism and reformist socialism but totally incongruous with Marxism, fascism, totalitarian democracy of Rousseau, technocracy, bureaucracy and even nationalism as practised in most of the third world countries. Politics ought not be confused either with ideology or with administration or with tradition and *utopia*. It is a purposeful contest between alternative programmes without violating the rules of the constitutional game played inside all pluralist-democratic societies. The liberal view of politics fights shy of such political possibilities as class struggle, revolution and dictatorship. Bernard Crick would like to reserve the usage of the term politics to the bargaining process that goes on among competing groups in the advanced capitalist countries of the west and even in these countries, he thinks that non-political Conservatives, a-political Liberals and anti-political Socialists do not know how to practise the art of politics.

Bernard Crick mentions the following conditions, which are necessary for the realization of a stable liberal system of politics:

(a) a society which recognizes plurality of interest and a division of labour;

(b) a society which recognizes that individuals are more real than groups, and as real in this life as in any next;

(c) a society which provides representative institutions for its citizens;

(d) a society in which the ruling elite is not exclusive of penetration from other groups;

(e) a society in which government is deemed to be predominantly a secular activity;

(f) a society in which some social conflict is recognized as normal and is institutionalized;

(g) a society in which there are no extremes of wealth; this need not imply the impossibility of a classless society;

(h) a society in which there is economic growth, at least in the long run;

(i) a society which can normally defend itself, but which can control its own military, the 'man on horse-back';

(j) a society in which a distinction is recognized in law, custom and thought between 'public life' and 'private life';

(k) a society where there is a tradition of political speculation and political action;

(l) a society in which the governing elite has the will to act politically;

(m) a society in which there is no universal consensus beyond a pragmatic agreement to do things according to the rules of the political game. (*187* : *74*).

Marxist View—Politics as a Form of Class Struggle

Marx approaches the question of politics from the point of view of social change, which is a dialectical process—a movement determined by the mode of production constantly interacting with its superstructural elements such as politics, culture and human nature etc. 'On the most general level', the Marxist view of politics, asserts that the separation between the economic, political, cultural and psychological aspects of the social whole is arbitrary and artificial. The notion of 'economics' as free from 'politics' or *vice versa* is an ideological distortion. The correct thing is to speak of 'political economy', in which the economic and political elements are dialectically united and of which Marx said: "The specific economic form, in which unpaid surplus-labour is pumped out of direct producers, determines the relationship of rulers and ruled, as it grows directly out of production itself and, in turn, reacts upon it as a determined element....it is always the direct relationship of the owners of the conditions of production to the direct producers—a relation always naturally corresponding to a definite stage in the development of the methods of labour and thereby its social productivity—which reveals the innermost secret, the hidden basis of the entire social structure, and with it the political form of the relation of sovereignty and dependence, the corresponding specific form of the state." (*223* : *772*). It is aften argued that for Marx politics is a very 'determined' and 'conditioned' activity. It gives politics a mostly subsidiary, derivative and 'epiphenomenal' character. It turns Marxism into a theory of 'economic determinism' depriving politics of any meaningful autonomy.

The fact is that both Marx and Engels explicitly rejected any rigid and mechanistic notion of 'economic determination' of the social and political process. Engels called it a 'meaningless, senseless and abstract phrase'. Marx said that the same economic basis, because of innumerable and different empirical circumstances, natural environment, racial relations, external historical influences etc. will show infinite variations and gradations in practice, which can be identified only by an analysis of empirically given circumstances. These variations obviously include the political elements of the superstructure. 'Economic base' and 'political-ideological superstructure' should be interpreted in terms of a 'historical bloc', a phrase used by Gramsci. The different elements which characterize a particular 'bloc' will vary in their relative weight in accordance with the time, place, circumstances and human factors.

The notion of class conflict characterizes the core of the Marxist view of politics. As Marx himself admitted, the idea of social classes and class war was not invented by him but existed in bourgeois-liberal literature even earlier. In the liberal view of politics, the class contradictions are not flatly denied. But the liberal treats them as so many 'problems' to be peacefully resolved. The assumption is that class conflict can be controlled and 'managed' by the exercise of reason and goodwill which bring about a compromise between hostile and conflicting interests. In the liberal view of politics, the political process is a continuous process of bargaining and accommodation, on the basis of accepted procedures between the parties who have agreed to settle all their disputes without recourse to violence. The Marxist does not deny that this is a valid description of the nature of politics in a stable, expanding bourgeois society at a given moment in history. However, Marx insists that class struggle, which remains dormant for some time, erupts again in the open in a period of economic crisis.

While the liberal views conflict as a 'functional' and stabilizing factor, the Marxist views it as a disequilibrating and revolutionary element in the historical situation. As Ralph Miliband puts it: "The Marxist approach to conflict is different. It is not a matter of 'problems' to be 'solved' but a state of domination and subjection to be ended by a total transformation of the conditions which give rise to it. No doubt conflict may be attenuated, but only because the ruling class is able by one means or another—coercion, concessions, or persuasion—to prevent the subordinate classes from seeking emancipation. Ultimately, stability is not a matter of reason but of force. The antagonists are irreconcilable, and the notion of genuine harmony is a deception or a delusion, at least in relation to class societies." (*235 : 17*). In Marxist view of politics, conflict is inherent in the objective situation of the class system.

Marx says that society does not consist of individuals, but represents the sum of inter-relations, within which these individuals exist. A member of one class may not feel any sense of hostility towards the members of the other classes and there may even be some mobility among the classes. But classes remain irreconcilably divided whether conflict is existent or non-existent at a given moment and irrespective of the forms which this conflict may assume from time to time. Revolts and revolutions are only the most visible expressions of permanent alienation and conflict. They only show that the contradictions of the social system are reaching the breaking-point.

Domination is a central theme of the Marxist notion of politics but Marx did not regard it as inherent in the human condition. In the same way, conflict is also not a feature of human nature as such. Domination and conflict appear only in class societies and are based on specific, concrete elements of their modes of production. They are rooted in the process of appropriation of surplus value generated by the labour of the working-class. Class domination is not merely a fact but a continuous process by which the dominant class maintains and extends its capacity for the exploitation of the subordinate classes.

In Marxist view of politics, the focus always is on class struggle though other types of struggles are not ignored. The ethnic, religious and national conflicts do take place in history but the Marxist writers generally link them to class conflicts. The class struggles in which these classes are engaged occur within the territorial boundaries of the nation-state, and the role of the state in class struggle, therefore, acquires an increasing importance in the Marxist view of the political process. The class struggles within a particular nation can also be influenced by external forces. This has been happening throughout the history of world capitalism. With increasing decolonisation of the former empires, the foreign intervention has assumed the form of neo-colonial domination through economic and military pacts.

The Marxist notion of class struggle was originally a model derived from the experience of the advanced capitalist countries. With suitable modifications, it is quite relevant for understanding the politics of the developing countries of the third world as well. The development of these countries has been distorted by colonialism and external capitalist domination. The indigenous capitalist class in these countries is relatively weaker and consequently, the industrial proletariat is also less developed. In effect, the mass of the working population is of peasant character and the main arena of class conflict is to be found in the relations between the landlord and the peasant.

Some Marxists argue that politics in the Soviet Union and East European countries is also characterized by a class conflict between a state bourgeoisie, that controls the nationalized industries as well as the state apparatus on the one hand and the mass of the working people on the other. Ralph Miliband does not agree with this view and says: "Whether the people in these regimes who are at the top of the pyramid are called a class, an elite, a bureaucracy or whatever, it cannot be analysed in the terms which are used to analyse the 'ruling class' of either advanced capitalist societies or under-developed one." (*235 : 31*). Gramsci has suggested a new term 'hegemony' to describe the ideological leadership of the ruling class. He felt that the capitalist class ensures its domination over the working-class not only through the use of a repressive state apparatus but also through the activities of a loyal intelligentsia which provides the ideology justifying the privileged position of the ruling class in society. The ruling ideas of a historical epoch, as Marx said, are the ideas of its ruling class. Just as feudal ideas dominated the minds of the people during the Middle Ages, so bourgeois ideas dominate the consciousness of the masses in the modern capitalist society. The working-class must first develop its own ideology in order to wage a successful political battle against the capitalist class. Georg Lukacs talked of 'class consciousness' as the most important condition for the historical emergence of a 'class': only when it acquires 'class consciousness' it would be able to participate in a revolutionary class struggle for its own emancipation.

Irving Zeitling sums up the Marxian paradigm of political analysis and Marxist view of politics as follows:

1. Consider first the economic order and, within it, the sphere of production of the society in question. Beginning with a definite base line in time, observe the main changes taking place. Such questions should be asked—How does the new technology affect the level of production? Is unemployment rising or declining? To what extent is the change a nation-wide or merely local phenomenon?
2. Locate the main classes in the economic structure. Determine the role of each in the processes of production, distribution, and exchange. Also locate the various sub-classes or strata in the economic structure.
3. Determine the objective economic interests of the respective classes and strata by asking such questions—Do the direct producers own or control the tools and other means of production? If not, who does own and control them? Does there exist an economic surplus of material goods over and above the subsistence requirements of the producers? Who has the control of the surplus? How is it used and which classes are benefited the most directly from it?

4. Are class-members aware of their objective position in the economic structure and the extent to which it determines their life-chances? One indicator of this awareness is the conflict among the classes in the economic sphere. A better indicator of class consciousness is the degree to which it finds political expression.
5. What form does conflict take among the classes and/or within the classes?
6. What is the role of the lumpen proletariat? How does its existence affect other classes? Who exploits them for their political ends?
7. Where political parties exist, it is necessary to determine their relationship with the respective classes and to assess the degree in which the parties express the interests of the various classes.
8. Which parties are in power? What is their relationship to the respective classes? Who controls the military order, the police etc.?
9. What patterns, regularities or trends can be observed in the changes within and among the classes? Which classes are growing or diminishing numerically?
10. What is the relationship among the major institutional orders of society, e.g., the economic, political, military, legal, religious etc.? Which of these determine the direction and speed of change in the society? Where are the key decisions made for the society as a whole? What is the relationship between the economically dominant classes and political office-holders in the government?
11. How do the external relations of a society affect its development? Such problems as international relations should not be overlooked. Marx never treated a society as a closed system.
12. Locate the radical and revolutionary elements in the society i.e. those classes putting forward radical demands for change and possessing an objective interest in revolutionary change. What are their explicit political aims? Conversely which classes have a predominant interest in preserving the *status quo*?
13. What representation or power do the subordinate classes have in the government? What is the political programme of each party i.e. their declared political aims? Contrast this with actual policies and actions.
14. Are there any coalitions, economic or political, among the classes and parties? What trends can be observed in these alignments? Which are the radical and which are the conservative elements?

15. What is the role of the 'great man' or the charismatic leader in the society? How does the role of such a leader affect the position of social classes? How is this role determined by the nature of class struggles in the society?
16. What are some of the central ideological themes of the society? Whose interests do these themes tend to serve?
17. Consider the historical context of the society in question. For example, in studying the western capitalist society, generalizations based on the period from 1914 to 1946 which included two world wars and a prolonged economic depression, would be quite different from those based on the period of 1946 to 1976 devoid of any such obnoxious event.
18. The role of tradition should not be ignored. Does a revolutionary, military or any other kind of tradition prevail? As Marx said, "Men make their own history, but they do not make it under circumstances chosen by themselves, but under circumstances directly encountered, given and transmitted from the past. The tradition of all the dead generations weighs like a nightmare on the brain of the living."
19. Consider the size and role of the state bureaucracy. Which of its administrative functions are necessary for the society as a whole? Which functions directly benefit only certain classes?
20. What is the role of the legislative body of the government? Is it an effective body or suffers from the disease of what Marx called *parliamentary cretinism*? Is its legislation, designed to improve the conditions of the subordinate classes enforced? (*182 : 79*).

Thus the Marxian view of politics is based on such concepts as the mode of production, class struggle and revolutionary transformation of society. But the relationship between the socio-economic base and political and ideological super-structures is not mechanical but dialectical. Linkages between politics and economics or ideology and politics have to be explored concretely. The contradictions inherent in any given situation can be revealed only through a dialectical method of investigation.

The Interdisciplinary Approach

The interest in the politics of developing countries enjoined upon the political scientists the responsibility to think in terms of the interdisciplinary approach by integrating the thinking and research in politics with the inter-related fields of history, anthropology, sociology, psychology and economics. The political scientist should know how changes in values, family structures or class relations studied by the sociologist can influence the direction of legislative and administrative policies or even the nature of ideology professed by the political elite. The stability and legitimacy of a political system ultimately depends upon the capabilities of the economic system which sustains it and for this the political scientist has to look up to research in economics. The researches of the anthropologists and psychologists are useful for the political scientist in understanding the motivations of citizens in their political behaviour. As an illustration Lipset says: "Politics will be different in caste and non-caste societies. It will vary among systems which have different concepts of kinship ties, and the nature of class and status relationships in various traditional societies will affect the possibilities for acceptance of a legal rational political order." (*239 : 26*). Both the Marxist and liberal-functionalist thinkers emphasize the need for an interdisciplinary approach in the study of politics. While the Marxists consider economics as the key social science, the functionalists draw our attention to the relevance of sociology, psychology and anthropology for the study of politics.

Take the concept and precept of globalization advocated by neoliberals today. It is a multi-dimensional social process with its economic, political and cultural dimensions. It is a two-way process in which national capitals are forging an alliance with international capital and global capital is penetrating national domains cutting across state boundaries. The NATO, the so-called regional alliance of the Atlantic bloc has assumed an international dimension to crush all opposition to policing powers claimed by the only super-power left after the demise of the Soviet bloc. Globalization signifies economic domination by American, European and Japanese capital, military domination by the NATO led by the United States and cultural domination by the knowledge industry and mass media controlled by the advanced capitalist countries. Politics, both national and international, has thus become a multi-dimensional social process even more than in the past.

CHAPTER 3

HISTORY, POLITICAL THEORY AND IDEOLOGY

Political scientists once described the intimate relation between history and political theory in terms of the maxim 'history is past politics and politics present history'. Paul Sweezy, who is a Marxist, analysed current American politics in an essay entitled *The Present as History*. Traditional political theory, both liberal and Marxist, recognised the interdependence of the two disciplines and emphasized the relevance of the historical method in the study of political theories and ideologies. While Marxist writers still use their materialist conception of history in political analysis, liberal writers of the behaviouralist school have abandoned the historical approach as either useless or harmful characterising it as historicism. As David Easton says, historicism gives a deterministic view of social and political developments in terms of historical *laws*, for which there is no adequate empirical support.

Behaviouralism and History. During the first two decades for the twentieth century, political scientists encountered the identity crisis. To differentiate political science from the work of jurists, historians and sociologists constituted an important aspect of this identity crisis. With respect to history, the crisis was resolved through progressive abandonment of historical analysis of the development of political institutions in favour of an emphasis on the description and comparison of current institutions. The First World War brought a legitimacy crisis over the goals and justifications for the study of politics. The careful detailed knowledge of the historical evolution of legal and governmental institutions did not seem relevant for the radically transformed social and political world after the war. As Richard Jenson puts it, "History no longer was important, for the tragedy of war and the opportunity for reconstruction had erased the past and focused all attention on the future. True understanding of the irrationality of man and of the power of government action for good or evil emerged as the proper goals for the research work of political scientists. Casting about for a new intellectual paradigm to guide their discipline in the modern age, political scientists fastened upon science—science as the key to planning, and the science of psychology as the key both to research methodology and to the nature of human behaviour." (*217* : 3). Since the historians did not attempt to write about the recent past, the separation of history from behavioural political theory was brought about without any methodological crisis.

As behaviouralists turned to social psychology or sociology, they increasingly rejected history. The new orientation of political theory was wholly empirical and experimental. Merriam, Thurstone, Lasswell, Gosnell, Quincey Wright, Almond and David Truman adopted the new behavioural paradigm declaring the old historical descriptive paradigm as obsolete. In one aspect, Charles Merriam was willing to use history i.e. in the psychological analysis of the character and leadership qualities of representative American statesmen. Harold Lasswell planned a developmental analysis of the psychological history of the modern world from a Freudian viewpoint. He observes, "The attention of one, who wishes to analyze social relationships, must play back and forth continually between the events that have receded into history, and to the future events destined to become history". (*217 : 10*). Though Lasswell used historical examples and case histories extensively in his work *Politics : Who Gets What, When, How,* he suffered from his lack of historical training.

Non-historical behaviouralism finally became the dominant research style of political science after the Second World War. Only the traditionalists pleaded that human values could be extracted from the study of history which could make the study of politics more meaningful. The behaviouralists looked askance at history because of all the disciplines history was at once the closest and most 'unscientific', while they were determined to make their own study of government absolutely 'scientific'. Most of the behaviouralists did not use any data which was more than a quarter century old, and thus avoided confrontation with historical problems. V.O. Key and Karl Deutsch, however, used older historical data in their studies of American elections, political mobilisation and international transactions. Some behaviouralists admired the work of sociologists with a historical orientation such as Alexie de Tocqueville, Ostrogorski, Mosca, Weber, Barrington Moore, Talcott-Parsons and Seymour Lipset.

The general attitude of the behaviouralist is that history is not important for his research. As the bulk of behaviouralistic political research concerns case studies of contemporary events and institutions, it cannot make use of historical studies, which deal with much older historical events. The style of history books is such that it does not enable the political scientist to formulate meaningful hypotheses for his own research work. The political scientist painfully discovers that he has to be his own historian. Analytic history of the social, political or cultural structure of a given society may be more relevant to analytic political science. Behavioural approach is, however, looked with suspicion by the mainstream historians. Intellectual exchange between the two disciplines is hampered by differences of methodology and terminology. Behavioural political scientists will insist on the need for a precise and scientific vocabulary which will be criticised by the historian as an obscure and useless jargon.

Despite these difficulties, the disciplines of history and political science are coming closer in the study of social crises. Crane Brinton's *The Anatomy of Revolution* and Barrington Moore's *Social Origins of Dictatorship and Democracy* represent this convergence. Historians generally deal with long-run economic and demographic changes that upset the equilibrium established in an earlier period leading to imbalance in social norms and growth of dysfunctional activities. As political scientists do not study such long-run changes, they will have to acquaint themselves with the relevant studies of the historians. Secondly, historians look for socio-economic conflicts between ethnic, religious and other groups reflected in the struggles for political power. But the political scientists of the behavioural persuasion are surprisingly backward in asking questions about the nature of the ruling elite or the identity and character of the opposition. Lastly, the historians show interest in the trends in the intellectual climate of opinion, which includes ideologies and beliefs of the different groups in society. Before 1965, political scientists did not pay attention to ideologies except in the analysis of communist political systems. When they studied democracy, they confined their inquiries to the study of voting behaviour of the electorate. But recently, the political scientists have realized that ideologies are implicit in all political systems including liberal-democratic societies.

Behaviouralism and Ideology. Among the early behaviouralist writers, V.O. Key emphasized the study of ideology, which can be approached in four different ways. One may look at it as a popular expression of a specific political tradition, a more or less coherent body of views, beliefs and ideas shared by a group. Liberalism, Marxism, fascism, nationalism or anarchism are examples of ideologies. These ideologies prescribe significant values, may possess some degree of internal logical consistency and may recommend a program of action.

Another way of examining an ideology is to identify its determining factors such as its social basis or ethnic or religious affiliation. Karl Mannheim in *Ideology and Utopia* was concerned with the social determinants of the ideological preferences of individuals and groups. One might study how a person's role or position in society affects his beliefs and values. From this standpoint, ideology can be studied empirically.

A third way of examining an ideology is to look at the psychological needs it fulfils for individuals and groups. For individuals, ideologies help in realizing their 'ego ideal' by satisfying their 'need for affiliation' by participating in an association united by commonly shared values and principles. So ideology is a way of relating the self to society and the ego to the environment.

The fourth aspect of ideology links the rulers to the ruled. In this sense, ideology represents the basis of legitimacy or justification for the use of power. It establishes moral principles on the basis of which the ruling elite justifies its coercive authority. If the people question the justificatory principles, the legitimacy of the rule is threatened. The French Revolution and the Russian Revolution were occasioned by the lack of legitimacy of the earlier regimes as the rebellious groups had rejected the ideological beliefs and principles subscribed to by the ruling elites.

Thus the four different ways of studying ideology enable us to get several perspectives on the effects of ideology on political behaviour. One can compare ideologies as relatively coherent doctrines in terms of their different ethical and philosophical preferences. One can analyse specific connections between broad doctrinal beliefs and the interests of socio-economic groups which prefer them. The significance or the intensity of an ideology to individuals can be studied in terms of the need people feel to establish their identity in relation to others specially regarding religion or nationality. Lastly, the relation between legitimacy and ideology may guide us in the analysis of conflict behaviour which, in extreme situations, may even endanger the basic consensus about principles of the regime itself. David Apter observes: "All four systems of study affect how people perceive themselves and others, what they consider to be important, who or what they will or will not support, when they will join parties or movements, when they can be relied on to sacrifice, support, and give loyalty to a cause, the character and intensity of their prejudices, and so on. In these terms we cannot divide public opinion into the ideas of true believers and non-believers. All people—in one or more senses of the term *ideology* as used above—have an ideological construction by which they mould their beliefs, whether they are active or passive or apathetic." (*172 : 223*).

Ideology differs in several ways from public opinion in general. The two can be distinguished on the basis of support that is, whether the belief is limited to a group or broadly shared by the public. A specific ideology, like that of the communist parties in Italy, France or India, is adhered to by a particular political elite and group. Their problem is to universalize the ideology in the masses through propaganda, agitation and confrontation so that it can control public opinion enabling them to capture state power. In democracies, political elites generally hold competing ideologies with which they hope to win support from the electorate, but public opinion is only loosely connected to these. Competitive elites seek middle ground between ill-conceived populist notions bordering on prejudices and more ideologically coherent ideas. Behavioural political science is interested in studying interconnections between popular public opinion and ideologies advocated by the elites.

Ideological labels may be imprecise but they do indicate and underscore alternative or antagonistic views of society and polity. Catholicism and Protestantism or Hinduism and Islam have shaped political opinions and moulded political behaviour in the context of contending religious ideologies in early modern European society or contemporary South Asian society respectively. Liberalism, conservatism, socialism and communism are their secular equivalents performing similar functions. Ideologies may be independent of political parties but all parties use them as instruments to link the broad views of mass publics to the more specific interests of various elites. Ideologies add some elements of principle to interests. Voting behaviour does not depend merely on perception of simple self-interests, but on other ideologically defined principles of fairness or justice as well. Those, who regard poverty as the fault of the social system, tend to vote for a radical party but those, who consider it a just punishment for defects of the individual, are inclined to support a conservative party.

Despite some ambiguities, ideologies enable people to judge political happenings. They are capable of being studied by content analysis, or can be interpreted as a symbolic language that encodes clues as how we think and behave in the political sphere. Flags, patriotic songs and other emotional symbols are ideological signs requiring interpretation. Robert Putnam in *The Beliefs of Politicians* used such a combination of subjective and objective analysis to compare the ideological preferences and values of political leaders and activists in Italy and England. He divided characteristic styles of thought into categories: inductive or deductive, vague or explicit, generalized or particularized, and so forth. Then he graded the political styles of different countries according to questionnaire responses gathered from a sample of the politicians. He then connected stylistic factors to personality characteristics such as degree of authoritarianism, willingness to compromise etc. linking them further to views about conflict situations, decision-making and democracy. Putnam's behavioural analysis reveals some difficulties political scientists have to face in using ideology as an explanatory variable. Some ideological elements correlate with political behaviour but the simplistic notion that makes ideological belief a consequence of class or status affiliation remains unproved. If one wants to predict the orientation of a politician towards social conflict or his commitment to social equality, his status or class background may be quite relevant. But if one wants to predict his position on economic planning or European integration, his social background may be much less indicative of his preference.

Of course, an explicit and passionate ideology like Marxism is behaviourally more significant. To motivate action ideologically it is necessary to stimulate a common group consciousness. This is what Mao's ideology could do in the People's Republic of China. There is a strong utopian element in radicial ideologies which can channel the energy of their supporters for purposive political action. Where ideology is vague, loosely knit and based on common sense, it cannot ensure loyalty to a set of fixed aims or values. Common sense ideologies may have contradictory elements. David Apter says: "While most Americans believe passionately in individualism as a fundamental part of a liberal ideology, in practice, many are influenced by what neighbours, peers, and associates think. People are often afraid to assert their individuality for fear of being regarded as peculiar or even anti-American. Hence the most individualistic of societies, in terms of ideology, is behaviourally among the most conformist". (*172* : *245*).

Debates on the End of Ideology. After the Second World War some social scientists in the United States started advocating the 'end of ideology' theory which was subsequently supported by West European writers as well. The other terms indicating the same concept or phenomenon were 'deideologisation' and 'the twilight of the era of ideology'. Some other concepts to strengthen 'the end of ideology' theme were: post-capitalist era, stages of growth theory, post-industrial society and convergence between capitalism and socialism. Some writers talked of 'people's capitalism' or 'socialism with a human face' declaring elimination of ideological conflict as an accomplished fact.

The cold war character of the end of ideology theory was evident from the fact that the Congress for Cultural Freedom, an American-sponsored propagandist agency, took a leading part in organising a seminar of writers, politicians, journalists and academicians in 1956 at Milan to pronounce the death of ideology in advanced capitalist societies. While some of the delegates were conservatives and reactionaries at one end there were also liberals, radicals and social-democrats of all varieties and hues at the other. It may appear that a conference of this nature would have produced intense political debates and ideological hostility. In fact, nothing of this nature occurred. The delegates assembled there displayed full doctrinal unity. Raymond Aron said that the rightists and the leftists in West European politics were converging towards each other disclosing new similarities in their attitudes and beliefs. Edward Shils pronounced liberation of mankind from 'obsessional visions and fantasies' and 'the harassment of ideologists and zealots'.

S. M. Lipset developed the end of ideology theme in *Political Man—The Social Bases of Politics.* Raymond Aron wrote an article entitled *Industrial Society, Ideologies and Philosophy* and a book *The Opium of Intellectuals* to prove that ideological thinking was confined to an intelligentsia with little relevance for acutal party politics or electoral behaviour in liberal countries. Daniel Bell wrote *The End of Ideology: On the Exhaustion of Political Ideas in the Fifties* to prove that a democratic liberal consensus has been reached in the Western democratic countries which has made all ideological conflicts anachronistic. The conservatives no longer opposed state regulation to pronote welfare and the socialists no longer advocated indiscriminate nationalisation. S. M. Lipset, therefore, concluded: "The change in Western political life reflects the fact that the fundamental political problems of the industrial revolution have been solved: the workers have achieved industrial and political citizenship; the conservatives have accepted the welfare state; and the democratic left has recognised that an increase in overall state power carries with it more dangers to freedom than solutions to economic problems. This very triumph of the democratic social revolution in the West ends domestic politics for those intellectuals who must have ideologies or utopias to motivate them to political action". (*216 : 406*). Lipset, however, maintains that bridging of ideological cleavage leaves ample scope for party controversy in democracies.

Barrington Moore thinks that in the United States, with the exception of the Negro, it is difficult to identify any group that has any ideological motivation for confrontation with the governing elite. David Reisman thinks that the general increase of affluence will put an end to the Madisonian bases for political conflict in developed capitalist countries. Lipset feels that these scholars confuse the decline of ideology with the ending of the economic class system, which, according to him, has sustained democratic controversy. The evidence on the voting behaviour in the United

States and West European countries proves that many voters continue to vote for different parties in accordance with their class images and perceptions of the role of these parties.

The end of ideology theorists, it has been argued by the critics, fully expresses the need of the ruling class in a liberal capitalist society to find ways of denying historical inevitability and the objective necessity of reconstructing its social system on new socialist foundations. The end of ideology theory has been criticised by C. Wright Mills on the following grounds: (a) It was a kindergarten fact that any political reflection of possible public consequence was *ideological*. In this respect, the end of ideology theme stands, negatively, for an endeavour to withdraw oneself and one's work from political relevance. Positively, it is an ideology of political complacency which appears to be the only way now available for many social scientists to acquiesce in or to justify the established social structure. (b) So far as orienting theories of history and of society are concerned, the end of ideology theory advocates a *fetishism* of empiricism, where political partisanship masquerades as methodological objectivity. (c) So far as the historic agency of change is concerned, the end of ideology theory rests upon the identification of such agencies with existing institutions and piecemeal reforms, but never upon the search for agencies which could be used for a structural change of society. Moreover, the problem of agency is never posed. Instead, there is ceaseless talk of the need to be pragmatic, open and flexible. (d) So far as human and political ideas are concerned, the end of ideology stands for a denial of their relevance. Merely, to hold such ideas seriously is in this view utopian.

C. Wright Mills characterised the end of ideology theory as the self-image of self-selected circles of intellectuals in capitalist countries, which constituted a fraction of mankind. To speak in such terms, he said, of much of Asia, Africa, Latin America or the Soviet Bloc countries was quite ridiculous. Mills observed: 'End of ideology is a slogan of complacency, circulating among the prematurely middle-aged....In the final analysis, it also rests upon a disbelief in the shaping by men of their own futures—as history and as biography". (*241* : *183*). According to David Aiken, the vision of the end of ideology as an end to rhetoric and rhetoricians, especially of revolution, is a utopian fantasy. It is an evil fantasy because it would mean a virtual end to discourse, to communication, and to argument.

Dialectical Materialism and History

The materialist conception of history is based on the application of the dialectical materialist method to the study of social and political change. For Marx, it was not just an academic theory aimed at interpreting the world, but practical guide for changing the world through a social revolution. Historical materialism has a contemporary significance. It is applicable here and now for explaining the present condition of men and society. Maurice Cornforth observes: "It is precisely in this contemporary application that historical materialism demonstrates its scientific character. For, in the last analysis, the test of social science, as of all science, can lie only in its practical application. If historical materialism makes history into a science, this is because the materialist conception of history is not only a theory about how to interpret history but also a theory about how to make history, and therefore the basis for the practical policy of the revolutionary class which is maing history today". (*184* : *21*).

For Marx, social and political theory was the outcome of a historical analysis of events and processes. The first principles of the historical approach to the study of political processes are to be found in the classical works of Marx himself e.g. *The Class Struggles in France, The Eighteenth Brumaire of Louis Bonaparte, The Civil War in France* and *Revolution and Counter-Revolution in Germany.* Marx went beyond an analysis of class relations and their influence on politics, for he examined the role of various strata or sub-groups of the same class, the struggle of individual groups and finally the role of individuals, leaders and ideologues. Marx combined his historical analysis with a wealth of supporting empirical data and statistics in his monumental work *Das Kapital.* Since then, serious Marxist scholars and revolutionaries have never tried to delink political analysis from its roots in history. All Marxist theorists and political activists study the modern social revolutions, the rise and decline of capitalist societies, the formation of the socialist bloc of nations, the disintegration of colonial empires and the rise of new national states, class and national conflicts, changes in military technology etc. in their proper historical contexts.

Fyodor Burlatsky identifies three approaches in contemporary Soviet political analysis: (1) the methodology of historical materialism, (2) the methods of political theory and (3) sociological case study techniques. This differentiation corresponds to three levels of analysis: the general methodology elaborated by historical materialism, the constructs of middle-range political theory and the methods employed in the study of specific phenomena in political life. The materialist dialectics bases its analysis on the study of contradictions. Without isolating the opposing tendencies represented by opposing social forces, it is impossible to forecast radical changes in the existing political structures. Contradictions may be studied at the highest level encompassing the entire historical process in all its mutual and mediative connections or at the middle level analysing the function of the system in specific historical conditions or at the empirical level.

Within the general framework of historical materialism, Burlatsky enumerates the following methods used in the study of politics: (1) *factor theory* which studies the influence of culture, economics etc. on the political process; (2) *differential* analysis of social communities; (3) *structure-functional analysis* of political institutions; (4) *systems* analysis of large and small political structures; (5) *composite* analysis of political administration and social leadership; (6) *Communications* analysis of the interaction of the elements of the political process; (7) analysis of *the correlation* of forces as a factor in shaping international relations; (8) analysis of political *dynamics*; (9) *comparative* analysis of related or opposing political systems; and (10) the method of political planning. (*180 : 34*).

Recently, Alan Wolfe has applied Marxist historical approach to study the liberal-democratic state in its successive historical incarnations. In *The Limits of Legitimacy* he discusses political contradictions of contemporary capitalism. "The history of politics", Alan Wolfe says, "is the history of the tensions between liberal and democratic conceptions of the state". Since the rise of an industrial bourgeoisie, a series of solutions have attempted to resolve these tensions (a) the *Accumulative State,* a compromise between the new liberalism and the active hierarchical state of the old regime; (b) the *Harmonious State,* the first capitalist theory of legitimation based on class harmony; (c) the *Expansionist State,* resolution of conflict between capitalism and democracy through imperialist expansion; (d) the *Franchise State,* attempt to solve class conflicts by granting public power to private agencies; (e) the *Dual State,* two faces of the same state, one responsible for accumulation and the other for legitimation; and (f) the *Transnational State,* attempt to transcend the national-state but not as far as a new world order. The late capitalist state finds itself trapped in its own contradictions. The major political struggles of the late capitalist period will "involve conceptions of the political world as much as concrete benefits". Karl Popper would, of course, dismiss the relevance of Marxist historical analysis attempted by Alan Wolfe as another example of economic historicism. But the author of *The Limits of Legitimacy* is not a determinist. He does not predict "the winners of the contest between liberal and democratic conceptions", though he forecasts that the battle for democrocy will be bitterly fought in the immediate future. (*258 : 9*).

Marxist Theory of Ideology. There is a radical difference between de Tracy's and Marx's use of the term ideology. But Plamenatz, Lichtheim and Richard Cox suggest that both of them had the same notion of ideology in their mind. Marx has merely refined the concept. Drucker regards this view as absurd. He observes: "de Tracy is propagating his science, 'his ideology'. Marx is largely condemning a characteristic of most social-political thought. Both wish to complete Bacon's task of uncovering ideals, Both are, in rather different ways, children of the Enlightenment. But it is precisely from the Enlightenment perspective that the difference between the two is so patent. de Tracy's 'ideology' is the Enlightened replacement for the idols of the market-place; Marx's 'ideology' is the idol of the market-plact". (*194 : 14*).

It may be asked why Marx used de Tracy's term. He was thinking about the reason why much political thinking goes astray. He was looking for an appropriate word which can describe this phenomenon. Ideology literally meant 'ideas' and 'logic'. Since one of Marx's objections to Hegel's thinking was that he paid greater attention to the logic of his ideas than to the practical, material world, the term ideology could suitably describe the concept he had in mind. When Marx regards a theory as ideological he is either commenting on the false consciousness, which has led the thinker to give a wrong interpretation of fact or suggesting the functional implications of theory such as serving the interest of a particular ruling class. In the first case, Marx wants to find out reasons for the theorist's misconception. In the second case, he wants to ascertain how the theory influences people's action. Thus, ideological thinking is either based on *false consciousness* or assumes the form of an *apology*. Sometimes, it can be a mixture of both these elements.

Marx's theory of ideology begins with his critique of Feuerbach's theory of religion. Religious dogmas, according to both these thinkers, are illusions. Marx applied Feuerbach's critique to all forms of thought, including political and economic thought. In the *Theses on Feuerbach* Marx presented a rough outline of his notion of ideology. Marx said that contemporary German philosophy centred on the state and not on property which was the real basis of society. This philosophy was by its nature mere *ideology*. It analyzed the various entities which made up the state but ignored or minimized the analysis of property relations. Marx has argued both in *The Holy Family* and *The German Ideology* that Hegel had transformed all objective class struggles into pure struggles of thought. Against this type of inversion, a feature of ideology, Marx set his scientific study of the technique and relations of production. (*238* : *26*).

The theory of false consciousness is Marx's explanation of the errors of previous social thinkers like Hegel and Proudhon. It also provided him with an explanation of how societies are ruled by a dominant class. The false consciousness of a ruling class, its ideology, guides it according to the direction of its own particular interest. The ideology of the bourgeoisie serves the economic and political needs of the capitalist class. On the whole the ideas which tend to justify and further the aims of the ruling class are also the prevailing ideas of that age. The ruling class controls all the products of property, material as well as ideological. Classical political economy developed by Adam Smith and Ricardo told the bourgeoisie how to expand its capital, increase production and earn more profits. This theory was unexceptionable, until the economic and social system guided by this ideology stopped expanding. At this stage, bourgeois ideology and the forms of material production came into conflict. At this stage, bourgeois ideology assumes the character of an apology. (*238* : *59*).

Marx praises those bourgeois thinkers, who have made scientific advances, particularly Adam Smith and Ricardo. Their thought was ideological in the sense of representing a false consciousness of the social reality. In Malthus, the spirit of inquiry was replaced by the evil intent and rhetoric of apology. Marx called Malthus a vulgar bourgeois economist, a deceiver of the working class and a plagiarist in the service of the reactionary ruling class. Thus Marx treated Hegelian philosophy, Proudhon's socialism and English political economy as examples of false consciousness but not of apology. Obviously, they deserved his respect as honest scholars, though they were in cognitive error. On the other hand, Burke and Malthus deserved his contempt because they were conscious and vulgar apologists of the bourgeois cause and the "hired prize-fighters" of the capitalist class. As Marx puts, it : "From the time of the conquest of political power by the bourgeoisie in France and England, the class struggle, practically as well as theoretically, took on more and more outspoken and threatening forms. It sounded the death knell of scientific bourgeois economy. . . . In place of disinterested inquiries, there were hired prize-fighters; in place of genuine scientific research, the bad conscience and the evil intent of the apologetic." (194:29).

As the new class conflict intensified, the capitalist class changed its attitude towards the state. Earlier the state was viewed with distrust. Now it became a useful instrument of class struggle with the proletariat. The capitalist class in power did not demand honest scientific criticism from its scholars any more. It became interested in 'apologetic' from its ideologists. Bourgeois thinkers can easily be divided into two groups : pre-revolutionary falsely conscious theorists and post-revolutionary apologists. Bentham occupies a curious position in Marx's thought. He is at once the archetypal bourgeois theorist and the worst of bourgeois apologists.

Karl Mannheim was impressed by Marx's theory of ideology as false conseiousness but he charges Marxist theory too of being biased in the same manner. Mannheim in fact believed that all social theories were environmentally determined and, therefore, possessed an ideological content. Drucker goes a step further accusing Marx of using the same style of scholarship which, he thought, the bourgeois apologists were using in their writings mixing propaganda with serious political analysis.

Marx, of course, described his theory as a philosophy which will emancipate the proletariat from capitalist oppression and exploitation. It was left to Lenin and other Marxists in general to explain what role 'ideology' could play in the revolutionary struggle of the working class. Obviously, ideology in the sense of 'false consciousness' could play no part in that struggle. The Communists visualize themselves as harbingers of true consciousness to the proletariat. But what of ideology as apology or creed ? Some Marxists such as Gramsci,. Lukacs and Mao Tse-tung have not shrunk from the use of the term 'ideology' in relation to Marxist theory. Gramsci and Lukacs have even argued for the need of an *ideological hegemony* of the proletariat in the revolutionary struggle against the political and ideological domination of the capitalist class.

Lenin, on many occasions, used the term ideology in the neutral sense without insisting that it ought to imply either apology or false consciousness. He said, "Since there can be no talk of an independent ideology formulated by the working classes themselves, in the process of their movement, the only choice is either bourgeois or socialist ideology. There is no middle course (for mankind has not created a 'third' ideology), and, moreover in a society torn by class antagonisms, there can never be a non-class or above-class ideology. Hence to belittle the socialist ideology in any way, to turn aside from it in the slightest degree, means to strengthen bourgeois ideology". (*194* : *103*). In calling Marxism an ideology, political activists like Lenin,

Gramsci and Mao Zedong emphasize its functional aspects in the clas struggle and revolution. Philosophical Marxists like Marcuse and Lichtheim persist in laying stress on the false consciousness aspects of Marx's theory of ideology.

C. B. Macpherson defines ideology as any more or less systematic set of ideas about man's place in nature, in society, and in history, which can elicit the commitment of significant numbers of people to political change. This does not exclude a set of ideas essentially concerned with merely a nation or a class, if it relates the place and needs of that section of humanity to the place of man in general. Ideologies contain, in varying proportions, elements of explanation of fact and of history, justification of demands, and belief in the ultimate truth or rightness of their cause. They are less precise and less systematic than political theories but they are necessary to any effective political movement and to any revolution. An ideology performs the triple function of simplifying, demanding and justifying. Political theory may interpret history, but ideologies shape it. (*185:301*).

This was the question which Gramsci posed when he spoke the hegemony of the dominant classes in civil society, by which is meant their ideological predominance over the subordinate classes. Marx's answer to this question was that the ideas of the ruling class are in every epoch the ruling ideas of that society. The specific ideological content of political socialization in capitalist democracies is "to faster acceptance of a *capitalist* social order and of its values, an adaptation to its requirements, a rejection of alternatives to it; in short ...... a process of massive indoctrination. " (*236* : *164*). "The striking characteristic of our contemporary ideological climate is that the 'dissident groups', labour, government, or academics, *all seek to accommodate their proposals for social change to the limits of adaptability of the prevailing business order.*" (*236* : *192*).

CHAPTER 4

THE NATURE OF THE STATE

The State is the most universal and most powerful of all social institutions. Wherever human beings have lived together for any length of time, there we find organization and authority. And where we find organization and authority, there we have the nucleus of the State.

As the Greek writers have taught us to think, the State is both a natural and a necessary institution. The State is natural in the sense that it has arisen out of the primary instincts of man and is a gradual growth. Aristotle declares that man by nature is a political being. To Aristotle, to live in the State and to be a man were identical, for whoever was not a member of the State or was unfit to be one was either a god or a beast; he was either above the State or below it. Modern writers sometimes speak of the political instinct of man. By that they mean that the State has its roots in the natural impulses of man and that it cannot be easily eradicated.

A great number and variety of definitions of the State have been attempted. We shall cite only some of the most satisfactory. Holland defines the State as a numerous assemblage of human beings, generally occupying a certain territory among whom the will of the majority or of an ascertainable class of persons is by the strength of such a majority made to prevail against any of their number who oppose it. Philimore, looking at the State from the point of view of international law, defines it as 'a people permanently occupying a fixed territory, bound together by common laws, habits, and customs into one body politic, exercising through the medium of an organized government independent sovereignty and control over all persons and things within its boundaries, capable of making war and peace and of entering into all international relaions with the communities of the globe'.

Among the definitions given by contemporary writers, those of Garner and MacIver deserve special mention.

Garner says: 'The State, as a concept of political science and public law, is a community of persons more or less numerous, permanently occupying a definite portion of territory, independent, or nearly so, of external control and possessing an organized government to which the great body of inhabitants render habitual obedience *(23:52)*.'

MacIver's definition which carries with it a pluralistic tinge is: 'The State is an association which, acting through law as promulgated by a government endowed to this end with coercive power, maintains within a community territorially demarcated the universal external conditions of social order *(55)*." This definition which, in many ways, is the best, emphasizes 'law', 'government', 'coercive power', 'communal unity', 'clearly marked territory', and 'the universal external conditions of social order'—elements which should enter into any sound view of the State.

DISTINCTION BETWEEN THE STATE, SOCIETY, GOVERNMENT, NATION AND NATIONALITY

1. The State and Society

The State is not identical with society.[1] Ernest Barker remarks that society and the State have the same moral purpose *(3:67)*. Consequently, they blend and borrow from one another. To the early Greek thinkers the State was indistinguishable from society. This identification of the State with society is to be explained by the peculiar circumstance that prevailed in the Greek city-state. The city-state was small in size and compact in population. The citizens knew one another personally and met together in common assemblies to pass laws and choose magistrates. They were knit together by common interests.

Whatever justification the Greeks may have had for the identification of the State with society, we, today, have no such justification. Interpreted strictly, the State is a political organization. It is society politically organized. Society is both broader and narrower than the State. It may be used to describe the whole community of mankind just as much as a small social group of a village. In its broader sense, it transcends the individual state and national boundaries; *e.g.*, the Islamic Society and the Free Masón Brotherhood.

The State is a part of society but is not a form of society. It is more than a number of loosely connected individuals who happen to live togehter. It is a number of people associated politically, organized under and through some form of Government, occupying a definite portion of the earth's surface. Society exercises authority largely through customs. The State exercises authority through laws enacted and enforced by Government. The State is the only instrument which can legitimately use force. Society, on the other hand, can use only moral persuasion or influence and social ostracism or expulsion. It cannot imprison a man for the violation of its requirements. To use the language of E. Barker, the area of society is voluntary cooperation, its energy that of goodwill, its method that of elasticity; while the area of the State is rather than of mechanical action, its energy force, its method rigidity. In the words of MacIver, 'the State is a structure not coeval and coextensive with society but built within it as a determinate order for the attainment of specific ends *(55:40)*'. The importance of the State to society is clearly brought out by E. Barker when he says, 'Society is held together by the State; and if it were not thus held together, it could not exist

1. **Prof. MacIver rightly says**: To identify the social with the political is to be guilty of the grossest of all confusions, "which completely bars any understanding of either society or the State." (55 : 4-5).

(*3:118-19*)'. Society may be compared to the many planks which comprise a wooden barrel, and the State to the iron band which goes around them holding them together in their proper places.

Prof. Barker in his book, *Principles of Social and Political Theory,* clearly brings out the difference between the State and society under three headings: (1) purpose or function, (2) organization and structure, and (3) method. From the point of view of purpose, the State is a legal association which acts for the single purpose of making and enforcing a permanent system of law and order. But society, comprising as it does, a plurality of associations, acts for a variety of purposes other than the legal purpose. These varied purposes are intellectual, moral, religious, economic, aesthetic, and recreational. The membership of the State and society may be the same. But they differ as regards purpose. "The State exists for one great, but single purpose; society exists for a number of purposes, some great and some small, but all, in their aggregate, deep as well as broad. (*87:42*)."

From the point of view of organization, the State is a single organization—legal, whereas society comprises within itself many organizations.

As regards method, as pointed out above, the State employs the method of coercion or compulsion; society employs the method of voluntary action. The purposes for which society exists, make the persuasive methods necessary; and the multiplicity of its organization gives ample opportunity to the members to relinquish one association and join another in case coercion is ever attempted.

Even though in theory we say that society depends mostly on persuasion, at times, it can be harsh tyrant. Witness, for example, the tyranny exercised by customs and fashions even in civilized societies.

A term which is becoming even more common and popular than society is "community". It suggests a group of people even more closely knit together than a society willing to help each other, and even die for one another when necessity arises.

J. Maritain writes: "A community is more of a work of nature and more nearly related to the biological, a society is more of a work of reason and more nearly related to the intellectual and spiritual properties of man". (*141:2*).

2. The State and Government

In our ordinary conversation we use the two terms interchangeably. Yet a moment's reflection is enough to show that they are not one and the same. Government is the instrument of the State. "The State itself is an ideal person, intangible, invisible, immutable. The government is an agent and within the sphere of the agency, a perfect representative, but outside of that it is a lawless usurpation."[2] In the words of Rousseau, government is

---

2. The Supreme Court of th U.S. in the case of Poindexter Vs. Green Show (114 U.S. 270).

'a living tool'. It is the practical organization of the State through which the will of the State is 'formulated, expressed and realized'. The ends and purposes of the State are executed through the instrumentality of the government. Without government the State has no existence. The State is largely an abstraction, but government is concrete. The State is permanent and fixed, while government is transitory. Changes in the form of government do not mean changes in the continuity of the State.

The authority of the government is not original. It is derived from the State. The functions of any government are executive, legislative, and judicial. Government is an expression of the genius of a people.

3. The State, Nation and Nationality

In political science these terms have often been used as synonymous terms. Even today political thinkers in general do not make a careful distinction between 'nation' and 'nationality'. For the sake of clarity of meaning and precision in the use of words, it is wise to employ these terms to describe distinct things. The State, as we have already seen, is a political organization. It may or may not be coexistent with nationality. Where a State is exclusively composed (or nearly so) of one nationality we get a nation State. But where we have a State which consists of more than one nationality, or where a nationality is spread over several states, the State and nation do not coincide. Nation means a self-governing nationality. Or, as Gilchrist puts it, a nation equals State plus nationality. The same writer goes on to say that the term nation today has acquired a definitely political meaning. 'It stands for the unity of the people organized in one State and acting spontaneously as a unity'. Nationality is primarily a cultural and ethical term. It is a spiritual sentiment or principle. Factors which make a people a nationality are geographical unity, common racial stock, common culture, common language, religion, customs and traditions, common history, common economic interests and political associations, common hopes and aspirations, and the like. It is not necessary that every one of these factors should be present in order that a people may become a nationality. Still without at least some of these factors nationality is unimaginable. On the political side, nationality may be defined as the disposition to act together politically.

Since the early part of the nineteenth century, there has been a growing feeling that every group of people who claim to be a nationality should be allowed to have an independent political organization. This movement received an impetus during World War I and expressed itself in such potent ideas as the 'self-determination of Nations', and, 'one nation one State.'[3]

The distinction that we have drawn between a 'nation' and a 'nationality' is not the one which is usually drawn. Gettell observes : 'Considerable confusion arises from the fact that publicists do not agree in their usage

---

3. The term nation is used here in the sense of nationality.

of the terms "nation" and "nationality". Some use the term "nation" to mean a population of ethnic unity, regardless of its political affiliation; others widen the term to mean a population having also political unity and identity of "nation" and "state". Some use the term "nationality" to signify the principle or characteristic that creates a nation. Others distinguish nation and nationality by using the former to mean a population of the same race, language and tradition inhabiting the same territory and constituting the larger part of its population and the latter to mean one of several distinct ethnic groups scattered over an area and forming but a comparatively small part of its population *(26:159)*'. Thus one may speak of the British nation and Welsh nationality.

ONE-SIDED OR FALSE VIEWS OF THE STATE

There is scarcely any term in political science which has given rise to more confused thinking than the primary term 'State'. Almost every writer of political science gives his own definition of the 'State', and there are hardly any two thinkers who agree on what they consider to be a satisfactory definition of the 'State'. MacIver in his *Modern State* sums up views of the state which are either narrow and one-sided or altogether false.

(1) According to writers like Oppenheimer, the author of *The State*, the State is essentially a class-structure, 'an organization of one class dominating over the other classes'. Or, as another writer puts it: "The State is the formal staff of the class which owns economic power". It is in line with the teaching of Karl Marx, according to whom the modern State is an agency for the exploitation of the poor by the rich. As a definition of the State, Oppenheimer's definition may be true of certain states at certain times, but we object to making it apply to all states at all times. It applies more to a diseased State than to a normal one. In a normal or well-ordered State, individual or class interests should be duly subordinated to the general interest or common good. However, the notion of the State as class-structure is today widely shared by many sociologists, political realists and socialist writers of different schools. Mosca, Weber, Sidney Webb, Laski, G. D. H. Cole and C. Wright Mills describe the state in terms of class relations.

(2) Some interpret the State as a power-system. They interpret it exclusively in terms of might. Machiavelli is the forerunner of this point of view. Many German writers such as Treitschke upheld the same view during World War I. We totally disagree with this view. Force is no doubt an essential part of the State, but it is not the foundation of the State. Might never makes anything right. It is right which can lend support to might. When used in the interest of right, might may be justifiable. T. H. Green aptly remarks, 'Will, not force, is the basis of the State'. Force is the distinguishing mark of the State. But the reason why we as enlightened citizens obey a well-ordered State is that we are conscious that in obeying such a State we obey the best in ourselves, we obey our own individual wills purged and purified of their selfishness. Obedience to the State is highly justifiable

when it arises out of the consciousness that, in obeying the will of the well-ordered State, one promotes a common good of which the individual good is an intrinsic part.

In criticizing the view that politics is 'the struggle for power', Hallowell rightly remarks that this view brings out the *fact* of power, but not the *purpose* for which it is exercised. The power of relationship, says he, is a two-way, and not simply a one-way, relationship.

Naked power or brute power can never justify a State. It is only when power is transformed into authority that it becomes a pillar of the State. Power becomes authority when it is well-organised, regularised, and is used for social ends. The rational transition is from force to power, and from power to authority. Many writers of the Behaviourist school prefer to discuss the State in terms of power relations.

(3) To thinkers like Grotius and Althusius the State is a welfare-system. One form of this theory is that the State is in the nature of a public utility company. We have no hesitation in saying that this is too narrow a view of the State. Promotion of public welfare is undoubtedly a very important duty of the State. But to identify the State with a public utility company, like the U.P. Electric Supply Company, is clearly a mistake. The State is not like a company at all. Membership in it is not voluntary. We are born members of the State. We cannot enter the State when we like and leave it when we like.

In India most people accept the 'Welfare State' as a praiseworthy end. It suggests the extension of State activity in several directions, particularly in the matter of social justice. Some businessmen and capitalists use the term as a cloak behind which to hide their individualistic propensities.

(4) There are a few writers whose number is happily diminishing today, to whom the State is in the nature of a mutual insurance society for purposes of mutual protection. Herbert Spencer was a staunch advocate of this theory. To him; the State is 'a joint stock protection company for mutual assurance'. We have already seen that the State cannot be compared to a company, much less can it be compared to an insurance company. Views like this do scant justice to the organic nature of the State, according to which, individual good and social good are intimately related and are not two clearly separable entities.

(5) Some interpret the State as entirely a legal construction. To them the State is a community 'organised for action under legal rules'. Once again, we would say that this is a very narrow view of the State. There is no doubt whatever that the legal aspect of the State is a very important aspect, but it is not the only aspect. The State guarantees to its citizens rights and it enforces duties. But that does not exhaust the nature or functions of the State. The legal view of the State ignores the higher life of the State altogether—the moral and spiritual.

(6) The individualists consider the State a necessary evil. They regard every action of the State as a subtraction from the freedom of the indivi-

dual. Hence, they say, the State is an evil, although it is rendered necessary by the selfishness and rapacity of man. If each individual were left to himself, they argue, he would seek his own self-aggrandizement at the expense of others and there would be no social peace and no social order. The State thus becomes a concession to human weakness. Spencer and even such an enlightened thinker as Bentham uphold this point of view. As for ourselves, we believe that it is a mistake to consider the State an evil, or even a necessary evil.

(7) Mild anarchists modify the position of the individualists to the extent of holding that the State is an evil, but that some day it will be unnecessary. They rely unduly upon the changeability of human nature, believing that with the increasing moral development of man the State will become less and less necessary and will eventually 'wither away'. The extreme anarchists such as those who subscribe to anarchistic communism hold that the State is an unmitigated evil, and that, therefore, the sooner we get rid of it the better it will be for the moral growth of man. While there is much that is appealing in the anarchist position, we must admit that it does scant justice to the fact that the State has its roots deeply embedded in human nature.

(8) Some modern writers prefer to regard the State as one in the order of 'corporations'. This is the pluralistic point of view in general which fortunately is practically dead today.[4] According to this view, the State is to be reduced to a position of equality with other permanent groups such as the family, the church, the trade union, the social club, etc., which cater to our varied interests. We realize that the time has come for us to recognize that the various permanent groups within society have a definite and distinct place to fill in the life of man and that, in order to do this satisfactorily, they should have as large a degree of internal autonomy as possible. Nevertheless, we need a superior organization to adjust relationships, and to keep the various subordinate orgnizations in their proper places. That organization is the State.

(9) The modern totalitarian view of the State regards the whole life of the individual as coming within the jurisdiction of the State. There is no part of man's life which he can call his own. If he lives, he lives for the State, and if he dies, he dies for the State. Mussolini stated the totalitarian view in the striking words: 'All within the State, none outside the State, none against the State.' The motto which he placed before the youth of his country was : 'To believe, to obey, to fight'.

The totalitarian view means regimentation of the life of the individual. It is a wholesale denial of the worth and dignity of human personality, leading to a system in which the individual becomes a cog in the wheel of the State.

---

4. Lipson writes : "The only genuine pluralist now left is the anarchist."

A POSITIVE STATEMENT OF THE STATE

1. Priority of the State

The State is the highest form of human association. Without it man's life is incomplete. It provides the environment for the self-realization and self-development of the individual. The State is thus prior to the individual. Men naturally tend to associate with each other. To paraphrase Aristotle, it is by the completion of civil society that man is the most excellent of all living beings. Without law and justice man would be the worst of beings. Only in the State does the individual really become a man. Without the State he might be potentially a man, but would be actually a brute.

2. The State as Will and Mind

Thus the State, as an idea, is prior to man. This does not mean that the end of the State is something apart from, or contrary to the end of the individual. Properly understood, the end of both is the same, *viz.*, the development of human personality. As Lord puts it, the State is an essentially necessary aspect of, or element in, the individual's own will. It is partly an external organization fulfilling the most universal and permanent needs of human personality and partly the individual nimself in a social capacity. It is the extension and completion of the moral and rational will of the individual. It is a rational organization of the various interests and purposes of the individual.

4. The State as Force

Physical coercion is an indispensable element in the constitution of the State. In the last analysis the State must have power to coerce the unsociable and recalcitrant will. Force, as used in this connection, does not mean mere physical or brute force. It means force *plus* reason, which unitedly means authority.

4. The Uniqueness of the State

The State is the one organization that represents the whole community. None of the other associations—social, religious, political, economic, educational—can include the whole of the individual. In the striking words of Miss Follett. 'The State cannot be composed of groups because no groups, nor any number of groups can contain the whole of me and the ideal State demands the whole of me. Again, the true State must gather up every interest within itself. It must take over many loyalties and find how it can make them one. I have all these different allegiances. I should indeed lead a divided and, therefore, uninteresting life if I could not unify them.'

5. The State as an Adjuster of Relationships

A corollary which follows from the above view of the State is that we require a supreme organization, *viz.*, the State to adjust the 'outstanding external relationships of man in society' (55). Life becomes a chaos without the State. It is the State which reconciles differenecs and gives unity and meaning to the many-sided life of man. In a complex and complicated world where there is an evergrowing conflict of loyalties, there is an urgent and increasing need for the State as an adjuster of relationships.

6. The State and Universal Interests

The State can concern itself only with those interests of man which can reasonably be regarded as universal. It cannot undertake the promotion of the sectional interests of its members. For this latter purpose, we have such organizations as the family, the church, the trade union and the cultural organization. As Garner puts it, while the purpose of a voluntary association is limited to the pursuit of one, or at the most, a few particular interests, the State is charged with the care of general rather than particular interests *(23:63)*.

7. The State and Morality

Finally, the State can regulate only the outer aspects of conduct. It cannot take motives into account, since they are altogether of an inner character. Thus gratitude to one's parents which is to be spontaneous if it is to be of any value at all cannot be enforced by State action.

The State may consider intentions, but motives fall outside its scope. T. H. Green rightly says: 'The only acts which it (the State) ought to *enjoin* or *forbid* are those of which the doing or not doing, *from whatever motive,* is necessary to the moral end of society' *(29)*. In simple language, it means that the State ought to undertake only those actions which are so absolutely indispensable to the good life of society that in enforcing them it can take the risk that some people will perform, or refrain from them, from a low and unworthy motive.

To sum up the discussion, the State is not an end in itself. It is a means by which the collective needs of man can best be secured in an orderly and just manner. Without the State, the individual sinks into insignificance. It is the State which holds the social order together. By a judicious use of reason and compulsion, persuasiveness and authority, it can promote the true well-being of society of which every individual is an intrinsic part. The State has no right to crush or hinder the individuality of persons. Nor has it a justification for existence so long as are absent the minimum conditions necessary for the good life of every individual.

ESSENTIAL ELEMENTS OF THE STATE

The essential elements of the State are population, territory, sovereignty, and government.

1. Population

It is obvious there can be no State unless people live together an associated life. The question relating to number of persons necessary to constitute a State is only of theoretical interest, although ancient writers laid much stress on it. Plato in his *Laws* fixed the number of citizens for an ideal State at 5,040. Aristotle considered 100,000 too many. In relatively recent times, Rousseau, who was an ardent admirer of the Greek city-state life, wanted to revive the ancient city-state with a compact population. According to him 10,000 would be an ideal number. Modern states vary in size and population as widely as Russia, China, and the U.S.A. on the one hand, and Monaco and San Marino on the other, the latter of which has an area of only 38 square miles. The Vatican City under the Pope, constituted in 1929, covers 109 acres in the heart of Rome. Iceland has meagre population of 132,000.

From the legal point of view, population as an element of the State includes both those who rule and those who are ruled. The people of a State possess a dual character. In the capacity of those who have a share in framing the will of the State, they are citizens, and in the capacity of those who obey the will thus formed they are subjects. This distinction we owe to Rousseau. As citizens, people possess rights and as subjects they have duties.

2. Territory

There can be little doubt that without fixed territory there can be no State. Yet not all political thinkers are absolutely agreed on it. The modern State undoubtedly requires a definite portion of earth's territory over which it can have undisputed authority. In contrast with the ancient State,. the modern State is essentially territorial in character. A nomadic people cannot be said to constitute a State, although they may have some form of political organization through common subjection to a leader or chief. In the words of Prof. Elliott : 'Territorial sovereignty or the superiority of the State over all within its boundaries and complete freedom from external control, has been a fundamental principle of the modern State life (19).'

A fixed territory is so much an essential factor of the modern State that no two separate and unrelated States can claim jurisdiction over the same area. The only apparent exception is that of the federal State, where two 'States' exercise authority over the same territory. Prof. Elliott says that it should be remembered that 'they are related States' and that 'the sphere of each is carefully determined by the provisions of the written constitution.'

As a rule, the territory of a State is contiguous. Yet there are exceptions. The far-away Alaska and the Hawaii have now been added to the American Union as the forty-ninth and the fiftieth states.

3. Sovereignty

Sovereignty and law are the two distinguishing characteristics of the State. By sovereignty we mean ultimate authority, an authority from which there can be no appeal. Associations other than the State may have population, territory, and even some form of compulsive organization, but they have no sovereignty. In the last resort, all individuals and groups of individuals with the State have to submit to the will of the State. This fact we express by the term internal sovereignty. In external relations, too, the modern State claims final authority. It may obey international conventions and understandings, but until world government becomes a reality there is no power on earth that can compel obedience of the State to a higher entity. This attribute of the State we express by the term external sovereignty. By virtue of its sovereign authority the modern State claims supremacy in internal matters and freedom from the control of external governments.

MacIver and many other modern writers dissent from this view. To MacIver, the State is an association, unique in its kind and of invaluable significance but still an association, like the rest *(55:ch.XII)*. We shall take up a criticism of this view in a later chapter.

4. Government

As seen already, government is the political organization of the State It is the instrumentality through which the sovereign will of the State finds concrete expression. If the ultimate sovereign in a democratic country is the people, the legislative sovereign is the government. A State without government is inconceivable, for the State wills and acts through the government. No particular form of government is essential. The form of government depends upon the nature of the State which in turn depends largely upon the political thought and character of people.

MacIver says that the State is the organization of which government is the administrative organ; and since the organization is greater than the government the State is the greater and more inclusive. To quote him directly: "A State has a constitution, a code of laws, a way of setting up its government. a body of citizens."

THE ORGANIC THEORY OF THE STATE

From the days of Plato down to the present day it has been the common stock-in-trade of political thinkers to compare society and, in turn, the State, to a living organism. Some have used analogy cautiously, while some have tried to apply it at every conceivable point, with the result that not a few among the most serious-minded writers on political science are inclined to dismiss the conception wholly as being useless, if not mischievous.

The nineteenth century political thought began with a reaction to the view that the State is an artificial creation of man. It tried to establish the truth that the State was no man-made, but a gradual, unconscious, and inevitable development of human nature. In this endeavour the familiar conception of the organic nature of society was revived and became a fundamental part of the thinking of German idealists especially Fichte, who belonged to this latter group of theorists, was the first to bring out clearly the interdependence of the individual and society. He held that the individual had no meaning and significance in and by himself, apart from society, but was an essential part of the social whole. In his own words: 'In the organic body each part constantly maintains the whole, and is in maintaining the whole thereby, itself maintained; just so stands the citizen in relation to the State.' Early idealists thus looked upon the State as a moral organism.

Herbert Spencer in the nineteenth century is the supreme example of a writer who works out to the minutest possible extent the parallel between an individual organism and social organism and yet misses the essential points of the comparison. He uses the organic analogy to prove his own preconceived notions of individualism. The analogy is used so very literally in an earlier essay that the up and down lines of a railway are compared to the arteries and veins of an animal.

Elements of Truth in the Organic Theory

Almost the first thing that needs to be said in the use of this conception is that an analogy is not the same as an argument. To establish a parallel between two objects is not necessarily to establish a logical connection between them. It is the failure to recognize this simple truth that accounts for the literal way in which the organic conception has been used by writers such as Bluntschli, Spencer, and Schaffle.

Society or the State is not an organism. It is *like* an organism in some respects and *unlike* an organism in other respects.

(1) Like a physical organism, it has in it the principle of life, growth, and development. We are not prepared to say with some writers that every State passes through youth, manhood, old age, decay, and death.

(2) In the social organism, just as much as in individual organism, there is present an inter-relation and inter-dependence of parts. The parts depend upon one another and upon the whole; the whole in turn depends upon the parts. The welfare of each is involved in the welfare of all. Individual good and social good are intimately related.

(3) Both the individual organism and the social organism embody the principle of differentiation of parts and the related principle of the distribution of functions according to fitness. Tools to the man who can use them is the underlying idea.

To press the analogy beyond the above general truths is sure to lead to confusion. The State is not an organism in the sense of being a physical structure.

Lipson brings out the limitations of the organic theory when he writes: "A human group (like the State) resembles an organism in that its members perform various functions and are interdependent. It differs from an organism in that it has no way of thinking, feeling, and acting as one". (*140:34*).

MacIver argues that the conception of the State as an organism is "a dangerous analogy". It has no proper place for the "autonomy, the initiative, the selfhood, the personality of the individual". It absorbs him totally in the great whole.

VALUE AND LIMITATIONS

To Gettell we owe the following points in summing up the value and limitations of the organic theory:

(1) The theory teaches the importance of the historical and evolutionary points of view.

(2) It insists upon the effects of the natural and social environment.

(3) It lays stress upon the inter-dependence of citizens and political institutions.

(4) It emphasizes the essential unity of social life and the intricate casual inter-relations of all its parts.

(5) It teaches that society is something more than an aggregate of individuals loosely thrown together without any unifying bond. It shows clearly that the members individually are in a peculiar sense dependent upon the whole and the whole in turn is conditioned upon the parts.

(6) It believes that men by nature are 'political beings' and that their universal tendency to social organization creates the State.

At the same time, many of the analogies between the State organism and the individual organism, while striking, are often far-fetched and contradictory.

(1) The will of the State is not always identical with the wills of its component units.

(2) In the individual organism, the laws of evolution are followed intuitionally. The growth of the State is in a large measure capable of conscious direction and control.

(3) The organic theory further runs the risk of magnifying the State as an end in itself, and of losing sight of the fact that the purpose of its existence is the well-being of its individual members. In other words, it is in danger of sacrificing the individual to soceity.

(4) The individual in the State does not exist solely to support and perpetuate the life of the whole. Each individual has to a large extent the shaping of his own life. He has a consciousness and a will of his own. All this is not true of the cells of the animal organism.

(5) A physical organism perishes and ceases to be living matter if the members are cut off. Such is not the case with a State, when a member separates himself from it.

In conclusion, it must be said that the organic theory, being of a flexible character, should be used with great caution. Analogy should not be pressed too far. To apply it at all points is certain to lead to illogical and even absurd results.

THE STATE ACCORDING TO LASKI AND MARX

Theory of State and Social Environment

Political philosophers have been reflecting upon the nature of the state and the processes of government from very early times. Confucius, Kautilya, Plato and Aristotle began a discussion of political affairs even before the commencement of the Christian era. Machiavelli, Hobbes, Locke, Rousseau, Hegel and Marx are some of the notable examples, who have tried to interpret the state in the modern age. Each political thinker has endeavoured to evolve his theory of the state in the light of his contemporary social experience.

The theory of Confucius is unintelligible except in the context of the social relationships prevailing in the ancient empire of China. Political ideas of Manu and Kautilya equally reflect the social conditions and caste prejudices of the ancient Hindus. Plato and Aristotle regarded the Greek city-states as the last word in political evolution and the latter justified the institution of slavery on account of its social expediency. Similarly, the theories of Machiavelli, Hobbes, Locke, Rousseau and Hegel have no meaning save in the context of the social environment in which they were propounded.

Marx, the founder of scientific socialism, was the first great thinker, who tried to build up his theory in the context of a world environment and his understanding enabled him to comprehend the social experience of millions of human beings of different classes in different countries. Among the many great political thinkers of history, he has exercised the greatest influence on Laski's political theory.

In England political theory has assumed three characteristic expressions during the preceding century. The early Victorian political thought was pre-eminently individualistic. Bentham, Adam Smith and Herbert Spencer were the prophets of English individualism. John Stuart Mill was also an individualist but he modified his outlook in his later years and showed a mild drift towards state interventionism. Political thought of the later Victorian period represented a swing towards idealist reaction and Green was its main exponent. The idealist reaction culminated in the philosophy of Bradley and Bosanquet, who reinterpreted Plato and Hegel for the contemporary generation of Englishmen.

Laski found that the *laissez-faire* philosophy of Mill and the collectivistic idealism of Bosanquet were equally unsuitable for the English society as it existed in the twentieth century. He regarded socialist professions of the Fabian Society as reformism, which could not solve the problems of the modern age. He was more radical in his socialist outlook than any of his English predecessors or contemporaries. His theory of the state is in effect a philosophical reconstruction of a cautious Marxist, who is prepared to revise Marxism in the light of local experience, which differs from country to country.

Laski's Theory of State

Laski's theory of the state is an unhappy blending of the political ideas of Mill, Maitland and Marx. The individualism of Mill, the pluralism of Maitland and the socialism of Marx have alike influenced his political thought. However, the influence of Mill and Maitland over his thought has gradually declined and has been replaced by that of Marx. It is significant that he did not become a convert either to the syndicalist philosophy of Sorel or to the guild-socialist theory of G.D.H. Cole, which was more in harmony with his early pluralistic ideas.

His break with the libertarian tradition of Mill is reflected in the rejection of the Fabian thesis of gradualism. When he realized the inadequacies of the pluralistic theory of the state as enunciated by him in the past, he openly acknowledged its limitations and imperfections. When he saw that the Fabian ideology of a libertarian socialism was unworkable, he unhesitatingly advocated the necessity of a thorough-going collectivistic state for a revolutionary refashioning of social relations.

James Sand's Criticism of Laski

Still the conversion of Laski to a revised form of Marxism was not a total surrender of his earlier presuppositions. This is evident from the criticism of James Sand, himself a true Marxist, of Laski's theory of the state. Laski attempted, he says, "to save the individual from the ravages of authority. Now he realizes that the problem is, not to put the State in its place, but to place the State in the hands of a new class. For one who in 1920 grew rhapsodical over the fact that French Socialism was founded upon Proudhon rather than Marx, this is truly a revolution. For one who has busied himself defending liberty and freedom, the discovery that there is only class liberty and class freedom, should mean a complete overhauling of his principles. He lets himself in for additional confusion by attempting to justify coercive power in terms of the measure of its satisfaction of maximum demand. This is arrant scholasticism. The justification for coercive power has always resided in itself. Only those who do not have it, or will not wield it when they have it, seek to justify it by anything but itself. Laski shrinks from the Thrasymachean view of justice as the will of the stronger because again he fails to ask the *ad hominem* question : who is the stronger ?"[5]

It shows that Laski's theory of the state remained "psychologically bourgeois" in the eyes of the Marxist commentators. It means that he could not abandon his early training in Mill's tradition and reverence for Maitland's jurisprudence. The inconsistencies in his outlook have arisen because he accepted the social goals of Marxism without surrendering his faith in the liberal method. This is the root cause of his pessimism and scepticism, which are conspicuous in the later formulations of his own doctrine. He ought to

5. Quoted by Professor G. Catlin in his ''Story of the Political Philosophers'', Chapter XX, p. 671, from James Sand's article in the ''Workers' Age'', August, 1935.

be a pessimist because he has accepted the goal of a classless socialist society without accepting the revolutionary method of achieving it and at the same time he is not sure that the constitutional means will finally bring about the desired social change.

Definition of the State.

The fundamental problem in all political inquiries is to determine the nature of the state. The state has now become the most important institution of the human community. Laski regards the state as the crowning point of the modern social structure and finds its special nature in its superiority over all other forms of human associations. Every state for him is a territorial society divisible into a government and its citizens. This government has the right and physical power to impose its legal imperatives on the body of citizens, whose normal obligation is to obey these commands.

This description of the state clearly shows that Laski has now discarded his pluralistic conception of the state. "In every state", he says, "there is a will which is legally pre-eminent over all other wills. It makes the final determinations of the society. It is, in the technical phrase, a sovereign will. It neither receives orders from any other will, nor can it finally alienate its authority. Such a will, for example, is that of the King in Parliament in Great Britain" (*48:12*). It clearly implies a return to Austinianism. In fact, Laski's acceptance of collectivism necessitated this change.

Even in "A Grammar of Politics", Laski had abandoned his pluralistic conception, when he said that every state in modern times claimed supremacy, within its territorial jurisdiction, over all other institutions and individuals. He called it "the final legal depository of the social will". The state provided the perspective of all social organisation established and functioning on its territory. It used its power to control all forms of human activity to the extent it desired. If it allowed a certain degree of autonomy and freedom for its citizens and their associations, this was done by its express permission. The state in England, he said, was gracious enough to allow the inter-marriage of cousins but prohibited the marriage of a brother with his sister which was a recognised royal prerogative in ancient Egypt. The state, therefore, was "the keystone of the social arch" which shaped and regulated the form and content of the life of all its citizens in its various aspects (*47:21*).

The State and Sovereignty

It is essentially a theory of the sovereign state conceived in Austinian terms. Laski draws a clear distinction between society and the state. He defines society as a group of human beings living together and working together for the satisfaction of their mutual wants which are primarily economic in charatcer. Theoretically, this society may embrace the entire humanity or it may be limited to a single nation on account of linguistic, cultural or political affinity. The State is merely an association within this society but it may be distinguished from all other associations by its possession of a supreme coercive power.

"This power", says Laski, "is called sovereignty and it is by the possession of sovereignty that the State is distinguished from all other forms of human associations. A municipality is a territorial society divided into government and subjects; so also may be a trade union or a church. But none of them possesses supreme coercive power. Each must normally subordinate its habits to those defined as legitimate by that supreme coercive power. Its will is, formally, an unchallenged will, since otherwise it could not be supreme. For the same reason, its will can suffer neither division nor alienation" (*50:21*). But the sovereign power of the State, as Laski would emphasize, is merely a description of its legal structure, which is valid strictly in the juridical realm. It has no ethical significance as attributed to it by the idealistic thinkers like Hegel or Bosanquet.

The State and Government

Just as there is a clear distinction between society and the State, there is, similarly, an important demarcating line between the State and government. Laski regards this distinction between the State and government as a fundamental axiom of political science. The government is the agent to carry out the objectives of the State. The coercive power resides in the State and the government uses it to carry out the aims of that power. The government is to be identified with the "mechanism of administration". But this distinction though quite valuable in political theory has very little importance in actual political behaviour. The State is an abstraction while the government is a concrete social reality. The State acts are really the acts of a particular government in power. Laws reflect the will of the State but they are lifeless if there is no government to enforce them. Political scientists say that the British State declared war on Germany on 3 September, 1939 but the fact was that the war was declared by the chief of the British government, who on that particular day was entitled to use the sovereign power of the British State. The State does not act, some persons who control its administration and formulate its policies act on its behalf.

Thus there is a functional identity between the State and its government despite their structural difference. The State is a wider term which includes the constitution, government and the people. But it is the government which alone provides a dynamic element to the State by operating its sovereign power. The constitution merely provides how that power is to be exercised by those who are legally competent to exercise it. The people are merely the objects over whom the sovereign power is exercised by the government on behalf of the State.

Sovereignty as Coercive Power of the State

As a realist Laski argues that sovereign power of the State, which is exercised through the agency of its government, means, in ultimate analysis, the right to use the armed forces of the State to suppress any opposition or rebellion which jeopardizes its existence. He points out that during every period of crisis in the development of the State, its survival depends upon its ability to dominate the adversaries of the regime by superior use of force. The basis of its sovereign power is the capacity to use the armed forces of the state to fight and suppress any challenge to its established authority. In every political society, the elements of conflict are inherent in its social structure and sovereignty is necessary to keep these hostilities in control. From this point of view the State means a method of organising "the public power of coercion" so that the will of its government prevails in all social antagonisms. It is a system of power which is outside and above the reach of the masses *(50:26)*. In this way the state is functionally a power organization and its armed forces are the instrument of enforcing its power. The heart of sovereignty lies in the armed forces of the nation.

Criticism of the Idealist View of State

Laski contrasts his realistic view of the State with the traditional ideal ist view of the State. While the idealist ignores the distinction between the State and Society and the State and government which are fused together into a single moral whole, Laski recognizes the fact that the State is only a factor, however important, within the social sphere and the government is merely an instrument of the State policy. He rejects the idealist conception of the general will as the basis of the State. The conception of the general will presupposes an inherent unity in the community and the possibility of purposive harmony between the conflicting claims of different classes and groups. It also presupposes that the government of the State, which is composed of fallible men, is capable of translating the general will of the community into actual administrative policies. Laski denies both of these assumptions.

In the first place, it is impossible to determine the general will out of the myriad wills of individuals and classes contending for supremacy in the community. Secondly, even if we accept for the sake of argument that such determination of the general will is possible, it is not at all certain that the State, which acts through the agency of a government composed of persons, who may be guided by their sectional interests, will truly translate its purposes into action. There is no explicit guarantee that the general will may not be distorted by those who are charged with giving expression to it.

Laski, therefore, concludes that the will of the State is, in fact, the will of a particular section in the society which is able to impose its decision upon the rest of the community by virtue of its possession of the political power in that community. "A working theory of the State", he says, "must, in fact, be conceived in administrative terms. Its will is the decision arrived at by a small number of men to whom is confided the legal power of making decisions" *(47:35)*. Thus a very large part of the citizens in every state has no real share in formulating the will of the state which is mostly the work of a small governing class of bureaucrats who are again guided by the sectional interests of the dominant economic class in the community (*131:152*).

Some vital facts emerge from Laski's analysis of the nature of the State. The State loses all its majesty and charm bestowed upon it by idealist writers. The individual need not approach the State in fear and trembling because it is no longer a moral demigod inspiring awe and reverence in its subjects. But the sovereign power of the State is restored not only in the traditional Austinian sense of a juridical formality but also in the Marxian sense which recognizes it as a factor of immense value in the struggle of warring classes for supremacy in the community. The state is defined as a power-system (*50:23*).

Though this power has always been exercised in the interests of a particular class, yet the ruling class never admits this fact and even seeks the justification of its policies in the common good. Aristotle justified the institution of slavery on the ground that it was beneficial both to slaves and their masters. The modern supporters of the institution of private property also justify it on the ground that it secures the general welfare of the community and every class is benefited by its retention in the existing form.

The Role of Popular Consent

Laski points out that though the basis of the state is force, yet the stability of a political system is maximized by obtaining consent of the governed in some way or the other. The emergence of representative institutions and the widening of franchise may be regarded as the best safeguards of its security as they have increased the social frontiers of its popularity, but even these have not basically altered the character of the state which remains an executive committee of the class that owns the means of production in a particular society.

Of course, the state system is not synonymous with the political system. The latter includes many institutions such as parties and pressure groups, giant corporations, Churches, the mass media. They wield considerable power which is integrated with the power included by the state elite of administrators, politicians, judges and military officers. The consensus between the political office-holders, the economically dominant class and the general mass of electorate is crucial. This is obtained through political socialization and ideological indoctrination.

CHAPTER 5

THE ORIGIN OF THE STATE

Various theories concerning the primary or pre-historical origin of the State have been propounded by historical and political writers. These theories are :

(1) The Divine Origin Theory;
(2) The Social Contract Theory;
(3) The Force Theory;
(4) The Patriarchal and Matriarchal Theories; and
(5) The Historical or Evolutionary Theory.

1. The Theory of Divine Origin

This is the oldest theory concerning the primary origin of the State. According to it, the State is established and governed by God himself or by some superhuman Power. God may rule the State directly or indirectly through some ruler who is regarded as the agent or viceregent or vicar of God. Such a State is known as a theocratic or God-ruled State. The Divine Origin or the theocratic conception is almost as old as the State itself and is found universally among early peoples. It is a well authenticated fact that early forms of political authority were believed to be connected with the unseen powers. The earliest rulers were a combination of priest and king or the magic man and king. According to MacIver, the magic man in early society was the priest and king all combined into one.

The chief exponents of the Divine Origin Theory in the early times were the Jews.

The theory of Divine Origin found some of its most earnest supporters among the early Church Fathers.

The teaching of the Old Testament and the Church Fathers profoundly influenced the mediaeval writers in the controversy between the Church and the empire. Some of these writers used the Divine Origin Theory to establish the supremacy of the Church over the State and others to establish the supremacy of the State over the Church.

The Protestant Reformation gave a great impetus to the Divine Origin Theory and to the related doctrine of passive obedience or non-resistance to governmental authority, although in religious matters it stood for individual liberty and the supremacy of individual conscience. The Divine Origin Theory more and more took the form of the theory of the Divine Right of Kings. This is particularly true of the sixteenth and seventeenth century England. The leading exponents of the latter doctrine were James I, the first Stuart king, and Sir Robert Filmer. Bousset in France elaborated this theory in supporting the despotism of Louis XIV, who proudly declared "I am the State".

The Divine Right of Kings

In his work called *The Law of Free Monarchies,* James I gives a clear exposition of this doctrine. He claims that the king has derived his authority directly from God. Therefore, he is above the people as well as above the law. He is subject to God and his conscience alone. He owes no legal obligation to the people. The only obligation that he has is a moral obligation to God to govern the people well. Kings make laws; laws do not make kings. The king 'is master over every person, having power over life and death.'

Even if the king be wicked, the subject has no right to rebel against him. To rebel against the king is to rebel against God Himself, for the king is God's chosen vassal.

To quote the forcible words of James I: 'Kings are justly called gods, for they exercise a manner of resemblance of divine power upon earth.' 'As it is atheism and blasphemy to dispute what God can do, so it is presumption and high contempt in a subject to dispute what a king cannot do or to say that a king cannot do this or that.' 'Kings are breathing images of God upon earth.'

The salient features of the doctrine of the Divine Right of Kings are:

(1) Monarchy is divinely ordained;
(2) Hereditary right is indefeasible;
(3) Kings are accountable to God alone; and
(4) Resistance to a lawful king is sin. (*G. P. Gooch*).

It is more than likely that even the supporters of this doctrine did not fully believe in all its extravagant claims. In supporting it, people failed to consider the danger of the king becoming a tyrant. Later, the theory was used against the growing political consciousness of the people and the rise of democratic ideas, and was made to support royal despotism. It was not until the end of the eighteenth century that it was rejected as unsound in theory and dangerous in practice. In countries like Austria, Germany, and Russia it lasted for a still longer time.

Today both the Divine Origin Theory and the Divine Right of Kings are without supporters among political thinkers. To refute them in great details is to flog a dead horse.

Some of the principal causes which brought about the decline of the theory are the rise of the contract theory, which rests political growth of authority on the idea of consent, the democracy which is opposed to absolutism, particularly royal absolutism and the secular outlook of the modern man which seeks, as far as possible, to separate religious and political issues.

As a doctrine of political philosophy, the Divine Origin Theory received its death blow at the hands of Grotius, Hobbes, and Locke. Yet the Divine Origin Theory had certain values, some of which are suggestive:

(1) At a time when man was emerging from semi-civilized conditions and was not accustomed to obedience to a secular authority or to a self-imposed law, the doctrine of the Divine origin of the State must have been a powerful factor in preserving order. It was a bulwark against anarchy and did much to strengthen the respect of man for person, property, and government.

(2) It may be interpreted to mean that the instinct for order and discipline is deep-seated in man and that it reveals itself in political organization.

2. The Social Contract Theory

I. Statement of the Theory. This theory holds that the State is the result of a deliberate and voluntary agreement on the part of primitive men emerging from a state of nature. It assumes that there was a period in human history when there was no State at all and no political law. This pre-civil or pre-political period is regarded by some writers as pre-social as well. In this state of nature the only law which governed human relations was the law of nature. Advocates of the Social Contract Theory are not agreed upon what exactly this law of nature was. The state of nature was either too idyllic to last long or too inconvenient and unbearable for man to put up with it. Hence men in this primitive state soon abandoned the state of nature and set up a political society through the instrumentality of a covenant. As a result of the covenant each man lost his natural liberty in part or in whole, and in its place he obtained the security and protection of the State provided by political law.

The contract is interpreted in various ways by its advocates. According to some, it is responsible for the institution of civil society alone, while others regard it in addition as an agreement between the rulers and their subjects, resulting in the institution of a particular government. The first type of contract is known as the social contract, the second is the political or governmental contract. The contracting parties of the original, or the social, contract are the individuals themselves, emerging from the State of nature agreeing with one another and with all. The parties to the second, or the governmental contract are the people in their corporate capacity on the one hand, and an agent or ruler on the other. A further difference which we find among the advocates of the Social Contract Theory is that while some regard it as an actual hitsorical fact, others consider it as a historical fiction which conveys a philosophical truth. An example of the former conception is found in Locke while Kant illustrates the latter conception. To Kant the contract is merely an 'idea of reason'. One other difference to be noted among the propounders of the theory is the varied use to which they put it. Hobbes uses it to justify royal absolutism; Locke to support constitutional government or limited monarchy; Rousseau to uphold the doctrine of popular sovereignty (*45:13*). On the whole, the theory has been used to justify the conception that governmental authority, if it is to be legitimate, must rest ultimately on the consent of the governed. The weight of its influence in general has been in the direction of safeguarding the rights and liberties of the people and of checking the arbitrariness of rulers. It has also engendered a general irreverence towards the State because of its assumption that the State is an artificial creation and that governmental authority is a restraint upon man's natural freedom.

II. Criticism of the Social Contract Theory. The Social Contract Theory has been attacked from three different angles, the historical, the legal, and the philosophical or rational.

In the words of Kranenburg, 'it employs too much deductive and too little inductive reasoning (*45:8*)'.

(a) **Historical :**

(1) The most obvious criticism that suggests itself to one is that the theory has no basis in fact. To assume that primitive men came together at some particular time and established a political society by means of a contract is to read history backwards. The idea too advanced for primitive man. No one has yet been able to give a single instance of a State coming into being as the result of a deliberate and voluntary agreement between individuals emerging from a state of nature.

(2) There have been historical examples of governmental or political contracts, but such contracts are contracts among people already living in the civil state. They do not by any means explain the historical origin of the State. They only define the rights and duties of the rulers and subjects. Governmental contract is a fact; social contract is a fiction.

(3) The theory assumes that primitive man was much of an individualist. It assumes that he was a free man who could enter into voluntary agreements with other free men. This is not what research into early times shows. Early law was more communal than individual. The individual was of little importance. The family was the unit. Property was held in common. Law took the form of customs. The individual had his prescribed place in society. In these circumstances the free contracting of individuals with one another, in so important a matter as the institution of the State, is an absurdity.

(b) Legal :

(1) Even if we assume for the sake of agrument that primitive man had advanced far enough in his social consciousness to enter into a contract, the fact remains that such a contract has no legal binding force whatever. A contract, in order to be valid, requires the force or sanction of the State. But for this contract there is no such sanction, for it precedes, and does not follow, the establishment of the State.

(2) Thus, if the original contract has no legal meaning and is invalid,

all subsequent contracts based upon it are equally invalid, and the rights derived from it have no legal foundation.

(3) A contract has binding effect upon only those who accept it voluntarily. But the social contract is supposed to bind generations of men who have had no say in the matter at all.

(c) **Philosophical :**

Philosophical objections to the Social Contract Theory are even more important than the historical and legal objections. As said already, several of the contract supporters admit that the contract notion is only a historical fiction and yet they use it in order to convey certain philosophical principles. The objections are—

(1) The theory assumes that the relation between the individual and the State is a voluntary one. This is a position which will not stand careful scrutiny. We are members of a state in the same way in which we are members of a family. The State is not an artificial creation of man. Membership in it is not voluntary. If the State were a voluntary organization like a company or firm, the individual would be at liberty to enter it or leave it at will. The obligations of the citizen to the State are not contractual at all. To use the oft-quoted and striking words of Edmund Burke : 'The State ought not to be considered as nothing better than a partnership agreement in a trade of pepper and coffee, calico or tobacco, or some other such low concern, to be taken up for a little temporary interest, and to be dissolved by the fancy of the parties.' If the State is a partnership at all, it is a partnership in a higher and more permanent sense.

(2) The entire conception of the state of nature and of the laws of nature is unsound. It assumes that whatever preceded the institution of the State is 'natural' and that whatever has followed it (including the institution of the State) is artificial. There is no warrant for dividing history into two parts with a hatchet, so to speak. Civilization is as natural today as was barbarism in the past. Man is a part of nature and the State is the highest expression of his nature. The State is a growth and not a manufacture.

Even if we grant that there was a State of nature governed by laws of nature, meaning thereby laws of inherent morality, the setting up of a State in such a situation is not a progressive step, but the opposite. To exchange laws of inward morality for the force of the State is a backward step.

Furthermore, if the state of nature is one in which a contract could be formed, it must have been a state where there was a consciousness of a common good, implying the ideas of social authority and individual obligation. But such a one, we claim, does not materially differ from a civil or political state. It is virtually, though not in name, a political state. The necessary elements constituting a political society are already present there.

(3) The Social Contract Theory implies a false notion of rights. T. H.

Green aptly remarks: 'The real flaw in the theory of contract is not that it is unhistorical, but that it implies the possibility of rights and obligations independently of society.' According to any sound view of rights, the basis of rights is *social recognition, i.e.*, recognition on the part of society of a common good of which the individual good is an intrinsic part.

III. Elements of Truth in the Theory. Although as a theory explaining the origin of the State or the right relations between man and man in society, the Social Contract Theory is defective and finds no support today, it contains certain elements of truth. If we are to understand the theory properly, as it was elaborated in the seventeenth and eighteenth centuries especially, we should know the practical aim which impelled its adherents to enunciate it, namely, to give a more satisfactory and human explanation of the fact of political authority and the duty of obedience rather than explanations based upon divine fiat. In the place of the Divine Right Theory which called upon subjects to render unquestioning obedience to the 'powers that be', the Social Contract Theory laid down the fundamental truth that obedience rested upon the consent of the governed and that the sovereign had no right to act arbitrarily. In working out this truth, the Social Contract Theory served as the basis for modern democracy. It emphasized 'the importance of the individual, the possibility of modifying political institutions by direct human effort, and the fact that ultimate political authority lies, at least potentially, in the people *(24:85)*.'

3. The Force Theory

According to this theory, the State is the result of superior physical force; it originates in the subjugation of the weaker by the stronger. It is natural to suppose that in primitive times the man of exceptional physical strength was able to overawe his fellowmen and to exercise some kind of authority over them.[1] The same is probably true also of superior tribes and clans in their relationships to other tribes and clans. On the basis of this supposition, advocates of the force theory contend that all States have come into being through physical coercion or compulsion.

In his book *The State*, Oppenheimer, who is a keen advocate of this theory, traces the origin of the State through various stages. Jenks, who is another prominent supporter of the theory, in his *History of Politics*, holds that there is not the slightest difficulty in proving that all political communities of the modern type owe their existence to successful warfare. According to this theory, it is war that begets the State. Advocates of the theory argue that what they regard to be fundamental features of modern political society—military allegiance and territorial character—are based on the relation between the war chief and his followers and on conquest which brings under the authority of a single ruler people of different countries and of different races.

---

1. Voltaire's aphorism is : '*The first king was a fortunate warrior*'.

Some writers use the term 'force' so very broadly as to include not only physical prowess but also power derived from intellectual and religious factors.

Like the Divine Origin and the Social Contract theories, this theory is advocated both as an explanation of the historical origin of the State and as a rational justification of the State to be; and like them, also, it is defective on both counts. In its practical form, it reduces itself to the position that government is the outcome of human aggression. Such a view is found in the earlier works of Herbert Spencer where he says, 'Government is the offspring of evil, bearing about it the marks of its parentage.' We admit that force must have been an important factor in the evolution of the State, but to regard it as the one and only factor is a clear mistake. Several other factors must have entered into the composition of early political societies. The State must have grown as much by voluntary amalgamation as by force and conquest. After conquest the State must have grown more as a result of conciliation and agreement than as a result of coercion. The force theory minimizes the element of co-operation and other such peaceful agencies which must have played an important part in the evolution of the State.

Force is an essential element of the State both for internal unity and for security against external attack. Without the element of force, the State would become a prey of disruptive factors and would soon cease to be.[2] But force alone cannot account for the historical origin of the State or for its continuance in modern times. 'Might without right can at best be only temporary. might with right is a permanent basis for the State *(28:79)*.'

The Force Theory, like the Social Contract Theory, has been used for a variety of purposes. Some have argued that since the State is the outcome of force, people should obey it absolutely. Such a position seems altogether illogical. As Rousseau has pointed out clearly, *(67: Bk. I, Ch. III)*, the right of the strongest is no right at all. Right based upon might lasts only as long as might lasts. But what kind of right is that which perishes when force fails? To quote Rousseau again, 'Force is a physical power.... To yield to force is an act of necessity, not of will—at the most, an act of prudence.' The individualists, as well as the socialists, have also employed the Force Theory to support their respective doctrine. The individualist argument is that just as the State is the result of superior strength, so within society itself the race should go to the swiftest. This means unrestricted competition and unlimited scope for individual efforts. The socialists attack this argument on the ground that individualism means an improper use of force and that the State, by means of its superior force, should check the exploitation of the weaker by the stronger and mete out justice to the workers.

---

2. Engels, the colleague of Marx, wrote : 'Without force and iron ruthlessness nothing is achieved in history.'

MacIver who brings a fresh point of view to bear on political questions adopts the Hobbesian view that one man is not much stronger than the other. He, therefore, discredits the theory that the State originated in the strong arm. Even such a man had to have the support of others. To use MacIver's own words: "The notion that force is the creator of government is one of those part-truths that begets total errors". (*142:15*) "Force alone never holds a group together". (*142:16*)

4. The Patriarchal and Matriarchal Theories

While there is general agreement that the origin of the State should be understood in terms of evolution, there is considerable difference of opinion as to the stages in this evolution. It is in this connection that we come across the patriarchal and matriarchal theories.

The Patriarchal Theory

Sir Henry Maine is a chief advocate of the patriarchal theory. He defines it as 'the theory of the origin of society in separate families, held together by the authority and protection of the eldest male descendant.' He believes that the State is the family writ large. He assumes that the original group consisted of a man and his wife and children and that this family soon gave rise to several families and that the original father or the eldest male descendant became the protector and ruler of this common patriarchal family. Relationship is traced in such a family through males, and from the same ancestor. The State is simply a further development of the patriarchal family. To state this development in Maine's own words: 'The elementary group is the family connected by common subjection to the highest male ascendant. The aggregation of families forms the Gens or House. The aggregation of Houses makes the Tribe. The aggregation of Tribes constitutes the Commonwealth (*28:85*).'

The theory rests on three fundamental assumptions: (1) That the patriarchal family was based on permanent marriage and kin relationships. (2) That the State is a collection of persons descended from the progenitor of an original family, and (3) That the ultimate source of all political authority is to be found in the extensive and unlimited power exercised by the head of the patriarchal family, who on his death-bed bequeathed to his successor all the legal rights that he enjoyed.

Criticism of the Theory. (1) Modern research into the history of early man shows that the patriarchal system was by no means universal. There are some who contend that the matriarchal system, where relationship is traced through the mother, was earlier, in point of time. McLennan, who is a staunch advocate of the matriarchal theory, claims that polyandry and the matriarchal family were the primary social facts and that polyandry later developed into the monogamous family, and the matriarchal family into the patriarchal state.

(2) Jenks, who is another strong supporter of the matriarchal theory,

asserts that the process by which families expand into clans and clans into tribes according to Maine's conception is, in fact, the reverse (*22:118*). According to Jenks, the tribe is the earliest and the primary group, then comes the clan, and finally comes the family. In support of his contention Jenks gives the examples of certain societies among primitive races such as those of Australia and the Malay Archipelago.

(3) The existence of polyandry and transient marriage relationships and kinship through females in uncivilized communities shows that the patriarchal family did not exist continuously.

(4) The most serious criticism of the theory is that it does not account for the origin of the State. It is simply a speculation into the beginnings of early society, particularly those of the family.

Adopting a slightly different point of view, MacIver holds that the family is the matrix of government, rather than of the State (*142:24*). Government, he says, may be regarded as "the continuation and expansion of the regulation developed within the family" (*142:24*). "Wherever the family exists—and it exists everywhere in society—government already exists" (*142:26*). The elements which lead to the formation of the State are, according to MacIver, the family, property, customary law, war and conquest.

The Matriarchal Theory

This theory is suggested by the institutions of savages still in existence such as the aborigines of Australia and certain communities in India. Savage life discloses a type of society which appears to be more primitive than the patriarchal society. The fundamental features of this society are:

(1) Transient marriage relationships,

(2) Female kinship,

(3) Maternal authority, and

(4) Succession of only females to property and power.

Some writers on the matriarchal theory consider all these four features as essential while others mean by the theory only 'mother-right' and 'mother relationship', and not 'mother rule'. It is the latter of these two views which seems more reasonable, according to which the mother does not rule herself but the right to rule on the part of a male is traced through the mother or the eldest female descendant.

According to the matriarchal theory, in the above restricted sense, the matriarchal family precedes the patriarchal family. It is natural to suppose that polyandry and transient marriage relationships were more common in primitive society than monogamy or polygamy. The Veemah marriage also existed, according to which the husband is incorporated into his wife's family. In these circumstances descent is traced through the mother; for, as Jenks points out, motherhood in such cases is a fact, while paternity is only an opinion. 'The woman here', says MacIver, 'is regarded as the agent of transmission, not the active wielder or even the participant of power." The system 'gave the woman, the wife and mother, a *social* rather than a *personal* standing (*55:29*).' It was at a later stage that 'mother right' gave place to the patriarchal society 'through the adoption of settled pastoral and agricultural habits in place of the purely wandering or hunting life of primitive men (*5:4*).'

Criticism of the Theory. (1) Although examples can be found of the polyandrous type of society in various parts of the world, there is no proof that it was universal or necessary to the beginning of society.

(2) Other forces and elements besides patriarchal and matriarchal relationship must have entered into the process of political organization.

(3) Both the patriarchal and matriarchal theories undertake to perform too big a task. They seek to enquire into the beginning of human society. Centuries must separate the most archaic society which we can picture to ourselves from the actual origin of mankind.

(4) Both theories are more sociological than political. They seek to explain the origin of the family rather than that of the State. The nature of the family and that of the State are different in essence, organization, functions and purpose.

The conclusion to which we are led with regard to both the patriarchal and matriarchal theories, can best be summed up in the words of Leacock: 'No single form of the primitive family or group can be asserted.' Here the matriarchal relationship, and there a patriarchal regime, is found to have been the rule either of which may perhaps be displaced by the other. Indeed one has to admit the fact that there is no such thing as a "beginning" of human society. All that can be asserted is that in course of time the monogamic family tended to become the dominant form, though even until today it has not altogether supplanted other forms of organization.

THE HISTORICAL OR EVOLUTIONARY THEORY OF THE STATE

5. The Evolutionary Theory: Factors in State Building

Over against the above five theories which are more or less speculative in character, is advanced the Historical or Evolutionary theory which furnishes a correct explanation of the origin of the State. According to it, the State is a historical growth or the result of a gradual evolution. It is a continuous development. It cannot be referred back to any single point of time. As Burgess puts it: 'It is the gradual realization.... of the universal principles of the human nature. It is futile to seek to discover just one cause which will explain the origin of all States. The State must have come into existence owing to a variety of causes, some operating in one place and some in other places. Whatever it is, the State is not the deliberate creation of man any more than language is a conscious invention. Political consciousness must have taken a very long time to develop and the primitive State must have grown along with the development of this consciousness.

More profitable than speculation, which seeks to reduce to a single theory the origin of all States, is enquiry into the factors which have gone into the building of the early State. As seen already, the State must have arisen from various causes and under varying conditions. Its emergence is almost imperceptible. The chief factors which have influenced its formation are:

I. Kinship,

II. Religion, and

III. Political consciousness.

I. Kinship. There can be little doubt that social organization had its origin in kinship. Blood relationship, either real or assumed, was the most important bond of union. It knit together clans and tribes and gave them unity and cohesion. But kin-relationship by itself could not have led to the formation of the State. People had to develop a common consciousness, common interest and common purpose. Kin-relationship must with great difficulty have given place to social relationship. 'Kinship', says MacIver, 'creates society and society at length creates the State (*55:33*)'.

The earliest kinship to be recognized was probably through the mother rather than the father. Man must have been a hunter and wanderer. Polyandry and transient marriage relationships must have been common. Yet mothers and children must have stuck closely together primarily for the sake of the security of children and because of economic necessity. As authority developed organization grew, men gained dominance of groups largely through physical superiority. Other factors which went to the establishment of such a patriarchal society were the domestication of wild animals, increased wealth, control of property, pursuit of pastoral industry, and the institution of slavery. Of these factors, control of wealth was probably the most important. Property had to be possessed securely and disposed of in an orderly manner. This meant the increasing social dominance of the male.

Patriarchal society was organized on the basis of kinship through males. Women came to be regarded more and more as a form of property. Wives had to be sought outside one's own group. Marriage relationships became more permanent and polygamy became common. The Patriarch or the House Father had complete control over the lives and persons of his descendants in the male line. When he died, authority passed to the eldest male descendant. The practice of adoption in order to continue the male line was widespread. This patriarchal community did not go on growing and developing till it became a nation. It broke up into several patriarchal groups, all recognizing some form of allegiance to the original group. The heads of these groups or clans probably formed a council of elders assisting the Patriarch, who later became the tribal chieftain, and this chieftain combined military, judicial and religious authority. The rulers or chiefs were more concerned with the privileges and powers of the dominant few than with the welfare of the community.

In the patriarchal society custom played a very important part, taking the place of law. As yet there was no conception of morality or a definite sense of legality. The sense of individual initiative and responsibility was altogether lacking. The patriarchal law was enforced by the Patriarch or the House Father who was both the judge and executioner. Custom governed both him and the accused. Custom was the king of men and was only gradually transformed into law. As yet there was no State in any accepted sense of the term, but some of its constituent elements were present. MacIver aptly says that it is a mistake to think 'that wherever we find a "headman" in a savage tribe we are in the presence of the State. We cannot say when or where the State begins. It is implicit in the universal tendency to leadership and subordination, but it emerges only when authority becomes government, and custom is translated into law (*55:42*).' To quote MacIver again: "Custom is always at work turning example into precedent and precedent into institution".

Patriarchal society differed fundamentally from modern society in the following ways (*39: Ch. VIII*):

(1) It was personal, rather than territorial. Membership in the community was based upon kinship—real or fictitious—rather than on locality. The entire group might migrate without disturbing its organization. Early kings were kings of their people, and not of their land.

(2) It was *exclusive*. It had no lust for numbers. Strangers had to live outside the ancient city walls. They could be admitted into the group only by adoption or as slaves.

(3) It was *non-competitive*. Its life was based on custom. It bound all alike and fixed the scale of social duties and rewards. The idea of change or of progress was looked upon with disfavour.

(4) It was *communal*, not necessarily communistic. It was a series of concentric groups, beginning with the single household, ascending to the village or guild, finally to the tribe or city. Interdependence rather than independence was the ideal. *Laissez faire* was wholly alien to it. It tended to repress individual effort and to restrict the free play of intelligence. The freedom of patriarchal society meant the freedom of the group rather than the freedom the individual.

The transition from the patriarchal society to modern society was marked by feudalism, and patriarchal ideas long existed after the State was well developed.

II. Religion. A second important factor in the creation of social consciousness and, in turn, in the emergence of the State is early religion. As Gettell observes, kinship and religion were simply two aspects of the same thing. Common worship was even more essential than kinship in accustoming early man to authority and discipline and in developing a keen sense of social solidarity and cohesion. Those outside were regarded as strangers and even as enemies.

Patriarchal religion, says Jenks, was almost universally ancestor-worship, *i.e.*, the cult of deceased ancestors. Patriarchal man must have believed in the continual existence of his ancestor, because he continued to see him in his dreams. He offered him sacrifices and worship and he adhered to all ancestral precedents lest he should in any way offend the deceased. Thus, offering to the dead became a characteristic feature of patriarchal religion. The patriarchal meal gradually came to occupy the place of a religious ceremony. Patriarchal religion was rigidly enforced on all members of the group.

Kinship and religion were so closely intertwined that the Patriarch, who later became the tribal chief, was also the high priest. He was the head of the family (later of the tribe), the guardian and interpreter of customs, high priest and often the magic man or the medicine man. Such a ruler was naturally looked upon with awe and reverence. He ruled with a rod of iron, and in this, religion was his powerful ally. Despotism in those early days was not an unmixed evil. It strengthened the tribal organization and accustomed men to authority and obligation. It was the best friend of progress and liberty in the early stages. All of this explains how religion and politics went together for a long time and are not completely separated even today.

When the patriarchal tribe began to expand by incorporation or conquest, patriarchal religion was not quite adequate to meet the new situation. It was at this point that nature worship began. Nature worship, in the form of crude animism, was present even in primitive times. But it now appeared in a somewhat advanced form and easily mingled with ancestor-worship and 'served as a sanction for government and law. Religious and political ideas were little differentiated, and obedience to law and to authority rested largely on the belief in the divine power of the ruler and in the sacredness of immemorial institution *(24:45)*.'

III. Political Consciousness. A third factor in the development of the State is the need that man felt at a very early time for order and protection, and along with it went the lust for power on the part of those who were strong and clever.

Once early man gave up his hunting and wandering habits and took to the pastoral and agriculture life, several changes took place. The population began to multiply. Contacts with neighbouring peoples increased. Wealth accumulated. The idea of property took root. The economic life advanced. All this necessitated some form of organization which would ensure internal order and give protection to person and property. Such an organization received further support from the need that man felt for an authoritative body to regulate social relationships such as those of the family and of marriage, as also from the need for concerted action for purposes of common defence and aggression.

The ambition for power was no doubt a strong motive in the formation of State-institutions. Military activity furnished the best opportunity for the realization of such ambition. In some cases at least 'war begot the king'. Earlier family organizations were gradually replaced by more purely political forms. Successful war leaders became kings and nobles, and society was stratified into classes. Power passed more and more into the hands of select classes who claimed prerogatives and superior rights.

Thus kinship, religion and the need for order and protection 'contributed the organization from which the state usually emerged *(24)*'. They necessitated some form of law and a government to enforce that law, and the State was the next step in this political evolution.

MACIVER ON THE EVOLUTION OF THE STATE

Looking at the question primarily from the sociological point of view, MacIver traces the State through the family, the institution of property, customary law, and war and conquest. He argues that wherever the family exists government already exists. The earliest type of economy is family economy. In course of time, the heads of families become the council of the community. "The family was the locus of the altar as well as of the workshop of the school as well as of the tribunal".

Customary law is another important factor in the evolution of the State. It precedes judges of courts of law. But if custom is to have authority it "must be hallowed and sanctioned by myth. If the myth is rejected, the custom collapses *(142:38)*".

War and conquest, says MacIver, have played their role not only in the extension of the area of government but also in the consolidation of political power.

MARXIST THEORY OF STATE ORIGIN

The Primitive Commune

According to Marx, Engels and Lenin, the early state gradually evolved as a result of the dissolution of the primitive communes which were stateless communities organized on the basis of a tribal, gentile constitution. The primitive commune was the primeval natural group based on common ties of blood, language and custom. The material basis of the commune's economy was hunting, fishing, fruit-gathering and cattle-grazing. It also implied a temporary communal appropriation of land. Man, according to Marx, was originally a social and tribal being, a herd animal, and he became an individual only through the process of history.

New forms evolved from the primitive commune with the transition to settled agriculture, stockfarming and craftsmanship i.e. with a development of the forces of production. When the people finally settled down, the extent to which the original character of the community was modified depended on various external, climatic, geographical and physical conditions as well as on their internal sex relations within the clan.

Marx and Engels mention several types of primitive communes: the Asiatic commune, the *polis* of the Greek and Roman world in its early form, the Germanic commune and the Slav commune. These communes in time gave rise to more complex socio-economic formations preparing the foundation for the rise of state. The most important point in this respect is the nature of private property that tends to emerge within the communal system when the social forces of production have developed beyond a certain level. As Engels says: "All civilised peoples begin with common ownership of the land. With all peoples who have passed a certain primitive stage, in the course of the development of agriculture this common ownership becomes a fetter on production." (*196:154*).

In the Asiatic commune individual property is an immediate part of communal property, and should, therefore, be described as possession rather than private property. In the Greek or Roman commune, private property is definitely established, and the individual breaks some of his ties with the community. Its social base is no longer the countryside but the city, as the seat of the landowning agriculturists. The Germanic commune differs markedly from both the Asiatic and the Graeco-Roman forms. Here the member of the commune does not share as such in communal property, as in the Asiatic form, nor is he simultaneously a private proprietor and interest-holder in the communal property, as in the Greek and Roman forms. The commune exists solely through the assembly of its members who are separate and autonomous landholders. In Asia there is an undifferentiated union between town and country with emphasis on rusticity. In Greece and Rome the city with its rural enclave is the economic totality with emphasis on urbanism. In the Germanic world the individual family dwelling, his rural home almost isolated in forest surroundings, is economically self-sufficient. The Slav commune was more or less like an Asiatic commune but it resembled the Greek commune in a limited development of private property.

Emergence of Slavery and Serfdom

The dissolution of the primitive communes as a result of the rise of private property and division of labour gave rise to new socio-economic formations such as the Asiatic society based on the "general slavery of the East" the classical society of Greece and Rome based on slavery under private law, and the feudal society based on serfdom. This transition is marked by the growth of clearly demarcated social groups, exploitative relations between these classes and ultimately the State.

The extensive development of the forces of production leads to significant progress in the sciences and arts, philosophy and religion, social organisation and legal structures, and political and ideological superstructures of the various socio-economic formations, which increasingly tend to assume divergent forms in various parts of the world. Thus, the so-called "civilized society" is born with all its benefits and drawbacks. Obviously, the impact of these developments is the greatest in the most dynamic communities, where there is inherently a basic contradiction between the common and private ownership of property.

The aim of these communities is survival in a hostile environment. The advance of population leads to colonisation and tribal wars of conquest. As

Marx puts it: "Warfare is one of the earliest occupations of each of these naturally arisen communities, both for the defence of their property and for obtaining new property.... If human beings themselves are conquered along with the land and soil as its organic accessories, then they are equally conquered as one of the conditions of production, and in this way arises slavery and serfdom, which soon corrupts and modifies the original forms of all communities, and then itself becomes their basis." *(224:414)*.

The more complex socio-economic formations which replaced the communes were based on slavery or serfdom as the mode of production. While slaves constituted the primitive property of their master, the status of the serf was relatively more vague and could be described as varying degrees of semi-slavery. As Rodinson says: "While slavery can be defined fairly clearly, serfdom is rather a vague notion which contains an infinite range of gradations and variations around the exploitation of a peasant enjoying varying legal rights, in particular over the land that he cultivates, by a land-owner who also enjoys variable rights, which are never absolute, over this peasant and his land". *(233:23)*.

It is possible to move imperceptibly from the status of a slave or that of a free contracting party such as farmer, sharecropper etc. to serfdom. Further, exploitation by the land-owner, the lord, is in many cases hard to distinguish from exploitation by the State through its officials. The pure concept of private property as an absolute right to use and abuse as it was defined by Roman laws, was rarely to be seen elsewhere. Everywhere, there was a hierarchy, a variety to multiple rights of the various communities, families, lineages, political and religious authorities etc. over the land and its produce.

Marx and Engels did not attach much importance to 'legal fictions' about property but always considered property relations as a significant expression of relations of production or relations between social classes. They also did not subscribe to the unilinear idea that slavery invariably preceded serfdom or that serfdom necessarily followed slavery. As Engels pointed out, serfdom and bondage were not necessarily medieval-feudal form and co-existed with slavery in classical Rome as well as semi-feudal Turkey and Russia in modern times. Similarly, slavery arose in classical Greece but co-existed with serfdom during the Middle Ages and the plantation economy of America in modern times.

When Marx contrasts slavery with serfdom, serfs with free workers, or the 'general slavery of Asia' with classical private law slavery of Europe, he is only analysing broad general categories. Actual historical instances in particular countries may differ from them in specific matters, nevertheless the distinction between slavery and serfdom or other forms of personal subordination has a precise economic, sociological and historical meaning. The Asiatic commune is transformed into a general slavery of village communities, which are subordinated to and exploited by a hierarchy of state officials. Here, the socio-economic formation leads to the creation of an oriental despotic state. Private law slavery gave rise to slave-owning city-states of Greece and slave-owning, imperial state of Rome. Germanic communes, with their independent household economies, did not practise slavery on any grand scale and were instrumental in founding the feudal state after the disintegration of the Roman empire.

From Matriarchy to Patriarchy

The main contribution to Marxist theory of the nature and origin of the State has come from Engels in his essay, *The Origin of the Family, Private Property and the State.* While MacIver and other liberal writers emphasize that the state emerged due to certain changes in man's consciousness, Engels gives primary importance to material factors such as production and reproduction. The desire for domination in one group such as the priests or the warriors and the desire for protection in another group such as peasants and craftsmen created the condition for the rise of State. This is the general explanation offered by liberal writers including MacIver for the origin of the state. Engels, however, puts forward a different point of view: "According to the materialistic conception, the determining factor in history is, in the last resort, the production and reproduction of immediate life. But this itself is of a twofold character. On the one hand, the production of the means of subsistence, of food, clothing and shelter and the tools requisite, therefore; on the other, the production of human beings themselves, the propagation of the species. The social institutions under which men of a definite historical epoch and of a definite country live are conditioned by both kinds of production: by the stage of development of labour, on the one hand, and of the family, on the other. The less the development of labour, and the more limited its volume of production and, therefore, the wealth of society, the more preponderatingly does the social order appear to be dominated by ties of sex. However, within this structure of society based on ties of sex, the productivity of labour power and others, and thereby the basis of class antagonisms: new social elements, which strive in the course of generations to adapt the old structure of society to the new conditions, until, finally, the incompatibility of the two leads to a complete revolution. *The old society based on sex groups bursts asunder in the collision of the newly developed social classes; in its place a new society appears, constituted in a state, the lower units of which are no longer sex groups but territorial groups, a society in which the family system is entirely dominated by the property system, and in which the class antagonisms and class struggles, which make up the content of all hitherto written history, now freely develop."* *(146:156)*.

Thus Engels introduces a new dimension to social transformation from primitive matriarchal social order based on sex equality and a certain prestige for the female sex into a patriarchal political order based on subordination and enslavement of women. Both Morgan and Engels believe that the women during the matriarchal age controlled the affairs of the family and the commune. They enjoyed real authority over men. The communistic household implied the supremacy of women in the commune. The exclusive recognition of a natural mother, in a situation where a natural father could not be identified with certainty, signified high esteem for the women. In the matriarchal clans, the women controlled the common stores and employed men as servants to gather fruits, to graze cattle or cultivate land. Women were often worshipped and ritually carried on men's shoulders on festive occasions. Engels says: "That woman was the slave of man at the commencement of society is one of the most absurd notions that have come down to us from the period of Enlightenment of the eighteenth century. Women occupied not only a free but also highly respected position among all savages and all barbarians of the lower and middle stages and partly even of the upper stage." *(146:189)*.

Arthur Wright testifies to the role which woman exercised in a matriarchal Iroquois clan: "The female portion ruled the house; the stores were in common; but woe to the luckless husband or lover who was too shiftless to do his share of the providing. No matter how many children or whatever goods he might have in the house, he might at any time be ordered to pack up his blanket and budge; and after such orders it would not be healthful for him to attempt to disobey.... The women were the great power among the clans, as everywhere else. They did not hesitate, when occasion required, to knock off the horns, as it was technically called, from the head of the chief and send him back to the ranks of the warriors." *(146:190)*.

Engels, agreeing with the above view, adds: "The communistic household, in which most of the women or even all the women belong to one and the same gens while the men came from various other gentes is the material foundation of that predominancy of women which generally obtained in primitive times." *(146:191)*. In the old Anglo-Saxon language, the wife literally meant the mistress of the house and the husband literally meant a servant who looked after the cattle or cultivated the land under his wife's command.

This situation changed with the transformation of group and pairing marriage customs into a durable monogamous relationship which made the determination of paternity easier and resulted in the establishment of patrilinear families and patriarchal gens. As Engels says: "The overthrow of mother right was the *world-historic defeat of the female sex*. The man seized the reins in the house also, the woman was degraded, enthralled, the slave of the man's lust, a mere instrument for breeding children." *(146:198)*.

Marx adds that the family is the mirror of society: "The modern family contains in embryo not only slavery but serfdom also, since from the very beginning it connected with agricultural services. It contains within itself in miniature all the antagonisms which later develop on a wide scale within society and its state." *(146:199)*. In the patriarchal family or clan, the chief owns his wife or wives as his property. In order to guarantee the fidelity of the wife, that is, the paternity of the children and inheritors of his property the woman is now placed in the absolute power of her husband. If he beats her or even kills her, he is merely exercising his right. Like the emergence of private property, slavery and serfdom, the enslavement of women under patriarchy was also a factor in the rise of the state. The state was *par excellence* a patriarchal institution. As Engels says, the state guaranteed that the wife remained the first domestic servant, pushed out of participation in public production and civic and political life. In the modern family, according to Engels again, the husband was the bourgeois and his wife represented the proletariat.

Origin and Nature of the State

According to Engels, the state in ancient Greece represented the purest, most classical form of evolution from the tribal *polis*. There the state arose directly and mainly out of the class struggles that developed within the Greek communes. In Rome, the tribal, gentile society became an exclusive aristocratic group amidst a large group of common people standing outside of it, having only duties but no rights. Later the victory of the commoners broke up the gentile constitution created a state which absorbed both the social classes. Finally, among the Germanic barbarian invaders of the Roman empire, the state emerged as a direct result of the conquest of large foreign territories, which the gentile construction had no means of ruling.

The gentile constitution had no coercive power except public opinion. But now a society had arisen that had split up into masters and slaves, into exploiting rich and exploited poor. This society could not reconcile class antagonisms and could only exist either in a state of continuous, open struggle of these classes against one another or under the rule of a third power which apparently stood above the classes, suppressed their open conflict allowing the class struggle to take place in the economic sphere within the bounds of law. As Engels put it : "The gentile constitution had outlived its usefulness. It had burst asunder by the division of labour and by its result, the division of society into classes. Its place was taken by the *State*." (*239:119*).

The state, according to Marx, Engels and Lenin, is neither the reality of the ethical idea, as Hegel said, nor it is a power forced on society from without, as some bourgeois writers argue. It was also not produced by a contract and cannot claim popular consent as its basis. Rather, it was a product of society at a certain stage of its socio-economic transformation. When the gentile society was entangled into an internal contradiction, which could not be solved within its framework, the state appeared on the historical scene to save the community from the intensity of the class struggles. Engels explains the origin of the state in these words : "In order that these antagonisms, classes with conflicting economic interests, might not consume themselves and society in sterile struggle, a power seemingly standing above society became necessary for the purpose of moderating the conflict, of keeping it within the bounds of 'order'; and this power, arisen out of society, but placing itself above it, and increasingly alienating itself from it, is the state." *(239:120)*. The Marxist theory of the origin and essence of state makes the following important points:

1. In contradistinction to the old gentile organization the state divides its subjects according to territory. The bonds of kinship were destroyed and citizens were allowed to exercise their public rights and duties wherever they settled irrespective of gens and tribe. This transformation was accompanied by long and arduous struggles.

2. The second point is the establishment of a *public power* which no longer coincided with the population organizing itself as an armed force. A self-acting armed organization of the people had become impossible because of class divisions. The slave-owners could not have trusted the slaves with arms. This public power included an army, a police force and a system of prisons and courts. The ruling class used it to keep the subject classes under its domination.

3. In order to maintain this public power, contributions from the citizen become necessary in the form of taxes. These were completely unknown in the tribal, communal society. The volume of these taxes goes on increasing with the multiplication of the instruments of coercion. The state may even make drafts on the future, contract loans and public debts.

4. The state creates a body of officials, who exercise the public power and claim the right to levy taxes. This bureaucracy now stands *above* society as a parasitical social stratum. The officials ensure respect for themselves by means of exceptional laws by virtue of which they enjoy special sanctity and inviolability. The shabbiest police constable of the state claims more 'authority' than all the organs of the gentile commune put together. The most powerful prince and the greatest statesman or general of a civilized state, says Engels, cannot compare himself with the humblest gentile chief who gets uncoerced and undisputed esteem from all members of his tribal commune. While the leader of the commune stands in the midst of society, the prince and the statesman have become alienated from their own society.

5. As the state arose from the need to hold class struggles under control, but as it arose, at the same time in the midst of the conflict of these classes, it became as a rule the state of the most powerful, economically dominant class. This economically dominant class, through the medium of the state also became the politically dominant class, and thus acquired new means of holding down and exploiting the subject classes.

6. The city-state of Greece or the imperial state of Rome was above all the state of the slave-owners for exploiting the oppressed class of slaves. The feudal state was the organ of the aristocracy for exploiting the oppressed class of serfs. The modern bourgeois state is, similarly, an instrument of exploitation of the working-class by the capitalists. The modern capitalist state, as Marx said, is an executive committee for managing the common affairs of the entire bourgeois class, which owns the means of production in modern society.

7. By way of exception, there are periods in history in which the war-

ring classes reach a balance so that the state temporarily becomes independent of both. It acquires the character of a parasite, such was the absolute monarchy of the seventeenth and eighteenth centuries which held the balance between the nobility and the bourgeois class. The French Empires under Napoleon I and still more under Napoleon III and the German Empire under Bismarck played off the bourgeoisie and the proletariat against each other.

8. . In most of the historical states, the rights of citizens are apportioned according to their status and class expressing the fact that the state is an organisation of the possessing class for ruling over the non-possessing class. It was so already in the Athenian and Roman classification according to property. It was so in the medieval feudal state, in which political power was granted in conformity with the amount of land owned. It is found in the electoral qualifications based on property in the modern representative state.

9. Yet this political recognition of property qualifications is by no means absolutely necessary. On the contrary, it marks a low stage of the development of state and politics. The highest form of the state is the democratic republic, which recognizes no property distinctions. In it wealth exercises its power indirectly, but all the more surely. This may be done by corrupting the bureaucracy or through an alliance between government and Stock Exchange. Under universal suffrage, the proletariat either forms a tail of the capitalist class or sets up its own revolutionary party and utilizes elections to spread class consciousness.

10. The state has not existed from all eternity. There were societies which had no conception of state or state power. The proletariat, after the socialist revolution, will establish a transitional state known as dictatorship of the proletariat. At this stage, the existence of classes and class divisions may become a positive obstacle to further development of the forces of production. The classes will, then fall as inevitably as they arose at an earlier stage. Along with them, the state will also decline and disappear. Under the final phase of communism based on a classless society, the state will not be needed i.e. it will wither away.

A Liberal Critique of the Marxist Theory

MacIver and Plamenatz do not accept the Marxist theory as propounded by Engels and Lenin as a valid explanation of the origin and nature of the state.

1. They reject the concept of primitive communism as the correct description of the pre-political tribal society. MacIver does not agree with Engels that matriarchal societies which were based on mother-right, actually implied any greater authority of women over men. There was no common ownership of the means of production; there was only common use of consumable articles. Neither communism and common ownership nor matriarchal authority can be accepted as adequate concepts to describe the

nature of the tribal and clan systems out of which has the state evolved.

2. The increasing division of labour does not necessarily create antagonistic classes in the Marxian sense. It only creates numerous occupations which need not be hostile to each other. As Plamenatz points out, Engels does not realize that the state will still be required even if there were no antagonistic classes: to settle non-antagonistic disputes between different occupational groups which arise in society.

3. Plamenatz feels that the real class structures arise after the state has already come into existence. The antagonistic classes of slave-owners and slaves, of feudal lords and serfs, of capitalists and wage labourers emerge when the state has already come into existence. The social classes are, therefore, a post-state phenomenon. The class structures have followed the creation of the state instead of preceding it.

4. Marx and Engels ignore the element of consent in the evolution of the state as well as the role of the state in promoting the common good. The state could have functioned as an instrument of class domination in ancient or feudal society or even under early capitalistic system. With the arrival of political democracy based on universal suffrage; the state has really emerged as an institution promoting the collective well-being of all social groups. The modern democratic state, therefore, cannot be described as an instrument of class domination.

5. The example of the Soviet State suggests that abolition of social classes in the Marxian sense does not lead to the weakening of the state as an instrument of domination. The state in all communist countries shows no signs of withering away, as Marx had predicted, but, on the contrary, has transformed itself into a totalitarian institution of regimentation and repression.

6. The state is not an organ of class rule in a liberal democracy. It is an organ that exists for the conciliation of divergent socio-economic interests. The liberal-democratic state creates a pluralist society in which both labour and capital can equally influence the decision-making process at the level of government.

In the words of a leading exponent of this democratic pluralist view, Robert Dahl, here is a political system in which "all the active and legitimate groups in the population can make themselves heard at some crucial stage in the process of decision" (*188 : 137*). This view of the state now dominates "political science and political sociology and ...... political life itself, in all..... capitalist countries" (*236 : 5*).

CHAPTER 6

THE HISTORICAL DEVELOPMENT OF THE STATE

THE EVOLUTION OF THE STATE

We have so far concerned ourselves with the speculative theories regarding the origin of the State and the factors which have gone into the building of the early State. We now turn our attention to the evolution of the State in historical times. Here we are on more solid ground.

1. The Early Empire in the Orient

Almost the first type of State which emerged from primitive and patriarchal conditions was the Imperial State, particularly that of the Orient. Patriarchal society did not have a large enough area or population to enable it to become a State. There probably existed loose alliances and confederacies of various tribes knit together by ties of blood, real or assumed. But these could not have produced the extended State. Conquest and domination were necessary before tribal man could accustom himself to larger loyalties and to political authority and obligation.

The warm and fertile plains of the Orient, watered by great rivers, and the plateaus of Mexico and Peru produced the earliest forms of citilization and the earliest State. These were regions where production was plentiful with the least amount of exertion. People multiplied rapidly and soon passed from the earlier family and religious systems to the newer political order. The rapid growth of population and the enervating climate of these warm regions led to the existence of a l rge servile class. Those who possessed surplus wealth, leisure, and power could easily domineer over the rest and establish despotisms. Social differences and caste distinctions came into vogue. From this state of affairs there soon arose vast empires—such as the Sumerian, the Assyrian, the Persian, the Egyptian, and the Chinese—all centering around cities. With the exception of the Persian empires which attained a degree of unity and stability, these empires were loosely knit together geographically, and loosely organized, and their authority rested on fear and despotism. For the most part they were merely tax-collecting and recruit-raising agencies. There was no common purpose and no common loyalty. As soon as the ruling dynasty became weak, powerful rivals contested for rule and authority.

2. The Greak City-State

The second important stage in the evolution of the State was reached in Greece. Although civilization arose later in Greece than in the Orient, it developed much faster once it got started. The country is peculiarly fitted by its physical environment for political growth and experimentation. The

Greek religion and outlook were naturalistic and the people had no awe for their gods. Since nature was not so profuse as in the tropical countries, people looked to colonization and trade. The patriarchal clans took possession of small areas and built their village communities around hills which could be easily defended. Some of these clans were fused by conquest, peaceful union, or ties of kinship. But they never developed a national unity. Local patriotism continued to the end.

In their self-government and self-sufficient city-states, or rather city-communities (the phrase used by MacIver), the Greeks developed a variety of political organizations. These communities contained the principle of growth. Sparta alone remained conservative and maintained 'a steady tradition of unbroken continuity in its government. In the other States the normal political evolution was from monarchy to aristocracy, from aristocracy to tyranny, and from tyranny to democracy *(2 Ch. 1)*.'

The Greek was passionately devoted to his city-state. The only life which mattered to him was a life of partnership in the city. 'Citizenship was a function, almost a profession *(55:84)*.' The Greeks looked upon the city as an ethical institution.

While the Greek city-state reached a very high level of political development and individual liberty, it had many serious drawbacks. For one thing, it rested upon a foundation of slavery. For another, the Greeks could not unite and form a common whole. They never felt a common political consciousness uniting all the Greeks together into a single political whole. The city-states formed loose confederations but nothing more. Frequent wars destroyed in turn the power of the leading cities.

Rome began her political career as a city-state, very much like the city-states of Greece. In the early days, her government was monarchic. The king was a magistrate, monarch, and high priest all in one. The nobility, known the Patricians, had a share in political authority. The landless, propertyless common people, known as the Plebeians had no share at the beginning but acquired the privilege later on.

In early Rome, as in the Greek cities, the tendency was towards a democratic form of government. About 500 B.C., monarchy fell and republic was established with two chief magistrates, who later came to be called consuls. For two centuries following the change, the patricians and the plebeians were engaged in a struggle for political control. The economic consequences of many wars intensified the struggle. Finally, the two fighting classes fused into one citizen body, having equal political and civil rights.

At this point Rome began to look outside her borders, with a view to annexing territories. The geographical conditions of Italy favouring conquest over those of Greece, Rome began the realization of her ambition with the incorporation of the neighbouring Italian States. As MacIver notes: 'From early times the Romans had the wit to distinguish between civil right—rights of equality before the law—and political right—rights of membership in the sovereign body *(55:97)*.' Some cities of Italy were given civil rights, but no political rights.

Soon atfer the conquest of Italy, Rome destroyed Carthage, her only rival in the West, and became a great naval power. A large part of the fragments of Alexander's empire came under her control. By the close of the first century B.C., almost the whole of the entire civilized Western world was united in a single political system.

An effective system of centralized administrative control was developed to hold the empire together. The conquered territory was divided into provinces and over each province was set up a Roman official known as the pro-consul, who had full powers in civil and political affairs. The only check which restrained him was the possibility of impeachment at home on his retirement from office. In Rome itself the republican form of government was replaced by military despotism. The emperor became all-powerful. Popular assemblies ceased to have any important functions. The Senate retained prominent position, but the emperor exerted control over it by securing a dominant influence in determining its position. The emperor's decrees finally came to be recognized as law.

By the end of the second century, Roman citizenship was extended to the provinces. All members of the State were equally subject to the rule of the emperor. During this period the old theory that the ruler received his power from the people gave place to the Divine Origin Theory. Thus the ancient democratic city-State became the autocratic world-empire. Emphasis was shifted from the Greek ideals of liberty, democracy, and local independence to the Roman ideals of unity, order, universal law, and cosmopolitanism.

Comparing the relative contributions and limitations of Greece and Rome, Gettell aptly remarks, "Greece developed democracy without unity; Rome secured unity without democracy *(24:59)*.'

3. The Feudal State

The downfall of Rome meant the death of the 'State' in Western Europe. A long period of confusion followed. The Teutonic barbarians who invaded Rome from the north were still living in the tribal stage, not yet having conceived of strong central authority. They were lovers of local independence and individual liberty and their kings were simply successful war chiefs. The freemen had a voice in all public affairs.

When such people came into contact with the Roman political system which was characterized by order, unity, and centralization, conflict was the inevitable result. Out of this conflict feudalism arose as a compromise—a compromise between the clan type of society represented by the Teutonic barbarians and the imperial State type represented by Romans. It is easy enough to decry feudalism and belittle its importance in the evolution of the State. It has been rightly said that it was not a system at all. But in the anarchic state into which society had fallen following the decline of Rome, it was feudalism which gave the people of Europe comparative peace and protection and preserved the machinery of the State. It was confusion roughly organized. It marked the transition from the imperialism of the Roman world to the nationalism of the modern world.

How Feudalism arose and What it Meant

On the decline of the Roman empire, the vast territories of Rome fell into the hands of powerful nobles. Each of these nobles became an authority unto himself and each by a process of 'sub-infeudation' of land created a community of his own around him. The supreme lord parcelled out his land among the tenants-in-chief, and the tenants-in-chief among the tenants, and the tenants in turn among the vassals and serfs. Thus a hierarchy was built upon the basis of land-holding. A rigid system of classes was established and the 'State' was swallowed up in the community. Services of various kinds, particularly military, were rendered to the immediate overlord, and the control of the supreme lord, or king, at the top of the social and economic ladder over the vassals and serfs at the bottom of the ladder was indirect and remote. The loyalty of each class was in the first instance to the class immediately above it. As a result of such limited loyalty, the idea of a sovereign power reigning supreme in a given territory remained foreign to the feudal period. In the place of a system of uniform and impartial law which the Romans had done so much to build up, there was reversion to custom as law. Real political progress was impossible as long as feudal ideas prevailed. Yet feudalism was not synonymous with anarchy. It justified its existence by providing peace and protection to the people of Europe. It was based upon personal loyalty and contract. In its later stage, particularly in England, where allegiance to the king took precedence over allegiance to the immediate lord, it helped the growth of the national State.

Another institution which survived the confusion following the downfall of the Roman Empire was the Christian Church. Christianity began as a humble faith among the lower classes of society, but in the course of a few centuries it reached mighty proportions, and about the year 337 A.D. the Roman Emperor Constantine was converted to Christianity. By the end of the fourth century it was the only recognized religion in the Roman world. It built its organization on the Roman imperial model and when the Empire fell to pieces, it was able to step into its place and give Europe order and peace. During long periods of the Middle Ages, it was able to control the State; and itself became a powerful temporal authority, holding in its possession considerable wealth, especially landed property.

In feudalism the Church found a valuable ally, for it was in the interest of the political aspirations of the Church that Western Europe should be kept divided with no common political superior to offer resistance to the extravagant claims of the Church. The Protestant Reformation which came soon after, in effect ended the secular supremacy of the Church, and the way was prepared for national monarchies.

5. The National State of Modern Times

The Renaissance and the Reformation are generally regarded as marking the beginning of the modern period. These movements quickened the life of Western Europe, which now entered upon a period of unparalleled expansion and conspicuous achievement. In the very nature of the case, feudalism could not have lasted long. It had a useful role to play so long as conditions were unsettled and there was general disorder and confusion everywhere. But once conditions became settled and the ethnic, linguistic, religious, and territorial bonds gave people a new sense of unity, feudalism was obliged to give way to a superior order of safety.

National States were coming into existence in England, France, and Spain. Cities grew and commerce developed. The pride of kings, mortified by the arrogant demands of the Popes, led to their breaking away more and more from Papal authority and making themselves masters in their own houses. Because they desired peace and security, the people gave them their loyal support. They looked upon the king as the visible symbol of the national spirit which was beginning to capture their imagination. The use of gunpowder, the rise of national taxation, and the setting up of standing armies freed the national monarchs to a great extent from their dependence upon the feudal nobility. The Hundred Years' War and the Wars of the Roses further weakened the authority of the feudal lords and diminished their political importance. By the close of the fifteenth century much of the feudal power was destroyed.

The immediate effect of the teaching of the Reformers was to strengthen the hands of national monarchs. The general tendency of the Reformation teaching was to strengthen the hold of the monarchic principle in monarchic lands and the principle of aristocracy in aristocratic lands. 'In both the effect was to strength absolutism in the political sovereign (*17*).'

Such absolutism, however, did not remain unchallenged very long. With the growth of enlightenment and understanding and realization of their power and importance, the common people began to question the duty of passive obedience to governmental authorities and to demand more and more political rights and privileges. This meant a prolonged contest for political control between the king and the people. In the transition from royal absolutism to democracy the Reformation idea of personal worth played a very important part. The common man acquired a new confidence in himself and he realized the fact that government existed not for its own sake but for the good of the governed. Thus, the ultimate effect of the Reformation teaching was to further the cause of individual liberty and democracy.

Royal absolutism was no doubt necessary to weld people together and to bring order and unity out of feudal disorder and disunity. But once that object was fulfilled, there was no reason for its continuance. The democratic movement started very early in England and its progress was on the whole gradual and peaceful. In France it meant a violent revolution. In other countries, the monarchs generally yielded to the popular will and were content to remain as historic-figureheads under a democratic government. The movement had taken such deep root and had worked so satisfactorily that, till recently, the democratic national State came to be regarded as the final stage in the evolution of the State. Bentham, for instance, hoped to better 'this wicked world by covering it over with Republics'.

6. World Federation

Undoubtedly a great deal can be said in favour of the Democratic National State. It would seem reasonable to suppose that every country with a well-defined natural boundary and having a homogeneous and united people should be allowed to govern itself and claim all the rights of a sovereign State, and that the formation of such self-governing and self-determining national States was essential to international peace and goodwill. But the history of the last century has shown that such a policy inevitably leads to rivalry, competition and even war. Colonial empires have well-nigh destroyed the geographic and ethnic unity on which the national State is based. Scientific discoveries of recent years, greater facilities of travel and greater inter-course among the people of the world, international trade on a gigantic scale and the world magnitude of present-day problems, all of which are causing 'the shrinkage of the world', tend to break down narrow ideas of patriotism and national sovereignty and point the way to some form of world federation. Just what form this world federation will take the future alone can show.

GENERAL FEATURES OF STATE DEVELOPMENT

A study of the evolution of the State, as stated by Gettell, leads to five broad conclusions (*24:65-67*).

(1) As in the case of organizations in general, the evolution of the State has been from the simple to the complex. Government has become more complex and complicated than in earlier times. But at the same time there has been an increasing unity and interdependence of governmental organs.

(2) The evolution of the State has meant 'the growth of political consciousness and purposeful action'. The first State came into being not through the deliberate action of man, but largely through natural causes. But with the evolution of the State and increasing intelligence, man was able to discover reasons for the existence of the State and mould the State according to his ideals. State authority came to be based on a more rational and stable foundation. The spread of political consciousness to the people led to the formation of democracies.

(3) As a general rule, the evolution of the State has meant the bringing together under a single state system larger areas and greater numbers of people. Among the factors which have made large states possible today are rapid means of transportation and communication, unprecedented economic

development, the growth of self-governing local institutions, and the increasing respect of modern man for law and order.

(4) State development has meant the curtailment of the power of the State in certain areas and the corresponding increase of it in certain others. Religion and the State evolved together in the early stages. But, at the present time, in all civilized countries, the Church and State tend to be entirely separate. It is generally admitted that the State ought not to interfere with such matters as domestic life and personal likes and dislikes as regards food, clothing, fashion, and the like so long as such freedom is not contrary to public order and safety or laws of decency.

On the other hand, there is an increasing demand for State action in the sphere of public welfare, where individuals cannot or will not help themselves. Thus education, sanitation, the care of defectives, the punishment and prevention of crime are justified by all modern States.

(5) In many ways, the most significant development has been the increasing measure of compromise which has been worked out between the sovereignty of the State and individual liberty. Modern totalitarian States are, however, an exception to the rule. Rigid enforcement of customs and despotic rule were necessary in the early days to make primitive man understand the importance of law and authority. But after this purpose was accomplished, they became rather a hindrance to individual liberty and the unity of the State.

The dominant pluralist view of Western-type societies and of the state upholds that there are elites in different economic, social, political, administrative, professional and other pyramids of power. But these elites altogether lack the degree of cohesion required to turn them into dominant or ruling classes. In fact 'elite pluralism' and competition between different elites guarantees that power in society will be diffused and not concentrated.

Nevertheless, advanced capitalism is all but synonymous with the existence of giant corporations. There is enormous *political* significance of this concentration of private economic power. Multinational corporations today dominate the world economy. They falsify the pluralist theory of governance not only nationally but also globally. (*236 : 15*).

CHAPTER 7

THE SOCIAL CONTRACT THEORY OF HOBBES, LOCKE AND ROUSSEAU

The names of Hobbes (1588-1679), Locke (1632-1704), and Rousseau (1712-1778) are inextricably interwoven with the social contract theory. Hobbes and Locke in England and Rousseau in France gave this theory its final form.

(A) THE STATE OF NATURE AND THE LAW OF NATURE

Hobbes. Hobbes presents a gloomy view of the state of nature. According to Hobbes, life of man in the state of nature is one of constant warfare on account of the essentially selfish nature of man. In his own forcible words, the life of man, is 'solitary, poor, nasty, brutish, and short'. 'Every man is enemy to every man *(35)*.' Man seeks pleasure, and to ensure pleasure he wants power over others. But he is not able to assert power over others, since, according to Hobbes, the bodily and mental powers of natural man are nearly alike. Hence men stand in natural fear of each other. From this state of fear there arises a state of constant warfare. This does not mean that men actually fight with one another all the time, but that the will to contend is ever present. In such a state there is no place for industry. 'Kill whom you can, take what you can' is the order of the day. There is no law to constrain such actions. Hobbes is not guilty of assuming that such a state of nature is one from which men actually started. All that he is concerned to show is that it is a state into which a country may lapse when there is no settled government for any length of time.

The Social Contract writers assumed that there were laws of nature in the state of nature, but they are not agreed on the nature or basis of these laws. To Hobbes laws of nature are laws of prudence or expediency, while to Locke they are laws of morality implanted in the human conscience. Hobbes plainly tells us that one's natural rights are one's natural powers. In the natural state, he says, there can be no morality and no consciousness of obligation. These are possible only after the establishment of law and government. Until laws exist all actions are equally good and right. The 'right of nature' is 'the liberty each man hath to preserve his own life'. The first law of nature is that everybody should aim at securing peace. The second law is that men should be willing, in concert with others, to give up their natural rights. The third law is that men should keep their contracts. The fourth and the last law is that men should show gratitude or return beneficence for beneficence. Duty in Hobbes' system, says Hallowell, coincides with self-interest.

Locke. The view of Locke on the state of nature and the laws of nature are very different. The state of nature to him is not a state of war. It is 'a state of peace, goodwill, mutual assistance, and preservation'. It is a state of liberty, but not of licence. The majority of people in this state obey the law of nature, *i.e.*, the law of inward morality. But there are a few recalcitrants who cause inconvenience to the rest. Consequently, the peaceable people are obliged to take the law into their own hands, and this is always irksome to the average man who wants to be left free to mind his own business. Besides, men are not good judges in their own case. Thus the only disadvantage of the state of nature is that there is in it no recognized system of law and justice.[1] To rectify this deficiency men abandom the state of nature and enter into a civil society by means of a contract. This view of Locke is far more unreal than that of Hobbes.

Rousseau. Rousseau's picture of the natural man, in his *Discourse on Inequality,* is that of a 'noble savage'. Men in the state of nature are equal, self-sufficient, and contented. They live a life of idyllic happiness and primitive simplicity. But, with the rise of civilization, inequality comes into being. Arts and sciences arise and private property is established. Division of labour, too, comes into existence. All this necessitates the establishment of civil society. The State is thus an evil, but is rendered necessary by the inequalities among men. In his *Social Contract,* Rousseau takes a modified view of the civil state and believes that the advantages of the civil state are greater than those of the natural state. In his own words : 'What man loses by the social contract is his natural liberty and an unlimited right to all which attracts him and which he can obtain; what he gains is civil liberty, and the property of what he possesses. To avoid error in the reckonings we must carefully distinguish natural liberty, which has no bounds but the powers of the individual, from the civil liberty which is limited by the general will; and possession, which is only the effect of force on the right of the first occupant, from property, which can only be founded on a positive title *(67:BK I, Ch. XIII)*.'

(B) NATURE OF THE CONTRACT

Hobbes. Hobbes posits one contract : the original or social contract: Locke posits two contracts : the social and governmental; and Rousseau posits one. While Hobbes speaks of a contract, it is of no consequence to him whether government really originated in the form of a contract or not. He

1. According to Locke, the three lacks in the state of nature are :
   (a) 'an established, settled, known law';
   (b) 'a definite and impartial judge'; and
   (c) 'power to back and support the sentence when right, and to give it due execution'.

is more or less aware that it is a historical fiction, but a historical fiction which conveys a philosophical truth. It is simply a device to show that government is not mere force, but in some respects rests on the will of the people. Locke, on the other hand, regards the contract as an actual historical fact. He thinks that there was a time when people did meet together and set up a government.

The contract, as conceived by Hobbes is between the people themselves who emerge from a state of nature. It is not between the people on the one hand and the sovereign on the other. It is a contract among the people themselves to set up a ruler. It is 'as if every man should say to every man, I authorize, and give up my right of governing myself to this man or this assembly of men, on condition that thou give up thy right to him and authorize all his actions in like manner *(35: Part II, Ch. 17)*.'

It is an absolute surrender of all of one's natural rights to the sovereign, although Hobbes does make some qualifications later on. The sovereign himself is not a party to the contract, but is a result of it. He is absolute. Once powers are conferred on him by the people, they cannot be withdrawn from him. Therefore, people have no right of revolution. The contract which is responsible for the institution of civil society is equally responsible for the establishment of government as well, for Hobbes makes no distinction between the State and government. The consequence of positing one and only one contract is that when a government is overthrown, the State also goes to pieces and society returns to anarchy, which is an illogical position to take.

Locke. By a first contract civil society is set up and by a second contract people get a government. The natural inference is that the first contract is among the people themselves and the second between the people in their corporate capacity on the one hand, and the ruler on the other. To Hobbes, as seen already, it is the setting up of a government that brings civil society into existence. To Locke setting up a government is a secondary transaction and the dissolution of the government does not mean dissolution of civil society. All that it means is that society will have to set up another government in its place. According to Locke, the surrender of natural right is not complete. People give up certain of their natural rights to a common authority in order that the remaining rights may be kept intact. When the ruler fails to maintain these rights, people are justified in overthrowing him and setting up a new government. In this way, Locke makes his theory the basis of limited monarchy, his object being to uphold the Bloodless Revolution of 1688. To Locke, then, the contract is a limited bargain. Thus in the chapter on property, he says that the government should take only what is necessary to carry on its business. It has not the power to take anything more without the owner's consent. This is quite an unreal view of government. Legislative power is not absolute.

Rousseau. According to Rousseau the contract is between the individuasl in their personal capacity and the individuals in their corporate capacity.

A, B, C, D, etc., surrender all their natural rights to the collective whole A+B+C+D, etc. No one is a loser; on the contrary, everybody is a gainer, for when anyone is attacked the whole society comes to his rescue. Each person in the state possesses an equal and inalienable portion of the sovereignty of the whole. In Rousseau's own words : "Each of us puts his person and all his power in common under the supreme direction of the general will, and in our corporate capacity we receive each member as an indivisible part of the whole.' Each man giving himself to all, gives himself to none, and remains as free as before. Rousseau does not believe that the contract is an actual historical occurrence.

(C) SOVEREIGNTY

Hobbes. Hobbes holds that men in the state of nature are simply a multitude of unconnected and warring individuals. Hence the problem which faces Hobbes is, how can a multitude of such individuals form a single body with single will ? The solution to it he finds in the social contract, by virtue of which a sovereign is set up with a *single will,* who will govern society continually. This single will takes the place of the individual will and at the same time represents them, in accordance with the terms of the contract.

The important point to note is that with whomsoever sovereignty rests, it must be absolute, indivisible, and inalienable. It is the setting up of a sovereign that creates society. Sovereignty is the supreme power on earth. In the sovereign resides the essence of the commonwealth. The sovereign, says Hobbes may be one, few or many, authough Hobbes' own preference is for the one. The advantages which Hobbes points out in favour of monarchy are—

(*a*) that the private interest of the monarchy is likely to be identified with the general interest of the people;

(*b*) that monarchy can work much more conveniently than other types of government; and

(*c*) that a monarchy is likely to remain fixed in his ways.

All these arguments have, no doubt, some amount of force. The practical purpose of Hobbes was to justify royal absolutism. But in doing this he received no thanks from the other supporters of royal absolutism in his day, because they wanted the king to rule by divine right. They argued that if the king's authority was not independent of the people's will, the same people who gave him absolute authority could hand over that authority by means of another contract to a few or to many. Nor would the opponents of monarchy have anything to do with Hobbes, because they wanted to limit the king's power.

The sovereign, says Hobbes, is the supreme law-maker. He cannot do any injustice to his subjects because he represents them. He may commit moral wrong, but he cannot do any legal injustice.

Locke. In Locke there is confusion of all the forms of sovereignty. A recent writer remarks: 'The more closely Locke's treatise is studied, the more clearly will it be seen that it is an attack directed far more against the idea of sovereignty, than against the claims of absolute monarchy (29).' The traditional view of sovereignty is that it should be absolute and indivisible. This view we find in Hobbes, Austin, and many others. But, according to Locke, sovereignty is neither absolute nor indivisible. It seems to be divided between the people on the one hand and the rulers on the other.

Locke's theory of sovereignty means in practice that the people have sovereign authority in reserve but that the actual power is exercised by the government, *i.e.*, by the king and the parliament as far as England is concerned, and that when the government violates its trust it becomes necessary for the people to withdraw their power from the government. Thus the people are in the nature of a sleeping partner. They let the government carry on the sovereign authority within certain limits till it begins to abuse its power, and when it does that, the sovereign people rouse themselves from their slumber, overthrow the existing government, and set up another government in its place. Locke's theory justifies revolution when it is the act of the whole community. The difficulty is in determining when it is such an act.

The serious error in Locke's theory of sovereignty is in his placing legal limits on the power of the sovereign.

Rousseau. As seen already, according to the terms of the contract, A,B,C,D, etc. surrender their natural rights to the collective whole A+B+C+D etc. Here we have the foundations of popular sovereignty and democratic government. Each citizen has a share in the sovereign power, and each is also a subject in that he has to obey the law, which he himself has made as sovereign authority. Rousseau adopts the view of Hobbes that sovereignty is absolute, inalienable and indivisible. While Hobbes locates it in the wrong place, *viz.*, in the monarch, Rousseau places it in the body politic as a whole. From Locke, Rousseau takes over the distinction between sovereignty and government but does not allow government as much authority as is allowed by Locke. To Rousseau government is only a derivative authority, always, subject to the will of the sovereign people. His sovereign is an ever-active or vigilant sovereign, unlike that of Locke; he does not wait till things are carried to an excess by the government before he rouses himself to action.

The greatest contribution made by Rousseau to political theory is his doctrine of the general will. The general will is the only manifestation of sovereignty. It is vested in the body politic as a whole.

[The doctrine of the general will is discussed in the note at the end of this chapter.]

(D) TYPE OF STATE AND GOVERNMENT

As regards the type of State, Hobbes' theory favours royal absolutism. Locke's theory favours constitutional government or limited monarchy while

Rousseau's theory results in popular government, and particularly in direct democracy.

In their conception of government, too, the three writers differ fundamentally. Hobbes makes no distinction between State and government. To him the *de facto* government is always *de jure*. Locke and Rousseau, on the other hand, distinguish between State and government and between *de facto* and *de jure* government. As said already, according to Hobbes, dissolution of government means dissolution of the State and return to primitive anarchy, which is absurd. Locke holds that the sovereign people have the right to choose their government and change it when it becomes unsatisfactory. Government is a trust or a moral responsibility. To Rousseau, government is simply an agent or a 'living tool' of the people. It is not the result of a contract. It has only limited authority and this authority is derived from the sovereign people. It has no original power. Its power can at any time be recalled by the sovereign will. The subordinate character of government is brought out by Rousseau in his conception that in their periodic assemblies people decide upon two questions *(67: Book III, Ch. XVIII)*.

(1) Do we want the present form of government to continue?

(2) If we do, do we want the present personnel to continue?

As regards the powers and functions of government, Hobbes gives absolute powers to the government which is also the sovereign. Locke gives the government only limited power, for according to his theory of the contract, people surrender only as much of the natural rights as is necessary to secure the benefit of civil society. Again, Locke distinguishes between the legislative and executive parts of government, which Hobbes had failed to do, and makes the legislative the supreme part of government. Hobbes makes order and security all important. Locke says that government should not only keep order, but govern well. The rulers should rule for the welfare of the subjects. Here Locke makes a definite advance upon Hobbes.

According to Rousseau, the business of government is only executive. Legislation is to be in the hands of the sovereign people. People cannot part with the power to make law without curtailing their sovereign authority. The essence of legislation is *will* and *will*, in its very nature, cannot be transferred or represented. On this ground Rousseau attacks representative government and makes a powerful plea in favour of direct democracy, such as that which prevailed in the small city states of Greece. In his own words: 'Sovereignty, for the same reason as makes it inalienable, cannot be represented; it lies essentially in the general will, and "will" does not admit of representation. It is either the same, or other; there is no intermediate possibility. The deputies of the people therefore are not and cannot be its representative *(67: Book III, Ch. XIV)*.'

Thus, according to Rousseau, the body politic has the will and the executive carries out the will. But this distinction is incapable of being stretched very far. For, if pressed too far, would mean that the executive has no will at all, which is a clearly impossible position. The executive is simply like a policeman who carries out orders. In every country the executive is given a considerable amount of discretion. Therefore, the executive does have a share in the general will.

A second distinction which Rousseau makes between the sovereign people who form the legislative and the executive which is the government, is that the former should concern itself with what is *general* and the latter with what is *particular*. This point of view is open to several difficulties. It is obviously difficult to draw a sharp line between what is general and what is particular. Even if we can say that a matter is general if it concerns the whole community equally, and is particular if it concerns a particular class or person, our difficulty is not solved by any means. In the modern State almost every piece of legislation is of a particular kind. There is hardly anything which concerns the whole community equally.

(E) INDIVIDUAL LIBERTY AND THEORY OF RIGHTS

Hobbes, on the whole, adopts the legal theory of rights; Locke bases his teaching on the theory of natural rights; Rousseau derives rights from membership in society and thus paves the way for the idealistic or personality theory of rights.

In Hobbes' theory the subject has all those rights which the law allows him. Wherever the law does not put a restraint, the subject retains his natural right. This does not mean that the sovereign's power over life and death is superseded. The sovereign can step in at any time and limit the liberty of the subject. The subject has power wherever the law does not regulate. In Hobbes' thinking, authority and liberty are opposed to one another.

According to Hobbes' view, there is no limit to what the sovereign may command, although there is a limit in extreme cases to the individual's obedience. This is in the very nature of the contract. The sovereign power was established for the security of life and happiness.

When we come to Locke, we find that he makes government depend upon the consent of the governed. The individual has all those rights which he has not surrendered to the State. The State exists mainly to protect life and liberty. Yet Locke so qualifies popular rights as to reduce them to nothing.

According to Rousseau's theory, the individual is as free in the civil state as he was in the state of nature (if not more so) because he does not surrender his right to any outside person. He surrenders them to himself and to others who form the body politic.

Thus we see that, according to Rousseau, man is a free person in the civil state. Whatever restrictions there may be are restrictions which he places upon himself. He obeys a self-imposed law, and this is not a denial of freeman. 'Obedience to a law which we prescribe to ourselves is liberty'.

The only criticism that we wish to offer of this view of freedom is that Rousseau assumes that a complete democracy means complete freedom. Experience shows that this does not always prove to be the case. Rousseau overlooks the possibility of the tyranny of the majority which J. S. Mill greatly apprehended in modern democracies.

TRUTH IN THE THEORIES OF HOBBES, LOCKE AND ROUSSEAU

Hobbes. The theory of Hobbes as a whole is very consistently developed. Once we grant his premises, his conclusions necessarily follow. Hobbes is an acute thinker. His chief contribution to political theory is his doctrine of legal sovereignty. The chief defect is that he does not supplement legal sovereignty by political sovereignty. Modern writers recognize the truth that behind the legal sovereign, and superior to it, is the political sovereign or the will of the people. Hobbes is mistaken in identifying the will of the state with the will of the *de facto* ruler. Such identification makes it difficult for him to distinguish the State from government. In fact, he goes so far as to say that the State is dissolved on the death of a ruler.

Hobbes claims that the sovereign is the representative of the people. But we are bound to say that Hobbes' term 'representative' is not used in its ordinary sense. There is no guarantee that the supposed representative sovereign will really represent the people, *i.e.*, will act for their public good.

It may be argued that the theory of Hobbes allows no liberty to the individual and leaves the individual to the mercy of the ruler. According to this theory, the individual should wait until his life is in danger before he refuses to obey the sovereign. Advocates of the rights of the people may say that whenever the sovereign acts in a tyrannical way, paying little attention to people's welfare the 'right of resistance' should be asserted. In reply to this argument it must be said that, even on Hobbes' own grounds, whenever the government is badly carried on the contract should disappear. But what is much more important is that Hobbes makes us see the fundamental necessity of a strong government. He realizes the danger of allowing the 'right to resistance' too soon. As Ivor Brown remarks, Hobbes was the first great philosopher of discipline.

For thinkers like Hobbes who start with absolute individualism, it is difficult to get a real insight into society. The starting point of Hobbes is defective. He assumes that man is essentially selfish and that he is actuated solely by the pleasure-pain motive. This is false psychology. Plato, on the other hand, starts with right assumption that the individual is not self-sufficient and that he has no meaning or significance apart from society. In Hobbes the only common element which unites people is their common fear of anarchy. So he is compelled to put the unity of society, apart from the people, in the will of the sovereign.

Locke. Locke is the philosopher of the English Revolution of 1688. His *Second Treatise on Civil Government* was very influential historically. It throws a great deal of light on the ideas of men during the Revolution. It is a political pamphlet rather than a scientific treatise on political theory.

It is not so closely argued as Hobbes' *Leviathan*. The central idea in Locke's theory is that the sole function of the government is to satisfy the needs of the people. If a thing works for the public good, Lokce does not care much about philosophical consistency. Hobbes makes order and security all important. Locke says that the government should not only keep order but should also govern well. The ruler should rule for the welfare of the subject. All this leads Locke to recognize the existence of political sovereignty, although he does not fully understand the implications of legal sovereignty. In bringing out the difference between Hobbes and Locke with regard to this point. Gilchrist observes: 'Hobbes gives a theory of legal sovereignty without recognizing the existence and power of political sovereignty; Locke recognizes the force of political sovereignty but does not give adequate recognition to legal sovereignty' *(28:63)*.

Rousseau: (1) Rousseau retains the language of the contract, but his ideas often surpass the ideas of the contract theory. In the words of MacIver: "Rousseau poured new wine into the old bottle, and the bottle burst." Writing in much the same vein, Lipson describes the *Social Contract* of Rousseau as "a work for the most part closely reasoned, yet containing illogical lapses and elusive concepts which have yielded equal inspiration to mutually incompatible successors."

(2) Rousseau combines the best elements in the theories of Hobbes and Locke. As one writer puts it, he combines the premises and temper of Hobbes with the conclusions of Locke.

From Hobbes he takes over the idea of sovereignty as absolute, inalienable, and indivisible, and from Locke he borrows the idea of public good as the test of a good government. The combination of these two ideas results in the doctrine of the general will. Unlike Locke, Rousseau is not content with insisting merely on the good of the people. He wants control of the people as a whole. 'Thus in Rousseau's hands the theory becomes fundamentally democratic and the claim is made that the people as a whole shall rule in fact as well as in name. . . . It was Rousseau, above all, who first made positive democracy a live doctrine in the world of politics *(Cole)*.'

THE DOCTRINE OF THE GENERAL WILL

The doctrine of the general will has played a very considerable part in recent political discussion. To some thinkers it is a meaningless, if not a dangerous, doctrine. To others it is the cornerstone of democracy and of political philosophy.

In order properly to understand the conception of the general will, it is necessary to go behind that conception and begin with the distinction between 'actual will' and 'real will'. At the very outset, it must be said that the terms 'actual' and 'real' are used in a technical sense in order to convey two different ideas. Therefore, to use the terms interchangeably, as we do in popular conversation, is not fair.

Those who use the term in the technical sense and make the distinction serve as a basis for the conception of the general will, avail themselves of the ever-present conflict that goes on in man between 'I' and 'better than I'. They use the term 'actual will' to describe man's impulsive and unreflective will. It is my will from moment to moment. It does not take into account life as a whole. It considers self-interest, but does not consider it in relation to the well-being of the community at large. It is the individual's rebellious will, his 'transitory' or 'trivial' will. It is narrow and self-contradictory. If I am a reasonable being at all, I try to free myself from this 'actual' will, however intense it may be, and bring myself under the subjection of my 'real' will. My 'real' will expresses my true freedom. It is my 'constant' will, not in the sense of being 'permanent' merely, but in the sense of giving me abiding satisfaction. It is a will purged and purified of at least some of its selfishness. It is my 'good' will. It no doubt takes self-interest into account, but it duly subordinates it to a common interest or common good.

Hobhouse is a vehement critic of the above distinction between the 'actual' will and the 'real' will. He claims that if the 'real' will were worked out it would be so remote from anything that we know that we would not be able even to recognize it. Despite what Hobhouse might say, the 'real' will is present to a substantial extent in the average citizen although we admit that in its fulness it is not complete even in the best of us. The mere fact that a certain desire of mine is intense does not make it 'real'. What makes it 'real' is its conformity to the common good of which the individual good is an intrinsic part. The average man's life is a mixture of the 'actual' and 'real' wills, with a more or less steady progress towards the 'real'.

It is upon the above conception of the 'real' or 'good' will that philosophers have built the doctrine of the general will. General will may be defined as the sum total, or, better still, an organization or synthesis of the 'real' wills of the individuals comprising society. It is the common consciousness of a common end or good. It is the most fundamental of Rousseau's political concepts, although his ideas on it are not always clear. For the original contract which brings civil society into existence, Rousseau thinks that unanimous consent is necessary; but after that, general will is enough. The term 'general will' suggests two ideas to him—the numbers voting and the common interest which it expresses. In one place he says clearly that common interest is more important. To quote his own words: 'What makes the will general is less the number of votes than the common interest uniting them' (*67: Bk. II. Ch. IV*). Yet there are times when he comes dangerously close to identifying general will with a numerical majority.

All of this means that general will is not identical with majority vote or public opinion. So long as genuine public interest is present, general will may be expressed by the vote of a majority, and even by the vote of a single person. For, the majority opinion may at times be little more than collective selfishness. Nevertheless, we are justified in saying that majority opinion is more likely to be general than the will of a single person or selected class of persons. It is a question of probability. Thus it is that the doctrine of the general will in practical terms leads to the democratic form of government. A democratic organization is likely to be more truly expressive of the general will of the community than an aristocratic or a monarchic organization. But even in an aristocratic or a monarchic organization so long as society holds together and there is no violent conflict, general will may be said to be indirectly present.

HOW GENERAL WILL IS GENERATED

In any society, according to Rousseau, we start with what he calls the Will of All, *i.e.* the particular wills of the members of society. Each member of society looks at any public question before him from his own particular angle. But if it is a decent type of society with the spirit of citizenship present in it, the selfish elements in the wills of the individuals cancel one another out; and as the result of such mutual cancellation we eventually get a general will. Thus we start with the Will of All and arrive at a General Will. This does not mean that the general will is simply a compromise, or the lowest common denominator. It is the expression of the highest in every man.

Such a general will is, according to Rousseau, the only manifestation of sovereignty. When sovereignty acts for the common interest, it is the exercise of the general will. So long as laws are in the common interest, they are an expression of the general will. General will is the key to self-government. When it is in operation, the individual can be 'forced to be free'. In such cases, the individual is forced out of a lower level of living and thinking, and is free to a higher level of living and thinking. It is like the 'freedom' of a man who is forcibly turned back from walking over a dangerous bridge, the peril of which he did not realize, or of a man who is constrained from contracting himself into a life of slavery.

CHARACTERISTICS OF THE GENERAL WILL

The first characteristic of the general will is its *unity*. The general will cannot be self-contradictory, because it is a reasonable will. It does not exclude variety. It makes for unity in variety.

Secondly, the general will is characterized by *permanence*. It is to be looked for directly neither 'in the tempests of popular feeling nor in the vagaries of statesmen. It is to be sought in the character of the people. It is more permanent than any particular act or movement in which it finds expression' *(54:140)*.

Thirdly, the general will is always a *right will*, because it always tends to the welfare of the whole. It aims at what is right and best under any given circumstance. This does not mean that it is infallible. As Rousseau points out the will is always sound but the judgment guiding it may be deficient. It may make errors of judgment, but cannot be morally vicious. People start out with the right aim, although they may be led astray.

Criticism : The doctrine of the general will has been subjected to several lines of criticism :

(1) The conception is said to be too abstract and narrow, unlike anything that we know in the world of practical affairs. If the general will is not to be determined by a majority vote, critics say that it is nothing. It is neither general nor a will.

(2) Some writers say that the doctrine may easily lead to State absolutism. In the name of the 'general will' the worst kind of tyranny may be perpetuated. The phrase 'forced to be free' opens the flood gates of absolutism. There is much force in this criticism.

(3) The doctrine of the general will hinges upon the conception of the common interest, and common interest, it is argued, is very difficult to define. Even the worst of tyrants can justify his action under the pretext of common good. Besides, we cannot always say in advance whether any particular expression of the general will will be in the common interest or not. Only the sequel can answer that question.

(4) The objection is raised by some that, even if we grant for the take of argument that the general will is always right, there is no guarantee that the State machinery will always be right. In reply to this objection we grant that the State machinery is imperfect. But we do not pretend that we can fully realize the general will. All that we can hope to do with the imperfect machinery at our disposal is to approximate to the general will as far as possible. It is in the educated or enlightened public opinion that we should look for the best approximation to the general will of the State.

TRUTH IN THE DOCTRINE OF THE GENERAL WILL

(1) It gives direction to political endeavour. It places before us a definite goal towards which we can strive in spite of temporay setbacks.

(2) It emphasizes the fact that society is an organic unity and not a mere aggregate of isolated individuals. It shows that the State has a will and unity of its own, in some ways different from the will and unity of its individual members. 'The State indeed has no life apart from the lives of its members, but it has or may have, a longer, broader, and fuller life than that of any individual or of any generation of its citizens' (*54:139*).

(3) It demonstrates the truth that 'Will, not force, is the basis of the State.' The conception of the general will does not call for the coercion of the minority *qua* minority. It shows that the policy of the majority can be modified according to the strength and sagacity of the minority.

(4) It teaches that the State is natural in that it has its basis in the will and the natural need of man. 'The State exists and claims our obedience because it is a natural extension of our personality (*Cole*).'

(5) It shows that the true basis of our democracy is not force, not even consent, but active will.

The reason why we ought to obey the general will is not because it is imposed upon us, but because it is an intrinsic part of ourselves. In obeying the general will of the State we obey ourselves, the very best in us.

LIBERAL IDEAS OF HOBBES, LOCKE AND ROUSSEAU

Hobbes as Founder of the Liberal Tradition

Hobbes, who superficially appears to be a conservative defender of monarchism, probably produced the most revolutionary theory of his age. His political theory was a defence of absolute government in an age of anarchy. A republican dictator would have been as welcome to Hobbes as a hereditary monarch if he could maintain social peace. His political theory did not recognize dynastic legitimacy or divine sanctions of monarchical rule. "His political philosophy", says Sabine, "had too wide a sweep to make good propaganda, but its drastic logic affected the whole later history of moral and political thought. Its positive influence was not fully developed until the nineteenth century, when his ideas were incorporated in the philosophical radicalism of the Utilitarians and in John Austin's theory of sovereignty. Hobbes's thought thus served the ends of middle class liberalism, a cause with which the philosopher would have had little sympathy." (*162:456*).

His conception of the state as utilitarian institution consciously designed by man for private security, his egoistic interpretation of human nature and atomic conception of society, the individualistic implications of his psychology and social theory and, finally, the idea of the state as the sovereign social institution were among the most important elements of the political theory of Hobbes which considerably influenced the later development of the liberal tradition.

Locke as Father of English Liberalism

While the support of Hobbes's political theory to middle class liberalism was unintentional, Locke may be regarded as the avowed father of English liberalism (*162:535*). He was not a profound philosopher as Hobbes had been. But he symbolized in his personality the classic temper of liberalism in the most characteristic fashion. He was the first consistent defender of constitutional government. His elaborate defence of private property, which was a part of his wider conception of rights, long remained an article of faith of the European liberals. Similarly, his belief that the protection of private rights of the individual is identical with the preservation of the common good of the community was shared by all good liberals of the succeeding generations. His suggestion that governmental authority should be based on the consent of its citizens was another contribution to the philosophy of liberalism.

Locke even preached the right of resistance against established authority. People could legitimately revolt against a government which failed to protect their natural rights. These natural rights consisted of—to use Locke's characteristic phrase—"life, liberty and estate." But this defender of the English Revolution was neither a democrat nor a radical in his political outlook. "The English Revolution", as Sabine says, "did not break violently the tradition of English government, and similarly Locke, its philosophical exponent, was the most conservative of revolutionists" (*162* : *535*). In spite of the obviously conservative import of his ideas and numerous ambiguities of his philosophy, Locke became the most important single influence in the development of radical political thought of both America and France in the eighteenth century.

Rousseau, Voltaire and Montesquieu

The centre of liberal political thought shifted to France in the eighteenth century. While Voltaire and Montesquieu continued Locke's tradition of individualism, Rousseau introduced a collectivistic element in the Liberal tradition for the first time. Montesquieu elaborated his conception of the separation of power as the necessary mechanism of constitutional government for the defence of liberty. Voltaire was the first bourgeois thinker to develop an elaborate conception of civil liberty in a middle-class state. But the representative French thinker of this age was Rousseau. His political thought represented the reactions of that section of the French middle class which was destined to play the most destructive role in enacting the drama of the French Revolution. His political philosophy was collectivistic because it was intended to stir mass action against an established system of tyranny.

There was a romantic element in Rousseau's ideas because they were propounded in an atmosphere which was not rationally suited to their birth. This is what Laski has to say about Rousseau's place in the history of European liberalism : "Radical in theory, with even a proletarian nuance to his thinking, in positive recommendations he added little to his time. It was his special genius less to determine what men thought in matters of social constitution than to disturb their minds so profoundly as to provide new foundations for their thinking. He incarnated in himself all the dissatisfaction and discontent of his time. He taught men to see their wrongs with new intensity. But it is not easy to say whether his influence, as a whole, was radical or conservative. If Marat and Robespierre were his pupils in one generation, Hegel and Savigny were among the greatest of his disciples in the next, and the link between him and the romantic reaction is, of course, direct and profound" (*132:112*).

Liberalism in the 19th Century

The nineteenth century is an epoch of triumphant liberalism. In England the utilitarian thinkers, Bentham and John Stuart Mill, made important contributions to individualistic liberalism. Following Hume, Bentham and other utilitarian thinkers rejected the theory of natural rights which was advocated by Locke but invented new utilitarian sanctions for the guarantee of fundamental rights of the citizen by the legal sovereign. Freedom of thought, speech, and action were now accepted fundamental liberal values although they were no longer called by the name of natural rights of man, Adam Smith propounded the economic theory of liberalism. The leading commercial and industrial nation of the world adopted the economic and political institutions of liberalism and operated them with a remarkable degree of success. With the emergence of another English-speaking nation on the other side of the Atlantic, the liberal ideas and institutions scored another success.

Idealistic and Collectivistic Elements in Liberalism

By the end of the nineteenth century, liberalism had become the unchallenged creed of all progressive nations of the world. But the individualistic content of the older liberalism was gradually modified by the intrusions of collectivistic ideas of Rousseau and Hegel into the main body of the liberal political thought. Green, Bradley and Bosanquet led the collectivistic revolt in English liberalism making an earnest effort to restate the principles of liberalism on the basis of an ethical idealism derived partly from the teaching of Plato and Aristotle and partly from the writings of Kant and Hegel (*50:63*). Tocqueville and Hobhouse manifested an intellectual drift towards collectivism without being idealists.

Contrary to the conventional liberal theories of the state, which originated with Hobbes and Locke, Hegel views the supreme institution not as an arrangement aiming at protection of man's self interest which is [illegible] at the level of civil society, but as transcending the egoism of individuals. "The state to Hegel", as Avineri says, "is universal altruism – a mode of relating to a universe of human beings not out of self-interest but out of solidarity." (*263 : 350*). According to Hegel, "the rationale of property is to be found not in the satisfaction of needs but in the suppression of the pure subjectivity of personality. In his property, a person exists for the first time as reason." (*263 : 351*).

CHAPTER 8

THE JUSTIFICATION AND END OF THE STATE

THE JUSTIFICATION OF THE STATE

Even more important than investigation into the origin and evolution of the State is the question relating to the justification and end of the State. Merely to show that the State has come into being due to one reason or another is not enough. What we are most concerned with is, why should there be a state at all? Has the State a rational basis?

The State is a way of regulating human conduct, by compulsion if necessary. The will of the State is in many ways superior to all other wills. The State has the power to take away the individual's life, liberty, and property. It commands him to surrender his property by means of taxes and his life upon the battlefield or in punishment for crime. Can all this be justified? Many attempts have been made to justify, and even condemn, the existence of the State in all ages. We shall sum them up under the following heads:

1. The Anarchistic View

Coker defines anarchism as "the doctrine that political authority in any of its forms is unnecessary and undesirable" *(93:192)*. Lao-Tse in China, five centuries before Christ, taught something like anarchism in his doctrine of non-assertiveness. Among Western thinkers, *William Godwin* (1756-1836), an Englishman, was one of the early advocates of anarchism. He was as much opposed to political authority as he was to private property.

Proudhon (1809-1865), a Frenchman, who, according to Coker, was probably the first to call himself an anarchist, declared property to be theft, particularly when it took the form of profits, interest and rent. He attacked both government and private property—the latter for its monopolistic and exploitative tendencies.

Thoreau (1817-1862), an American anarchist, advocated civil disobedience, the non-payment of taxes and the like, thus anticipating Mahatma Gandhi by half a century.

For some reason or other anarchism found a fruitful soil in Russia and France. Coker attributes it to the anti-clericalism of these two countries. In Russia it was expounded by *Bakunin* (1814-1876), *Kropotkin* (1842-1921) and *Tolstoy*. The former two advocated organized revolution and attacked the centralized control of the Marxist system.

According to Bakunin, who founded a kind of proletarian anarchist movement, anarchism is the natural goal of man's moral evolution. Political authority, private property, and religion belong to the lower stages of his development. The State, Bakunin held, debases man's moral nature, because an act done under compulsion has no moral or rational quality. To quote from Coker, "The state makes tyrants or egoists out of the few and servants or dependants out of the many" (*93:204*).

Bakunin holds that anarchism could be realized both by evolutionary and revolutionary methods, *i.e.,* by education and intrigue. When the State is destroyed, its place is to be taken by a free society based on contract and voluntary association.

Kropotkin, who followed Bakunin, some years later stated his ideas in terms of biology and "human geography". He stressed the co-operative principle in man and animals as against the competitive. He believed in a society of mutual aid. Like Bakunin he thought that the State, private property, and religious authority stood in the way of the realization of the anarchistic goal. Man has not always lived under a State and, therefore, political authority is a later innnovation. Ancient habits and usages based on co-operation and instinct of justice are enough to hold men together. Laws formulated by the State have a class bias. Even when they are based on ancient customs, they are such customs as bear heavily on the poor and unfortunate. The modern State thus is not "the guardian of the inherent rights of the individual". Standing armies and prisons are immoral because they help to debase human nature. "Economically, the new order will be that of complete communism" (*93:212*). Each man is to choose his own work and put in four to five hours of labour at some socially useful service. Man, left to himself prefers work to idleness, order to disorder, social morality to conventional morality, and natural religion to dogmatic religion. In all that he wrote Kropotkin placed emphasis on social responsibility and human brotherhood.

The doctrine of Bakunin and Kropotkin made some appeal to the working classes in the last century, but it was shortlived. In fairness to Bakunin and Kropotkin, it must be said that though they believed in revolution, they never advocated "the terrorism of assassination". They did not go so far as did the Nihilists. Their teaching was that "private property, the state and the church must be got rid of, but not property owners, politicians, and priests" (*93:221*).

Like the Marxists, anarchists believe in a classless and stateless society, with this qualification that the Marxists and Leninists believe in the need of the State during the transitional period.

Leo Tolstoy was a philosophical anarchist. He was not an arm-chair philosopher, but a literary man who tried to put his socio-philosophical ideas into practice. He was opposed "to a life of luxury, sophistication, and oppression" and exalted "honest labour and simple living" (*93:223*).

Even though he did not adhere to dogmatic Christianity, his ideas were imbued with Christian ethics. The major Christian principle which he emphasized was love. He opposed the State because it was based on force and not on Christ's teaching, "Resist not evil; but overcome evil by good"

Tolstoy was equally opposed to the institution of private property which he held was contrary to the Christian ideal of love and brotherhood.

As to how the anarchistic society was to be brought about, Tolstoy's emphasis was on the regeneration of the individual and not on violent revolution. The anarchistic society, according to him, was to be realized through such means as passive resistance, the non-payment of taxes, refusal to serve on juries, and defiance of laws which do not accord with one's conscience. Two of Tolstoy's anarchistic writings are "The Kingdom of God Within You" and "What Shall We Do Now".

The Anarchistic Theory

The anarchists find no justification whatsoever for the State. They believe that the State has no rational purpose to serve and that the sooner we eliminate it the better it will be for man's growth and development. The revolutionary anarchists want to subvert the present social order by violent methods. With these anarchists we are not much concerned in a serious study of political science. The type who merit our attention are the philosophical anarchists such as Tolstoy and Kropotkin. Their objection is not so much to the State as such, but to force used by the State. They claim that the truly moral life is realized by one's own effort and that the authority of the State is a hindrance to the development of such morality. They see in this authority a destruction of all moral values. The State is to them like a red rag to a mad bull. Instead of making man moral, it makes him immoral by the force that it wields. Instead of trusting the individual to do the right thing, it distrusts him and threatens him with punishment. Government, they argue, is therefore not only useless, but also mischievous. According to them, voluntary organization can very well undertake the work of society and, if the State is to be retained at all, it should become a voluntary organization. Laws should take the form of suggestion and advice; and taxes the form of voluntary contribution. As Garner puts it, according to Kropotkin, there is to be "no compulsion, no law and no Government exercising force" (*23:448*). The "coercive" state is to be replaced by voluntary associations which look after internal order, national defence, and the enforcement of contracts.

The philosophical anarchists believe that society should be governed by love and not by the 'irrational' principle of force. Man should be so educated that he will voluntarily and almost instinctively do that which is true, good, beautiful, and noble. The perfect society they conceive in terms of a love-knit family, untouched by authority. The only kind of government that they are prepared to support is the perfect and unfettered self-government of the individual. Recent anarchists have usually been opposed to the institution of private property as well as to organized religious authority. Bakunin (1814-76) wanted a society which would be anarchistic, collectivistic and atheistic. If his type of society can be called anarchistic communism, that of Thoreau can be called anarchistic individualism.

Criticism. Several lines of criticism suggest themselves in considering philosophical anarchism.

(1) We are prepared to concede to the anarchists that true morality is largely self-earned. But this is not to admit that State action means a complete destruction of moral values. The State cannot *directly* promote or enforce morality. Yet it can so order external conditions as to make it possible for the individual to live the good life.

(2) The anarchist is mistaken in thinking that liberty is the greatest of all political goods. Liberty, we need to remind ourselves, is not an end in itself. It is simply a means to an end. Liberty and authority are not opposed to one another, as the anarchist conceives them to be. They are supplementary to and complementary of each other. No human association leaves the individual completely free. Every group implies some restraint upon individual freedom.

(3) The anarchist gives us a faulty picture of human nature. His assumption is that organised political society has debased human character and that once it is removed, man will once again become a noble being. This is very much like the assumption of Rousseau in his essay on *Inequality* that man in the state of nature lived an idyllic life and that the development of civilization has brought about all our present ills. However, Rousseau himself considerably modified this view in his later *Social Contract* and came to the conclusion that the balance of advantage is on the side of the civil state.

The anarchist assumes that we can effect tremendous improvement in human nature by education, persuasion, and moral teaching and that in some far-off day at least, we can entirely rid ourselves of the State. While we do not want to deny that human nature can be greatly improved by the means suggested and that the scope within which it is possible to improve human nature has not yet been fully discovered, we fear that the abolition of the State at present or in any conceivable future will lead to general disorder and chaos. The brute in man cannot be easily destroyed and it is the coercive authority of the State which keeps it in check.

(4) The anarchist assumes that there is nothing but love in the perfect household. This is a false assumption. Authority, law, and restraint are not evident on the surface in an ideal family. Nevertheless, they are there. As Hearnshaw observes, in order to curb criminal tendencies in the natures of all, it is necessary to have the might of the State in reserve. Therefore, at least for the present, we cannot dispense with the tutelage of government and the sanity of law.

It is wrong to assume that all government means force and aggression. Many of the activities of modern government are in the form of aid and assistance.

(5) The anarchist proposes to do away with the authority of the State and substitute for it the authority of the individual conscience. But the

individual conscience, as has been aptly remarked, is an extremely tricky and capricious sovereign.

(6) From the practical point of view, it must be said that the voluntary associations proposed by the anarchists for the defence of the country, police protection and enforcement of contracts, would be found to be totally inadequate if not altogether unworkable.

(7) Destruction of the State would not result in a state of pristine purity but in a state of affairs where the strong would dominate the weak. Or, it may mean reversion to patriarchal or clan type of society and mankind will have to start all over again the upward climb of centuries.

2. The Religious View

From very early times people have justified the existence of the State on the supposed ground that it is the creation of God and that obedience to the State is in accordance with Divine purpose. Oriental monarchies were for the most part theocracies. The conception of theocracy was most highly developed among the Hebrews who regarded themselves as God's chosen people. The Jewish State was conceived as the direct result of Divine will and was justified wholly on religious grounds.

The Greeks, too, justified the State in religious terms, although they did not carry the theocratic conception so far. Among the Greeks the worship of common goods lay at the foundation of State life.

Like the Greek city-state, the Roman State had a religious origin. The Romans, too, had their special divinities and the Roman tribes were knit together by a common religious worship. Later on when Rome became an empire, divine attributes were assigned to the Emperor.

Martin Luther, with whom the Protestant Reformation began, wrote: 'It is in no wise proper for anyone who would be a Christian to set himself up against his government, whether it acts justly or unjustly.' Unfortunately this view is still held by many Christians in Western lands.

Criticism. In this age of scientific enquiry the argument that we should obey the State merely because it is supposed to have been created by God does not carry much conviction. There is no positive proof to show that any State is the direct creation of God. The most that even religious-minded writers are prepared to admit is that State-life is in accordance with a divine purpose. Even if we assume for the sake of argument that the State is divinely created, such a theory does not help us to distinguish right forms of political authority from wrong forms.

3. Physical Force

From the very early days of political speculation attempt has been made to justify the existence of the State on the ground that it possesses superior physical force. The Sophists held that the State was either the rule of the strong for the oppression of the weak or the combination of the weak, who formed the majority, against the physically strong but less numerous. To Machiavelli the State is only a power system. Yet towards the close of his celebrated book, he admits that the power of the State is not for its own sake, but for the sake of the prestige, honour, and well-being of the people.

In modern times, Spinoza, Marx, Engels, Nietzsche, and Spencer have given currency to the view that the State is the embodiment of force. Spinoza held that the state expressed superior physical strength and that its right was limited only by its power. Marx and Engels regarded the State as an instrument of the ruling class. Nietzsche built his theory of the Superman on the basis of physical strength. Spencer held that the State was an expression of mere brute force and that its power should be curbed in the interest of individual liberty.

Criticism. To say that we must obey the State merely because it is the rule of the strongest seems absurd.

The force theory is in essence a revolutionary theory. For, if it is fully worked out, it will mean that any group is justified in asserting itself and securing control of the government as soon as it is physically able to do so. The force of the State is justifiable only so long as it is able to repel other forces. But the moment one of these forces is able to establish itself successfully, it becomes right and the original force ceases to be right. We may, therefore, ask with Rousseau, 'What kind of right is that which perishes when force fails?'

To add one further point, a State in the last resort must use force; but it must be capable of support on moral grounds. In the words of Lipson: "The State must either monopolize the force of the community or risk surrender to whoever can muster counter-force for its overthrow....Power must be clothed with moral approval if it is to receive our willing consent" *(140:54)*.

Agreeing with the above view, MacIver labours the point that power is not the same as authority. He says that "because Gandhi had authority he had power". "Power alone has no legitimacy, no mandate, no office" *(412:83)*. In early society, power depended on property, status, prestige, etc. Today it is multiform in nature. The mistake made by the Marxists is their over-emphasis on power. "The Marxist teaching is that economic power is always primary in the capitalistic society and that political power is both its offspring and its servant" *(142:91)*.

4. The Contract View

In the 17th and 18th centuries in Western Europe, the contract view was the most popular in justifying the existence of the State. According to it the authority of the State is justifiable because we have set it up ourselves by free choice. At first sight, it would appear that there was no better way of justifying the existence of the State than this view. The State, it might be argued, is the product of the will of the individual and, therefore, obedience to it is thoroughly reasonable.

Criticism. A moment's reflection, however, is enough to show that to base political authority on a contract is to base it on shifting sand :

(1) History knows of no State which came into being as the result of a deliberate agreement among men. The State was not deliberately created by particular individuals; it has evolved gradually.

(2) If subjection to the State is justified on the ground of free consent, it is reasonable to demand unanimous consent for every law of the State before it can become operative. Mere majority opinion is not enough. There is no reasonable ground for the coercion of a dissenting minority by the majority. The force of this criticism is clearly brought out in the political theory of Herbert Spencer.

(3) Even if literal consent is possible in any matter, it is ruled out in the modern State by the fact that representative government in some form or other is the only way by which the will of the State can find expression. Direct democracy is impossible under modern conditions. To say that tacit consent is enough in these cases, according to the argument of the contractualists, is not justifiable. 'Because consent involves the notion of a deliberate act of will, something more positive than this (*viz.*, tacit consent) is required' (*48:31*).

(4) If consent is freely given, it is logical to argue that it might be freely withdrawn and that those so withdrawing might freely unite again to form another State. Hobbes realized this difficulty and attempted to solve it by declaring that it was a law of nature that men should keep their covenants when made. It is obvious that such an argument carries with it no conviction whatever. It is a pure assumption on the part of Hobbes, which has no support in experience or reason. Other contractualists have argued that people who want to withdraw their consent from the law of the State may be regarded as 'strangers within the State'. This is sheer nonsense.

5. The Utility Theory

Many thinkers have tried to justify the existence of the State on utilitarian grounds. They argue that the rationale of the State lies in the fact that it provides law and order, protects the individual against internal and external enemies, enforces contracts, adjusts relationships between individuals and groups, fosters literature, art and science, and provides, in short, the framework within which the life of society can be carried on with the least possible friction and the maximum advantage possible.

Criticism. There isno doubt that the above justification of the State is much more satisfactory than those that we have previously considered. Nevertheless, it too is open to criticism.

(1) Theories based upon utility are apt to take too narrow and materialistic a view of the State and regard the State as 'a mere public utilities company'. We have considered this point of view in an earlier chapter and have said that the State is not a mere partnership for the attainment of certain material ends. The State should undoubtedly secure the material well-

being of its members. But at the same time it has a moral and spiritual function to fulfil.

(2) The utility theory is apt to regard the State as a mere means to the welfare of the individual, while as a matter of fact, it is both a means and an end. The State considers the welfare not only of existing generations but also that of generations yet to be. In this latter respect it may be regarded as an end in itself.

6. Necessity of Organization

A particular form of the utilitarian justification of the State is expressed by some who emphasize the need for organization. Primitive man did not know the value of organization. What organization he had was of an elementary character, and more or less instinctive in origin. But civilized times have witnessed the establishment of organization for every conceivable purpose. Experience has taught us that the group can do certain things more successfully than the individual.

Criticism. While there is no objection to this justification of the State, it must be said that the criticisms mentioned above in connection with the utilitarian theory hold good here as well. Besides, it is too narrow and inadequate view of the State.

7. The Psychological View

Attempts have been made since the days of Aristotle to show that man has a political instinct and that it is a part of man's nature to be ruled. Man, it is said, is a 'political animal'.

Criticism. If this be so, how do we account for the fact that there are those who deny that they have an instinctive sociability or political sentiment? As Willoughby has aptly pointed out, our problem in political theory is to justify political as humanly exercised, and to harmonize it with man's personal freedom. The psychological view does not help us in this task, for it does not show how, or by whom political authority is to be exercised and how it is to be reconciled with individual freedom.

8. The Idealistic View

According to the Idealistic view, obedience to the State is justifiable because the State expresses the best in us. It is not an enemy of man, not even a disinterested observer, but the true friend of the individual. In obeying the will of the State we are obeying our own wills, purged and purified of their selfishness. In their true being, the State and the individual are identical. To use the language of Hegel, the State is the 'actualisation of freedom' or 'the embodiment of concrete freedom.'

From the idealistic point of view, the State is an ethical institution. It makes possible free social life, without which man cannot realize himself fully. Hence obedience to the State becomes a moral duty.

It is in this manner that T. H. Green justifies obedience to the State.

He controverts the popular belief that the root of morality is man's conscience and that of political subjection is force.

Criticism. (1) It will no doubt be said that the view presented here is fanciful inasmuch as there is no actual State which answers to the picture painted. We do not argue, as Hegel did, that the ideal State is identical with the Prussian State of Hegel's day or with any other State. Nevertheless we contend that the State embodies, however, imperfectly, the conception of a common good, and it is this conception which is the true source of political subjection.

(2) Those who are opposed to the idealistic justification of the State will probably argue that force creates the State and habit perpetuates it or that political subjection is in the interest of social expediency. There is no doubt that self-interest, force, and fear have played a considerable part in the creation and perpetuation of the State, but they have produced good results only so far as they have been 'fused with and guided by some unselfish element' (*29:XVI*).

(3) It may be further said that even if it be granted for the sake of argument that will is the basis of the State, it can be the basis only of the democratic State. How can people have a feeling for the State and an appreciation for the common good unless they actively participate in the legislative and administrative function of the State? This is a forcible criticism, and we are bound to accept it as generally valid.

THE END OF THE STATE

The justification of the State is incomplete without a consideration of the end or purpose for which the State exists. In discussing this theme it is usual to distinguish between the immediate or proximate end, and the final or ultimate end. While it is easy to determine the former, the latter is more a matter of faith than of knowledge.

To the Greeks the purpose of the State was self-sufficiency. The State, they said, should provide for its citizens all that was necessary for their highest development and happiness. Plato regarded the State as a macrocosm in which the individual could find his proper place and perform the duties for which he was best fitted. The rulers and warriors should give their undivied attention to the highest well-being of the State, and to this end Plato laid down a communistic way of life for them. To the mind of Plato the State was a well-developed organism in which each individual and each class had a particular place to fill and was happy in so doing.

Aristotle believed that the purpose of the State was to secure the development of virtue in the citizens; but he, too, believed in the self-sufficiency of the Greek city-state, which was to produce the greatest happiness in the individual. Thus in his *Politics* Aristotle devotes a whole chapter to this theme. A free paraphrase of the chapter is as follows:

The State exists not for the sake of wealth or security or society, but for the sake of a *good life*. If life were the only object of the State, slaves and brute animals might form a State, but they cannot, for they have no share in happiness or in a life of free choice. If alliance and security from injustice or exchange and mutual intercourse were the only objects, all who have formed commercial treaties would be citizens of the State. They do not have common magistraceis, are not concerned with the wrongs and wickedness of the other States, and do not endeavour to make the citizens what they ought to be. The State also takes into consideration *virtue* and *vice*. It is more than a mere alliance designed for the protection of life and property.

Political society therefore exists for the sake of noble actions, and not for mere companionship, and those who contribute most to such a society have the greatest claim to power.

According to Hobbes, the purpose of the State was to maintain order and the right of property. Hobbes took such a gloomy view of the state of nature preceding the establishment of civil society that he held that any State was better than no State. Tyranny was to him preferable to anarchy. Locke, likewise, claimed that the purpose of the State was to maintain life, liberty, and property, by means of a known law and a common judge. When we come to Rousseau, we find a revival of the idea that the State exists in order to make good life possible for the individual, although he does not state it in this particular form. He is convinced that the State is not a mere matter of convenience for the gaining of utilitarian ends, but the highest expression of the best in man.

1. The End as General Happiness

Jeremy Bentham in the early part of the 19th century popularized the idea that the purpose of the State was the promotion of the 'greatest happiness of the greatest number'. This utilitarian view is strongly held even today. It was largely responsible for a great number of reforms in the social and political life of the nineteenth century England. In particular it brought about reforms in the poor law, land law, prison management, divorce law, franchise, and popular education. As Gilchrist observes, it is 'a commonsense expression of the ends of legislation but as a complete expression of the end of the state it breaks down on close examination' (*28:427*).

2. The End as Maintenance of Order

In the nineteenth century many other views were proclaimed regarding the end of the state. One of the most popular of these was the individualistic view that the State existed merely to maintain law. Some writers extended it to include order and security. It was argued that each individual should be left to work but his own salvation free from the activity of the State and that the State should simply provide external and internal protection so that men might live together peaceably.

3. The End as Progress

Some have defined the end of the State as progress. This theory does not say much. It does not state clearly what the end is. The term progress is meaningless apart from the end or goal towards which progress is made. We must determine the end in order to make progress possible.

4. The End as Social Service

Those with a socialistic turn of mind claim that the State exists in order to promote 'certain social services, which have nothing to do with protecting the individual from external attacks, nor the maintenance of law as between the individuals in the State, but which have to do primarily with the social interests of the community' (19). Such an end, we find, is coming more and more to the forefront in the practice of modern states, which undertake the care of public health and public morals and the promotion of the economic interests of the people. A large group of these writers propose to extend the power of the State so as to include the ownership and management of the means of production and distribution.

5. The End as Justice

A great many modern writers regard justice as the end of the State. These are usually idealists but not all idealists accept justice as the political end.

While we are prepared to accept the general statement that the end of the State is ethical, we cannot help feeling that justice as a political end is too narrow a view.

Lipson skilfully combines the second and fifth points of view. He claims that the State exists in order to provide protection, order and justice. To quote his own words: "Protection grows into order and order seeks to blossom into justice" (*140:61*). "If order is to culminate in justice, power must be transmitted into authority" (*140:61*). Force must take the form of protection; power that of order and authority that of justice.

Is the State an End or means? A question which has engaged the special attention of modern writers is this: 'Is the state an end in itself or is it only a means?' The ancients, particularly the Greeks, regarded the State as the highest fulfilment of human life and as an end in itself.

The view that the State is an end in itself was revived in recent times by Hegel, who identified the will of the individual with the will of the State. This view has been carried to its logical conclusion by Fascism.

Over against such absolutism is the view of individualists, to many of whom the State is only a means for the promotion of the welfare of the greatest number of individuals. The chief objection to such a view is that the State does not concern itself entirely with the welfare of any one generation.

Therefore, the general consensus of opinion today is that the State is both an end and a means. Thus Willoughby, in *The Nature of the State*, argues that if we look at the state purely from the individualistic point of view, 'it is only a means, instrumentality, or an expedient through which the highest possible development of humanity is obtained. But if the state is considered an institution distinct and apart from the citizens who compose it, it is, of course,.... an end in itself' *(81:70)*.

According to Garner, the triple end of the State is: firstly, the advancement of the good of the individuals; secondly, the promotion of the collective interests of individuals in their associated capacity; and finally, the furthering of the civilization and progress of the world.

In recent times, in his violent reaction to idealism, Laski has emphasized the State as a means rather than as an end. Laski writes: "For its citizens, a state is what it does; it is not justified merely because it is a state" *(50:18)*. "The philosopher may, like Burke, think of the State as a partnership in all virtue and all perfection; the common man thinks of it as a way of being ruled which satisfies his expectation of legitimate satisfactions" *(50:18)*.

THE STATE AND CLASSES

Moderation of Class Struggle as the Purpose of the State

Laski claims that he has adopted the Marxian view of the end, nature and history of the state with certain modifications which were necessary on account of the so-called excessive simplicity of the Marxian analysis. In his famous essay, "The Origin of the Family, Private Property, and the State", Engels said, "The State is therefore by no means a power imposed on society from the outside; just as little is it "the reality of the moral idea", "the image and reality of reason", as Hegel asserts. Rather, it is a product of society at a certain stage of development; it is the admission that this society has become entangled in an insoluble contradiction with itself, that it is cleft into irreconcilable antagonisms, which it is powerless to dispel. But in order that these antagonisms, classes with conflicting economic interests, might not consume themselves and society in sterile struggle, a power apparently standing above society became necessary for the *purpose* of moderating the conflict and keeping it within the bonds of "order"; and this power, arising out of society, but placing itself above it, and increasingly alienating itself from it, is the state".

Lenin fully agrees with Engels in his essay on "The State and Revolution"' when he says, 'The state is the product and the manifestation of the irreconcilability of class antagonisms. The state arises when, where and to the extent that class antagonisms cannot be objectively reconciled. And, conversely, the existence of the state proves that the class anatgonisms are irreconcilable". Laski has admitted that this analysis of the end of the state is basically correct and no alternative theory has been able to explain its character and justification in a better way.

Coercive Power as the Essence of the State

Both Marx and Laski think that the essence and justification of the state is its coercive power and the armed forces, the police and bureaucracy are the instruments of that coercion. "The basic struggles", says Laski, "are always struggles between economic classes to secure control of the sovereign power. An economic class may be defined as a group of people whose special place in the productive process is differentiated sharply from that of other groups. That place is defined by the system of economic relationships which the state maintains. The state puts at the service of any dominant class in the society that supreme coercive power which is its essence; unless it possesses this, no class can alter fundamentally its position in the society. A class, therefore, which seeks such a fundamental alteration is bound to capture the state *(50:117)*.

Class Domination as the End of State

In this connection, Engels has remarked, "As the state arose from the need to hold class antagonisms in check, but as it arose, at the same time, in the midst of the conflict of these classes, it is, as a rule, the state of the most powerful, economically dominant class, which, through the medium of the state, becomes also the politically dominant class, and thus acquires new means of holding down and exploiting the oppressed class. Thus, the state of antiquity was above all the state of the slave-owners for the *purpose* of holding down the slaves, as the feudal state was the organ of the mobility for holding down the peasant-serfs and bondsmen and the modern representative state is an instrument of exploitation of wage-labour by capital". This shows that historically, the task of the state has been to safeguard the exploitation of one class by another.

The State and Revolution

When Laski accepts the Marxian argument that every state is basically a class state, he has also to accept, somewhat grudgingly, the need for a violent revolution. He says, "The conclusion we have reached is the grave one that in a society where the instruments of production are privately owned the main fact of significance is the struggle for the possession of the state-power between the class which owns those instruments, and that which is denied access to the benefits of that ownership. The conclusion implies that the state is always biased in the interest of the former, and those in whose interests its authority is exercised will not surrender their advantages unless they are compelled to do so.... The view here taken is one that naturally disturbs many generous minds. It postulates the inevitabality of revolution as the midwife of social change; and it admits that there are phases of human evolution in which men cease to settle their differences in terms of reason, and resort to force as the ultimate arbiter of destiny" *(50:138)*.

Differences in the Approaches of Laski and Marx

But there is a difference between the approaches of Laski and Marx to revolution. He suggests the recourse to a violent revolution only when the constitutional methods have either been given a fair trial or their employment has been rendered impossible by the ruling class *(126:233)*. On the whole, he takes a brighter view of capitalist democracy than what strict adherence to Marxism would have permitted him to take. "A democratic republic", says Lenin, "is the best possible political shell for capitalism, and, therefore, once capital has gained control of this very best shell, it establishes its powers so securely, so firmly, that no change, either of persons, of institutions or of parties in the bourgeoisie democratic republic, can shake it"[1].

Dictatorship as the Essence of the State

According to Lenin, the forms of bourgeoisie states are extremely varied, but in essence they are all the same because, in the final analysis, they reveal themselves as the dictatorship of the bourgeoisie. Similarly, there is bound to appear a great variety of political forms of the proletarian states during the transitional phase between capitalism and communism, but they will necessarily be just different forms of the dictatorship of the proletariat. Laski admits that every state including a liberal democracy has a class content but he shirks from what he calls the "excessive simplicity" of this explanation.

Anarchism as the Goal of Communism

As the Marxian thesis assumes, the state and class antagonisms have a reciprocal relation. It logically follows that with the abolition of class antogonism in a communist society, there will be no need of a state as it has existed in history. In Marxian terminology, the state will wither away. Thus the ultimate goal of communism is anarchism *i.e.* the achievement of classless and stateless society shared equally by Marx, Lenin, Bakunin and Kropotkin.

Engels on Classless, Stateless Society

As Engels has significantly remarked, "The state, then, has not existed from all eternity. There have been societies that did without it, that had no conception of the state and state power. At a certain stage of economic development, which was necessarily bound up with the cleavage of society into classes, the state became a necessity owing to this cleavage. We are now rapidly approaching a state in the development of production at which the existence of these classes not only will have ceased to be a necessity, but will become a positive hindrance to production. They will fall as inevitably as they arose at an earlier stage. Along with them the state will inevitably fall. The society that will organise production on the basis of a free and equal association of the producers will put the whole machinery of state where it will then belong: in the Museum of Antiquities, by the side of the spinning wheel and the bronze axe" (*146*: *Vol. II, 292*). In the past, the state had been an instrument of class exploitation and oppression. In the socialist

1. Lenin : "Selected Works", Vol. II, His essay on "The State and Revolution," p. 149.

society of the future, such a state will have no reason to exist because the exploitation of one class by another will be abolished.

In his essay on "Communism", Laski has dismissed this part of the Marxian theory of the state as irrelevant to this central thesis. It is that utopian element of the Marxian prophecy which a realisic political thinker like Laski need not consider. As a matter of fact, the theory of the withering away of the state is the logical outcome of his contention that the state is a necessary product of class antagonisms in society.

Laski's Partial Acceptance of the Marxian View on Withering Away of the State

In "The State in Theory and Practice", Laski somewhat revises his earlier attitude towards this aspect of the Marxian doctrine. "This is the truth in the Marxian argument," he now admits, "that in a classless society the state, as we know it has always had the function not of preserving law and order as absolute goods seen in the same broad way by all members of the state; the function of the state has always been to preserve that law and that order which are implicit in the purposes of a particular class-society. And since the character of a given class-society is always set by the interests of those who own the instruments of production, it follows that the law and order maintained serve, at every critical point, those interests and those interests only. If, then, the instruments of production were owned by society in comm on, it follows that the state-power would protect the interests of the who e society and not the interests only of a class in it. Under those circu stances the habits of the state, as we have known them, would clearly undergo a profound transformation. A common organ of government would still be necessary. But the postulates on which it would proceed would not involve the elevation of supreme coercive power to maintaining the economic interests of the property-owning class" *(50:206)*.

This is partial acceptance of the Marxian view that the state becomes superfluous in a socialist society. There is no longer any need of the state as a repressive machinery. In Marxian terminology, the government of persons is replaced by the administration of things and the direction of the process of production by the voluntary efforts of the people.

Conceptions of Individual Liberty and Group Autonomy Revised

There are certain important consequenecs of Laski's acceptance of the Marxian conception of the State as an instrument of class domination. In the first place, it has compelled him to revise his earlier notions of liberty conceiving it in the manner of Mill's tradition *(49:161)*. Secondly, Laski has been obliged to withdraw his former support for the principle of autonomous groups standing on an equal footing with the state. Lastly, he has endeavoured to evolve a comprehensive theory of law in the light of his new Marxian thesis *(50:122)*.

The liberty protected by the capitalist state is merely a liberty for the capitalist class. The judgments of the courts are always biased in favour of the capitalists, and the workers cannot expect equal protection of law on account of the various disabilities imposed upon them. The fundamental cleavage in society is not between one social group and another but between one economic class and another. Everything has now a class perspective. Religion, culture, laws and politics have a distinct class character. All other distinctions and conflicts lose their significance in comparison with the basic social conflict of the warring classes (*126:129*).

Ralph Miliband says, "More than ever before men now live in the shadow of the state. What they want to achieve, individually or in groups, now mainly depends on the state's sanction and support. But since that sanction and support are not bestowed indiscriminately, they must, ever more directly, seek to influence and shape the state's power and purpose, or try and appropriate it altogether. It is for the state's attention or for its control that men compete; and it is against the state that be at the waves of social conflict. It is to an ever greater degree the state which men encounter as they confront other men. This is why, as social beings, they are also political beings, whether they know it or not. It is possible not to be interested in what the state does; but it is not possible to be unaffected by it. The point has acquired a new and ultimate dimension in the present epoch; if large parts of the planet should one day be laid waste in a nuclear war, it is because men, acting in the name of their state and interested with its power will have so decided, or miscalculated. " (*236 : 3*).

CHAPTER 9

THE PROPER SPHERE OF STATE ACTION

The question of the proper sphere of State action was not of such primary importance in the early days of political speculation as it is in modern times.

1. THE INDIVIDUALISTIC THEORY

The *laissez faire* theory arose as a natural reaction to the mischievous and meddlesome interference which characterized the relation of the State to the individual prior to the eighteenth century. There was also undue restriction on the freedom of trade. With the coming of the industrial revolution in the eighteenth century there was bound to be a reaction against all these forms of State action. There were new inventions revolutionizing the economic life of the people. Goods were being produced on a gigantic scale and new markets were being won where these goods could be sold. In these circumstances, it was natural for men of industry, enterprise, and originality to claim the right to be left alone as far as possible so that they could utilize their powers to the maximum advantage. "Let things alone because the world is self-regulating" was the slogan of the eighteenth century individualism.

In the light of this background, it is not surprising to find that individualism holds that the State is an evil, but an evil, necessitated by the selfishness and rapacity of man. It is a concession to human weakness. Individualism assumes that but for the restraining power of the State there would be no social peace and order. The State should therefore give its undivided thought and attention to the protection of the individual, but the promotion of his welfare falls outside its scope. Its main business is the suppression of violence and fraud. The guiding principle of the individualist 'is maximum possible individual freedom and minimum possible State action'. In the words of J. S. Mill: 'Over himself, over his own body and mind, the individual is sovereign.'

Individualists are not all agreed on what constitutes the legitimate functions of the State. Extreme individualists such as Spencer limit the sphere of State action to

(a) the protection of the individual against external enemies;

(b) the protection of the individual against internal enemies; and

(c) the enforcement of contracts lawfully made.

Individualists of the moderate type are prepared to go much farther. The functions of the State as conceived by them are neatly summed up by Gilchrist as follows:

1. Protection of the state and individuals from foreign aggression.

2. Protection of individuals against each other, that is, from physical injury, slander, and personal restraint.

3. Protection of property from robbery or damage.

4. Protection of individuals against false contract or branch of contract.

5. Protection of the unfit.

6. Protection of individuals against preventable evils such as plague or malaria (*28 : 397-8*).

The individualists support their position from three different points of view: ethical, the economic, and the scientific.

1. The Ethical Argument

It is admitted that freedom of action is essential to the development of character. Without such freedom the individual becomes a mere automation. What gives joy and meaning to life is the liberty to mould one's life according to one's ideals. The highest development of the individual is possible only when there is opportunity for self-reliance. When the individual is thrown upon his own resources, a powerful incentive is provided for the exercise of his powers of initiative, enterprise, and originality. If he possesses any intrinsic worth, it has an opportunity to manifest itself.

Government action is legitimate up to a certain point. But beyond that it cramps the individual. Over-government kills his sense of initiative and substitutes reliance on government for self reliance. It creates a pauper mentality, for the individual is tempted to be lazy and indolent and expects others to do for him what he should do for himself. He receives no stimulus for the development of his talents; the consequence is that both the individual and society are losers.

2. The Economic Argument

From the point of view of the economic life of man, individualism assumes that every man is self-seeking and that he knows his interests best. Therefore, the argument runs, if every person is left to himself he will make the best use of his opportunities, benefiting himself directly and society indirectly. Thus if the capitalist is left alone he will look around to see where he can invest his capital to the best advantage. Likewise, the labourer will look around to see where he can get the most advantageous terms for his services and offer his services there. Free competition and unrestricted operation of the law of supply and demand are thus in the economic interests of society. Prices, wages, rent, and interests should all be unfettered so that they can adjust themselves to the prevailing economic conditions. Similarly foreign trade should be left free. Artificial aids such as high tariffs and bounties to infant industries should be discouraged. Beyond providing that the market is kept free and open and that fraud and treachery are not practised on one another by the members of society, the State has little to do in the economic field.

3. The Scientific Argument

Individualism is said to be in accordance with the biological law of the struggle for existence and survival of the fittest. Herbert Spencer is a chief exponent of this argument. He holds that the law by virtue of which life has evolved in the case of the lower animals and the subhuman species is this law of the struggle for existence and survival of the fittest and argues that the same law should be allowed to operate in the case of man, too, if we are to evolve a race of strong, able and virile human beings. The natural course of progress means that the poor, the weak, and the inefficient must go to the wall. Although such a course means injustice for some individuals, the interests of society demand it.

To these theoretical arguments certain practical reasons are added by the adherents of individualism.

4. Practical Reasons

It is argued that when the government attempts to do many things it does them badly. It means red tape and routine, resulting in unnecessary delay and much waste. A great deal of necessary work is left undone. Experience shows that governmental interference produces bad results in many cases. As contrasted with private management, government management produces numerious failures. It lays the door open to jobbery and corruption.

Besides, the administration of law is not seldom irksome to the people, either on account of the natural aversion of man to official interference or on account of the nature of the law.

Criticism. Individualism contains an important truth, but it grossly exaggerates it. It over-emphasizes one aspect of man's social life at the expense of others. In reacting against petty laws and meddlesome legislation, it goes to the other extreme. The arguments sketched above in its favour are decidedly one-sided and, to some extent, even false.

Complex modern civilization makes it difficult, if not impossible, for the individual to develop all his powers harmoniously. There are many situations in the life of today which the individual himself cannot control and for which he requires the action of the State. Without extended State action, there seems no hope for the vast majority to develop themselves fully.

The basis of individualism is unsound. It assumes that man is fundamentally selfish. It bases itself on the hedonistic theory which has long since been exploded. Man possesses not only self-regarding impulses but also other-regarding impulses. Egoism and altruism are present in every man in varying degrees. Therefore to build an entire theory of State action on a single aspect of human nature is not proper. Individual welfare and social welfare are not opposed to each other. They are dependent upon one another. H.G. Wells is not wrong when he says: 'Self-interest never took a man or country to any other end than damnation.'

Individualism assumes that every man knows his own interests best. Experience shows that this is not true in a large number of cases. The individual may know his present, but there is no assurance that he knows his future interests, too. Further, even if the individual is the best judge of his interests, it does not follow that he is necessarily the best judge of the means to such interests. Even such an ardent champion of individual liberty as J.S. Mill admits that society should protect a man against himself when he tries to cross an unsafe bridge or contracts himself into slavery.

The individualist argument is that if each man is allowed to pursue his own interest, everybody will be happy and society will become prosperous. This will be true if the interests of men run parallel to each other and there is no contradiction between them. But experience shows that they are often at cross purposes with each other. We, therefore, require the might of the State to adjudicae differences and to see that no undue advantage is taken of individual weakness.

The starting point of individualism is 'the atomic individual with fringe of right' (9 : 245). Such an individual, it need hardly be said, is only a figment of the imagination. Society is an organism. Therefore, the interests of the individual are not entirely different from those of his fellowmen. The State is not an evil, but a positive good. It is not an artificial creation, but a natural growth. Governmental regulation does not necessarily mean the curtailment of individual freedom.

The individualist places implicit faith in the law of supply and demand and free competition. It is a well-known fact that the law of supply and demand is not as scientific as it is made out to be. Often it is freakish. As for free competition, there is very little of it in practice. It leads to monopolies, trusts, and combinations, the opposites of free competition. The need for a policy of non-intervention in industrial matters is not even half as great today as it was at the time of the Industrial Revolution.

The scientific argument advanced by Spencer is open to several objections.

Survival of the *fittest* does not necessarily mean survival of the *best*. All that the law of the survival of the fittest seems to mean is that that which survives deserves to survive. This is clearly absurd. For, 'if the sole test of fitness to survive is found in the fact of survival then the prosperous burglar becomes an object of commendation and the starving artisan a target of contempt (51 : 346).' Hallowell writes 'Spencer made the fatal mistake, which many continue to make, of transferring concepts that are appropriate to one science to another where the phenomena are quite different.'

Moreover, what is true of the lower animals is not necessarily true of man, the noblest of creatures. For, when we arrive at man in the scale of evolution we arrive at a startlingly new stage of development. The lower animals passively allow themselves to be adapted to nature. Man, on the other hand, on account of his superior intelligence, is able actively to adapt nature to his needs.

In answering the practical difficulties, it may be said that the fact that governments make mistakes is not necessarily a condemnation of all State action. Individualists point with much satisfaction to the many mistakes made by the government and its officials. They forget that private agencies, too, commit errors. But their mistakes are not so patent or so well known to the public. Those of the government, on the other hand, are generally known to everybody.

As Gilchrist points out, with the advance of democracy the need for individualism is not as great today as at an earlier time. Where democracy prevails and where local government is strong and capable, the line between socialism and individualism tends to become less clear. The objections of individualists to centralized regulation do not have much force with reference to local regulation. In other words, 'municipalization' is not open to some of the objections to which 'nationalization' is open.

Some individualists tend to confuse individuality with eccentricity or oddity of character. This is particularly true of Mill, who treats the individual as a self-centred entity rather than as an intrinsic part of society.

If prevention is better than cure, the State should prevent injury to society as well as cure injury. Pure non-intervention in the conduct of government is impossible. Its logical conclusion is anarchism. To use the language of Leacock, it divorces individual from social rights. It overlooks the plain advantages of co-operative and regulated efforts.

Among the various arguments advanced against the individualistic theory by Laski, the principal one is that it is morally inadequate. Laski observes that it means 'poor health, undeveloped intelligence, miserable homes and work in which the majority can find no human interest. Undue advantage is taken of weakness. The bargaining capacity of the labourer not being the same as that of the capitalist, the labourer often loses out in the economic race. The higgling of the market is the apotheosis of inequality' (47 : 191). Supply and demand do not in any way indicate a social value in the reward secured. Great fortunes are made in the advertising enterprise, in slum houses and the like. The higgling of the market so far from being a measure of social values, is likely to destroy all social values.

Summing up the case for and against individualism, Gilchrist notes the following points:

(1) Individualism emphasizes self-reliance.

(2) It combats needless governmental interference.

(3) It urges the value of the individual in society.

(4) It has helped to destroy useless laws of petty interference.

'But it exaggerates the evils of state control when it forgets that there are more instances of good state actions than of bad. It gives a fundamentally false conception of individuality, and finally, it has proved quite unfitted for the complexity of modern life' (2 : 408).

A 'negatively regulative' State is altogether out of date. We want a State which, while conserving individual freedom and initiative, will at the same time undertake many positive measures in the interest of society as a whole—particularly in the economic, educational and social fields.

2. THE SOCIALISTIC THEORY

The socialist regards the State as a positive good. Therefore, instead of minimum possible State action, he wants the maximum of it. He believes that this is the only way by which social justice can be made possible for the bulk of mankind. He aims at a 'co-operative commonwealth controlling all the means of production and regulating distribution according to some method of joint control'. Under socialism there would be a common ownership of the means of production and exchange and wages would be according to needs. Some socialists advocate equal distribution, others equitable distribution.

The chief merits of socialism may be briefly outlined as follows:

'Socialism protests against the obvious evils of our present social system and urges the need for a radical change. Money and power are concentrated in the hands of a few, and the labourer does not receive his proper due. Since the bargaining capacity of the labourer is not equal to that of the employer, the working man is often obliged to make a forced agreement. The present system leads to grave inequalities of wealth and opportunity. It is also responsible for enormous waste and the duplication of services. There is no planned economy on a nation-wide scale. Unrestricted competition leads to lower wages, over-production, cheap goods, and unemployment. The present system further tends to beget materialism, unfairness, dishonesty, and a general lowering of the standard of individual character' (22 : 302).

Careful planning under socialism will avoid duplication, over-production, unnecessary advertisement, and the production of harmful goods. The socialistic ideal places a much-needed emphasis on altruism and on the cultivation of a desire for social usefulness and for the love of activity for its own sake. Collective ownership and collective management, it is claimed, are thoroughly democratic. According to its supporters, socialism is the next step in democracy. Where socialistic policies and programmes have been adopted in practice, they have succeeded on the whole.

There is no gainsaying the fact that many of the evils pointed out by socialism in our present industrial system are true. We may further concede to the socialist that the only remedy for those evils lies in the substitution of a new economic and political system for the present. But all of this does not mean that socialism has proved its case. The practical difficulties in making it a living reality are too many to be ignored.

The difficulties of administration will probably be stupendous under socialism. The post office, the telegraph, the telephone and railway systems are no doubt managed with considerable success in most countries.

But in the absence of competition, we cannot say that they are run on the most economic lines possible. Critics of socialism say that a multiplication of State activities means that the governmental machinery will break down under its own weight. The socialist, it is rightly contended, is over-optimistic in the matter of governmental management.

At the present stage of man's moral development, socialism would mean a tremendous increase of opportunities for corruption, intrigue, and personal spite.

Socialism, it is said, is not conducive to progress. The incentive to labour will probably be destroyed. The activities of the average man today are determined for the most part by the desire for gain and not by any altruistic motive nor by the desire for social usefulness. The socialistic State is likely to check individual initiative. Life would become uniform and even stagnant. New wants would not be stimulated under a governmental regime.

The working man is not as powerless as he is sometimes pictured. Through trade unions and other forms of combination he is not infrequently able to strike a bargain advantageous to himself.

Socialism is likely to mean a restriction of individual freedom and a deterioration of individual character. Herbert Spencer believes that each member of the community as an individual would be a slave of the community as a whole. Socialism would repress individuality. Genius would be satisfied and citizens would become lethargic. Individual spontaneity and responsibility would be sapped by bureaucracy and departmentalism would reign supreme.

Production might suffer both in quantity and in quality.

Evaluation of Individualism and Socialism. Both Individualism and Socialism contain an important truth; but they grossly exaggerate it. Both of them, further, are theoretical and doctrinaire. Just as pure individualism is an impossibility, so is pure socialism. What we need is a system which would somehow preserve our individualities and yet keep society intact as an organic whole. Burns is right when he declares: 'If we could imagine an ideal at once individualistic and socialistic such would be the effective ideal for most thinking men' (10 : 275). For, to quote the same writer again: 'If on the one hand we tend to isolation and selfishness, on the other we tend to lose our individualities in the flood and complexity of "The Great Society"......The individualist is right in aiming at the variety of individuals, and so is the socialist in impressing on all their common interest; for the fullest development of each is to be found in the performance of his function in the life of the whole' (10 : 275).

Notwithstanding the obvious defects of socialism, it is perhaps the part of wisdom to adopt a policy of judicious and gradual extension of State activities in the direction of the socialistic ideal,[1] aiming at the same

1. Hobson remarks: 'The State has assumed the duties of a doctor, nurse, school-master, trader, manufacturer, insurance agent, house builder, town planner, railway controller, and a hundred other functions.'

time at the moral elevation of mankind. Free competition may be allowed at the lower levels of production, but when we come to large-scale production which affects the lives of many people, State ownership and control might well be the order of the day.

3. THE IDEALISTIC THEORY

Leaving out the extreme forms of idealism as found in Hegal and confining ourselves to the English idealists, we find there a theory of State action which merits serious consideration. The idealists take an exalted view of the State, regarding it as the embodiment of the best in every man. The State is to them an ethical institution and in obeying it we obey ourselves. Seeing that the idealists give such a glorified place to the State, one would expect them to assign a very wide range of activities to it. Yet, as a matter of fact, they narrowly limit its sphere. The explanation for this seeming contradiction is not far to seek.

To the idealists, the end of the individual and the end of the State are one and the same, viz., the realization of the 'best life' or the promotion of the excellence of human souls (Bosanquet). This end, however, is of such a personal and inward character that for the most part it can be realized by individual effort alone. Moral good is essentially a self-earned good. A further reason for leaving the individual to earn his own moral life is that the instruments at the disposal of the State—force and compulsion are of so external a character that they cannot very well promote such an inward grace as moral perfection. In the words of Bosanquet, 'the general will (of the State) when it meets us as force and authority resting on force, and not as a social suggestion which we spontaneously rise to accept, comes to us *ex hypothesi* as something which claims to be ourself, but which, for the moment we more or less fail to recognise', with the result that we are abandoned to automatism or stirred to rebellion (5 : 201-202)).

The sphere of State action is therefore negative. The State should provide an opportunity for the individual to earn the best life possible for him by removing the obstacles which stand in his way. This means that the function of the State is the 'hindrance of hindrances' to the best life or an 'adjustment of all adjustments'. To undertake more than that would mean a frustration of the moral purpose of the individual.

In the language of T. H. Green, 'only external actions can be matter of obligation. The ideal of law must be determined by reference to the moral end which it serves. Law *can* only enjoin or forbid certain acts; it cannot enjoin or forbid motives. And the only acts which it ought to enjoin or forbid are those of which the doing or not doing *from whatever motive,* is necessary to the moral end of society' (29: p. IX).

On the basis of this principle, Green condemns much legislation which has tended to weaken religion, self-respect, or family feeling. Applying his formula of 'removal of obstacles to good life' to the conditions prevalent in England in the latter part of the nineteenth century, Green makes a powerful plea for compulsory education, regulation of liquor traffic, greater control of land ownership, and interference with freedom of contract in cases where the contracting parties are at different levels of bargaining power.

Among those who do not subscribe to the idealistic view of State action, there are many who are quite willing to recognize that higher goods like religion and morality are incapable of enforcement by the State. But they see no reason why the State should not regulate economic and social relations with a view to the promotion of the general good. Bosanquet's answer to this interpretation of State action would be that economic and social life is not entirely different from moral and religious life. Economic and social goods have a close relation to moral and spiritual goods.

The State is to protect, to encourage, to organize, but not to promote the good life directly. This is one of the reasons why we place the State above all other institutions and give it the power to keep them in their proper places. Our social, political, economic, and religious organizations are the laboratories in which we try experiments in better life. It is only after preliminary experimentation and success in rousing public conscience in favour of this or that undertaking that we can look to the State for aid. It is only then that we realize a good life.

Criticism : This view of State action seems to exaggerate the distinction between law and morality. While much morality undoubtedly falls outside the sphere of law, the extent to which moral duties are covered by law is not sufficiently realized. The criminal law, for example, exerts moral influence over a wide area.

The idealist places undue emphasis on the negative character of State action. The State, we believe, should undertake both negative and positive measures, taking care, of course, not to deaden spontaneity in its individual members. Provision of free education, for example, is a measure more positive than negative. Green and Bosanquet are mistaken in assuming that every positive measure will lead to automatism and the weakening of character. That will depend, at least partly, upon time, place, and circumstance.

Moreover, this theory of State action is open to the danger that the State might wait too long before taking any effective step to 'hinder hindrances to good life'. If the State were to stand aside as a detached observer, letting us struggle for the good life as best we may, it might easily fall into a lethargy from which it would be difficult to rouse it.

A further objection which may be raised is that 'the idealist is so concerned with the spiritual foundation of society in the human conscience, so occupied with the inward man and the autonomy of his free-will, that he is blind to the need of reform of material conditions'. In reply to this objection, it may be said that the ideal and the actual, the spiritual and the material, are not locked up in separate compartments, but are correlated. However true this may be in theory, in practice the correlation is not always clear.

Finally, the formula 'hindrance of hindrances to good life' is so indefinite and vague that it is capable of being used both by the individualist and by the socialist to support their respective theories of State action.

In spite of these limitations the idealistic theory is sound in insisting that whatever the State may or may not do, it should not interfere with the free or disinterested performance of moral acts.

4. OTHER THEORIES

General Welfare. This view underlies the actual operation of Government in most modern states. It is practical and concrete and is capable of easy adaptation to varying circumstances. The strength of this view is due chiefly to the fact that the modern temper is distinctly against purely theoretical arguments and is in favour of practical results. Liberty is no longer regarded as freedom from law, nor is individual freedom measured by the narrowness of the range of state functions. The eighteenth century doctrine of the inherent and inalienable rights of man is practically dead and the emphasis is on Social Welfare. Utilitarian and opportunistic considerations play a conspicuous part in determining the functions of the State. Care is taken to keep in view from a utilitarian stand-point, the best interests of the individual and society. Thus, we find that Jeremy Bentham, the founder of Utilitarianism, enquired into the practical utility of all institutions and laws before he would justify their existence.

Advocates of this view rightly claim that no hard and fast line can be drawn between legitimate and illegitimate State action. Whether the State ought or ought not to interfere in any situation must be decided on the merits of each case. Certain general principles, however, may be laid down governing State action.

(1) Does the proposed action make for the common good?

(2) Is it likely to be effective?

(3) Can it be done without doing more harm than good?

Garner's View. With general welfare as his guiding principle, Garner draws up his view of State action in the following terms: Police duty is not the sole mission of the State. The State ought to do more for its citizens than merely prevent them from robbing or murdering one another. It should contribute to the perfection of the national life, to the development of the nation's wealth and well-being, to its morality and its intelligence. It should secure for every man as effectively as possible those essentials of rational human living which are really each one's right. It should encourage literature, art and science. It should, in general, be an instrument of social and economic progress. It ought to intervene and protect society against the evils of private monopoly. The presumption in general, however, is against State interference. Freedom should be the rule and interference the exception. The State should not ordinarily undertake to do for society what the individuals themselves can do as well, or better. Interference should be made, not on any special or doubtful grounds, but only when it can be clearly made out that it will be productive of public advantage. The policy of *laissez faire* is impossible today, much more so now than in the eighteenth and nineteenth centuries. Liberty is not the end of all human associations. It is merely a means for the realization of the fulness of individual life.

MacIver's View (55 : Ch. 5). His view, which is tinged with pluralism, is that the sphere of State action should be determined by what the State *can* do as *an* organ (but not *the* organ of the community). The question for him is not what the State should or should not do but what the state is permitted to do by other social organizations and by the limited nature of the State itself. The practical working of this view, however,. results in much the same conclusions as those of the general welfare theory. The positive and negative tasks of the State, says MacIver, are to establish order and to respect personality. To begin with, the State should not seek to control opinion, *no matter what the opinion may be* (*55:150*), although there are some exceptions.

(1) Incitement to break laws of the State or to defy its authority should be taken cognizance of by the State. Citizens may properly criticize existing laws. They may use peaceful persuasion to convince others and employ all constitutional methods in bringing about the desired change. But law-breaking cannot be tolerated. All this does not mean, however, that the State ought to punish every offender who preaches disloyalty.

(2) 'Like considerations apply to literature which clearly instigates such immoral acts *as are at the same time prohibited by law*' (*55*: *Ch. 5*). Care should be taken to see that the instigation is direct, and not constructive.

(3) Freedom to express opinion does not mean freedom to express libellous or defamatory opinion or publish comments on a case which is *sub judice*.

1. Law and Morality

MacIver agrees with the idealists in holding that it is necessary to separate the inner sanction of morality from political law. Law cannot prescribe morality. It can prescribe only external actions. It should prescribe only those actions whose mere fulfilment, *from whatever motive*, the State adjudges to be conducive to welfare—such actions as tend to promote the physical and social conditions requisite for the expression and development of free—or moral—personality. To turn all moral obligations into legal obligations would be to destroy morality. 'Puritanic' legislation stands self-condemned because it claims that its own morals should be those of all, even to the point of destroying all moral spontaneity that is not its own. 'The ethical appeal is always to the individual's own sense of what is right and wrong, in the last resort always to his sense of what is good and evil' (*55* : *155*). Morality has for its basis the fact of choice. It is inward. It comprehends the unity of personality. The sphere of morality, therefore, can never be coincident with the sphere of political law.

Although law differs from morality, the citizen has a moral responsibility towards political law. He ought to obey it as a general rule. In MacIver's words: 'We obey the law not necessarily because we think that the law is right but because we think it right to obey the law. Otherwise the obedience of every minority would rest on compulsion, and there would be so much friction in the State that its working would be fatally embarrassed. Political obligation is based on the general recognition of the universal service of law and government, for the sake of which we accept specific enactments which in themselves we disapprove (55 : 156).

2. Law and Religion

If morality cannot be enforced directly by law, much less can religion. The church ought not to appeal to the State to coerce those whom the church itself cannot persuade. To do so means to distrust its own moral powers.

3. Law and Customs

Customs are the 'enforced natural growths which reveal the underlying conditions of belief and mode of life' (55 : 160). A State cannot legislate away the rooted customs of its citizens. Conflicts between law and customs are more likely to arise in democracies than in autocracies. Democracies are less homogeneous and more unstable in respect of custom. Therefore they are ready to abrogate customs practised by minority groups. But experience shows, as in the case of prohibition in the United States, that the custom of minorities stubbornly resists the coercion of law. 'Custom, when attacked, attacks laws in turn; attacks not only the particular law which opposes it, but, what is more vital, the spirit of law-abidingness, the unity of the general will' (55 : 161). 'Dangerous customs may have to be rooted out by legislation. But such instances show at least that the main body of social customs is beyond the range of law and is neither made nor unmade by the State' (55 : 161).

4. Law and Fashion

'Over that minor and changeful form of custom called fashion the State has even less control' (*55 : 161*). 'Here we have a curious illustration of the limitations of the State. A people will follow eagerly the dictates of fashion proclaimed by some unknown coterie in Paris or London or New York, but were the State to decree changes in themselves so insignificant, it would be regarded as monstrous tyranny–it might even lead to revolution' (55 : 161). Witness what happened in Afghanistan when Amanullah tried to change the customs and the traditional costume of his people.

5. Law and Culture

'In general the whole of that living culture which is the expression of the spirit of a people or of an age is beyond the competence of the State. The State reflects it, and does little more. The State orders life, but does not create it. Culture is the work of the community, sustained by inner forces far more potent than political law' (55 : 161-2). Art, literature, and music do not come directly within the purview of the State. In all these activities, 'a people or a civilization goes its own way, responsive to influences and conditions for the most part unknown to itself, and where known for the most part uncomprehended and uncontrolled by the State' (55 : 162).

6. State and War

The State 'has the power of life and death over all associations no less than over persons—because of its unabated right to make war and peace'. It 'claims the right to settle political disputes by force. In so doing it elevates political interests to complete supremacy over all oher interests'. In declaring war the State puts a particular political object above the general ends of the family, of the cultural life, and of the economic order. MacIver believes that this absolute power of the State should be limited, because it is, according to him, a limited organization and cannot be identified with the nation or the whole community.

The conclusion to which MacIver is driven on the whole question of State action is that, in general terms, the business of the State includes those external conditions of social living which are of universal concern in view of the acknowledged objects of human desire. In particular, it means the preservation of *order* 'for the sake of *protection* and of *conservation* and *development*' (55:185). Order for its own sake is futile. It is justified only to the extent to which it serves the needs of the community and it is limited by the ideals of the community, particularly by the ideals of justice and liberty.

In practical terms, the functions of the modern State include all those activities which the State can pursue more efficiently and thoroughly than can individuals or private organizations. It includes the protection of the weak, establishment of a minimum standard of living, maintenance of the minimum conditions necessary for a healthy and decent living, vast works of constructive enterprise such as town planning and town building whose benefits will be shared by future generations, preservation of the countryside, of the beauties of the forest, lake and mountain, fruitful experiments in irrigation, utilization of the soil, breeding of plants and animals, control of insect pests, etc.; promotion of the establishment of industries by mutual aid, control over currency, credit, etc.; encouragement of industry, trade and commerce; conservation and development of human capacities, education, and general promotion of the cultural life. In undertaking all these activities the State should take care not to repress the inner springs of conduct.

CLASSIFICATION OF GOVERNMENTAL FUNCTIONS

Several writers have attempted a classification of governmental functions on the basis largely of what actually prevails in most modern States. These functions are divided into :

(1) Essential or fundamental, and
(2) Optional or ministrant.

1. Essential Functions

These include functions which are necessary for the continued existence of the State, for the guaranteeing of the civil and political liberty of the individual, and for the protection of his life, liberty and property against other individuals. They are determined, in other words, by the three-fold relations of State to State, of State to citizen, and of citizen to citizen (*24* : *364*). Woodrow Wilson (*39* : *613-41*) sums up the essential functions as follows:

(1) The keeping of order and providing for the protection of persons and property from violence and robbery.

(2) The fixing of the legal relations between man and wife and between parents and children.

(3) The regulation of the holding, transmission and interchange of property, and the determination of its liabilities for debt or for crime.

(4) The determination of contract rights between individuals.

(5) The definition and punishment of crime.

(6) The administration of justice in civil cases.

(7) The determination of the political duties, privileges, and relations of citizens.

(8) Dealings of the State with foreign powers; the preservation of the State from external danger or encroachment and the advancement of its international interests.

While approving of the above classification, Gettell holds that there are two branches of administration—financial and military—which call for special attention. Under the financial functions he includes the imposition of taxation, the regulation of tariffs, liquor, coinage and currency, and administration of public property, such as public lands and forests, public buildings, and munitions of war and of State monopolies such as post offices and, in some State, of railways and telegraphs. The management of the public debt is an allied function.

Military functions include the maintenance of an army, a navy, and an air force. 'Ordinarily both armies and navies are considered safeguards of peace rather than direct challenges to war; armies being used to maintain internal order, and navies to protect commerce and colonies' (24 :400-1). In all the leading States a very large proportion of the national income is spent on the army and navy. Even in the United States, where the danger of war in the thirties was comparatively remote, three-fourths of the expenditure of the federal government was used for the army, navy and pensions.

2. Optional Functions

These are functions which are considered to be non-essential for the existence of the State or for the maintenance of individual liberty and security. Yet they are generally undertaken by most States as being necessary for the promotion of general welfare. The line between essential and optional functions is not easy to draw and the two merge into each other. The classification is bound to vary from time to time and from place to place.

Optional functions are divisible into socialistic and non-socialistic functions. The socialistic functions are those which can be left to private enterprise, but which are usually undertaken by the State in order to avoid the evils of private control or on account of the greater efficiency of governmental agencies in certain tried fields. Examples of such functions are the ownership and management of railways and telegraphs in some States and the municipal control of water, gas, and electricity.

Non-socialistic functions are those which, if not undertaken by the State, are not likely to be undertaken at all. 'Under this head come care of the poor and incapable, maintenance of public parks and libraries, sanitation, certain forms of education, and the large amount of investigating and statistical work, the purpose of which is to improve the environment and give information by which further improvement may be made' (*24 : 396*)

Woodrow Wilson sums up the optional or ministrant functions under the following heads:

'(1) The regulation of trade and industry.

'(2) The regulation of labour.

'(3) The maintenance of thoroughfares—including State management of railways and that great group of undertakings which we embrace within the comprehensive term 'internal improvement'.

'(4) The maintenance of postal and telegraph systems, which is very similar in principle to (3).

'(5) The manufacture and distribution of gas, the maintenance of water works, etc.

'(6) Sanitation, including the regulation of trades for sanitary purposes.

'(7) Education.

'(8) Care of the poor and incapable.

'(9) Care and cultivation of forests and like matters, such as the stocking of rivers with fish.

'(10) Sumptuary laws, such as "prohibition" laws' (*28 : 433*).

STATE ACTION IN INDIA

The State in India is neither individualistic nor communistic. If anything, it is nearer to socialism than to other theories of State action. It provides for external and internal protection and operates a postal system like any other State. But in addition, it runs the telegraph and telephone system, owns and operates railways and aeroplanes, and is increasingly bringing bus transport under its management. Several heavy industries and steel plants are directly under its control. Life insurance and banks have been nationalized. Government builds ships, railway engines and wagons, and other railway equipment. It makes electric goods of various kinds. It conducts a dozen or more Scientific Laboratories and hundreds of experimental stations and projects of different kinds. It has several river valley schemes under its control, as also coal development. While the State does not undertake all these services directly, it manages some of them through public corporations.

In addition, the State in India has the major responsibility for the improvement of agriculture, fisheries, cattle and poultry, and for the preservation of forests and wild life and the establishment of national parks. It carries on a vast network of construction programmes—irrigation works, public buildings, roads and bridges. It also has the major responsibility for the education and culture of the people. It carries on extensive archaeological excavations and looks after national monuments and ancient works of art in the country. With the help of the rural people rural uplift is being undertaken through community development projects. Co-operative farming has been introduced in some areas and the Zamindari system has been abolished practically all over the country.

Yet considerable scope is left for private enterprise. Except for some amount of state trading and the control of articles in short supply much of the trade and commerce of the country is in private hands. The entire newspaper business and practically the whole of book production are also in private hands. Similar is the case with regard to the manufacture and sale of drugs and toilet requirements. Private bodies still have a considerable share in education, hospital service and the like.

It is customary these days for the private sector to blame the public sector for all its ills and claim that it is receiving a step-motherly treatment at the hands of the Government. This is not a fair charge. The fact of the matter is that the private sector not infrequently suffers from greed and does not scruple to use unethical methods on certain occasions, while the public sector suffers from indifference and lack of initiative. The cure for both types of ills is the cultivation of a high degree of civic sense and patriotism and the translation into daily life of lofty moral and spiritual principles. A friendly competition between the two will be all to the good.

LIBERAL THEORY OF STATE INTERVENTION IN ECONOMIC LIFE

Liberal thinkers of the twentieth century such as Graham Wallace and Bertrand Russel became even more collectivistic in their outlook as they were confronted by a growing challenge of socialism which represented the ideology of the working class now bent upon to overthrow the economic and political institutions of a middle-class state. The Liberal theory now cast off its revolutionary fervour and became a polite defence of the *status quo.*

Liberal Economic Doctrine

"What produced liberalism", says Laski, "was the emergence of a new economic society at the end of the middle ages. As a doctrine, it was shaped by the needs of that new society; and, like all social pholosophies, it could not transcend the medium in which it was born. Like all social philosophies, therefore, it contained in its birth the conditions of its own destruction" (*132 : 17*). The basis of the liberal state should be sought in the economic system which produced it. The first principles of the liberal political philosophy are rooted in its economic doctrines. But the various economic doctrines that were propounded during the Liberal era were not logically cohesive. The only logic behind them was the logic of the class interest that they faithfully served in spite of the apparent contradictions involved in their theory.

Mercantile Theory

Mercantilism was the first expression of the liberal theory in economics. It justified strong absolute government which should actively intervene in economic affairs in order to safeguard and promote the interests of commercial and industrial classes. The strong rule of the monarch had already secured social peace in his kingdom. The question was why the absolute power of the state should not be utilized to achieve economic prosperity for the people. The state was strongly urged to remove feudal restrictions on trade, to promote national industries in every way, to reform the currency, to establish a system of protective tariff, and finally, to safeguard the right of commercial and industrial property by every possible means.

With the emergence of the Mercantile theory, the Church ceased to exercise any determining influence on the economic ideas of the mercantile middle class. This class now looked towards the state as its new benevolent master. It felt the need of new legislation that would enable it to earn more wealth. It adopted a frankly materialistic and utilitarian outlook of life. The most characteristic part of the Mercantile theory was reflected in its attitude towards the poor and unemployed who were regarded as nothing short of social criminals deliberately avoiding honest work and effort. Laski rightly thinks that the whole trend of the theory was to construct a state which could adequately answer the needs of the industrialist and trader in the sixteenth centruy (*132:143*).

Physiocratic Theory

But the Mercantilist doctrine of state intervention was reversed by the Physiocrats who demanded that the state ought not to regulate business. The Physiocrats tried to apply the utilitarian ideas of Helvetius in the economic sphere and regarded enlightened self-interest as the basis of a well-regulated society. They pleaded that the legislator must not interfere with the natural operation of economic laws because the only way to secure social happiness and prosperity is to allow each individual to pursue his enlightened self-interest. The purpose of legislation should be restricted to prevention of invasions on individual liberty. But this does not mean that the Physiocrats were against despotic government in general. They were quite content with absolute monarchy if it would guarantee economic liberty to its citizens. They failed to develop any conception of political rights. They also failed to appreciate the necessity of constitutional government. The limits they sought to impose on the action of governments were the limits of nature. As they assumed that the economic laws they sought to vindicate belonged to the realm of nature, the state was naturally required to refrain from interfering with them.

It is to be noted that the Physiocratic theory was primarily designed to protect the interest of the French farcer and proprietor. There was a definite agrarian emphasis in the economic theory of the Physiocrats which showed that they had not sufficiently realized that feudalism was fast changing into capitalism. There was another defect in the Physiocratic theory. The defect was that it still adopted a purely rationalistic procedure in social theory without attempting an analysis of empirical facts. They opposed state intervention in economic affairs because it was inconsistent with the commands of natural law. They did not oppose it because it was found wanting in empirically observed practice. Curiosly enough, Adam Smith made the same mistake by accepting natural law as a valid deterrent to state action.

Adam Smith's Economic Liberalism

Adam Smith is considered as the most representative exponent of the ideas of economic liberalism. The theory of Adam Smith was more scientific and less sectarian than the Physiocratic theory and interpreted the meaning of contemporary economic transition from feudalism to capitalism in a better way. But Adam Smith was not alone in working out the theory of classical economics which is also known as the theory of *laissez faire*. Ricardo and Malthus made important contributions to the classical theory of economics by developing new theories of population and rent. The views of these writers were not only important in the sphere of economic theory but exercised a determining influence on the development of social and political theory throughout the nineteenth century. The basic creed of *laissez faire* implied the separation of politics from economics because the state was asked to mind its own business and not to interfere in business affairs. The characteristic feature of liberal political thought is this artificial separation of the economic from the political sphere which was not at all practicable in real life. The theory of classical economists was essentially a bourgeois theory which signified the distrust of the English middle class in a state which was still effectively controlled by feudal elements. It was on the other hand an expression of self-confidence which the rising English bourgeoisie felt about the glory of its economic mission.

Two Assumptions of the Classical Theory of Economics

The classical theory of economics was based on two important assumptions which were not quite logically compatible. In the first place, it conceived society simply as the market where a free exchange of goods produces a natural harmony of interests because the individuals are free to purchase and sell goods to the best of their advantage. Secondly, it involved a theory of distribution of social wealth in the form of rent, profits and wages which implied corresponding class conflicts. Ricardo's labour theory of value clearly showed this. He argued that in a free and competitive market the value of commodities is determined by the amount of labour involved in their production. The price of a commodity in exchange fluctuates about its value on the basis of temporary conditions of supply and demand. The operations of a free market will usually enable the producers to get just price of their goods and the consumers will likewise have the satisfaction of having just returns on their money. Malthus and Ricardo in their analysis of rent came to the conclusion that there are singular exceptions to this rule. "The interest of the landlord," as Ricardo said, "is always opposed to the interest of every other class in the community."[1] The rent which the landlord receives cannot be said to be a just return on his labour. Sometimes the value of land increases due to factors with which the landlord has nothing to do and yet he claims all the resultant benefits for himself. While the traders, industrialists, workers and farmers actually work to increase the wealth of the community, the landlord sits tight as a social parasite living on the labour of others. The Malthusian theory of rent based largely on his theory of population argued that the rent which the landlord received was ultimately extracted from the profits of the capitalist since the labourer would get a fixed amount of wages in any case.

Criticism of the Classical Theory

It is clear from this analysis that the classical theory of economics purported to be a defence of the interests of the commercial classes against land-owners. Besides this, it was simultaneously a defence of the privileges of capitalists against wage-earners. There was another anomaly in this theory. While it accepted natural rights in economics, the defenders of this theory denied them in ethics and politics. While their general philosophical outlook was utilitarian and empirical, their method in economics was rationalistic and doctrinaire. They even failed to examine the logical conclusions of their own premises in the light of facts of daily observation.

Even a liberal critic like Sabine is compelled to remark, "In so far as the labour theory of value was turned into a defence of the natural justice of a competitive labour-market, it was most unfairly applied. Goods were asserted to exchange according to the amounts of labour contained in them. But in a system of capitalist production what was denominated labour had to include capital invested in machinery and the like. This the theory called "accumulated labour", but it was obvisouly not the capitalist's labour that was accumulated in it. The wage-earner, therefore, was supposed to be justly compensated for his own labour, while the capitalist was compensated for all the accumulated labour of other men that he had in some way got his hands on. Both wages and property-rights to capital were defended as natural, neglecting the fact that the latter especially were the result of historical and institutional accident. It was these qualities of partiality and lack of historical sense that exposed the classical economics to the criticism of Marx" (*162 : 661*).

---

1. See Erich Roll's, "*A History of Economic Thought*", Chapter IV, pp. 175-97 for an illuminating discussion of Ricardo's Theory.

In the same way, Laski also concludes, "The fact is that, granted its assumptions, economic liberalism was a doctrine limited to the service of a narrow section of the community. The price for its operation was paid by the factory operative and the landless worker who, forbidden to combine, largely deprived of the franchise, subject to the courts of law which regarded the preservation of bourgeois ownership as the chief end of life, were largely helpless before the new dispensation" (*132 : 195*).

MARXIST THEORY OF THE FUNCTION OF THE STATE

Evolution of Marx's Ideas on the State

Karl Marx first formulated his views on the nature and function of the State as a result of his direct experience of the repressive policies of the imperial Prussian State, which censored his articles of the *Rheinische Zeitung*. At this time Marx conceived the possibility of a true democratic state, an idealised state of the Hegelian model representing reason. By 1843 Marx realized the importance of socio-economic factors in the framing of legislation and developed a critique of Hegel's theory of state. According to Hegel, the state was ethically superior and logically prior to its two constituent elements, the family and civil society. Marx now said that it was wrong to believe that the state had a universal character capable of reconciling the discordant elements of civil society and synthesizing them on a higher plane. All state institutions—monarchy, representative assemblies and bureaucracy were actually instruments of sectional interests of socio-economic groups.

The State, therefore, was no more than an empty ideal sphere which created the illusion of belonging to the whole society. Marx said that this opposition between civil society and the state was the feature of the existing bourgeois social structure though not of feudalism. In contrast to Hegel, he now recommended a form of government where there was no separation between civil society and the state and which directly corresponded to 'the essence of socialised man'. He called this true democracy in which the state, the law and the constitution were self-determined by the people.

With his conversion to communism in 1844, Marx concluded that the state was essentially the negation of man. In the *Paris Manuscripts,* Marx described the state to be an expression of human alienation similar to religion, law and morality, and equally based on a particular mode of production. He viewed the state, like religion, as a statement of man's ideal aims and also a consolation for their failure to achieve them in practice. The state was limited precisely because its aims remained illusory. The French and American revolutions, which claimed to liberate man as a political citizen, left him in servitude as a man, or member of civil society, i.e. the economic sphere.

Marx felt that the bourgeois state was not capable of solving society's problems because of its alienated condition. As he puts it, "The state cannot abolish the contradiction which exists between the role and good intentions of the administration on the one hand and the means at its disposal on the other, without abolishing itself, for it rests on this contradiction. It rests on the contrast beween public and private life, on the contrast between general and particular interests. The administration must, therefore, limit itself to a formal and negative activity, for its power ceases just where civil life and work begin." (*232 : 181*).

Class Domination Theory of State

Although Marx at no stage abandoned the idea of the state as alienated and parasitical social power, he later concentrated his attention on an analysis of the function of state in society. While in his earlier writings he had emphasized the gap between the state and society, he later considered the state as a part of society. In *The German Ideology*, Marx traced the origin of state to the division of labour. The state was an illusory community serving as a screen for the real struggles fought by antagonistic classes. In the course of history each mode of production gave rise to a particular type of state structure promoting the interests of the dominant economic class. The large-scale modern industry and universal competition of capitalist society also created their own political superstructures—the modern state which was dependent on the capitalist class for taxes and credits. The state in turn moulded other social institutions. Marx says :—

> "Since the state is the form in which the individuals of a ruling class assert their common interest and the entire civil society of an epoch is epitomised, the state acts as an intermediary in the formation of all communal institutions and gives them a political form. Hence, there is the illusion that law is based on will, that is, on will divorced from its real basis, on free will. In similar fashion, right in turn is reduced to statute law". (*232 : 182*).

The class domination theory of state was summed up by Marx and Engels in the *Communist Manifesto*, which stipulated that the executive of the modern state was but a committee for managing the common affairs of the entire class of bourgeoisie. Marx, however, did not consider this correlation between economic substructure and political super-structure in any dogmatic fashion. For example, he pointed out that though England's mode of production was more advanced than that of France, yet the political system of France was more developed than that of England in many respects.

Marx also admitted that there was certain exception to his general characterization of the State as an instrument of class domination. McLellan observes :—

> "Sometimes Marx says that the state need not be representative of the whole of a class but only of a section of that class (for example, the financiers under Louis-Philippe); or that one class can control the state for the benefit of another (for example, the Whigs on behalf of the middle class in England). In relatively backward countries, where classes were not fully developed, Marx thought

that the state could play an independent role, also in the European absolute monarchies in the transition between feudal and bourgeois classes." (*232 : 183*).

Louis Bonaparte's regime in France and Bismarck's regime in Germany were also cited by him as examples of 'independent' states. And yet, he felt, that the state power cannot remain suspended in mid-air. Bonaparte too represented the most numerous class of French society, the small-holding peasants. Yet his policies ultimately benefited the bourgeoisie by encouraging the industrial development of France. It was only in North America that the classical bourgeois state had been formed, which from the very beginning had been subordinated to bourgeois society and bourgeois forces of production.

The second broad exception to the Marxian idea of the state as an instrument of class domination occurred in Asian societies—China, India, Persia, and to some extent Russia. Owing to the inadequate development of private property in land, the Asian despotic ruler appeared as the protecting father of all the numerous village communities, representing the common unity of his subjects. Yet this Asian state also created a bureaucratic group, which exploited the servile peasant masses through the exercise of public power of the coercive state machinery.

Bureaucracy and Coercive State Apparatus

Marx regarded bureaucracy to be the most essential part of the modern state apparatus. In *The Eighteenth Brumaire of Louis Bonaparte*, Marx explained that bureaucracy emerged with the rise of absolute monarchies in modern Europe. It was, to begin with, a progressive institution which destroyed the power of medieval corporations and introduced an element of rationality and equality in administration.

In his *Critique of Hegel's Philosophy of the State* Marx pointed out how the Prussian bureaucracy had finally emerged as a privileged caste which claimed an absolute right to define the interests of the state. Thus the bureaucracy itself became an exclusive club of privileged men working in an atmosphere of secrecy, hierarchy and authority. In France, the bureaucracy played an independent role in the transition from feudalism to capitalism but later it came under the full control of the bourgeois class. The bureaucracies in England and America were less powerful as they were controlled by stronger parliaments and had played no role in the bourgeois transformation of these societies earlier. Under Louis Bonaparte, bureaucracy was able to dominate state institutions owing to the weakness of the French bourgeoisie and the isolated existence of the peasants who constituted the social base of Bonaparte's political power.

Any successful revolution, therefore, involved the breaking of the power of the bureaucratic state apparatus. In 1871, Marx reaffirmed his position, specified earlier in *The Eighteenth Brumaire*, where he had maintained that the destruction of the bureaucratic-military machine of the state was the first condition of any real popular revolution on the

European continent. Lenin further developed the same theme in the context of socialist revolutions of the twentieth century in his essay *The State and Revolution.*

Function of the State in Capitalist Society

The chief function of the state in a capitalist society is repression of the working class movement. In *The Eighteenth Brumaire,* Marx explains the nature and function of the state in the following words:

> "This executive power with its monstrous bureaucratic and military organization, with its artificial state machinery embracing wide strata, with a host of officials numbering half a million, besides an army of another half million, this appalling parasitic growth, which enmeshes this body of French society like a net and chokes all its pores, sprang up in the days of absolute monarchy, with the decay of feudal system, which it helped to hasten." (*241* : *158*).

The first French Revolution developed centralization of the bureaucratic power further. Napoleaon also prefected this state machinery through a legal code. The parliamentary republic finally, in its struggle against the radical elements, further strengthened the repressive state machinery of the French government. As Marx puts it, all bourgois revolutions in France perfected the coercive state apparatus instead of smashing it up. The parties that contended in turn for power regarded the possession of this huge bureaucratic structure as the chief spoils of the victor.

As Lenin points out, the development, perfection and strengthening of the bureaucratic and military apparatus proceeded during all the numerous bourgeois revolutions which Europe has witnessed since the fall of feudalism. Lenin says: "It is precisely the petty bourgeoisie that is attracted to the side of the big bourgeoisie and is subordinated to it to a large extent by means of this apparatus, which provides the upper strata of the peasantry, small artisans, tradesmen and the like with comfortable, quiet and respectable jobs which raise their holders *above* the people." (*214* : *160*).

Through repression and gradual reform, the function of the state in capitalist society is to unite the small, medium and large property-owners so that the entire bourgeois class benefits from the new techniques of production. Lenin, however, says that this situation also unites the working-class in its opposition to the domination of the bourgeoisie. He says: "The more the bureaucratic apparatus 'redistributed' among the various bourgeois and petty-bourgeois parties, the more clearly the oppressed classes, with the proletariat at its head, becomes conscious of their irreconcilable hostility to the whole of bourgeois society. That is why it is necessary for all bourgeois parties, even for the most democratic and revolutionary democratic parties, to increase their repressive measures against the revolutionary proletariat, to strengthen the apparatus of repression i.e. the state machine that we are discussing. The course of events compels the revolution *'to concentrate all its forces of destruction'* against the state power, and to regard the problem, not as one of perfecting the state machine, but one of *smashing and destroying it*". (*214:161*).

The state in capitalist society during the last five decades has assumed two major forms—the bourgeois-democratic regime and the fascist regime. Despite the existence of a competitive party system, universal suffrage and elected legislatures, the executive power of the governing elites in these countries has increased tremendously. The military and bureaucratic elites have become firmly entrenched in the political system. Ralph Miliband has shown in his book *The State in Capitalist Society* that economic elites of capitalist countries still constitute a dominant social class which exercises considerable control over the state systems of these countries. C. Wright Mills has argued that the United States today is ruled by a power elite which consists of an alliance of three powerful elites represented by big corporate capitalists, top military officers of the American armed forces and the top leaders of the two political parties. The working class, though highly organised into trade unions, has very little influence over the decision-making process.

The fascist regimes emerged in Europe during the inter-war period in Italy, Germany and Spain. The capitalist classes of these countries, frightened by the economic crisis and prospects of a socialist revolution welcomed the overthrow of bourgeois-democratic regimes and the establishment of fascist dictatorships. The fascist state uses its coercive apparatus to suppress the trade unions and the political parties of the working class. While the bourgeois-democratic state permits the working-class to conduct its economic and political struggles through legal methods so long as these struggles do not threaten the survival of the capitalist mode of production, the fascist state does not allow the working class to engage in such activities, which are legally banned and brutally suppressed by the government. The bourgeois state machine under fascism uses terror to suppress the revolutionary proletariat.

The Marxist view of the function of the state in capitalist society has been re-stated by Gramsci and other European communists. Gramsci has argued that the ruling class in a capitalist society does not govern by repression alone. It also establishes its ideological hegemony over the proletariat through its control of the sources of knowledge, the mass media and educatinal institutions. The emancipation of the working class requires the establishment of proletarian hegemony in the ideological sphere. The party of the working class should first make an attempt to break up the monopolistic control of the bourgeois class in the sphere of art, literature, science and other forms of culture.

The Function of the State in Socialist Society

Engels, speaking about the function of the state in socialist society, says: "The proletariat seizes the state-power and transforms the means of production in the first instance into state property. But in doing this, it puts an end to itself as the proletariat, it puts an end to the class differences and class antagonisms, it puts an end also to the state as the state .As soon as there is no longer any class of society to be held in subjection; as soon as, along with class domination and the struggle for individual existence based on the former anarchy of production, the collisions and excesses arising from these have also been abolished, there is nothing more to be repressed, which would make a special repressive force, a state, necessary." (*215* : *127*).

According to Marx, Engels and Lenin, the state would be required as a dictatorship of the proletariat during the transition from capitalism to communism. It will wither away during the communist phase of social development. As Engels put it: "The first act in which the state really comes forward as the representative of society as a whole the taking possession of the means of production in the name of society—is at the same time its last independent act as a state. The interference of the state power in social relations becomes superfluous in one sphere after another, and then ceases of itself. The government of persons is replaced by the administration of things and the direction of the process of production. (*215* : *128*).

The function of the state in socialist society is to consolidate the public power of the proletariat by smashing the bourgeois state machine. Once this has been accomplished, the state loses its historical character as an instrument of class domination though it may continue as an administrative agency for directing the process of production. The revisionists and social-democrats talk of transforming the bourgeois class-state into a free people's state and the anarchists want to abolish it immediately after the socialist revolution. Disagreeing with the above stand-points of the revisionists and the anarchists, Engels presents his point of view in the following words: "The state is not 'abolished', it withers away. It is from the standpoint that we must appraise the pharse 'free people's state'—both its justification at times for agitational purposes, and its ultimate scientific inadequacy—and also the demand of the so-called anarchists that the state should be abolished overnight." (*215* : *129*).

Marx also outlined the main features of a socialist state in the following words: "The standing army should be replaced by a people at arms. Responsible councillors, mostly workers or recognised representatives of the working class, should form an assembly that would be essentially a labour body rather than having purely legislative or decorative functions; election would be by universal suffrage and could be revoked at any time. The police should be converted from being a component of the central government into a responsible agency of the assembly, deprived of any political assignments and liable to suspension at any time. Every branch of administration should be converted in a similar way. Public office should be made really democratic, ceasing to be the private preserve of the central government and its creatures and being discharged at all levels by workers for a wage." (*233* : *141*).

The function of the state in socialist countries has not entirely conformed to the visions of Marx and Engels. All socialist countries have large standing armies and powerful bureaucracies. Property has been nationalised but the state has come under the domination of bureaucratic, army and party elites. In Trotsky's opinion, the Soviet bureaucracy is in the full sense of the word the sole commanding and privileged stratum. The means of production belong to the state but the state, so to speak belongs to the bureaucracy. Today, many Marxist as well non-Marxist critics argue that the state in Soviet Russia exhibits the features of bureaucratic collectivism and cannot be considered as genuinely socialistic. Umberto Melotti, speaking about the Soviet Union and other East European countries, says: "One cannot in all honesty call those countries socialist, since there are clear-cut class distinctions, and exploitation persists. Nor can one talk of a society in transition towards socialism, since such a society requires that the proletariat should hold power with the conscious aim of steering society towards socialism." (*233* : *143*).

Melotti, who is an Italian Marxist, argues that the proletariat is really an oppressed class in Russia, exploited and dominated by the bureaucracy. Pizzi says: "We naively tell ourselves that property is 'nationalised'. For scientific Marxists that is not very much. We wonder what kind of 'nationalized' property this is, when it is exclusively controlled by a single class which then appropriates its fruits in just as blatant a fashion as did the former bourgeoisie. In practice there is in Russia an exploiting class that holds sway over the means of production and acts just as if it owned them. Although it is not divided up into individual owners, its members as a class, *en masse*, are the real owners of all the 'nationalised' property." (*233* : *143*).

According to Carlo, the main features of bureaucratic collectivism as practised in the Soviet Union are as follows:

1. Property is owned by a class as a whole, and not its individual owners.
2. The economy is run in accordance with a central plan and is insulated from the market competition.
3. The commanding position is occupied by state machinery for the extended reproduction of use-values, and not exchange values, as in capitalism.
4. The exploitation of man by man is a direct process, operating by the appropriation and distribution of part of the total surplus product through the plan.
5. Political and economic power is completely centralized.

These features put bureaucratic collectivism in a totally distinct category from all precapitalist modes of production, capitalism, or genuine socialism, and make a completely new type of socio-economic formation, with its own laws, completely different from those identified by Marx for all other types of society.

State in Developing Societies

Marx characterized the pre-capitalist societies of Asia as based on the Asiatic mode of production. Melotti describes its feature in the following words: "Private land ownership, if exists at all, is very limited. Class distinctions exist on purely spurious lines, and are sometimes distorted further by the caste system, whose outstanding feature is a tendency to create accepted inequalities. The form of exploitation is less rigid, owing to the absence of private slavery or personal bondage and the educated ruling bureaucracy's capacity to create illusions, and hence more able to secure considerable growth of productive forces within the existing social structure. Town and country form a unity, free from distinctions. And, above all, tht State is all-powerful." (*233 : 101*).

Unlike Europe, the Asian societies did not experience social revolutions and did not produce states based on slavery, serfdom or wage labour. Neither feudalism nor capitalism could develop out of the stagnant, self-perpetuating village communities ruled by a despotic state bureaucracy. China provided the classic example of the centralized bureaucratic state based on the Asiatic mode of production. European colonial intervention brought about the first social revolution in Asian and African societies. As Marx put it: "England has broken down the entire framework of Indian society, without any symptoms of reconstitution yet appearing. This loss of the old world....separates Hindustan....from all its ancient traditions, and from the whole of its past history." (*146 :: 313*). It was much the same story with China. Marx condemns the exploitative aspects of modern colonialism but at the same time stresses the progressive nature of the capitalist penetration of Asian and African societies. Summing up the impact of British colonial conquests, Marx said: "All the English bourgeoisie may be forced to do will neither emancipate nor materially mend the social conditions of the mass of the people, depending not only on the development of the productive powers, but on their appropriation by the people. But what they will not fail to do is to lay down the material premises for both; has the bourgeoisie ever done more? Has it ever effected a progress without dragging individuals and peoples through blood and dirt, through misery and degradation." (*146 : 323*).

The response to colonial rule was the awakening of nationalities. Colonial societies were gradually transformed into nation-states with underdeveloped economies which combined pre-capitalist social relations with capitalist relations. Political sovereignty for the Afro-Asian states did not imply economic sovereignty for many of these nations. According to Helio Jaguarib, three types of states have emerged in the developing societies: the colonial fascist state, the national reformist state and the socialist state.

In the colonial fascist state, the political power is in the hands of a coalition of foreign capitalists, native land owners, native capitalists, the military elite and the bureaucracy. The state assumes the form of a military dictatorship or a landowner's oligarchy. In Latin America, Chile, Brazil, Argentina etc. may be cited as examples of the colonial fascist type. They have generally assumed the form of military dictatorships. The military elite is recruited from the landowning class as well as the bourgeoisie. They have ties with foreign capitalists, whose capital is invested in these countries.

The Catholic Church in Latin America generally supports this combination of landowners, capitalists, militarists and bureaucrats. The United States, as an imperialist and neo-colonial power, supports the existence of these colonial fascist states in the Third World. Indonesia, the Philippines and Saudi Arbia are the Asian examples of the colonial fascist type.

The second category consists of the national reformist states. In these countries, sovereignty is exercised by a combination of the bourgeoisie, intelligentsia, army officers of the middle rank who may seize power through a *coup d'etat,* and the bureaucracy. Peru, Bolivia and Mexico are described as national reformist states in Latin America. India, Sri Lanka, Burma, Iraq, Egypt, Algeria, Tanzania and Guinea are cited as examples of national reformism in Asia and Africa. These states make an attempt to defend themselves from neo-colonial pressures and also try to curb the privileges of the landowning class and promote industrialization by supporting private capitalists and by creating a sector of nationalized industries.

The third category consists of socialist states such as China, North Korea, Vietnam, Laos, Cambodia and Cuba. These countries have abolished precapitalist and capitalist social relations in their economic life and have reorganised their economic systems on a predominantly socialist basis. With the exception of Cuba, these were predominantly peasant societies. China under Mao Zedong made an attempt to establish an egalitarian social structure. Vietnam under Ho Chi Minh made a similar effort simultaneously struggling against French and American imperialism. The function of the state in these societies is to uplift a predominantly peasant population to the position of a self-sufficient industrialized community through centralized economic planning. Only future development will show whether the socialist states in the developing countries will be able to avoid the social and political contradictions, which have now surfaced in the Soviet and East European societies. Nicaragua is the latest example of an emerging socialist state in the Latin American segment of the third world.

Jaguarib's classification has lost its relevance now. The social-fascist dictatorships have acquired democratic facade and some legitimacy as bourgeois neo-liberal states. National reformist and socialist states have given up statist planning and are following market-oriented models of economic growth. Even China is now pursuing the path of capitalist development though she still calls it "socialism with Chienese characteristics."

CHAPTER 10

THE WELFARE STATE

The term 'the welfare state' is so much in vogue in present-day India that it seems advisable to devote a chapter to it. The idea of a welfare state is deeply embedded in the Indian Constitution in the part dealing with the Directive Principles of State Policy.

Article 38 says: "The State shall strive to promote the welfare of the people by securing and protecting as effectively as it may a social order in which justice, social, economic, and political, shall inform all the institutions of the national life". Article 39 speaks of (a) adequate means of livelihood; (b) distribution of natural resources so as best to subserve the common good; (c) opposition to the concentration of wealth; (d) equal pay for equal work for both men and women; (e) conservation of health and strength of workers—especially of women and children; and (f) the non-exploitation of children. Article 41 speaks of the State securing the right to work, to education, and to public assistance in cases of unemployment, old age, sickness, and disablement.

The articles following feelingly refer to provision for just and humane conditions of work and for maternity relief: a living wage for workers; provision for free and compulsory education until the children are fourteen years old; promotion of the educational and economic interests of Scheduled Castes, Scheduled Tribes, and other weaker sections; and the duty of the State to raise the level of nutrition and the standard of living and the duty to improve public health. A wet blanket, however, is thrown on all these desirable things by Article 37 which says that none of them is enforceable at a court of law.

THE ORIGIN AND DEVELOPMENT OF THE WELFARE STATE IDEAL

While every State today would like to call itself a welfare state almost up to the end of the nineteenth century most states contented themselves with being "police" State. Their primary business was merely to provide law and order. The promotion of welfare was left to individuals and groups of individuals. Among political thinkers in our day, Laski more than anyone else was the first to turn the attention of the world from the police state idea to the welfare state idea.

The welfare state ideal took strong root in England. Its development, however, was different from the development in Germany. In England Trade Unions, ably supported by Fabian and other types of socialists, played an important part in developing the ideal.

The National Health Service whose foundations were laid by earlier governments received its final shape during the Prime Ministership of Mr. (Later Lord) Attlee. Besides, a series of measures were passed resulting in the nationalization of railways, coalmines and steel; nationalization of the Bank of England, and nationalization of transport. When the Conservatives came in power the only measure on which they have gone back is the nationalization of steel. The rest of the programme has come to stay.

A vast social insurance scheme is in operation today in Britain. According to it, all persons of working age contribute to it except housewives. Provision is made for old age retirement benefits, widow's benefits, unemployment benefits, family allowances for families with two or more children, milk for school children, milk and special food for expectant and nursing mothers, free medical service, free secondary education, and liberal scholarships for higher education.

This vast programme has been made possible by steep graduated taxes, by the high degree of self-discipline practised by the people, and by their conscientiousness in the payment of taxes. Surprisingly enough, national production has increased in spite of high taxes. There is a high level of economic satisfaction in the country.

When we turn to the U.S.A. we find that on account of the strong individualistic tendencies of that country the term 'welfare state' is anathema to a great many, although there are several welfare schemes in operation in the broad sense of the term such as the Tennessee Valley Authority. elaborate social security schemes, public works and excellent roads, price support for agricultural products, free education up to the college stage and state and federal aid to education. The Social Security Scheme is so very comprehensive as to include even white-collar workers, University teachers, and self-employed persons.

Among the Continental countries, Sweden, Norway, and Denmark have extensive welfare schemes supported by high taxation. We are reliably informed that in some of the welfare states of Europe the inequality between the highest and lowest incomes is less than ten times.

The socialist states also are welfare states; but here welfare is planned and executed from above. More attention is paid to material welfare than to moral and spiritual welfare. Russia has been the first modern country to have a planned economy. Her successive Five Year Plans have been a remarkable success and paid her a good dividend during World War II. There is in general a pooling of wealth.

The aspiration of the Indian State has been to provide full employment to all its citizens, free and compulsory education at least up to the eleventh year, public assistance in cases of unemployment, old age, sickness, disablement, and even of undeserved want, a decent standard of life, full enjoyment of leisure and social and cultural opportunities, adequate housing, and health facilities. In spite of the best efforts of the Government, full employment still remains a mere will o' the wisp, the mounting population of the country serving as a deterrent. Free and compulsory education has made some advance, but is nowhere near the goal. Half-hearted attempts have been made at the limitation of population.

The five giant evils of India which need to be tackled are want, disease, ignorance, squalor and idleness. Time is of the essence in tackling these evils since time waits for no man.

The three Five Year Plans and yearly plans of Plan holiday periods have helped to improve the agricultural and individual conditions of India, but much leeway has yet to be made. In the Fourth Plan still greater stress is laid on all out development. Many spectacular schemes have been started, and some completed, in the harnessing of turbulent rivers for purposes of power and irrigation, in the production of steel and cement, in the manufature of railway engines, coaches, telegraph and telephone equipment etc. But a detailed description of it will take us far afield. The emphasis on the public sector has been so great that the private sector complains of a stepmotherly treatment. Nehru at one time said: "the public sector must grow and dominate".

DEFINITION AND NATURE OF THE WELFARE STATE

From the above description of the welfare state in many lands, we may now proceed to a definition of it. Adopting a rather narrow and restricted view of it, Abraham defines it as "a community where state power is deliberately used to modify the normal play of economic forces so as to obtain a more equal distribution of income for every citizen, a basic minimum irrespective of the market value of his work and his property". Suffice it to say that this definition looks at the matter from a purely economic point of view. T. W. Kent attempts a more inclusive definition when he says that a welfare state is "a state that provides for its citizens a wide range of social services." Kent goes on to say that the primary purpose of the state is to give the citizen security, but the welfare state undertakes to help him, if he loses his ordinary source of income.

Hobman describes the welfare state as a compromise between communism on the one side and unbridled individualism on the other. As such, Hobman believes that in spite of all its imperfections, the welfare state sets a pattern for any humane and progressive society. To sum up his views somewhat extensively, the welfare state guarantees a minimum standard of subsistence without removing incentives to private enterprise, and it brings about a limited redistribution of income by means of graduated high taxation. Yet it does not pretend to establish economic equality among its citizens. All are assured of adequate help in case of need, whether the need is due to illness, old age, unemployment or any other cause.

In the light of what has been said above, it is somewhat unfortunate that in India at present the welfare state is used so very broadly as to include every activity of the State which makes for a better state of affairs. Strictly speaking, the welfare state has reference to such items as social insurance of various kinds, old age and other kinds of pensions, free primary education, housing—particularly for those coming within the

11—17 149

lower brackets of income, medical assistance, poor relief, etc. Therefore, it is not quite accurate to describe the multi-purpose river valley schemes, public corporations, and nationalized industries as coming within the purview of the welfare state. A welfare state is not a catch-all term for every kind of improvement.

So far as the nature of the welfare state is concerned, the first important thing to remember is that welfare is not a matter of *charity,* but of *right.* Welfare, as understood here, does not carry with it any stigma of pauperism.

Secondly, if welfare is to be genuine welfare, the ground for it should have been prepared earlier by the various agencies at work in the State. Unless the minds and attitudes of men and women are attuned to the idea of a welfare state, they are apt to look upon welfare as manna from heaven falling into the mouths of an expectant people.

In the third place, if the welfare state is to be a blessing and not a curse, it should not produce a pauper mentality on the part of its recipients. In whatever is done by the State, care should be taken not to dry up the wells of initiative and self-help.

HINDRANCES TO THE REALIZATION OF A WELFARE STATE AND THEIR REMOVAL

So far as India is concerned the greatest hindrance is the low level of production. It is obvious that before there can be a more equitable distribution, there should be a phenomenal rise in national production. While the per capita income of the U.S.A. is about $ 1800 a year, that of India is as low as $ 100.00 a year. Millions do not get even that amount.

If national production is to increase, we need far-reaching moral and institutional changes. On the moral side, we need somehow or other to impress upon people that work is worship. Through our homes, our educational and religious institutions, civic associations, our recreational and social clubs, and our party cells we must instil in people a keen desire for honest, sustained and arduous work. We must make it clear that anyone who shirks his work is unworthy of his country. Something like this has been done in Russia by bestowing the 'Order of Lenin' on good workers and the 'Order of Tortoise' on bad workers.

Side by side with a zeal for work, we need to create in people an enthusiasm for the welfare state. Nehru is right when he says, "Little men cannot work for great causes". A welfare State should be characterized by a spirit of self-discipline.

The fear of high taxes which is found all over the country is another hindrance to the realization of the welfare state. "One cannot have the cake and eat it too". This means that some amount of self-sacrifice is necessary if a welfare state is to become a reality. No one pretends that he enjoys paying taxes. But once the common man's traditional attitude to material things changes, he can become an honest and cheerful tax-payer. In this connection it is gratifying to find that the Estate Duty went through without much difficulty. An indirect result of the many taxes which are being imposed upon India is that people are gradually changing their old attitude towards property.

When we turn from the moral to the institutional changes required to make the welfare state a success, several ideas occur to a person. The first among these is the nationalization of key or heavy industries. As has been said already, mere nationalization is not an *open sesame* to prosperity. Yet one fails to see how a welfare state can be realized without a gradual and judicious nationalization.

As regards the ownership of land, India is not yet socially or morally advanced enough to launch upon a nation-wide scheme of collective farming. Yet a limited amount of experimentation can be made with co-operative or joint farming; and if it succeeds there can be further extension of it. The establishment of a wide network of small-scale and cottage industries has a definite place in the expansion of production; as also the expansion of transport and communication facilities.

A minimum wage legislation is one of the earliest steps which a welfare State should undertake. A corollary of that is that the quantity and quality of work performed should be commensurate with the wages received. To this end, it is the responsibility of the State not only to impart free and compulsory primary education, but also vocational and technical education to all those who can benefit by it. It is the elementary duty of every democratic State to teach some kind of skill or other to every citizen. Basic education is another such duty. It should be related to actual life conditions.

The heedless increase of population in India, five million a year, is a great hindrance to the welfare State. What economic improvement is made is more than cancelled by the reckless multiplication of population. It is far better to have fewer children to whom one can give the best possible opportunities of life than to have a multitude to whom even the barest needs of life have to be denied. Gorwala rightly observes, "Failure to solve the population problem can ruin all attempts to obtain welfare."

Every welfare measure enacted in good faith opens up opportunities for illicit gain. This means that those who administer welfare as well as those on whose behalf it is administered should develop a high degree of personal integrity. If a large percentage of the money spent on welfare is consumed by a top-heavy administration or is diverted into wrong channels as is the case at times, the game is not worth the candle. In the name of 'welfare' we may drive ourselves into national bankruptcy.

A hindrance to the welfare state particularly applicable to India is the wide prevalence of such narrow loyalties as those of the family, caste, tribe, religious community and linguistic groups. When these loyalties clash with national loyalties, the latter should prevail if the benefits of the welfare state are to be shared by all alike.

THE WELFARE STATE AND SARVODAYA

A question of special interest to Indian readers is whether these two deals can be reconciled. There is no gainsaying the fact that the welfare state, as understood and practised at present, is essentially foreign to our culture. It is like a ripe fruit tied to a tree which has not produced it. The remedy for it is to prepare the minds and hearts of the masses and classes for it. The welfare state may be an excellent ideal, but neither the political leaders of India by and large nor the people as a whole at the present stage are good enough for it.

The welfare state, as it is envisaged at present, seems to call for large outlays of money, an army of public servants of various categories who can easily become birds of prey, a good amount of centralized government control, red tapism and routine, and ample opportunity for corruption and nepotism. One additional disadvantage we find in India today is that the welfare state is creating new vested interests such as the Scheduled Castes, Scheduled Tribes, Backward Classes, peasants, labourers, etc. New classes of exploiters also are being constantly created.

By contrast it seems that Sarvodaya is free from these defects. It stands for decentralization in production and administration, simplification of life standards, reduction in the number of public servants, and a self-regulating community operating through non-violence. While all of this is admirable, Sarvodaya is still a dream and has not yet been accomplished even partially; and when it begins to function it is bound to give rise to its own set of problems, some of which may be the same problems which confront the welfare state but in new clothes. Anyhow, since the needs of the people are stupendous we cannot afford to throw away the tangible gains of the welfare state for the probable gains of Sarvodaya. The part of wisdom is to allow both systems to compete with each other peacefully—a kind of "peaceful co-existence" until we are absolutely sure as to which one of them can produce better results.

THE CONCEPTION OF A SOCIALIST SOCIETY AND WELFARE STATE

Laski's Welfare State Ideal Closer to Fabianism

Laski's conception of a socialist society and welfare state is essentially closer to Fabianism than to Marxism. It is somewhat more radical than the Fabian conception but certainly more conservative than the tpye of socialist society the Marxists have created in their countries. Laski, however, thinks that minor reforms within the limits of the capitalist system may promote popular welfare in a limited way but cannot solve the crisis of capitalism. As he says, "The fact is that, in the circumstances we have reached, it is necessary to go outside the postulates of the capitalist system in order to achieve significant and lasting reform. Concessions of the older type are only possible when the margins of capitalist achievement are wide enough to permit them to be made without detriment to those postulates. We do not confront that condition. We have reached the stage of economic evolution which Marx foresaw when he predicted that the contradictions of capitalism would result in the emergence of a permanent and growing body of workers for whom no prospect of profitable employment can be found. Technological unemployment, the increasing power of finance-capital, the growth of economic imperialism, his prediction in each of these realms has been fully substantiated. Within the framework of the existing legal order, we cannot control the implications of these tendencies" (*50 : 278*).

Laski thinks that a fundamental change in the ownership of the means of production is necessary to meet the present crisis of capitalism. All solutions, which fall short of this necessary change in the ownership of the instruments of production, will be of no avail ond cannot touch the heart of the crisis.

The Present Crisis of Capitalism

The crisis of capitalism has permeated every sphere of human life. Describing the magnitude of this crisis, Laski says, "We are in the midst of the profoundest crisis our civilization has known, at least since the Reformation, and perhaps since the fall of the Roman Empire. On our ability to act upon an understanding of what the crisis is, may well depend the peace and the well-being of the human race for centuries to come. It is not a crisis which any simple or single remedy can resolve. For there are in dispute amongst us not only the ultimate character of the relationships of men but also the faith, or system of values to which those relationships give birth. There is no plane of thought or of action that is exempt from the influence of the crisis. Religion, politics, economics, science, culture, these in the massive totality of their interaction upon one another are all deeply affected by it" (*131 : 305*).

Implications of a New Socialist System

Laski thinks that the inauguration of a new socialist system will imply significant changes in every sphere of human life. It will equally affect our social, political, cultural, economic and intellectual values. The change in the methods of production is bound to be reflected in social relationships, political forms, cultural patterns and mental habits of the people. The differences of rank and status and the privileges associated with birth, caste, creed or class will have to be abolished.

Abolition of Discriminatory Privileges

The political institutions which protect the privileges of one class against another will have to be suppressed. The institution of monarchy in any form, a hereditary second chamber like the House of Lords, a discriminative franchise, an irresponsible judiciary which can over-ride the will of the legislature, a bureaucracy drawn from the members of a single class—all these are declared to be incompatible with the announced purposes of socialism. Education will be universalized and the avenues of knowledge and the highest cultural development will be open to all on the basis of an equalized opportunity. Science and technology will be placed at the service of the common people which will put an end to the economics of scarcity and inaugurate a new era of planned progress for all.

Defeat of Fascism and Social and Political Change

Laski thought that the defeat of fascism in the Second World War was bound to release new social forces for the overthrow of capitalism and the eventual victory of socialism. As he said, "Given the victory of the United Nations, the overthrow, that is, of those forces in the world which have deliberately made war in the interest of counter-revolution, the individualist capitalism of the classical economists is bound to be revealed as obsolete. It has, indeed, long been known as an anachronism by all who have watched the growth of industrial combination, on the one hand, and the emergence of a caste of economic directors, mainly remarkable for their skill in financial manipulation, who are the masters alike of their shareholders and of the consumer, and are not seldom in a position to hold even states to ransom. Their power is as massive in volume as it has largely been irresponsible in operation. We have reached a state in historical evolution where either their power must be subordinate to the interest of the community or the interest of the community will be a tragic pseudonym for their power. Precisely as in the nineteenth century, the irresponsible privilege of rentier and aristocrat was broken by the development of democracy in the political field, so, in the twentieth century, we have to break the irresponsible privilege of rentier and plutocrat by the development of democracy in the economic field" (*131* : *206*).

Democratisation of Economic Power and Planning for People's Welfare

Thus he concludes that the power of the financial oligarchy must be broken to lay the foundations of a new socialist order. The economic power must be democratised and the masses must get an opportunity to determine their own economic future. A socialist planning for people's welfare can begin only by breaking the control of capitalistic monopolies. (*121* : *180*).

It should be noted that Laski does not contemplate the necessity of immediate state control of all industries and agriculture as was done by the Communists in Soviet Russia. He only wants that the fundamental bases of the economic power should be transferred to the ownership and control of the community. The most important step in this direction is the nationalization of banks and insurance companies to regulate the supply of capital and credit. Secondly, the state must own and control the land. Thirdly, the control of imports and exports must be the responsibility of the community. Lastly, he recommends the nationalization of transport, fuel and power such as the coalmines or the production of electricity.

Laski, however, does not consider the above programme as the achievement of socialism. He only regards it as the most initial and preparatory stage to start the process of further socialization. He believes in the achievement of socialism by stages and through the traditional methods of parliamentary democracy.

Democratic Freedom and Socialist Planning

Thus Laski thinks that the achievement of a planned socialist society is compatible with the atmosphere of democratic freedom. He thinks that only fascist planning should be regarded as a negation of democratic freedom. He says that even Russian system of planning, although it has been achieved under the leadership of a communist party, has widened the scope of human freedom in some important respects while restricting it in certain other equally important respects. But if the transition from capitalist anarchy to socialist planning is achieved within the limits of a parliamentary system, Laski does not think that the community will be a loser in any sphere of freedom.

As he says, "I see no evidence to suppose that the transition from capitalist democracy to planned democracy involves any temporary or permanent loss of freedom. But the defence of this hypothesis requires precise analysis of the content of freedom. I have already quoted the profound aphorism of Marx that freedom is the recognition of necessity. There is no point in crying for the moon....The essence of freedom, given the framework of necessity within which each of us must discover it, is, I think, to be found in what I have called the sense of continuous initiative, the conviction that each of us, even if involved in a social purpose which transcends our private purpose, can yet contribute to its definition some emphasis which is our own. Freedom, in short, is the knowledge that each of us counts as and, as well as instrument, that there is elbow-room in the society which gives us power to make our own choices, to experiment with ourselves. So that our freedom comes of a sense of spacious horizons we are empowered to scan, of opportunities unbarred in which we can find significance. A man is free in society when the operation of its institutions gives him that mood of creative hope which spurs him on to achieve a fulfilment in which he finds significance and exhilaration" (*131* : *342*). This definition of freedom is far in advance of his earlier notion of freedom as absence of restraint and shows how far Laski has travelled on the road of collectivism.

New Collectivistic Conception of Freedom in a Welfare State

It is on the basis of this new collectivistic conception of freedom that Laski concludes that there has been a real extension of human freedom in the Soviet Union hitherto unknown in the capitalist world. He points out that the Russian worker has got the freedom of criticising his foreman or the manager of his factory in a way that is not open to the British or American worker. His employment is secure, his health is insured, his children get free education, his work has been given a social dignity, he continuously shares in the general increase of the standards of living—all such things are denied to his counterpart in the capitalist countries (*169* : *495*).

Communism and the Ideal of People's Welfare

"Communist dictatorship", as Laski says, "may plan the growth of the individuality of the citizens; and it may punish with harshness those who seek to escape from the fundamental rules of the plan. But that the communist dictatorship has in fact achieved for millions the sense of a capacity for growth seems to be beyond the possibility of serious denial. That sense of a capacity for growth, which enables its possessor to affirm his or her personality, is the very secret of freedom" (101 : 343).

This shows that a social system which is based upon the common ownership of the means of production is bound to increase the scope of human freedom and people's welfare in several ways. Laski thinks that it will result in a comprehensive transvaluation of values creating new individual and institutional perspectives for the idea of freedom. Moreover, he is convinced that socialist planning can be attempted and realized without the support of a political dictatorship as was the case in Soviet Russia. In this way freedom in the social and economic sphere and people's welfare can be achieved without endangering the political freedom.

A Socialist Commonwealth of Nations can Promote Welfare of the Peoples of the World

Ultimately Laski's ideal of socialism and popular welfare is not nationalistic but universal. He does not think that socialism is a creed only meant for the advanced industrial nations in the orbit of the Western civilization. He has been a consistent champion of colonial movements for international independence and freedom. He has declared capitalist imperialism as incompatible with his ideal of a socialist commonwealth of nations. Laski, however, does not prescribe any uniform path to be followed by all countries in their journey towards the final destination of a welfare state based on socialism. Every nation will advance towards the final goal of socialism in its own way because the national traditions and the cultural prepossessions of the people differ from country to country.

He criticizes the Communists rather unjustly for being dogmatic and narrow-minded because they want to impose a uniform system over all races and peoples without any regard for the differences in national histories and psychology. Laski wants to trust the methods of internal evolution rather than those of imposition from without. But he is convinced that all nations must ultimately seek their welfare and salvation in the adoption of some form of socialism, which they will evolve according to their own national genius.

Lastly, it should be pointed out that Laski as well as Sidney and Beatrice Webb believed that even the Soviet system of dictatorship has the natural propensities of liberalizing itself in the course of time. He

was, therefore, quite hopeful that in a not very distant future a world federation of socialist nations will emerge on this unhappy planet which will finally banish from its midst the twin scourges of war and scarcity. The ideal of welfare state will become, then, a universal ideal bridging the existing gulf between the standards of living of the citizens of economically advanced nations of Europe, Japan, and North America on the one hand and economically underdeveloped countries of Asia, Africa and Latin America on the other.

Professor Lipset says: "The fundamental political problems of the industrial revolution have oeen solved. The workers have achieved industrial and political citizenship; the conservative have accepted the *welfare state*; and the democratic left has recognized that an increase in overall state power carried with it more dangers to freedom than solutions for economic problems." (*216 : 406*).

Miliband points out a miscarriage of the notion of welfare: "In no field has the notion of the 'welfare state' had a more precise and opposite meaning than here: there are no more persistant and successful applicants for public assistance than the proud giants of the private enterprise system." (*236 : 72*). Labour, socialist and social-democratic regimes brought into being a comprehensive system of social insurance and other services which were regarded as the pillars of the 'Welfare State'. But conservative regimes of Thatcher and Reagan started a process of dismantling these welfare structures which has emulated in all capitalist countries. Mafia capitalism of Yeltsin has abolished all social welfare benefits which were earlier available under socialism.

CHAPTER 11

THEORY OF STATE : ITS COMPARATIVE DIMENSIONS

Empiricist Attack on the Notion of State

The disruption of the notion of the state is a significant feature of the 'new science' of politics, whose very claim to scientific dignity is based on a strictly empirical approach to political facts and on a strict adherence to ethical neutrality. This approach completely alters the perspective of traditional political thought. Empirical political theory tends to dissociate the study of political phenomena from traditional concentration on the concept of the State. Being concerned in general with distribution of power and influence in any social context, it can afford to take little notice of the specific label or 'name' given to institutionalized power in a particular society at a particular moment.

Bentley in the *Process of Government* denied the relevance of the concept of the State for political analysis. His thesis is that government is 'first, last and always activity' in the shape of a 'process' not of ideas or institutions. The task of political science lies in singling out the purposes or 'interests' which determine men's action and which link them together in an infinite variety of relations or 'groups'. In fact, it is impossible to separate the notion of group from that of interest. But political phenomena do not consist only in activities that embody an interest. They are further characterized by the presence of an element called force or pressures.

Pressure is always a group phenomenon, which indicates the push and resistance between groups. The balance of the group pressures determines the existing state of society. It is precisely at this moment that Bentley comes out with his repudiation of the concept of the State. The term state does not coincide with what is meant by political phenomena in general. The idea of the state, as Bentley puts it, "has been very prominent, no doubt, among the intellectual amusements of the past", which might have served "at particular places and times....to help give coherent and pretentious expression to some particular group's activity", but its claims are based on "too minute a factor" to deserve our special attention in political inquiry. In a comparative study of legislation, administration, adjudication or even the constitution, political science "must go behind the formal element" to find "what are the real interests that are playing on each other through this agency". (*192* : *61*). Ultimately, there is nothing left of the pompous notion called the state except the bare fact that some groups succeed in carrying out their will by determining the behaviour of others.

It is easy to trace in the above attack on the concept of the state the clear influence of positivism or pragmatism and a reflection of an absence in American linguistic usage of a precise connotation for the term 'state' Bentley's arguments are still echoed by contemporary writers such as David B. Truman, Harold Lasswell and David Easton. Truman feels that the "group interpretation of the political process....inevitably must ignore some greater unity designated as society or the state" and that "the institutions of government" are nothing else than "centres of interest-based power". Lasswell and Kaplan dissolve "such political abstratctions as 'State' and 'sovereignty' into concrete interpersonal relationship of influence and control" but grudgingly admit that we may still speak of a group as a state, "whenever a certain pattern of identifications, demands, and expectations with regard to power exceeds some selected frequency in the group". (192 :63) However, the most severe assault on the conception of the State is found in David Easton's work, *The Political System*. Easton suggests that the political scientist, who is interested in meaningful empirical research, should scrupulously avoid the use of the term State in view of the variety and confusion in its connotation in traditional political theory. Political Science is concerned not with description or comparison of institutions for organizations but with analysis and understanding of the activities involved" in the formulation and execution of social policy, in what has come to be called elliptically....the policy-making process". Comparative political analysis should focus attention not on the nature and role of the state in different societies but on differentiation and classification of political systems in terms of "the authoritative allocation of values for a given society as influenced by the use and distribution of power" (*195* : *129*).

Behind this sophisticated language, we receive again the message of the political realist "to tear the veil of verbal illusions and to look at the facts". Alexander P. d' Entreves observes : "Indeed, with the final disruption of the notion of the State at the hands of the modern empiricists, one conclusion seems to stand out as the inevitable outcome of any approach to the problem of politics in strict realistic terms. The conclusion can only be that, from a purely empirical standpoint, the state does 'exist' only as kind of force-relation among men—however much disguised the ultimate datum of force may be by such broader and milder expressions as 'pressure', 'influence', control, and so forth, expressions prefered by modern writers to the crude old language of might, the language of Thrasymachus and Machiavelli". (*192* : *63*). He further argues that force admits of a qualitative, and not merely a quantitative differentiation. It is precisely this qualitative difference which may possibly give some sense to the notion of the State which has fared so badly in contemporary political science and has been discarded as a conceptual tool for comparative political analysis.

The political realist is perhaps justified in maintaining that the State, when interpreted from empirical point of view, is just one group among other groups, one system of force among others. But to argue, as modern positivists also do, that the notion of the State is an abstract or formal concept is to admit that the notion represents a conceptual elaboration or the empirical datum of force, a specific way of interpreting certain facts which enables the political theorist to single them out among the large variety of the power-relations existing in the social context. The State regarded as 'power' is the State of legal theory, where power means force qualified by the law.

The state regarded as 'authority' is the state that requires a justification or legitimation which is not provided by mere force or by the sole exercise of legal power as an attribute of sovereignty. Political realism views the state as simply an expression of force. Where force is lacking, there is no State, only chaos and anarchy. The legal theory of the State is chiefly concerned with the validity or loyalty of commands. The power of the state is a legal power, conditioned by the existence and the observance of law. But legality should not be confused with legitimacy. The notion of the State will become clear and intelligible only when we are able to explain how force, first legalized as power, becomes in turn legitimate as authority.

The socio-political dimension of force, the legal dimension of power and the philosophical dimension of legitimation are closely interwoven in the concept of the State. The philosophical, legal and socio-political aspects, representing three attributes of the state viz. legitimacy, validity and 'efficacy' respectively, ought to be taken into account in any fruitful comparative study of modern political systems. The legitimating principles, according to Alexander d' Entreves, could be divine right, consent, law and order, negative and positive liberty, country and nation or the common good. The legality or validity of state power could be expressed through such phrases as the rule of law, the 'mixed state' and the 'division of power', government by men and government by laws, constitutionalism, sovereignty or justice. The element of force or efficacy in the concept of the state was recognized in Thrasymachian theory of justice, the 'new principality' of Machiavelli, 'reason of state' and *Machtstaat* of the German philosophers, theories of the ruling class and governing elites, and all political doctrines based on realism, pessimism, positivism and empiricism. The above approach is based on a re-statement of the 'classical view' about politics which regards contemporary empirical approaches to comparative politics as one-dimensional as they are entirely occupied in analysing the force-relation, which is a characteristic of political realists in every age and every country.

Some Recent Perspectives on the State

In European academic circles, the state has been the subject of considerable discussion in recent years. Theoretical analyses are now rather more sophisticated, though sometimes conceptual clarity may be lacking. There is often the predominance of complex 'formalism' which fails to be empirically grounded. This is evident in the writings of

N. Poulantzas, particularly his *Political Power and Social Classes* and *Social Classes in Contemporary Capitalism.* As Richard Scase points out, analyses and considerations of the state now go beyond the rather vague perspectives which tended to polarise the debate during the late 1960s and the early 1970s. Then, it was possible to identify two basic approaches: the 'liberal-democratic' and the 'Marxist'.

The 'liberal-democratic' tradition conceptualized the state as "an autonomous complex of institutions, politically neutral and external to structurally-determined social forces". This conception of the state was outlined by R. Dahl in *A Preface to Democratic Theory* and by S. Lipset in *Political Man*. The state "is then, up for grabs, to be 'captured' by elected regimes and used as an instrument for their own specific political purposes." Within the liberal-democratic perspective, the state is considered "necessary for the purpose of creating, defining and enforcing 'the rules' within which various socio-economic and political forces operate". It is also regarded as the institutional "basis for the 'political' as distinct from the 'economic' sector of social life. There are two basic assumptions within this perspective. First, that western capitalist systems are 'pluralistic' because political and economic powers "are institutionally separated". Secondly, that the political power "is structurally and internally differentiated not only in terms of the functions exercised by the executive, the legislative and the judiciary, but also because of the existence of various pressure groups and political parties." Richard Scase further observes: "The 'political', then is regarded as irreducible to the 'economic'; indeed, this is seen to be one of the major differences between Western capitalist and East European societies. Within the former, there are 'economic' and 'political' rights, roles and obligations which are quite separable both instituionally and legally. Any social forces that would be likely to lead to an erosion of this distinction are seen as 'dangerous' since they would undermine the essential characteristics of the liberal-democratic state". (*251 : 11*)

The above perspective includes two tendencies: 'conservative-liberal' and 'social-democratic'. The former regards the role of the state as 'facilitative' i.e. to provide the general framework within which capitalist enterprises can operate and, if necessary, to ameliorate the problems created by the market economy. The state is essentially considered to be a 'passive' instrument, unsuitable as a force for social change. The social-democratic perspective views the state as an institution which can be 'captured' and used for obtaining 'reforms' within a market economy and also for effecting 'gradual changes' in the capitalist mode of production. Within the Labour, Social-Democratic and Socialist Parties of Western Europe, 'a rhetoric' has grown which emphasizes the virtues of 'welfare capitalism', 'parliamentary socialism', 'democratic socialism' and incremental change. In fact, these ideologies owe very little to Marxism, out of which some of these parties developed, and can be placed squarely within the liberal-democratic tradition.

The Marxist perspective of the European writers of the late 1960s and early 1970s viewed the state simply as an 'instrument' of the ruling capitalist class. The State, according to them consciously and unequivocably served the ideological and economic interests of capital. Contrary to right-wing socialist beliefs, the 'capitalist' state cannot be 'captured' through election and then used as an agency for social change. Many Marxist theorists of 'state derivation' argued "that the structure and function of the state can only be adequately explained by reference to the global requirements of capital". The changing role of the capitalist state, for example, its increasing intervention in the process of production, can be interpreted as an answer "to the tendency for the rate of profit to fall", brought about in late capitalism by "an increase in the organic composition of capital, the over-extended capacity of productive process, and the heightened intensity of class struggle". Consequently, the state must involve itself in renewing and maintaining the forces of production such as technological developments and reproduction of labour power. With this reasoning, the Marxist writers explain "the increase in functions of the state" in capitalist systems, such as "health and social welfare facilities", promotion of "technological research," expansion of "state subsidies to capitalist corporations and the growth of state capitalist enterprises". *(251 : 13)*

In an ultimate sense, the state in any capitalist society would try to satisfy the needs of capital. It has to provide conditions which facilitate the process of accumulation. But this does not mean that there will always be a congruence between the functions of the state and those of capital. One defect of the derivation theory is its under-estimation of the tensions that may develop between a fraction of capital and the state. Capital is often internally divided in terms of the interests of large and small capitals, industrial and financial capitals, or national and transnational capitals. Therefore, the state representing the needs of capital in general may come into conflict with one or more of its specific segments.

As a result, the state is now increasingly viewed to be 'relatively autonomous', partially removed from the immediate control of capital and its vested interests. This alone can explain the persistence of 'important structural variations' between 'different national formations'. The state cannot be simply conceived as a servant of capital. It has to cope with the *general* needs of capital but the manner in which it does this will greatly vary depending upon the conjuncture of economic, political and cultural forces operating within 'the context of specific national social formations.'

This point may be explained by an example. A necessary precondition for capitalist production is the existence of propertyless workers who can sell their labour power. This is a *universal* feature of capitalist mode of production. However, the conditions under which labour power is sold and the character of workers available to various units of capital are determined not only by capital but also by the state. In providing these conditions, the state is only 'relatively autonomous' since it is also influenced by various economic, political and cultural forces. Every capitalist state does not follow the same policy regarding different sections of workers such as immigrants or women and these differences cannot solely be explained by reference to *logic* of capital. Richard Scase says: "Although the capitalist mode of production predominates within the national economies of such countries as the United States, Sweden and West Germany, the state has not met similar 'needs' of capital in a uniform manner. Witness, for example, the differences that exist between countries in the extent to which the state has directly intervened in determining contracts of employment, systems of industrial relations and wage bargaining structures, as well as in the provision of facilities necessary for the reproduction of labour power, such as housing and education". *(251:14)*. This shows that there is *sufficient autonomy* to enable the state to implement .policies which are not always reducible to the needs of capital except at the general level.

Comparative Dimensions of the Theory of State

It is within this context that we can study the comparative dimensions of the concept of state in contemporary social life. The nature of political regimes has to be explained as the expression of specific interest and forces within particular national states, which can take important decisions for the operation of an economy. When social-democratic regimes implement legislation in such areas as health, housing, education and employment, the basic relationship between capital and wage labour remains unchanged but the material circumstances of the workers improve. Reformist political regimes may reinforce a crisis within the accumulation process by increase in the costs of production. A consequence of social-democratic policies may be the creation of various corporatist and state-capitalist structures.

The above comments indicate the need for shifting from general, formal theories of state to more particular and policy-oriented theories in relation to specific national social formations. Within this framework, it is necessary to relate the structure and functions of the state to the development of the forces of production and class relations. Obviously, the role of the State in a dependent, 'peripheral' or underdeveloped economy will differ substantially from its role in a developed, metropolitan capitalist economy. Any theory must recognize that the state is shaped by civil society i.e. the conjuncture of a wide range of social, cultural, economic and political forces. A historical analysis of these alone will enable us to grasp the nature of the state in terms of its structure, function and legitimacy. In order to investigate the origins and characteristics of present-day states, it is necessary to consider their political history and also the dynamics of the mode of production, capitalist or socialist. In addition, the conjunctures of socio-economic and political forces have created 'national cultures' which legitimate the role of the state and prescribe the limits of its intervention in the sphere of social and economic activity. In this sense there are considerable *differences* not only between states based on *different* modes of production but also between political regimes situated within *similar* modes of production.

The assumption made here is that if civil society shapes the nature and role of the state, it is also to be recognized that the state too conditions civil society. It does so as a relatively autonomous entity, not merely as a *tool* of the dominating class. In other words, the state represents an 'uneasy compromise' of class interests in which some of the demands of the dominated classes become, at least partially, incorporated. In a capitalist society, this may be the case when wage labour is well organised in trade unions and represented by 'reformist' social-democratic parties in state institutions.

This shows that there is need for more 'theorised historical analyses' of specific national states. Detailed *comparative* studies are also necessary in order to explain differences and similarities in terms of the *structure* and function of national states, the *development* of their specific institutions, their varying *autonomy* in relation to various social and economic forces and their internal *contradictions* and dynamics of *social change.* However, this emphasis on specific national states should not detract from the consideration and 'comparison' of broader socio-economic forces that differentiate or join together clusters of states. Indeed, a comparative study of these forces should provide the framework within which any particular state formation should be analyzed. Increasing internationalization of capital has brought about the existence of numerous dependent national economies in the third world and has also created a wide range of supranational economic and political institutions. Therefore, it is possible to indicate a number of common trends in the development of national states, which ought to be considered in any specific analysis. Richard Scase has noted five similar trends in his comparative study of the Western democratic states.

First, the state has increasingly taken over functions necessary for the maintenance and reproduction of labour power such as the provision of education, health, housing and welfare. This has created a controversy about the 'legitimate' area of state intervention and the extent to which the 'benevolent' acts of the state are, in fact, further extension of state 'repression'. In a number of countries this has led to popular reaction resulting in the election of rightist political regimes committed to dismantling of the welfare structure. The welfare 'state' of the social-democrats has also "rendered as problematic the liberal-democratic distinction between 'private' and 'public' spheres highlighting the basic contradictions inherent in the provision of these resources.

Secondly, the state has become explicitly more repressive reinforcing its functions of 'control' and 'surveillance'. This has been the result of 'rationalisation' within the accumulation process causing the mobility of labour and the destruction of family structures. Informal sources of control have been replaced by formally prescribed agancies of the state, not only the police but social functionaries too. Such developments have created new danger to 'human rights' and 'political freedoms' revealing an essential contradiction of the state as a 'protector' and a 'despot' simultaneously.

Thirdly, the state has become more centralised. In every Western democracy there has been the rationalisation of the iocal and regional state activities and their "integration within centralized, national boureaucracies". As part of this trend political parties have become less relevant as effective power has become concentrated in the executive. This has led to the crisis in the legitimacy of political institutions such as parliament. Strategies of protest have emerged ranging from peaceful mass movements to acts of terrorism by *revolutionary,* conspiratorial societies. While the accumulation process requires greater centralisation within the state apparatus, the grass-roots social movements have intensified demands for decentralisation and self-management highlighting yet another source of contradiction in late capitalism.

Fourthly, the state has increased direct intervention within the productive process. There has been "a shift from general Keynesian macroeconomic management to direct state intervention through loans, subsidies and the formation of state capitalist enterprises". It has become involved in the 'modernisation' and 'rationalisation' of the forces of production i.e. labour power as well as technology. It appears that late capitalism is developing 'corporatist' structures. It attempts to reduce the intensity of class struggle "by the institutionalisation of industrial relations and the incorporation of the subordinate classes". Corporatism is a response to the crisis of 'profitability' but this, in turn, has created a *fiscal* crisis for the state. Its activities have become 'over-extended' but the sources available for financing its operations have become more scarce. Deficit budgeting causes inflation; irrational expenditure on defence must continue as a 'patriotic' duty; and a reduction in the living standards of wage labour is the only feasible alternative but this source for additional revenue has a strictly limited scope.

Fifthly, there is a growing contradiction between the internationalisation of capital and the existence and survival of independent national states. Within the international division of labour, there is increasing economic and political dependence of 'peripheral' states upon the 'central' capitalist state especially the United States. Even among the highly developed capitalist economies, "the dynamics of the accumulation process have questioned the relevance of the national state". Consequently, 'supranational' institutions have been created to regulate the financial, industrial, and political relationships among traditionally sovereign nations. But the states must 'compete' with each other in order to attract international capital by guaranteeing conditions for its profitable investment. In fact, a moderate reformist policy of a social-democratic regime such as protection of employment legislation "may lead capital to perceive of a particular national economy as an inappropriate site for investment." (*251 : 16*).

A Liberal Typology of Contemporary States

While American political scientists have discarded the usage of the term state in favour of 'government' or political system, European writers like S.E. Finer still find the traditional usage useful in their typology. According to S.E. Finer contemporary states fall into three main categories: (1) The liberal democratic state, (2) the totalitarian state, and (3) the third-world states. The third category includes three sub-types: (i) the *facade*-democracy, (ii) the *quasi*-democracy and (iii) the military regime. Finer suggests the following criteria for his typology: (a) how far the mass of the public are involved in or excluded from the governing process—this is *participation-exclusion* dimension; (b) how far the mass of the public obey their rulers out of commitment or how far out of fear—this may be called the *coercion-persuasion* dimension; and (c) how far the arrangements are designed to cause the rulers to reflect the actual and current values of the mass of the public or how far they may disregard these for the sake of continuity and future values—this may be called the *order-representativeness* dimension.

Certain assumptions underlie the liberal-democratic state. Obviously the first of these is that it is 'democratic'. The primary meaning of 'democracy' is government which is derived from *public opinion* and is accountable to it. This public opinion, it must be presumed, is overtly and freely expressed. In matters of contention between sections of public opinion, it is the majority opinion which prevails. But the liberal-democratic state is also 'liberal' and hence a *qualified* democracy. The first qualification is that government is *limited*, which operates in a world of autonomous spontaneously self-creating, voluntary associations. The second qualification is that it is *pluralistic*, which means that the government rules, not in the interest of any one group or alliance of groups, but in the general interest. This indicates the third qualification of the liberal-democratic state: it denies that there is any *objective science of society or morals*. On the contrary, it asserts that truth is a matter of individual consciences, where all consciences are held, by an act of faith, to be equal. Two working conclusions flow from this, namely, toleration and the qualification of majority rule.

The liberal-democratic state has *four* characteristic features. S. E. Finer observes; "First, all governments of this type contain a representative organ in an elected legislature—and in some cases, too, an elected head of state or president. Secondly, and accountable to these representative organs, there goes a stabilizing and expert organ, both advising it and executing its instructions; this is the 'executive'. Thirdly, there exists a system of social and economic checks and balances, a network of centres of private power which acts as a brake upon the activity of the government. And fourthly, this system of social and economic checks and balances is paralleled and assisted by a system of political checks and balances." *(200 : 66)*

Finer considers a state to be totalitarian when two conditions are fulfilled: first, the entire society is politicised as no private areas of life are exempted from the control of the state; secondly, the viewpoints which so politicise it do not tolerate dissidence. It is therefore "the veritable contradictory of the liberal-democratic type" of state. The scope and authority of government is 'not limited' but, just the reverse, is *total*. The plurality of view-points, the hall-mark of the liberal-democratic state, is here suppressed in favour of one 'objective truth'.

In principle, a totalitarian state may be ruled by a single despot. Hitler or Stalin, says Finer, was such a dictatorial ruler. In practice, the characteristics of a totalitarian state may be summarised as follows: the authority of the ruling elite is unlimited in scope, a single political party exercises *de facto* or even *de jure* 'monopoly of power; the structure of authority is 'hierarchical'. The party controls and directs the organs of administration, formulates and interprets the official ideology of the state and transmits and enjoins this upon the rest of the population through persuasion, coercion or even terror. Fascist Italy, Nazi Germany and the existing communist states in Russia and China are *totalitarian* in accordance with Finer's definition of the totalitarian state.

The communist variant of the totalitarian state is consciously based on the Marxist-Leninist philosophy but it also incorporates, though unconsciously, a doctrinal imspiration from Rousseau as well. It regards society as a 'monistic' structure. It pursues a transcendental end, a consummatory value called communism. The party is in possession of an objective science of society and morals which will guide its progress towards its ulitmate goal. Democracy is not majority rule but rule by the vanguard in the interest of the majority. The party, therefore, basing itself upon the scientific principles of Marxism-Leninism always expresses what the majority 'wants' even when popular opinion as actually and freely expressed is flatly opposed to what the party proposes to do.

In the Fascist and Nazi conceptions of the totalitarian state, "there was not even the nominal bow to democracy which the communist party of the U.S.S.R. felt obliged to make." Mussolini said: "Three conditions are necessary for the full, complete, integral and revolutionary fulfilment of the Corporate State: a single party by means of which there shall be effectuated political control as well as economic control and which shall be above the competing interests a bond which unites all in a common faith. Nor is that enough. We must have, as well as the single party, the totalitarian state, i.e. the state which absorbs in itself, to transform and make them effective, all the energy, all the interests and all the hope of a people. The third is to live a period of the highest ideal tension." (*199:231*)

In the totalitarian state, the government propagates the official myth or ideology. The ruling party controls all the mass media. The state relies heavily upon secret and security police forces. The judiciary is totally subordinate to the executive in the totalitarian state, the hegemonic party controls the administrative apparatus at all levels from top to bottom. Inside the party, there is no inner party democracy. The central committee or the polibureau or the supreme leader exercises real authority. S. E. Finer observes, "The decision-taking in the totalitarian state is concentrated, not dispersed. All sections and associations in society are emanations of and colonies of the party. Nothing throughout society escapes the party except through accident or administrative incapacity. the single party in a totalitarian state becomes the leading and directing institution, and inside that party, policy is not decided by the rank and file but by the leading oligarchs." *(200 :94)*

One basic defect of Finer's comparative analysis of the states is that it totally disregards their socio-economic basis i.e. the modes of production with which they are associated. He forgets to mention that *both* the liberal-democratic and Nazi-Fascist totalitarian states *share* a common socio-economic basis in the *capitalist* mode of production while the states governed by communist parties are based on an essentially different *socialist* mode of production. Thus a socialist state is *qualitatively* different from both the Nazi-Fascist and liberal-democratic variants of the capitalist state.

The third-world states are transitional in nature. According to S.E. Finer, the *facade* democracy is that type of regime where "historic *oligarchies* of lineage and wealth govern from behind a facade of liberal-democratic forms which serve as a cloak or screen to their rule". He defines *quasi-democracy* as "largely improved and pragmatic system of single or hegemonic party rule" of a modernising elite. The third type of regime arising from the failure of the other two types of rule mentioned above is the *military regime* where state power is captured by a military elite. The third-world state is essentially an authoritarian, though not a totalitarian structure. It claims legitimacy in terms of a 'liberal-democratic' rhetoric but is unable to implement its institutional norms. Finer, however, fails to relate the structure and functioning of the third-world states with their socio-economic foundations. Political underdevelopment of the third-world states is a consequence of their economic underdevelopment for which the past *colonial* and present *neo-colonial* policies of the Western liberal-democratic states are also responsible in no small measure.

Modern *democracy*, as Samuel Huntington says, emerged in *three waves*. The *first* began in the aftermath of the French and American revolutions. It was mainly a European affair. The Depression of 1930s, reversed the process. The *second* wave, a short one, began with the defeat of fascism and decolonisation in the third world. Communist dictatorships flourished in the second world and military dictatorship thrived in the third world with India as the sole exception. The *third* wave began in mid-1970s, toppled right wing dictators in Europe, Latin America, Asia and Africa. Finally, communist regimes were also overthrown after 1989 in quick succession in Eastern Europe.

sublimates politics into nothingness nor places it on a high pedestal beyond analytic reach". The state should be restored into the domain of political theory and the reality of political action. Neither mystification of the state nor glorification of its power can make the real nature and role of the state in capitalist society intelligible to us..

Stages in the Evolution of the Capitalist State

The political history of capitalist systems has followed neither a simple nor a linear path of development. Liberal democratic state, characteristic political formation of capitalism, symbolizes a contradiction, which can be expressed as an essential tension between the needs of accumulation and of legitimation. The liberal ideology was the product of the demands of a private system of accumulation that structured public conceptions about the state. The desire for popular acceptability and obedience gave rise to democratic ideas about political life which were inconsistent with earlier liberal notions. Contradictions between these two expectations were "temporarily resolved through six different 'ideal types' of capitalist states, each of which corresponded to a particular historical 'moment' over the course of the last two hundred years". *(258 : 247)*

The *Accumulative State* corresponded to the first wave of capitalist industrialization. It made accumulation its own mechanism of legitimation. Since any means required to achieve the accumulation of wealth was justifiable, the Accumulative State was not ideologically committed to *laissez faire* but instead promoted active government intervention into the economy and social order such as (i) defining the parameters of the emerging capitalist society; (ii) preserving discipline among the workers; (iii) adjusting macro-economic. conditions; (iv) providing subsidies to capitalists; (v) fighting colonial wars; and (vi) supporting miscellaneous eclectic activities. The Accumulative State was a transitional compromise between the authoritarian mercantile state and a relatively more flexible state appropriate for the needs of industrial capitalists. When the task of legitimation became necessary with the rise of a working class, its contradictory character became manifest. Although some features of the Accumulative State persist today, the 'pure' form vanished by the middle of the nineteenth century.

The *Harmonious State*, which had a preoccupation with legitimation, arose during the second phase of capitalist industrialization. Two different strands of thought joined to stress that under capitalism all social classes will benefit by allowing the bourgeoisie to control the state. One such strand promised ultimate harmony if matters were kept out of the hands of government. The other developed an ideological rationalization for state action in response to working-class threats from below. Those two strands of thought are often viewed as polar opposites, their common attempt to use theories of harmony to justify capitalistic arrangements makes them essentially alike. The first one was internally inconsistent, led to Social Darwinism and failed as a legitimation mechanism. The latter led to concrete reforms but at the cost of disproving the notion of harmony between antagonistic interests. Politics of the *Harmonious State* in the last part of the nineteenth century was dominated by the bourgeois politician, who institutionalized corruption. Theoretical weakness combined with practical corruption discredited the doctrines of harmony as well as the capitalist state founded upon them.

The *Expansionist State* made its appearance when the contradictions between capitalism and democracy reached the breaking point. Although an imperialist policy of expansion carried out in the interest of finance capital seemed to relieve domestic pressures from the working-class, expansionism symbolized the end of the classical liberalism. The end of free trade, unrestricted immigration and export of capital to colonies and semi-colonies were accompanied by efforts to indoctrinate and control the labouring classes through education and mass culture. It took some time for the contradictions of imperialism to mature but, even so, the *rationale* of the Expansionist State was disappearing by the end of the First World War. The war revealed that class conflict was not the only cause of paralyzing the capitalist state. It was also caused by bitter conflicts within the ruling classes and strata as well. Politics of the post-war period tried to harness discontent in both of these areas. It led to various types of corporatist solutions.

The *Franchise State* emerged to regularize conflicts between classes and strata by delegating public power to private bodies. The Franchise State offered a fairly long period of stability particularly when its basic priniciples were extended to groups outside of industrial sectors that had organised enough political power to make their claims on the state. The ideology of the Franchise State was based on the pluralist dispersal of power. The state of 'pluralist-democracy' was supposed to give away power, not to exercise it. This was a mystification. With the failure of private interest groups to regulate themselves effectively, the Franchise State began to decline by the end of the Second World War, when its contradictions became too evident. Economic planning in European capitalist countries and military spending in the United States led these states to assume enormous powers, which belonged to them theoretically even earlier. This made the Franchise State, based on delegation of public power to interest groups, a thing of the past rather than a solution for the future.

The *Dual State* was created to resolve the inherent tension between capitalist and democratic conceptions of the state at this stage. Instead of one state trying to do two different things, two states with parallel structures were created, one charged with keeping order and the other with preserving a democratic *facade*. The military-bureaucratic establishments and secret intelligence bureaus constituted one arm of the diarchy and the electoral-parliamentary apparatus, more visible to the public eye, formed the other arm of the same. The Dual State required of its political leadership, at the level of cabinet or presidency, a difficult balancing act. The covert face of the Dual State grew smaller and less visible as the need for secrecy became larger. Alan Wolfe says, "In addition, the Dual State found itself caught between the vested interests of its component parts and its general interest in secret intelligence. These internal difficulties would have existed regardless of who was in power, but the Nixon Administration, through general ineptitude, exacerbated them. The fate of the Dual State is unclear at this time, but even if it successfully defends itself in the face of the publicity around Watergate and revelations about CIA, it will still confront internal and external contradictions that will limit its general applicability as a permanent solution to the contradiction between liberal and democratic principles". (*258 : 249*)

The *Transnational State* is the latest model of the capitalist state. It is the product of the internationalization of capital which gave rise to multinational corporations that regarded the world, and not any particular state, as their market. However, this development did not transcend the problems of nation-state because multinational corporations required government aid in a way not seen earlier in the political history of the capitalist state. The experiences of supranational bodies such as the European Common Market do not resolve the contradiction between accumulation and legitimation but raise it to a new level. The transnational political arrangements extend the historical limitations of the capitalist state to a new plateau. Hence, the Transnational State is also unable to resolve the political contradictions of contemporary capitalist society. The political system is no longer capable of resolving the tasks which the economy imposes upon it. Each of the six major forms of the capitalist state created to resolve the tensions between accumulation and legitimation within the framework of liberal democracy has shown its incapacity to do so. In late capitalism, therefore, the major political issues will arise not within the parameters of liberal democracy but over them.

Contemporary Debates about the State in Late Capitalism

Liberal scholars assume that power in advanced capitalist societies is competitive, fragmented and diffused. In these societies, citizens enjoy universal suffrage, free and regular elections, representative institutions and effective civil liberties. Both individuals and groups take ample advantage of these rights under an independent judiciary and free political culture. As a leading exponent of the democratic-pluralist view of the capitalist state, Robert Dahl has said, "all the active and legitimate groups in the population can make themselves heard at some crucial stage in the process of decision". (*188 : 137*) Other pluralist writers, Professor Dahl has also noted, "suggest that there are a number of loci for arriving at political decisions; that businessmen, trade unions, politicians, consumers, farmers, voters and many other aggregates all have an impact on policy outcomes; that none of these aggregates is homogeneous for all purposes; that each of them is highly influential over some scopes but weak over many others; and that the power to reject undesired alternatives is more common than the power to dominate over outcomes directly." (*189 : 36*)

Parliament is seen as the focal point for the pressures which are exerted by interest groups throughout the nation either directly through lobbies or through the mediation of political parties. The pluralist thesis dominates political science in all advanced capitalist countries. It excludes, by definition, that the state might be a rather special institution, whose main purpose is to defend the privileged position of a particular class. In developed capitalist countries, there are no such privileged classes, interests or groups. There are only "competing blocs of interests", whose competition, which is allowed by the state itself, ensures that power is diffused and balanced, and that no particular group is able to dominate the government. There are elites in different economic, social, political, administrative, professional and other pyramids of power. But these elites lack the degree of cohesion necessary to elevate them to the position of a ruling class. In fact, 'elite pluralism' ensures that power in society will not be concentrated in any dominant class.

The state, subjected as it is to a multitude of conflicting pressures from organised groups and interests, cannot show any market bias towards some and against others. Its special role is to accommodate and reconcile them all. The dominant pluralist view of capitalist state does not preclude a critical attitude to some aspects of the political system or of the social order. But criticism is directed towards the improvement and strengthening of a system whose basically *democratic* credentials are beyond doubt and to which the notion of 'power elite' or ruling class is absurdly irrelevant. The ideological and political climate of the Western capitalist countries has tended to make subscription to the democratic-pluralist thesis a test not only of political wisdom but of social morality as well. Yet, the general acceptance of a particular view of the contemporary capitalist state does not prove its truth. It will be presently argued that 'democratic-pluralism' does not reflect the social reality of the late capitalist state. According to Ralph Miliband, "the pluralist-democratic view of society, of politics and of the state in regard to the countries of advanced capitalism, is in all essentials wrong". Instead of providing a guide to reality, this view "constitutes a profound obfuscation of it." (*236* : *6*)

Despite a vast scatter of small and medium-sized enterprises in all developed capitalist countries, a few large corporations are of overwhelmingly disproportionate importance in their economy. As Galbraith says, "The five largest industrial corporations in the United States....possessed over 12 per cent of all assets used in manufacturing. The fifty largest corporations had over a third of all manufacturing assets. The five hundred largest had well over two-thirds". (*203* : *74*) Much the same situation prevails in other capitalist countries. The enormous *political* significance of this concentration of private economic power, including its impact upon the state, cannot be doubted. But the giant corporation is not only a national but a transnational phenomenon encompassing developed as well as underdeveloped economies. Extension of multinational firms to Asia, Africa and Latin America has become an important feature of the foreign policies of capitalist states.

In these countries, the other end of the social scale is occupied by a working class mostly composed of industrial workers, which remains everywhere a distinct social formation. It is from their ranks that are recruited the unemployed, the aged poor, the chronically destitute and the sub-proletariat of capitalist society. Despite the superficial claims of "classlessness', the proletarian condition remains a hard and basic fact of capitalist societies in the work process, in levels of income, in opportunities or lack of them, in the whole social and cultural definition of existence. The economic and political life of capitalist societies is primarily shaped by the relationship between the capitalists, who own the means of production, and the working-class which sells its labour power for its living. The political process of these societies is mainly about the confrontation of these two social formations. In Britain one per cent of the population owned 42 per cent of personal wealth, five per cent owned 75 per cent and 10 per cent owned 83 per cent. In the United States two per cent of American families owned 29 per cent of personal wealth and just one per cent of adults owned 76 per cent of corporate stock. The inequality in income will be reflected in inequality in political power.

Apart from the giant corporations, there does exist a plurality of economic elites but 'elite pluralism' does not prevent the separate elites in capitalist society from constituting a dominant economic class, possessed of a high degree of cohesion and solidarity. This dominant class, according to the Marxist view, also constitutes the ruling power in the contemporary capitalist state. In fact, its ownership and control of strategically important sectors of the economy ensures its control and domination of the means of political decision-making in the particular political environment of advanced capitalism as well.

The State System and the State Elite

The state in this context stands for a number of political institutions which together constitute its reality and which interact as parts of what may be called the state system. The first element of the State is the *government* which is formally *invested* with state power but it does not follow that it also effectively *controls* that power. A second element of the state system is the *administration,* which now extends far beyond the traditional bureaucracy and also includes public corporations, state banks, regulatory commissions etc. possessing different degrees of autonomy. The third element represents the *military* and *police* constituting the coercive apparatus of the state. In most capitalist countries, it constitutes a vast, sprawling and resourceful establishment, whose professional leaders are men of high status and great influence, inside the state system and in society. The fourth element of the state system is the *judiciary* which is formally independent but practically an integral part of the state system, which affects profoundly the exercise of state power. The fifth element of the state consists of the various units of *sub-central government,* which have remained power structures in their own right notably in federal systems such as that of the United

States. The sixth element is provided by the *representative assemblies*, which are formally independent but in practice subordinate to other elements of the state system.

Besides the government, the administration, the military and the police, the judiciary, parliamentary assemblies and sub-central government, the state system includes parties and pressure groups and non-political institutions like the giant corporations, Churches, the mass media and even cultural and educational institutions. The social composition of the state elite and the relationship of the state elite to the economically dominant class must be understood in order to explain the role and purposes of the state in advanced capitalism. Ralph Miliband suggests that businessmen today constitute the largest single occupational group in cabinets of all capitalist countries. Business predominance over other groups is found in the top layers of bureaucracy and specially in the financial and credit institutions of the state. However, the point to be noted is that the state elite is exclusively drawn from the upper or middle classes to which the businessmen also belong. It applies not only to the administrative, military and judicial elites, which are insulated from universal suffrage and political competition, but to the political and elective ones as well. Ralph Miliband concludes: "In an epoch when so much is made of democracy, equality, social mobility, classlessness and the rest, it has remained a basic fact of life in advanced capitalist countries that the vast majority of men and women in these countries has been governed, represented, administered, judged, and commanded in war by people drawn from other, economically and socially superior and relatively distant classes". (*236* : *62*).

The reason for attaching considerable significance to the social composition of the state elite in advanced capitalist countries lies in the strong presumption which this creates as to its general outlook, ideological dispositions and political bias. Despite the impressive diversity of views, attitudes and policies advocated by different sections of the state elite, there is a consensus among them on fundamental issues i.e. the validity and virtues of the capitalist system. Even the presence of 'social-democratic' leadership as a component of the state-elite does not disturb this consensus. The state elite itself does not see its commitment to capitalism as a case of class bias. In its consciousness and speech, Hegel's exalted view of the state as the embodiment of social morality and the common good lives again. From this point of view 'what is good for General Motors is good for America' because the interest of *Business* is equated with *national* interest while *Labour* represents a *sectional* interest, the viewpoint of a minority only. Governments may be solely concerned with the better running of 'the economy'. But the description of the system as 'the economy' is an ideological idiom which obscures the real process, because what is being improved is a *capitalist* economy. This ensures that whoever may gain or lose, capitalist interests are most likely to benefit from any scheme of development in any sector of the economy.

Quite naturally, this partiality of the capitalist state assumes an even more pronounced and organised character in relation to all movements, groupings and parties dedicated to the transformation of capitalist societies into socialist ones. The manner in which this antagonism is expressed has varied over time and between countries, but the hostility itself is a permanent feature of all capitalist state systems. The leaders of all governmental parties, whether in office or in opposition, including nominally 'socialist' ones, have always been deeply hostile to the socialist and militant left advocating repressive policies to crush all left-wing dissidence. In this instance too, liberal-democratic and pluralist writers, in their celebration of the political competition which is supposed to exist in capitalist societies, and in their insistence on the political neutrality of the capitalist state, "quite overlook the fact that the governments of advanced capitalist countries, far from taking a neutral view of *socialist* competition, do their level best to make it more difficult". Ralph Miliband points out: "In some countries, for instance Federal Germany, Communist and other left-wing parties and organisations are suppressed altogether, and membership made a crime punishable by law; in others, such as the United States, left-wing organisations, of which the Communist Party is only one, operate in conditions of such harassment as to narrow rather drastically, in their case, the notion of free political competition". (*236* : *75*) In other countries like France or Italy, electoral manipulation is used to deprive their Communist parties of the legitimate parliamentary or governmental representation to which their electrol support entitles them.

The suppression of left-wing, anticapitalist groups and parties reaches its culmination in the totalitarian fascist state. Despite the rhetoric of total transformaion and renewal and some anti-bourgeois slogans, the Fascist and Nazi states were essentially capitalist in character. Of course, capitalist enterprise was subjected to state control in the corporative economy of the Fascist and Nazi varieties. But this did not disturb the profit-oriented, capitalist character of the fascist economies in any fundamenal sense. Members of the business and bourgeois classes continued to occupy important positions in the state hierarchy as well as the corporative economy. Ralph Miliband observes: "The most telling fact of all about the real nature of the Fascist systems is surely that, when they came to an end, twenty years after Mussolini's 'March on Rome' and twelve years after Hitler's assumption of the chancellorship, the economic and social structure of both countries had not been significantly changed. The classes which occupied the higher reaches of the economic and social pyramid before the Fascists came to power were still there; and so was the capitalist-system which sustained these classes". (*236* : *84*) The Christian Democratic parties of Italy and West Germany inherited the capitalist structures of their economy from their Fascist and Nazi predecessors without any visible damage.

The capitalist states of the fascist variety in Italy, Germany and Japan have been transformed into liberal-democratic ones after the Second World War. However, it is to be noted that the leading conservative party representing the capitalists has been permanently in office in Japan and the predominantly conservative party of Italy, the Christian Democratic party, has been the main constituent of all coalition regimes that have ruled Italy after the war. The Christian Democratic Union, the party of the West German bourgeoisie, has ruled West Germany for most of the time either unilaterally or as a leading group in a coalition regime. In the United States, both the ruling parties are patronized by the capitalist class equally. In Great Britain, France or Germany social-democratic regimes are voted into office for short periods and their essential function is 'crisis management'. Even the Communist parties may occasionally be admitted as junior partners in a coalition government in France or Italy for the same purpose. When the 'reformist' regimes are in office, the working-class is prevented from fighting its class battles in the political arena due to false hopes created by an electoral victory of right-wing socialist leadership, which then occupies state institutions. The occasional victories of the Labour party in Britain, of the Socialist Party in France and of the Social Democratic parties in West Germany and Sweden should be seen in this perspective. In Sweden, the social-democratic regimes have failed to change the basic character of the capitalist state despite the fact that they have been in office much longer. In the peripheral capitalist states of Spain, Portugal and Greece, the Socialist parties face hostile competition not only from indigenous bourgeois parties but also from international capital which has greater strangle-hold on their less developed economices.

Miliband observes: "Capitalism .... is now more than ever an international system, whose constituent economics are closely related and interlinked. As a reult, even the most powerful capitalist countries depend.... upon the goodwill and cooperation of the rest and of what has became, notwithstanding..... national capitalist rivalries an independent international capitalist 'community'..... central bankers, enjoying a high degree of autonomy from their governments, have come to assume extraordinary importance.... A *conservative* government in a strong economic and financial position, such as the government of President de Gaulle long enjoyed, may play rogue elephant without undue risk of retribution. A radical government, on the other hand, would be unlikely to be given much shrift by these representatives of international capitalism." (*236 : 138*).

CHAPTER 13

NATURE OF STATE IN SOCIALIST SYSTEMS

Theoretical Basis of the State in Socialist Societies

Socialist societies are those where the capitalist mode of production has been replaced by a new mode of production based on social ownership. Invariably, such societies have come into existence as a result of revolutionary overthrow of the capitalist state. The revolution was carried out by a Marxist-Leninist party, which became the ruling party in the new socialist state. Marxist theory of state, therefore, remains an important key to the understanding of the nature of State in Socialist societies. Marx first formulated his theory of the state as a result of his direct encounter with the repressive policies of the Imperial German State which censured his articles of the *Rheinische Zeitung.* At this time Marx conceived of a true democratic state, an idealised state of the Hegelian model representing reason. By 1843, he realised the importance of socio-economic factors in the framing of legislation and developed a critique of Hegel's theory of state. He rejected Hegel's view that the state had a universal character capable of reconciling discordant elements of civil society and synthesizing them on a higher plane. All state institutions—monarchy, parliament and bureaucracy were actually instruments of sectional interests of socio-economic groups. In contrast to Hegel, he now recommended a form of state which directly corresponded to "the essence of socialised man". He called this *true democracy* in which the state, the law and the constitution were self-determined by the people.

In his *Economic and Philosophic Manuscripts* Marx described the state to be an expression of human alienation and based on capitalist mode of production. The bourgeois revolutions, which claimed to liberate man as a political citizen, left him in servitude as a man, or member of civil society. Although Marx at no stage abandoned the idea of the state as alienated and parasitical social power, he later concentrated his attention upon the role of the state as an instrument of class domination. In the *Communist Manifesto,* Marx and Engels called the state as a committee for managing the common affairs of the bourgeoisie. He admitted that in exceptional situations, the state could play a neutral or autonomous role such as the Bonapartist regime in France. Marx regarded bureaucracy to be the most essential part of the bourgeois state apparatus. In the *Eighteenth Brumaire,* Marx pointed out that the destruction of the bureaucratic-military machine of the state was the first condition of any real popular revolution.

Engels, speaking about the nature of the State in socialist society, observes: "The proletariat seizes the state power and transforms the means of production in the first instance into state property. But in doing this, it puts an end to itself as the proletariat, it puts an end to all class differences and class antagonisms, it puts an end also to the state as a state. As soon as there is no longer any class of society to be held in subjection; as soon as, along with class domination and the struggle for individual existence based on the former anarchy of production, the collisions and excesses arising from these have also been abolished, there is nothing more to be repressed, which would make a special repressive force, a state, necessary". (*198 : 127*) This fiirst act in which the state really comes forward as the representative of society as a whole the taking possession of the means of production in the name of society–is at the same time its last independent act as the state.

The function of the state in socialist society is to consolidate the public power of the proletariat by smashing the bourgeois state machine. The state will be required as a dictatorship of the proletariat during the transition from capitalism to communism. Marx outlined the main features of a socialist state in the following words: "The standing army should be replaced by a people at arms. Responsible councillors, mostly workers or recognised representatives of the working class, should form an assembly that would essentially be a labour body rather than having purely legislative or decorative functions; election would be by universal suffrage and could be revoked at any time. The police should be converted from being a component of the central government into a responsible agency of the assembly, deprived of any political assignments and liable to suspension at any time. Every branch of administration should be converted in a similar way. Public office should be made really democratic, ceasing to be the private preserve of the central government and its creatures and being discharged at all levels by workers for a wage." (*233 : 141*).

The function of the state in socialist societies like the Soviet Union, Poland, East Germany or China has not entirely conformed to the visions of Marx and Engels. All socialist countries have large standing armies and powerful bureaucracies. Property has been nationalised but the state has come under the domination of bureaucratic, military and party elites. In Charles Bettelheim's opinion, the state elite in socialist countries has become a dominating and priviliged class. Umberto Melotti observes: "We naively tell ourselves that property is 'nationalized'. For scientific Marxists that is not very much. We wonder what kind of 'nationalized' property this is, when it is exclusively controlled by a single class which then appropriates its fruits in just as blatant fashion as did the former bourgeoisie. In practice there is in Russia an exploiting class that holds sway over the means of production and acts just as if it owned them. Although it is not divided up into individual owners, its members as a class, *en masse,* are the real owners of all the 'nationalised' property." (*233 : 145*). Charles Bettleheim even designates the ruling elite in Russia as the 'state bourgeoisie' and characterizes the Soviet social system as based on 'state capitalism' rather than true socialism.

For liberal critics, the socialist state ruled by a Communist party is essentially totalitarian in character. Like the Fascist and Nazi states of the inter-war periods, the communist states put an end to democracy aiming at total control of the social, economic, political and cultural life. **Bourgeois writers reject the democratic credenials of not only contemporary** Communist doctrines prevalent in Russia and China but also of classical Marxism which never defined dictatorship of the proletariat as the rule of one political party. Karl Popper characterised Marxist theory as essentially historicist and totalitarian in conception. Hence, the Stalinist or Maoist totalitarian state is not an aberration but the logical outcome of the basic assumptions of the Marxist ideology.

Characteristic Features of the State in the Soviet Union

The first and probably the most distinctive feature of the Soviet state is its socialist basis. The Soviet Union is a socialist society in terms of its property relations and its economic system. Consequently much of the substance of captalist states does not exist there. Soviet industrial ministries may wield some influence within the party leadership but they cannot exercise any power independently. They do not exert the political power of the large corporations in a capitalist society. Like the workers, the farmer and rural business interests acting as pressure groups are also non-existent there. All sections, which have separate interets, should advance them through the Communist Party.

Economic planning of a socialist state is more direct and more comprehensive than the planning of capitalist states. The end of planning is also different i.e. the reconstruction of society into communist society through a series of long-range plans. Not only the economy but the entire society is subject to close control and direction. The usual distinction between the state and society or between the political and non-political spheres of life, is very difficult to make in a socialist system. The long-range objective of establishing communism requires the remaking of man and of society, not merely the achievement of a more efficient and more productive economy.

The second important characteristic of the Soviet state is the monopoly of political power exercised by the Communist Party. It also prescribes an official ideology, which is the only operative political doctrine. Consequently, the Western writers frequently describe the Soviet state as totalitarian and monolithic. Earlier the term totalitarian was applied to Fascist Italy, Nazi Germany and militarist Japan. The ascription of the same term to Soviet Russia was the product of the Cold War psychology during the post-war era. Some American political sociologists now find the concept of totalitarianism as inadequate to explain the changing character of the state in the post-Stalin period. Some western writers have applied group theory to Soviet politics. But in the absence of rival classes, parties or pressure groups, it is hardly relevant to use the group approach. There is widespread and active participation by citizens in officially approved collectives or groups. But this group life is not competitive in the Western sense of pressure groups trying to influence political decision-making to their own advantage and to the disadvantage of others.

A third important feature of the Soviet state is its multi-national character. Ethnic groupings play a marginal role in American political system but the entire state structure of the Soviet Union from the central level to regional and local levels has been deliberately related to 'nationality' groupings. This has brought about the integration of the non-Russian, particularly Asian nationalities with the Soviet state. The spread of Russians throughout the USSR is a legacy of the Tsarist period. Rapid industrialisation and socialisation have heightened this process. Whether this process deserves to be called 'colonisation' is open to question but it has surely resulted in curbing nationalism and in considerable social and economic dislocation. In Kazakhstan, the Russians constitute over 40% of the total population and Kazakhs themselves have been reduced to a minority. On the other hand, the raising of the cultural and educational standards of formerly backward nationalities has enabled many Asians to migrate to the cities of European Russia.

A fourth feature of the Soviet state is the universal application of the principle of 'democratic centralism' to the governmental and administrative structure. The Soviet state is formally federal but in practice unitary since higher executive bodies may direct, supervise and modify the work of lower bodies. The executive branch of government at every level is responsible to a directly elected soviet of the same level but it is simultaneously responsible to next higher executive body in the administrative hierarchy of the Soviet system. Even the Council of Ministers of a Union Republic is subject to supervision from the USSR Council of Ministers even in spheres recognised by the constitution as righfully belonging to the Union Republic.

A fifth characteristic of the Soviet state is its participatory basis not in the Western sense of voting but in terms of Marx's vision of the participation of masses in actual administration as members of a collective group. It implies the steady involvement of an ever increasing number of Soviet citizens in carefully selected social, political and administrative work under the guidance of the Communist Party. While the Soviet system does not ignore professionalism in government, it places less emphasis on it at the lower administrative levels than do most capitalist states. The extent, quality and value of this 'mass participation' is still subject to much controversy.

A sixth feature of the Soviet state is its revolutionary origin and tradition which demarcates it from all other capitalist states. The socialist revolution of 1917 was anti-feudal, anti-capitalist and anti-colonial in nature which put an end to exploitation of the peasants by the landowners, of industrial workers by the capitalists and of the oppressed nationalities by the Russian imperialists. The new Soviet State abolished all traditional forms of inequality based on class or race. The new revolutionary state aimed at the reconstruction of society on a socialist basis and then the eventual transformation of a socialist society into communism. In this sense the revolution initiated by the Bolsheviks in November, 1917 is still in progress.

The seventh and final feature of the Soviet state is its increasing bureaucratisation. Capitalist states too have become increasingly more and more bureaucratic in their organisation. We may count the Soviet Union as a bureaucracy along with other modern industrial societies but to do so without examining the peculiarities of Soviet bureaucracy is surely misleading. While bureaucracies of capitalist states are conservative, the Soviet bureaucracy has been the principal instrument of social transformation. It is continually torn between routinization of its functions and the political duty to lead an entire society into a higher stage of socialism. Another specific feature of Soviet bureaucracy is its duality i.e. the existence of two parallel bureaucracies of the state and the Party from the top to the bottom. The fact that the Party is superior to the state in theory as well as practice complicates the rational functioning of the state bureaucracy. Lastly, Soviet bureaucrats do not enjoy a permanent tenure unlike their counterparts in parliamentary capitalist states. The party operates bureaucratically but it is not bound by the restraints, checks and norms observed in constitutional bureaucracies. Autonomous public controls are also weak. In a capitalist society, parliaments, labour unions or business groups exert some countervailing power against the state bureaucracy. In the Soviet Union, this is done through the Procuracy and the Ministry of People's Control, which are themselves bureaucratic agencies. At lower levels, involvement of amateurs in aministrative work is a popular check on bureaucratic power.

Development of the Theory of Soviet State

The basic governmental unit of the Soviet state is the Soviet, a revolutionary organisation of the workers, peasants and soldiers at the inital stage but now transformed into a directly elected representative institution at several levels. The role of the initial revolutionary soviets was explained by Lenin in the following words: "In Russia the bureaucratic apparatus has been completely smashed up, razed to the ground; the old judges have all been expelled, the bourgeois parliament has been dispersed—and *far more accessible* representation has been given to the workers and peasants; *their* Soviets have replaced the bureaucrats, or *their* Soviets now control the bureaucrats, and *their* Soviets new elect the judges. This fact alone is enough to cause all the oppressed classes to recognise the Soviet government i.e. the present form of the dictatorship of the proletariat, as being a million times more democratic than the democratic bourgeois republic". (*214 : 136*).

As the Soviets were considered to be based on the revolutionary masses, the workers and peasants who constituted four-fifths of the population, they were claimed to be more democratic than any parliamentary regime, which despite liberal forms of representation remained an instrument of capitalist minority rule. Hence, we face a paradoxical claim that a dictatorship of the proletariat, which is practically a single party government of the

Communist Party, is the most democratic state in existence. Stalin observes: "The Soviet power is a new form of state organisation different in principle from the old bourgeois-democratic and parliamentary form—a new type of state, adapted, not to the task of exploiting and oppressing masses, but to the task of completely emancipating them from all oppression and exploitation, to the tasks facing the dictatorship of the proletariat." (*253* : *47*). The republic of soviets is thus the transitional state, within the frame-work of which the socialist mode of production will be developed and consolidated. However, the celebration of the soviets at an ideological plane continued long after the Soviet state bureaucracy had established considerable immunity from Soviet control in actual fact.

The fullest statement of Stalin's theory of the Soviet state is contained in his report to the 18th Congress of the Soviet Communist Party in 1939. Stalin accepted the classical Marxist view that the state would wither away under communism, when there was no longer any class to be held in subjection but he pointed out that Marx had not considered the possibility of socialism being established in one country ahead of others. Since the Soviet socialist state was surrounded by several capitalist states, the Soviet socialist state cannot be expected to wither away. In fact, the Soviet and other socialist states will continue unless the danger of foreign military attack from capitalist states has disappeared. However, the form of the state would continue to change with the productive development of the Soviet economy and with changes in the international situation. He said that the Soviet state has already passed through two phases of development. The first phase from 1917 to 1931 was characterised by the founding and consolidation of the revolutionary Soviet state and the second phase was characterised by socialist economic construction and the emergence of a developed socialist state. Stalin theorized the function of the state in developed socialism in the following words: "Now the main task of the state inside the country is the work of peaceful economic organization and cultural education. As for our army, punitive organs and intelligence service, their edge is no longer turned to the inside of the country but to the outside against external enemies." (*254* : *637*). This remark sounds a little strange in the context of the obvious increase in the coercive role of the Soviet state during the period of the purges of political opponents and dissidents.

Criticism of Stalin's theory has been attempted by Soviet scholars at three points: the class basis of the Soviet state, the periodization of the Soviet state and its functions in the various stages of development and the role of the socialist state in the transition to communism. While some writers have argued that there were elements of antagonistic contradiction i.e. class struggle still operating in Soviet society, none of them has openly admitted, as has Mao Tse-tung, the possibility of antagonistic contradictions operating between government and people because it is a part of the Soviet ideological myth that both the Soviet state and the Communist Party represent the interests of the whole of Soviet society. It is only some foreign Marxists like Charles Bettelheim who recognise the antagonistic contradictions between the ruling 'state bourgeoisie' and the working masses.

Piskotin and Romashkin have elaborated on the question of periodization and functions of the Soviet state. They attribute the repressive policies of the Soviet state to defects of Stalin's personality and emphasize the constructive role of the Soviet state in building socialism from the day Lenin captured political power in 1917. Regarding the role of the Soviet state in the post-Stalin phase, Khrushchev emphasized the view that there was no 'impenetrable barrier' separating the two stages of socialism and communism and that the transition to communism will be accelerated in future. The development of the socialist state into communist administration will be brought about through gradual transfer of functions from the state to social organisations. The Soviet leadership under Brezhnev has claimed that such transfer of functions in the spheres of health and other social services has been progressively realized. Still there is a wide gap between the ideal of communist self-administration and the political reality of a monolithic state apparatus.

The ideology of the transition to communism has been stated dialectically by a Soviet writer as follows: "The state of socialist society, with the greater and greater development of socialist democracy, gradually transfers functions of administration to different democratic institutions. It follows that the withering away of the socialist state should be understood as the transfer of separate state functions of different social organisations and the transformation of the state as a social and political organ into social communist self-administration. This of necessity is a prolonged process and cannot be completed as a result of the victory of communism in one country or even in a group of countries. However, the tendency is such that the very strengthening and development of the functions of the socialist state leads to the transformation step by step of different state functions into founctions of social self-administration." (*221 : 244*).

As with the state, the role of the Communist Party will also be strengthened during the transition to communism. The Party will outlast the state, when it withers away, under a classless communist social order. Chesnokov observes: "The party will occupy the leading position for a long time under the communist society. Even in the early stages of the victory of communism on a world scale the party as the embodiment of all that is most progressive and original will need to exist. The people will need many years, decades of life under communism while all the new mechanism of social organisation is sorted out and coordinated, till at length the conditions will be created for the withering away of the party. This process will be long and protracted." The usefulness of the above theorisation by Soviet writers for the correct interpretation of the Soviet State is doubtful in view of its contemporary transformation into a huge military-bureaucratic complex with its repressive role internally as well as externally. Most Western critics would regard Soviet theories about the withering away of the state and the party as irrelevant, if not deliberately misleading.

People's Democracy as a Transitional State

The concept of people's democracy arose in connection with East European states which were established after the defeat of Nazi Germany in the Second World War. In all these countries, which were at various stages of economic and political development, coalition regimes consisting of communist, socialist and liberal parties were established. They constituted the transitional forms of the state and their purpose was to bring about a 'democratic' transformation of the social system and thus prepare the ground for the subsequent socialist state, which could then function as a dictatorship of the proletariat under the exclusive leadership of a Communist Party. The people's democratic state was needed in East European countries because the revolution there was brought about by the conquering armed forces of the Soviet Union and not by indigenous Communist revolutionaries. The indigenous Communist parties were either very weak or practically non-existent. Hence, a multiparty coalition regime led by the Communist party functioning under the close supervision of the Soviet occupation authorities became a historical necessity. Within less than a decade the transitional form of state defined as people's democracy was transformed into a dictatorship of the proletariat on the Soviet pattern.

Yugoslavia, however, evolved its own pattern of socialist state, which was a little more pluralistic than the usual Soviet model instituted in other European countries. The revolts in Poland, Hungary and Czechoslovakia showed the unsuitability of the Soviet model in these states and though they were crushed by Soviet armed intervention, yet they had an impact on subsequent political development in these countries resulting in the tolerance of somewhat greater plurality in their state systems. In Poland the trade unions and the Catholic Church enjoyed a degree of autonomy not allowed elsewhere in any communist system. The Solidarity movement of the Polish trade unions became so strong as to threaten the rule of the Communist party, which could not contain it and was forced to surrender its power to a military regime. This is the first instance of a Communist party abdicating its authority in favour of a military dictatorship to suppress a movement of its own working-class after three decades of the socalled proletarian rule.

From New Democracy to Socialist State in China

While the concept of people's democracy in Eastern Europe was pragmatic, Mao Tse-tung's theory of 'new democracy' in China can be described as essentially ideological. As China was an underdeveloped, semi-colonial society, the Communist Party had to carry out a 'democratic' revolution first to put an end to the domination of imperialism, feudalism and 'bureaucratic' capitalism on the Chinese state. This revolution would be different from the bourgeois-democratic revolution of the Western countries because it was to be carried out not by the bourgeoisie but by the proletariat in alliance with the peasants, the petty-bourgeoisie and the national bourgeoisie under the leadership of the Communist Party. Mao Tse-tung described the Kuomintang regime in China as a dictatorship of the big *comprador* bourgeoisie in alliance with the rural landowners. After the Second World War, the Kuomintang regime became a satellite of American 'imperialism.' The Chinese Communists succeeded in setting up a 'new democratic' state in 1949 after smashing the Kuomintang dictatorship in a victorious civil war. Mao Tse-tung observes: "The Chinese democratic republic that is to be built can be nothing but a democratic republic of joint dictatorship of all the country's anti-imperialist and anti-feudal elements. It will be a republic of new democracy.... The republic of new democracy also differs from socialist republics of the USSR type, the latest republics of the dictatorship of the proletariat."

Mao Zedong identified the new democracy period with the transitional form of the Chinese state, which it would assume before its transformation into a socialist state. He thought that state power at that stage would take the form of a dictatorship of several 'democratic classes', rather than the revolutionary dictatorship of the proletariat. The democratic classes that were to wield political power were the peasantry, the working class, the national bourgeoisie and petty bourgeoisie. In view of capitalist underdevelopment in China, the working-class in China was numerically small and politically less conscious of its historical role. It lacked the capacity to play a leading role on its own in the form of a dictatorship of the proletariat at that early stage. The peasants had played an important role in the Chinese revolution and could not be denied a legitimate share in the joint dictatorship. The national and petty bourgeoisie too, if appropriately regulated, could join the working class and the peasantry in completing the establishment of a political system, economy and culture in a state of new democracy.

According to Mao Zedong, the new democratic state would confiscate the property of 'bureaucratic' and monopoly capitalists, which owned the banks, railways, airlines etc., but would not abolish capitalist mode of production itself. He said that the foreign and feudal yoke in China fettered the initiative and development of 'national' private capital. The task of the new democratic state in China was to protect and encourage development of legitimate private property. The Common Programme of the Chinese People's Political Consultative Conference laid down the goals of the new democratic state as follows: "The basic principle for the economic construction of the People's Republic of China is to develop production and bring about a prosperous economy through the policies of taking into account both public and private interests, of benefiting both labour and capital, of mutual aid between the city and countryside, and circulation of goods between China and abroad." *(252 : 21)*.

But the policy of benefiting both labour and capital could not go on for more than a short period until the launching of wide-scale socialist construction. The class contradictions were growing more acute after the tasks of economic rehabilitation and agrarian revolution were completed by 1952. Thus the preparatory stage for future socialist industrial development had been completed. The state sector became paramount in the pluralist Chinese economy, which comprised various forms of ownership of the means of production such as state property, cooperative property and capitalist private property. In 1954 the state sector amounted to 47% of industrial production. The state also owned about half the assets in the joint sector accounting for 10% of industrial production. The state was already in control of the main raw material sources, banking, foreign trade and the key industries. Radical structural socio-economic changes had also been effected in agriculture. The conditions were thus created for the development of a socialist economy by introducing new socialist relations in agriculture as well as non-socialist sectors of industry. The transformation of the new democratic state into a socialist state i.e. a dictatorship of the proletariat became a historical necessity in China at this stage of its economic and political development.

While the constitution of 1950 has defined the Chinese state as people's democratic dictatorship, the constitution of 1975, taking cognizance of the socialist transformation of its economy having long since been completed, described the Chinese People's Republic as a "socialist state under the dictatorship of the proletariat, led by the working class and based on the alliance of workers and peasants." By describing China not simply as a socialist state but as one under the dictatorship of the proletariat, the constitution obviously sought to emphasize Mao Zedong view that the economic overthrow of the bourgeoisie does not mean the end of class struggle, "that it is absolutely necessary to consolidate the dictatorship of the proletariat so as to carry through the socialist revolution and the socialist construction; and that the theory of 'the dying out of class struggle' and the clamour for the substitution of 'a state of the whole people' for a state under the dictatorship of the proletariat are nothing but subterfuges used by the bourgeoisie to prepare public opinion for the restoration of capitalism." (*261 : 236*).

Like any other socialist state, the Communist party enjoys the monopoloy of state power in China. However, for historical reasons the people's liberation army has a close relationship with the Communist party and may be regarded as a co-sharer in political power. During the Cultural Revolution, Mao Zedong used the armed forces to suppress the 'capitalist roaders' in the party and the state. However, the Communist party continues to assert and maintain its supremacy in the Chinese state system.

Unlike the Soviet Union, China does not claim to be a multinational, federal state. It is a unitary political system with a limited degree of autonomy accorded to regions inhabited by minority nationalities. Like the Soviet Union, the Chinese state and the Communist party function on the basis of the principle of democratic centralism. As compared to the Soviet political system, the Chinese state accepts greater pluralism and larger sub-system autonomy. Another characteristic of the Chinese state is its participatory basis. The mass campaigns and the cultural revolution gave opportunity to thousands, even millions, of Chinese citizens to participate in the political process. The quality and value of this kind of 'mass participation' is still subject to considerable debate. The radical and revolutionary image of the Chinese Communist party has suffered a great deal, since the moderates assumed its leadership after Mao Zedong's death. The new moderate leadership of the Chinese state has called 'the cultural revolution as a great national disaster disrupting its economy and damaging the party and state structures.

The main question regarding the state in socialist societies is how to make it more democratic and more participatory in conformity with the classical Marxist ideal of democracy. Whatever may be the status or quality of 'socialism' established by the Socialist States, they have failed to democratise their political institutions. Civil liberties and democratic rights are still non-existent in socialist political systems. The state continues to reflect authoritarian tendencies. Before the socialist state withers away under communism, let it first become democratic during the period of transition, not just in rhetoric but in reality.

Demise of Soviet-style state socialism

The overthrow of communist regimes after 1989 in quick succession put an end to Soviet-style socialist political systems in Eastern Europe and led to the disintegration of the Soviet Union too. These states are now in various stages of transition from statist socialism to managerial capitalism and from single party hegemony to multi-party, neo-liberal democracy. In the Russian Federation, you have the curious spectacle of a President of the Republic, who does not have a political party of his own, and the government party still remains the single largest party in the Russian parliament and its candidate can still poll more than 40 per cent votes against Yeltsin, the partyless President, who presides over a failing economy and mafia capitalism where the GNP has come down by 47% during the last decade.

CHAPTER 14

COMPARING THE NATURE AND ROLE OF THE STATE IN DEVELOPED AND DEVELOPING SOCIETIES

Nature of the State in Developing Societies

The concept of development has acquired considerable importance in contemporary social science. More than a century ago, Marx said: "The country that is more developed industrially only shows to the less developed the image of its own future." (*223 : 13*). Assuming that the developed nations show to the underdeveloped the portrait of their own futures, the question arises, do the developing countries accept this image? Are they willing to accept modernisation or industrialisation without qualifications? Does this include latest innovations in technology, consumerism, alienation and privatization? Do the less developed nations adopt the strategy of evolutionary reform or revolutionary change? Will they follow the capitalist path or choose the socialist road to economic prosperity? Is their underdevelopment a consequence of the policies of developed states? Answers to these questions are necessary before we can discuss the nature and role of the state meaningfully in the contexts of developed and developing societies.

The emergence on a mass scale of new nations with different cultural traditions, new political forms and new economic systems has created new issues for our times. No underdeveloped nation rejects the goal of development but the 'image' of a developed nation has been fragmented into 'images' of developed nations. In the consciousness of a developing nation lives the example of the socialist Soviet Union no less than the capitalist United States. The *existence* of a development process is a social fact. The *recognition* of a need for development is a social value. The *belief* that the development process is economically and socially experimental, neither socialist nor capitalist but a fusion of both, is an ideology. The nature and role of the state in a developing society will be determined in terms of the social reality and ideological aims of development. A related question which ought to be considered is the degree of independence available to a developing nation to choose the strategy and goals of its development. Experience has shown that for various reasons, the underdeveloped societies are unable to break the vicious circle of their stuctural *underdevelopment* without a social revolution.

In the third world, the *formal* state systems are almost everywhere republican in character, while their *real* political systems are nearly always authoritarian. They are neither monarchies nor total dictatorships. They have constitutions but their constitutionalism is at the mercy of the dynamic leader of the single or dominant party. They have a higher political elite often controlled by an even more conservative military elite. There is neither a developed parliamentary system nor the kind of stable and competitive political parties found in developed capitalist states. Where parliamentary regimes have been permitted to exist, they have become a conservative force which has served to fragment the political power of progressive social groups. Parliamentary rule is often established in some Latin American countries, which have achieved formal independence much earlier than their Asian or African counterparts. Here, the rural working masses have been systematically excluded from effective participation either through denial of suffrage or through electoral frauds of various kinds. In such circumstances, the legislature becomes the front for the property-owning class.

In Africa and Asia, some developing states have avoided this situation by abandoning the multi-party system. Thus, in Syria, Iraq, Egypt, Algeria, Tunisia, Kenya, Tanzania and Guinea, there has been the gradual erosion of parliamentary norms in the name of mass participation. Irving Horowitz observes: "The Parliament has become an upper-class forum, while the President has become the hope of the masses. This struggle is simply another way of describing the differences between formal and real political systems in emerging nations." (*206 : 27*). In a developing society, the national state is often identified in the minds of the people with the nationalist party which led the struggle for independence. Hence, the Congerss Party, despite its amorphous structure, has been able to retain monopolistic control of state power in India with just a brief interruption. This is even more true regarding the P.R.I. which has been ruling Mexico since 1911 without interruption.

Thus, even in those states which are identified with Western liberal values, parliamentary systems are more formal than real. To achieve even a minimum rate of growth or to enter the 'take-off' stage, the state in a developing society must undertake central planning. The politics of planning necessitates an authoritarian state structure, not particularly concerned with the observance of parliamentary norms. A parliament is a forum of conflicting interests and contrasting opinions. As such, it is deemed incapable of serving the whole people. Military dictators, taking advantage of parliamentary rifts, proclaim their authoritarian rule and abrogate the constitution.

Horowitz observes: "Parliamentary development can be afforded as a splendid luxury when time and history allow. This was the case for the United States in the nineteenth century. Whether there is a margin for parliamentary developments in the Third World depends on the role that parliaments perform in these nations. The case histories presently available are hardly encouraging. In Latin America they have tended to preserve the *status quo* and to retard the development of central planning. It is hard to imagine the new African states following such a model. Therefore, there is within the Third World a development of radical political orientations without many constitutional safeguards." (*206:28*). It is because of this that the radical elites of the third world have rejected the Western social democratic ideology and prefer to speak in Rousseau's idiom.

The authoritarian nature of the state in developing societies has resulted from the rapid growth and consolidation of the one-party state or the military regime without parties. Yet this rarely spills over into totalitarianism i.e. total control of the social and economic system. Technological backwardness and bureaucratic inefficiency make this impossible. A verbal commitment to liberal-democratic norms is retained. While an authoritarian state structure is declared necessary for the transition period from underdevelopment to development, democracy remains a goal to be attained in future. Almost every state in the developing countries has a written constitution and a formal legislature. This constitution is literally drawn from elements found in the written constitutions of developed capitalist countries and occasionally those of the Soviet Union. The constitution and formal parliamentary institutions serve to legitimize the auhoritarian rule of the dictator.

Role of the State in Developing Societies

The state plays a major role in directing and regulating economic development in practically all underdeveloped countries. It generally promotes a mixed economy with both private and public sectors. While in Brazil and India, public sector accounts for less than 25% of the economy, it accounts for 75% share in the national economies of Algeria and Eygpt. Economic policies of the state reveal a conflict between desire for integration based on self-sufficiency, and external aid for developmental purposes. It faces a dilemma between strong internal regulation and moderate external regulation and ability to implement development schemes. One additional problem in this connection is the difficulty which the state encounters in controlling the richer classes inside the country and in negotiating for better overseas arrangement in aid. There is a decline in terms of trade and a balance of payment problem. The state has to choose between a variety of planning techniques. Planning may be total, budgetary or project-based.

Although the typical economy is based on the peasant sector and basic economic production is agricultural, the state policy stresses industrial development and a premium is placed on heavy industry. The state desires contraction of the primary sector. It promotes mechanisation of agriculture either on cooperative or capitalist basis. The quality and efficiency of state planning will decide whether a successful shift from a predominantly agrarian economy to an industrialised society is possible or not. The state tries to control growth in consumerism by following inflationary policies. In planning, the state has to rely on finances, which are limited and variable. So it has to depend on foreign aid, credits and investment. The state makes an attempt to control imbalances in the economy through governmental regulation. The desire of the private sector to maximise its short-run profits vitiates the effects of long-run public-sector planning. Frequent strikes by radical labour unions also affect production. Growth rates may be high in percentage but not in terms of per capita production.

The state has to deal with the problems created by the growth of middle-sized and metropolitan cities. Though industrial growth is still attaining the 'take-off' stage, the imbalance between cities and villages has already become acute. Traditional status differentiation is diminishing in urban areas and occupational mobility is increasing. The state promotes mass literacy as well as technical and scientific education with planning to integrate industrial needs into educational programms. Despite lack of funds, the state facilitates the growth of mass media but tries to enforce conformity in opinions. High birth rate and a declining death rate, though mortality rate is still quite high by the standards of developed countries, creates the problems of rising population, depressing consumption rates which are already very law. The state tries but faces difficulties in promoting birth-control policies. Islamic, Catholic, Buddhist and Hindu ideologies resist policies of birth-control and other modernisation programs of the ruling elites in developing countries. Sometimes, the ruling elites are themselves opposed to secularisation and may promote theological or fundamentalist policies.

Despite their commitment to the objectives of disarmament and non-alignment and opposition to power blocs and their military alliances, the states in developing countries try to develop a strong military establishment. But the basic feature of the military elite in a third world country is its politicisation. The military elite soon becomes a rival to the political-bureaucratic elite as a formulator and executor of political decisions at state level. Horowitz says, "The 'new nations' witness the rise of military politics, either as a prime mark of sovereignty or directly, as the ruling political group. The armed forces have specific ideological commitments—in pre-revolutionary Third World countries to conservative. Caesaristic models and in post-revolutionary Third World countries to radical-charismatic models. The organizational code of the military is ambiguously defined, with an extreme emphasis on personalities, on the military leader as a national redeemer." (*206*:*70*).

The standing army of a state in developing countries is relatively small in numbers, but with a top-heavy ratio of officers to soldiers. But the level of financial expenditure on the armed forces is quite high considering the small size of the standing army. In part, this is a consequence of the need for purchasing arms from developed industrialized countries. But this is also the consequence of maintaining a potential agency for exercising maximum coercion with minimum numbers. The centres of military operations are concentrated in or near the capital cities or the industrial regions so that they could be used for repressive acts against a rebellious popular movement more easily. This also enhances the possibility of 'palace revolutions' and seizures of state power by the military elite. Political activity is restricted usually to the officer caste in the armed forces. Service rivalries are quite high, with the naval and air force elites often displaying more conservative attitudes than those of the army. Factionalism is often noticeable in pre-*coup d'etat* situations. In periods of crisis or discontent, politicisation may reach ordinary soldiers. The state, then uses its repressive powers to crush the protest actions of the politicised soldiers with the same intensity as it would do in the case of protest movements intiated by peasants or workers.

The state in developing societies makes use of Rousseau-style 'mass democracy' legitimated through 'highly articulated and politically grounded ideology of nationalism and socialism with charismatic leadership. The political idiom is radical and socialism with considerable variation, polycentric rather than monolithic, deriving inspiration from Islam, Christianity, Gandhism or half-baked Marxism. The state promotes centralization and aims at maximum control and suppression of conflict groups without distinguishing between 'policy-makers and policy-implementers'. It may fail to achieve this objective due to low level of party discipline and lack of efficiency on the part of the bureaucrats. Source of change in state policies should be located in multiple interest articulation and application rather than in opposition of minority parties. The state's capacity to achieve economic growth or social change is often affected adversely or otherwise by the proper or improper roles of the military, political and bureaucratic elites in the political system of a developing country. Often 'independent and over-participant role of military, executive branch, and/or prematurely over-developed bureaucracy' and sometimes much too underdeveloped bureaucracy may prevent the state from achieving its developmental goals. Except in revolutionary circumstances, the state in the third world country formulates its policies by adjusting the interests of a modernising bourgeoisie with those of a conservative, traditional land owning class.

The State in Developed Capitalist Societies

The state maintains the capitalist mode of production based on private ownership of property and a free market. The typical economy is capitalistic which is based on 'individual entrepreneurial initiative', limited centralized planning, generally 'in social welfare sectors'. There is a tendency towards monopolistic control of finance and industries with a phenomenal development of corporate wealth. There is stress on consumer goods production and services. The state regulates the economy in a general way but relies on market forces to keep internal balance. High international integration has been created by financial and commodity markets with slight regulation. The state encourages voluntary savings on the part of individuals through a liberal tax system. The state does not attempt to restrict or coordinate private investments. Source of finance is variably based on autonomous decisions taken by 'business, bank credit, and international capital market'. The state tries to maintain stable currencies.

The protectionist ideology has considerably influenced the trade policies of the states in developed capitalist countries but they are less fatal in their mutual relations than for underdeveloped countries. Growth rates tend to be low reaching a period of zero growth recently and a prolonged recession. The agricultural sector is five to twenty percent of the GNP and labour force engaged in agriculture varies from six to twentyfive per cent. Agricultural sector does not grow because of international competition. Technological and industrial level of development is quite high though growth rate has now levelled off with the notable exception of Japan. Consumption is encouraged through advertising and other means as necessary stimulus to production and growth creating the psychology of 'consumerism'. Labour unions are strong, highly organised which agitate for economic demands within the framework of capitalist society.

The state maintains parliamentary democracy, which is established by constitutional authority and based upon 'economic law of market.' The government follows policies which are either conservative or moderately reformist. The state permits conflict within the rules of the game. The national character of the state is not stressed ordinarily but it may come on the surface occasionally. A recent example is Britain's war with Argentina to regain the control of the Falkland Islands. The number of political parties in the states of advanced capitalism is restricted, which are divided on pragmatic lines much more than ideological. Political parties and interest groups articulate and aggregate policies to be implemented by the state. The range of party activity is narrowly political. The membership of the party elite is small. The party elite is inactive except at the time of elections. The party organisation is highly bureaucratised and membership does not exactly correspond to class or ethnic divisions in the national community. The basic unit is the party caucus. Elected representatives forming party leadership exercise oligarchical control over the party apparatus and policies, while remaining sensitive to fluctuations of public opinion.

At the state level, the political executive makes policies which are to be implemented by the bureaucrats. Judiciary is independent of the executive but the two may be united by a common ideology of the *status quo*. The state is secular based on separation of politics and religion though, paradoxically, the Christian Democrats are today the ruling parties of West Germany and Italy and the only Catholic President of the predominantly Protestant United States, Kennedy, was assassinated. The army is regarded as subordinate to the democratically elected civil government though the military elite may wield enormous influence behind the scene. According to C. Wright Mills, the military elite is an indivisible component of the Power Elite which rules America today. The Corporate Rich and the Political Directorate are the two other constituent elements of the power elite.

The basic property of the military caste in advanced capitalist society is its professional character. Its role is confined to the execution of decisions made by a non-military civil body. The armed forces are not expected to have any ideology of their own apart from the defence of the nation as this is interpreted by the civilian political elites. As a matter of fact, the beliefs and motivations of both civilian and military elites in the countries of developed capitalism are deeply ideological. The capitalist ethos and anti-communism unite the political and military elites into a common front to defend the interests of the capitalist corporations. The standing army is not very large but the stockpile of armaments, both nuclear and conventional, is continuously increasing. Three of the advanced capitalist states are nuclear powers and one of these three, a nuclear super-power with a capability to destroy the entire human race.

The military elite in developed capitalist society does not pose a direct threat to parliamentary democracy. The centres of actual military power are dispersed throughout the nation, the naval power floats on the oceans of the world, the military bases may be distributed all over the globe. But there is no direct military intervention in the parliamentary system operating within the national frontiers. Engagement in formal political activities is prohibited for members of the armed forces. Service rivalries exist but they are normally confined to allocation of funds by the state for development of different sectors. Unlike the military elites of the third world states, the military elites of developed capitalism have no ambition to assume direct responsibilities of government.

The state of developed capitalism has to administer a highly urbanized population living in large metropolitan cities and numerous middle-sized towns. The middle class, both professional as well as entrepreneurial, is increasing in proportion to the total population. The working class is contracting and employment opportunities are declining. There is great status differentiation through occupation and income. Inequality has increased due to increasing bureaucratisation in society and economy. The State provides increased social welfare programs and benefits but is unable to check widespread unemployment of workers during recessions. As the birth and death rates are low, the state has few official demographic policies. The state, which claims to be a guardian of a pluralist social order, permits a proliferation of highly organised, functionally specific, autonomous groups.

The State in Developed Socialist Societies

The state in a developed socialist society recognises only the socialist mode of production, which is based on public or state ownership of property in a rigidly controlled internal and external market. The state controls all sectors of the national economy through centralized planning. The typical economy is geared to proletarian values. Emphasis is on heavy industrial development to create the preconditions for diversified industrialisation. Internal and external markets are regulated primarily in accordance with economic considerations. The trade agreements are largely between and within the socialist bloc countries. The state determines the savings policies. Investment is through the public sector, restriced and coordinated by the state. Source of funds is stable, based as it is on the state budget. Currencies and prices are generally stable. Production is need-oriented in a non-market society. Growth rates are generally high. Imbalances are controlled through economic regulation. Agricultural sector constitutes fifteen to thirty per cent of GNP and about forty per cent of the total labour force. Individual private agriculture is prohibited or severely restricted. Industrial level of development is high and growth rates have just begun to level off. The state exercises direct and numerous controls on production and distribution of consumer goods. Consumerism is discouraged as deterrent to industrial development. Labour unions are subordinate to the state structure. The state allows the worker councils a minor consultative role.

In developed socialist societies, the state is organised as a pyramid like structure of soviets based on the principle of democratic socialism. The state is legitimated by rationalized authority derived from a formal constitution and based upon 'economically grounded ideology of communism-socialism' interpreted by the Communist Party with a high degree of doctrinal uniformity. Very strong emphasis is put on building common forms of socialism in all socialist countries particularly when a particular member of the socialist bloc announces an independent strategy of development. Political dissidence is suppressed. Strong single-party system dictates all interest articulation. The party and state structures are highly centralized from top to bottom. The party has a large membership ranging from five to ten per cent of the total population. Leadership is based on bureaucratic principles of selection. The activities of the party extend to all social spheres and are carried on continuously. The political system of developed socialism does not provide for separation of powers. The bureaucrats legislate functioning under the direction of political executives. Judiciary is a branch of administration. Religion and Church activities are discouraged. The army is entirely subject to civil authorities.

The basic property of the military elite in developed socialist societies is its professional ethos. While it is generally engaged in implementing policies determined by the party and state leadership, it works closely with the elite at the level of decision-making as well. The armed forces do not have a specific ideological commitment apart from the general social commitment to the socialist ideology as defined by the civilian political elites. The military generals may assume the responsibilities of government only in an exceptional case i.e. when the Communist Party finds itself unable to govern and proclaims martial law inviting the military to assume administrative powers. This happened in Poland when the labour unions led by Solidarity leaders made it impossible for the civilian rulers to govern in peace.

The armed forces operate within a well-defined organizational code, with a minimum emphasis on personalities. The standing army is generally larger than its counterpart in a capitalist country. The stockpile of armaments, both nuclear and conventional, has been constantly increasing in the Soviet Union and to a lesser extent in China. The Soviet Union is a superpower and has acquired nuclear capability to destroy the entire human race. In terms of military power, it has achieved parity with the United States. The centres of actual military power are dispersed throughout the nation. In the case of the USSR, the Soviet navy is present in all the oceans and Soviet military bases exist on the territories of its allies and satellites. Engagement in political activities is permitted to officers and soldiers on conformist lines. Service rivalries are discouraged and loyalty to the Party and the State is emphasized for all branches of the military.

Deliberate promotion of industrialization by socialist states has resulted in the growth of urbanization. Large and medium-sized towns have sprung up. Yet a sizeable peasant sector has survived in all socialist countries.

High pace of industrial growth has resulted in the growth of industrial workers and substantial increase in the number of professional employees. Technological development has created a high degree of social mobility. There is a lower degree of status differentiation as compared to situations existing in a developed capitalist country or any non-socialist underdeveloped country. The state promotes technical-scientific mass education. As Horowitz puts it, "The educational sphere is unique in that it alone can claim manpower priorities over economic production. This is based on notion of education as postponed economic improvements." (*206:67*). The State provides for high social welfare programs and benefits and has banished unemployment and recessions. Consumption levels are lower than those of capitalist societies. Due to low birth rate and low death rate, socialist states, with the exception of China, have few official demographic policies. China, which is not yet a fully developed socialist society, follows an active demographic policy to keep its population under control. The Chinese state has prescribed a single-child norm and promotes its adoption by offering material incentives to the couples who adhere to it.

Comparing States in Developed and Developing Societies

According to C. B. Macpherson, three types of *democratic* states are co-existing in the present-day world. He calls them the liberal, communist and nationalist variants of democracy. He observes "that democracy is not properly to be equated with our unique Western liberal-democracy, but that the clearly non-liberal systems which prevail in the Soviet countries, and the somewhat different non-liberal systems of most of the underdeveloped countries of Asia and Africa, have a genuine historical claim to the title democracy." (*219:3*). The liberal-democratic state exists to enforce a certain set of social relations based on property rights, Capitalism and the liberal state have developed together. In capitalist societies, democratic franchise was installed only after the market society and the liberal state had been firmly established. Democracy, as Macpherson says, came as a top-dressing. It had to accommodate itself to the conditions of a fully developed market economy and individualist enterprise. In its earlier phase, the liberal state had freely competing parties, but they were essentially oligarchical in character. It was this liberal state which was later democratized by extension of suffrage to all people and in the process democracy was also liberalized and became identified with market society and capitalist enterprise.

In the existing socialist societies and newly liberated countries of Asia and Africa, the democratic state came as the result of a revolution against the liberal-capitalist state, which was also imperialist in relation to colonial societies. The communist and nationalist movements which came to power there had a self-image of being democratic. For them democracy had something like its original meaning i.e. government by or for the common people, by or for the hitherto oppressed classes and masses. Democracy in classical Western thought meant rule by the common people, the plebeian majority over the patrician minority. It was very much a class affair. It meant the rule of the poorest and largest class. That is why democratic state was feared and rejected by the upper classes. Plato, Aristole, Cromwell, Locke and even J. S. Mill rejected *democracy* which could give power to the labouring class. Marxism in socialist countries and Afro-Asian nationalism have revived this original meaning of the term 'democratic state'.

Marx called the proletarian rule as democratic. This seems outrageous to the liberals. Of course, proletarian dictatorship has nothing liberal about it, but to call it 'democracy', as Marx did, was simply to use this word in its original and then normal sense. This was Marx's meaning when he talked of winning the battle of democracy against the capitalists. Democracy was to be a class state; it was to use its power to abolish the legal basis of capitalism and put the productive powers of the whole society, including its accumulated capital, at the service of the entire community. The Marxian idea of democratic state started from the age-old notion of democracy as a form of class rule. The vanguard state of the existing communist countries claims to be democratic in the non-liberal sense i.e. it represents the interests of the majority class. But this is only the first step in the direction of the humanisation of the whole society and conversion of the proletarian state into a state of the whole people.

Macpherson insists that the *nationalist* state of the third world is also democratic in its own distinctive way. The nations of Asia and Africa have achieved independence from capitalist-colonial rule only after a revolutionary struggle. These national revolutions are the product of an organised popular movement under a leadership which is able to get mass support for the national democratic ideal. The national-democratic state of the third world neither corresponds to the liberal-democratic state of capitalist societies nor resembles the proletarian-democratic state of the communist countries. As Macpherson points out, the national-democratic state rejects the basic ideas of liberal-individualism as well as the class analysis of Marx which constitute the ideological bases of the other two varieties of democracy. Its own ideological basis can be seen in Rousseau's doctrine of the general will and mass democracy.

Regarding the nation-state in Asia and Africa, Macpherson observes: "To call it democratic is to put the emphasis on ends, not means. It is to make the criterion of democracy the achievement of ends which the mass of the people share and which they put ahead of separate individual ends. And this of course is the classic, pre-liberal, notion of democracy. The classic formulator of this democratic doctrine was Rousseau, and there are strong echoes of Rousseau in many of the theoretical statements made by leaders in the underdeveloped countries. Like Rousseou, they find the source of their social ills, of moral depravity, of dehumanization and loss of human freedom, in the institution of inequality. Like him they believe that men can be restored to full freedom and humanity by, and only by, the operation of a general will." (*219 : 29*). The nationalist vanguard party, representing the general will of the nation, pursues the two national goals of modernization and socio-economic progress.

Andre Gunder Frank in his work on *Capitalist Underdevelopment* has tried to show that underdevelopment of neo-colonial states in the third world and development of metropolitan capitalist states are the simultaneous results of a unified historical process. Paul Baran in *The Political Economy of Growth* agrees that the process of ever growing development in the countries of advanced capitalism is structurally related to growing underdevelopment in the third world states and that it is a continuing trend which has relevance for the present and future too. There is just one capitalist system of which the developed and developing countries are an integral part. The terms 'colonial', 'imperialist' and 'capitalist', as Andre Gunder Frank suggests, "refer to a set of relationships, in which domination, super-subordination, exploitation, and of course, development and underdevelopment, play a central part.... they must all be understood to refer to the same system which may be described by the phenomenon they all have in common, might best be called *capitalist*". (*202:3*). According to this theory, underdeveloped countries are *dependent* capitalist societies constituting the exploited and dominated sections of an integrated world capitalist system.

For purposes of development and underdevelopment, it is important to know that the semicolonial society not only loses a certain amount of wealth in absolute terms to the metropolitan capitalist society, actually this constitutes the loss of present and future capital. While the developing countries are denied the developmental potentialities of this capital, the developed country can use it for its own economic development. The landowning and commercial classes in a number of Latin American, African and Asian states are today highly dependent on the economic and political power of developed capitalist states. They have a vested interest in preserving indefinitely the system and pattern of industrial backwardness and *underdevelopment* in their countries. Commercial agriculture replaces traditional subsistence farming to a considerable extent and manufactured commodities from the developed capitalist countries invade the market of the native artisans and craftsmen, Paul Baran observes: "In the now backward areas this sequence did not unfold 'according to plan'. It took a different course; such division of labour as was bred by the initial division of labour resembled the apportionment of functions between a rider and his horse. Whatever market for manufactured goods emerged in the colonial and dependent countries did not become the 'internal market' of these countries. Thrown wide open by colonisation and by unequal treaties, it became an appendage of the 'internal market' of Western capitalism." (*174 : 323*)

The requirements of the world capitalist market or one of its monopolized sectors result in the relatively rapid expansion of a primary export product such as petroleum in Saudi Arabia, copper in Chile or coffee in Brazil. To get the process started, the foreign interests of a developed capitalist state seek a concession from the government in an underdeveloped country. A military dictator is more likely to give such a concession. If such a dictator does not exist in the concerned state, the general procedure is to set him up. But some time later, the concession has been secured, business is looking up, foreign capitalist corporation has earned enormous profits and the national clients of the export sector are progressing economically. The time has come to throw out the military dictator and set up a liberal-democratic government. The circumstances change. The quantity of exports starts declining. As no secondary manufacturing sector was built, the economy faces a disaster. The local ruling elite and foreign interests demand restoration of dictatorship to protect their profits.

Andre Gunder Frank remarks: "The cycle leaves its mark. It leaves a structural heritage. The cycle is not a circle. It is a spiral. The extractive export industry has, in its phase of glory, literally extraced a part of the national riches......A portion of the country's best resources have been used up. The fruits of these resources have been invested not to create alternative facilities in that country; they have been shipped aboard for consumption in the metropole, or for investment to further develop the metropole......Economically .... the underdeveloped country is more underdeveloped than ever and less easily able to develop than before." *(202 : 38)*

According to Paul Baran, the liberal parliamentary state and the fascist military state in the Third World are linked with the structure of their underdevelopment on account of their economic dependence on the developed capitalist states. He says, "The principal impact of foreign enterprise on the development of the underdeveloped countries lies in hardening and strengthening the sway of merchant capitalism, in slowing down and indeed preventing its transformation into industrial capitalism....What results is a political and social coalition of wealthy compradors, powerful monopolists, and large landowners....Ruling the realm by no matter what political means—as a monarchy, as a military-fascist dictatorship, or as a republic of the Kuomintang variety—this coalition has nothing to hope for from the rise of industrial capitalism which would dislodge it from its position of privilege and power. Blocking all economic and social progress in its country, this regime has no real political basis in city or village, lives in continual fear of the starving and restive popular masses and relies for its stability on Praetorian guards of relatively well-kept mercenaries." *(174:338)*. In most countries of Latin America, Africa and Asia, these neo-colonial regimes could have been toppled through social revolutions by now but for the military and economic aid and support extended to them by developed capitalist states.

In some third world states, the national bourgeoisie may be strong enough to resist pressures of external capitalist states and may try to meet a potential threat of an internal social revoluion by making an all-out effort to lay the foundations of an indigenous industrial capitalism and to create a modern capitalist state. Such a nationalist elite may also create a state-capitalist sector along with a co-existing private capitalist sector to expedite economic growh. The national state of this type may proclaim 'socialism' as its official ideology though the outcome of state-capitalist planning within the framework of a market society is bound to be capitalism and not socialism.

Paul Baran sums up the achievements and failures of the independent national-democratic state in India in the sphere of economic development in the following words: "There the united front of anti-imperialist forces is still—if only precariously—intact, and provides the broad political basis for the government of the national bourgeoisie. Yet this breadth of the national coalition which accounted for the enormous strength of the Congress Party in the days of its struggle for national independence at present nearly paralyses the administration that it supports. Although still enjoying approval of the overwhelming majority of the articulate part of the nation, it encounters unsurmountable difficulties in attempting to formulate and to carry out a programme of economic and social regeneration. Setting out to promote the development of industrial capitalism, it does not dare to offend the landed interest. Seeking to mitigate the most outrageous inequalities of incomes, it refrains from interfering with the merchants and moneylenders. Looking for an improvement of the wretched position of labour, it is afraid to antagonize business. Anti-imperialist by background, it is courting favours from foreign capital. Espousing the principles of private property, it promises the nation a 'socialist pattern of society.' Fancying itself to be *au-dessus de la melee*, standing above the struggle of antagonistic classes, it merely reflects the stage which the class struggle has reached in Indian society. Anxious to reconcile irreconcilable needs, to compose radical differences, to find compromises where decisions are inevitable, losing much valuable time in bridging recurring conflicts within its own fold, this government substitutes minor reforms for radical changes, revolutionary words for revolutionary deeds, and thus endangers not only the very possibility of realizing its hopes and aspirations but even its very tenure in office. Handicapped by the heterogeneity and brittleness of its social foundations and by the ideological limitatons resulting therefrom, the essentially petty-bourgeois regime is incapable of providing genuine leadership in the battle for industrialization, is powerless to mobilize what is most important: the enthusiasn and the creative energies of the broad popular masses for a decisive assault on their country's backwardness, poverty and lethargy. (*174 : 369*).

The example of developing socialist states within the Third World shows that only the elimination of the capitalist structure and introduction of socialism have so far enabled an underdeveloped society to escape either from imperialism or from underdevelopment. If the capitalist path of development is unable to liberate underdeveloped countries today from their traditional situation of underdevelopment, the nations of the third world may be obliged to seek development through a social revolution. However, this trend has been reversed during the last few decades when China dn other socialist states of the third world have opted for market-oriented policies of economic growth with considerable success.

CHAPTER 15

THEORIES OF RIGHTS

We may preface our discussion of the subject by three preliminary observations which should underlie any sound view of rights. In the first place, rights and duties are correlative conceptions; that is to say, every right carries with it a corresponding obligation. They are like the two sides of a coin. Rights depend upon duties. 'It is only in a world of duties that rights have significance' (*81 : 119*).

Our second observation which is a corollary of the first is that every right requires social recognition. Without such recognition, rights are empty claims. Rights do not exist in a vacuum, so to speak. They require the sanction of society.

Thirdly, a right is not a selfish claim. It is a disinterested desire. It is something which is capable of universal application. In asserting my right, I am really rendering a public service, and when I fight for the rights of others I may do so at great personal loss or inconvenience to myself.

Older societies as a rule did not recognize rights to any great extent. They had only petitions and charities. Modern democratic societies, on the other hand, give a very important place to rights. 'The Revolution (French) did not ask for charity; it demanded the rights of man' (*10 : 152*). Some of our present-day constitutions such as the Irish and Indian constitutions guarantee certain fundamental rights to their citizens. Rights have a tendency to grow. New rights frequently come into being e.g., the right to work, the right to strike, the right to retain one's job when one is on a strike, etc.

Among the various explanations of rights which have been offered from time to time, we can distinguish five main theories. These are:

(1) the theory of natural rights;

(2) the legal theory of rights;

(3) the historical theory of rights or the theory which bases rights on customs;

(4) the social welfare or the social expediency theory of rights; and

(5) the idealistic or personality theory of rights.

1. The Theory of Natural Rights

This is the earliest theory of rights. It goes back to the Greek times. It holds that rights belong to man by nature. They inhere in him. They are self-evident truths. One simply asserts them dogmatically. Rights are absolute. They are pre-civil and, according to some, even pre-social. They are inborn. They can be asserted anywhere and everywhere. Thus, Locke says, all men are born free and rational. God has given authority to no man to compel another to carry out his orders. Likewise, the right of life, the right to liberty, the right to judgment, the right to carry out one's judgment, etc. are all natural rights.

This theory of natural rights has played a very important part in the history of human development. Among Western writers, John Locke and Thomas Paine made much use of it. In practical politics it exerted great influence on the constitutional struggles of America and France. Thus the Virginian Constitution declares: 'That all men are by nature equally free and independent, and have certain inherent rights, of which, when they enter into a state of society, they cannot by any compact deprive or divest their posterity; namely, the enjoyment of life and liberty, with the means of acquiring and possessing property, and pursuing, and obtaining happiness and safety' (*66* : *5*).The French Declarations of 1791 and 1793 use similar language. The Declaration of 1793 names liberty, equality, security, and property as among the important natural rights of man. The American Declaration of Independence (1776) holds these truths to be self-evident that all men are created equal, that they are endowed by their Creator with certain inalienable rights, that among these are life, liberty, and the pursuit of happiness.

The social contract writers in general are advocates of the theory under consideration. They assume that man had certain natural rights to start with, and that, at the time the contract was formed, he surrendered some of those rights to a superior auhourity in order to be able to safeguard the rest. This point of view is clearly seen in Locke.

Herbert Spencer, whose political theory has a very strong resemblance to the thought of the social contract writers, asserts that his study of the evolution of life in both the animal and man leads him to the conclusion that the one fundamental right of all men is the right to equal freedom, according to which, every man is free to do that which he wills, provided he infringes not the equal freedom of others.

Criticism: (a) The most obvious criticism of the theory is that it is very difficult, if not impossible, to define the term 'natural'. D.G. Ritchie has written a whole volume on Natural Rights and brings out clearly the various senses in which the term has been used. Some of the senses, which he finds, have been assigned to the terms are:

(1) Nature = the whole universe
(2) Nature = the non-human part of the universe
(3) Nature = the ideal (or completed purpose)
(4) Nature = the original (the incomplete)
(5) Nature = the normal or average.

At this point we naturally ask, 'In which of these various senses are we to understand the term 'nature' in speaking of natural rights'?

(b) Seeing that the terms 'nature' and 'natural' are indefinite and are used rather loosely, we are not surprised to find that, among the supporters of the theory of natural rights, there is an ambiguity as to what these rights are. There is no official or complete or generally agreed-upon list of natural rights. Some justify slavery as natural; others condemn it as being unnatural and artificial. Some assert that by nature men and women are equal; others deny it. Some hold that men are naturally good; others believe that by nature they are wicked. Some regard private property a natural right; others deny it altogether.

(c) The so-called natural rights conflict with one another. The French Revolution declared liberty, equality, and fraternity to be the absolute rights of man. They are supposed to be self-evident truths. But when we begin to apply them in practice, we are faced with endless difficulties.[1] In no rational system can there be a place for absolute liberty and absolute equality. If we begin society with absolute liberty, we soon get inequality. On the other hand, if we start with absolute equality, liberty soon vanishes.

Or, turn to the question of property. If property belongs to all, as is assumed by supporters of the theory of natural rights, we must know what that right implies. Does it mean private property? If it does, does it include the right to dispose of one's property as one wills; the right to do exactly what one wills with one's own, even to the extent of abusing it?

(d) The implication of the theory of natural rights is that the State and social institutions in general are artificial and that they have robbed man of certain inherent rights which belonged to him in a state of nature. The logical conclusion to which the theory of natural rights leads is extreme individualsm. It is capable of being used both by anarchists and conservatives.

(e) The real flaw in the theory is that it assumes that we can have rights and obligations independently of society. This is an erroneous conception. We have rights only as members of society. Apart from society, we may have powers but not rights. Rights antecedent to society are meaningless, for the simple reason that a right is nothing without a correlative obligation.

2. The Legal Theory of Rights

According to this theory, rights are creations of the State. What the law gives me is my right, and what the law does not give me is not my right. Rights are not absolute. They are not inherent in man at all. They are relative to the law of the land. My right to life, liberty, property, etc., is determined by the State. Rights are artificial.

This theory is opposed to the theory of natural rights. Its advocates argue that the so-called natural laws either agree with the laws of the land or disagree with them. If they agree, they are superfluous, and if they disagree, they are futile. Therefore, in either case, they can be ignored. It is no wonder that Bentham, who is an advocate of the legal theory, ridicules natural rights as being 'nonsense upon stilts'.

We find a trace of this theory in Thomas Hobbes, who holds that the

1. Even such an obvious right as the right to worship is not conceded by all modern States.

fundamental right of every individual is that of self-preservation. This right, Hobbes believes, can be better maintained by the State than by the individual.

Criticism: (a) Spencer's point of view is that the State does not create rights; it exists in order to maintain rights. N. Wilde remarks: 'The law does not create our rights, but only recognizes them and protects them. The rights themselves exist whether they are thus legalized or not. They are enforced because they are rights, and are not rights because they are enforced.' For ourselves, we believe, that what makes a claim a right is not the mere fact that it is recognized by law, but that it is morally justifiable. A typical right should combine legal and moral recognition.

(b) To say that the State is the sole creator of rights is to make it absolute. However high a place we may be prepared to give to the State, we are not prepared to go so far as that. Technically, no doubt, the sovereignty of the State is supreme. But there are certain practical limitations imposed upon it by customs, traditions, history and morality. Law is often determined by the customary rule of the community. Not infrequently it is simply the formulations of customs. Justice in very many cases follows customs. Therefore, to argue that all rights are derived from law is unsound.

(c) Some of the advocates of the legal theory of rights seek to overcome the difficulty by saying that the State is only the creator of legal rights. But when they say this they are not saying anything profound. They are guilty of tautology. It is like saying man begets a human child. The defect with the legal theory is that it does not cover the whole scope of rights. Whether rights are derived from history, customs or laws, they all require a moral basis. The legal theory does not enable us to decide whether the rights that are recognized are the rights that ought to be recognized.

Truth in the Theory. (a) While the arguments advanced above go to show that the legal theory cannot give us a satisfactory view of rights, the theory cannot be dismissed lightly. We are not prepared to go to the extent of saying that rights are possible apart from the State. Claims which are essential to the moral development of man, and which are violated or ignored by the State, can at best be only potential rights. They are the raw material or ground of rights, but are not full-fledged rights. It is desirable that in democratic countries, at least, where presumably the general will of the people can bring about necessary changes in a peaceable manner, all our rights should win legal recognition. But this is not the same as saying that whatever has legal recognition behind it is necessarily a right. It may be only a technical right.

(b) As said already, a right should have both a legal and a moral aspect. To quote from Bosanquet: 'A right....has both a legal and moral reference. It is a claim which can be enforced at law, which no moral imperative can be; but it is also recognized to be a claim which ought to be capable of enforcement at law, and thus it has a moral aspect....A typical 'right' unites the two sides. It both is, and ought to be, capable of being enforced at law' (*5 :187*).

3. The Historical Theory of Rights

This theory can be summed up in the sentence: 'History makes right.' It holds that rights are the crystallization of customs. We are familiar with the phenomenon of long-standing customs assuming in course of time the form of rights. If a person has been receiving a birthday present from a friend for number of years, he soon comes to imagine it as a right. What is a pure gratuity becomes a custom, and one expects it as a matter of course. The right of way on the public road is a customary right. In cases of divorce the amount of alimony is adjusted not according to the cost of living, but according to the kind of life to which a person is accustomed. As Ritchie remarks, we often find that 'those rights which people think they ought to have are just those rights which they have been accustomed to have, or which they have a tradition (whether true or false) of having once possessed. Custom is primitive law' (*66* : *82*). Many of the so-called natural rights, when scrutinized carefully turn out to be claims which have 'the sanction of the longest and the least broken custom,' (*66* : *82*) while claims, which are of quite recent growth or are not widely adopted, are regarded as 'conventional'.

Edmund Burke has observed that the French Revolution was based on the abstract rights of man, while the English Revolution was based on the customary rights of Englishmen. This statement contains much truth. While as a historical fact the French Revolution was provoked by the conditions which prevailed in the 18th century France, it had for its battle-cry the abstract principles of liberty, equality, and fraternity, applicable to all men. The English Revolution, on the contrary, was simply a reassertion of the rights that Englishmen had enjoyed from very early days and which had found expression in such documents as the Magna Carta and the Petition of Right. In fact, the entire constitutional history of England is summed, up by some writers as a struggle for 'liberties', as against liberty.

Criticism : No doubt a large number of our rights are rooted in customs. But to say that all our rights can be traced back to ancient customs is a clear exaggeration. The late Prof. Summer of Yale claims that the mores or customs of people can make anything right. We do not accept this point of view. In criticizing it, Hocking asks: 'Was slavery right when it was lawful? Was infanticide right?' And the obvious answer is in the negative. According to him, although slavery was customary in most parts of the world, it was never right. The weight of academic opinion, however, is that slavery was a relative right, i.e., right at one time, but not right now when the moral sense of man is more fully developed. The difficulty with this point of view is that if right is always in relation to custom, reform is impossible. The abolition of *Satee* and polygamy, the Sarda Marriage Act, and temple entry for the depressed classes (the Harijans) are to a large extent violations of the well-established customs of the country.

Yet enlightened public opinion has no hesitation in supporting such reforms.

4. The Social Welfare or the Social Expediency Theory of Rights

From the point of view of this theory, rights are conditions of social welfare. They are the creations of society. Advocates of the theory like Roscoe Pound and Prof. Chafee hold that law, custom, natural right, etc., should all yield to what is socially useful or socially desirable. Rights, says Prof. Chafee, are determined by a balance of interests. The right of speech, for instance, is not unlimited. It is determined by considerations of social expediency.

The Utilitarians in general support this theory of rights. Bentham and Mill expressly advocate the principle of utility 'in opposition both (1) to the mere following of custom or external authority, and (2) to the arbitrary appeal to the voice of nature speaking in the human heart—an appeal which can be made in support of abuses, as well as in support of the revolt against them' (*66* : *87*). They set up the principle of 'the greatest happiness of the greatest number' as the criterion by which to judge of what ought to be. They believe that utility can be determined by means of reason and experience.

Criticism : The social welfare theory of rights no doubt has a great deal to commend it. Nevertheless, it has some serious defects.

(a) Public welfare is undoubtedly a good test of rights. But difficulty arises when we begin to define the term 'public welfare.' Does it mean 'the greatest happiness of the greatest number,' majority interest, public opinion or what the government of the day considers to be the common good? Even if it means any of these, it does not help us much, because these terms are equally vague and indefinite. 'Greatest happiness', as such, cannot be measured. The community, as such, has no feeling.

(b) Another defect of this theory is that social welfare may infringe on what we call our individual rights. It may lead to the position that it is right to do a little injury to an individual in order to do a great deal of good to the community—to the doctrine that the end justifies the means. It may mean in practice general welfare overruling what is admitted to be a private right. The principle of social expediency is a dangerous principle with which to work. Fortunately, in a good many cases individual right coincides with general welfare. Trouble arises only when the two conflict. When such conflicts arise, advocates of the social welfare theory are bound to prefer common interest to individual good.

5. The Idealistic or Personality Theory of Rights

From the point of view of this theory, rights may be defined as the outer conditions, essential to man's inner development. The supreme right of every man is the right of personality. By this we mean that it is the right and duty of every human being freely to develop his full potentiality. Every other right is derived from this one fundamental right. Even such important rights as the right to life, the right to liberty, the right to property, etc. are not absolute rights. They are conditional or presumptive. They are relative to the right of personality. Thus, I have a right to life only to the extent to which it is necessary for my highest development. I have no right to commit suicide, for I can never tell with certainty that I have reached the highest perfection possible for me. The moment I abuse my right society is perfectly justified in taking it away from me. Green speaks of rights as powers 'necessary to the fulfilment of man's vocation as a moral being' (*29 : 43*).

This theory looks at rights from a highly moral point of view. Rights are powers which I can claim from society on a moral plane. They are rooted in the mind or soul of man. They are powers granted to me by society in order that I may, with others, realize a common good of which my good is an intrinsic part. This truth we expressed earlier by saying that every right requires social recognition.

Stating the same truth in other words, we may say that every right has for its basis a rational or responsible wish. Whimsical or irresponsible wishes can never become rights. My wish for anything should be coincident with some wish of the person or persons to whom I address my claim. Dr. Hocking remarks whenever one person claims a right against another, he says to that person: 'If you infringe my rights you hurt yourself in a very central place.' Slavery injures the slave-holder even more than it injures the slave, what the slave suffers is to a large extent physical, while the injury sustained by the slave-holder is moral. In recognizing the rights of others I honour my own strength. In killing an innocent person I kill something of myself.

Criticism and Appreciation: (a) On the whole, the idealistic or personality theory of rights seems the most satisfactory. Difficulty may arise when we begin to reduce the conception of personality to practical terms. It may be asked: by what standard is the State to judge the conditions required by each of its citizens for his fullest self-development? Is not the idea of personality after all a subjective idea? What do we know of other people's destinies? These are no doubt weighty objections.

(b) It is conceivable that to a very large extent the social welfare theory and the idealistic theory, in their relation to rights will go hand in hand because individual good and social good are intimately related[2]. But if and when individual good and social good come into conflict, the idealistic theory will go one way and the social welfare theory another. The idealistic theory refuses to sacrifice any human being to the development of someone else. It believes with Kant that no man is to be treated as simply a means to another's end: it calls upon everybody to treat humanity in his own person and in the persons of others always as an end and never merely as a means.

(c) One of the chief merits of this theory is that, unlike the theory

2. Laski is right in saying: "I do not exist solely for the State; but neither does the State exist solely for me." (37 : 94). They exist for one another and promote each other's good.

of. natural rights which posits too many absolutes, and the other three theories which posit no absolutes whatever, it lays down one absolute right, viz., the right of personality and derives every other right from it. Because there is only one absolute right there is no inner contradiction, as in the case of the theory of natural rights. Besides, this theory furnishes a safe test of rights which can be applied at all times, and herein it is superior to the legal, historical, and social welfare theories. Then one absolute right of all human beings is the right of personality. It is invariable.

RIGHTS, LIBERTY AND EQUALITY

Laski's Conception of Rights

The conception of rights occupies an important place in Laski's political theory. He is interested in the problem of rights both as a liberal and as a socialist. As a liberal, he is a great champion of individual liberty. As a socialist, he is also a believer in the ideal of social and economic equality. Laski's interpretation of rights in his earlier phase shows a pluralistic tinge when he argues that a decentralized system of government is a necessary condition for an adequate conception of rights. In his later socialistic phase, he revises his opinion when he advocates nationalization of industries to bring about social and economic equality in society which is now regarded by him as an essential fulfilment of the conception of rights.

It is, however, clear that Laski never accepted that atomistic conception of rights which was advocated by such individualists as Bentham, Adam Smith and Herbert Spencer in the nineteenth century. Yet he is as enthusiastic as Mill was in his defence of intellectual liberty or freedom of the mind. He welcomes Green's innovations in the individualistic tradition of liberalism and agrees with him in saying that liberty cannot be negatively defined as absence of restraint. But he is not prepared to accept Green's defence of private property. Laski, in fact, regards capitalism as a system based upon discriminatory privileges rather than upon equal rights. The true conception of rights can be realized only under conditions of socialism.

Rights Denied Under Fascism

Laski's passion for rights is evident from the vehemence with which he has denounced the fascist theory. He has reserved his unqualified condemnation only for the fascist system amongst the various ideologies prevailing in the world because the fascist state implies the total repudiation of civil liberties. He regarded the fascist dictators as essentially executioners brought to power by the abnormal circumstances of their countries. He thought that the fascist governments were essentially gangster governments securing obedience from an unwilling people by the use of gangster methods.

As he says, "What Mussolini called the decaying corpse of liberty is the index to their view of human nature. They have no respect for it; they deny its capacity for self-mastery. They believe that the masses are sheep to be used for whatever purposes they may determine. They deny the validity of any aspiration or belief which threatens their right to power. They insist upon a slavish obedience to their will which, at the best, makes hypocrites and sycophants, and, at the worst, turns the dignity of which man is capable into a fawning imitation of their own cruelty" (*131* : *107*). Thus he concludes that a regime which denies the enjoyment of rights to its citizens converts human beings into robots. Therefore, rights must be regarded as the necessary conditions of proper development of human personality.

Danger to Rights in the Modern State

But the danger to an adequate philosophy of rights in modern times does not come from fascism alone. Liberty, which may be regarded as the quintessence of rights, is neither perfectly secure in a capitalist democracy like America nor, according to him, in a socialist dictatorship like Russia. As Laski points out, "When attacks on liberty are political or economic, it is their motive rather than their nature that changes. A political pattern has the same hold upon its votaries as a religion; the enthusiasts of Moscow and of Washington differ only in the object of their worship. An economic system defends itself in just the same way: the devotees of Marxism in its extreme form have never doubted their right to impose their outlook upon the recalcitrant, even at the cost of blood. In a constitutional state like America the suppression of liberty is called the inhibition of license; in a dictatorship like Moscow it is termed resistance to the admission of incorrect 'bourgeois' notions........A scrutiny of history, moreover, makes it plain that the right to liberty will always be challenged where its consequencte is the equalization of some privilege which is not generally shared by men" (*49* : *213*).

In fact, Laski does not believe that any political or economic system can be considered as the embodiment of final truth and so there is always a scope for its just criticism and reform. Liberty consists in the affirmation of this right as absolute and inviolable. That this right should be equally shared by all is also quite self-evident.

Rejection of the Theory of Natural Rights

Laski has very carefully distinguished his conception of rights from certain other conceptions which have been widely accepted by political philosophers in different ages. He totally repudiates the view that the rights are those historic conditions which man possessed in the very dawn of civilization but lost in the process of time. He rather takes an evolutionary view of rights and concludes that a modern democratic state provides greater scope for the enjoyment of rights than any preceding state in history has done. The theory of natural rights is simply absurd because it conceives rights not as the product of a developing social life of the community but as those prepossessions of human beings which were inherited by the human race from its pre-civic past.

The rights are not static simply because human civilization is not static. If we regard them as the reflections of a natural order, we shall have to deny their essentially dynamic character. In Greek city-states, a free citizen possessed the right to own slaves. Aristotle defended this practice as the reflection of natural principle. In modern times, none can agree with Aristotle in regarding slavery as natural.

Partial Validity of the Legal Theory of Rights

As regards the legal theory of rights, Laski does not deny its validity in the realm of jurisprudence but considers it as inadequate for the purposes of political science. As he says, "It is an attractive theory; for since the courts enforce the will of the State as they discover that will, we know that claims are immediately entitled to recognition. But so purely legalistic a view has nothing to contribute to an adequate political philosophy. A legal theory of rights will tell us what in fact the character of a State is; it will not tell us, save by the judgment we express upon some particular state, whether the rights there recognised are the rights which need recognition" (*47 : 90*).

Law does not create rights; it merely defines and recognizes them for a particular legal community. Therefore Laski does not agree with the views of Hobbes and Austin who defined rights as the expression of the will of the sovereign. To do justice with the Austinian view, it is necessary to admit that rights acquire a practical meaning only when the will of the sovereign supports them. In the absence of this support, they remain simply pious wishes or moral aspirations of certain liberal minds in the community.

Rights as Conditions for Self-Realisation

According to Laski, the rights may be defined as those social conditions which are necessary for self-realization. In this way, the source and content of rights should be sought in a moral realm. Here Laski and Green hold a similar point of view. Both of them regard the development of moral personality as the goal of an adequate system of rights. "But the possession of rights, in the sense here used," says Laski, "does not mean the possession of claims that are empty of all duties. We have rights to protect and to express our personality. We have rights to safeguard our uniqueness in the vast pressure of social forces. But our rights are not independent of society. We have them because we are members of the State. We have them by reason of an organization through which in the world as it is, the contribution of that uniqueness can alone be made. Our rights are not independent of society, but inherent in it" (*47 : 93*).

Thus the purpose of rights is two-fold. In the first place, they aim at the enrichment of human personality. Secondly, they promote social cohesion and collective progress by enabling each individual to shoulder his special responsibility in the communal effort.

Inadequacy of the Liberal Theory of Rights

It is to be noted that Laski's enumeration of rights does not follow the old liberal and individualistic pattern. He regards the individualistic theory of rights as unfit for the present age and pleads for new socialistic value in our social and political life. "The decay of our political system," says Laski, "is due to its failure to embody a new spirit different from that which it was devised to contain. That new spirit brings within its own sense of values, its affirmation of a plane of rights antithetic to the old. It is, like its predecessor, a plea for variety in unity, a search for a new balance between order and freedom. Like its predecessor, also, it seeks the means for the affirmation of individual personality. But its way of attaining its ends is wholly different from that which marked the previous path" (*126* : *61*).

Laski thinks that we must discover a new basis of defining rights in the light of changed social conditions. As he points out, "The error which was inherent in capitalist democracy was its atomic conception of social life. That error, regarded historically, was intelligible enough. It was a protest against controls upon individual behaviour exercised in the name of a small oligarchy whose actions were rarely referable to rational principle. Its exercise of authority made government itself seem a necessary evil. The more narrow the sphere of its operations, the greater, it was argued, would be the freedom of citizens" (*126* : *62*). In fact, the antithesis between the state action and individual rights evolved by the liberal thinkers was based upon a misconception of the relationship between the individual and the community.

Rights as Privileges of the Ruling Class under Capitalism

When the liberal writers were pleading for individual liberty, they were only in search of an ideological justification for the *laissez faire* economy. As Laski says, "The liberal state, though it represented a definite gain in social freedom upon any previous social order, was in fact no more than the exchange of one privileged class for another. And its refusal to link political liberty with social equality had grave consequences. It brought into the control of authority a race of men whose idea of good was built in the association of material success with civic virtue. The 'private war' of which Sir Henry Maine spoke was for them morally beneficent. They equated effective economic demand with right. They argued that for the weaker to go to the wall was a law of nature to which we were disobedient at our peril" (*131* : *305*).

The area of freedom was strictly confined within the social borders of the ruling capitalist class and the majority of toilers did not enjoy any rights in substance. "The liberal state," says Laski, "began in a condition of society in which the few were rich and the many poor; it ended in a condition in which the few were still rich and the many poor. Its explanations of this situation were hardly satisfactory. No one believed that the difference between rich and poor was really due to ability or moral worth. Few could see why, if wealth was scarce, the recognition of an equal claim to its benefits did not represent the maximum social advantage" (*126 : 63*). Thus Laski wants to indict capitalist democracy for its failure to bring about social and economic equality.

Denial of Economic Equality in Capitalist Society

In a capitalist democracy, the absence of social and economic equality results in a practical differentiation and discrimination in the enjoyment of rights, by different groups and classes in the community. Laski points out that people in a class-ridden society do not share equally "in the gain as well as in the toil of living." Capitalist society of today provides greater opportunity for moral and material development of human personality than any previous social system but even then this opportunity for self-realisation is limited to a small section of the population. The state is not neutral or impartial in the distribution of rights. It favours those who are economically powerful. The courts discriminate between the rich and poor while administering these rights. Not only wealth but knowledge is shared unequally by people. Liberty is protected on a class basis and it is a privilege of the rich.

The masses are asked to maintain order because disorder may threaten the liberty of their rulers. The islands of prosperity are created in the midst of popular misery, unemployment and starvation. "Our knowledge", says Laski, "increases by leaps and bounds; but those who have genuine access to the intellecual heritage of the race are still but a fragment of the people......The rule of the rich, whether of landed men or of those who owned industrial capital, has been devoted firstly to the accumulation of wealth, and secondly to preventing its diffusion. The whole character of social life, and, therefore, the whole character of the state, is above all determined by its division into a small number of wealthy persons and a large number who dwell upon the margins of subsistence. We enjoy security and order. But the security we enjoy means the protection of most in their importance, and the order is, very largely, the safeguarding of the few against the demands of the many for a richer and fuller life" (*47 : 98*). Thus an adequate conception of rights can be realized only in an egalitarian society from which class privileges have been banished.

Safeguards for Property Rights

The most important indictment that Laski advances against the capitalist democracy is directed against its conception of property rights. In his critical analysis of the working of parliamentary institutions in England, he plainly admits that they are based on an anachronistic conception of the sanctity and inviolability of private property. "Our political system", he says, "takes for granted the private ownership of the means of production; the consequences of that assumption cover every nook and cranny of the law. All the great categories of our jurisprudence are soaked in the traditions of individualism. They assume property-rights which, save in the absence of direct contrary prescriptions from Parliament, are to be safeguarded from invasion. They are based, not upon the collectivist and corporate habits of the twentieth century, but on the liberal atomic principles worked out from the seventeenth to the midnineteenth century. They were the work of men who believed. that, with the triumph of the businessman, a term had been put to the need of revolutionary change" (*130* : *22*). This clearly shows that Laski regards the individualistic view of property rights as predatory and out of tune with the time.

It should be noted how the judicial system of a capitalist democracy safeguards the institution of private property. "No one can honestly examine", says Laski, "the history of the relations between labour and the courts without seeing that their result is to give the vested rights of property a special place in the American system. That is positively apparent in the ideas of Hamilton and Marshall, of Webster and Taney and Story, and of Chancellor Kent long before the Civil War; it is still more apparent after it. The view of John Adams that unequal property is the necessary outcome of liberal institutions has found a wide echo on the judicial bench. But once that has been assumed, the next step is quite naturally to argue that laws which seem to invade that inequality are themselves a source of danger to the stability of the commonwealth. The main technique has been to due process of law; and this has been interpreted to mean not what a normal reasonable man would be justified in regarding as just, but rather as a method of protecting the property the wealthy class has acquired and, therefore, the laws under which that property is safe. Due process of law is not a road, but a gate; and those to whom it bars admission are the masses in the community. It is a way of protecting the past legal rights of the few against the present legal claims of the many" (*121* : *211*). This clearly shows the inadequacy of the system of rights that a capitalist democracy maintains. The primary purpose of law in a capitalist society is to protect the privileges of the capitalist class instead of securing the rights of the common people (*50* : *76*).

CHAPTER 16

PARTICULAR RIGHTS

A. THE RIGHT TO LIFE

The particular rights which we take up for detailed consideration are the Rights to Life, Liberty, Property, and Equality, Political Rights, and the Right of 'Resistance' to the State.

The most fundamental of all rights is the right to life, for without it man can have no other rights. According to T. H. Green, the right to life and the right to liberty together constitute a single right, viz., the right to free life. Life without liberty is useless and conversely, it is the use made of life that gives one the right to life.

The bases of the right to free life are the instinct of self-preservation natural to man and the instinctive aversion of the average person to take the life of any sentient being. Of course it is very difficult to build a system of rights merely on the basis of instincts and emotions. Before any right is conceded, society must be convinced that it is necessary for the individual's self-development as well as valuable to itself. Again, if rights rest merely on instincts and emotions, how are we to explain the readiness with which people kill their own fellowmen in warfare or the ever-present phenomenon of wilful murder? The right to life, therefore, is not unconditional. Only to the extent to which it is used in the interest of one's self-development and in the interest of society can it be justified.

IMPLICATIONS OF THE RIGHT TO LIFE

1. The Duty to Live

The right to life implies the duty to live. Neither from the point of view of himself nor from that of society is an individual justified in taking his life. Hence it is that attempt at suicide is punishable in all States.

Suicide stands condemned from the side of society also. As Gilcharist remarks, every life is valuable from the point of view of general welfare. Therefore, to take one's life or that of another is to eliminate 'an individuality which has rights as well as duties'. A few of our present-day thinkers, however, are in favour of the right to suicide. Suicide or attempt at suicide does not meet with such strong disapproval in Japan as in some other countries.

2. The Duty Not to Commit Murder

If one has the right to life, it is one's duty to refrain from taking the lives of others. Murder is not only a moral wrong, but also a serious legal offence. Is capital punishment a violation of the right to life of the murderer ? Strictly speaking such a person has no right to life at all. He has forfeited his right by the 'unassociable will' which he clearly demonstrates.

Those who are opposed to capital punishment argue that not infrequently a wrong man is sentenced to death and that most cases of murders are committed under extreme provocation or in a fit of insanity. They further argue (a) that death penalty has had a bad effect upon society in tending to cheapen human life and make people callous to human suffering; (b) that it is a relic of the barbarous times when vindictiveness characterized the dealings of men; (c) that many a murderer is an irresponsible person and does not realize the gravity of his crime; and (d) that death penalty has not acted as a sufficient deterrent. The conclusion which they draw from all this is that society should cure or restrain the criminal, not hang him.

In evaluating these arguments, it must be said that they are based on a false sentiment for life as mere physical existence. Society is not obliged to maintain the life of a member in society if he deliberately injures the lives of other members. A man who murders another for the sake of his property obviously forfeits his right to life.

Sir Herbert Stephen opines that capital punishment gratifies, as no amount of imprisonment can, the natural and healthy resentment of the relations and friends of the murdered man, and that it is an effective check on murder. It is his opinion that a good many murders are committed after methodical calculation. If allowed to haave his way; he would lightly extend the present law so as to include despicable acts of villainy under crimes punishable with death.

The conclusion to which we are led is that in clear cases of murder, death penalty is justifiable at least at the present stage of human development. We should take special care, however, to see that capital punishment is as rigidly restricted as possible.

3. The Right to Self-defence

It is generally assumed that hte right to preserve life includes the right to defend life. As to whether in a given case the force used in the defence of oneself was justified or not is left for the law courts to decide. The prevailing belief is that self-defence is justifiable, but not aggression. The difficulty with this view is that it is not always easy to define such terms as 'self-defence' and 'aggression.'

War. A question which arises at this point is in reference to war. Is the State justified in calling upon the individual citizen to lay down his life on the battlefield ? Is this not an interference with his 'right to life' ? Most wars, as noted by Green, have arisen from despotic ambition or national vanity and from a desire of economic gain.[1] Therefore, to speak of an inevitable conflict between States is an absurdity.

1. These days wars are due to ideological differences, real or imaginary, hiding many other reasons behind.

Hegel takes a different view. 'The state of war shows the omnipotence of the State in the individuality.' This belief in the divinity of the nation convicts of nullity the independence of individuals. The only things which matter are country and fatherland.

Suffice to say that all this is least convincing. Modern warfare involves rapid and often secret action. It is normally accompanied by cruenlty, fraud, and treachery. It is an economic drain and involves waste of life and thought. It is an incentive to individuals and groups of individuals to use force for the gaining of private ends. Modern warfare in particular, with its weapons of colossal destruction, is morally indefensible, economically inexpedient, and politically suicidal. In the light of all this, we have no hesitation in concluding with Burns: 'Democracy and war are irreconcilable, and therefore, the ideal of democracy must provide an alternative to war as an institution' (*10 : 295*). So long as nations feel that, in the last resort war is the best means of settling international differences, they live on a primitive level of existence.

4. The Right to Reproduce Life Coupled with the Right to be Born Without Heavy Handicaps

A primary instinct of man which is to be placed alongside of the instinct of self-preservation is the instinct of sex. From this it would appear that the right to reproduce life was almost a 'natural' right. Yet it is not a right which can be claimed absolutely. In modern society, it is not unreasonable to demand that in the interest of society in general and of the offspring in particular, such people as hereditary and incurable lunatics, idiots and imbeciles, hereditary deaf, mutes, lepers, etc., should be prohibited from marrying and prevented from propagating their kind.

In close connection with the right to reproduce life we may discuss a right which is not yet asserted to any great extent, but which, in some form or other, will have to be included in the organization of progressive societies—the right to be born without undue handicaps. The fact that children do not have a voice in the choosing of their parents places a grave responsibility upon parents and society to see to it that no child comes into the world which is unable by virtue of its birth to take its proper place in the common life of society. If the population of a country keeps on increasing recklessly, it is not unreasonable for the State to put some workable checks on it. Modern Japan goes to the extent of legalizing abortion, which is morally indefensible. China is now following suit.

B. THE RIGHT TO LIBERTY

1. MEANING OF LIBERTY

The ideal of liberty has made its powerful appeal to man in all ages; and in the name of liberty have been performed great acts of heroism as well as despicable acts of crime. Even today there are very few ideals which can move men more readily than the ideal of liberty. Liberty is the essential quality of human life.

From what has been said earlier, it is obvious that there can be no absolute freedom anywhere in society. The only 'absolute' right of any normal human being is the right to the full and free development of his personality. The right of liberty is relative to this end. No man has the right to pursue his inclinations irrespective of consequences.

Freedom in the negative sense means the mere absence of restraint. But it does not say whether such freedom is good or bad. What is wanted is positive freedom which may be defined as the positive opportunity for self-development or for the continuous expression of one's personality.

J. S. Mill on Liberty. The word 'liberty' is rich in connotation and suggests new ideas at every turn. In the olden times, as J. S. Mill *(61)*. points out, liberty meant protection against the tyranny of political rulers. The rulers, however essential their presence was for the continuance of the body politic, were regarded as holding interests antagonistic to those of the people, and so the limitation of monarchical power was what was meant by the liberty of the people. This limitation took the form of winning recognition for certain immunities and political liberties and the establishing of constitutional checks. In course of time, it was found that it would be better to have representatives or delegates of the people as magistrates of the States. Even this proving inadequate, the further step was taken of identifying the rulers with the people, and making their interests and will coincide with those of the people. Thus the power of the State became the power of the nation, concentrated in a form convenient for exercise. In short, 'liberty' came to mean the popularizing of government.

But liberty soon proved a mirage, and there came to be the anomaly of a 'tyranny of the majority'—tyranny of the prevailing opinion and feeling. This tyranny was found to be more thorough-going and even more deadly than the tyranny of the individual ruler. And in its attempt to come once again to the forefront was born a new form of liberty, individual or personal liberty. It is to this form of liberty that Mill gives his chief attention in his celebrated essay 'On Liberty', his aim being to safeguard the individual, even his eccentricities and oddities, against the attacks of society.

2. TYPES OF LIBERTY

1. Natural Liberty

The conception of 'natural liberty' is a euphemism for the freedom of the jungle. Those who uphold 'natural liberty' argue that man is by nature free and that civilization is responsible for his increasing bondage. They quote with approval the words of Rousseau, 'Man is born free; and everywhere he is in chains', forgetting that Rousseau himself, after weighing the arguments for and against the state of nature and the civil state, had no hesitation in deciding in favour of the civil state. Man in the state of nature is subject to physical impulses, while in the civil state he becomes a rational creature governed by laws of justice and morality. 'What man loses by the social contract is his natural liberty and an unlimited right to everything he tries to get and succeeds in getting; what he gains is civil liberty and the proprietorship of all he possesses' (*67: Bk. I, Ch. VIII*).[2] Absolute freedom therefore equals absolute anarchy.

2. Personal Liberty

Every normal human being desires personal freedom. He wants to be able to plan his life in his own way. He values highly the right to exercise his faculties and to determine the general conditions of his life. He does not relish undue restrictions on his freedom to go about his business the way that he thinks best. Interference with his particular mode of living, tastes, and pursuits is particularly resented, especially when these personal preferences are not contrary to the social order or public morality. In the U.S.A. prohibition of liquor by state legislation was keenly opposed by many a law-abiding citizen because it was construed to be an undue interference with his personal freedom. In India too, the law relating to prohibition is flouted by many—particularly by those at the top and those at the bottom of the economic and social ladder. Some think it smart to break this law. In England every man regards his house as his castle, inviolable against all outsiders. Even the officers of the State cannot force entrance into it, except as provided by ordinary law.

Mill values the right of personal freedom so greatly that he goes to the extent of saying that the individual should be free to experiment with his life, so long as his actions do not directly and definitely affect others. Mill is even prepared to allow people to experiment in extravagance, viciousness, and drukenness, subject to consequences. This is an extreme point of view.

Like Mill. Bertrand Russell attaches much importance to personal freedom, which he regards as the greatest of all political goods. Thinkers who adopt this point of view value their personal freedom much more than any political rights, for, they say freedom of thought, freedom of speech and expression, and the like are much more essential to a person's real development than the privilege of voting or holding an office. It is this view of personal liberty which underlies much of the thought of philosophic anarchism. In the trenchant words of Rousseau, 'To renounce liberty is to renounce being a man, to surrender the rights of humanity and even its duties.' Slavery is universally condemned today because it robs human life of all its meaning and makes man 'an animated tool'.

---

2. A. J. Carlyle claims that the first important contribution of Rousseau was 'his emphatic assertion of the long tradition of the Stoics and the Christian Fathers that men in their primitive condition lived in a happy and innocent anarchy'. Instead of lamenting the passage from the state of nature to civil society, Rousseau thinks political subjection legitimate because in Carlyel's words, 'man to be man must live under the rational and intelligible authority of his fellow-men in the great community of the state' (91 : 182ff)

3. National Liberty

Although the conception of nationality is comparatively recent in its origin and development, from very remote times men have been prepared to lay down their lives for the safety and security of their group. The love of one's country is deep-seated in man, and patriotism, even in its narrow form, evokes feelings which cannot be easily awakened by other ideals. Thus it is that liberty in the sense of national independence has played a very conspicuous part in world history. Wars of independence are still applauded by the bulk of mankind in spite of the fact that there is a growing revulsion of feeling against war as a means of settling international disputes. So long as we are governed by the conception of sovereign nation-states and so long as internationalism is a little more than a pious hope, freedom from the control of other states is essential to the conception of liberty in its fullest sense.

4. Constitutional Liberty

Freedom in the twentieth century means not only self-government but also popular government. The term 'National Independence' is beginning to be used more and more as a synonym for democracy or popular government. There is little disposition to substitute for the arbitrary rule of the foreigner an arbitrary rule exercised by one's own countrymen. Thus liberty, in one of its essential forms, stands for a government chosen by, and responsible to, the general body of the people; and this we call 'constitutional liberty'.

5. Civil Liberty

This may be defined simply as liberty in society. 'It includes liberty to free action and immunity from interference' (*24 : 111*). 'It consists of the rights and privileges that the State creates and enforces, such as:

(a) freedom of the person;
(b) equality before law;
(c) security of private property;
(d) freedom of opinion and expression; and
(e) freedom of conscience.'

It is, in brief, a safeguard against physical and moral coercion whether it be from the side of the individual or of the government. It includes personal freedom.

6. Political Liberty

As contrasted with civil liberty, political liberty stands for the share that the individual has in the management of the State; or, at least in the direction of the manner in which the power of the State shall be exercised. In particular, it implies such rights as the right of franchise and the right to stand for public offices.

7. Economic Liberty

Even after attaining all the foregoing types of freedom, a person may not be much better off than a slave so long as he has no control over the economic conditions governing his life. In recent years much has been written, and more said on the virtual slavery of the toiling masses. What is uppermost in the minds of these people when they contemplate their lot in life is not political nor civil nor constitutional liberty. It is an economic freedom which will ensure to the labourer a just reward for his labour. It is a freedom which will destroy all cut-throat competition' and blind-alley jobs and remove such artificial regulations of manufacture and trade as result in the demoralizing of the worker. It is a freedom which will help to create that harmonious industrial system in which every man will produce only that which he is best capable of producing and the community will have need for what he produces. And unless and until this freedom is achieved, it cannot be said that we have solved the problem of liberty in its fulness. Economic liberty implies, says Tawney, the absence of such economic inequalities as can be used as a means of economic constraint.

8. Moral Liberty

A person may have all the kinds of freedom considered above. Yet if he does not have moral freedom, he is among the most deplorable of men. A moral slave is one who habitually wills and acts against his universal or rational self. Without it social and political freedom is of little value. T. H. Green and Bosanquet pay much attention to it. To Hegel in particular and to the idealists in general, freedom interpreted in this manner is objectively realized in the State.

3. LIBERTY AND AUTHORITY

Our natural impulse is to regard liberty and authority as mutually exclusive of one another. The eighteenth century individualism gave expression to this impulse by regarding every action of the State as an infringement upon individual freedom. This is a profoundly mistaken view. Experience clearly shows that authority in some form or another is necessary for the maintenance of liberty. As Willoughby puts it, freedom exists only because there is restraint. The only liberty possible for civilized man is a defined and limited liberty.

Far from liberty and authority contradicting one another, they supplement and complement each other. Locke discovered long ago that 'where there is no law there is no freedom'. Hocking goes so far as to say that the greater the liberty a person desires, the greater is the authority to which he should submit himself.

What we have said about authority in general applies with equal force to the relation of man to the State. The State is a servant to do our will, and to the extent to which it carries out our will faithfully, we are free and have positive political liberty.

Liberty and Law

The close relation between liberty and authority in the political field is expressed by the statement that sovereignty, far from being opposed to liberty, is essential to it. Without law there is no true freedom. As Ritchie remarks: 'Liberty in the sense of positive opportunity for self-development is the creation of Law and not something that could exist apart from the action of the State' (*66 : 139-140*). Certain restraints are necessary in the interest of general well-being. But they should be applied impartially, and society should be convinced of their reasonableness. Otherwise, liberty and authority remain opposed to each other. So long as one has the feeling that law is an external compulsion devised for the benefit of some particular person or class, there is bound to be profound discontent and unhappiness leading at times to rebellion. Therefore, if liberty is to be reconciled with authority, the authority which we are called upon to obey should be reasonable, and obedience to that authority should be voluntary. To quote Rousseau: 'Obedience to a law which we prescribe to ourselves is liberty' (*67 : 19*). Green says that man is free when he obeys the law of which he is the author and obeys it from the impulse for self-perfection.

All of this does not mean that a voluntary and literal consent of all citizens is essential to every law before it can be rightly enforced. The individual has no intrinsic right to disobey every law of whose worth he is not personally convinced. To concede such a right will lead to general anarchy.

4. LIBERTY AND EQUALITY

Such ardent lovers of freedom as De Tocqueville and Lord Acton hold the view that Liberty and Equality are opposed to each other. This seems to be a mistaken view. The French revolutionists were neither mad nor stupid when they made 'Liberty, Equality, and Fraternity' their war cry. All these terms are logically related. If liberty is to move to its appointed end, it is necessary that it should be accompanied by equality in some form. In saying so, we do not mean that society should provide a dead, mechanical level for everybody. Nature has not endowed all men alike. Equality does not mean identity of treatment, reward or functions.

There is a tremendous wastage of talent today, and in the ideal society talent must not be allowed to 'perish for want of encouragement' (*47 : 154*). Opportunity should be given to everyone to realize the implications of his personality. Inequalities there may be but only after a minimum basis of civilization has been assured to everybody. There may be varying rates of payment for effort. Still, great inequalities of wealth make the attainment of freedom impossible.

All of this implies that deliberate social restraints be placed upon individual freedom. Bentham's maxim. 'Each to count or one and no one for more than one', is fairly widely observed in political relations. Experience shows that Political Equality is valueless unless it is accompanied by virtual Economic Equality. Prof. Pollard puts the truth in a nutshell: 'There is only one solution of the problem of Liberty. It lies in Equality.' 'The liberty of the weak depends upon the restraint of the strong; that of the poor upon the restraint of the rich....Every man should have this liberty and no more, to do unto others as he would that they should do unto him; upon that common foundation rest Liberty, Equality and Morality' (*76 : 247-8*).

So far as India is concerned, the principle of equality calls for the distinctions of sex, caste, language and province to be eliminated as early as possible. Since Independence the position of women has considerably changed for the better. They can vote on equal terms with men and stand for public offices. A few of them have been taken into the administrative services of the country. Increasingly equal opportunities are being provided in the realms of education, work opportunities, marriage, property, and inheritance. Much is being done to raise the status of those of depressed class origin. Liberal scholarships are being provided for their education, and more are being employed in public services. The practice of 'untouchability' is against the law of the land, but the law is not properly enforced because of the lack of strong public opinion in support of it.

5. STATE REGULATION OF LIBERTY

1. The Right of Personal Security

This is the most elementary condition of personal liberty. No one has a right to assault me or to use my body as it pleases him or to restrain me from moving about as I please. The law protects us against menaces of violence—e.g., the angry shaking of one's fist as well as against threats of future violence. It likewise recognizes the right of self-defence.

In England, the right of personal freedom means that no one may be imprisoned, arrested or coerced except in accordance with the ordinary law of the land. This right is safeguarded by (1) redress for wrongful arrest; (2) the Habeas Corpus Act; and (3) the Rule of Law in general.

(1) Redress for arrest means that a person who has been wrongly arrested can either have the wrong-doer punished, or exact damages in proportion to his injuries. Such action may be taken against any person in the realm, official or non-official.

(2) A Habeas Corpus writ demands that a man who is kept under restrainst should be produced before the open court for proper trial. This is a very great check on the arbitrary action of the executive government. It makes it incumbent upon the police and the executive to act in accordance with the law of the land.

(3) The Rule of Law, in normal times,
   (a) subjects all persons in the State, including officials, to the ordinary civil courts.
   (b) opposes prerogative or the discretionary authority of the government, and
   (c) deduces constitutional liberties, such as the liberties of

speech, writing, and of public meeting from the ordinary private law relating to private persons.

2. Liberty of Thought, Speech and Writing

In a sense, everyone has the liberty of thought, and nobody can restrain it. A person may shut himself up in his room and say or wish to himself anything that he likes. Nobody is affected by it so long as no attempt is made to communicate it to others or to translate it into practice. But this is not the ordinary interpretation of freedom of thought. If liberty of thought is to have meaning, it is necessary that to some extent it be accompanied by liberty of speech ond action. To think what one pleases and not be free to express it in speech and action is oppression. It 'becomes a torture which eats away the soul' (*66 : 168*).

Freedom of thought and discussion has been valued as a sacred possession of man from very early days. Socrates preferred death to restrictions on his freedom to speak his mind. He took the position that the established order should, to some extent, be threatened by the advocacy of new ideas. In England the case for freedom of thought and discussion has been stated in immortal language by Milton, Sidney, Locke, and J. S. Mill. Milton held that liberty of thought and speech was the very foundation of all other liberties.

Mill's Views. Mill justified the fullest liberty of thought, speech, and **writing in the form of a sorites. He believed that liberty of thought should** have for its corollary liberty of speech and that liberty of speech should have for its corollary liberty of writing. His well-known argument is that the received opinion may be altogether true or altogether false or, what is more likely, partly true and partly false; and that in every one of these cases, there is a very strong reason why complete freedom of thought and discussion should be permitted. If the received opinion is altogether true, why should one be afraid of giving others a chance to refute it, if they can? To limit freedom in such a case may mean that one is not sure that the received opinion is, after all, true. It is certain that to refuse permission to have one's creed openly discussed is to make it a dogma. If, in the second place, the received opinion is altogether false, it is our privilege and duty to give up our error for the truth that we can get from others, by free discussion. Finally, if the received opinion is partly true and partly false, there is all the more reason why there should be full freedom of thought and discussion in order that each one may learn of the other. To suppress opinion in such cases is to claim infallibility, and experience shows that nobody is infallible.

In setting forth the above argument, Mill naively believes that mankind is so reasonable that truth will always meet with warm reception. He overlooks the fact that more often than not people decide not according to reason but according to emotion; and that even in a civilized community one finds a percentage of people incapable of using liberty aright.

It is admitted on all sides that there are limits to the free expression of opinion. These limits are fixed by society through public opinion and by the State through laws relating to libel, slander, defamation, blasphemy, sedition, etc. The general principle followed in restricting freedom of speech is that expression of opinion should be within the limits of decency and not be contrary to the social order and public morality.

Libel and Slander. Aggression on the personal liberty of the individual is not merely physical. It may take the form of causing mental suffering. It is obvious that the law cannot protect us against this form of suffering, for both the proof of the suffering and the measurement of it are alike too indefinite for the law to take into account. Nevertheless, the law does protect one's reputation by providing against libel and slander.

The Right to Criticize Government. While in a sense the State is the creator and guarantor of liberty, liberty always demands a limitation of political authority. To be able to call to account one's rulers is one of the essential safeguards of liberty. But no state can allow law-breaking and, therefore, acts of violence and disloyalty come under the laws of sedition and treason. When the danger is indirect and remote, statesmanship requires toleration.

Liberty of the Press. The laws relating to the press in England and France represent two different types altogether. Which of the two systems—the English or the Continental—is superior is a debatable question. According to Lord Mansfield, in England the 'liberty of the press consists in printing without any previous licence, subject to the consequences of law'. There are no special courts for the trial of press offences. Newspapers are under no more special liabilities than private individuals.

In France and the Continental countries in general, however, there are not only special press laws, but also special tribunals for trying press offences. The French theory of government is that government should not only punish those guilty of exceeding the limits of freedom of speech, but that it should also guide public opinion in the proper channels. It is based on the principle that prevention is better than cure.

No such right as the liberty of the press has ever been recognized by law in England. Even though there is no censorship of the press, there are laws relating to sedition, treason, blasphemy and the lie, and these laws circumcribe the liberty of the press. Under these limitations it is generally assumed that freedom of discussion is ensured by jury trial. However true this assumption may be as regards the past it does not have the same validity at present owing to changed conditions. In earlier days the class from which jurymen were drawn had a tendency to give verdicts against the government. But today the majority of jurymen are not particularly noted for the love of freedom of thought or discussion. Hence it may be that the system which was once a guarantor of individual liberty may have to be abandoned unless it can be radically transformed.

3. Liberty of Action

Individual Action: Mill's Views. Mill's essay on *Liberty* is an eloquent plea not only for liberty of thought and expression. but also for liberty of action. Mill divides conduct into self-regarding and other-regarding conduct. Self-regarding conduct is, according to him, conduct which concerns the individual and the individual alone, while other-regarding conduct is conduct which affects others besides oneself. In the former sphere, Mill argues, there should be no interference of any kind. It is purely a matter of individual preference. In the latter sphere, however, the State may interfere by means of laws and society by means of public opinion, although there are cases in which it is not expedient for either to interfere. In other words, Mill argues for absolute liberty in one sphere and limited authority in the other.

This division of conduct is open to serious criticism. No weapon has been forged which is sharp enough to divide conduct into self-regarding and other-regarding spheres. If there is any truth at all in the organic theory of society, it is that individual good and social good are interdependent. Even acts which appear to be altogether personal in their bearing sooner or later touch society at large. According to Mill, extravagance, drunkenness, gambling, etc. are self-regarding acts, so long as they do not lead to the non-payment of debts, neglect of one's work, or laxity in the performance of one's duties to one's family. However sound such a distinction may be in theory, in practice it is bound to break down in most cases.

Notwithstanding these obvious defects, it must be said that Mill's distinction has a tremendous practical value as a rough and ready rule of action. As far as possible, society should regulate only such conduct as directly and definitely concerns others; but this is not an absolute law. In these days of unlimited bureaucracy and blind worship of the State, Mill's theory needs to be re-stated with all the force that it contains.

Collective Action. The liberty of collective action includes the right of public meeting, the right of association, and the right to boycott, strike and picket.

The Right of Public Meeting. In Belgium there is no interference with indoor meetings, which can be assembled even without permission from the police, open air meetings come under the police law. The English law recognizes no such distinction, and there is no law at all recognizing the right of public meeting. The rights of public meeting are derived from the right of private individuals to go where they please and say what they like, subject to the law of the land. As Dicey puts it: 'No better instance can indeed be found of the way in which in England the constitution is built upon individual rights than our rules as to public assemblies.'

The Right of Association. Like individuals, associations have their rights and duties. No association has a right to wage war against the State or secretly endeavour to overthrow it. Whatever local autonomy associations may possess, the final authority rests with the State. Associations which extend beyond the frontiers of any one State and which command the ready loyalty of its members, in course of time, lead to the undoing of the modern nation-State and to the foundation of an international

State. Whatever the future may have in store, it is clear that the modern State should safeguard the liberty of the individual against the ever-increasing authority of associations and should prevent associations from coming into conflict with one another. As far as powerful organizations like trade unions are concerned, it is the business of the State to be impartial as between unionists and nonunionists.

The Right to Boycott, Picket and Strike. Most modern States allow the practice of boycott within limits. It may be undertaken for social, economic or political reasons. It is primarily an offshoot of the modern industrial civilization. When boycott is resorted to by an individual or individuals it is not a serious matter: but when undertaken by an association on a large scale, it calls for social regulation. Ordinarily the State does not interfere with cases of boycott because of the inconvenience involved in 'imposing severe and dangerous restraints on the freedom of industrial intercourse' (*72* : *579*). In India, however, there was a curbing of the right of boycott when used, as a political weapon against Great Britain.

Most States have no objection to peaceful picketing. Peaceful picketing, however, can shade off into disorderly picketing, and any well-constituted State will seek to draw as careful a distinction as possible between the two. Persuasion is justifiable, but not molestation. It is not always easy to say whether lying down in front of a shop in order to prevent a person from buying articles prohibited by public sentiment is persuasion or molestation.

The right to strike has been recognized only in recent times. It is generally recognized that when all other means of settling the issue have failed, the only effective weapon left is the strike. Sympathetic strikes and the general strikes are variously considered. Laski upholds the right to a general strike. He believes that the general strike is in extreme cases, the only way of rousing the inert public to its responsibility towards the labouring masses. 'A government which meets the threat of a general strike is not entitled to public support merely because it meets the threat' (*49* : *133*).

However justifiable strikes may be in the industrial field, it is widely maintained that civil servants, policemen, postmen, railwaymen and others engaged in public services have no right to strike. Here again Laski holds a different view. 'The civil servant is not merely an employee of government; he is also a citizen' (*49* : *138*). Therefore, Laski argues that the community is not entitled, on any terms, to put its convenience before the worker's freedom. In order to diminish the number of strikes, Laski proposes that the State regulate the basic wages and basic hours of labour so as to make the conditions of each vocation materially and spiritually adequate, and to confer a large amount of self-government upon each vocation.

4. Liberty of Religious Opinion and Practice

This is essentially a modern right. Whatever conflict may have existed in the past between the Church and State, the present relation is generally one of friendly recognition not only between the Church and State, but also among the various religions and sects in the same State. We agree with Rousseau when he says: 'Tolerance should be given to all religions that tolerate others, so long as their dogmas contain nothing contrary to the duties of citizenship' (*67 : Bk. IV, Ch. VIII*).

India today claims to be a secular democratic State, where there is no state religion and where everybody is free "to profess, practise, and propagate" his religion. In actual fact, however, some over-zealous individuals and groups seek to restrict this freedom. Attempts are being made to give official patronage to the religious practices of one particular faith. A secular State should be free from all religious and sectarian preferences and prejudices.

The Right of Conscience. While the right to profess and practise any religious belief within limits of decency and public order is widely recognized, the right of conscience has not yet won such recognition. The individual can decide for himself in the light of his conscience what is good and what is bad; and with such freedom no power on earth can interfere. But the State can, and must, interfere with outward actions inasmuch as they affect the safety and welfare of the people at large.

Most modern States allow conscientious objectors to wars to refrain from fighting. This they do on grounds of expediency, and not on the general ground of allowing each citizen freedom to pursue the dictates of his conscience, wherever his conscience may lead him.

5. The 'Right' to Resist the State

This "right" closely follows the right of conscience and in discussing it we shall state the point of view contained in T. H. Green's *Principles of Political Obligation,* Section H. The individual must indeed judge for himself whether a given law is for the common good or not. Even if he judges it not to be, he ought as a general rule to obey it especially in a country where there is popular government, and where there are legal or constitutional ways of bringing about the desired change without much difficulty. Till bad laws are repealed the individual should conform to them for that is his social duty. But where there is no legal way of getting bad laws repealed, or where the government of the day is so corrupt that it deliberately prefers private interest to public good, or where it invades the sphere of personality, it may be the duty of the individual to resist. Even in such extreme cases, resistance is not a right but a painful duty.

Before embarking upon resistance, the good citizen, especially if he be a leader, should place before himself the following considerations:

(a) Have I exhausted all constitutional methods of bringing about the desired change?

(b) Are the people whom I call upon to resist keenly conscious of a flagrant wrong done to them, or am I simply exciting their passions? Is the wrong done by government of such a serious nature as to demand resistance? Do the mass of the people appreciate the grounds on which resistance is to be made?

(c) What about the character and temper of the people with whom I have to deal? Are they emotional and easily excitable, or are they reasonable and self-possessed persons who know where to stop? For once resistance is started, there is no knowing where it will stop.

(d) What about my own character? Have I divested myself of all egotism, and am I actuated by an unselfish desire for common good?

(e) What about the consequences? Is the second stage likely to be worse than the first? Will law-breaking lead to a condition of general anarchy?

Green realizes that times of revolution are not the times when questions like these are likely to be impartially considered. Times of revolution are times for action. Besides, in many cases, whether a certain line of action is for the common interest or not, only the sequel can tell. Further, repeated attempts and repeated failures may be necessary before a good cause succeeds. A majority has no right to resist simply because it is a majority. It may often be the duty of a helpless minority to resist, even when there are no chances of success.

The practical conclusion to which Green is led as a result of these considerations is that whichever side the individual may decide to take, he is sure to do more good than harm provided his character is sound and his motives are pure and unalloyed. On the whole, the best character is likely to produce the best result, notwithstanding appearances to the contrary.

As is to be expected, Laski takes a more radical view of the "right" to resist the State as seen in some of the following quotations: "My duty......to the State, is above all, my duty to the ideal the actual State must seek to serve" (*47 : 96*). "The State, clearly, has a right to self-protection, but it should be in obvious danger before it is given leave to act" (*47 : 123*). "Liberty is nothing if it is not the organized conscious power to resist in the last resort" (*74 : 142*). Laski places more emphasis on the individual conscience in resisting the State than does Green—to the point of "conditional anarchism".

PUNISHMENT

The Right of the State to Punish

Redress of grievance in early times rested with the aggrieved individual or the clan to which he belonged. But today it is universally recognized that it is the duty of State to punish offenders, although it may not be expedient for the State to punish every offender. Outwardly, punishment is a limitation of the liberty of the individual.

It has been said repeatedly that the right of the individual to free life depends upon his capacity for membership in society. A criminal displays an anti-social will, therefore, society is justified in interfering with his right to free life. In the interest of society it is necessary that the criminal tendencies in every one of its members be curbed. To neglect this will lead society back to primitive chaos and anarchy.

On the theoretical side, punishment has been justified from various points of view. Theories of punishment can be grouped under: (1) the retributive theory, (2) the preventive or deterrent theory, and (3) the reformatory theory.

The Retributive Theory. The first of these has an unfortunate name. It suggests the idea of retaliation or revenge, though historically it is the oldest conception of punishment. Among the ancient Israelies, the recognized practice was 'an eye for an eye, and a tooth for a tooth'. It represented a primitive standard of justice. No one was to take in turn more than what he had suffered.

Two natural perversions of the theory as brought out by Bosanquet, are: (1) the confusion of punishment with personal vengeance, and (2) the claim that punishment be equivalent to offence. While the feeling of vengeance can be understood in relation to the individual or even in relation to nations, it is inexplicable when applied to the relation between the individual and the State. Green begins his treatment of punishment by disclaiming the association of punishment with the idea of revenge.

As regards the second perversion, it must be noted that there is no way by which the State can measure either the pain of punishment or the moral guilt of the crime. Punishment cannot be adapted to factors which cannot be ascertained. As Green notes, even if the State could work out a proportion between the pain of punishment and the moral depravity of the crime, the result would be that the State would have to punish every case differently. This would mean an end to all general rules of punishment' (*20*: *191*).

The Deterrent Theory. This theory is expounded at great length by Green and Bosanquet. According to these writers, though a sound view of punishment should include all these elements—retribution, deterrence, and reformation, stress is laid by them more on the second than on the other two. According to this theory, the primary aim of punishment is to prevent other possible criminals from committing the same crime. In the words of Green, the object which the State has in punishing 'is not to cause pain to the criminal for the sake of causing it, nor chiefly for the sake of preventing him, individually, but to associate terror with the contemplation of the crime in the minds of others who might be tempted to commit it' (*29*: *192*). The purpose of punishment, in other words, is to provide society with an object lesson.

We are unable to agree with Green when he claims that the primary aim of punishment is the future prevention of crime by associating terror with it in the popular imagination. If we accept this view, it will mean that the seriousness of a crime is to be measured not by the amount of suffering it causes to society, but by the amount of terror which needs to be associated with it in order to bring about its prevention. It will mean, for instance, that if offences against property become more common than offences against life, the former class of offence will have to be dealt with more severely than the latter, which is clearly absurd. We measure the gravity of the crime by the gravity of the right violated.

The Reformatory Theory. This theory has been very prominent in recent discussions. According to it, the primary purpose of punishment is to restore the individual to society by bringing about lasting reform in his character so that he will become a self-respecting and independent member of society. Some of the advocates of this theory regard the criminal as a patient to be cured rather than as an anti-social individual to be punished. The followers of Lombroso claim that crime 'is a pathological phenomenon, a form of insanity, an inherited or acquired degeneracy'. According to this view, 'prisons must be superseded by hospitals, asylums, and reformatories'. Other advocates of this theory blame social conditions for the existence of crime and argue that crime would vanish almost completely if we could have more just social conditions.

To the extent to which the reformation theory is a reaction against the unrelenting and unreasonable spirit of vengeance of an earlier age, it is a sound theory. But, at the same time, it is subject to certain serious limitations. To regard all crimes as pathological phenomena is wide of the mark. Not all criminals are insane or feeble-minded. We distinguish cases of mental insanity from cases of crime proper. A criminally insane person is confined and given treatment, but a normal person is not, except as he requires rehabilitation. He is punished because he is a responsible person, accountable to society for his actions.

There is no doubt that for certain classes of crimes society is more responsible than is the criminal himself. But such people are abnormal, and we are not justified in basing a theory on exceptions. Most crimes arise out of an indisciplined will.

Reformation is certainly an important element in punishment but is not the only element. We agree with Bosanquet when he says that punishment must be deterrent for others as well as reformatory for the offender, and, therefore, in some degree painful. To place all emphasis on reformation is to disregard the interests of society. If reformation were the only sound theory, there would be no justification for the indefinite imprisonment of those criminals who are altogether incorrigible; for punishment in their case is useless.

James Seth uses the term 'discipline' to describe the view of punishment which we have adopted, a view which combines into an indissoluble unity the best elements of Retribution, Deterrence, and Reformation. Punishment must be firstly preventive of injustice. It should have no trace of vengeance or vindictiveness. The goal in punishing should be 'to bring home to a man such a sense of guilt as shall work in him a deep repentance for the evil past, a new obedience for the time to come' (*71 : 323*).

For ourselves we believe that punishment should punish, but this need not take the form of physical pain in every case. The deprivation of freedom to move about as one pleases and the social disgrace associated with imprisonment are enough of a punishment to a sensitive individual. But in all cases, punishment should aim at recreating the individual, in full co-operation with him, with the help of all the devices that society has at its disposal—knowledge of modern psychology and psychiatry, the teaching of skill or vocation, inculcation of a love of the family and a changed attitude towards society, and moral and religious instruction, which appeals to the highest in the individual.

C. THE RIGHT TO PROPERTY

The Importance of Property

The attachment of man to property is so great that many of our laws relating to property are much fuller, more precise, and more exacting than even laws relating to life and liberty. The idea of property lies at the root of the economic, legal, and political sciences. Economics for the most part is concerned with exchange values, involving property. Jurisprudence makes the idea of ownershop even more fundamental. Political science considers not only the protection of person but also that of property.

The long history of human civilization on its material side centres in the idea of property and ownership From the days when semi-civilised man began to claim possession of his tools, ornaments, and such other personal things to modern times when the thoughts and activities of the average man hinge on such matters as income, dividend, and inheritance, idea of property has been a supreme factor in the evolution of civilization. Modern civilization falls to pieces if we remove from it the institution of property. Individualism, nationalism, and imperialism—all embrace the concept of property.

The Evolution of Property. The instinct of acquisition is common to both animals and human beings. A dog becomes ferocious when anyone tries to deprive it of its bone. Wolves hunt in packs and share the prey among themselves and fight any intruder. Children collect all sorts of objects—birds' eggs, pebbles, bright-coloured rags, etc. Even fully grown people are not free from this instinct, though they may collect more worthy objects such as rare pictures, stamps and books. The attachment to private property and the enjoyment derived from it are much more intense than the care of public property and the enjoyment which it gives.

To prove that acquisition is instinctive with man is not a difficult task. What is much more important is to show whether any particular form of acquisition such as private property is more natural than other forms. Hocking argues that all of man's instincts are resolvable into 'the will to power' and when that is satisfied it is not necessary to satisfy every instinct as such. The 'will to power', however, in many cases may and will demand private property within limits.

Hobhouse makes a significant distinction between 'property for use' and 'property for power'. Historically viewed, it would seem that in very early times property was held for use and not for power. It is generally assumed that private property is comparatively recent in origin and that communal property was the universal order in early days. The investigations of Hobhouse, however, lead him to think that there was private property as regards personal belongings, but no universal rule as regards land. To use the words of Hobhouse himself, in early society land may be communal property, or it may be personal, or the two principles may be intermingled, but in any case it is held for use and not for power.

With the development of agriculture, however, appropriation of land must have become more and more exclusive and permanent. To begin with, ploughing was on a co-operative principle but in course of time the process of individualism led to the division of land into narrow strips for individual owners scattered over a vast area. The history of the evolution of property thus shows that it is not simply the 'creature of the State'. It had its beginnings even before the definite appearance of the State. It is instructive to note that the law of theft is earlier than the State. While, broadly speaking, the State did not create property, it has done much to protect and develop it. So far as the future of property is concerned, Jenks is right in saying that the State should refuse to protect or favour any appropriation without a due return to the community; it should restrain abuses of property and raise the necessary revenues of the State from those best able to contribute to it.

Characteristics of Property. Property may be defined as the control by man over things, or an appropriation of material objects recognized by society. It does not mean mere possession which confers only a delegated right. It calls for exclusive and permanent control over things. As Sidgwick observes, the right to property when used without qualification means 'the complete right of exclusive use, including the right to destroy and the right to alienate, but not necessarily the right of bequest' (*72 : 70*). He is right when he says that the right of excluding all others permanently from interference with a particular portion of matter is the most essential element in the right of property.

Like all other rights, the right to property requires the recognition of society to make it valid. A right is nothing if it does not have behind it the sanction of society. This is particularly true of property, which is largely the result of co-operative endeavour in our presentday society. The argument that property is a natural right carries with it no conviction any longer. The socialist goes to the other extreme and claims that property is entirely the creation of society. For ourselves, we believe that property has an important social aspect and that the right to property is relative and never absolute. Property is a form of regulated control and cannot be claimed against the well-being of society.

In modern society property has come to mean power. In one sense it spells freedom, inasmuch as it is a corollary of the right to free life. In another, it means the restriction of freedom, particularly the freedom of the toiling masses. It confers upon the owner almost unlimited power over the lives and destinies of human beings. Property which strictly meant control over things has come to mean control over persons through things. Hobhouse emphatically asserts that modern economic conditions have virtually abolished property *for use* for the great majority of people and have brought about the accumulation of vast masses of property *for power* in the hands of a relatively narrow class.

THEORIES OF PROPERTY

1. The Occupation Theory

In very early times when the sense of right and wrong was still undeveloped, the view which based property on first occupation marked a great improvement. In the case of newly discovered countries such as the United States and Australia, this view certainly had its value. Among political thinkers, it was advanced by some of the social contract writers with reference to private property rights in the state of nature.

However sound the occupation theory may have been in primitive times for providing a rough-and-ready measure of justice, in a settled state of society it is practically useless. As Willoughby observes, rights in a completely non-social and non-civil state are an impossibility.

2. The Legal Theory

According to this theory, 'the civil law is able to furnish not only the legal, but the ethical basis for the institution of private property' (*28 : 83*). Quoting approvingly from Cicero, Hobbes writes: 'Take away the civil law, and no man knows what is his own, and what is another man's'. His argument is: private property is a part of the political order; maintenance of this order is essential to human happiness, it is man's ethical duty to seek his own happiness; therefore he should accept the law of property along with the other laws of the State as binding upon him both morally and legally.

Like Hobbes, Bentham takes the legal view of property. As a utilitarian, he recognizes the general beneficence of the laws which secure men in the possession of their property. 'Property and law', he writes, 'are born together. Before laws were made there was no property; take away laws and property ceases'. Rousseau adopts the general view 'that it is only as an institution made secure by the protection of the political authority that the foundation of property is to be found in law' (*82 : 90*).

In evaluating this theory of property, it must be said that while law confers upon property-owners a secure sense of possession, it does not afford any clue as to the ultimate justification of property. Law is not our final standard. It protects only those who have property and the propertyless are practically excluded from acquiring any wealth. As Rousseau observes, under bad governments law 'serves only to maintain the poor in misery and the rich in his usurpation'.

3.. The Labour Theory

John Locke in the seventeenth century advanced what has come to be known as the Labour Theory of property, according to which, that with which a man mixes his labour is his. This right is limited by two considerations, that there should be 'enough and as good left in common for others', and that a man's right to the fruits of his labour is determined by his power to use. As regards the first, Locke himself realized there was not 'enough and as good' for others anywhere in the world except in the Americas of his day. The second consideration Locke intended to serve as a basis of individualism. But Karl Marx made it the basis of socialism, advancing the claim that 'the labourer has a right to the whole produce of his labour'. Both Marx and Locke forget that material goods with which a man can 'mix his labour' do not lie about unclaimed in the modern world. Nevertheless, the labour theory contains certain valuable elements: every man has a right to the opportunity of labour; he has a right to the fruits of his labour; and from the point of view of commonsense and morality, no one has a right to anything more than he can use in the best interests of himself and society at large.

While conceding these elements of value, it must be said at the same time that labour does not create all value. The social order is just as important for the peaceful production and disposal of property as labour itself. Most labour is social labour. Socialist advocates assume that labour alone is the standard of distributive justice.

4. The Individualistic Theory

The extreme individualistic position that each man should be left free to acquire all that he can in the open market and do what he pleases with that acquisition does not accord with the idea of social control which is gaining ascendancy everywhere nor with the organic conception of society. The law of supply and demand would no doubt furnish a true index to income if there were an equal opportunity for everybody, but it is a patent fact that there is little of such opportunity in modern society. We admit that in all ordinary cases there seems to be no other practical way of rewarding a man than that of letting him gain what he can in a fair and open market. But the conditions of such competition do not prevail in the modern world. In the words of Laski: 'The higgling of the market is the apotheosis of inequality' (*47* : *191*). The bargaining capacity of the labourer not being the same as that of the capitalist, the labourer often loses out in the economic race. This means, as Laski notes, poor health, undeveloped intelligence, miserable homes, and work in which the majority can find no source of human interest. To pay according to marginal worth is bourgeois justice. The communist slogan is that each should be paid according to his needs. Regarding the social control of property, Laski believes that a state which holds the lives of its citizens at its disposal is entitled in a far higher degree to hold their property at its disposal also. In other words, if conscription of men for war is justified, why not conscription of property for the sake of social justice?

5. The Socialistic Theory

Socialism in general is not opposed to private property, but is opposed to private capital. Unlike communism, it believes in rewarding the labourer in proportion to the *value* of his labour, and here it is in agreement with the individualistic theories of distribution. To Marx and his followers, labour alone has worth since labour alone, according to them, produces wealth. But socialists who differ from Marx understand the term 'worth' or 'desert' to mean 'socially useful labour' as determined by Government officials, while to individualists the same term means result or value as determined by the law of supply and demand. The substitution of the phrase 'socially useful labour' does not really help the socialist since it raises the difficult question of measuring a person's worth in concrete terms. Is assessment to be on the basis of time or piece work or in terms of the agreeableness or disagreeableness of the task, etc. ?

In spite of these criticisms, we have no hesitation in agreeing with Sidgwick that advance in the direction of the socialistic ideal by a *judicious* and *gradual* extension of governmental functions is not opposed to sound economic theory. A more equal distribution is, in a broad and general way, productive of an increase of happiness and is thus an aid to the good life of the community.

6. The Communistic Theory

On its economic side, communism attacks the institution of private property. It not only seeks to nationalise the means of production and distribution but also to bring consumption under State control. It is a radical attempt to confine property to use. Communists espouse the theory : from each according to his ability; and to each according to his need. The Russian constitution of 1936 substitutes the word 'work' for 'need'.

There is no doubt a *prima facie* justice in a social order in which members of the group can live together as members of a family, with no material goods which they can call exclusively their own. Nevertheless, it must be admitted that difficulties raised by communism are of too serious a nature to consider it a workable proposition. It may be just and reasonable in a community besieged on all sides or temporarily cut off from foreign supplies. It might be just also in a society which has reached its highest possible well-being. But we know of no such society today.

A further difficulty is that of fairly apportioning among its members the labour of the community. The usual answer which used to be given by Communists to the difficulty is that all should be made to work at every description of useful work. But as Mill says : 'All persons are not equally fit for all labour; and the same quantity of labour is an unequal burden on the weak and the strong'. Nowhere in society, except in a crude and barbarous state, backed by supernatural fears, can it be right to have a group of despotic officials who would assign men to their work and reward them according to their own sole pleasure and judgment. To quote Mill again: 'The chief criticism of communism and socialism is whether there would be any asylum left for individuality of character, whether public opinion would not be a tyrannical yoke'. Once more, communism calls for a cataclysmic change, for a sudden reconstruction of society resulting in serious dislocation of the present economic and social order. Justice, in one of its phases at least, means the fulfilment of expectations arising naturally out of the established order of society. Finally, the maxim 'From each according to his ability and to each according to his need' is more a moral injunction than a canon of legal justice. Neither individual needs nor capacities can be easily measured. Since real needs and real abilities vary, it seems unjust to reward all alike. Nevertheless, the idea of equality which the theory embodies is too precious to be slightingly rejected. That all should start on exactly equal terms is certainly inconsistent with any view of justice, but in the treatment of individuals justice demands absolute impartiality—what Rashdall calls equality of consideration. In the absence of any special reason for inequality, equality is the only right rule for distributive justice.

7. The Idealistic Theory

The idealists support private property on the basis of personality. Among German philosophers, Kant accepted the institution of private property and laid the foundation of the idealistic theory of property, according to which property is necessary for the realization of one's will. Hegel carried this view to its logical conclusion and said that property is 'the first reality of freedom'. It is a necessary condition for the fulfilment of personality. But the trouble is, as MacIver points out, "it is also an extension of the personality of one over the personalities of others". (*142 : 12*).

According to Green appropriation of property is an expression of will and is an effort of the individual to give reality to a conception of his own good which is at the same time a common good. Property does not rest on contract or on supreme force. It is an instrument of expression and satisfaction.

To Bosanquet, property is essential for the development of character, for without some property there can be no liberty, and without liberty there can be no proper development of character. Thus viewed, property becomes an ethical institution.

This way of interpreting the meaning of private property is not to be taken as a justification of the capitalistic system. Personality is not isolated and self-contained, but can exist only in fellowship. Therefore, a legitimate development of personality involves a legitimate development of fellowship. Applied to property it means that nobody can claim an absolute right to his possessions. Property is a trust and is relative to the common weal. Since all men have a right to develop a worthy human life, all should have in reasonable measure enough 'property to use'.

Further, as Rashdall points out, while we must regard property as essential to the development of character, we must not close our eyes to the bad effects upon character of the present almost unlimited competition and facility for accumulation. If, on the one hand, property is an aid to character, on the other it fosters intense selfishness.

The Case for and against Private Property Summed up

The possession of private property gives man a sense of security. The fate of the propertyless, landless man in the industrial society today is, in some ways, worse than that of the slave. Belonging to no one in particular who may take a proprietary interest in him, the freedom which he enjoys is not seldom the freedom to starve. Property enables a man to provide for the future and affords a sound basis for family independence.

A man of property is said to be one who has a stake in the country. As such he is not likely to be swept off his feet by every new-fangled doctrine leading to violent change. He is a man of deliberation and prudence.

Property promotes a sense of independence. A man who has means at his disposal does not need to accept the work which he does not desire. He can devote his means to the fostering of art, science and literature. He has direct access to the social heritage of the ages and is enabled to have a share 'in the life creative'.

According to Aristotle, private property gives its owner opportunity to be liberal and hospitable. As the idealists contend, it is an aid to the development of character and the expression of personality. The individualists are right when they claim that private property gives a man the most effective stimulus to exertion. It is the fear of want and starvation that often keeps a man's nose close to the grind-stone. Raleigh observes that 'there are many operations connected with the management of land and capital, which are most efficiently performed by private persons, working at their own risk and for their own advantage' (*64 : 111*). He further notes that it is a matter of common knowledge that officials are less active, less frugal, and less eager for improvement than private traders (*64*).

Further, private ownership gives the individual a deep sense of pleasure and satisfaction which no other form of ownership can give. The magic of private property can convert sand into gold. At least within limits, private property is a measure of a person's ability. It is an extension of the sound economic and moral principle, 'Tools to the man who can use them'.

While these and other arguments may be advanced in favour of private property, the case against it is even stronger. The socialists argue that many of the defects are inherent in the system and cannot be removed by mere education, enlightened public opinion, or social legislation.

There can be no gainsaying the fact that the institution of private property perpetuates the division between the rich and the poor. Inequality begets inequality and divergences breed divergences. While property gives its owner a sense of security, it often leads to luxury and indolence. Those who are freed from the necessity to labour do not generally devote their time and energy to creative effort. While a certain amount of private property may be necessary for the development of character, the same argument cannot be applied to unlimited private capital or to the control which it gives over the lives and destinies of human beings. There is no logical reason why a person should claim property in the instruments of production. To justify private property in all its aspects—unlimited wealth, bequest, inheritance, etc.—is as dishonest as it is unconvincing.

Further, private gain need not be the only incentive to labour. Lord Haldane remarks that the desire to distinguish himself in the service of the State is as potent a motive with the brain workers as the desire to amass a fortune. Plato was neither a fool nor a visionary when he claimed that the satisfaction derived from performing a congenial task or from rendering public service was a reward in itself.

It is generally admitted that ownership is justifiable only when it is correlated to service to society. But even the staunchest supporters of private property cannot but admit that, at best, there is only a very rough correlation between ownership and service. The law of supply and demand does not always work scientifically. At times it is freakish. As Laski argues, just because there is a demand for slaves in Abyssinia and for obscene literature all over the world, it does not mean that those who supply these needs are rendering great service to society.

Furthermore, if we trace the history of property, we find that property, particularly in land, has not had a respectable ancestry. Some of it is rooted in robbery.

Private property in modern times has certainly meant colossal production, increased prosperity and comfort, maximum utilization of the natural resources of the world, and marvellous growth of material civilization. But such progress in the material field has not meant equal progress in the moral and spiritual fields. Values have been vulgarized to a large extent, and there is a widespread tendency to worship power and wealth as such. Modern society is so organized as to whet the desire for personal gain. It teaches a man to compete with his fellow-men and scramble for power and wealth rather than to co-operate with him in achieving common ends. It makes effective citizenship for the masses practically impossible of attainment.

Laski sums up the case against the present order in these trenchant words : 'The present system is inadequate from whatever angle it is regarded. It is psychologically inadequate because, for most, by appealing mainly to the emotion of fear, it inhibits the exercise of those qualities which would enable them to live a full life. It is morally inadequate, in part because it confers rights upon those who have done nothing to earn them, in part because where such rights are related to effort, this in its turn has no proportionate relevancy to social value. It makes a part of the community parasitic upon the remainder; it deprives the rest of the opportunity to live ample lives. It is economically inadequate because it fails so to distribute the wealth it creates as to offer the necessary conditions of health and security to those who live by its processes. In the result, it has lost the allegiance of the vast majority of the people. Some regard it with hate; the majority regard it with indifference. It no longer infuses the State with that idea of purpose through which alone a State can prosper' (*47 : 216*).

PARTICULAR RIGHTS ACCORDING TO LASKI

Laski's conception of rights can be made more explicit by a reference to particular rights which he advocates. The particular rights advocated by him may be considered in three distinct aspects. In the first place, they indicate the position of the individual in relation to the civic community of which he is a member. Secondly, they require a discussion of the meaning of liberty and its compatibility with the notion of equality. Lastly, they also determine the character of political structure and institutions necessary for their adequate fulfilment.

He believes that the personality of the individual cannot be submerged in the corporation known as the state and so his rights are distincly claims which have validity even against the state. He regards liberty as the cumulative product of the system of rights that a state maintains and comes to the conclusion that liberty can thrive only in an atmosphere of equality. Finally, he envisages a political structure which at once combines the merits of Anglo-Saxon political democracy with the gains of the Soviet system in the sphere of economic opportunity.

Right to Work

In "A Grammar of Politics", Laski begins with the right to work as the first important right of a citizen. As he says, "The citizen has a right to work. He is born into a world where, if rationally organized, he can live only by the sweat of his brow. Society owes him the occasion to perform his function. To leave him without access to the means of existence is to deprive him of that which makes possible the realisation of personality" (*47 : 106*).

The right to work implies that there should be a system of national insurance against unemployment. It also implies that there should be some form of economic planning to utilize the productive labour of the whole populace. Similarly, the right to work implies the right to be paid an adequate wage which should be sufficient to guarantee a citizen the basic minimum of comforts. "The contrast in the modern world", says Laski, "between men and women who have never known a decent house, a decent meal, and clothing that barely protects them against the elements, and those who have never known what it is to have unsatiated a want that the possession of property can supply is an intolerable one" (*47 : 107*).

Laski thinks that the realization of this right is not impossible. If we cannot realize it in a capitalist system, he would suggest that we should adopt the socialist system. The example of Soviet Russia has proved how a socialist system guarantees full employment and an increasing standard of living for all citizens. As Laski says, "Either the State must control industrial power in the interest of its citizens, or industrial power will control the state in the interest of its possessors. The first need of the masses is to realize the right to adequate payment for their effort. The first principle, therefore, of industrial organisation is a system of institutions directed to that end" (*47 : 109*).

Lastly, the obvious corollary of the right to work is the right to leisure. The amount of work and leisure should be equitably distributed in the community. There should be no bifurcation of society into a working-class on the one hand and a leisured class on the other.

Right to Education

The second right which Laski emphasizes is the right to education. A citizen cannot contribute his best self to the community in the absence of proper intellectual training. Mere literacy is not enough. Every citizen must possess that basic knowledge of the arts and sciences which may make him conscious of his own place in the civilization.

"There is no more fundamental division in the modern state," says Laski, "than that between those who have the control of knowledge and those who lack such control. In the long run, power belongs to those who can formulate ond grasp ideas. Granted that such ability exists in a wide range of inequality, there is yet, once more, a minimum basis of education below which no one of average intelligence can be permitted to fall" (*47 : 114*). Even the advanced capitalist states have failed to guarantee this right of education to their citizens.

Both in England and America, some school-children break their education at the primary level. In Russia free and compulsory education is provided up to the high school level for every boy and girl and education up to the high school level is considered as the basic minimum for every citizen.

Right to Political Power

Thirdly, Laski emphasizes the right to political power which may be said to contain three derivative rights. In the first place, it implies the right to the franchise. Laski favours universal adult suffrage and considers Mill's test of education as irrelevant in determining the competence of a voter. Secondly, it implies the right to be elected to office without any discrimination on the basis of caste, creed, colour, or sex. Finally, it means selection of the members of bureaucracy on the basis of comparative merit. Laski is aware that the system of representative democracy as practised in capitalist countries is heavily biased in favour of the capitalist class and the right of the workers to exercise political power of any kind is reduced to the minimum. But he shows no preference for the Soviet system in this respect as he thinks that this right is non-existent there.

Right of Free Speech

In the fourth place, Laski is very much concerned with the right of free speech. In defending this freedom of the mind, he has shown himself as a true and ardent disciple of John Stuart Mill. He is opposed to persecution of opinion in any form. All opinions, whether in the sphere of religion or morality, science or art, literature or politics, should be allowed to be expressed freely and no penalty should be inflicted for a mere expression of opinion.

He is prepared to allow a fascist, a communist, a Catholic, a Jew, or a Negro the same amount of freedom to express his opinion as would be available to a law-abiding liberal and a constitutional socialist or a pious Quaker and a member of the Anglican Church in England. Laski is so enthusiastic in defending this freedom that he also severely condemns its usual curtailment in times of emergency such as a war. It should be noted that no state has so far found it advisable in practice to grant the right of free speech to its citizens in this absolute form. However, nobody can dispute its desirability as an ideal. Moreover, Laski points out that this freedom can be protected only by full judicial safeguards. He regards preventive detention as inconsistent with the right of free speech. The right of free speech implies the genuine independence of the judiciary and its complete separation from the executive.

Limited Right to Property

Finally, Laski has to say some controversial things about the right to property. "In the absence of other considerations", he says, "a political system in which rights are built upon property is one in which the propertyless man will have no rights" (*47 : 174*). In a capitalist society, there is no economic planning in the sphere of production and distribution. The community is divided into the 'haves' and 'have nots' which means that the distinguished few possess private property in abundance while the overwhelming majority is reduced to the position of landless and propertyless proletariat.

Laski is not against the right to property as such but is only opposed to its unequal distribution. But this reform in distribution can be brought about by changing the ownership of the means of production. In other words, the present capitalist system must give way to a new socialist system. The right to property will have meaning only when it is related to the value of one's effort and nobody is allowed to collect unearned income in the form of rent, interest or profits. It will have significance only when the exploitation of man by man and of class by class cease to take place.

Conception of Liberty

The conception of liberty is closely related to the conception of rights because the former is regarded by Laski as the product of the latter. Laski rejects the idealist view of liberty as a logical contradiction. Liberty does not consist in mere obedience to law as Hegel presupposes. Rousseau also failed to understand the meaning of liberty when he paradoxically stated that man is forced to be free by the command of the general will.

Laski defines liberty as absence of restraint in a moral sense. It implies a freedom for the individual to plan his life according to his own choice. It necessarily requires that some limitations be placed on the mode of operation of the political authority represented by the state. Finally, liberty means that law must provide adequate means of protecting the rights of the individual from the encroachment of the government.

Political Liberty and Economic Equality

Laski, however, does not believe that there is any antithesis between the concepts of liberty and equality. By equality, he does not mean the identity of reward but the creation of equal opportunity for all to develop their faculties. It denies the existence of special privileges for certain classes at the expense of others. Laski also implies by equality a certain levelling process in the economic sphere as well. Economic equality can be brought about only in a socialist society. Laski's attempt to harmonize the concepts of liberty and equality is the theoretical foundation of his democratic socialist philosophy.

Marx on the Nature of Civil Liberties

Speaking about liberties in a bourgeois constitution, Marx wrote in "The Eighteenth Brumaire" as follows, "The inevitable general staff of the liberties of 1848, personal liberty, liberty of the press, of speech, of association, of assembly, of education and religion etc., received a constitutional uniform which made them invulnerable. For each of these liberties is proclaimed as the absolute right of the French citizen but always with the marginal note that it is unlimited insofar as it is not limited by the "equal rights of others and the public safety" or by "laws" that are intended to mediate just this harmony of the individual liberties with one another and with the public safety......The constitution, therefore, constantly refers to future organic laws that are to put into effect those marginal notes and regulate the enjoyment of these unrestricted liberties in such manner that they will collide neither with one another nor with the public safety. And later, these organic laws were brought into being by the friends of order, and all those liberties were regulated in such a manner that the bourgeoisie in its enjoyment to them finds itself unhindered by the equal rights of other classes, where it forbids these liberties entirely to the others or permits enjoyment of them under conditions that are just so many police traps, this always happens solely in the interest of "public safety", that is, the safety of the bourgeoisie, as the constitution prescribes. In the sequel, both sides accordingly appeal with complete justice to the Constitution; the friends of order, who abrogated all these liberties, as well as the democrats, who demanded all of them. For each paragraph of the constitution contains its own antithesis, its own upper and lower houses, namely, liberty in the general phrase, abrogation of liberty in the marginal note. Thus, so long as the name of freedom was respected and only its actual realization prevented, of course, in a legal way the constitutional existence of liberty remained in fact, inviolate, however moral the blows dealt to its existence in actual life."

The Marxist Theory of Property

Marx, Engels and Lenin have adopted a historical approach to the question of property. The concept of property has not been the same in all ages and all societies. The primitive communes of the tribal society, for example, had no notion of private property. With changes in the mode of production, there emerged in history various forms of private property, which co-existed with certain forms of community property under slavery and feudalism. Private property became the dominant form of economic organisation with the arrival of commodity production under capitalism. Marx, Engels and Lenin hoped that the proletarian revolution would put an end to commodity production and also to private property in the means of production. Private property, they argued, would finally disappear even in the sphere of consumption with the establishment of a classless communist society.

Thus according to Marx, the various stages of development in the division of labour are just so many different forms of property i.e. the stage reached in the division of labour also determined the relation of individuals to one another with respect to the materials, tools and products of labour. The first form of property is communal property of the primitive tribes. It corresponds to an undeveloped stage of production in which a tribe lives by hunting, fishing, cattlebreeding, or at the last stage, by primitive agriculture. In the latter case a large area of cultivable land is pre-supposed. The division of labour at this stage is very elementary and is based on the natural division of labour occurring within the family. The social structure is just an extension of the family, with a matriarchal or patriarchal chief at the top, below them the members of the tribe and finally, a later stage, servants and slaves recruited from the defeated tribes in tribal warfare. The slavery i.e. property in human beings develops gradually with the increase of population, and with the growth of external relations through trade and war.

The second form of property is the communal and State property of classical Greece and Rome, which results from the union of several tribes into a polis, either by conquest or confederation of tribes, which is accompanied by slavery on a large scale. Alongside community property, personal and later real private property also develops and co-exists with community property for a long time. The citizens, who are mostly slave-owners, use the organised power of the polis to hold down the slave masses. Marx says : "The whole structure of society based on communal property, and with it the power of the people, decays in proportion as private and real property develops.....The class relation between citizens and slaves is now completely developed." (*179* : *102*). The third form is feudal property. Like tribal and communal property, it is also based on a community, but the directly producing class which confronts it is not, as in the case of the ancient community, the slaves but the enserfed small peasantry—half free and half-slave. The hierarchical system of land ownership, and the armed bodies of retainers with it, gave the feudal lords power over the serfs. The feudal structure of landownership had its counterpart in the towns in the form of guild property, the feudal organization of trades and the corresponding class division between guild-masters and labourers. Thus, in the feudal period, the chief forms of property consisted of landed property with serf labour chained to it and individual labour with small capital commanding the labour of the town craftsmen.

From the serfs of the Middle Ages, there emerged the chartered burghers of the earliest towns. From these town dwellers, the first elements of the bourgeois class, owning and acquiring private property through trade, banking and industry, were developed. The discovery of America, the capturing of the Indian and Chinese markets, the colonization of backward areas, trade with the colonies including the slave trade in African Negroes, the increase in production of commodities for the market etc. created the condition for the rapid growth of the wealth of the bourgeois class. Private capital of the merchant, banker, industrialist and plantation-owner became the dominant form of property in the modern society. As Marx points out, the bourgeois form of property is the product of a long course of development, of a series of revolutions in the modes of production and of exchange. What Marx emphasizes is the ***purely historical*** character of the existing forms of bourgeois property. They are not eternal and in no way rooted in human nature.

In a class-divided society private property arises as a result of the surplus value appropriated by the slave-owner, the feudal lord or the capitalist by denying the direct producers the full value of their labour. While the slave-owner or the feudal lord owns his slaves and serfs (under some limits) as his private property, the capitalist is able to exploit the wage workers by controlling the means and instruments of labour. The worker is forced to sell his labour power as a commodity in the market. The capitalist does not pay him the full value of his work and earns profits. These profits enable him to accumulate capital which gives him continuously increasing opportunities for further exploitation of the working-class. Marx predicted the evolution of competitive capitalist system into monopoly capitalism with increasing concentration of capital in a few big corporations.

The bourgeois forms of property were progressive in relation to earlier forms of property but in the existing stage of capitalist development, they have become fetters in the further development of the forces of production. The proletariat consisting of the landless and propertyless masses of workers will rebel against the existing class relations, which justify the bourgeois system of property, and bring about through a revolution a new system of socialized property. The Soviet Union, China and other socialist countries have already put an end to private ownership of property. The bulk of property in these countries is in the form of the state property or cooperative and collective property of the direct producers belonging to the working population

Unlike Laski, Marx does not offer a mere ethical critique of the bourgeois system of property and does not foresee any merit in reforms carried within the framework of the capitalist mode of production. The Marxist theory of property has a dialectical view of property relations. As Charles Bettelheim says, the creation of state sector under capitalism does not put an end to capitalist forms of private property, which dominate the economy in other fields and mould the state sector in the capitalist image. He is also doubtful whether the state sector controlled by the ruling bureaucratic class in the Soviet Union really represents the true Marxist concept of socialist property relations as the organised working class in the Soviet Union has hardly any influence on the decision-making process for the management of the nationalized industries in particular and the government in general.

Beltelheim's view of Soviet-style socialism that it had developed the features of bureaucratic capitalism has been partly demonstrated by the ease with which the communist regimes were overthrown. During the transition from statist socialism to entrepreneurial capitalism, the people have lost even those socio-economic rights which they were granted by the previous regimes. Millions of women lost their jobs, so today we have a party called "Women of Russia" with representation in the Duma to agitate for women rights. Right to work, medical aid, old age pensions etc., has been abolished. Civil liberties have been formally granted but with mafia capitalism dominating the scene, the common people have hardly benefitted from them. In Russia, the workers have not received their wages for months, even a year, but they are not able to protest in the absence of an organised trade union movement.

CHAPTER 17

LIBERTY AND EQUALITY

H.J. Laski : Liberty and Equality in Political and Economic Spheres

The conception of liberty and equality occupies an important place in Laski's political theory. He is interested in the problem of defining these concepts both as a liberal and as a socialist. As a liberal, he is a great champion of individual liberty in the political sphere. As a socialist, he is also a believer in the ideal of social and economic equality. Laski's conception of liberty and equality can be more fruitfully studied by considering the development of his ideas in this respect during the pluralist, Fabian socialist and pro-Marxist phases.

Concepts of Liberty and Equality During the Pluralistic Phase

Laski, who proclaimed himself to be a pragmatist during the early phase of his intellectual evolution, nevertheless based his entire analysis of rights, liberty and equality upon an idealistic theory of the end and purpose of the state. This view of rights does not conform to his general anti-idealistic and anti-statist position at this time. He said, "We start from the theoretic purpose we admit in the state. It aims at the development of the fullest capacities for good possessed by its members. That implies at once liberty and equality." (*129:85*). Laski believes that the dominant purpose of the contemporary state should be to secure for the humblest of its citizens "a certain minimum standard of civilized life" and to secure the economic conditions which can guarantee that standard. In particular, the state must ensure general equality of educational opportunity. As Laski puts it, "If the object of the state is to enrich the social heritage through the enlargement of individual personality, then individual personality, must be given that power of adequate expression which comes through knowledge to make its needs known." (*211:13*).

The concept of the state's purpose, according to Laski, implied both liberty and equality. He defined liberty as "the positive and equal opportunity of self-realisation." He agreed with T. H. Green's definition of freedom as a positive power of doing or enjoying something worth doing or enjoying, and that, too, something that we do or enjoy in common with others. Laski also supported Acton's conception of liberty as "the assurance that every man shall be protected in doing what he believes his duty against the influence of authority and majority, custom and opinion." (*122:55*).

The major defect of Laski's conception of freedom is its unreflective electicism and his disinclination to undertake a rigorous analysis of the idea of freedom. His notion of freedom combines Acton's individualistic view with Green's collectivistic interpretation. He does not accept the idealist definitions of the self, reality and rationality. His difficulty arises from the fact that he is using the idealist formula of "self-realization" after having rejected the entire philosophy upon which that formula is based. As a result, he defines freedom as the opportunity to express any of men's "creative impulses", without recognizing any ethical distinction between different kinds of impulses. He also affirms that the concrete meaning of liberty will vary from age to age and that in each different period of history the substance of liberty would be found in what the dominating social forces of that period greatly desire. In this interpretation, the individual loses his identity in the struggles and movements of competing social classes and groups. Coming to modern times, the real point which Laski intends to stress in his discussion of freedom is that the existing hierarchically organised social and political structure denies opportunities for self-expression to an overwhelming majority of the citizens. Laski feels that freedom defined in this manner is not compatible with the present system of property relations as it results in a concentration of economic and political power in the hands of a small minority.

Freedom thus implies equality. Liberty and equality are not contradictory but "different facets of the same ideal." He defines equality as the expression of "an opportunity for the full development of personality, while freedom was defined by him earlier as "the positive and equal opportunity for self-realization." Hence, it is obvious that liberty and equality are incapable of contradicting each other. As Herbert Deane says, "Indeed since they are identical, there can be no problem of how or to what extent they are or can be related; this is surely the neatest, if not the most satisfactory, solution ever devised for a perennial problem in political philosophy". *(191:46)*.

The major demand of our epoch is reduction of the existing inequalities in the social and economic sphere, "which challenges the legal rights established by prescription in the name of equality for which our institutions are unsuited." *(129:29)*. Every citizen should be guaranteed right to work and a minimum standard of material well-being. He maintains that his demand for equality does not necessarily involve the abolition of private property but it does mean its limitation in the context of social justice. Property, according to Laski, must be made conditional upon the performance of socially useful function.

Laski does not pay adequate attention to the fact that his proposals for control over distribution of incomes in order to realize equality require a strong, centralized state, which cannot conform to his self-proclaimed pluralistic ideal. Moreover, the drive towards social equality would obviously curtail the liberties of others who intend to satisfy their creative impulses by accumulating wealth. Herbert Deane says, "Clearly the relationship between liberty and equality.... is far more complicated than Laski's single identification assumes. While liberty and equality are not simple contradictories, they are not the same thing. In the actual situations that we confront, we may be forced to curtail some liberties of some people in order to achieve wider equality of opportunity, and we will have to impose certain restrictions on one group in order to safeguard or promote certain freedoms for another group. When we attempt to deal with these problems, we will not find Laski's over-simple formulations of the concepts of liberty and equality and of their interrelation particularly useful." (*191*:*48*).

At this stage, Laski supported the conception of natural rights. Like Locke, he had criticized the doctrine of unified state sovereignty and like him again he postulated certain natural rights of the individual. He called them fundamental notions of each age and deduced them from the general purposes for which the state existed, which could change in the course of historical evolution. Laski said: "When the realisation of these hopes is keenly enough felt to be essential to the realisation of the purpose of the state we have a political right. It is a right natural in the sense that the given conditions of society at the particular time require its recognition. It is not justified on grounds of history. It is not justified on grounds of any abstract or absolute ethic." (*122*:*43*).

Laski is here asserting that rights are the demands or needs of an individual or a group of individuals, which must be satisfied if the state wishes to fulfil its theoretic purpose. Citizens are likely to resist if any of these rights is denied to them. He rejects the idea of an absolute ethic from which rights could be logically inferred. The concept of the theoretic purpose of the state is quite vague. Hence, Laski sometimes falls back on the historical explanation of such rights, in spite of his earlier assertion that they are not to be justified on grounds of history. Deane, however, affirms: "A theory of natural rights based upon the appeal to historical experience can give no warrant for changes in the content of rights. The past cannot be called upon to validate new demands or new claims to rights; tradition offers little or no support for most of the rights listed by Laski as the conditions that are necessary to the fulfilment of the duties of citizenship—free speech, a living wage, an adequate education, a proper amount of leisure, and the power to combine for social effort." (*191*:*50*).

Liberty and Equality During the Fabian Socialist Phase

In the late twenties, a significant change took place in Laski's view of liberty. In the preface to the second edition of *A Grammar of Politics*, written in 1929, he said: "In 1925 I thought that liberty could most usefully be regarded as more than a negative thing. I am now convinced that this was a mistake and that the old view of it as an absence of restraint can alone safeguard the personality of the citizen." In 1930, Laski elaborated his new conception of freedom in *Liberty in the Modern State*. He stated at the outset: "I mean by liberty the absence of restraint upon the existence of those social conditions which, in modern civilization, are the necessary guarantees of individual happiness" *(49:1)*. This definition, despite its deceptive appearance, does not embody the traditional, negative view of freedom as the absence of restraint upon the actions of the individual. In substance, it is the same as Laski's earlier view that liberty is the system of social conditions which enable the citizen to achieve self-realization by satisfying his demands. Later, he accepts the traditional, negative conception of freedom in the main body of his work.

Laski now insisted that there was an antithesis between liberty and authority and that "a man's freedom is born of a limitation upon what his rulers may exact from him." *(49:14)*. He also admitted that, while freedom might be illusory if a man had no security of job or insufficient education to enable him to give expression to his needs, economic security could not be equated with liberty and deprivation of knowledge was not a denial of freedom, though it could be a denial of power to use liberty for great purposes. He further conceded that "equality is not the same thing as liberty.... men might be broadly equal under a despotism, and yet unfree." *(49:7)*. But he argued that freedom could not be realized in the absence of certain equalities. Only when the economic power of all citizens was nearly equal, an individual could succeed in seeking his own happiness in his own free way. He regarded freedom as "essentially an expression of an impalpable atmosphere among men. It is a sense that in the things we deem significant there is the opportunity of continuous initiative, the knowledge that we can, so to speak, experiment with ourselves, think differently or act differently, from our neighbours without danger to our happiness being involved therein." *(49:29)*.

While democracy was a precondition for the realization of freedom, Laski now argued that even under a democratic form of government, it was necessary to discover ways and means of protecting the minority against a majority which sought to invade its freedom. Liberty became in those circumstances an "inescapable doctrine of contingent anarchy." In the last analysis, liberty meant being loyal to one's own set of values and convictions.

Though Laski emphasizes the importance of liberty, he does not regard it as an end in itself but as a means for the achievement of a larger goal. The freedom desired by the workers is "the freedom to enjoy the things their rulers enjoy. The penumbra of freedom, its purpose and its life, is the movement for equality." *(49:218)*. He does not advocate identity of reward for individuals irrespective of their needs and functions but he does demand "identity of response to primary needs", and a guarantee of an economic minimum for every citizen. As Laski puts it, equality is "an insistence that there is no difference inherent in nature between the claims of men to happiness. It is therefore an argument that society will not construct barriers against those claims which weigh more heavily upon some than upon others." *(49:9)*. This means that approximate equality of personal incomes is necessary if political equality and justice are to be implemented. Differences in incomes or status are to be justified only in the context of the enhancement of general well-being. Laski rejects the communist plea for complete economic equality as this would be destructive of development of talents and skills.

Herbert Deane says: "Laski's concrete proposals for attaining 'economic equality' are a good deal less dramatic and revolutionary than his abstract discussions of the subject. The concept of a basic minimum income, adequately to satisfy the primary needs of the individual which has been a familiar ideal in the Western democracies since 1900, has, with the development of programmes of unemployment and old-age benefits, extensive free social services, and full-employment and minimum-wage legislation, to a large extent now been translated into practice, even in the United States, the last stronghold of *laissez-faire*.... Progressive taxation has curtailed the right of property to an extent that does not fall far short of Laski's suggestions.... Laski invites confusion by his constant use of the term 'economic equality' when he means equality of opportunity and a minimum income to provide for each citizen's basic needs. His rejection of the theory of equal incomes for all demonstrates that he is not, in fact, advocating equality. His principle that, above the basic minimum, each worker should be paid in proportion to his output is obviously not egalitarian." (*191:112*).

Laski's main thesis, as a Fabian socialist at this stage, is that inequality is an inherent feature of a market economy based on capitalism. Equality of his conception, therefore, can be realized only through.... gradual introduction of socialism. Deane's view that Laski was basing his analysis at this stage in terms of simple dichotomous concepts such as 'capitalism' and 'socialism' is not correct because Laski, unlike the Marxists, believed in the gradual transformation of capitalist society into a socialist society bringing about gradual approximation towards the ideal of equality through a mixed economy.

There is also no reason for finding fault with Laski's remarks that "any society, in fact, the fruits of whose economic operations are unequally distributed will be compelled to deny freedom as the law of its being." (*49:220*). The rise of fascism in Italy and Germany and erosion of civil liberties in other capitalist countries at any period of social stress is a clear testimony to correctness of Laski's view. Similarly, Laski is justified in saying that "discussion of inessentials can be ample and luxurious; discussion of essentials will always, where it touches the heart of existing social arrangements, meet at least with difficulty and probably with attack." (*49:224*). Laski believes that freedom is meaningful only to the small privileged class in capitalist society, that owns and controls the means of production. The masses, he thought, have been so brutalized by the sytsem of inequality that their only response to their degradation is apathy or impotent rage.

Laski says: "In an unequal society it is necessary to repress the expression of individuality. Every attempt at such expression is an attempt at the equalization of social conditions; it is an attempt to make myself count, an insistence on my claim, an assertion of my right to be treated as equal in that claim with other persons. To admit that I ought to have that freedom is to deny that the inequality upon which society rests is valid. And, accordingly, every sort of devious method, conscious and unconscious, is adopted to prevent my assertiveness." *(125:221)*.

Herbert Deane, however, disagrees with Laski's above formulation. According to him the inequalities which at present exist in the Western capitalist countries do not crush the growth of individuality. On the contrary, opportunities for individual self-expression are maximum in democratic societies based on market economy. A rigidly egalitarian society, Deane argues, is destructive of individual initiative and vitality. The so-called unequal societies of the United States and Western Europe, in fact, provide for a great deal of social mobility, advance in industrial technique, higher per capita income and a large degree of political freedom.

Liberty and Equality During the Pro-Marxist Phase

The concept of liberty was not one of Laski's chief concerns during the pro-Marxist phase of his thought. His continued criticism of Hegel's view of freedom based on idealist premises implied that he still adhered to the definition of freedom as the absence of restraint. But he also argued that a socialist society, which has abolished private property, can alone implement real freedom. But this commitment to Marxian conception of freedom is not consistent with his Hobbesian view of liberty, which he has failed to renounce. In a capitalist society, Laski now argues, the liberty that exists under a democratic régime is purely formal and lacking in substance except for the property-owning minority. The bourgeois liberty of capitalist democracy, he says, means that the government must not interfere with the privileges enjoyed by this class. He observes: "The liberty of capitalist democracy is essentially an aristocratic conception. It is an attempt to deny the right of government to invade certain spheres of behaviour in which the dominant members of society wish to be left alone." *(126:202)*.

The contrast that Laski draws between the political equality characteristic of a democratic system and the inequality and despotism implied in a capitalist economy is intelligible and significant, as Deane argues, only on the assumption that political liberties of the average citizen are far more substantial than he consciously recognizes. Laski believes that the ethos of capitalism is "an effort to maximise material well-being for the owners of capital; their liberty means that restraints will not, so far as possible, be laid upon the conditions of that maximisation." (*132* : *204*). Capitalist democracy is "the prisoner of the end it had been destined to serve. For the men who served it did not believe in its claims apart from that end.... the liberty they cherished was, in sober fact, a freedom denied to the overwhelming majority of their fellow-citizens." These assertions, according to Deane, ignore the important checks imposed upon capitalist enterprise and profit making in the Western democracies during the last fifty years. The rise of labour and socialist parties to power in a number of capitalist countries also shows, according to Deane, that the capitalist class may remain faithful to the democratic system and peaceful constitutional processes even when its class interests are adversely affected.

Criticizing Laski's approach to liberty and equality at this stage, Deane remarks: "The confusions and contradictions that mark Laski's analysis arise from his use of the terms 'capitalist democracy' and 'liberalism' to cover three distinct periods and their different political and social philosophies—the period of *laissez-faire* liberalism and the negative state, the new liberalism and the positive state that developed in England after the 1870's and, finally, the period of what Laski calls 'the decline of capitalism' and the movement towards Fascism after 1929. Because he makes no distinction between these three phases of 'capitalist democracy', Laski alternates between the position that real liberties are confined to the few who own property and the thesis that the present capitalist crisis inevitably means the destruction of the significant political liberties as well as the economic and social gains of the positive state." *(191:180)*.

During the pro-Marxist phase, Laski was inclined to sacrifice, at least temporarily, the ideal of liberty for the achievement of socialism. Only in a classless society, we can realize the ideal of equality and only when equality is established. we can give liberty positive content for the masses and create a true democratic society. Laski believes that there is a "constant drive of human impulse towards the establishment of greater equality in society.... Men take the view that differences in the state require justifications; their exclusion from same privilege always leads to a demand for either its abolition or its extension to themselves." *(50:58)*. By equality, Laski means primarily its economic dimension i.e. equality of income and property. He believes that other inequalities as those of influence, status and power are derived from the basic inequality of material circumstances. Laski also argues that an egalitarian social structure is quite consistent with the operation of a modern industrial system. Finally, the most crucial assumption in this respect is that the elimination of private property is essential if economic inequalities are to be eradicated and that the working-class is now conscious that it is the capitalist system, which prevents the workers from getting the equal share in the fruits of social production.

Criticizing Laski's assumptions, Deane points out: "His discussion of equality involves several assumptions, all unproven and some, at least, highly dubious. He offers no evidence to demonstrate the existence of universal impulse towards equality.... In fact most men in any democratic society do not desire the abolition of differences in rewards and in the privileges associated with status." *(191:187)*. Regarding his second assumption that economic inequality is the root of all other inequalities, Deane observes: "While we have not yet observed a classless society in operation, we see in societies that have eliminated the system of private property no sign of the disappearance of marked differences in power, status, and opportunities for education.... And the attempt to achieve economic equality by revolution and dictatorship, advocated by the Bolsheviks and accepted as virtually inevitable by Laski, is certain to intensify differences in the political power of individuals and groups within the society." (*191:188*).

As regards the compatibility of economic equality with the working of a modern industrial society, Deane further says, "The experience of such different societies as the Soviet Union and the United States indicates that the gradations of payment necessary to maintain output and to obtain the proper number of skilled workers at each level of the complex industrial hierarchy render impracticable any rigidly egalitarian system of reward.... Soviet experience thus fails to support Laski's assertion that a state founded on equality can not only succeed in operating a modern system of production, but also achieve a development of its productive capacity that far surpasses that of a competitive and unequal society." (*191:190*).

Regarding Laski's last assumption that elimination of private ownership is essential for removal of economic inequalities and that the working-class is consciously aiming at this goal. Herbert Deane makes the following judgement: "But many workers in capitalist society do not accept the conclusion that socialism is the proper remedy for such inequalities as they resent ....they have used the power of their unions and their ability to influence governmental action in order to increase their share in national income, while accepting the basic framework of the capitalist system." (*191:189*).

In his discussion of liberty during Second World War, Laski abandoned the view that freedom meant the absence of restraint. In its place, he used a confused mixture of idealist and Marxian conceptions of liberty. He now admitted that liberty is not necessarily self-determination as opposed to the determination of one's actions by the state. He uses the Marxian phrase 'recognition of necessity' as well as Green's term 'self-realization' to formulate his own concept of freedom. It is obvious that Laski now has a very low opinion of the liberties that exist in capitalist democracy. They operated on a narrowly political plane and its benefits are monopolized by a small class. Occasionally, he admitted that the social services provided by the modern state have meant striking additions to the positive freedom of the citizens but his general position is that there has been a marked decline in the content of freedom during the contemporary era of crisis-ridden capitalism. According to him, liberty is a function of "the security men feel about the foundations of the social order; and that security in its turn, is a function of the capacity for economic expansion of that social order." (*212:162*).

Laski now defines equality as "the admission of a plane of general satisfactions in social organization where the minimum satisfaction of equal needs is at a level which permits the increasing fulfilment of personality." (*131:208*). To make freedom real for the common people, we must establish an equal society based on social ownership of the means of production, where the goods of civilization are open to all, not merely to the owners of capital. We must build this equal society as early as possible or abandon the democratic process because democracy cannot continue under the impact of that "class war which is the normal condition between citizens who have the security that property gives and citizens who have nothing but their labour-power to sell." *(128:89)*.

In order to realize this equality, Laski suggests that we must move from the negative conception of liberty towards a new, positive definition of freedom. He says that "every society is built upon a system of postulates the continuing life of which its members must agree to respect; and their freedom is only available within the limits of that respect. *(131:382)*. This is Laski's translation of the Marxist view that freedom is a recognition of necessity. Laski further observes: "If the introduction of planning into a capitalist democracy is to be compatible with the maintenance of freedom it must have behind it the general consent of citizens. . . . When a society accepts the decision to plan it is, thereby, providing itself with an overriding purpose to the general principles of which the mass of citizens must conform. Their freedom becomes a function of its necessities; the limits of their permissible initiative are set by the logic it implies." *(131:383)*.

Laski also insists that "citizens who participate in a great end about which they are agreed find a freedom in its service which makes right and duty reciprocal terms." *(131:396)*. He cites the examples of the Soviet Union since the Revolution and of Britain during the anti-Nazi war to prove that men find freedom in the service of a great purpose. Laski observes that "the Bolshevists regarded freedom as the positive organization of opportunities for ordinary people to exercise a creative initiative" *(128:57)*. Hence, the sense of a capacity for growth, which enables its possessor to affirm his or her personality, is the very secret of freedom.

Ralph Miliband says, "Historically, labour and socialist movements have been the main driving force for the extension of the democratic features of capitalist societies; and it is also they who, from very necessity, have been the strongest defenders of civil and political liberties against infringements primarily directed at them..... But their performance of this role has been very substantially and very negatively affected by the constantly more pronounced ideological and political integration of social democratic leaers into the framework of capitalism." Soviet-style test socialist societies have also failed to meet the test pescribed by Laski and democratic transition has yet to prove its capabilities.

CHAPTER 18

THE CONCEPT OF EQUALITY

R. H. Tawney : The Right to Equality

Probably, the last important work written exclusively on the theme of equality was by R. H. Tawney, who published his book entitled *Equality* in 1931. He was a close friend of Sidney and Beatrice Webb and like them a democratic socialist and a leading member of the British Labour Party.

As we all know, Tawney was the teacher of the generation of Attlee, Stafford Cripps, Herbert Morrison, Cole and Laski. His work on Equality, which he himself described as a 'sermon on the mount', still remains a classic of socialist literature. Since then, no one has written another sermon on the mount though more than fifty years have passed after Tawney published the first edition of his memorable work on equality.

Any comprehensive and serious debate on equality raises three important questions. The first question relates to the social ideals of equality. What forms of equality are desirable and what forms of inequality are undesirable and on what grounds? The second question is fact-oriented. What are the social realities of inequality? What are the findings of the empirical research on distribution of incomes in contemporary societies? The last question is related to the impact and bearing which the answer to the second question will have on the answer to the, first question. How does social reality affect social ideals about equality? What is the most desirable *essence* of equality in the light of the actual and what appears possible?

The ideal of equality, as Tawney points out, has always been central to the socialist tradition. In assessing the validity of the socialist idea of equality the three questions raised above need convincing answers. First, why is greater equality in the conditions of life desirable? Secondly, how unequal are such conditions in contemporary industrial societies, capitalist as well as non-capitalist, and what explains these inequalities? Thirdly, are these inequalities ineradicable, or eradicable only at an unacceptable cost? Concerning the first question, which is philosophical in nature, Tawney has suggested a reformulated Kantian ethical basis for the social, political and economic equalities that socialists like him have traditionally wanted to establish. Regarding the second question, which is sociological in nature, he refers to historical and contemporary facts about actual inequalities and the range of possible explanations for them. With regard to the third question, Tawney has examined the arguments generally advanced by advocates of inequality indicating logical fallacies involved in them.

The Social Ideals of Equality

Talking about the religion of inequality, R. H. Tawney says that the British people consider hierarchy as natural. They may disapprove destitution but turn a blind eye on privilege. The inequalities survive, as Tawney puts it, not merely because the rich exploit the poor under capitalism, but also because too many of the poor admire the rich and legitimise the cult of inequality. The ideal of equality may be declared to be ridiculous in two different ways by those who subscribe to the religion of inequality. First, it may be interpreted as based on the principle of absolute and unconditional equality—treat everyone equally in every respect. In fact, few serious thinkers, let alone socialists, have advocated this simplistic view. Secondly, it may be interpreted as based on the empty formal principle —treat people equally unless there are relevant or sufficient reasons for treating them unequally. Tawney has tried to put substance into this formula in two ways: positively, by advancing a set of reasons for treating people equally; and negatively, by rejecting certain reasons as justifications for treating people unequally.

Historically, the struggle for equality has taken the form of attacking specific inequalities and their alleged justifications. Inequalities of privilege and power in the legal, social, political and economic spheres have been attacked as unjustifiable because they are capricious, irrational and arbitrary in nature. It has been suggested that all inequalities are irrational unless they satisfy the criteria of merit, need or social benefit. On such a basis it would be hard to justify the present extreme inequality of inherited wealth in any capitalist society. Steven Lukes observes, "But, quite apart from the difficulty of interpreting these criteria, especially the last, such an approach always presupposes a view of what is justifiable, that is, what are relevant and sufficient sorts of reasons for unequal treatment, and over this individuals, classes and cultures conflict." (*209:75*).

Another influential argument for treating people equally and for according them equal income and wealth is the utilitarian argument for attaining the maximum aggregate satisfaction on the assumption of diminishing marginal utility. As Tawney says, unequal distribution of a given amount of purchasing power among a given number of people is likely to be a wasteful distribution from the point of view of economic welfare. In economic terms this means that people with low incomes value extra income more than people with high incomes. If we want to maximise the aggregate satisfaction of the nation, the best way to distribute the national income is to give every citizen an equal share. Income disparities, except those based on variations in need, will always reduce overall satisfaction, because individuals with low incomes will lose more than individuals with high incomes gain. But this utilitarian argument may be challenged. There is no reason to assume that a given amount of purchasing power yields equal utility for everyone and that it diminishes as income or wealth increases.

In any case, a socialist like Tawney has not rested his case for an egalitarian social order on the utilitarian basis alone. There is an alternative tradition of thought on the subject of equality, of which Rousseau is the classical exponent and Rawls the major contemporary advocate. R. H. Tawney, with some reservations, belongs to the same tradition and offers an interpretation of equality which is inspired by deeper values than the utilitarian. Tawney's interpretation of equality is based on the assumption that all human beings have certain basic characteristics which entitle them to be considered or respected as equals, and this is seen as implying practical policies for establishing substantial social, political and economic equality.

What, then, are the basic features of human beings which command equal consideration or respect. For Christians the answer is that they are all children of God, for Kant they are rational wills and thus members of the Kingdom of Ends, for classical liberals that they share common natural rights, for many socialists and anarchists that they share a common human essence and dignity. These transcendental answers, whether religious or secular, do not impress Tawney, who defends the principle of equality in the context of satisfaction of human needs and realization of human capacities. He says that there are basic human needs such as the means to life and health without which men and women could not function in a recognizably human manner. On the other hand, there are certain basic capacities of human beings, whose realization is essential to their enjoyment of freedom. It may be objected that since people may have unequal needs and capacities, they should be accorded unequal respect and consideration. The answer to this objection, which Tawney gives, is that it is the existence of the needs and capacities, not the degree of their satisfaction or realization, that elicits the equal respect which precisely consists in doing all that is necessary and possible to satisfy their basic needs and to promote and develop their basic capacities.

The principle of equal respect for needs contradicts all humanly alterable economic and social arrangements which discriminate between individuals' access to the means of sustenance and health. But need is a concept to which appeal cannot be made beyond this basic, if rising, minimum level. Beyond that point, it becomes a question of individuals' entitlement to the means of realizing certain basic capacities. There is, first, the capacity of human beings to think and act with relative autonomy. Secondly, human beings have the capacity to develop involvements and engage in relationships to which they attach value. Thirdly, each man has the capacity to develop in himself some characteristic human excellence—whether intellectual, artistic or moral, theoretical or practical, personal or social.

Tawney has argued that these three characteristics of persons entitle them to equal respect and consideration. This involves treating them as autonomous, as requiring a free space for the pursuit of valued activities, and as capable of self-development. It points towards as society with substantially reduced inequalities, both of material and symbolic rewards and of political power. We fail to respect someone by denying his autonomy not only when we control or dominate his will, but also when we put unreasonable restrictions on the range of alternatives between which he can exercise his choice. Such control can be social, economic or political arising from the family status, the work situation, educational and employment opportunities or the relation between the citizen and the state.

There is an intimate relation between the concept of man's autonomy and his freedom to choose on the one hand and the principle of social, economic and political equality on the other. R. H. Tawney observes, "Freedom for the strong is oppression for the weak; and oppression.... is not less oppressive when its strength is derived from superior wealth, than when it relies on a preponderance of physical force. Hence, when steps to diminish inequality are denounced as infringements of freedom, the first question to be answered is one not always asked. It is : freedom for whom ? There is no such thing as freedom in the abstract, divorced from the realities of a particular time and place. Whatever else the conception may imply, it involves a power of choice between alternatives, a choice which is real, not merely nominal, between alternatives which exist in fact, not only on paper. Because a man is most a man when he thinks, wills and acts, freedom deserves the sublime things which poets have said about it; but, as part of the prose of everyday life, it is quite practical and realistic.... The second question which arises, therefore, is not less simple. It is whether the range of alternatives open to ordinary men, and the capacity of the latter to follow their own preferences in choosing between them, have or have not been increased by measures correcting inequalities or neutralizing their effects. If an affirmative reply be given, liberty and equality can live as friends, if a negative one, they are condemned to be foes." (*76:259*).

The Essence of Equality

If we interpret correctly, the essential meaning of equality is inseparable from the notion of human freedom and dignity. We violate the principle of equality and human dignity when we fail to treat a person as a self from which actions and choices emanate, when we view him as merely the bearer of a title or the performer of a role, or merely as a means to securing a certain end. We deny a person equality if we define his human essence in terms of what Tawney called "tedius vulgarities of income and social position" (*76:153*). This denial of equality persuaded him to recommend universal and equal political participation so that the slavish feelings that shrink up the human soul in the presence of an imagined superior will disappear. Agreeing with William Morris, he wrote of socialism as a condition of equality in which a man is neither known by his dwelling, nor by his office, nor by his property but only by his human qualities. Tawney wanted an egalitarian society in which there is no boss-class, no menial-class, no beggars, no prostitutes, no lawyers, no priests, no boot-licking, no cap-touching and no undue respect for money and position.

Distinguishing between different connotations of the concept of equality, R. H. Tawney says, "It is obvious that the word 'Equality' possesses more than one meaning, and that the controversies surrounding it arise partly, at least, because the same term is employed with different connotations. Thus it may either purport to state a fact, or convey the expression of an ethical judgement. On the one hand, it may affirm that men are on the whole, very similar in their natural endowments of character and intelligence. On the other hand, it may assert that, while they differ profoundly as individuals in capacity and character, they are equally entitled as human beings to consideration and respect, and that the well-being of a society is likely to be increased if it so plans its organisation that, whether their powers are great or small, all its members may be equally enabled to make the best of such powers as they possess" *(76:35)*.

Respecting the autonomous character of human personality points towards what Tawney calls a 'single status society' which rejects the ideal of a stable hierarchy. He observes, "It is the fact, that, in spite of their varying characters and capacities, men possess in their common humanity a quality which is worth cultivating, and that a community is most likely to make the most of that quality if it takes it into account in planning its economic organisation—if it stresses lightly differences of wealth and birth and social position, and establishes on firm foundations institutions which meet common needs, and are a source of common enlightenment and common enjoyment." What keeps a stable hierarchy entrenched is the idea of its necessity, that it is somehow inevitable for the functional success of a social and economic order. The people's reflective consciousness must undermine this legitimising belief in inequality. Tawney points out, "A society which is convinced that inequality is an evil need not be alarmed because the evil is one which cannot wholly be subdued. In recognizing the poison it will have armed itself with an antidote. It will have deprived inequality of its sting by stripping it of its esteem" *(76:47)*.

Secondly, one obviously fails to implement equal respect for persons if there is any external interference with their valued activities and relationships. Liberals characteristically attack such violations of equality or equal liberty, especially in totalitarian societies, when they take the form of bureaucratic tyranny, single party dictatorship, racial or religious persecution or social pressures to conformity. But Tawney points out that interference with valued activities and relationships may occur in other ways such as through class discrimination, remedial economic deprivation and insecurity and the hard discipline of the market where formally equal economic freedom is unequally operative because of unequal but equalizable conditions and opportunities. Tawney remarks, "A society which values equality will attach a high degree of significance to differences of charatcer and intelligence, and a low degree of significance to economic and social differences between different groups. It will endeavour, in shaping its policy and organisation, to encourage the former and to neutralize and suppress the latter, and will regard it as vulgar and childish to emphasize them, when unfortunately, they still exist. A society which is in love with inequality will take such differences seriously, and will allow them to overflow from the regions, such as economic life, where they have their origin, and from which it is difficult wholly to expel them, till they become a kind of morbid obsession, colouring the whole world of social relations" *(76:49)*.

Lastly, one also fails to recognize the principle of equality and equal freedom if one limits a person's opportunities to realize his capacities of self-development. It is the systematic and cumulative denial of such opportunities to the less favoured citizens of stratified societies, both capitalist and non-capitalist, that probably constitutes the strongest argument against the structural inequalities they maintain. This argument really has two parts. The first part is simply an argument against discrimination, against the failure to bring the means of a good life within the reach of all citizens. Tawney says, "It is not surprising that the temper which had as one of its manifestations humanism, or the perfecting of the individual, should have had as another manifestation an outlook on society which sympathized with the attempt to bring the means of good life within the reach of all, and regarded the subordination of class to class, and the arrogance and servility which such subordination naturally produces, as barbarian or gothic, as the mark of peoples which were incompletely civilized" *(76:87)*.

Thus the main argument against a discriminatory educational system is not that it creates social inequality but rather that it blocks the self-development of the less-favoured and thereby fails to make some work more challenging requiring greater skill, talent or responsibility, it is a denial of human respect to confine workers within menial, onesided and tedious tasks creating a feeling of alienation in them. Again, when workers are denied real participation in the formulation of decisions affecting them, they are thereby denied the right to develop the human excellence of active self-government celebrated by classical democratic theory and contemporary socialism. The second part of the argument is that structured inequalities provide an unfavourable environment for the self-development of ordinary people. Mathew Arnold claimed that for the majority of common people, living in a society of equals tends in general to make a man's spirits expand, and his faculties work easily and actively, while to live in a society of superiors, though occasionally good for learning discipline, generally tends to tame the spirits and makes the play of the faculties less active and secure. Tawney made the same assumption, arguing that "individual differences, which are a source of social energy, are more likely to ripen and find expression if social inequalities are, as far as practicable, diminished" *(76:49)* His case was that establishing the largest possible measure of equality of environment, circumstance and opportunity was a precondition for ensuring that the diversities of gifts, skills and talents may develop.

Tawney has drawn a distinction between his notion of equality of consideration and respect and that of 'equality of opportunity', as normally advocated by some socialists and non-socialists alike. The latter principle is *not* generally taken to refer to equality of opportunity to develop individual capacities or gifts, but rather equality of opportunity to achieve scarce social rewards. Thus understood, it contradicts the principle of equal respect, since it focuses attention on forms of differentiation and grading which carry status and prestige. It perpetuates those very structures of inequality, characterized by competition and emulation, which Tawney's doctrine of equality of respect would like to abolish. Showing the limitation of the notion of 'equality of opportunity', Tawney remarks, "So the middle classes acquiesced in sharp distinctions of wealth and power, provided that, as individuals, they were free to scale the heights. The upper classes were glad to be reinforced by individuals of means and influence, who sprang from below, provided that, as a class they remained on their eminence.... What neither understood nor admired, what, indeed, with rare exceptions, they feared and despised, were the aspirations that found expression, not merely in the claim for an open road to individual advancement, but in collective movements to narrow the space between valley and peak" (*76:107*).

An opposite view to that of Tawney is held by C. A. R. Crosland who **says that there is nothing improper in either a high continuous status ladder** or even a distinct class stratification if opportunities for attaining the highest status or class position are equal at the starting point. By contrast, Tawney as an egalitarian socialist focuses on equalizing the rewards and privileges attached to different positions, not on widening the competition for them. In fact, both the notions are often combined in socialist theory and practice. Though there are well-known arguments to support the view that unequal rewards, together with equal opportunity to achieve them, have essential social and economic functions, they contradict the social, political and economic assumptions of Tawney's doctrine of equality of respect which points towards greater equality in the conditions of life i.e. of status, income, wealth and political power.

The Social Realities of Inequality

Contemporary industrial societies, whether capitalist or state socialist, still permit structured inequalities in relation to educational opportunity, social services, economic security, income and political power. Three myths which are widely propagated are belied by evidence. The first is that of convergence according to the logic of industrial development. There is actually no continuing trend towards great overall economic equality or towards the congruence of middle incomes and middle class life style and status. The second myth is that 'affluence' in capitalist societies has eroded inequalities of income, wealth and security of life. It is not true that the power of private capital has been tamed by 'managerial revolution', nationalization of some banks or industries and pluralistic competition among different sections of the ruling elite. The third myth is the official communist interpretation of state socialist societies which acknowledges the existence of non-antagonistic classes and the stratum of intelligentsia and the existence of inequalities of income,-consumption goods, education etc. but maintains that these inequalities are in process of steady decline and denies that there is a structured hierarchy of status and political power.

According to Tawney, the occupational structure in a capitalist society constitutes the basis of the principal dimensions of social stratification and the connecting link between different institutions and spheres of social life. The hierarchy of economic classes has its roots in the occupational structure and the same is true of the hierarchy of political power and authority as government has become a full-time vocation. Of the inequalities characteristic of capitalism, the most obvious is that of wealth. It has been justly said of capitalism that capitalism produces extremely rich people with a great deal of capital, which means high income, luxury, comforts, security, leisure, prestige and political power. The most recent studies of income distribution in advanced capitalist societies show that the top 5 per cent of wealth holders own between one-half and three-quarters of the total persosonal wealth in the country. Its impact is accentuated by the fact that the very rich tend to hold their wealth in the form of company shares and real property yielding a higher return than the assets owned by small savers. The concentration of share ownership is even greater than that in the distribution of wealth as a whole, which is significant since shares convey not only income but also rights of control.

Income inequalities, as Tawney noted in the fourth edition of his book *Equality*, have remained unaffected by the rise of the Welfare State. Overall taxatión appears to be almost neutral in relation to income and in certain cases directly regressive, while redistribution through the welfare State, although it helps the poor more than the rich in relative terms, is paid for by workers themselves. It takes the form of a life-cycle transfer within social classes. Moreover, these welfare measures tend to favour more privileged groups. In general the Labour Party 'welfare approach' brought little changes in the class system of British Society. With the growth of an underclass of unemployed and unemployable, inequality has probably increased at the base. The welfare schemes discriminate between manual and non-manual categories of work. Status and income disparities, which survive, have disproved the thesis of accommodative *embourgeoisment* of the 'affluent' workers bringing about an increasing polarisation in capitalist societies.

Inequalities of political power are directly related to the disparities in status and income, since these represent the power of the dominant class to command a disproportionate share of rewards and privileges in relation to the subordinate class. The dominant class uses all the means at its disposal to preserve its rewards and privilages, not only within state institutions, but within the administrative service, the educational system, industry, the law, mass media etc., not only through coercive power but also through mobilization of the bias, operating anonymously through the structure of institutions, especially private property and the market, the rituals of social and political life, and ideological assumptions and beliefs.

The inequalities typical of state socialist societies, as Tawney admits, display a different pattern. Property, in the sense of legal ownership is largely non-existent. There is no private property-owning class in Soviet-type societies and so great concentrations of personal wealth are not found there. One can argue that the intelligentsia and the bureaucrats above all "exercise rights of control over the use and products of collective property" and "expropriate surplus value from the subordinate class" *(209:91)*. There is no direct inheritance of such rights, as with private property, though there is evidence of *de facto* inheritance of educational and vocational privileges. However, the analogy between legal ownership and sociological control cannot be carried too far, but there is a considerable hierarchy of monetary privilege and political authority. The pattern in relation to economic inequality is this: a highly egalitarian phase of socialist reconstruction, followed by a substantial widening of income and wage disparities in order to provide material incentives, followed by a subsequent move towards greater equality. The current picture is one of a substantially narrower range of money incomes in socialist than in capitalist societies. Thus the status hierarchy does not reflect and reinforce a dichotomous class structure on the Western capitalist model. However, the most important difference between the two systems lies in the hierarchy of political power. Here, despite some minor pluralistic tendencies identified by certain Western writers, "the explicitly hierarchical, monistic and all-pervasive structure of party control, increasingly manned by the white-collar intelligentsia, is altogether distinctive" *(209:88)*.

Tawney prefers a collectivist strategy for achieving greater equality in capitalist societies. Increase in money wages is no solution for social misery and deprivation under capitalism. Tawney observes, "The result is the paradox of rising pecuniary incomes and deepening social misery both attested by equally incontrovertible historical evidence—which has emerged in all industrial revolutions, to the confusion of those who forget that 'the timid, staring creature, man', is so compounded as to require, not only money, but light, air and water, not to mention such uneconomic goods as tranquillity, beauty, and affection. It is not till it is discovered that high individual incomes will not purchase the mass of mankind immunity from cholera, typhus and ignorance, still less secure them the positive advantages of educational opportunity and economic security, that slowly and reluctantly, amid prophecies of moral degeneration and economic disaster, society begins to make *collective* provision for needs for which no ordinary individual, even if he works overtime all his life, can provide himself" *(209:135)*.

The Realizability of the Egalitarian Goals

Tawney certainly believed that his ideal of an egalitarian society was realizable. While criticising the religion of inequality, he had examined the biological, genetic and psychological arguments in defence of inequality and refuted them. Tawney also rejected sociological arguments which maintain that inequalities are functional to, or inherent in, all possible social systems including contemporary industrial societies. The genetic and psychological studies, which justify inequality and hierarchy, display an ethnic and cultural bias and are scientifically unreliable. Steven Lukes rightly points out, "The principle of equal respect requires, in Tawney's words, that society's organization be planned so that 'whether their powers are great or small, all its members may be equally enabled to make the best of such powers as they possess.' Since this requires the equalization of rewards and privileges biological differences would correlate with social positions but not with unequal rewards and privileges attaching to those positions (*209:91*).

Sociological arguments for the inevitability of inequality are of two broad types. One is that inequalities are functionally necessary for any society, the other that they are inherent in the very nature of social life. Tawney regards both these arguments as rationalizations of the *status quo*. He observes, "When clever people, therefore, dismiss the idea of equality as monstrous and visionary, we may comfort ourselves with the thought that there is one humble aspect of it, which, though still far from being realized, is capable of realization.... If it is practicable to equalize the conditions of life required for physical development, may it not be practicable also to equalize those needed for mental development? If it is possible to secure to all, not equal health, but an environment equally favourable to its preservation, may it not be possible also to secure them, not indeed equal culture or intellectual attainments, but equal opportunities of cultivating the powers with which Nature has endowed them" (*76:152*).

Refuting the sociological arguments for retaining hierarchy and inequality, Tawney concludes that a stratified society is inconsistent with the norms of human civilization. In an emotional vein, he says: "What matters to a society is less what it owns than what it is and how it uses its possessions. It is civilized in so far as its conduct is guided by a just appreciation of spiritual ends, in so far as it uses its material resourecs to promote the dignity and refinement of the individual human beings who compose it. Violent contrasts of wealth and power and an indiscriminating devotion to institutions by which such contrasts are maintained and heightened, do not promote the attainment of such ends, but thwart it. They are therefore, a mark, not of civilization, but of barbarism, like the gold rings in the noses of savage monarchs, or the diamonds on their wives and the chains on their slaves" (*76:78*).

The fact that the civilizing ideal of equality, which is central to the socialist tradition, has found only very limited expression in the advanced industrial societies highlights an unresolved dilemma; namely, whether it is possible to establish the political conditions for an egalitarian society while also guaranteeing civil rights to all citizens within a system of socialist legality or to reconcile the contradiction between liberty and equality within the constitutional framework of a capitalist democracy. Let us hear

Tawney again on this unresolved dilemma; "The criticisms upon equalitarian policies which most deserve respect are not those which raise the loudest cries. They come from opponents who challenge such policies on their own dogmatic ground. They relate to the ends proposed, not merely to the difficulties and dangers in pursuing them. They assert that the values which the pursuit of equality must inevitably destroy are out of all proportion greater than the gifts which even if successful, it could confer, and denounce them, therefore, not merely as inexpedient or superfluous, but as vicious in principle and essence" (*76:255*). According to these detracters of equality, the supreme political good is 'liberty' and an appetite for equality with the inevitable restrictions that pander to it, is the deadliest foe of freedom. While inequality of power, says Tawney, is the condition of liberty, since it is the condition of any effective action, it is also a menace to it, for power which is sufficient to use is sufficient to abuse.

The Concept of Equality

The theory of natural rights is related closely to the idea of equality. The state of nature, declared Locke is also a state of equality. The law of nature teaches "all mankind who will but consult it, that being all equal and independent, no one ought to harm another in his life, health, liberty, or possession." The American Declaration of Independence proclaimed "that all men are created equal, that they are endowed by their Creator with certain unalienable rights." The French Declaration of 1789 also declared: "Men are born and live free and equal in their rights." As Barker puts it: "The principle of Equality accordingly means that whatever conditions are guaranteed to me, in the form of rights, shall also, and in the same measure, be guaranteed to others, and that whatever rights are given to others shall also be given to me" (*175:151*).

Equality, in short, means the equal enjoyment of rights by all citizens and absence of any discrimination based on status, race or sex. As Benn and Peters, in *Social Principles and the Democratic State*, point out: "The universality claimed for natural rights strongly suggests the criterion of impartiality for a moral rule. If, for instance, democratic rights were to be accorded to white men.... one must show good cause to deny them to black men. Where there are no relevant differences it would be unfair—or we might say *unjust*—to treat people differently" (*177:107*). In political theory, equality cannot be used in a descriptive-comparative sense. It is difficult to think of a human quality—physical, intellectual, or moral—of which it could be true. Women are generally lighter in weight than men but this cannot justify denial of legal or political rights to them. The phrase—all men are equal—is prescriptive. It does not mean that they possess certain attributes in the same degree but that they ought to be treated in the same manner in certain vital respects. A poll tax which prevents the poor from exercising their equal right to vote is a denial of the principle of equality but an income tax imposed on people earning higher incomes does not violate the principle of equality in the same way.

The difficulties arise in understanding the conception of equality when the question is posed in a wrong manner. For instance, Hobhouse explains the concept in the following words : "As a matter of the interpretation of experience, this is something peculiar to human beings and common to human beings without distinction of class, race or sex, which lies far deeper than all differences between them. Call it what we may, soul, reason, the abysmal capacity for suffering, or just human nature, it is something generic, of which there may be many specific, as well as quantitative differences, but which underlies and embraces them all. If this common nature is what the doctrine of equal rights postulates, it has no reason to fear the test of our ordinary experience of life, or of our study of history and anthropology" (*205:95*).

Benn and Peters believe that the terms like human nature, reason, soul or even the capacity for suffering do not explain anything in relation to the concept of equality. They observe : "Hobhouse seems to be making a distinction between all the particular differences between men, which he would treat as accidentals, and some essential or fundamental quality of 'men as men'—something called 'human nature', 'human dignity', 'personality', 'soul', etc.—by virtue of which they must be treated as fundamentally equal. But if we strip away all the qualities in respect of which men might differ, what is left ? If from human nature, we abstract talents, dispositions, character, intelligence, and all other possible grounds of distinction, we are left with an undifferentiated potentiality" (*177:109*).

Benn and Peters suggest three criteria in this respect (a) equality of consideration, (b) relevance, and (c) equality of proportion. The only universal right is the right to equal consideration. Equal consideration really means impartiality of treatment. It implies that 'none shall be held to have a claim to better treatment than another, in advance of good grounds being produced.' Kant expressed the same idea when he said : "Treat humanity, whether in your person or in that of any other, in every case as an end, never solely as a means." When we have to decide between claims, impose burdens or distribute benefits, the rational basis for treating them differently is that they differ in some way that has same relevance to the discrimination or distinction we want to make. To do otherwise is to treat a man purely as a means for some one else's satisfaction. Even when we agree in a given case about what distinctions are relevant, disagreement may arise about the relative weight and importance of such differences. A tentative answer can be that differences in treatment should be *proportionate* to the degree to which individual differ in relevant respects.

Speaking about the concept of equality, Harold J. Laski says : "Equality, broadly, is a coherence of ideas each one of which needs special examination. Undoubtedly, it implies fundamentally a certain levelling process. It means that no man shall be so placed in society that he can overreach his neighbour to the extent which constitutes a denial of the latter's citizenship. It means that my realisation of my best self must involve as its logical result the realisation by others of their best selves. It means such an ordering of social forces as will balance a share in the toil of living with a share in its gain also.... Equality, therefore, means first of all the absence of special privilege.... Equality means, in the second place, that adequate opportunities are laid open to all" *(47:153)*.

Lastly, as Benn and Peters argue, the claims to equality are, in a sense always negative, denying the propriety of certain existing inequalities. Egalitarians have been eager to oppose existing discriminations in a given area without asking for equality in other spheres. For example, the liberals who asked for equal right to vote did not demand equal distribution of wealth in society. The jurists, who asked for the removal of status differences in the legal or judicial sphere, remained unconcerned about distinction of social class in the sphere of production. Marx, therefore, maintained that equality, like liberty and other rights, was a bourgeois concept which merely established a formal equality of citizenship without putting an end to class domination and economic exploitation of man by man.

Legal Dimension of Equality

While feudal society was based on legally sanctioned differences of status, the modern industrial society has no use for legally sanctioned inequalities and hierarchy. In a liberal regime, every person is given equality before the law and can claim equal protection of the laws. Feudal law allowed certain privileges to the nobility and rights and duties of different ranks were in proportion to their wealth in the form of landed property. Law in a modern democratic state does not allow special privileges to any particular class and does not confer unequal rights on, or claim unequal obligations from different categories of citizens. Women, who were earlier denied certain legal rights like inheritance to property, may not suffer from these disabilities now.

As Benn and Peters point out, law, despite protecting the principle of equality in a general sense, does recognize certain differences in rights and duties which are reasonable from the point of view of the particular context. They observe: "Law creates classes with special rights and duties. Landlords have different right from tenants, policemen from sanitary inspectors, Members of Parliament from judges. As law is a system of rules for a society in which there is considerable specialization and division of function, such differences in right are inevitable. In such a differentiated society strict equality of rights is not simply a Utopian ideal; it is incompatible with the existence of such a society" *(177:122)*. Ernest Barker has used a phrase "equality of legal personality" to explain the legal dimension of equality. Legal personality is a legal term devoid of any non-technical implications regarding its meaning. It merely implies that the citizen is granted certain rights by law specifying the nature and extent of these rights. A slave for example has no legal personality and, therefore, no legal capacity. Benn and Peters do not find Barker's phrase as quite adequate.

Hobhouse defines equality before the law as equal enjoyment of certain fundamental rights and duties. Though he admits that if we go into a deeper analysis, we notice that law does create categories involving differences in rights and duties, yet he emphasizes one type of equality i.e. universality of rules. For instance, in the modern law, we do not distinguish the crime of homicide on the ground of the murderer's caste, class, sex or nationality and so on. In every case the rule is universal for the cases to which it applies, and this means that all persons whose cases conform to the rule are treated equally. Benn and Peters regard this view of Hobhouse also as inadequate. In their view, the equality before the law is a practical ideal on condition that we give up the search for a universal basis of equality, and interpret it negatively, as a denial of the rationality of making distinctions of a particular type.

Laws may apply equally and impartially to all persons who come within a certain category. The impartiality of the men, who may have social, communal or class biases, cannot be guaranteed in the application of these laws. Benn and Peters point out : "The colour of a man's skin may have no legal relevance to a charge of rape, but it would be rash to assume that it would make no difference to an Alabama jury's assessment of the evidence.... Inequality in the administration of the law may arise not only from the partiality of judges and juries, but from defects of a different sort. If poor men are kept from the courts by the cost of a legal action; if a rich man can force a settlement on less favourable terms than a poor opponent would get in court, by threatening to carry the case to appeal; if the former's case is put by more skilful—and more expensive—counsel than the poor man can afford; then the formal equality in law of rich and poor is contradicted by a substantial inequality of access to justice" (*177:126*).

Political Dimension of Equality

The liberal view of equality also emphasizes the political dimension of equality alongwith its legal dimension. It implies equal access to political power through the exercise of the right to vote. Explaining the implications of political equality, Laski says : "In the penumbra of equality, it means, in the political sphere, that my will, as a factor in the counting of heads, is equal to the will of any other. It means that I can move forward to any office in the State for which men are prepared to choose me. It means that I am not to find that there are persons in the State whose authority is qualitatively different from my own. Whatever rights inhere in another by virtue of his being a citizen must inhere, and to the same extent, in me also. There is no justification in such a view for the existence of an hereditary second chamber" (*47:253*).

Political equality, therefore, is intimately connected with a liberal-democratic regime. Feudalism, oligarchy, absolute monarchy, totalitarianism etc. are incompatible with the principle of political equality. Even a liberal-constitutional government organised on aristocratic basis does not provide for political equality. When franchise is limited to property-owners, it is a denial of political equality to the property-less working people. A totalitarian regime may provide votes to every citizen but elections in these countries become a farce due to the existence of a single party. The ruling elite nominates all the candidates and the existence of an opposition party is disallowed. This means that there is no equal access to political power for all in such a regime. A large number of countries in the Third World are ruled by military dictators. The regimes of these countries also deny equal access to political power to their citizens.

There are some writers, who doubt the reality of genuine political equality in the modern democratic state. The advocates of the elitist theory like Mosca, Pareto and Michels argue that ordinary citizens, even when they have votes, have no real access to political power because the political process results in the usurpation of power by a governing elite which is oligarchical in nature. Michels has propounded "the iron law of oligarchy" which asserts that political parties even in a democracy are controlled by a clique of self-appointed leaders. Laski also feels that political equality "is never real unless it is accompanied by virtual economic equality; political power, otherwise, is bound to be the handmaid of economic power." Marx also maitnained that there could be no real political equality in a society based on capitalism. The bourgeois parties, supported financially and organisationally, would not allow a proletarian party to win elections, or to form a government which may change the captialist system. The members of the working-class may have equal voting rights in a formal sense but owing to lack of resources, they cannot send their true representatives to Parliament.

Socio-Economic Dimension of Equality

It is now generally accepted, even by contemporary liberal writers, that the legal and political interpretation of equality is not adequate because it ignores the basic aspect of equality i.e. its socio-economic dimension. As Barker says, the poor citizens now tell those who are superior to them in wealth or culture : "We are now equal to you in legal capacity; it is therefore fair that we should also be equal in general capacity—in wealth and the opportunities it brings: in culture and the grasp it gives; in the general equipment and endowment of our faculties and the legal equality should thus be crowned by social equality" (*175:152*).

A cardinal question which confronts us today is how far the liberal capitalistic state can go in promoting equality of culture and equality of material rewards. In the matter of educational opportunities, the welfare state in advanced countries has already secured an educational minimum open equally to all but this is hardly true of underdeveloped countries in the Third World. The welfare state in the West also enables some of the meritorious students to pursue higher education with state support. But there is no genuine equality of opportunity in the sphere of higher education and culture even in advanced capitalist countries. Barker even justifies this in the following words : "We can hardly dream of absolute equality for all in education and culture. We have to face two obstinate and irreducible facts. One of them is the natural existence of individual differenecs in mental interest and mental capacity. The other is the social necessity of different social functions, ranging from ploughmen and smiths to scholars and Ministers of State, and requiring for their performance a difference of mental equipment." *(175:154)*. Capitalist countries still preserve an elitist bias in education. The problem of social equality has been more satisfactorily resolved in socialist countries. They provide for much greater equality of opportunity in the sphere of education and culture.

The principle of social equality is also critical of discrimination based on racial origin, religion or sex. In many countries, discrimination and persecution is the lot of racial and religious minorities. Nazi Germany persecuted the Jews. South Africa enforces *apartheid*. The United States does not grant social equality to its Negro population. In India social equality is denied to the people belonging to scheduled tribes and scheduled castes. The racial discrimination is practised in England against the Indian immigrants.

The case for equality of the sexes is also connected with the socio-economic dimension of equality. While there are admitted physical and psychological differences between men and women, there is no evidence that women as a class are inferior to men in intelligence, administrative capacity, moral character, soundness of judgement etc. The biological differences between the sexes cannot justify discrimination in the sphere of voting rights, entry to the professions, educational opportunities; levels of remuneration, or rights to hold the highest offices in government or industry. Of course, the feminists need not complain if the national law forbids the employment of women as coal-miners or if the municipal byelaw does not allow women to work as rickshaw-pullers, because the admitted difference in physique between the sexes makes this distinction reasonable. As Benn and Peters say, the biological difference however, "does not justify elevating the husband into a lord and master, nor the complete sacrifice of the women's personality to the demands of the family. The emancipation of women has expressed itself not only in law and economics, but also in changes in conventional marital relations. Many husbands now recognize that the domestic burden carried by mothers of families in previous generations was out of all proportions to the difference in function implied by the difference in sex. Their readiness to share the chores and the baby minding is a sign of a practical extension of the principle of equal consideration." *(177:118)*.

The socialist advocates of equality stress its economic dimension and argue that without changing the capitalist mode of production, one cannot really think of economic equality. The equality of opportunity is just an element in the ideal. What is criticized as 'inequality' is basically the disparity in economic power. The capitalist, who owns the means of production and exchange, cannot be brought at par with his worker, who has merely his labour power to sell, by any levelling process within the general frame-work of the capitalist mode of production. He thinks that genuine economic equality is possible only under socialism i.e. a society based on abolition of private property and social ownership of the means of production. The wide inequalities of income and property cannot be abolished in a capitalist society. The capitalist welfare state, as Ralph Miliband and Macpherson point out, has improved the living conditions of the workers in advanced capitalist countries without bridging the wide gulf that divides the owners of capital from their workers in terms of incomes, life-styles and property of the two social classes. But the question is whether abolition of private property and its replacement by state property is a sufficient condition for bringing about socio-economic equality. In the Soviet Union, a new class-system has emerged which differentiates the state bureaucratic elite from ordinary citizens in terms of both incomes and life-styles.

The ideal of classless society is directed as much to eliminating social inequalities based on status, prestige and political office as to an economic restructuring of the relations of production. In an ideal society, the respect owed to a man should be determined by the qualities of his personality, not by social graces. Hence, the socialist advocate of equality is suspicious of public schools and other institutions fostering the visible differences which are the badges of social class. Benn and Peters rightly conclude : "The term 'social equality' has been adopted by socialists largely to distinguish their objective from the earlier egalitarian ideals of the French Revolution. The men of 1789 sought 'equality before the law', which for them meant eliminating aristocratic legal privileges and feudal obligations. The Jacobins and the nineteenth century Republicans on whom their mantle descended, sought 'political equality' or universal suffrage. To socialists these ends by themselves seem inadequate; they are at best ways of achieving 'real' equality—social equality. Without that, "political equality, is an illusion. A wealthy elite would continue to exercise effective political power; judges and legislators would still be drawn from its ranks, and predisposed to favour it. Legal costs would put justice beyond the poor man's reach. Without social equality, equality 'before the law' would remain an empty form". (*177:121*).

Liberty and Equality

Ernest Barker, like all liberals attaches more significance to liberty and considers equality as of secondary importance. He observes : "Equality, after all, is a derivative value. It is derived from the supreme value of the development of personality—in each alike and equally, but in each along its own different line and of its own separate motion. It has to be adjusted to that supreme value. What is derived must not divert, the source from which it comes. But any equality which spelled uniformity would necessarily divert and defeat the spontaneous development of all the varieties of human personality." (*175:155*). Barker, however, does not regard the two concepts as antithetical to each other as was customary with aristocratic critics of the idea of equality.

Laski attaches equal importance to the concepts of liberty and equality and considers economic equality as a pre-condition to political liberty. He criticizes Lord Acton and Tocqueville for saying that liberty and equality are contraditcory concepts and that liberty can thrive only in an unequal society. By equality, Laski does not mean the identity of reward but the creation of equal opportunity for all to develop their talents and capacities. He criticizes the existence of special privileges for certain classes at the expense of others. The exploited and the exploiting classes do not enjoy equal freedom. If we want to make liberty a universal category, we must accept a certain levelling process in the economic sphere. Political freedom and economic equality are, for Laski, complementary concepts which not only co-exist but support each other. Marx maintained that only under communism we can build a genuinely egalitarian society which would simultaneously guarantee the maximum realization of human freedom.

In *Democracy in America*, Alexis de Tocqueville talked of his religions dread of the democratic egalitarianism promoted by the American revolution. But Professor Kalko says that "no significant trend towards income equality" can be discerned there and H.P. Miller feels "that our 'social revolution' has not only been marking time for twenty years, but that it is also beginning to move backwards". Professor Meade is more frank when he talks of "a really fantastic inequality in the ownership of property" in all advanced capitalist contries. "As for the United States..... the share of wealth accruing to the top 2 per cent of American families ...... amounted to 29 per cent." (*236 : 25*).

CHAPTER 19

SOVEREIGNTY

1. DEFINITION OF SOVEREIGNTY

'Sovereignty' is derived from the Latin word *superanus* meaning supreme. It means that in every full-fledged or independent State there is an ultimate authority, an authority from which there is no appeal. This authority is supreme both in internal and in external matters. Internally, no individual or group of individuals has the legal right to act contrary to the decisions of the sovereign power. In external matters, too, the sovereign State is supreme.

Definitions of sovereignty are many and varied (*22:159*). Bodin, the first Western writer to develop a systematic doctrine of sovereignty, defines it as 'the supreme power over citizens and subjects, unrestrained by law'.

Among modern writers, Duguit, a French professor, says that sovereignty as generally understood in his country is the 'commanding power of the State: it is the will of the nation organized in the State; it is the right to give unconditional orders to all individuals in the territory of the State.' Burgess, an American writer, describes it as 'original, absolute, unlimited power over the individual subjects and over all associations of subjects'.

Giddings, the well-known American sociologist, in *The Responsible State* writes: "In all the dictionaries there is no other word that has more disastrously been conjured with by the metaphysical juggler.... Jurists and political theorists, losing sight of concrete fact, gave their minds to abstractions. And sovereignty became for political science a thing that never was on sea or land."

Soltau describes sovereignty as the exercise of "final legal coercive power by the State". Finally, Roucek, Huszar and others, in their *Introduction to Political Science* say "In any theory of politics, the concept of sovereignty must be near the centre." Or, to quote them again, "Theories of sovereignty....are reflections of the social facts, political institutions and cultural backgrounds which they are intended to explain and to justify."

2. CHARACTERISTICS OF SOVEREIGNTY

Writers on the traditional doctrine of sovereignty have summed up its attributes as under:

(1) absoluteness;
(2) universality;
(3) inalienability;

(4) permanence;
(5) indivisibility.

1. Absoluteness

The sovereign power is said to be absolute and unlimited. There is no power on earth which can bind it. (a) Internally, the sovereign power has absolute power over all individuals and groups of individuals within the State. Whatever limitations there may be are self-imposed. (b) Externally, too, the sovereign authority is considered supreme. It is absolutely 'independent of any compulsion or interference on the part of other States' (*24:95*). Treaties, international understandings and conventions, etc., do not destroy sovereignty, inasmuch as there is no compelling power behind them.

The remaining attributes of sovereignty are corollaries of this.

2. Universality or all-comprehensiveness

The sovereign power, as seen already, is supreme over all persons, associations, and things within the State. This does not prevent the State, however, from waiving its right of jurisdiction in certain matters. No person or body of persons can claim exemption as a matter of right. A well-organised world-wide association such as the Free Masons is not superior to any State. It is subject to the laws of individual States.

3. Inalienability

If sovereignty is absolute and unlimited, it stands to reason that it should be inalienable. A sovereign State, cannot give away any of its essential elements without destroying itself. An American writer, Lieber, says: "Sovereignty can no more be alienated than a tree can alienate its right to sprout or a man can transfer his life and personality without self-destruction". A State may cede part of its territory to another State. By so doing it surrenders its sovereign rights over that particular territory without destroying its sovereignty as such.

Rousseau, who upheld the inalienability of sovereignty, claimed that power could be transferred, but not will. Sovereignty is the essence of the personality of the State and to alienate it is equivalent to suicide.

4. Permanence or perpetuity

Sovereignty is as permanent as the State itself. So long as the State lasts sovereignty lasts. The two are inseparable. The death or dispossession of a king or president does not mean the cessation of sovereignty. Sovereignty shifts immediately to the next bearer. 'It is only a personal change in the government, not a break in the continuity of State' (*28:111*).

5. Indivisibility

The indivisibility of sovereignty is a logical deduction from its absoluteness. Thus Gettell writes: 'If sovereignty is not absolute, no state exists; if sovereignty is divided, more than one state exists' (*24:95*).[1]

To sum up the discussion in the forcible words of Calhoun: 'Sovereignty is an entire thing: to divide it is to destroy it. It is the supreme power in a state, and we might just as well speak of half a square or half-a triangle as of half a sovereignty' (*22:173*). Or, again, 'there is no difficulty in understanding how *powers* appertaining to sovereignty may be divided and the exercise of one portion be delegated to one set of agents and other portion to another or, how sovereignty may be vested in one man, in a few, or in many. But how *sovereignty* itself, the supreme power, can be divided....it is impossible to conceive' (*22:177*).

3. DIFFERENT MEANINGS OF SOVEREIGNTY

1. Titular Sovereignty

The term sovereignty is used in different senses, and failure to distinguish them results in much confusion. The term 'titular sovereignty' is used with reference to a king or other monarchical ruler who at one time was a real sovereign, but who for a long time has ceased to be such. The king of England is officially referred to as the 'sovereign', although his sovereignty is only nominal. Real power passed to other hands long ago. Therefore, the sovereignty of the king is a harmless fiction.

2. Legal Sovereignty

A distinction is often made between legal sovereignty and political sovereignty. The legal sovereign is the supreme law-making body in the State. Only its commands are laws. It can override prescriptions of divine law, the principles of morality, and dictates of public opinion. Such a sovereign is found in England in the King-in-Parliament. Legal sovereignty is the lawyer's conception of sovereignty. It is 'the determinate person' referred to in Austin's definition of sovereignty. Courts recognise only those laws which emanate from such a sovereign authority.

3. Political Sovereignty

This term is not so easy to define. In a democratic country, while the legal sovereign is the supreme law-making and law-enforcing body, there is behind it the will of the people which is the ultimate and final source of all authority. It is the authority from whose verdict there can be no appeal. In the words of Dicey, 'Behind the sovereign which the lawyer recognises there is another sovereign to whom the legal sovereign must bow.' To quote the same authority again: 'That body is politically sovereign, the will of which is ultimately obeyed by the citizens of the state' (*15:66*). Gilchrist

1. Treitschke writes: "A State where sovereignty is divided would be impossible; only political dilettanti like Cicero would dally with such eclectic fooleries." (*166* : *vol. I* : *136*).

defines it as 'the sum total of the influences in a State which lie behind the law."

Much confusion arises when we attempt an exact definition of the term 'political sovereignty'. It is vague and indeterminate. It is not something which can be located with exactness. In a country in which direct or pure democracy prevails, legal and political sovereignty are almost coincident. But most countries where democracy prevails are of the representative or indirect type. Therefore, legal sovereignty and political sovereignty are different. Some writers identify political sovereignty with the collective community, some with the mass of the people, some with the general will, some with public opinion, some with the physical power of that part of the people who can bring about a successful revolution.

4. Popular Sovereignty

From political sovereignty to popular sovereignty there is a natural transition. According to the doctrine of popular sovereignty, ultimate authority rests with the people. In the eighteenth century it became the cornerstone of the teaching of Rousseau, who proclaimed it 'as with a trumpet blast' *(22:164)*. The doctrine received further impetus in the nineteenth century with the growth of democracy so much so that, in all self-governing countries, it is taken for granted that the people are the ultimate custodians of political authority. The legal sovereign cannot last long if it deliberately and continuously opposes the wishes of the people, for the people in the last resort can have recourse to force and establish a new government by means of revolution.

While the doctrine of popular sovereignty is a very attractive doctrine and satisfies the vanity of the people, difficulty arises when we attempt to analyze the concept and give it a precise meaning. The more we ponder over it, the more difficult we find it to define. It is open to all the criticisms to which the conception of political sovereignty is exposed. The two possible meanings that can be given to the term 'people' in defining popular sovereignty are (a) 'the total unorganised indeterminate mass', (b) the electorate. People, as understood in the first sense, connot obviously be the sovereign, As regards the second, people can act only through legal channels if they are to be regarded as sovereign in any sense at all. In the words of Garner: 'Unorganized public opinion, however powerful, is not sovereignty unless it is clothed in legal form, no more so than the informal or unofficial resolution of the members of legislative body in law.' In actual practice, popular sovereignty seems to mean nothing more than public opinion in time of peace and the might of revolution 'in the case of a conflict' *(24:100)*.

Whatever difficulties we may encounter in defining 'popular sovereignty', the doctrine contains several valuable ideas:

(a) Government does not exist for its own good. It exists for the good of the people.

(b) If people's wishes are deliberately violated, there is the possibility of revolution.

(c) Easy means should be provided for a legal way of expressing public opinion.

(d) Government should be held directly responsible to the people through such means as frequent elections, local self-Government, referendum, initiative, and recall.

(e) Government should exercise its authority directly in accordance with the laws of the land and not act arbitrarily.

5. De jure and de facto Sovereignty

Sovereignty being a question of fact, a distinction is sometimes made between *de jure* and *de facto* sovereignty. The *de jure* sovereign is the legal sovereign and the *de facto* sovereign is the actual sovereign—a sovereign which is actually obeyed by the people whether it has a legal status or not. *De facto* sovereignty may rest purely on physical force or religious influence, while *de jure* sovereignty has the legal right to command obedience. The distinction between the two comes out sharply in times of revolution. Some revolutions mean a mere change in the personnel or organisation of government, while others result in a complete destruction of the old legal sovereign and the establishment of a new one. Austin refused to recognize the distinction between *de jure* and *de facto* sovereignty, because the adjectives 'lawful' and 'unlawful' cannot be applied to the term "sovereignty". According to Austin's view governments may be *de facto* or *de jure* but the latter terms are inapplicable to sovereignty.

To give an example, soon after the overthrow of the Chiang Kai-shek's regime in China, Communist China became *de facto* sovereign. But now that it has been in power for more than two decades and there is none to challenge its authority, and a good many States (including India) have recognized it, it may be regarded as both *de facto* and *de jure*.

4. LOCATION OF SOVEREIGNTY

One of the most difficult questions for a student of political science to answer pertains to the location of sovereignty in the State. There is diversity of opinion among reputed thinkers on this question. Gettell notes that among these thinkers sovereignty is located respectively in:

'(1) The people of the State.

'(2) The organization which has a legal right to make or amend the constitution of the State.

'(3) The sum total of the legal law-making bodies in the government of the State' (*24:98*).

The first of these views need not detain us long. In dealing earlier with the conception of popular sovereignty, we have mentioned the several criticisms to which it is open. The other two views, however, cannot be so easily dismissed. Difficulty in locating sovereignty is not a serious question so far as the United Kingdom is concerned, where no distinction is made between constitutional law and statutory law. The English constitution is flexible and is not hemmed in on all sides, as is the American constitution. In the United Kingdom, legally speaking, the Parliament including the King, Lords and Commons is supreme. It can make and unmake any laws. It is, therefore, described as legal sovereign. The political sovereign is the people as a whole, or, strictly speaking the electorate.

In the United States, owing to its rigid constitution, it is not so easy to locate sovereignty. Neither the President nor the legislatures, federal or State, enjoy absolute legal powers. Every act of theirs which goes beyond the limits of the constitution can be questioned by the appropriate courts. Sovereignty, therefore, is not vested in them but rests in that body which is legally entitled to change the constitution.

Gettell and a few other writers take exception to the point of view which regards legal sovereignty as vested in that body which can make and amend the constitution. Their chief argument is that 'the constitution-making organs act intermittently and at infrequent intervals, in some cases never', while the sovereignty of the State must be constantly exercised. They, therefore, locate sovereignty in 'the sum total of all law-making bodies in the government', including (*24:102*) :

'(1) *Legislature*—National, commonwealth, or local.

'(2) *Courts*—in so far as they create law, not when merely interpreting or applying law.

'(3) *Executive officials*—In so far as they create law, by ordinances, proclamation, etc.

'(4) *Conventions*—When acting legally as law-making bodies, as in the case of a constitutional convention properly assembled.

'(5) *Electorate*—When exercising powers of referendum or of plebiscite' (*24:103*).

Notwithstanding the merits adduced by Gettell, the theory under review does not seem to be satisfactory. It rests on a profound confusion between the State and government. The various law-making bodies are manifestations of the organic unity of the State and are not divisions of the sovereignty of the State. Their powers of law-making are delegated powers. Therefore, sovereignty does not rest in them, but is vested in that body which can make and amend the constitution and allot its powers among the various organs which express its will.

5. JOHN AUSTIN'S THEORY OF SOVEREIGNTY

In his *Lectures on Jurisprudence*, Austin writes : The notions of sovereignty and independent political society may be expressed concisely thus : 'If a *determinate* human superior not in a habit of obedience to a like superior, receives *habitual* obedience from the *bulk* of a given society, that determinate superior is sovereign in that society; and the society (including the superior) is a society political and independent'. Laws are defined simply as the command of a superior to an inferior. In Austin's words : 'Law is the aggregate of rules set by men as politically superior, or sovereign, to men as politically subject'. The chief reason for the bulk of a given society rendering habitual obedience to a determinate human superior is the power it possesses 'to put compulsion without limit on subjects or fellow subjects' (*Volume I 226, 1869 ed.*).

One of the most important things to note in Austin's theory of sovereignty is that he makes power or might the determining factor. There is no question of laws or right. If Rousseau places the emphasis on *will,* Austin's emphasis is on *force* (*57:350*).

The legal view of sovereignty has been best expounded by John Austin. It carries with it a certain scientific precision and finality which is highly impressive. It can be summed up under the following four simple propositions :

(1) In every State (or 'society political and independent' as Austin calls it) there is a 'determinate human superior', who receives habitual obedience' from 'the bulk' of its citizens.

(2) Whatever this superior commands is law, and without him there can be no law.

(3) The power of this superior, which is known as sovereignty, is indivisible.

(4) This sovereign power is absolute and incapable of limitation.

Criticism

(1) All of these propositions have been severally handled by critics. Yet, as Lord points out, every one of them contains a truth or a half truth which is of importance.

(a) The first proposition was attacked by Sir Henry Maine in his *Early Institutions,* in which he shows that in many of the Empires of the East there is nothing to correspond with 'the determinate superior' of Austin. In the Sikh kingdom of the Punjab, for instance, Ranjit Singh exercised despotic power over his subjects. To disobey even his smallest commands meant death or mutilation. Yet even he was subject to the customary laws of the community, and never issued a command in the Austinian sense of the term. Customs are the outcome of ages and do not proceed from any 'determinate person' or body of persons.

(b) It is relatively easy to locate the 'determinate superior' in the United Kingdom, but when the theory is applied to ancient despotisms of the East or to the constitution of the United States, it is not very helpful. Nevertheless, we agree with Lord in holding that because it is difficult to locate the supreme power in a given State we should not deny its presence altogether.

(2) Austin's second proposition is that the sovereign in the sense of a

'determinate human superior' is the supreme law-maker. Whatever he commands is law. As regards long-standing customs and immemorial traditions which exist in every community, alongside of positive laws, the Austinian position is 'What the sovereign permits he commands'. Taking for example, the English common law 'which exists in customs, which are explained, modified or expanded when the courts apply them' *(28:115)*, it may be said that the king in Parliament permits the common law and as such can alter it in the way it pleases. But this is largely a theoretical power, for the sovereign cannot alter much of the common law without endangering its own safety.

Austin's theory, in brief, errs in regarding all laws as merely 'commands and in overemphasizing the single element of force. The supremacy of his sovereign is only in respect of positive law : and it is only in the legal, and not in the moral or physical, sense possible to apply his theory. Only as a maker of positive law the sovereign is supreme and uncontrolled.

From all this it would appear that the Austinian sovereign is not the sole creator of laws. Duguit goes so far as to say that it is not the State which creates laws, but it is laws, which create the State. 'Laws', he says, 'are merely the expression of social necessity'.

(3) The third proposition is that sovereignty is indivisible.

(a) From one point of view, as Lord points out, this is an untenable proposition. In every political society there is a division of functions though not of will, and without such division no government can be conducted effectively. In the British constitution, there is not only Legislative Sovereign, but also an Executive and a Judicial Sovereign. From this it would appear that sovereignty is divisible. In reply to it, the Austinians would say that the legislative sovereign is the real sovereign because it is habitually obeyed by the executive and the judges. But what about countries such as the United States which have a fundamental law, unalterable by the ordinary process of legislation ?

(b) The distinction between legal and political sovereignty also has at times been construed to mean the divisibility of sovereignty. Austin was aware of the fact that the people of England or 'the numerous body of the commons', as the described them, had a share in sovereignty. But, not being able to anticipate the later distinction between legal and political sovereignty, he fell into the error of believing that people formed a part of the legal sovereign.

(4) The fourth proposition is that the sovereign power is absolute and unlimited. This position has been vehemently attacked by pluralists. Even non-pluralists recognize that though the sovereign may be legally unlimited, there are political and historical limits on every side. They consider the unlimited authority and infinite right of the sovereign power as mere abstractions of jurisprudence.

THE PLURALISTIC CRITICISM OF THE THEORY OF SOVEREIGNTY

Political pluralism which criticises the doctrine of sovereignty is the logical consequence of a pragmatic analysis of the dynamics of power. The concentration of power at a single central source results in a tyrannical social order. The dispersion of power to peripheral points of the body politic is the basis of free societies. Laski's theory of the pluralistic state is essentially based on a federal conception of political authority. The federal conception of political authority is the indispensable condition of a really democratic political system. The pluralist thinks that the state should not monopolize power in society but should share it equitably with other groups and associations. It should not try to reduce the varied aspects of its citizens' lives to a wooden uniformity. Instead of threatening force to secure the total acquiescence of all dissenting groups in its own majestic will, the state should respect their reasonable autonomy and regard social diversity as the conclusive proof of a really healthy community[2]. In the interest of society as a whole, the state is asked to renounce its claim for sovereignty.

Reinterpretation of the Doctrine of Consent

Besides, this argument involves a re-interpretation of the doctrine of consent in politics. It regards the traditional doctrine of consent as "a specious intellectualism" which does not express the governmental process adequately. "We do not choose our governors", Laski says, "in the sense of actively making certain persons govern by our deliberate choice. We do not accept their legislation in the sense of finding it expressive of what is one with our own sense of our needs. Between us and our rulers there lies a vast abyss which is filled by the devices that power and its varied mechanisms bring into being. We are told that public opinion wills this and desires the other. But we have no satisfying channels either for the garnering of public opinion or for placing before it the materials upon which it may build an edifice of demand which represents its wants. Consent may in practice mean any of a score of things from blank ignorance through dumb inertia to deliberate coercion" (*47:241*). If the liberal dogma of consent as the basis of government be impracticable, what is its proper substitute? The alternative that Laski suggests is the maximum association of the organised interests within the community with the dynamics of government.

Revision of the Theory of Representation

The participation of organised groups in the actual formulation of state policies can be secured only by reorganizing the representative mechanism of the modern state. Walter Lippmann once said that the classical theory of representation assumes that the successful candidate of a constituency represents the best wisdom of his constituents and that the legislature

2. Harold J. Laski : ''The Problem of Sovereignty'', Chapter I; p. 25.

composed of such delegates is the best repository of national wisdom.[3] Disagreeing with the classical theory Laski says, "Obviously, nothing of the sort occurs. The wisdom of most men is simply never made available to their representatives in a central legislature. Those who choose are, often enough, unable to say what that wisdom is; those who are chosen are not seldom unable to interpret, sometimes from self-interest, sometimes from stupidity, the wisdom that does express itself. The idea that my will and my experience are, in some mystic fashion, embodied in the will and experience of my representative is contradicted by all the facts at our disposal. My will cannot, as Rousseau saw, ever be represented at all" (*47:264*).

Rousseau, Laski and G.D.H. Cole

Rousseau suggested direct democracy as a substitute for representative democracy. But direct democracy can properly function only in small communities. Laski does not agree with Cole's view of functional representation either. "It is true", he says, "that I cannot be fully represented as a citizen, but it is also true that I cannot be fully represented as an engineer or a doctor or a carpenter" (*47:266*). Instead of a functional parliament replacing the territorial assembly of the present, he would like the creation of a system of advisory councils of interest groups to aid and advise the territorial legislature as well as the administrative departments of the state, "Because society is federal", says Laski, "authority must be federal also That involves......the making of decisions out of the interests which will be affected by them, and in turn, their application by those interests. It means making the mining industry a unit of administration in the same sense as Lancashire. It means surrounding the Ministry of Education with bodies entitled to speak on behalf of the parties to the educational process...... It means the abandonment of the sovereign state in the sense which equates the latter with society and gives it, thereby, the right to dictate to associations within society" (*47:271*). The basic problem that confronts the pluralistic theory of the state revolves round the conception of sovereignty. The validity of the pluralistic theory as a whole depends upon the effectiveness of its charges against the classical conception of sovereignty which was so admirably put forward by Austin and his disciples.

Lindsay, Barker and Krabbe on Sovereignty

While the anarchists believe in the abolition of the state, the pluralists like Laski are prepared to retain it but on condition that it surrender its sovereignty. "If we look at the facts", wrote Lindsay, "It is clear enough that

---

3. Walter Lipmann : "Public Opinion", p. 288. Writing in an American context, Lippmann says, "The theory is that the best man of each district brings the best wisdom of his constituents to a central place and that all these wisdoms combined are all the wisdom that Congress needs". (Quoted by Laski in "A Grammar of Politics", p. 264).

the theory of the sovereign state has broken down".[4] Barker agreed that "no political common place has become more arid and unfruitful than the doctrine of the sovereign state".[5] Krabbe similarly pleaded that "the notion of sovereignty must be expunged from political theory."[6] Echoing these words, Laski argued that "it would be of lasting benefit to political science if the whole concept of sovereignty were surrendered" (*47:44*). There ought to be grave reasons, one is led to believe, that have provoked in the pluralist mind so violent an attitude against the doctrine of state sovereignty.

Three Aspects of Sovereignty

The classical theory of sovereignty, according to Laski, demands a critical investigation from three different aspects. One of the aspects is historical. The sovereign state is essentially a product of certain historical circumstances in a definite epoch. The history behind the sovereign state should be carefully scrutinized and the various factors that gave rise to it should be scientifically analysed. This kind of historical examination of the doctrine of state sovereignty would alone explain its present strength and its future utility. In the second place, the theory of sovereignty involves a conception of law which regards it as the command of the sovereign. It should be carefully examined how far the juristic postulates of Austin are valid for political philosophy. Lastly, the modern theory of sovereignty is based on a theory of political organisation which insists that in every political society there ought to be a definite human superior who is habitually obeyed by all administrative agencies and all private citizens. In other words, it insists upon a centralized administrative structure in industry and in government with little scope for group autonomy and individual initiative. The traditional views regarding sovereignty expressed successively by Bodin, Hobbes, Rousseau, Hegel and Austin should be reconsidered from all the three angles. Laski examines the theory of sovereignty from all these aspects and arrives at the startling conclusion that it is completely valueless for modern political theory.

Historical Aspects of Sovereignty

Historically, the sovereign state is the product of the religious struggles of the western world in the sixteenth century. The emergence of the sovereign state gave rise to the monistic theory of the state. "We must ceaselessly remember", says Laski, "that the monistic theory of the state was born in an age of crisis and that each period of its reverification has synchronized with some momentous event which has signalized a change in the

4. A. D. Lindsay: "The State in Recent Political Theory", in "Political Quarterly" Vol. I (February 1914), pp. 128-145.
5. Ernest Barker: "The Superstition of the State", in "London Times Literary Supplement", (July, 1918), p. 329.
6. H. Krabbe: "The Modern Idea of the State" (Translation by George H.. Sabine and Walter J. Shepard, New York and London, 1922), p. 35.

distribution of political power. Bodin, as is well known, was of that party which, in an age of religious warfare, asserted, lest it perish in an alien battle, the supremacy of the state. Hobbes sought the means of order in a period when King and Parliament battled for the balance of power. Bentham published his "Fragment" on the eve of the Declaration of Independence; and Adam Smith, in the same year, was outlining the programme of another and profounder revolution. Hegel's philosophy was the outcome of a vision of German multiplicity destroyed by the unity of France. Austin's book was conceived when the middle classes of France and England had, in their various ways, achieved the conquest of a state hitherto but partly open to their ambition" (*129:233*). The monistic political thinkers, who evolved the doctrine of state sovereignty, did so in order to reinforce the authority of the state in a period of crisis.

Luther, Grotius, Bodin and Locke

Externally, the theory of the sovereign state represented the protest of national monarchies in Europe against the papal claims of overlordship. Luther was the first protagonist of princely sovereignty as the success of the Reformation and his struggle against the Pope depended on the support and alliance of the princes who were waging a similar struggle in a different sphere. Grotius was the first jurist who evolved his theory of international law on a clear recognition of the principle of state sovereignty in the international field. But the recognition of state supremacy in the international field was not enough. The existence of national monarchies was jeopardized by the religious feuds and the consequential division of the national communities into warring sects. The ruling princes applied their sovereign rights to secure internal peace by suppressing and persecuting the members of the rival sects in the beginning. When this policy failed to achieve necessary results, the political thinkers like Locke recommended a policy of religious toleration so that the religious minorities could be gradually assimilated within a nation. Bodin was the first political thinker who suggested the extension of sovereignty in the internal sphere.

Hobbes, Rousseau, Bentham and Austin

Originally the sovereign state emerged to vindicate the supremacy of the political authority against ecclesiastical claims. Subsequently it extended its supremacy to every department of human activity, religious or otherwise. The social groups, economic classes, religious sects and even cultural associations were brought under the iron heel of the all-conquering state. In the hands of Hobbes the theory of sovereignty became an instrument of monarchical despotism. Rousseau glorified the sovereign people but his ideas were utilized by the French bourgeoisie to establish its own dictatorship in France. In the name of sovereignty, Hegel asked the German people to surrender their liberty and rights to a feudal-militarist clique that ruled Prussia in the name of the Emperor. Bentham was the spokesman of the

English middle-class that aspired to control the English state by way of parliamentary sovereignty. Austin, as Laski thinks, emphasized the dogma of parliamentary sovereignty as a device to perpetuate *status quo*. Chief Justice Marshall interpreted the doctrine of national sovereignty for the benefit of the American bourgeoisie struggling against state particularism.

Limited Validity of the Theory of Sovereignty

The conclusion that Laski draws from this analysis of the historical evolution of the sovereign state is that the theory of sovereignty might be considered valid for particular societies in a particular epoch but it could not be regarded as valid for all societies in all ages. The conception of state sovereignty was completely unknown to ancient Greeks and was quite out of place in medieval politics. Even in modern times, the doctrine of state sovereignty was successively challenged by organized groups within the community either religious or economic. A historical survey of the successive conflicts between the British Parliament and the various religious sects on the question of secular control over doctrinal affairs or internal discipline of the sects has conclusively proved the inadequacy of the theory of parliamentary sovereignty as conceived by Austin. The misrable failure of Bismarck's experiment with the *'Kultur-Kampf'* proves the same thing under German conditions. Laski further holds that the operation of sovereignty remains suspended in times of civil upheaval when different factions fight among themselves for the control of state sovereignty but none of those factions is able to claim that it commands it. The theory of sovereignty is, therefore, on its internal side a doctrine of doubtful validity.

International Aspect of Sovereignty

In modern times, the theory of sovereignty has become anachronistic on its international side also. "Internationally", says Laski, "it is not difficult to conceive the organisation of an allegiance which reaches beyond the limits of the state. To leave with a handful of men, for instance, the power to make war may well seem anachronistic to those who envisage the consequences of war. When State sovereignty in international affairs was recognized, there was no authority existent to which that type of control might be entrusted. It is at least arguable now that an authority predominant over states may be conceived which is entrusted the regulation of those affairs of more than national interest.... It involves, at any rate on the international side. the abolition of State Sovereignty". He thinks that the emergence of a world organization like the former League of Nations was essentially a development in this direction.

Juristic Aspects of Sovereignty

Secondly, the theory of state sovereignty as developed by Austin and his disciples does not even give a true explanation of the legal order of those political societies for which it has largely been conceived. In the sphere of jurisprudence Laski finds the views of Montesquieu, Sir Henry Maine, Durkheim, Duguit and Krabbe as of far greater value than those of the analytical jurists like Austin. "Political philosophy," says Laski, "must, doubtless, consider law as an important factor in the life of the State. But it must also bear ceaselessly in mind that the method of approach to the nature of law is, for itself, either akin to that suggested by Montesquieu, or else more likely to deceive than to assist. Law, for the student of politics, is built upon the general social environment. It expresses what are held to be the necessary social relations of a State at some given period. The organ by which it is declared to be law is, for politics, incomparably less important than the forces which made that organ act in the particular way" *(47:55)*. Laski is, therefore, convinced that Austin's conception of the legal order as a formal hierarchy, in which the political superior is entitled to receive habitual obedience to its commands from all who happen to reside within its territorial jurisdiction, is inadequate because it does not inquire into the substance of those commands which are to be canonized as law by the fiat of the sovereign.

Positivistic Conception of Jurisprudence

In this way, Laski is led to develop his positivistic or historical conception of jurisprudence. Like Sir Henry Maine, he regards law as the embodiment of custom and moral outlook of a given society. In other words, it is an expression of social relations of a given period. The political superior of Austin's conception, when deprived of its conceptual majesty, is actually an agent of the dominant social groups for registering their will which is conditioned by the social environment in which it is formulated.

Pragmatically speaking, the will of the sovereign is never absolute because it is in a continuous process of modification due to the resistance put up by the corporate wills within the state. The corporate wills as necessarily define the content of law as the will of the political sovereign. The King-in-Parliament may be sovereign in a formal sense but the factory legislation of England would be unintelligible purely in terms of the will of the political sovereign. A realistic conception of law must concede that the corporate wills of trade unions have played as effective a role in the actual formulation of labour legislation as the will of the political sovereign expressed through parliamentary leaders.

Personality Theory of Corporations

Laski is attracted by the juristic conceptions of Gierke and Maitland although he does not fully agree with the personality theory of corporations advanced by them. But he agrees with them in regarding the corporation as autonomous bodies sharing alongwith the political sovereign in the legislative process and legal life of the community. The classical theory of sovereignty denies that the sources of law are essentially plural. Laski as a pluralist recognizes the inherent plurality of the legal order.

Federalism and Sovereignty

The emergence of federal politics further shows the inadequacy of Austin's conception of sovereignty. It is difficult to locate a determinate human superior as the political sovereign in the American body politic. "The Congress", says Laski, "is a limited body the powers of which are carefully defined; the separate states are similarly combined within the four corners of the Constitution; and even the amendment of the Constitution is limited by the exception that no state shall, without its own consent, be deprived of its equal suffrage in the Senate. In the theoretic sense, therefore, the United States has no sovereign organ; for the Judges of the Supreme Court, being overridden by Constitutional Amendment, are clearly only a penultimate court of reference. A peculiar historical experience has therefore devised the means of building a state from which the conception of sovereignty is absent" (*47:49*). But this type of difficulty is not confined to those states which have adopted a federal form of government. The peculiar structure of the Belgian constitution is cited by Laski as an example of a unitary state which also lacks a sovereign organ in the Austinian sense.

Complexity of the Law-making Process

The sociological conception of law clearly points out that the law-making process is too complex to be adequately explained by the simple Austinian hypothesis. "The most perfect example of the Austinian view," says Laski, "is, of course, the position held by the King-in-Parliament. Any command which issues therefrom will, as Dicey pointed out in a classic analysis, be obeyed by enforcement through the courts. But every one knows that to regard the King-in-Parliament as a sovereign body in the Austinian sense is absurd. No Parliament would dare to disfranchise the Roman Catholics or to prohibit the existence of trade unions. If it made the attempt, it would cease to be a Parliament" (*47:52*). Laski is of opinion that Parliament can behave as an Austinian absolute only in a conceptual world. If it tried to act in the same manner in the world of realities, it is bound to be destroyed by the organized will of the nation as a whole or that of the powerful dissenting groups.

Dicey's View on Political Sovereignty

But when Laski says that the will of the King-in-Parliament may be superseded by the will of the nation, he is merely echoing Dicey's words that there is a political sovereign behind the legal sovereign. This political sovereign, as Dicey said, is the electorate. Laski has, however, restated the same thing in a pluralistic form. "There is probably a larger degree of obedience," he says, "from the sovereign Parliament to its constituents than there is the other way round; a series of by-elections, for instance, produce with amazing rapidity a change in the will and temper of the sovereign. Behind.... the legally omnipotent authority it is not very difficult to discern an electorate to whose opinions and desires increasing deference must be shown.

That notion of an increasing deference is important. As the community becomes organized into associations with the end of bringing pressure to bear on government, the sovereign organ becomes, as a general process, little more than a machine for registering decisions arrived at elsewhere. All the forms of an Austinian arrangement are preserved; but it is upon their saving condition that their substance is surrendered" (*47:53*). The pluralistic state is thus a state without sovereignty. It is just an association among other associations advancing no particular claims of legal majesty for itself.

The Fiction of Popular Sovereignty

The reaction of Laski to Rousseau's conception of popular sovereignty is equally hostile. He thinks that the theory of Rousseau is an impossible fiction. The hypothesis of Rousseau is that unlimited power in society should be vested in the people as a whole. Laski admits that the myth of popular sovereignty has been the theoretical basis of a number of popular revolutions—the most important of these being the American and French Revolutions. But the real criticism of the theory of popular sovereignty is that it always remained a myth. The sovereignty of the general will could not operate, as he thinks, even under the modern conditions of representative government.

According to Laski, administrative application of Rousseau's theory of popular sovereignty is not in the realm of a working hypothesis. Rousseau tried to distinguish between the state and government by assigning unrestricted power to the former. In the absence of representative institutions, the government was to be carried on either by perpetual plebiscites or frequent meetings of the assembly of all citizens. Laski thinks that "so frequent an elicitation of the sovereign's will" was not possible even in small states. The business of the modern state is too complex to be conducted in this way. In practice, democracy can mean no more than majority rule through elected parliaments and this was not acceptable to Rousseau. Laski feels that Rousseau's political system was likely to lead to oligarchical rule of "that minority" which is able to manipulate the will of the mass of the population. The conception of popular sovereignty in the sense of the whole people legislating, adjudicating and administering themselves was, therefore, an impossible fiction (*129:213*). It shows that Laski is neither prepared to accept the doctrine of sovereignty as a legal postulate of Austin's conception nor would he accept it in the form of Rousseau's myth of the general will.

CHAPTER 20
POLITICAL PLURALISM

Though pluralism and a pluralistic universe are long-established terms in philosophy, pluralism in political science is a relatively modern term.

Definition of terms

The pluralistic theory of the State is opposed to the monistic theory. Mabbott distinguishes between absolute monism and concrete monism. According to the former theory, the State is the only legitimate association and all others are to be suppressed by the State if necessary. No one in his senses would support such a theory today. Concrete monism, on the other hand, admits the need of functional associations, but wants to subordinate them to the State. This theory of the State has many followers among political thinkers. Pluralism, in the strict sense of the term, argues that the State and other associations are on a par with each other and that the State is not to have any superior value or status. Extreme pluralists would want to abolish the State altogether and transfer all its functions to other associations. In this respect pluralists are no different from anarchists. Most pluralists, however, do not go that far. They stop with guild socialism or at the most with syndicalism. Mabbott takes the view that the State is "a specialized association among others" (*141:119*).

In his well-known work *Political Pluralism,* Hsiao defines the monistic state as "one which possesses, or which should possess, a single source of authority that is theoretically comprehensive and unlimited in its exercise". By contrast, the pluralistic state is defined by Hsiao as "one in which there exists no single authority that is all competent and comprehensive, no unified system of law, no centralized organ of administration, no generation of political will".

Factors responsible for the rise of Pluralism

Among the factors, responsible for the rise of pluralism, the generally held opinion is that pluralism is a reaction to the absolutist conception of the State as held by Hegel in the nineteenth century and as it influenced the idealists, militarists and fascists. Hegel raised the State to a mystical height, viewing it as 'God on earth' and investing it not only with supreme legal but also with supreme moral authority. Coker regards this factor as secondary when compared with such factors as the rigid legal view of sovereignty as advocated by the analytical jurists since the days of John Austin. Critics remind us that Hegel interpreted the State primarily in terms of its moral supremacy and was not averse to the idea of functional representation, so dear to the hearts of pluralists particularly the guild socialists.

The legal view of sovereignty is often regarded by pluralists at any rate as the principal factor responsible for the rise of pluralism. But as impartial critics have pointed out there can be no gainsaying the fact that within the limits prescribed by Austin, sovereignty is supreme and that such sovereignty cannot be shared with other associations.

Closely connected with the legal approach to sovereignty is the conception of law as laid down by the analytical jurists. Pluralists such as Duguit and Krabbe object to the entire approach and hold that law as such (the spirit of law) is superior and anterior to the law laid down by the State. They forget that Austin and his followers are concerned only with positive law, legal law or statutory law; and are not directly concerned with such conceptions as moral law, natural law, and the sense of law embedded in the minds and consciences of people.

A fourth factor put forward by some writers for the rise of pluralism is the rise and rapid spread of federalism in the field of constitutions. Their argument is that the experience of federal states is that sovereignty in the Austinian sense of the term is difficult, if not impossible, to locate in a federal state. Therefore, they jump to the conclusion that pluralism is the only logical solution. One cannot very well agree with this view because, however difficult it may be to locate sovereignty in a federal state, it is not absent. As Hsiao says "Federalism and monism are not incompatible terms" (*113*:*7*).

The urgent need there is for an effective international law and international morality is often cited as a reason why sovereignty should undergo modification in the direction of pluralism. This argument too does not carry much conviction. It is possible to interpret the limitations of international law and international morality as auto-limitations or self-limitations. If the British Constitution can function satisfactorily on the basis of conventions, so can states with limited external sovereignty in a rapidly shrinking world. Internationalism and sovereignty are not incompatible with each other.

Pluralistic Thinkers

Pluralism in the western world may be said to have had its dim beginnings in the guild system of the Middle Ages.[1] In the unsettled conditions of those times, the merchant, trade, and craft guilds of the period came to enjoy considerable autonomy and assumed the character of corporations. *Otto Gierke* in Germany and *F. W. Maitland* in England, in the last quarter of the nineteenth century, may be regarded as the originators of pluralism in modern times, on the side of permanent groups within society. Both these writers look upon these groups as having a consciousness and a will of their own, as distinct from those of their individual members.

1. For ideas in this section the author is indebted to F.W. Coker and Hsiao.

Much the same doctrine of the 'real personality' of groups has been advocated by *J. N. Figgis* in relation to the Church. The Church, he says. does not exist by an act of grace on the part of the State but has 'powers of self-develepment like a person'. Its corporate personality is neither granted nor withheld by the State but has simply to be recognized. Human society, says Figgis, is not a 'sand heap of indiduals related only through the State, but an ascending hierarchy of groups'. The traditional doctrine of sovereignty is, therefore, according to him, 'a venerable superstition'. The general trend of his thought is that there are different spheres of action in which different groups should function exclusively.

Pluralism in England

Pluralism has found its support in England in the writings of the Webbs, G. D. H. Cole, H. J. Laski, A. D. Lindsay and E. Barker. They do not all adopt the same approach nor do they place the same emphasis on pluralism.

Cole may be regarded as the most vigorous upholder of pluralism among English writers; but even he toned down his views in his later years. According to Webbs and Cole, legislative power must be divided between several bodies or 'parliaments' so that the legislative function, as a constitutional instrument, becomes a system of balance of powers, not between a parliament and a supreme court but between many independent "functions" or organized interests so that every one of them should be in its own sphere supreme (Hsiao).

The Webbs, like Cole, envisage a "Social Parliament" and a "Political Parliament", the former to represent individuals as members in a "Social Democracy" and the latter to represent them in the capacity of citizens in a "Political Democracy". Suffice it to say that this is an impracticable division.

According to *A. D. Lindsay*, "the State.... can have control over the corporations within it only if, and so far as the citizens are prepared to give it such power". The State has no personality of its own, for the idea of a 'gruop mind', a 'group will' or a group personality in reference to corporations in an absurdity. The State is 'an organization of organizations'. While other organizations have a voluntary and selective membership, the State has a *compulsive* and *comprehensive* membership. But this uniqueness alone is not enough to justify the doctrine of a sovereign State.

Ernest Barker rejects the conception of the 'real personality' of groups. But he admits the juristic claim that the permanent groups within society existed prior to the State and that each of them has a corporate character and function of its own. 'The State', says Barker, 'as a general and embracing scheme of life, must necessarily adjust the relations of associations to itself, to other associations, and to their own members—to itself in order to maintain the integrity of its own scheme; to other associations in order to preserve the equality of associations before law, and to their own members in order to preserve the individual from the possible tyranny of the group'. The State is interpreted as a group of groups or a community of communities.

Pluralism in N. America

While there is no logical connection between pragmatism and pluralism in general, in the thought of *William James* the two seem to be linked together. James looks upon pragmatism as offering a middle course between absolute monism and absolute pluralism. Commenting on it, Hsiao observes that James loves a pluralistic universe, but that his reason tells him to choose a monistic order.

Miss M. P. Follet in her excellent book, *The New State,* shows distinct pluralistic tendencies, but refuses to take an extreme view. She looks upon the State as a unifying agency. It acts upon the individual not only through the various groups to which he belongs but also directly. In the striking language of the author herself: 'the state cannot be composed of groups because no group nor any number of groups can contain the whole of me, and the ideal state demands the whole of me. . . . My citizenship is something bigger than my membership in the vocational groups. We want the whole man in politics. . . . . The ideal unified State is not all-absorptive. It is all inclusive. . . . . The true State must gather up every interest within itself. It must take our many loyalties and find how it can make the one. The home of my soul is in the state'. This notable tribute to the uniqueness of the State from one who shows distinct pluralistic tendencies is indeed significant.

R. M. MacIver (originally a Canadian), in his *The Modern State,* advances the familiar pluralistic conception that the State is one association among many within the community, although exercising functions of a unique character. The State has the essential character of a corporation. It has 'definite limits, definite powers and responsibilities' (*55:473*). As a Corporation, 'it is the subject of rights and obligations which belong to it as a unity' (*55:473*)'. Other associations being as native to the soil of society as the state itself, the state is not their creator. 'It stands for the common interest of all individuals and associations, but not for the whole of the common interest' (*55:473*). 'The partial interests of a thousand associations, cultural and economic, are also parts of the common interest' (*55:476*). 'The business of the State is merely to give 'a form of unity to the whole system of social relationships'.

MacIver goes on to say that the legalistic conception of sovereignty is false and inadequate to explain the nature of sovereignty. In the first place, it is formal. Legally, the State is unlimited because it is the source of legal enactment. But so is the case with regard to the Church, because it is the source of ecclesiastical law. Secondly, the legalist doctrine speaks in terms of power, and not of service. Service is the end of the State, and power is its means. The service of the State is not unlimited and, therefore, the conception of unlimited sovereignty is 'dangerously false'.

The two writers who merit our serious attention under this heading are *Leon Duguit* of France and *H. Krabbe* of Holland.

Pluralism in Europe: Sovereignty and Law

Duguit is totally opposed to the theory that law is a command of an absolute and unlimited sovereign. Law, he says, is 'independent of, superior and anterior to political organization, and is objective, and not subjective' (Coker). Laws are the conditions of social solidarity or the interdependence of man. They are obeyed because they are the formal expression of social rules. They are necessary for the attainment of social solidarity. Law is not force. Law limits the State, and not the State, law. 'The State does not command but humbly serves'. Therefore, emphasis is to be laid on the duties of the State, rather than on its rights. Public service rather than sovereignty is to be its essential characteristic.

Law is certainly not the command of the State, according to Duguit. It emanates from many sources and this plurality, Duguit calls, legal decentralization.

Duguit further attacks the personality of the State which he considers is mere fiction. His argument is that the State has no real existence apart from the persons who comprise it and who are bound together by social interdependence.

Krabbe's point of view is essentially similar to that of Duguit. The starting point of his thinking is that law and political sovereignty were distinct entities in the eighteenth century, but gradually became amalgamated. His endeavour is to separate the two once again. The only sovereignty which Krabbe is willing to recognize is the sovereignty of law. Law, he argues, is independent of, and superior to, the State. It does not arise out of social solidarity, as in the case of Duguit, but is the outcome of the *sense of right* of the majority of the community constituting the State.

Law, according to Krabbe, is subjective and spiritual in origin. Power is not the essential feature of the State. The characteristic mark of the State is that it is a legal community. 'The State is nothing except a legal community....a portion of mankind having its own independent body of legal relations. Hence the State performs no function whatever except to impute legal value to certain interests'.

Unlike Duguit, Krabbe carries his idea of law into the realm of international relations. According to Krabbe, the sense of right should extend to international affairs as well, and to the extent to which progress is made in this direction, the legal activity of existing State should contract. Eventually, Krabbe believes that the present States will become provinces of one supernational State, but before this supernational plane is reached, the 'international community must pass through the phase of the idea of sovereignty' (*44:217*).

CRITICISM AND APPRECIATION

From what has been said-above it will be clear that the traditional doctrine of sovereignty has been assailed from three different angles : the angle of permanent groups or associations; the angle of international relations, and the angle of law. We shall deal with them one by one.

State Sovereignty and Group Autonomy

Pluralism contains a large element of truth, although it grossly exaggerates it. It is a welcome reaction against the glorification of the State. Whatever legal supremacy the State may possess, it should be subject to moral limitations.

In her admirable book, *The New State*, Miss Follett sums up the merits of pluralism as follows : (1) The pluralists prick the bubble of the present State's right to supremacy. (2) They recognize the value of the group and see that the variety of our group life today has a significance which must be immediately reckoned with in a political way. (3) They plead for a revivification of local life. (4) They see that the interest of the State is not always identical with the interest of its parts. (5) Pluralism is the beginning of the disappearance of the crowd. (6) It has seized upon the problem of identity, of association, and of federalism.

In spite of these merits, we cannot accept political pluralism for the following reasons :

(i) The logical conclusion of pluralism is anarchistic individualism although pluralists as a whole do not admit this truth. To divide sovereignty is to destroy it. Even after dividing sovereignty between the State and other associations, the pluralist is eager to assign to the State the function of coordination and adjustment. The State is viewed as a 'society of societies' or an association of associations' endowed with the function of adjusting relationships.

To perform this function satisfactorily, the State should be given supreme legal control. It should not tolerate the existence of any association which is hostile to general welfare and state policy which aims to promoting that end.

(ii) When the pluralist clamours for a slice of sovereignty for each of the permanent groups functioning within society, the most which we are prepared to concede to him is as much of local autonomy as will be consistent with the safety of the State and general welfare. Mabbott is right when he says, "Every association in its corporate capacity must keep the peace, be subject to criminal law, submit its disputes to the civil law, obey such regulations as are necessary for the achievement of those aims which only the State can secure, and contribute to the taxation which makes all the above State action possible" (*141:124*).

The Church, like any other association, is subject to the civil and criminal law of the country. There is no justification for extending any kind of immunity to the clergy as in medieval times or for tolerating clerical parties in politics as in certain European countries. "The Church.... can claim absolute freedom for her doctrines, her forms of worship, and the inculcation of her moral standards. She must render absolute obedience in the fields where the State is supreme—peace, security, order, health and contract" *(141:137)*.

(iii) The pluralist naively assumes that the various groups within society run along parallel lines and that there is no overlapping of functions among them. If this assumption were sound, there might be no occasion for a sovereign State. But the facts of social life are the overlapping of functions, the clash of interests, and the conflict of loyalties. For the settlement of this state of affairs we require an authoritative State. The guild socialists forget that no sharp line can be drawn between economic and political questions:

(iv) The monistic enemy whom the pluralists attack is, to a very large extent, an imaginary figure. We are not apologists for Hegelian absolutism. But very few monists today are Hegelians. None of the traditional supporters of sovereignty, barring the Hegelians, claim omnipotence for the State. They acknowledge the fact that the actual power of the State is limited by the possibilities of effective disobedience, as well as by restrictions of a moral and rational character. Such admission, however, does not entitle the pluralist to draw the conclusion that the State is not sovereign and that it has no superior claim to a person's allegiance.

The main tenets of monism, as summed up by Coker, as (a) that inter-relations between individuals and groups require an organization of unification and co-ordination, (b) that the organization should have the right to compel membership within a given territory, (c) that it should be endowed with coercive authority to carry out its orders, and (d) that there cannot be more than one organization of this kind in a given territory. All these contentions seem so sensible that we cannot conceive of serious opposition to any of them.

(v) The one unique feature of the State is that it is compulsive and comprehensive in its membership. Dr. Lindsay admits this uniqueness, but claims that it is not enough to constitute a sovereign State. We fail to see the logic of this position if sovereignty is interpreted, as in the preceding paragraph. The State, says Miss Follett, is a unifying and not mere co-ordinating, agency

(vi) Not only Miss Follett, but many other pluralists, fail to go clear over to the pluralistic goal of a non-sovereign State. This means that, in spite of their eagerness to establish a position of absolute equality for all essential associations, the logic of the situation compels them to give a supreme place to the State *(F. W. Coker)*. Thus we find that Gierke and Maitland, while ascribing real personality to groups, recognize the fact that the State is above other social bodies.

(vii) Pluralists do not make it absolutely clear just what it is that they want. If the State is to become an association like other associations, will the pluralists abolish compulsory taxation and compulsory citizenship? One thing which is clear is that the pluralists attack the sovereignty of the State in order that the various permanent groups within society may have as large a degree of local autonomy as possible. To such a legitimate desire no monist can rightly object: it is eminently just that a larger share in the control of industry and government should be given to those who are at present excluded from such control.

As a theory which corrects the excess of the traditional doctrine of sovereignty and supplements what is lacking in it, pluralism is a valuable theory. But when it seeks to supplant it altogether, it becomes dangerous, if not futile.

It is curious that in spite of their loud protestations against State authority, many pluralists ardently support, or at least complacently tolerate, other forms of social coercion. Even such an ardent lover of liberty as Laski declares: 'Legally no one can deny that there exists in every State some organ whose authority is unlimited.'

State Sovereignty and Internationalism

Here we find ourselves in substantial agreement with the point of view of internationalists. It seems to us that the need for external sovereignty is not so urgent as the need for internal sovereignty. The time has come for the States of the world to set up a strong, impartial and universally respected international body and abide by its decisions in all matters of common interest. The League of Nations and the Hague Tribunal were steps in this direction. The United Nations today has the potential power of becoming an instrument of world co-operation and peace, but before this can come about, the nations of the earth will find it incumbent to modify current adherence to absolute State sovereignty.

Already virtual limitations are placed on sovereignty by the Charter of the United Nations in Article 2, paras 4 and 7 and in Article 24, para 1. It is interesting to note that in the Nuremberg trials after World War II, the waging of aggressive war was not admitted to be a prerogative of State sovereignty.

If States are to surrender their sovereignty, either partially or wholly, in international relations, it may well be asked, what is to become of the doctrine of absolute, unlimited and indivisible sovereignty? Our answer is that the well-being of humanity is of infinitely greater importance than the forcible fitting of world situation into a preconceived theory in order to save face.

State Sovereignty and Law

The point of view of Duguit and Krabbe is something which we cannot very well accept. No organization in any community 'makes' the content of laws. Both in the way in which laws are made and in the way in which they are enforecd, they often reflect a will other than that of the formally constituted legislatures. If law were to be true to itself, it must possess the essential element of reason in it. The monist has no hesitation in accepting this point of view. Yet he cannot accept the pluralist definition of law.

(i) 'Social solidarity' is a term which does not have the precision conveyed by the term 'legal sovereignty'. If applied in a thorough-going fashion, it will substitute 'a social monism for political absolutism' (Hsiao) *(113:20)* It will mean the absolutism of existing social power. Furthermore, there is no reason to suppose that there is among human beings a unanimity of individual wills to justify an expression like 'social solidarity'.

(ii) The term 'sense of right' used by Krabbe is not any better. It is too subjective. Even if an objective interpretation could be given to it, it would lead to 'a logical monism of the most thorough-going sort'. Merely to use the magic expression 'community of interests', as is done by Krabbe, does not produce harmonious correlation within society.

(iii) The main defect in Duguit's theory is that he does not grasp the meaning of legal sovereignty. A legal system presupposes a legal sovereignty. Hsiao rightly remarks that a flat denial of legal sovereignty does not yield anything like a sound theory of politics as Duguit seems to think. 'Even the general rules of nature have to be interpreted and applied by a legal sovereign.'

(iv) Coker is right when he reminds Duguit, Krabbe, and other jurists that law is something which is *prescribed;* it is not merely what a commonsense of right demands or what the community demands. Outside a determinate person or legislature, we can speak of the spirit of laws, 'a common will', and the like, but we cannot speak of laws in their generally accepted connotation. 'Social solidarity' and 'sense of right' are incapable of giving us specific laws which can be interpreted and enforced by the judges.

(v) The theory under consideration seems to reopen the question of natural law and natural rights from which political theory has been comparatively free in recent times. To revert to natural law and natural rights will lead us into a labyrinth out of which political theory cannot easily find its way.

(vi) There is evidence to show that when these jurists attempt to limit the sovereignty of the State by means of law, what they really have in mind is the organs of government, and not the State itself. Duguit, in particular, fails to distinguish between State and Government.

CONCLUSION

(a) Pluralism, as said already, may be regarded as a welcome reaction against the excess to which the traditional theory of sovereignty has been carried by such of its supporters as Hegel. To attribute moral sovereignty to the State, as Hegel does, is a dangerous procedure to adopt. In so rejecting the State absolutism of Hegel, however, we do not necessarily become pluralists.

(b) Pluralism has rendered a great service to modern political theory by inviting the pointed attention of States to the reality of group life. There is no doubt that economic, professional, social, and religious groups play a vital and unique part in the life of the community. But all of this does not mean that the State should be reduced to a level of equality with other associations. The State should continue to be in a class by itself. It should remain supreme.

(c) Even after granting complete internal autonomy to the essential associations in the community, we require a superior organization for purposes of co-ordination and adjustments. If the State is only one association among many associations having similar power and similar status, it is difficult to see how it can satisfactorily fulfil its unique function of adjustment and adjudication.

(d) The innumerable groups which function in society do not exhaust all the services required for the well-being of man. They serve only partial interest. The State is the only organization which is competent to deal with the universal needs of the members of society.

(e) If we reject the monistic theory of sovereignty, the only logical position to take is that of the anarchists and syndicalists. Pluralism attempts an impossible middle position. Pluralistic doctrines are, in the long run, anarchistic doctrines.

(f) If the term 'sovereignty' is open to abuse and cannot be freed from the kind of absolutism assigned to it by Hegel, the term 'supremacy or final authority' will serve just as well from the point of view which we have adopted.

(g) The conclusion to which we have been led may be stated in the striking words of Sabine: 'For my own part, then, I must reserve the right to be a monist when I can and a pluralist when I must'.

THE PLURALISTIC VIEW OF LASKI

In contemporary political thought, the monistic theory of the state has been vehemently criticized by a number of political thinkers belonging to the pluralist school. Laski himself played an important part in the formulation of the pluralistic doctrine in the formative years of his political philosophy. Laski's pluralism was fundamentally a revolt against the philosophy of Hegel and the jurisprudence of Austin. It implied a complete reversal of the classical tradition in western political thought which regarded political authority as essentially monistic in nature.

The monistic conception of the state is at least as old as the modern state itself. Its leading exponents are Bodin, Hobbes, Rousseau, Hegel, Bentham and Austin. The monistic philosophers have argued that the state possesses a single source of authority that is by definition comprehensive and unlimited in its exercise. This supreme authority in the state is known as sovereignty. The monistic theory makes certain legal, sociological and philosophical assumptions which help the state in obtaining for itself a position of unrivalled moral supremacy in society. The pluralist wants to dislodge the state from its high moral pedestal by rebutting the legal, sociological and philosophical arguments of the monist. In the legal sphere, pluralism denies the doctrine of state sovereignty. On the sociological plane, it contests the organic conception of the state and society. In the philosophical arena, it fights the idealist philosophy of state worship. In the administrative field, it stands for decentralized government providing full freedom for the associative life of its citizens.

A Theory of Economic Organisation

But the scope of pluralism is not confined to the spheres of jurisprudence and political philosophy. It is at the same time a theory of economic organisation. Both Laski and Cole have emphasized the economic aspects of pluralism. They criticized the totalitarian tendencies of monopoly capitalism and advocated reorganisation of industry on pluralistic models. Cole developed this line of argument into a comprehensive philosophy of Guild Socialism. Laski's pluralistic notions in the realm of economics did not develop into any consistently pluralistic system as the guild socialist philosophy of Cole. Before his conversion to Marxian socialism, Laski advocated a vague conception of industrial federalism.

A Plea for Religious Freedom

The place of religious organisations in the modern secular state was another important problem to which Laski gave his particular attention. His pluralism is a passionate plea for religious freedom ever put forward in the history of political philosophy. His ideas in this respect were considerably influenced by those of Figgis who was an equally passionate supporter of religious freedom against the encroachments of the secular sovereign state.

Lack of Coherence in Laski's Theory

Laski's pluralism is not in itself a coherent sytsem of philosophy. It is rather a creative effort of great practical value in search of a political philosophy—a search which is still incomplete. As Norman Mackenzie says, Laski "left no finished body of tidy doctrines. On the contrary, his work is rather the record of a succession of dilemmas, each created by his effort to reconcile the march of hisotry conceived in Marxist terms with human dignity and liberty." If he failed to produce a rounded system of political philosophy in his life-time, we do not expect him to do better in his early years when his writings had been the product of a comparatively less mature intellect.

Pluralism represents the initial and tentative phase in his political theory. But it is an important stage in the evolution of his thought process. It has also left its impress on the successive phases of his political thought. Even when he became almost a Marxist, he did not abandon his emotional admiration for pluralism. It was his pluralistic past which prevented him from supporting the Marxist theory of proletarian dictatorship even when he acknowledged the Marxian analysis of capitalist society as fundamentally correct. Besides, both pluralism and Marxism refuse to accept the state as an institution of ultimate reference in social conflicts. The Marxian conception of communist society as a stateless society based on the co-operation of voluntary associations has a certain resemblance with the spirit of Laski's pluralism.

Intellectual Roots of Pluralism

The pluralistic theory of the state has sometimes been described as a doctrine of revolt in political theory. The intellectual roots of pragmatic pluralism can be discovered as early as in the scepticism and sensationalism of Hume. But the doctrines of Hume also influenced the ideas of Bentham and Austin who so shaped their conceptions of state sovereignty as to result in a legal monism of the most thorough-going type. The monistic tradition in English political thought was reinforced by the writings of the Oxford idealists who adapted the doctrines of Hegel and Kant to English conditions. The main current of the pluralistically inclined but not substantially pluralistic revolt in modern English political philosophy began with Hobhouse who repudiated the "metaphysical theory of the state" and laid the basis for further attacks by Barker, Figgis, Lindsay and Laski. The pluralistic point of view is clearly noticeable in Barker and Lindsay and is even more pronounced in Figgis and Laski. Even Dicey, a professed disciple of Austin, pointed out the practical limitations of state sovereignty.

Sovereignty as a Fiction

The doctrine of state sovereignty was questioned by Laski from a pragmatic point of view which saw in it a theoretical fiction which could not be realized in practice. In his writings, we may find probably the best statement of the pluralistic doctrine. "In all the varied current of contemporary political theory", says W. Y. Elliott, "which seems to have set against the conception of unitary sovereignty as the basis of the structure of the state, the work of Mr. Laski stands out sufficiently to command general attention. Perhaps this is as much because of the arresting fashion in which he has challenged the traditional doctrines of political theory as it is from the positive content of his theories" (*102:143*).

Gierke, Maitland and Figgis

In developing his criticism of the sovereign state, Laski made use of the theory of corporations as developed by Gierke, Maitland and

Figgis. The individualists opposed the absolute state in order to protest individual liberty. The pluralists wanted to discredit the sovereign state as they wanted to protect group autonomy. Laski agrees with the Gierke-Maitland theory that corporate persons are real moral persons and it is in the interest of these corporate persons within the state that the doctrine of state sovereignty is hotly contested.

Juristic Doctrines of Duguit

The juristic doctrines of Duguit also exercised a considerable influence on Laski's pluralistic interpretations of the state and law. Duguit developed a sociological view of jurisprudence which sought in the conception of *"solidarite sociale"* a justification for placing limitations upon the sovereign power of the state. Duguit regarded law as the expression of social solidarity and rejected the Austinian view that it was a command of the political superior. Laski did not sufficiently realize that Duguit's jurisprudence merely substituted a new doctrine of social monism in place of the old doctrine of political monism. Duguit's ideas as developed by Durkheim and Krabbe provided the basis of new monistic conclusions both in the spheres of legal and social theory. Duguit's conception of social solidarity was also exploited by the fascists to discredit the liberal state and establish their totalitarian regimes. Thus there was a latent contradiction between Duguit's jurisprudence and Laski's pluralism.

Pragmatism of William James

As Laski is a professed disciple of William James, he proposes a pragmatic test for the theory of state sovereignty. The pragmatic test of truth is its workability. A doctrine is true if its fruitfulness or workability can be proved in given circumstances. Laski says that the theory of state sovereignty fulfilled a great pragmatic need in the past in securing the independence of the secular state from papal dominance. It unified the political allegiance of the people to a common sovereign and produced a united nation out of warring religious factions. But Laski thinks that the theory of sovereignty has lost its pragmatic validity in modern times particularly in view of the growing challenge of powerful groups from within and some kind of international organization from without (*129:233*).

The State as First Among Equals

In the company of other groups, the State is only first among equals and nothing more. The State is only a particular group for Laski who says, "We then give to this particular group (i.e. the State) no peculiar merit. We refuse it the title of creator of all else. We make it justify itself by its consequences. We stimulate its activities by making it compete with the work of other groups co-extensive with or complementary to itself. As it may not extinguish, so it may not claim pre-eminence. Like any other group, what it is and what it will be, it can be only by virtue of its achievement. So only can it hope to hand down undimmed the torch of its conscious life."[2]

Criticism of the Austinian View

It is clear that Laski is attacking the Austinian conception of sovereignty not on a legal plane but on an extra-legal or moral plane. He is himself convinced of the technical correctness of the Austinian conception of absolute and legally unlimited sovereignty. He explains his position in these significant words, "It implies only that for the courts the will of the sovereign body, the King-in-Parliament for example, is beyond discussion. Every judge must accept unquestioningly what fulfils the requirements of the forms of law. But, for the purposes of political philosophy, it is not so abstract and *a priori* a definition we require. What we desire to know is not what has the legal right to prevail, but what does in actual fact prevail and the reasons that explain its dominance. Here, it is clear enough, the legal theory of sovereignty is worthless. Once we are in the realm of actual life it is upon the limitations of sovereignty that attention must be concentrated. What then impresses us is the wide divergence between legal right and moral right" (*122:40*). In this manner the discredited state is reduced to the position of a Church or a trade union or even a golf club. If the idealists erred in their cult of state worship by going to one extreme, there is no doubt that the pluralists like Laski also erred in their iconoclastic zeal of discrediting the state by going to the other extreme.

The State as a Power System

The state, as conceived by Laski, is a power system. "The monistic state," he says, "is an hierarchical structure in which power is, for ultimate purposes, collected at a single centre. The advocates of pluralism are convinced that this is both administratively incomplete and ethically inadequate" (*129:240*). The accumulation of power at a single centre of authority is the characteristic of a monistic state. In a pluralistic society, the power should not accumulate at the centre but should be diffused into the entire body politic reaching all peripheral points as well. Administrative decentralization is necessary for the general health of the community.

Administrative Decentralization

Administrative decentralization is the only remedy to check the despotic tendencies of a centralized administration prevailing in the monistic states. "The division of power", says Laski, "makes men more apt to responsibility than its accumulation. A man, or even a legislature, that is overburdened with a multiplicity of business, will not merely neglect that which he ought to do; he will, in actual experience, surrender his powers into the hands

2. Harold J. Laski: "The Problem of Sovereignty", in the "Harvard Law Review", Vol. XXIX, p. 426.

of forceful interests which know the way to compel his attention. He will treat the unseen as non-existent and the inarticulate as contented. The result may, indeed, be revolution; but experience suggests that it is more likely to be the parent of a despotism" (*129:241*). The pluralistic theory of government is essentially federalistic. But Laski does not think of federalism merely in the conventional territorial terms. It is applicable no less to functions than to territories.

Industrial Federalism

In the economic sphere, Laski's suggestions about the so-called industrial federalism have not been put forth in explicit terms. However, the emphasis on the autonomy of the trade unions is quite clear. Laski's defence of trade union rights is essentially pluralistic at this stage. The class war thesis of Karl Marx is still beyond his consciousness. He is compelled to defend the corporate rights of trade unions as a part of the general defence of the corporate rights of all associations and groups. His economic theory is at present a minor part of his general sociological doctrine. Defining his conception of social organisation, he says that this implies a federalistic conception of society in the economic as well as political spheres. He repudiates the paramount character of the state and affirms that its scope of activity is strictly limited. If it extends the areas of intervention, it will bring about definite disadvantages to society. He is not thinking in terms of division of powers in a federal political system. He rather pleads for a division of "power upon the basis of functions". He is trying to visualize "a society in which authority is not hierarchial but co-ordinate."

Structure of the Pluralistic State

When the state is to be theoretically divested of its sovereignty, the practical question that arises is what the actual sructure of the pluralistic state should be and how it should function. Laski's conception of political authority is based on pragmatic conception of the state and government. According to this pragmatic theory, the state is what it does and the state always acts through its government. For practical purposes, there is no effective distinction between the state and government. The doctrine of state sovereignty has been practically an instrument which is used by the government of the day to exercise supreme coercive authority over its subjects. When pragmatically considered, the sovereignty of the state in effect becomes the sovereignty of a particular government. The fundamental problem of political pluralism is to devise ways and means for preventing the absoluteness of governmental authority. The organization of power in the body politic should be such as to prevent the accumulation of power at any specific place. The concentration of absolute power in a single central organ results in the denial of liberty to the citizens and brings about gross inefficiency in administration.

Democratisation of Administration

Administrative decentralization is thus a necessary condition of the pluralistic state. Laski thinks that decentralization is the only way to democratize the administrative process because it enables a larger number of citizens both in their individual and corporate capacity to associate with the process of government. In a monistic state, the government is a set of persons set apart and above the people. The arrival of representative institutions has not obliterated the fundamental distinction between the governors and the governed. As Rousseau pointed out, the citizens of a representative democracy are free only at the election hour and even this freedom is limited to choosing their new enslavers for the next four or five years. Laski thinks that this weakness of representative democracy can be remedied, if the administrative machinery of the modern state is so reorganized as to provide the greatest opportunity for continuous consultation between the government and the people in their various associative capacities. The government ought not to be authorized to undertake any important decision of policy without consulting the group of the people most affected by it.

Laski recommends a radical change in the existing institutional machinery of the state. The existing institutional machinery puts an undue emphasis on administrative centralization. The central organs of the state have shown an increasing tendency to tighten their grip over the life of the community. They are not prepared to share administrative power on terms of equality with local administrative organs. They refuse to give even a consultative status to organized groups of public opinion in the community. A centralized state may be democratic in its external form but it is essentially oligarchical in its operative processes. The failure of representative democracy can largely be attributed to centralizing tendencies of the modern state.

The Federal Theory of Constitutional Organisation

The federal theory of constitutional organization represented a sharp break from the traditional theories of unified sovereignty which regarded the constitution of a centralized monistic state as the last word in political science. The emergence of federal politics has shown that there was no finality about the constitutional structure of a unitary state. Federalism became a pragmatic necessity for all those political societies which included in their fold peoples divided among themselves on grounds of race, religion, language and local loyalties. It also represents a greater fulfilment of the democratic idea because by dividing power it enables a larger number of citizens to snare it. Lastly, federalism is a practical ally of pluralism. Even James was aware of this kinship when he said, "The pluralistic world thus is more like a federal republic than an empire or kingdom. However much may be collected, however much may report itself present at any effective centre of consciousness, something else is self-governed and absent and unreduced to unity."[3] The pluralist thinks that federalization is a necessary stage in the establishment of a real pluralistic state. But this belief is not warranted by facts. The tendency towards centralization is visible in all the states which have adopted federal forms of constitutional organization. No realist can now argue that the United States or any other federal polity is likely to transform itself into a pluralistic state in any conceivable future.

Recent Trends in Federalism

It is obvious that Laski at this stage completely misunderstood the trends of development in federal constitutions which were leading towards centralization rather than towards decentralization. It appears that he was preoccupied with federal theory rather than with federal practice when he welcomed federalism as an ally of pluralism.[4] "Federalism", says Elliott, "which divides legal sovereignty by the terms of a constitution accepted by all the members of the body politic so created, in practice has tended to increasing unity, as is the case in the United States, or to a sovereignty in fact and in law, more and more completely absorbed by the constituent states, as is the case with the British Empire" (*102:163*). The division of powers implicit in federalism has never led to the so-called division of sovereignty which is regarded by Laski as a welcome transition to pluralism.

Decentralisation and Nonpluralistic Writers

The case for administrative decentralization has been argued even by certain non-pluralistic writers. "With centralization", says M. Lamenais, "you have apoplexy at the centre and paralysis at the extremities".[5] The most important advocates of territorial decentralization are the Distributists in England and the Regionalists in France. Belloc is the leader of the English Distributists. Deschanel, Hennessy and Ribot are among the more famous Regionalists. They think that a devolution of power from the central government to local units of administration is the only way to prevent apoplexy at the centre and avoid paralysis at the periphery. There are certain writers like Willoughby and Paul-Boncour who have advocated devolution of powers on functional basis. They propose that special administrative problems should be entrusted to autonomous and self-governing agencies. Independent commissions and autonomous boards should be created to administer specialized functions. Laski is not much interested in the Distributist or Regionalist scheme of territorial decentralization. But he is a strong advocate of functional decentralization on the lines suggested by Willoughby and Paul-Boncour.[6]

---

3. Quoted by Laski from James' "Pluralistic Universe" in "The Problem of Sovereignty", p. 10.
4. W. Y. Elliott : "The Pragmatic Revolt in Politics", Chapter V, pp. 162-63.
5. Quoted by Buel in his "Contemporary French Politics", p. 383.
6. C.H. Kung : "Political Pluralism—A Study in Contemporary Political Theory", Chapter IV, pp. 91-96.

Territorial Decentralisation in England

It is evident that administrative decentralization on a territorial basis has no logical connection with the pluralistic theory of the state. The devolution of powers to local administrative organs may be attempted without touching the monistic legal structure of the state.[7] England is the classical instance of a state based on a monistic legal structure. But in spite of parliamentary sovereignty, the local bodies in England have enjoyed the widest administrative autonomy in practice. In the United States, which is the classical home of federalism, the tendencies towards administrative particularism have not only been checked but the facts show that the American constitution has been developing in an opposite direction. The dualistic legal structure of the United States is gradually developing into a monistic legal structure necessitating readjustments in the administrative sphere as well.

Pluralism and Functional Decentralisation

Laski and the pluralists in general do not regard administrative decentralization as an end in itself. They want to utilize it only as a means for the attainment of a higher end which is the achievement of a pluralistic society. The pluralistic social order envisages the division of a political community into small functional republics cutting across the nation vertically and horizontally. Each functional republic of this kind, as the pluralists suggest, should administer its own affairs autonomously. The state should administer only that minimum residue of functions which are of common concern to the community as a whole and cannot legitimately be entrusted to any other social agency except the state.[8] The pluralistic state will be a state only in name because most of its existing functions will be entrusted to autonomous groups of various kinds. As the pluralistic state has not been realized in practice so far, the pluralistic ideals have largely remained utopian and impractical. The emergence of totalitarian states in the last few decades and the emphasis put on centralization even in the traditionally liberal states conclusively show that the world is not yet ripe for the pluralistic experiments in political and social re-organization.

Self-Government in Industry

No theory in political science can now claim a wide hearing which does not take into consideration the economic environment in which it is propounded. The pluralistic writers in general have criticized the authoritarian tendencies of monopoly capitalism which they regard as the negation of economic democracy. Sidney Webb, G. D. H. Cole and Harold J. Laski are the well-known leaders of the pluralistic revolt in economics. Sidney Webb in the beginning was a strong advocate of economic decentra-

7. *Ibid*, p. 97.
8. *Ibid.*, pp. 95-98.

lization but gradually he became an exponent of collectivistic socialism. His suggestion of a dual organization of society under two parallel bureaucratic hierarchies regulated at the top by 'political' and 'economic' parliaments respectively formed the basis of other pluralistic schemes of reorganizing industry on a pluralistic basis.

Guild Socialism and Syndicalism

Cole developed his theory of guild socialism which is probably the most comprehensive scheme of reconstructing the industrial world on pluralistic lines.[10] The syndicalist and anarchist theories have carried the pluralistic idea to its farthest logical limits. Laski's conception of industrial government does not wholly agree with either of these theories. As it stands somewhere between state socialism and guild socialism, it is much less pluralistic than either guild socialism or syndicalism. Of course, there can be little comparison, between anarchism and Laski's ideas of industrial reconstruction which recognize the necessity of ultimate supremacy of the state in the industrial sphere.[11]

Industrial System in Capitalist Countries

The purpose of industrial organization is to secure the regular supply of certain commodities to citizens as consumers and to safeguard what Laski calls the natural rights of men throughout the operations of the industrial process. The industrial system prevalent in capitalistic countries is defective in both these respects. It does not satisfy the principles of abstract justice as it is heavily biased in favour of the capitalists against the workers engaged in industry.[12] The worker has no guarantee of security of employment, of adequate livelihood or reasonable conditions of work under the existing industrial system. Nor has he any right of participation in the organizational control of the productive processes. "The broad characteristic of modern industry", says Laski, "is the almost absolute separation of management from labour. The area of consultations is narrowed down to the conditions attaching to the price to be paid for labour and the physical conditions of its employment. The worker has no right to express his ideas upon methods of production. He has no organized opportunity for suggestion. Even when he has demands to make, or grievances to put forward, their formulation usually involves a test of power in which the thing of import is not the moral quality of the demand or the grievance, but the strategic condition of the parties to the industrial relation. Nor, finally, has

9. For Webb's views, see his "A Constitution for the Socialist Commonwealth of Great Britain", Chapters I-IV.
10. For G. D. H. Cole's views, see his "Self-Government in Industry", Chapters I-III.
11. Harold J. Laski: "A Grammar of Politics", Part II, Chapter IX, pp. 433-520.
12. *Ibid.*, Part 1, Chapter V, pp. 201-11.

the worker any claim upon the product of his work. Once his price has been paid he is insignificant in relation to it. He is, in a full sense, that animate tool which to Aristotle was the essence of the slave" (47:733).

Responsibility of the State in the Economic Sphere

But it is not the producer alone who is in a deplorable plight. The interests of the consumer demand as much vigilance of the state as those of the producer. The industrial organization should be capable of satisfying the maximum cultural and material needs of the citizens. The economic needs of the community can be classified into three broad categories. In the first place, the community required certain commodities to preserve itself or to perpetuate the life of its members. The state must ensure an adequate supply of such commodities and the industries connected with their production should be run on a non-profit basis and their control be vested in the nation as a whole. Secondly, the community also needs certain commodities which are necessary to raise the standards of physical comfort and cultural attainments of its members. In the production of such commodities, the individual producer can play an important role alongwith cooperative forms of production. Lastly, there are commodities which have no universal demand and usually cater to the whims of a significant minority. The state, according to Laski, cannot take any responsibility for the supply of such commodities. It should only see that adequate standards in wages and reasonable conditions of work are maintained by the industry. It is evident from the above that Laski does not advocate anything like the disappearance or abolition of private enterprise. As a pluralist, he only wants to mitigate the monopolistic tendencies of modern capitalism.

Opposition to Nationalisation Policy of the Communists

Laski does not agree with the Communist programme of what he terms as "catastrophic nationalisation". He thinks that the process of nationalisation should be a piecemeal one so that the experience of one nationalised industry may be pragmatically used in the operation of other industries which are to be nationalised subsequently. If his programme of trial and error is followed, it will take a number of decades or even a century to establish a socialist sector in important branches of the national economy. The socialist and capitalist sectors will exist side by side for an unknown period. Laski does not consider complete abolition of the capitalistic system even as an ultimate goal to be achieved in some remote future.

It is obvious that Laski's advocacy of state socialism is in direct contrast with the spirit of pluralism. He rejects the syndicalist argument that the producers alone have the right to control their respective industries and expropriate its profits. "We reject", says Laski, ". . . .any purely syndicalist plan of industrial organisation. It is not less objectionable in principle than any other plan of private ownership. There is no reason to suppose that the ownership of the American mines by the United Mine Workers of America would be more careful of the public interest in coal than has been the case under their ownership by corporations like the present interests. The fact is that all exclusive control of this kind is morally vicious" (*47:439*).

Laski's State Socialism Incompatible with Pluralism

He, therefore, wants that the ownership of the major industries should be vested in the State or the community as a whole. "That is necessary," he says, "for two reasons. It emphasises where the ultimate incidence of control must rest. It enables us to insist that the producers in the industry are not entitled to regard it as existing solely for their benefit; they cannot therefore, claim such a level of prices as will give them a wage disproportionate either to need or to the result of effort. It emphasises also that the surplus value created by the industry, over and above cost of production and the distribution of the product to the ultimate consumer, belongs to the community as a whole" (*47:439*). By disagreeing with the syndicalist plan of industrial organisation which is more pluralistic than his own plan, Laski proves that he is not an uncritical adherent of the pluralistic dogma in the economic sphere.

Proposed Structure of Nationalised Industry

As regards the administrative structure of the nationalised industry, the internal operations of the industry will be controlled by a governing board at the apex. It will represent three distinct types of interests *i.e.* the management, the workers and the consumers. But the direction of general policy will still be vested in the legislative assembly. It is true that in the vast majority of cases, important administrative decisions will be made by the governing board and other subordinate administrative organs of each nationalized industry. All questions of practical importance and the details of administration will be worked out by those engaged in a particular industry. Laski is in favour of a large amount of practical autonomy in industrial government but this autonomy is to be exercised within the limits placed by the sovereign legislature. As the critics of Laski have pointed out, it involves an important contradiction in Laski's political theory. By placing the final control of nationalised industries in the hands of the legislative assembly, he implicitly admits the utility of the doctrine of sovereignty in practice despite the fact that he has attacked the theoretical aspects of the doctrine with great vehemence. It also shows that Laski's conception of industrial self-government is entirely different from the guild socialist or syndicalist conceptions which are based on much broader conceptions of industrial freedom.[13] It is very likely that Laski's State socialism will appear

13. See Bertrand Russell's exposition of 'Syndicalism' and 'Guild Socialism in his "Proposed Roads to Freedom", (New York, 1919).

in guild socialist and syndicalist eyes as a charter of new industrial tyranny rather than as a manifesto of true industrial liberty.

Cooperative and Private Sectors of Industry

In Laski's scheme, the nationalized industries will occupy only a fragment of the total industrial field. He envisages that a considerable part of national production will be carried on by private enterprise or through consumers' co-operation. But here the real point of significance is that he recommends a large amount of state control both in the cooperative and private sectors of industry. Moreover, his entire programme of industrial refrom can be successfully carried out only by a socialistically inclined Labour government on the condition that it remains continuously in power for some decades. If his programme is implemented to the full, it will democratize the present oligarchical organization of capitalist enterprise to a considerable extent. But the point is that the state which will actively intervene to implement his comprehensive programme of industrial change cannot be called pluralistic by any standards. Elliott has pointed out that it will be direct antithesis of the pluralistic State.[14] Government regulation of private industry on the scale recommended by Laski will require the assistance of a highly inflated bureaucracy. It implies a vast increase in the functions and coercive power of the state.

Criticism of Guild Socialism and Syndicalism

The guild socialist and syndicalist vision of autonomous communities of producers regulating their own affairs has no meaning for a collectivist like Laski. He thinks that the Guild Socialist and Syndicalist ideas are not likely to work in practice because they intend to carry the process of decentralization too far. Laski, on the other hand, favours a large amount of centralized control. The centralized control will not be limited to nationalized industries alone. The state control of private enterprise will be exercised through the Ministry of Production and national councils of each industry. The purpose of this kind of control will be to prevent private enterprise from operating in an anti-social way. But the Ministry of Production, governing boards and national councils will work as th instruments of a highly centralized, collectivist state.

Economic Democracy and Social Justice

The economic institutions of such a collectivistic state will no doubt be infused with a greater amount of economic democracy and social justice.[15] The position of the worker as a citizen will be much more dignified in collectivistic society than what it is in the existing individualistic society. In comparison with the *laissez faire* regimes of the past, the collectivistic state is decidedly far superior not only in its administrative technique and

14. See his article on Laski in his "Pragmatic Revolt in Politics", where he justifies his view by an elaborate analysis of Laski's economic theories.
15. *Ibid*, pp. 539-40.

economic results but also in its ethical basis and cultural potentialities. But this is not the real point at dispute. The question is whether the collectivistic state as contemplated by Laski can possibly be organized by eliminating the conception of sovereigenty from it. Judging from the nature and functions of a collectivistic state, it seems reasonably certain that it cannot continue to exist as a non-sovereign state. The state which refuses to assert its sovereignty cannot be expected to bring about that revolutionary change in property relations which Laski considers as necessary for the establishment of a new social order.

According to Rober Dahl, pluralist writers "suggest that there are a number of loci for arriving at potential decisions; that businessmen, trade unions, politicians, consumers, farmers, voters and many other aggregates all have an impact on policy outcomes; that none of these aggregates in homogeneous for all purposes; that each of them in highly influential over some scopes but weak over many others; and that the power to reject undesired alternatives is more commom than the power to dominate over outcome directly. " (*263 : 103*).

While the dominant model of pluralism is related to elite behaviour in liberal-democratic societies of developed capitalism, some writers apply it to ethnic, religious, and cultural groups competing for power and influence in the political systems of the transitional or developing societies. This is called the *primordial* pluralist model. Sometimes, primordial affiliations can assert themselves in highly industrialized countries, such as the Blacks in the United States. (*263 : 105*).

CHAPTER 21

LAW

Just as the idea of sovereignty is central to the idea of the State, so the idea of law is central to the idea of sovereignty. We may go one step further and say that the idea of justice is central to the idea of law.

The evolution of law may be dealt with from the narrow legal point of view or from the broad philosophical point of view. We shall deal with it in both ways taking up the philosophical aspect first.

The Philosophy of Law: Historical Treatment

From the very beginning of political speculation, thinkers have been at pains to discover the significance of law to the State and society. In his *Republic,* Plato posed the question whether a State should be governed by men or by measures (law) and gave his verdict in favour of the former. But at Plato grew older and became more practical he gave greater importance to law. In the *Statesman* he makes government by law and government by wise men two alternatives. Law rather than knowledge is to be the ruling force. This idea is carried still further in Plato's *Laws,* where the balance is tilted in favour of laws.

Aristotle who was a realist in politics emphasized law from the very start. He taught that "uniform laws uniformly administered" was the mark of a good state and defined law as "reason unaffetced by desire". According to him, a ruler who rules according to law is different from a dictator. He rules by consent.

More than any other people in the ancient world, the Romans developed the idea of law to a remarkable extent. To Cicero we owe the well-known sentence: "For as the laws govern the magistrate, so that magistrate governs the people, and it can truly be said that the magistrate is a speaking law and the law a silent magistrate."

Justinian's *Digest* is a landmark in the evolution of law. In developing the concept of law, the Romans evolved three closely related concepts, *jus naturale* (natural law), *jus gentium* (law common to nations) and *jus civile* (civil law).

Although natural law and the law of nations were distinguished from each other for some time, later on they merged together to form the beginnings of international law at the hands of Grotius.

In the Middle Ages the common law of the Church carried forward the tradition of the natural law and adjusted it to a Church-centred society. In the economic and social fields where feudalism held sway for a few centuries, there were different laws for different classes of people. This pernicious system continued in France up to the Revolution.

Coming to the modern period in Western political thought, we find Grotius (1583-1645) defining law as a "dictate of right reason". "The mother of law," he wrote, "is human nature itself". As Hallowell states it, right is what is in accordance with reason. Law is to follow the dictates of reason rather than the impulses of subjective and particular desire.

Hobbes defined law as the "command of that person....whose precept contains in it the reason of obedience" (*162:400*). The law of nature is law only in a figurative sense. What limits the sovereign is not the law of nature, but the power of his subjects. Locke looked upon natural law as the law of inward morality. Law in the State is law made by the King-in-Parliament but it is limited in scope. The State cannot make any and every law it pleases. It was a flash of genius which made Rousseau write "Obedience to a law which we prescribe to ourselves is liberty". In this short sentence one finds the true meaning of law and liberty and the basis of democracy.

According to Bentham, the object of law is to promote the greatest happiness of the greatest number. All laws are evil because they are an infringement on liberty. In deciding what he should do, the legislator should use the calculus of pleasure provided by Bentham.

After Bentham came John Austin (1790-1859) who is regarded as the founder of the analytical school of jurisprudence. According to him, law is a command and the principal reason for obeying it is fear. Positive law is the only true law. True to the tradition set by Rousseau, Green claimed that in obeying the will of the well-ordered State, one obeys one's will purged and purified of selfishness. MacIver writes, "Without law, there is no order, and without order men are lost, not knowing where they go, not knowing what they do" (*142 : Ch. IV*).

Schools of Jurisprudence

In studying the approach made to law by different writers, one can broadly distinguish three schools of thought. In connection with Austin, we have already used the term, the *analytical school.* Besides Austin, Machiavelli, Bodin, Hobbes and Holland also belong to this school. According to this school, sovereignty is vested in a determinate person or body of persons and law emanates from such a body. The law-givers may be a legislature or a judiciary; but whoever they may be, they should be capable of location. The primary reason for obeying law is force and restraint.

The defect of this theory is that law becomes static and lacks the drive for progress. Sir Henry Maine and Savigny questioned the assumptions of the analytical school and put forward the view that law was the result of a long historical process. For this reason they are said to belong to *the historical school of jurisprudence* : Hallowell sumps up their teachings as follows :

(1) Law is relative to time and place and to particular people. (2)

Since law is found not in reason or in conscience but in the historical process, the individual has little or no responsibility for shaping the content of law; (3) the idea of individual natural rights is replaced by the idea of the historic rights of Englishmen, Frenchmen, Germans etc.; (4) since reform is impossible, it is better to allow the historical process to work itself out without hindrance; (5) the idea of a transcendental natural order is replaced by the idea of an order immanent in the historical process; and (6) the sanction of law is conceived less in terms of the inherent justice of the rule and more in terms of the social pressure behind it.

According to Savigny law is embodied in the folk-spirit or folk-mind of a people. It is rooted essentially in customs and is linked up with nationality. History can tell us not only how we have come to be what we are, but also to anticipate our future destiny.

To the *Sociological School* belong such writers as Duguit, Krabbe, and Laski. They regard the traditional view of law as futile. According to Duguit, laws are obeyed not because there is someone to enforce them, but because they are the conditions of social living. "Social solidarity" is the key phrase and laws are relative to it. They are so vital to social living that it is in the self-interest of the individual to obey them. Laws, "in the fundamental sense are the rules of conduct which normal men know they must observe in order to preserve and promote the benefits derived from life in society" (*117:172*). The sanction behind law is primarily psychological "resting in each individual's awareness of the social approval or reprobation of his conduct according to its conformity or non-conformity to fundamental social lures" (*117*).

In the thought of Krabbe, man obeys laws out of a sense of right. Laws are above the State and independent of them. They are rooted in man's standards of value and judgment. "The rule of law....is due to human reaction to the sense of justice and is not a matter of eternal legal authority but an internal human matter".

As against this view, it is possible to argue that "sense of right" is only a thin veil for "self-interest". Even if "sense of right" can be given something like a precise meaning it is bound to vary "from century to century, from nation to nation, from group to group, indeed from man to man" (*45:142*).

In coming to our own conclusion with regard to the above three schools, it seems fair to say that none of them contains the whole truth. They supplement and complement each other. Laws are not merely a fiat of the State. They are not just commands of a determinate human superior. They are dependent on the social, moral, economic, and religious outlook of the people. They are also dependent on what the community considers to be fair and just. No law will be obeyed very long if it does not accord with the people's ideas of right and wrong.

Yet law is a command. Even bad laws, if democratically formulated have to be obeyed until they are democratically abrogated. They require physical compulsion behind them in the last analysis. Without such compulsion, great many whose moral and social sensitivity is poorly developed will not obey laws.

From the above discussion of law more or less in the philosophical sense of the term, we now proceed to a discussion of law from other points of view especially from the point of view of positive law.

The Nature of Law

The term 'law', points out Gilchrist, is derived from the old Teutonic root 'lag' which means something which lies fixed or evenly. Its English equivalent is 'that which is uniform'. In the words of MacIver "Law in its broader significance reigns everywhere. Where life exists there are universal laws of life, and for each form of life after its kind" *(55:250)*.

The word 'law' is used in a variety of senses. (1) Scientific law is law in which can be traced the sequence of cause and effect. Examples of such law are the laws of motion and the laws of gravitation. Unlike human laws they are universal and eternal. (2) Social laws are laws or customs for the guidance of the individual as a member of society. (3) Moral laws are laws which deal with matters of intrinsic right and wrong, of good and bad; they deal with motives of conscience. (4) Political laws are laws regulating man's behaviour as a member of the State. For the most part, they deal with external conduct and are enforced by "a system of compulsions".

Between social laws and political laws there is much in common. However, social laws do not carry with them the same kind of coerciveness contained in political laws. To quote MacIver: "Every association makes laws, but the laws of other associations, in the developed state, bind the members of them only in so far as they prefer to accept them rather than lose the benefits of membership" *(55:17)*. The impulse to obey social laws lies wholly within us, but political laws are external and must be accepted if order is to be insured.

Definitions of Law

Definitions of law are many and varied. The following will serve as samples. According to Montesquieu, a law means "the necessary relations arising from the nature of things". Woodrow Wilson who seeks to harmonise the analytical and the historical approaches to law defines law as "that portion of the established thought and habit which has gained distinct and formal recognition in the shape of uniform laws backed by the authority and power of government".

Holland who on the whole seems to follow the Austinian tradition defines law as "a general rule of action taking cognizance only of external acts, enforced by a determinate authority, which authority is human and among human authorities is that which is paramount in a political society; or briefly, a law is a general rule of external action enforced by a sovereign political authority".

Salmond defines law as "the body of principles recognized and applied by the State in the administration of justice".

From the above definitions of law it is possible to deduce certain essentials of law. They are: (1) laws imply the presence of a civic community; (2) they reflect the social conditions of that community; (3) they are a set of rules, (4) they regulate the external or the outer conduct of man; (5) they imply coercion, more physical than moral.

The Sources of Law

In a vital sense all laws proceed from the State. But behind State enactment one can detect several factors which have entered into the making of laws. Holland mentions six of them which are custom. religion, adjudication, scientific discussion, equity, and legislation.

(1) *Custom*: The earliest form of law in every community is custom. A still earlier variation of it is folkways. As MacIver *(142: Ch IV)* writes, no individual person makes or unmakes folkways.

Folkways gradually transform themselves into custom in early society which has transcended the primitive level. In such a society custom is the king. It is obeyed for a variety of reasons such as the force of habit, its social utility, and the security which it provides. Even today custom accounts for a considerable part of law. But behind such blind obedience one can often detect a social utility. Apropos of this, MacIver writes: "In the great book of law the State merely writes new sentences and here and there scratches out an old one. Much of the book was never written by the State at all" *(55:478)*. The customary law of India and the common law of England are good illustrations of the notable part played by customs in the evolution of law.

(2) *Religion*: Customary law, particularly in early societies, is closely related to religion. In such societies it is very difficult to draw a sharp line between religious prescriptions, customs, and laws.

Writing on the broad distinction between laws in the East and those of the West, Gilchrist pertinently remarks: "In the West law tended to become political; in the East, religious" *(28:162)*. The Hindu Law draws its inspiration from Manu just as the Muslim Law draws it from the Shariat. It is desirable that in time to come there should be a single system of law of all the members of a state since so many of the so-called religious laws have become out of date and tend to be a divisive, rather than a unifying force.

(3) *Adjudication*: As social organization became more and more complex, custom had to be supplemented by adjudication or legal decision. When tribes came together for trade, marriage or other such purposes, conflicts of customs arose. Cases of this nature were referred to the wisest men of the community.

Even today the interpretation of law is an important instrument in the making of law. The case law or common law of England and decisions of the Supreme Court of the U.S.A. are illustrations of this method. By it laws are expanded and made to fit into changing conditions and the new demands of the day. Thus judges have an important part to play in law-making. Chief Justice Hughes of the U.S.A. is said to have remarked that the constitution is what the judges say it is.

(4) *Scientific Commentaries*: These are the works of eminent jurists who collect and compare past customs, decisions and laws. They also point out the omissions and suggest ways by which improvements could be effected. Such treatises natually do not have the force of law or even of judicial adjudication But lawyers and judges have great respect for them if what they say has intrinsic worth and are scientific in their approach.

Illustrations of writers who have left their impress on law are, Coke, Hale, Littleton, and Blackstone in England; and Storey and Kent in America. A position of similar respect is assigned to the Mitakshara and the Dayabhaga systems of India.

(5) *Equity*: The term means equality, fairness or justice. In a sense, it is a judge-made law and an extension of adjudication. While adjudication is concerned with interpreting and applying existing law to cases as they come along, equity breaks new ground altogether. Where the existing law does not apply properly, the judge is expected to give his judgement according to commonsense or fairness.

Gilchrist speaks of three types of equity: (1) exclusive, (2) concurrent, and (3) auxiliary. "Equity is exclusive where it recognizes rights not recognized by the common law, it is concurrent, where the law recognizes the right but does not give adequate relief; and auxiliary, where the necessary evidence cannot be procured" (*28:167*).

(6) *Legislation*: In modern society this is the most direct and most prolific source of law. In democratic countries laws are made by popularly elected representatives and are thus said to reflect the will of the people. Not all laws made are wise or necessary. Some of them are superfluous and even futile. But that is the price one has to pay for the luxury of democracy.

While equity, legal decisions, and scientific commentaries still have an important part to play, the laws made by the legislature are coming to occupy a superior place. If legislators were more wisely chosen and did not have to work under the necessity of initiating a new bill or clause in a bill or amendment in order to justify their existence, more wise and really essential laws are likely to be passed.

The whole process of the development of law is ably summed up by Woodrow Wilson as follows:

"Custom is the earliest fountain of law, but religion is a contemporary, an equally prolific, and in the same stages of national development an almost identical source. Adjudication comes almost as authority itself and from a very antique time goes hand in hand with equity. Only legislation, the conscious and deliberate organization of law, and scientific discussion, the reasoned development of its principles, await an advanced stage of its growth in the body-politic to assert their influence in law-making".

TYPES OF LAW

MacIver classifies laws as follows :—

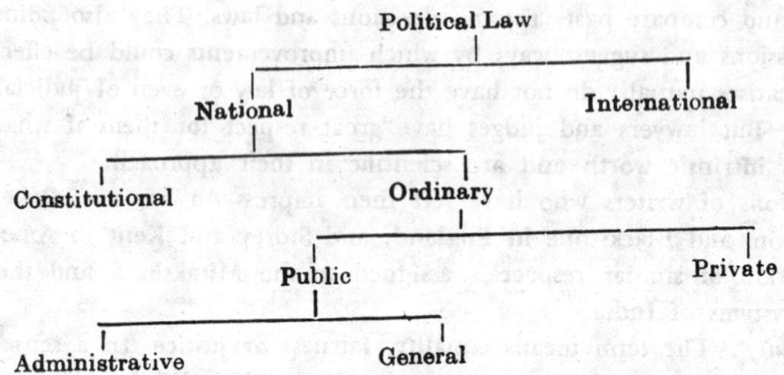

(1) *Constitutional Law* : Distinction is often made between the fundamental law which governs the organization of the State and government and the law by means of which the State governs the people. The former regulates the powers of the government, the rights of the governed, and the relations between those who govern and the governed. The latter deals with all other matters. Constitutional law may be written or unwritten. Where it is written, it is usually done by a Constituent Assembly like the one which India had in evolving the Act under which she is governed today. The ordinary law-making body also may be used for the purpose as was the case in India. Parliament was at the same time the Constituent Assembly. Customs and usages also play their part. In whatever way it is enacted, constitutional law carries with it a special sanctity and is not frequently amended.

(2) *Ordinary Law or Statue Law* : This is the most important type of law, which governs the everyday life of the individual. It is the law made by the King-in-Parliament in the United Kingdom, by Parliament in India, and by Congress in the United States. In the U.K., it needs to be remembered that the same Parliament by the same procedure can pass both ordinary laws and constitutional laws. Such is not the case elsewhere. Ordinary law is divided into (a) public law and (b) private law.

Holland describes public law as law in which the State or a delegated authority of the State is concerned. This would include administrative law of which we shall speak later. Private law, on the other hand, deals with cases where the parties involved are private persons and neither of them represents the State directly or indirectly.

Public law, says Holland, is concerned with the organisation of the State, the limitation of governmental functions, and the relations of the

State to the individual. "In private law the parties concerned are private individuals, above and between whom stands the state as an impartial arbiter. In public law also the State is present as arbiter, although it is at the same time one of the parties interested".

(3) *Ordinances* with which India is all too familiar are issued by the executive branch of the government within the limits laid down by law. As a rule, they are not permanent and are issued for the sake of administrative convenience, particularly during an emergency. The Ordinance (July 1960) to deal with the strike of the Central Government Employees and the other dealing with the Bank Nationalization (1970) in India are illustrations in point.

(4) *Municipal Law* is national law in contrast with international law. It includes both public and private law. It applies to all individuals and associations of individuals within the territorial limits of a given State. It has no jurisdiction over those living outside.

(5) *Internatonal Law* relates to the dealings of States with one another. We shall deal with it separately on account of its growing importance in the world.

(6) *Judge-Made Law*[1]. *Case-Law or Common Law.* In some countries at least the courts make and develop law. Where statutory law is not always clear or full or not free from ambiguities of language, the meaning, spirit and implications of law have to be spelt out by courts. Where the existing law is silent, the judge may consult customs, equity, and the like. This is the way that the Common Law of England has been built up. This type of law is known as "case law" or "judge-made law".

In Latin countries, this procedure is known as jurisprudence. In Anglo-American countries,[2] it means the right of the judges to constitute and interpret statutes. It also means the right to decide what the common law is when the statute law is silent. Judges are to interpret not only what the legislature meant by a statute but what it would have said if a point which was not present there had been present.

In France where the law is silent, obscure or insufficient, the judge is compelled by law to do justice. This is the way that the Roman law was built up from its humble beginning in the Twelve Tables.

As regards the content of judge-made law or common law in England, Garner writes: "It includes the greater part of the law of the contract, almost the whole of the law of torts, all the rules or doctrines of equity, and the body of law known as the conflict of laws; or, as it is sometimes called the body of private international law" (*23:777*). Such common law is not found in any statute books, but in the reports of the courts. In France

1. For the material in this section the author is indebted to J.W. Garner (23 : 775).
2. Countries which have followed the Anglo-Saxon system of law to a greater or lesser extent.

the whole of the administrative law has been built up by the decisions of the Council of State, which is the supreme administrative court of the country.

Bentham was opposed to this method of explaining and expanding law by judges. He regarded it as an encroachment on the functions of the legislature. Bryce, on the other hand, upholds it as providing the necessary loophole for "the expansion or extension" of law.

The decisions of the courts constitute precedents and these exercise a great influence, especially in Anglo-Saxon countries. They are regarded as a source of law and the courts are bound to further them. There is no such moral compulsion in the continental countries in general where even inferior courts may depart from them. In the Anglo-American countries, the superior courts can depart from or overrule precedents, but they do not do it generally.

(7) *Administrative Law* has been defined as "that part of public law which fixes the organization and determines the competence of the administrative authorities and indicates to the individual remedies for the violation of his rights".

Administrative courts are found in France, Germany and several other European countries, parallel to the ordinary courts (but not in India). They deal with cases involving claims against the State and apply laws different from the civil law. The idea of separate courts and separate laws for administrative cases arose in France. The argument was that a State officer applying law is different from ordinary individuals in private cases. The administrative issues involved could not very well be grasped or taken into full account by ordinary courts and ordinary judges. Therefore, for such judges to deal with the above cases would mean "interference with the operations of the Government and impair the efficiency of administration". Special administrative tribunals or courts were therefore set up for the purpose. The Council of State is the highest court under this system. Just as the English courts have built up a large body of common law, the Council of State has built up a large body of administrative case law. Originally meant to prevent the interference of ordinary courts in administrative cases, today their major function seems to be to protect the individual against "the arbitrary and illegal acts of government and its administrative agents" *(23)*.

In England and the U.S.A. an aggrieved individual cannot generally sue the State, but only the particular officer or agent concerned who is supposed to be personally responsible. This method has not often been very effective. The Council of State in France decides thousands of cases with speed and little expense to the person concerned.

In the Anglo-Saxon countries and others which follow their system, the State can be proceeded against only by petition of right. A public official has to be proceeded against as though he was another private individual. Even though the British system does not admit special administrative courts, yet there are many subordinate administrative tribunals, boards, commissions and authorities performing much the same function. But the theory is that in Anglo-Saxon countries any public official can be called up before an ordinary court for his public acts.

Criticism: For a long time there was a general prejudice in the Anglo-Saxon countries against administrative courts. But such prejudice is not so strong now. In every country the ordinary citizen has a different status from that of the government official as regards privileges and immunities. Judges of administrative courts, contrary to the popular opinion, are not at the mercy of the government of the day, but have shown considerable independenec of action. In hundreds of cases they have decided in favour of individuals against government officials. Considerations of equity are often taken into account. Garner says that for the French people the Council of State has come to have a position of respect similar to that enjoyed by the Supreme Court in America.[3]

INTERNATIONAL LAW

Definitions of International Law

Lawrence defines international law as "The rules which determine the conduct of the general body of civilized States in their mutual dealings". According to Brierly, it is "the body of rules and principles of action which are binding upon civilized States in their relation with one another". To Fenwick it means "the body of general principles and specific rules which are binding upon the members of the international community in their mutual relations". Pitt-Cobbett holds that international law is "the sum total of the rules accepted by civilized States as determining their conduct towards each other and towards each other's subjects". Oppenheim defines it as "the body of customary and conventional rules which are considered legally binding by civilized States in their intercourse with each other".

The paramount question is how far are the claims of international law to be called law justified in the light of the nature of law? To an answer to this question we now turn.

Is International Law law at all?

If law is interpreted as "the will of the sovereign" in the sense interpreted by Hobbes and Austin, then the claim of the law of nations falls to the ground. Oppenheim (*International Law*, p. 7) rightly holds that such a narrow, legalistic definition of law ignores the existence of customary law; and that at the same time it wrongly presupposes that a law must always have 'a law-making authority' prior to its existence and that "it must receive recognition" before it is called a law. Furthermore, the conception of law under question is only partially correct as it ignores the totality of its "essence and comprehension".

---

3. For further details of Administrative Law and Administrative Courts see chapter on Organization of Government under the Judiciary.

Oppenheim solves the tangle by giving a more scientific definition of law as "a body of rules of human conduct within a community which, by the common consent of the community, shall be enforced by external power". This means that law has three essential components : (1) a community; (2) a body of rules for human conduct within that community (both customary and conventional), (3) enforcement of these rules by external power. Oppenheim says that "a community may be said to be a body of a number of individuals more or less bound together through such common interests as create a constant and manifold intercourse between its members". This means that there can be a true international community, as distinct from a mass of humanity. Where there is such a community we find certain customary conventional rules of conduct. Trouble arises, however, with regard to enforcement. It is obvious that the execution of international law as compared to the execution of domestic law is weak because of a lack of "a permanent machinery" to give expression to the "common consent" of the community. But where such common consent is present, as is often the case, the enforcement of international law becomes possible.

Those who object to the above interpretation may hold that the so-called international law is no more than international morality. Oppenheim gives a fitting reply to it when he says : "A rule is a rule of morality, if by the common consent of the community it applies to conscience and to conscience only; whereas, on the other hand, a rule is a rule of law if by the common consent of the community it will eventually be enforced by external power".

Thus for the existence of law neither a law-giving authority nor a court of justice is absolutely indispensable, however important they may be. In spite of this truth, it may be said that the law of nations is a weak law, when compared with the municipal law. Even if this be true, the admission does not take away from the law of nations the character of law. The weakness is due to the fact that international law is a law *between* sovereign states and not *above* them.

Sources of International Law

The common consent of nations is the basis of the law of nations; but this does not mean simultaneous consent. It simply means that no single nation can unilaterally alter existing international law.

Consent can be both *express* and *tacit,* respectively known as conventional and customary international law. Article 38 of the Statute of the International Court of Justice directs the court to apply the following canons, which, in turn, form the source of the law of nations (See Brierly : The *Law of Nations*, p. 576) :—

(a) International conventions, whether general or particular, establishing rules expressly recognized by the contesting states.

(b) International customs, as evidence of a general practice accepted as law.

(c) The general principle of law recognized by civilized nations.

(d) Subject to the provisions of Article 59, judicial decisions and the teachings of most highly qualified publicists of various nations as subsidiary means for the determination of rules of law. Pitman Potter considers the following as the principal sources of international law:—agreement and consent, international treaties, legislative action taken in international conferences, decisions of judicial bodies, both national and international, and writings of jurists.

Theories of the Nature of International Law

(a) One of the oldest of theories is that of the *Naturalists.* Pufendorf is the father of this school. His ideas were developed in the eighteenth century by Rutherford. According to this theory, the law of nature is the sole source of the law of nations. It denies the claim of customary international law to be called law at all. According to it, the law of nations is only a part of the higher law of nature.

(b) The *positivists* led by Richard Zouche (1590-1660) as interpreted by Oppenheim. According to them international law is not *above* states but *between* states. In other words, the chief source of the law of nations is the consent of the state, and so the law of nature has little to do with it.

(c) The Grotian school adopts a middle position between the above two theories. It was developed by Wolfe (1679-1754) and Vattel (1714-1767). In the words of Oppenheim, "Just as the law of nature applies to men taken individually so also it must apply to them, taken collectively, *i.e.*, as organised states" (*153:93-94*). Thus while conceding the claims of national sovereignty, this school asserts the existence of external limiting factors of the same in the law of nature.

Of the three schools, the Naturalist school held the field until the close of the Middle Ages. It received considerable support from the writings of the Greek, Roman, and mediaeval writers such as Aristotle, Cicero, and Aquinas. The consolidation of the principle of sovereignty beginning with the modern period witnessed the rise of the positivist school which received further support in the writings of Bodin, Hobbes, and Austin.

Twentieth century developments can well be called a revival of the Grotian school in a more rationalized form due to two factors. The first of these is the growth of international organizations and conventions, limiting the absolutist claims of national sovereignty such as the Hague Conventions (1899, 1907); the Covenant of the League of Nations (1919), the Pact of Paris (1928); the Charter of the United Nations (1945); the Geneva Convention (1949); and the Panchsheel (1955). The second factor is the re-emergence of humanist philosophies in rationalized forms, as in the writings of Laski, Russell, and M. N. Roy. Resting on a world outlook, the doctrine of Marxism too, in a negative way, has done much to counter the old positivist conceptions of international law.

The twentieth century has further witnessed the codification of international law, making for precision as well as elaboration.

Public and Private International Law

Public international law relates to the rights and duties of States. At times it relates also to sub-state entities. Private international law, says Potter, "consists essentially of principles for resolving conflicts of law or jurisdiction among States over individuals, their activities, and their property".

The Relation between Municipal Law and International Law

As on most issues, there are two points of view with regard to this question : (a) the dualistic and (b) the monistic view. According to the dualistic view, the two types of law differ (i) because their sources differ. Whereas municipal law develops through customs and enactments *within* a State and is enforced by the *sovereignty* of the State, international law develops through customs which have grown within the family of nations and law-making treaties concluded by the members of that family (*153 : 35-36*).

(ii) The two systems differ as regards the relations they regulate. Whereas municipal law regulates the relations between individuals under the control of a State, international law regulates the relations between the member-States of a family of nations.

(iii) The two systems further differ as regards substance. Whereas municipal law is the law of a sovereign over the individuals subject to its control, the law of nations is a law, not 'above' but 'between' sovereign states.

In view of these differences, advocates of the dualistic view regard municipal law and international law as altogether different from each other and hold that international law, neither as a whole nor in part, can be regarded as a part of municipal law. They further argue that just as municipal law cannot make or alter international law, so international law cannot create or change municipal law. Needless to say that this is an extreme point of view and is correct only partially.

(b) *The Monistic View.* According to this view, the subjects of law under the two systems are not essentially different. While municipal law regulates the conduct of the individuals under it, international law regulates the conduct of states between each other. In the second place, in both cases law is essentially "a command binding upon the subjects of the law independently of their will". Thirdly, according to the monistic view, as interpreted by Oppenheim, international and municipal law, far from being essentially different, must be regarded as manifestations of "a single conception of law." That is to say, international law cannot be comprehended without the assumption of a superior legal order from which the various systems of municipal law are, in a sense, derived by delegation (*153:36-37*).

Even though an international order of the kind described here is not in full operation, yet it is not a mere phantasy. The development has been from the city state to the nation and empire states, and may we hope that the next stage will be towards a world state ? Thus the conclusion to which we are driven is that it is international law which determines the judicial limits of the personal and territorial competence of the state. Furthermore, it is only by reference to a higher legal rule in relation to which states are equal. This means that the equality and independence of sovereign states are derived from the equality of states as a *political* concept, and not as a *legal* concept.

We admit at the same time that municipal courts are not bound by the law of nations and that they may even enforce laws which are contrary to international law. But this merely shows the weakness of international law and organization. The fundamental problem, therefore, is to evolve a rational relationship between the two systems of law so that progress in international law may not be hampered by the deadweight of a stagnant municipal law.

The Content of International Law. The three broad divisions of international law are the law of war, the law of peace, and the law of neutrality. Some important aspects of international law are diplomacy, commercial and personal intercourse, postal and electrical communications, health, morals, intellectual life, etc. The scope of international law is expanding all the time; and conventions are coming to play a greater and greater part.

Sanctions. International law does not generally have the automatic sanctions enjoyed by municipal law. Yet there are sanctions of an indirect character. Among these must be listed (1) respect for principle; (2) pledges given by states in advance, as in the case of the "Optional Clause"; (3) considerations of mutual convenience; and (4) fear of retaliation. "International Police Action" is no longer an empty phrase, as seen in connection with situations tantamount to war in Palestine (1948 and later), Egypt (1956) and the Congo Republic (1960).

To conclude the discussion on international law, we agree with Potter when the says, "The integration of international law with national law, or the subordination of the latter to the former, is likely to continue, along with the integration of international organization and administration with national government".

LAW AND MORALITY

In general terms, it may be said that law is a subject of study of political science, while morality as a subject of study is assigned to the field of ethics. Yet there is considerable overlapping between the two. Gilchrist rightly observes that "both political science and ethics deal with man as a moral agent in society" (*28:178*). The end of the State, says another writer, "is to establish order and to respect personality". According to MacIver, the State creates those universal, external conditions of social order necessary for the expression and development of free, moral personality. But it is obvious that it cannot promote the moral end directly, since morality is for the most part a self-earned good. While the State cannot *make* a person moral, it can *induce* him to be moral or *surround* him with those social and physical conditions where the spontaneous living of the moral life becomes possible.

Law and morality differ from each other in content, sanction, and definiteness. Political law is chiefly concerned with the outward acts of man, but not with his inner motives. As a recent writer puts it, it does not touch his thought or his inner springs of conscience. In the words of Ernest Barker, "In matters of conscience there is no compulsion." Law touches only a segment of human life, whereas morality includes the whole of life, *i.e.*, man's thoughts, motives, and actions. Law can prescribe external acts, but it cannot prescribe morality. It is only when thoughts and motive translate themselves into action that they come within the purview of law. Falsehood, meanness, envy, jealousy, ingratitude, and cunning are morally wrong, but not legally. One may be a habitual liar in his personal life, but so long as he does not cheat some one or break a contract, law does not come into operation.

The sanction behind law is force—often physical; whereas the force or sanction behind morality is one's own conscience, social indignation, and the fear of incurring God's wrath. The State makes use of fear of legal punishment and hope of reward in the carrying out of its behests. Morality, on the other hand, rests on a person's intuitive ideas of what is good and what is bad as well as on the motive of social approbation and disapprobation. In general terms, it may be said that public censure is behind morality, while physical punishment is behind law.

Law and morality differ further in their scope and definiteness. Law is universal. It is more exact, consistent, and definite than morality into which enter elements of uncertainty and vagueness. In the last analysis, an individual is the best judge of what is right and what is wrong for him. Therefore, standards of moral judgment are bound to vary from person to person. Apropos of this, MacIver writes: 'The sphere of morality can never therefore be coincident with the sphere of political law. Morality is always individual and always in relation to the whole presented situation, of which the political fact is never more than an aspect" (*55:156*).

Moral duty and legal obligation do not always coincide with each other. Thus what is morally unjustified is not necessarily legally wrong. Nor is what is prohibited by the State necessarily morally wrong. Thus traffic to the left is legally right in India, the U.K., and a few other countries. But there is nothing morally right about it except in a remote way. As a matter of fact, in the U.S.A. and the continent of Europe traffic keeps to the right of the road. Self-indulgence is morally reprehensible, but not legally wrong. As has been rightly said, law follows standards of convenience or expediency, whereas morality prescribes absolute standards of right and wrong, of justice and injustice. A compromised morality is no morality.

Political law is objective, while ethical law is subjective. The former deals with what is permitted and what is not permitted by the law of the land. Morality, on the other hand, is rooted in universal values as conceived and interpreted by the individual. "To turn all moral obligations into legal obligations would be to destroy morality" (*55:157*). This means that the State cannot dictate morality, because State-directed morality is no morality at all. As said above, morality is a matter of inner conviction and conscience and, as such, it does not easily lend itself to outer regulation.

COMMON GROUND BETWEEN LAW AND MORALITY

Yet, there is considerable common ground between law and morality. If the people are good, the State is good and *vice versa*. In the well-known words of Plato, "The best State is that which is nearest in virtue to the individual. If any part of the body politic suffers, the whole body suffers." To put the matter in other words, man can fully develop his personality only within the State. It is the supreme condition of his moral life.

The State can positively promote the conditions of morality and negatively remove conditions inimical to morality. Gilchrist states the matter as follows: "As a positive moral agent, the State makes good laws, i.e. laws which are in accord with the best moral interests of the people. Negatively, the State must remove bad laws."

The connection between law and morality is so close that it is not always easy to draw a sharp line between the illegal and immoral. Thus theft is both a moral and legal offence. Further, what is immoral today may become illegal tomorrow and *vice versa*. Thus drunkenness is immoral, but not illegal until a prohibition law is passed. Compulsory education when it is enacted is legal but not necessarily moral. But as people's ideas regarding their responsibility to their children advance, not to send one's child to school becomes immoral. In every case, care should be taken not to let the State assume that it has an end of its own apart from the enrichment of personality.

LAW AND THE STATE ACCORDING TO LASKI

Legal Norms and Economic Power

It is necessary to recognize the close relationship between Laski's theory of the state as the administrative instrument of a class and his conception of law. In his "Introduction to Politics", Laski says, that in every social system, a struggle goes on for the possession of economic power. The section of the community which controls this power can also make its wants effective. Law is therefore "a system of relations giving the expression of legal form" to these wants. The patterns of distribution of economic power in a given society decide the nature of legal norms of that society. Law, in these circumstances, reflects the wants of those who own or control the means of production in the state. Political authority uses the legal structure to serve the economic interest of the owners of land or capital or both depending upon the ascendancy of a particular interest in a given social system. The state does not exist to realize any abstract concept of general justice or common good. Its function in its actual historical role has been to promote the particular interests of the dominant economic class in society.

Justice and Class Interest

Thus the purpose of law is not to secure absolute justice but to safeguard the political ascendancy of the economically dominant class. The legal structure of every society has a distinct class basis. The function of law in a feudal society is to consolidate the social, economic and political power of the nobility. In a capitalist society, the legal system administers to the needs of the capitalist class. In a socialist society, the legal structure is again modified and adapted to the needs of the working class. Thus law can never be an impartial body of rules mediating between the conflicts of different classes in the society. Laski does not agree with those liberal jurists who regard the law as a neutral agency of mediation established by the state for the preservation of social peace and order.

Criticism of the Austinian View

Laski regards the Austinian theory of law as inadequate for the purposes of political science although he admits its formal consistency in the realm of jurisprudence. In fact, Austin has only sought to develop a self-consistent theory of the juridical order in which neither ethical nor sociological considerations have been taken into account. "Law, on this view" says Laski, "was completely separated from justice on the ground that this latter concept introduces non-juristic postulates foreign to the nature of law. On this view, the authority of law ultimately derives from the final norm in a series—the state, and this norm, in its turn, is a postulate incapable of examination since, as the supreme source of authority, it cannot be called into question. Granted its postulates, I believe the pure theory of law to be unanswerable, but I believe also that its substance is an exercise in logic and not in life. For we know in fact that the law of any given society is the expression of the push of social forces in that society".[4]

Some Pertinent Questions

He therefore makes an attempt to define the content of law as distinct from its source or mode of operation. This he does by asking a few pertinent questions. If law is grounded in utility, Laski at once asks to whom it is useful. If it is the expression of reason, he asks whose reason it embodies. If it is an embodiment of the common good, he would ask who conceives that common good. If it is a fulfilment of certain social purposes, he would like to know who has defined those purposes. To all these questions, the answer would be that the law is useful to a particular class only which

4. Laski : "A Grammar of Politics", Introductory Chapter, p. 6.

owns the means of production in that society. It embodies the reason of that class alone to the exclusion of other classes. The common good is conceived by the representatives of that class which often identifies its sectional interests with the common good. The social objectives which the legal order serves are the objectives defined by the members of the ruling class and administered by them either directly or through their trusted agents in the state bureaucracy and the courts *(50:31)*.

The Content of Law

There is no place in Austin's theory of law for an objective analysis of its content as Laski has attempted. But he no longer attacks Austin's view on pluralistic grounds. As Laski has accepted the principle of the sovereign State, he must accept it with all its implications in the legal system. He is quite conscious of this when he says that the law cannot be anything else except the will of the sovereign State. Law is not just a body of rules and regulations existing independently of the will of a particular State. Law is, therefore, a system of commands which the State is willing to enforce. From this point of view the content of law becomes of secondary significance. The law may be foolish or unjust but it is nevertheless law because the sovereign has commanded it. Citizens ought to obey the law because disobedience is punishable. Its title to obedience depends solely on the source from which it emanates. If disobedience is permitted, the State would not be regarded as sovereign.

Laski compares Austin's theory of law with Euclid's system of geometry both of which are self-consistent systems whose validity cannot be challenged within their respective spheres of discourse. As he says, "It is, so to speak, an abstract conceptualism in which, for certain clearly defined purposes, law is divorced from justice and made simply a final term in a hierarchy of wills behind which it is impossible to go. The jurist here is engaged on a purely formalistic analysis. He excludes from his field of discourse all considerations of what is ethically right or socially expedient and considers only as law that which emanates from a will whose source may be traced to the sovereign. For him, as jurist, the only problem involved is whether the sovereign sanctions the particular form of behaviour which presents itself as legal. Any other question is, in Maitland's happy phrase, metajurisprudence, and so outside his province" *(50 : 32)*. Thus Laski admits the formal validity of Austin's analysis but he is more concerned with the sociological content of the law and its relation to an ethical norm of justice.

Two Discordant Elements in Laski's Theory

In Laski's theory of law, two rather discordant elements have been unhappily combined. In the first place, he has defined the sociological content of law in a Marxist way regarding it as an expression of the needs of a particular class. Secondly, he has revived the traditional theory of natural law as an ethical test of any legal system. According to Marx, morals as well as laws have a precise class basis and there is no absolute morality by which the ethical quality of particular laws may be tested. Thus Laski's belief in the theory of natural law is not consistent with his sociological analysis of its content.

Legal System and Class Structure

The content of a legal system is judged by its reference to the class structure it supports in a given society. Laski, however, does not argue that all law is a product of the class struggle. There does exist a great body of legal rules in every community which may be deemed socially neutral and are adopted for the general convenience of the citizens. But the most important elements of any legal system do exhibit a clearly defined class character.

"The idea of the class struggle", says Laski, "permeates legal notions at every point of pivotal importance. The law of sedition is unintelligible except as an effort to protect the *status quo* from the threat of invasion. It is a safeguard, we say, of law and order; but the law and order it safeguards are that which maintains a particular system of class-relations from the threat of challenge. The attitude of our courts in trade union cases is, again, unintelligible except as the expression of a mental climate which has never freed itself from the belief that trade unions are organisations threatening the equalibrium of a society built upon the principle that the means of production must remain in private hands. The use of the injunction in labour disputes by the American Courts is as a weapon in class warfare" (*50:174*).

Judiciary in England and America

On the basis of a detailed examination of the judicial processes in England and the United States, he has come to the obvious conclusion that the judiciary cannot transcend the class-structure of the society in which it operates. While in capitalist countries the legal system operates in favour of the capitalist class, in Soviet Russia the legal structure is similarly biased in favour of the working-class. Besides, Laski thinks that there is not only an inherent bias in the substance of law discriminating the rich against the poor, there is also a procedural inequality between different classes on account of the financial question involved in securing the justice from the courts.

As Laski points out, "Broadly, there is equality before the law only when the price of admission to its opportunities can be equally paid; and there is no administrative equity to redress this balance. It is simply inherent in a society with the class-relations of our own. And it is those class-relations also which mean that, as a general rule, the ablest lawyers will be at the service of those only who are able to afford them. The successful lawyer—the class from which, in the Anglo-American system, the members of the judiciary are mostly drawn—spends his life in ministering to the needs of the dominating class of our society" (*50:175*). Thus Laski concludes that the principle of the so-called equality before the law is completely vitiated in practice by the inequality of economic opportunity in a capitalist society.

Ethical Test of the Legal System

Finally, Laski wants to determine the ethical test by which the validity of a legal system may be adjudged. Neither Austin nor Hegel gives any adequate answer to this question in his opinion. Law does not become morally desirable because it has been willed by the sovereign. If the sovereign commands compulsory conscription for the Quakers who are conscientious objectors to war, the act of the sovereign will be legal but it will at the same time be morally inadmissible. Nor does he agree with Hegel that the law as it really exists as a bequest of history is an embodiment of rationality.

According to Hegel and the idealists in general, the law becomes ethically desirable simply because it has been widely accepted by the community. Laski points out that the law of a fascist State is generally accepted by the community because the decrees of the totalitarian state are backed by a tremendous amount of force. But people accept these decrees not because they regard them as the embodiment of morality but because they have been enacted by a coercive authority against which resistance is not possible. The ethical test of the law lies in the judgment of the individual conscience.[5]

Law, Rights and Conscience

"Law to be ethically valid," says Laski, "must conform with the requirements of the system of rights the purposes of which the state exists to maintain. And since law is a command seeking to control my behaviour in some particular way, I must judge that conformity for myself as the test of its ethical adequacy. The roots of valid law, that is, are, and can only be, within the individual conscience. I make law legal, so to say, by giving to its operation the consent of my conscience" (*50:82*). This conception of the ethical test of law rests upon an atomistic conception of society which is in direct contradiction with the collectivistic basis of the Marxian doctrine which regards the class rather than the individual as the supreme factor in the legal system. Laski has obviously not realised this contradiction in his theory of law because he has generally interpreted the protest of the individual not in his personal isolation but as a member of the class to which he socially belongs.

---

5. See Professor Coker's remarks about Laski's conception of law in his "Recent Political Thought", Chapter XIX, pp. 537-539.

CHAPTER 22

THE CONCEPT OF JUSTICE

In determining a nation's rank in the scale of political civilisation, no test is more decisive than the degree in which justice as defined by the law, is actually realised in its judicial administration and social and political life, both as between one private citizen and another, and as between private citizens and the wielders of governmental authority. MacIver rightly observes that the original justification of the king's power was found in the society's need for justice. Whenever some men were involved in disputes, they needed an arbitrator of their rival claims. The customs and moral sense of the community provided the criteria for rendering justice. Gradually the customary law was transformed into a written code and the king's authority was dispersed among several magistrates. Until recently the same officials of the state exercised law-making, administrative and judicial functions. With the emergence of liberal democracy, the judicial function was entrusted to the separate hierarchy of officials known as the judges who were required to render justice to the citizens of the community without fear or favour.

Development of the Concept of Justice

The Sophists in ancient Greece had defined justice as the interest of the stronger. They argued that in every society the social group, which was militarily strong or economically rich was able to impose laws on the weaker and poorer sections and justice actually meant the enforcement of these laws by the magistrates. Since then, the realistic theory of justice has always emphasized its inherent class basis.

The idealist theory of justice, first conceived by Plato, emphasized the moral element in justice. Justice was a virtue to be cultivated by society through subordination of the irrational masses of producers to the brave class of warriors and the rational class of philosopher-rulers. Aristotle held that justice consists in an equality of proportion between person and things assigned to them, i.e. that differences in treatment should be proportional to the degrees to which individuals differ in relevant respects. As Benn and Peters point out this definition of justice may be useful if we grant a loose or metaphorical sense to the term "proportionate", but in a stricter sense, it is misleading. The standards of "proportion" differ from age to age. Slavery for the Greeks and the Romans was an example of proportionate justice just as unequal incomes bebtween capitalists and wage-earners constitute proportionate justice in the modern society based on market economy. (*177 : 112*).

The liberal concept of justice emphasizes its legal and political dimensions. The rule of law, as distinguished from the rule of men, is the first condition of justice. Equality before law and equal protection of laws are two judicial principles enshrined in the Anglo-Saxon judicial system. Civil and political rights, which allow the citizens of a democratic community to participate in the political process, are also the necessary attributes of a political system based on justice. As for social and economic dimensions of justice, the liberals insist that the rights of private property should act as constraints over them.

Sources of the Idea of Justice

As Barker has pointed out, the literal meaning of the Latin term *Justitia* from which justice has been derived is the idea of joining or fitting, the idea of bond or tie. Primarily, the joining or fitting implied in the idea of justice is that between *man and man* in an organised system of human relations. Barker, however, extends the meaning of justice by including in it the idea of a joining or fitting between *value and value* in a general synthesis of values. Since the French Revolution, the modern liberal society recognises liberty, equality and fraternity as three supreme values necessary for a just system of human relations.

All these values are present in different degrees in any legal system and there is a constant process of adjustment and realignment between the rival claims of liberty, equality and fraternity according to the prevailing notions of justice. The claims of liberty have to be adjusted to those of equality; and the claims of both have to be reconciled with those of fraternity. As Barker says: "Justice is the reconciler and the synthesis of political values; it is their union in an adjusted and integrated whole." (*175 : 102*).

Justice is thus the general and controlling idea of the right and the just which we feel that the law of the state ought to express. We expect justice to justify law to us and that by this act of justification it will oblige us to obey its precepts. But what are the grounds on which people generally consider a legal system just or unjust? According to Barker, four different answers have been given to this question. The first is that the source of justice and its obliging power is religion. The second is that the source of justice is nature. The third answer finds its source in economics. Barker's own view is that the source of justice should be sought in the realm of ethics.

The medieval Christian writers like St. Thomas Aquinas held the view that God has planted the notion of justice in the human mind which is preserved through the authority of the Church. The Church is the source of laws which are declared and implemented by its secular arm i.e. the state. With the separation of the Church and the state in modern times, the religion has lost its importance as the source of the notion of justice. The standards of religion can only be applied in the area of voluntary life which lies outside the State. The norms of justice set up by religion ought to be applied without any shadow of legal coercion. If the state enforces them through legal prescriptions, the attempt is very likely to fail. Barker admits that religion as a source of ethical principles may be regarded as an ultimate source of the notion of justice but cannot be considered as its immediate validating principle.

The idea of nature, and of a natural order of things, as a source of justice, is at least as old as the Stoics. The Stoic conception of nature which was transmitted to the Roman jurists and finally to the Christian writers of the middle ages, is a conception belonging to a mixed world of religious belief and moral philosophy. The term "nature" from the age of the Stoic Zeno to the times Rousseau was the keyword of a religious-ethical conception relating to a spiritual world. Natural justice was not an engineering concept relating to reconstruction of the material world at all. Justice was identified with the rule of reason or God. It was a bridge between the religious notion of justice as ordained by the divine law and the ethical notion of justice as conceived by a modern rationalist lawgiver. When this school appeals to nature as the source of justice, its real appeal is to a code of ethics conceived as proceeding purely and solely from human reason and rationally calculated to the sum of human happiness. Blackstone, indeed, identified ethics and natural law. The rational pursuit of happiness, he said, is the foundation of what we call ethics or natural law.

Duguit and Proudhon are cited by Barker as examples of those thinkers who regard economics as the most important source of the notion of justice. Marx also emphasizes the economic and social dimensions of justice. These dimensions of justice will be considered presently. As an idealist, Barker upholds the view that law, as the expression of prevailing ethical ideas, determined the order of economics much more than it has itself been determined by that order. The true soource of justice, therefore, for all idealist thinkers such as Plato, Aristotle, Hegel, Kant, Green and Barker is to be found in ethics. The moral standard of the community, sanctioned and enforced by the general moral conscience, constitutes the real basis of the idea of justice. The system of values accepted by a community will be in its trun the impersonal source of positive law enforced by the State.

Legal Dimension of Justice

Positive law as the declared will of the state is the most obvious dimension of justice. Positive law includes customary law as well as statutory law. Together it constitutes the general body of rules recognised and enforced, and in that sense, imposed by the courts. Legal codes enacted by the state and supplemented by customary rules observed by the community define the content of justice in any given society. The constitution as well as acts of legislature delimit the legal dimension of justice prevalent in any country. When the Indian Constitution abolished untouchability, it was a legal way of promoting justice. Law defines the rights and obligations of individuals and groups in a community. The executive branch of the government enforces these rules and the courts ensure that these rules are applied properly to all. The legal dimension of justice implies faithful adherence to declared rules. Some values are no doubt implicit in every system of positive law but a lawyer does not inquire into the ethical foundations of existing legal rules. He is concerned only with the validity of particular law in terms of its enactment by a legitimate authority. The jurist is neutral regarding the value-components of any existing law considering justice as synonymous with application and adjudication of declared formal rules. (*175* : *108*).

Political Dimension of Justice

While the legal dimension of justice is concerned with formal rules, the political dimension of justice is concerned with actual policies through which the political process realizes the norms of justice. The constitution, parliament and the courts give shape to the legal dimension of justice. But the bureaucracy and political parties, the interest groups and voluntary associations etc. try to translate the legal norms of justice into pragmatic political programmes. The law abolishing untouchability or prohibiting forced labour or fixing a ceiling on land may remain unimplemented or partially implemented due to absence of the required administrative measures. The preamble and directive principles enshrined in the Indian Constitution envisage the creation of a just social order in the country. The directive principles of state policy are fundamental in the governance of the country but they remain pious ethical platitudes so long as the ruling elite lacks the political will to implement them.

Social Dimension of Justice

The legal ideology and political practice reflect a given social structure. Traditional societies were hierarchical in which the division of the community into ranks, castes or orders was regarded as an expression of justice. Some were born as lords and masters destined to rule over others who were slaves or serfs by birth. This was justified in terms of God's will, reason and morality. In India, the caste hierarchy was sanctioned by the law of *Karma* and ordained by *Dharma*.

In modern times, social justice has been defined as a concept which requires elimination of all kinds of discrimination and privileges based on **birth, race, caste, creed or sex. Social roles ought not to be determined by** status but by capacity. Social mobility between different types of occupations *should replace rigid stratification of roles* inherited from the past. As Max Weber pointed out, capitalist society conceives social justice in terms of social relationships based on contract. The actual working of a capitalist democracy has shown that though it enlarges the social dimension of justice by abolishing feudal ranks and caste distinctions, it fails to remove the class character of justice as it sanctions and institutionalises the exploitation of the working-class by the owners of capital.

Economic Dimension of Justice

With the development of modern industry, the theory began to be advanced by utopian socialists, anarchists and Marxists that the origin of the idea of justice should be discovered in the economic structure of a given society. Proudhon wanted to establish a just social order by developing an economic system based on the principle of mutual co-operation among different groups of producers. Following Proudhon, Duguit developed his theory of social solidarity as the basis of a just economic order. The basic fact of every economic system is the existence of different occupational groups, producing different commodities, but bound to one another by a system of mutual exchange. The co-operation should replace competition in order to maximise production and to achieve equitable distribution of commodities so produced among different classes of society.

Marx criticised utopian socialists, syndicalists and anarchists as bourgeois social reformers and idealists whose notion of justice was a sentimental play with empty and meaningless words. Mutual cooperation and solidarity are impossible to achieve in a society divided between two hostile classes of the capitalistic exploiters on the one hand and the exploited proletarian masses on the other. A just socio-economic order was possible only when the proletariat put an end to all modes of bourgeois exploitation by smashing the bourgeois state apparatus through a successful socialist revolution. Justice in capitalist society was a narrow class-oriented concept. True justice would be realised only in a classless communist society of the future.

Relation between Liberty, Equality and Justice

Justice, as we are now in a position to conclude, is a term of synthesis. It is the final principle which regulates the general distribution of rights and the various principles of their distribution. It is, in a word, the general right ordering and adjustment of social relations by the authority of the State. It gives to each person rights, as his share in the whole system, and it thus reconciles the claims of one person with another. It also gives to each principle of distribution—liberty, equality and fraternity—its share and weight in determining the distribution actually made, and it thus adjusts principle to principle.

Barker has described the relation between liberty, equality and justice in the following words: "Justice is a joining or fitting together not only of persons, but also of principles. It joins and knits together the claims of the principle of liberty with those of the principle of equality....Equality may quarrel with liberty; for if its application be pushed to the length of what is called a classless society, with absolute equality of possessions.... Civil liberty may be pleaded in support of claims which run contrary to those of economic liberty; and similarly political liberty may be on occasion the enemy of either civil or economic liberty. There must therefore be some final principle transcending that of liberty, as it also transcends the principle of equality and co-operation, a principle which can balance each of these principles against the others....that final principle is justice." (*175* : *160*).

The personified figure of justice in the folklores of many peoples shows her as a goddess holding a balance in her hand and with eyes blindfolded as a sign of her impartiality. However another visual representation of justice shows her as *Shakti* wielding the power of the sword for punishing the evil-doer. Both the representations have found their place in the vocabulary of political scientists today.

As MacIver says, no thinker has argued that politics is merely a power system. But many writers have exalted the state as a power-agency, making the exercise of power as the primary condition of social order. Against these views, other writers have always protested, invoking the claims of justice and human personality as such, denying the master-servant relation as properly applicable in the political sphere and minimizing the value of coercion as a means to welfare. As men naturally appeal from force to justice, they oppose the idea of politics as justice to the idea of politics as power. While MacIver thinks that private property can co-exist with social justice, Laski thinks that social justice requires social ownership of the means of production. According to the socialist view, private property is a negation of the socio-economic dimension of justice.

Justice and the Distribution of Income

The general principles discussed above have practical implications for the ethics of income distribution. A society, from an economic point of view, is an organisation for the cooperative production and distribution of goods and services. It is a process governed by rules. In the nineteenth century, it was regulated by contractual relationships under a market economy. In the twentieth century collective joint negotiating machinery fixes wage rates and a powerful state organization also redistributes income by progressive taxation and provision of social services. Can we call these arrangements just and fair ? To justify them it would be necessary to demonstrate that inequalities in income were related to criteria which are rational and relevant. Justice consists in treating equals equally, and in adopting as criteria by which men are to be considered equal or unequal.

According to Benn and Peters, the rational criteria for income distribution are (a) desert, (b) needs, and (c) property ownership. *Desert* is a normative term. Its use presupposes a rule having two components; (i) a condition to be satisfied; (ii) a mode of treatment consequent upon it. We cannot estimate desert without reference to some rule or standard from which what reward an individual deserves can be adequately measured. It is generally held that greater skill and responsibility are adequate reasons why some persons should get more than others. It might be said that a scientist deserves more than a miner. Sometimes, a higher payment is made for dirty or dangerous work. In every society, there is a socially accepted hierarchy of occupations with a traditional scale of income and prestige. Drastic alterations in the traditional scale would meet popular resistance. Existing inequalities are justified on the criteria of desert. The Saint-Simonions attached great importance to the desert criteria and adopted the maxim: "From each according to his capacity, to each according to his work." This was mainly in protest against large incomes from landed property.

Just as Saint-Simon stressed the criteria of desert, Babeuf and Louis Blanc adopted the slogan : "From each according to his ability, to each according to his need." Marx paid homage to this ideal which was to be realized during the final communist phase of development but was not relevant for the transitional, socialist phase. Benn and Peters observe : "Distribution according to need has a kind of moral persuasiveness which distribution by desert seems to lack. There is something attractive in the vision of a society in which financial incentives would be unnecessary, and in which incomes would be proportionate to needs, none enjoying luxuries until the necessities of all had been satisfied." (*177 : 141*).

It appears that the criteria of needs are more specific and determinate. Human needs such as food, clothing, shelter would seem to be factual, whereas deserts depend on norms. Benn and Peters regard this as a mistaken point of view. Needs are not simple matters of fact, but presume norms as much as do deserts. While the need for food may be determinate, a need for leisure or artistic enjoyment or constructive occupation is normative in nature.

Biological needs are the most palpable. These are related to the need for survival. In addition, there are some basic needs connected with the general living standards of a particular community, which yield norms like 'subsistence level' or 'a decent standard of living'. Finally, there are functional needs, which must be satisfied if a man it to do his particular job. It would be possible to imagine about a system, by which, once the above-mentioned biological, functional and minimum needs are satisfied, the surplus was distributed equally so that everyone would have the same amount of money for satisfying the artistic and cultural needs according to taste. Equal distribution of the surplus would not be distribution according to need as every one may not experience the need or equal need for artistic and cultural enjoyment.

Benn and Peters conclude : "It is fairly generally agreed that, property incomes apart, our system of distribution by desert, supplemented by redistribution according to need, is right in principle. Differences of opinion arise mainly about the proper weight to be given to these criteria. On the one hand, some people complain that we so emphasize need at the expense of desert that initiative and enterprise are seriously discouraged...... Economic egalitarians on the other hand, believe that we are too much bound up in our traditional assumptions, and that the gap between the extremes of income could be narrowed still further, stressing need more and desert less.... They believe that this could be done without disastrous consequences; that on the contrary a greater equality of incomes would eliminate snobbish distinctions, and create a stronger sense of fraternity and social harmony." (*177 : 154*).

This controversy is closely related to the problems of ownership of property, which has been dealt with in an earlier chapter

JOHN RAWLS : A THEORY OF JUSTICE

A Concept of Distributive Justice

The most widely acclaimed theory of justice, that of John Rawls, is devoted to working out a general principle of distribution which will justify the class difference in life prospects which any society, capitalist or noncapitalist, is bound to produce. Macpherson characterizes it as "a general theory of distributive justice" which is "scarcely recognizable as a theory of economic justice." He says : "For it starts from the claims of dissociated individuals, not of individuals as members of society, and assumes market-maximising behaviour as their innate or essential attribute, whereas the hallmark of the concept of economic justice has been its assumption that social norms and ethical values should prevail over, or not be eroded by, impersonal market values." (*220 : 12*).

It may be argued that Rawls's theory does meet the criteria for a theory of economic justice since it does propose to regulate distributive arrangements in society by an ethical principle. This argument cannot be sustained because Rawls places a severe limit to the amount of redistribution of income allowed by his ethical norm. This limit is dictated by the market economy. His ethical principle of distributive justice prescribes that transfers of income from the rich to the poor should not reach a point at which "greater taxes interfere so much with economic efficiency that the prospects of the least advantaged in the present generation are no longer improved but begin to decline." (*249 : 286*).

The test of economic efficiency, as Rawls visualizes, is to be applied explicitly in the 'competitive economy' and it logically must be completely dominated by market in which the unfavourable reaction of the capitalist to increases in taxation reduces the productivity of the entire economy. Rawls wants to implement his distributive justice within the constraints of the classical model of the competitive capitalist market economy, in which impersonal market forces determine the level of productivity and investment. Macpherson points out : "Thus Rawls's ethical distributive principle does not prevail over, but is overriden by the capitalist market relations of production. And indeed this is the only position consistent with his fundamental Hobbesian assumption of unsocial maximising individuals as the irreducible units of modern society." (*220 : 13*).

According to Rawls, justice is the first virtue of social institutions, as truth is of systems of thought. A theory however attractive should be rejected if it is untrue. Similarly, institutions and laws however efficient or well-arranged must be reformed or abolished if they are unjust. In a just society the liberties of equal citizenship are taken as settled. The rights secured by justice are not subject to the calculus of social interests or to political bargaining. A well-ordered society, he says, is effectively regulated by a public conception of justice. It is a society in which everyone accepts and knows that the others accept the same principles of justice, and the basic social institutions satisfy these principles. Rawls observes: "If men's inclination to self-interest makes their vigilance against one another necessary, their public sense of justice makes their secure association together possible. Among individuals with disparate aims and purposes a shared conception of justice establishes the bonds of civic friendship; the general desire for justice limits the pursuit of other ends. One may think of a public conception of justice as constituting the fundamental character of a well-ordered human association." (*249* : *5*).

Rawls does not consider "the institutions and social practices generally" or "relations between states" as subjects to which his theory of justice can apply. "The political constitution and the principal economic and social arrangements" such as "the legal protection of freedom of thought and liberty of conscience, competitive markets, private property in the means of production and the monogamous family" must be accepted as given. Unfortunately, this system breeds "deep inequalities" which "cannot possibly be justified by an appeal to the notions of merit or desert." Rawls says: 'It is these inequalities, presumably inevitable in the basic structure of any society, to which the principles of social justice must in the first instance apply....The justice of a social scheme depends essentially on how fundamental rights and duties are assigend and on the economic opportunities and social conditions in the various sectors of society. (*249* : *7*). Thus Rawls is interested in developing a conception of justice which can provide a standard by which the distributive arrangements of a given society can be assessed but which need not concern itself with the fundamental question of ownership of the means of production.

His aim is to present a conception of justice which generalizes and carries to a higher plane the familiar theory of the social contract as found in Locke, Rousseau and Kant. The guiding idea is that the principles of justice for the basic structure of society are the object of "the original agreement." These are the principles that "free and rational persons concerned to further their own interests" should accept "in an initial position of equality as defining the fundamental terms of their association." They will regulate all further agreements, specify the modes of social cooperation and determine the form of government. Justice as incorporated in these principles can simply be called *fairness*.

This contractarian concept of justice is elaborated by Rawls in the following words: "In justice as fairness the original position of equality corresponds to the state of nature in the traditional theory of the social contract. This original position is not, of course, thought of as an actual historical state of affairs, much less as a primitive condition of culture. It is understood as a purely hypothetical situation characterized so as to lead to a certain conception of justice. Among the essential features of this situation is that no one knows his place in society, his class position or social status, nor does any one know his fortune in the distribution of natural assets and abilities, his intelligence, strength, and the like. I shall even assume that the parties do not know their conceptions of the good or their special psychological propensities. The principles of justice are chosen behind a veil of ignorance." (*249* : *12*).

In the Anglo-Saxon ethical tradition, two important schools of ethical theory were utilitarianism and intuitionism. Each of these schools "has strengths, from Rawls's point of view, but each also has fatal weaknesses. Rawls revives a version of the theory of the social contract as a way of discovering a *via media* between utilitarianism and intuitionism." (*259* : *11*). Morally, he is "more comfoıtable with the intutionists" but methodologically "his heart is with the utilitarians and with the neo-classical economists." (*259* : *12*). R. P. Wolff says: "Rawls proposed to construct a formal model of a society of rationally self-interested individuals, whom he would imagine to be engaged in what the modern theory of rational choice calls a bargaining game. His intuition was that if he constituted the *bargaining game* along the line suggested by the contractarian tradition of political theory ....then with a single additional quasi-formal, subsantively empty constraint, he could prove as a formal theorem in the theory of rational choice, that the solution to the bargaining game was a moral principle having the characteristics of constructivity, coherence with our settled moral convictions, and rationality, and making an independent place for the notion of the right while acknowledging the dignity and worth of moral personality. Rawls would, if he could prove his theorem, be in a position to say to a reader: *If you are a rationally self-interested agent, and if you are to have a morality at all, then you must acknowledge as binding upon you the moral principle I shall enunciate.* (*259* : *16*).

The task of the parties to Rawls's hypothetical Original Position is to choose principles of justice which will play a central role in their life. As is well-known, Rawls proposes the following Two Principles as those the parties would prefer:

First Principle

Each person is to have an equal right to the most extensive total system of equal basic liberties compatible with a similar system of liberty for all.

Second Principle

Social and economic inequalities are to be arranged so that they are both: (a) to the greatest benefit of the least advantaged, consistent with the just savings principle, and (b) attached to offices and positions open to all under conditions of fair equality of opportunity.

First Priority Rule (The Priority of Liberty)

The Principles of justice are to be ranked in lexical order and therefore liberty can be restricted only for the sake of liberty. There are two cases: (a) a less extensive liberty must strengthen the total system of liberty shared by all; (b) a less than equal liberty must be acceptable to those with the lesser liberty.

Second Priority Rule (The Priority of Justice over Efficiency and Welfare)

The second principle of justice is lexically prior to the principle of efficiency and to that of maximizing the sum of advantages; and fair opportunity is prior to the difference principle. There are two cases: (a) an inequality of opportunity must enhance the opportunities of those with the lesser opportunity; (b) an excessive rate of saving must on balance mitigate the burden of those bearing this hardship.

General Conception

All social primary goods—liberty and opportunity, income and wealth, and the bases of self-interest—are to be distributed equally unless an unequal distribution of any or all of these goods is to the advantage of the least favoured." (*249 : 302*).

Is Rawls right? Are his two principles really the principles of justice? Despite the enormous length of *A Theory of Justice*, Rawls says little about the concrete facts of social, economic and political reality. R. P. Wolff characterizes it as an example of "utopian liberal political economy" and as "a philosophical *apologia* for an egalitarian brand of liberal welfare-state capitalism." The device of the bargaining game and the veil of ignorance may preserve the self-consistency of his abstract doctrine but this drains away its "empirical specificity". What is left is "ideology, which is to say prescription masquerading as value-neutral analysis." (*259 : 195*).

Laissez-faire liberals, neoclassical advocates of the welfare-state, democratic socialists and Marxists will dispute about the answers, but all would agree that any theory of social justice must include a coherent account of the sources, organization, distribution and workings of political power. Rawls seems to have "no conception of the generation, deployment, limitations, ,or problems of political power. In a word, he has no theory of the *state*." (*259:202*). Another way to get at the source of the inadequacy of Rawls's theory is to recognize its failure to focus squarely on the structure of *production* in the economy rather than on alternative patterns of distribution." He is, therefore, unable to explain "the ways in which the organization of production determines the distribution of power and thereby establishes systematic patterns of exploitation and domination." (*259 : 207*). Looked at more broadly, Rawls's failure "grows naturally and inevitably out of his uncritical acceptance of the socio-political presuppositions and associated modes of analysis of classical and neo-classical liberal political economy. By focusing exclusively on distribution rather than on production, Rawls obscures the real roots of that distribution." Marx highlights this point in his critique of the Gotha Programme: "Any distribution whatever of the means of consumption is only a consequence of the distribution of the conditions of production themselves. The latter distribution, however, is a feature of the mode of production itself." (*259 : 210*).

A Theory of Liberal Democratic Justice

John Rawls, in the course of a close and protracted discussion of justice, has set out a mode of a liberal-democratic society which he believes satisfies the concept of justice as propounded by him. Rawls's substantive doctrine is a rather pure form of egalitarian democracy. Its controversial elements, according to Thomas Nagel are "its egalitarianism, its anti-perfectionism and anti-meritocracy, the primacy it gives to liberty, and the fact that it is more egalitarian about liberty than about other goods." The common good "is measured in terms of a very restricted, basic set of benefits to individuals: personal and political liberty, economic and social advantages, and self-respect." (*190* : *3*).

A Theory of Justice was published on the heels of a period of intense political questioning, a period of serious challenge to liberalism. In the United States, the Civil Rights and Black Liberation movements, followed by the Anti-Vietnam War movement, brought millions of people into conflict with existing political institutions and policies. They raised fundamental questions about the justice of the existing social order, questions about unequal distribution of income and questions about the just use of power. Liberal ethical judgements were pitted against liberal political institutions and these institutions were in turn justified by a revisionist liberal logic. Marshall Cohen says : "All the great political philosophies of the past—Plato's, Hobbes's, Rousseau's—have responded to the realities of contemporary politics, and it is therefore not surprising that Rawls's penetrating account of the principles to which our public life is committed should appear at a time when these principles are persistently being obscured and betrayed." (*190*:*XV*).

According to Norman Daniels, it would be wrong to conclude that, because Rawls's work has this timely, ideological significance, he is merely a polemicist for the *status quo*. His 'ideal theory' of juctice does challenge to some extent existing social and political institutions and his style is not that of a polemical ideologue. Rawls even claims that his theory of justice is, in principle at least, compatible with both socialism and capitalism. However, these neutralist credentials of Rawls are not acceptable to Steven Lukes. He says: "In the end, the 'Archimedean point for judging the basic structure of society' that Rawls seeks eludes him. Every political theory, and every theory of justice, expresses a particular political and moral perspective. Rawls's achievement, which is considerable, is indeed to have produced a theory of justice—a theory of liberal democratic justice. (*190*:*XVII*).

The controversy regarding his monumental work on the theme of justice has taken many forms. Some have argued that the particular version of Liberalism that Rawls projects is wrong, believing it too egalitarian or not egalitarian enough. Some have claimed that it shows little concern for other classical notions, like merit or entitlement, guilt, innocence or reribution connected with the concept of justice. Some liberal critics find fault with his contractarian approach to justice from their utilitarian or intuitionist points of view. Others, who think that all forms of liberalism are inadequate, would now have the task of attacking and refuting a powerful theoretical defence of it. Bernard Crick remarks on the nature of this challenge: "Rawls is profundly wrong but almost perfectly relevant.

Truly he forces us to see that theories of socialism without a critical moral philosophy are as undesirable as they are impossible. Who can answer him fully and go beyond? *(190:XVII)*. Rawls's theory of justice, "which avoids discussing possible Marxist objections, nevertheless provides Marxists with a serious and sophisticated challenge." *(190:XX)*.

This challenge has been accepted by Milton Fisk in his essay "History and Reason in Rawls's Moral Theory" and by Richard W. Miller in his essay "Rawls and Marxism". C. B. Macpherson offered a critique of Rawls's theory of distributive justice in his essay on "Revisionist Liberalism". Arguing from a Marxist point of view, Milton Fisk tries to show that Rawls's biases in the original position are a general feature of social contract theories. Though Rawls claims that he can earn justificatory force for the contract position by stripping men down to ther natural characteristics of 'freedom' and 'equality', these characteristics, according to Fisk **reflect a class rationality based on the liberal ideology. Rawls believes that** men are naturally free, by which he means they choose their life prospects without external restrictions, like those imposed by a concern for the interests of others. Milton Fisk argues that abstracting man from his real material condition, which always involves group interests, especially class interests, is an irrational distortion. This distortion has three bad consequences. It leads to selecting ideologically biased principles which really favour the privileged class. It also leads to a misrepresentation of the nature of the state, which is viewed as a check to individual selfishness and not as an instrument of class domination. Lastly, this distortion makes genuine 'community' impossible.

Milton Fisk further argues that another major distortion of human nature is embodied in the claim that people are 'equal'. In reality, Fisk claims, people are unequal due to existence of class divisions. They are 'equally' members of classes, not members of society as a whole. Adopting a universalistic view of society, Rawls enunciates principles which seem to treat all people equally, but which really have different effects on different classes. Daniels points out: "Fisk's overall argument has the form, then, of granting the analytic function of the original position but denying its justificatory function. Rawls reduces liberal moral and political theory to a problem of individual rational choice. But Fisk rejects the model of the individual who makes the choice as itself ideologically biased." *(190:XXI)*.

According to Milton Fisk, the Locke-Kant-Rawls concept of human nature is a falsifying abstraction. A revolutionary view of human nature, like Marx's claims that human nature is not being realized until human activity becomes an end rather than a means. If one sells one's labour skills on the market, then the man possessing these skills has been reduced to the status of an object. What can be greater injustice than this degradation of man? In a class-divided society, justice cannot be achieved without struggle. Fisk, therefore, concludes: "Struggle is constantly shattering illusions and changing the participants. Struggle is thus antithetical to the idea of a contract. For an enduring agreement requires an enduring concept of human nature. And struggle will change this concept. The conclusion to all this is not that contract theory is restricted to situations of stability and compliance. It is rather that because of the structural guarantees of conflict in the relevant sorts of societies, the situation of stability and compliance that must be possible for contract theory to be credible is excluded in advance." (*190 : 80*).

Richard Mill argues that the difference principle as suggested by Rawls cannot appeal to those who will end up as members of an upper income group. Suppose that some existing societies display these three characteristics: (a) no institutional arrangement acceptable to the upper class is acceptable to the lower classes; (b) the upper class is also a ruling class; and (c) the upper class has a more acute desire for wealth and power than is typical of the lower classes. If these features of class-divided society, as depicted in Marxist theory, exist, then Rawls will not be able to show that representatives of the richer classes would tolerate the constraints of the difference principle. Rawls will also fail to prove that the difference principle constituted minimization of risk. So, Rawls must be assuming "that societies have only moderate class conflict, no ruling class, and no class differentiated basic desires, at the very least a controversial, if not false, set of assumptions." (*190:XVIII*).

Macpherson believs that the model of justice proposed by Rawls has put him, whether or not he so intended, among the revisionist liberals. Rawls's arguments, he says, are so elegant that the narrowness of some of his postulates may easily be ignored. But when examined they appear inadequate to a justifying theory of liberal democracy. He proposes and defends his principles of justice as criteria for judging the moral worth of various distributions of rights and income *only within a class-divided society*. His explicit assumption is that institutionalized inequalities are inevitable in any society and he is here referring to inequalities between classes by income or wealth. The assumption that such class division is inevitable does narrow his principles of justice severely. Rawls's principles designed to show when class inequalities are just do not go very deep.

Rawls has argued that class inequalities are consistent with a substantial equality in liberty and personal rights, in any society, including a capitalist market society. Macpherson has argued, on the contrary, "that these are inconsistent in a capitalist market society, where class inequality of income or wealth is the result and the means of an inequality in power which reaches to the liberties, rights, and essential humanity of the individuals in those classes." Non-capitalist models which utilize or permit differences of income or wealth are of course possible, and may result in classes by income or wealth. But "these need not create unequal liberties and rights since they are not necessarily either the result or the means of domination, of gaining at the expense of others." Macpherson says: "Rawls's principles of justice, applied to such a society, would probably make very good sense. But as we shall see, he applies them to a capitalist society, where they become a charter for revisionist liberalism." (*218 : 90*).

The model which Rawls proposes as conforming to his two principles of justice is a *constitutional democracy* in which "the government regulates a free economy in a certain way. More fully, if law and government act effectively to keep markets competitive, resources fully employed, property and wealth widely distributed over time, and to maintain the appropriate social minimum, then if there is equality of opportunity underwritten by education for all, the resulting distribution will be just." (*249* : *69*). It is obvious that Rawls like Chapman, is assuming the inherent rationality of capitalist system and is dealing with justice only within the limits imposed by it. He assumes that inequalities of income will always be necessary as an incentive to efficient production and therefore welfare. state transfer payments must be limited to an amount which will still leave one class much better off than another.

Rawls, however, fails to see that the class inequality in his market system is bound to be an inequality of power as well as of wealth and that it permits one class to dominate another. In his later model of a competitive market society, he does refer to a tendency for concentration of wealth and admits that excessive concentration of economic power is detrimental to equal liberty and equality of opportunity. But he considers that it is so when inequalities and concentrations of wealth go beyond a certain limit. But the limit will still permit class differences in life prospects. Moreover, where this limit lies, Rawls tells, "the theory of justice has nothing to say." (*249* : *71*). Macpherson points out: "That is indeed the case with a theory of justice which does not recognize that in a competitive market system where capital and labour are in separate hands, all capital, whatever its degree of concentration, is power which controls and impedes the lives of others. Capital in that society is extractive power, and the extractive power of the owners of capital diminishes the developmental powers of the non-owners." (*218* : *92*).

We find that Rawls's principles of justice, as they would operate within his model of market economy, are self-contradictory. His first principle requires continual income transfers from the upper to the lower class, and also requires various steady administrative measures to control the normal market tendencies towards concentration of capital. These transfers and the controls must not, by his second principle, surpass a point at which their amount would reduce the efficiency and productivity of capitalist enterprises. The limit must be low enough to maintain the incentive system of classes with different life prospects. But it is impossible to find a limit on transfers and controls which is low enough to do the one thing and high enough to do the other. Macpherson says: "There has to be *some* limit on transfers and interferences, to comply with the second principle; but if there is *any* limit on transfers and interferences, they will not prevent concentrations of private capital detrimental to equal liberty and equality of opportunity. . . .Put otherwise, the limit on transfers and interferences cannot coincide with the limit on accumulation of capital because the limit beyond which accumulation of capital becomes detrimental to equal liberty and equality of opportunity is zero, whereas the limit on transfers and interferences cannot, by the second principle, be zero." (*218* : *93*). Rawls sees some inconsistency in his principles when he admits that the principle of fair opportunity can only be imperfectly carried out so long as we accept the institution of the family as accidents of birth can create unequal chances of achievement and culture for different persons. Since he is still attributing the difficulty to the institution of the family rather than to the institution of capitalist market, it cannot be said that he sees the full contradiction.

Liberal political theory has traditionally attempted to provide a two-fold justification. On the one hand, liberal theorists, from Locke to Mill, have argued for the equality of various political liberties. On the other hand, while justifying some degree of equality in the political sphere, these liberal theorists at the same time accepted and justified significant inequalities in income, wealth, power and authority between both individuals and classes. Norman Daniels says: "Despite the highly divergent theoretical frameworks used to justify these political equalities and socio-economic inequalities, including appeals to natural rights, to social contracts, and to different forms of utilitarianism, there was always a shared assumption. Liberal theorists uniformly assumed that political equality is compatible with significant social and economic inequalities......A similar assumption is implicit in John Rawls's 'special conception' of justice as fairness and in his powerful and sophisticated arguments for it." (*190* : *253*).

The crucial point here is that economic and ideological factors are explicitly excluded from among the constraints *definitive* of liberty. He says: "The inability to take advantage of one's rights and opportunities as a result of poverty and ignorance, and a lack of means generally, is sometimes counted among the constraints definitive of liberty. I shall not, however, say this, but rather I shall think of these things as affecting the worth of liberty, the value to individuals of the rights that the First Principle defines." (*249* : *104*). Rawls also remarks that greater authority and wealth implies having greater means to achieve aims and thus greater worth of liberty. Thus the full range of economic factors, and not just abject poverty, are excluded, from the category of constrains defining liberty. Daniels regards Rawls's distinction between liberty and worth of liberty as arbitrary and believes that equal liberty which co-exists with unequal worth of liberty inevitably leads to unequal justice.

CHAPTER 23

CLASSIFICATION OF STATES AND CONSTITUTIONS

CLASSIFICATION OF STATES

There has been considerable discussion among political thinkers as to whether one should speak of 'the classification of states' or 'the classification of governments'. Willoughby, Gilchrist, and Garner prefer the latter term on the ground that in essence all states are alike and that they all possess population, territory, sovereignty and government. Writers like Leacock, on the other hand, do not agree with this argument and claim that a State is known by the structure of government and by the end which it serves. They, therefore, prefer the term 'classification of states' or 'classification of constitutions' to the term 'classification of governments'.

1. Plato and Aristotle

The classification of states is not a modern idea. It goes back to those two masters of political thought, Plato and Aristotle.

Being a pioneer in the field, Plato is not consistent in his classification. He offers two different versions in his *Republic* and the *Statesman*. In general, he speaks of three types of states :—

(a) The State of the sovereign idea or reason. This is the *state of perfect knowledge,* where the real sovereign is knowledge. Such a State Plato believed never existed anywhere. Yet it is an ideal towards which political efforts might be directed. This ideal is sometimes stated as rule by an all-wise philosopher, *i.e.,* ideal monarchy. At other times it is stated in terms of an ideal aristocracy.

(b) States where there is *imperfect knowledge*. In such states laws are necessary. Human imperfection necessitates laws. This is decidedly the point of view of Plato's *Laws.* In his earlier work *The Republic,* the preference was for an ideal monarchy (or an aristocracy) in which there would be no laws, but only occasional decrees issued by the all-wise philosopher-king; but failing to discover such kings, in his later work, *The Laws,* Plato turns in the direction of laws.

(c) States where there is *lack of knowledge*. These are the states of ignorance. Here laws exist, but they are not obeyed.

Thus the criterion of Plato's classification is States where laws are obeyed and States where laws are not obeyed.

Gilchrist states the matter in the form of a chart :–

	States in which law is obeyed	*States in which law is not obeyed*
Rule by One	Monarchy	Tyranny
Rule by Few	Aristocracy	Oligarchy
Rule by Many	Moderate Democracy	Extreme Democracy

Aristotle, who followed closely on the heels of Plato, was more of a realist than his master. The bases of his classification were quantitative and qualitative; that is to say the number of those in whom sovereign power was vested; and the end or purpose towards which the power was directed. States which seek the good life of all are the true or normal states. Those which deviate from that end are the perverted states. Thus his classification in the form of a chart is as follows :–

Form of constitution	*Normal State seeking the common welfare*	*Perverted State where the common welfare is ignored*
Rule by One	Monarchy	Tyranny
Rule by Few	Aristocracy	Oligarchy
Rule by Many	Polity	Democracy

To explain the matter in detail, pure monarchy or royalty is government by the one in the interest of all. When it degenerates into the selfish rule of one, it becomes tyranny. When a few rule for the common good, it is aristocracy. But when they rule in their own self-interest, aristocracy is perverted into oligarchy. When the many rule in the interest of everybody it is called polity or mild democracy. But when they rule with a view to promoting their own class interest, it becomes democracy or ochlocracy (*i.e.* mob rule). It is necessary here to make note of the fact that where the modern world uses the term 'democracy', Aristotle uses the term 'polity'. What he calls 'democracy', is what we today would call mob rule. An equivalent of polity used by Aristotle is 'constitutional democracy', which is defined as the unselfish rule of many for the common welfare. These types of governments, according to Aristotle, follow one another in the form of a cycle.

The above classification given by Aristotle is more realistic than that of Plato and covered the field adequately until recent times. Commenting on it, Gilchrist writes: "The classification is not sufficient for modern forms of government: but it has provided the historical basis of practically all classifications made hitherto". (*28* : *228*).

According to Aristotle, the question of numbers is only accidental compared to the end or purpose for which a state exists. Thus an oligarchy is the rule of the rich, be they few or many, in the interest of the rich; and democracy likewise is the rule of the poor, be they few or many, in the interest of the poor. All of this is not very helpful to us today.

Dealing with the thought of Plato and Aristotle as a whole it may truly be said that Aristotle begins where Plato leaves off. Plato started with an ideal monarchy and ended with a mixed aristocracy, i.e. an aristocracy of ability modified by an aristocracy of landed property. Aristotle began with such an aristocracy as his ideal but ended with a mixed constitution which is much the same as polity as the most practical ideal. Between mild democracy and mild oligarchy he does not draw too much of a distinction. On the other hand, he devotes a great deal of space and attention to the preservation of different types of constitutions. Here he sounds more like the realist Machiavelli than the idealist Plato.

2. After Aristotle

Some other writers of the past who have attempted a classification of states are Polybius, Cicero, Machiavelli, Bodin, Hobbes, Locke, Montesquieu, Rousseau, and Bluntschli.

Polybius adhered to the traditional classification of states into monarchy, aristocracy, and democracy and tended to believe that they together with their corresponding corrupt forms followed one another in the form of a cycle. Thus the order was monarchy, tyranny, aristocracy, oligarchy, democracy, and mob rule. When the last stage became unbearable it gave rise to monarchy again and the cycle repeated itself.

Cicero who followed Polybius was no innovator. Like Polybius, he paid his tribute to the mixed constitution and the system of checks and balances. The only addition he made was to interpret the three organs of government as representing the three principles necessary for stability; thus monarchy represents the principle of force or authority, the senate, the principle of prestige and influence, and popular assemblies, the principle of liberty.

Coming to the beginning of the modern period in European history, Jean Bodin may be regarded as the first important political philosopher of modern times to base his classification solely on the number of men in whose hands sovereign power resides. When sovereign power rests in the hands of one man it is a monarchic state; when in less than a majority of citizens, it is aristocratic; and when in the majority, it is democratic. Bodin further classified monarchy into (1) royal or pure, (2) despotic, and (3) tyrannical.

In his *Leviathan* (pp. 96-97), Hobbes writes "When the Representative is one man, then is the Commonwealth a Monarchy: when an Assembly of all that will come together, then it is a Democracy, or Popular commonwealth: when an Assembly of a Part only, then it is called an Aristocracy". Suffice it to say that there is nothing new in this classification.

Locke does not differ substantially from Hobbes. He classifies states as monarchies, oligarchies, and democracies and subdivides monarchy into the hereditary and elective types.

Montesquieu classifies states into (1) republics (a) democratic and (b) aristocratic (2) monarchies and (3) despotisms. All these governments have a sustaining and driving power behind them. Democracy has the spirit of public service behind it. Aristocracy is based on the principle of moderation, monarchy on honour, and despotism on fear.

Coming to more recent writers, we find that J. A. R. Marriott classifies constitutions as :—

1. Unitary and federal
2. Rigid and flexible
3. Monarchical and presidential.

He also speaks of parliamentary and responsible or the cabinet type of Government.

Leacock draws a sharp line between despotic and democratic states and further divides democratic states into (a) limited monarchies and (b) republics. Each of these (a) and (b) in turn he subdivides into unitary and federal; and these again are divided into parliamentary and non-parliamentary types. The following table as drawn up by Gilchrist puts the matter clearly.

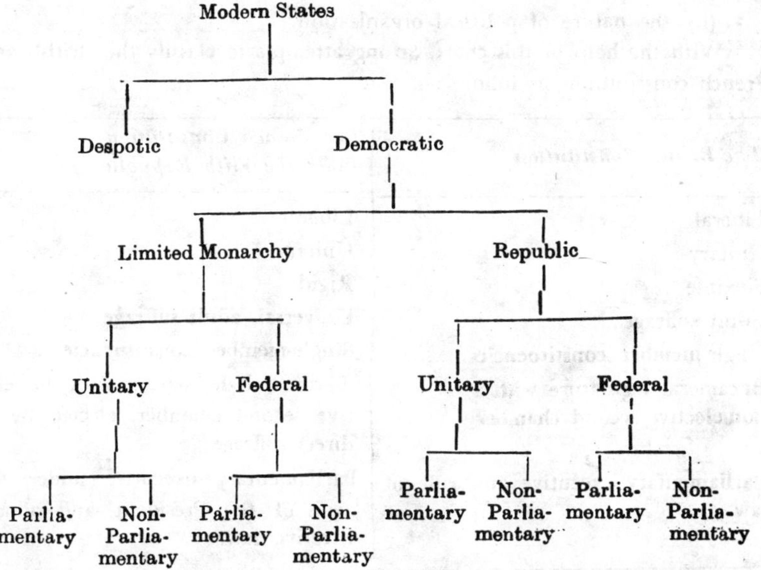

A CLASSIFICATION OF MODERN STATES AS SUGGESTED BY BRYCE, JENKS AND MARRIOTT (*164*)

	Basis of Division	*A*	*B*
I	The conception regarding the sphere of the State	Liberal	Totalitarian (*a*) Communist (*b*) Fascist
II	The nature of political organization		
1	The nature of the State	Unitary	Federal
2	The nature of the Constitution	Flexible	Rigid
3	The nature of the electorate	(*i*) Adult suffrage (*ii*) Single member constituency	(*i*) Restricted suffrage (*ii*) Multi-member constituency
4	The nature of the Legislature	Bicameral (*a*) Elective or partially elective second chamber (*b*) Non-elective second chamber	Unicameral
5	The nature of the Executive	Parliamentary	Non-Parliamentary
6	The nature of the Judiciary	The rule of law	Administrative Law

This classification is based on two major ideas :–

(i) the sphere of state action; and

(ii) the nature of political organization.

With the help of this chart, Strong attempts to classify the British and French constitutions as follows :–

The British Constitution	*The French Constitution under the Fifth Republic*
Liberal	Liberal
Unitary	Unitary
Flexible	Rigid
Adult suffrage	Universal, adult suffrage
Single-member constituencies	Single-member constituencies
Bi-cameral legislature with a non-elective second chamber	Bi-cameral legislature with an elective second chamber, elected by indirect suffrage
Parliamentary executive and rule of law.	Parliamentary executive under the aegis of the President and administrative law.

George Schwarzenberger classifies states into national and multi-national states. The latter, he says, are divisible into (1) the dynastic state (e.g. Austria-Hungary, prior to World War I); (2) the religious state (e.g. the Ottoman Empire as it was up to 1919); (3) the colonial state; (4) the Commonwealth state; (5) the federal state; and (6) the pseudo-federal state.

THE NATURE AND DEFINITION OF CONSTITUTIONS

The Nature of the Constitution

Inasmuch as modern states are constitutional states, they have been classified according to their nature as to whether they are written or unwritten, rigid ot flexible. Although we generally tend to think of a constitution as a written document, it "may be un-written and yet serve the same general function as a written constitution" *(94:299)*.

Definitions of Constitution

Bouvier, in his *Legal Dictionary,* defines a constitution as "the fundamental law of a state, directing the principles upon which the government is founded, and regulating the exercise of the sovereign powers, directing to what bodies or persons these powers shall be confined and the manner of their exercise" *(94:299)*. George Cornewall Lewis writes: "The term 'constitution' signifies the arrangement and distribution of the sovereign power in the community, or the form of government" *(138:20)*.

A constitution fixes the general structure of the State. It is, so to speak, the skeleton of the State. Charles Borgeaud, a noted Swiss authority on the subject, says: "A constitution is the fundamental law according to which the government of a state is organized and agreeably to which the relations of individuals or moral persons to the community are determined. It may be a written instrument, a precise text or series of texts enacted at a given time by a sovereign power; or it may be the more or less definite result of a series of legislative acts, ordinances, judicial decisions, precedents, and customs of diverse origin and of unequal value and importance"[1].

H. Finer defines the constitution as "the system of fundamental political institutions" or as, "the autobiography of a power relationship". *(20:116-17)*.

The Necessity of a Constitution

During the period before the American Revolution, the idea of a constitution as a necessary and fundamental document was very much to the forefront. As the nineteenth century wore on, the idea became firmly rooted that every state must have a constitution and that it must rest on the approval of the whole people. Today constitutionalism has become the bed-

---

1. "The Origin of Written Constitution", Political Science Quarterly, Volume I, p. 613.

rock of democracy. A constitution is desired for a variety of reasons :—

1. To curb the powers of government by a fundamental law.
2. To restrain the government on behalf of the individual.
3. To limit the vagaries of present and future generations. John Adams, James Madison, and a long succession of the Supreme Court Justices of the U.S.A. emphasized this viewpoint. In contrast to it, Jefferson preferred to set a limit to the duration of any particular constitution (*94:302*).

Today most scholars will agree with Schulze when he says "every community entitled to the name of state must have a constitution, *i.e.,* collection of norms by which the legal relations between the government and its subjetcs are determined and in accordance with which the power of the state is exercised, A state without a constitution is unthinkable."[2]

KINDS OF CONSTITUTIONS

(a) The written Constitution

The American Constitution heralds the era of constitutionalism. The American example has been followed by several other nations. Constitutionalism provides for a philosophy of change which is rationalized legally as well as morally and socially. According to Finer, "France set the example of written constitutions in Europe, and the soldiers of the Revolution and the Empire carried the notion into Italy, Belgium, Spain and the South German States" (*20:122*). Written constitutions, says the same writer, "secure a firm basis for political life".

A written constitution is one in which most of the provisions are embodied in a single formal written instrument or instruments. "It is a work of conscious art and the result of a deliberate effort to lay down a body of fundamental principles under which a government shall be organized and conducted" (*116*).

A written constitution may be comprised within a single document bearing a single date such as the constitutions of the U.S.A., India, and Burma or may be written in a series of documents such as those of France and Austria. In states having written constitutions there are generally two bodies of law, one cnostitutional and paramount, and the other statutory and subordinate. This distinction, however, is not always found in states with written constitutions (*23:505-10*).

(b) The unwritten Constitution

An unwritten constitution is that in which most, if not all, of the prescriptions have never been reduced to writing and formally embodied in a document or collection of documents. It consists mainly of customs, usages, and judicial decisions together with a smaller body of legislative enactments

2. ''Deutsches Statsrecht'', Vol. I, p. 19.

of a fundamental nature created on different dates. The constitutions coming under this category cannot be struck off at once by a constituent assembly or any other body. They illustrate Sir James MacIntosh's dictum that "Constitutions grow, instead of being made" (*23:508*). The British constitution is the best example of such a constitution. Nobody has the legal authority to declare an Act of Parliament or of the executive unconstitutional.

Even Britain has certain written documents such as the Magna Carta, the Petition of Right, the Bill of Rights, the Act of Settlement, the Franchise Acts, the Parliament Act of 1911. But the most important part of the British constitution is contained in "conventions" or "understandings". As Finer puts it, "they are taken for granted but not formulated".

The classification of constitutions as written and unwritten has been criticized as inadequate and as lacking in political significance. The distinction between them is said to be one of degree rather than of kind since all written constitutions "become overlaid with an unwritten element" after a lapse of time and written constitutions, as Bryce remarked, become "developed by interpretations, fringed with decisions, and enlarged by customs". Moreover, experience shows that it is impossible to embody all the principles in a written document, and conventions do grow in spite of there being a written document.

Therefore, classifying constitutions as written and unwritten is said to be not only unscientific but also confusing as it results in placing certain unwritten constitutions under the category of written constitutions and *vice versa*. Consequently, it has been suggested that a more useful and scientific classification of constitutions would be on the basis of the relation which the constitution bears to ordinary laws rather than its source. On the basis of this test constitutions are classified as flexible and rigid.

(c) Flexible Constitutions

All those constitutions which possess no higher legal authority than ordinary laws and which can be changed or amended by the same procedure as ordinary laws, whether they are enshrined in a single document or in a large number of conventions, are classified as flexible or elastic constitutions. Such constitutions, though written, possess flexibility and can be altered at will as easily as an ordinary law. The constitution of Great Britain and, to some extent, that of India come under this category.

(d) Rigid Constitutions

Those constitutions which are enacted by a different body, which have a higher status than ordinary laws, and which can be altered only by special procedure, are classified as rigid, stationary or inelastic constitutions. This fact is made clear if the method of amending the American, Australian or Swiss constitutions is carefully studied.

Written constitutions are generally rigid and unwritten constitutions are generally flexible. We may now examine the merits and demerits of rigid and written constitutions on the one side and those of flexible and unwritten constitutions on the other.

The *merits* of a written constitution are that they are :

(1) clear and definite;

(2) drawn up with great care and deliberation;

(3) free from being bent and twisted easily according to popular emotions or legislative despotism;

(4) stable and steady.

They further (5) afford protection to the individual and guarantee people's rights. Written constitutions usually incorporate fundamental rights.

Demerits

(1) A written constitution attempts to compress into one document all the ideals and political principles of a nation. It is an attempt to fit the garment to an individual without taking into consideration his future growth and changed size, as Garner has put it.

(2) Written constitutions are as a rule difficult to amend. When rigidity and conservatism are carried too far, they prove to be elements of weakness and are detrimental to the national interest and may even lead to revolution.

(3) Under a written constitution the main concern of the judiciary is to see whether the law conforms to the provisions of the constituency or not. Since judges are generally conservative in their outlook, they tend to disregard the spirit of the times.

The merits of an unwritten constitution are as follows :–

(1) They are easily adaptable to the changing conditions of a dynamic society.

(2) Elasticity removes the temptation to violate the constitution but provides a legal means for satisfying popular passions and preventing revolutions.

(3) In the words of Bryce, "they can be stretched or bent so as to meet emergencies without breaking their framework; and when the emergency has passed, they slip back into their old form like a tree whose outer branches have been pulled aside to let a vehicle pass (*116*)".

The defects of an unwritten constitution are the following :–

(1) They are unstable and in a state of perpetual flux.

(2) They can be amended according to the whims and fancies of individuals or parties.

(3) They sometimes become "the plaything of judicial tribunals".

(4) According to some, they are meant for aristocratic societies rather than for democracies.

Both Esmein and Judge Jameson are of the opinion that an unwritten constitution "is suitable to a people who have a strong sense of tradition and a profoundly conservative spirit". Our own experience leads us to think that a nation lacking political consciousness and vigilance in the safeguarding of democratic rights must have a written constitution. Finer, however, argues that a written constitution does not have any great advantage over the unwritten. His argument is "At the most, the written constitution is a standard of reference, and it is valuable only in proportion to its clarity and the extent to which it has not been altered by interpretation" (*20:127*). Since such conditions seldom last more than a decade, the advantages of the written over unwritten constitutions are practically nil.

An ideal *written constitution* should contain the following elements :—

(1) A set of civil and political rights which demarcates the area of freedom for citizens and sets a limit to the authority of the State.

(2) Provisions outlining the structure and organization of the government, allotting powers and functions to each of it, and determining their mutual relation and defining their relations to the electorate.

(3) A suitable method of amending the constitution. The prevailing view is that "constitutions ought not to burden the present generation with the legal conceptions of the past" but that they provide easy modes of amending the constitution, consulting the people periodically.

As regards the length of the constitution, there is no fixed rule about it. Earlier constitutions such as the American constitution confined themselves to stating the general principles of fundamental law. But later constitutions have incorporated even items which may properly be called ordinary law. As a result of this tendency modern constitutions have become lengthy and unwieldy. The Indian Constitution (1949) with its 395 articles and 8 schedules is the longest constitution in the world.

UNITARY AND FEDERAL STATES

Modern governments are classified as unitary and federal on the basis of the concentration or distribution of powers and on the relations between the central and local authorities.

In a unitary system of government the entire governmental power is vested by the constitution in a single central government, and local authorities not only derive their power and autonomy from it but owe their very existence to it. In such a system :

(1) There is only one state and one government, and there is no constitutional division or distribution of powers between the central and local governments. There is only one source of power, and one will.

(2) For the sake of administrative convenience, unitary states are divided into units known variously as departments, provinces, countries, communes, etc. They are given a certain amount of autonomy and limited

powers of local government. But their creation as well as continuance depends on the will of the central government and is not determined by the constitution.

(3) Another way of stating this truth is that the power and autonomy possessed by these local bodies is not an original power, but is derived from the central government which may enlarge or restrict it at its will.

(4) In short, in a unitary state the local authorities are merely parts of the central organization created by the latter to act as its agents for the purpose of local administration.

Merits of a Unitary State

(1) A unitary state can bring about a uniformity of law, policy, and administration throughout the length and breadth of a country. By so doing it can help to bring about a unified and integrated governmental machinery.

(2) In matters of defence and international relations, the strength of the unitary state is especially manifest because in such a state there can be no conflict of authority, no conflict or confusion of responsibility for work to be performed, no overlapping of jurisdictions, no duplication of work, plant or organization which cannot be immediately adjusted *(170:177)*.

(3) A unitary state has the advantage of being simple in structure and less expensive than a federal state because of the absence of duplication of governmental departments and services.

(4) A unitary constitution is particularly suited for a small country with a homogeneous population such as England.

Demerits of a Unitary State

(1) A major weakness of the unitary system is the absence of strong provincial and regional institutions and the regulation of local policies and affairs by distant and far-off authorities.

(2) Such added responsibility for local and provincial affairs places an additional burden on the central government and leads to greater red-tapism and bureaucratic administration.

(3) Central authorities often lack the necessary knowledge of local conditions and needs; and the consequence of it is that local interests suffer.

(4) A unitary state tends to suppress local initiative and discourage interest in social problems. It is unacceptable to a people accustomed to vigorous self-government and a love of local liberty.

The Federal State

As Garner remarks, a federal state as distinguished from a unitary state is a system in which the totality of governmental power is divided or distributed by the national constitution or organic Act of parliament creating it, between a central government and the governments of the individual states or other territorial sub-divisions of which the federation is composed (*23:348*). In the words of Hamilton, a federal state is "an association of states that forms a new one". Or, as Dicey defines it, "it is a political contrivance intended to reconcile national unity with the maintenance of state rights". It combines the respective advantages of unity and diversity.

The chief features of a Federation are :—

(1) The existence of one state, but many governments.

(2) A formal division or distribution of governmental powers between the central and state or provincial governments.

(3) A written constitution which is supreme.

(4) The *ultra vires* of any law of the state or central legislature or any act of government which is contrary to the constitution. The setting up of a Supreme or Federal Court to decide cases, such a such often being known as "the guardian of the constitution".

(5) Comparative rigidity of the federal constitution in order to prevent hasty and ill-digested legislation.

(6) The derivation of state or provincial authority not from the central government, but directly from the constitution.

K. C. Wheare considers that government to be a federal government which predominantly embodies "as division of powers between general and regional authorities, each of which, in its own sphere, is coordinate with and others and independent of them". (*Federal Government*, 1963, p. 33).

Wheare considers the independence of the governments in their respective spheres as hallmark of the Federal Government. Recent opinions are that the general and regional governments are linked in a mutually interdependent political relationship; that neither level of goveernment becomes dominant to the extent that it can dictate the decision of the other but each can influence, bargain with and persuade the other. Emphasis is thus laid on interdependence of the two levels of governments.

Dual federalism was commonly used to describe the American federal system. The Depression (1930) inaugurated the era of modern or cooperative federalism. The concept of dual federalism was current throughout the nineteenth century and referred to in the decisions of the U.S. Supreme Court. The division of the power between the federal and state governments formed the "Key to the entire concept of dual federalism", and both sets of governments had exclusive area of authority and jurisdiction. This doctrine holds no more good. The new federalism or cooperative federalism has arisen "which can be traced back to Wilson's administrations or at the latest to the second Roosevelt's". The old barriers between the federal government and the states have broken down. Separation has been replaced by cooperation. This is a major departure from the traditional system of dual federalism.

Requisites of Federation

Historically speaking, federations have been created by the coming together of a number of small sovereign states with the object of establishing a common government either for better military or economic security, *e.g.*, Switzerland, the U.S.A., and Australia. The Indian federation of our day is an exception to this rule. For it has been created by breaking up a unitary state into autonomous units.

Whatever be the mode of its formation, a federation can be firmly established and continued if the following conditions exist:

(1) *The desire for union.* Among the people of various political units a desire to create a common government for their own common interest must exist before a federation can be created.

(2) *The desire for union, but not for unity.* The component units must cherish a strong desire to maintain their individual freedom in all but essentially common matters. It should not, however, be of such a nature as to swallow up individually and lead to a unitary state.

(3) *Geographical contiguity.* Geographical nearness of various units desirous of forming a federation strongly favours a federation. If the units are widely separated, the desire for union cannot very well materialize.

(4) *Absence of inequality among the units.* No unit should be so powerful and domineering as to become the master of the joint enterprise (*15*).

(5) *Political education of the people.* It should be of very high order inasmuch as a federation demands ability on the part of the people to appreciate and reconcile loyalty to two governments. They should exhibit a willingness to obey the laws of the two governments and a particular readiness to yield to the authority of the law courts. Violent events in India in connection with the reorganization of states have shown that many in India still have too much of a provincial and parochial loyalty and too little of a national loyalty.

Distribution of Powers in a Federation

The principle on which the distribution of governmental power takes place in a federation is that those affairs which are of national importance and which require uniformity of regulation are delegated to the central government whereas subjects which are not of common interest are left with the local governments. Generally, any one of the following three methods may be adopted in distributing the powers between the centre and the units.

(1) Powers allotted to the central government may be specifically enumerated in the constitution and all the remaining powers, with the excep-

tion of those specifically prohibited to them, may be left with States, as in the U.S.A.

(2) Just the opposite procedure may be adopted, as in the case of the Canadian federation where the powers of the State are specifically enumerated in the constitution, while the residuary powers are left with the centre.

(3) Specific powers may be assigned to the centre and the states respectively, with the residuary powers belonging to the centre, as in the Indian Union. In India, in addition to the two lists, there is a third list of subjects known as the concurrent list on which both the governments have jurisdiction. In cases of conflict the Union government is given priority. Two or more States may request the centre to frame legislation for them on certain specific matters.

Merits of a Federation

(1) It affords opportunity to small and weak states to unite into a powerful state without losing their independent and separate existence.

(2) By combining in it the twin advantages of national unity and local independence, a federation becomes particularly valuable to big states with vast population and with racial, cultural, and linguistic diversities.

(3) In such a state only a federal system can maintain an equilibrium between centripetal and centrifugal forces. For a country like India with its linguism, provincialism and casteism, federation has a special value.

(4) Federation makes it possible for a uniformity of policy, legislation and administration where it is necessary and for diversity where such diversity is desirable.

(5) Federation is the best system of government for trying our political, social, and economic experiments. In India, prohibition and several other social and economic schemes are being tried out in limited regions, and their results are being carefully watched and assessed.

(6) By giving local independence to the people of the units, it stimulates their interest in public affairs.

(7) On account of the distribution of powers, the central government in a federation is relieved of the burdens and congestion created by a top-heavy administration. This, in its turn, discourages red-tapism and bureaucratic administration.

(8) According to Lord Bryce, there is no danger of a despot usurping the rights of a people.

Defects inherent in the Federal System

(1) Leacock opines that "politically and on its external side it has

proved itself strong, but economically and in its internal aspect it is proving itself weak". This view is untenable in view of the growing strength and economic prosperity of the U.S.A.

(2) Some writers claim that a federation is weak in the conduct of its foreign affairs. Recent experience shows that this is not true. No one can claim that the foreign policy of the U.S.A., the Soviet Union or of India is weak and vacillating.

The genuine defects of federation are :—

(1) The diversity of legislative policy and administration.

(2) Duplication of governmental organization, the civil service and departments; and their complexity.

(3) The danger of possible conflict of jurisdiction between the national and state governments.

(4) Heavy costs of administration.

(5) The danger of secession.

Outlining the main difficulties of federalism, particularly American, Finer says that (1) It is financially expensive since there is much duplication of administrative machinery and procedure. It is wasteful of time and expenditure. Much time is spent on negotiation. Transport, public utilities, health, employment, etc., could not be administered smoothly and economically because of the multiplicity of authorities.

(2) It is confusing to the public and has awkward results on personal rights and obligations. (The use of federal troops in Little Rock, Ark, in enforcing desegregation in schools is a case in point. It brought into sharp conflict state right and federal responsibility).

Modern Tendencies in Federal Government

Tendency towards centralism is evident in all federal governments. The power of the central government is growing at the expense of the consequent unity of the federation. Four factors, according to K. C. Wheare, are responsible for this development, namely war, economic depression, the growth of social services and the mechanical revolution in transport and industry. Growth of welfarism and technological revolution are permanent factors. The centralising tendency, however, is counteracted by localism which finds expression in linguistic, cultural and regional loyalties. U.S. is moving swiftly towards a unified economic and social system, coextensive with its whole territory. Inter-state commerce, agriculture, education, health, morals, labour laws, migration etc. are all coming more and more under federal regulation, with the system of federal grants-in-aid playing an important part in the process.

A Confederation

Here it is proper to distinguish between a federation and confederation as the latter is also an association of states, with the difference that it is the union of sovereign states formed for realizing certain definite objects.

The chief features of a confederation are as follows:

(1) Confederating states or units retain their sovereignty. There are as many states as there are members.

(2) In a confederation there is no common government.

(3) The various units make their own laws and administer them in their respective territories.

(4) A confederation is unstable and may be broken up at any time.

(5). A confederation is the result of an agreement whereas a federation is based on a constitution.

(6) Confederating units have an international status and can establish diplomatic relations with other sovereign states, while this is not possible in a federation.

(7) If a war breaks out in a confederation it is an international war; whereas in the case of a federation it is a civil war.

(8) In a confederation the common organ established deals with the governments of the units, and not with the people; while in a federation the central government deals directly with the people.

A confederation, in the very nature of the case, is weak and unstable. Faced by a common enemy, the American States formed a confederacy in 1781 known as a "firm league of friendship". But in actual fact, in the words of Finer, it became "a league of disgruntled independents". Few and limited powers were conferred on the Congress. It had no direct power over individual. Nor could it levy direct taxes or regulate commerce.

The history of confederations in the U.S.A., Switzerland, and Germany shows that as a general rule a Federal Union follows a confederation. Experience shows that a confederation is no permanent halting place in the history of constitutions. It has either to go forward and become a federation or go backward and become a unitary state.

Presidential and Non-Presidential Forms of Government

In the Presidential form of Government, the executive head is independent of the legislature. He is usually elected directly by the people or by a college of electors. He is not only the real executive, as against a nominal executive, but is also the ceremonial Head of State. Under certain circumstances he can be impeached, but his term cannot be shortened. He is not a member of the Legislature, but sends to it messages and recommendations. For the passing of measures he has to depend upon legislative committees and his own party men, and other legislators who sympathize with him for one reason or another. His term of office is not the same as that of the legislature. He has the power of limited veto. He can call special sessions of the legislature. The budget is prepared by his office.

Members of the Cabinet are subordinate to him. They are his personal assistants. They are not members of either house of legislature and as such not responsible to it. The legislature has a share in the making of appointments and treaties and in supervising administration. The chief executive is also the Head of Administration. He is the Supreme Commander-in-Chief and has extraordinary powers given to him in times of war or other emergencies.

In the non-Presidential system of government the nominal executive is a President or King, whereas the real executive is the Prime Minister. He as well as other members of the Cabinet are members of the legislature, a majority being from the Lower House. They are the parliamentary leaders of the party in power. They formulate national policy, initiate all important legislation including the budget, defend the acts of the Government, and stand together as a single unit. This last-mentioned feature is described as collective or joint responsibility. When an adverse vote is passed against the Government in a matter which the latter regards as important, there is no alternative left for the Government except to resign. The Prime Minister recommends to the King or President, as the case may be, the dissolution of Parliament and in consultation with him fixes the date for a new general election.

In relation to his colleagues, the Prime Minister has been "the first among equals". But the stress and strain of modern times has made him more than that, but less than dictator. Members of the Cabinet are also heads of administrative departments, although there is room for some who have no administrative responsibility.

In Italy the Cabinet is responsible to both Houses which makes it weak. In Britain and India the responsibility is only to the Lower House.

The Collegiate or plural type of executive is what prevails in Switzerland, Uruguay, and Soviet Russia. In Switzerland, the Federal Council is completely subordinate to the National Parliament and acts as its agent. In Soviet Russia, on the other hand, the presidium enjoys complete authority over the legislature.

Democratic and Dictatorial Governments

Monarchies of the functioning kind are practically out of the picture today. Where monarchies still exist, limited monarchy is the order of the day. Even Japan and Iran have only constitutional monarchies. More and more countries are joining the ranks of democracies, however defectively they may function.

Since the close of World War I several countries have witnessed dictatorship of one kind or another. Even today Spain and Portugal have a dictatorship of the right. The communist countries in general are under a dictatorship of the left. The Latin American States in general have one form of dictatorship or another. During the last few years Indonesia, Pakistan, the United Arab Republic, and Iraq swung to the side of dictatorships, and sometimes, with good results.

Underlying modern dictatorships is a distrust of democracies and a belief that quick results in government could be attained through the rule of a single dictator assisted by a body of consecrated men and women dedicated to the service of the State. Mussolini and his followers as well as Hitler and his followers referred to themselves as the *elite*. In Soviet Russia and countries following the Soviet system the party in general and the top ones of the party in particular constitute the *elite*. While at times they may act, tyrannically and sometimes in their own self-interest, their main aim is the strengthening and glorification of their own countries. Dictatorship at times may be a temporary cure for the ills of democracy, but never a permanent cure.

FORMS OF GOVERNMENT ACCORDING TO LASKI

Economic Basis of Political System

There is a saying of the French utopian socialist Saint-Simon, which Laski quotes with approval at several places, that "the law which constitutes the powers and the form of government is less important and has less influence on the happiness of nations than that which constitutes property and decides its use."[3] Accepting the truth of this contention, Laski attaches greater importance to the economic structure than to political forms because he regards the latter simply as super-structures of the former. In fact, he has never made any attempt to classify the forms of government as other political thinkers from Aristotle onwards have usually done. The reason is, it appears, that he probably considered such classification as devoid of any practical significance.

The traditional classification of governments into monarchical, aristocratic and democratic forms has no meaning for Laski except in terms of **property-relations which they maintain. He is concerned with the socio-**economic foundations of a government rather than with its political superstructure. The content of government is always more important than the form in which that content is expressed. The civic politics of ancient Greece adopted various constitutional forms verging from despotic governments to direct democracy. Yet all of them remained just so many versions of an oligarchical rule of the slave-owners over the slaving masses. The modern capitalist states have similarly ranged from absolute monarchies to representative democracies, and yet all of them have uniformly signified an oligarchical government of the bourgeoisie over the proletariat (*127:24-27, 29-35*)

The Rise of the Middle Class

In "The Rise of European Liberalism" Laski has made an important analysis of the various forms of government which have come into existence in the wake of the rise of the middle class to economic ascendancy.

---

3. For example, Laski has quoted it in his "Rise of European Liberalism", the concluding Chapter, p. 242-3 and again in his "Parliamentary Government in England", Introductory Chapter, p. 22.

"In the period between the Reformation and the French Revolution", he says, "a new social class established its title to a full share in the control of the state.... To achieve its ends, it effected a fundamental change in the legal relationships of men.... The control of politics by an aristocracy whose authority was built upon the tenure of land came to be shared with men whose influence was derived solely from the ownership of movable capital. The banker, the trader, the manufacturer, began to replace the land-owner, the ecclesiastic, and the warrior, as the types of predominant social influence" (*132:11*).

Class Character of Absolute Monarchy

Analysing the nature of absolute monarchies of the sixteenth century in Europe, Laski says that these monarchical governments were based on the alliance of the ruling monarch with the merchants and manufacturers. "The sixteenth century prince is allowed wide powers", he points out, "because, the greater his authority, the better the chance of the economic revival which conflict hinders. And none are so eager for peace as the new merchants. It is their alliance with the monarchies that is most helpful in extinguishing the effort of the great feudatories to retain some vestige of independent authority. The rising bourgeoisie sees in a strong central authority the best guarantee of its own survival, the best hope of its own prosperity. The princes recognized the value of that alliance; and their legislation is, in large part, a deliberate effort to establish the conditions the bourgeoisie requires. The greater the wealth the bourgeoisie can attain, the more powerful will be the state. The prince should encourage and protect manufactures, give them peace and a cheap and rapid justice, a disciplined working-class schooled to work" (*132:81*).

Feudal and Bourgeois Monarchies

But Laski emphasises that this type of absolute monarchy has merely curbed the power of the landed aristocracy in the interest of the bourgeoisie without eliminating it completely. The new bourgeois monarchy differs from the old feudal monarchy in some significant respects. In the first place, the private armies of the nobles are suppressed and a national army is created. The political power is now concentrated in a central government and the authority of its executive officers and judges replaces the more or less autonomous authority of the nobles. A certain degree of separation between the state and the church is brought about with an increasing emphasis on the secular nature of government. The representatives of the new middle class are now associated by the monarch with the work of administration, who act as ministers, officers, and judges replacing the priests and landlords in a gradual manner.

But the creation of an absolute monarchy was only a stage in the process of the advance of the middle class towards the final and total capture of the state apparatus. It was essentially based on a compromise between the declining power of the nobility and the rising prestige of the bourgeoisie which in itself shows its inherent instability. "The rising bourgeoisie," says Laski, "adapts, first, religion, then culture, to its purposes; the state is the last of its conquests.... It makes of the state first ally, then enemy, in the pursuit of its objectives.... That means a century and a half of warfare during which the Crown and middle class in partnership make a new discipline to replace the old. At this stage, the bourgeoisie is not ready for a total redefinition of legal relationships. The Crown is strong; the landowning aristocracy is strong; the traditional belief in regulation is still implicit in all the major social experience. It is only when the new order of things has firmly established its foundations, when freedom in the economic sphere seems an obvious inference from its attainment elsewhere that the bourgeois moves to the final assault. He has then supreme coercive power in his hands. The chief use of the state to him is merely as a police agency. He bids it keep outside that realm of economic action he now proposes to exploit on his own terms" (*132:145*).

Class Origin of the Democratic Republic

What does this final assault on the state signify? It signifies that the middle class now wants to replace the absolute monarchy by a constitutional monarchy or a democratic republic to secure greater freedom and power for itself. This is the meaning of the English Revolution of the seventeenth century and the French Revolution in the eighteenth century. The establishment of constitutional monarchies and democratic republics implies that the middle class has now taken over all effective channels of government. It organises itself into political parties, sends its representatives to legislative assemblies, exercises executive power through responsible cabinets, delivers justice through its loyal henchmen in the courts, and carries out the smallest details of public administration with the help of a faithful and subservient bureaucracy.

Executive Responsibility to Legislature

In Europe, the form of government which a constitutional monarchy or a democratic republic usually adopts is known as the parliamentary type of government, which is based on the idea of a conciliar executive collectively responsible to an elected legislature. In "Parliamentary Government in England", Laski has tried to analyse the nature of parliamentary democracy as practised in England. In the marriage between capitalism and democracy," he points out, "which has given us our system of parliamentary government, the capitalism is more important than the democracy because the relations of property that it imposes give the democracy its constitutive principle. The democracy cannot deny that principle without, as it were, dissolving the marriage that has given it birth. It may survive the dissolution, but that will be on the condition only that it is a divorce by consent" (*130:68*).

Capitalist Basis of Parliamentary System

Thus he argues that the constitutive principle of the British parliamentary system has been its capitalist basis. In "Democracy in Crisis", Laski explains the economic basis of capitalist democracy in a lucid way. "Political democracy", he rightly says, "developed in response to the demand for the abrogation of privilege. In modern European history its cause was the liberation of a commercial middle class from domination by a land-holding aristocracy. To free itself, that middle class formulated a body of liberal generalisations which culminated in the widespread grant of universal suffrage. Their underlying philosophy was the well-known Benthamite argument, that since each man in a political democracy was to count for one and not more than one, and since each was, on the whole, the best judge of his own interest, universal suffrage would permit the translation of the majority will into the substance of legislation.... The flaw in the argument was an obvious one. It assumed the absolute validity of the form of the political state regardless of the economic character of the society it was supposed to represent. It did not see that each economic *regime* gives birth to a political order which represents the interest of those who dominate the *regime,* who possess in it the essential instruments of economic power.... In a capitalist society, quite similarly, sovereignty belonged to the owners of capital. It is in the perspective of these general truths that the history of parliamentary democracy must be set" *(126:49)*. This clearly reveals Laski's view of the parliamentary democracy as a bulwark of capitalism.

Capitalist Democracy in America

His analysis of the American form of government follows a similar pattern. Despite the difference in the organisation of the political institutions, the political democracy in the United States manifests the same characteristics as it does in England. "Ever since its emergence as an independent political community", says Laski, "America has been a political democracy; and the idea of majority rule through representative institutions has been deeply embedded in its tradition. But we must be careful not to embody in the idea of this political democracy more than it in fact implies. It is essentially a democracy of the middle class, which assumes, though it does not announce, the authority of wealth, and has been careful, throughout its history, not to permit its informing idea to jeopardize the claims that men of property invariably put forward as the boundaries beyond which democracy may not pass.... The forms of political democracy obscured, but did not conceal, the fact that they were being based on an economic foundation which was growingly oligarchical in character" *(121:17)*.

It is evident from this analysis that Laski regards democratic government both in its European and American forms as the expression of the capitalist way of life which is equally reflected in the organisation of its political parties and in the working of its legislative, judicial and executive organs. The constitutional fabric of a capitalist democracy always remains a defence mechanism for protection of the vested interests of the property-owners. The fundamental rights are defined in such a way as to emphasize the basic bourgeois right of the possession of private property

Distinction between Fascist and Communist Forms of Dictatorship

In his comments upon totalitarian governments, Laski equally insists that we must judge them on the basis of the class relations which they maintain. He condemns a fascist government absolutely because it prefers dictatorship to democracy as a form of government and uses its dictatorial authority to maintain the capitalist way of life. His condemnation of a communist government is qualified by his partial appreciation of the social purposes for which that dictatorship is exercised, as the goal of a communist dictatorship is the creation of classless society on a socialist basis. Laski stands for a redefinition of class-relations in the existing legal order but is equally insistent that this transformation should be brought about without jeopardizing the form of political democracy.

Socialist Democracy as Laski's Ideal

Economic considelrations apart, Laski prefers a parliamentary system with a single chamber to other forms of government. In his comments upon the English monarchy, he also doubts the constitutional neutrality of a hereditary monarch in the existing social conflict and suggests a thorough revision of his position. He also proposes the abolition of the House of Lords and considers it not only as a superfluous luxury but also as a weapon of momentous significane in the hands of the capitalist class. In fact Laski wants to remodel the political institutions of England in order to facilitate a constitutional victory of the party of socialism. He also wants to remove some of the constitutional hindrances from the path of a socialist government in power. Laski regards the American system of the checks and balances as inconvenient from the point of view of a democratic socialist and suggests the need of a stronger Presidency less dependent upon Congress in finance and foreign policy and a stronger Congress less subservient to the authority of the Supreme Court in its legislative powers.

His primary object in the constitutional reform of this type is to create favourable conditions for the working of a positive state. A socialist cabinet functioning with the support of a loyal majority in the House of Commons can bring about a greater and more rapid transformation of England into a socialist society in the absence of an obstructionist House of Lords and a racalcitrant monarch, who still remain the last two reserve powers of the conservative capitalist class in England, than would be the case if they were allowed to obstruct the process by utilizing their own accumulated prestige in favour of the vested interests of the English bourgeoisie.

CHAPTER 24

ORGANIZATION OF GOVERNMENT

THE EXECUTIVE

The executive plays such an important part in the modern State that very often it is described by the inclusive term 'government'. In non-democratic States, the executive authority is all in all. Even in democratic countries it exercises much greater authority than is generally believed. Finer says that the executive is the residuary legatee in government after other claimants like Parliament and the law courts have taken their share. It performs many functions besides the execution of laws as laid down by the legislature and interpreted by the courts.

The Nominal Executive. It is usual to distinguish three aspects of the executive. These are the nominal or ornamental executive, the political executive, and the permanent executive. In England, the nominal executive is the monarch, the political executive is the Prime Minister and his Cabinet, while the permanent executive is the administration. In the self-governing British Dominions it is the same, except for the fact that the king is represented by the Governor-General. In the United States the line of demarcation is not so clear. The president is the chief of State as well as the political executive and performs several administrative functions in addition. Several of the appointments which he makes are limited to his term of office.

In countries where the parliamentary system of government prevails, the nominal executive has little to do with the actual governance of the country. While government is carried on in his name, all his acts have to be countersigned by a minister, who is responsible to the cabinet, to the legislature, and to the people at large. Many of the functions performed by the nominal executive are ceremonial in character, as in the case of the King of England. He summons Parliament, prorogues and dissolves it, but all this is done in accordance with the arrangements made by the ministry of the day. The king is a titular sovereign. He reigns, but does not govern. It is true that he does play some part in the choice of the Prime Minister, especially when there is more than one recognized leader of a party or when no party has an absolute majority in the lower house. But even here his discretion is restricted to narrow limits. His constitutional rights are, in the words of Bagehot, 'the right to be consulted, the right to encourage, and the right to warn'. As far as the British Empire (and now the Commonwealth countries) are concerned, he is the visible symbol of unity and the most important link which holds together countries and peoples scattered over the different parts of the world

The nominal executive in France up to the Fifth Republic was the President, who was elected for a term of 7 years by the two houses of legislature sitting together for the purpose. In theory he had all the powers of the American President except the veto, as well as many powers which belong to the king in England. But in actual practice he neither reigned nor governed. As has been well said, he was a prisoner in an iron cage Every act of his had to be counter-signed by a minister, who in turn was dependent on parliament.

Under the Fifth Republic the President is elected for seven years by an electoral college consisting of members of Parliament, the General Council and Assemblies of the Overseas Territories and the elected representatives of the Municipal Councils.

It is his duty to see that the Constitution is respected. He appoints the Prime Minister and other ministers on his advice. He presides over the Council of Ministers and promulgates laws. He signs the ordinances and decrees decided upon in the Council of Ministers. He may ask Parliament to reconsider any of the clauses of the law, which Parliament cannot refuse. Certain types of bills he may submit to a referendum. He may dissolve Parliament not more than once a year after consulting the Premier and the Presidents of the Assemblies. He enjoys many other powers not only in theory but in practice.

The nominal executive in Germany under the Weimar Constitution was the President. He was elected by the people who also had the power to recall him. He was given wider powers than those enjoyed by the French President before the Fifth Republic. He could submit to a popular referendum bills passed by the Reichstag but which did not meet with his approval. He had no power of veto. He could also declare a state of siege, suspend various constitutional rights of the citizen and govern virtually as a dictator. Whereas in France the President before the Fifth Republic could dissolve the lower house only with the consent of the Senate, the German President could do it on his own authority.

Under the present constitution for the Federal Republic (Western Germany) the Federal President is elected, without debate, by the Federal Convention. The Federal President thus is not elected directly by the people as under the Weimar Constitution, but as in France, by a joint parliamentary body consisting of the members of the Bundestag and an equal number of the members elected by the Laender.

The Political Executive. Turning from the nominal to the political executive, we find at least four distinct forms, *viz.*, the English, the American, the Swiss, and the French. In England, the Prime Minister and the Cabinet constitute the political executive. They can remain in office only so long as they command the confidence of Parliament. They are members of one or the other house of the legislature and play a leading part in initiating legislation. They are also administrative heads of departments and, in that capacity, are responsible to Parliament not only for policy but also for the details of administration. They work together as a team and, in their relation to Parliament, stand or fall together. The Prime Minister is not the master of his Cabinet. In this respect he is quite unlike the American President. Hs is the first among equals and is responsible to the king and country for the work of the Cabinet as a whole. It is his business to act alone or with the other members and to make the necessary adjustments. The complex conditions of the world today make it necessary for the Prime Minister to assume more and more responsibility. From this point of view it may be said that he is more than *primus inter pares,* but less than a dictator.

The British system of government works for smoothness and harmony between the executive and the legislature. By their personal day-to-day contact with parliament and their responsibility to it, the Cabinet ministers are kept in the strait and narrow path. Whatever praise or blame they deserve is administered to them at the time it is deserved, although the general election is the real testing time. Parliament in turn cannot afford to be irresponsible because the Cabinet can always threaten it with dissolution before its normal term of five years is over and can actually carry it out. In spite of all these merits, what we find in actual practice is that when the party in power has an overwhelming majority in the Commons, it tends to become indifferent to the criticism of the Opposition and to public opinion in general. It even becomes lethargic and self-satisfied resting on its oars.

Summing up the importance of the British Cabinet, Finer writes: 'On the whole.... the British Cabinet system offers quick, vigorous, thoughtful and responsible leadership; it is controlled, but not stultified; threatened but not executed; questioned, but not mistrusted; politically partisan, but not pesonally malicious; restrained as much by the spirit of responsible power as by its institutions and sanctions; and Janus-like, it looks at once to the people and to the Senate' (*20:994*).

In the American sytsem of government, the President is the political as well as the ornamental executive. Even today in form he is elected by a body of electors representing the various states in the Union. In actual practice, however, he is popularly elected. His term of office is four years, and he cannot be removed before that time except for treason. He is *not* a member of the Legislature, and so whatever legislative programme he wishes to carry through he can do only with the help of individual legislators or committees of Congress. He also sends periodical messages to Congress outlining his policy and legislative programme. In the nature of the case, this is an unsatisfactory method, and is conducive to lack of harmony and friction between the executive and the legislature. The President is almost entirely independent of the legislature. He possesses the power of suspensive veto, which is not used unless there is reason to think that there is popular support behind the action of the President. When the party which has the majority in the legislature happens to be different from the party to which the President belongs, there is endless trouble as under President

Truman in 1946. Good measures are at times thrown out by the legislature in order to discredit the President.

The President nominates his own Cabinet members who are directly responsible to him and not to Congress. They are not members of the legislature, and as such their responsibility is to the President alone. In the absence of parliamentary questions and answers or interpellations, which are a prompt and effective way of checking administrative irregularity and of eliciting information on matters of current importance, the American Congress depends upon resolutions of enquiry, which are a round about way of securing the desired end.

In spite of the fact that the President's power is somewhat weakened on account of his lack of contact with the legislature, he is one of the strongest political officers in the world. Wilson considered the office to be almost unlimited in its influence. As the executive or administrative head of the government, as the leader of his political party, and as the guide of the nation in legislation and policy-framing, the President enjoys wide powers and influence. He is the only one who can be regarded as the spokesman of his country and the platform from which he can address the country is the national platform. In times of emergency he is given wide powers.

The Swiss executive is indeed of a very unique kind. It consists of a board or council of 7 members elected for a fixed term of three years by the two houses sitting together. It is controlled by the legislature, and there is no question of resigning because of 'no-confidence' motion or vote of censure. If the legislature does not approve of the policy or measures of the Council, the Council makes the necessary adjustment and goes on with its work. It is not a party government and there is no prime minister at the head of it. One of the seven is elected annually as the president. He is only a chairman and is not the 'first among equals' as the British Prime Minister. He has no more power than his colleagues. He performs the ceremonial duties of the executive. The work of the Council is divided into departments and each member is in charge of a department. Since the final control of the Council does not belong to a single individual, the Swiss executive council is usually described as a collegiate or plural executive. Although a plural executive generally means lack of unity, direction, and shifting of action, the people, for long accustomed to plural executive in their cantons, have made a success of the Council. Besides, the Swiss temperament does not run along strong party lines.

In France before the Fifth Republic, the executive was a parliamentary executive. On account of the group system it was almost always a coalition of some kind and was more dependent on the legislature than is the British Cabinet. The French ministers had the right of entry to both Chambers and could speak in either. French ministries were notoriously unstable, the average life of a ministry between 1878 and 1928 being nine and a half months. In the words of Finer there was no ministry in France; there was only a collection of ministers. And these had no real administrative control on account of their precarious tenure. The commissions played a large, and even a rival-part in the legislative, financial, and administrative work of government. The Council of Ministers presided over by the President deliberated on *policy*, while the Cabinet presided over by the Prime Minister deliberated on *tactics* *(20:1063)*. All of this has now been changed and the President of the Fifth Republic is all in all. He has a firm grip on the government and the ministers are subordinate to him.

The Governor-General of India and Governors of the Indian Provinces under the 1935 constitution were in a totally different category from their counterparts in the British Dominions. They were far from being nominal executives, possessing as they did special powers which they could exercise at their discretion or individual judgment, in addition to being the custodians of the interests of certain classes of peoples and of public officials.

Mr. S. Srinivasa Iyengar advocated a non-party political executive for India, elected by the legislature. Earlier, Late Mr. Jayaprakash Narayan revived the idea. Some others have wanted an executive representative of the different parties in the legislature. In our judgement, neither a non-party nor an all-party executive will really be a satisfactory solution. An all-party executive will mean continuous conflict and friction both within the Cabinet and outside. It will mean lack of unity and cohesion, vacillation, and constant wrangling. As for a non party executive, it seems to be outside the range of practical politics. Accustomed as we are to British parliamentary tradition, the safe course will be not to launch upon untried and novel experiments. A non-party executive can well function in a country where there is a high degree of public political education, and where pepole are well-disciplined and leaders do not hanker after positions. It is needless to say that none of these conditions is widely prevalent in India at present.

THE CABINET, PARLIAMENTARY OR RESPONSIBLE EXECUTIVE

This may be defined as a system of government in which the real executive, *i.e.*, the ministry or the Cabinet is legally and directly answerable to the legislature for all its acts of omission and commission and through it to the electorate, while the nominal executive occupies a position of complete irresponsibility.

The chief characteristics of a cabinet executive are :—

(1) *A nominal head.* In a cabinet government a clear distinction is made between the nominal head who may be either hereditary or elected and the real executive. The former possesses only nominal powers.

(2) *The real executive.* The popularly elected ministry is the real executive and shoulders the responsibility for all official acts. It guides and supervises administration.

(3) *Political homogeneity.* All the members of the ministry or the

Cabinet are normally members of the same political party, generally the one having a majority in the legislature. Exceptions are made in times of emergency or in the case of exceptional individuals. A coalition ministry naturally draws its membership from the various parties making the coalition.

(4) *Collective responsibility.* This means that all policy decisions are collectively taken. All the ministers sink or swim together. For the blunders of a finance minister, for example, a capable war minister will have to resign along with others if they forfeit the confidence of the legislature.

(5) *Ministerial responsibility.* The ministry is responsible to the legislature for all its acts. It can remain in office only so long as it enjoys the confidence of the legislature. This responsibility is made effective by requiring that all ministers must be members of one or the other house of parliament. This provision brings about harmony and co-operation between the legislative and executive organs in a Cabinet system of government.

(6) *The Prime Minister as Leader.* As the leader of the majority party, the Prime Minister supervises and co-ordinates the work of the ministry. Though *primus inter pares* (the first among equals), he is the real chief executive. As has been rightly said, "he is central to its (ministry's) birth, central to its life, and central to its death."

The Merits of a Cabinet type of Executive

(1) It ensures harmony between the legislature and the executive and thus avoids deadlocks and the working at cross purposes.

(2) It is flexible and elastic, for, under this system the legislature can "choose a ruler for the occasion." (Bagehot).

(3) It recognized the ultimate sovereignty of the people since the ministers, through their responsibility to the people's representative in parliament, keep their fingers on the pulse of the electorate.

(4) It has a high executive value as it cannot succeed without organized political parties. The party system, the election process, and propaganda make people politically conscious.

Demerits of the Cabinet System

(1) The cabinet system violates the theory of the separation of powers.

(2) Sidgwick, among others, is of the view that ministers are distracted from their executive duties by the amount of legislative work imposed upon them.

(3) The Cabinet system of government is said to be unstable since its term of office depends upon the mood of the legislature. Due to the growing strength and consolidation of individual political parties, however, this defect has been minimized.

(4) Opposition parties too frequently oppose every move by the ruling party just for the sake of opposition.

(5) The Cabinet system of government is said to be a government by amateurs, which is another way of saying that it is inefficient.

(6) With the growth of the party system and its rigid party discipline, it tends to reduce cabinet government to a mere party government.

(7) The Cabinet system lacks promptness and vigour in taking immediate action in times of emergency.

THE PRESIDENTIAL EXECUTIVE

The Presidential system of government is that in which the executive is constitutionally independent of the legislature in respect of the duration of its tenure and irresponsible to it for its political policies. In such a system—

(1) The chief executive is not merely the titular head, but he is the real executive and wields all the powers granted to him by the constitution.

(2) He is the elected representative of the people and his office goes by the calendar. He cannot be removed from office with the same ease with which a Prime Minister can be removed, impeachment being a difficult process.

(3) He is neither dependent on the legislature nor is responsible to it.

(4) There is a complete separation of powers between the three branches of government.

(5) The executive and the legislative organs do not always cooperate. There is often a friction between the two as members of the executive are not members of the legislature.

(6) The legislature cannot be dissolved.

Merits of the Presidential system of government

(1) Without being responsible it retains a representative character.

(2) The President being elected for a fixed term with the possibility of being re-elected there is a continuity of policy and a great sense of stability.

(3) There being a single individual armed with all powers, there is vigour in action and promptness of decision.

(4) The Presidential system is of great advantage to states with diverse interests, cultures and the like.

(5) Ministers are not obliged to put in constant attendance in the legislature and, therefore, have more time for departmental duties.

(6) Legislatures are likely to be less dominated by party discipline.

Demerits of the Presidential System

(1) Esmein says that the system appears to be autocratic, irres-

ponsible, and dangerous because the president is empowered to act more or less as he pleases, although within the limits of the constitution.

(2) The executive lacking initiative in legislation leads to the dissipation of energy. Deadlocks between the legislature and the executive become the order of the day.

(3) The existence of multiple committee system in the legislature, says Bryce, results in delay, confusion, and working at cross purposes.

(4) Bryce further says that "the separation of powers has turned out in practice to be the forcible disjunction of things naturally connected."

(5) The presidential system of government leaves more to chance than does the Cabinet system.

(6) The presidential executive is inelastic as government must be carried on according to constitutional provisions.

SINGLE AND PLURAL EXECUTIVE

It is agreed by all reputed thinkers that a single executive is preferable to a plural executive. As Napoleon has well said one bad general is better than two good ones. In ancient Athens, the executive power was broken up into fragments. The Romans for a long time had two consuls with no clear division of powers between them so that one could veto the actions of the other. In modern times, Switzerland alone has a plural executive, but even there, one does not find an overlapping of powers and functions among the members of the executive council. The Commission form of municipal government in the United States, which divides responsibility among the commissioners, is being replaced by the City Manager type, where there is one strong city administrator.

Plurality in the executive means a division of responsibility. It tends to conceal faults and militates against promptness of decision and singleness of purpose. It lacks unity and energy. In its favour it may be said that it is a check upon the abuse of power and the possibility of a *coup d'etat.* It may also bring to the service of the State a higher degree of ability than is possible under the single executive. But the fact that it lacks unity, directness, and swiftness of action is enough to condemn it. It is possible, however, to combine the principles of single and plural executive. Modern administration is so complex that no individual, however gifted he may be, can be an expert in every branch of administration. What is wanted is responsibility at different levels of administration working up to a single executive at the top.

TENURE OF EXECUTIVE

In the case of a hereditary executive, tenure is for life The question concerns elected or nominated executives, whose tenures at present vary from 1 to 7 years.

Under modern conditions a short tenure of one to two years is worse than useless. It is detrimental to a continuity of policy. The executive is not given enough time to gain experience or to plan in a large way and execute big schemes. Frequent elections have a disturbing effect on public life. Very often they lead to abuse and corruption. The executive is placed at the mercy of the people, especially when it is entitled to seek re-election. It becomes weak and vacillating and is afraid to act boldly and independently.

A period of 7 years is, on the other hand, too long a period for an elected executive, even for a nominal or ornamental executive. For political executives as well as for many nominal executives a period of four to five years seems to be the proper duration. It is interesting to note that among the framers of the American constitution, Hamilton advocated good behaviour for the President.

Whether the chief executive should be eligible to succeed himself is a debated question. In the U.S.A., according to convention, the President is eligible for re-election only once, but this convention was set aside by the election of President Roosevelt to four consecutive terms. The present constitutional arrangement is that no President can be re-elected more than once continuously. In favour of re-election it may be said that 'it secures the continuance of good policy'. Against it, it is said that it leads to pandering to the public, the executive being too timid to act independently.

POWERS AND FUNCTIONS OF THE EXECUTIVE

The legislature expresses the will of the state, and the executive carries it out. Garner classifies the powers of the executive under five heads. These are the diplomatic power, the administrative power, the military power, the judicial power, and the legislative power.

(1) The diplomatic power includes the conduct of foreign relations. The executive appoints diplomatic represntatives to foreign States and receives representatives from them. This latter power is construed to mean the right to recognize or the refusal to recognize the independence of foreign States and their governments.

Treaties and other international agreements are concluded by the executive alone or in conjunction with one or both houses of legislature. In order to secure secrecy, the legislature is kept out of the negotiations, at least in the early stages.

In Great Britain even today the treaty-making power is largely in the hands of the executive. Parliament has no share in it except 'where legislation may be necessary to perfect the treaty or carry it into effect.' The executive both negotiates and concludes treaties. In many of the other States ratification by the legislature is required. In the United States certain classes of international agreements, such as reciprocal trade agreements, may be concluded on the authority of the President alone. As regards other treaties, the rule is that they should be ratified by the Senate. This power has been interpreted by the Senate to mean not only the right to ratify or reject the draft submitted to it, but also to amend it. The House of Representatives has only an indirect share in treaty-making through the power of the purse. It may refuse to sanction the appropriations necessary to put the terms of a treaty into operation. It may also refuse assent to treaties which deal with the regulation of foreign commerce. In Switzerland, provision has been made for submission to popular referendum of treaties of more than 15 years' duration.

(2) The administrative power means the execution of the laws and the administration of the government. In some countries this latter power is exercised in a detailed manner, and in others in a general way. It includes financial, commercial, agricultural, and educational administration. In France, a useful distinction is made between the *political* or governmental functions of the executive and the purely *administrative* functions. In many states appointments made by the executive are to be ratified by one or other of the two Houses. In the United States they require ratification by the Senate, but the President alone has the power of dismissal. In the states, cities, and countries of the United States many public offices are filled by popular election. In Switzerland, on the other hand, choice by the legislature is a common practice.

As for the power of direction, we find that it varies in different States, and sometimes in the same State itself. In countries where the monarchical tradition has persisted, the power of the ministry is very great. In the United States the President's power of direction is often restricted by legislative acts. He has, however, the power to issue instructions and orders to departmental heads. In Great Britain, the permanent civil service works in close contact with the ministry.

(3) *The Military Power.* In countries with a monarchical tradition like England, the military power of the executive includes the right to declare war. In the United States, Congress alone can declare war, but in the conducting of foreign relations the President may bring the country to such a pass that declaration of war becomes inevitable. The President has the supreme command of the army, navy and air forces. In times of emergency he may declare martial law and suspend the constitutional right of citizens, including such an important right as the writ of *habeas corpus*. He can suppress newspapers. During World War II a series of Congressional Acts practically gave him dictatorial powers. Similar powers were conferred upon the executives of other belligerent countries too.

(4) *The Judicial Power.* One of the important powers of the executive under this head is the right of pardon or clemency. Montesquieu considered it as quite out of place in republics. In Great Britain this power is exercised by the Crown on the advice of the Home Secretary. The American President has the power of pardon before as well as after conviction. He can remit fines and forfeitures, grant reprieves and commutations, and exercise the right of amnesty to large numbers of persons convicted of crime.

Under a democratic constitution departments of government acting under the general supervision of the executive are given wide powers of a semi-judicial character. Thus the Ministry of Health in England in the exercise of its administrative functions can impose fines, recover costs, and the like. More and more states today are abolishing capital punishment.

(5) *The Legislative Power.* In all constitutions, both the legislature and executive have control over each other. In parliamentary countries the executive has the power to summon, open, adjourn and prorogue sessions of the legislature. This power of the executive is limited in the presidential system of government, where regular sessions of the legislature meet automatically. In parliamentary constitutions the executive has the power to dissolve the legislature and call for new elections; it also has a ceremonial opening. All this is found lacking in the presidential form.

The power of the executive in the sphere of legislation is strictly limited in countries with the presidential system of government. It consists in furnishing the legislature with information concerning the legislative needs of the country; in recommending measures for its consideration; sometimes, though rarely, in the initiation of legislative projects, in approving or disapproving its acts and in promulgating those which are approved' (*23:726*).

An extraordinary power of the executive in the presidential system is the power of veto. In the United States it is a suspensive veto, which can be over-ridden by a 2/3rd votes of each house. It is considered to be a check on hasty and ill-digested legislation. In declaring his veto, the President is required to state his reasons for dissent, and the legislature is given an opportunity to reconsider its decision.

In most modern States the executive is given the power of subordinate legislation known as the Ordinance power. This power takes the form of decrees, orders, rules and regulations, some of which require parliamentary approval. The usual qualification in the exercise of this power is that it should not modify or suspend statutory law but should be calculated to promote the execution of statutory law or fill in the details. Occasionally, extraordinary power is given to the executive in times of emergency to issue regulations for securing the public safety and the defence of the realm. This power is almost unlimited. Under it the country may virtually be placed under martial law.

In the United States there is not much scope for ordinances since the Congress frames statutes in great detail. Nevertheless, there is a large number of presidential proclamations and executive orders and regulations governing the transaction of business in each of the executive departments, besides a large body of specialized rules, regulations and instructions issued by the various departments.

In England the king no longer enjoys the inherent power of law-making by means of proclamations and ordinances. Nevertheless, the power to issue regulations may be conferred on the servants of the Crown for proper conduct of public affairs. Ordinances are made in the form of 'statutory rules and orders', and these have the same binding effect on the community as statutory laws. The filling in of details is often left to administrative departments, especially in such matters as education and public health.

Tests of a Good Executive. The tests of a good executive are promptness of decision, unity, finality, and sometimes secrecy of procedure. In the very nature of the case, the executive should be small in size. Otherwise quickness of decision and promptness of action become impossible. It is here that dictatorships score over democracies. It is a significant fact that in times of emergency the American President is given extraordinary powers. In England a War Cabinet of six was formed to ensure promptness of decision and action.

Immunity of the Executive. Immunity of the executive from judicial process is considered necessary in the interest of good government. In England the theory is 'the king can do no wrong'. The American President is not subject to the jurisdiction of the ordinary courts during his term of office. For his criminal acts the Senate may try him, acting as a court of impeachment, and remove him from office, if found guilty. After that he may be tried for criminal acts by the ordinary courts. During the term of office the President cannot be arrested or compelled to appear in person before a court or obey any judicial process.

THE CIVIL SERVICE

1. Definition and history

The Civil Service constitutes the permanent executive in the modern State. While the Parliament, the Cabinet and the President may reign, it is the civil service which really governs. Doctrines of popular sovereignty, Parliamentary supremacy, and cabinet control have a theoretical value to the academic students of political science. But the doings of administrative officials concern him as well as the ordinary citizen in his daily life and contacts.

Finer defines the civil service as 'a body of officials, permanent, paid and skilled'. All these features are essentially modern in character. For a long time, even in some of the advanced States of the world, the task of administration was performed by amateurs in the intervals of their occupations. This was the case in England up to the end of the eighteenth century, but since then public service has become a skilled profession.

In modern times Russia has been a pioneer in organizing public services. Infinite care was bestowed in that country upon the proper methods of recruitment and training of public servants, and elaborate rules were framed to make the service as efficient and useful as possible. Even today Germany has the best system of rights and guarantees for civil servants.

On the side of liabilities, it must be said that the German services still carry with them an authoritarian tradition, but everything possible was being done, until the advent of the Nazis, 'to smooth the rough edges and convert officiousness into good service'. The Bourbon kings of France did something to build up public service traditions in Europe, but appointments and dismissals remained arbitrary.

One of the finest public services in the modern world is found in England, dating from the middle to the last century. Finer describes the British Civil Service as the envy of the world. It combines 'technical efficiency and humane serviceability as no other civil service does'. In the words of Graham Wallas: 'the creation of this Service was the one great political invention in nineteenth century England'.

In its origin and development, it is a necessary counterpart to the amateurishness of the British cabinet government. In nine cases out of ten the British Cabinet Minister who is placed in charge of the administration of a department knows little or nothing of the inner working of the department. He brings to his task a fresh mind free from preconceived notions and bureaucratic inhibitions, while the civil servant brings expert technical knowledge. A combination of the two results in good government. But writers like Lord Hewart, Ramsay Muir and C. K. Allen condemn the system saying that it makes the permanent civil service too important. According to Ramsay Muir, in legislation, administration, finance, and enunciation of policy, the body which really directs affairs, though from behind the scenes, is the civil service. He is alarmed to find that bureaucracy thrives under the cloak of ministerial responsibility.

Conditions of public service in the United States began unsatisfactorily on account of the prevalence of the 'spoils system', according to which hundreds of civil service posts were filled at the end of every presidential election by supporters of the victorious party at the polls. The person who was responsible for this policy of rotation of offices, and of giving a political colour to public offices was Andrew Jackson who, as President (1829-36), declared: 'The duties of all public officers are so plain and simple that men of intelligence may readily qualify themselevs for their performance; and I cannot but believe that more is lost by the long continuance of men in office than is generally to be gained by their experience. No one man has any more intrinsic right to official station than another'. Today, except for some top officials in some departments, all government workers are under Civil Service and much is being done to weed out party politics and nepotism.

2. Recruitment and training of Civil Servants

One of the most important questions to consider in evolving a sound type of civil service is recruitment and training. Till the middle of the last century, both in England and India, patronage played a dominant part.

According to the system prevalent in England and India today, recruitment for the most part is by open competition supplemented by an interview, both conducted by a Public Service Commission. For recruitment to certain departments, the competition is 'limited' as in the case of the Foreign and Diplomatic Service in England. The *viva voce* test which was established in England in 1917 is given a prominent place in all competitive examinations.

Civil servants as a rule are recruited at an early age because of the pliability and receptiveness of youth to new ideas. The Civil Service Commission in England consists of three members directly appointed by the Crown by an Order-in-Council. Similar commissions function in India both at the Union and state government levels.

While the examination in England are designed to test general ability, in the United States they test technical efficiency. For many appointments there is a qualifying examination, rather than a competitive examination with the result that the American Civil Service is not sought after by capable and highly educated men. For many classes of posts one does not require much more than 'the ordinary high school education, together with some practical efficiency'.

3. Conditions of Service

If the State is to secure the best possible service from its servants, it should provide them an adequate salary, and relieve them from the fear of insecurity and want, especially in old age. Security of tenure till the time of superannuation is a recognized rule in England and India. In the U.S.A., where civil service traditions are still in the making, it is not uncommon for civil servants to be on the look out for other and more lucrative posts.

Salaries for public servants in England before 1940 were low compared with the abnormally high salaries and allowances in India. The maximum pay for administrative heads in England (about 40 of them) was £3,000 a year, although many of them could easily command £10,000 a year in the City. The Indian Collector received a maximum of Rs. 2,650 per month including overseas pay. But here was a number of posts 'above the time scale'—divisional, financial, and judicial commissionerships, the posts of provincial Chief Secretary, posts of Secretaries of the Government of India, etc., the salaries for which posts ranged from £2,700 to £3,600 a year.

Besides security of tenure, adequate salary, and liberal leave privileges, the civil servant should be given a reasonable chance of promotion, work suited to his capacities, and protection in the faithful performance of his duties. In Great Britain manipulative and clerical services are distinguished from the executive and administrative services, and different types of entrance examinations are held for the two types of services. Superior services are recruited not only by direct recruitment but also by the promotion of the most capable from the lower grades. Since 1920 transfer and promotion from one department to another has been possible.

Promotion according to seniority is a sound policy for many situations. It at least saves considerable administrative inconvenience. But seniority alone is not enough. There should be opportunity for men of capacity to rise rapidly from one grade to another. Finer claims that the least amount of evil in the State service is produced by the best classification of civil servants according to efficiency and by correlating efficiency with rises and falls in salary promotion, demotion, and dismissal.

The civil service is a silent and anonymous service. In the nature of the case, it cannot come out in the open and defend charges made against it. Such being the case, it is necessary to give to the civil servant the necessary protection for the faithful performance of his duties. France and other continental countries, recognizing this fact, have set up special administrative courts for the trial of cases in which public officials are involved. In the English-speaking countries, on the other hand, the same system of law and the same system of courts obtain for both private wrongs and wrongs in which officials are involved, although Australia in recent years has departed from this practice.

According to Finer, the civil service in Germany has a well-defined body of rights accorded to it by law and by the ultimate assent of the people. There are also ways whereby the civil servant can challenge any but the smallest amount of disciplinary measures against him.

The civil service is not only a silent service; it is also subjected to strict discipline. In England particularly it is expected to serve whichever political party may come into power with equal respect and equal earnestness. In order to attain this end, civil servants are forbidden to take an active part in public political affairs. They are not allowed to stand as candidates, although they have the right to vote as they please.

Practice varies on the question of the right of association and the right to strike which civil servants may claim. In Great Britain up to 1917, individuals and associations in the civil service could get their grievances redressed mainly by means of memorial which had to go through various hands before reaching the Head of the Department and finally the Treasury. England provides a special court for interpreting the clauses relating to the pay and working conditions of the civil servants under this category. But the final interpreter of the terms of the judgments of the courts is the Treasury. A civil servant in England has no legal sanction against his dismissal inasmuch as the ultimate interpreter of the Superannuation Rights is the Treasury, and not any law court.

If civil servants require to be protected against the public, the public in turn requires protection against the arbitrary use of authority by civil servants. Such protection is provided by a system of checks and balances, by certain legislative controls over administration, and by certain judicial controls, namely through the issue of such writs as mandamus, injunction, *habeas corpus, quo warranto* and *certiorari* which are orders by courts to public officers commanding them to do or not to do certain things. In this respect of affording protection to the public, Finer considers that France and Germany occupy the most enviable place, while England occupies the least enviable place, with the U.S.A. occupying somewhat of a middle position.

4 Functions of Civil Servants

It is the business of civil servants to carry out the law entrusted to their care. In this respect they are literally the servants of the legislature and the supreme executive. Whatever indirect share they may have in framing policy in their personal contact with the political executive, direct share they have none, at least in fully self-governing countries.

In the nature of the work performed, the British and Indian civil servants differ fundamentally. Though a collection of experts, the British civil service does not determine the political policy of the country. That is done by the ministry of the day. The permanent Under-Secretary and his assistants give all the necessary advice and suggestion, but they do not dictate. Specialists are not consulted directly by the ministers. A weak minister may easily be led by the civil servant. But a strong man can always have his way.

The civil servant today is not a policy maker. His chief function is to advise and administer. Practice of sound parliamentary government requires that ministers decide the policy while officials carry it out faithfully whether or not they agree with it.

Whether it be in India or elsewhere, pure administration is not the sole task of civil servants. They are given semi-legislative and semi-judicial powers. Officials of departments are empowered to make rules and regulations binding upon their subordinates and the general public. Some of these, especially in war-time take effect even before Parliament has given them its formal approval. The permanent executive fixes in detail the manner in which the requirements of parliamentary statutes are to be met and how the rights created under them are to be enjoyed. In the matter of delegated legislation, England stands midway between France and the United States. Summing up the causes for the increasing amount of delegated legislation given to administrative departments, Marriott writes : 'Partly owing to the increasing complexity of industrial and social conditions, partly under the subtle influence of Fabian Socialism, partly from the general abandonment of the principle of *laissez faire* and the growing demand for governmental guidance and control in all the affairs of life, partly from sheer despair of the possibility of coping with the insistent cry for legislation, parliament has manifested a disposition to leave more and more discretion to administrative departments' (*58: Vol. II, 233*).

Administrative departments in many countries enjoy semi-judicial functions, e.g., the Inter-States Commerce Commission in the United States. They are given the power to investigate into the truth or justice of the complaints made by the public against the official acts of their subordinates. Thus the 'Income-Tax Commissioner alone is empowered to hear complaints raised by a private individual over the assessment made by a subordinate of the Department.'

Similarly, a high official of the Industrial Department decides cases of compensation to workmen in factories for injuries sustained in the course of their work.

One further question which merits our attention in connection with the work of administration is the chaotic way in which departments and their sub-divisions have been allowed to grow. If economy and efficiency are the touchstones of sound public administration, it is necessary that departments of governments should be carefully organized so as to avoid overlapping and bring together closely-related departments under common control. Undue centralization, as in France, as well as undue decentralization, are defective. Integration offers a *via media* in that it calls for co-ordination at different levels of administration, working towards a final head.

5. Tests of a Good System of Civil Service

Public administration, unlike business administration, is not a money-making concern. Its chief aim is to render service wherever it is most needed. In doing that, civil servants must be fair to everybody. They should not favour one individual or one class of individuals against another. They must be guided only by the application of equal law to everybody. They should consider themselves servants of the people in the real sense of the term. One of the charges frequently levelled against the Indian Civil Servants was that they were supercilious and overbearing in their attitude to the public. The Indian Administrative Service of today is more approachable and does not have the same degree of 'superiority complex', but is gradually moving in that direction. It is more subservient to ministers, deputy ministers, legislators, and politicians in general than was the case with the I.C.S.

Finer holds that the civil service should possess life, inventive power, ability to serve the needs of the population and enterprise. A besetting sin of civil servants is tendency to fall into a rut, to rise out of which they do not have the necessary disposition or strength. A certain amount of routine and red tape is no doubt essential in the management of public affairs, but it should not be allowed to occupy the foreground. Care for human values should be given the first place in all planning and execution of official tasks.

The civil servant should do everything possible to remove the attitude of fear and hostility which the public often has towards government servants in general. Speaking in general terms, Finer says : 'The public is hostile to the official, it is afraid of him, misunderstanding him, occasionally admires him'.

While the administrator should act without fear or favour, he should not purposely defy public opinion because of his exalted position. In no circumstances should he usurp the powers of the political executive or of the legislature.

Communal representation was insisted upon as a condition of a good system of administration in a country like India with its rival communal groups. All that needs to be said is that public administration should not become a plaything of politicians if its honesty and efficiency are to be kept unimpaired. Other things being equal, there should be a due proportion between the strength of any one community in the country and its representation in the services. But it must be remembered that the right of the citizen to be safeguarded against inefficient and worthless officials is much greater than the right of every caste and community or linguistic group to have its mathematical percentage in the various services.

The duties of the civil servant in Germany, as stated by Finer, are :

1. The civil servant must discharge his duties in accordance with the constitution and the laws and obey the official orders of his superiors, in so far as they are not contradictory to the law.
2. He must carry out the duties of his office with the greatest sincerity and probity without regard to private advantage, with the greatest impartiality with all industry and care. He must be specially on his guard against partiality.
3. He must keep punctuality to the hours of arrival at and departure from his work.
4. Without claiming extra pay, he must be prepared to undertake additional duties or other duties to which his training and capacity fit him.
5. He must be truthful in his official doings. He must not pass over in silence important facts the disclosure of which is of concern to the department.
6. Respect for superiors is demanded, outside as well as inside the office, even when the superior is objectionable in character and demeanour.
7. In their intercourse with the public, officials must always be courteous.
8. The civil servant must not allow insults to pass unnoticed, lest the Service should suffer degradation.
9. No official may take on any additional offices or employments, other than those for which he has asked and obtained permission of the appropriate departmental authority.
10. The civil servant must observe official secrecy.

26—17 149

THE LEGISLATURE

Among the organs of government, especially in democratic countries, the pride of place is given to the legislature. But such has not been the case always. In the olden days, as Jenks points out, laws were not made but discovered. They were folk laws based upon the customs of the people, and it was the business of what governmental and religious authorities there were to discover these laws. As time advanced folk laws became less important, and laws took the form of ordinances or decrees issued by the executive for the maintenance of peace. These were not as permanent as folk laws and did not cover such a wide range. At a still later stage came laws by established estates which were more or less representative assemblies. Finally, there came into being parliaments and parliamentary overeignty.

When parliaments were first summoned, the object was not to secure their help in law-making but to vote supplies for the carrying out of the king's policy. Membership in Parliament at this time was not a position of honour and influence to be coveted, but an onerous responsibility to be avoided. Soon, however, representatives in Parliament realized that before supplies could be voted they could insist upon the redressal of grievances, which a harassed king, involved in foreign wars and domestic difficulties, felt obliged to do. From this time on began the continuous history of law-making by the legislature.

Laws made by Administrative Departments of Government

In the modern State the legislature alone does not make laws. The executive head in the United States, for example, negotiates treaties subject to ratification by two-thirds vote of the Senate. The British Parliament does not have the time or the necessary knowledge to draft all the details of every legislative measure, and hence what it does in several instances is to content itself with passing the broad outlines of the measure, leaving the administrative departments to fill in the details by means of administrative orders, rules and regulations. Some of these are provisional in character and require the approval of Parliament, while others do not even require this formality. This species of 'delegated' or 'subordinate' legislation has assumed such great dimensions that Chief Justice Hewart described administration in England by the telling title, 'the New Despotism'.

Legislation by People

Switzerland, which is the home of several novel political devices, has made experiments in direct legislation by means of the referendum and initiative, and other States such as the Commonwealth of Australia and some of the state constitutions have followed suit. Referendum simply means that a piece of legislation, after being passed by the legislature, has to be approved by a specified majority of the voters before it can become valid.

While the referendum is negative in character in that it approves or disapproves of legislative measure, the initiative is positive in that it enables the voters themselves to take the lead in law-making. According to this system a certain number of voters have to ask for legislation on a given question. They may themselves formulate the details of the legislation or give the general aim of the projected legislation to the legislature, and ask it to fill in the details. In either case it is submitted to the vote of the people and becomes effective if ratified by a majority voting at the poll.

The Plebiscite is resorted to in ascertaining the wishes of the inhabitants of a territory in transferring territory from one State to another or in creating new states. This practice has been in operation in Europe since the end of the 18th century. In 1935, the Saar region was restored to Germany as the result of a plebistice. We have witnessed the holding of a plebiscite in India also in recent times when in 1947 the people of the princely state of Junagadh and its tributary states were asked to indicate their choice between joining India and joining Pakistan. As a result of that plebiscite, Junagadh state was merged with India.

Reviewing the value of direct legislation as a whole, it may be said that while small areas long accustomed to free democratic institutions, like the Swiss communes and cantons, can make it a success, it is likely to do more harm than good in large countries lacking the Swiss traditions of democracy and local self-governemnt.

The Organization of Legislature

Both in political theory and practice the organization of the legislature has been a much-discussed question. Bi-cameral legislature is the usual practice everywhere, especially as regards the centre. In provinces and the component units of federation bi-cameralism is not uniformly found. Several of the Indian states in the new constitution possess bi-cameral legislatures. England has had a bi-cameral legislature more because of historical circumstances than as a result of deliberate design.

Where there are two legislative chambers, it stands to reason that they should be organized differently, as regards both their composition and powers and functions, in order to avoid conflict and jealousy. The lower house, which is also called the popular house, is usually elected by the people themselves, and representation is on the basis of population and a wide franchise. The upper house, also known as the second chamber, usually represents interests in the community, or the states in a federation, and is usually not directly elected.

The British House of Lords is largely hereditary, and possesses larger numbers than the House of Commons. The Senate in the United States consists of 100 members, two from each of the 50 states, and has been directly elected since 1913. It is a continuous body, each member sitting for six years, one-third of the total number retiring every two years. It is one of the strongest, if not the strongest, second chambers, in the world. Second chambers in Switzerland and the Commonwealth of Australia are constituted on the same principle as the American Senate. Each of the Swiss cantons sends up two representatives and each of the six Australian States sends up six representatives to their representative federal second chambers. The Reichstag under the Weimar Constitution (1919) of Germany represented the states, as opposed to the people, both in legislation and administration, but did not give them equal representation. The French Upper Chamber known as the Senate today is indirectly elected. It ensures the representation of the territorial units of the Republic. Even Frenchmen living outside France are represented on it.

India has two chambers at the federal centre and in some of the States. The two houses of the Indian Parliament are known as the Lok Sabha (the House of the People) and the Rajya Sabha (the Council of States). The maximum number of members of the Council of States is 250, of whom 12 are appointed by the President for their distinction in the fields of art, literature, social service, etc. The rest are indirectly elected by the State legislative assemblies under a system of proportional representation. The seats are distributed according to the Fourth Schedule of the Constitution. It is a continuous chamber. Its members are elected for six years, one-third retiring every two years. There are 232 members at present including the 12 nominated.

If second chambers are necessary at all, they should be distinctive from the popular house, act independently and responsibly, and possess the necessary capacity and impartiality effectively to revise the work of the lower house.

Are Second Chambers Necessary?

It does not follow that because second chambers are virtually universal, they are indispensable. The usual reasons given in favour of second chambers are (1) that they are a useful check upon the hasty and ill-digested legislation of the lower house and (2) that in federal constitutions, they safeguard the interest of the component units. Both these arguments have been seriously questioned, and the last word on them has not yet been uttered.

Writing in the latter half of the last century, J. S. Mill feared that one house alone might become 'despotic' and 'overweening' and that a second chamber was necessary in order to prevent 'the corrupting influence of undivided power'. Sir Henry Maine went so far as to say that 'almost any second chamber is better than none', on the ground that a well-constituted second chamber provided not a 'rival infallibility' but an 'additional security'. According to Lord Acton, a second chamber is the essential security for freedom: it provides the necessary balance of power in legislation, gives protection to the minorities, and is a good revising chamber.

From all this it would appear, as Marriott points out, that there is a singular uniformity in favour of two legislative chambers. Mr. S. S. Iyengar, on the contrary, holds that bicameralism in democracy is 'an outworn creed'. According to him, the institution of bicameralism is due to 'a hesitant faith in democracy, and a desire to conciliate minorities', and there is no valid reason 'why the popular will should seek two channels of expression, why democracy should speak in two voices'. In this view second chambers are retained 'to provide scope for the ambitions of party men who may not be accommodated in the first, to lessen rivalries in leadership within the party itself, and generally to enlarge the circle of party influence'. Their introduction in the Indian provinces in the past, it would seem, was to bolster up vested interests and to put a brake on the possible radical tendencies of the lower house, especially as regards landed property.

The classical argument against bicameralism was stated by Abbe Sieyes when he said : 'If a second chamber dissents from the first, it is mischievous; if it agrees with it, it is superfluous.' The fitting reply to this dilemma which so paralyzes thought is in the words of Finer : 'If the two Assemblies agree, so much the better for our belief in the wisdom and justice of the law; if they disagree, it is time for the people to reconsider their attitude'.

On theoretical grounds, there is no doubt whatever that a good case can be made out for a properly constituted second chamber. As a revising body, it can play a very useful part in legislation. On account of the nature of its composition, longer term of office, greater experience, and comparative freedom from the prejudices and passions of the popular house, it can consider measures in all their aspects in a more or less detached manner. But what practice shows is that it is likely to become a bulwork of conservatism and even of reaction in politics.

The argument that a second chamber is necessary in order to check hasty and ill-digested legislation does not strike us as weighty. The various readings of a bill, submission to special committees, consultation of the public through the press and the platform, etc., seem to be sufficient safeguards against any hasty action being taken. Besides, on most urgent reforms, to give the power of delay to the upper house is perhaps to court disaster in the long run, and pave the way for popular revolution.

The further argument that a second chamber is a fundamental part of the federal principle can also be questioned. Matters which are purely local are dealt with by the local legislatures, and a second chamber is not necessary to protect state interests as against national interests. Taking the United States as an example, we find that the Senate has not been any less 'national', or less progressive than the House of Representatives. It is wrong to assume that one house will think only in terms of provincial or state interests and the other in terms of national interests.

To conclude, whether second chambers are necessary or not, our reply is that no uniform answer can be given which will be applicable to all cases. A great deal depends on historical antecedents. The United States and France would undoubtedly be the poorer if their Senates were abolished. Both of them have attracted to themselves men of mature wisdom and experience, who have played a notable part in law-making and policy-framing.

Even Great Britain would be the poorer by the abolition of the House of Lords, which has been a reservoir of ministers, and a store-house of knowledge and administrative experience, and has made possible unhurried and dispassionate discussion of some of the great questions of the day. Canada, on the other hand, is not likely to lose much if her Senate is abolished. So far as constitution-making for the future is concerned, a second chamber should be an exception rather than the rule. In order to avoid waste, it may be provided that controversial measures should be passed twice over by the lower house, with a general election intervening if necessary, before they take effect.

Powers and Functions of the Legislature

Law-making is not the only function of legislatures. They have to consider the budget, vote supplies, and exercise general supervision over administration. In the matter of legislation, the usual practice is to give a more important place to the lower house than to the upper. Finance bills can be introduced only in the lower house. This is the case in India too. Non-finance bills in many countries can be introduced in either house, but when there is a deadlock between the two houses, the upper house has usually to yield. In many constitutions arrangements are made for a joint sitting of the two houses or committees of the two houses, where the final decision is reached by a specified percentage of votes; and since the popular house is almost everywhere the more numerous body, the dice is loaded in its favour.

The British Parliament is one of the most powerful legislative chambers in the world. Its powers are as wide as public opinion and the will of the electorate will tolerate. It has both constituent and legislative functions. In the United States and Switzerland, on the other hand, an elaborate machinery is set up for changing the constitution. In Australia, too, constitutional changes require a special procedure. The process of amendment in France is considerably easier than in the United States, although the procedure sounds far more complicated.

In countries where the parliamentary system of government prevails, parliament exercises control over administration through questions and answers or interpellations. Writers on public administration draw a parallel between the legislature and the board of directors of a business concern, in that both are responsible for the function of direction, supervision, and control, as against execution. In the United States it is the legislative branch of government which 'possesses the final authority to determine how the administrative branch of government shall be organized, how duties shall be distributed among the several parts, and what methods of procedure shall be employed by them.'

The legislature, particularly the upper house, also possesses a few judicial functions. Even today the Lord Chancellor, the presiding officer of the House of Lords, is the highest judicial authority in England, and together with the six law-lords, constitutes the highest court of the realm. In the United States the Senate tries cases of impeachment preferred by the House of Representatives.

The upper house in certain countries has some executive functions. In the United States appointments of ministers, judges of the Supreme Court, ambassadors, consuls, and other such officers made by the President require ratification by the Senate. In the United States the upper chamber is exceptionally strong, enjoying almost the same power as the lower house. While the American Senate cannot initiate money bills it can amend them. It exercises more influence in foreign affairs than does the House of Representatives. On account of its maturity of experience, longer term of tenure, its continuous nature, small size, connection with the political machine, and the powers conferred upon it by law, it enjoys greater reputation in the country.

LEGISLATIVE PROCEDURE

Law-making in modern times is not an easy process. It requires the service of expert draftsmen and careful consideration of the general principles of the bill as well as the details, clause by clause. In Great Britain, a bill has to go through the first reading, second reading, committee stage, report stage, and third reading. In order to prevent the dilatory tactics of the opposition. and to save the time of the House, recourse is had to 'guillotine' and various types of closure.

Political parties and 'pressure groups' exercise much influence on the course of legislation. Candidates have to promise to support the programme and policy of their party before they are officially accepted. At times groups of voters interested in some scheme or other obtained the written promise of candidate as a condition of their support. In some constitutions, such as the state constitutions of the United States, when a legislator loses the confidence of his electorate in part or in whole, he may be obliged to stand for re-election by a protest known as recall before his term is over.

The power of parties and 'pressure groups' and of public meetings is so great today that the old question whether the representative is a mere delegate, or one who can use his discretion, has lost much of its force.

While there is no general rule regarding the circumstances when it should be obligatory for a representative to resign, it is generally agreed that he should resign and seek re-election when he changes his party, or adopts a line of conduct or policy totally opposed to the express wish of his constituency, or violates his fundamental election pledges.

Similar considerations apply also to a government in power in the parliamentary system. Finer discusses three circumstances in which dissolution is considered advisable in England :

(1) when it is proposed to launch upon a new policy of fundamental importance as Baldwin did in 1923 when he wanted to introduce protection as a remedy for unemployment after Bonar Law (from whom Baldwin had taken the premiership) had promised at the General Election not to raise tariffs;
(2) when a government sees convincing signs that it is no longer trusted by the country;
(3) when the position of parties is such as to produce a deadlock, preventing necessary legislation from being passed, and when severe criticism makes it impossible for the government to maintain itself in power with dignity.

The Committee System

Modern legislatures do much of their work through committees. In the United States all business in Congress is done by means of committees because of the separation of the executive and the legislature. The committees deliberate in private. While both parties are represented on them, the majority party has the larger share, and the chairman belongs to that party. There is a tendency for the members of the party to act together. Members of the Cabinet are sometimes asked to appear before these committees, but their advice need not be accepted. The chairmen of some of the important committees occupy in effect the position of ministers such as the chairmen of the committees on Ways and Means and on Appropriations.

Duration of Parliament

There is no cut-and-dried answer to the question of how long parliaments should sit. In general, it may be said that the duration should be short enough to keep the representative close to the people, and long enough for the representative to gain experience, and not subject the people to frequent elections. A four-year period with the right of earlier dissolution seems best for parliamentary governments. In Great Britain the Crown dissolves parliament, but the authority for dissolving it is located in the cabinet.

As regards second chambers, leaving aside hereditary bodies, bodies which are directly or indirectly elected should not last for more than five years. Second chambers which are continuous bodies may last six years, one-third retiring every two years, as in the case in the United States and in the Rajya Sabha of India. Mr. S. S. Iyengar, quoted above, holds that no member should be eligible to be a representative of the people in any legislature more than twice, inasmuch as it leads to professionalism in politics and encourages the operation of mercenary motives. Over against this point of view something can be said for experience and continuity in office. Besides, if a person is allowed to be a representative for only two terms, that will effectively shut out the non-leisured classes, and those who look forward to an honourable career in politics. The problem is to weed out the ineffective and hopelessly selfish and docile members of the legislature.

Salary of Legislators

Most modern governments pay salaries to their legislators. Mr. S. S. Iyengar thinks that this practice of payment is pernicious on the ground that it makes many of the legislators servile to the party. They look to pay rather than to service, throwing aside their convictions for the sake of an emolument. On the other hand, it must be said that if all classes of citizens are to carry their proper share in the work of Government, payment for service rendered is the only logical principle to follow. At the same time the salary paid should not be so large as to rule out motives of selfless service.

Privileges of Legislators

Certain privileges are usually extended to members of the legislature in all countries. In their original form they were won by the British Parliament as the result of a struggle with the king. The important privileges are freedom of speech and freedom from arrest for civil causes. Nobody can be punished for what he says on the floor of the house. This does not mean the use of unparliamentary language which is regulated by the Speaker of the House, nor does it mean endless speaking, which is restricted by rules relating to closure and 'guillotine'.

RELATION BETWEEN THE LEGISLATURE AND THE EXECUTIVE

This takes four different forms. (1) According to the British model, the cabinet is the steering committee of Parliament. It regulates the time, the policy, the law, and financial burdens of Parliament. (2) In the French model (prior to the Fifth Republic) which was also of the Parliamentary type, the cabinet was entirely dependent on the legislature even for its existence. The fate of the ministry depended upon the whims of the legislature, which had no settled principles in offering its co-operation or non-co-operation. (3) In the Swiss model the executive is non-partisan and collegiate and enjoys a fixed term. If its measures or policies are turned down by the legislature, it does not go out of office, but makes the necessary adjustments to the legislature. (4) In the American model there is no legal relationship between the President and the House of Representatives. The legislature and the executive have no vital points of contact for close co-operation, but have several points (especially as regards the Senate) where they can come into clash with each other.

THE ELECTORATE

This is the body of people in any country who have the power of vote. By the exercise of this power they make and unmake governments in the last analysis. It is only seldom that an entire country acts as a single consti-

try into easily manageable constituencies with nearly equal population. Where a constituency is entitled to one and only one representative, it is called a single-member constituency. Constituencies sending up more than one representative are called multi-member constituencies. England and India have single-member constituencies for the most part.

In India before independence we had separate constituencies for minorities and for special interests such as commerce and the landed aristocracy, as well as University constituencies. All this was undemocratic and stood in the way of India evolving into a genuinely national and democratic State. Communalism is a survival of tribalism, and representation of special interests is a vestige of feudalism.

Representation by estates was common in several of the European countries till comparative recent times. Political reformers in England agitated for a long time for the principle of 'one man, one vote'. In the words of J. Bentham, the prince among reformers, 'Each (was) to count for one, and nobody for more than one'. This reform has come to pass in all democratic countries, in spite of a few anomalies here and there. Plural voting existed in England until 1950 according to which a person could vote as a member of the constituency in which he lived as well as an occupier of business premises worth £10 a year. University graduates, too, could exercise a second vote in voting for the member for whom the constituency was entitled. The present law is, one person one vote.

Women were denied the franchise until very recent times, especially for national elections. Partly as a result of continuous and even militant agitation and partly as a result of the notable part played by them during the Great War, women above 30 secured the vote in England in 1918. In 1928 this age discrimination was abolished and both men and women were placed on the same footing. The United States extended the franchise to women by the 19th Amendment to the Constitution in 1919, and Germany provided for women franchise in the Weimar constitution. France until 1945 and Italy until 1948 refused the right of vote to women, one reason being the fear that it might unduly strengthen the influence of the clergy on politics. Spain, another Catholic country, removed the restriction some time earlier. Soviet Russia treats both men and women alike as regards the franchise Even foreign residents are allowed to vote. In India women enjoy the franchise for all elections on the same terms as men. In Switzerland women have acquired voting rights in national elections since January, 1971.

The extension of the franchise to women was heralded by many as inaugurating an era of purity and social justice and humanitarianism in politics. However, women as a whole have not exercised the vote any more discriminately than men. After fighting for the vote, many have failed to use it. Still, as a result of the presence of women representatives in the legislature and of the increasing interest of individual women and women's associations in the civil life of the country, greater attention is being paid to social questions and, in a country like India, to the removal of the legal and social disabilities of women and to the satisfaction of the needs of children.

The age at which a person is entitled to vote varies in different countries, the prevailing age being 21, as in Great Britain and India. Turkey and Soviet Russia enfranchise their young people at 18 when a great many are still immature. The German constitution of 1919 threw open the franchise to men and women above 20. In some countries the right to vote is not given until a person is 25. Some have argued that it is a mistake to enfranchise youth who are often irresponsible and radical in their outlook. But the prevailing opinion is that by the time youth reaches 21 he has enough knowledge of the world around him to exercise his vote intelligently. Even his alleged radicalism is not to be frowned upon in view of the preponderance of conservation in positions of authority. Besides, youth is bound to learn by experience.

The age at which a person may contest a seat to the national legislature is usually fixed at a higher level than the age at which he can vote. Thus in the United States, Germany, and France a candidate has to be at least 25, in Japan he has to be 30. In Great Britain and Russia the same age is fixed for both candidature and voting. In India under the present constitution the qualifying age for the candidate is 25 for the House of the People (Lok Sabha) and State assemblies and 30 for the Council of States (Rajya Sabha) and State councils or upper chambers where such exist. No maximum age limit seems to be fiixed anywhere. In England a candidate is not required to be resident of the constituency from which he proposes to stand, but not so in the United States.

Modern theory and practice are in favour of universal, equal and adult suffrage. But certain classes of people in some countries are excluded—such as the insane, certified mental defectives, certain classes of criminals, paupers, and insolvents. Aliens are excluded from the franchise in all countries, except in Russia. Most countries lay down rules for the naturalization of aliens. The usual qualification is residence in the country for a period of years. In the United States each state has its own rules regarding electoral qualifications. Some states require a citizenship and literacy test in England in addition to residence. The 15th amendment to the Constitution provides that no person may be excluded from the vote merely on the ground of race or colour. But the southern states which are colour-ridden have devised several subterfuges by which to keep the Negroes out. In the South African Union the black people, who form nearly 4/5ths of the population, have no vote. The coloured (half-caste) voters were removed from the general roll in 1956. Germany, under Hitler, denied all political rights to the Jews. In several of the European countries national minorities are excluded from the vote. Certain classes of government servants such as election officers and soldiers are excluded from the vote in some countries.

Property and educational qualifications are usually insisted upon as conditions for voting. But with the advance of democracy these qualifications are fixed at as low a level as possible. The earlier theory was that only those who had 'a stake in the country', that is, propertied classes should vote. But this resulted in the creation of many vested interests and the perpetuation of much injustice. The Reform Bills of 1832 and 1867 in England fought against restrictions based on high property qualifications. Until 1919 the three-class system based upon the direct amount of taxation paid, prevailed in Prussia, according to which a voter in the first class roughly possessed four times the political power of a man belonging to the second class and sixteen times that of a member of the third class.

As regards educational qualification, simple literacy in the language of the area is considered adequate. While literacy is no doubt a great advantage, mere illiteracy ought not to be considered a serious disqualification. Political parties can do a great deal in educating the electorate. But what they actually do is to diseducate the public by giving it perverted information and by rousing its passions.

We no longer subscribe to the old theory that the right to vote implies the duty to back up one's vote by physical strength, if necessary. No one claims today that women should be excluded from the vote because they do not bear the brunt of the battlefield as much as men. Therefore, military qualification for voting is irrelevant today. Everybody has a right to good life and as such every normal person who is not an enemy of the State should have the vote.

In the view of many thinkers the right to vote is not a right which automatically belongs to every citizen. It is a privilege which can be conferred only upon those who are capable of exercising it for public good. This being so, some argue that the duty to vote is not only a moral duty but also a legal obligation. Thus we find that some of the cantons of Switzerland, Australia, Belgium and the Argentine Republic make voting compulsory. In Mexico a person who has failed to exercise his vote once without sufficient excuse is barred from voting at the next election. Compulsion in this matter, as in many other matters, is undesirable and defeats its own end. The proper remedy for non-voting is not compulsion but the stimulation of interest and the avoidance of too many and too frequent elections.

The old theory of representation was 'Community' representation. People were grouped according to classes or estates, and each class voted eparately. The system which has been in vogue in modern times is territorial representation. Recently this system has come in for much criticism. It has been argued by guild socialism, syndicalism, etc., that the mere fact that people live together in a given locality does not mean that their interests are common or tend to become common. A coal-miner, for instance, is certain to have more in common with another coal-miner living fifty miles away from him than with a commercial traveller or a school master who may be his next-door neighbour. On the basis of this argument, it is said that a truer form of representation is the vocational. The system was tried in the corporative State of Italy under Mussolini. It is not at all certain that the system will work more efficiently than territorial representation. One of the chief criticisms of vocational representation is that it is not always easy to say what occupations should be recognized as entitled to representation and what amount of representation should be given to each of them. Besides, this system is likely to multiply rival interests and groups and militate against the creation and maintenance of a spirit; of true citizenship. 'Neighbourhood' is just as important a factor in man's social life as 'profession'. The primary function of a legislature is not to protect the interests of rival economic groups, but to secure and advance the interests of the nation as a whole.

THEORIES OF SUFFRAGE

According to Professor Shepard[1], three theories of suffrage have prevailed at different times:—

(1) The primitive tribal theory prevailed in the city states. It regarded the right to vote as a necessary attribute of membership in the State.

(2) The feudal theory regarded suffrage as a vested right usually accompanying the ownership of land.

(3) The ethical theory regards suffrage as a necessary and essential means for the development of individual personality.

This last theory is what holds the field today. According to it, voting is a natural and inherent right of every citizen and belongs to a person by virtue of his membership in the State. It is increasingly regarded as a public office or function, without which no person can adequately exercise his citizenship.

The idea that suffrage is a public function has led to the theory that it is a public duty which every citizen may be compelled to fulfil. Accordingly, compulsory voting was created in Balgium (1893), the Netherlands (1917), and some of the Swiss cantons. The penalties imposed for failure to vote are generally light.

The system of compulsory voting has been opposed on two grounds:

(1) If the electorate is made to vote for fear of punishment, the right is likely to be exercised without any regard to public good, thus lowering its character.

(2) Compulsory votes could be easily purchased. In spite of these fears, compulsory voting in Belgium has proved beneficial.

Universal Suffrage

Adult suffrage has been slow in making itself a universal law. It was first extended gradually and reluctantly to men only; and only after many years of agitation did women get the suffrage. An advanced country like

1. American Political Science Review: Supplement to Vol. VII.

England did not have woman suffrage until 1918, and when it was given to them it was only to women above thirty years of age. This age disparity between men and women was set right in 1928 when all were allowed to vote at 21.[2] The triumph of the masses in the matter of voting has not been without its opponents.

(1) Lord Macaulay opined that universal suffrage would lead to one "vast spoliation" and "a few half naked fishermen would divide with the owls and foxes the ruins of the greatest of European cities" (*103:325*).

(2) In the extension of suffrage to the masses, Lecky saw the danger of government by the ignorant masses and, therefore, advocated restricted franchise based on education and property. He asked the rhetorical question whether "the world should be governed by its ignorance or by its intelligence" (*136: Vol. I:13*). It was his belief that the masses would cast their votes as directed by individuals or selfish organizations.

(3) Sir James Stephen thought that universal suffrage "tended to invert what I should have regarded as the true and natural relation between wisdom and folly" (*143:36*).

(4) Pointing out the opposition of the masses to modern progress, Sir Henry Maine argued that "universal suffrage which today excludes free trade from the United States would certainly have prohibited the spinning jenny and the power loom. It would certainly have prohibited the threshing machine" (*143:36*).

(5) The Belgian publicist, Emile Lavaleye, held that the parliamentary system of government would lead to "the loss of liberty, of order, and of civilization" (*135: Vol II: 51-52*). "Give the suffrage to the ignorant", he said, "and they will fall into anarchy today and into despotism tomorrow".

(6) Bluntschli thought that to vest the power of choosing those who are to rule the state in the hands of incapable and unworthy classes would mean state suicide.

Along with the movement for adult franchise has gone the movement for the extension of this right to women also. Several arguments were advanced against the political emancipation of women. These were—

(1) That active participation of women in politics would unsex them and destroy their feminine qualities;

(2) That the home, rather than the political arena, was the proper place for women and that women suffrage would strike at the foundation of home life;

2. The minimum voting age was lowered to 18 in Great Britain before the general elections of 1970, enfranchising three million young boys and girls in the 18-21 age group. Some of the other countries where the minimum voting age is already 18 years are U.S.S.R, Yugoslavia, Rumania, **East Germany, Sri Lanka, North Korea, North Vietnam, El Salvador, Egypt and India.**

(3) That woman suffrage would create discord and division in the family;

(4) That in Catholic lands it would open the way for Catholic influence in politics; and

(5) That women could not discharge all the principal duties of citizenship such as military service.

All these arguments, however, have been ably and convincingly rebutted by Sidgwick, John Stuart Mill, Esmein and others. They have defended woman suffrage on the following grounds:

(1) That the basis of the right to vote is moral and intellectual, and not physical;

(2) That the physical weakness of women demands greater dependence on law and society and hence women require the vote even more than men;

(3) That women require the franchise for self-protection against the tyranny and unjust laws of men;

(4) That logically women's political emancipation should follow their civil enfranchisement; and

(5) That the admission of women to political life would purify, ennoble, and refine politics.

Earlier opposition to adult suffrage has now subsided so much so that universal suffrage is regarded as a sign of political maturity. The ominous warnings uttered by Macaulay, Maine, Lecky, and others have not come true. Nevertheless, the fears entertained by them have to be countered by positive measures if democracy is not to become a mockery.

In order to mitigate or neutralize some of the evils of universal franchise, such methods as weightage and plural voting have been tried.

The Weightage System

The weightage system was the practical application of Maine's doctrine that voices should not be counted but that they should be weighed. It was based on the assumption that there are some whose opinions should be given more weight in electing public officials. John Stuart Mill supported it on the ground that it would be "a counterpoise to the numerical weight of the least educated".

Objections to the Weighted Vote System

(1) Any criterion by which votes may be counted is arbitrary.

(2) The possession of property is not infrequently the result of an accident and hence it is unjust to base political rights on it.

(3) It establishes a class system of government.

(4) According to Esmein, it is based on "a principle which is a logical contradiction". He asked the question whether it would not be logical

to refuse entirely the electoral right to the masses if weightage is intended to counteract the evils emanating from adult franchise.

Plural Voting

Under this system one may cast two votes in certain circumstances. For example, a University degree holder may vote in a constituency where he resides as well as in his university constituency. Again, an occupier for business purposes of premises worth £10 per annum in a constituency different from that in which he resides may vote in both the constituencies. Plural voting once prevalent in England, India and Germany is now practically gone.

Minority Representation

Certain methods are in vogue by means of which a minority can get some representation, even though it may not be proportionate to its numerical strength.

One of these is the *Cumulative Vote System.* Under this system.

(1) the constituency must be multi-membered : and

(2) an elector is allowed as many votes as the number of representatives to be elected.

The voter is allowed to cast all his votes in favour of one representative or of different representatives according to his choice. By this method a well-organized minority is in a position to elect at least one representative by cumulating all its votes in favour of its candidate.

Under the Limited Vote system too

(1) the constituencies must be multi-membered; but

(2) voters are allowed one or two votes less than the number of representatives to be elected.

(3) The electors are required to cast their votes in favour of different candidates.

These conditions make it impossible for a majority party or community to monopolize all the seats. A minority is enabled to elect at least one or two of its representatives.

Proportional Representation. Single member constituencies often lead to anomalous results when there are more than two candidates contesting for a seat. Votes are so divided that the successful candidate frequently represents the minority, and not the majority, of the electorate. In the General Election of November, 1935, in Great Britain the pro-Baldwin group secured 430 seats in the House of Commons, although their total voting strength in the country was only 11,764,660; while the parties opposed to the Baldwin ministry, though securing 10,071,993 votes, obtained only 185 seats. To remedy such an anomalous state of affairs, several devices have been put forward such as the Second Ballot, the Alternative Vote, the Cumulative Vote, he Limited Vote, and proportional representation by single transferable vote.

Of these the last mentioned, known also as the Hare plan, seems best fitted for producing the most equitable electoral results. But as yet there is no great enthusiasm for it, although it has been tried in India, the Dominions, and certain constituencies of Great Britain such as University Constituencies.

According to this scheme, the quota required for the election of any candidate is fixed beforehand in accordance with the formula.

$$\text{Quota} = \frac{\text{Valid votes}}{\text{Number of candidates} + 1} + 1$$

In the voting paper the elector indicates his preference with numbers 1, 2, 3, 4, 5, and so on. After the polling is over, the first preferences are all counted and candidates securing more than the quota are declared elected. As the effect of no vote is to be lost, the superfluous first votes (that is votes above the quota) of any candidate or candidates are passed down the list in accordance with the order of preference indicated in the ballot paper. Votes are transferred according to the order of preference indicated not only from those candidates who have enough and to spare but also from those who have no chance of being elected at all on account of the few first votes cast in their favour. Their ballot papers are scrutinized to find out their second, third, fourth preference, etc., and the votes are transferred accordingly. This two-fold transference of votes is kept up among the 'continuing' candidates till a point is reached when the number securing the quota is equal to the number of candidates to be returned from the constituency, in question. At this point the process of transfer stops and the results are announced. The transference of votes from the bottom is resorted to at a later stage in the process than transference from above since it means the exclusion of certain candidates.

There is no doubt that, more than any other system, the system of Proportional Representation will more accurately represent the relative strength of the parties in the country. But it has certain defects. Instead of reducing the number of parties in a country to two or three main parties, it has a tendency to multiply them and stereotype the existing ones. Every small group is encouraged to maintain its own peculiarity without seeking to find points of contact with other groups and eventually be merged in them. The system is likely to increase the importance of the party machine. The successful candidate is not likely to take the same personal interest in the welfare of his constituency, as his election depends upon the working of a mathematical formula and not upon his having successfully wooed a definite body of known voters. With a heterogeneous group of representatives in Parliament, a strong, united and homogeneous cabinet becomes well-nigh impossible. Besides, there will be no periodical by-elections which provide a rough indication of the degree of confidence in which the government of the day is held by the electorate. Furthermore, the process is too complicated for the average voter.

All these arguments have been countered by the advocates of proportional representation. In smaller bodies such as the municipal councils in Canada and the United States, the system has proved useful. While the Liberal party in England was a staunch supporter of the proportional representation system, the two major parties did not take to it kindly.

Article 80 (4) of the Indian Constitution provides for proportional representation in the election of representatives of A and B States to the Council of States. The article provides "the representatives of each State specified in Part A or Part B of the First Schedule in the Council of States shall be elected by the elected members of the Legislative Assembly of the State in accordance with the system of proportional representation by means of the single transferable vote".

Speaking in broad terms, it may be said that the system of proportional representation is not of much value to a country like India because of the vastness of its size and population, the apathy and illiteracy of the people, the absence of sound political training and experience, and the lack of well-organized political parties.

POLITICAL PARTIES

W. B. Munro aptly writes: "Government by free political parties is merely another name for democratic government. Nowhere has there ever been a free government without political parties. Political parties existed even in ancient republics and mediaeval cities; although they were not known by that name. There were Lancastrians and Yorkists, Cavaliers and Roundheads in England long before the American Revolution. There were Whigs and Tories in the thirteen colonies. These rival factions sometimes settled issues by breaking heads rather than by counting them, but they were the ancestors of our political parties at the present-day" (*151:113*).

Political parties are considered to be indispensable for the successful working of modern democracy. By a political party we mean an organized body of people who stand for certain principles and policies in the political life of the country by whose operation they seek to promote the interests of the country as a whole. Burke defines a party as 'a body of men united for promoting by their joint endeavours the national interest upon some particular principle in which they are all agreed'. A political party, it must be borne in mind, does not mean a faction; and sharp differences of opinion among party leaders are not to be interpreted in terms of a personal quarrel. A political party without definite political principles and a clear programme is not worth the name.

Parties with differing policies and programmes under despotism are not tolerated. Modern dictatorships are all governments by one party, party being a euphemism for the arbitrary rule of a few people. Parliamentary government on the other hand, is essentially a party government. It allows full freedom of thought and discussion within, of course, the limits of constitutional propriety and ordinary decency. As a consequence; people divide themselves into such groups as Conservatives, Liberals, Labourites or Republicans and Democrats. Owing to periodical changes in the general life and thought of the country, party labels do not always clearly indicate the programmes for which the parties stand. Thus at one time in the history of England the Liberals stood for a policy of non-intervention in the industrial life of the country and the Conservative stood for considerable regulation of indutsray and for programmes of social reconstruction. Later on, however, the two parties changed places almost completely. Even on such fundamental issues as free trade and protection the attitudes of parties have not been consistent. Whatever major difference in principle there may have been between the Republicans and Democrats of the United States of America in the past, they have largely disappeared today.

The party system is especially valuable in countries which have adopted parliamentary democracy, for it helps to bring about a harmonious relation between the executive and the legislature which is the bedrock of successful party government. The party in power in the legislature is the party from which the executive is drawn. When, owing to a national crisis, a coalition government is formed, the parties are represented in the Cabinet or ministry, roughly in proportion to their strength in the popular house. This happened in England during World War II with Winston Churchill as Prime Minister.

This advantage of a harmonious relation between the executive and the legislature is found lacking in the constitution of the United States where it is possible to have those two organs of government controlled by the two rival parties in the country. Even in such a country, parties play a very important role in creating public opinion on the momentous questions of the day.

There can be no doubt that under the complex conditions which prevail in modern states, parties render a valuable service in clarifying issues and policies. The party system helps a person to see his way through a maze of conflicting policies and intricate details. The issues before any modern government are so complex and difficult of comprehension that without the systematic guidance offered by political parties, the average voter will find himself entirely at sea. Parties perform in politics a function similar to that performed by lawyers in arguing the different sides of a case. Just as it is possible for a clever lawyer to make right appear wrong and wrong appear right, a party by means of false propaganda, catchwords, and shibboleths may mislead the public altogether. But such tactics do not always succeed, especially if the electorate is educated, well-read and discriminating.

To sum up the discussion so far in countries which have adopted the parliamentary system of government, parties help to make the government strong and stable; and in both parliamentary and non-parliamentary forms of democratic government they help to make the opinions of the electors articulate.

Some recent thinkers, however, have seriously questioned the validity of the party system. Against the continuance of the party system, it is said that party mentality is very often a partisan mentality and that parties lead to bribery and corruption and exercise a tyranny of the most thoroughgoing kind both over their representatives in the legislature and over the general public. All these charges no doubt contain enough truth to make them appear plausible, but it must be remembered that it is easy to exaggerate them.

The primary aim of a party is to succeed and in its keenness for success, a party frequently adopts dubious vote-catching devices. The party platform is made as broad and as nebulous as possible so as to catch the largest number of votes. Promises are made which are never meant to be fulfilled. Political opponents and rival political programmes are misrepresented, if not ridiculed. The choice before the voter is so limited that at times he is forced to choose between a knave and a fool. Party corrupts even the administration in a country like the United States where the 'Spoils System' reigned supreme for generations. Voters are bribed, flattered and cajoled. In the words of Lord Bryce, the party system has 'demoralized politics and made them sordid'.[3] The party machine is controlled by a few selfish individuals and 'bosses' who declare a secret or open war upon ability and integrity of character.

The fair-minded student of public affairs is bound to admit the weight of many, if not all, of these criticisms. Yet he may not be prepared to throw out the baby along with the bath water. Mr. S. S. Iyengar is much concerned about the loss of freedom of the average member of the legislature. But it must be remembered that not all legislators are power-houses of ideas. Many of them are probably happier to have a party programme and policy which they can blindly follow than take the trouble of examining every detail for themselves for which they may not have the requisite qualification. Besides, it is always possible for an active member to influence policies and decisions in party meeting. Party discipline is undoubtedly a check upon the egotism of individual members. It curbs their ambitions and eccentricities and enables them to take their proper place alongside of others who think and act with them. In a country like India as elsewhere, to destroy parties altogether would mean undue development of individualism, each person playing the game for himself. If undue regimentation is bad, so is undue individualism. To the charge that the party system leads to dictatorship, our answer is that dictatorship is not the result of a well-organized party system working within the constitutional framework. It is the result of the disintegration of the party system, as was the case in Fascist Italy and Nazi Germany. Without a well-organised party system with adequate

3. The politics of defection in India is a testimony to the above view of Lord Bryce. For selfish interests the members of legislature have been very often shifting their loyalties from one party to the other.

resourecs behind, able but poor candidates have little chance of being elected.

Conditions for the successful working of parties. The party system has worked well in countries which have a strong two-party system. A strong government and an almost equally strong opposition presenting alternative programmes of public interest seem to be necessary if parties are not to degenerate into cliques. The opposition in England plays a very vital part in the conduct of public affairs. By its responsible criticism of measures proposed by the government, it not only keeps the government alert and watchful, but also renders a great public service. It is no wonder, therefore, that it is described as 'His Majesty's Opposition'.

France has demonstrated in no uncertain terms the weakness of the multiple party system. Government is formed by continuous bargaining and trafficking among members of different groups who have no scruples in changing their allegiance on the slightest pretext possible. It is no wonder that French governments have been exceedingly unstable, altogether at the mercy of the legislature. It is more than likely that the historian will find in the French multiple party system a potent case for the defeat of France at the hands of Nazi Germany.

If public opinion is not able to prevent the formation of frivolous or avowedly selfish parties, we may have to resort to legislation. Our constant endeavour should be to integrate groups which are similar to each other in order that there may not be more than two strong parties in the country. No tolerance should be shown to a party whose avowed object is to break up all other parties and establish a dictatorship of its own.

Parties founded merely on difference of caste, religion or community have no abiding place in politics. They are a fruitful cause of national weakness. By perpetuating fissiparous tendencies they place themselves entirely at the mercy of the interested outsider. Even broad national questions which should be judged purely on their own merit are approached from the caste or communal angle. The caste and communal spectacles distort the vision with regard to economic, social and political policies and programmes. At times of national crisis parties should be prepared to lay aside their differences and work together as a single unit.

In no circumstances should a party be allowed to maintain a private military force, knowing as we do that the Nazis in Germany and the Fascists in Italy rode to power on the backs of their private armies. The only legitimate weapons which a party may use in winning adherents are persuasion and conviction. The long tongue and recourse to physical force are signs of barbarism. Democracy can function only if political minorities defeated at elections accept their defeat manfully. Their only constitutional right is to convert themselves into a majority by argument and persuasion.

If party government should succeed, it is necessary to keep the administration outside the reach of parties and politicians. Government officers from top to bottom should be elected on the basis of merit by a body which commands the respect of everybody by its stern impartiality. Government officials who are found guilty of favouring men of their own caste or community should be dealt with mercilessly. Recruitment, transfer, and promotion of public servants should follow the recognized canons of public service.

Everything possible should be done to break up the control of party 'bosses' and time-servers. Those who seek to control the party machine for their own selfish ends should be hounded out of the party. For accomplishing this end sound public opinion is necessary. Leaders of outstanding ability and unimpeachable character are the life breath of a party.

The failure of the party system is partly a reflection on the people themselves. If the electorate is not intelligent, critical and discriminating, party dictatorship is inevitable. It is absurd to say that a person should vote in a particular way because his father and grand-father before him voted that way; or because the members of his class or profession want him to vote in that manner. The intelligent voter should be prepared to defy customs and conventions when necessary and vote according to the dictates of his conscience and judgment.

The party system is bound to fail if there is a lack of character among politicians and the people at large. A high degree of public-honesty and honour is the first requisite of successful party government. Without character of a very high order widely prevalent among the people, any type of government, particularly the democratic, will come to grief. An honest and well-informed press and platform can do much in making the party follow the narrow and strict path of public morality.

THE JUDICIARY

1. The Importance of the Judiciary

A country may have a very good legislature and an excellent executive, but if it does not have an independent and impartial judiciary, its constitution is not worth much. Protection against arbitrary rule is a condition which every citizen expects a civilized government to provide for him; and a properly constituted judiciary is one of the best means by which this condition can be secured. It is for this reason that it is often said that the excellence of a country's judiciary is a measure of the excellence of its government.

While people greatly value the importance of the judiciary, its evolution has indeed been slow. The kind of justice which prevailed in early times was a tribal conception of justice. It did not matter whether the guilty person was punished or not. The ends of justice were supposed to have been met when punishment was inflicted upon members of the offending clan or tribe.

All through this period justice was personal and private. The aggrieved individual or tribe had to take whatever action it was possible to take. Besides, in many cases there was no way of enforcing a decision.

Gradually there developed the idea of the King's peace. It first included 'bootless' crimes, i.e., crimes for which atonement could not be made by money payment. Later on theft and other such crimes came to be included under King's peace. Feudal lords and the Church continued to administer their own kind of justice for a long time, and it was not without a struggle that they gradually gave place to the King's justice.

In the modern State all crimes are crimes against the state, although we speak of private law and public law. While various social organizations may use persuasion, moral pressure, and social ostracism in reference to their members in enforcing a certain line of conduct, they have no right to imprison people, award capital punishment or do the like. Justice is a function of the State.

The greatest enemy of an independent judiciary has been an all powerful executive Under the first two Stuarts in England endeavour was made to subordinate the judiciary to the executive and even some of the judges of the time were a party to this unholy endeavour.

2. Conditions required of an Efficient Judiciary

The first condition required of a good system of judiciary is independence. The manner in which a judge is appointed and the term of service under which he works should all be such as to enable him to act in an independent manner. Fear of the executive or of the people at large should not influence him in any way in the performanec of his duties.

Impartiality in the administration of justice is as important as independence. It is commonly said that in England 'there is one law for all' and that 'all men are equal before the law'. Differences in wealth, influence, and social position should not weigh with the judge. Under no circumstances the executive should be allowed to dictate to the judiciary the kind of judgment to give especially when it is one of the interested parties.

Besides being independent and impartial, the judge should be learned and skilled in his profession. An incompetent judge is bound to reduce popular regard for the judiciary. A judge should be absolutely incorruptible, upright and fearless in the discharge of his duties.

Passing from judges to courts, it must be said that justice should be swift and sure. To the attainment of this end, the number of judges should be large enough to prevent delays. In the United States it is said that justice is neither swift nor sure. There are so many loopholes in the law and its processes that it is possible for a clever lawyer or client to delay justice unduly, if not to thwart it altogether. If the poor people are to benefit by the judiciary, it is necessary that justice should not be as costly as it is today in many countries, including India. The judicial process should be simple, direct, and inexpensive. While ample provision should be made for the correction of judicial errors by a well-organized system of appeals, everything possible should be done to prevent prolonged and vexatious litigation. Strenuous efforts should be made by courts to effect reconciliation and arbitration wherever possible. In this matter of the amicable settlement of disputes the lower courts in India might be instructed to play a useful part which they are not playing today.

3. Functions of the Judiciary

(1) The primary function of the judiciary is to apply the law to specific cases, both in civil controversies and in cases in which persons have been accused of crime. This function is not as easy as it may seem on the surface. There are many cases where the law is not clear, or altogether free from ambiguity. Therefore, the judge is asked to interpret the meaning of laws, and in so doing judges have built up a great body of 'judge-made law' or 'case law'.[4] In Anglo-Saxon countries, in dealing with cases which are not covered by statute law, judges declare what is the common law. In France, almost the whole body of administrative law has been built up by the decisions of the Council of State, the supreme administrative court of the country.

While precedents are not binding on future decisions, much respect is attached to them. Both lawyers and judges make use of them. In the Anglo-Saxon countries precedents are not merely evidence of the law, but are a source of law. In France, Germany, and on the Continent generally, however, judicial precedents do not bind even the inferior courts.

(2) A second important function of the judiciary is the protection of the individual against the encroachment of the State. No special provision is made for this purpose in the English-speaking countries or in Belgium where the rule of law prevails, according to which there are the same laws and same courts for both officials and private individuals. What special courts there may be are subordinate to the ordinary courts. In France, Germany, Italy and other Continental countries there are special administrative courts applying administrative law.

Controversy has raged over the question as to whether the rule of law is superior to administrative law or *vice versa.* A. V. Dicey is largely responsible for the exaggerated importance given to the rule of law and for the prevailing opinion in English-speaking countries that the rule of law alone can adequately protect the liberties of the individual against public officials. More intimate knowledge of the special administrative courts of France that was available in the days of Dicey has convinced thinkers that administrative courts and administrative law do not necessarily mean arbitrary rule. There is no solid foundation for the popular belief that in administrative

4. U.S. Chief Justice Hughes once said: "We (the Americans) are under a constitution, but the constitution is what the judges say it is." For this reason, the judges of the Supreme Court in the U.S.A. are called "the Judicial Oligarchy", "the Aristocracy of the Robe", etc.

courts justice is perverted for the sake of administrative convenience or in order to oblige those in authority. Judges of the administrative courts are not only well-versed in law but also have had administrative experience which enables them to take into account both the public and private aspects of a case in which State officials are involved. In the course of years they have become the protectors of the individual against the arbitrary and illegal acts of government and its administrative agents.

One respect in which administrative law is superior to the rule of law is that, in a country like France, the individual can sue the State and obtain an indemnity if he has suffered injustice at the hands of its officials. In England, on the contrary, the individual cannot generally sue the State. He has to sue the officer concerned for damage which may not be forthcoming if he is insolvent or is unable to pay. When some high official is to be sued, permission has to be sought by means of a petition of right, and this is not always easy to obtain.

A significant development in recent years is that both the rule of law and administrative law have undergone changes in the direction of each other, thus minimizing the sharp differences between the two. As seen earlier, a great many administrative departments in England such as Health and Labour enjoy semi-judicial powers, and in some cases there is no appeal to higher authority. Continental administrative courts, in their turn, have become more and more judicialized with a definite procedure regarding evidence, judgment, etc. There is no country in the world where the public official is on a footing of absolute equality with the private citizen as regards his privileges and immunities. This being the case, it seems best to accept frankly the French view that the public official in the performanec of his duties is in a different category altogether from the private individual in his relations with other private individuals. It is an English writer, C. K. Allen, who says: 'The remedies of the subject against the State in France are easier, speedier, and infinitely cheaper than they are in England today. It has become a maxim of constitutionalists, and a bulwark of French democracy that the *Counseil d' Etat* is the great buffer between the public and the bureaucrat.'

The Council of State, the supreme administrative court of France, is presided over today by a non-political head instead of by the Minister of Justice, as before. The Council of State further exercises the function of judicial review over the ordinances and rules which do not have their source in the legislature.

(3) An important function of the judiciary in federal constitutions is the interpretation of the constitution and declaring invalid statutes which are at variance with the constitution. As has been well poined out, there are in the United States four kinds of laws possessing various degrees of authority. There are (a) the Federal constitution, (b) Federal statutes, (c) State

constitution, and (d) State statues. Of these the first prevails against all the rest.

The Supreme Court Judges are the guardians of the federal constitution. This does not mean that they scrutinize the constitutionality of every statute law before it can become operative. It is for the aggrieved party to bring the alleged violation of the constitution to the notice of the Supreme Court. As a recent writer observes: 'The court has no authority to interfere until its office is involved in a cause submitted to it in the manner prescribed by law'.

The power of judicial review given to the Supreme Court enables the judiciary to act as a guardian of the constitution against the possible inroads of the Executive or the Legislature. On the whole the system has worked admirably, in spite of the fact that there have been occasions when the class prejudices of the judges have contributed much to the rejection of essential legislation under the pretext of defending the constitution. Thus, the Employers' Liability Act, Workmen's Compensation Act, Minimum Wages Act, Act to Prevent Child Labour, etc., passed by the Federal Congress and approved by the President, have been at one time or another rejected by the Supreme Court, although today these acts have succeeded in becoming the law of the land.

(4) Other functions of the judiciary as summed up by Garner are (a) the issuing of writs and injunctions of various kinds; (b) the pronouncing of declaratory judgments regarding what is right or what the law requires when such opinions are requested by interested parties; (c) the giving of advisory opinion on questions of law when requested by the executive or the legislature; (d) the adjudication of disputed cases of jurisdiction in federal constitutions; (e) the appointment of certain local officials of the court, the choosing of clerical and other functionaries, the granting of licences, the appointing of guardians and trustees, the admission of wills to probate, the administering of the estates of deceased persons, the appointing of receivers, etc.

4. Organization of the Judiciary

The judiciary is organized differently from the legislature and executive. As Garner points out: 'The judicial power.... is exercised neither by a single magistrate nor by an assembly, but by a series of magistrates or collegially constituted tribunals usually hierarchically organized one above another with a supreme court of review or cessation at the apex' (*22:780-1*).

In the Anglo-Saxon countries, except in the case of the courts of an appeal, the usual practice is for each court to consist of a single judge. In France, Germany, and several other European countries the collegiate principle generally prevails. Plurality of judges, it is believed, is a protection against arbitrariness. But it is very expensive. In Great Britain and the

United States, the number of judges in the lower courts is relatively small.

Another different between the Anglo-American and Continental courts is that in the former judges go 'on circuit' from county to county, holding court in different places for the convenience of litigants. On the continent of Europe, on the contrary, courts are 'sedentary' or localized; and litigants are to go to them.

A valuable feature of the Continental courts, when contrasted with the state courts of the United States, is that their judicial system is unified and integrated. It is highly desirable that all the state courts should be organized into one system so that there will be one great court with severai branches under it.

In federal States, such as the United States, 'there are usually two separate and distinct series of judicial bodies, one to exercise national or general jurisdiction, the other local jurisdiction' (*22:783*).

Such diversity is not necessary, as can be seen in the case of Germany under the Weimar constitution where there was 'a single uniform system for the federation and the States' (*22:783*).

No division of jurisdiction was observed between the federation and the states; nor was there any diversity of law. In the United States, on the other hand, in spite of a certain degree of uniformity and similarity as regards essentials, the different states possess different systems of judicial organization and law procedure. This does not mean that the courts of the various states regard each other as foreign. On the contrary, they give full faith and credit to the records and judicial proceedings of each other.

The two general types of courts, as distinguished by Garner, are the ordinary or regular courts and extraordinary or special courts such as administrative courts, military, commercial, and industrial courts, labour arbitration courts, courts of claims, conciliation courts, probate courts, customs courts, courts of impeachment, consular courts, etc. Many of the courts under the second category exercise only voluntary or non-contentious jurisdiction.

The federal judicial system of the United States consists of district courts, the Circuit Court of Appeals, and the Supreme Court, in addition to several special courts. The Supreme Court consists of a Chief Justice and eight associate justices. Six form a quorum. The original jurisdiction of the Supreme Court is 'determined by the Constitution and includes only cases in which ambassadors of States are parties; its appellate jurisdiction is determined mainly by statute, and includes all cases from state courts involving conflicts between State Law and Federal Law, all cases involving the interpretation of the Federal Constitution or any Federal Law, or Treaty, cases involving a conflict between a State Constitution and the Constitution of the United States, and all cases where the decision of the Circuit Court of Appeals is not final (*58: Vol. 2:301*). There are other kinds of appeals also received by the Supreme Court which need not detain us. While in England judges are never called upon to interpret the constitution, in the United States the Supreme Court judges are frequently called upon to do it. They have the right to declare the legality of the law itself and are, in a literal sense, the guardians of the constitution. Their appointment rests with the President subject to the approval of the Senate. Once appointed, they hold office for life there being no statutory age of retirement. They can be removed only by impeachment.

'The Federal courts, like the Federal Laws, operate directly upon the individual citizens' *(58:307)*. In Switzerland, on the other hand, the execution of the laws and decrees made by the executive Council is left to the cantonal administrators and courts of justice.

The State courts are wholly distinct from the Federal courts, the bifurcation of judicial administration being absolute and complete. 'Each State has its own series of courts, and appeals from those courts, to the Federal courts of the United States lie only in cases involving Federal law, or in cases where one of the parties to the suit belongs to a different state' *(58:308)*.

The British courts consist of the central courts located in London and local courts scattered throughout the country, such as County Courts, Coroner's Courts, Assizes, and Quarter Sessions. The High Court of Justice in London consists of 25 judges. It does not sit as one body, but meets in three branches *viz.*, the King's Bench, the Chancery, and the Probate, Divorce, and Admiralty Division. These courts have both original and appellate jurisdiction. 'The Court of Appeal is solely concerned with the hearing of appeals from persons all over Britain and cases tried in the first instance at other subordinate courts. The Judicial Committee of the Privy Council tries appeals coming from different parts of the Empire'.

For purposes of local judicial administration, Britain is divided into eight circuits and sub-divided into several counties. Offences which are non-indictable, also known as 'petty' offences, receive a summary jurisdiction. There is no jury trial in such cases. The presiding officer of such courts is very often an honorary Justice of the Peace, assisted by a clerk well-versed in law. Indictable offences are tried by Assizes and Quarter Sessions, the jury acting as a complement of the judge. Rigorous proof of crime is required before a person standing the trial is condemned.

While in criminal cases the State appears as the complainant, in civil cases both sides appear in their private capacity. The Circuit Courts or Assizes deal also with civil disputes, but with different procedure and in a different hall.

In France there is hierarchy of ordinary courts as well as administrative courts. They combine original and appellate jurisdiction. The highest administrative court is the Council of State. Below it are the Councils of Prefecture which deal 'with complaints regarding direct taxation and transactions of the lower public officials with private individuals' *(65:356)*. Administrative courts deal also with election petitions.

The High Court for ordinary law in France is called the Court of Cassation. It is the supreme court of appeal as well as the court which annuls all decisions contrary to the laws of the land. Cases where disputes of jurisdiction arise as between the ordinary courts and the administrative courts are decided by the Court of Conflicts. The French Justices of the Peace in the cantons are concerned more with persuading parties to arrive at an amicable settlement of disputes than with delivering judgments.

The federal judiciary in Switzerland does not occupy the high place occupied by the Supreme Court of the United States. It has the power of judicial review only over cantonal statutes and cantonal constitutions and not over federal statutes and the federal constitution. It can compel the obedience of the cantons, but not of the citizens of the cantons, to the federal constitution and federal statutes. It can approach the citizens of the cantons only through the cantonal administration. There is no hierarchy of federal courts in Switzerland, as in the United States, but only a single federal court of 24 Judges at Lausanne.

Discussion of the organization of the judiciary cannot be complete without a word about the part assigned to laymen in the judicial system. For petty cases laymen are employed as unpaid, honorary judges for short periods. In England this function is performed by Justices of the Peace and in India by honorary magistrates. On the whole, the system has not worked satisfactorily. There is a lack of uniformity in the decisions given. In Britain the 'Justice of the Peace' is rather slipshod, lacking in uniformity. On the other hand, this system gives opportunity to well-to-do citizens with leisure for political education and social service, although there is a possibility of the power given being abused.

Akin to the system of honorary magistrates is the jury system which is used widely in many countries. Its object is to help the judge to appreciate the facts of a case. It originated in England and has been widely adopted in other lands. In favour of the system it is said that it acts as a check upon bribery and other corrupt motives influencing the judges. It is also said to be a valuable means of education in civic duties and responsibilities. By its spirit of disinterestedness and application of commonsense, it is argued that the jury can help the judge in a proper appreciation of the facts of the case.

In actual practice, however, the jury system has not been a great success. There are many cases where an upright judge has been hindered in his work by a partial and prejudiced jury. This has notoriously been the case when Negroes in the United States had to be tried before juries composed exclusively of white men. An unpaid jury is reluctant to give its time when the case prolongs for days and weeks together. In cases where technical issues are involved, an ordinary jury is worse than useless.

The jury system was introduced into India in 1861. In spite of its trial for many years it must be said that it has been more a failure than a success.

Another practice which has even less justification than the jury system is the system of trial by assessors. In the criminal courts of India the system of assessors has not served any useful purpose. As a well-known judicial authority puts it: 'The assessors are not anxious to be there. Judges are not anxious to have the assessors.'

5. Appointment, Tenure, and Removal of Judges

There are three principal forms of appointment of judges, *viz.* (1) election by the legislature, (2) election by the people, (3) appointments by the executive by itself or under certain conditions such as appointment from a list of nominees submitted by the courts or on the basis of a competitive examination or with the approval of an executive council or the upper house in the legislature.

(1) *Appointment by the legislature* prevails in Switzerland. The judges of the federal court who number 24 are elected by the two houses of the legislature at a joint session for a period of six years and can be re-elected any number of times. This system was popular in the United States for some years after the Revolution. Since then all but four states have abandoned it. The defects of the system are that the judiciary is made unduly dependent on the legislature and appointments are made by the party caucus. Political and geographical considerations are given greater weight than technical qualifications. Notwithstanding these defects which particularly apply to the United States, the system has worked well in Switzerland on account of the small size of the legislature and the comparative lack of partisanship in politics.

(2) ***Election by the People.*** This system was first introduced in France in 1790 and was much abused in 1793 when stone-cutters, clerks, gardeners, and common labourers were elected as judges. Napolean abolished it so far as France was concerned.

The system prevails today in the cantons of Switzerland and in many states of America. It is the worst method of securing good and efficient judges. Condemning the system, Garner writes: 'It lowers the character of the judiciary, tends to make a politician of the judge, and subjects the judicial mind to a strain which it is not always able to resist'.

The evils of the system have been partially overcome in the United States by non-partisan primaries nominating candidates and by the bar recommending suitable candidates to the electors.

(3) *Appointment by the Executive*. This seems the best method. It prevails in Great Britain and the British Dominions as well as in the Federal Government of the United States and in six of the part-states and in India. Though political considerations play a part in making the selection, when once appointed the judges are independent and are not under the influence of the executive. In France the executive is not given a free hand. A competitive examination is held to fill up vacancies in the lower grades, and

from there promotion is by seniority. In England and the United States practising lawyers are often chosen to judgeships.

Appointment by the executive is the best method on the whole. The executive is a better judge of the merits of those appointed than either the legislature or the people can be.

Tenure of Judges. Short-term tenure is the usual practice in the United States. The term varies from 2 to 21 years, while the average is from 6 to 9 years. In Switzerland the federal judges are elected by the two houses of the legislature for a period of six years, but can be re-elected and number of times. Outside the United States good behaviour tenure is almost universal. This is a sound practice because is secures 'a steady, upright, and impartial administration of the law'. It also secures experience and knowledge of judicial precedents.

The United States practice of fixing no age limit for the retirement of the Supreme Court judges is indefensible. It keeps in the saddle too many old men who are terribly conservative and incapable of adjusting themselves to new conditions.

Removal of Judges. In every constitution there must be provision, for the removal of corrupt and inefficient magistrates. In England judges can be removed by the Crown upon an address of both houses of Parliament. The usual practice in the United States is impeachment whereby the lower house makes the charge and the upper house tries it. The process is rather cumbersome. It is capable of being used for party purposes. Several states have adopted the popular recall of judges and of decisions. In many of the countries of continental Europe 'Judges may be removed only by the court of which they are members, or by the supreme court sitting as a disciplinary tribunal, and after a regular trial, and for reasons expressly stated in the laws' *(22:802)*.

THEORY OF THE SEPARATION OF POWERS

The traditional classification of the organs of government has been into the legislative, the executive, and the judicial; but this classification is considered to be too simple to suit modern conditions.

Aristotle, the father of Western political thought, distinguishes between the deliberative, the magisterial, and the judicial powers. Although in theory Aristotle found it easy to separate these three powers, in practice they were all exercised by the same persons in ancient Greece.

Bodin, one of the earliest thinkers of the modern period, sees the importance of separating executive and judicial powers. He insists that the Prince should not administer justice himself, but should delegate this power to an independent tribunal, his argument being that not to separate the two powers would mean the indiscriminate mixture of justice and mercy, of strict adherence to law and arbitrary departure from it.

In his *Civil Government* Locke makes a casual reference to the theory of the 'Separation of Powers'. According to him civil society was constituted for the protection of life, liberty, and property, and the means for the attainment of these ends are as definite as the ends themselves. These means express themselves in a three or four-fold division of governmental activity, namely legislation, which provides for a 'standard interpretation' of the law of nature which fixes these rights; the judicial side of governmental activity, namely the provision for an authority just and impartial for applying the interpretation of the Laws of Nature as among the individuals in a community; and the executive side of it, the provision for employing the force of the community in enforcing by penalties the prescriptions in the laws. The function of maintaining the interest of the community and of its individuals in relation to other communities Locke calls the 'Federative' duty.

Locke's doctrine of the separation of powers breaks new ground. The functions of legislation and execution must needs be separated; and certainly it is unwise to invest the makers of laws with the duty of enforcing them, for either they may exempt themselves from the operations of such laws or may suit the laws to serve their own ends.

As to Locke's treatment of the theory, the principle is merely suggested as a determinant of the relations between the Legislature and the Executive. The 'tripartite' divisions of functions, familiar today, and the complementary doctrine of mutual checks and balances which it entails, do not find a place in the speculation of Locke, but owe their development to Montesquieu, the French philosopher, who expanded the English philosopher's suggestions.

It was Montesquieu (1689-1755), the celebrated French writer, who made the doctrine his own in his *Esprit des Lois* (*1748*). Curiously enough, after studying the working of the English constitution on the spot for two years. Montesquieu gave it as his considered judgment that the stability of the English constitution was due to its adherence to the separation of powers. It is agreed by all today that Montesquieu was mistaken in his interpretation of the English constitution. Even though the cabinet system of government which is a direct violation of the separation of powers was not fully developed in the eighteenth century when Montesquieu wrote his work, there was no clear separation of powers even in the England of his day. It is instructive to note that even the English jurist, Blackstone, who wrote twenty years later, repeated the error committed by Montesquieu in holding that the fundamental principle of the English system of government was its clear-cut distinction betwen the legislative, executive and judicial powers. The fact of the matter is that both Montesquieu and Blackstone concerned themselves with the principle of the English constitution and not with its actual practice, thus laying themselves open to the charge of being superficial.

By temperament and upbringing Montesquieu was an aristocrat. Nevertheless he had a profound respect for liberty, which he considered to be the greatest of all human goods. It was for the securing of this good that Montesquieu advocated the separation of powers. He realized that it was in the nature of authority to abuse itself and that unless, therefore, clear limitations were laid down, arbitrary rule would be inevitable. Moderation in exercise of governmental authority, he considered, was the *sine qua non* of good government. In the interest of such moderation, he enunciated his well-known theory of the separation of powers, according to which each power should be exercised by a different organ of government and among the various organs of government there should be a system of checks and balances so that no one organ might become all-powerful. The doctrine as stated by Monstesquieu himself is:

> 'When the legislative and executive powers are united in the same person or body, there can be no liberty.... If the power of judging were joined to the legislative power, the life and liberty of the subject would be exposed to arbitrary control.... if it were joined to the executive, the judge might behave as an oppressor'.

Montesquieu particularly emphasized the separation of the executive and legislative powers. Within the legislature itself there were to be two chambers, one acting as a check upon the other.

The doctrine had a profound influence on the framers of the American constitution as well as upon revolutionary France. Whereas in France the theory broke down, leaving only administrative courts as a tribute to the doctrine of separation of powers and the cabinet system was adopted by the 1875 constitution, in the United States of America it has come down to modern times. Even today the legislature, the executive, and the judiciary are organized independently of each other. Thus, the President of the United States who is the chief executive, and his cabinet are not members of the legislature, and the close contact between the legislature and the executive found in countries which have adopted the British system of government is unknown in America. The two houses of the legislature are separately constituted with different periods of tenure and with different powers. The judges of the Supreme Court are appointed by the executive with the consent of the Senate, but the terms of appointment are such as to make the judiciary virtually an independent branch.

Not only are the organs of government separate from each other, but each organ exercises certain checks upon the rest. Thus, the consent of the Senate is required to all the appointments of chief officials made by the President. War and peace are to be declared by the Congress, and treaties entered into by the executive require ratification by the Senate. The President is empowered to send messages to the Congress outlining his legislative programme, but a convention of the constitution prevents him or any of the members of his cabinet from appearing on the floor of the Congress to elucidate or defend the government policy. The President has the power of vote on the acts of the legislature, but it is a suspensive, and not an absolute veto.

Criticism

While the principle of the separation of powers is generally admitted as valid, embodying as it does the scientific principle of differentiation, the practical difficulties experienced in working it make it of little value to us today. Even the United States does not possess a rigid separation of powers. In modern governments every legislature performs some executive duties; and the executive has certain judicial functions. The chief value of the theory is in emphasizing the independence of judiciary; but this end is attained more easily by other means such as security of tenure to the judges, liberal salaries which are independent of annual budgetary provision, and freedom of the judges from party alignments or control.

Another value of the theory is that it lays down the sound principle that government must act according to well-established rules or laws. Arbitrary rule is a negation of good government. The theory admonishes the executive and administrative officials not to interfere with the processes of law and justice. In the words of Finer, it imposes upon each power the need to explain itself.

In justification of the doctrine, some have argued that while functions may be combined, powers should always remain supreme. This seems to us to be a distinction without a difference. How functions can be performed without the necessary power to perform them it is difficult to see.

The doctrine of the separation of powers was of great value against the despotism of the king at one time and, at a later date, against the despotism of Parliament. But there is no danger of either of these despotisms today. In democratic countries we may require protection against the domination of parties and the 'despotism' of civil servants, while, in countries with a dictatorial form of government we need protection against the dictatorship of the party and the leader. Against none of these types of domination, the separation of powers is of any avail. It is too mechanical in nature. The best safeguard of individual liberty in a democratic country is a well-informed and vigilant electorate.

The smooth working of government under modern conditions calls not so much for separation of powers as for the 'co-ordination' or 'articulation' of powers. Each organ should regard itself as a servant of the public and do everything in its power to advance its end. Apropos of this H. J. Laski writes :

> 'Legislatures could not fulfil their task unless they were able both to interfere in the execution of law, and also, on occasion, to overrule by statute the decisions of the judges the results of which are widely felt to be unsatisfactory. An executive is bound, in applying the law, to clothe the general principle in the garment of detail; and in the modern State, this function covers so wide an ambit

that it is often difficult to distinguish it from the work of the legislature. The judiciary, finally, which settles either the competence of the executive (in which case it determines the substance of legislative will) or dispute between two citizens (in which case it extends the legal imperatives of a state to cover new ground, or denies that the ground involved comes within the ambit of those imperatives) is in fact performing a function which is legislative in character' *(22:63)*.

As against what Laski writes, the doctrine of the separation of powers, while making for a certain degree of efficiency, places a premium on jealousy, suspicion, and internal friction. The nature of power is such that anybody entrusted with it wants to press it to the utmost limit and prevents others from exercising their power. The serious limitations of the doctrine of the separation of powers were clearly brought out during the second term, as president, of Woodrow Wilson, when the State refused to ratify the treaty which the President had concluded.[5] In the picturesque language of Finer, the theory of the separation of powers throws 'government into alternating conditions of coma and convulsion'. In modern democracies the legislature, representing the people as it does, occupies a more important place than that occupied by the executive or the judiciary.

There is no doubt that the British system of government which knows of little or no separation of powers as understood by Montesquieu, and in which there is an intimate and continuous relation between the executive and legislature, works more efficiently than the American system. It provides for 'a single focus of government'. Writing on the contrast between the two systems, Ramsay Muir says: 'If the Separation of Powers is the essential principle of the American constitution, Concentration of Responsibility is the essential principle of the British constitution'. Another writer has said: 'Separation of powers means confusion of powers'.

Willoughby, who adopts a slightly different point of view, argues that in the English government there is a separation of powers organically but a union of powers personally, while in America there is a union of powers organically, but a separation of powers personally. The principle strictly adhered to in England is that of vesting the exercise of each power in a distinct organ, but this distinction is ignored in the United States. What prevails in this latter country is a personal separation of powers, but not an organic separation.

In the British ministry or cabinet we find a good illustration of union of persons *(28:254)* but a separation of organs. The ministry acts as an executive organ, a legislative organ, and an administrative board. When it acts in one capacity it keeps in abeyance its power in other capacities. To

5. Several of President Truman's plans for the welfare of the country were torpedoed by an unsympathetic legislature, specially in the fields of price control and fair employment practices between 1946 and 1948.

paraphrase Willoughby on this question: when the ministry acts as an executive organ, it acts independently of Parliament and as representative of the Crown. When it acts as a legislative organ, it keeps within the legislative field and does not seek to take to itself strictly either executive or administrative function. When it acts as an administrative board, it does not seek to exercise either executive or legislative powers, but confines itself strictly to the problems of administration.

Thus in the British constitution the several branches of government are kept separate. But they are made to realize that they are part and parcel of a common mechanism by placing the same persons in charge of several organs.

As regards the American constitution, Willoughby writes that many people imagine that the public liberties of the American people are safeguarded by a strict separation of powers. But the fact of the matter is that there is considerable union of powers. The difficulty of working the American constitution is not due to the separation of powers but is due to a joint exercise of powers by two or more authorities.

In the American constitution, says Willoughby, neither the union of powers nor the separation of powers is consistently carried out; and the consequence has been a chronic struggle between the executive and legislature. This struggle has been intensified by the failure of the American constitution to realize the importance of administration as a separate branch of government.

In broad terms, the doctrine of the separation of powers is a valuable doctrine. But even with its companion doctrine of checks and balances, it has not proved to be a great safeguard of liberty. Nor has it been favourable to the smooth working of government as a whole. McCarthy and McCarthyism, for instance, have not been conducive to the protection of the liberty of the American people. On the other hand, they held a good many innocent people in fear and mortal dread of legislative committees of enquiry which practised smear tactics and "hit and run" policies. They interfered too much with administration. President Truman in his turn in his 1948 election spared no pains in belittling the House of Representatives and in hauling it over coals of fire. Instead of producing unity and harmony in the working of government, the doctrine of the separation of powers, has frequently produced friction and disharmony. Considering facts such as these, Sabine observes that Montesquieu "was guilty of extreme oversimplification" (*162:551*). "He united his theory to a hasty and superficial analysis of the constitutional principles of liberty" (*162:551*).

Seeing the futility of a rigid application of the theory of the separation of powers to modern conditions, H. Finer divides the powers of government into *resolving* powers and *executive* powers, the former including the electorate, political parties, parliament, cabinet, and the chief of state; and the latter including the cabinet, the chief of state, the civil service and the courts of justice.

In modern democratic States, there are not three, but seven organs of government, closely related to each other and capable of being grouped under 'policy-making' organs of government and 'policy-enforcing' organs of government.

LIBERAL POLITICAL THEORY AND ORGANISATION OF GOVERNMENT

Laski's analysis of the liberal political theory is closely related to his analysis of its economic doctrine. Marx regarded the methods of production as the key to all political institutions. The political institutions of a capitalistic state such as the legislature, the presidency, the cabinet, the judiciary and the bureaucracy have to uphold the class interests of the ruling capitalist class. The legislature may in theory be elected by majority vote under a system of universal adult franchise but political parties which participate in elections depend on financial support of the capitalists to achieve electoral success. The executive branch of the government, though elected directly or indirectly by the people, has to pursue policies which are approved by the capitalists, whose non-cooperation by paralysing economy may bring down any elected cabinet from power.

The judiciary and bureaucracy similarly show a bias towards the interests of property-owners. Laski almost agrees with the Marxian view and this leads him to argue that the key to political institutions of the liberal state will be found in the capitalistic methods of production. But he does not believe in economic determinism as an inflexible dogma. He thinks that the social process is too complex to be adequately explained by a simpie formula.

The political theory of liberalism was formulated partly on the basis of abstract writings of some political thinkers mainly English, French or American and partly as a generalization from the working of political institutions of those countries. England has been the pioneer home of liberal thought and practice. The United States and France also joined the fraternity of liberal states by the close of the eighteenth century. While the character of liberal political thought remained comparatively moderate in England, the expression of liberal political ideas in France and America showed a much more radical bias. The reason behind it was that the English people had already established constitutional government in their country which the French and Americans had yet to wage a violent struggle to achieve the same in their respective countries. Moreover, if the continental political thinkers emphasized dialectical conflicts and logical extremes, the British people had evolved the philosophy and technique of reasonable compromise and practical adjustment.

Liberalism in England

In England the political objective of the liberal writers like Bentham,

James Mill and John Stuart Mill was to secure a reform of Parliament in which the landed interests still exercised a preponderant influence. It was pointed out that both the ruling parties represented a small circle of feudal families and this defect could not be remedied unless the basis of representation was widened to include the suffrage of the middle class. They advanced new theories of representative government and advocated practically universal suffrage. The earlier utilitarians like Bentham and James Mill were more interested in good government than in individual liberty. John Stuart Mill attached equal importance to both. Herbert Spencer was more devoted to individual liberty and could not sacrifice it at the altar of good Government. Thomas Green suggested positive checks to regulate individual liberty in the interests of social welfare. It shows that the liberal political theory was not static but considerably dynamic which had to adjust itself to continuously changing surroundings.

Liberal Thought in France and America

In France and America the liberal political thought was mainly cast in the form of republicanism. While in England the liberals had refrained from making any frontal attacks on monarchy, the French and American liberals regarded monarchy as inconsistent with liberal principles. The reason for this divergence was not difficult to explain. The British monarchy was no longer a hindrance in the path of representative government which the English middle class secured through Parliament and the cabinet system. In France and America, the monarchies had been instrumental in withholding from their peoples the right of democratic self-government which they could win for themselves either through a revolution as in the case of France or through a successful war of liberation as in the case of America.

Two Aspects of Liberalism

The political implications of Liberalism can be described in its two broad aspects. In the first place, Liberalism is a theory of *political organization*. Secondly, it is a theory of the *rights of the individual.* Both these theories form a unified pattern because both of them have been derived from the economic exigencies of the middle class which has established its supremacy in the economic field and is trying to consolidate its victory in the political sphere as well.

A Theory of Political Organisation

As the middle class had no use for the feudal particularist state, the liberal theory came forward as a champion of state sovereignty. Bentham and Austin developed the conception of absolute, indivisible and inalienable sovereignty but this sovereignty was to be exercised by an elected legislature in which the middle class ought to have a preponderant representation. In England the Liberal theory became a *defence of responsible, par-*

liamentary government. In America the institutional pattern was different from that of England but the triumph of the representative principle was even more emphatic in the American constitution. The trusted representatives of the middle class exercised effective law-making power through Parliament or Congress and the executive power similarly vested in the President or a cabinet in whom the middle class had an equal confidence. In the judicial sphere, the courts were emancipated from feudal control and securely placed in middle class hands. The lawyers and judges, who operated the judicial system, used it as the instrument of middle class conceptions of justice.

A Theory of Rights

The second constituent element of the Liberal theory has been its characteristic theory of rights. Laski is of opinion that the Liberal theory of rights was as much the product of the particular class interests as the Liberal theory of political organization. In order to understand the Liberal theory of rights, it is necessary to define Laski's own conception of rights in general. Rights, as Laski would say, do not mean "the grant of some historic conditions possessed in the childhood of the race, but lost in the process of time.... Nor do we imply by rights the reflection of a natural order which lies behind the shifting appearance of contemporary society" (*47:89*). The legal theory of rights, as developed by Hobbes, Bentham and Austin, also does not appeal to Laski. "A legal theory of rights," says he, "will tell us what in fact the charatcer of a state is; it will not tell us, save by the judgment we express upon some particular State, whether the rights there recognized are the rights which need recognition" (*47:91*). What Laski thinks is that the conception of rights cannot be static which may be applicable to different political societies indiscriminately. "Rights are asserted in a new from", says he, "as the rights which have gained the cognisance of law become inadequate or outworn. They have a content which changes with time and place" (*47:92*).

Defence of Private Property

The liberal theory of rights in this way asserts only those rights which were necessary for the realization of the peculiar interests of the middle class. In the first place, it asserts the right of private property but the interpretation of this right is strictly in conformity, with the middle class norms (*49:36*). The liberal writer, who waxes eloquent on sanctity of bourgeois property, does not show the same respect for the feudal right in land. After the French Revolution, the large landed estates of the French nobles were taken away from them and were distributed among the French peasantry. The French liberals regarded this act of appropriation as quite just and normal. Similarly, the liberal conception of liberty was formulated from the point of view of the middle class. How circumscribed this view was is evident from the fact that the liberals considered the workers' right of forming a trade union as a negation of individual liberty while the capitalists enjoyed full freedom of organizing themselves. In England, the Common Law has always interpreted rights in such a way as to favour the richer classes against the poorer sections of the society. In the U.S.A., the Supreme Court has performed this discriminatory function with the similar zeal and efficiency.

It is quite evident that Laski could not be satisfied with the liberal theory of rights which views them from the stand-point of the middle class. He has suggested a redefinition and reinterpretation of rights from the point of view of the community in general and the working-class in particular which constitutes a large majority of every nation. He thinks that privilege and liberty cannot exist side by side. In a capitalist society, there can be no genuine freedom because the freedom of the many is circumscribed by the privileges of the few. True liberty for all can develop only in an atmosphere of socialist equality. Laski, therefore, evolves a new conception of socio-economic rights in place of the old conception of liberal-individualistic rights.

PRESSURE GROUPS

Pressure groups, unlike political parties, do not participate directly in the political process. But the analysis of political systems remains incomplete so long as we do not take note of the influence and pressure exerted by organised groups on the political process. These pressures may be indirect, ordinarily invisible and intermittent. Yet no student of political science can today afford to neglect the study of their functions and role in politics. As Jean Blondel explains: "The study of groups raises very serious practical and theoretical problems. This is because groups are not as such part of the study of politics : we are interested in groups to the extent that they enter the political process, but not in the groups themselves. Some of them may be involved so often in politics that they cannot easily be separated from political life : but even these are not wholly in politics. Conversely, however, any group, or almost any group, is involved from time to time in the political process. Thus we become concerned with practically all the groups which exist in society".

Arthur Bentley in *The Process of Government,* which appeared in 1908, laid the foundation of the group theory in politics. The group theory, as David Truman says, assumes that society is a collection of numerous groups living in interaction with one another. The groups make certain demands on the government and the government, in turn, acts as the balancer of the interests of the divergent social groups. As a result each of the major interest groups associates itself with a distinctive interpretation of politics and its demands may be justified in terms of a particular ideology. Today, two major groups are organised labour and organised business. Statesmanship is an art of keeping balance between the competing groups, especially between the competing interests of the owners of capital on the one hand and trade unions on the other. As Oran Young suggests the emphasis in the group theory on the dynamics and activities of social groups is basically a criticism of the legalistic and static approach of the institutionalists to political analysis. In addition, the insistence of the group theories on the functions and role of the interest groups was a reaction to the atomistic indidivualism of classical liberals from Locke to Bentham and also against the narrow psychologism represented by the writings of Pareto and Durkheim.

Oran Young has mentioned the following ten features of the group approach to politics :

1. The group is viewed as a combination of activities and not as a collection of persons and also as a dynamic entity and not as a stationary institution.

2. The group lives in the midst of interactions among divergent groups. The actions and reactions of the group can be organised into a definite pattern.

3. The group has a specific interest of its own. This should be studied empirically on the basis of its policy-oriented decisions and actions.

4. The genuine group has to be distinguished from an accidental combination of individuals. The individuals hold simultaneous memberships in several groups with different degrees of involvement.

5. The fundamental assumption of the group theory is that real knowledge of the social system can be obtained by the analysis of the interaction of a very large, almost, all interest groups that exist in a society.

6. The condition of a social system at any given moment can be understood only in terms of the nature of balance of the group pressures.

7. The power of a group to influence the political process depends upon the numerical strength of the members, the intensity of their involvement and the forms of organization and mobilization.

8. All group activity does not have a bearing on politics. It may be non-political activity as well. Group activity becomes political only when they make certain demands on political parties and governmental institutions.

9. The government and political parties establish regularised balancing instruments for processing the claims of the rival interest groups.

10. The government may itself harbour a variety of group interests such as bureaucracy or army that are themselves often in conflict and competition with each other.

Hitchner and Harbold define the pressure group as "any collection of persons with common objectives who seek their realization through political action to influence public policy". Still more simply, a pressure group is a lobby that wants something from the legislature or administration.

The pressure group is an organised aggregate of interests and attitudes, which desires to influence the context of legislative and administrative decisions without attempting to place its members in formal governmental institutions. Henry Turner describes them in the American context in the following words: "By definition, pressure groups are non-partisan organisations which attempt to influence some phase of public policy. They do not themselves draft party programmes or nominate candidates for public office. Pressure associations do, however, appear before the resolution committees, of the political parties to urge the endorsement of their programmes as planks in the parties platforms. They often attempt to secure the endorsement of both major parties and thus remove their programme from the arena of partisan controversy. Many groups are also active in the nomination and election of party members to public offices".

Today, pressure groups play their part in every political system, democratic as well as non-democratic. The characteristic features of pressure groups are as follows: 1. The formation of a pressure group depends upon the pressure of *a specific interest.* Unless there is a specific interest forcing the individuals to resort actively to political activity for promoting that interest, the pressure group will not come into existence. 2. A pressure group *does not function openly* on the political arena. It shuns the limelight and avoids clear alignment with political parties. 3. A pressure group sometimes acts as a *faction* within a political party but generally keeps its *separate* organisational identity. It prefers to remain an extra-political grouping. 4. A pressure group may be termed either as an interest group or an attitude group. The basis of unity is *economic* for an interest group. The members of an attitude group are motivated by a *moral, religious* or *humanitarian* objective.

Considered from a broader perspective, pressure groups can be institutional, anomic, non-associational or associational. Bureaucracy, army and departments are examples of *institutional* groups. Demostrations, riots, spontaneous violent actions, etc. are the activities of *anomic* groups. Groups based on class, kinship, religion, race etc. are *non-associational* pressure groups. The trade unions or business associations are the examples of *associational* pressure groups. The function of associational groups is to *articulate* and publicise the demands of their members.

Pressure groups in the U.S.A.

Some of the well-known pressure groups in the U.S.A. are the National Chamber of Commerce, Standard Oil Company, American Federation of Labour, Congress for Industrial Organizations, the Farm Bureau, American Association of Railway Executives etc. These groups appoint regular and whole-time officials or representatives in Washington who perform lobby functions for them. Lobbies were created before 1920 for propagating prohibition and extension of voting rights to women. Today, a pressure group exists to promote the case of civil rights for the Negroes and another pressure group demands equal rights and opportunities for women. Before 1970 there was a China lobby to oppose U.S. recognition of the Communist regime in China.

The pressure groups in the U.S.A. maintain regular contacts with members of the Senate and the House of Representatives, with the administrative heads of departments and with the bosses of political parties. They try to influence them to pass laws and take decisions which would serve their interests. They spend large sums of money in propagandist activities. They create public opinion by using such mass media as newspapers, radio and television. They also publish books and pamphlets written by experts to propagate their views.

Before the presidential election, the pressure groups may enter into a bargain with one of the candidates and try to get him elected with the collective support of their members. Before the Congressional elections, the pressure groups give financial assistance or electoral support to those candidates, who are likely to work in their favour in the Senate or the House of Representatives. As Laski points out, there are instances when some pressure groups have secured their objectives by offering bribes or other advantages to legislators and officials. The pressure groups, which possess great resources, give financial support to such research institutes which do research work and collect necessary statistics for their use. They arrange seminars and conferences to publicize their views on issues which concern them.

The number of pressure groups, which are active at federal and state levels in the U.S.A., can be counted in thousands. They have been sometimes described as "the extra-constitutional third chamber of the Congress" in the U.S.A. Some of the highly powerful pressure groups have been formed by the corporate capitalist groups. The workers also are organised into powerful national federations of trade unions. The pressure groups appoint ex-Senators, ex-bureaucrats and clever lawyers as their agents in federal and state capitals. Several members of the Senate, some members of the President's cabinet and numerous officials at various levels of administration work as disguised spokesmen of different pressure groups.

Pressure Groups in India

In India pressure groups arose even during the colonial period. British and Indian capitalists set up separate pressure groups. This reflected a contradiction in their mutual objectives. Later, they also established a joint organization known as the Mill Owners' Association. The pressure groups were initially set up by British industrialists and businessmen and the Indian merchants and manufacturers followed their example in due course. Some of the early pressure groups were the Indian Mining Federation, the Indian Collieries Association, the Indian Sugar Mills Association, the Indian Soapmakers' Association etc. The aim of these pressure groups was to secure economic and political concessions for themselves. They also combined together to determine prices, wage rates, bulk purchase of raw materials, and the quantity of production.

The trade unions of the working class also came into existence during the colonial period. The All-India Trade Union Congress was the first countrywide pressure group of the organised Indian working-class. The trade unions in India have come under the influence of political parties. After independence the Congress promoted a separate pressure group of the workers, which was known as the Indian National Trade Union Congress. Today, the major parties of India have created separate all-India federations of workers.

The Indian capitalists have two major pressure groups: the Employers' Federation of India and the All-India Organization of Industrial Employers. A parallel organization of these two is the Federation of Indian Chambers of Commerce and Industry—FICCI. This represents the interests of corporate capital in India. Its representatives are included in several boards and commissions of the Government of India. They exercise considerable influence on policies dealing with imports and exports, plan targets and the entire process of planning and other important economic matters. The pressure groups, representing the interests of corporate capital, control a large part of the national press and exercise a great deal of influence on the Indian government.

Bentley and C. Wright Mills have admitted that in the U.S.A. and other capitalist countries, the pressure groups representing *capital* wield much greater power and influence than the pressure groups representing *labour*. The same remark applies equally to conditions prevailing in India.

Critical Assessment of Pressure Groups

The emergence and articulation of organised pressure groups has been condemned by some idealist writers as a sinister development. It enables an organised minority to crush the will of the majority and promotes corruption in political behaviour. The shrewd and corrupt leaders of pressure groups promote sectional interests at the expense of the common good. The behaviour of pressure groups is hardly democratic and tolerant towards unorganised masses and classes. The battle between producers and consumers or between capital and labour is fought on unequal terms.

As a result, many advocates of genuine democracy view these pressure groups with a sense of moral indignation. They are alarmed by the extent of penetration of these sinister interests into the mechanism and processes of modern representative government. It is also argued that the techniques of lobbying, as practised by the pressure groups, involve abuses, frauds and corrupt practices on such a scale as to destroy the credibility of popular government for ordinary citizens. Woodrow Wilson once remarked that the will of the Congress was really the collective term for the wishes of the organised pressure groups. Carl Friedrich in *Constitutional Government and Democracy* remarks : "The genuine representative significance of all organisations arising in connection with man's activities within the total context of modern industrial life has become sufficiently apparent to make it necessary to reckon them (pressure groups) as pretenders to the throne of government. Where the interests are sharply divided, certain of these groups have proceeded to take over the government and to revolutionise it in such a way as to suit their particular needs and conceptions. Such efforts have been accompanied by dictatorial methods–relapses into crude techniques of government which violate the fundamental premises of constitutional limitations."

Despite the above criticism, the utility of the pressure groups for the working of a modern liberal-democratic state, standing on the economic foundations of capitalism and class divisions, cannot be deniad. The pluralistic democracy can maintain its equilibrium only when various interest groups are permitted to act as a check upon one another in order to sustain the system of checks and balances. Verney has observed : "The use of the term 'pressure groups' suggests that outside interests are obtaining special favours at the expense of the public, but it is also true that groups help to prevent Government from imposing unfair burdens on the unorganised masses. Moreover, where party programmes tend of necessity to be general group policies and proposals can be usefully specified." When politics in a modern democratic state is viewed as a balancing activity of the competing elites, the function of the pressure groups will be to articulate sectional interests and partial causes and the political parties will be required to formulate a general policy through *aggregation* of these partial causes and sectional demands into a rational synthesis

Ralph Miliband says. "What is wrong with pluralist democratic theory is not its insistence on the fact of competition but its claim (very often its implicit assumption) that the major organised 'interests' in these societies, and notably capital and labour, compete on more or less equal terms, and that none of them is therefore able to achieve a decisive and permanent advantage in the process of competition. This is where ideology enters, and turns observation into myth." (*236 : 131*).

CHAPTER 25

DEMOCRACY

1. DEMOCRACY UNDER REVISION

It is a commonplace observation that the world today is not as hopeful of democracy as it was in previous generations. Its attitude is one of caution, if not of criticism. World War I, in the words of Woodrow Wilson, was fought to make the world 'safe for democracy'. But the problem which has confronted it since then is, how to make democracy safe for the world? The years succeeding World War II have shown clearly that democracy is not an open 'sesame' to peace, prosperity, and progress. In the multitude of voices, we do not necessarily find wisdom. We no longer hope with Bentham that we can radically improve 'this wicked world by covering it over with Republics'. We are more sober now, if not, altogether disillusioned.

Democracy is being attacked today from various angles, both by reactionaries and revolutionaries. It is attacked with much vehemence by believers in autocracy and dictatorship. Many of these advocate the gospel of direct action, according to which a well-organized, strong-willed, and assertive minority should impose its will upon the helpless majority by remorseless terrorism, if necessary.

Therefore, majorities should be disregarded and coerced for their own good. Direct action, in one of its phases, means the unreserved use of industrial power. 'It is a clear assertion of the antagonistic principle of oligarchy and ultimately of despotism'.

H. G. Wells is convinced that there has been a growing distrust and discontent with politicians and the political method evolved by parliamentary democracy.

The ranks of the critics of democracy are being fortified by those who believe in the doctrine of the *elite*. According to them, democracy is founded altogether on wrong premises. It assumes that the common man understands political issues in all their complexity and that he has the capacity to govern himself. Both of these assumptions are challenged by the advocates of the doctrine of the *elite*. According to them, a vast majority of people are incapable of understanding political problems and are thoroughly incompetent to govern themselves. Therefore, government should be vested in the hands of the few who are wise and capable.

2. THE MEANING OF DEMOCRACY

Democracy is not a mere form of government. It is a type of State as well as an order of society. Even friends of democracy have at times interpreted democracy to mean only a form of government. Thus J. R. Lowell says that democracy is only 'an experiment' in government. Lincoln defines it as 'government of the people, by the people, and for the people.' Seeley describes it as 'a government in which everyone has a share'. Dicey defines it as a form of government in which, 'the governing body is a comparatively large fraction of the entire nation'. Even Lord Bryce, in his monumental work *Modern Democracies,* treats it as only a form of government.

Democracy is not a mere form of government; it is not primarily a form of government. A democratic government implies a democratic State, but a democratic State does not necessarily mean a democratic government. As Hearnshaw remarks, all that a democratic State means is that the community as a whole possesses sovereign authority and maintains ultimate control over affairs. 'Democracy as a form of State is merely a mode of appointing, controlling, and dismissing a government'.

In addition to being a form of government and a type of State, democracy is an order of society. A democratic society is one in which the spirit of equality and fraternity prevails. Such a society does not necessarily imply a democratic State or a democratic government. The Mohammedan society is on the whole democratic, although it does not generally possess a democratic State or a democratic government. The new state of Pakistan calls itself an Islamic Republic. In the opinion of many, theocracy and democracy are mutually exclusive of each other.

The meaning of democracy is not exhausted even after interpreting it as a form of government, a type of State, and an order of society. It invades the realm of industry too. There are many today who claim that the battle for democracy will not be complete till industry is entirely democratized. They argue that, while democracy has made great strides in the social and political fields, it has made very little advance in the economic or industrial field. Some of these look forward to socialism as the next step in democracy. Whether their claim is right or not, we must admit that no society can call itself entirely democratic if it uses democratic methods in some fields and autocratic methods in others.

In the last analysis democracy embodies a moral principle. It means that every man has value. It enshrines the truth that government does not exist for its own sake, but for the enrichment of personality. No government has a right to be called a democracy if it does not bring out the best in man.

Direct and representative forms of democracy. Democracy in its narrow sense means rule by the many. For its origin it goes back to the old Greek city States, all of which enjoyed complete local autonomy. They experimented with different forms of Government—monarchy, tyranny, aristocracy, oligarchy, and democracy. There was considerable speculation as to which one of them was the best. After weighing the arguments for and against the various forms Aristotle gave his verdict in favour of policy or a moderate form of democracy. The type of democracy which prevailed in the Greek city-states was pure or direct democracy. All the freemen met together in general assemblies, passed laws and executed them, received ambassadors, and acted as jurymen. This type of democracy was revived in mediaeval times by Italian city States. The Forest Cantons of Switzerland also had direct democracy which has come down to modern times. Rousseau in the eighteenth century was a powerful advocate of this type of government. He deprecated indirect or representative democracy. But even he saw the difficulty of realizing direct democracy on a large scale under modern conditions. Thus he says that pure democracy presupposes many things difficult to combine. It presupposes:

(1) a small State, in which people may be easily assembled, and in which every citizen can easily know all the rest;
(2) great simplicity of manners:
(3) considerable equality in rank and fortune; and
(4) little or no luxury.

Present-day experience shows that democracy of the pure and direct type is an absolutely unattainable ideal. The only type which is possible for us today is the indirect or representative type. According to it the actual administration of affairs is taken from the hands of the people and is vested in delegates. The nearest approach that we find to direct democracy in some modern States is in the form of the referendum, initiative, and recall. These devices are by no means capable of universal application. Some of the other devices which are much more common are the widening of the electorate, responsibility of government to the majority party, frequent elections, and local self-government. Democracy and Parliamentary government are not necesarily identical, although for England and other countries which have adopted the English political model, democracy is indissolubly connected with Parliament.

Forms of Government. The time-old classification of government into monarchy, aristocracy, and democracy does not have much value for us today. Most governments at present are of a mixed type. They include the monarchic, aristocratic, and democratic elements in various degrees. The English constitution may appear to be monarchic on the surface, but it is fundamentally democratic, with a strong tinge of aristocracy. What experience shows is that a sound democracy should make room for, and include, a sound aristocracy—not an aristocracy of birth or wealth, but an aristocracy of intellect, ability and character. Bryce remarks that all governments are in fact aristocracies, in the sense that they are carried on by a relatively small number of persons. Another recent writer says that every form of government which has ever existed is aristocratic.

There are different types of democratic governments today. Bryce says:

(1) they can exist under republic or a nominal monarchy.
(2) they can exist under a rigid or flexible constitution.

But they are all based on the doctrine of popular sovereignty. As a consequence of this feature, the right of raising revenue and appropriating it to the several services of the State belongs in all these systems to the representatives of the people. They are all worked by political parties.

Democracy in its broder sense. In its broader sense democracy is 'a political status', 'an ethical concept', and 'a social condition'. It means faith in the common man. Or, as A. D. Lindsay states it, it implies that all beings have a worth in themselves. No one is a mere means to another's end. The well-known formula of Kant in this connection is, 'So act as to treat humanity, whether in your person or in that of any other, in every case as an end, and never merely as a means'.

The value of personality which is the crux of democracy does not mean that all individuals are alike or equal. 'Democracy in practice', says C. D. Burns, 'is the hypothesis, that all men are equal which is used in order to discover who are the best'.

Democracy, we believe, is a practical manifestation of the enthusiasm for humanity. It is a concrete attempt at the reconciliation of the apparently contradictory principle of liberty, equality and fraternity, in order that every individual in the community may be enabled to attain the highest good possible for him.

3. THE CLASSICAL CASE FOR DEMOCRACY

1. *The Precautionary Reason.* Democracy gives us a guarantee that the will of every one in the community shall be duly considered, and that no one shall be neglected in what is done by the government. If efficiency were the only test of good government, a bureaucracy or even a dictatorship might be a better form than democracy. But efficiency is not the only test. The best government is that which makes the best possible citizens. In an autocracy or a bureaucracy, individuals and groups of individuals may suffer here and there without affecting the rest of the community. In a democracy, on the contrary, at least in theory, there is not a single man who can suffer without the rest of the community sharing in his suffering. An autocracy or a bureaucracy, in other words, is partially paralyzed. A democracy, on the other hand, is considered to be equally sensitive to the wishes and sufferings of all its members. Democracy, says Prof. Hocking, ties a nerve to every individual. It makes a connection between him and the centre. In it there are as many incoming connections as there are outgoing connections. 'In a complete democracy no one can complain that he has not a chance to be heard.' (A. L. Lowell).

2. *The Psychological Reason.* Efficiency, as said above, is not enough. Soulless efficiency killed Rome. In every form of government, we shall always try for government by specialists. But specialists do not know the whole mind of the people. Specialization warps the intellect. The specialist knows his side of the case exceedingly well. But he does not always know how his prescriptions affect the people at large. It is the wearer who knows

where the shoe pinches. What good government requires is a co-operation or working alliance between the specialist and the layman, and democracy best fulfils this condition. Prof. Hocking goes so far as to say that to be governed by the highly educated man alone is a calamity. Such a ruler is apt to be too abstract and doctrinaire, far removed from the concrete situations of life.

3. *The Educational Reason.* Democracy is a large-scale experiment in public education. It stimulates interest and is informative. It tends to create a higher type of mentality among the people whom it governs. When a general election takes place every reasonable opinion is given a chance to express itself. Issues are discussed in all their bearings, and what was private soon becomes public. Speeches are delivered, articles are written, programmes are outlined, and policies are propounded. The result of all this is a phenomenal rise in the popular understanding of the problems of government. C. D. Burns writes: "All government is a method of education, but the best education is self-education; therefore the best government is self-government which is democracy'.

4. *The Moral Reason.* Democracy ennobles the people. It rests on the principle that what a man earns for himself by his own efforts is of much greater value to him than what is handed down to him by someone else. It is the best aid to self-help, initiative, and the cultivation of individual responsibility. The supreme merit of democracy, says J. S. Mill, lies in the fact that 'it promotes a better and higher form of national character than any other polity whatever'. Bryce likewise says that the dignity of individuals is enhanced by political enfranchisement. Democracy, we may add, is conducive to the development of all-round man. Under no other form of government is self-realization as easily possible as under democracy.

5. *The Practical Reason.* From the practical point of view, democracy has several advantages:

(1) It promotes patriotism. The French people, says Laveleye, never really loved France until after the Revolution when they were admitted to a share in the government. Since then, they have become passionate lovers of their country.

(2) A corollary of the fact that democracy promotes patriotism is that it reduces the danger of revolution. Democracy is government by persuasion. Every other form of government rests to a greater or less extent on force. Democracy believes in discussion and deliberation, and this is the only method which is bound to succeed finally.

In addition, democracy is the only form of government where both order and progress can easily go together. This fact constitutes another check on the possibility of revolution. Dictatorship gives us order, but not much progress.

A further way in which democracy acts as a check on revolution is by emphasizing the principle of equality. It knows of no sharp social cleavages and provides, on the whole, an open road to talent. Social inequality and social discontent which often prevail in other forms of government are bound to take a revolutionary turn when an opportune moment presents itself.

(3) Some writers claim that democracy makes for greater efficiency than any other form of government. They argue that 'popular election, popular control, and popular responsibility are more likely to insure a greater degree of efficiency than any other system of government' (*23:390*).

4. THE CASE AGAINST DEMOCRACY

Whatever the merits of democracy may be in theory, there is no doubt that it has been accompanied by many evils in daily practice.

1. The attacks on democracy in its early stages took an aristocratic turn. There were many who felt that democracy meant rule by the irresponsible multitude. Aristotle regarded it as a degenerate or perverted form of constitutional government. Mill feared the tyranny of the majority. Lecky thought that democracy was opposed to liberty. Even today there are those who claim that democracy attaches undue importance to quantity rather than to quality. Votes are counted and not weighed. Social training, conscientious judgment, and expert knowledge receive little consideration. It is a government by crowds. It exalts mediocrity and inferiority. It makes the majority supreme, even if it be a very narrow majority. The minority which may have greater knowledge and better judgment is spurned. In a democracy it is difficult to secure enforceable responsibility.

2. There are others who adopt somewhat difficult line of argument from the one sketched above. They argue that democracy in practice leads to oligarchy of the worst kind. Talleyrand describes it as 'an aristocracy of blackguards'. Power in a democracy falls into the hands of the demagogue, the grafter, and the 'boss'. Leaders of first-rate ability are not chosen. People are jealous of superiority. Therefore, they choose popular men rather than able men to lead them. Stating the case against democracy, Maxey says that it easily falls a prey to demagoguism, bossism, and vicious pressure politics.

The average voter, it is said, in not much interested in matters of State. On many subjects that are discussed, there is no general will or common mind. The apathy of the voter in many democratic countries is proverbial.

3. In close connection with this argument it is often said that democracy means in practice the evils of party politics and that political parties constitute an invisible oligarchy. While the party system is indispensable to a democracy, it

(1) encourages hollowness and insincerity;

(2) carries the national divisions into local elections;

(3) leads to the 'Spoils system'; and

(4) debases moral standards (*7: Vol. 1, Ch. XI*).

The party machine is so well-worked that the individual citizen who wants to exercise his judgment is given little or no freedom. He has to choose between two or more candidates who may be either knaves or fools and for none of whom he cares, and decide between two or three issues, none of which meets with his approval.

4. The French writer, Faguet, describes democracy as the cult of incompetence. It is a government by amateurs or those who are hopelessly immature. It rests upon a broken reed inasmuch as it rests upon the common multitude which is ungrateful, emotional and passionate. The common people do not reason much. Today they laud a man to the skies and tomorrow they cast him down in the mire. They are inconstant and fickle in their attachment both to principles and to persons. They are not swayed by any consistent and unifying ideals. At times they are given to idealism and hero-worship; they are easily swept off their feet by such shibboleths as 'self-determination of nations' and by such catchwords as 'Hang the Kaiser'. At other times they become obscurantists and obstruct all progress. In the words of Hearnshaw, they are like school masters elected by their pupils and liable to be punished and dismissed by them. Majority rule, it is claimed, always tends to become majority tyranny.[1]

5. Those who attack democracy from the psychological standpoint argue that people, in the words of Maxey are sheep-minded, ape-minded, and wolf-minded. In other words, "they are credulous, impulsive, panicky, intolerant, unconscionable, cruel, unjust, stupid, and everything but rational". The democratic government, it is further said, is "prone to indecision, feebleness, instability, and stupidity because of the volatility, irrationality, and ineptitude of the masses."

6. It is claimed that democracy is a government by the people. The critic asks whether this is really so in practice. Who are these people in whom wisdom, justice and power are supposed to be embodied? Does it mean a majority of electors? Even if it be granted for the sake of argument that a majority vote often represents majority opinion in the country, we have to face the further query whether the majority is necessarily right? The voice of the people may very well be the voice of the devil. To assume that representatives always 'represent' the will of the people is a mistake. They may consciously or unconsciously misrepresent it. They are not always free men. They are subject to strict party discipline and are at times more afraid of newspapers and of vested interests than of their electors.

7. One of the forcible arguments used by Faguet against democracy is that it is a biological misfit or a biological monstrosity. What Faguet means by this criticism is that democracy is not in line with the process

1. For a detailed criticism of Democracy see Hearnshaw : *Democracy at the Crossways*.

of evolution. He argues that the higher we ascend in the scale of evolution the greater is the degree of centralization. Casting off figurative language, what Faguet means is that government should be in the hands of an intelligent oligarchy and that the many should implicitly obey it. He interprets the democratic form of government to mean extreme decentralization and thorough incompetency.

Those who adopt the biological and ethnological argument at times claim that non-white races are incapable of practising democracy in comparison with the white races.

8. A serious charge laid at the door of democracy is that it is a very expensive form of government. Democracy means organization of opinion, propaganda, and frequent elections. All this involves a great deal of expenditure. Money which should be used for productive purposes is spent on electioneering and 'nursing the constituency'. The wastefulness of democracy is a fact which cannot be easily controverted. There is waste not only of money, but also of time and opportunity. According to some thinkers, says Maxey, democracy is the most inefficient and extravagant, the most factional and intolerant, the most hostile or indifferent to progress.

9. Even the moral value of democracy has been seriously questioned by some. These critics say that there is always in democracy a temptation to falsify. Issues are to be vulgarized and popularized before they can make an appeal to the people. Questions are not discussed dispassionately. They are discussed in such a manner as to catch votes.

Bribery and corruption are said to be the common abuses of democracy. In his chapter on 'The Money Power in Politics' (*9:Ch. LXIX*), Bryce shows that there are several instances of electors, members of legislatures, administrative officials, and even judicial officials succumbing to the temptation of illicit gain. This abuse, however, is on the whole on the decline today. In India, however, since Independence the opportunities for illicit gain have become greater and because of that, the numbers taking advantage of them larger.

10. Democracy, it is said, is a process of diseducation, rather than of education. It flatters people. It produces a pretentious proletariat. It hides from people their deficiency. It engenders in them a false sense of equality. Every man thinks that he is as good as anybody else, for the governance of his country. It calls for no special effort and training. It lowers standards. It makes people think too well of themselves in literature, science, and art. Appeal is made to mob psychology, and every effort is made to pander to the people. People as a whole are indifferent, if not hostile, to the advancement of education, science, literature and art. They are more apt to run counter to scientific conclusions than are the privileged classes. The civilization which a democracy produces is said to be 'banal mediocre or dull' (Burns).

11. Democracy, it is said, is not friendly to liberty and individuality. It is meddlesome. McCarthyism in the U.S.A. in recent years being a supreme

example of it. Several critics have drawn attention to the fact that there is in democracy a 'large and increasing mass of hasty and ill-digested legislation' (*54:613*). The average representative not infrequently feels that the only way in which he can justify his existence in the legislature is to help to place some new law or another on the statute books.

12. There are many instances in democratic countries of local interests tending 'to obscure and to defeat the interests of the State at large' (*54:164*). In the scramble for power and patronage, the general well-being of the State is apt to be brushed aside in order to do some good to a limited number of people. Representatives vie with each other in obtaining whatever they can, irrespective of its effect on the welfare of the country at large in order to curry favour with their electorate. The recent furore over the creation of linguistic States in India is an excellent example of the part taking the place of the whole and of one part savagely fighting another.

Lord Bryce sums up the chief faults observable in modern democracies as follows:

(1) 'The power of money to pervert administration or legislation.

(2) 'The tendency to make politics a gainful profession.

(3) 'Extravagance in administration.

(4) 'The abuse of the doctrine of equality and failure to appreciate the value of administrative skill.

(5) 'The undue power of party organization.

(6) 'The tendency of legislators and political officials to play for votes in the passing of laws and in tolerating breaches of order' (*9: Vol. II, p. 504*).

5. EVALUATION OF THE CRITICISMS AGAINST DEMOCRACY

Many of the above criticisms undoubtedly contain elements of truth. But for the most part they are mere caricatures. It is interesting to note that some of them mutually cancel each other. Thus, according to some writers, democracy means hero-worship and idolatry, while, according to others, it means insubordination and anarchy. Some say that democracy is given to idealism and worship of abstract theory, while others contend that in a democracy there is no place for sentiments and principles. These mutual contradictions contain their own refutation.

1. If democracy is a bad form of government, we are justified in asking, what is the way out? Is there any other form of government which is as good as democracy, if not better? Our answer is in the negative. The world has tried aristocracy and oligarchy at various times and has found them to be generally failures. We cannot go back to them; for, in the striking words of C. D. Burns: 'No one denies that existing representative assemblies are defective; but even if an automobile does not work well, it is foolish to go back to a farm cart, however romantic' (*9:80*). The world is not yet fit to inaugurate the type of society which the philosophical anarchists have

long dreamed about. The tendency for some time past has been in the direction of dictatorship. Whatever be the merits of dictatorship, there is no gainsaying the fact that, inasmuch as dictatorship is a denial of individual liberty and initiative, it is contrary to the development of personality, which we conceive to be the supreme end and destiny of man. Dictatorship suppresses all criticisms and all organizations which are not its own.

2. Democracy is blamed today for many of the evils which two wars have brought about. The world-wide depression and unemployment of the thirties and the inflationary trends of today are the result of the unsettled conditions of the world for which democracy alone is not responsible. The sad plight in which the world finds itself today, economically, politically, and internationally is not one in which the true merits of democracy can be impartially judged. As A. L. Lowell observes : 'It is not fair to rate the soundness of a man's judgment by his behaviour when fighting, when drunk, or when scared. Nor can we measure democracy by events that occur under highly abnormal conditions.'

3. Faguet describes democracy as an unbiological arrangement and claims that it expects the brain to be located anywhere and everywhere in the social organism. This is not a sound criticism. Democracy is not a plea for the dissipation of authority. As said above, a sound democracy makes room for and includes, a sound aristocracy. In the words of Mazzini democracy is 'the progress of all, through all, under the leading of the best and wisest'. Modern democracies realize that government is an art, and that it can be safely entrusted only to those who have made a speciality of it. Democracy, we repeat, does not exclude government by experts. While in an aristocracy the expert may hold himself aloof from the people, in a democracy he is expected to possess the necessary social virtues which will enable him to feel at home with the people whom he is called upon to govern. It is needless to say that the difference is in favour of democracy. British democracy abounds in men of ability and distinction although the British cabinet government is often described as a 'government by amateurs'.

In the light of all this, we refuse to believe that democracy is an incompetent form of government.

As regards the biological and ethnological assumption that democracy is a speciality of the white races, Maxey is right when he says : "There is no credible scientific proof that the white races are innately superior in political genius or any other mental quality to the black, brown, or yellow races" (*Ibid.*, p. 687). Ancient India and China had well-developed and well-conducted forms of local self-government.

4. Those who are uncompromisingly opposed to democracy point the finger of scorn at the common people and say that they are incapable of governing themselves. We demur to this point of view. We admit that the choice of leaders in a democracy has not always been happy. But for this the people are not altogether to blame. Choosing the wrong type of leaders may be partly the result of autocracy, and not of democracy. Pres-

tige attached to wealth, power, and rank in society is not yet dead. The remedy is not to lessen democracy but to increase it. It is mistake to think that people always make wrong choices. Experience in democratic countries shows that people are better judges (a) of men than of measures; (b) of negative measures than of positive ones; (c) of questions involving general policies than of technical and detailed questions; (d) of matters which involve ethical principles (*e.g.*, questions of foreign policy) than of those which arouse their emotions and passions.

In reply to those who claim that the average man is not interested in governing himself and that the greatest indictment of democracy is the apathy of the voter, we may say that other forms of government do not show better results. If there are periods of apathy in popular interest in a democracy, there are also periods of intense interest and keen devotion. A non-democratic form of government is sure to win the support of people as long as it confers boons upon them but the moment it imposes burdens, there is profound discontent.

5. Although some of the present-day critics of democracy decry the principle of representation, they are unable to free their minds of it entirely. No reputable thinker today is prepared to justify unadulterated autocracy. It is instructive to find that even the most ardent supporters of dictatorship justify it on the plea that it is truly representative of the people. Whether we agree with their interpretation or not, the point is that the principle of authority on the basis of representation has become a permanent part of political philosophy today. If we are agreed on this point, the further question concerns the most effective way in which people can be represented. We demur to the point of view which claims that dictatorship is truly representative of the people, especially when we take into account the fact that it stifles criticism and a free expression of opinion.

6. To the charge that democracy necessitates party government and that party government is an unsatisfactory way of dividing opinion, our reply is:

(a) Parties are inevitable, for without them it is impossible to operate a democratic government. Parties bring order out of chaos. They mould and educate public opinion. As Bryce remarks, 'parties keep a nation's mind alive, as the rise and fall of the sweeping tide freshens the water of long ocean inlets'.

(b) 'Party discipline', to quote the same writer again, 'puts a check on self-seeking and corruption'.

7. To the charge that democracy means diseducation, there is perhaps no satisfatcory answer on the basis of facts. The diseducation of the masses can be gradually overcome by instilling into people a spirit of teachableness. Already we see signs in that direction. We concede to the opponents of democracy that there is considerable waste and extravagance in a democracy. But our plea is that this is not a necessary evil. Education of public opinion will go a long way in overcoming it.

8. Alongside of waste and extravagance, bribery and corruption are common in most democracies. But for these, we have to blame the general life of the country and not democracy alone. Lowell is right when he says that we cannot fairly attribute to democracy evils tolerated in the commercial life. 'Right and wrong have always existed and always will. A lack of probity in public life is no new thing'. 'There is certainly less corruption among office-holders now than there was in Europe in the eighteenth century, but popular forms of government will hardly be rid of it until a higher standard is exacted on the street, and those who violate it are socially tabooed'.

9. It is almost a fashion today to proclaim the death of democracy. Like many other fashions, it is possible that this fashion has no solid foundation. In countries like England and the United States, where democracy has been developed and where it has functioned successfully for a long period there seem to be no serious signs of its abandonment. All that the enthusiasm for dictatorship indicates is that democracy should adjust itself to changing condition. As pointed out by Dr. A. D. Lindsay : 'A democratic society sure of itself can be indefinitely elastic in its methods. It can, as in a time of crisis, give enormous powers into the hands of its government, in cheerful confidence that, the crisis past, it can take them back' *(52:17)*. The way in which Churchill in England and President Roosevelt in the United States acquired enormous powers in the course of a relatively few years and the way in which their countrymen calmly and confidently acquiesced in such an extension are a sign not of the weakness but of the strength of their democratic faith. Much the same thing may be said of the extraordinary influence of the late Nehru over the people of India during the past decade.

10. Some say that democracy is a myth and that there is nothing like it on land or sea. One possible answer to it is that men live by myths. If so, why not they live by the myths of democracy, natural rights, equality of man, and general will ? Dewey says, "The foundation of democracy is faith in the capacities of human nature; faith in human intelligence and in the power of pooled and co-operative experience".

6. REMEDY AND CONCLUSION

The conclusion to which we are inevitably led is that democracy has no absolute worth, it has only conditional worth. It does not contain a panacea for all the ills of the world. The worst failings of democracy are due to immaturity and are likely to be overcome with growing experience. Its supreme value is ethical and educational. The foundation on which it rests *viz.,* the worth of every human personality is unshakable. We believe that De Tocqueville is right when he says : 'The progress of democracy seems irresistible, because it is the most uniform, the most ancient, and the most permanent tendency which is to be found in history'.

Democracy, we believe, is a right organization, embodying a sound principle. The evils which we see in it are not inevitable. They can be cured by the people themselves by proper education, reflection, and experience. We do not agree with those who say that the only way to cure the evils of democracy is to end democracy. What needs to be ended is the prevailing international anarchy, using such means as an effective world government, planned economy, disarmament, and the removal of tariff and racial barriers.

If, as we believe, democracy requires to be made genuinely democratic, and not ended, what are the specific ways by which this process can be accomplished?

Prof. Hearnshaw lays down the following conditions:

(1) *A high standard both of honesty and of honour*. Moral soundness is absolutely necessary. Without clean hands and a pure heart, particularly in the leaders, democracy is bound to fail. A corrupt democracy is the vilest and most hopeless of political organizations. There should be equal rights for everybody, equity in law, and equality of opportunity.

(2) *A high level of intelligence and a sound system of education*. Lack of commonsense is dangerous in a democracy. Without a spirit of 'normal reasonableness on the part of the people at large', democracy will degenerate into mob rule or lead to dictatorship

(3) *A clear consciousness of the community*. Democracy calls for a strong sense of solidarity, an intense conviction of unity, a pervasive feeling of communal life.' Racial feuds, religious schisms, class conflicts, and social cleavages are bound to weaken democracy.

(4) *A sound public opinion, a sensitive social conscience, and an effective general will*. Democracy cannot be much better or much worse than the prevailing public opinion. Therefore, when and where democracy fails, one of the potent causes for it is unsound or ineffective public opinion. To these conditions, we may add

(5) *Social and industrial democracy*. If democracy is to succeed, it should invade man's social relationships as well as his economic life. Maxey rightly observes that an industrial democracy should be set up within, or parallel to, political democracy. It is a welcome sign that Indian democracy stresses the importance of democracy in both the political and the economic fields.

J. W. Garner lays down the following as the essential conditions of democracy:

(1) 'A relatively high degree of political intelligence and abiding interest in public affairs, a keen sense of public responsibility, and a readiness to accept and abide by the decision of the majority' (*23:405*), coupled with respect for the rights of minorities.

(2) Facilities for elementary education.

(3) Education in political matters and training in the habits of government.

(4) A high moral level.

Among the practical suggestions advanced for improving the machinery of the democratic organization, the views of the following writers deserve mention :

Lord Lothian says :

(1) That government should be conducted under guarantees of freedom of speech and criticism, and political and economic initiative for the individual; and

(2) That it should be changeable without violence, at the ultimate decision of an adult electorate.

Andre-Maurois suggests 'an individual leadership for a defined purpose and a fixed period' as a check upon dictatorship. Others suggest a strong executive. Lord Eustace Percy claims that 'the British constitution saves itself by the Monarchical Prime Ministership and that the day when he (the Prime Minister) falls under the domination of party caucus there will be no alternative to dictatorship'. 'Parliament's first and supreme duty is, therefore, to make strong Prime Ministers. Their freedom is its freedom; their strength its strength'.

Other suggestions made by Lord Percy are :

(1) Parliament should concern itself with broad questions of policy and not lose itself in petty details. It should deal with taxation and expenditure as broad issues of policy, and voice grievances arising out of the misdirection of expenditure and the unfair incidence of taxes.

(2) Parliament should take the initiative in formulating bills. It should not depend too largely on overdriven government departments for formulating legislative proposals. It should constitute a series of committees of the House for this purpose.

(3) Other committees of Parliament should be constituted 'to watch the administrative action of particular departments, to examine departmental orders and regulations before their issue, to investigate individual complaints and to make representation of ministers'.

(4) An economic council should be constituted by Crown nominations, as nearly as possible representative, not of economic opinion, but of economic power.

Writing on 'Parliament as it Should Be' Sir Stafford Cripps claims that the three attributes of democracy are :

(1) That the people must have a free and unfettered choice of their representatievs, with a right of recall at stated periods;

(2) That the people must signify their choice of the policy that they desire to be carried out;

(3) That representatives must be able to carry through the desired policy

without undue delay and without outside interference from any particular interest or persons.

To give effect to these practical attributes of democracy, Sir Stafford Cripps recommends:

(1) The abolition of the leisurely methods of nineteenth century law-making;

(2) The House of Commons taking a bold line when it has the support of the country behind it and effectively controlling the manner and *tempo* of the nation's progress, not being browbeaten by a non-democratic Second Chamber; and

(3) The formation of functional committees to supervise the legislative and administrative activities of the ministers.

Lord Bryce concludes his discussion on the relative merits and demerits of democracy in the following terms:

If the optimists overvalued the moral influence of democracy, the pessimists undervalued its practical aptitudes. It has reproduced most of the evils which have belonged to other forms of government though in different forms, and the few it has added are less serious than those evils of the older governments which it has escaped.

(1) It has maintained public order, while securing the liberty of the individual citizen.

(2) It has given a civil administration as efficient as other forms of government have provided.

(3) Its legislation has been more generally directed to the welfare of the poorer classes than has been that of other governments.

(4) It has not been inconstant or ungrateful.

(5) It has not weakened patriotism or courage.

(6) It has been often wasteful and usually extravagant.

(7) It has not produced general contentment in each nation.

(8) It has done little to improve international relations and ensure peace, has not diminished class selfishness, has not fostered a cosmopolitan humanitarianism nor mitigated the dislike of men of a different colour.

(9) It has not extinguished corruption and the malign influences wealth can exert upon government.

(10) It has not removed the fear of revolutions.

(11) It has not enlisted in the service of the State a sufficient number of the most honest and capable citizens.

(12) Nevertheless, taken all in all, it has given better practical results than either the Rule of One Man, or the Rule of a Class, for it has at least extinguished many of the evils by which they were defaced.

CONDITIONS FOR THE SUCCESSFUL WORKING OF DEMOCRACY

1. If democracy is to work successfully, the first important condition

is the inculcation of faith in certain fundamental democratic principles. Among these principles, the pride of place must be given to the value of every human being. Democracy, in theory, at least means that every individual is as important as any other individual and that nobody should be neglected in what is done by government. A second important principle to be borne in mind, particularly in present-day India, is that democracy means government by discussion. It is government by consent. This rules out violence and direct action. The one important right which a minority has in a democracy is to convert itself into a majority by constitutional means.

2. Without popular education no democracy can long endure. It is not claimed that education alone can make a democracy successful, but it is a great help. History has known of educated crooks. Barring such people who are more the exception than the general rule, it may be said that education helps a person to be well-informed, balanced, and discriminating. With eighty to eighty-two per cent of illiterates in India, the prospect for democracy is not too bright unless speedy steps are taken to liquidate illiteracy.

3. Popular education should be supplemented by a high degree of citizenship and a spirit of law-abidingness. No democracy can long endure unless both leaders and the people possess clean hands and a pure heart. If democracy is to succeed, the average citizen should be prepared to play his part in the civic life of the community. He should be willing to vindicate the rights of others, and not simply stand on the sidelines and allow the innocent to suffer. If eternal vigilance is the price of liberty, it is equally the price of democracy.

4. In modern times stress is laid on economic equality and equality of opportunity as far as possible. While economic equality need not mean identical reward for everybody, it certainly rules out great disparities in income. The successful working of democracy these days requires that there should be no great wealth on the one hand and no abject poverty on the other. Aristotle discovered an important truth centuries ago when he said that a strong middle class was the backbone of a democracy. It makes for both stability and progress.

5. Democracy, in one of its important phases, means social equality. Caste and class differences and social distance between one person and another mean the undoing of democracy. One of the most encouraging things happening in India at present is the general disappearance of caste exclusiveness among the educated and city-bred people. It still raises its ugly head in the rural areas; but even there it is only a question of time when it will disappear altogether. Linguistic and state differences, however, are not declining to any considerable extent. In a democracy there should be an open road to talent and talent should not be allowed to perish because of lack of opportunity. Such a situation can be created by providing free education, a liberal system of freeships, and scholarships, and public offices being

filled purely on grounds of ability and character. That the latter is still not the general rule in India has to be admitted with regret.

6. If democracy is to succeed, there is need for carefully selected leaders. Once they are chosen the people should trust and respect them. The flouting of leaders is just as bad as kowtowing to them. Flattery and adulation of those in power can never make a people great. Yet the general rule in India is "the gods may change, but the worshippers remain the same". There is need for people to distinguish political principles and policies from personalities, and not be unduly tied down to individuals. Leaders in their turn should have convictions of their own and stand by them and not be swayed back and forth by every gust of public opinion. A reason why Kennedy in the U.S.A. and Nehru in India were tremendously popular among their respective peoples was that they refused simply to bow to crowd mentality.

7. Too many popular elections are not conducive to the successful operation of democracy. In this connection one must look askance at the election of judges and heads of administrative departments for short periods, as well as of members of school boards, all of which is common in several of the states of the American Union.

8. If the electorate is not to be burdened with too many elections, neither should it be bothered with the submission of too many issues to it. At the same time the electorate should be consulted on principal issues No Parliament or a member of Parliament has a right to go against the deliberately expressed wishes of the electorate at the previous election or in some other equally effective manner. While in doubt, Parliament or its individual members should go back to the people for a mandate.

9. It is often assumed that people are fair judges of issues involving moral principles such as the issues of war and peace, international friendship and understanding, the communal harmony. But recent happenings have tended to shake this faith. It is possible, however, that with the removal of the extraordinary conditions under which mankind is living today, such faith can be restored.

10. If a democracy is to work well, the people must have easy access to accurate and unbiased information on both domestic and international matters. That such is not the case in a good part of the world has to be admitted with sorrow. Freedom of thought, freedom of speech and writing, and freedom of association are the very life breath of democracy.

Our conclusion of the whole discussion on democracy may well be that of Edward Carpenter: 'O, disrespectable democracy, I love thee'. In the words of T. V. Smith : 'If one cannot gain heaven, it is foolish to despair if there still remain in one's hands the means of avoiding hell'.

A NOTE ON PUBLIC OPINION

There can be no doubt that modern democracy and public opinion are very closely intertwined. The extension of franchise, the organization of political parties and of legislatures constituted on a popular basis have all tended to highlight the importance of public opinion. A renowned Spanish writer, Jose Y. Gassett, rightly remarks: "Never has anyone ruled on the earth by basing his rule essentially on any other thing than Public Opinion" (*107*).

Although the term 'public opinion' is used widely, particularly by politicians and public men, like other terms in political science, it is open to different and, at times, confusing interpretations. As a recent writer puts it, it is often a vague stereotype tossed about by writers and speakers, while dealing with economic and political matters. Roucek strikes a note of caution when he says: "Care must be taken to clarify the concept of public opinion and propaganda—always keeping in mind that the term is something to be studied rather than just defined" (*160:355*).

Various definitions have been attempted of public opinion. L. W. Dobb writes: "Public opinion refers to people's attitudes on an issue when they are members of the same social group" (*97:35*). To Roucek "public opinion is in the nature of a consensus arrived at on the basis of the predominating cross-currents of view that prevail in a given time or place.... It is a relatively homogeneous expression of preference by members of a group concerning issues which though debatable, concern the group as a whole" (*97:358*).

Wilhelm Bauer distinguishes 'public opinion proper' from 'opinion which is voiced in public'. The latter is essentially personal in character, whereas public opinion "is a deeply pervasive organic force, intimately bound up with the ideological and emotional inter-play of the social groupings in which since the earliest times gregarious individuals have come together; it articulates and formulates not only the deliberative judgments of the rational elements within the collectivity but the evanescent common will, which somehow integrates and momentarily crystallizes the sporadic sentiments and loyalties of the masses of the population".[2]

Morris Ginsburg, a noted sociologist says, "public opinion is a social product due to the interaction of many minds" (*109:145*). Kimball Young, an American psychologist, writes: "Public opinion consists of the opinions held by a public at a certain time" (*171*).

An analysis of these views, says Roucek, suggests that public opinion implies four things. In the first place there is a group of members or a 'public'. Secondly, these members of the group have issues of common interest about which they communicate with each other, although at times they may differ from one another to some extent. Thirdly, there is a leader, or leaders of the group, who take upon themselves the task of formulating opinion on certain important issues at a given time and of drawing the attention of the members of the group to that opinion. Fourthly, comes the adop-

2. Wilhelm Bauer : Public Opinion (Article contributed to the Encyclopaedia of Social Sciences, Vol. XII, p. 670).

tion of this opinion by the members of the group and of acquiescence in the action necessitated by such opinion.

Another writer says that controversy is the very essence of public opinion. In the formulation of it there is the interplay of ideas and conflicting forces. When opinion has behind it the support of a large percentage of the group it appears as truth for the time being. But when this truth is contradicted by new facts and observations, it once again becomes opinion. Thus there is a see-saw relationship between truth and opinion at a given time in a given group, the distinction being that "truth is accepted as fact; opinion only as a belief".

There seems to be an inherent contradiction in public opinion. As one writer puts it, as 'public' it is good, but as 'opinion' it is bad. For this reason some describe it as confusing, incoherent, amorphous, and varying like shifting sand from day to day. Yet out of this diversity and confusion there arise certain consolidated and clarified views which may be called public opinion and which determine the action of a great many citizens in a country. It is worthy of note that such a noted writer as Walter Lippman who in his *Public Opinion* (1922) had regarded the public as irrational modified his views in favour of the public in his later work, *The Phantom Public* (1925).

There can be no doubt concerning the educative character of public opinion. 'The people can only learn to think by thinking'. Ordinarily, no government today would flout public opinion; for to do so in the last analysis might mean the invoking of the wrath of the people.

Another important consideration in favour of government giving heed to public opinion is the well-known argument that it is the wearer who knows where the shoe pinches. The best judge of a thing is not the expert who makes it, but the person who uses it. To use Aristotle's language, the guest is a better judge of the dishes served than the cook. To lay aside all figurative language, that opinion which is formulated by the people is likely to serve them better and last longer than any other opinion.

Evaluation of public opinion. It is not always easy to detect public opinion and when detected to be sure that it is both 'public' and 'opinion'. If public opinion is to be a blessing and not an engine of oppression, it is necessary to distinguish between true public opinion and false public opinion. In modern society a great deal of what passes for public opinion is manufactured under highly artificial conditions. It is the opinion shaped and moulded by pressure groups and vested interests of one kind or another. These groups and interests often operate in such a subtle and insidious manner that the public comes to regard it as its own opinion in its own interest, whereas in reality it is the opinion of a few in their self-interest. Those who manufacture public opinion in this manner often play upon the known facts of mass psychology. They play upon people's fears and hatreds, their prejudices and inhibitions. Sometimes they flatter the public; and at other times they cajole it.

Among the agencies which mould public opinion, a prior place should be given to newspapers. People are often influenced in their thinking by the particular slant of their favourite newspaper. While the conscientious person would want to find out something of the background of the one editing or managing it or of the interests, individual or chain, which own it, the bulk of newspaper readers do not exercise such care. This means that newspapers and news agencies such as the Reuter and the Press Trust of India come to have undue control over the minds of readers.

Equally important as newspapers are well-organized political parties, communal groups, and pressure groups of one kind or another. In Soviet Russia members of the Communist Party constitute only a small percentage of the total population. The rest are inert and may or may not support the opinions of the Communist Party. Yet what passes as 'public opinion' in that country is often the views of the inner clique within the party. Although the same is not true in India to the same extent, it is possible to argue that on many issues public opinion may be synonymous with the views of the Congress High Command. This does not mean that views are necessarily selfish or anti-national. All that it means is that it may not be truly representative. In Communist China such public opinion as there may be is the result of careful 'brain-washing'. It may be that many in that country applaud the achievements of their government without applauding the means of those achievements.

In a country like India where communal and sectarian loyalties are still strong, the public opinion of a given group may often run counter to the well-being of the country as a whole. This means that in a given country, instead of one public opinion there may be a rising gradation of public opinions—local, state, linguistic, communal or sectarian, national, and international. Many enlightened people today believe that national and international loyalties should be given a higher place and the lesser loyalties should be integrated into them so long as they are not diametrically opposed to them. Integration is the magic word in this connection. If a lesser loyalty or lesser public opinion cannot be integrated, it should be rejected.

The Roman Catholic countries as a whole and in many Moslem lands the Church or the Mosque takes a leading part in moulding public opinion. An instance in point pertaining to Catholic countries is the practically uniform opinion held by Catholics on the question of birth control. Many Moslem lands still adhere to medieval ideas concerning the State, property and inheritance, marriage and women, and the treatment of 'infidels'. In such countries enlightened public opinion has an uphill task to perform.

The influence of pressure groups is best seen in a country like the United States where there are lobbies of various kinds trying to influence legislature at all levels. There are lobbies representing chambers of commerce, the National Association of Manufacturers, farmers, organized labour, minority groups of different kinds, such as the Jews and Negroes, churches etc. The influence of these groups is not necessarily bad or underground. In the case of some at least there is reason to think that their influence is not all to the good.

Even government may become a pressure group. This is particularly true when a war is on or when the people are to be whipped up to the acceptance of a certain plan or programme sponsored by the government. Practically every government today has a well-organized department of information, publicity or public relations. Not satisfied with that they are setting up information services in other lands with the approval of the countries concerned. Government propaganda is often highly coloured and is not always completely true to facts. A high degree of selective process is resorted to in the selection of news and views; and such news and views as are selected are presented in the most plausible manner.

All of this does not mean that government or other pressure groups are impervious to the feeling, wishes, and inchoate ideas of the people. In a well-ordered government care is taken to find out what people think and feel and how they react to certain policies and measures before decisions are taken. At the same time, it must be said that governments are not so customer-sensitive as big business is. In the United States big departmental stores, restaurants and hotels conduct intensive research into the needs, desires, and reactions of the consuming public. They even create needs where there may be none. Governments generally are bureaucratic and believe that they know what is good for the people without conducting a minute and painstaking research into customer needs and reactions.

One of the checks upon the possibility of a government running amuck and ignoring the people is the fear of revolution. Where people feel keenly conscious that deliberate wrong has been done to them, they may be driven to revolution. Such revolutions are rare in the English-speaking world because mistakes are corrected before such proportions are reached. In the Latin American countries, on the other hand, where people seem to be more volatile and emotional, revolutions are more frequent. But revolutions there do not always mean a clear-cut verdict in favour of public opinion.

It is desirable that public opinion and general will should be synonymous conceptions. But under the conditions described above they are not necessarily the same. In some extreme cases public opinion may be the collective selfishness of a few or even of many. As Aristotle pointed out long time ago, the rule by the many in the interest of the many is not true democracy; nor is it a manifestation of the general will. It should be in the interest of all.

The formulation and promulgation of sound public opinion calls for the following :—

(1) Free access to facts, to all facts and not only to one set of facts favourable to those setting them forth;

(2) Objectivity of outlook, calm reflection, and mature judgment on

the part of the leaders as well as the led. If people are to have an important share in the creation of public opinion, people should be well-educated, reflective, and free from prejudices, with a certain amount of leisure for the weighing of evidence and the reaching of well-reasoned conclusions.

(3) Individuality or independence of character. One should be willing to stand up for one's convictions and not simply swim with the current.

(4) Relative freedom from the rigid control of political parties, trade unions, ecclesiastical or sectarian authorities, and communal or linguistic groups.

Though public opinion may be hard to discover, it is the only solid basis on which an enduring democracy can be built.

CRISIS IN LIBERAL DEMOCRACY

According to G. D. H. Cole and Laski, the twentieth century is an epoch of critical transition when a new social order is struggling to be born replacing the old order of capitalism. The emergence of this new social order has necessitated a reorganisation of our legal system and political institutions. There has developed a fundamental conflict between the economic purposes of capitalism and the political aspirations of a representative democracy. The logic of social evolution requires the abandonment of capitalistic methods of production and their replacement by socialistic methods. Laski is in search of a formula which can remodel the liberal state in such a way as to bring about the intended socio-economic changes in a peaceful way. How far he has succeeded in finding this formula is a matter of controversy and Laski himself is sceptical whether the formulation of such a technique is really possible.

Merits of the Liberal Democratic State

It was widely believed in the nineteenth century that the superiority of a liberal democratic state over other polities lay in its performance of three specific functions. In the first place, it secured order in the community and its coercive power was exercised with the consent of the majority. Secondly, it provided a technique of peaceful change whereby the community could elect the rulers of its own choice after each general election. Thirdly, it worked for the benefit of the largest possible majority of the nation. Laski is of opinion that the liberal democratic state no longer provides the technique of peaceful change in the existing era of transition from capitalism to socialism. It is also an illusion to think that the liberal state has worked in the interests of an overwhelming majority in the community.

Class Character of the Liberal Democratic State

It is true that the state secures order apparently with the consent of a majority of the electorate. As a matter of fact, this consent is fraudulently obtained. The coercive power of the state is always exercised in the interest of those who own the instruments of production. As Laski says, "The State expresses a will to maintain a given system of class-relations. It does so by the use of its supreme coercive power to that end. In the last analaysis, this power consists of the defence forces of the state. These are used, in ultimate challenge, to impose the will of the owners of the instruments of production upon those excluded from such ownership" *(47:3)*. Thus Laski clearly emphasizes the class character of the liberal democratic state. Moreover, it also implies that any fundamental alteration of class relations cannot be achieved by peaceful means because the owners of the instruments of production are bound to resist it by the use of force including the military force at the command of the state. In these circumstances, any substantial change in the existing class relations of a capitalist society can be achieved only by means of social revolution involving the necessary use of force.

Profit Motive and Economic Inequality

The claim of the liberal democratic state that it secures the benefit of an overwhelming majority is also unjustifiable in the light of historical facts. In a capitalistic society, the incentive to production is the motive of maximum profit for the capitalist which is obtained by exploiting the workers. While the capitalist takes for himself the maximum profit, the worker never receives the just reward of his labour. Thus the opulence of the rich goes side by side with the misery of the many under a capitalistic system. The liberal state has continuously maintained this unjust distribution of wealth in the community. The legal postulates of the liberal state effectively protect private ownership of the means of production and support the glaringly unjust system of differential rewards to labour and capital. The state under the conditions of liberal democracy brings benefit only to a handful of capitalists who are permitted by its legal postulates to exploit the rest of the community. Thus both the assumptions of liberalism that the liberal state provides a technique of peaceful change and that it secures the benefit of an overwhelming majority have been falsified in practice.

The Marxian Criticism of the Liberal Theory

This type of criticism of the liberal theory was first advanced by Marx and Engels in their classical formulation of the doctrines of scientific socialism. "Broadly speaking", says Laski, "the Marxian theory of the state has so defined its nature and functioning as to enable us to predict with assurance the course its operations will follow. As an index to the problems of our age it decisively, in my judgment, holds the field" *(47:5)*. About the idealist theory of the state, Laski says that it is a theory of the conceptual state which has nothing to do with the real states as they exist in this imperfect world. About the liberal and anti-idealist standpoint of Hobhouse, he says that his theory is based on an unproved conviction that reason will always be victorious in matters of social conflict.

Law and Class Relations

Laski regards Austin's theory of law as inadequate for the purposes of political science. He thinks that this theory only gives a formal view of the nature of law without explaining its substance. "In the last forty years", says Laski, "there has been a growing movement towards a less formal, and more realistic, jurisprudence. The relation between sociology and law has grown ever more intimate; and a jurisprudence of formal concepts now satisfies few save the veterans of an earlier age" (*47:6*). To say that the law is a command of the sovereign merely explains the mode of its formulation. The content of the law can be known only by a reference to the economic relations of a given society. As Laski puts it, "Law in a feudal state is made as law because it is useful to the owners of land; the reason it embodies is their reason; the general end of society it seeks to fulfil is their conception of what that general end should be; the canons of behaviour it will seek to enforce will derive from their conception of how demand may best be maximised. In a capitalistic society, like Great Britain, for instance, the substance of law will similarly, be predominantly determined by the owners of capital. In a socialist society, like Soviet Russia, the substance of the means of production subordinates the interest of a class to the interest of the society as a whole" (*47:7*).

In a capitalist society, law has consistently served the purposes of capitalism. The proceedings of the British and American courts contain numerous examples to show that the laws of the liberal democratic state have been designed to protect the interests of the capitalist class. Laski does not agree with the liberal view that the purpose of the law in the liberal state is to secure the common good. He criticized Dean Pound's theory of law as essentially Hegelian in character which ignores the class basis of the legal postulates of the liberal state. Social revolution can succeed only when the entire legal structure of the existing society is changed. The socialist way of life requires a new set of legal postulates in the absence of which it cannot operate with success.

Alliance of Liberalism with Capitalism

The fundamental weakness of the liberal theory is that its legal postulates and political institutions have been wedded to an economic system which is oligarchical in character. Liberalism in practice meant an uneasy alliance between a political democracy and an economic oligarchy. The liberal democratic states, which functioned as capitalist oligarchies in their own countries, became imperialistic tyrannies in relation to their colonies. When capitalism was in its early phase of expansion, the alliance between the capitalist oligarchy and the representative democracy worked successfully. The masses accepted the capitalist leadership of the state because their condition also improved on account of a partial share given to them in the rich booty obtained from the colonial countries. When capitalism entered into a period of contraction, when there were no more colonies to be conquered and shared, the old alliance could not be maintained for the simple reason that the masses now wanted to redefine economic relations in their own favour. In certain countries like Italy and Germany, the capitalist class resolved this crisis by withdrawing the institutions of liberal democracy and installing fascist dictatorships in their place. The capitalist class thus showed greater love for its vested interests than for the institutions of liberal democracy.

Need for Socialist Democracy

Laski thinks that socialist democracy is the only correct answer to the liberal democracy of the past. But he is a bit pessimistic about the achievement of socialism by peaceful means. The example of Soviet Russia shows that the violent means alone could establish socialism. But Russia before the socialist revolution was an autocracy. Will it be possible to achieve socialism by constitutional means in parliamentary democracies? The examples of Italy, Germany and Spain have shown that the ruling classes resort to fascism whenever they see a real danger to their vested interests. Laski does not believe in the Communist methods of insurrection and civil war because they lead inevitably towards an authoritarian government or dictatorship. He is a democratic socialist who wants to bring about socialism without destroying the parliamentary institutions of liberalism and without resorting to a dictatorship of the Communist type.

But as a realist Laski knows that the parliamentary victory of a socialist party does not necessarily mean the victory of socialism in the social and economic sphere. Such an electoral victory is only a beginning of the march towards the distant goal of socialism. Any socialist party, which is successful at the polls, must know that important branches of government like the civil service, the army, the police and the judiciary still remain in the hands of those who will zealously act to defend the *status quo* and resist any radical change in the economic structure and social habits of the community.

Laski does not clearly suggest how a successful socialist party is to overcome this concerted opposition of the army, the bureaucracy and the courts. However, he entertains an intuitive belief in the superiority of the constitutional method to the insurrectionary method so long as the capitalist class itself does not resort to fascism. Laski thinks that the insurrectionary methods, if adopted by the working class, might themselves lead to the establishment of fascism by the ruling class. Thus he retains his faith in the fundamental liberal values of constitutionalism, individual liberty and parliamentary government despite his passion for social justice, economic equality and a collectivistic utopia in which all men will live as brothers.

CHAPTER 26

THEORIES OF DEMOCRACY

The Elitist Theory of Democracy

Mosca propounded the elitist theory of democracy in his famous work *The Ruling Class.* After him, Pareto discussed the elite theory of democracy in his book *Mind and Society.* Roberto Michels analysed the elitist role of political parties in a democracy in his book *Political Parties.* The views of Mosca and Pareto are generally identical with each other. Both emphasized the application of the sociological method to the study of politics and democracy. While Mosca displayed great interest in political analysis, Pareto was more interested in general social analysis and the study of social problems as a whole. Both of them rejected the classical theory of democracy as a government of the people and argued that society is invariably divided between a minority which rules and the majority which is subject to its rule. Both emphasized the irrational basis of politics and believed that talent and intelligence was a monopoly of the few who constituted the elite. Both thought that war and revolution were inevitable in every age. History shows that there is a continuous change of ruling classes from time to time. They proposed the law of the circulation of elites in history. No political system or regime could be regarded as stable or permanent.

According to Mosca, classification of governments into monarchy, oligarchy or democracy was not at all meaningful. There has been essentially one type of government in history, that is oligarchy. He says that starting from early underdeveloped social structures, when the elements of civilization were barely visible, up to the highly developed social structures of today, we can always distinguish between the elite which governs and masses over which the elite exercises its authority. The elite, which is a minority, enjoys all the privileges and comforts which flow from its monopolistic control of power in society. The masses, who constitute a majority, obey the commands of the elite. These commands may be enforced legally as well as illegally. The masses work in order to satisfy the wants of the ruling class.

This ruling class need not be autocratic. Irrespective of the character of a regime, the common people do influence the political behaviour of the elite. In a democratic regime, this influence is exercised through peaceful elections and formation of interest groups. In an aristocratic regime, the elite can be pressurized through agitations and violent rebellions. However, no elite can go on ruling permanently. Heredity, ideology and force are used by the elite to maintain its power but ultimately all elites are dethroned. Perpetual exercise of authority makes the ruling elite lazy, weak and luxury-loving. When this happens, a group of talented and industrious individuals revolts and captures power from the enfeebled elite. They now constitute a new ruling elite.

Every ruling elite uses a political formula to stabilise its rule. Political elites of a civilized society do not want to justify their right to rule in terms of naked force. They prefer to legitimize their authority in terms of legal and moral principles and popularly accepted traditions and beliefs. The basis of the political formula legitimising the rule of an elite is invariably a half-truth or a myth acceptable to the highly gullible masses. The political formula is a device to preserve the unity and solidarity of races, cultures and political regimes.

The elites, which can adapt themselves to changing environments, may retain their authority. This was the case with the British aristocracy after the democratic revolution. The elites which fail to transform themselves in accordance with the changing circumstance, fall from power. The French aristocracy lost power because it failed to adjust itself to new democratic surroundings. Mosca says that a clever elite would allow gradual expansion of its membership by recruiting new members from the subject classes on the basis of talent and merit. The elite ought to include all important elements representing wealth, military power, religion, education, science etc. in order to survive successfully. Mosca admired the Prussian ruling elite in Germany as the best possible combination of ideal traits required for a ruling class. He admired the anti-democratic ideas of Bismarck, Cavour and Hegel. According to Mosca, the democratic elites of England, Switzerland and the United States also possessed the qualities of a good ruling class. The apparent success of these democratic regimes was essentially the success of a highly talented ruling class which governed all of them.

Pareto also thought that democracy was unrealizable. He regarded socialism and humanism, the inevitable allies of democracy, as hypocrisy and delusion. He regarded men as weak and depraved beings, who neither knew the art of self-government nor understood the principle of social control. According to Pareto, man is guided by his sentiments and passions. He uses logic merely to justify and rationalize his irrational behaviour. Man is basically a creature of impulses and instincts.

Every society has two types of individuals : foxes and lions. The foxes are bold and courageous; they are not cautious but use their cunningness to survive. In the economic field, individuals with foxlike qualities are prepared to take risks, involve themselves in speculation and other schemes of earning profits. On the contrary, the lions are strong, conservative, tradition-loving, orthodox and loyal to the ideals of family, religion and country. They prefer to use force to using cleverness. They like stable income from rent or interest. People get their rulers from these two categories of lions and foxes in accordance with their own sentiments and passions.

According to Pareto, society can be divided between an elite and a non-elite. The elite can be further sub-divided between a governing elite and a counter-elite. The counter-elite includes individuals who aspire to govern in future due to their success in non-political areas of activity. According to Pareto, elites are formed in all professions including the prostitutes and thieves. There is an uninterrupted cycle of the rise and decline of elites in history. In every society, the talented and more meritorious members of the lower classes become new claimants for elitist status and privileges. Thus the elites rise and fall from power. History is virtually a graveyard of the numerious fallen elites. In capitalist society, private enterprise helps the transformation of the existing elites but democracy, which encourages the labour syndicates to pressurize the government and persuade it to regulate and control economic life in new directions, prevents progress.

Pareto's main interest was in the nature of the governing elite. In democracy, top leaders of political parties constitute the governing elite. Their power is based partly on force and partly on consent but the element of force in this mixture is more significant. The governing elite uses bribery, deceit and cunningness to secure the consent of the subject classes. The rulers can secure obedience from dissatisfied minorities by the use of money but they must use force to keep the masses under their control. An elite, which is not capable of using force, does not deserve to continue as a ruling elite. A weak elite is easily overthrown by a new counter-elite, which becomes the next ruling elite. Generally, new elites come to power by using force and preserve their authority with the help of superior force. Even the ruling elite of a democratic regime has to use violence and force whenever it is challenged by the organised power of the masses.

Michels, who agrees with Mosca and Pareto in his elitist view of democracy, disagrees with them on one point. He argues that no elite loses its power and rights completely when it is overthrown. Both in France and England, members of the bourgeoisie penetrated the ranks of the aristocratic elite gradually and overthrew it ultimately. Even then, the members of the overthrown aristocracy continued to enjoy many of their privileges as associates of the new bourgeois elite. They continued to occupy top positions in the government.

The most important contribution of Michels was in the field of political parties, which were essentially oligarchical structures according to the analysis of this author. He propounded the famous law known as the iron law of oligarchy about the structure and functioning of parties in a democracy. Every political party needs a small clique of leaders and officials to run its organisation. With the expansion of the size and activities of the party, the controlling power of the leaders also increases. The leaders are always anxious to preserve their exclusive control of the party apparatus. They become accustomed to a life of luxury and comforts. Even the leaders of the German Social Democratic Party claimed and received salaries which were equal to the highest paid civil servants in the government or managers in industry.

According to Michels, the power of the elite depends upon the peculiar psychology of the common people. Many people are indifferent, lazy and servile by nature. They dislike freedom and feel secure in the presence of a leader who can lead them. They are superstitious, timid and habitually obedient. This gives an opportunity to the elite to ride on their shoulders and command them to march in the desired direction. As Michels says, the rules aimed at reducing the power of leaders in the party remain ineffective because the masses feel a masochistic delight in being whipped.

The Pluralist Theory of Democracy

Today, some Western writers have propounded a pluralist theory of democracy based on the competitive character of governing elites in modern democracies. Lipset advocates this view of democracy in his book *Political Man.* Dahrendarf supports the same view in his *Classes in Industrial Society.* Robert Dahl has explained his pluralist theory of democracy in *A Preface to Democratic Theory* and *Polyarchy*. According to these writers, society consists of diverse interest groups and the elites which lead them. They raise their demands directly or through the mediating agency of political parties on the political system. No group or elite is so powerful as to dominate the government to such an extent that it may implement all its demands completely. No social class can really control the machinery of government to the total exclusion of all other competing classes or groups.

As Robert Dahl says, there are several places where decisions are being made. Merchants, industrialists, trade unions, farmers' associations, consumers, politicians, voters and many other groups and associations influence policy-making in government. No one succeeds in obtaining full satisfaction of its demands. Some groups may be more influential than others though it is difficult to measure the different degrees of this influence exactly. Moreover, the groups have greater power to resist policies which are not wanted and relatively less power to get desired policies implemented by the government.

Robert Dahl admits that the formation of elites is quite natural even in a democratic society but he rejects the notion of the power elite and the ruling class. The theory of the ruling class is based more on imagination than on empirical facts. In his empirical survey of New Haven in his book *Who Governs,* Robert Dahl concluded that the city was governed by a combination of elites in the cultural and economic fields but none of these competing elites could be described as a ruling elite. They together also did not constitute a power elite. The political elite of the United States both at national and local levels is a democratically competing pluralist leadership drawn from a large number of elites in different fields of activity.

As R.P. Wolfe says about the American Congress, the diverse interest groups of the nation either through the two national parties or through their own pressure groups try to influence the course of legislation there. The laws, which are ultimately passed and implemented by the government, represent a compromise between the forces of labour and capital as well as the organised power of other intermediary groups. C. Wright Mills does not agree with the pluralist theory of democracy. He believes that the United States is today ruled by a power elite which represents an organic fusion of three elites—the big corporations, top leaders of the two national parties and the military leaders.

The Marxist Theory of Democracy

Marx was a democratic republican for about two years 1842-43 before his conversion to communism and this period coincides with his journalistic work for the *Rheinische Zeitung*. He wrote twelve essays during this period to express the principal tenets of his democratic convictions. There is no evidence that Marx rejected his basic beliefs about democracy when he embraced the socialist philosophy. His defence of the freedom of the press and opposition to the Prussian institution of censorship is well-known. Marx saw no danger in diversity of opinion but regarded as natural that a politically mature nation would have a press representing the various "doctrines of the people and its parties". He justified the existence of several parties in a democracy and said: "Without parties there is no development, without division, no progress". Richard N. Hunt says: "Even after becoming a communist, Marx never repudiated these early articles in which he defended freedom of expression with such fervour and wit. Indeed, in 1851, he had them all published in book form without altering their substance in even the smallest detail." (*207 :34*).

For Marx, philosophy was a critical activity of applying free reason to human problems. Thus human institutions, as they ought to be, could be discovered by extracting from imperfect existing institutions their inner rational principle or essence. The essence of Marx was not the Absolute Idea of Hegel but a human conception developing through man's life-process. Freedom is surely the species-essence of man and critical philosophy as paraxis is the liberator of mankind. Free press in a democratic state is the condition of other freedoms and also the principal instrument for achieving general emancipation of man.

Philosophy demands that the state should be the state of human nature, that is, that society should conform to man's essence and serve his essential needs. Absolute monarchy cannot establish such a state. Only democracy can help establishing the state on a rational basis. Marx criticized the arbitrary laws of the monarchical state as representing irrational privileges. Only democracy can make laws based on reason and universal rights. As Richard N. Hunt puts it: "In dealing with the formulation of law, Marx combined his strict rationalism with an unquestioning belief in popular sovereignty. True law will emerge only when 'law is the conscious expression of the will of the people, created, with and through it'. Implicitly assumed was his faith that the people, given the choice, would will the rational ......The problem which so exercised Rousseau and his totalitarian-democratic disciples concerning possible differences between the "will of all" and the "general will" did not engage Marx's attention." (*207* : *39*).

In these essays, Marx contrasted the sham Parliament of Prussia and other provincial diets with the representative assemblies of Britain and France saying: "In Britain and France, deputies do not speak for estates but are elected as representatives of the people......Because of their peculiar composition, the provincial diets are nothing but a society of special requirements against the state." (*207* : *40*). He also criticised the principle of aristocratic heredity, domination of the landed interest, property qualifications for franchise, under-respresentation of the urban communities etc. in tht Prussian political system.

Marx was a principled democratic republican at this time who demanded equal territorial representation for the people on the basis of universal suffrage. Marx wanted the popular will to permeate the executive as well as the legislative branch of the government. Within the executive branch of government, the character of the bureaucracy attracted Marx's special attention. He argued that bureaucrats in the Prussian state were not neutral and had become a party in social conflict. He also assailed the bureaucracy on the ground that in a non-democratic state, it emerged as self-interested party within society opposed to its general interest. Marx said: "If the official charges that the private individual is elevating his private interest into the interest of the state, so the private individual may charge that the official debases the interest of the state into his own private interest, an interest from which all others are excluded as laymen, so that even the clearest reality appears illusory to him as against the reality presented in the official reports." (*207* : *43*).

Marx's love for democratic freedom and his hatred for barbarian despotic rule of the Prussian absolute monarchy has been thus expressed: "Freedom, the feeling of man's dignity, will have to be awakened again in these men. Only this freedom, which disappeared from the world with the Greeks and with Christianity vanished into the blue mist of heaven, can transform society into a community of men to achieve their highest purpose, a democratic state. The people, though, who do not feel themselves to be men, grow attached to their masters, like a herd of slaves or horses. The hereditary masters are the purpose of this whole society. They stand where their feet have grown, on the necks of these political animals that know no other destination than to be attached to their masters and subject to them to be at their disposal. The world of the Philistine is the *political animal kingdom,* and if we have to recognize its existence, we simply must acknowledge the *status quo.* Centuries of barbarism created and formed it, and now it exists as a consistent system, whose principle is a *world dehumanized*.... Despotism's only idea is contempt for man, dehumanized man, and this idea further has the advantage over many others of being fact. A despot always sees men as degraded. He sees them drown for him in the mud of common life from which they again and again emerge like toads... Once one has reached the threshold of the political animal kingdom, no further movement and no other withdrawal are possible than to leave its basis and enter the human world of democracy." (*207* : *47*).

Marx's early critique of despotism was based on his concept of humanism. He had not yet developed the class perspective on democracy. As Richard N. Hunt says, the central ideas of 'totalitarian democracy' as mentioned by Talmon, cannot be found in the writings of young Marx. As yet, there is no concept of an organized vanguard party, no appeal for terror in any form, no call for revolution of any type and no desire to silence dissent. On the other hand, his devotion to the goal of human freedom, his respect for law as a human need, his concern for separation of powers in a democratic state and his passionate defence of individual rights against bureaucratic tyranny can safely place this young Marx within the liberal-democratic tradition.

The Class Perspective on Democracy

After his conversion to communism, Marx developed his concept of bourgeois democracy with a class perspective on democracy. He now distinguished between the political emancipation and the general human emancipation. "Political emancipation", he said, "is indeed a great leap forward. It is not, to be sure, the final form of universal human emancipation, but it is the final form *within* the prevailing order of things." Throughout his life, as we shall see, formal democracy without socialism i.e. bourgeois democracy was for Marx not *worthless* but *inadequate.* Democracy without socialism was certainly superior to feudal, monarchical and absolutist forms of government. So long as the civil society was organised on the basis of private property, bourgeois democracy was the best possible political system—the perfected political state.

The bourgeois state, like religion, represented a form of human alienation. Marx said : "By its nature of perfected political state is man's species-life in opposition to this material life. All the presuppositions of this egoistic life remain in *civil society outside* the state, but as qualities of civil society. Where the political state has achieved its full development, man leads a double life, a heavenly and an earthly life, not only in thought or consciousness but in *actuality.* In the *political community* he regards himself as a *communal being*; but in *civil society* he is active as a *private individual,* treats other men as means, reduces himself to a means, and becomes the plaything of alien powers. The political state is as spiritual in relation to civil society as heaven is in relation to earth." (*207* : *70*).

Just as religious man imagines a heaven of ideal communal life, so the political man aspires to see in a democratic republic a vision of ideal communal living. But both are illusions, which do not conform to the tragic reality of the egoism and class conflict of the bourgeois economic order, which Marx calls the civil society. The practical application of the right of liberty is the right of private property, to enjoy and dispose of one's possessions as one wills, without regard for other men and independently of society. In bourgeois democracy, it is the right of self-interest, or the organised self-interest of the bourgeois class as a whole.

In his *Paris Manuscripts* of 1844 Marx tried to put forward his concept of true democracy which accomplishes general human emancipation. He regards political freedom of bourgeois democracy only as a first step in the direction of man's total freedom. Though he is contemptuous of the so called rights of bourgeois democracy on the whole, yet he feels that the rights of free expression, free assembly, free association etc. coupled with universal suffrage would enable the oppressed masses to organise and struggle for their general human emancipation. Marx was still to develop his economic doctrines, but his moral commitment to communism is quite clear in the *Paris Manuscripts.* Marx wanted true democracy to be classless and propertyless and in the final analysis it was a social concept which could be realized by abolishing the coercive state apparatus.

Marx had criticized earlier the law of primogeniture and feudal forms of property. He now declared that all forms of private property including bourgeois property were inconsistent with man's freedom in a true democracy. Marx's hatred for the hereditary caste system of medieval Europe, which he called as "the animal history of mankind, its zoology" has already been pointed out. He had welcomed the French Revolution which eliminated these legal estates and their political functions. Political classes now become merely social classes where wealth and education determined the social ranks. But equality hardly characterized the new social system. Just as the Christians are equal in heaven yet unequal on earth, so the individuals in a bourgeois democracy are equal in the heaven of their political world but unequal in their earthly existence and possessions.

Bourgeois democracy may abolish property qualifications for voters and their representatives but it cannot abolish private property and unequal possessions. It declares birth, social rank, education, occupation and class as *non-political* distinctions and proclaims that irrespective of these distinctions, all citizens are equal partners in political sovereignty. The fact is that bourgeois democracy presupposes these actual differences and considers them ever-lasting. True democracy, says Marx, demands the negation of private property i.e. the negation of all non-political distinctions in actuality. True democracy demands an end to class structure based on the capitalist mode of production. True democracy demands an end of the alienated condition of man exemplified by wage labour, money, private property, division of labour and religion. True democracy provides the radical critique of the existing society and in its political and ideological superstructures. Marx said : "To be radical is to grasp things by the root. But for man the root is man himself......The criticism of ruling ends with the doctrine that *man* is the *highest being for man,* hence with the categorical imperative to overthrow all conditions in which man is degraded, enslaved, neglected, contemptible being." (*207 : 77*).

True democracy of Marx is not only anti-class, it is also anti-state. He started with the premise that popular sovereignty is the underlying authority of the people to form and reform their own institutions. He criticized Hegel for his assertion that the people, even if they wanted to, had no right to alter the monarchical constitution. To Marx it meant another instance of the man allowing himself to be ruled by an alien power that was in reality his own creation. Marx said : "The question is simply this : Does the people have the right to give itself a new constitution ? The answer must be an unqualified yes, because the constitution becomes a practical illusion the moment it ceases to be a true expression of the people's will........Just as it is not religion that creates man but man who creates religion, so it is not the constitution that creates the people but the people which creates the constitution....Democracy is the resolved mystery of all constitutions. Here the constitution is returned to its real ground, actual man, the actual people, and established as its own work. The constitution appears as what it is, the free product of men." (*207* : *78*).

To Marx a popular revolution is needed to bring about the social order based on true democracy. Civil society and the state will be destroyed through a popular revolution in their old forms and will be transcended in a higher unity, where neither would be distinguishable from the other. As Richard N. Hunt puts it: "The chief characteristic of the old order, egoism, would disappear in favour of the species-life. In civil society this would mean the disappearance of private property, the legal recognition of selfishness–in favour of communal property. In political life it would mean the disappearance of the self-interested state as an institution standing over civil society and alienated from it." (*207* : *79*).

The dissolution of the old state does not mean that there would be no arrangements at all for making and carrying out collective decisions. Marx did not think that the socialist commonwealth will merely be conventional democratic republic supervising a nationalised economic system, which became the social-democratic concept after some time. Marx advocated a thoroughgoing democratisation of executive power not only at the top but at all levels and in all departments. He wanted to destroy the bureaucratic state by eliminating the profession of governing i.e. professional politicians, professional army and police and professional officials and judges. In short, it had no place for Hegel's universal class, the bureaucracy. His ideas on the legislative branch were equally radical and democratic. He expected that the people would vote on important legislative matters by referendum in addition to holding elections for the representative assembly. He wanted the judiciary to be elective as well.

In purely political terms, Richard N. Hunt feels that Marx's vision of true democracy ran parallel to the conception of democracy prevailing in Periclean Athens i.e. direct, participatory democracy of classical *polis* minus its class structure based on slavery: "Communist men would no longer separate their own collective power from themselves and turn it over, as alienated 'political' power to the professionals who run an institutionalized state. And their own activities as citizens would no longer be infrequent and unreal, but would become a meaningful part of their daily lives–they would have absorbed the abstract 'citizen' back within themselves. It is in this sense that Marx embraced communism to resolve the political as much as the socio-economic dilemmas of modern society." (*207* : *82*).

Concept of Proletarian Dictatorship

Unfriendly critics of Marx suggest that advocacy of violent revolution is undemocratic *per se*. We forget that Marx and Engels lived most of their lives in the pre-democratic era of European history. Moreover, all communist revolutions have occurred in countries–Russia, China, Cuba etc.–which were undemocratic earlier. The strategies for socialist revolutions advocated by Marx, Engels, Lenin and Mao Tse-tung have been based either on the concept of the *proletarian majority revolution* or on the concept of the alliance of the *majority classes*. Even some bourgeois writers have endorsed the initial popular character of almost all major communist revolutions. It should not be forgotten that bourgeois democracy is itself a product of violent revolutions e.g. the English Revolutions of 1649, the American Revolution of 1776, the French Revolution of 1789 and the European Revolutions of 1848. Unlike Babeauf and Blanqui, the Marxists have never advocated a strategy of minority revolution. The following pronouncements by Marx and Engels in this respect deserve attention : "Democracy has become a proletarian principle, a principle of the masses. . . .The democratic masses can safely be counted in the reckoning of communist forces. The first basic condition for the introduction of a community of goods is the political liberation of the proletariat by means of a *democratic* state constitution. . . . in the first place it will draw up a *democratic constitution* and by means of this establish directly or indirectly the political rule of the proletariat. . . . The first step in the revolution by working-class, is to raise the proletariat to the position of the ruling class, to win the battle of democracy." (*207 : 135*).

Marxism thus should be distinguished from Blanquism, which suggested a strategy of minority revolution as well as defined post-revolutionary regime as the dictatorship of the revolutionary elite. Marx himself complained that his concept of revolution was being unjustly associated with that of Blanqui : "The proletariat rallies more and more round *revolutionary socialism,* round communism, for which the bourgeoisie has itself invented the name of *Blanqui.* This socialism is the *declaration of the permeance of the revolution, the class dictatorship of the proletariat* as the necessary transit point to the *abolition of class distinctions generally.*" (*207 : 302*).

The Communist League, which Marx and Engels had formed, was not a vanguard party for master-minding a minority revolution by an elite. Marx's concept of the revolutionary party was based on the principles of internal structural democracy and not the "iron law of oligarchy". Though Lenin and Mao Tse-tung did develop the concept of a vanguard party, they too did not want to create a totalitarian party structure and did not believe in the strategy of a minority revolution imposed from above.

If Marx and Engels really stood for a *democratically* organised party and a *democratic* majority revolution, why did they want to follow it all by dictatorship ? What sort of dictatorship did they want to institute ? Are their statements on the post-revolutionary state so confusing as to permit any inference from Bernstein to Kautsky to Joseph Stalin. Hal Draper says that Marx used this phrase at eleven places only in the forty odd volumes of his collected works and a study of the concept in the context of its appearance proves adequately the *democratic* credentials of the two founders of classical *communism.*

Marx used the term dictatorship in the sense of the rule of a particular social class and not as a government of a single party, a clique or an individual. He used the term dictatorship of the bourgeoisie to signify different forms of bourgeois government varying from absolute monarchy to constitutional monarchy and democratic republic. Similarly, he used the term dictatorship of the proletariat to signify different forms of proletarian government. Engels once clearly distinguished his own conception of proletarian rule as a rule of the entire class of the proletariat and Blanqui's conception of dictatorship of the proletariat as a dictatorship of one or several individuals. Engels said: "From Blanqui's conception that every revolution is a surprise attack by a small revolutionary minority, there follows of itself the necessity for a dictatorship after the success of the venture. This would be, to be sure, a dictatorship not of the entire revolutionary class, the proletariat, but of the small number who have made the surprise attack, and who are themselves previously organized under the dictatorship of one or several individuals." *(239 : 237)*

Unfortunately, the historical experience of the dictatorship of the proletariat has not been in keeping with the conception of proletarian rule as developed by Engels and Marx. Lenin developed the concept of the vanguard communist party and so dictatorship of the proletariat in Russia was transformed into the 'government of a small number' under his leadership. Rosa Luxemburg said that the Bolshevik government under Lenin became the dictatorship of the Central Committee of the Communist Party. Stalin transformed the so-called proletarian dictatorship into a dictatorship of an individual. Richard N. Hunt feels that this was done in violation of the classical Marxist theory of dictatorship of the proletariat as the rule of an entire social class. Under the present rulers of Soviet Russia, the dictatorship of the Central Committee of Communist Party has been restored. The social base of the Russian government today is to be found in a bureaucratic social stratum in the process of becoming a new class.

One reason for this degeneration of the concept of proletarian dictatorship in practice is that socialist revolution has yet to materialize in advanced capitalist societies with bourgeois-democratic state structures. When revolutions occurred in industrially less developed or ex-colonial predominantly agrarian societies, the Communist Parties had to undertake the task of rapid industrialization of these countries on a new socialist basis. This required a more authoritarian, even totalitarian party and state structures than those which could be found in the classical Marxist model of proletarian dictatorship and actual historical experience of popular municipal democracy under the Paris Commune, which failed to survive.

Revolutionary dictatorship of the proletariat represents in Marxist theory the historical epoch of transition from capitalism to socialism to communism. Marx, Engels and Lenin distinguish two phases in the development of socialism and communism. The first or lower phase is still stamped with the birthmarks of the old society from whose womb it emerges. This is the socialist phase, when the available consumer goods are to be distributed among the members of the society according to principle of performance or work. The second phase is called communism in which the sources of production are already flowing so abundantly that distribution of consumer goods is on the principle of human needs. This is the phase when the dictatorship of the proletariat as a state withers away. Ernest Fischer rightly points out: "From the context of Marx's whole body of ideas it emerges with certainty that he imagined the victory of the revolution and of socialism as a more or less simultaneous process in the advanced capitalist countries, and the social order he had before his mind's eye was the one of which the *Communist Manifesto* had said: *the free development of each is the condition for the free development of all.*" (*201:142*).

Marx's vision of a classless society represented a negation of both aspects of the historical state i.e. its parasitical character as well as its social class basis. Speaking about the conception of communism as developed by Marx and Engels, Richard N. Hunt rightly concluded: "Their vision of the ultimate classless society likewise included both states in negation: it would have no institution of government separate and estranged from the people, and it would have no organized coercive force, for none would be needed. Human emancipation and full human freedom would be attained when no external or coercive power existed, and when the *res publica* became the part-time collaboration of all the people rather than the full-time profession of a special body of coercers. Marx and Engels both allowed for the non-professional delegation of authority but insisted on the democratic election of all such officials and appropriate safeguards for their continual accountability, particularly the right of recall. This very radical conception of democracy was linked with a still more radical aspiration to transcend the division of labour altogether. Thus Marx and Engels' version of democracy goes as far beyond today's conventional parliamentary republic as it does beyond the professional non-party dictatorships of the present-day communist world. However much one might like further details and specifications, and however rashly optimistic one may find their aspirations for the mankind, there can be no real question of Marx and Engels' profound democratic conviction." (*207 : 130*).

Karl Popper, Hannah Arendt and Talmon are not convinced that Marx was really a democratic thinker and do not agree that Lenin or Stalin modified his conception of the state. While Popper and Arendt describe Marxism as a totalitarian doctrine, Talmon calls Marx as a totalitarian democrat, who upholds the concept of totalitarian democracy in the tradition of Rousseau, Robespierre, Bebeuf and Blanqui. Isaiah Berlin and George Lichtheim argue that Marx and Engels went through two distinct phases of development and that they were *communist* revolutionaries up to 1850 but matured into *democratic* socialists thereafter. The truth is that no such dichotomy can be detected and proved in classical Marxism, which has presented a thoroughly consistent theory of socialist democracy transcending the assumptions and vision of bourgeois democracy.

Liberal Dimension of Democracy

There is considerable confusion about the concept of democracy, partly because of its use as an ideological weapon. In the history of western political thought, the term 'democracy' has changed its meaning more than once, and in more than one direction. Democracy once used to be a hated word. Nearly all men of culture and intelligence from the earliest historical times down to about a century ago thought that democracy as a rule of the bulk of the people, who were poor and ignorant, was fatal to individual freedom and to all the graces of civilized living. Then, democracy was transformed into a noble ideal. Its full recognition into the ranks of respectability was conceded by the close of the nineteenth century. The First World War was fought by the Allies to make the world safe for their version of democracy. Since then, democracy has remained a noble object and everybody claims to pursue and practise it. Revolutions have been made against the liberal version of democracy in the name of proletarian democracy or people's democracy or several varieties of Asian and African democracy. In these circumstances, democracy has beome an ambiguous thing, with different and mutually contradictory meanings for different nations and their political elites.

It is obvious that the conception of democracy has changed and it will go on changing. After the Second World War, socialist countries have emerged in Europe and Asia, which have rejected the liberal-democratic pattern of political development. On top of this, most of the underdeveloped countries of Asia and Africa have achieved independence in circumstance which have led them to become one party states. Though they have decisively rejected both the ethos and the actual institutions of liberal democracy, yet these countries consider themselves to be democratic in their own unique way. It is obvious that in the changed circumstances, the concept of democracy should not be equated with Western liberal political systems only. The non-liberal systems which prevail in the socialist countries and some third world countries have also a genuine historical claim to the title of democracy.

Another fact about liberal democracy is that it is a system of power by which people can be governed, by which power is exerted by the state over individuals and groups and by which a certain set of relations are enforced between individuals through their rights to property. These relations themselves are relations of power as they give different people in different capacities power over others. History shows that liberal democracy and -capitalism go together. We find that liberal-democratic state coexists with an economic system which is either entirely or predominantly based on capitalist mode of production. With some exceptions such as the rise of fascist regimes between the two world wars, every capitalist country generally has a liberal-democratic political system. This close correspondence between capitalism and liberal-democracy is not merely co-incidental.

In all Western countries the democratic franchise was not introduced until after the liberal society and liberal state were firmly institutionalized. Democracy came as an ornament. It had to adjust itself to the competitive, individualist, market society and to the liberal polity functioning through a system of freely competing oligarchical political parties. Thus the liberal state was gradually democratized by extension of franchise but in this very process, democracy was also liberalized reconciling itself with capitalism.

The liberal state was firmly based on the market economy. In its fully developed form, when most individuals offered their labour on the market to those who possessed accumulated capital on which they hired other people's labour, it is called the capitalist system of production. Capitalist economy was a great liberalizing force. It created a society based on individual mobility, on contract, and on impersonal market allocation of work and rewards in response to individual choices. This society based on individual choices had some defects. There was, nothing democratic about this market economy but it was liberal in its basic assumptions.

To make this society work, a non-arbitrary or responsible government was needed. There had to be certain other liberties such as freedom to form political parties and pressure groups, or freedom of speech and publication. These freedoms could not be limited for ever to men of propertied classes. The essence of the liberal state was the system of alternate or multiple parties whereby governments could be held responsible to different sections of the class or classes that had political voice. Macpherson says, "The market society did produce, after a time, a pressure for democracy which became irresistible. Those who had no vote saw that they had no weight in the political market....So finally the democratic franchise was introduced into the liberal state. It did not come easily or quickly. In most of the present liberal-democratic countries it required many decades of agitation....The female half of the population had to wait even longer for an equal political voice......So democracy came as a late addition to the competitive market society and the liberal state." (*219* : *9*).

By the time democracy came in capitalist countries, it was no longer opposed to the liberal society and the liberal state. It was, by then, no threat to liberal institutions as the working class had now taken its fully and fairly competitive place in the political system. The liberal-democratic state became a welfare state and a regulatory state without transforming the capitalist character of its economic system. Macpherson concludes, "What the addition of democracy to the liberal state did was simply to provide constitutional channels for popular pressures, pressures to which governments would have had to yield in about the same measure anyway, merely to maintain public order and avoid revolution. By admitting the mass of the people into the competitive party system, the liberal state did not abandon its fundamental nature; it simply opened the competitive political system to all the individuals who had been created by the competitive market society. The liberal state fulfilled its own logic. In so doing, it neither destroyed nor weakened itself; it strengthened both itself and the market society. It liberalized democracy while democratizing liberalism." (*219* : *11*).

The Empirical Theory of Democracy

Liberal-democratic theory has been recast in an empirical mould today.

The empirical theory of democracy, also known as the pluralist theory, was first clearly formulated by Joseph A. Schumpeter in his work *Capitalism, Socialism and Democracy* and has been restated by Robert A. Dahl in *A Preface to Democratic Theory* and *Polyarchy*. Both Schumpeter and Dahl have severely criticized what they called the classical theory of democracy, traced back variously but generally represented by J.S. Mill, T. H. Green, Ernest Barker and A.D. Lindsay. They had defined democracy as an ethical concept intended to improve the moral condition of the citizens. Dahl and Schumpeter argue that democracy is a mechanism by which the political system maintains its equilibrium. Macpherson, however, suggests that the pluralist-empirical concept of democracy is quite inadequate as a general theory of democracy. It is regressive even as a general theory of Western democracy. It has done considerable harm to the traditional, normative theory of democracy.

The model of democracy as a competitive struggle among different sections of the political elite has become a part of the orthodoxy for American political scientists. But it destroys the original meaning of democracy as popular or majority rule. This notion, in fact, defines democracy as minority rule and repudiates the egalitarian and developmental content of the original theory of democracy. It proclaims competition between two or more elite groups for the power to govern the whole society as the only adequate and accurate model of democracy. Macpherson says, "Democracy is held to be consistent with, and even to require, a low level of citizen participation : Only so, it is said, is the political system likely to stay in equilibrium. Democracy is reduced from the humanist aspiration to a market equilibrium system. And although the new orthodox theory claims scientific neutrality, its value judgement is clear enough : whatever works, is right—that is, whatever enables the existing class-stratified society to operate without intolerable friction is best." (*218 : 78*).

The pluralist theory of democracy propounded by Dahl, Sartori and other behaviouralists represents a striking reversal of the original nineteenth-century liberal democratic theory. It is an even more striking departure from the truly classical concept of democracy. From Plato to the early nineteenth century, democracy was defined both by its supporters as well as its adversaries as the government of the poor and oppressed and their claim for recognition as equally human beings. Both in the classical and the nineteenth-century traditional concepts of democracy, it meant a social and political order in which all men could enjoy and develop their human qualities and capacities. All this is dismissed as irrelevant by the empiricist theoreticians of pluralist democracy. For them, democracy is simply a mechanism by which citizens can register their demands as voters in the political market. Schumpeter says, "We now take the view that the role of the people is to produce a government, or else an intermediate body which in turn will produce a national executive or government. And we define : the democratic method is that institutional arrangement for arriving at political decisions in which individuals acquire the power to decide by means of a competitive struggle for the people's vote." (*278 : 173*).

Schumpeter claims the following merits for his theory of democracy: (1) It provides "a reasonably efficient criterion by which to distinguish democratic governments from others" because it stresses "a *modus procedendi* the presence or absence of which it is in most cases easy to verify." (2) While the classical theory ignored the phenomenon of leadership, it recognises the vital fact that "collectives act almost exclusively by accepting leadership" which "is the dominant mechanism of practically any collective action which is more than a reflex." (3) It emphasizes the role of "genuine group-wise volitions" in the democratic process and explores the "interaction between sectional interests and public opinion". (4) It defines democracy as "free competition for a free vote" and asserts that "the electoral method is practically the only one available" for conducting this "competitive struggle". (5) It clarifies "the relation that subsists between democracy and individual freedom" and implies the existence of civil liberties. (6) It points out that the only significant manner in which the electorate controls the government is by "refusing to reelect them or the parliamentary majorities that support them". (7) It distinguishes between the will of the majority and the so-called will of 'the people,' which is an abstraction, and then asserts that even the majority has a limited function of choosing "any of the competing individuals or teams" to exercise the power of governance." (*248* : *175*).

Sartori has proposed a similar theory of democracy when he says, "The unorganized majority of the politically inactive becomes the arbiter in the contest among the organized minorities of the politically active. So, no matter how oligarchic the organization of each minority is when examined from within, the result of the competition between them is democracy." (*50* : *124*). Like Robert Dahl, he defines democracy as "an elective polyarchy" but adds that it should not be described as "an *egalitarian* polyarchy" as Dahl suggested but simply as "an *electoral* polyarchy." For Sartori, democracy is "a political system in which *the influence of the majority is assured by elective and competitive minorities to whom it is entrusted.*" Democracy is thus "*a polyarchy of elected elites*" or "*a selective system of competing elected minorities.*" (*50:126*). Robert Dahl believed that minority rule was implied in the notion of democracy as elective polyarchy. He observes, "If we cannot expect citizens always to check leaders...... then we are forced to rely on checks by other leaders." (*189* : *62*).

Unlike Schumpeter or Dahl, Sartori claims that his theory of democracy does not reject the classical doctrine, which, according to him, has a prescriptive validity. The competitive theory merely seeks to develop it to its logical end by adding a descriptive or empirical dimension. The classical conception, he says, is simply an unfinished portrait. He wants to complete this picture by adding "the principle of leadership openly, without the usual guilt complexes." Otherwise, the theory of democracy "will remain unbalanced, only prescriptive and not sufficiently (if at all) operational." (*250* : *127*). Sartori concludes, "One might say that this is an aristocratic theory of democracy as against its *demolatric* version. However, what is the value of the *demolatric* theory of democracy? The voting studies and the opinion polls have confirmed beyond the point of doubt that we have to reckon with a leader-seeking and leader-needing public. On the other hand, our findings prove that the imagery of a self-governing *demos* is either a deceptive myth or a demagogic device, and that in both cases it can only foster the bankruptcy of the system........I therefore venture to suggest that the democratic theory of elites is in the light of present-day factual knowledge the core of democratic theory itself." (*250* : *128*).

Though the elitist view of democracy has been criticised by its opponents as self-contradictory, yet it exposes one of the two contradictory assumptions on which the traditional liberal-democratic theory was based. The traditional theory of democracy failed to distinguish between two concepts of power, or between two concepts of the essence of men. When it tried to reintroduce the pre-Hobbesian concept of the power of a man as his ability to use and develop his specifically human qualities, it could not abandon the contradictory concept of a man's power as his ability to command the services of others.

Macpherson offers the following critique of the contemporary pluralist theory of democracy: "The Schumpeter-Dahl axis is based on the implicit postulate that man is essentially a consumer of utilities, and it proceeds by assuming that any realistic and honest liberal-democratic theory will treat men so. The point is, of course, that where and when and in so far as men do behave as consumers rather than as exerters, democracy is reduced to a means of letting people have some indirect say in who gets what, when, and how: in that case, the Schumpeter-Dahl model makes very good sense." (*218* : *80*). The contradiction in the traditional liberal-democratic theory is that, while it has always tried to propound a nobler democratic concept of man, it has simultaneously accepted a model of society which assumes that men behave primarily as consumers. If contemporary advocates and revisers of the normative theory of democracy are to rescue democratic theory from its behavioural perversions, they will have to re-examine the self-contradictory model of man and society that characterizes the traditional theory. As Macpherson says, the empirical theorists like Schumpeter, Sartori and Dahl have indirectly contributed to the retrieval of democratic theory as their *reductio ad absurdum* of democracy is simply the logical outcome of their sticking to assumption that man is basically a consumer of utilities.

Lasswell, Kaplan, Friedrich, Easton and Dahl have all defined political power as power *over* other men. Unlike the classical theorists, these empirical theorists do not associate political power in a market society with the economic power of land and capital. Criticising their approach, Macpherson says, "They see that political power is power over others, the ability to make others do what you want. Then, looking for differential of political power, they are apt to fasten on the state's monopoly of physical coercive power. What is interesting then is the means by which those who have political power manage to maintain it? Attention is focused on the source of the power-holders' power: how do they recruit and renew their power? Hence the main interests of current political theory: analysis of models of democratic elitism, pluralist equilibrium analysis, systems analysis. What is lost sight of is that political power, being power over others, is used in any unequal society to extract benefit from the ruled for the rulers. Focus on the source of political power puts out of the field of vision any perception of the necessary *purpose* of political power in any unequal society, which is to maintain the extractive power of the class or classes which have extractive power." (*218 : 47*).

Revival of a Normative Theory of Democracy

Rejecting the empirical theory of democracy as inadequate and narrow, Macpherson has tried to develop a new normative theory of democracy. He has opened a new path of inquiry by analysing the limits and possibilities of liberal democracy and liberal democratic thought. This type of analysis leads to propose a broad theory of democracy, of which liberal democracy is a particular example. As Weinstein says, "He has related this general theory of democratic politics to a vision of the contemporary human condition and has suggested some ways of moving from the present competitive social order to a future society marked by the enhancement of creative freedom. Thus Macpherson is a theorist in the grand style. Following the central theme of clarifying contemporary democracy, he moves from a concern with methods of inquiry to recommendations for social change." (*186 : 253*).

Macpherson's theory of democracy is based on a humanist vision which aims at putting an end to human alienation and exploitation. This vision he shares with all contemporary radical theorists of democracy. Macpherson's distinctive method places him outside both behavioural and traditional approaches and provides some clues about the nature and objectives of a humanistic science of politics. This necessitates both fresh empirical inquiry and fresh philosophical thinking. This view has led him to argue that the goal of a contemporary theory of democracy should not be limited to an empirical or positivistic analysis of the *status quo* but to "rethink a political philosophy adequate to the new moral problems posed by changes in society." The positivistic models interpret democoratic politics as a market and offer justifications of liberal democracy which ignore basic class conflicts. Macpherson deplores that "the trouble with the equilibrium theory of democracy" is that "like the economists' marginal utility theory, it leaves out of account the historical determinants of effective demand." This theory treats "class interests in advanced countries, as just one among many kinds of political pressure." In this way, the empirical theory "averts its thoughts from the most serious problems of democracy." (*183 : 256*).

In capitalist economy, labour is a commodity which can be purchased and sold in the market. This brings about an exploitative system of property relations because the owners of capital impose a heavy toll for access to the means of production. As Macpherson points out, the most freely competitive capitalist economy, apart from its basic tendency towards the formation of monopolies, involves the amassing of huge capital in the hands of a small class, which gives it unlimited economic power over the working class. The economic failing of capitalism consists in the appropriation of surplus value by the owners of capital. But the moral failing of capitalist democracy consists in sanctioning the condition of alienated labour which prevents the majority of the working people from using their energy and skill creatively and in an atmosphere of freedom. The power of a horse or a machine may be defined as the amount of work it can do whether it is set to work or not. But a human being is a purposive creature who should be able to use his labour and capacity for the realization of goals he has formulated consciously.

The ontological assumptions of Western democratic theory are contradictory because they consist of two incompatible notions of human essence. One of those notions is the liberal, individualist concept of man as basically a consumer of utilities, an infinite desirer and infinite appropriator. This idea played a significant role in the development of capitalism in the pre-democratic stage. The other notion of man regards him as an enjoyer and exerter of his uniquely human attributes and capacities. This view challenged the market view of man with the establishment of a democratic polity and became an integral part of the justifying theory of liberal democracy. Thus the Western democratic ontology has two aspects—its individualistic basis and its egalitarian complement.

The individualistic aspect of the democratic theory made the criterion of good society the maximization of individual utilities and made the essence of man the desire to maximise his utilities. Man was inherently a bundle of appetites demanding satisfaction. His happiness consisted in the limitless increase of the aggregate of material goods. Man was first and foremost an appropriator and consumer of material utilities. The right of unlimited appropriation was an important incentive for maximising production in a market soicety. While the postulate of man as infinite consumer does not necessarily make him an infinite appropriator, only a simple additional minor premiss is required to transform him into that. The premiss needed is merely that capital and land should be privately owned in order to be productive. Then, to realize his essence as consumer man must be an appropriator. Thus, man the infinite consumer is converted into man the infinite appropriator.

The egalitarian complement of democracy was introduced at a time when the liberal individualist theory was challenged by a politically conscious working class resenting the inequalities created by the unregulated development of market society. Thinkers as different as Marx and Mill, Carlyle and Green, Ruskin and Saint-Simon criticized the individualistic basis of liberal democracy. They thought that it was morally justified to assert a higher set of values than those of the market. This meant an equal right of every individual to develop his personality. It emphasized a concept of man as essentially an enjoyer and exerter of his own powers. The end of man was to develop his uniquely human capacities. Man was viewed as an infinite developer of his human attributes. The liberal-democratic thinkers who took this view were going back to a much older tradition based on classical Greek humanism and medieval natural law. They were reasserting the old values but on a new and more democratic plane.

It can be argued that a liberal-democratic state would have the best of both worlds—the individual freedom of the liberal society and the equality of a democratic society. This is, in effect, the claim of liberal-democratic theorists like Dahl and Sartori. But according to Macpherson, Marcuse or Sartre, this claim has not yet been made good. In practice, the two concepts of the essence of man cannot be reconciled. The concept of man as infinite consumer and infinite appropriator is still needed to justify the power relation of a capitalist market society and the Western liberal-democratic systems still function as capitalist market societies.

Macpherson, however, believes that the scientific and technological revolution of our age, for the first time, has created a social condition in which it is possible to reject the concept of man as an infinite appropriator. It can be expected to bring all nations of the world up to a level of production where they can start realizing the Marxian vision of man freed for the first time in human history from compulsive and alienated labour. He says, "The technological revolution could provide the means of realizing the democratic concept of the human essence (which is fundamentally the same as the Marxian concept). It could, that is to say, by releasing more and more time and energy from compulsive labour, allow men to think and act as enjoyers and developers of their human capacities rather than devoting themselves to labour as a necessary means of acquiring commodities. At the same time the technological revolution could enable men to discard the concept of themselves as essentially acquirers and appropriators." (*218* : *37*). Macpherson is here arguing for the substitution of one ontological postulate by another. The *individualistic* value postulate should be replaced by an *egalitarian* value postulate. It is not a factual question but a question of value preference. For him democratic society means an egalitarian socialist society which has discarded the market concept of the essence of man.

The normative theory of democracy should make a distinction between the *extractive* and *developmental* concepts of power. A man's power may have two components: his ability to use his own capacities, and his ability to use *other* men's capacities. The latter ability is power over others, the ability to extract benefit from others. That is why it can be described as *extractive* power. On the other hand, a man's ability to use and develop his capacities may be called his *developmental* power. The reduction of power to *power over others* was not a product of intellectual carelessness on the part of empirical theorists. It was a factual description of power relations in a market society where the power of non-owners of property is *negligible* in the developmental sense and *zero* in the extractive sense. On the other hand, the power of owners of land and capital is roughly in proportion to the value of land and capital which they own and by which they can buy and use the manual and intellectual power of the workers and the intelligentsia respectively for their own benefit.

The developmental concept of power is the true basis of an egalitarian theory of democracy. It represents a man's ability to develop his truly human capacities such as capacity for rational understanding, for moral judgement and action, for aesthetic or artistic activity, for love and friendship and of course the capacity for materially productive labour. The above list of human capacities is not exhaustive. It treats man as a creator, an exerter of energy and an actor. A man's developmental power in the sense required in a democratic theory, is to be measured in terms of the absence of impediments to his using his human capacities. Macpherson mentions three impediments to the maximization of a man's developmental power : lack of adequate means of life, lack of access to the means of labour and lack of protection against invasion by others. The problems created by the scarcity of the means of life as well as the scarcity of the means of labour are technological and material on the one hand and cultural and ideological on the other. Macpherson is quite convinced that they cannot be resolved within the framework of a market society based on capitalist social relations. The uninterrupted transfer of developmental power of the non-owners to the owners of land and capital is inevitable under capitalism and can be stopped only under a socialist mode of production which combines civil liberties with developmental freedom.

According to Weinstein, there are three major inconcistencies in Macpherson's theory of democracy. First, he argues that "liberal society frustrates human development" but holds at the same that "liberal-democracy is justified by a commitment to human development." Secondly, he believes that "liberal-democracy is maintained by economic factors" but at the same time he argues that it "should be reformed by changes in consciousness". Thirdly, he suggests that "liberal society debases human beings", but at the same time he argues that "liberal-democracies need not face the problem of imposing moral regeneration." (*186 : 269*). Macpherson's radical critique of liberal-democracy does not postulate the need for a violent revolution or a vanguard dictatorship of the Soviet type. The normative theory of democracy proposed by him looks paradoxical because so far no nation has succeeded in transcending capitalist social relations through peaceful and evolutionary methods.

> Miliband says, "The point of the socialist critique of 'bourgeois freedoms' is not .... that they are of no consequence, but that they are profoundly inadequate, and need to be extended by the radical transformation of the context, economic, social and political, which condemns them to inadequancy and erosion." (*236 : 239*).

CHAPTER 27

LIBERALISM AND UTILITARIANISM IN POLITICS

THE RISE OF LIBERALISM

The Meaning of Liberalism

It is not easy to define Liberalism because it does not represent any coherent body of doctrine. It is rather a historical tendency embracing diverse and even contradictory currents of thought that manifested in certain countries at a given epoch. Liberalism in this wide sense should not be confused with the programme or creed of a particular party which adopts the Liberal designation but may or may not represent the essential philosophy of Liberalism.[1] It is also somewhat difficult to state what exactly constitute the essential principles of Liberalism. In the first place, the representative political thinkers of the liberal school themselves are not agreed about it. Secondly, the circumstances under which the Liberal state emerged in different countries have been so various that they have necessitated a corresponding change in the liberal outlook in those countries. Lastly, the liberal state has been susceptible to changing economic patterns in the same country requiring a restatement of the Liberal ideology.[2]

Laski's Interpretation of Liberalism

Among the contemporary writers Laski has presented us in "The Rise of European Liberalism" with a coherent analysis of the philosophy of the European Liberal movement in its proper social perspective. This analysis is all the more valuable as it has made a sustained attempt

1. ''Liberalism'', as Laski says, ''is the expression less of a creed than of a temperament. It implies a passion for liberty; and that the passion may be compelling it requires a power to be tolerant, even sceptical, about opinions and tendencies you hold to be dangerous, which is one of the rarest human qualities.'' (''The Social and Political Ideas of some Representative Thinkers of the Victorian Age'', Chapter V, p. 100).
2. In this connection, Tocqueville rightly observes, ''The more I study the former condition of the world, and see the world, of our own day in greater detail, the more I consider the prodigious variety to be met with not only in laws, but in the principles of law, the more I am tempered to believe that what we call necessary institutions are often no more than institutions to which we have grown accustomed, and that in matters of social constitution the field of possibilities is much more extensive than men living in their various societies are ready to imagine.'' Tocqueville's ''Recollections,'' p. 99; quoted by Laski in his essay on (Tocqueville).

to utilize the Marxian method of social research in tracing the economic foundations of Liberalism. But it is not as a friend and admirer but rather as a critic that Laski has volunteered to discuss and interpret the philosophy of Liberalism for the contemporary generation.[3] Even then he shows considerable sympathy in his treatment of the various aspects of the Liberal philosophy. It appears that Laski's own political outlook was far more in harmony with the fundamental spirit of Liberalism than he himself cared to admit. Even when he declared himself to be a convert to Marxian socialism, he did not abandon or even mitigate his enthusiasm for some of the most fundamental assumptions of liberalism. Liberalism had in fact become an ingrained habit with Laski's political behaviour and it was simply impossible for him to effect a complete break with the liberal tradition of his country in which he was brought up. Liberalism is a habit of mind no less than a political creed or doctrine. Laski may reject some or most of the doctrinal aspects of liberalism but as a mental attitude Liberalism never deserts him. Even when he is talking pure socialism, a liberal under-current of thought can easily be discerned.[4]

Philosophy of the Middle Class

Liberalism was primarily the philosophy of the victorious middle class in Europe that came into power and prominence after the eclipse of the feudal classes. Sabine has lamented the fact that the doctrines of the Liberal philosophers from Locke to Adam Smith suffer from grave logical inconsistencies.[5] But the vitality of the Liberal doctrines depended less on their logic than on their agreement with the interests of the class that mainly produced them. It is really curious to note that liberalism has found its adherents and spokesmen with equal ease in persons professing such varied creeds as Christians and atheists, monarchists and republicans, aristocrats and democrats, idealists and utilitarians, rationalists and empiricists, or even individualists and collectivists. But even these strains have not been able to destroy the inner unity of the Liberal doctrine. This inner unity is derived from the fact that it always remains the ideological instrument of a particular class in social evolution. That class is the capitalist class. The capitalists first utilized the body of liberal ideas in their ideological offensive against the landowners. As time went on the opposition between landowners and capitalists became a vanishing issue. A new opposition arose between the capitalists and the wage-earners, with the result that liberalism tended to become more and more a defence mechanism of the capitalist class against proletarian attacks. Liberalism no longer remained an ideology of progress and radical change. It was

3. Laski is decidedly not the first political thinker to apply the principle of economic determinism in interpreting and evaluating the philosophy of liberalism. Tocqueville, the great French Liberal, adopted a similar attitude in his "Democracy in America".

4. See Laski's Introduction to his "Liberty in the Modern State", (New Edition, 1948).

5. Sabine : "History of Political Theory", Chapters XXVI and XXXI.

now transformed into an ideology of conservative decadence and reaction. The consistency of the Liberal doctrines should be sought in the social purpose which they serve and not in the philosophical assumptions which they make.

The Liberal Tradition

If we examine the various historical forces and intellectual trends that have shaped the evolution of the Liberal doctrines in the period between the Reformation and the Russian Revolution, we realize that the number and character of such influences is bewildering.

Laski believes that liberal ideas were propounded and developed sometimes by political thinkers, who were not even conscious of what they were doing. Liberalism as a school of political philosophy did not evolve in a direct and straightforward manner. The doctrines of liberalism lack clarity and precision because they have been derived from several sources with little internal affinity. People, who were otherwise indifferent and even antagonistic to the obectives of liberalism, have contributed, without being conscious of it, to the theory and practice of the liberal state. The liberal tradition has been enriched by such important men as Machiavelli, Calvin, Luther, Copernicus, Henry VIII and Thomas More in the sixteenth century and by Hobbes, Jurieu, Louis XIV, Richelieu, Pascal and Bacon in the seventeenth century. Besides this, the liberal outlook was also generated by constantly changing social environment in Western Europe during that period". (*132* : *12*).

The rise of a new social class to political power has always synchronized in history with radical adjustments in the social philosophy of the people of that period. The advent of the middle class to the position of political supremacy was no exception to this rule. It signified a violent break from the intellectual conceptions of the feudal past. Theology and ethics, jurisprudence and politics, arts and science were reconstituted on a new basis. The entire outlook of the age was so changed as to become receptive to new norms of social behaviour and new forms of social organisation.

The Breakdown of Feudalism

The breakdown of the medieval society was not achieved by peaceful means. The liberal capitalistic state was born in the midst of violent struggles and factional fights which culminated in the liquidation of the feudal state system in a large part of Western Europe. "Revolution and war", says Laski, "presided over its emergence from the womb; and it is not beyond the mark to say that there was hardly a period until 1848 when its growth was not arrested by the challenge of violent reaction. Men fight passionately to retain those wonted habits in which their privileges are involved; and liberalism was nothing so much as a challenge to vested interests rendered sacred by the traditions of half a thousand years" (*132* : *13*). The destructive role of liberalism in this period is as important as the constructive role which it assumed subsequently.

In the sixteenth century, the liberal state was only slowly emerging. The commercial and industrial classes first allied themselves with the cause of monarchical absolutism in order to secure national freedom from papal control on the external side. Absolute monarchy was favoured on the internal side because by crashing the feudal particularist state it provided better facilities of trade for them. Machiavelli was the first political thinker of some repute through whom the hopes and desires of the rising middle class of Europe found a concrete expression. The secular outlook of Machiavelli ultimately became an important element of the creed of Liberalism. It is true Machiavelli's secular conception of politics was far in advance of his age. As the subsequent history of Europe showed, religion was yet destined to play a far greater part in European politics than Machiavelli had imagined.

Machiavelli's Liberal Ideas

Machiavelli's conception of human nature as that of the English philosopher Hobbes was also strikingly modern.[6] His view that human beings are fundamentally egoistic long remained the acknowledged creed of individualistic Liberalism. His conception of a supreme law-giver gave rise to the later liberal theories of sovereignty. His interest in stable government led him to favour absolute monarchy for the moment but he was not a monarchist by conviction. Once the causes of perpetual anarchy were removed, the popular and republican form of government was the desirable ideal. This appreciation of popular government coupled with his condemnation of nobility and aristocracy entitles Machiavelli to be counted as one of the founder-philosophers of Liberalism.

As the first prophet of Italian nationalism, he became the author of another item on the Liberal programme because the Liberal state was destined to become a nation-state in course of time. Thus the contribution of the Italian philosopher in building up the liberal tradition was not insignificant.

The Reformation and Liberalism

Liberalism derived indirect support from the Reformation as well. Max Weber believes that the Protestant doctrines facilitated the triumph of the Liberal ideals to a very great extent. But the alliance between Liberalism and Protestantism was accidental rather than consciously designed. It is true that the social philosophy of Luther and other leaders of the Reformation was essentially conservative. But their protestant mood in the realm of theology could not but have repercussions in other fields of intellectual inquiry.

By questioning the Catholic tradition of revering the papal authority, it produced a violent earthquake in mass psychology. Protestantism brought about immense changes not only in theological doctrines but also effected

6. See Laski's article on "Machiavelli and the Present Time", in "The Dangers of Obedience and Other Essays", pp. 238-53.

far-reaching changes in the distribution of wealth by transferring ecclesiastical property to lay hands. It also facilitated the growth of the secular state by opposing papal interference in national affairs. Protestantism aided the emancipation of the individual by creating rationalist temper although it was only a by-product of the Reformation and could in no case be called its essence. There were even trends like Calvinism which were definitely hostile to everything Liberalism has stood for.

Bodin's Liberal Ideas

In the development of the Liberal theory, Jean Bodin and Hobbes played an important role. Their theories of sovereignty were pleas for the supremacy of the liberal state in social affairs. They dismiss the claim of the Church to dispute its sovereignty. But Bodin unlike Hobbes could not completely eradicate the influence of the medieval doctrine of natural law. He maintained that even the sovereign was bound by the moral conventions of his generation, a view rejected by Hobbes completely.

Another distinctive feature of Bodin's philosohpy as that of Hobbes or Locke was his conscientious respect for bourgeois property which the sovereign should consider as inviolable (*129* : *16*). In Bodin's time the struggle between ecclesiastical and civil power was finally decided in favour of the latter and against the former. In the sphere of theory, it implied the victory of the secular over the theocratic ideal. But the secular state that emerges at the end of the sixteenth and seventeenth centuries is still a paternalistic state and has yet to travel a long way before it can properly be called a Liberal state.

Liberal Ideas of Hobbes, Locke and Rousseau

In the seventeenth and eighteenth centuries the liberal state was further consolidated. The battle for liberal ideas assumed a violent struggle in the civil war of England and the French Revolution of 1789. Hobbes, Locke and Rousseau were the main advocates of the Liberal theory of state during this most interesting age in the history of western political thought.[7]

Utilitarianism is essentially an English school of thinking. It played a notable part in England in the nineteenth century, particularly in the earlier half, in effecting reforms of a far-reaching character. According to Hallowell, it had its basis in the nineteenth century liberalism when "freedom was conceived less and less as a natural right and more and more as a social utility". To quote the same writer again : "Utilitarianism was an attempt to establish ethical and political theory upon a thoroughgoing scientific empiricism" (*31* : *198*).

1. STATEMENT AND CRITICISM OF UTILITARIANISM

Utilitarianism is primarily an ethical theory based upon the psycho-

7. See chapter 5 of this book for Political Ideas of Hobbes, Locke and Rousseau.

logical doctrine known as Hedonism. According to the teaching of Hedonism, every man, as a matter of fact, seeks pleasure and avoids pain. Other motives may enter the calculation, but the ultimate motive is that of pleasure *versus* pain. The hedonistic teaching is by no means new. It goes back to the Greek times, especially to the teachnigs of Aristippus, the founder of the Cyrenaic school, and, in a modified form, to the teachings of Epicurus. While modern Hedonism differs widely from the ancient, both forms regard pleasure as the guiding principle. Earlier Hedonism was egoistic in character, while the modern is altruistic. Utilitarianism bases itself on the latter form. Hence it is sometimes called altruistic or universalistic hedonism. Its goal is the greatest happiness of the greatest number, or simply, general happiness; and the scoffer adds, 'the greatest number is one'.

It is generally admitted today that the psychological and ethical foundations of Utilitarianism are unsound. Self-abnegation is as natural to man as may be the pursuit of pleasure. Therefore, to reduce everything to the pleasure-pain principle is to force human motives into a Procrustean bed. Bentham is guilty of using round-about argument when he affirms that the production of pain is wrong, unless it be to diminish future pain or promote future pleasure.

In making the above criticisms, we do not forget that Utilitarianism claims to make a powerful appeal to the altruistic impluses of man. But our condition is that, in so doing, it is inconsistent with itself. Universalistic hedonism is a contradiction in terms. If a thing is 'universalistic' it cannot be hedonistic; and, conversely, if it is hedonistic it cannot be 'universalistic'. Pleasure is individualistic in nature. It is subjective experience. Therefore, to speak of general happiness as meaning general pleasure, as the Utilitarians do, is meaningless.

Although Utilitarianism is an unsound ethical theory, it has been instrumental in bringing about a large number of valuable reforms in practical politics. How do we account for this seeming contradiction? The answer is to be found in the fact that the Utilitarian performs a somersault when he passes from ethics to politics.

As a political thinker, the Utilitarian interprets general happiness in a loose manner to mean general well-being or social welfare. He minimizes the conception of pleasurable feelings and fastens attentions upon utility. It is obvious that terms like 'social welfare' and 'utility' are of such a general and practical character that anybody using them as the foundation of his political programme is bound to do immense good. Thus we find that it is the inconsistency of the Utilitarians in the interpretation of their end which accounts for the great good which they accomplished in the realm of practical politics. Their political theory was a theory of government rather than a theory of the State.

2. ESTIMATE OF UTILITARIANISM (*13 : Chapter 1*)

Criticism of Utilitarianism as a psychological and ethical theory does not prevent us from giving due praise to it in the political field. Utilitarianism represents interest in the welfare of mankind. With this interest it combines practical efforts to improve the conditions of human life on rational principles. It believes in the possibility of raising the condition of the masses through effective State legislation. All Utilitarians have at heart the general welfare. Their first and great concern is human life, human activity, human well-being. They are the strenuous opponents of tyranny and injustice, and the 'champions of individual freedom.' They are opposed to all 'sinister' interests. Hence Utilitarianism is emphatically practical. It is reformatory. It is simply another name for humanism.

Utilitarianism is often unjustly criticized as the utility theory or expediency philosophy. Utility means serving a purpose or end. In popular conversation, it often means a low purpose or end. The Utilitarian conceives man not only as an individual, but as an individual who is by nature social. 'Utility for him means what is best for all the elements of his nature, and what can most effectively promote his full and ultimate good, and the full and ultimate good of his fellows'. The Utilitarian doctrine is expressed in such phrases as 'the greatest happiness of the greatest number', 'enlightened benevolence', and 'general happiness' (*13 : 13*).

In like manner, Utilitarianism has sometimes been regarded as synonymous with materialism of the worst type. In order to avoid misconception it is proposed that we substitute such terms as 'welfare' and 'well-being' for 'utility' and 'happiness'. Commenting upon Green's treatment of Utilitarianism, D.G. Ritchie writes : 'There is no reason why the Idealist, after making clear his objections to Hedonism, should not join hands with the Utilitarian'. Green's ethical system, says the same writer, is Mill's Utilitarianism plus a secure basis and a criterion.

The supreme consideration of the legislator, says the Utilitarian, should be the welfare of people in general. Proper legislation has a negative and a positive aspect. Negatively, it should get rid of degrading or untoward circumstances. Positively, it should put favourable inducements in their place.

The ideals that the Utilitarian cherishes are of an essentially practical and human kind. The ideals rejected by him are those which appear to him either undesirable or unrealizable, or both. He is neither a fanatic nor a dreamer. His feet stand on solid ground.

Utilitarianism is founded on experience. It appeals to experience as the ultimate test. Consequences are everything to the Utilitarian. He regards experience as the source and origin of knowledge and the ultimate criterion of truth. He is opposed to mere abstraction or speculation.

Utilitarianism is thus an intensely human and intensely practical philosophy.

Carlyle was wrong in describing Utilitarianism as 'pig philosophy' or 'pig trough philosophy'.

T.H. Green who had considerable sympathy for Utilitarianism wrote : "Whatever the errors arising from the hedonistic psychology, no other theory has been available for the social and political reforms containing so much truth with such ready applicability"..

3. UTILITARIAN THINKERS

1. Jeremy Bentham, who lived from 1748 to 1832, laid the foundations of the Utilitarian School of thinking. He played a conspicuous part in removing injustice and in bringing about lasting reforms. The keynote of his philosophy is: 'Nature has placed man under the governance of two sovereign masters, pain and pleasure......They govern us in all we do, in all we say, in all we think: every effort we make to throw off our subjection will serve but to demonstrate and confirm it.' The principle of utility, he says, recognizes this subjection, because it approves or disapproves of every action whatsoever, according to the tendency to promote or oppose happiness. This principle he later describes as 'the greatest happiness principle'. In the apportionment of lots of happiness, the principle to be applied, he says, is 'each to count for one and no one for more than one.'

According to Bentham, pleasures differ in intensity, duration, certainty, and propinquity or nearness, but are one in quality. This means that we cannot regard one pleasure as 'better' or 'higher' than another. The Benthamite doctrine is undoubtedly narrow and psychologically false. Nevertheless, as Ivor Brown remarks, it 'has an immense value because it denies the infallibility of the superior person who endeavours to foist his own morality or his own type of happiness upon others whom he believes to be the pitiful dupes of ignorance' (*6 : 96*). 'Benthamism, shorn of its crudities, is simply humanism' (*6 : 102*).

The primary concern of Bentham was the good or welfare of the community. He believed that his principle of utility could be applied with advantage to all social questions and particularly to constitutional, legislative, and law reform. 'He had a living and practical interest in view, and was not merely concerned with a barren speculative theory' (*13 : 48*).

At the time that Bentham appeared on the scene as a great reformer and thinker, the theory of natural rights and the pompous generalizations of Blackstone regarding the greatness of the English constitution and the English law held the field. Upon both of these Bentham poured his scorn, and exposed them to merciless criticism. Natural rights he described as 'simple nonsense: natural and imprescriptible rights rhetorical nonsense—nonsense upon stilts'. For the theory of natural rights he substituted the principle of utility.

In his first work of any importance, *A Fragment on Government*, published in 1776, Bentham bitterly criticized Blackstone who praised the English law as a slow, natural growth in accordance with Divine providence. 'Bentham showed that it was a shameless tyranny which worked only for the misery of the weak and poor, an elaborate mechanism for helping the educated and the powerful to keep down the ignorant and the oppressed' (*6 : 102*). He further attacked Blackstone for basing political obligation upon an original social contract. He argued that there was no such contract in the past and that, even if there were one, it did not bind the present generation. The only valid reason for obedience was utility or the general good. Governments exist because they are believed to promote the happiness of those living under them. In Bentham's own characteristic language, 'The probable mischiefs of obedience are less than the probable mischiefs of disobedience.' Man obeys political authority not because of an original contract or natural rights or any other 'fiction', but because of 'the habit of obedience'. Thus, as Dunning points out, among the venerable principles and practices of conservative England's law and politics, Bentham became 'a veritable bull in a china shop' (*27* : *212*).

Theory of Government. Far from extolling the English constitution, as his contemporaries had done, Bentham attacked it in forthright earnestness. He pleaded for annual parliaments, vote by ballot, and universal male suffrage, subject to the test of ability to read. He went still further and attacked the utility of the House of Lords and of monarchy on the ground that the interests of these institutions were not compatible with the interests of the people at large. He was convinced that a single-chambered legislature, renewable every year was most in accord with democratic principles. Bentham's faith lay in a Republic, which he thought would be conducive to 'both efficiency and economy and the supremacy of the people'.

Legislation. It was in this field that Bentham made his greatest contribution. On the publication of his *Principles of Morals and Legislation*, he became a sort of 'new Moses' of legislation. The ends of legislation are, according to him, security, subsistence, abundance, and equality. In simple language, the object is the good of the people. If laws are to be obeyed, says Bentham, it is necessary that legislation should carry the people along with it.

The number of practical reforms which Bentham advocated is legion. The principal ones among them, as summarized by Davidson, are : reform of the corrupt and restricted parliamentary system; thorough-going municipal reform; humanization of the terribly cruel criminal law of the time; improvement of prisons and prison management; abolition of imprisonment for debt; elimination of the usury laws; repeal of the religious test; reform of the poor law; suppression of 'sturdy beggars'; utilization of able-bodied paupers; training of pauper children, establishment of a vast scheme of national education; institution of 'frugality banks' (now known as savings banks) and friendly societies; forming of a code for merchant shipping; protection of inventors; encouragement of local courts; comprehensive system of health legislation; creation of public prosecutors and advocates for the poor; thorough-going revision of hereditary rights; supervision of scientific and philosophical foundations; and recall of public officials. It is needless to add that many of the reforms for which Bentham ardently pleaded have since been incorporated into the laws of the various lands.

Law Reform. Bentham aimed at being a great law reformer. He was eager 'to see justice administered, and happiness secured to the deserving and the oppressed' (*13* : *92*). Sir Henry Maine pays a generous tribute to Bentham's place in the history of judicial reform when he writes : 'I do not know a single law reform effected since Bentham's day which cannot be traced to his influence'.

Bentham realized that the laws of the day were in a chaotic condition and he took upon himself the task of codifying them, but no encouragement was given to him in his own country. Encouragement came, however, from foreign lands, particularly from France and Russia. Applying his utilitarian principles to the laws of these countries, Bentham demonstrated how his theory would work in concrete instances.

Education. Bentham had unswerving faith in the power of education to improve mankind. He sketched two systems of education—one for pauper children, another for upper class children.

Punishment and Prison Reforms. Bentham held that the chief end of punishment was to prevent crime. It should not be merely vindictive. It should secure the good of the community. If capital punishment were necessary for the safety and security of society, it was justifiable, otherwise not. Whether or not capital punishment was to be administered in cases other than murder, Bentham held, should be determined by considerations of utility, i.e., their effect upon the general good.

On the whole, Bentham's emphasis is on the deterrent theory of punishment. But this does not exclude the reformation of the criminal, which Bentham regards as 'a part of the calculation of the balance of consequences in meting out punishment' (*13 : 101*). Bentham believed that a great many criminals and evil-doers were capable of improvement and that they could be restored to society as useful and self-respecting members.

Estimate of Bentham. It is a well-known fact that Bentham was not the originator of Utilitarianism or of the "greatest happiness principle" He got it form Priestley's *Essay on Government;* and Priestley in turn had got his principle of the "greatest happiness of the greatest number" from Hutcheson.

In the use of the greatest happiness principle Bentham was dogmatic. In the striking words of Wayper, Bentham swallowed his first principles without digesting them.

'The utilitarian calculus' which meant summation of pleasures or the balancing of pleasures against pains became a wooden and unrealistic doctrine, a mere figment of the imagination.

In spite of his social passion, Bentham never ceased to be an individualist. His attitude towards state action was negative in spite of the large area of activity which he assigned to the State. To the end he held on to the atomistic view of society and could not see how the individual and society are intimately wrapped up together and are not poles apart. As has often happened in other cases, his uncriticized individualism led him to an uncritical collectivism.

Moreover, Bentham over-rationalized everything. It looked as though emotion was an ingredient lacking in his nature. He frowned upon asceticism, claiming that those who practised it suffered from a perverted notion of pleasure.

Yet Bentham was a great reformer. The times in which he lived needed a person like him. Burke had been unduly harsh upon the French Revolution; and consequently the middle classes in England were frightened of revolution. Yet the time was ripe for reforms in all directions; and Bentham met that need. His attack on "sinister interests" under the inspiration of James Mill was most timely. It is the considered opinion of Ebenstein that "Bentham changed the character of British institutions more than any other man in the nineteenth century". (*98*).

Bentham's greatest contribution was in the realm of practical reform and legal thought. The word 'codification' which has become a household term in the legal world was his coinage. Bentham undertook the codification of laws for more than one country. He clearly anticipated Austin's theory of sovereignty. As a matter of fact, some of the key phrases in his definition of sovereignty, Austin owes to Bentham. In the estimation of Dicey, Bentham was "in very truth the first and greatest of legal philosophers."

2. James Mill (1773-1836) was a devoted follower of Bentham to the end of his life. He regarded a sound representative system as a check upon the self-interest of governments. While not advocating the abolition of the House of Lords, as Bentham did, he proposed drastic measures for the curtailment of its power, closely anticipating the 1911 Act. He believed that political power, when vested in the middle ranks of society, would be most conductive to order and progress. In every way, as Davidson remarks, James Mill was 'the leader of the Utilitarian Radicals after Bentham, and the chief operative force in effecting the practical reforms of the school' (*13* : *142*).

3. John Stuart Mill (1806-73), son of James Mill, is the better known of the two Mills. His father who was a strict disciplinarian and an ardent believer in Utilitarianism brought him up in that creed. At one time he told Bentham that his son was "a successor worthy of both of us". Mill was over-educated and over-drilled in Utilitarianism. But at the same time when he reached maturity and began to reflect on things for himself he clearly saw the serious defects of Utilitarianism. Besides, he was a man with a catholic outlook willing to see the merit in other points of view. In this process of self-liberalization Mill was helped by his wide reading of contemporary works such as those of Augustus Comte, Thomas Carlyle, S. T. Coleridge, etc. The influence of Mrs. Taylor who many years later, on the death of her first husband, became his wife was also important. She helped to rouse in Mill his feelings and emotions which lay dormant under the stern eye of his father. In his dedicatory note to *Liberty,* Mill pays her (who had died a few years earlier) a glorious tribute which only a man in deep love could have paid. He claims that the essay was as much a work of hers as his. In accounting for his passing from individualism to "qualified socialism," in the later editions of his *Political Economy,* Mill pays a similar tribute to the memory of his wife.

In spite of all the concessions he made to his critics, Mill remained a Utilitarian to the very end. To abandon it altogether, which he should have done in accordance with the profound modifications he had made in it, he thought was sacrilege to the memory of his father and Jeremy Bentham.

Yet Mill admits that pleasures differ not only in quantity, but also in quality. He does not subscribe to the Benthamite formula that quantity of pleasure being the same, "push-pin is as good as poetry." In his oft-quoted words: "It is better to be a human being dissatisfied than a fool satisfied, better Socrates dissatisfied than a fool satisfied. And if the fool, or the pig, is of a different opinion, it is because they only know their own side of the question. The other party to the comparison knows both sides." (p. 9 Everyman's Library ed.)[1]

While Bentham recognized only external sanctions for constraining the individual to promote general happiness, Mill admitted both external and internal sanctions. In this respect Mill was closer to the organic theory of society than Bentham ever was. He realized that individual happiness and general happiness are closely intertwined, and that, therefore, it was not necessary to force oneself to pursue the pleasures of others. Mill was of the opinion that every man possessed 'a feeling for the happiness of mankind' and that, consequently, he should desire and promote general happiness. Among the sanctions, Mill mentions "the religious motive," "The internal sanction of duty", "the desire of virtue," etc.

Summing up Mill's Utilitarian position as a whole, Wayper holds that the changes that Mill introduced into Utilitarianism were "of such a wholesale kind that when he had finished reinterpreting and refurbishing Utilitarianism, Utilitarianism was singularly hard to find". (*93 : 107*). "Yet perhaps because he is the least logical, he is also incomparably the most satisfactory of the Utilitarians". (*93 : 107*). Wayper further says that in spite of all his faults, Mill remains "far and away the most satisfactory of the Utilitarians." According to Ivor Brown, Mill "made Utilitarianism at once more human and less consistent." (*6 : 119*).

On Liberty. Mill was as much interested in political and social reform as he was in philosophical speculation. His well-known essay on ***Liberty,*** together with Milton's *Areopagitica* stand out as the two most noble defences of the freedom of the individual in the English language. In ***Liberty*** Mill first traces the growth of political liberty from the days of royal despotism to the days of popular government with its attendant evil of the tyranny of public opinion.

Holding the view that democracy does not necessarily ensure opportunity for the development of individuality, Mill devotes a major part of ***Liberty*** to the defence of individuality, even to the extent of justifying eccentricity and oddity of character. His own striking words are: "It is not by wearing down into uniformity all that is individual in themselves,

1. In so modifying Utilitarianism, Mill virtually repudiated it. Some pleasures are, according to his thinking, more valuable than others. It is no wonder that once when he was asked to attend a meeting in honour of Bentham, he said, "And I am Peter who denied his master."

but by cultivating it and calling it forth, within the limits imposed by the rights and interests of others, that human beings become noble and beautiful objects of contemplation."

The three types of liberty with which Mill is vitally concerned are liberty of thought, liberty of expression (which includes speech and writing) and liberty of action. Liberty of thought is something which does not require an elaborate defence. But if it is to mean anything at all, it must include liberty of expression and action.

So far as free discussion is concerned, Mill would practically place no limits on it, so long as it is within the limits of public order and decorum. His well-known argument is that the received (i.e., traditional) opinion may be altogether true or altogether false or what is most likely, partly true and partly false. In every one of these cases, Mill holds that there is a powerful case for absolute freedom. If the received opinion is altogether true, no one should object to its being openly challenged by anybody. Not to allow it is to assume infallibility for oneself. The received opinion in such a case is nothing more than a dead dogma, which is not a part of one's own thinking or conviction. If the received opinion is altogether false, which is the second alternative, freedom of discussion gives a person the opportunity of substituting his error for some one else's truth.

Not to do it means that one continues to be a victim of his own errors and prejudices. The third alternative which is the most likely is that the received opinion may be partly true and partly false. In such a case, permitting free discussion means that what is true in one's own position becomes stronger still and what is false in one's position is given up for the truth one can receive from others.

It was Mill's belief that in the struggle of ideas, truth will ultimately prevail. There was something like the survival of the fittest in the world of ideas. To us this seems to be a questionable proposition. Not everybody is endowed with a high degree of reasoning or discrimination. Modern history is full of instances where a specious idea, skillfully presented, is accepted as gospel truth by a large majority of people, even when they are intelligent and well-educated. How else is one to interpret the Nazi propaganda which hypnotized millions of people into a belief concerning the superiority of the Nordic race and the right of the Germans to conquer and rule over as much of the world as possible?

Mill rightly points out the fallacy of the argument that no sound idea can be suppressed for all time and that it is bound to come back to life sooner or later. The fact is that persecution has at times succeeded in crushing truth for a long time, thereby checking its normal growth and development. Social vitality, Mill believed, should precede social calm.

As regards freedom of action, Mill marks out an area of individual preference where the State should not interfere by means of law or society by means of public opinion. This is the area of "self-regarding conduct." It is conduct which concerns oneself and not others. But the moment an act directly impinges upon others, either the State or society or both may interfere. In Mill's own striking words: "The only part of the conduct of any one, for which he (the individual) is amenable to society, is that which concerns others. In the part which merely concerns himself, his independence is, of right absolute. Over himself, over his own body and mind, the individual is sovereign." (p. 73). Thus a soldier or policeman drunk at home should not be punished or made an object of ridicule. But if the same man gets drunk while he is on duty, he should be punished.

The particular fields assigned to individual preference are (1) the inward domain of consciousness, liberty of thought and feeling, including the liberty of expressing public opinions; (2) tastes and pursuits, like what a man may eat or drink or what he may put on; and (3) voluntary combination among individuals (such as trade unions) so long as it does not involve harm to others.

The two principal mistakes made by Mill in this connection are (1) his assumption that all the distinctions that he makes are in accordance with the principle of utility; and (2) his naive belief that self-regarding and other-regarding conduct can be clearly separated from each other.

Barker's harsh judgment on Mill is that he remained to the end "a prophet of an empty liberty and an abstract individual".

In portions of his essay on *'Representative Government'*, to use the words of Wayper, Mill appears in the role of a "reluctant democrat". The reasons are (1) Mill's fear that democracy tends to crush individuality and mould people according to a single pattern, (2) his fear of demagogism under the guise of democracy, and (3) his distrust of the masses. On the last point he writes: "Ordinary human nature is so poor a thing." "Men are stupid and selfish as individuals and stodgy as a mass." Where the necessary conditions exist, Mill is convinced that democracy is the best of all governments. Yet it is not suited for all people.

It is Mill's claim that while democracy may not make people happier, it makes them better. In the sphere of practical politics, Mill was a Philosophical Radical. He was an ardent champion of the rights of women and wanted to 'emancipate' them from the 'subjection' of men. He believed that differences between sexes were not fundamental and inevitable. As a Radical member of Parliament from 1865 to 1868 he strenuously advocated the interests of the labouring classes, woman suffrage, reduction of the national debt, and land reform in Ireland. He opposed all class interests and one-sided legislation. He believed that minorities were not adequately represented in the British Parliament and so advocated the system of proportional representation associated with the name of Thomas Hare. While favouring universal suffrage for all tax-payers, Mill advocated plurality of votes for men of superior intellect and high character. Giving equal votes to all, according to Mill means that inexperience sits in judgment over experience and ignorance over knowledge.

When he stood for a seat in Parliament he would not canvass himself nor would he pay agents to canvass for him. After election he would not attend to the local business of the community. He was opposed to the idea that a member of Parliament was a delegate who had to consult his constituency on every important issue before recording his vote.

While maintaining the superior legislative authority of the House of Commons, Mill favoured a strong House of Lords in the form of a Chamber of Statesmen.

Mill put forward the idea of Legislative Commissions for the drafting of Bills. Once the Bill had been drafted and submitted to Parliament, it could accept it or reject it or return it to the Commission for reconsideration. But it had no right to amend it.

Mill favoured open competition to public services. The details of legislation and methods of enforcement were to be worked out by administrators. According to Mill, Parliament was to control the business of government, but not actually do it. Parliament was to lay down the general lines of policy, but the actual execution was to be in the hands of administrators.

Mill was in favour of compulsory education provided by the State, although he found that it might result in turning out people after a single pattern determined by a governmental bureau.

In the *economic field,* Mill was far from being a bigoted individualist. He approved of extensive State action when it was in the interest of social welfare. In his later years he looked forward to the socialistic ideal when there might be 'a common ownership in the raw materials of the globe, and an equal participation of all in the benefits of combined labour'. He combined political liberalism with economic socialism. Ivor Brown says: "Mill's political ideas are perfectly compatible with socialism, so long as that socialism is based on a philosophy of individual welfare." (*6* : *129*).

Summing up the entire social and political thought of Mill, R. H. Murray aptly writes : "A Free Trader, he allowed protection of infant industries thereby letting in Protection. An individualist he turned to socialism. A radical, he proved as imperialist as Carlyle. An empiricist be drifted towards idealism. A utilitarian, he refuted it and then transformed it so greatly that Bentham could not have recognized it."

Even today utilitarianism or 'the greatest happiness principle' is capable of doing much good if it is not interpreted too literally. It is possible to combine idealism with utilitarianism, as does T.H. Green in the realm of political theory. In the field of practical politics such a combination can well lend support to a mixed economy or the welfare State ideal of India.

CHAPTER 28

IDEALISM AND PRAGMATISM IN POLITICS

THE IDEALISTIC TRADITION IN POLITICS

The idealistic theory of the State is known by various names. Some call it the absolutist theory, some call it the philosophical theory. MacIver goes to the extent of describing it as the 'mystical' theory, and still some the metaphysical theory. Whatever the name may be, the idealistic tradition had a long, though somewhat broken, history. Its earliest traces are found in the writings of Plato and Aristotle. These Greek thinkers, along with many others of the time, regarded the State as natural and necessary. To them the State was all in all, and apart from it man could not attain the highest possible perfection for him. Aristotle held that the State first came into being in order to meet the needs of mere life, but was continued through the necessities of a moral life. To both Plato and Aristotle the State was supremely an ethical institution. The true State was a partnership in a life of virtue.

This way of looking at the State from the moral point of view and of approaching political theory through ethics has profoundly affected later idealistic thinkers. Another respect in which Greek philosophy has left a deep impression on some of the recent idealists is in the practical identification of the State with society. This tendency is particularly marked in the thinking of Bosanquet. A third way in which Greek thought, particularly the thought of Plato, has influenced later idealists is in conceiving the State as an organic unity. The idealist starts from the position that the State is a central social system, in which the individual must find his proper place.

It is with Rousseau that Greek political theory begins to exercise a steady and continuous influence on modern thought. For this reason Rousseau may rightly be regarded as the re-discoverer of the great truths discovered by Greek philosophers centuries ago.

Plato was a dominant influence in his thought, and with his help he liberated himself from the individualist theory of Locke, and arrived at the collectivist theory of State expounded in the *Social Contract.* In his epoch-making work, the *Social Contract,* Rousseau advances the conception of the State as a moral organism and the doctrine of the general will. The State in his judgment is not primarily a legal association for the safeguarding of citizen's legal rights. It is essentially a moral association, through whose common life man reaches his moral perfection. Rousseau preached the doctrine of the general will and of every individual having a share in its formulation.

The profound teachings of Rousseau influenced the thought of Kant and the other German philosophers of the time and, through them, the thought of the British idealists.

Factors that led to the rise of idealism in modern times. Modern idealism had its origin in Germany. It arose on the ashes of the earlier theories which had completely discredited themselves. Among these were the social contract theory which had been smashed to pieces by such writers as Bentham and Hume; and the eighteenth century individualism with its emphasis on unrestrained liberty and the theory of *laissez faire*.

Among the factors which went a long way to change the earlier views of the State and society were the French Revolution and the Napoleonic Wars. They pointed the way to a more positive view of the State which would call for a devotion and allegiance to the State, which was not dreamt of by the individualists. The imperialist expansion of the period also discredited individualism to a certain extent.

A factor which paved the way for idealism was the growth in various branches of knowledge such as history, economics, ethics, psychology, and jurisprudence. In the ethical field, need was felt for laying down certain norms or standards both for the individual and society. It was against this background that idealism made its appearance.

STATEMENT OF THE IDEALISTIC THEORY OF THE STATE

The idealists believe that the State is an ethical institution. In the words of Bosanquet, it is the embodiment of an ethical idea. Other important ethical institutions in society are the family and the Church. The State is the most important among these institutions. In a sense it includes all the others. Interpreted strictly, the State is a legal organization. But interpreted broadly, it is a moral organism practically identical with society.

The State is indispensable to the fullest growth and development of human personality. Man is by nature a social being and the State is the effective organization of society for the realization of a moral end. Between the end of the individual and the end of the State there is no true contradiction.

Viewed in this manner, the State is man's best friend. The conception of Man *versus* the State is entirely erroneous. The anarchists who regard the State as an unmitigated evil and the individualists who look upon it as a necessary evil, both fail to understand its true significance.

While the ethical unit is the person and the State exists for the sake of the person, the idealists believe that the State has a will and a personality. It has a past, a present and a future, and is thus in some ways different from the individuals who comprise it at any one time. It has a continuity of purpose and steadiness of aim.

The basis of the State is, according to the idealist, will and not force. The State no doubt uses force, but that is not its primary or most significant quality. It is the embodiment of will. We ought to obey the

State, says the idealist, because of the consciousness that in obeying it we advance a common good of which individual good is an intrinsic part.

In practical language, it means that the State should remove obstacles to good life. It cannot and ought not to enforce religion and morality. It should constantly keep before itself the supreme end of the individual which is the development of personality, also known as self-realization or self-satisfaction. It should maintain those conditions of freedom which are necessary for man's good life by enforcing a system of universal and impartial right. And rights, as mentioned earlier, are the outer conditions necessary for man's inner development.

As a general rule, the individual should obey the State. This does not mean that he may not criticize the political order. He is both sovereign and subject. But when the State invades the sphere of personality, he has the right of rebellion. Rebellion in such a case becomes a public duty. Even in his rebellion the individual should remember that he is still a citizen loyal to the best for which the State stands. There are two situations, says James Seth, in which the individual may rightly rebel: (a) When the State acts as a private individual or a body of individuals; (b) When present formulation of the general will becomes so inadequate as to require reformation.

(a) The English and French revolutions are good illustrations of the former case. At these times 'the actual State contradicted the ideal, seeking to destroy those rights of personality of which it ought to have been the custodian, and before which it was called to give an account of its stewardship.' Hence revolution was eminently justifiable.

(b) England before the Reform Bills provides a good illustration of a situation in which the general will needed to be re-formulated. In cases of this kind, re-formulation does not need to take the form of revolution. Reformation is enough. Such reformation goes on continuously in the good State where there is an articulate public opinion.

A. The German Idealists. The first to claim our attention among these is *Immanuel Kant* (1724-1804), who is generally admitted to be the father of idealistic philosophy in modern times. There are some writers, however, who would confer that distinction upon his successor, Hegel. Kant, like his political guide, Rousseau, marks the transition from eighteenth century individualism and the philosophy of 'natural rights' and the social contract to nineteenth century idealism and the conception of the State as a moral organism.

There is not much that is original in Kant's political philosophy. Rousseau and Montesquieu were the two great formative influences in his political thinking. Dunning states the matter in these words: 'His doctrine as to the origin and nature of the State is merely Rousseau's put into the garb of Kantian terminology and logic; his analysis of Government follows Montesquieu in like manned' (*17*: *131*).

In the field of morals as well as in politics, Kant adopted Rousseau's doctrine of the 'moral will' and made it the cornerstone of his whole thinking.

Respect for personality is the core of Kant's philosophy. Every individual, he tells us, is an end in himself, and no one is to be treated as though he were simply a means to another's end. The categorical imperative which should guide the actions of every rational individual is: 'Act in conformity with that maxim, and that maxim only, which you can at the same time will to be a universal law'.

From the supreme worth and dignity of man Kant deduces liberty and equality as the necessary attributes of all rational beings. His passion for individual liberty is so great that he is not prepared to sacrifice it on the altar of the State.

Passing from the ethical foundations of Kant's political philosophy to definitely political questions, we note that Kant deals with the following subjects:

(a) *The Social Contract.* Kant does not concern himself with the question relating to the historical origin of the State. He considers it as irrelevant and dangerous. Nevertheless he keeps the social contract on the ground that no man can rightfully be compelled to obey a law he has not accepted of his own accord. But it is kept as a 'mere idea' as in the case of Rousseau.

It is worthy of note that none of the idealists following Kant uses the conception of the social contract even as a 'mere idea'.

(b) *Society and the State, Civilization and Culture.* To German thinkers, society is a technical term which means something empirical or external. The State, on the other hand, is conceived as a moral entity, 'the creation of self-conscious reason operating on behalf of the spiritual and ideal interests of its members'. Its function is cultural and educative.

A similar distinction is made between civilization and culture. Civilization is a natural and largely unconscious growth when people live close together. It is external. Culture, on the other hand, is deliberate and conscious. It is internal. It is the working of man's inner spirit. Morality is necessary for its development

(c) *Property.* Like the idealists in general, Kant accepts the institution of private property. He does not adopt the Lockian teaching that a thing with which a person mixes his labour is his. He rejects the extreme individualistic doctrine of property as untenable. The ground on which he supports private property is that it is necessary for the expression of man's will. It is a derived right and does not belong to man by nature.

(d) *Punishment.* Kant realizes that the maintenance of the supremacy of justice through a system of rights necessitates compulsion and punishment. Right must be upheld for its own sake. Therefore, the primary object of punishment is to punish.

Kant does not defend punishment, either in theory or in practice, as a means of striking terror into the hearts of prospective criminals, as do Bentham and Green.

(e) *Rights and Duties.* As is to be expected, Kant lays much stress on the rights and duties of the individual. His interpretation of rights is in the spirit of Rousseau. Right is synonymous with moral freedom. 'The only original right', he says, 'belonging to each man in virtue of his humanity is freedom'. Elsewhere he writes, 'Liberty consists in the power to do anything which inflicts no injury on one's neighbour'.

As between rights and duties Kant's emphasis is on the latter. Bernhardi says, 'While the French people in savage revolt against spiritual and secular despotism had broken their chains and proclaimed their rights, another quite different revolution was working in Prussia—the revolution of duty', and the apostle of this revolution was Kant. Duty is to him self-imposed. It is purely a matter of inner consciousness.

(f) *The Sphere of State Action.* Kant is not a blind worshipper of the State. The general tendency of his political philosophy is individualistic. Hence we find that he does not assign a wide sphere to State action. The State is justified in repelling whatever force is opposed to freedom. The force used by the State is different from other forms of force. 'It has a sort of sacred import; for it represents force consecrated to the assertion and expansion of final goods which are spiritual, moral, rational' (*14*).

(g) *The Right of Revolution.* Having lived during the days of the French Revolution, Kant's chief political work, *Rechtslehre*, published in 1797, bears on it the influence of the Revolution. Kant had a horror of revolution and, in his horror, he preached 'a stagnation which even Burke would have regarded as excessive' (*79 : 28*). The existence of the State is so essential to man for the realization of moral purpose that there can be no right of revolution.

(h) *Forms of Government.* It is interesting to note that the German idealists as a whole, in spite of their advocacy of the general will and the supremacy of the people, find it impossible to abandon their superstitious reverence for monarchy. Kant in particular, 'an aged professor in a royal university of the Kingdom of Prussia', could not bring himself to believe that the King was merely a chief executive; he had something at least of sovereignty inhering in him.

(i) *World Peace.* Kant was enough of a child of the eighteenth century to adopt cosmopolitanism as his creed. Nationalism as yet was a negligible factor so far as Germany is concerned. Kant conceived humanity as a whole and advocated a federal league of nations, 'each subject to the adjudication of the general collective will' (*3 : 27*). He believed that enduring peace could be secured among nations on the basis of such a federated union of mankind. The title of one of his important political works is *On Perpetual Peace.*

CRITICISM OF KANT'S THEORY OF THE STATE

The following are the chief criticisms to which Kant's theory of the State is open:

(a) The ideal that Kant sketches is, as said above, an ideal without a content. It is too abstract and intellectual. It does not make an adequate use of the empirical method.

(b) The German interpretation of the State and culture, including that of Kant, is liable to much abuse. In a sense it is right to speak of the State as the body which embodies the spirit of the people. But German thinkers use this idea too literally. World War I, e.g., was regarded by the Germans as 'an outer manifestation of a great spiritual struggle'. They regarded World War II in the same light.

(c) In spite of his abundant use of the conception of 'moral freedom', Kant never made up his mind whether he wanted to use freedom in the ordinary sense of 'being left alone' or in the higher sense of providing opportunity for the development of man's higher faculties. 'He failed', says Vaughan, 'because he hovered between two entirely different conceptions of the State.' He wavered between eighteenth century individualism and later idealism.

Fichte (1762-1814) was a practical idealist. His political philosophy was largely influenced by the historical events of his day. He began as a cosmopolitan and ended as a nationalist. The disasters of the Napoleonic conquest were responsible for this change.

As far as his theory of the State is concerned, he follows Rousseau very closely in his earlier works. The individual and his rights occupy the central place. In the latter works, there is a decided shifting of interest. The people and the nation are placed at the centre of the scene and a scheme of state socialism is set forth as the ideal of a national State.

Unlike Hegel and his followers, Fichte takes care not to merge the individual in the sovereign State. In this respect he is like Kant and Green.

On the question of property, the starting point of Fichte is much the same as that of Kant, but he goes beyond the cautious limits laid down by his distinguished predecessor. Property, says Fichte, is not mere possession. It has deep moral significance.

In his Closed Commercial State, Fichte supports State Socialism. He supports it not on economic but on moral and idealistic grounds. Every individual has a right to labour and to a certain amount of property for the development of his moral personality. According to Hallowell, as Fichte grew older, he accepted more and more a degree of State control and Collectivism. Like Kant, Fichte upheld the independent position of the hereditary monarch in a democratic constitution.

Hegel (1770-1831). Among German idealists Hegel has had the greatest influence in his own country. There are many who claim that he, more than anyone else, was responsible for World War I of 1914-18. The philosophy expounded by him elevated the State to a mystical height and held that the German people had a divine mission to fulfil in their relation to the rest of the world.

Although proclaimed to be a typical idealist, Hegel was in a genuine sense a realist. 'He had no patience with the "Idea" or the "Absolute" whose foundations are laid in heaven'. His ideal State was not something to be realized in the distant future, but was practically identical with the German State of his day. In his attitude to the State, Hegel was an Absolutist, almost a **'Brutalist'.**

The starting point of Hegel's philosophy is that the real is rational and the rational real. Essentially, God or the Absolute is Thought and Thought is the ultimate reality. Thought is Life and Life is Thought. (Condensed from Hallowell).

1. Kant and Hegel. While Kant had adopted the *a priori* or deductive method, Hegel pursued the historical and evolutionary method. As Vaughan writes: 'Analytic criticism is the dominant idea of Kant; the keynote of Hegel's achievement is evolution'.

Hegel glorified the national State and rejected international morality without any ceremony. Kant, on the other hand, was a believer in world peace and in a federal league of nations. Both, however, were firm believers in monarchy and distrusted representative institutions.

2. Fichte and Hegel. Fichte, as we have said already, marks the transition from eighteenth century cosmopolitanism, as seen in Kant, to nineteenth century nationalism embodied in Hegel. In him also we find an attempt to blend the German philosophy of the State with its philosophy of history.

These basic ideas of the State and of history are taken over into the philosophy of Hegel, and these appear in a more accentuated form in such works as *Outlines of the Philosophy of Rights* (1820) and *Outlines of the Philosophy of History* (1822-31).

3. The Philosophical Implications of Hegel's Political Theory. As in Kant and Fichte, so in Hegel, political theory is developed as part of a comprehensive system of philosophy. The keynote of this philosophy is that 'what is rational is real; and what is real is rational'. Although the historical and evolutionary method is used by Hegel at great length, it is used an an appendix to a vast body of abstract speculation.

Freedom being the essence of man, Hegel conceives man's will as free. Will, then, is free and absolute and manifests itself in various forms by applying right reason. The first of these forms is law, the second is inward morality and the third is 'the whole system of institutions and influences that make for righteousness in the national State' (*2 : 27*). Under Law, Hegel discusses the idea of personality, property and contract, and shows that all of them are manifestations of the free will. A living creature becomes a person only so far as it exercises free will to be a person. Material objects are property because they are expressions of man's free will and have no will of their own. A slave is little better than property because he lacks the free will to be free. Throughout his discussion, Hegel judges laws and rights 'not by a fixed standard, but with reference to the various stages of culture and self-consciousness that history reveals' (*17: Vol. III : 157*)

The second phase is subjective morality. Here Hegel discusses 'those aspects of self-determination in which the individual is affected by a consciousness of other like individuals' (*17 : Vol. III : 175*).

The third and final phase which Hegel conceives as the highest of the three is *Sittlichkeit,* variously translated as 'Social Ethics', 'The Ethical System,' 'the moral life,' and 'Conventional or Customary Morality'. This is the sphere where the mere externality of law and the mere inwardness of morality are reconciled. It is the sphere of concrete morality or conduct.

The successive phases of this final phase of the moral consciousness (*Sittlichkeit*) are the family, the civil or Bourgeois society, and the State.

The family. Hegel's views on this question are the conventional views of his day and are for the most part incorporated into the teachings of Green. The modern family is a necessary element of society and the State, and is at the same time distinct from both. Like other institutions, it represents an element of mind. It reveals an intelligent purpose. It is not founded on mere feeling or on mere contract. It has an ethical and public side. On the ethical side it implies monogamy and equal and permanent relations between the husband and wife. The non-monogamous family is unethical. The modern monogamous family represents a higher stage of civilization than the ancient tribal system or any other system in which 'the whole bond of union rests on mere natural feeling, kindness, generosity, or affection' (*5 : 250*).

The Civil Society. This presents itself to Hegel as 'the opposite extreme of life and mind to that embodied in the family' (*5 : 225-3*).

The Civil society stands for the economic and industrial world in which men appear as bread-earners. For the successful pursuit of their economic interests they demand police functions and administration of justice. A society of this kind does not materially differ from the State. Yet Hegel insists on this distinction, partly with a view to giving an artistic symmetry to his system by dividing it into three stages and giving the highest place to the State. The Civil Society, to Hegel, 'is not a separate society, but only an appearance within a larger system' (*5 : 355*). It is only within the State proper, and resting on its solid power, that such a world as that of Bourgeois society could arise or be conceivable.

The third phase is the Political Organization or the State in the strict sense of the term.

The Idea of Development. From the above treatment of Hegel's philosophical tenets, it is clear that the idea of development is germane to them. The development which Hegel traces is not the development of events or of institutions, but of the speculative idea. The idea—and not the facts—is the real object of our study. 'The idea, like all other things, has a history; and it is only by following its growth in time, that its true nature can be understood' (*79*). The two central ideas of Hegel's system are :

'(a) There is nothing in the whole world of men's experience which is not the creation of reason;

'(b) Reason being essentially a principle of growth, no one of its manifestations is intelligible, unless it be studied along the lines of its continuous development.'

Progress and Freedom. Progress is to be measured in terms of a fixed end, which is the realization of the spirit in accordance with the principle of freedom. Freedom is an idea. It is the ideal to be realized by all men; progress means the gradual realization of the idea of freedom. Freedom does not mean the mere absence of external restraints. It is not synonymous with the liberty of the individual to do what he wills with his own faculties and his own possessions. It stands for the free development of man's power—moral, intellectual and spiritual—according to the fundamental laws of his own nature.

History. To Hegel history is the pilgrimage of the spirit of man in search of itself. History is reasonable. The course is governed by reason, or Providence. The individual plays an important part in history which through the community provides ample opportunity for the free development of his personality. Man's very existence as a moral being demands the community.

World history is world judgment (Hegel). Judgment, as used by Hegel, means victory for one people and defeat for another. Victory is the final proof that the world spirit has passed from one nation to take up its residence in another. To be defeated in such a way that a nation is obliged to take a secondary place among nations is a sure sign that divine judgment has been passed upon it. This is the way that God works in human history. World history reveals four distinct stages in the realization of the idea of freedom. These stages are marked respectively by the ascendancy of the Oriental, the Greek, the Roman, and the German State systems. 'The Orient knew, and to the present day knows, only the *one* (i.e. the despot) is free, the Greek and Roman world that *some* are free, the German world knows that all are free' (*43:104*).

4. Hegel's Theory of the State. Hegel treats the State as the system in which the family and the civil society 'find their completion and their security' (*5 : 159*). The State is the individual in history. It is to history what a given individual is to biography. It is the actualization of freedom because it is the embodiment of reason. Therefore, true freedom for the individual consists in obeying the laws of the State and in cultivating 'the everyday habit of looking on the Commonwealth as our substantive purpose and the foundation of our lives' (*5 : 267*).

The State represents the best in the individual will. It has a will and personality of its own, apart and superior to the wills and personalities of the individuals who compose it. The individual can attain his higher freedom only as a member of it. Rights are derived from the State and no individual has rights against it.

From these premises Joad draws three somewhat paradoxical conclusions.

(a) The State can never act unrepresentatively; thus the policeman who arrests the burglar and the magistrate who locks him up express the real will of the burglar as a member of the State to be arrested and locked up.

(b) The bond which binds the individual to other individuals in the community and to the State as a whole forms an integral part of his personality.

(c) The State contains within itself, and represents, the social morality of all its citizens. This does not mean that the State is itself moral, or that it is bound by moral relations to other States or to any groups within the State itself. It is supra-moral.

All this easily leads to the absolutism, omnipotence, and infallibility of the State. It is the march of God in history. 'It is the divine idea as it exists on earth'. 'It is the divine will as the present spirit unfolding itself to the actual shape and organization of world.' It enriches the personalities of its individual members, purging them of petty aims and all selfishness.

5. War and Internationalism. The nation State is the object of Hegel's veneration. He does not want it to be absorbed in the whole of humanity. An international federation he considers a mere will-o-the-wisp, because, in his judgment, the essential principle of the nation State is struggle, and this is in accordance with the divine purpose. The State can attain its uniqueness and perfection only in relation to other States. Only one nation at a time can be the fullest realization of God. The movement of God in history is seen in the way in which supreme power passes from one nation to another. War is the best illustration of such a flight of the divine spirit in its outward movement. 'The state of war', says Hegel, 'shows the omnipotence of the State in its individuality'. War is an evil, but not an absolute evil. Hegel does not aim at exalting war, but at justifying it.

International law is properly no law, since there is no superior power which can enforce its will upon the State. It represents merely certain usages which are accepted so long as they do not come into conflict with the supreme purpose of the State.

6. Constitution. According to Hegel, the State manifests itself as a constitution or internal public law, as external public law, and as world history. Each one of these reveals a progressive realization of freedom—the synthesis of the universal and individual will. The three important powers in Hegel's rational State are the legislative, the administrative (including the judicial), and the monarchic. Of these three the monarchic is the most important. It is the unifying force in the State, which prevents, the other two from disrupting the State.

Sovereignty, as a philosophical conception belongs to the State as a whole. It does not reside in any one element. It resides only in the organized whole acting as organized whole. Nevertheless, in practice, sovereignty means determination by some person, though this may mean only the signing of one's name. Such a sovereign, says Hegal, is the monarch; and the monarchic principle is thus present and active in every State.

Sovereignty must therefore be assigned scientifically to the monarch, and not to the will of the people, which is vague and indefinite.

The legislature includes the prince, the administration, and the people Without the participation of the first two elements, the unity of the State is sure to be destroyed. The popular element in the legislature must be representative of interests and classes, rather than of masses of individuals.

As for the division of power the legislature lays down general principles, the executive applies them to particular cases and the prince brings 'to a point the acts of the State by giving them the final shape of individual volition' (*5 : 263*). True freedom is possible only in a monarchy of the kind described by Hegel. Landed aristocracy is best fitted to govern because of its economic independence.

7. **Theory of property.** Hegel supports the institution of private property on the familiar ground that it is the material means upon which the individual will can exert itself. It is essential to the fulfilment of personality.

8. **Theory of Punishment.** Hegel, like Kant, looks at the question from the point of view of right and morality. When a right has been violated, says Hegel, it is the duty of the State to reassert it by means of compulsion and punishment, if necessary.

9. **Value of Hegel's Work.** To C.E. Vaughan we owe the following points:

(a) Hegel grasped the connection between politics and morals more clearly, and handled it with far greater insight than any of his predecessors.

(b) He exposed to merciless criticism the popular belief in a sharp cleavage between the individual and the State. The State, he showed, includes the whole circle of man's life. The individual, therefore, cannot be conceived apart from the community of which he is an intrinsic part.

(c) He was the first thinker to grasp the full scope of the historical method.

(d) He was the first to recognize the debt of the individual conscience to the instinctive sense of the community.

10. **Hegel's Limitations.** Notwithstanding these valuable contributions, Hegel's theory is subject to serious limitations:

(a) It easily leads to the absolutism and omnipotence of the State. If the seventeenth century thinkers extolled the Divine Right of Kings, Hegel extolled the Divine Right of the State. As Barker remarks, Hegel exalted the national State to a mystical height. The State is conceived by him as an end in itself and the citizen is called upon to fall down and worship it. Such sacrifice of the individual to the State is not in consonance with our ideas of liberty and democracy.

(b) In spite of his advocacy of the historical method, Hegel deals with the State not as a historical phenomenon but as an intellectual concept. He constructs his view of the State on the basis of his philosophical speculations and, curiously enough, identifies the ideal State with the German State of his day. In politics especially, he insists that the actual is the rational.

(c) There is in Hegel 'a disposition to applaud the existing fact just because it is a fact and to deify successful brutality just because it has succeeded'. It is no wonder that Hegel's disciples in Germany transformed his Idealism into Brutalism.

(d) Hegel's interpretation of world history and of the divine spirit is least convincing. We cannot help feeling that it is forced to fit into Hegel's preconceived notions with a view to glorifying the German State.

(e) Green criticizes the Hegelian conception of the State as a realization of freedom in the following words: 'To an Athenian slave, who might be used to gratify a master's lust, it would have been mockery to speak of the State as realization of freedom, and perhaps it would not be much less to speak of it as such to an untaught and underfed denizen of a London yard with gin shops on the right hand and on the left......Hegel's account of freedom as realized in the State does not seem to the facts of Society as it is, or even as, under the unalterable conditions of human nature, it ever could be' (*29 : 8*). The real flaw in Hegel's theory lies in mistaking tendencies for accomplished facts.

(f) Hegel's denial of the principles of State morality and of the sanctity of international law is not in keeping with idealism, as commonly understood.

(g) Hegel identifies the State with Society. This is a profound mistake. However closely interrelated the State and society may be, the distinction between the two should be kept clearly in view if we are to avoid State despotism.

(h) The Hegelian theory as a whole is abstract and metaphysical and far removed from the realities of life.

Hegel's Disciples. Certain elements in the Hegelian conception of the State were advocated in an exaggerated form by later German political writers and militarists, notably by Neitzsche, Treitschke, and Bernhardi. 'All these taught the indispensability and even the nobility of war; they deified and apotheosized the State; they maintained that it sets its own standards of morality; that it is not bound by the rules of international law except in so far as it chooses to be bound by them; and that every State is itself the judge of its own international obligations, etc.' (*23 : 232 : 33*).

T. H. GREEN AS A SOBER IDEALIST

(1) Sources of Green's Thought. The sources of his thought are Plato, Aristotle, Rousseau, Kant and Hegel. With the Greek philosophers Green agrees in regarding the State as natural and necessary and the life of the individual as an intrinsic part of the life of the community. At the same time he differs from them as regards the aristocratic view of life held by them. While the life of self-satisfaction or self-realization was viewed by Greek thinkers as belonging to the few, Green adopts the democratic point of view that the life of citizenship can be realized by all who are capable of a common interest.

From Rousseau, Green, like Kant and Hegel, borrows the conception of 'moral freedom' as the peculiar and distinctive quality of man. He assumes the free will of man—although within certain limits—and distinguishes between 'negative' and 'positive' freedom.

Freedom in its true sense does not mean the freedom of being left alone. When the satisfaction that man seeks is not his true satisfaction, it may be said that his will is not free. There is no moral freedom in such a case. Such a man is under bondage. True satisfaction may be described as the state of peace or blessedness. It is a state of mind in which the whole man has found his object. It is not the satisfaction of this or that particular desire. It is the realization of the whole self of man.

Green does not accept without qualification Hegel's dictum that the State is the realization of freedom or freedom objectified. Green does not endorse the Hegelian dictum : 'The Actual is the Rational and the Rational is the Actual'. Nor does he give such an exalted place to established morality.

In more ways than one Green departs from the teachings of Hegel and approaches the standpoint of Kant. Witness, for example, his view on individual liberty, war and international morality, where he is more Kantian than Hegelian. Like Kant, Green believes that the only good thing is a goodwill. Freedom is not something negative. It is positive. On questions of resistance to the State, the value of representative government, the place of the monarch in the constitution, the rationale of punishment, etc., he differs from both the German writers. He is at the same time a Hegelian in that he emphasizes the moral value of the majesty of the State. But this emphasis is not at the expense of the 'liberty of the subject'.

(2) Green's Theory of the State. The political philosophy of Green, says E. Barker, can be stated in the form of three related propositions : human consciousness postulates liberty; liberty involves rights; rights demand the State.

Green is convinced that the best way in which the State can help its individual members in the life of self-realization is by providing them with a system of impartial and universal rights. Rights, he holds, are the outer conditions necessary for man's inner development. Natural rights in the sense of pre-social rights are a meaningless conception. But natural rights in the sense of moral or ideal rights are full of meaning. 'They are necessary to the end which it is the vocation of human society to realize' (*29 : 34*). The basis of rights is not mere legal recognition. It is a common moral consciousness. Rights are relative to morality rather than to law. They are the conditions necessary to the fulfilment of man's moral end.

True to the idealistic tradition, Green regards the State as natural and necessary. It is an ethical institution essential to the moral development of man. Its primary purpose is to enforce rights, even by compulsion, if necessary. The State is justified in using force because it expresses the general will of the people, and by general will Green means the common consciousness of a common end. "Will, not force, is the basis of the State".

According to Green, the State is neither absolute nor omnipotent. It is limited from within and without. From within (a) it is limited by the fact that law can deal only with external acts and intention and not with motives. Therefore, the State cannot promote the good life directly. It can only remove obstacles to good life. (b) It is limited also by the fact that in exceptional circumstances the individual has duty of resistance. (c) Green further recognizes that the various permanent groups within society have their own inner system of right and that the right of the State over them is one of adjustment. As E. Barker observes: 'The State adjusts for each (group) its system of rights internally and it adjusts each system of rights to the rest eternally' (*3 : 43*). Because of its power of adjustment, the State, says Green, has ultimate authority. For not adopting the pluralistic position wholesale, MacIver criticizes Green in these words: 'All through he is considering what the State can and therefore should do to secure the conditions within which man can act as a free moral being. But the poles of his thought are still the individual and the State. He does not consider how both are affected by the existence of other associations with other instrumentalities than political law. Had he done so he would have seen that the problem is not simply what the state should do but also what the State is permitted to do, surrounded as it is by other powers, limited as it is by definite organizations of other kinds, fulfilling functions of their own in ways of their own. Green remains on the verge of the modern problem of sovereignty' (*55 : 41*).

From without, Green holds, the State is limited by international law. Unlike Hegel and like Kant, Green believes in a universal brotherhood of men. The right of every man as man to free life involves the conception of a common humanity and of a common social organism.

(3) War. (29) Holding the above point of view, Green's attitude towards war is entirely different from that of Hegel and his German disciples. War, says Green, is never an absolute right. It is at best a relative right. It violates the right of man to free life. It may be 'cruel necessity'.

Nevertheless, war is a moral wrong. The argument that those who kill in war do not intend to kill anyone in particular, does not make the violation of right any less serious.

A second argument which is often used in defence of war is that in a war between civilized nations soldiers may incur the risk voluntarily and that, therefore, there is no violation of the right to free life. Green refutes this argument. His refutation is that it does not rest with a man to retain or give up his right to life at his pleasure. (It is for the same reason that suicide is condemned everywhere).

A third argument sometimes used by those who defend war is that the right to physical life may be overridden by a right arising from the exigencies of moral life. Green is not convinced by this argument. He holds that all that the argument in question does is to shift the blame of war to those responsible for those exigencies. War remains a wrong just the same. The destruction of life in war is always wrong-doing, whoever be the wrong-doer.

A fourth argument used by some people in defence of war is that war calls out certain virtues, such as heroism and self-sacrifice and that it is the only means of maintaining the social conditions of the moral development of man. As such, they argue that war is a necessary factor in human progress. While admitting the force of this argument, Green holds that destruction of life in war is always wrong-doing. Caesar's wars of conquests in Gaul and the English wars in India were certainly followed by beneficent changes. But these changes, Green believes, could have been brought about by other means just as well.

Hence it follows that the State, so far as it is true to its principle, cannot have to infringe the rights of man as man by conflicts with other States. War is not an essential attribute of the State in its perfect condition. It may belong to the State in its imperfect actuality. But as the State becomes more perfect, there will be less and less need for war.

Therefore, we do not accept the further argument used by the supporters of war that conflict between States is inevitable. It is not because States exist, but because they do not fulfil their functions as States in maintaining and harmonizing general rights, that such conflicts are necessary. The conclusion to which Green is driven is that no State as such is absolutely justified in doing a wrong to mankind, though a particular State may be conditionally justified. War cannot be condemned on the ground that it is a necessary incident of the existence of States. There is no ground for holding that a State is justified in doing whatever its interests seem to require irrespectively of its effects on other men. War at best is only a relative right.

The sixth and the final argument used in defence of war is that Green's consmopolitan view will destroy patriotism and national life and necessitate a universal empire. Green's reply to this argument is that public spirit, to be real, must be national, but the more a nation becomes a true State the more does it find outlets for its national spirit in ways other than conflicts with other nations.

The identification of patriotism with militarism is a survival of the times when States in the full sense did not exist. Patriotism and militarism are by no means identical. Standing armies are a proof that mankind is not yet thoroughly organized into political life. They are due not to the development of a system of States, but to circumstances which witness the shortcomings of that system.

(4) State Action. As said earlier, Green conceives State action in negative terms. Good life is for the most part self-earned. The State cannot promote it directly. All that it can and should do is to remove obstacles that lie before human capacity as it seeks to do 'things worth doing'. A good act is good only when it is done spontaneously, that is, from a disinterested motive. Acts done under compulsion lose their moral value. What the State must do, therefore, is only to enforce those acts the doing of which, *from whatever motive,* is necessary for the good life within society.

Applying the theory to the practical conditions of his day, Green considers ignorance, drink, and pauperism obstacles to the free expression of human capacity, and is, therefore, in favour of a considerable range of State action in the removal of these obstacles. This point needs stressing because idealism is sometimes criticized as being a high sounding justification of hidebound conservatism. Sabine writes: "What Green added to liberal theory was the conception of collective well being as a pre-condition of individual freedom and responsibility."

(5) Punishment. Green's treatment of this question is an intrinsic part of his theory of State action. The criminal's will, which is anti-social, constitutes a force opposed to freedom. Punishment in such a case is a force directed against that force. Punishment is not inflicted with any direct reference to the moral guilt of the offender in the past, or to his moral reformation in the future (*3 : 48*).

(6) Property. On this question, as many others, Green takes a liberal view for his day. He is neither a defender of private property in all its aspects nor an out-and-out critic of it. To use modern terminology, he is neither an individualist nor a socialist. He defends property in general on the ground that it is indispensable to the expression of man's personality. It is a corollary of the right to free life. It is the external means by which the invisible self of man is made visible. It provides man an opportunity to give a concrete expression to his ideas, and ideals, his aims and aspirations, whether he actually uses it to that end or not. Every man should have the opportunity to earn property, because every one has the capacity to partake of a common social good. But this capacity varies from man to man. Therefore, property should be unequal. Different men have different functions to fulfil in the life of the social whole, and inequality of property is a necessary condition of it. When, however, some people acquire or retain property in such a manner as seriously to interfere with the realization of the wills of others, the State should step in to redeem the situation. On this ground Green justifies the restriction of private property in land, and opposes family settlements. His ideal is 'a class of small proprietors tilling their own land'. The State is not to appropriate unearned increment. Green defends freedom of inheritance and freedom of trade.

(7) Representative Government and Practical Politics. Unlike Kant and Hegel, Green was a firm believer in representative government and an advocate of a wide franchise. He was an active liberal in politics and not a mere academician. 'He had always a lively sympathy for the middle class and non-conformity. He had, besides, a keen interest in education and licensing reform....In the civic politics of Oxford he took a share which has made his name a tradition and an example in the university. In national politics, he was a liberal of the school of John Bright, and from 1867 onwards he appeared on political platforms' (*3 : 31*).

(8) Criticism and Appreciation. Among those who have adopted the idealistic point of view Green seems to be the most sober. His justification of property in capital, his depreciation of any attempt on the part of the State to appropriate unearned increment, and his stress on the deterrent theory of punishment, may not commend themselves to us today. 'But what matters is rather his principles than analysis of a particular set of conditions or his suggestions of a particular policy. If his principles are true, each age can progressively interpret their meaning to meet its own needs'. His firm hold on the worth of persons, his deep sense of the liberty of the individual, his conviction that individual good is an intrinsic part of social good, his refusal to raise the State to a mystical height, his recognition of a universal brotherhood and international law, his eagerness to place limits on the power of the State so that spontaneity in the performance of moral acts may not be deadened, his emphasis on rights, his view that property is a means for the expression of personality, and his admission that in extreme cases the individual has the duty of resistance–all these are as sound today as they were when Green's lectures were delivered (1879-80).

In the striking words of E. M. Burns (*Ideas in Conflict*, p. 251), "Green was the most liberal of the new idealists. In fact, he is sometimes considered the real father of the liberalism of the twentieth century. It is not concerned essentially with the life, liberty, and pursuit of happiness of atomistic individuals, but with the welfare of the whole society and especially with the welfare of its less privileged members. Green owed almost nothing to the natural rights, *laissez faire* philosophy of his English predecessors".

F. H. Bradley (1846-1924) is more Hegelian than Green ever was. In his chapter on *My Station and its Duties in Ethical Studies,* Bradley expounds his theory of the State. E. Barker regards this theory as a combination of the Platonic conception of justice with the Hegelian conception of *Sittlichkeit.* Without going into the details of Bradley's view of the State, we may say that the conception of a moral organism is the central feature of it. The sum of relations in which man stands constitutes his position or station in society. It is the duty of every man, says Bradley, to find that position in society and fulfil the functions attached to it. In so doing, he obeys the law of his being. All this means that for the individual morality consists in the fulfilment of his station and its duties.

Bradley realizes that no given State is a perfect embodiment of the ideal which he sketches. At any given time the morality of the State may be on a lower plane than the public conscience of the people or ideal morality. Again, individuals may desire to rise above the narrow limits of their station in the community and realize a cosmopolitan morality. All this may lead to the realization of 'all humanity as a divine organic whole' (*3 : 66*).

The chief criticisms to which Bradley's theory is open, are:

(1) No careful distinction is made between the State and society. The State as described here is really society as well as the State.

(2) 'My station and its duties,' is a phrase difficult of interpretation. It may be construed to mean that the individual should be satisfied with whatever lot has befallen him and should carry out the duties of that station without complaining, even as the law of *Dharma* has meant in relation to caste. Such an interpretation would, of course, make idealism synonymous with hide-bound conservatism.

B.Bosanquet (1848-1923). Hobhouse characterizes him as Hegel's 'most modern and most faithful exponent.' This is somewhat of an exaggeration. We are safe in saying, however, that Bosanquet begins with Rousseau and Green, and ends almost in Hegel.

The starting point of Bosanquet's theory is the conception of the free moral will of man expounded by Rousseau. True freedom, to all idealists, consists in willing rational, universal objects. The exposition of Bosanquet's doctrine falls into three stages: (1) distinction between the 'actual' will of the individual and his 'real' will; (2) connection between the 'real' will of the individual and the 'general' will of society; (3) the State as the supreme expression of the general will.

(1) Using the 'actual and 'real' in a technical sense, Bosanquet consistently uses the term 'actual' to describe man's impulsive, unreflective, or recalcitrant will, and the term 'real' to describe his rational or 'constant' will.

(2) The 'real' will of the individual does not stand alone. It is bound up with the 'real' wills of other individuals in society and becomes the 'general' will. This means that the individual can make the best of himself only in society.

(3) The State is the perfect embodiment of the general will. The common life of society depends upon the law and political order provided by the State.

The various ethical institutions in society are the family, the neighbourhood group, the nation State, and the like. Of these the State is the most supreme. It is *the* ethical ideal. It is a source of all-pervading adjustments. It is an operative criticism of all institutions. In its narrow sense, it is a political organization using force. It put its seal of approval on all those social efforts which are beneficial in their nature.

In a broad sense, it stands for the general organization and synthesis of life and is practically synonymous with society. This latter interpretation of the State as a working conception of life as a whole brings Bosanquet very close to Hegel.

Green and Bosanquet. A close study of these two writers reveals not only striking resemblances, but also striking differences.

Resemblances

(1) Like Green, Bosaquet assumes the indispensability of the State for the realization of man's higher life. But unlike him, he comes close to the Hegelian conception of the free absorption of the individual in the spirit of a nation.

(2) On the nature of the State and the proper sphere of State action, there is little to distinguish Bosanquet's theory from that of Green. Both writers believed that while the State is an ethical institution, it cannot, in the very nature of the case, promote morality directly.

(3) Unlike the German idealists, and particularly Hegel, neither Green nor Bosanquet is a believer in absolute monarchy. True to the English tradition, they both believe in representative government as the best form. But Bosanquet's reverence for the State is so great that it may easily lead to State absolutism.

Differences

(1) On the question of resistance to the State, Bosanquet adopts a more conservative point of view than that adopted by Green. The State as representing the will of the community, has the sole right of judging when the expressions of the individual conscience are dangerous to the welfare of the community. His general conclusion is that the orderly processes of the State 'as sole organizer of rights and as guardian of moral values' are so important that the 'right of rebellion' may be regarded as almost negligible.

(2) In his theory of punishment, Bosanqquet departs to some extent from Green. Both thinkers adopt the element of deterrence in punishment as the most essential. However, Bosanquet's view is somewhat more positive than that of Green.

(3) In his treatment of war and international morality, Bosanquet parts company with Green most decidedly. As seen already, Green condemns war as wrong because it violates the rights of every rational being to free life. Bosanquet adopts a totally different point of view. He makes a distinction between the acts of the State as such and the personal acts of individual statesmen and insists that it is altogether inappropriate to apply to acts of the former category moral terms like murder and theft.

To the question whether or not it is possible to remove these conflicts which arise out of the many-sidedness of life by recognizing humanity as a unit, Bosanquet returns a negative. His answer is that at present there is no organization of humanity, no connected communal consciousness. States are not united to one another in the way that individuals in a State are united together. The League of Nations, he contends, was just a means to make international law more effective. It was not a single community. There were no common aims and common life. Humanity is an aggregate rather than an organism. Our primary loyalty is to a quality and not to a crowd; it is to the best life of our own community. From a religious point of view one might say that both these loyalties should coincide but not in the practical secular life.

Criticism and Appreciation of Bosanquet's Theory

(1) Hobhouse, who is a vehement critic of Bosanquet, criticizes him for his doctrine of the will. He holds that the distinction between the 'actual' and 'real' will is altogether false and claims that the actual is the real and the real is the actual.

Hobhouse says that there is strictly no part of the individual which is more real than any other part. But we know from experience that one act is not exactly the same as another. We constantly differentiate between moods and act. By 'actual' Hobhouse means that all the acts expressive of the will—good and bad—are there. No one denies that. The question is, do they all have the same quality or value ?

Calling to his aid the average man, John Jones, Hobhouse argues that if Jones is to give up his selfish will, his will must be transformed. Bosanquet would not use the word 'transformed', because the individual is rational even at the beginning. What Bosanquet calls 'real', Hobhouse calls 'good', 'rational' or 'harmonious'.

Passing from the distinction between the 'actual' and the 'real' will to the conception of the general will, Hobhouse asks, what ground is there for assuming that the harmony between the individual and society will express the true will of the individual ? Suppose an individual desires to get the better of others. How are we to show him that this is not his 'real' will ? Hobhouse answers it by saying, 'Consistency be hanged ! I'II do what I please.'

When Bosanquet uses the phrase 'the general will', he has in mind a general scheme running through a common nature or a common structure. Common nature does not mean that all are identical. General will stands for a common social nature determining the lives of individuals. But it is not identically the same in everyone of the people. Hobhouse says, 'In quality and character, these real wills are indistinguishable.'

A little later Hobhouse attempts a definition of 'self'. In this definition he emphasizes physical, bodily things. He forgets that the things that unite us with other people are not private, personal things. Bosanquet, on the other hand, places it in the higher spheres. According to him, individuality expresses itself in the share it takes in the common life of society. Bosanquet can quite as well work with Hobhouse's phrase 'individual of a higher order' as with general will. The point to remember is that we cannot draw hard and fast lines between two individualities, although we can draw those lines on the bodily side.

(2) Bosanquet's conception of the social mind or social will, together

with the related conception of a social organism, has also been questioned by critics. Here, again, it seems to us that Bosanquet stands on a much more solid ground than do his critics.

Bosanquet is right in insisting that only in society the individual can make the most of his life. No one can develop his human nature in a well-rounded way apart from society. This, however, is not the same as saying that there is no conflict between the individual and society in practice, as Bosanquet is apt to hold. Ivor Brown, who criticizes Bosanquet, says, "This conception of the State as a social organism, transcending all the individual organisms that compose it is......fundamentally undemocratic' (*6 : 144*). Nevertheless, there is some justification for Brown's charge that, in his doctrine of the general will, Bosanquet 'puts into the hands of the governing class and of those who can worm their way into that charmed circle a weapon of infinite menace' (*6 : 145*). 'If the concept of the social organism is rigorously applied the result is State-slavery on an unparalleled scale' (*6 : 148*).

(3) As shown above, Bosanquet practically identifies the State with society and comes very near to a belief in the free absorption of the individual in the rational State. These are blemishes in his theory against which we cannot defend him.

(4) Neither can we defend Bosanquet's views on war and international morality. The State is responsible for the actions of its agents. It is quibbling with words to say that the actions of the State as such are different from the acts of its accredited representatives. Both the State and its agents are responsible to the moral judgment of the world. As Ernest Barker puts it, 'If a citizen can....treat his own State as legally responsible for damage, it is difficult to see why a State, which can undergo legal responsibility, should not also undergo moral responsibility if there is any body of moral opinion to affix responsibility (*3 : 78-9*).' Bosanquet is too full of enthusiasm for the State when he claims that the State 'has no determinate function in a larger community, but is itself the supreme community, the guardian of a whole moral world, but not a factor within an organised moral world' (*5 : 302*).

Many and varied are the criticisms which have been levelled against the idealistic interpretation of the State.

Criticism of Idealism and Defence

(1) Critics of idealism say that it is a purely abstract and metaphysical theory and that it does not deal with realities. The conceptions which it presents are far removed from the actual conditions of life. Thus William James describes the idealistic theory as 'a rationalistic philosophy that indeed may call itself religious, but that keeps out of all definite touch with concrete facts and joys and sorrows'. It is a purely intellectual theory. It considers man as a rational being and leaves out of account the other aspects of human nature. The State is presented in terms of conscious reason and will, and such factors as habit and imitation, feelings and passions are entirely ignored.

We admit that a considerable part of the teaching of the idealists is abstract and metaphysical. It gives a theoretical basis to practical facts. Political science being a normative science will be failing in its duty if it does not provide us with ideal types and standards. It is not a mere descriptive science. Apropos of this, Garner writes: 'Like ethics political theory is concerned with what ought to be as well as with what actually is; the real nature of a thing is what the thing is when its growth is fully developed; the political philosopher, therefore, may very properly idealize the State and deal with it in its imaginary splendour and perfection' (*23 : 238*).

When the idealist claims that the State is the product of reason and the rational will, he does not pretend that political life and political institutions have come into being as a result of careful reasoning. What he means is that, looking at the development through the ages, it is clear that man's reason has been in operation all the time even though in an indirect and implicit manner. 'If it had not been present, the development would have ended not, as it has done, in a rational system of organized life which our reason can understand, but in a confused amalgam of taboos and instincts and habits which would have no meaning, no connection, and no reason' (*3 : 83*).

The idealist admits that even today, in spite of the great advances that man has made in various directions, his actions are not often dictated by conscious reason. They are frequently the result of habit or unconscious limitation.

(2) Even those who admit the importance of reason and will in a consideration of State life, feel at times that idealism mistakes ideals for actual facts. Instead of realizing the ideal, it idealizes the real. This tendency is particularly marked in Rousseau and Hegel. Hobson goes so far as to describe idealism as 'the tactics of conservatism.' The social reformer despairs of it, because it seems to preach 'the divine right of things as they are'.

This criticism is not without its justification. Aristotle idealizes slavery; Hegel glorifies war; and Green is able to reconcile private ownership of capital with his liberal tendencies. Our only defence is that there is no necessary connection between idealism and conservatism. It is quite possible to argue for a radical social programme on the basis of idealism as it is to argue for conservatism. The phrase 'removal of obstacles to good life is so broad as to include extensive State action, depending of course upon external circumstances and the predilections of the persons employing the idealistic theory.

(3) In close connection with the above criticism, it is sometimes said that the idealistic theory is too negative in character, especially in the sphere of State action. The idealists hold that the State can deal only with external acts since it uses compulsion. It cannot deal with motives. There is no way by which the State can directly promote moral excellence or perfection.

In defence of idealism, it may be said that, while the theory of State action is stated in negative terms, the results are positive. Individualism glorifies the individual and treats him as the end to which society is only a means. Socialism and Hegelianism go to the other extreme and claim for the State 'the glamour which belongs to the highest self-expression by which man transcends his isolation (*5* : p. *XXXIII*)'. English idealism, on the contrary, takes the middle course, although we cannot help feeling that both Green and Bosanquet exaggerate the purely negative aspect of State action.

(4) The idealistic theory, remarks Bosanquet, is said to be too narrow and rigid. Critics say that this theory may have been applicable to the simple conditions of ancient Greek City-States where no distinction was made between the State and society. But under the changed conditions of today, it is said that the State should be carefully distinguished from society and that a more adequate place should be given to the permanent associations within society than has been given by the traditional monistic theory.

We admit that many of the idealists fail to separate the State from society and that this failure leads to the sacrifice of the individual to society. At the same time, we are not prepared to admit the pluralistic point of view which seeks to reduce the State to a place of absolute equality with other associations in society.

Another sense in which idealism is said to be too narrow is in its alleged emphasis on the moral and spiritual goods of life to the exclusion of the material. The end of the State is assuredly good life or the excellence of souls. But this does not mean that the idealist advocates the direct promotion of good life by State action. Nor does it mean that he is altogether oblivious of the material needs of man. A perusal of Green's theory, for instance, is sufficient to show how close this writer keeps to the concrete facts of social life.

The ground on which idealism is said to be too rigid is in connection with the difficulty of locating the general will. Pluralists either deny the conception of the general will altogether or claim that each permanent association within society has a general will and personality of its own. The idealist does not refuse to a limit that groups or associations other than the State can have a will and personality of their own. All that he wants is that the State should be given unique place in society on account of the special tasks which it is called upon to perform.

Joad denounces idealism as unsound in theory, untrue to fact, and liable to extend a dangerous sanction to the more unscrupulous actions of existing States in the sphere of foreign policy.

(a) Both Joad and MacIver claim that the idealists identify the State with society and that this is a serious flaw in their theory. This criticism is no doubt applicable to the German idealists and to such British idealists as Bradley and Bosanquet; but is not applicable to such sober idealists as Green. MacIver argues that the community may be regarded as possessing 'an enduring mind (*55 : 451*).' but not the State.

(b) We agree with Joad when he argues that to say that man cannot develop himself fully apart from the State is not to accept the omnipotence of the State. But the assumption that he makes that the idealists as a whole believe in the omnipotence of the State is a mistake. We have already seen how narrowly Green and Bosanquet limit the sphere of State action. Joad draws a false contrast between the individual and the State when he writes: 'The State exists for individuals, individuals do not exist for the State (*41 : 18*)'

(c) Both Joad and MacIver consider the distinction between the 'real' and 'actual' will as unsound in theory and unreal in practice. Joad defines 'real' will 'as a will to carry out every decision of the majority of an association to which I belong' (*41 : 19*).

(d) MacIver, in particular, attacks the idealistic doctrine of the personality of the State. **His argument is that a State consists of persons, but that does not make the State a person any more than a grove of trees is itself a tree or a colony of animals an animal.**

Many of the criticisms of MacIver and other opponents of idealism apply to individual governments, but do not apply to the State as such. The mistake made by some idealists is in identifying the actual government of the day with their ideal State.

Appreciation of Idealism

While not apologizing for extreme forms of idealism, as found in Hegel, we believe that the sober idealism of the type presented by Green has much to commend it.

(1) It maintains a close connection between ethics and politics, and rightly holds that no political progress is possible apart from the application of the highest moral principles to our individual and social lives. Separation of politics from ethics is disastrous to both.

(2) It insists on the organic unity of society and shows clearly how society is held together by the State. Individual development is impossible in isolation. The true good of the individual is to find his proper place in the common life of society.

(3) It holds that the highest form of good is a self-earned good. Any form of State action which is a hindrance to the spontaneous performance of morality stands self-condemned. Individual initiative, enterprise, and originality should have free scope for their manifestation in every well-ordered society.

(4) Idealists are justified in placing before us a goal towards which political progress may be directed. To the extent to which this ideal is a mere Utopia or the product of one's fancy, it is futile. But to the extent

to which it is based upon what we know of human nature and the practical conditions of social life, it is valuable. The ideal presented by the idealists is capable of realization. It is not an idle dream.

Summing up the case for idealism, Garner writes: 'It may be said of much of the criticism which has been directed against the idealistic theory that it is unfair, exaggerated and based upon a misconception of the theory itself. In so far as the idealists exalted the State above all other human associations, regarded it as indispensable to the realization of the good life, and held that, as such, it is entitled to the loyalty of the citizen and may demand sacrifices of him to preserve its existence, that it is the sole source of law and of rights, and that in it alone, is the individual capable of realizing fully the ends of his existence, and that without it human progress and civilization would be impossible, the theory is entirely sound and irreproachable' (*23 : 238*).

PRAGMATISM IN POLITICS

Pragmatic Criticism of the Idealist Theory

It should be made clear at the outset that Laski was not a profound philosophical thinker. He was not interested in metaphysics and never devoted himself to a serious study of the problems of speculative philosophy. But in his youthful days he became temperamentally associated with the pragmatic movement in contemporary American philosophy.[1] The ideas of the American pragmatists influenced his outlook at this stage to a considerable extent. He acknowledges a profund intellectual indebtedness to the pragmatic philosophy of William James who was a source of great ideological inspiration to him.[2] Laski, therefore, criticizes the idealist theory from the point of view of pragmatism.

It is from William James and other pragmatists that Laski borrows his empirical method which he regards as the only adequate method in scientific inquiry. He considers the work of these philosophers in discrediting metaphysical absolutism as of lasting benefit to humanity. He feels that the monistic dogma has been a stumbling-block in the way of all progress. Absolutism has always been a rationalized plea in favour of the *status quo.* Ethically, it has always endeavoured to bridge over the distinction between good and evil because the absolute must be a harmonious whole. Idealism has always preached acquiescence in the evil rather than struggle against it. Laski recoils from the wooden unifomity of monistic systems in order to seek comfort in the pluralistic universe of James.

Scientific Method and Pragmatism

Laski once himself explained the cause of his unusual interest in the pragmatic philosophy. "The real cause of the sudden interest in prag-

1. W. Y. Elliott : "The Pragmatic Revolt in Politics", Chapter V—"The Politics of Mr. H. J. Laski" : 142-76 (1st Ed. 1928).
2. Harold J. Laski : "The Problem of Sovereignty," p. 23, "The Foundations of Sovereignty", p. 169; "A Grammar of Politics", p. 261.

matism," he tells us, "was the impact of scientific method and its immense social consequences upon a pure metaphysics which, in the cloistered atmosphere of academic life, made a futile distinction between thought and deed, between theory and practice. Pragmatism was an attempt at their integration. It urged the need to recognize that thought is an instrument of life, and that in life the process of which thought is a part seeks to verify hypotheses which are expected to prove capable, as they are applied, of satisfying the demands men make out of their experience" (*121* : *726*).

A Philosophy of the Modern Age

Pragmatism is essentially a philosophy of the modern age, having its rise within the twentieth century. It is essentially a philosophy of life as distinct from the philosophy of abstractions. It is not only a philosophy but also a movement, a programme of action and a way of life.[3] "It makes philosophy", as Laski says, "an activity for the market-place and not a debate upon definitions confined to the cloister. Indeed, it may well claim that it has the immense merit of insisting upon the importance of philosophy to ordinary people instead of depriving them of its instruction by transforming it into a monkish vocation for a handful of scholars. In its essence, it urges upon the philosopher the need, if he would find the meaning of truth and good, to find them in the experience of daily life" (*95* : *726*).

Pragmatism of William James

The fundamental message of pragmatism is the spirit of youth, adventure, and experimentation. "A pragmatist," says James, "turns his back resolutely and once for all upon a lot of inveterate habits dear to professional philosophers. He turns away from abstractions and insufficiency, from verbal solutions, from bad *a priori* reasons, from fixed principles, closed systems, and pretended absolutes and origins. He turns towards concreteness and adequacy, towards fact, towards action and towards power. That means the empiricist temper regnant and the rationalist temper sincerely given up. It means the open air and possibilities of nature, as against dogma, artificiality, and a pretence of finality in truth."[4] The importance of the ideas of James can be judged from the serious controversy they immediately precipitated in the contemporary philosophical world and from the loud denunciations they received from the idealist philosophers.[5]

3. W.Y. Elliott : "The Pragmatic Revolt in Politics" Chapter I, pp. 45-68.
4. William James : "Pragmatism", p. 51.
5. Laski makes an interesting comment on this controversy :—"I venture the guess that no small part of the angry debate which centred around the discussion of pragmatism forty and fifty years ago is set in a social framework of very considerable interest. The major exponents of pragmatism, William James in the first place, and John Dewey in the second, were both Americans who so restated the central problems of philosophy that for the first time since the great debate between official theology and the Darwinians they

Idealism and Pragmatism Compared

There is a world of difference between the traditional idealistic and the new pragmatic approach to philosophy. While idealism is monistic, determinist and rationalistic in outlook, the pragmatism of James is pluralistic, evolutionary, voluntaristic and empiricist in temper. The idealist takes a highly abstract but quite conservative and stationary view of the world. The pragmatist on the contrary interprets the world in a positivistic, experimentalist and progressive way. While idealism is a philosophy of the *status quo,* pragmatism is a philosophy of social change, evolution and progress (*121 : 446*).

Pragmatic Theory of Knowledge

Reality, as conceived by the pragmatists, is fluid, changing, evolving and constantly transforming itself into something new. It is neither mental nor material but vital. The pragmatic epistemology denies the correspondence and coherence theories of truth and evolves its own instrumental theory of truth.[6] Laski is attracted by the pragmatic epistemology as its necessary consequence is the empiricist outlook that condemns as unwarranted the rationalistic search for cosmic unity. In other words, the pragmatic epistemology enables him to formulate his pluralistic conception of the world. The world of the pragmatists is pluralistic not only in the spatial sense but also in the temporal sense. James says, "Mind engenders truth upon reality. Our minds are not here simply to copy a reality that is already complete. They are here to complete it, to add to its importance by their own remodelling of it, to decant its contents, so to speak, into a more significant shape. In point of fact, the use of most of our thinking is to help us to change the world".[7] Thus the purpose of James to rouse the philosophers from their 'monistic slumber' is fulfilled.

Pragmatism as Unconscious Ally of Idealism

The most serious criticism that can be levelled against the pragmatic theory is that it is an unconscious ally of idealism which it wants to refute. It is true that the idealist writers have taken grave objections to certain aspects of the pragmatic theory but the whole controversy seems artificial when the broad results of the two theories are critically examined. As

---

commanded the interest and attention of the whole civilized world''. (Quoted from ''The American Democracy'', chapter XIV, p. 726).

6. William James : ''Pragmatism'', p. 201. ''True ideas'', says James, ''are those that we can assimilate, validate, corroborate and verify. False ideas are those that we cannot......The truth of an idea is not a stagnant property inherent in it. Truth *happens* to be an idea. It becomes true, is made true by events. Its verity is in fact an event, a process; the process namely of its verifying itself, its verification. Its validity is the process of its validation.''

7. William James : Letter to the ''New York Times''. November 3, 1907 quoted by Ralph H. Gabriel in ''The Course of American Democratic Thought'', p. 286.

Laski himself later realised, the idealist and the pragmatist arrive at similar conclusions by travelling a different route (*121 : 447*). Josiah Royce was the most prominent American idealist who criticized vehemently some of the new assumptions of William James. But to an independent observer, the differences between their philosophies seem quite superficial and the points of similarity really remarkable. While Royce justifies his belief in the Absolute on rationalistic grounds, James is prepared to revere the Absolute as pragmatic need of the finite human beings. Thus even monism appears in the philosophy of James from the side-door. "Is not James," asks Laski in disillusionment, "driven to admit that we all end in the bosom of the Absolute, even if he permits himself to hope that the Aboslute is—if we only will hard enough—perhaps a little less Absolute than Royce had prophesied? And if that be the right conclusion, are we not bidden to find fulfilment less in the arrival at our own end than in the journey down that road which is the way to which the Absolute compels us" (*121 : 449*).

It seems that much of the sound and fury of the pragmatist fails to hit the mark. It is all the more ridiculous when it is understood that this sound and fury is directed against an idealism which is most probably its ideological ally. It has been rightly pointed out that 'radical empiricism' of the pragmatic thinker logically leads to subjective idealism and solipsism. Pragmatism also compromises its position by acknowledging the Absolute as the fulfilment of finite wills. It means that the pragmatist substitutes a voluntaristic route for the rationalistic one of the Hegelian idealist but, nevertheless, arrives at the same destination. Thus it seems that the victory gained by the pragmatist over his idealistic adversary is at best a pyrrhic victory.

Liberal Temper of Pragmatism

Pragmatism became a popular philosophy primarily due to its liberal temper opposed to the conservative temper of contemporary idealism. But the distinction suggested here is mainly a distinction of emphasis and not that of quality. Sometimes it has been suggested that pragmatism is a philosophy of "cosmic republicanism". But this description is nothing more than a figure of speech. To equate idealism with evolution and stability may be correct but to identify the pragmatic creed with a cult of revolution and anarchy cannot be justified. The ideas of James and Dewey may be less conservative than those of Bradley and Bosanquet but they are certainly not more liberal or radical than those of Royce or Green who are both idealists.

Middle-Class Philosophy

As Laski subsequently realised, pragmatism and neoidealism in modern philosophy represent the same social background. They are both essentially middle class philosophies. They are both byproducts of the same economic and social forces. While the philosophy of the Oxford idealists symbolizes the spirit of a triumphant English bourgeoisie, the struggling American bourgeoisie has chosen the pragmatic cult of James as the intellectual medium of its self-expression (*121* : *166*). It is to be noted that pragmatism remained a source of ideological inspiration to Laski only during the pluralistic phase of his political outlook. The influence of James on Laski's thought declined as his political theory drifted away from pluralism.

Impact of Pragmatism on Laski's Thought

There are three important points of contact between the pragmatic philosophy of James and the pluralistic political theory of Laski. In the first place, the argument against the sovereign power of the state sounds peculiarly like the protest against the all-inclusiveness of the Absolute. Secondly, it is submitted by both Laski and James that the "experimentalist" method is the only valid method of scientific inquiry in their respective spheres of study. Thirdly, the pragmatic cult of James and the pluralistic theory of Laski are essentially the dogmas of conservative reconciliation. They can in no case be regarded as radical doctrines having any kind of revolutionary potentiality. It cannot be inferred from the above that there is a logical or necessary connection between philosophical pragmatism and political pluralism. It merely shows that both these theories have been cast in a kindred psychological temper.[8]

Inadequacy of Pragmatic Pluralism

Finally, we find that both James and Laski had to modify or even abandon their pluralistic views in philosophy and politics respectively which they so tenaciously upheld in their youth. James modified his pragmatic pluralism to profess a conditional belief in the Absolute as a moral holiday.[9] Laski abandoned his political pluralism because it did not explain the impact of economic forces on political evolution. He adopted a revised form of Marxism because it alone could give a satisfactory answer to contemporary problems in various spheres. The conversion of Laski and James to new monistic ideals demonstrated the insufficiency or incompetence of the pluralistic ideal in the realms of political and philosophical theory to a great extent.

Rejection of the Ethical Conception of the State

Laski has rejected the ethical conception of the state as propounded by various thinkers of the idealist school from Hegel to Green. But he does not suggest, as Machiavelli and Hobbes did, that ethical questions are irrelevant in political science. This is evident from the fact that he pleaded resolutely for the 'sovereignty' of the individual conscience as against the sovereignty of an impersonal brute force called the state. Thus the pluralistic protest against state sovereignty is basically a protest of the moralist.

The ethical ideas of Laski have been set forth in relation to his conception of conscience and the theory of allegiance. His approach in ethics

8. C.H. Kung : "Political Pluralism—A Study in Contemporary Political Theory", Chapter VIII : 206-7.

9. *Ibid*, p. 203.

is similar to that of an intuitionist but not identical with it. His theory of allegiance is in essence a doctrine of moral pluralism.

Internal and External Standards of Moral Judgment

There are two important standards by which the actions of human beings are judged to be right or wrong. The standard of moral judgment may be either external or internal. If it is external, it may be custom, law or the state. If it is internal, it is intuition or conscience. Laski prefers the internal standard of moral judgment to the external standard and thus adopts an intuitionist position in ethics. The external standard leads to moral determinism leading to regimentation of personality. It preaches obedience to some form of authority. Laski believes in libertarian ethics which proclaims the sovereignty of conscience. "Freedom means self-expression," says Laski, "and the secret of freedom is courage. No man ever remains free who acquiesces in what he knows to be wrong. His business as a citizen is to act upon the instructed judgment of his conscience."[10]

Pluralism as an Ally of Individualism

It is obvious that Laski's conception of conscience as the supreme factor in moral action involves an individualistic attitude to human personality. In the moral sphere, pluralism appears as an ally of individualism. Laski's ideas are in this respect in fundamental harmony with those of John Stuart Mill as propounded by him in his brilliant essay on *Liberty*. In opposition to Bradley, Bosanquet and Green, Laski continues in contemporary British thought the individualistic traditions of Locke and Mill. Attachment to individual liberty conceived primarily in intellectual and moral terms is the characteristic feature of Laski's political thought not only during the pluralistic phase but also after his adoption of a Marxian approach to world problems.

The Source of Moral Sanction in the General Will

The idealists think that the standard of moral judgment cannot be left to the capricious wills of individuals which are many and conflicting. The source of moral sanction should be sought in an ideal fixed by an external authority which harmonises and transcends the conflicts of actual wills. As the organized expression of the general will of the community, the state is the most adequate moral agency to prescribe morality for its citizens. While the conscience or the actual will of the individual may be capricious, irrational and immoral, the general will is by definition precise, moral and rational. The citizen, therefore, cannot rationally and morally disobey the state. This is the monistic ethical position in political theory. The reply of Laski would be that only a conceptual state having cerebral existence in the minds of the idealist philosophers can represent the so-called general will. The states as they exist in the world of the empiricist can represent only the will of those individuals or groups who form the

10. Harold J. Laski : "The Dangers of Obedience", p. 7 (1930 Ed.).

ruling class at a particular moment of history. Pragmatically speaking the will of the state at a particular time is the will of the government of the day.

Irrational Acts of Government

As the government is compopsed of fallible men, the will of the state which expresses itself through the law, orders and decrees of its government cannot always be rational and moral. History shows that there can be no *a priori* moral distinction between the governors and the governed. There are circumstances when acquiescence in the will of the State is immoral. There are indeed situations in which resistance to the will of the state becomes a moral duty of its citizens. A Negro citizen in the United States is morally bound to resist the state that passes discriminatory laws against his race. A colonial subject is similarly entitled to rise in rebellion against the imperialistic state that oppresses his people. Thus the moral superiority of the conscience as the standard of moral judgement is obvious.

The Doctrine of Plural Allegiance

This repudiation of the monistic ethical position in political theory enables Laski to formulate his theory of plural allegiance. The theory of plural allegiance is an immediate consequence of his conception of conscience the standard of moral judgment. Laski thinks that the state is not entitled on moral grounds to claim the total allegiance of its citizens. The moral pre-eminence claimed by the sovereign state for its own will over the wills of all other groups in all circumstances cannot be justified rationally. Man is a creature of competing loyalties and Laski cannot accept on *a priori* grounds that loyalty to the state is the highest loyalty irrespective of the circumstances in which that loyalty is demanded. A pacifist is morally justified to defy the law of conscription. A miner can similarly resist the state if it attacks his trade union rights. A citizen who is persecuted for his religious convictions cannot be expected to acquiesce in that persecution on moral grounds. There are a number of circumstances in which loyalty to group ideal may be morally far superior to loyalty to state ideal. The state must prove the moral wholesomeness of its command before it expects the allegiance of its citizens to the purpose of that command.

The doctrine of plural allegiance is in essence Laski's protest against "a world in which the supporters of conventional morality are anxious at all costs to legislate against the diversities of which they disapprove" (*125 : 9*). He feels that diversity is sign of a vital social order. The monistic ideal which suppresses this diversity creates morally depraved individuals. The doctrine of absolute allegiance to the state retards the moral aspirations and sentiments of its people. A worker who is imprisoned for participating in a strike, a Jew who is persecuted for his religious belief, a writer whose book is banned for containing dangerous thoughts, or the Quaker who is punished for his opposition to warfare cannot give their absolute allegiance to the state which treats them in that manner. This kind of monistic state is the antithesis of all morality (*125 : 11-30*).

Objections to the Theory of Plural Allegiance

There is a logical difficulty in Laski's moral assumptions. The conception of conscience as the moral standard of judgment does not explain the fact that society also consists of people having essentially depraved consciences and these people may create chaos and anarchy if left free to follow their consciences. He does not suggest a demarcation line between vulgar opposition of a depraved conscience and the honest protest of a beneficial dissent.[11]

Whatever the merits of the doctrine of plural allegiance as an ethical ideal, it is impracticable as a sociological formula. In practice it may result in mutual conflicts of loyalties sometimes leading to violent clashes between hostile groups. Thus it will perpetuate a system of doctrinaire anarchy.[12] Laski himself foresaw this objection to this argument when he wrote, "It is objected that this is a doctrine of anarchy. If men are to disobey because they disbelieve, there is, it is said, an end of social peace; and in a period of violence it is never justice that triumphs. To argue, therefore, that a man must act upon the dictates of his conscience, to insist that there are times when the law may be rightly disregarded, is to attack the foundations of public well-being. We must approach the state in fear and trembling. We must remember that its habits, its traditions, its purposes are born of the inherited wisdom of the past. Who are we, it is said, with what Burke called "our little stock of reason", to pit our judgment against the immense induction for which it stands" (*125 : 21*). This is the classic case against his theory of plural allegiance and the subjectivist standard of moral judgment.

The Conservative Argument Refuted

This kind of argument has been the traditional line of defence of all conservatives in moral and political philosophy. "The argument", says Laski, "has the appearance of power; but, in fact, it is wholly void of substance. The present conditions are not just merely because they are the present conditions; they are just to the degree that justice is inherent in them. An American would not condemn Washington for 1776; few Frenchmen would doubt the justice of 1789; fewer Englishmen would deny the common sense of 1688. But Washington and all other revolutionaries have had, at some moment, to make the decision to disobey; and the decision has involved the judgment that their view of the future must be pitted against that for which traditional authority has declared. Obviously enough, we must make our protest proportionate to the event. We need not march out with machine guns because the income-tax

11. C. H. Kung : "Political Pluralism—A Study in Contemporary Political Theory", Chapter IX : 240-41.
12. *Ibid*, Chapter IX : 241-47.

inspector has assessed us wrongly. But if the state to which we are reduced is that of the French peasant in 1789, or the Russian peasant in 1917, it is difficult to see why the wisdom of our ancestors should be dignified by the name of wisdom" (*125 : 21-22*).

Laski's Ethical Ideals more Radical

It cannot be denied that the ethical ideals of Laski are more progressive and radical than those of the idealists. They are also valuable as instruments of social and political change although to a limited extent. But the grave defect of the pluralistic ideal of Laski's ethics is that it suffers from an undue subjectivistic bias. While emphasizing the subjective source of moral judgment, he ignores the importance of the objective content of that judgment. The conscience of a democrat resisting the fascist state and the conscience of a fascist revolting against the liberal state cannot be equally moral. There ought to be an objective moral criterion for the ethical evaluation of political attitudes.

Let us consider a concrete case of strikes by workers in a capitalist democracy. Trade unions are expected to defend their 'sectional' interests against the employers and the state. But the state and 'public opinion' expects them to act 'responsibily' and in 'national interest'. Dr. V.L. Allen comments: "Strikes take place within a hostile environment even though they are a common every-day phenomenon. They are conventionally described as industrially subversive, irresponsible, unfair, against the interests of the community, contrary to the workers' best interests, wasteful of resources, crudely aggressive, inconsistent with democracy and, in any event, unnecessary." (*2236 : 142*), yet without these struggles, the workers would have been unable to achieve social justice and mitigate the worst consequences of their exploitation and oppression.

CHAPTER 29

NATIONALISM, IMPERIALISM AND INTERNATIONALISM

DEFINITION OF TERMS–NATION AND NATIONALITY

Writers on political science are not all agreed on the precise meaning of the terms 'nation', 'nationality', and 'Nationalism'. The word 'nation' is derived from the Latin word *'natio'* which means 'birth' or 'race'. This does not mean, however, that nationalism and racialism are identical conceptions. In the seventeenth century the term 'nation' was used to describe the population of a State in respect of its racial unity, and this meaning, says Bernard Joseph, has in a large measure persisted up to this day. During the French Revolution the term 'nation' came into great popularity and was used to mean 'patriotism'. 'Nationality was at this period a collective sentiment' *(43:20)*.

Since the nineteenth century, however, the terms 'nation' and 'nationality' have assumed quite definite meanings. The term 'nation' conveys the ideals of political independence or sovereignty (either actually attained or desired); while 'nationality' is largely a non-political concept and can exist even under foreign domination. It is a psychological quality, although it is often used to convey an ethical and cultural conception as well. Interpreted in this manner, 'nation' and 'nationality' are not identical conceptions. A nation, meaning the population of a self-governing State, may very well include several nationalities. Thus, while Great Britain is a single nation, it consists of four distinct nationalities–the English, the Scots, the Welsh and the North Irish. As soon as a nationality acquires political unity and sovereign independence, it becomes a nation. According to Lord Bryce, 'The sentiment of nationality is that feeling or group of feelings which makes an aggregate of men conscious of ties, not being wholly either political or religious, which unite them in a community which is, either actually or potentially, a nation' *(7:118)*. The term 'national group' is used to designate a community in which nationality is still in the making and the 'will to live' as a nation is still lacking.

The terms which are confused most are 'nationality' and 'nationalism.' 'Nationalism' is at times used to describe an exaggerated sentiment of nationality bordering on aggressiveness. This perverted sentiment which sees nothing but good in one's own nation and its deeds is not true nationalism. Rightly understood, nationalism stands for the historical process by which nationalities are transformed into political units and for the legitimate right of a people who form a distinct and vigorous nation or nationality to a place in the sun.

The Meaning of Nationality. A. E. Zimmern writes : Nationality, like religion, is subjective; psychological; a condition of mind; a spiritual possession; a way of feeling; thinking and living.' According to the same author, nationality is not a political but an educational conception. Broadly speaking, if a people feels itself to be a nationality, it is a nationality. Nationality is only accidentally a political question, but primarily it is a spiritual and educational question. According to Ernest Renan, a nation is a soul, a spiritual principle. "To have suffered, rejoiced, and hoped together" makes a people a nation.

Bringing out the difference between a 'national state' and 'nationality', C. J. H. Hayes writes : 'A national state is always based on nationality, but a nationality may exist without a national state. A state is essentially political, nationality is primarily cultural and only incidentally political' *(23:5)*.

Factors of Nationality. Writers on political science have discussed at great length the factors which constitute nationality. But they are all agreed that none of the factors which they discuss is absolutely essential, although without some of them at least, no nationality can truly exist. There is no universal law which can be laid down regarding the relative importance of these various factors. In the Western world, religion has long since ceased to be a factor of nationality. But in the East, particularly in India, it is still a force to be reckoned with. Where certain factors of nationality are weak in a given country, it is necessary to strengthen other factors if nationality is to survive at all.

(i) *Geographical Unity.* There can be no doubt that a naturally defined territory or geographical unity, often described by the name 'homeland', is a powerful tie in the formation and continuance of nationality. Several exceptions to this statement may, however, be found. For ages the Jews had no national home of their own. Yet the hope that some day Palestine would be restored to them kept alive and gave strength to the Jewish nationality. The boundary between Germany and France is artificial : and yet in both these countries there are very strong nationalities.

Where there is no national home or no hope of securing one, it is difficult to acquire or develop the spirit of nationality. The gypsies have never had a settled abode, accustomed as they are to wandering from place to place. The Romans of old, in exchanging their homeland for a world empire lost their nationality.

Naturally marked geographical boundaries are an immense aid to nationality owing to various reasons. In the first place geography and climate have a definite bearing upon the character and physique of a people. They tend to create common physical, mental, and psychological traits, thereby aiding co-operation and mutual understanding among people.

In the second place, human sympathies are limited, and at the present stage of man's development a national home seems to be the most suitable geographical unit for the drawing out of the altruistic feelings and emotions of man. There was a time when such feelings and emotions were confined to one's village or tribe. But in all progressive countries these narrow loyalties have given place to a national loyalty.

A third reason for stressing a naturally defined territory as an important factor of nationality is that human beings share with animals a love of their habitat. There is an instinctive attachment on the part of every human being to the land of his birth. The love of one's country is intensified during exile.

So far as India is concerned, it was a distinct geographical entity, marked off from the rest of the world until the partition in 1947. 'Country' is the most suitable geographical unit for the calling out of the highest patriotic feelings. If India is to survive in the modern world, it is necessary that we should at once replace village politics, caste politics and tribal politics by national politics.

Mr. Ruthnaswamy rightly argues that if the people of India have their rights, so has the land of India. It 'has its own rights and liberties, its own interest and importance'. India is our national home, a sacred land; and it is the duty of every son of India to protect his country so that the people will become zealous of the country, of her freedom and progress. The figure of India, its form, beauty, rivers, sand, hills, its flora and fauna must be made known to every man, woman and child in India. Tourist and travel agencies must organize tours of common folk to all parts of the country.

(ii) *Identity of Racial Type or Racial Unity.* Racial integrity is put forward by some writers as a helpful factor in the formation and strengthening of nationality. Zimmern gives it a high place but Bryce regards it as merely one of the factors in creating the sentiment of nationality. Mazzini, on the other hand, holds that race is not essential to nationality. Renan is of opinion that 'race is something which makes and unmakes itself and has no application to politics'. J. H. Rose claims that only in a very crude form does nationality depend on race. 'Purity', says Hayes, 'if it exists at all, exists nowadays only among uncivilized tribesmen'. Pillsbury writes, 'In the determination of national lines, in general, race is no more important. There is no pure race in any nation. Man is everywhere a mongrel.' Even Mussolini once said : 'Race is a feeling, not a reality. Nothing will ever make me believe that biologically pure races can be shown to exist today.'

The weight of academic opinion thus seems to be on the side of those who give a relatively low place to race. Modern Switzerland and Canada are frequently quoted as examples of people of different racial origins living together and forming a strong nationality. For several generations the United States has been 'the melting-pot of nations'. For ourselves, we believe that racial unity is a powerful tie of nationality, but it is not indispensable to it. It is a more important factor in the earlier stages of nationality than in the later. In the United States there is a great diversity of racial stock, but at the same time there is a dominant racial group, descended from the

'Old Immigrants', which is able to give a tone to the national life of the country.

When we are dealing with unity of race as a factor aiding nationality, it is well to remember that racism in the modern world is an enemy of mankind. Apropos of this, E. M. Burns writes, "From the ancient Hebrews to the descendants of the Boers in South Africa exponents of the doctrine of master race have sought to bolster their rights to conquer and rule by claiming for themselves inherent superiority over their victims" (*90:487*). The French aristocrat, de Gobineau (1816-1882) stood for the superiority of the so-called Aryan race, including the Greeks, Romans, Persians and Teutons. H. S. Chamberlain (1855-1927), an Englishman who lived in Germany, picked up the idea of race supremacy from Gobineau and applied it to the **Teutons. He excluded the Persians and Indians from his purview of Aryans.** It was his ideas that largely contributed to the growth of Nazi fascism.

(iii) *Unity of Ideas and Ideals or a Common Culture*. If nationality is primarily a cultural conception, unity of ideas and ideals is indeed an important element in it. Unity of culture includes common customs and manners, common traditions and literature, common folklore, epics, and art. It also stands for 'a certain dominant view of life with its common standards, duties and prohibitions'. Unity of ideas and ideals draws people close together and creates in them an *esprit de corps* which cannot easily be destroyed.

National literature, education, culture and art may be both the cause and effect of nationality. While national literature does not, by itself, create nationality, it can strengthen the sentiment of nationality. In recent times, national literature has played a notable part in the rejuvenation of Bohemian and Serbian nationalities. 'National literature makes a large contribution to the development of nationality by striving to create and maintain national traditions and by endearing the national history to the nationality. It is the vehicle of national traditions" (*43:114*).

National education can play an important part in creating a similarity of outlook on life and in setting up the same or similar standards. The teaching of citizenship in the form of 'Americanization' has gone a long way in moulding the diverse racial and cultural groups of the United States into a single powerful nationality. When mishandled, as in the case of Nazi Germany, national education can easily lead to national bigotry and prejudice. National education, if rightly used, 'serves the necessary purpose of creating a moral unity, a common understanding of right and wrong a community of ideas in most mattres and social intercourse amongst all the members of a natioality' (*43:118*).

National history and tradition also become vital factors in the creation of national culture. Ramsay Muir says : 'Heroic achievements, agonies heroically endured, these are the sublime food by which the spirit of nationhood is nourished.' A legitimate pride in the past, a wholesome confidence in the present, a buoyant hope for the future, all strengthen and sustain the national spirit.

If Indian nationality is to become a plant of vigorous growth, stress should be laid on the unity of ideas and ideals which underlies Indian culture. Both Hindu and Muslim cultures have influenced each other so much so that Indian or Pakistani Islam today is not the Islam of Arabia or of other Muslim countries nearby. Therefore, our cultural differences need not be exaggerated; and if only proper understanding between the two major communities can be secured many of these differences will sink to the background. A national system of education is the supreme need of the hour. There is an urgent need for the rewriting of our history, omitting all exaggerated references to bloody wars and persecutions in the relations between the two communities. In this connection it may be noted that the Catholics and Protestants in some of the European countries have fought more bloody battles than the Hindus and Muslims have in India, but have settled down peacefully now.

(iv) *Unity of Language.* The most obvious element of nationality is language. Ramsay Muir believes that language counts for more than race in the moulding of a nation. Common language means also a common literature, a common inspiration of great ideas, and a 'common heritage of songs and folk-tales'. Rose considers common language to be the most powerful political influence. Joseph holds that a common language enables people to express the same ideas and same sentiments, creates common standards as regards morals, manners and justice, preserves common historical traditions, and creates a common national psychology. In modern times, the Polish people, more than others, have demonstrated the value of a common language in keeping alive the national spirit. When there is a determination on the part of a people to keep together culturally and socially, unity of language is of great value. In spite of the manifold advantages of a common langauge, it is obvious that several nationalities do not possess a common language. Thus the people of Switzerland speak at least three distinct languages. If other factors of nationality are strong, it is possible to dispense with a common language. The German-speaking population of Alsace is attached more to France than to Germany Likewise, in spite of the fact that the Americans and Canadians speak the same language and live next door to each other, there is no disposition on their part to fuse into a single nationality.

So far as India is concerned, diversity of language has been a hindrance to national unity. The designation of Hindi as the official language will, in time, rectify this situation. The trend should be in the direction of developing one mother-tongue, using it in the schools and on the streets, utilizing it in the dissemination of culture and making it a fine-tempered instrument not only for traditional and modern literature and the arts, but for current technical and scientific thought. This does not mean, however, the obliteration of one's mother-tongue, when it is different from Hindi which is the case as regards Telugu, Tamil, etc. The English language became the *lingua franca* of a portion of the population under British rule but in the nature of the case, it could not become the language of the people. However, students in higher education will still profit by gaining a sound working knowledge of this language, stressing not so much on English literature, as recent scientific discoveries and social and economic facts.

The indications are that the regional languages will come to prevail as the medium of instruction right up to the University, but that English will continue as an associate official language for some years to come. For cementing state differences and for the purpose of providing a window on the outside world it is desirable that the well-educated Indians should continue to write and speak English fluently. At present English serves as a useful link language between the different parts of the country. It will be a bad day for India when English is relegated to an insignificant place in the life of the country. The present emphasis on regional languages as the medium of instruction is likely to place a severe strain on Indian unity.

(v) *Unity of Religion.* The history of nationalities shows clearly that religion played an important part in the early stages. Early communal life centred in religious customs and practices. Among the Jews, for instance, religion has been the mainspring of their national life. It has been the warp and woof of their common life. A similar statement can be made of the Japanese, the Poles, and the Irish of today. During centuries of oppression, it was the Greek Catholic Church which enabled the Greeks to persist as a people.

Common religion is no longer a factor of much consequence, although in a few exceptional cases it is still the basis of nationality on account of peculiar historical antecedents. 'Most modern nationalities', says Hayes, 'manage to flourish without insisting upon uniformity of religious belief or practice'. Most States today practise religious tolerance, and diversity of faith does not interfere with their national life. In all progressive countries religion is becoming more and more an individual affair. In the United States it has hardly entered into the national life of the people at all. In 1960 Kennedy who was a Catholic was elected President, in spite of the fact that a good majority of the people are Protestants. In India, on the other hand, religious differences are grossly exaggerated so as to benefit interested parties. It is not widely recognized that religious fanaticism and bigotry can never make a people great. 'Religion in danger' is a meaningless cry. It is time that the educated people of India realized that what is required in the interest of national unity is genuine religious tolerance born of sympathy and understanding, and not a flabby kind of indifference which consists in being all things to all men. The educated people at least should cultivate a profound respect for each others religious beliefs and susceptibilities. Politics should be secularized.

(vi) *Common Economic Interest* has been one of the strongest factors in the maintenance of the Japanese and Australian nationalities. The economic motive among other factors, undoubtedly welds a people together and creates in them 'a consciousness of kind'. Behind 'the White Australian policy' which was strenuously advocated even in the midst of war by Australian politicians, there is the fear, real or imaginary, that Australia will be flooded by Mongolians and Indians who might imperil the economic life of the Australians if the immigration bars are removed or lowered.

However important common economic interests may be in the holding of a people together, we do not believe that such interests alone are capable of creating the sentiments of nationality. The European Common Market of our day is not likely to transform the people of Western Europe into a single nationality. During times of war one finds that the spirit of nationality cuts across economic distinctions and unites people with different economic interests.

(vii) *Common Subjection* to a firm and systematic government has at times proved to be a powerful factor of nationality. The strong rule of Britain has to a certain extent precipitated Indian nationalism. In a similar way unquestioning obedience to a single ruler has at other places fostered the national spirit, though of a morbid kind, as in the case of Germany under Hitler and Italy under Mussolini. However important a part a strong government may play in reference to nationality, it cannot by itself produce nationality. Ramsay Muir rightly observes : 'Mere unity of government, however admirably welded, will never of itself produce nationhood'.

(viii) *Common Suffering* has at times been a powerful stimulus to nationality. History furnishes several examples of nationality being intensified under persecution. 'In Europe', says Zimmern, 'Nationality is an instinct which has been stung into morbid and acute self-consciousness by political oppression' (*84:74*). After the Franco-Prussian war of 1870, the national spirit in France became acute. The Moorish oppression and Napoleonic wars roused the sentiment of nationality among the Spaniards. The partition of Poland quickened the national spirit and preserved it under the most adverse conditions. Irish nationalism developed into an exaggerated and even undesirable form under English oppression. In spite of these illustrations, as Joseph notes, 'oppression of a group does not itself transform it into a nationality'. It may split the people into several selfish communities, each trying to win the favour of the oppressor, as was frequently the case in Indian history.

(ix) *Political Sovereignty*. It is sometimes argued that it is the State which creates nationality, and not *vice versa*. This is a position which it is difficult to uphold. Despite the fact that Great Britain is under a single political sovereignty, it comprises four distinct nationalities. A general remark which we may venture to make at this point is that while nationalities have existed even before modern States assumed a permanent form, political sovereignty has contributed to the strengthening of growing nationalities. Leaving aside such exceptional cases as Switzerland where perhaps a common political sovereignty has given birth to nationality, the most that political sovereignty can do is to fortify existing national consciousness by means of common laws and political institutions. It cannot produce nationality as we have defined it.

(x) *Popular Will.* We cannot easily pass over the importance of the will to co-operate and the 'will to be a nation' on which Dr. Ambedkar places so much emphasis in relation to Indian nationalism. To quote his own words: 'It is a feeling of corporate sentiment, of oneness which makes those who are charged with it feel that they are kith and kin'. Toynbee regards 'the will to be nation' as the principal element of nationality. Likewise, Mazzini regards popular will as the basis of nationality.

Renan who is instructive on the whole question of nationality rejects the view that the essence of the nation lies in the unity of race, language, religion, community of interest, or geographical unity. He holds that the nation is a "a spiritual principle" and that it is based primarily on (a) a rich "heritage of memories" and (b) a keen "desire to live together". People are a nation because they want to be a nation.

The Self-determination of Nationality. A question which interests both the student of political theory and the practical politician is whether every nationality has an intrinsic right to be a self-governning, sovereign state. Since the days of the Congress of Vienna (1815) all through the nineteenth century the principle which dominated European politics was "one nationality, one state'. This principle received further stimulus during World War I (1914-1918) when the idea of 'the self-determination of nations' came to the forefront. The contention has been that to group together people of different nationalities into a single State will lead to a lack of patriotic feeling and internal dissensions. It is further contended that a nationality spread over several States can never be happy and contented and that such a nationality is like a dismembered social organism. All these contentions are seriously questioned today. It is admitted by many that, other things being equal, political boundaries should be drawn where national lines are drawn. Thus J. S. Mill in his *Representative Government* writes: It is in general a necessary condition of free institutions that the boundaries of government should coincide with those of nationality'.

Lord Acton and several others take the opposite view. According to Acton, 'the theory of nationality (*i.e.* one nation, one State) is more absurd and more criminal than the theory of socialism'. He foresaw how the identification of the State with nationality might lead to political absolutism. In his view, the multi-national state is "one of the chief instruments of civilization" (*99:636*). Zimmern writes, 'In the long run the theory of a national state will go the way of Henry VIII's and Luther's theory of a national church'. Bernard Joseph holds that 'one nationality one State' is a dangerous principle and constitutes a chief obstacle to world progress. He argues that 'nationality' and 'State' are different conceptions and that a nationality can continue to exist even after the State has been destroyed. Either a single

State includes more than one nationality, or a single nationality is spread over several States. National and State loyalty are two different things and, according to Joseph, they can exist side by side with each other, for all that nationality requires is freedom for cultural and social life and a certain measure of group autonomy, particularly in communal matters. He believes that 'the only hope of order and peace in world affairs is to be sought in the ultimate recognition of the principle that several nationalities may live together in harmony and co-operation within a state, each at the same time following its own national life' (*43:331*).

Is Nationalism a Blessing? Many thinkers have idealized and idolized nationalism and see nothing but virtue in it. Others find that, in practice, It has led to many evils and they are convinced that, as it is practised today, it is the greatest enemy to international peace and goodwill. Rabindranath Tagore, in his essay on 'Nationalism', has no hesitation in condemning it. He calls it the 'organized self-interest of a whole people'; 'self-idolatry'; 'the organization of politics and commerce for selfish ends'; an organized power for exploitation. Nationalism so embitters relations between countries that a systematic study of one another's culture and civilization becomes almost impossible. Hayes condemns that form of nationalism which is 'a proud and boastful habit of mind about one's own nation accompanied by a supercilious or hostile attitude towards other nations'. He finds that nationalism in the nineteenth and twentieth centuries has been unable to give a creditable account of itself. In the words of Shillito, it has become 'man's other religion'. It is 'sentimental, emotional and inspirational'. It has more devout followers than almost any living religion. It claims to have a mission for the rest of the world. In the name of national rights, national honour, and national policy millions of lives and billions of treasure have been wasted in recent times. Nationalism easily leads to hatred of the foreigner, and this aggressive kind of nationalism which is aptly described as 'wolf-pack' nationalism is the breeder of war and easily shades off into imperialism of the worst kind. Striking illustrations of this 'wolf-pack' nationalism were to be found in militarist Japan, Fascist Italy and Nazi Germany.

Writing on how nationalism which was a power for good in its early days, has become degenerated. Ebenstein writes: "Since the French Revolution at least, nationalism has been one of the driving forces of domestic, imperial, and international politics. Complex in its origins, it has developed along many, and often contradictory, lines. In its name some of the greatest acts of heroism and liberty have been committed, but also crimes of cruelty and fanaticism. In the first half of its existence—from the late eighteenth to the middle of the nineteenth century—nationalism was essentially inspired by humanitarian, democratic ideas; this was the story of early French, American, Czech, Italian, Irish, and Polish nationalism. In the last eighty years, on the other hand, nationalism has tended to ally itself with parochialism, intolerance, bigotry, persecution of minorities, racialism, and finally imperialism and aggression—the recoil of Pan-Germanism, Hungarian imperialism, Japanese militarism, and finally Fascism" (*99:635*).

We cannot grasp the full meaning of nationalism unless we interpret it in the cultural, economic, and political fields. While nationalism in the cultural field has been on the whole a unifying factor, in the economic and political fields it has been a divisive factor. In its extreme form, economic nationalism known as 'Autarchy' aims at complete economic self-sufficiency. Beyond a certain point economic nationalism is a fruitful cause of war. It is like a boomerang, bringing infinite harm upon its own head. Autarchy is a folly. Past years have witnessed the spectacle of wheat being burnt in Canada, apples and milk being dumped into rivers in the United States and coffee being thrown into the sea in Brazil while millions were starving.

From the kind of aggressive nationalism described earlier we have to distinguish a redemptive kind of nationalism whose motto is 'Live and help others to live'.

So far as India is concerned, nationalism is not luxury but a necessity. It is the very basis of our existence, a matter of life and death to us. While it is utter folly to place all our misfortunes at the door of the foreigner, there can be no doubt that foreign domination over a long period of time produces certain slave vices for which self-determination has been the only genuine remedy. Political nationalism alone can curse such vices as fear, cowardice and dissimulation.

Now that India has attained her political freedom, she must give more attention to cultural and humanitarian nationalism. 'Above all nations stands the ideal of Humanity as a goal and guiding principle' (Hallowell). Because of her economic backwardness, India is bound to favour her own industries for years to come. But the goal must be well-thought-out national planning which is an integral part of world planning.

Only such a nationalism can become a road to internationalism. 'An ideal international world means a world of nations living at their best' (*43:338*). The future well-being of the world requires the education not only of our minds but also of our wills and emotions in internationalism. 'It must be an education, which aims to surmount exclusiveness and to inculcate mutual understanding and co-operation, an education which seeks to overcome docility, to foster the critical spirit and to encourage independence of judgment' (*32:272*). Exclusive nationalism and the doctrine of racial superiority are some of the curses of the modern world.

Despite the disparaging views of nationalism held by men like Lord Acton and Tagore, we believe that nationalism still has its value, if it does not take an aggressive and militaristic turn. We cannot go as far as Theodore Roosevelt when he says that loving other nations as much as one loves one's own nation is like loving other woman as much as loving one's own wife. Nor can we endorse the chauvinistic nationalism of Rudyard Kipling or J. A. Cramb, the latter of whom practically equates the nation with God.

IMPERIALISM

The Meaning of Imperialism. According to Ebenstein, imperialism is a chief distortion of nationalism. Writes he : "Love of oneself becomes hatred of others, and enslavement of others is clothed in such masks as 'the white man's burden', or the need for 'living space'. Even highly democratic nations have at one time or another fallen victims to the disease of imperialism". (*101:637*).

To some imperialism is a synonym for the economic exploitation and political domination of weaker races and for gross materialism. To others it is a sacred duty which must not be shirked by the advanced countries of **the world in their relation to backward countries. Both of these views are** extremes. A well-planned and carefully worked out programme of the ruthless exploitation of backward regions is as foreign to the general history of imperialism as a conscious civilizing mission typified in the much abused phrase 'the white man's burden'.

In the very nature of the case, it is difficult to give a definition of imperialism which will fit both ancient and modern empires. Even in modern times imperialism has assumed various forms. There is no *a priori* way of deciding whether 'trade follows the flag' or 'flag follows the trade'. Some empires have been almost accidental in origin, while others are the result of deliberate planning. Earlier empires were largely 'tax-collecting and recruit-raising' agencies. They were an expression of the superior military strength of the conqueror over the conquered. Modern empires are largely for economic and strategic purposes.

C. D. Burns claims that imperialism is a name given to a 'single system of law and government in many different lands and races', a half-way house to internationalism, and an antidote to provincial nationalism. The latter part of the definition is certainly not accurate. 'Imperialism', says Prof. Schuman, 'is the imposition by force and violence of alien rule upon subject people, despite all moralizing and pretensions to the contrary".

With modern Western imperialism in mind, Parker T. Moon, a well-known authority on the subject, defines imperialism as "the domination of non-European native races by totally dissimilar European nations" (*154:181*). Schumpeter defines imperialism as an "atomistic force, ancient in inception, decadent and self-conscious in an age of nationalism, yet still powerful enough to lord it over its rival, the upstart capitalism".

A good working definition of imperialism as found in the Encyclopaedia of Social Sciences is that it is 'a policy which aims at creating, organizing and maintaining an empire : that it is a state of vast size composed of various more or less distinct national units and subject to a single, centralized will'.

In studying modern imperialism, we find that colonization is not as important a factor as the economic and political control of the backward regions of the world. Hence attention is directed more and more to trade, investment of surplus capital, and political control. In other words, exploitation colonies are valued more than settlement colonies.

Causes of Imperialism. Imperialism has come about as a result of various factors. In its earlier and more primitive forms, parallels to which are not lacking even today, it was a manifestation of the predatory instinct of man. In the movemnet of races from one part of the world to another in search of pasture, food, and the like, and the conquest of one tribe by another, we find ample evidence of the predatory character of man's nature in one form or another. Sometimes it takes the form of ruthless aggression and bloody warfare, sometimes of gradual displacement by superior skill and intelligence.

When we turn from the earlier types of empire to the later ones, we find that thirst for conquest and the competitive struggle for power have played a notable part in their development. It was the boast of Cecil Rhodes that he thought in terms of continents. Colonial possession and military success are often taken to mean national strength and glory. Prof. Schuman believes that modern imperialism is a new expression of the will to power and the drive for conquest. This ideal was forcibly expressed by Mussolini in 1932 when he said : 'The Fascist State is a will to power and an empire. The Roman tradition is the idea of force. In the Fascist doctrine, the imperial idea is not only a territorial, military, and mercantile expression but also one of spiritual and moral expansion. For Fascism, the tendency to the imperial idea means expansion of the nation and is a manifestation of vitality'. Imperialism means expansion. It is interlocked with nationalism.

Colonial possessions are also desired as an outlet for surplus population. This was the constant plea of Japan till 1941, when other motives such as domination, too, entered into her calculation. Italy, also, claimed for years that her 'narrow but adorable peninsula' was unable to house her teeming millions and that, therefore, she had to look out for fresh colonies. The surprising fact with regard to the argument that imperialism is a remedy for over-population is that it has not so worked in practice.

One of the most fundamental causes of imperialism today seems to be economic. The imperialist nations of the world at present are for the most part highly industrialized countries depending upon backward countries for raw materials. 'The fight for raw materials,' says Dr. Schacht, 'plays the most important part in world politics, an even greater role than before the war (1914)'. Statistics, however, show that no imperial country, with the possible exception of Great Britain, can solely depend upon its colonial possessions for the supply of a major portion of her raw materials. Parker Moon contends that there is no truth in the common notion that an imperial country receives most of the raw materials which its colonies produce. He writes: 'Raw materials, in general, are colour blind. They recognize no national flag. They follow the law of supply and demand, and of distance and transportation costs. They obey economic rather than political control'. Great Britain has joined the European Common Market, even if it means the snapping of the ties that bind her to the Commonwealth.

Colonies are valued even more as markets for finished products than as producers of raw materials. The Empire, says Joseph Chamberlain, 'is commerce'. Preferential tariffs and commercial discrimination are often resorted to in order to favour the finished goods of the mother country. But these devices have not been a complete success. According to Andrew Carnegie, trade does not follow the flag, but the lowest current price. " Buell estimates that only one-fifth of the world trade is with countries wh. come under imperial sway. The remaining four-fifths is with independent States. Nevertheless, 'imperialism affords an additional margin of marketing facilities for an industrial nation's goods' (*63:351*). The most important point to note is that those who benefit by imperialism are not the masses, in general, but a few industries such as cotton, iron, steel and oil. The explosive situation in Iran a few years ago is an interesting study, involving imperialism, socialism, the struggle of an impoverished nation for true State sovereignty and for the fruit of its own resources—oil.

An empire is valued not only as an outlet for surplus goods, but also for surplus capital. The United States is able to exert a powerful influence over the economic and even political conditions of Central and South America, as well as of other parts of the world, by means of her vast investments. This kind of diplomacy, known as 'dollar diplomacy', is almost as effective as a foreign army of occupation. If 'money talks', the American dollar shouts. Government agencies and diplomatic channels are used to persuade, if not coerce, backward countries to borrow money from advanced countries.

Capital may be lent not only by imperialist countries but also by their individual citizens and private companies. This tendency is particularly marked where labour is cheap and abundant and is not able to defend itself. One of the arguments often used in defence of this form of imperialism is that if a country is unable to exploit its own natural resources to the full, some advanced country has an intrinsic right to do so on the ground that the world's resources belong to those who can best use them. But this argument is never conceded by the stronger nations to the weaker. If it were allowed, large tracts of land lying uncultivated in Canada, Australia, and parts of Africa would, of right, belong to the teeming, industrious and frugal millions of Japan, China, and India. But it is too much to expect imperialists to apply to themselves the arguments which they apply to others in the process of exploitation.

Imperialism offers advantages of various kinds to a select few. It provides ample opportunities for the investment of foreign capital and for the utilization of the services of foreign pro-consuls and diplomats, foreign civil servants, and foreign army at a prohibitive cost to the people of the dependent country. It is very well for Mr. Amery, a former Secretary of State for

India, to have said with righteous indignation that India paid no tribute to Britain; but he conveniently forgot the statement of the semi-official Institute of International Affairs that one Englishman out of every four lived by India directly. In a country under foreign domination the civil and defence services are invariably hampered, and foreign merchants, traders, planters, and joint-stock companies constitute a solid wall of opposition to every attempt in the direction of self-government.[1] Others who benefit by imperialism and constitute vested interests are ship-owners and manufacturers of arms and armaments, of military and railway uniforms, and of railway, cable, and telegraph materials.

A further important cause of imperialism in modern times is diplomatic. Imperialism breeds imperialism. The vital interests of Britain in the Suez Canal, her indirect control over Egypt, her efforts to establish some form of authority and friendly relations in West Asia, and her partial occupation of Iran, until a few years ago, are all to be explained in relation to her former control over India.[2] The British naval base at Singapore was a forcible reminder to Japan that she could not with impunity set foot in Australia or other parts of the British Empire in the Orient. For the same kind of military and naval reasons, France for a while controlled Djibuti. She valued her African possessions as troop reservoirs. Annexation in most cases has for one of its objects the increase of military strength.

Religious and humanitarian considerations are sometimes adduced in favour of imperialism. In the seventeenth century the missionary motive was an important factor of imperialism. The name of David Livingstone in Africa is the most outstanding name in the history of missionary empire builders. The London Missionary Society was closely linked up with the spread of British imperialism in Africa. Even Calvin Coolidge, a former President of the United States, said, 'The legions which (America) sends forth are armed not with the sword but with the cross'. General MacArthur advocated a similar policy with regard to Japan after her military defeat in 1945. Imperialism today is generally indifferent to converting the peoples of backward countries to Christianity. At times they even oppose the work of missionaries, for it might give the subject people a new dignity and new freedom. Where Christian missions were the open or secret allies of imperialists, as in the past, they received a warm welcome, from empire-

---

1. Witness what happened in Algeria where for more than a decade the French setters known as the 'Colons' put up a stiff resistance to every attempt at self-government for the people of the country as a whole. The virtual civil war with the mother country ended in 1962 when Algeria got its independence.
2. The situation has changed today. Egypt is completely free and has the Suez Canal under her control. Iran is free to govern herself and exploit her oil resources under an international consortium. To make up for all this loss Britain concluded the Baghdad Pact including herself, Turkey, Iraq, Iran and Pakistan. In 1958 Iraq dropped out of the Pact, now known as the Middle East Defence Organization.

builders. There have been many instances where the missionary was the forerunner of the trader and the ruler.

A particular form of humanitarian motive is expressed in the hackneyed phrase. 'the white man's burden'.[3] It also goes by the name of 'Imperialism of Responsibility'. It carries with it a subtle suggestion of racial superiority and prestige. At its best it seeks to supplant ignorance by enlightenment, crude forms of government by settled and progressive forms of it, and primitive ideas of justice by modern ideas of it. It aims at abolishing cannibalism, slavery, serfdom, and usury. Whatever the case may be today, humanitarianism was certainly not the original cause of imperialism, but is only an afterthought. Increasing emphasis is placed on this aspect of imperialism today, although much of it is only lip service. Those who speak of it with great enthusiasm conveniently forget that if 'the white man's burden' is a plausible theory, 'the black man's burden' is a solemn reality for which he has had to pay in hard cash, in the destruction of the power of self-help, and in the loss of dignity and national self-respect.

Despite humanitarian professions, the amount of money spent on the public education, sanitation, and the general improvement of the people is notoriously small. According to Julian Huxley, African infant mortality ranges from 1 in four to 1 in two; probably every adult Negro is infested with one or more kinds of worms, usually including hookworm, and often with malaria as well; in some areas up to 90 per cent of the population suffers from venereal disease, a disease imported by the white man; gross malnutrition as well as vitamin deficiency is frequent. Over most of Africa not one per cent of the children ever attend school. In the light of all this, one is inclined to agree with Schuman's observation: 'It is no more the "purpose" of imperialism to confer benefits upon its victims than to confer benefits upon the home country' *(70:426)*.

Until World War II prestige played an important role in the annexation of other people's land. Since the scramble for Africa began in the last quarter of the nineteenth century, possession of colonies became a hallmark of respectability in the international world. Thus Italy held on to Libya, although it meant no material gain to her. Until a few years ago, as a recent writer points out, the bosom of the average Englishman swelled with pride at the thought that he was a part-owner of a mighty British empire even though he did not possess even six feet of ground in which he could be buried when he died. Apropos of this, Hans Kohn quoted by Palmer and Perkins, *(op. cit.* p. 188) writes: "Besides the economic urge, psychological motives played a great role in imperialism—the lust for adventure and/for power, the added prestige and glory which seemed to accrue from a vast colonial empire not only to the governing classes but even to the masses of the colonizing nations, the new sentiment of pride and superiority

3. The current American equivalent of it is "the moral leadership of the world".

which animated even the lowest members of the white races in their dealings with the 'backward' races".

According to Lenin, capitalism is the sole cause of imperialism. In his own words: "If it were necessary to give the briefest possible definition of imperialism, we should have to say that imperialism is the monopoly stage of capitalism".

The desire to transplant to new countries one's own culture and civilization has played an important part in the history of imperialism. It is an expression of parent-offspring relationship.

The United States, especially since World War II, has indirectly pursued an imperialist policy. Her main object is the securing of strategic naval and aerial bases and allies all over the world in her effort to contain communism, of which she is mortally afraid. American imperialism may be described as imperialism by proxy or a "hitch-hike" imperialism, as was the case in Indo-China. If it were not for the material support given to the Netherlands government, Indonesia would have attained her freedom sooner than she did. In recent years the United States has entered into a military alliance with Western Europe known as the NATO and has forged military links with Japan, the Philippines, Australia, New Zealand and Pakistan. Several countries in Europe and Asia such as the Philippines, South Viet Nam, Thailand, and Pakistan have been brought within the sphere of her influence primarily through military aid and secondarily through economic assistance. The lend-lease agreement has been an important item in this form of control. Moreover, the United Nations is so manipulated as to carry forward American foreign policy, England having become the latest 'colonial possession' of the United States.

American people still have a holy horror of imperialism. They still remember what happened to American colonies in the days of George III. But they do not realize that in the present contest for world power, they might indirectly be a party to the crushing of nationalist aspirations particularly in Asia and Africa and to the setting themselves up as the sole judge of what is good for other people. The current American policy of arming Pakistan and training Pakistani military personnel has brought the cold war to the doorsteps of India.

Modern Imperialism. Imperialism in the twentieth century assumes more indirect forms than in earlier times. Reliance is placed more on diplomacy and international agreement than on the sword, though downright conquest and annexation are not altogether foreign to the spirit of the age. As one writer puts it, the stakes today are commerce, industry, railroads, ports, strategic bases, raw materials, and markets for goods and for capital.

The indirect forms of imperialism which prevail in many parts of the world are:

(1) *Leasehold.* For commercial or for strategic reasons, weak or backward countries are persuaded or compelled to part with the jurisdiction of

portions of their territory for a certain number of years, usually 99 years. Nominal sovereignty still rests with the country granting the lease, but actual jurisdiction is with the lessee. For all practical purposes 'a leasehold is a colony until the lease expires' (*8:443*). Examples of leasehold are the Manchurian ports given by China to Russia in 1898 for a period of 25 years, Port Arthur and Dairen in Ghina formerly held by Japan, and Wei-hai-wai held by Great Britain. The United States possesses lease of the Panama Canal which extends to five miles on either side of the Canal. By virtue of this lease, the United States has practically established a semi-protectorate over the Republic of Panama.

(2) *Protectorates and Semi-protectorates.* These may be of various kinds. In all protectorates foreign relations and defence are controlled by an imperialist power, and in many cases control is exercised even over financial affairs and other matters of internal administration. In the British Empire a protectorate is virtually the same as a Crown Colony, although from the point of view of international law these two are different. In the case of protectorates, old treaties with foreign powers continue, but not so in the case of a colony. Protectorates generally end in annexation or independence.

The best example of a protectorate in recent times was Egypt. Though the 'independence of Egypt was declared on February 28, 1922, it was so hedged and qualified that up to the Anglo-Egyptian Treaty of Alliance of 1936 Egypt was to all intents and purposes a disguised protectorate'. According to the 1922 declaration, four points were absolutely reserved; the security of the communications of the British Empire in Egypt; the defence of Egypt against all foreign aggression or interference, direct or indirect; the protection of foreign interests in Egypt and the protection of minorities; and the Sudan. Some writers preferred to regard Egypt as a semi-protectorate. Today she is completely free.

Examples of semi-protectorates have been Cuba and Haiti, which could make certain treaties in their own name but the foreign power could act as a check. Another type of protectorate is the international protectorate, an example of which was Abyssinia some years ago. According to the 1906 Convention between Great Britain, France, and Italy, these three powers agreed to protect the integrity of Abyssinia and not to compete with each other for concessions. But this convention proved to be a mere scrap of paper.

(3) *Spheres of Influence.* A sphere of influence means that the State holding the territory is given 'preferential or exclusive rights to make loans, construct railways, operate mines, or develop public works' (*8:447*). Spheres of influence are generally the thin end of the wedge, ultimately resulting in protectorates or outright annexation, although they are neither colonies nor dependencies. These are sometimes carved out even without the consent of the backward countries in question. 'This form of control', says Buell, 'has probably led to more disputes than it has settled' (*8:448*). In Asia, Africa, and the Pacific, spheres of influence have been a convenient instrument

of Imperialism in recent times. England and France held spheres of influence in Siam.

A distinction is sometimes made between a 'sphere of influence' and a 'sphere of interest'. The latter is strictly economic, while the former may imply certain vague political privileges, short of a protectorate. Spheres of influence have been more common in Africa than in Asia.

(4) *Condominium* or joint government means control by two or more powers over a disputed territory in order to prevent colonial rivalry. Such control was exercised by Great Britain and Egypt over the waters of the Nile in the Sudan; by France, Spain and Britain over the city of Tangier in Morocco; and by France and England over the New Hebrides. This form of jurisdiction satisfies neither the foreign powers nor the native people over whom the control is exercised. International control of this type is almost always unsatisfactory and is usually unsuccessful in the long run. It means divided responsibility. This is the reason why no serious attention was ever paid to the suggestion that Kashmir might become a condominium of India and Pakistan.

(5) *Financial Control.* 'In a number of cases capitalist countries either through government officials or representatives of banks, control the revenues and expenditures of the governments of backward countries which are otherwise independent' *(8:458)*. This form of control may be exercised by several States together or by a single State alone. Examples of the latter kind are found in the financial control of the United States over certain Caribbean and Central American countries, as well as over Liberia and Persia.

(6) *Tariff Control.* With a view to benefiting themselves, Western powers have frequently compelled backward countries not to raise their tariff duties on foreign goods beyond a certain limit. This kind of control was exercised over Japan till 1911. Such control has been exercised over China, Turkey, Morocco, Siam and Persia, the object of this control being to enable Western countries to dump their goods upon backward regions and prevent the development of indigenous industries.

(7) *Extra-territoriality.* This means the right of a foreign government to establish courts of its nationals residing in backward countries on the ground that these countries do not possess a reasonable brand of justice which can be applied to all. This right of extraterritoriality was claimed and established in almost all Muslim countries which give few rights to Christians, as well as in Japan, China, Korea and Siam. When, however, those countries adopt western standards of justice, the foreign powers gradually drop their extra-territorial claims. Thus in 1894 the United States relinquished her claims over Japan, and the Soviet Union over China in 1924. Turkey has abolished all extra-territorial claims. After World War II began Great Britain and the United States abolished their extra-territorial claims in China. These rights are usually exercised by consular or international courts and, as is to be expected, they are frequently abused. Extra-territoriality

may be interpreted to mean even exemption from local taxation. Sometimes it may be extended even to natives adopted as their proteges by foreigners.

(8) *Informal Control.* Sometimes foreign countries acting together in unison refuse to recognize the government of a backward country until it fulfils certain conditions laid down by their diplomats. This method of control is described by Buell as 'extra-legal' or 'backstairs' method. In the exercise of this control, various devices are adopted. The United States has used her marines in Nicaragua, Santo Domingo, the Caribbean, etc.; Great Britain has had recourse to the device of foisting her nationals as advisers, especially in matters of finance, on Persia, Egypt, and Iraq.

(9) *Interventions.* In the name of the Monroe Doctrine, the U.S. has at times intervened in the Latin American countries. The doctrine came to be regarded as the juridical basis of interventions.

The Open Door and Closed Door. Several wars fere fought with China in the last century to impose the policy of Open Door on her. According to this policy, all foreign powers wishing to trade with a backward country are given equal facilities. No discrimination is practised against the goods of nations of any foreign country. The 'open door' is sometimes extended to shipping and settlement as well. It means 'equality of opportunity' for both the imperial and other foreign countries. The traditional policy pursued in the British Empire has been that of the 'open door', but today it is considerably modified. The mandatory system required the maintenance of the open door in the A and B classes of mandates. Any member of the League could have 'complete economic, commercial, and industrial equality' in these areas. Since 'open door' frequently leads to cut-throat competition among foreign powers, recourse is sometimes had to international co-operation. Thus, in China, prior to the new government, no single state or group of states was allowed to make loans in return for political privileges.

The 'closed door' is the opposite of the 'open door'. It means preferences, discriminations, and monopolies not only as regards trade and commerce, but also as regards shipping, investment and settlement. Its purpose is to strengthen the economic ties between the mother country and the colony and shut out foreigners from any appreciable share in the profits. For many years the United States followed this policy with regard to the Philippine Islands. It is, says Schuman, survival of the old mercantalistic system. In the C class mandate there was no obligation to keep the door open.

The closed door usually takes three forms (a) tariffs, (b) shipping and (c) concessions. Some countries adopt tariff assimilation by which free trade is maintained between the mother country and the colony; but both have the same tariff system in their relation to other countries. Some other countries adopt tariff preference by which the mother country and the colony have different tariff systems, but extend special concession to the goods of each other.

As Buell writes: 'From the standpoint of the consumer the closed door means high prices, from the standpoint of a native it is but one more phase of the policy of exploitation; from the standpoint of the world at large, it means the perpetuation of the worst form of nationalistic imperialism' (*8:426*).

Military Alliances. While these have always existed, they assume new importance today. Member states entering them usually retain their sovereignty, but carry through a common military policy, often under the hegemony of a powerful nation. Examples of such alliances are found in the standardization of arms among the American countries and a common military policy–mutual military aid found among the group of countries represented by the NATO, SEATO, and MEDO.

The Mandates. The idealism engendered by Woodrow Wilson during World War I took a concrete form in the Mandatory system, provision for which was made in Article 22 of the League Convenant. While previous wars between European nations often meant the outright annexation of the colonial possession of the defeated powers, at the Peace Conference at Versailles it was said that the rights of the backward peoples should be the first concern of the Allies, that no single allied power should be allowed to become the sole possessor of any of the colonial territories of the former enemy countries. Hence there was brought into existence the Mandatory System whose object was (1) to safeguard the interests of the native population and (2) to avoid friction and rivalry among the imperial powers which, if not checked, would lead to future wars. The idea of 'trusteeship' on behalf of 'people not yet able to stand by themselves' was definitely asserted. Much against the wishes of President Wilson, the mandates were grouped into three classes, A, B and C, on the plea that not all the territories taken from the former enemy countries were at the same level of development. Hence it was argued that different systems of government were required to meet their differing needs. The A class mandates were considered the most fitted for the attainment of self-government in the near future and the C class mandates were considered the least, while the B class was placed in between. The tutelage of these mandates was entrusted to 'advanced nations' which were required to submit annual reports of their work to the League Council, which was working through a Permanent Mandates Commission for this purpose.

Although the mandatory system was devised in good faith, it did not justify the high hopes entertained at the time of its inception. The mandatory powers, instead of regarding the mandates as 'trusts of civilization' imposed upon unwilling nations, proceeded to regard them as annexations. 'For all practical purposes', Schuman says, 'the C mandates (were) treated as annexations and the B mandate administration (was) scarcely distinguishable from that which would have been provided for outright conquest. The A mandates (were) also under effective control of the mandatories' (*8:617*). Except in Iraq the mandatories ruthlessly crushed the legitimate aspirations of the people towards independence and self-government. Even in the matter of choice of the mandatory, the wishes of the mandates were set aside, as in the case of Syria which declared the United States to be her first choice and England next; and yet she was assigned to France. In 1932 Iraq was declared an independent British Protectorate, but her 'independence' was no more real than that of Egypt. The situation in Syria was much worse. The French and the Syrians seemed to be temperamentally incapable of understanding and helping each other.

Is Imperialism Justified? It is too late in the day to try to justify imperialism by roundabout and circumlocutory methods. Very few people today are prepared to believe with C. D. Burns that imperialism breaks down the mere narrowness of village politics and leads to internationalism and world brotherhood. If anything, it has precisely the opposite effect. The essence of imperialism is exploitation and domination. It is no heresy to say that imperialism has not had a respectable ancestry, although a stage comes in the histroy of its development when ruthless exploitation is clothed behind such high-sounding conceptions as 'trusteeship' and 'the civilizing and humanizing mission' of the West to the East. Many a modern empire had its origin in piracy and slave trade. Even the British Empire, says Barnes, is no exception to this rule (*4:11*).

The supporters of imperilaism, generally place emphasis on such factors as law and order, roads and railways, medicine and sanitation, schoolhouses, trade and instalments of self-government. But those who are opposed to it call attention of such concomitant factors of imperialism as brutality and ruthlessness, exploitation, misery, poverty and degradation, racial arrogance and unbrotherliness. J. A. Hobson regards imperialism as being rapacious and immoral, in addition to tending to destroy free government at home. According to Jawaharlal Nehru, the crisis of our time in Asia is colonialism *vs.* anti-colonialism.

(1) *Does Imperialism Benefit the Colonial People?* For a few cases of genuine humanitarianism, there are many cases of ruthless exploitation. As late as the mid 1920's European states possessed colonies with twice their own population and twenty times their own area. (*154:202*). Leonard Barnes is right when he paints the British Empire as 'a composite jumble, ramshackle in some parts, repressive in others, aimless in most, and beneficent in a few' (*4:21*), as against the familiar picture of 'a perennial spring of universal justice and benevolence on which the sun never sets' (*4:20*). It is true that in out-of-the-way places in Africa, imperialism has abolished cannibalism, slavery and crude forms of justice and government. But over against these benefits of imperialism we must weigh such facts as the culture system followed by Holland in the former Dutch East Indies, the atrocities committed by the Belgians in the Congo, indentured labour and virtual slavery which prevail in many parts of the tropical empire, and the confiscation of enormous tracts of land by a handful of whites in South Africa and Kenya. In South Africa, a million and a half whites own 280 million acres, while 5½ million Negroes possess 27 million acres.

In pursuing the policy of *Apartheid* or segregation, Negroes, Indians, and other non-whites in South Africa are being driven to the *ghettoes*. The situation has worsened considerably since the end of World War II. A few universities which were formally open to non-white races are becoming increasingly closed to them. In 1958 there took place the Sharpeville massacre when 67 Negroes were shot to death in cold blood and many were seriously injured when the Negroes protested against the law which compelled them to carry pass cards.

Barnes points out that in the mining districts of Africa 'conditions analogous to slavery' prevail. Native labourers are recruited for the most part by deception, and the compound system under which many of them live is detrimental to health, morals, and economic uplift. A compound, Barnes defines, as a 'cross between a barrack and a jail'. Conditions of agriculture in Africa are not any better. In the last few years, as Barnes points out, a system of native policy has been built up in the Union of South Africa which is a calculated outrage upon every tradition of fair dealing. In the Transvaal and Natal, 'no male native may be employed outside the farm on which he resides, unless he carries a document from the farmer permitting him to seek employment' (*4:256*) ! Brutality is added to oppression.

It is a notorious fact that imperialist countries spend very little money upon improving the conditions of the people over whom they are the self-appointed trustees. Leonard Woolf says that in the year 1924, out of an estimated revenue of two million pounds, the Kenya Government spent £44,000 on prisons and £37,000 on education. The whole policy pursued by the Government is to favour some 10,000 Europeans at the expense of 25,00,000 Africans and 36,000 Asians. All the desirable land is reserved for them and the 'native is on the road which leads to economic slavery' (*83:86*).[4] Conditions in South and East Africa show that the fate of the native population is much worse when entrusted to the white settlers on the spot than when it is in the hands of the Colonial Office in the mother country. This is the one reason why the natives in Northern Rhodesia, Southern Rhodesia, and Nyasaland were unalterably opposed to the formation of the self-governing Central African Federation out of these territories.

When we turn from Africa to India, we find that conditions under the British were not very much better, although Great Britain was a better master than most imperial powers. The economic exploitation and drainage of the country went on apace without much let or hindrance. Parker Moon wrote: 'The reason why the British first entered India, and the primary reason they have remained there was not to benefit India, but to benefit Great Britain' (*63:290*). In spite of more than 175 years of British rule in

4. One result of it has been the rise of the Mau Mau rebellion, a terrorist organization among the Kikuyu tribe killing the Whites and White sympathizers and informants. It has now been suppressed.

India, the average wage of the Indian labourer was, at the end, about six annas a day. The appalling poverty of the masses is still the most hideous fact that strikes the attention of any observer. In the words of Mahatma Gandhi : 'The Government established by law in British India is carried on for the exploitation of the masses. No sophistry, no jugglery in figures can explain away the evidence the skeletons in many villages present to the naked eye' (*106:753-34*). Besides poverty, there was still ignorance of the worst kind, 87 per cent of the people having been illiterate in 1940, although the new free Indian government is now doing everything possible to educate its people.[5] Public health was very poor, with a high rate of mortality and a high birth-rate, although the imperial power was not to blame for all of it. A disproportionately large percentage of the revenue of the country was spent on an expensive army and as equally expensive civil service and a host of pensioners, with the result that nation-building departments such as education and public health were obliged to live a hand-to-mouth existence. The flow of capital from England to India in the form of investment brought no relief to the masses. As Barnes notes : all that it did was to tighten the grip of the rich upon the poor and of Great Britain upon India.

By controlling currency and the military budget and, to some extent, the tariff and fiscal policy of the country England was able to favour her own people at the expense of the poverty-stricken masses of India. The indigneous cottage industries of India, which provided a living to many thousands and gave them opportunity for the expression of their personalities in creative work were practically wiped out under the stress of imperialistic competition. It is a well-known fact that the widespread textile industry of India was destroyed early last century by, among other things, the imposition of prohibitive import duties in England on fine Indian fabric. In the light of all this, it seems a mockery to speak of imperialism as a purely humanitarian task. Cecil Rhodes was nearer the truth when he said : 'Pure philanthropy is very well in its way, but philanthropy plus 5 per cent is a good deal better'. Schuman contends that profit motives, power motives, and prestige are skilfully concealed in terms of humanitarianism, civilizing missions, religious conversion, and material benefits conferred upon the backward people (*70:422*). The same writer says that in the countries under the heel of imperialism, very little money is spent as a rule on removing illiteracy and in promoting education. Much money is spent for military purposes, administration, and railway building. The white settlers take the lion's share. Beggary, starvation, and social disorganization stare one in the face everywhere. Head taxes and hut taxes are levied in Africa primarily not to raise revenue, but to compel the natives to work for white employers.

Even if it be granted, as it is, that certain indirect economic benefits

5. Illiteracy percentage today is about 70.

accrue to the victims of imperialism, it must be said that these benefits are often at the expense of their political independence, self-respect, and dignity. Political subjection is as intimate a part of imperialism as is economic exploitation. The nature of power is such that those who are kept under its yoke for long years come to love their very chains. As Rousseau points out: 'If there are slaves by nature, it is because there have been slaves against nature'. The recent history of Egypt, Syria, Palestine, India, Burma and Ceylon goes to show that imperial powers are most loath to part with authority and responsibility, and can be depended upon to place as many hindrances as possible in the way of a people being able to govern themselves. Imperialist powers have not yet learnt the truth that 'no man is good enough to be another's master'.

When the agitation on the part of subject peoples for self-government and independence becomes persistent, the imperial power adopts one or more of the following devices (*70:624-29*):

(a) It crushes native resistance by force and devises means by which to enfeeble the victims.

(b) It uses persuasion, education, and coercion to make a people loyal subjects of the empire.

(c) It replaces the language and culture of the people by those of the conquerors.

(d) It makes 'a pretence of colonial participation in the national government', substituting such an arrangement for national self-determination.

(e) It provides for various forms of autonomy, protection, and native participation in local governments, taking care to retain the substance of power in its own hands.

(f) It uses native princes and other vested interests as agent of colonial government.

(g) It sees to it that executive power is not allowed to be controlled by the legislature.

(h) In exceptional cases, it relinquishes power without war, as in the case of the British Dominions and India.

'So long as those who resist alien rule are weaker than the foreign conquerors, resistance merely intensifies foreign oppression and prolongs the dictatorial regime imposed from without' (*70:629*). Public disorders, intercommunal rivalries and frictions, illiteracy, low moral standards, and the like, are used as excuses for indefinitely postponing self-government, without any attempt being made to remove these hindrances. The backward countries are not given a chance to develop themselves and to learn by making mistakes. In this respect, the African native has probably been the most unfortunate, at least until very recent years.

Another fact of which Schuman reminds us in connection with the alleged benefits of imperialism is that Western civilization is not an unmixed blessing. The white man's religion, morals, language and social institutions have not infrequently resulted in the destruction of indigenous culture and in social chaos and demoralization. We are told that the native population of the South Seas is dead or dying on account of its contact with the West, which at its worst, has meant rum, guns and syphilis. In other parts of cult, world people living under imperial sway have lost their own cult, arts, morals and folk ways and have, become 'grotesque and debased caricatures of western whitemen' (*70:592*). While ancient imperialism touched the lives of the people only at a few points and left the people for the most part to develop their own native genius, modern imperialism is thoroughgoing in its application to the. lives of the people and is destructive of the best in their culture and civilization. It brands them as people of 'lesser breeds without the law' and equates military superiority and superior technology with cultural superiority.

Imperialism has much to answer in the matter of racial relationships. Racial frictions which mar the relationships of people in Asia and Africa are a direct legacy of imperialism. C. F. Andrews asks the question : 'How can you be a friend of the man who insists on always keeping you in a semi-inferior position'?

Furthermore, war is a necessary feature of imperialism—in the first instance with the backward peoples, and later with other imperial powers. Hardly a single colony has been won without some bloodshed. A recent writer observes that the path of empire is red with the blood of its victims Another writier says : 'Diplomacy, coercion, and military force are the necessary accompaniments of imperialism.' Even after subjugating a backward country, the imperial power is obliged to maintain a large army of occupation, partly for the sake of asserting its prestige, partly because of the fear of native revolt, and partly because of the fear of the possibility of rival imperial powers grabbing an ill-gotten gain. An imperial power is always on pins and needles, and the mentality which it exhibits is inimical to the maintenance of normal human relations.

(2) *Does Imperialism Benefit the people of the Mother Country?* It is often assumed that imperialism brings great material advantages to the people of the mother country. A careful analysis of the situation does not support such an assumption. On the emotional side, there is no doubt that imperialism is a good tonic for a people smarting under an inferiority complex. But it does not help the masses materially.

As a general rule, the pecuniary gains resulting from imperial adventures go to a favoured few. The nation as a whole pays the piper without calling the tune. Thus, for instance, the direct gain to the British masses from their possession of India was probably slight, in spite of the fact that 'India is by far the greatest market ever acquired as a colony by any industrial empire' (*63:520*). Particular industries such as cotton and iron may benefit, but not industry in general. If the huge capital which had been invested in India and other colonial possessions had remained in Britain itself, the condition of the British working classes might have been much better than it is today. Leonard Barnes writes: 'Colonies, in particular, are normally class assets, which bring advantages *e.g.*, to investors and manufacturers; but disadvantages, *e.g.*, to wage-earners' (*4:21*).

Advocates of empire often say that the imperial country obtains a bulk of the raw materials which its colonies produce. Actual facts, however, do not support such a contention. Raw materials, as Parker Moon puts it, are colour-blind. They obey economic rather than political laws. Trade generally follows the lowest price level, and not any patriotic exhortations.

The imperial preference idea which gained strength in the British Empire after World War I and which reached its climax in the Ottawa Agreement of 1932 did not bring much relief to the empire. *The Times* wrote, 'in the seven years between Ottawa and the outbreak of war, Great Britain and the Dominions simultaneously learned that their most pressing economic problems and the hopes of solving them turned on their trade relations not with one another but with the rest of the world.' Britain today seems to have learnt that lesson to perfection when she is willing to scrap a large free trade area in which she occupied a central place in favour of the European Common Market.

Notwithstanding the above arguments, the lower classes in the mother country benefit indirectly. Foreign trade and importation of cheap raw materials make for greater general well-being and greater buying power. This is true of the United States, even though she is not an imperialist power in the sense in which Great Britain, France, Belgium and Portugal have been or are.

In order to protect a far-flung empire, Britain was obliged to maintain a large army, navy, and air force. And this means that the British tax-payer had to bear the brunt of the burden; and whatever indirect gains he may have derived from Britain's imperial possessions was possibly more than offset by the burden of taxation. This economic burden is possibly one of the reasons why since the close of World War II, Great Britain has been busy conferring independence of self-government on several of her erstwhile possessions.

The plea that imperialism is a remedy for over-population is not supported by facts. The people of Italy and Japan who complained of overcrowding did not find colonies a solution to their problem. Adjustments in industry, agriculture and finance as well as international co-operation can perhaps solve the problem much better.

Imperialism further results in the lowering of wages and standards of living among the people of the imperial country. When the capitalist finds that he can get quick returns for his money by investing it in backward areas where labour is cheap and abundant, he naturally diverts his capital there. Before long he finds that a great variety of goods can be produced there at a much smaller cost than at home. The result of all this is that the labouring classes in the mother country suffer reduction in wages as well as unemployment.

The moral effects of imperialism upon the victors are very grave indeed. Prof. Hocking is right when he says: 'It is especially dangerous for any people to live long among a population which it holds in contempt'. It leads to lower standard of morality and debases conscience. It is not uncommon to find the white man using one set of standards for himself and another for the coloured. Even the law of the country is made to do service to such perversions. The white man hypnotizes himself into the belief that the coloured man belongs to a lesser breed, that he does not require the comforts that he demands for himself, that he can live on next to nothing, that his manners and morals are not worthy of attention, that his sentiments and feelings need not be scrupulously considered, and the like. It is this kind of veiled contempt which accounts for the fact that few Englishmen in India have real insight into the culture and civilization of the people of the country. They know a great deal about elephants, tigers, and snakes, social clubs and palaces, but not much about the inner life and genius of the people. The beauty of Indian philosophy, poetry, literature and art is a closed book to many of them.

A century ago (in 1860) Cobden asked the thoughtful question whether repression and injustice tolerated in the colonial possession by Britain may not corrupt her own domestic politics, "just as Greece and Rome were demoralized by their contact with Asia". A lesson which mankind learns very slowly is that injustice tolerated abroad soon comes to roost in one's own backyard. In our own day, J. A. Hobson, writing about administrators, soldiers, and businessmen returning to their mother country after years of stay in the colonial possessions says: "Everywhere they stand for coercion and for resistance to reform.... It is, indeed, a nemesis of imperialism that the arts and crafts of tyranny, acquired and exercised in our unfree Empire, should be turned against our liberties at home." (Quoted by Ebenstein, W., p. 667).

Imperialism is at its best a benevolent despotism so far as the so-called 'backward' regions are concerned. Repression is the very breath of its nostrils. Experience shows that repression practised in a colonial possession soon comes to roost at home. It is probably true that the freedom-loving Englishman has lost some of his original zeal for freedom, partly because of the changed mentality brought about by the militray excesses of his countrymen abroad and by the serious restrictions placed on freedom in various parts of the dependent empire.

The unnatural relation prevailing between the imperial country and its possessions is altogether inimical to the possibility of the two learning from each other. Receptivity to new ideas and suggestions and the drawing out of the innate capacity of the learner are difficult of attainment so long as the master-servant relation prevails between two peoples.

(3) *Does Imperialism Help to Avoid Friction Points Among Nations and Make for World Peace?* The answer to this question is, for the most part, in the negative. Imperialism means international rivalry and compe-

tition. It means a struggle for markets, raw materials, and places for capital investment. As long as there were plenty of open spaces in Africa and Asia for settlement or exploitation, the Western powers were able to parcel them out among themselves without much friction. Today almost all available space is taken up, and the future promises to witness a period of struggle between the imperial powers for colonies and markets. Germany and Japan sought to justify their part in World War II as an attempt at equalization in the imperial world. Writing before the commencement of the War, Leonard Barnes said: 'It is true and fair to say that Britain's possession, on the present privileged terms, of a vast dependent Empire is incompatible with peace' (*4:21-22*).

It is claimed by Prof. E. Barker, for instance, that, while the British Empire originally signified overseas expansion for the two-fold purpose of settlement and business, it is revealing a process of sublimation which is leading to the totally new idea of a community of self-governing nations based on voluntary adhesion to the English ideas of law and liberty. It is needless to say that this statement about a free association of self-governing nations may apply to the Dominions, but not to the colonies and dependencies which till recently constituted 6/7ths of the whole Empire.

Even if it be admitted for the sake of argument that the British Empire secures peace, order and contentment over vast territories, it does not follow that world peace is secure. Britain may be honest in her desire not to engage in wars and aggression as well as in her desire to fit her colonies and dependencies for self-government as speedily as possible. But so long as the non-British capitalistic countries of the world harbour the grievance that they do not have an adequate share in the trade and territories of the world, world peace rests on slender basis. Therefore, our conclusion is that imperialism in practice, and not the imperialism of the philosopher, is not conducive to peace. At best it means armed neutrality.

(4) *Is there an Alternative to Imperialism?* Imperialism, we are convinced, is not *finally* possible. Schuman believes that the days of empires are numbeerd, even though their decline will inevitably be slow and gradual.

A very useful suggestion made by Barnes is that, inasmuch as imperialism and capitalism are intimately linked together, it is necessary to substitute socialism for capitalism in the 'mother country', if imperialism is to undergo profound modification. In the author's words: 'Some sort of socialistic revolution in Britain is a precondition of every tolerable imperial system'. The 'liberation and development of the colonies is interdependent with the socialization of Britain. Neither can take place without the other. They are two aspetcs of a single interlocked process.' According to R. Fox: 'The issue of the struggle of the British working class, the question of socialism in England, cannot be considered apart from the liberation of the peoples of the Empire'.

INTERNATIONALISM

Thoughtful people everywhere are coming to realize the urgent need of replacing international anarchy by international order. The world is no longer a huge place, as we once imagined it to be. Distance has been annihilated by rapid means of transport and communications. Economically the world is a unit. The radio and television have annihilated the sense of space and the mysterious fear which accompanied it. 'From the point of view of news and views', as Madariaga says, 'the world has attained the unity of the market place.' We are surely living in an interdependent world in which what concerns one people sooner or later has its repercussion upon every other people. If mankind is to save itself from the catastrophe which awaits it, it should replace national exclusiveness by international inclusiveness; the doctrine of national sovereignty by the doctrine of international solidarity.

Internationalism stands for a family of self-respecting and self-governing nations, united to each other by ties of equality and living at peace and concord with each other. At the present stage of human development at least, a sound nationalism is a prelude to a sound internationalism. In the words of Joseph: 'Nationality is the necessary link between man and humanity'. Militarism and jingoism or what has earlier been described as 'wolf pack nationalism' is surely an enemy of internationalism. The fact that I love the group to which I belong does not in any way mean that I should despise other groups. Nationalism of the cultural, moral and spiritual kind is an ally of internationalism. In the words of William Lloyd Garrison, 'Our country is the world, our countrymen are all mankind. We love the land of our nationality as we love all other lands.'

Internationalism in the Twentieth Century: The League of Nations. The greatest advance in internationalism was made in the first quarter of the twentieth century, at least from the point of view of machinery. What was lacking was the will to international co-operation and international control. Nevertheless, public opinion was gradually veering round to internationalism, and it was reasonable to hope that before long internationalism would become as much a natural and normal part of man's thinking as nationalism and imperialism had been hitherto.

The League of Nations saw the light of the day on January 1, 1920. Although it was not the work of any single individual or of any single generation, Woodrow Wilson, more than any other statesman of the day, helped to give it a practical reality. It was in pursuance of the last of his famous fourteen points which declared, 'A general association of nations must be formed under specific covenants for the purpose of affording mutual guarantees of political independence and territorial integrity to governments and small States alike.'

The general purpose of the League as set forth in the preamble to the Covenant is as follows:

'1. The High Contracting Parties

In order to promote international co-operation, and to achieve international peace and security;

by the acceptance of obligations not to resort to war,

by the prescription of open, just and honourable relations between nations,

by the firm establishment of the understandings of international law as the acutal rule of conduct among Governments,

and by the maintenance of justice and a scrupulous respect for all treaty obligations in the dealings of organized peoples with one another,

Agree to this Covenant of the League of Nations'.

A close study of the Articles of the Covenant shows the objects of the League to be:

(a) Preservation and maintenance of the *status quo* as established by the Peace Conference;

(b) Fulfilment of certain administrative and supervisory functions, such as the protection of national minorities, the supervision of the free city of Danzig, the administration of the Saar valley, and the operation of the Mandates system;

(c) Concern with problem of health, social questions, finances, importation, communication and the like; and

(d) Prevention of war and the pacific settlement of disputes.

Membership in the League and Withdrawal. The League started with forty-two original members. According to the provisions made in the Covenant, admission of new members required a two-thirds vote of the Assembly The condition of membership was the promise to observe international obligations and disarmament regulations laid down by the League. Very small states such as San Marino and Armenia were excluded from membership, while Switzerland was admitted in spite of her unwillingness to fulfil her military obligations because of her neutralized status. The United States never became a member because of the failure of the Senate to ratify the Covenant. In spite of it, the United States co-operated with the League in many of its activities. Some of her eminent sons served as judges of the Permanent Court of International Justice and some were closely associated with the scaling down of reparations.

Withdrawal from the League required two years' notice, except in cases where an amendment made to the Covenant was unacceptable to the member withdrawing. Before withdrawal a member was required to fulfil all its obligations. A member violating the Covenant could be expelled. Three significant withdrawals before the commencement of World War II were those of Japan, Germany and Italy.

The Organs of the League—(a) The Assembly. Each member of the League had one vote. This meant in theory at least that the League was controlled by the small States, since they formed a majority. Each member of the League was allowed to have three delegates, collectively exercising one vote. India and the self-governing Dominions of the British Empire were counted as separate States for this purpose. The delegates to the Assembly were chosen by the executive governments of their countries, and hence represented governments rather than peoples.

Till World War II began, the Assembly met once a year at Geneva. Provision was made for special sittings. Business was conducted in English and French. Much of its work was done through committees, there being six standing committees to deal with the important aspects of the League's work. Final debate took place in the Plenary Assembly. The agenda of the Assembly was prepared by the Secretary-General in consultation with the President of the Council. Questions proposed by an earlier Assembly, by the Council, or any member of the League were included. The Assembly was presided over by an elected President, who was assisted by twelve Vice-Presidents, six of whom were presidents of the standing committees.

One of its functions was that of admitting new members to the League by a two-thirds majority. It also elected annually three of the nine non-permanent members of the Council by a majority vote. Once every nine years, in conjunction with the Council, it elected by a majority vote fifteen judges and four deputy judges of the permanent Court of International Justice. It further approved by a majority vote the Council nomination for the post of Secretary-General. It had the power to amend the Covenant in accordance with Article 26.

As a deliberative body, it exercised very wide functions. It had the competence to deal with any matter 'within the sphere of action of the League affecting the peace of the world'. Any member of the League could bring to the attention of the Assembly or the Council any matter threatening 'to disturb international peace or the good understanding among nations upon which peace depends'. The Assembly had the right to advise members to reconsider treaties which had become inapplicable.

A special function of the Assembly was the approval of the annual budget, which was about one-fifth the cost of a single modern battleship. According to Madariaga, in 1936 the world spent more than 10 billion dollars on armaments, while the average League budget was 8 million dollars or 1/2500th. The budget was prepared by the Secretariat and was subject to revision by the Assembly, which apportioned the share of the expenses among the member States. The total expenses were divided into a thousand units and a certain number was assigned to each member in accordance with its size, population and political importance. Of the total income, approximately half was spent on the Secretariat, one-third on the International Labour Office, and one-tenth on the permanent Court.

In the very nature of the case, the work of the Assembly was of a general character. Its size and importance made it difficult to act as swiftly as the Council. Nevertheless, it exercised a general supervision over the work of the Council.

Both the Assembly and the Council were assisted by a number of 'Technical Organizations'. One of the limitations of the Assembly was that it could not arrive at any decision without a unanimous vote of the members present at the meeting. But since most of its acts were in the nature of recommendations, a simple majority vote was deemed sufficient. The representatives at the Assembly were delegates of their respective governments. Therefore, they could not vote independently but under instructions from their foreign offices.

In spite of these limitations, the Assembly was a valuable body. It provided a ready platform for the discussion of international grievances and disputes. Even 'domestic questions' which were not matter for arbitration by any League body could be discussed by the Assembly under Article XI, and, if they had an international bearing they could be made the basis of a treaty binding those powers which ratified it. Although the Council was a more influential body, in the case of the Japanese occupation of Manchuria at least, the Assembly was able to deal with the situation much more effectively.

(b) **The Council. It consisted** of three classes of members (i) permanent, (ii) non-permanent, and (iii) special. The permanent members were the allies who won the war in 1918. Germany was admitted to a permanent seat in the Council in 1926, but lost it on her withdrawal from the League.

The Council held four regular meetings a year, and provision was made for special sessions. At the beginning of each session the Secretary-General of the League presented a report on the action taken on the earlier decisions of the Council. The President and Vice-President of the Council were elected annually by a majority vote of the Council. They were not eligible for election continually for two years.

The most important function of the Council was the settlement of international disputes. In cases where the disputants refused arbitration or adjudication, as well as in cases where these methods of settlement were inapplicable, the Covenant required that the matter be referred to the Council for action. This meant that 'non-justiciable' or 'political' disputes fell within the jurisdiction of the Council. During the time that a dispute was under consideration by the Council or Assembly the parties concerned were required not to go to war.

The power of the Council could be increased by treaty agreements among the member States. The Council was vested with authority to mobilize sanctions against a Covenant-breaking State. Together with the Assembly, it elected the judges of the World Court, appointed Secretaries-General, and increased the number of members on the Council. As in the case of the Assembly, a unanimous vote was required for all decisions and agreements. But on matters of procedure and similar matters a majority vote was sufficient.

The precise relation between the Assembly and the Council was not laid down in the Covenant. Some have compared the two bodies to the two houses of a modern legislature while others have compared the Assembly to a Parliament and the Council to a Cabinet. Both these comparisons are misleading; while the Assembly concerned itself largely with questions of 'legislative policy', the work of the Council was mostly semi-judicial and administrative.

(c) **The Secretariat.** It was the permanent administrative organ of the League machinery. It may be regarded as an International Civil Service. While not in itself an executive body, it was vested with administrative powers. At the head of it was the Secretary-General who was appointed by the Council with the approval of the majority of the Assembly. He in turn appointed other Secretaries and members with the approval of the Council. There was no competitive examination for admission into the service, but in making appointments, professional competence and the need for fair distribution of posts among the member States of the League were borne in mind. Once a person was appointed he was to regard himself as a servant of the League of Nations, and not of the State to which he belonged. The duties of the members of the Secretariat were not national, but international. During the period of service they were not allowed to accept any honour or decoration from their governments.

The work of the Secretariat was to collect data, prepare the agenda for the meetings of the Council and the Assembly, summon meetings, keep records, communicate decisions and agreements to the member States for ratification, transmit recommendations for information and action, prepare drafts, and make suggestions for the solution of current international problems. It prepared and published the Official Journal of the League which contained minutes of the Assembly and Council proceedings. It was the permanent adviser on international affairs.

(d) **The Permanent Court of International Justice.** Prior to the formation of this Court in 1920, there was no genuine 'International Court', much less a Permanent International Court. This Court had the competence to decide all cases of an international character submitted to it by the parties concerned. It also gave advisory opinion upon all questions submitted to it by the Council or the Assembly. Although such opinion had no binding effect, it was generally accepted. The interpretation of the League Covenant did not belong to the Court, but to the member States.

The powers of the Court were much wider than those of the old Hague Tribunal. The Court had the power to interpret treaties and questions of international law, decide the extent and nature of reparations to be made for breaches of international obligation, and determine the existence of any situation which if established would constitute a breach of such obligations. But the jurisdiction of the Court in these matters bound only those member States which signed the 'Optional Clause'. Members of the League agreed to submit to the Council for either arbitration or investigation such matters as could not be settled by the Court. On questions arising with regard to ports, waterways, railways, and the like, the Court had compulsory arbitration.

Judgments were delivered by a majority vote and there was no appeal. If, however, a party to a dispute discovered a new fact which was relevant to the case, it could appeal for revision of the judgment 'within six months after the discovery of the fact and within ten years after the judgment' (*8:588*). In arriving at decisions the Court used international conventions and rules established under them by the agreement of the contracting States, international customs, the general principles of law recognized by civilized States, and judicial decisions and teachings of eminent publicists.

The number of judges in 1930 was 15 and their term of office was nine years. The system of electing was such that both big and small nations were represented on the Bench. In the case of a State to a dispute which did not have its own national on the Bench, it was allowed to select a judge. For failure to fulfil the conditions of his appointment a judge could be removed from office by a unanimous vote of his colleagues.

(e) **The International Labour Organisation.** It consisted of (a) General International Labour Conference, (b) a Governing Body, and (c) an International Labour Office. The General International Labour Conference was composed of four delegates of each co-operating government. Two of these represented the Government, one represented capital, and one labour. Although capital and labour representatives were chosen by each government, they were chosen in consultation with the industrial organization concerned. The delegates were given the privilege of voting individually. This made it possible, for instance, for all the labour delegates of the conference to vote against the employers' delegates. Non-members of the League also were allowed to send representatives.

The chief object of the International Labour Organization was to promote uniform labour legislation throughout the world, although certain exceptions were made in the case of Japan, China and India on account of differing climatic and other conditions. One of the useful conventions passed was the eight-hour day and forty-eight hour week. Another convention was the prohibition of children under fourteen from being employed in gainful occupations. As regards India, children under fourteen were prohibited only from working in mines, factories and transportation.

Appraisal of the League of Nations. Even the most enthusiastic supporters of the League cannot claim that it was an unqualified success. While it did much good, it failed to prevent war and injustice in many cases, especially in China, Abyssinia and Spain. Nevertheless, it was a movement in the right direction. Its failures lay largely in the domain of 'high politics', while in the field of international co-operation in non-political matters, and more particularly in matters pertaining to labour, it achieved considerable success. It was an association of sovereign nations. What was required was an association of peoples. A confederation of governments alone, each striving for its own ends, could never attain success.

Many who judged the value of the League judged it by its ability to prevent war and settle international disputes by pacific means. From this point of view, the League was largely a failure. It is unfortunate that the League was linked up with the Versailles Treaty, one of whose clauses imposed 'war guilt' upon Germany and made her responsible for the whole cost of the war. The sordid story of reparations and the occupation of the Ruhr as a part of that story did much to discredit the League. Other factors which contributed to the same end were the League 'trusteeship' of the Saar Valley in the interest of France, the joint protectorate of the League and Poland over Danzig, and the League administration of Memel, a port given to Lithuania.

Leonard Woolf observes: "The statesmen who 'worked' the League for fifteen years or so did not believe in it; they thought themselves to be realists and the League either an Utopia or a convenient or inconvenient instrument—it depended upon circumstances—of national policy." (Quoted by Ebenstein, W., *op. cit.*, p. 739).

Disarmament. If the attempts to outlaw war were not a great success, neither did attempts in the direction of disarmament succeed. The League worked for disarmament through the Permanent Advisory Commission and the Temporary Mixed Commission, but both efforts failed. A general Disarmament Conference of the League of Nations met at Geneva in 1932. A multitude of proposals came up before the conference, but nothing materialized. At one stage in the conference Soviet Russia proposed complete and immediate disarmament, but this was not acceptable to the other members.

Sanctions. The League Covenant provided for economic, military and political sanctions. During the Italo-Abyssinian war, economic sanctions were applied by several States in regard to various commodities, but not in regard to oil, the most important commodity required by Italy. The League could not force any of its members to apply sanctions. Military sanctions—*i.e.*, the use of armed forces belonging to the members of the League on the recommendation of the Council—were never applied. Political sanctions referred to exclusion from membership of the League for violation of the Covenant. This was done in the case of Russia in 1939.

NATIONALISM, IMPERIALISM AND INTERNATIONALISM TODAY

The Rise of Internationalism

Just as the nineteenth century was an epoch of triumphant nationalism, the twentieth century may be regarded as an epoch of new resurgent internationalism. As Laski thinks, the inadequacy of the sovereign nation-state has been demonstrated by the tragic occurrence of two world wars in a period of three decades. The emergence of the League of Nations after the first world war and the establishment of the United Nations Organisation after the last war are the steps in a right direction but they are nothing more than the initial steps in the direction of a world federation based on complete abrogation of the sovereignty of nation-states as the only remedy of the myriad ills caused by the existing anarchy in international affairs.

New Basis of International Law

He stands for a total reconstitution of the traditional basis of international law which regards sovereignty as an essential characteristic of every nation-state. "The concept of an absolute and independent sovereign state", says Laski, "which demands an unqualified allegiance to government from its members, and enforces that allegiance by the power at its command, is incompatible with the interests of humanity. If we are to have a morally adequate theory of political obligation, we must approach the problem from a different angle. In a creative civilization what is important is not the historical accident of separate states, but the scientific fact of world-interdependence. The real unit of allegiance is the world. The real obligation of obedience is to the total interest of our fellowmen'" *(47:64)*.

International Government in a Unified World Society

Laski thus believes in the ideal of a unified world society with an international government exercising authority over the national societies in their mutual relations. This will result in an alienation of the sovereign power from the national societies such as Russia, England or India to an international body like the United Nations Organization which will be converted into a genuine world federation by the possession of a coercive power over its constituent units. The advent of international government will no doubt cure the present lawlessness in international relations but its attainment still seems in the realm of remote possibility.

Greater Awareness of International Solidarity

There are at present several trends leading towards a greater awareness of the sense of an international community. The progress of science specially in the means of communications, has brought one nation closer to another. The technological advance resulting in the growth of large-scale mechanized industries created new opportunities for the development of international trade. The imperialist drive of the capitalist countries, though a sad event for the victims of imperialism, created new linguistic, cultural, economic and political bonds between the European nations and the races and peoples of other continents.

Capitalism and an International Market

Capitalism created an international market supplanting all national barriers and breaking the iron bars of isolation in one country after another. If it led to competitive wars between capitalist nations, it compelled the generous minds in every nation to pause and think and find out the means of outlawing war as such. Moreover, the growth of an international labour movement may be regarded as an inevitable by-product of the rise of capitalism. Laski recognizes the fact that all these factors have produced a greater consciousness of international solidarity. The birth of such organizations as the League of Nations or the present United Nations Organization is a proof of this consciousness.

National Sovereignty as a Threat to Internationalism

But it must be admitted that the forces which resist internationalism are still powerfully entrenched in various spheres of social organization (*50:258*). The doctrine of national sovereignty is still a positive hindrance in the effective realization of a broadly agreed international policy. This is evident from South Africa's denial of human rights and equal treatment to its coloured citizens although the overwhelming majority of the world public opinion has condemned its policy through the successive resolutions passed by the United Nations Organization for the last several years. The tendencies such as racialism, colonialism or fascism still act as powerful deterrents to international unity and cooperation. Laski even declares capitalist imperialism as incompatible with the ideal of a cooperative world order.

War as a Legal Right of the State

Since Grotius formulated his conceptions of international law, war has been regarded as the legal right of every sovereign community for the settlement of disputes with any fellow member in the community of nations. Laski regards the reconstruction of the Grotian theory of international law a vital part of his political theory.

As he says, "A theory of the State, that is to say, must be, from one angle a philosophy of international law. It must explain why states should regard themselves as bound by the rules of international intercourse. It must build itself upon postulates which satisfactorily fit the kind of world to which we belong. It must be wide enough, in its foundations, to weigh the significance of the immense changes we have witnessed in the relations of states since Grotius, some three hundred years ago, first formulated a scientific approach to the problems of international law. No foundations for such a philosophy can be adequate, unless they provide for the rules of international intercourse the assurance of that continuity of application which enables the state, within its own community, to make its law the measure of the behaviour of all other associations with which it has contact" (*50:218*).

Machinery for Pacific Settlement of Disputes

In other words, Laski is pleading for a revision of the traditional basis of international law which makes every state the sole judge of its disputes with other states and permits it to seek its settlement by a trial of arms. He wants to evolve an effective international machinery which may secure the pacific settlement of disputes between different states without any need of recourse to war. In short, war should be banned by international law as an instrument of national policy. Considering the present tensions and ideological conflicts between the communist bloc of nations and the capitalist countreis under American hegemony, legal outlawry of war still remains an idealistic dream of the pacifists with little possibility of its practical realization.

National Sovereignty as a Doctrine of the Capitalist Era

It is a historical fact that the sovereign nation-state of the modern times is essentially a product of the capitalist era. In the context of international law, the doctrine of sovereignty has found expression in two ways. In the first place, it is a logical formula which regards the rules of international law as the product of independent wills of the sovereign states. No state is considered bound by any rule to which it has not given its prior consent. This logical formula is further reinforced by a philosophical justification of this position. The state is regarded as a supreme moral community which cannot be externally bound by any moral or legal consideration against its own will. Moral relations presuppose an organised life and it is claimed that such an organised life can be found only within the borders of a single nation-state. We cannot claim the same type of organised life for the states in their external relations with one another.

National Sovereignty as the Basis of the League of Nations

Hence the rules of international law can have no validity against the will of particular states. Laski points out that the organisation of the League of Nations was based on clear recognition of the fact of sovereignty of individual states. It was this emphasis of sovereignty of each state, which prevented the evolution of a consensus in the field of disarmament. Every state regards the pursuit of self-interest as the basis of foreign policy both in peace and war. Self-interest can be pursued only with the support of armed forces and armaments, which a state maintains. The right to wage war is an expression of the sovereign power of each state. Therefore, no state is prepared to relinquish sovereignty in the interest of international order. The armed forces and armaments are not only valuable in times of actual war but they serve the national self-interest in times of formal peace as well because a more powerful state can impose its will on weaker states simply by threatening the use of force. Such matters as tariffs, migration, persecution of national minorities, nationalisation of foreign companies etc. may create differences of opinion between two states and the stronger party is always likely to use diplomatic pressures, subversion and intervention to resolve such disputes in its own favour.

War as a part of the World Order

Laski therefore concludes that the war or an armed peace threatening the outbreak of actual hostilities at any moment has become an essential feature of the world order, which has recognized the existence of a multiple number of sovereign nation-states.

It is obvious that the most important single barrier in the path of realizing an ever-lasting world peace is the doctrine of national sovereignty. Laski does not agree with the views of those international jurists, who think it is possible to abolish national sovereignty in the context of the existing class-relations of a capitalist country.

National Interests and Capitalism

The purpose of sovereignty in a capitalist state is to maintain and protect the interests of a capitalist class both internally and externally. The so-called national interests are always the sectional interests of the ruling capitalist class. The modern capitalist states have waged a series of imperialist wars only for the benefit of the capitalist rulers of those countries. The numerous wars of colonial conquests in Asia, Africa and America waged by the capitalist states of Europe may be cited in support of this fact. Even the war of 1914 was a struggle between two blocs of capitalist countries fighting for the control of markets and colonies.

War Inherent in Capitalist System

Laski therefore concludes that the doctrine of sovereignty is a weapon in the hands of the ruling class of a capitalist state to safeguard its interests by diplomacy and war in the international sphere. As he significantly remarks, "The State in a capitalistic society needs to remain sovereign in order to protect the interests of capitalism. In the last resort, these interests have to be protected by war, which is the supreme expression of sovereignty in international relations. So long, therefore, as the effective purpose of the state, internally regarded, is to protect the principles of capitalism, so long, in its external aspect, will it require to retain the use of war as an instrument of national policy. If sovereignty and an effective world-order are incompatible ways of life, then, also capitalism and world-order are incompatible; for war is rooted in the capitalist system in our experience of its necessary functioning" *(50:229)*.

World Peace Depends on Abolition of Capitalism

It is an important conclusion because it regards the abrogation of the capitalist system as a precondition for the abolition of national sovereignty which alone can guarantee peaceful relations between different communities of the globe. All attempts at international organisation, which ignore this fundamental hypothesis of Laski, are almost predestined to failure. Realistically speaking, international government is impossible in face of the serious antagonisms that have historically divided the capitalist world. With the emergence of the Soviet Union and other Communist states on the world scene, there has emerged another source of antagonism between states *i.e.* the antagonism between the Capitalist and Communist blocs of nations.

Sovereignty and the Communist State

Laski thinks that the Communist state does not threaten the peace of the world in the way the capitalist states have been doing in the past and are likely to do the same in future at any suitable opportunity. He is convinced that the fundamental interest of a Communist state is the preservation of international peace. As he says, "it is, I think one of the clear lessons of the inter-war years that while the interest of a Communist state, like that of Russia, is peace, since peace is the condition of the success of its experiment, the interest of capitalist states is held to be threatened by its successful development. That is why, as I have already argued, even the statesmen of the capitalist democracies did not, in its early phases, at least, regard the anti-Bolshevik crusade of Hitler as unwelcome" (*131*:*209*).

Soviet Russia and Colonialism

He thus emphasizes the fact that a socialist society like the Soviet Union does not suffer from those contradictions which compel a capitalist state to pursue a policy of colonial aggrandizement bringing in its wake the inevitable cycle of imperialist wars. There are no vested interests in the Soviet Union seeking control of foreign markets and colonies. Thus a Communist state does not require a sovereign power for aggressive purposes as the other capitalist states do require it. The Russian state needs sovereignty only to defend its frontiers against an invasion by some capitalist state" (*121*:*537*).

Contrast between Foreign Policies of Russia and Capitalist States

Laski says that a socialist state like Soviet Russia does not require the attribute of sovereignty in the sense other capitalistic states need it. In Germany, Japan, the U.S.A. or Great Britain supreme coercive power of the state is in possession of a privileged social class which governs in order to safeguard its class interests. Surrender of sovereignty by these states will endanger these interests. Externally the vested interests of these countries use the sovereign power to wage "the war of steel and gold" and "invoke the half-rational sentiment of nationalism" to protect their privileges in foreign countries. Such vested interests do not exist in Soviet Russia and, therefore, the motive to aggression in the case of the Soviet regime can never be attributed to economic imperialism. Soviet Russia, unlike a capitalist country, will wage wars only in self-defence. But a capitalistic state, threatened by economic crisis inherent in the system, will use its sovereign power for aggressive purposes in order to protect or expand its economic empire.

Socialism and Sovereign Power

Laski in this way shows that socialist societies do not require the sovereign power for aggressive purposes, and the transformation of the existing capitalist societies into socialist societies can alone bring about that atmosphere of peaceful intercourse between nations, which is the first condition for installing an international government which can control the external relations of the national communities.

Capitalism, War and Sovereignty are Related

The contemporary history of the major capitalist countries abundantly proves Laki's thesis that capitalism, sovereignty and war are intimately connected with one another. Every capitalist society by its unequal distribution of income in the community creates a contradiction between its production and consumption. The capitalist class does not meet this crisis by a change in the relations of production but by a policy of economic imperialism. This brings one capitalist government in conflict with another for the possession of colonies, protectorates, the spheres of influence, or the zones of legitimate aspiration which can serve as sources of raw materials, as markets for the finished goods, or as areas where the surplus capital may be exported and reinvested. This has been a history of England, France and Holland in the nineteenth century. This has, also, been the history of Germany, Italy and Japan in the first half of the twentieth century. As Laski foresaw, this may as well be the history of the United States of America in the second half of the present century.

America's Drive towards Aggressive War and Imperialism

As he says, "American economic expansion, in the classic sense, is over, the relations of production deny the possibilities of the forces of production in the same way as in Great Britain. The standard of life of the masses does not satisfy their established expectations.... Meanwhile the power of American production increases without any parallel power, within the domestic market, to consume the commodities so made available. There develops the classic need to capture foreign markets to satisfy that profit-making motive which is the drive of capitalist production. But since America, like Europe, has, as the great depression after 1929 made obvious, entered upon the period of econmic contraction, its democracy, in its present form, can only survive either by becoming imperialist or by transcending its capitalist relation. If the future of America were to lie in the first direction it could not surrender its sovereignty. For, if its will as a state could be bound by the wills of other states, it would be unable to develop an imperialism. That would force it to choose between capitalism and democracy; and, if it chose the first, America, like Hitlerite Germany, would be driven to aggressive war".[6] The transition from the New Deal regime of President Roosevelt to the

6. Laski: "Reflections on the Revolution of Our Time", Chapter VI, pp. 215-16. "His final question to the united States", says Kingsley Martin, "was whether it would realize in time that its democracy was unreal unless plutocracy was dispossessed, or whether the propertied class would destroy democracy and resort perhaps to Fascist methods to maintain their power and their privileges". (Harold Laski: *A Biographical Memoir*, p. 195).

reactionary administrations of Johnson and Nixon implies that America has finally chosen the path of economic imperialism leading inevitably to international violence and war (*127:108:116*). There is no chance now of that socialist transformation of the American society which Laski regards as the basic condition of a peaceful American foreign policy. America cannot abandon an aggressive use of its sovereignty as is evident from her aggression in Viet Nam because it has now clearly embarked upon a policy of economic and military imperialism to solve the internal crisis of American capitalism.

Imperialist Phase of Capitalism

"My argument therefore", says Laski, "is the simple one that the postulates of the imperialist phase of capitalist development necesssarily involve war; and that an effective international order is, *a priori*, incompatible with it. That international order must fit the categories of a unified economic world, and this has completely outgrown the limitations which the sovereign state, as a political category, puts upon it" (*50:243*). In other words, Laski concludes that the sovereign capitalist state must be sent to the dust-bin of history, a place where it now truly belongs, before any serious attempt to define the nature of an effective world organization, which can successfully safeguard world peace, may be made.

The Conception of a World Organisation

When the League of Nations was brought into existence as a consequence of the Treaty of Versailles, Laski regarded it as an important forward step in the direction of the erosion of national sovereignty. In the beginning he regarded it as a super-state but he later on accepted that it was an erroneous interpretation of the position of the League of Nations. Even then he thought that this international organization was bound to become a super-state in the course of time. In "A Grammar of Politics", he wrote, "Nor need I dwell upon the purely technical issue of whether the League is juristically a superstate or merely an association of sovereign nations. I believe myself that it is inevitably destined to become the former and that this character will become increasingly obvious as its functioning becomes more adequate. For it has, in fact, the power to bind its members; and there are already spheres of activity within its ambit of authority in which evasions of the obligations it creates are, if not theoretically impossible, at least sufficiently difficult to be impossible in practice" (*47:588*).

The League of Nations as an Association of Sovereign States

The subsequent histroy of the world events falsified Laski's prediction in this regard and the League of Nations remained merely as association of sovereign nations till it met its final doom in the outbreak of the Second World War. The League failed to impose its decisions on the sovereign states against their will. This was revealed on the question of registration of treaties, the problem of a readjustment of national boundaries, the question of disarmament or limitation of armaments, the issue of the treatment of racial and religious minorities, and, finally, on the question of the claims of subject races for better administration and self-government.

The League Failed as an Instrument of Collective Security

When the League failed in these matters, it was bound to fail as an instrument of collective security. When Japan, Italy and Germany embarked upon a policy of international adventurism and brigandage, the League of Nations could not even compel its members to impose economic sanctions against the aggressors. On the other hand, the major capitalist countries of the League condoned the aggressive acts of the fascist governments and pursued a policy of appeasement towards them bringing about the inevitable collapse of the League as an instrument of collective security.

The U.N.O. also as an Association of Sovereign States

The contemporary history of the world abundantly shows that the state retained its sovereignty not only after the coming into being of the League of Nations but the legal status of a state in international law remains basically unaltered even after the establishment of the present United Nations Organization. The state is still the sole judge and executing authority of its internal and external policies. It still makes war and concludes peace in its discretion. It decides for itself the nature of its foreign alliances. It determines how large or small armed forces are needed for its defence or offence, necessary. If it possesses colonies, it must itself decide how to govern or misgovern them.

Even the United Nations Organisation cannot compel the sovereign state of South Africa to show a better consideration for its coloured citizens than what it has been doing in the past. Nor can it ask the United States of America to desist from the policy of building its military, naval and air bases in every part of the world and of stationing its armed forces in such far-flung places as Western Europe, North Africa and East Asia, because this policy is likely to disturb international peace. Similarly, it cannot ask Great Britain or Portugal to wind up the remnants of their empires, say in South Arabia or Central Africa where the people have unmistakably shown a desire to be free of colonial control and are even waging a relentless struggle for their national liberation.

Lessons of the Manchurian and Abyssinian Crises

Laski realized this fact after sixteen years of ineffective functioning of the League of Nations climaxed by its utter collapse in face of the Manchurian and Abyssinian crises. As he significantly remarks, "For what the experience of the last sixteen years has surely shown is the incompatibility of the League with the coexistence of sovereign states; and the latter display no sign of a serious willingness to abandon their sovereignty. They need it, in fact, for the protection of interests which cannot be promoted or maintained save by the technique of war. The ambitions of Japan and Germany, of Italy and Hungary, to take some obvious instances, assume a period when they will make demands upon other states which only the arbitration of the sword can enforce; and recent experience seems decisive that they are willing to break legal obligations, however morally profound, in order to realise them. The answer of the League should be opposition in terms of collective security; but both the Manchurian and the Abyssinian incidents make it plain that collective security assumes the existence of an international community able and willing to act as an effective unit against an aggressor. No such possibility appears to exist within the framework of the present system."[7] In short, the League failed because it had no coercive power over its members which could obey or disobey the decisions of the League as they pleased.

National Sovereignty Cannot be Abolished without Abolishing Imperialism

But the fundamental question, which remains to be answered, is whether it is possible to construct an international system on the basis of abolition of the fact of national sovereignty. Laski finally came to the conclusion that it is impossible to abolish national sovereignty without abolishing the capitalistic structure of society. It is impossible to build an international system based on mutual cooperation of the national communities so long as a capitalist class formulates the foreign policies of the nation-states.

As he says, "An international order, to be effective, must control things like currency, tariffs, labour standards, migration, access to raw materials, the penetration of backward areas, and so forth. But to control these things, it must be able to override the existing vested interests which use the sovereignty of the state for their protection. It cannot override them as the world is at present organised; for they arise inherently from the class-relations of a capitalist society. The forces which protect them are exactly the same as the forces which protect the power of the capitalist inside the national society to which he belongs. Exactly as the sovereign state protects, in the internal sphere, a system of legal rights intended to safeguard his supremacy, so, externally, its authority by the sheer logic of his relationships with it, must be used to impose that supremacy, so far as may be, upon others. It is only as these class-relations are transformed that state-antagonisms become capable of any fundamental reconciliation. Upon the existing basis the utmost goodwill in international relations can only postpone, without being able to avoid, the ultimately inevitable conflict *(50:244)*.

The seeds ot the present international unrest are rooted in the inner drive of capitalism towards imperialist expansion and the League of Nations failed to preserve international peace because of the imperialist ambitions and rivalries of the major capitalist countries. Laski is therefore right

---

7. Laski : "A Grammar of Politics", the Introductory Chapter, p. XVIII.

in regarding capitalist imperialism as incompatible with the foundations of a peaceful world order.

World Peace Not Compatible with Capitalism

The problem of a lasting organization for world peace cannot be discussed on a legal or political plane alone. "The organization of peace", says Laski, "therefore presents us with problems the main emphasis of which is on the economic plane. Peace depends upon the resumption of the conditions of an economics of expansion. That economics is unavailable to us within the framework of the present relations of production.... The root of economic crises lies in the conflict, which is permanent in any capitalist society, between productive power and consumptive power. Hence arise not only the perpetual tragedies of the trade cycle, but, in the long run, domestic revolution and war. Given a mal-distribution of individual income within a community, and of productive resources in nation-states competing in the world-market, and there is no escape from the ultimate arrival of any capitalist system of production at an epoch of conflict because its contraction of available welfare is bound to breed war and revolution.... It is at least certain that within the historic framework of capitalism a stable and peaceful international society cannot be built" (*131*:*219*).

Capitalist Peace as a Temporary Interval between Wars

Laski therefore concluded that a reconstitution of another international organization after the Second World War on the pattern of the League of Nations could not be a lasting solution for world peace. He regarded capitalist peace as only a breathing-space between wars. The advent of the United Nations Organization and the post-war armament race between the major countries of the world have abundantly proved the correctness of his thesis in this respect. No international organization can check the imperialist drive of the capitalist states, which leads them finally to the inevitable policies of aggression and war. This has been clearly revealed by the post-war foreign policies of the major capitalist countries. Laski was therefore quite justified in saying that the transformation of the capitalist relations of production into socialist relations must precede any serious attempt to establish an international association of mankind from which we can legitimately hope to realize a lasting world peace.

This is an important conclusion for Laski to make because it is a complete reversal of his earlier position taken by him in "A Grammar of Politics" in 1924. He laid no such condition at that time and welcomed the League of Nations as that super state which would prohibit the occurrence of any future war. No such optimism swayed his judgment when the United Nations Organization was born after the conclusion of the Second World War. The reconstitution of an international association of the sovereign states was no guarantee for a stable world peace so long as the capitalist system itself was not overthrown.

Socialism Alone Can Guarantee World Peace

As he pointed out, "In my view, therefore, the high road to an effective international order lies through the reconstruction of the class-relations of modern society. The more effectively this is pursued the less interest states possess in the pursuit of an imperialist policy. To develop the productive power of the Community so that men share equally in its results is to prevent the perversion of its political authority to the interest of a small number of its members. Its sovereignty is then no longer a cloak for that interest. Its direction of capital investment is no longer a technique of exploitation abroad which proceeds regardless of domestic need. Its foreign relations express a commercial connection which does not require the inherent militarism of a policy built upon the ideal of economic empire. A society of socialist states is in a position, to which no other order of life can pretend to consider its economic problems upon a basis of genuine mutuality and goodwill.... We cannot build a system of cooperation upon principles which, as they are applied, live on the exploitation of man by man" (*50:254*).

International Commonwealth of Socialist Nations

Thus only an International Commonwealth of socialist nations can bring about those conditions, which alone may be regarded as the foundation of a genuinely peaceful world society. A new Society of Nations, Laski argues, must be built on the basis of the liquidation of imperialism, alike in its political and economic aspects:[8] It must encourage and bring about a rapid industrialization and modernization of the colonial and semi-colonial areas of the world. Lastly, it must ensure an equitable distribution of wealth in every national community. If these central conditions are fulfilled, the international government is bound to be successful and prevent the possibility of a future war.

This ideal of a socialist commonwealth has receded with the disintegration of the socialist bloc of nations during the last decade. Old style imperialism has been liquidated but a new type of international domination is reappearing in the form of neo-libral globalisation. The capitalist superpower and the NATO can attack small nations like Iraq or Yugoslavia at their will.

8. In a letter to Justice Frankfurtur, Laski wrote in 1931, "The truth is, dear Felix, that we ought not to stay in India. Literally and simply, we are not morally fit for the job." (Quoted by Kingsley Martin in "Harold Laski : A Biographical Memoir", p. 64).

CHAPTER 30

THE EVOLUTION OF COMMUNISTIC THOUGHT

"Whether or not we agree with Marx's analysis of industrial society, it is safe to say that no one can study Marx as he deserves to be studied....without recognizing the fact that, perhaps with the exception of Ricardo, there has been no more original, no more powerful, and no more acute intellect in the entire history of economic science."—Professor E.R.A. Seligman in his *Economic Interpretation of History*, p. 56.

"There is little merit in socialism as a matter of pure economics. Nationalism and all the rest of it is so much mere machinery, though essential machinery : the aim is, or should be, the enhancement of personality. A technically socialist state, in the economic sense, can be as illiberal, as materialistic, as inhumane as a capitalist one : indeed, it can be more so. In other words, socialism is valuable only in so far as it serves Western (human) values". (Victor Gollancz : *Our Threatened Values*).

Both modern socialism and communism stem from the same source, *viz.* Karl Marx, who lived from 1818 to 1883. His parents descended from Jewish rabbis, and the Jews have been known throughout the ages for their passion for social justice. Marx's father was a convert to Protestantism. Marx had known hard days, and this seems to have left a deep influence on his thought on social questions. Early in his life there grew up friendship between him and Engels; and this led to a close collaboration between the two in political activity as well as in research and writing. Because of his revolutionary activities, Marx was forced to spend many years of his life as a political exile from Germany, Holland and France. Much of his time was spent in the British Museum in London. In his life time he was regarded as the unquestioned leader of the European working class movements. Even today he is considered to be the father of modern socialism. Together with Engels he published "The Manifesto of the Communist Party" in 1848. His monumental work, "Das Kapital (Capital)" was published in 1867.

The important influences on Marx's thought were those of Hegel and Feurbach (1804-72). From Hegel he borrowed the idea of the dialectic, which means that progress comes about as a result of an interaction between opposites. According to Hegel, history proceeds by a dialectical path to its predetermined goal. Hegel had taught the dialectic in the realm of ideas, whereas Marx applied it to matter. While Hegel had taught dialectical idealism, Marx taught dialectical materialism. Writing on this difference, Marx claimed that he was placing Hegel "right side up". To quote his own words "with him (Hegel) it (the dialectic) is standing on its head. It must be turned right side up again." To Hegel the primary thing is the evolution of the idea. To Marx, however, matter is primary. Spirit, thought, and consciousness are derivative. The material life of society determines the spiritual.

Adapting the highly speculative conception of the dialectic to man's economic life, Marx contended that the earliest stage in man's economic development was one of primitive communism and that this economy later came into conflict with feudalism and capitalism, and that out of this interaction between the two, a scientific communism was coming into existence.

From Feurbach Marx learned that it is not God who creates man, but it is man who creates God. In his own words, "Man makes religion; religion does not make man". Religion, he said, is "the opiate of the people"; and these words have become widely known throughout the world. According to Marx, God exists only in man's mind.

Interpreting this thought, Hallowell writes that history in Marx's thought is not a conflict between spirit and matter, it is not the unfolding of the spirit of the Absolute. It "is nothing else than the activity of man pursuing his own aims."

Collectivism. The Encyclopaedia of Social Sciences defines Collectivism as a general name for theories opposed to individualism. "It is broadly a term for a trend in social development, a programme of economic reform, a theory of general welfare and a utopian order for mankind; technically, a general label for comprehensive schemes of authoritative control such as socialism, communism, syndicalism, and Bolshevism and specifically, a name for the trend away from the extreme *laissez faire* of the nineteenth century."

As time went on, individualism came to centre round free enterprise and capitalism as against socialism or communism. It was at this stage that men turned towards collectivism which emphasizes large-scale State action and the replacement of the motive of gain by the spirit of service.

According to Hamilton, individualism tried to keep up the fiction of private business in the form of "corporations", but the collectivists are not enamoured of it. They want the business of the community to be collectivized. In the nature of the case, Hamilton holds that "empirical collectivism" cannot be reduced to "the clear-cut lines of a blueprint."

Discussing the issue between individualism and collectivism, MacIver says that the latter stands for the collective action of the community. J. S. Mill was a good example of an enlightened individualist and he tended to speak of liberty as an ultimate end of life. But experience soon showed that liberties conflict. Hence it is that collectivism came into the field in the economic world.

Joad equates collectivism with State socialism which has lost its favour in recent years. On p. 55 of *Modern Political Theory,* he says, "Collectivist Socialists have insisted that society is capable only of gradual change, and that each change must be conditioned by the nature of the social structure that preceded it." The Fabians, according to him, set the pace for Collectivist Socialists.

Of the three writers quoted, it is obvious that Joad takes a restricted view of Collectivism. Hamilton and MacIver, on the other hand, take a broader view with which we agree.

THE TEACHINGS OF MARX AND THE IDEOLOGY OF COMMUNISM

Communism in the twentieth century is said to be an answer to the inherent evils of capitalism which have become more and more apparent in recent times. It is the nemesis of capitalism, the chief features of which are private ownership of the means of production, private enterprise, and private profit. Under capitalism goods are produced not for use, but for profit. As Fox puts it: "The social product is appropriated by the individual capitalist". Although production is a social act, exchange and appropriation continue to be individual acts. The tragedy of our times is that in the midst of plenty there is want and privation. Overproduction is coupled with under-consumption.

According to Julius Hecker, modern capitalism is unable to meet the three great needs of the world: economic security, social or national security, and freedom for self-expression. Communism, he claims, promises to meet all these needs.

Marx and Marxism

Modern communism, no less than socialism, owes its inspiration to Karl Marx. His book, *Das Kapital*, and his joint work with Engels, *The Communist Manifesto,* form the basis of Communism. The teachings of Marx and Engels were later elaborated by Lenin, the founder of Russian communism and adapted to the conditions presented by modern imperialism. In the teachings of Marx for the first time, socialism and communism shed their utopianism and became scientific and realistic.

1. *The Dialectic.* The starting point of Marxism is the Hegelian dialectic. To state the dialectic in simple language, human progress is by means of contradictions. It is in the form of thesis, antithesis, and synthesis. It is a unity of opposites. History is not a smooth continuous evolution. Human evolution is like the ascent of a spiral staircase. It is a zigzag movement. It consists of contrast, negation, and contradiction. According to Marx, the three stages through which society passes are (1) primitive communism, (2) historical society (present industrial), and (3) higher communism. The third stage combines the communism of the primitive epoch with the technical science and achievements of the historical epoch. The transition from the first to the second is slow and gradual. But the transition from the second to the third is bound to be sudden and sharp.

With the dialectic as his starting point, together with the influence of Ludwig Fuerbach, Marx developed the theory of dialectical materialism, the economic interpretation of history (or economic determinism), the iron law of wages, the theory of surplus value and the class war. To these Lenin added a special emphasis on the doctrine of imperialism as the final phase of capitalism and the idea of the dictatorship of the proletariat. Catlin writes : "The Marxian philosophy is a coherent whole. It is massive because revolutionary action is built upon class war theory; the class war upon the economic theory of surplus value; this economic theory upon the economic interpretation of history; this interpretation upon the Marxo-Hegelian logic or dialectic; and this upon a materialistic metaphysic". *(92:569)*.

For ourselves we believe that the dialectic is an artificial way of forcing history into a pre-conceived pattern. If the dialectic process has no end, scientific socialism should itself become a thesis in turn.

2. *Dialectical Materialism.* Progress is dialectical (the literal meaning of dialectic is "discussion"), but its nature is materialistic. Marx writes, "with me.... the ideal is nothing else than the material world reflected by the human mind, and translated into forms of thought". Commenting on this statement, Catlin argues that the metaphysic of Marxism is materialism. "There is nothing other than the material universe. There is nothing other; and that which is other is no thing, nothing".

According to materialism, says Engels (quoted by Catlin), "nature is primary. It exists independently of all philosophy. It is the foundation upon which we human beings, ourselves products of nature, have grown up......". Even Hegelianism which is a dialectic of ideas is to the Marxist really a form of materialism turned upside down in method and content.

As indicated above, Marx not only taught materialism, but a particular species of it known as dialectic materialism. Sabine holds that this dialectic materialism forms the most important part of Marx's social philosophy. Matter evolves according to the dialectic process which is revolutionary in nature. The evolution implied is a social revolution which is of a higher order than a political revolution. The latter simply transfers power from one class to another, whereas the former aims at the abolition of all classes. Rights brought about by a political revolution are *bourgeois* in nature, whereas those wrought by the social revolution anticipated by Marx are human. "The classless society which will result will abolish the division of labour and indeed all compulsory labour". (Sabine, *op. cit.,* p. 635).

The dialectical materialism of Marx, Catlin contends, is not a mere crude materialism. It is not mere sensuousness. Object is not conceived subjectively. If circumstances change men, men change circumstances. Social life is thus essentially practical. Marx's striking words in this context are : "The philosophers have only interpreted the world in various ways; the point however is to change it".

According to Marx, ends are determined by the historical process, and the most desirable end is a classless society.

3. *The Economic Interpretation of History.* According to Marx, history is to be interpreted purely in materialistic terms, and not in terms of God, purpose or design. The central point in Marx's theory is that forms of production and exchange of commodities determine social and political insti-

tutions. To use the language of Sabine, legal relations and forms of state are all rooted in the material conditions of life.

To state Marx's contention in different words, economic forces influence human affairs much more than any other force such as morals, religion or nationalism. Thus, the abolition of slavery in America was, according to Marx, not due to any humanitarian reasons, but due to economic causes. The northern states discovered that slave labour was less economical and less efficient than free labour. Therefore, they went to war and emancipated the slaves. The four stages through which society passes are slave society, feudal society, capitalist society, and communist society. One of Marx's most famous sayings is that men's social existence determines their consciousness and not, as had been generally accepted before Marx, that "the consciousness of men determines their existence".

To Marx economics is a historical science. It is a combination of history and an analysis of economic factors which determine the process of history. In the succinct words of Sabine : "any system of production (according to Marx), by an inexorable logic of its own, must determine the distribution of the social product". (*op. cit.*, p. 639).

Turning to the evolution of the economic order, Marx and Engels claim that the earliest stage was primitive communism. There was common ownership of lands as well as of handicrafts. With the coming of monogamy there came into existence private ownership of property and division of labour. This change in turn brought about increased production which in turn gave rise to trade, commerce, and navigation. All this meant that society came to be organized on a class basis and parasitism appeared on the scene.

At the earlier stage feudalism became the prevailing order and man's place in society was determined by the place he occupied in the economic ladder of land ownership and cultivation. Feudalism gradually gave way to capitalism and labour became a commodity to be bought and sold like any other commodity. Instead of destroying slavery, capitalism perpetuates it in a disguised form and the wage-earner becomes a 'wage-slave'.

In the evolution of this type of economy, a middle class emerges which serves as a buffer between the capitalists and the proletariat. But in course of time it sinks to the level of the proletariat, leaving the bourgeoisie and the proletariat to wage a deadly battle which could only be resolved by the complete destruction of the former and the state assuming the ownership of the means of production. When this happens coercion is replaced by voluntary co-operation and a classless society comes into being.

Capitalism thus contains within itself the seeds of its own decay. It produces its own grave-diggers. Marx held that the material conditions necessary for the realization of the goal of socialism exist within the womb of the capitalist society. Capitalism is chaotic. It means excess of supply over demand, overproduction, the glutting of the market, business crisis, unemployment, underemployment, and misemployment. It means also that private capital is gradually replaced by joint stock companies and trusts and later by monopoly-capital and finance-capital. When this happens capitalism reaches its climax, and is destined to decline rapidly after that.

4. *The Doctrine of Surplus Value.* Marx distinguishes between value in use and value in exchange. The first consists in the satisfaction of human needs and the second in what one exchanges for other commodities. Exchange value is determined solely by labour spent. Marx defines capital as the sum total of all the privately owned means of production employed for the acquisition of surplus value. The essence of capital is the exploitation of labour.

According to Marx, labour creates all values, and whatever is left after paying for raw materials and a subsistence wage to the labourer goes into the pocket of the capitalist in the form of profit, rent and interest. This surplus is used by the capitalist to acquire greater quantities of surplus value by expanding production and employing more labour.

Surplus value is defined as the value which labour produces beyond that which is socially necessary to sustain itself. Appropriation of it by the capitalist is a form of theft. Surplus value is "concealed labour" or labour not paid for.

Marx also uses the significant expression "the iron law of wages". The idea behind it is the supposition that what the labourer receives for his services is only a pittance to enable him to hold body and soul together and to induce him to return to work the next day. Whatever is earned more than that is misappropriated by the employer.

Marx further argues that capitalism results in the overproduction of capital and of commodities. The home market shrinks because of the decreased purchasing power of labour. Hence resort is had to foreign markets, and this results in imperialism and war.

The remedy proposed by Marx in preventing capitalist exploitation is the nationalization of all the means of production, distribution, and exchange. Land, factories, machinery, means of transportation and the like are to be owned and controlled by the State.

It is instructive to note that Lenin, the great disciple of Marx, hardly mentions surplus value in his discussion. In the words of Sabine, it is today "a relic of the teaching of the master rather than a serious part of the system." *(162:657)*.

Sabine further points out that Marx considers labour in the abstract. It is unique among commodities because in being used up, it creates more value. "The labour power used produces value beyond replacement of the labour power consumed".

On the whole question of surplus value, a final criticism which needs mention is that in spite of his great adherence to materialism and materialistic considerations, Marx used ethical principles right through. As Sabine states it : "In fact the labour theory of value never altogether lost the ethical connotation that it had in Locke; it remained in some degree the theory of a just or natural price". (p. 658).

5. *The Doctrine of Class War.* Capitalism is the thesis; organized labour is the antithesis; classless society is the synthesis. In Marxian terminology the classless society represents the synthesis. Marx pictures human life as a grim struggle between the capitalists and wage-earners; that is between the bourgeoisie and the proletariat. In the *Communist Manifesto* the proletariat is defined as "that class of society which derives its substance solely from selling its labour and not from any profit on capital". In modern parlance, the proletariat is the landless, propertyless masses.

Marx's thesis is that so long as the present wage system lasts, based as it is on minimum wage and maximum profits, exploitation of the proletariat by the bourgeoisie is bound to continue. Besides, the working of capitalism requires multiplication of the number of propertyless labourers on the one hand and concentration of capital in the hands of fewer and fewer individuals. Such a dual process alone, says Marx, can ensure safe profits to the capitalist. This tendency eventually leads to monopoly capital and slump of increasing severity inasmuch as the purchasing power of the masses is greatly diminished. Periods of boom which become shorter and shorter in duration are followed by periods of slump till the system ultimately breaks down, paving the way for the replacement of the bourgeois regime by the dictatorship of the proletariat. In the forceful words of Marx himself: "Capitalist production begets, with the inexorability of a law of nature, its own negation". Or, again, "the history of all hitherto existing society is the history of class struggles".

Instead of leaving the collapse of the capitalist order to the operation of natural forces indicated by Marx himself Marx and his followers advocate the complete wiping out of the bourgeoisie and the creation of a classless society. Though classless, the ideal society is bound to have such distinctions as those between skilled and unskilled labourers and between government officers and those who obey orders. But distinctions based on birth, wealth and position would find no place. No one would be allowed to exploit another or remain idle. The State itself would gradually 'wither away' for, as constituted at present, it is, in the words of Lenin, but 'a machine for maintaining the rule of one class over another'. What the proletariat would do would be to capture the army and the administrative machinery with a view to smashing the State and establish revolutionarily the Communist class order. Later in his life, Marx admitted the possibility of workers in England, America, and Holland obtaining their end by peaceful means. But the general rule, he believed, would be force. In his own words: "Force is the midwife of every old society pregnant with a new one". In fairness to Marx it must be said that according to Marx, the communist end could be brought about by evolutionary as well as by revolutionary methods, although his preference was for the latter.

In reply to Marx's prophecies, it must be said that not many of his forebodings have come true. In most industrial countries while the rich have become richer and richer, the poor have not become poorer and poorer.

On the other hand, they are becoming less and less poor. The chief reason why communism and, for that matter, even socialism have not taken root in the U.S.A. is the comparatively prosperous condition of the working classes.

It is possible to argue, on the other hand, that the relative prosperity of the working men in the United States is due to the strength of the trade union movement and that the prosperity of the country as a whole is due to the fact that the United States has gathered in the economic wealth of the world. If the latter contention can be substantiated, it is possible to apply the Marxist theory to the inter-relation between nations, rather than to the individuals of any one nation, reaching the unpleasant conclusion: the richer the U.S. becomes the poorer the world becomes, thus paving the way for world communism.

Another aspect of Marx's theory concerning economic classes is that the peasantry and *petit-bourgeoisie* which were politically inert would finally coalesce with each other, because, according to Marx, both of them had the same ideology and same interests. As Sabine points out, recent history has belied this anticipation, Fascism showed how stoutly the lower middle class of Italy resisted any attempt at a merger with the proletariat.

A further conviction of Marx with regard to the class struggle is that the working classes of the whole world will join together against their common exploiters. The closing words of the *Communist Manifesto* which carry with them an oratorial flourish are: "The Communists disdain to conceal their views and aims. They openly declare that their ends can be attained only by the forcible overthrow of all existing social conditions. Let the ruling classes tremble at the prospect of a communist revolution. The proletarians have nothing to lose but their chains. They have a world to win. Working men of all countries, unite". "The working men have no country".

Suffice it to say that this naive belief in the solidarity of the working classes has not turned out to be true. World War II showed clearly that people are more loyal to their nation and country than to their social and economic classes. Therefore, to insist on a working class solidarity all over the world is more romantic than realistic. Even in India the Communist Party has openly declared its unqualified opposition to the Chinese aggression against India.

6. *Dictatorship of the Proletariat*: This was another of the anticipations of Marx and Engels. The privileged classes who were in the saddle would not surrender their power without a revolution on the part of the proletariat. When this revolution takes place and the upper classes and rich peasants are being eliminated there would be a dictatorship of the proletariat. It would capture the army and the rest of the machinery of the State in order to destroy the State and the capitalist system, the ultimate goal being a classless society living under collective ownership and having

a complete control over the economic system. To quote Marx himself: "When, in the course of development, class distinctions have disappeared, and all production has been concentrated in the hands of a vast association of the whole nation, public power will lose its political character.... in the place of the old bourgeois society, with its classes and class antagonisms, we shall have an association, in which the free development of each is the condition of the free development of all".

According to Marx and Engels, this dictatorship is only for a temporary or transitional period when the proletariat is consolidating its position. We are bound to cast doubt upon the accuracy of this anticipation **in view of the fact that although seventy-two years have lapsed since the Russian revolution and forty years since the Chinese revolution, there** is no sign of either dictatorship or the State disappearing from these countries.

The programme of communism during the transitional period is not as revolutionary as it must have been when it was first announced by Marx:

(i) abolition of property in land and application of all rents from land to public purposes;

(ii) heavy progressive or graduated income tax;

(iii) abolition of all rights of inheritance;

(iv) confiscation of the property of all emigrants and rebels;

(v) centralization of the means of communication and transportation in the hands of the State;

(vi) extension of factories and instruments of production owned by the State; the bringing into cultivation of waste-lands and the improvement of the soil, according to a common plan;

(vii) equal obligation of all to work;

(viii) combination of agriculture with manufacturing industries and a more equitable distribution of population between town and country;

(ix) free public school education and the abolition of child labour.

During the transitional period labour is rewarded according to work. In other words, differences in pay are to be according to differences in skill. This will not mean exploitation inasmuch as the means of production in the new society will be owned by the State and not by individuals. The ideal to be realized eventually is "From each according to his ability and to each according to his need".

7. *The Withering Away of the State.* Under communism the State will gradually wither away, as it has been from the beginning "an instrument of class coercion". In the words of Engels, the State is "the product of society at a certain stage of development". When the perfect, classless society is established, the State disappears. It is not abolished, but it just fades away. Its place is taken by administrative apparatus which controls and manages the instruments of production. To quote Engels: "The government of persons is replaced by the administration of things".

8 *Disappearance of the Family, Religion etc.* According to the Marxist theory, since private family and private property came together they are bound to disappear together. The only basis on which marriage will be based in the future is "mutual affection". It will have no moral, religious or economic significance. With the disappearance of the family will also disappear religion, which is an opiate of the people". In the socialist state, religion "dies a natural death". What morality there is will be relative morality, relative to particular economic conditions. There will be nothing like an absolute morality. "Bourgeois morality" will be replaced by proletarian morality. Law based upon *a priori* principles will also disappear.

By way of criticism it may be said that even though Marx denounced religion and prophesied its complete disappearance, his own teaching "struck the world like a flaming religion" (*148:574*).

To quote somewhat extensively from Maxey: "It was a religion even more than a philosophy, and was offered as a substitute for all existing loyalties. Patriotism was an emotional snare to enslave the workers; religion was 'the opium of the people'; the family was a bourgois institution for perpetuating property rights. The one supreme loyalty was loyalty to humanity as a whole, symbolized by the red flag, which proclaims the universal brotherhood of men.

Scientific Socialism : To Communism of the kind described above Marx gives the name 'scientific socialism'. He contrasts it with the idealistic and utopian socialism of More, Owen, Fourier, and Saint Simon. In this new society exploitation ends and everybody's wants are satisfied. Man becomes for the first time the master of his destiny. Christopher Dawson (quoted by Hallowell) rightly describes all of this as "a secularization of the coming of the Messianic Kingdom".

A Critique of Marxism : (1) It is wrong to assume that the economic factor is the only factor in man's life or in the interpretation of history. Man is not only a biological organism, but also a spiritual creature. Therefore, the economic interpretation of history is an over-simplification and does not take into account all the aspects of man's life. It ignores in particular certain psychological and spiritual factors. Man strives not merely because of his acquisitiveness but also because of motives of vanity, rivalry, love of power, joy of service, and a sense of fulfilment. Marxism exaggerates the economic factor in man's life and does not take into full account such factors as human passions, sentiments and emotions.

(2) Marxism is mistaken in denying the eternal and universal principles of moral conduct. Moral judgments are relative, but moral principles are absolute.

(3) Marxism is too abstract and doctrinaire. It is a rapid generalization on the basis of slender evidence. Several of the predictions of Marx, such as the poor becoming poorer and poorer, have not come true. It is apocalyptic in nature in that it builds a beautiful vision of the future with-

out taking into account some of the baser elements of human nature. Marxism uses the langauge of determinism.

(4) Marxism is mistaken in assuming "the withering away of the State". As a matter of fact, in the Communist states of today it is daily increasing in power and authority.

(5) Marxism is wrong in giving undue prominence to class war. A classless society brought about by strife and annihilation of the opposite group is not worth the trouble. In his treatment of classes Marx did not anticipate a new class of managers and technical advisers or of innumerable stockholders. His theory of a classless society is a kind of Utopian dream.

(6) Marx overlooks the important fact that man co-operates as well as competes. MacIver rightly says that men can live without competition, but they cannot live without co-operation. It is wrong to assume that all important social changes are accomplished by force.

(7) Theory of surplus value has proved to be wrong. As said above, Lenin hardly refers to it. A recent writer has said that what Marx teaches on value is not a theory of value, but one of prices.

(8) There is no historical foundation for Marx's four stages; nothing to substantiate the theory of primitive communism.

(9) The State has not withered away. It is becoming stronger instead of weaker.

(10) Marx's anticipation that the proletarian revolution would first break out in a highly industrialized country like Germany or England has not turned out to be true. It broke out in the backward Tsarist Russia and the agrarian society of China.

(11) Marxism fails to take into account the forces of nationalism and even racialism. World War I and World War II have proved conclusively that the working men of the world do not all unite together in putting down wars which are largely capitalistic in character. Instead, they side the governments of their own countries and bring about untold hardships to the working classes everywhere.

(12) Although Marxism attacks religion mercilessly, it has become a rival religion of man. Hallowell writes : "In theory Marxism rejects religion but in practice the passion which informs it is religious in character."

(13) "Like all dogmas, Marxism is strong in what it asserts and weak in what it denies." Marx did not have a proper understanding of social psychology, religion or ethics. "He was at his best only when he was thundering as a prophet against the capitalists".

Appeal of Communism. In spite of its failures and shortcomings, both theoretical and practical, communism makes an appeal to an increasing number. Hallowell writes, "We may reject the programme of Marxism but we cannot ignore the indictment which it makes of capitalism." *(31:446)*.

R. B. Gregg, who is by no means a communist, in his *Which Way Lies Hope,* says that Communism appeals to people with a sense of social justice. A sensitive person has a sense of personal guilt for having enjoyed comforts and privileges at the expense of weaker and poorer people. Some other reasons for its appeal, are, according to Gregg, the following:

(1) It gives persons a clear and strong realization of the evils done by capitalism in contrast with the justice and fairness promised by it.

(2) The communistic interpretation of history (dialectical and philosophical materialism) gives a sense of scientific sureness, of truth, and right, similar to the assurance that Roman Catholicism gives to many of its followers.

(3) The communist theory seems to give one a sense of understanding reality, of man, and of what has happened and is now happening in the world. It seems to give a key for the unlocking of history.

(4) It marks a revolt against the past and gives to the individual the thrill of new adventure.

(5) It places before the individual certain captivating ideas:

(a) that society is more important than the individual;

(b) that ends are more important than means; and

(c) that environment is more important than ideas.

(6) Joining the Communist Party gives the individual the feeling that he is becoming a part of a supremely important cause. It calls for strenuous action and the exercise of courage, fortitude, and daring. It provides a common discipline and a sense of order and self-integration. The individual joining the party is said to experience a relief and happiness which come from complete commitment to a great cause. Communism, it is claimed, offers no superficial choices.

Estimate of Marx. However much we may disagree with Marx and his teaching, there is no gainsaying the fact that he gave a philosophy which has revolutionized the world. He "shunned delights and lived laborious days" in promoting the ends of a class to which he himself did not belong. He was not simply an abstract philosopher, but a political economist and social thinker.

COMMUNISM AFTER MARX

Lenin and Leninism

Lenin (1870-1924) was the author of the Russian revolution of 1917 and the father of the present Russian nation. He was both a theorist and a man of action. He joined the revolutionary movement as early as 1890 and spent many years abroad studying Marx and Engels. By a happy coincidence of circumstances he was brought back to his motherland by the Germans during World War I, and this opportunity he utilized to overthrow the Tsarist regime and effect a thoroughgoing revolution. He was the acknowledged leader of the Soviet party since November 1917 until his death in 1924. He applied Marxism with masterly brilliance to Russian conditions. A great service which he rendered to Marxism was to restore to the working classes their revolutionary zeal.

Alongside of Lenin, Trotsky too made a great contribution to the development of the communist theory; but for political reasons the Marxists have not given the credit due to him. In making a comparative study of Lenin and Trotsky, it is obvious that Lenin in 1917 came to some of the conclusions that had been reached as long ago as 1905 by Trotsky.

On the question of revolution, Lenin held to a middle position up to 1917, whereas Trotsky took a revolutionary stand all along. He knew that the bourgeoisie was timid and would not initiate any genuine revolution, which could be brought about only by the proletariat with the full co-operation of the peasants. In time to come the two revolutions—that of the proletariat and that of the peasants—would coalesce or be concurrent. Trotsky called this "the law of combined development". Lenin, on the other hand, thought that the two revolutions would be continuous. At the same time, like Trotsky, he realized that without the passive co-operation of the peasants no great revolution was possible in Russia.

A second point of difference between Lenin and Trotsky is that in 1905 and after Lenin held to the orthodox Marxist view that political democracy was a necessary precursor to Socialism, whereas Trotsky was under no such illusion. He wanted the abandonment of democracy and the full acceptance of the socialist revolution. Lenin came to the same conclusion during the revolution of 1917. By that time he came to believe that democracy was "hypocritical to the core" and that it had no value for anybody except for a small minority of exploiters.

Speaking on it Sabine says that this depreciation of liberal political institutions was a complete reversal of the valuation set upon them by the tradition of Western Marxism. Karl Kautsky held on to it.

After dismissing liberal democracy as useless, Lenin tried to discover a purer and higher form of democracy in the commune and the Soviet. This endeavour, rightly says Sabine, was "a mere self-deception". Later on Lenin called his brand of democracy "democratic centralism". To any impartial student it is obvious that it was centralism no doubt, but precious little of democracy.

Resemblances between Marx and Lenin

1. Like Marx and Engels, Lenin believed in *dialectical materialism.* He believed that every philosophy must be either idealist or materialist. Anything other than that was a confusion and a pretence. Lenin, says Sabine, looked upon idealism or clericalism as he called it, as "a bad product of a bad social order."

Lenin believed that dialectical materialsim could be applied to every field of science. From this belief he drew the conclusion that philosophy and social studies were all partisan in character. He regarded professors of economics as "scientific salesmen of the capitalist class" and professors of philosophy as "scientific salesmen of theology." Within the framework of dialectic materialism, says Lenin, there are social scientists of different classes—social scientists of the bourgeoisie and social scientists of the proletarian varieties. In the words of Sabine: "whether he is a proletarian or a bourgeois, every social scientist is a special pleader". This unscientific way of looking at science and history coloured Soviet thinking until recent times when Russian leaders spoke as though history, science and philosophy were all written from the point of view of different social and economic classes; there was nothing objective about them. Even morality was interpreted by Lenin in relativist terms. It is always a class morality. To quote Lenin himself: "We deduce our morality from the facts and needs of the class struggle of the proletariat."

2. Like Marx, Lenin adopted the materialistic interpretation of history and economic determinism. He believed in class war and the ultimate victory of the proletariat. As in the case of Marx, again, religion had no place in Lenin's system. He wanted religion to be regarded as a private matter. Once more, like Marx he held the view that the state was a class organization. It was the organization of one class for the domination of the other classes and as such it will gradually wither away when exploitation ceases and the means of production and distribution are taken over and administered by the people themselves.

Lenin's Contribution to Marxism

In spite of certain resemblances, Lenin reinterpreted Marxism to suit Russian conditions. Sabine is of the opinion that the unique contributions of Lenin were as regards his theory of revolution, organization, party and leader. All of these contributions were essentially practical in nature. Confronted as he was with the opportunity of establishing communism in Russia, Lenin's mind naturally turned to the practical ways by which this end could be realized. But he was keen enough and brilliant enough to clothe them in terms of communistic theory and communistic ideology. A recent writer says that Lenin's contribution was not so much to precision of theory, but to the dynamic leadership of his country at a time of crisis. According to Sabine, Lenin's Marxism was "at once intensely dogmatic and highly pragmatic (*137:668*).

To the points made by Sabine mentioned earlier and to other points we shall now turn the reader's attention. Although Marx had anticipated imperialism to be the last phase of capitalism, it was Lenin who gave the idea full form and shape. Leninism is, as defined by Stalin, "Marxism of the era of imperialism and of proletarian revolution". One of the main endeavours of Lenin was to explain why capitalism had not collapsed. It found an ally in imperialism. The reason why the lot of the working classes in the industrial countries which were also imperialistic, had not deteriorated is that the whole nation, including the proletariat, benefited at the expense of the people under colonial rule. Colonialism, in other words, gave to the capitalist countries a shot in the arm which was very much needed for their survival. It particularly helped those engaged in skilled trades.

From this phenomenon capitalists drew the conclusion that the interests of the bourgeoisie and the proletariat could be reconciled, which was an absurdity in Lenin's thinking.

Lenin not only contributed the idea of imperialism being the last phase of capitalism, but also the ideas of monopoly capital and finance capital. According to Lenin, it is the nature of capitalism to keep on expanding until it drives out the smaller capitalists and becomes a monopoly. At first nationalist in scope, it soon spreads its tentacles all over the world and becomes international. In this process of expansion Lenin visualizes three stages. In the first place there is a struggle within the imperialist country itself where there is big gulf between the rich and poor, and an apparent prosperity. This struggle between the proletariat and the bourgeoisie becomes more and more intensified as time goes on. A second form of struggle is an inter-capitalist and inter-imperialist rivalry. A struggle takes place between the old-timers and the "newcomers" in the field of imperialism; between the "haves" and the "have nots". This means a scramble for raw materials, markets, spheres of influence, and the like. A third form of struggle is a struggle on the part of the national liberation movements in Asia and Africa against European colonialism.

In this fierce competition, tariffs are no longer used to protect infant industries, as they were originally intended, but as a weapon of international warfare. Industrial combinations on a world scale mean that the control of industry passes out of the hands of those who produce commodities into the hands of financiers and bankers. Commercial capital and banking capital become fused in the hands of a financial oligarchy. Capital itself becomes a commodity of export and the world becomes enslaved to a few financiers. In these circumstances, according to Lenin, parliamentary liberalism becomes a sham and mockery. Interpreted in this manner, the Leninist thesis, as stated by Sabine, is that World War I was not a war for democracy, but a war between rival financial groups for the control of Africa—syndicates of German capitalists with their subsidiaries on the one side and syndicates of Britain and France with their subsidiaries on the other. The smaller capitalists on the sidelines pick up what they can, but this is only a passing phase. In the words of Sabine: "Fundamentally, however, monopoly- and finance-capitalism is the logical outcome of free competitive capitalism, political imperialism is the logical outcome of monopoly-capitalism, and the war is the logical outcome of imperialism. Imperialism is 'the highest stage of capitalist development,' and a part of the process by which a still higher, non-capitalist or communist, economy and society are evolving." (*162:684*).

Lenin interpreted the period 1871 to 1914 as "the age of capitalist domination and incipient decay". During this period there was a sense of false harmony between capital and labour in the industrial countries of the world, but all along finance-capital was riveting its hold upon the people. Therefore, there was nothing left for the masses except to bring about a revolutionary overthrow of finance-capitalism. World War I was interpreted by them as a part of the game being played by international financiers. It was correlated with "the increasing frequency and severity of crises". Looking upon World War I as an imperialist war, Lenin welcomed the defeat of his own nation under the Tsar and wanted to "turn the imperialist war into a civil war" *i.e.* into a proletarian revolution. He wanted class consciousness to take the place of national patriotism.

1. *Revolution.* In his *State and Revolution* (published in 1918), Lenin attempts a picture of state under proletarian conditions. In the course of it he lays down his theories of finance-capitalism, the imperialist war, and of social revolution under capitalism. He makes bold to say that every form of state represents a class struggle. Even the new state brought about by revolution is bound to be an instrument of power and repression. Only when the proletariat brings about a genuine communism will the state gradually wither away. Lenin scoffed at the idea of some Marxists that the capitalist state would gradually wither away by a process of evolution. He does not face the question of how a dictatorship of the proletariat is to eventuate in a classless society. By way of concession to Marx he conceded the view that the democratic republic represented the highest stage of government in bourgeois society.

Lenin posited two stages of communism. The first or the lower stage he sometimes called socialism as distinguished from the second called communism. Under the first, exploitation will be substantially eliminated, but not wholly. Under the second, the more perfect form, there will be reward according to need and the complete withering away of the state.

To quote Lenin's own words on revolution, exploitation, democracy, and communism: "In capitalist society, we have a democracy that is curtailed, wretched, false, a democracy only for the minority. The dictatorship of the proletariat, the period of transition to communism, will, for the first time, produce a democracy for the people, for the majority, side by side with the necessary suppression of the minority constituted by the exploiter". Under capitalism the state is "a special instrument for the suppression of one class by another, and of the majority by the minority at that". During the transition from capitalism to communism suppression is still necessary; but in this case "it is the suppression of the minority of the exploiters by the majority of the exploited".

According to the teaching of Lenin, the ideal posited is not only a *classless* society, but also a *stateless* society. "Only under communism will the state become quite unnecessary, for there will be *no one* to suppress—'no one' in the sense of a *class,* in the sense of a systematic struggle with a definite section of the population.

For the complete extinction of the state, says Lenin, complete communism is necessary. While the state exists there can be no freedom. When there is freedom, there will be no state. The state will gradually wither away when it realizes the formula: "From each according to his ability and to each according to his need."

2. *Organization, Party and Leader.* The practical revolutionary that Lenin was, he fully understood the importance of organization and party. His philosophy was that instead of the usual democratic procedure of the majority forming the Government, a revolutionary party was first to seize power and then build up a majority. This, says Sabine, was practically the position of Trotsky in 1905.

For the dictatorship of the proletariat Lenin substituted dictatorship of the party. This party was to be made up of carefully picked people who are the intellectual and moral *elite* of the community. Not only are they to be carefully selected, but carefully trained. They are to be distinguished from the body of workers. They are the nucleus or the vanguard of the community. In the words of Sabine: "The party thus becomes the staff organization in the struggle of the proletariat to gain power and to retain it after it has been gained." *(162:673)*. "Marxism is the creed that holds it together, and organization is the principle that makes it powerful".

During the transitional period when the proletariat comes into its own, the only instrument it has at its disposal is the organisation. Inasmuch as this party, backed up by the people, knows what it wants for the country, there is no room for a second party. In Lenin's own words (as quoted by Sabine): "In the U.S.S.R. there are only two classes, workers and peasants, whose interests—far from being hostile—are, on the contrary, friendly. Hence there is no ground in the U.S.S.R. for the existence of several parties, and consequently, for freedom for these parties".

No Soviet or other mass organization was to take a decision without directives from the party. Stalin said in 1928, "the dictatorship of the proletariat is substantially the dictatorship of the party". Freedom of criticism, Lenin regarded as "opportunism, eclecticism, and lack of principle;" and hence "a form of disloyalty". The party is not only to decide questions of policy, but also pass upon the correctness of opinions in the light of the "Marxist-Leninist theory". While some questions are open to criticism, others are closed. When the party speaks *ex cathedra* it speaks infallibly.

Lenin thoroughly disapproved the idea of the party being merely an expansion of the trade union. It undoubtedly included it, but was much more than that. It was an extra-legal society. Even from the point of view of ideology, socialism (in the sense of communism) was not to be identified with trade unionism. According to Sabine, Lenin regarded trade unions in the way in which Marx regarded the *petit bourgeoisie* and the peasantry.

Lenin wanted the party to be strongly centralized or hierarchical "from the top downward". Democracy in party organization was described as "a useless and harmful toy". Lenin consistently opposed any form of decentralization or federalism. To describe the kind of centralization he wanted, Lenin, as said earlier, coined the term "democtratic centralism". Within the party itself, Lenin was willing to allow criticism and self-criticism in order to keep alive "inner party democracy". But no criticism was allowed of the party itself or of the central Marxist principles. The party was to serve as the instrument of the dictatorship of the proletariat and was to be the embodiment of the unity, will, and wisdom of the working classes. Finally, it was to strengthen itself by periodically purging itself of opportunist elements. Rigid discipline was to be enforced within the party.

As indicated earlier, Lenin emphasized the idea of leader in the party. To the end of his life he was "the leader of the Bolshevik faction of the Marxian Social Democratic Labour party". To the credit of Lenin, it must be said that "he combined personal dictatorship with complete selflessness".

Summing up Lenin's views on party, Sabine writes that "a socialist party supposed to draw together the workers of the world, becomes a closed organization of professionals hierarchically organized from top down and composed of a self-selected and self-perpetuating *elite*".

Years ago Trotsky who was in opposition to Lenin made the following remarkable prediction: "The organization of the party takes the place of the party itself; the Central Committee takes the place of the organisation; and finally the dictator takes the place of the Central Committee".

3. *Communism first in Russia.* Lenin took great pains to show how communism broke out first, not in a highly industrialized country as Britain, but in a feudal country like Russia. Lenin's explanation is that although Russia had no experience of capitalism at its height, yet she had experienced capitalism and industrialism "vicariously", that is the experience of the highly industrialized countries of the time. The Russian society at the time was highly feudal, militarist, and despotic deriving its strength from French capital, and people were ready for any kind of a change which would give them relief. This adroitness on the part of Lenin is characteristic of communist ideology and tactics as a whole.

It appears that Lenin took up his idea of socialism in a backward country from the history of Russian socialism which had agrarian and humanitarian character. These socialists, says Sabine, believed that socialism in Russia might develop from the communism of the *mir* or village without passing through industrialism. Lenin took up the idea and used it in his own way—an example of Lenin's flexibility of thinking. It was Lenin's argument that "by conscious planning and the will of the proletariat communism was to be introduced into the least industrialized of European countries".

4. *National Interpretation.* Lenin revised Marx by giving a national interpretation to Marxism which had been primarily international. He invented the theory of the possibility of "socialism in one country". His explanation was that just as capitalism was uneven in its development in the several parts of the world where it was found, so socialism too would spread unevenly. There was nothing like universal communism at one stroke. It was bound to come about in an uneven and spasmodic way. Lenin believed

that a socialist island in the ocean of capitalism would serve as a "beacon" for the revolutionary movements of tlre proletariat all over the world. On this issue of "socialism in one country" Stalin and Trotsky later differed sharply. The latter was driven away from his country, and his head was smashed to pieces in Mexico by an assassin. The new leadership in Russia since 1956 has been trying to restore Trostsky to his rightful place in the history of the Russian revolution. Conversely, attempts had been made by Khrushchev and his cohorts to haul down the flag of Stalin which had been flying aloft for thirty years. The extraordinary reverence shown to Stalin in the past was condemned as 'personality cult'.

5. ***The New Economic Policy.*** Lenin was enough of a practical thinker not to ride a hobby horse to death. When he found that the War Communism of 1917-21 met with the vigorous opposition of certain elements in the population he had no hesitation in going back on it and introducing the New Economic Policy, making several concessions to capitalism. Individual initiative and personal profits were reintroduced within limits.

After Lenin's death, personal and ideological differences between Stalin and Trotsky shook the party to its depths. Trotsky wanted complete collectivization of peasants, whereas Stalin wanted further concessions to them. According to Stalin, socialism was to be made a success in Russia first, although he gave his support to all attempts at the establishment of world communism.

Criticism and Appreciation. (i) Even though Lenin made certain departures from the teachings of Marx, he held firmly to the Marxist teaching concerning dialectical and historical materialism. At the same time he held the courage to adapt Marxism to the conditions of his day. He gave a free rendering of Marxism, (ii) He invented the idea of "socialism in one country" which is a far more practicable idea than World Communism brought about by revolution and sustained by revolution. (iii) Lenin's chief contribution was not so much to the precision of theory as to the dynamic leadership which he gave to his country at a time of crisis. (iv) As pointed out above, in 1905 he held the view that political democracy was a precondition of socialism, but by 1917 he came to the conclusion that the Soviets themselves were "the highest type of democratic state". He called the communes and the Soviets a higher form of democracy. Proletarian democracy was to him "a million times more democratic than the most democratic bourgeois republic". According to Trotsky, traditional forms of democracy are merely "the ultimate hypocrisy of the bourgeois social order". (v) Such an important Marxist thesis as "reward according to need" or the more popular idea of equal pay was described by Lenin as a "slander on Marxism". (vi) Lenin never paid much importance to the idea of a national culture. However, he sympathized with the aspirations of minorities for cultural equality. Under his influence a human and enlightened policy was adopted towards national and racial minorities. Lenin agreed with Marx in regarding national patriotism "as a bourgeois virtue that depended ultimately on economic causes."

Stalin and Stalinism

1. Stalinism is said to be a continuation of Leninism in the period of socialist reconstruction within Soviet Russia since 1927. In so far as Stalin stuck to the cause of the revolution he was faithful to Leninist principles. But in his overweening desire to capture power for personal aggrandizement he deviated from Leninism. He continued to pay lip service to the "democratic centralism" of Lenin, but in his hands it became more centralism and less democracy. The idea of criticism and self-criticism within the party, advocated by Lenin, was set aside in favour of centralism. The world knows only too well of the periodical purges which he enacted in getting rid of rivals and political suspects. Even people who were close to him lived in constant fear of him, never knowing when their turn will come for liquidation.

2. Stalin subscribed to the Leninist thesis that imperialism was the last phase of capitalism and that with the disappearance of imperialism would also disappear capitalism. According to this belief, as Sabine points out, Stalin thought that Russia could insulate herself and practise socialism while waiting at the same time for the collapse of capitalism in accordance with the rigid canons of Marxism. Unfortunately for Stalin this never happened.

3. Stalin stuck to the Leninist dictum of "socialism in one country" and was ruthless in curbing remnants of capitalism within Russia. There was a keen rivalry between Stalin and Trotsky as to who was the true exponent of Leninism. Trotsky regarded Stalin as a muddle-headed, ill-mannered, and crafty politician who only wanted to capture power and retain it. He considered Stalin's ideas as leading to a counter-revolutionary reaction. Trotsky advocated the idea of a world communism and a permanent revolution.

4. Even though Stalin was an advocate of "socialism in one country", he kept up the form of the third international, created by Lenin in guiding world proletarian movements. The myth of "the international solidarity of the proletariat" was kept up in order to serve the interests of Soviet Russia. In 1943 Stalin had no scruples in dissolving the Comintern as being "superfluous" and a deterrent to Soviet war efforts. There is no single case of the "International" having precipitated a successful revolution anywhere. Communists of other countries were often looked upon as 'fifth columnists' trying to undermine Russian foreign policy.

5. The idea of "socialism in one ocuntry" has turned out to be nothing more than fierce nationalism which is characteristic of the present-day world as a whole. Sabine is right in thinking that there is no clear line of demarcation between communism as a driving force in politics and nationalism which is the other great drive in politics.

What is more, in the case of Russia and China, the other large communist country of our day, nationalism has become blended with imperialism. John Strachey who was a leftist in politics for many years and sympathetically inclined towards communism now believes that the world may yet see a great Russian and a great Chinese Empire.

6. True to the Marxist tradition, Stalin held to the idea of "the withering away of the state", but the phrase did not mean much on his lips. Stalin held that the withering away will come about only when the higher stage of communism was reached which was impossible so long as communism was like an island surrounded by an ocean of capitalism. Without the liquidation of the capitalist state, the state in a communist society was bound to remain. All of this, rightly observes Sabine, was a clever device to postpone the disappearance of the Russian state.

7. Stalin changed the character of Marxism by introducing the idea of wages according to labour. The formula "from each according to his need" was replaced by the formula "from each according to his labour". Stalin considered equality of consumption an idle prattle. He wrote "even under socialism 'wages' would be paid according to labour performel and not according to need." "Equalization in the sphere of consumption and personal life is reactionary petty-bourgeoisie nonsense." Under Khrushchev incentives were given a place in production, as also certain other techniques of American production under capitalism.

8. Stalin took great pride in the 1936 constitution of Russia. He regarded it as the only true democratic constitution in the world. He overlooked the fact that no country which does not allow opposition parties to function and does not provide freedom of speech and association can be called a genuine democracy. Lord Attlee (quoted by John Strachey) compares elections in a communist country to a horse-race in which only one horse runs!

Yet Stalin may rightly take pride in the fact that however indirect and remote the control of government by the people may be in Russia, their system of Soviets is an improvement upon pre-existing conditions. The party conclave, the politburo, and the presidium are still the most powerful groups in whose presence the Soviets of peasants and workers pale into insignificance.

9. As a theoretician, Stalin was not the equal of Lenin. He did not possess the massiveness and nimbleness of Lenin's mind. He temporized with communism in certain matters, but for the most part he saw the world "through thick Leninist lenses." (Strachey). He was too inflexible and rigid in his thinking to see the world as it was. As late as 1952, a year before his death, he wrote in the *Economic Problems of Socialism in the U.S.S.R.*:

"The U.S.A. has put Western Europe, Japan, and the other capitalist countries on rations. Western Germany, Britain, France, Italy, and Japan have fallen into the clutches of the U.S.A. The major vanquished countries, Western Germany and Japan, are now languishing under the jackboot of American imperialism."

Suffice it to say that Stalin did not have sensitivity to understand the feelings of some of the Finns, the Poles, the Czechoslovakians, the Hungarians, etc. under "the jackboot of Russian imperialism".

10. Whatever the inconsistencies and contradictions of Stalin as a Marxist may be, there can be no question that he is the architect of modern Russia. From 1924 until 1953 he was the predominant voice in Russian affairs. He modernized Russia in the agricultural, industrial, and military fields, making her a great power in world affairs, rivalling the U.S.A.

In the economic field as a whole, Russia has made rapid strides through her carefully drawn and rigidly executed five year plans. There are still shortages as regards consumer goods, but this is nothing to regret when we take into account the surfeit of goods in some highly industrialized capitalist countries of the world. For any country to have reached the economic level that Russia has reached, building herself up from the scratch during a short space of forty years is nothing short of a miracle.

Militarily, Russia is one of the front-ranking countries of the world. During World War II Russia gave an unusually good account of herself, despite early reverses, and much of the credit for it goes to Stalin. By clever strategy and iron discipline over his people as well as through such devices as the scorch-earth policy, Stalin led his people to victory.

Positively as well as negatively, Stalinism has demonstrated that nationalism continues to be a stronger force than communism. Russia is no longer the insulated country that she was under Stalin's leadership. Since Stalin's death, Russia's relations with the outside world have improved considerably, despite cold war rivalries and frictions. Even in relation to China, it is only after communism there had become a *fait accompli* did Stalin recognize that country as a partner in world communism, having regarded Chinese communism in its earlier stages as 'a rightist deviation'.

Maoism may be regarded as Leninism applied to conditions of a predominantly agrarian civilization. The main problem of China has been one of land hunger and Marxism is regarded as an answer to it.

Revolutionary tendencies in modern China began with Dr. Sun Yet-sen who in 1911 put forward his three principles of Nationalism, Democracy, and People's Livelihood or Socialism. The enunciation of these principles alone did not bring about a new heaven and a new earth. By 1919 the situation in China had worsened and just at this time the star of Bolshevism was in the ascendancy in Russia. The Chinese intelligentsia began to look with favour upon communism, and a communist society was founded in Peking as early as 1918. At this time Li Tao-chao was a famous philosopher who was turning to communism and Mao Tse-tung, his library employee, deeply impressed by his mentor, joined the communist society as a student member.

In the meantime exchange of personnel was taking place between China and Russia and Dr. Sun Yat-sen himself was turning sympathetically towards communism. By July, 1921, there was a communist party existing in Peking, Canton, Shanghai, and Hunan. A mighty proletarian surge was on the way under the leadership of the communist party.

Sun Yat-sen was deeply influenced by the positive measures of party organization on Leninist lines. In attaining Nationalism, one of the three principles, he began to organize the party along Leninist lines. The Kuomintang, the party founded by Dr. Sun, was represented as a coalition of all the classes and the communists were urged to enter it and make it a driving force of revolution. Individual communists entered the party while at the same time a separate communist party was maintained. Borodin, a Russian communist leader, who had arrived in China by now, and Sun Yat-sen were the chief actors.

By this time the Chinese were organizing themselves for leadership. Mao Zedong who himself was of peasant origin began to organize the peasantry for revolution. He knew how to create mass discontent. Student groups, journalists, and other such people joined the party. The communists at first won many positions in the K.M.T. and an anti-imperialist and anti-feudal revolutionary programme was set up.

Meanwhile Dr. Sun had died, and his successor, Chiang Kai-shek, a rightist military general, turned against the communists and revolutionaries. Large numbers of revolutionaries were expelled from the K.M.T. and all suspects were ordered to be shot. Borodin made a [illegible] exit to Russia.

When Chiang Kai-shek was carrying on his ruthless methods a close alliance was being worked out between the peasants and workers and plans were being made for the establishment of a "democratic dictatorship". Fearing that nothing effective could be done without military force, Red armies were being established here and there.

From 1927 the lines were sharply drawn between the Nationalists (K.M.T.) and the Communists Stress was laid on agrarian reforms and armed uprisings. The communists were bitterly persecuted and civil war aged in the country. But Mao Zedong managed to strengthen his force and in 1931 became the chairman of the newly-established Soviet Provisional Government.

Now came the Japanese attack on Manchuria. The abandonment of Mukden and the Jehol province by the K.M.T. in 1931 was a source of great help to the communists. While the Nationalists were busy fighting the Japanese, the communists organized a vigorous anti-K.M.T. campaign. The K.M.T. not being able to cope with the situation, there arose a demand for national unity in 1935. The two parties laid aside their differences and worked together for the defeat of the common enemy, Japan. But even during World War II, Chiang kept his crack troops in reserve to fight the communists when the war was over.

After the war, Chiang Kai-shek's party was discrediting itself more and more because of its nepotism and corruption. The agrarian needs of the people continued to be neglected. This gave the opportunity for the communists to push forward. Bit by bit they took over China and in 1949 drove Chiang and his followers to Formosa (also known as Taiwan), from where with American aid, they have been continuing the fight with the communists from time to time. The New Chinese government has been recognized by the U.K., and U.S.S.R., and several Asian countries, including India. It has now been admitted to the United Nations. The U.S.A. has not only recognised it but is frantically trying to win it over to its side.

Mao's addition to Marxist-Leninist teachings

1. The organization of Communist Russia has been closely followed in Communist China. Vigorous attacks have been levelled against feudalism, capitalism, and imperialism. But the most important change has been in the reorganization of the peasants. While Communist Russia had gone a long way in the collectivization of farms, in China it would appear that peasant proprietorship was the general order in the early days of the movement. No one was allowed to hold land if he could not cultivate it. This meant the virtual elimination of the middle class Mao did much to distinguish the rural proletariat from the urban proletariat; and his communism was for some years at least largely made up of the former group. In recent years, however, China began to collectivize her farms through her communes.

2. Mao Zedong and his followers consider themselves to be the true Marxist-Leninists and regard the Soviet leaders as rightist deviationists. A few years ago Mao spoke of hundred flowers blooming and hundred schools of thought flourishing at the same time, but this was only a temporary lapse from his communist line of thinking. Chinese communists are rigid and unbending in their Marxist convictions. In the matter of world revolution, they are more Trotskyite than Leninist.

3. Mao keeps up the Hegelian-Marxist idea of inner contradictions in the realm of ideas as well as of institutions. Like Marx he believes that ideas develop out of matter. Speaking of post-war world situation, Mao recognizes that the world is divided into 'socialist' and 'capitalist' blocs. Both of them have their inner contradictions. The only difference, according to Mao, is that while the inner contradictions of capitalism can only be resolved through war and revolution, those of the socialist world will be resolved peacefully.

4. As is true of communism elsewhere, so in China rigorous methods have been followed in dealing with opposition and even with those who may have honest difference of opinion. Yet Mao's genius has been to absorb rivals and not liquidate them, as was the case with Stalin. Not only peasants and the urban proletariat, but even the middle classes and the patriotic bourgeoisie have been allowed to join the party. In this way, the older idea of the hegemony of the proletariat has been modified in the direction of

'the collaboration of classes'. In his book, *A New Democracy* (1938) Mao argues for a new alliance based on the concept of "democratic dictatorship of the peoples against the reactionary remnants of feudal lords and traitor capitalists".

5. Although an outstanding military leader, Mao Tse-tung believes in the subordination of the military to the civilian. It is his determination to see that the communist movement does not become a 'plaything of ambitious generals', as was the case for years after the death of Dr. Sun Yat-sen.

6. At the time of writing, the relations between Chinese Communism and Russian Communism are not too cordial. Among the European Communist countries, Albania seems to be the only wholehearted supporter of China, which regards itself as more truly communist than Russia.

According to Chinese communists Russia is compromising too much with the capitalist world.

LASKI'S CRITICISM OF MARXISM

In modern times the liberal democratic state has been challenged by the fascists on one extreme and by the Communists on the other. Laski's answer to the imperfections of the old capitalist democracy has been the adoption of a new socialist democracy. Both the socialist and communist movements of the present day derive their inspiration from the writings of Karl Marx.[1] While the Communists regard themselves as the true followers of Marx, the socialists have sought to revise some of the important aspects of the Marxist theory and practice. Laski as a democratic socialist *accepts* the *basic assumptions* of Marxism but *differs* as regards its *theoretical details* and *methodology*.[2] He agrees that Marx was a great thinker and his social philosophy has an important message for the civilization of our contemporary generation. As Laski says, "from whatever aspect it be regarded, the work of Karl Marx is an epoch in the history of social philosophy. It is easy to show that he was less original than he believed, and that his debts to his predecessors were greater than he was anxious to admit. The vital fact about him is that he found communism a chaos and left it a movement. Through him it acquired a philosophy and direction. Through him, also, it became an international organisation laying continuous emphasis upon the unified interest of the working classes of all countries" (*123:22*). There is no doubt that Karl Marx has been the most important single influence in shaping the world labour movement and in providing that movement with a coherent socialist ideology.

1. In his first essay on Karl Marx, he underrated the value of his political philosophy dismissing it as sheer propagandist literature. At this stage, Laski was deeply under the spell of Proudhonism.
2. In his subsequent pamphlet entitled "Socialism and Freedom", Laski's approach towards Marxism is that of a Fabian, who accepts the social objectives of Marxism without agreeing to its methods.

Rejection of the Utopian Approach by Marx

Karl Marx, as Laski has recognized, was the first socialist thinker to realize the futility of formulating a *utopian* constitution of socialist society. He concentrated his attention mainly on charting the road which may lead towards the establishment of a socialist society. This involved the necessity of a detailed analysis of the working and growth of the capitalistic system. "Marx," says Laski, "wrote at once the epitaph of the new capitalism and the prophecy of its ultimate outcome. The first aspect of his work, both by reason of the materials he used and the theses he deduced from them, put the defenders of economic individualism finally upon the defensive; the second provided an inspiration to his followers which has increased in profundity as the years have gone by" *(123:23)*. However, Laski does not entirely agree with the sociology and economic theory of Marx. "It may be true", he points out, "that Marxian economics is in no small degree self-contradictory and it is certainly true that much of the Marxian sociology bears the obvious stigmata of its special time" *(123:23)*. It shows that he is not **prepared to accept every aspect of the Marxian doctrine uncritically. He** wants to examine and revise it in the light of his own observations.

Laski on Lenin's Strategy of Revolution

Laski's attitude towards communism is also reflected in his appreciation and criticism of the various aspects of the Russian Revolution. Lenin, as the architect of the Russion Revolution, applied the doctrine of Marx in practice and brought about the transformation of the Russian society from capitalism to socialism. Laski is prepared to accept that the Leninist interpretation of Marxism might be valid for the particular conditions obtaining in Russia but he certainly denies its claim for a universal validity. The conditions which enabled the Bolsheviks to seize power in the Russian Revolution cannot be reproduced in other countries. Lenin himself said that insurrection is an art which should be practised with great caution. In these circumstances, Laski did not favour the adoption of revolutionary tactics by the socialists of Western Europe. While admitting the mistakes of the socialist parties of Western Europe, he did not like the introduction of Communist parties in the labour movement of those countries. He was also critical of the "terrorist" and dictatorrial methods of the Russian Communists in consolidating the gains of the revolution. Laski's views about communism may be conveniently divided into two parts for the sake of a proper study. In the first place, we may deal with his analysis and interpretation of the Marxist theory. Secondly, we must study his opinions and attitude towards the tactics and strategy of the communist movement both before and after Marx.

Marxist Theory—Historical Materialism

One of the most important elements of the Marxian doctrine is the materialist interpretation of history. Laski does not define his attitude regarding the philosophical position of Karl Marx as a materialist. As a pragmatist, Laski had no interest in the traditional controversy between the idealists and materialists about the nature of ultimate reality. Similarly, Laski has refused to comment upon the dialectical method of Marx which he probably regards as irrelevant to his social philosophy. He is only concerned with the materialist conception of history which appears to Laski a valuable contribution of Marx to contemporary social theory. Marx derived his materialist conception of history from his general philosophical position as a dialectical materialist. Laski takes no notice of this logical derivation. He is only interested in the Marxian interpretation of history as a formula for explaining social change.

He thinks that the materialist interpretation of history adequately explains the directions of social evolution. "The Marxian philosophy of history", he says, "is the insistence that the primary motive force in social change is the system of economic production which obtains at any given time. To its needs, all other forms of social effort will adjust themselves, whether consciously or unconsciously. Law, religion, politics, philosophy, all these are born of the reaction upon the human mind of the methods by which men wrest from nature the necessary means of life" (*123:26*). This, in brief is Marx's conception of history.

Laski's View on the Materialist Conception of History

What is Laski's verdict on the materialist conception of history? "In this simple form", he argues, "it is impossible not to regard the theory as in the main true.... There is no department of human life in which the governing ideas and institutions will not be found, upon examination, to be largely a reflection of a given set of economic conditions" (*123:77*). But Laski agrees with the view of Bertrand Russell that the theory is valid only under certain limits. As he warns, "We must be careful, indeed, not to push the theory too far. There are particular sets of facts in which it is not helpful as an explanation; and there are others where the obvious requirements of an economic environment cannot be met through the pressure of non-economic factors" (*123:79*). It is, however, to be remembered in this connection that Marx himself reorganized certain exceptions to the general rule" (*123:83*).

Criticism of the Theory of Class Struggle

The second important element of the Marxian doctrine is the theory of class struggle. Marx declared in the Communist Manifesto, "The history of all hitherto existing society is the history of class struggles. Freeman and slave, patrician and plebeian, lord and serf, guild-master, and journeyman, in a word, oppressor and oppressed, stood in constant opposition to one another, carried on an uninterrupted, now hidden, now open fight, a fight that each time ended, either in a revolutionary reconstitution of society at large, or in the common ruin of the contending classes".

Laski agrees with the Marxian theory of class struggle as an explanation of social relations in their broad aspectes. But he is not prepared to accept that the class antagonisms must necessarily express themselves in violent contests for the seizure of the state power. The communist regards the conflict between the classes as a definite war with an unlimited use of the war-like methods. Laski interprets the class antagonism as a clash of interests, which may or may not manifest itself in an armed conflict.

In the existing capitalistic system, the class conflict has developed between the capitalists and workers. The Communist thinks that the emancipation of the working-class from the yoke of the capitalist class can be brought about only by a successful armed uprising of the organised workers. There is no other road which may lead to the liberation of the proletariat from the economic and political subordination to the bourgeoisie. It is here that Laski adds his footnote of dissent.

Criticism of the Theory of Surplus Value

The most serious criticism that Laski advances against the Marxian doctrine is directed against its economic assumptions. Marx reinterpreted the classical labour theory of value in such a way as to prove the injustice of the distributive process in a capitalist society. He defined the profit of the capitalist as the surplus value extracted by him from the labourer, whom he does not pay the full price of his labour in the form of his wages. Laski does not agree that the labour theory of value is a correct explanation of the determination of prices. He points out, for instance, that competition between different capitalists also influences the prices of commodities and is a factor in the determination of the rate of profit. "It does not mean", says Laski, "that labour is not an essential element in price; but it does mean that other factors must be taken into account" (*123:97*). The theory of surplus value which has been derived from his labour theory of value is also untrue to the same extent.

Ethical Aspect of the Theory of Surplus Value

Even though the Marxian theory of surplus value be inadequate from the point of view of an economist, yet Laski is quite in agreement with the ethical purpose of the theory. Marx wanted to explain the parasitical character of the capitalist class and also the extent of exploitation of the common people that is being carried on under the capitalistic regime. In this endeavour he has brilliantly succeeded. Besides this, the theory of surplus value even if it be partially valid illustrated how the class conflict is going on in capitalist society. Laski says that the broad features of the Marxian analysis of capitalist society are correct despite the fallacious theory of value. Marx is right when he insists that the exclusion of the workers from the control and ownership of the instruments of production is bound to result in an unjust system of distribution. He is also right when he asserts that the capitalist system cannot avoid periodical crises in the form of depressions.

These depressions are caused by a steady decrease of the purchasing power of the masses resulting in an artificial crisis of overproduction. The depressions bring about the insolvency of the banks, the suspension of business, the forced closure of factories, large-scale unemployment of the workers and an intensification of the class struggle of the workers against the capitalists. Marx was also justified in pointing out that capitalism has led to imperialist wars by its need for the control of foreign markets, the supply of raw materials and the regulation of tariff policies. By pointing out these contradictions of capitalism, Marx showed that capitalism was a disintegrating force in the modern society. Laski admits that these conclusions of Marx have been verified by contemporary experience.

Laski's Views on Marxian Theory of State

Lastly, the Marxian theory of the state is a logical development of his interpretation of history on an economic basis. The state in history has been an instrument of the ruling class for oppressing and dominating the rest of the community. Laski agrees with Marx in this analysis of the historical states. "That there is a bias in state operations", says Laski, "will be denied by no one who scrutinises the historical evidence. The Greek city-state was biased against the slave. The Roman empire was biased against the slave and the poor. States in the medieval world were biased in favour of the owners of landed property. Since the Industrial Revolution the state has been biased in favour of the owners of the instruments of production as against those who have nothing but their labour power to sell" (*50:104*).

The Marxian View of the Capitalistic State

This shows that Laski has adopted the Marxian view of the pre-capitalist and capitalist states as his own. The Marxian view of the capitalist state is that it is essentially an executive committee of the capitalist class despite the fact that it may externally assume several forms from an absolute monarchy to a democratic republic and back again to a fascist dictatorship. The pre-Soviet autocracy of Russia, the constitutional monarchy of England, the democratic republics of France and America, and the fascist states of Italy and Germany embodied the same class essence despite important differences in their internal organization. They were all designed or have been designed to protect and promote the interests of the capitalists and to perpetuate the slavery and exploitation of the workers.

The Marxian View of Liberal Democracy

Laski has also largely accepted the Marxian view of the functioning of liberal democracy. The representative institutions of the liberal democratic state do not provide any opportunity for a real overthrow of the capitalist system by constitutional means alone. Laski agrees with Marx that it is difficult to achieve socialism by peaceful methods, yet he is not prepared to admit the inevitability of an armed conflict. He differs from Marx in believing that constitutional methods are worth giving a fair trial before we jump to the rash conclusion that revolutionary violence is indispensable for the emancipation of the proletariat. Laski accepts a greater part of the Communist criticism of the liberal state and yet he is not prepared to concede the Communist alternative of a dictatorship of the proletariat in place of the institutions of liberal democracy.

Laski's Verdict on the Communist Theory of State

His own alternative is the introduction of socialism by gradual means through the agency of a parliamentary socialist party. As a final summary of Laski's view about the Communist theory of the state, it is necessary to quote the following passage from his essay on "Communism". "The first comment one is tempted to make upon Communism as a theory of the State is that, like most philosophies, it is strong in what it affirms, and weak in what it denies. Obviously enough, its criticism of the assumptions of the classical theory of the State is, in part at least, well-founded; the margin between the ideal and the real is a large one. It is, moreover, true that no ruling class in history has so far surrendered its privileges, or utilised its authority for the common good, without a struggle. Men cling to power even after the grounds which make its tenure intelligible have passed away; and there is a real basis for the assumption that the holders of power in a capitalist state are no exception to the rule. And, not less certainly, there is substance in the communist criticism of formal democracy; the mere conference of universal suffrage and the creation of representative institutions will not, of themselves, secure the kind of State which adequately safeguards the claims of men upon the common good' (*123:166*).

Laski's Opposition to Violent Revolution

Laski argues that Marx may be right in pointing out the imperfections of the existing economic structure of society but he is certainly not correct when he affirms that these imperfections can be removed only through a catastrophic change brought about by a violent revolution. The classless, ideal society will not emerge out of revolutionary chaos and revolutions cannot be stage-managed in accordance with certain preconceived principles. In the course of revolutionary effort, the original purpose of the revolution gets distorted and so the final outcome rarely corresponds the vision of the prophet.

Criticism of the Tactics and Strategy of Communism

The latter part of Laski's argument involves a criticism of the tactics and strategy of Communism. Besides, it shows his disbelief in the "prophetic" aspects of the Marxian theory. Marx predicted that the state will gradually wither away after the abolition of classes from society and the achievement of Communism. Laski thinks that the transitional dictatorship of the proletariat will become a permanent rule of the Communist Party and Communist rulers like all ruling classes of the past will not abdicate from power voluntarily. The Communist answer to this criticism would be that the Communist Party is not an economic class with its own vested interests which may be opposed to the general interest of the community.

Communist Practice—Revolution and Dictatorship

While Laski accepts a larger part of the Marxian interpretation of history and his analysis of the nature of society and the state, he emphatically disapproves the strategy and tactics of the Communists for capturing the state power and subsequently using it in a dictatorial way. Marx and Lenin believed that a violent revolution is the only way by which the downfall of capitalism can be brought about. The task of the Communists is to prepare the ground for such a revolution. Even in a democratic republic, the Communists think that they cannot seize the state power by an electoral victory. Even if they secure an electoral victory, the capitalists will not permit them to direct that state machinery because in no case they will be prepared to part with their privileges peacefully.

The Communists recognize the fact that a democratic republic with universal suffrage is, among the various forms of bourgeois states, most suitable for organising the movement and struggles of the working-class. It provides an opportunity for organising the workers into trade unions and a mass political party of the proletariat. But the formation of a political party of the workers does not guarantee that it will be able to capture the power of the state by constitutional means alone. Historically, force has been an indispensable condition of every successful change in the class structure of a community. The capitalist state itself was born out of fierce internecine struggle of the contending classes in which the capitalists were victorious over their feudal masters. The history of the failure of the Paris Commune of 1871 and the success of the Russian Revolution of 1917 equally show the necessity of the exercise of superior force by the proletariat in its struggle with the enemy.

Laski's Argument Against Insurrection in a Modern State

The argument of the inevitability of a violent revolution for the overthrow of the capitalist class does not appeal to Laski for various reasons. In the first place, he thinks that it is not possible to organise an insurrection in a modern capitalist state. An insurrection can be successful only when the army and navy are won over to the cause of the working-class. This task is almost impossible in conditions of international peace. The Russian working-class was able to win the support of the Russian army because of the Russian defeats on the battle-field in the war against Germany. This situation cannot artificially be reproduced in other countries for the purpose of "engineering" a proletarian revolution.

Unsuccessful Insurrection Leads to Fascism

Moreover, he argues that the working class attempts of an insurrection, which is not successful, may lead to the establishment of fascism (*131:90*).

Fascism means an oppressive dictatorship of the capitalist class, which destroys democratic liberties and suppresses all working class organizations in a ruthless way. The trade unions and the working class political parties are thoroughly suppressed by the iron hand of the fascist dictatorship. Finally, Laski is opposed to insurrectionary methods because they may easily lead to an end of civilized life and bring about anarchy instead of a dictatorship of the proletariat. To employ a phrase used by Marx, it may as well lead to "the common ruin of the contending classes". A perpetual class war waged with the modern weapons may be a total catastrophe for human civilization. It may as well restore the conditions of medieval barbarism instead of opening the gates of socialist millennium. Laski, therefore, opposes the employment of insurrectionary methods by the working class in a liberal democracy. The progress towards socialism may be slow but it should be steady. The constitutional means do not guarantee an effective march towards socialism but they, at least, preclude the pitfalls involved in the insurrectionary method.

The Communist Party as Revolutionary Vanguard

The Communists believe that a proletarian state would necessarily be a dictatorship of the workers in alliance with other exploited sections of the society over the capitalists and other exploiting classes (*104:101-127*). The Communist party as the revolutionary vanguard of the proletariat will exercise effective political power in a proletarian state on behalf of the exploited masses. The Parliamentary institutions of the liberal state have no place in the Communist scheme of political reorganization. The example of the Russian Revolution shows that the Communists show a greater preference to association of the workers with the apparatus of the state than to the technicalities of the universal adult suffrage. They believe in indirect elections or plebiscites with no real choice of candidates. The Chinese Communists have adopted similar principles in their constitution.

Proletarian Dictatorship and Socialist Transformation

The primary purpose of the proletarian dictatorship is to suppress the capitalist and precapitalist methods and relations of production and bring about a socialist transformation of the society and economy. Another important function of the proletarian state is to thwart the counter-revolutionary efforts of the former exploiting classes by reorganising the army, the police, the administration, and the courts on popular and revolutionary basis so that they can properly defend the gains of the socialist revolution (*131:46*). The Communist state will not permit any opposition party because the only function of such an opposition party will be to work for the restoration of capitalism. In Soviet Russia, the only legal party is the Communist Party. In China and Eastern Europe, there are other political parties besides the Communist Party but they must accept the leadership of the Communist Party in a national front. These parties are merely junior partners in a fellowship of parties, where the seniority of the Communist Party is unquestioned. Therefore, these parties can in no case be considered as opposition parties.

Marx and Lenin on Withering Away of the State

But the dictatorship of the proletariat is not a permanent feature of the Communist scheme of things. Ultimately, the state will become redundant with the abolition of classes in the community. Marx said that the proletarian state will wither away with the achievement of communism. Lenin developed this theory further and said that the state cannot wither away in a single socialist country like Russia so long as other capitalist states exist in the world surrounding and threatening the security of Soviet frontiers from all sides. The Communist practice, therefore, assumes that the transitional phase of the proletarian dictatorship will continue till the triumph of the socialist revolution in the major countries of the world.

Laski's Criticism of the Communist Theory of Dictatorship

Laski is opposed to the entire theory and practice of the proletarian dictatorship. It is a natural corollary of his criticism of the insurrectionary method. The dictatorship of the proletariat, he feels, is in reality a dictatorship of the Communist Party.[3] The Communist Party, Laski argues, controls the state machine by its monopoly of elections, by its control of the channels of public opinion, by its supervision of education, art and science, and, finally, by its management of the entire apparatus of the national economy. The centralized discipline of the party, he alleges, enables a small "bureaucratic caucus" to monopolize all power in the state. Any breach of party discipline, any slackness in an official of the government or industry, and any criticism of the Communist doctrine is considered an act of treason to the state. The state in this context means the small bureaucratic caucus of the Communist Party (*127:161*). This, according to Laski, explains the periodical purges and execution of even prominent national leaders in Communist countries and the concentration of a large number of political offenders in the corrective labour camps provided they escape execution in the first instance. Such methods of the Communist dictatorship, as Laski says, are hardly in consonance with the announced purposes of communism which include the creation of a new society based on the principles of social justice and brotherhood. "It is a common place of history," says Laski, "that power is poisonous to those who exercise it; there is no special reason to assume that the Communist dictator will in this respect be different from other men. Indeed no group of men who exercise despotic authority can ever retain the habit of democratic responsibility" (*123:174*). This shows the undesirability of dictatorship as a form of government.

---

3. Laski : "Reflections on the Revolution of Our Time", Chapter II, p. 57. As he says, "The dictatorship of the proletariat, in fact, became necessarily the dictatorship of the Communist Party; for every serious purpose, the party has been identical with the apparatus of the State".

Communist Dictatorship Incapable of Voluntary Abdication

Moreover, the Communist defence that the proletarian dictatorship will be necessary only during the transitional period between capitalism and communism does not convince Laski in any manner. He thinks that communist dictatorship will not part with its power on its own initiative and allow the state to wither away. "To sit continuously in the seat of office," says Laski, "is inevitably to become separated from the minds and wants of those over whom you govern. For any governing class acquires an interest of its own, a desire for permanence of power, a wish to retain the dignity and importance of its functions; and it will make an effort to retain them. That, after all, is only to insist that the exercise of power as such breeds similar habits in its operators. The corollary of dictatorship appears to be that which follows from all other systems that it is incapable of voluntary abdication" (*123:175*).

Thus Laski thinks that force will be necessary to "dethrone" a Communist dictatorship. Otherwise, it will perpetuate its authority for a very long period in history. In his criticism of this aspect of the Communist practice, Laski shows the undeviating faith of a Liberal, who is not prepared to exchange the gains of individual liberty with those of economic security and social justice.

International Strategy of Communism

Lastly, we must consider the internationl strategy of the Communist movement in view of the fact that it is movement with an international objective. This objective is the achievement of proletarian revolutions in all countries and the creation of an international Socialist Commonwealth. Marx thought that proletarian revolutions will first occur in industrially advanced countries. Lenin, however, pointed out that in the existing imperialistic phase of capitalism, the chain of world capitalism may be broken in any country. The present international strategy of Communism assumes two forms. In the first place, it is a struggle of the working-class of every country against its own capitalist rulers. Secondly, it is a struggle of every colonial and semi-colonial people against its imperialist exploiters.

The Communist International and World Revolution

Besides this, the world strategy of the Communists must include the problem of defending and consolidating the socialist part of the world against any attack or interference by the capitalist states. After the victory of the Communists in the Russian Revolution, a Third International was created to spread and coordinate the Communist movement in different countries. The Communist parties of various countries were affiliated to the Third International with its headquarters at Moscow. The Russian Communists naturally played the leading role in formulating the strategy and tactics of the Communist parties outside Russia and this was interpreted by the opponents of the movement as an unwarranted interference by a foreign state in the domestic affairs of the capitalist countries.

Laski's Opposition to Communist Strategy and Tactics

As member of the British Labour party, Laski stood in consistent opposition to the strategy of world communism and the Communist movement inside his own country. In the first place, he argued that there was too much Russian domination over the national Communist parties, which almost converted them into instruments of the Russian foreign policy. Secondly, the emergence of the Communist parties disrupted the unity of the working-class by dividing it into two warring factions. The foreign affiliations of the Communist parties, says Laski, prevented them from seeking sincere cooperation with the socialist parties despite their opportunistic tactics of the united front. The insurrectionary tactics of the communists in certain countries and the division which they created in the ranks of the working-class facilitated the rise and victory of fascism in those countries.

United Front of Socialist Parties Against Fascism

However, the ever increasing menace of fascism, which suppressed the Communist and socialist parties with equal ruthlessness, enabled the Communists and socialists to forget their ideological differences and enter into popular fronts against fascism. Laski welcomed this achievement of unity between the two working class parties for resisting the common danger of fascism.

Unfortunately, the Nazi-Soviet non-aggression pact ended the brief period of cooperation between the socialist and Communist parties of the West European countries. Laski here unjustly accuses the Soviet foreign policy and the Communist advocacy of peace as the appeasement of Hitler forgetting the fact that rejection of the Soviet plan of collective security by England and France and their policy of appeasing Hitler by concluding the Munich Pact had left no alternative for Soviet Russia but to ensure its defence by concluding a non-aggression treaty with Germany.

During the war of resistance against Hitler, the European socialists and Communists acted as the most resolute fighters against fascism. This unity of the two working-class parties could not continue during the post-war period when the rightwing European socialists chose the side of America in its struggle against world communism.[5] Laski died before he could see the consequences of this new development and nobody can exactly say what would have been his reaction to it if he had lived longer. Most probably, he would have supported a policy of neutrality in the cold war between Russian Communism and American capitalism.

---

4. Laski, however, gives a more pro-Soviet interpretation of the Nazi-Soviet Pact of 1939 in his "Dilemma of Our Times", p. 166.
5. For Laski's criticism of the pro-American foreign policy of the Labour Government, see his "Dilemma of Our Times", Chapter II pp. 44-51.

CHAPTER 31

MARXIST THEORIES OF ALIENATION, FREEDOM, STATE AND REVOLUTION

MARX'S THEORY OF ALIENATION

Nature of Alienation

Marx defined human freedom as absence of man's alienated condition. For him alienation and freedom were historical negations. Man expresses his humanity through productive labour which can be of economic, social, artistic, literary or scientific nature. Man as a subject transforms the material objects around him to express his creative capacities. In capitalist society, man's productive activity is deformed in such a way as to cause his alienation and estrangement. In *Economic and Philosophic Manuscripts,* Marx mentioned four aspects of estrangement: alientation from the product of work, from the work itself, from one's fellow-beings and from human species-life. Estrangement or alienation is a radical loss of freedom because it is the negation of free genuinely human creative activity.

In the first place, the worker in the capitalist mode of production does not own and control the products of his own labour. The proletarian does not use the wealth which he creates. Thus he is alienated from his own product. The life which he has given to the object sets itself against him as an alien force. The labourer himself becomes a commodity whose value is equal to the bare means of his subsistence. The capitalist, who purchases the labour-power of the proletarian, is the real owner of the wealth which he creates.

Secondly, Marx affirms that the alien relationship of the worker to the product of his labour is only a manifestation of the alienated nature of the productive activity itself. The labourer, who sells his labour-power for a wage, produces commodities under orders from the capitalist. His work is, therefore, neither free nor voluntary because he does not satisfy any creative urge of his own by working in a factory owned and managed by his bourgeois employer. The bourgeois institution of private property reduces him to the status of a wage-slave.

Thirdly, alienated labour results in the estrangement of the proletarian from his fellow-beings. It results in the hostility between the employed and unemployed workers who look upon each other as alien forces. The worker similarly sees in the manager and the proprietor alien forces profiting from his alienated work. The basis of genuine social relation is thus totally destroyed in capitalism.

Fourthly, the above three aspects of man's alienation produce his **estrangement from his species-life. The egotistic, self-centred existence of** the estranged proletarian alienates him from man's entire cultural heritage. As Marx points out, the oppressed members of the working-class are scarcely aware of the artistic, scientific, literary and other cultural achievements of the human race. They lack the capacity to understand and enjoy these beautiful and valuable gifts of human creativity. Man is thus cut off from the life-history of his own species. By dehumanizing his existence, man becomes a slave to his own alienated activity. What is true of the worker, is equally applicable to those who live parasitically on appropriations, the products of estranged labour. The capitalist, who rides on the backs of the proletariat, also leads an alienated life because he is also not personally engaged in any creative work and is a victim of the fetishization of the commodities. In a society based on unfreedom, the slave and his enslaver are equally unfree.

Marx believed that this condition of man's alienation can be fully overcome under communism which abolishes commodity production. In communism, there will be no private property and, therefore, no alienated labour. Economic planning will reverse the existing domination of the product over the worker and distribution according to need will remove the worker's existing concern for his physical survival. The division of labour existing under capitalism will be replaced by a new system of assigning work through which an individual can engage himself in several types of productive and creative activity according to his own aptitude and choice. In capitalist society, the working-class cannot hope to achieve its freedom because it cannot put an end to the phenomenon of alienation without abolishing the capitalist method of production itself.

The historical concept of freedom, which was worked out by Marx in connection with his theory of the development of social forces in history, is not a replacement for the humanistic concept of freedom as outlined above, but a complement to it. Marx realized that the realm of freedom represented by communism has to be made possible by the age-long struggle of man to control his natural and social environment. Man's struggle for the realization of the realm of freedom is a process of liberation itself. The freedom of self-realization under communism could be achieved by the mediation of freedom as power, that is, the proletarian revolution.

Different Forms of Alienation

Marx's theory of alienation was derived directly from Hegel, though its roots go much earlier. Alienation, for Hegel, consisted in man's failure to realise that the world was not external to spirit. When men saw this, they would become free and this freedom has been realized in history. Marx's main criticism of Hegel was that man's alienation would not end with the hypothetical abolition of the external world. The external world, was, in fact, part of man's nature and only the establishment of right relationship between man and his environment could put an end to the condition of alienation. Marx thus rejected the idealist notion of spirit and substituted its supposed antithesis to the external world by the real antithesis between man engaged in alienated labour and his social self eager to achieve fulfilment through creative work under conditions of freedom.

In his early writings Marx discussed several forms of alienation starting, like other young Hegelians, from religious alienation to philosophical, political and economic categories of alienation. As labour was man's most significant activity, economic aspects of ailenation were regarded by Marx as more important than its ideological and political aspects. David McLellan points out, "In all fields the common idea was that man had forfeited to someone or something what was essential to his nature—principally to be in control of his own activities, to be the initiator of the historical process. In the different forms of alienation some other entity obtained what was proper to man." (*322 : 106*). In the religious form of alienation, God or gods have usurped man's position. Religion serves the dual purpose of a compensation for suffering and a projection of man's hopes and desires. Marx believed that the abolition of religion as the illusory happiness is the demand for their true happiness. The demand to give up the illusions about their condition, Marx felt, is a demand to change the material condition that requires illusions to sustain it. Philosophy too could constitute a form of alienation. Here Marx was alluding to Hegel's idealist philosophy. Speculative philosophy reduced history and man to a mental process, and replacing God by the Absolute was no better than a secularised theology. Marx said, "In Hegel the appropriation of man's objectified and alienated faculties is thus firstly only an appropriation that occurs in the mind, in pure thought, i.e. in abstraction." (*231 : 163*).

Marx analysed the form of political alienation in a similar manner. The state, he said, contained a true description of human nature but at the same time it deprived men of the opportunity of achieving it. Speaking about political alienation, Marx observed: "The political constitution was formerly the religious sphere, the religion of the people's life, the heaven of its universality over against the earthly and real existence. This political sphere was the only state sphere in the state, the only sphere in which the content as well as the form was a content of the species and the genuine universal; but at the same time this was in such a manner that, because this sphere stood over against the others, its content too became a formal and particular one. Political life in the modern state is the scholasticism of the people's life. Monarchy is the perfected expression of this alienation. Republicanism is its negative inside its own sphere." (*231 : 67*).

In Economic and Philosophic Manuscripts, Marx analysed the economic aspects of alienation. Starting from the concept of alienated labour, Marx highlighted four related aspects of human alienation under capitalism. He said, "The worker is related to the product of his labour as to an alien object. The object he produces does not belong to him, dominates him, and only serves in the long run to increase his poverty. Alienation appears not only in the result, but also in the process of production and productive activity itself. The worker is not at home in his work which he views only as a means of satisfying other needs. It is an activity directed against himself, that is independent of him and does not belong to him. Thirdly, alienated labour succeeds in alienating man from his species. Species-life, productive life, life creating life, turns into a mere means of sustaining the workers' individual existence, and man is alienated from his fellow men. Finally, nature itself is alienated from man, who thus loses his own inorganic body." (*232 : 107*).

The members of the proletariat were obviously the most alienated section of capitalist society. Marx, however, applied the concept of alienation to all social classes including capitalists. In the *Holy Family,* Marx observed, "The propertied class and the class of the proletariat represent the same human self-alienation. But the former feels comfortable and confirmed in this self-alienation, knowing that this alienation is its own power and possessing in it the semblance of a human existence. The latter feels itself ruined in this alienation and sees in it its impotence and the actuality of an inhuman existence." (*232 : 113*).

Thus it is the division of labour with all its effects, private ownership of the means of production and the products of labour, fetishism of commodities, the power of money, State, church and other institutions confronting the individual as alien forces, which produce the condition Marx described as alienation. Men, with the exception of a few individuals engaged in creative activity, cannot recognize themselves in their own works. In a world dominated by private property, alienation is generalized. Not only the worker who sells his labour but also the capitalist who appropriates the product of his work and the merchant who sells the commodity in the market, the 'haves' and the 'have-nots', the rulers and the ruled, are, in such a system, alienated from their work, from themselves, from others and from nature. In many ways, it is a topsy-turvy world in which the commodities, appropriated by a few individuals, acquire the strange power of enslaving and owning human beings.

In a society of alienation the relationship of a man with other men is not that of a human being to his fellow human beings but that of a servant to his master, of an exploited man to his exploiter, of a petitioner to a man of privilege, of a subordinate to his boss, and so forth. The worker's alienation is the most extreme form of alienation because it is the very nature of his activity. For the non-worker, the master, the owner, the idler, the priest, the philosopher, the general or the ruler, alienation is not an activity but a condition. It should be noted that everything which appears to the worker as an activity of alienation, would appear to the non-worker as a condition of alienation.

While Althusser has argued that the concept of alienation was a romantic humanist notion of the young Marx, which he renounced after his epistemological break from Hegel, other writers like Meszaros, Fischer, McLellan and Ollman insist that there are enough passages in the *Grundrisse* and *Capital,* which prove the continued acceptance of the concept of alienation by Marx during the period of intellectual maturity. Marx wrote in the

Grundrisse, "This process of *objectification* appears in fact as a process of *alienation* from the *standpoint of labour* and as *appropriation* of alien labour from the *standpoint of capital* (*234* : *64*). But it is true that the hope that the 'objective moments of production can be divested of alienation' was supplemented in the last volume of *Capital*, which was Marx's final testament, by the thought that man can only become a whole man by overcoming his condition or activity of alienation, when he has progressed beyond the sphere of production for the sake of necessity.

In the *Manuscripts*, Marx proposed communism as his solution to the problem of alienation in the following words, "Communism is the positive abolition of private property and thus of human self-alienation and therefore the real reappropriation of the human essence by and for man. This is communism as the complete and conscious return of man conserving all the riches of previous development for man himself as a social, i.e. human being. Communism as completed naturalism is humanism and as completed humanism is naturalism. It is the genuine solution of the antagonism between man and nature and between man and man. It is the true solution of the struggle between existence and essence, between objectification and self-affirmation, between freedom and necessity, between individual and species. It is the solution to the riddle of history and knows itself to be this solution." (*232* : *216*).

As David McLellan points out, the counterpart of alienated man, the unalienated or total man of the *Manuscripts*, "the fully developed individual, fit for a variety of labours, ready to face any change of production, and to whom the different social functions he performs, are but so many modes of giving free scope to his own natural and acquired powers," (*232* : *109*) also appears in *Capital*. Meszaros sums up the originality of Marx's theory of alienation as follows: "(1) the terms of reference of his theory are not the categories of *Sollen* (ought), but those of *necessity* (is) inherent in the objective ontological foundations of human life; (2) its point of view is not that of some *utopian partiality* but the *universality* of the critically adopted standpoint of labour; (3) its framework of criticism is not some abstract (Hegelian) speculative totality, but the *concrete totality* of dynamically developing society perceived from the material basis of the proletariat as a necessarily self-transcending universal historical force." (*234* : *65*).

Conclusion

Marx summed up Hegel's views on alienation in the following words: "For Hegel, the human essence, man, is the same as self-consciousness. All alienation of man's essence is therefore nothing but the alienation of self-consciousness. The alienation of self-consciousness is not regarded as the expression of the real alienation of man's essence reflected in knowledge and thought. The real alienation (or the one that appears to be real) in its inner concealed essence that has first been brought to the light by philosophy, is nothing but the appearance of the alienation of the real human essence, self-consciousness." (*231 : 165*).

Marx rejected Hegel's idealist interpretation of alienation and discovered its roots in the commercial spirit and particularly in the importance ascribed to money. He observes: "Money is the universal, self-constituted value of all things. It has therefore robbed the whole world, human as well as natural, of its own values. Money is the alienated essence of man's work and being, this alien essence dominates him and he adores it...... under the domination of egotistic need man can only become practical, only create practical objects by putting his products and his activity under the domination of an alien entity and lending them the significance of an alien entity—money." (*231 : 114*).

Discussing various dimensions of alienation, Marx pointed out: "Religion, family, state, law, morality, science and art are only particular forms of production and fall under its general law. The positive abolition of private property and the appropriation of human life is therefore the positive abolition of all alienation, thus the return of man out of religion, family, state etc. into his human i.e. social being. Religious alienation as such occurs only in man's interior consciousness, but economic alienation is that of real life and its abolition therefore covers both aspects." (*231 : 149*).

According to Marx, capitalists and workers are both affected by alienation, though in different ways. He says: 'The propertied class and the class of the proletariat present the same human self-alienation. But the former class finds in this self-alienation its confirmation and its good, its own power: it has in it a semblance of human existence. The class of the proletariat feels annihilated in its self-alienation; it sees in it its own powerlessness and the reality of an inhuman existence. In the words of Hegel, the class of the poletariat is abased and indignant and that abasement, an indignation to which it is necessarily driven by the contradiction between its human nature and its condition of life, which is the outright, decisive and comprehensive negation of that nature." (*229 : 51*).

Within this antithesis, the capitalist is the conservative side and the proletarian is the destructive side who rebels againt his alienated activity. Marx says: "This is the *process of alienation* of man's own labour. From the start, the worker is superior to the capitalist in that capitalist is rooted in his *process of alienation* and is completely content therein, whereas the worker who is the victim finds himself from the beginning in a state of rebellion against it and experiences the process as one of enslavement." (*232 : 119*).

In feudal society, the lord and the serf were both under the grip of alienation. Marx says: "Already in feudal land-ownership the ownership of the earth appears as an alien power ruling over men. The self is the product of the land. In the same way the heir, the first born son, belongs to the land. It inherits him." (*227 : 114*).

Distinguishing the alienation of the bourgeois from that of the proletarian, Marx affirms:

"It should be noted first that everything which appears to the worker as an *activity of alienation* appears to the non-worker as a condition of alienation." (*201* : *46*).

MARX'S VIEW OF MAN AND FREEDOM

The Concept of the Whole Man

Marx's social philosophy underwent a continuous evolution in the course of his intellectual development and revolutionary activities, but what had served as his starting point in his early work, *Economic and Philosophic Manuscripts,* remained intact : the concept and possibility of the whole man. Since the success of the industrial revolution based on the capitalist mode of production at the end of the eighteenth century, the fragmentation of man as a consequence of the division of labour, mechanization, exploitation and money economy had become the basic European experience. The longing for unity with one's own self, with nature and with one's own species was cherished by all thinkers who entertained humanist sentiments and thoughts, Marx shared this longing with them.

In his revolt against a world which turned everything into a commodity and degraded man to the status of an object, Marx complained that man had become a fragment of his own self, had been crushed by the products of his own work, and had fallen away from himself. As Marx points out, both the aristocratic and the plebeian critics of the rising bourgeois society protested against the dehumanization of man brought about by extremes of wealth and poverty, greed of capital and misery of the proletariat, ever-increasing luxury and conspicuous consumption at one end and ever-growing material and spiritual wretchedness and starvation on the other. But there was a fundamental difference between the reactionary and progressive opponents of capitalism. While the reactionaries looked to the feudal past as a time of human dignity and unity, the radicals turned their vision to the future, hoping for the resurgence of the whole, the *total* man in a communist society which will be a realm of freedom, abundance and abolition of alienated labour.

The political revolutions of the bourgeoisie had proclaimed man's right to liberty and the doctrine of 'free personality'. The contrast between such proclamations and the social reality was quite painful. Man in bourgeois society had become an atomized individual engaged in harsh competition with other men. "Liberty as a right of man", said Marx, "is not founded upon the relations between man and man, but rather upon the separation of man from man." (*179* : *24*). Marx is here commenting upon the bourgeois view of liberty which isolates man from his fellow beings. He adds, "None of the supposed rights of man, therefore, go beyond the egoistic man, man as he is, as a member of civil society; that is, an individual separated from the community, withdrawn into himself, wholly preoccupied with his private interest and acting in accordance with his private caprice." (*179* : *26*). The problem, therefore, was to turn these fragmented men, reduced to an empty individuality, away from their pursuit of selfish interests, to integrate them with a community based on the freedom of all rather than on the dominance of a class.

Marx saw the denial and mockery of the nature of man in the wretched figure of the proletarian representing the quintessence of dehumanization. But precisely in this negation of the human essence, Marx saw the hope of overcoming it. He felt that the proletariat was forced by its very poverty to liberate itself from inhuman conditions by overthrowing its exploiters. In liberating itself, the proletariat would become the liberator of mankind. Marx described the negation of man as found in the proletarian of his time in the following words: "Labour certainly produces marvels for the rich, but it produced privation for the worker. It produces palaces, but hovels for the worker. It produces beauty, but deformity for the worker. It replaces labour by machinery, but it casts some of the workers back into a barbarous kind of work and turns the others into machines. It produces intelligence, but also stupidity and *cretinism* for the workers." (*179 : 124*).

Hegel's radical disciples thought that atheism would liberate man by bringing his spirit back from an imaginary heaven into the real world. Marx's view of religion was more profound. He was conscious of the need for liberation both from material and spiritual bondage. He saw religion both as 'the expression of real misery' and as the 'protest against real misery'. As Marx put it, "Religion is the sigh of the oppressed creature, the sentiment of a heartless world, and the soul of soulless conditions. It is the opium of the people." (*201 : 20*). The quotation is sometimes twisted to imply that religion was opium for the people, a narcotic given to them by the ruling class which for Marx is only a half-truth. Atheism, through a negation of God, asserts the existence and dignity of man. Socialism does not require such a roundabout method. It begins from the theoretical and practical sensory perception of man and nature as essential beings. It is positive human self-consciousness, not a self-consciousness acquired through the negation of religion. The real life of man is also positive to be attained through communism, which is more than a mere negation of private property.

Thus religion, atheism and communism were, for Marx, stages or features of development rather than its end. The end was positive humanism, the real life of man as a liberated being in harmony with nature and the community to which he belonged. The existence of the proletariat was the most striking contradiction of such a life; but the 'ruptured reality' of capitalism did not express itself in the alienated worker alone. Marx's scientific analysis of capitalist industrialisation proved that it dehumanized the exploited and the exploiters alike in a new heartless world of machines, profits and paupers. Even the state in bourgeois society is a dehumanizing instrument.

The fundamental principle of religion is God. Hegel's philosophy was rooted in the State. The central theme of Marx's socialism is Man. Hegel proceeded from the State and made man the State subjectified. Marx proceeds from man and makes the State man objectified. According to Marx, man does not exist for the law's sake but law exists for man's sake. The decisive thing for Marx is man—concrete, real, individual man. The object of his scientific inquiry, of all his revolutionary efforts, is the whole man, the reality of man and positive humanism.

The Concept of Human Freedom

Man needs the community in order to develop into a free individual. In the previous and existing substitutes for the community and in the bourgeois state in particular, personal freedom has existed for the atomised individuals who developed within the relationships prescribed by the ruling class, and only in so far as they were individuals of the class. Individuals who behave as though they were free are actually conditioned by the circumstances of their tradition, upbringing, occupation and class identity. In fact, their personality is in many ways determined by quite definite class relationships. In bourgeois society, men and women wear what Marx calls 'social character masks'—not as specific individuals but as standardized average individuals.

But Marx is not exactly a determinist who denies the notion of human freedom. James J.O.'Rourke in *The Problem of Freedom in Marxist Thought* says, "The notion of freedom plays a central role in the thought of Karl Marx.....his notion of freedom often figures significantly in the background which gives meaning to his more specific and immediate concerns. It is for him one of those fundamental categories which are constantly assumed, and often too obvious to be explained. For example, one can easily forget that the ultimate meaning of history is not the mere development of socio-economic forms but the progressive liberation of mankind. Similarly, the notion of freedom lurks behind the critique of religion and the whole description of the forms of alienation....the theme of the freedom of men has a pervasiveness and extent in the long development of his thought which marks it as one of these basic themes providing continuity to his work." (*243* : *9*).

The articles written by Marx for the *Rheinische Zeitung* are quite significant for understanding his concept of freedom. According to the young Marx, freedom is the generic essence of man. Ethics, law, the state and the press must make an effort to realize freedom and this is the measure of their goodness. The foundation of all human thought, history, and institutions is the daily concrete existence of empirical human beings. There is nothing more fundamental than man. In the liberal conception, freedom consists in the maximum absence of restraints on the activities of atomized individuals. Marx rejected this view because it mistook the negative tendencies of man, his selfishness, for his true essence. Man is not correctly defined as an egotistic being in the Hobbesian tradition. The liberal view of individual liberty emphasizes the negative relation of men to one another; which does not distinguish them from animals. Marx's view of freedom puts a stress on men's positive relation to each other which is genuinely human. Its distinguishing feature is men's *social* character.

It should, however, be clearly understood that Marx's concept of human freedom does not subordinate men ontologically to society. On the contrary, the process by which man becomes a species-being and secures his emancipation is founded upon his concrete individuality. Marx says, "Only when the real, individual man has taken back into himself the abstract citizen and as an individual in his empirical life his individual work and his individual relationship, has become a species being....... only then is human emancipation achieved." (*207 : 74*). Marx believes that freedom consists in the ability to follow the inborn laws of one's own nature, rather than to be determined by external factors. Since man is essentially a social being, he achieves his freedom by positively developing his capacities in the family, the community and society.

Marx's defence of the freedom of the press and opposition to the Prussian institution of censorship is well-known. He saw no danger in diversity of opinion but regarded as natural that a politically mature nation would have a press representing the various 'doctrines of the people and its parties'. He defended the existence of several parties in a democracy and said, "Without parties there is no development, without division, no progress." Richard N. Hunt says, "Even after becoming a communist, Marx never repudiated these early articles in which he defended freedom of expression with such fervour and wit. Indeed, in 1851, he had them all published in book form without altering their substance in even the smallest detail." (*207 : 34*).

For Marx, philosophy was a critical activity of applying *free* reason to human problems. Thus human institutions, as they ought to be, could be discovered by extracting from imperfect existing institutions their inner rational principle or essence. The essence of Marx was not the Absolute Idea of Hegel but a human conception developing through man's life-process. Freedom is surely the species-essence of man and critical philosophy as *praxis* is the liberator of mankind. Free press in a democratic state is the condition of other freedoms and also the principal instrument for achieving general emancipation of man.

Marx's love for democratic freedom and his hatred for despotism has been expressed in the following words, "Freedom, the feeling of man's dignity, will have to be awakened again in these men. Only this freedom, which disappeared from the world with the Greeks......can transform society into a community of men to achieve their highest purpose, a democratic state. The people, though, who do not feel themselves to be men, grow attached to their masters, like a herd of slaves or horses. The hereditary masters are the purpose of this whole society......They stand where their feet have grown, on the necks of these political animals that know no other destination than to be attached to their masters and subject to them, to be at their disposal. The world of the Philistine is the *political animal kingdom* and if we have to recognize its existence, we simply must acknowledge the *status quo.* Centuries of barbarism created it and now it exists as a consistent system, whose principle is a world *dehumanized*.... Despotism's only idea is contempt for man, and this idea further has the advantage over others of being fact. A despot always sees men as degraded. He sees them drown for him in the mud of common life from which they again and again emerge like toads." (*207 : 47*). Once one has reached threshold of the political animal kingdom, there can be no further movement and no other withdrawal except to rupture its basis and enter the human world of democratic freedom.

Conclusion

Marx's writings up to the end of 1843 show a development through successive stages of idealism—romantic and then Hegelian—to liberal rationalism and his first critique of Hegel's philosophy, where many of the basic concepts of Marx's radical thought appear for the first time. Marx now applied Feurbach's critique of Hegel's metaphysics to his political philosophy as well.

Marx says: "Hegel proceeds from the state and makes man into the state subjectivised. Democracy proceeds from man and makes the state into man objectivised. Just as religion does not create man, but man creates religion, so the constitution does not create the people, but the people create the constitution......Democracy is the essence of every constitution, socialised man as a particular constitution......Recently the French have conceived of this in such a way that the political state disappears in true democracy." (*231 : 159*).

In his comments on democracy Marx now outlined a position that was humanist, since man was viewed as the basic factor in society. Marx was a libertarian in that man was viewed as a free subject. He was also a socialist because man realized his freedom as a communal being in true democracy after the abolition of the repressive state. Man's social emancipation was not possible under capitalist society.

Marx says: "Man has a life both in the political community, where he is valued as a communal being, and in civil society where he is active as a private individual, treats other men as means, degrades himself to a means and becomes the plaything of alien powers." (*231 : 94*).

With great passion, Marx condemned the dehumanization of woman. Under a regime of private property, the love-based relationship between man and woman has been distorted into a relationship of ownership and domination. This has resulted in the woman's debasement and reduction to a *thing*.

Marx observes: "In the relationship with woman, as the prey and the handmaid of communal lust, is expressed the infinite degradation in which man exists for himself.....From this relationship man's whole level of development can be assessed. It follows from the character of this relationship how far *man* has become, and has understood himself as, a *species being*, a *human* being. The relationship of man to woman is the *most natural* relation of human being to human being. It indicates, therefore how far man's *natural* behaviour has become *human*, and how far his *human* essence has become *natural* essence for him, how far his human nature has become nature for him. It also shows how far man's needs have become *human* needs, and consequently how far the other person, as a person, has become one of his needs, and to what extent he is in his individual existence at the same time a social being." (*227 : 154*).

Marx discovers the roots of dehumanization in the institution of private property and regards its negation as the condition of a truly human society. He outlines in almost lyrical tones his conception of a truly humanist method of production.

He observes: "Supposing that we had produced in a human manner: each of us would in his production have doubly affirmed himself and his fellow men. I would have: (1) objectified in my production my individuality and its peculiarity and thus both in my activity enjoyed an individual expression of my life and also in looking at the object have had the individual pleasure of realising that my personality was objective, visible to the senses and thus a power raised beyond all doubt. (2) In your enjoyment or use of my product I would have had the direct enjoyment of realising that I had both satisfied a human need by my work and also objectified the human essence and therefore fashioned for another human being the object that met his need. (3) I would have been for you the mediator between you and the species and thus been acknowledged and felt by you as a completion of your own essence and a necessary part of yourself and have thus realised that I am confirmed both in your thought and in your love. (4) In my expression of my life I would have fashioned your expression of your life, and thus in my own activity have realised my own essence, my human, my communal essence." (*[illegible]*).

In his last work, the third volume of *Capital,* Marx described the future communist society as the realm of freedom. Marx observes: 'In fact, the realm of freedom actually begins only where labour which is determined by necessity and mundane considerations ceases: thus in the very nature of things it lies beyond the sphere of actual material production......Freedom in this field can only consist in socialized man, the associated producers, rationally regulating their interchange with nature, bringing it under control, instead of being ruled by it......But it nonetheless remains a realm of necessity. Beyond it begins that development of human energy which is an end in itself, the true realm of freedom, which, however can blossom forth only with this realm of necessity as its basis." (*223 : 799*).

Thus not only the young Marx of the *Manuscripts* but also the mature Marx of *Capital* is equally committed to the humanist goal i.e. development of the human potential through creative work in various fields in an environment of freedom.

Marx's vision of the whole man can be summed up in the following words: "Man appropriates his manifold being in an all-inclusive way, and thus as a whole man. All his *human* relations to the world—seeing, hearing, smelling, tasting, touching, thinking, observing, feeling, desiring, acting, loving—in short, all the organs of his individuality, like the organs which are directly communal in form are in their objective action (*their action in relation to the object*) an appropriation of this object, the appropriation of human reality. The way in which they react to the object is the confirmation of *human reality*. It is human effectiveness and human suffering, for suffering humanly considered is an enjoyment of the self for man." (*227* : *159*).

MARX AND ENGELS : THEORY OF STATE

The State as Parasitical Social Power

Karl Marx first formulated his ideas on the nature of the State as a result of how direct confrontation with the imperial German State which censored his critical articles for the *Rheinische Zeitung*. At that time, he regarded the state as the most characteristic institution representing man's alienated condition. In contrast to the repressive, antidemocratic state of Prussia based on unreason and brute force, Marx conceptualized the possibility of a true democracy, an idealized state of the Hegelian model representing reason and freedom. By 1843 Marx realised the inadequacy of the concept of 'true democracy' as a result of his intensive study of political economy which led to his epistemological break from Hegel's idealism. According to Hegel, the state was logically prior and morally superior to its two constituent elements, the family and civil society. Marx now argued that Hegel was not justified in claiming that the state had a universal character capable of reconciling the discordant elements of civil society and synthesizing them on a higher plane. All State organs i.e. monarchy, parliament and bureaucracy were actually parasitical structures of social power.

The state, therefore, was no more than an empty ideal sphere which created the illusion of belonging to the whole society. Marx felt that the opposition between the civil society and the state was an attribute of the existing capitalist society though not of the feudal social formation. In opposition to Hegel, Marx now recommended a form of Government which can overcome the separation between civil society and the state and which directly corresponded to the essence of socialised, unalienated man. In this higher form of democracy, the law, the constitution and the state were salf-determined by the people. In *Economic and Philosophic Manuscripts,* Marx concluded that the state was essentially the negation of man, an expression of human alienation similar to religion, law and morality and equally based on a specific mode of production. Like religion, the state was viewed by Marx as an embodiment of man's ideal aims and also a consolation for their failure to achieve them in practice. The state was limited precisely because its ideals remained illusory. The bourgeois state, which claimed to liberate man as political citizen, left him in servitude as a man, or member of civil society i.e. in the economic sphere.

The state under capitalism was not capable of solving society problems because of its alienated condition. Marx pointed out, "The state cannot abolish the contradiction which exists between the role and good intentions of the administration on the one hand and the means at its disposal on the other, without abolishing itself, for it rests on this contradiction. It rests on the contrast between public and private life, on the contrast between general and particular interests. The administration must, therefore, limit itself to a formal and negative activity, for its power ceases just where civil life and work begin." (*232* : *181*). If the modern state wished to do away with the importance of its administration, it would have to do away with the contemporary private sphere by abolishing the alienated condition of man.

The State and the Ruling Class

Although Marx at no stage abandoned his theory of the State as alienated and parasitical social power, he later concentrated his attention on an analysis of the function of state in society. While in his earlier writings he had emphasized the gap between the state and society, he later considered the state as a part of society. In *The German Ideology,* Marx traced the origin of the state to the division of labour. The state was an illusory community, which according to Marx and Engels, served as a screen for the real struggles fought by antagonistic classes. In the course of history each mode of production gave rise to a particular type of state promoting the interests of the dominant economic class. The large-scale modern industry and universal competition of capitalism created their own political superstructures in the form of a modern state in which the dominant capitalist class emerged as the new ruling class replacing the aristocracy. The state in turn moulded other social institutions.

Marx observes, "Since the state is the form in which the individuals of a ruling class assert their common interest and the entire civil society of an epoch is epitomised, the state acts as an intermediary in the formation of communal institutions and gives them a political form. Hence, there is the illusion that law is based on will, that is, on will divorced from its real basis, on free will. In similar fashion, right in turn is reduced to statute law." (*232* : *182*). The class domination theory of the state was summed up by Marx and Engels in the *Communist Manifesto,* which stipulated that the executive of the modern state was but a committee for managing the common affairs of the entire bourgeois class. Marx, however, did not consider this correlation between economic substructure and political superstructure in any dogmatic fashion. For example, he asserted that though England's mode of production was more advanced than that of France, yet the political system of the French democratic republic was more developed than that of the English bourgeois monarchy in several respects.

Marx also admitted that there were certain exceptions to his general characterization of the state as an instrument of class domination. McLellan observes, "Sometimes Marx says that the state need not be representative of the whole of a class but only of a section of that class (for example, the financiers under Louis-Philippe); or that one class can control the state for the benefit of another (for example, the Whigs on behalf of the middle class in England). In relatively backward countries, where classes were not fully developed, Marx thought that the state could play an independent role, also in the European absolute monarchies in the transition between feudal and bourgeois classes." (*232* : *183*).

Louis Bonaparte's regime in France and Bismarck's regime in Prussia were cited by Marx as examples of independent states. Yet he pointed out that the state power could not remain suspended in mid-air. Bonaparte too represented the most numerous class of the French society, the small holding peasantry. Yet his policies ultimately benefited the bourgeoisie by encouraging the industrial development of France. It was only in the United States that the classical bourgeois state had been formed, which from the very beginning had been subordinated to bourgeois society and bourgeois forces of production.

The second important exception to the Marxian idea of the state as an instrument of class domination occurred in Asian Societies—China, India, Persia, and to some extent Russia. Owing to the inadequate development of private property in land, the Asian despotic ruler appeared as the protecting father of all the numerous village communities, representing the common unity of his subjects. Yet this Asian state also created a bureaucratic group, which exploited the servile peasant masses through the exercise of public power of the coercive state machinery.

Modern State Apparatus and Bureaucracy

Marx considered bureaucracy to be the most essential part of the modern state apparatus. In *The Eighteenth Brumaire of Louis Bonaparte,* Marx explained that bureaucracy emerged with the demise of feudal monarchies in modern Europe. It was initially a progressive force which destroyed the power of medieval corporations and introduced an element of rationality in administration. In his *Critique of Hegel's Philosophy of the State,* Marx explained how the Prussian bureaucracy had finally become a privileged stratum which claimed an exclusive right to define the interests of the state. Thus the bureaucracy itself became an elitist group of privileged persons working in an atmosphere of secrecy, hierarchy and authority. In France, the brueaucracy played an independent role in the transition form feudalism to capitalism but later it was fully subordinated to the bourgeois class. The bureaucracies in England and America were less powerful as they were controlled by stronger parliaments and had played no role in the bourgeois transformation of these societies earlier.

Under Louis Bonaparte, bureaucracy was able to dominate state institutions owing to the underdevelopment of French bourgeoisie at that time and the isolated existence of the peasants who constituted the social base of Bonaparte's political power. In Bismarck's Germany, the bureaucracy acquired power as a balancing force between the dominant aristocracy and the rising bourgeoisie. Marx, therefore, aruged that any successful revolution involved the breaking of the entrenched power of the bureaucratic state apparatus. In 1871 Marx reminded Kugelmann of the passage in the *Eighteenth Brumaire of Louis Bonaparte* where he talked of the bureaucratic-military machinery and described it as the precondition of any real popular revolution on the European continent.

The chief function of the state in capitalist society is repression of the working-class movement. For this purpose, it requires an ever-growing military bureaucratic complex. Discussing the nature of executive power in the French bourgeois state, Marx says, "This executive power with its monstrous bureaucratic and military organisation, with its artificial state machinery embracing wide strata, with a host of officials numbering half-a million, besides an army of another half million, this appalling parasitic growth, which enmeshes this body of French society like a net and chokes all its pores, sprang up in the days of absolute monarchy, with the decay of feudal system which it helped to hasten." (*214 : 158*). The first French Revolution developed centralization of the bureaucratic power further. Napoleon also perfected this state machinery through a legal code. The parliamentary republic, in its struggle against the French proletariat, further strengthened the repressive state machinery. As Marx puts it, all bourgeois revolutions and regimes in France perfected the coercive state apparatus instead of smashing it up. The political parties that contended in turn for power regarded this huge bureaucratic structure as the chief spoils of the victor. All bourgeois states have subsequently strengthened their military-bureaucratic structures to such an extent as to render the French state structure of the nineteenth century quite moderate and libertarian by comparison. The dialectical impact of this is visible in socialist societies too.

The Nature, Origin and Essence of the State

Marx and Engels make the following important points about the nature origin and essence of the state. In contrast to the organisation of a primitive commune, the state is a territorial organisation which allowed its subjects to exercise their public rights and duties wherever they settled irrespective of gens and tribe. This transformation was accompanied by long and arduous conflicts.

The second point is the establishment of a *public power* which no longer coincided with the population organizing itself as an armed force. Because of class divisions, a self-acting armed organisation of the people had become impossible. The slave-owners could not have trusted the slaves with arms. This public power included an army, a police force and a system of prisons and courts. The ruling class used it to keep the subject classes under its domination.

In order to maintain this public power, contributions from the citizens become necessary in the form of *taxes*. These were completely unknown in the primitive communist society. The volume of these taxes goes on increasing with the multiplication of the instruments of coercion. The state may even make drafts on the future, contract loans and public debts. The state creates a body of officials, who exercise the public power and claim the right to levy taxes. This bureaucracy now stands *above* society as a parasitical social stratum. The officials ensure respect for themselves by means of exceptional laws by virtue of which they enjoy special sanctity and inviolability. The shabbiest police constable of the state claims more 'authority' than all the organs of the gentile commune put together. On the other hand, the most powerful ruler of a modern civilised state cannot compare himself with the humblest tribal chief who gets undisputed and uncoerced esteem from all members of his tribal commune. While the leader of the commune stands in the midst of society, the prince and the statesman have become alienated from their own society.

As the state arose from the need to hold class antagonisms under control, but as it arose, at the same time in the midst of the conflict of these classes, it became as a rule the state of the most dominant class in society. The economically dominant class through the medium of the state also became the politically powerful class, and thus acquired new means of holding down and exploiting the subject classes. The city-state of Greece and the imperial state of Rome was above all the state of the slaveowners for exploiting the oppressed class of slaves. The feudal state was the organ of aristocracy for exploiting the oppressed class of peasant serfs. The modern bourgeois state is, similarly, an instrument of exploitation of the proletariat by the capitalists who own the means of production and, thereby, convert the workers into their hired wage-slaves.

By way of exception, there are periods in history in which the warring classes reach a balance so that the state temporarily becomes independent of both. It acquires the character of a parasite. Such was the absolute monarchy of the seventeenth and eighteenth centuries which held the balance between the nobility and the bourgeoisie. The French Empire under Napoleon I and still more under Napoleon III and the German Empire under Bismarck played off the bourgeoisie and the proletariat against each other.

In most of the historical states, the rights of citizens are apportioned unequally according to their class position. It was so in the Athenian and Roman classification according to property. It was so in the feudal system in which political power was determined by the amount of land owned. The early bourgeois state limited the right to vote on the basis of property qualifications. The advanced form of the bourgeois-democratic state does not recognise property distinctions in franchise. In it wealth exercises its power indirectly but all the more effectively. This may be done by corrupting the bureaucracy or through an alliance between the ruling political party and forces of capital. Under universal suffrage, the proletariat either forms a tail of the capitalist class or sets up its own revolutionary party, which utilizes the electroal process to spread class consciousness.

The state has not existed from all eternity. There were societies which had no conception of state or state power. The proletariat, after the socialist revolution, will establish a transitional state known as dictatorship of the proletariat. At this stage, the existence of classes and class divisions may become a positive hindrance to further development of the forces of production. The classes will, then fall as inevitably apart as they arose at an earlier stage. Along with them, the state will also decline and disappear. Under the final phase of communism based on a classless society, the state will not be needed as a repressive institution i.e. it will wither away.

Conclusion

Engels describes the nature of the State in the following words:

"With the difference in distribution, class differences emerge. Society divides into classes; the privileged and the dispossessed, the exploiters and the exploited, the rulers and the ruled; and the state......acquires the function of maintaining by force the conditions of existence and domination of the ruling class against the subject class. (*196* : *204*).

Explaining the nature of class domination, Engels adds : "The possessing classes...... keep the working class in servitude not only by the might of their wealth, by the simple exploitation of labour by capital, but also by the power of the state—by the army, the bureaucracy, the courts." (*193* : *251*).

In this sense, politics is concentrated economics, the state is the political superstructure, which rests on the socio-economic organisation of society Marx observes : "The power of the state is the concentrated and organized force of society......the summing up of bourgeois society." (*223* : *751*).

Engels elucidated the same point in greater detail : "The state...... is a product of society at a certain stage of development, it is the admission that this society has become entagled in an insoluble contradiction with itself, that it is cleft into irreconcilable antagonisms which it is powerless to dispel. But in order that these antagonisms, classes with conflicting economic interests, might not consume themselves and society in sterile struggle, a power seemingly standing above society became necessary for the purpose of moderating the conflict, of keeping it within the bounds of 'order', and this power, arisen out of society, but placing itself above it, and increasingly alienating itself from it, is the state". (*193* : *252*).

Discussing class basis of the state in European history, Engels sums up his analysis as follows :

"Thus, the state of antiquity was above all the state of the slave-owners for the purpose of holding down the slaves, as the feudal state was the organ of the nobility for holding down the peasant serfs and bondsman, and the modern representative state is an instrument of exploitation of wage-labourer by capital." (*193* : *257*).

The best-known summary statement about the rise of the modern bourgeois state is in the *Communist Manifesto,* where Marx emplains : "Each step in the development of the bourgeoisie was accompanied by a corresponding political advance of that class. An oppressed class under the sway of the feudal nobility, an armed and self-governing association in the medieval commune; here independent urban republic (as in Italy and Germany), there taxable 'third estate' of the monarchy (as in France); afterwards, in the period of manufacture proper, serving either the semi-feudal or the absolute monarchy, as a counterpoise against the nobility, and, in fact, corner-stone of the great monarchies in general, the bourgeoisie has at last, since the establishment of Modern Industry and of the world market, conquered for itself, in the modern representative state, exclusive political sway. The executive of the modern state is but a committee for managing the common affairs of the whole bourgeoisie." (*232* : *192*).

The state will continue as dictatorship of the proletariat during the transition from capitalism to communism. When classes disappear, the state will wither away. Marx says: "By anarchy all socialists understand this: once the aim of the proletarian movement, the abolition of classes, is attained ......the state power disappears and governmental functions are transformed into simple administrative functions. (*232* : *194*).

This merely means that the repressive state apparatus will become superfluous under communism but not during the socialist phase of transition.

MARX AND ENGELS: THEORY OF REVOLUTION

Marx's Approach to the Study of Revolution

In modern times the most significant contribution to the study of revolutions has been made by Karl Marx. By synthesizing the far reaching implications of the French Revolution, which for Marx was the classical example of a bourgeois democratic revolution in the political sphere, with the causes and consequences of the Industrial Revolution in England, which was for him the classical model of a bourgeois democratic revolution in the economic sphere, Marx created a coherent system of social and political thought, which still dominates our civilization. As Jean Paul Sartre has remarked, almost everything since Marx has essentially been a commentary on his philosophy. Because Marxism does not merely interpret the world but also seeks to change it, almost every important revolution in the twenthieth century has been carried out in his name. To study revolution is therefore largely to deal with Marx and his influence.

In Marx's time the impact of the French Revolution was still very real, and he shared with Tocqueville and many other thinkers the view that it was a world historical event which had transformed the social structure based on the pre-eminence of the aristocratic class. It demonstrated to Marx that social progress would have to come about through a violent struggle between classes. By progress Marx meant the expansion of the productive capacity of both society and individual human beings. This would ultimately lead to greater freedom and equality and to the realization of man's capacities.

The dramatic conflict of classes intensified during a period of social upheaval reached its climax in a political revolution. The fundamental cause of any revolution was the desire and endeavour of a subject class to capture the state power from the ruling class by force and to reorganise the state apparatus to suit its own specific needs. The final struggle takes place in the political realm but the social and economic objectives which divide the warring class formations are really the true causes of a revolution. A successful revolution will remove those social, economic and political institutions which obstruct the development of the class for whose benefit the revolution has been carried out. Just as France witnessed the sudden victory of the bourgeois class over its aristocracy, so too will other nations will carry out their own bouregois-democratic revolutions. Marx has developed this general prognosis of class conflict and general and specific causes of revolution in such works as *The German Ideology, The Communist Manifesto* and *A Conrtibution to the Critique of Political Economy.*

When Marx discussed specific revolutions, he enriched his general theory with a wealth and empirical facts. In his *Eighteenth Brumaire of Louis Bonaparte,* Marx produced a masterpiece of contemporary French revolutionary history taking account of the complexity of the revolutionary events, wherein a multitude of classes interacted changing continuously their alignments. Moreover, Marx clearly recognized the crucial role played by individuals in promoting or thwarting the course of revolution. In his brief analysis of the English Revolution, he singled out the class alliance of the English bourgeoisie with large land-owners as its unique feature which paved the way for the Industrial Revolution. Quite obviously, this was a development at variance with the French model where the bourgeoisie forged an alliance with the peasantry against the large landowners.

History and Revolutionary Theory

Some people are not aware that Marx recognised the importance of historical accidents as a causative factor in revolutions. We notice this flexibility of approach in his analysis of the Paris Commune of 1871. He even lent his public support to this first abortive socialist revolution despite the fact that it occurred in a not yet fully industrialized society, with a poorly organised working class and a leadership consisting of largely petty-bourgeois groups. He even predicted that the Commune could never succeed. Marx in his essay entitled *The Civil War in France* explained the accidental circumstances which enabled the working class of Paris to liberate itself from the capitalist government of France.

Explaining how accidents can become the cause of success or failure of a revolution, Marx said, "World history would indeed be very easy to make, if the struggle were taken only on condition of infallible favourable chances. It would, on the other hand, be of a very mystical nature if 'accidents' played no part. These accidents themselves fall naturally into the general course of development and are compensated again by other accidents. But acceleration and delay are very dependent upon such accidents, which include the accident of the character of those who at first stand at the head of the movement." *(225 : 86)*.

The Marxist theory of revolution is the consequence and the concentrated expression of Marx's view of historical development, that is to say of the sequence of social formations in history. He saw the driving force of social development in the historical tendency towards establishing property relations which corresponded to the level of development and character of the techniques of production at a particular period. Marx found the key to understanding the sequence of the various modes of production in the law of motion, which was activated by social classes whose interests coincided with the developing tendency. For Marx, social revolution is an ongoing process in which causes and effects are dialectically related. The old social order includes in its womb certain elements which contradict its dominant features.

Marx said, "In the social production of their life, men enter into definite relations that are indispensable and independent of their will, relations of production which correspond to a definite stage of development of their material productive forces .... At a certain stage of their development the material productive forces of society come into conflict with the existing relations of production, or what is but a legal expression for the same thing—with the property relations within which they have been at work hitherto. From forms of development of the productive forces relations turn into their fetters. Then begins an epoch of social revolution." (*201 : 126*).

When in past history the fetters of the relations of production were broken by the developing forces of production, the resulting revolutions were partial in nature. The transition from the feudal relations of production to bourgeois relations of production, accompanied by a social and political constitution adapted to it, represented a *partial* revolution only. Marx observed, "What is the basis of a partial, purely political revolution? It is that a part of civl society emancipates itself and attains to universal domination, that a particular class undertakes the general emancipation of society from its particular situation. This class frees the whole of society, but only under the presupposition that the whole of society is in the same situation as this class, that it possesses, or can easily acquire for example, money and education." (*231 : 125*).

Why had the French Revolution, that seemed so progressive, entirely failed to cure social evils and in particular to achieve a redistribution of the wealth of society? Marx saw much that was positive in the French Revolution: it had destroyed feudalism and status-based hierarchy and proclaimed men's equality as citizens. But Marx's central criticism was that men's common membership of the state had no influence on their real life which was antisocial in the extreme. Here, liberty was based on the separation of man from man and not on the association of man with man.

Political and Social Revolutions

This contradiction between the principles of the state and the real economic life of the citizens was what, for Marx, characterised a merely political revolution. Marx says, "Political intelligence is political just because it thinks inside the limits of politics. The sharper and livelier it is the less capable it is of comprehending social evils. The classical period of political intelligence is the French Revolution. Far from seeing the source of social defects in the state, the heroes of the French Revolution see in social defects the source of political misfortunes." (*231 : 214*). Thus although the theory of the merely political revolution held that it was open to everyone to emancipate himself by becoming a bourgeois, not everyone could do so in reality and the inevitable consequence was the exploitation of the workers by the capitalists.

The unfinished character of the bourgeois revolution was itself the cause of the next stage in revolutionary process. The most important characteristic of the next revolution was that it would be social and not merely political. It would not only proclaim abstract rights that in fact only a minority could enjoy, but achieve a general emancipation by penetrating to the real life of man—his socio-economic existence. This would be the first revolution to involve the whole society. The cause of the socialist revolution, its determining motive force, was located by Marx in the proletarian movement of protest against capitalist exploitation. He points out, "All previous historical movements were movements of minorities, or in the interest of minorities. The proletarian movement in the self-conscious, independent movement of the immense majority, in the interests of immense majority. The proletariat, the lowest stratum of our present society, cannot stir, cannot raise itself up, without the whole superincumbent strata of official society being exploded into the air." (*232 : 198*).

Thus the radicalism of the revolution depended on the class that was instrumental in causing it. The proletariat alone could represent the interests of society as a whole, a society in which class struggle was so intensified and polarised as to permit its abolition through a social revolution. For Marx, the Paris Commune was the 'political form of social emancipation.

The Proletariat as a Revolutionary Class

It is necessary to remember that Marx emphasized the human causes of revolution. He was at pains to point out that he did not conceive of revolution as a mechanical result of the conflict of economic forces; it was something that had also to be accomplished by human beings. He says, "of all the instruments of production, the greatest productive force is the revolutionary class itself. The organisation of the revolutionary elements as a class presupposes the existence of all the productive forces that could be engendered in the womb of the old society." (*230 : 196*). But the proletariat had to undergo a massive transformation through its own education in the school of class struggle before it could become a fit agent of revolution. In making the revolution, the proletariat will acquire the capacity of undertaking the task of socialist reconstruction.

Marx observes, "Both for the production on a mass scale of this communist consciousness, and for the success of the cause itself, the alteration of men on a mass scale is necessary, an alteration which can only take place in a practical movement, in a revolution; this revolution is necessary, therefore, not only because the ruling class cannot be overthrown in any other way, but also because the class overthrowing it can only in a revolution succeed in ridding itself of all the muck of ages and become fitted to found society anew." (*228 : 87*).

The name that Marx gives to this activity is 'revolutionary praxis.' It embodies through a dialectical unity of theory and practice the subjective and objective causes of revolution. He sums this up in the following words, "In revolutionary activity, the changing of oneself coincides with the changing of circumstances." (*228 : 234*). It implied that the proletariat must become a class 'for itself' by developing class consciousness which is a necessary cause and precondition of a successful social revolution.

Marx on Strategy and Tactics of Revolution

Despite what Karl Popper says, Marx did not believe in revolutionary prophecy. He did not go into detail concerning the exact nature, strategy and tactics of the socialist revolution he thought to be imminent. He did, however, say something about when he felt there might be a revolution, where it could break out, and whether it would involve violence or not. Concerning the possibilities of a successful revolution, Marx adapted his views according to the historical situation in which he found himself. He was very optimistic during the European revolutions of 1848 but his hopes faded gradually thereafter except for a brief revival during the Paris Commune of 1871. In 1846 Marx said, "There can be no talk at the present moment about the inauguration of communism; the bourgeoisie must first take over the rudder." (*232 : 199*). On the eve of the 1848 revolution, he declared in the *Communist Manifesto,* "The bourgeois revolution in Germany will be but the prelude to an immediately following proletarian revolution." (*201 : 162*).

Even in March 1950 after the failure of the revolution. Marx, in his *Address to the Communist League,* still advocated the idea of 'permanent revolution.' After the attainment of the aim of the petty bourgeoisie, it was the task of the working class to make the revolution permanent until all the property-owning classes were deprived of their state power so that the proletariat could eventually use the apparatus of the state for socialist transformation. It is difficult to reconcile this approach with the idea of the gradual development of political systems in accordance with the economic basis of society present in other contemporary writings of Marx.

By 1851 Marx had become convined of the primacy of economic factors in determining the possibilities of revolution. His considered view about revolution now was that only a severe economic crisis caused by a falling rate of capitalist profits in a slump could precipitate it. The effective cause of the revolution has to be located in the economic situation and nowhere else. A new revolution is possible only as a consequence of a worsening trade cycle leading to increasing misery of the proletariat. It is just as certain as this crisis. Marx became so convinced of economic determinism of the revolutionary process at this stage that he was prepared to dissolve the *Communist League* when it appeared to be falling under the control of leaders who believed in attempting a revolution irrespective of the economic situation.

During the next decade, he expected the capitalist crisis to break out that would provoke a socialist revolution. David McLellan says, "Later he took a more long-term view of the economic causes of revolution. In the *Grundrisse* the impression is given that capitalism has a very long way to go before it exhausts its capacities to exploit the enormous possibilities of automated machinery; on the other hand the Drafts of the *Civil War in France* and Marx's remarks on Bakunin indicate that Marx conceived of the possibility of a successful proletarian revolution in countries where the majority of the population were peasants." (*232* : *200*).

International Dimensions of Revolution

This problem was connected with the question of where the revolution would take place first. Marx's materialist view of history would indicate that it was most likely to break out in the most advanced industrial countries like Britain, France or the United States. Yet he realised by 1860 that European revolutions were becoming more dependent on the general world situation. In a letter to Engels in 1859, Marx mentioned capitalist expansion in the colonies, the opening up of California, Australia and the Far East and added, "Revolution is imminent on the Continent and will also immediately assume a socialist character. Can it avoid being crushed in this small corner, because the movement of bourgeois society is in the ascendent over much larger areas of the earth ?" (*232* : *200*).

But Marx also believed that in some undeveloped countries such as Germany a bourgeois revolution could spark off a subsequent socialist revolution. Later in his life, he came to believe that backward Russia might prove the starting point of a new European revolution, initially bourgeois but ultimately proletarian in character. Lenin implemented this Marx's theory of two-stage revolution in his own way in the Russian Revolution of 1917 and Mao did the same in his own characteristic way in bringing about the Chinese Revolution. Marx was certainly well aware of the importance of colonial exploitation for the coming revolution as well as of the role that the peasantry could play in expediting the revolutionary process. About Russia, Marx said a year before his death, "If the Russian revolution becomes the signal for a proletarian revolution in the West, so that both complete each other, then the present Russian system of community ownership of land could serve as the starting point for a communist development." (*232* : *201*).

While Marx generally regarded force as the midwife of revolution, he conceded that socialism could come about as a culmination of a peaceful mass movement in some of the capitalist democracies. In 1872 he spoke of the possibility of a peaceful revolution in America, England and Holland. In 1879 Marx said, "A historical development can only remain "peaceful" so long as it is not opposed by the violence of those who wield power in society at that time. If in England or the United States, for example, the working class were to gain a majority in Parliament or Congress, then it could by legal means set aside the laws and structures that stood in its way." (*232* : *201*).

Marx was opposed to the use of revolutionary terror as it weakened the cause of revolution. He strongly criticised the use of terror by the Jacobins in the French Revolution. Physical force, however, as opposed to terror, was to Marx a perfectly acceptable revolutionary weapon provided that the economic, social and political conditions were such as to make its use successful. It was also Marx's view that a successful revolution in one country could not be stabilized if it remained confined to the borders of a single country. But he was equally convinced that the working class organisation necessary to produce an international revolution could only be achieved by building up revolutionary proletarian parties within existing nations. The outstanding Marxist revolutionaries of the twentieth century have benefited from Marx's analysis of the causes, strategy and tactics of revolution and creatively applied them to make their own revolutions in the specific socio-economic milieu of their countries.

Conclusion

Describing the partial character of political revolution, Marx says: "Political revolution dissolves civil life into its component parts without revolutionising and submitting to criticism of these parts themselves. Its attitude to civil society, to the world of need, to work, private interests, private law is that they are the foundation of its exisence, its own presupposition that needs no further proof." (*231* : *107*).

Comparing the social revolution with political revolution, Marx observes: "Every revolution is social in so far as it destroys the old society. Every revolution is political in so far as it destroys the old power...... A political revolution with a social soul is as rational as a social revolution with a political soul is paraphrastic or nonsensical. Revolution in general—the overthrow of the existing power and dissolution of prèvious relationships—is a political act. Socialism cannot be realised without a revolution. But when its organising activity begins, when its peculiar aims, its soul comes forward, then socialism casts aside its political cloak." (*232* : *204*).

Describing the nature of the communist revolution, Marx points out: "In all revolutions up till now the mode of activity always remained unscathed and it was a question of a different distribution of this activity, a new distribution of labour to other persons, whilst communist revolution is directed against the preceding *mode* of activity, does away with *labour*, and abolishes the rule of all classes with the classes themselves, because it is carried through by the class which no longer counts as a class in society, is not recognised as a class, and is in itself the expression of the dissolution of all classes, nationalities etc., within present society; and both for the production on a mass scale of this communist consciousness and for the success of the cause itself, the alteration of men on a mass scale is necessary, an alteration which can only take place in a political movement, a *revolution*; this revolution is necessary, therefore, not only because the *ruling* class cannot be overthrown in any other way, but also because the class *overthrowing* it can only in a revolution succeed in ridding itself of all the muck of ages and become fitted to found society anew. (*228* : *87*).

According to Marx, the breakdown of the capitalist system is inevitable due to its inherent contradiction between the forces of production and class relations. He says: "The monopoly of capital becomes a fetter upon the mode of production, which has sprung up and flourished along with, and under it. Centralisation of the means of production and socialization of labour at last reach a point where they become incompatible with their capitalist integument. Thus integument is burst asunder. The knell of capitalist private property sounds. The expropriators are expropriated." (*223* : *763*).

Marx was not dogmatic about the strategy of revolution. He oriented the members of the First International towards both possibilities. He said :

"We must declare to the governments : we know that you are the armed power which is directed against the proletariat; we shall proceed against you by peaceful means where possible; and by force of arms if necessary. (*201* : *132*).

In the eleventh thesis on Feurbach, Marx affirmed the need for a synthesis of political philosophy with revolutionary practice. He said :

"The pholosophers have only *interpreted* the world differently, the point is, to *change* it." (*201:158*).

Marxism, therefore, can be summed up as a philosophy of social revolution rooted in the science of political economy.

The demise of Soviet-style socialism has put a question-mark on the significance of Marxism as a critique of capitalism. But classes continue to exist and class struggles in different forms continue to characterize the politics of advanced capitalist countries as well as under-industrialized countries. Class struggles have reappeared in the former socialist countries where capitalism has been restored. Marxism as a critical philosophy of soviet revolution and rooted in the science of political economy has a secure future. Marxism as an ideology of the working class and Marxist parties as the representatives of all exploited classes have not yet exhausted their historical roles in developed, developing and transitional societies.

CHAPTER 32

SOCIALISM AFTER MARX

1. GERMAN SOCIAL DEMOCRACY

After Marx's death, his teaching bifurcated into the evolutionary and revolutionary forms. The evolutionary form in Germany and the Continent on the whole was represented by the Social Democratic Party which lacked the fire and vigour of Marxism. The programme of the Social Democratic Party of Germany was a mild one. As outlined by Hallowell, it meant

(a) universal, direct, and equal suffrage,
(b) representation according to population,
(c) direct legislation by the people through the right of initiative and referendum,
(d) popular militia in the place of standing armies,
(e) popular referenda on the declaration of war,
(f) abolition of the use of public funds for religious purposes,
(g) secularization of schools,
(h) popular election of judges with free legal counsel,
(i) abolition of capital punishment,
(j) free medical attendance,
(k) progressive income taxes,
(l) eight-hour work day,
(m) prohibition of night work and child labour and the establishment of a system of social insurance.

This mild programme became even milder after 1925.

Karl Kautsky (1854-1938) was a principal spokesman of the Social Democratic Party after World War I. He ranged himself on the other side of Lenin and the Russian revolution. He upheld Marxist teachings as being sound in principle. He believed that revolution was the ultimate means for realizing the socialist goal, but thought that the end could be realized with minimum violence. In the words of Hallowell, he looked with favour upon the growth of the trade union movement, the extension of co-operatives, participation in parliament, and legislation designed to ameliorate the worker's condition. These reforms, he said, were not socialism itself, although they prepared the way for it.

The *Revisionists* of this period were in favour of a doctrine of gradualness and socialism "by evolution". Kautsky claimed that he was not a Revisionist. This was true only in theory. In practice he was very near to being one. He supported democracy and democratic methods and seemed to argue that democracy was more important than socialism. He opposed both rightist and leftist deviations. According to Hallowell, he read Marx to mean the controlling of government by the proletariat through universal suffrage. He opposed Bolshevism as being a minority government, representing rule by force. In his book *The Proletarian Revolution and Kautsky, the Renegade.* Lenin attacks Kautsky mercilessly. Kautsky laid the foundation for the activities of the Social Democratic Party. The Communists were opposed to this party all through the days of the Weimar Republic. It was a weak-kneed party and it is on the backs of such weak parties that Hitler and Nazism rose to power. The same weakness in Italy accounted for the rise of Mussolini and the fascist party.

2. SYNDICALISM

Syndicalism is essentially a French school of thought and is the offspring of the French labour movement. Its important intellectual leader was Georges Sorel (1847-1922). It was popularized by the French Confederation Generale du Travail (C. G. T.), the General Federation of Labour. It repudiates Marx's political programme, but retains his revolutionary doctrine of violence. In this respect, it is a child of anarchism and Marxism. The word 'syndicalism' is derived from the French word *syndicat* which means trade union. In some respects, it is a reaction to the French revolutionary ideals of "liberty, equality, and fraternity." The working man in France found that the great Revolution had brought him little liberty of action. The commercial and manufacturing classes took control of the reins of government and denied to the working classes the usual economic and political devices for bettering their lot. Even the legitimate trade union weapons were not allowed to them. The French law hampered the activities of trade unions. This meant that when the French working man became strong he dissolved both trade unionism and political socialism and looked for his salvation in more radical directions, such as unrelenting class war, general strike, sabotage, and "go slow" methods. His aim was to weld the working classes of the world together and wean them away from national patriotism.

Definitions of Syndicalism. C. E. M. Joad writes: "Syndicalism may be defined as that form of social theory which regards the Trade Union Organizations as at once the foundation of the new society and the instrument whereby it is to be brought into being." F. W. Coker says: "Syndicalism, loosely defined, holds that the workers alone must control the conditions under which they work and live; the social changes they need can be achieved only by their own efforts, by direct action in their own associations, and through means suited to their peculiar needs" (*93 : 229*). According to Laidler, syndicalism places "positive emphasis on the trade and industrial union movement as the basis of the new industrial structure, on the producer rather than the consumer as the controlling factor in industry, and on the general strike and other forms of 'direct action' as the means of social transformation, with its negative emphasis on the need for abolishing the political state and on the impotency of political action as a means of working class emancipation." G. E. Hoover, writing in the *Twentieth*

Century Political Thought, says, "As now employed, (syndicalism) means the theories and programmes of those revolutionists who would utilize the economic power of industrial unions to destroy capitalism and organize a socialist society."

Teachings of Syndicalism. From the above definitions, the teachings of syndicalism can be clearly delineated.

(1) Syndicalism is unalterably opposed to the State and looks upon it as a bourgeois and middle class institution. Whatever its form may be, the State is an instrument of capitalist exploitation. All states are instruments of class rule. Thus workers cannot succeed unless they destroy the power of the State. Reforms and concessions conceded by the State are mere palliatives. They hide from the worker the real facts of inequality and of class distinction. Therefore, even the democratic State cannot bring about harmony, and state power needs to be broken.

Service of the State as government workers, makes men bureaucratic and unsympathetic to the needs and aspirations of the workers. Furthermore, State action means dead uniformity and routine, and there is no place for imagination. No attention is paid to local needs or for the bringing out of individual enterprise.

(2) The syndicalist regards trade unions organized on a functional basis as the cornerstone of future society. A system of producers' societies is to take the place of the State. Under the present system the **vote, exercised once in five years or so at the time of the general election,** is of no value. Under syndicalism, it is claimed that the worker will take a personal interest in his work and that both the quantity and quality of goods produced will improve. The ideal of the syndicalist is 'free work in free society'. His belief is that when the workshop is free, society would be free.

(3) As pointed out by Hallowell, all of this means that class struggle is given the central, if not exclusive, importance. Syndicalism seeks to promote class solidarity. There is to be no collaboration with other political parties, and labour is to have no country of its own. In the words of Hallowell, syndicalism regards itself as a trade union reading of the Marxian economic doctrine and the class war.

Methods of Syndicalism. Syndicalists differ from Marxists in believing that the time is not far off when the proletariat would rise in revolt against the possessing classes. Marx, they believe, was unduly optimistic in believing that employers would fight the workers and thereby bring about their own self-destruction. What they would do is to make compromises and bargains. Therefore, the only way to deal with them is to carry on a perpetual offence against them through strikes, sabotage, destruction of machinery, boycott, label, and 'go slow' methods.

Syndicalists are ardent believers in direct action. They are distrustful of political methods. Direct action, it is claimed, is the only means of educating the worker and of preparing him for the final struggle. In this struggle there is no place for intermediaries. The methods pursued may be violent, but not always so. The general strike is the chief weapon. It is not to be confused with ordinary strikes, political strikes or sympathetic strikes. It comes about after the workers have been well-trained in a series of particular strikes. The general strike is a final and mighty weapon which would paralyse the state and make the wage-earners the masters of society.

Syndicalists are unscrupulous in the methods they advocate for the realization of their ends. They advocate in particular the doing of bad work, the breaking of machinery, spoiling work and 'Ca canny' methods which consist in sleeping over one's job or doing it with such minuteness as to waste time.

The boycott of goods produced by non-union labour and the placing of the union label produced by the syndicates themselves are some of the other methods advocated by the syndicalists. All of this is in preparation for the general strike which may fail today, but 'today's failure is a preparation for tomorrow's success" (*119* : *292*).

The Structure of Society under Syndicalism. The syndicalist plan of action is direct, vigorous, and well-defined. But the state of society under it is extremely nebulous. Syndicalism is mainly a creed of opposition. It is negative. As one writer puts it: "It offers primarily a policy of revolution and not of administration." Under syndicalism, the syndicate is to be the basis of industrial organization. Workers assume control of production and private capital is to be replaced by collective capital. National services like highways, railways and post offices are to be placed in the hands of the National Federation of Workers. Prisons and courts are to be abolished, and punishment is to take the form of social boycott.

In short, the syndicalist aims at a stateless society. This implies that the means of production would be owned by society and syndicates would regulate and control production.

Syndicalism and Socialism. While most socialists want to retain the State and make the maximum use of it, the syndicalists want to abolish it altogether. Socialism generally takes into account the welfare of both producers and consumers. Syndicalism, on the other hand, is only interested in promoting the interest of the producers. In this respect it is an antithesis of socialism. Furthermore, socialism generally believes in constitutional methods whereas syndicalism is a creed of violence, revolution, and direct action.

Criticism of Syndicalism. Syndicalism made little headway outside France and Italy because of its intrinsic weakness. It overstates its tactics and is deliberately vague in its objectives. It is "too doctrinaire, too extreme and too logical" to appeal to those who believe in natural compromises in a world of practical politics. It antagonizes the consumers by paying too much attention "to the rights and responsibilities of producers and too little to those of consumers" (*119* : *310*). General strike is only a myth. It is nothing more than "organized anarchy". Once direct action is resorted to, nobody knows where it will end. It is, therefore, wise to adhere to well-tried constitutional methods. Violence is always irksome to the saner elements in the population. Hallowell writes, "The kinship between

Syndicalism and Fascism is a close one and it is no accident that Mussolini was an avid reader of the works of Sorel."

3. FABIAN SOCIALISM

Fabianism. It is the product of British intellectuals and differs sharply from Marxism in that its methods are flexible and in that it believes in attaining socialism by the slow process of persuasion.

The word 'Fabianism' is derived from the name of the Roman general, Fabius Cunctator, who waited patiently for the opportunity of striking hard at his opponent, Hannibal, when the opportune time came for the attack. H. G. Wells, himself a Fabian, has remarked that Fabius never struck hard.

The Fabian society saw the light of day on January 4, 1884 and adopted the following as its convenient motto : "For the right moment you must wait, as Fabius did, most patiently, when warring against Hannibal, though many censured his delays; but when the time comes you must strike hard, as Fabious did, or your waiting will be in vain and fruitless" (*155 : 32*).

The basis of Fabianism was hammered out in 1887 and was restated in 1919 with slight modifications. The latter statement reads as follows :

"It therefore aims at the reorganization of society by emancipation of land and industrial capital from individual ownership, and the vesting of them in the community for the general benefit. In this way only can the natural and acquired advantages of the country be equitably shared by the whole people.

The society accordingly works for the extinction of private property in land, with equitable consideration of established expectations, and the provision as to tenure of the home and the homestead, for the transfer to the community, by constitutional methods, of all such industries as can be conducted socially; and for the establishment, as the governing consideration, in the regulation of production, distribution and service, of the common good instead of private profit" (*155 : 239*).

This means, says Laidler, (*120 : 184*) that Fabianism (1) regards the transition from capitalism to socialism as a gradual process; (2) it looks forward to the socialization of industry by the peaceful economic and political agencies already at hand; (3) it sees in the middle class a group that can be utilized in developing the technique of administration on behalf of the new social order; and (4) it feels that an important step in the attainment of socialism is the rousing of the social conscience of the community in favour of the socialist ideal.

Unlike syndicalism, Fabianism believes in attaining its end through parliamentary government. It advocates a peaceful revolution. Land, industry, and financial institutions are to pass from private ownership to the State by peaceful methods. In the words of Hallowell, Fabian Socialism aims "at the reorganization of society by the emancipation of land and industrial capital from individual and class ownership and the vesting of them in the community for the general benefit". There is to be no private property in land, and no rent. Industrial capital is to be transferred to society as conveniently as it can utilize it.

The chief exponents of this type of socialism have been Sidney and Beatrice Webb, Graham Wallas, Annie Besant, E. R. Pease, H. G. Wells, G. B. Shaw, and G. D. H. Cole. Their chief method of approach has been through the publication of numerous pamphlets and essays addressed to the intelligence and social conscience of people The Fabian essays were edited by G. B. Shaw and delivered as lectures in 1888. Sidney Webb, writes Hallowell, envisaged the emergence of a socialist society as the result of democratic, gradual, peaceful, and constitutional means. A significant phrase which we owe to the Fabians is "the inevitability of socialism".

Difference between Marxism and Fabianism. Whereas Marxism rests largely on the labour theory and class struggle, Fabianism rests on the extension of the theory of rent and the growth of the social conscience of the nation. Marxism is revolutionary, whereas Fabianism is evolutionary.

Defections in Fabian ranks. Fabians have never been large in numbers. Fabianism has been confined mostly to the intellectuals. Even at the height of its popularity in 1943, it had only 3,600 members. During the numerous controversies of the twenties several younger intellectuals left the movement and joined guild socialism. The Webbs turned their sympathies towards the Russian experiment and wrote a monumental work called 'Soviet Communism—a New Civilization'. Cole restated Fabianism in 1942 as follows :

"We believe there is need, somewhere in the socialist movement, for a body which is entirely free to think out and to give publicity to new ideas, even when they run counter to socialist orthodoxies inherited from the past. Socialism is not a set of fixed dogmas, always ready to be applied irrespective of time and space." Cole goes on to say, "The Fabian society is organized for thought and discussion and not for electoral action which it leaves to other bodies......Fabians should specialize in their chosen task of writing and research. But now that no one is doing this wider job (the socialist propaganda within the party) Fabian tract-making and research.. ....are unable to make their needed impact on the party as a whole.... The Fabians will have to go out and preach socialism far and wide, if no one else will." (*95 : 164*).

Applicability of Fabianism to India. Because of India's attachment to non-violence, Fabianism, together with the programme of the British Labour party, to which it gave rise, is more in keeping with Indian temperament and needs than any other form of socialism. We want the transition from the capitalistic to the socialistic society to be effected by peaceful methods. As we gain in knowledge, experience and character, the public sector will more and more replace the private sector, and all means of production will be owned by the community. Violence and social justice have nothing in common.

The British Labour Party. Starting from very humble beginnings, it has reached great heights within the last fifty years, holding office four times in 1924, 1929-31, 1945-51 and 1964-70. During the first two periods, not having an absolute majority, it had to depend on the mercy and goodwill of the other parties. But during 1945-51 and 1964-70, it was not only in office, but also in power and brought about a great many changes in the socialistic direction as well as in loosening the knots of British imperialism and in transforming it into a democratic commonwealth.

From the beginning the strength of the Labour Party has been in its Trade Unions and in the moderate policy which it has followed. As early as 1889, a Scottish Labour Party was founded by Keir Hardie, a Scottish coal-miner. He founded with others in 1893 an Independent Labour Party, one of whose early members was Mr. Ramsay Macdonald who became the first Labour Prime Minister in 1924. He was again Prime Minister during 1929-31, but after that he deserted the Labour Party.

The Parliamentary Committee of the Trade Union Conference was named the British Labour Party in 1906. It is a federation of labour groups rather than a party of individuals. It is after 1906 that the British Labour Party had a real start. In that year it forced through the Trades Disputes Act in Parliament. This Act extended to the working classes the right to picket and ruled out collective fines for damages. Because of its minority position, the Labour group in Parliament could not push through other reforms. But it gave its support to the Liberal Party in its advocacy of the Irish Home Rule Bill, the Suffrage Bill, and the Welsh Disestablishment Bills.

Prior to World War I, though looking in the direction of socialism, the Labour Party did not definitely commit itself to the socialist position. In 1918 it adopted the programme of *Labour and the New Social Order* based on four fundamental points:

(1) The universal enforcement of a national minimum.
(2) The democratic control of industry.
(3) Revolution in National Finance.
(4) Surplus wealth for the common good.

In 1929 the party issued another manifesto known as *Labour and the Nation* which committed the party to the socialization of coal, land, transport, and life insurance as well as to the nationalization of the Bank of England. In 1929 the party won 288 seats, but that was 20 less than a majority. Therefore, it had to depend on the Liberal Party to keep itself in office for two years. Because of its minority position, it could not introduce much legislation of a socialistic character.

After Macdonald and Snowden crossed the floor to the Conservative Party, there was nothing for Labour to do except to form His Majesty's Opposition. In the early years of World War II, in 1940, the party issued its programme known as *Labour, the War and Peace*. In the same year it entered into a coalition with Churchill and remained in office as a junior partner until Germany was destroyed. In the general election of July 1945, contrary to the expectations of everyone, Labour was elected by a comfortable majority and was able to push through some of its programmes.

In the 1942 Congress the party had urged:

"The socialization of the basic industries and services of the country, and the planning of production for community consumption as the only lasting foundation for a just prosperous economic order in which political democracy and personal liberty can be combined with a reasonable standard for all citizens".

The accomplishments of the Labour Party after it came into power in 1945 under Clement Attlee are the nationalization of the coal and steel industries, the nationalization of the Bank of England, of civil aviation, power-transmission, telecommunication, railways and road transport, London transport, waterways and gas. Subsidies also have been given for bread and milk. Progress has been made with housing schemes and provision for old-age pensions. Twenty per cent of the national economy has been brought under public control. Provision of National Health Service is one of the greatest accomplishments of the Labour Party.

It was during the days of Labour acsendancy that India, Pakistan, Burma, and Ceylon gained their independence.

For some time when Labour went out of office there arose an acute controversy between the Rightists and Leftists within the party. The latter who formed the minority, were led by Mr. Aneurin Bevan until his death. The acknowledged leader of the Labour Party then was Mr. Hugh Gaitskell. The Conservatives who succeeded tried to undo some of the work of Labour. Steel was de-nationalized but the Labour Government renationalised it after coming to power in 1964.

British Labour recognizes both manual and brain workers. It conceives reconstruction in socialist terms on the basis of democracy and justice. It rejects dictatorship of both Right and Left. Members of the party call their policy and programme "revolution by consent". There is a conflict between "liberalism" and "totalitarianism". It is believed by some that a number of high-handed steps may have to be taken in order to attain socialism.

4. GUILD SOCIALISM

Guild Socialism. This has been a fashion in radical thought for a while in England. Rockow describes it as "the intellectual child of English Fabianism and French Syndicalism". (*157 : 150*). Hallowell, who is more hard on it, writes : "Guild socialism was and remains a kind of anaemic version of French syndicalism". In origin it is a purely English theory. Some describe it as a halfway house between syndicalism and collectivism. It does not agree with syndicalism in wanting to abolish the State by direct action. Nor does it want the State to control all of industry, as does collectivism. It adopts a middle course. It wants to establish guilds of producers and guilds of consumers within the framework of the State. A guild is defined as "a self-governing association of mutually dependent people organized for a responsible discharge of a particular function of society".

The chief advocates of guild socialism are A. J. Penty, who was practically its founder, A. R. Orage, the editor of the *New Age,* S. G. Hobson, the veteran of the movement, and G.D.H. Cole, its most effective and prolific thinker and popularizer.

Influences which have brought about Guild Socialism are :

(1) The socialist attack on the wage system and the profit-making of the capitalist.

(2) The influence of such literary men as John Ruskin, Thomas Carlyle, and William Morris, all of whom waged a campaign against the monotony of mass production.

(3) The French syndicalist movement with its bias against the State.

(4) The influence of the famous Churchman, Figgis, who exploded the myth of state sovereignty and described political authority as "an association, not a lordship".

(5) Functionalism, according to which property should be functional and its control should pass out of the hands of functionless owners to those of workers.

Progress of Guild Socialism. Its two main items are (i) the abolition of the wage system and (ii) "the establishment of self-government in industry through a system of national guilds working in conjunction with the democratic organizations in the community" (*41* : *75*).

The guildsmen support the Marxian theme that the wage system should be abolished. It is bad morally, psychologically, economically, and aesthetically. It produces a slave mentality and curbs the creative instinct of the labourer. A person, says the guildsman, should be paid as a human being, and not as a mere contributor of so much labour power. Society should pay him when employed as well as when unemployed, in health as well as in sickness. Besides, the organization of production is to be controlled in conjunction with workers.

Joad calls guild socialism functional democracy. Industry is to be controlled by both brain and manual workers. Power and responsibility in society are to be proportionate to the functions performed.

Functional Representation. It is the key phrase of guild socialism. It is argued that no one person can represent another. Guildsmen believe that "although a man cannot represent his neighbour, he can represent a group of purposes which his neighbours have in common". This is possible through 'functional representation'. Such representation is to be on a local as well as a national basis. National affairs such as taxation, defence, and education would be represented by a national body, while local bodies would look after such matters as gas, electricity, and the police force.

Elected factory committees would decide questions of wages, hours of work, and amount of output. Consumers' councils in conjunction with factory committees would decide questions of costs, prices, and the extent of production.

Democracy, says the guildsman, is to come first in the economic field and is to be extended to the political field later on. Today it seems to be the other way round. According to guild socialism, modern industrial conditions are so chaotic and exploitative that unless they are first remedied, no change is possible in other departments of social life.

Under guild socialism, further, there would be not only industrial guilds but also consumers' guilds and civic guilds, as well as guilds for the various arts and professions. All these would be organized locally, regionally, and nationally.

The State is to be replaced by the commune. It is to have limited functions. Tools of production are to be handed over to the guilds as trustees of the State.

Methods of Guild Socialism. Unlike syndicalism, guild socialism believes in evolutionary methods. At the same time, however, it has limited faith in parliamentary action. It wants to make much use of the Trade Unions. "The trade unions of today will become the guilds of tomorrow." They have to wrest power little by little from the hands of the possessing classes. In this respect they differ from syndicalism which resorts to direct action and general strike.

Criticism. (1) Guild socialism idealizes and idolizes the guild system of the Middle Ages. (2) Functionalism would mean the atomization of society. (3) Guild socialism is impractical since it is not possible to draw a sharp line between producers and consumers. Even if they are clearly demarcated, the former are likely to dominate the latter. (4) An economic parliament cannot easily take the phase of a political parliament or function side by side with it. At best it can only serve as an advisory council.

Merits. In spite of the above weaknesses, it must be said that guild socialism has rendered considerable service by calling pointed attention to the importance of democracy in industry; to the dangers of bureaucratic control; to the desirability of producers' participation in the management of the workshop; and to the value of functionalism in both politics and industry.

5. SOCIALISM IN INDIA

The Socialistic Pattern of Society or the Socialist Structure for India

Ever since Jawaharlal Nehru returned from China in 1954, he had been full of enthusiasm for a socialistic society in India. The Avadi session of the Indian National Congress held early in 1955 adopted the realization of such a society as a goal for India. The 1956 session held in Amritsar has substituted the expression 'the Socialist Structure'. This change probably meant that the pattern which was lying like a blueprint on the table hitherto had begun to stand up on its feet like a structure. The term 'socialistic society' or 'socialist structure' is deliberately vague, in view of the fact that neither in theory nor in practice does socialism mean the same thing to all people. Thus the socialism of the British Labour Party is, in many ways, different from Continental Socialism; and both in turn differ from Russian and Chinese Communism. Even in India itself, socialists are not all agreed as to what their creed means. Their party is probably more divided within itself than any other party in the country.

In addressing the National Development Council some time ago, Nehru said that what he had in mind about "Future India" was "definitely and absolutely a socialistic picture of society". He went on to say that he had no intention of eliminating private enterprise, but averred at the same time the acquisitive instinct was not only out of date, but was also immoral. The new society, according to him, is to be based on equality of opportunity, and, strangely enough, this is practised to a very large extent by a capitalistic society such as the American. Nehru further says that the Constitution of India lays down that the goal of the Indian people is the Welfare State in which the individual shall live for the community, and the community for the individual. In practical terms, a socialist society, according to Nehru, means "the right to live; the right to work for a living; and the right to receive what one has earned".

Dr. John Matthai, the well-known Indian economist, scholar, and man of affairs, says that the two ideas central to socialist society are freedom and equality. Declining to describe socialism as a creed or as a type of organization, Matthai urges that it is "a way of life and an attitude to society which aims at the widest practicable diffusion of social justice by methods which may be regarded as appropriate to a free.....democratic community". The instruments by which this socialist society is to be realized are the recognition of (1) the sacredness of individual human personality; (2) the principle of love; (3) the idea of fellowship.

Surprisingly enough, Dr. Matthai does not think that nationalization or the "State taking over the means of production" is essential to socialism, because, to quote his own words, "many of the objectives which those who ask for nationalization have in mind could be achieved by measures other than nationalization by legislation, by executive order, and by fiscal measures". It is not likely that Nehru and many others, including the present writer, would agree with this point of view. But it is unlikely that they will differ from him sharply when he goes on to say "I do not think it is an essential part of Socialism that individual enterprise and initiative should be controlled or suppressed".

Dr. Matthai would apparently support the present bifurcation of Indian economy into the public and private sectors, although he has a fear that if care is not taken, in the name of an economic democracy, severe limitations may come to be placed upon the freedom of the individual citizen. He wants that a proper balance should be kept between the small producer and the large producer so that neither may be sacrificed on behalf of the other. Another fear which he entertains is that the financial resources of the country, not being able to cope with the demands made by the First and Second Five Year Plans and the plans to come, may lead to a period of rise in prices and "a definite inflationary trend" That this is not a mere imaginary fear can be seen by opening one's eyes to the situation around oneself.

In the socialistic society there is to be a minimum reward for work, adequate leisure for everybody, and care of the old and infirm. As regards the principle of equality, Dr. Matthai stressed "equality in justice, equality before the law, equality in opportunities of growth and development, education, enterprise, and choice of occupation". He raises the question of "equality in respect of income and wealth", but does not seem to be in favour of it at the present stage of development in India. On the question of reform of land tenures too he declines to express a firm opinion. He lays special stress on the fair treatment to be accorded in a free society to women and children; on such voluntary service as is rendered by the Social Service Board, the Bharat Sevak Samaj, and the Community Projects; on fellowship in study; and on religious *ashrams,* and international fellowship.

While this is an admirable picture of the socialist society from a more or less conservative and religious point of view, the radicals would want the State to go much farther. Mr. U. N. Dhebar, a former President of the Congress, has addressed himself to the task of spelling out the meaning of the socialistic society. On the economic side, he says that it means at least three things, viz., (1) the national ownership or national control of certain basic industries; (2) an equitable distribution of wealth; and (3) equality of opportunity. On the social side, we may add on our part that a socialistic society should mean a casteless and classless society, a society from which all present-day artificial distinctions between man and man are eliminated. And it is our conviction that neither economic nor social changes of a far-reaching character are really possible unless there be a wholesale change in human motives and desires and in national character.

Turning to the economic side first, while 'nationalization' is an attractive term to many, it is not a mere magic wand by the waving of which a new society can be created overnight. A socialistic society is already on its way in India through its several multi-purpose river valley schemes, including irrigation works, reclamation activities, and fertilizer plants, through the development of inland fisheries, the improvement of the cattle of the country, the nationalization of railways, aeroplane assemblage and civil aviation, nationalization of life insurance, attempts at the abolition of landlordism, the setting up of machine tool shops, and government subsidies given to small-scale and cottage industries. The Second Five-Year Plan contemplated a much larger outlay on the public sector (Rs. 4,800 crores) than on the private sector (between Rs. 1,500 and 1,700 crores). The third Plan is even more ambitious, although it may have to be modified because of the war forced upon us by China, which is bound to consume a great deal of our resources. Much greater attention than in the past is to be paid to education in all its phases, to public health, housing and social welfare, as well as to employment.

Prof. John Saunders writes that the socialistic pattern of society calls for justice (in the sense of a more equitable distribution), social security, and a fuller life. According to him priority is to be given to land reform, debt relief, and scientific farming. Food production is to be increased by double cropping, irrigation, manuring, etc. It is strange that land revenue in socialistic India amounts to a smaller percentage of government funds than was the case in India under Britain. Landlords are making use of the parliamentary machinery for keeping down land revenue.

John Strachey rightly argues that in a heavily populated country with limited cultivable land as India, tractors, combine-harvesters and other large-scale agricultural implements cannot increase production to any remarkable extent. What we need is scientific farming with its emphasis on improved seeds, fertilizers, rotation of crops, intensive cultivation and the like, and not mammoth agricultural machinery.

Next to land reform and related subjects, Saunders places full employment and the raising of living standards as the immediate goals to be reached. He deplores the fact that among agricultural labourers the number of idle days ranges between 82 and 115 days a year. Side by side with unemployment is the mounting evil of over-population. While birth-rate in several advanced countries is either stationary or receding, it shows no sign of falling in India, where new births account for 2 p.c. increase to the population of the country every year. Death-rate, on the other hand, is falling.

Vinoba Bhave seeks to bring about a new order of society through voluntary methods. With the help of a few going on foot from place to place, he has been able to secure more than four million and a half acres of land for distribution among the poor. In spite of it the lot of the poor does not seem to be appreciably different. It is Bhave's conviction that before a community project is started in any place, the land should first be redistributed. For ourselves we believe that Bhave's movement has a beautiful symbolic meaning, but so far it has not gone very far in alleviating rural poverty. It is an appeal to man's heart and conscience.

The *Sarvodaya Movement* concentrates attention on the 550,000 villages of India. It looks askance at the great industrial plants and irrigation works sponsored by the Government of India. Its ideal is the revitalization of village life. It advocates aproducer-and consumer-centred economy whose first object is the earning of foreign exchange and dollar assets. The existing village tanks should be renovated and deepened and fed by small feeder tanks in the neighbourhood. There should be canals and cross-canals all over the country. States should be reorganized along riverine valleys, centring around economic factors. There should be small generating stations for hydro-electric schemes. At the higher levels of the rivers industries are to be concentrated, and at the lower levels, cultivation. River transportation is to be so enormously expanded as to care for internal trade and commerce as well as to provide employment for millions of people. Roads are to be built primarily to meet the needs of the villager and his bullock-cart. Large-scale industries should not be left in private hands. Coal and electricity should be made easily available to the villager. The handloom and hand spinning, oilpressing and other hand industries are much stressed by the Sarvodaya Movement.

India's contribution to world economy is said to be her villages. Apropos of it, Mahatma Gandhi says, "If the village perishes, India will perish too. It will be no more India. Her mission to the world will be lost."

On the organizational side, the community projects of India, 55 in number, inaugurated on October 2, 1952, are said to fall in line with the socialistic pattern of society. They are described as a plan of the people, by the people and for the people. It is the hope of the sponsors that they will become pilot projects throughout the country. About 64 p.c. of the expenditure on these projects is said to come from the people in the form of cash, kind or voluntary labour. What a contrast to forced labour which is said to prevail in some parts of Russia, and certainly in China. Each project is divided into 3 blocks and each block covers 100 villages. At the village level there is village level worker who is assisted by a stockman. For each block there is a Block Project Officer. The District Collector serves as Deputy Development Commissioner. All of this is in strange contrast to the administrative set-up under British days. It is estimated that at the end of the Second Plan period, 60 p.c. of the villages in the country had been covered by the scheme.

The Welfare State. It is interesting to note that the welfare state ideal with which India inaugurated her Constitution in 1950 has become gradually blended with the conception of the socialistic society of today, although it is clear that a welfare state need not necessarily be socialistic. In the Ajmer session of the All-India Congress Committee held on 23rd July, 1954, a resolution was passed to the effect "The objective of the Congress is the establishment of a co-operative commonwealth and a welfare state." Welfare since has been interpreted mostly in economic terms.

Dr. Abraham (quoted by Professor S. Ghosh) defines welfare state as "a community where state power is deliberately used to modify the normal play of economic forces [illegible] a more equal distribution of income for every citizen, a basic minimum real income irrespective of the market value of his work and of his property." T. W. Kent (also quoted by Prof. Ghosh) says that "it is a state that provides for its citizens a wide range of social services. The primary purpose is to give the citizen security. The State undertakes to help him if he loses his ordinary source of income."

According to Ghosh, economic justice, security against unemployment, old age, etc., and freedom for the individual are the three pillars of the welfare state. Welfare is to be conceived not only in material terms, but also in terms of human freedom and progress. The Ajmer resolution, referred to above, defines welfare state in terms of the elimination of unemployment, greater production, and equitable distribution.

A welfare state, however conceived, must include many social services such as education, old age pensions, unemployment pay, and public assistance. Even though the U. S. Government renders many of these services, the term 'welfare state' is anathema in that country since it is regarded as a next door neighbour to the socialistic state.

A grave danger which besets the welfare state everywhere is that it may easily transform itself into a totalitarian state. Ghosh is right in thinking that material good has meaning only as a means to the moral freedom of man. "If the welfare state or the socialistic pattern of society is to be properly realized in India, it should be realized non-violently and democratically. Democratic and welfare ideals must be harmonized. According to some writers, planning and democracy cannot go together.

Planning anywhere is in danger of becoming bureaucratic. If it is to be effective, it must be total. If the present day linguistic rivalries are overdone, the likelihood is that planning will be partial and defective, and will defeat itself. Planning in order to be effective must be free from too much centralism and party dictatorship and must be continuous. Writing on the last point, Barbara Wooton says: "If the existence of political parties does mean the right to change our mind every six months then I am afraid it is incompatible with long-term planning". As things stand at present, Prof. John Saunders opines that India's greatest danger is not economic dictatorship but futile democracy.

An equally imminent danger is the apathy of the people. Unless people have a zeal and passion for a socialistic society and are willing to work for it with honesty and integrity, it is impossible to get the full benefit of planning.

Summing up the issue in all its phases, Prof. Ghosh wisely writes: "We should plan for plenty but not at the cost of freedom; we should execute our plan not through the coercive power of the state or the government-appointed officers but through the active and enthusiastic participation of the people in the plan; we should have political parties not to suppress other parties outside or its own members inside, but to educate the people about matters of public importance and enthuse them to participate in the actual execution of public policies; we should have a state which is not a monolithic structure, but one which is a co-ordinated network of small democracies in which the people can directly and actively participate, not so much to help the (abstract) state but to train themselves as sovereign citizens"[1].

The Ideologies of Socialism and Communism. Socialism and Communism are by no means identical concepts. Marx describes socialism as the first or lower phase of the communist society. It is a half-way house to Communism.

The main differences between Socialism and Communism are: (a) While, according to Socialism, there is to be a social ownership of producers' goods, according to Communism there is to be in addition social ownership of some or all forms of consumers' goods as well. (b) Under Socialism wages are reckoned according to services rendered or socially useful labour performed; whereas under Communism reward would be according to individual needs, the motto of Communism being 'from each according to his ability and to each according to his needs'. (c) Socialism believes in attaining its goal by evolutionary or constitutional methods. Communism, on the other hand, pins its faith on revolution, its teaching being that revolution is a part of evolution, comparable to the biological jumps in the lower world. (d) While Socialism aims at preservation of the State and the utilization of it in gaining social needs, Communism believes in the gradual 'withering away' of the State. (e) Communism in theory at least believes that world revolution and world Communism are necessary for

1. *Indian Journal of Political Science,* Oct-Dec. 1954, p. 338.

its successful working anywhere, while Socialism for its most part is satisfied with a nationalist programme.

6. LASKI AS A DEMOCRATIC SOCIALIST

During the transitional period, Laski as a Democratic Socialist realized that the pluralistic theory of the state was not very satisfactory as the doctrinal basis of a radical philosophy of political reorganisation. His intellectual loyalty to the pluralistic ideal still continued but the institutional pattern that he unfolded in "A Grammar of Politics" was far more monistic than, perhaps, he himself realized (*102 : 167*). The impress of collectivitistic ideas on Laski's political thought at this stage is obvious. His opposition to syndicalist and guild socialist proposals of a decentralized state and his rejection of the Webbian bi-parliamentarism clearly reveal his drift towards a unitary theory of the State. But his collectivism is different and much less rigorous than the collectivism envisaged by the Marxist political theory (*102 : 167-68*). It appears that the under-currents of pluralism and individualism soften the monistic edges of his collectivistic state.

Pragmatic Basis of His Political Theory

There is no doubt that the political grammar of Laski is a brilliant attempt to restate the principles of political science in pragmatic terms. This is one of the very few books of Laski which have a sure future. "Despite its great length", says W. Y. Elliott, "and despite a tendency to treat subjective wishes and opinions as if they were objective facts, it may well be the most important contribution that has been made to recent political theory. To this distinction it has several claims of a unique order, the chief being that it is the first sustained attempt on the part of the accepted leader of contemporary political pluralism to state an adequate basis for political reconstruction. Its claim may rest also upon one fact that it is the most ambitious survey of the essential problems of politics yet undertaken by any modern writer of English—and this in spite of the confessed omission of the whole bearing of the agrarian problem. Within the scope of a single volume, Laski has managed to get in not only a treatise upon political ethics but a very richly suggestive outline of the political and economic institutions which he holds to be the best means of realising an ethical world order, as well as of realising the "new state" that will extend the area of freedom in industrial society" (*102 : 166-67*).

Ethical Foundations of a New Political Order

The aim of Laski in his Political Grammar is to suggest the ethical foundations of a new political order. The great question in political science, as Lord Acton said, is to discover not what governments prescribe but what they ought to prescribe as no prescription can be valid against the conscience of mankind. He has made an earnest effort to answer Lord Acton's ethical question but the ethical motive in his political inquiry has introduced an essentially utopian element in his political thought. Where this utopian element is singularly absent, Laski appears as a conservative defender of existing institutions with only minor proposals of structural or functional reform. He appears to be a progressive philosopher because of his vague socialistic aspirations interspersed in his writings during this period. But he is practically a conservative who is afraid of the revolutionary social effort involved in the realization of those socialistic ideals.

A Revision of Marxism

In his treatise on "Communism", which was first published in 1927; Laski has produced a detailed analysis of the Marxist political philosophy. But it is as an opponent and not as a friend that he has voluteered to discuss it. "Communism", says Laski, "has made its way by its idealism and not its realism, by its spiritual promise, not its materialistic prospect. It is a creed in which there is intellectual error, moral blindness, social perversity. Religions make their way despite these things. Mankind in history has been amazingly responsive to any creed which builds its temple upon spiritual heights. The answer to the new faith is not the persecution of those who worship in its sanctuary, but the proof that those who do not share its convictions can scan a horizon not less splendid in the prospect it envisions nor less compelling in the allegiance it invokes." (*123 : 250*).

Marxism as a Social Science or Religion

It is difficult to agree with Laski who attributes the success of Communism to its "perverse idealism". Marxism has nothing to do with 'idealism', religious or philosophical. It succeeded bacause it bases its programme of action on a scientific understanding of historical facts and processes. It is neither a dogma nor a faith. It is historical science developing continuously through social experience of the masses, and an intellectual discipline based on scholarly researches in sociology and economics. Communism has not made its way, as Laski thinks, by its so-called 'idealism' or 'spiritual promise'. An objective analysis would show that it has grown as a mass movement by its sober realism and an essentially materialistic prospect of a rising standard of living for the peoples of all countries. Laski's alternative at this stage to Marxian socialism which is both scientific and materialist, is a vague sort of utopian socialism or a kind of cooperative capitalism. It is his own utopian socialism which constructs its doctrinal edifice on the foundations of idealistic and spiritual promises which may not work successfully in face of hard political realities.

The General Will and the Common Good in a Class-ridden Society

In a class-ridden society, the functioning of the State tends to preserve and promote the sectional interests of the dominant class or classes. Laski is right when he rejects the idealistic conception of the general will as an end of the state. But at the same time he asks the state to pursue the common good. If the state cannot represent the general will, it logically follows that it will be unable to pursue the common good. But he somehow thinks that the capitalist state, which does not represent the general will, nevertheless, be persuaded to pursue the good of society as a whole. He has specially the British conditions in mind where the existence of a Labour party participating in the constitutional politics of the country is the guarantee of an inherent harmony of state purpose. But the conception of the common good to be realized by a capitalistic state is essentially un-Marxian in character.

Conception of Individual Liberty

There are other inconsistences in Laski's "A Grammar of Politics". His conception of liberty is as *a priori* and uncritical as that of John Stuart Mill. He treats liberty as a static concept which can operate only in settled and stationary political societies. This individualistic conception of liberty is an anachronism in the modern collectivistic era. It is also inconsistent with his passion for a collectivized state operating the nationalized industries of the community.

Conception of Authority as Federal

Similarly, his conception of political authority as federal is inconsistent with his demand for the grant of larger economic functions to the state. His rejection of state sovereignty as a part of political theory is inconsistent with his proposal for an omnicompetent single chamber as the sovereign legislative power in the realm. The only concession to pluralistic sentiment is the provision of advisory councils and consultative committees representing the various group interests in the nation. But these advisory councils having only a consultative status cannot affect the omnicompetence of the sovereign legislative chamber. As W. Y. Elliott points out, Laski's theories discussed in the first part of the political grammar cannot be logically reconciled with his proposals of institutional reform put forward in the latter half of the book.

Anarchic Pluralism and Utopian Socialism and other Contradictions of Laski's Theory

These contradictions are due to his attempt to reconcile artificially the conflicting notions of an anarchic pluralism inherited from his intellectual past and a collectivistic socialism revealed to him as utopian dream of the future. His conception of the League of Nations as a super-state which would bring peace and justice to mankind proved to be most conspicuously utopian. Laski visualized in the League of Nations a kind of world federation and used its existence as an empirical argument to deny the sovereignty of the nation-state. He did not clearly understand that nationalism had not yet fulfilled its historical mission specially in colonial and semi-colonial countries. The peoples of these subject countries aspired for separate sovereign states where they could enjoy the fruits of their own national freedom. They were not willing to surrender their sovereignty, after winning it from the hands of their imperialistic overlords, to an international organization which was bound to be dominated by the major imperialistic powers of the world. Moreover, the constant rivalry between the major imperialistic powers prevented any international organization from becoming an instrument of unified international policy much less of a liberal or progressive policy as envisaged by Laski. The fate of the League of Nations is a sufficient commentary on his utopian interpretation of the functions of that world organization.[2]

Constructive Elements in His Political Thought

In spite of these deficiencies, the significance of the constructive element in Laski's political thought during the transitional phase should not be minimized. His criticism of the general will, his emphasis on the class character of political institutions, his argument for the refashioning of property relations in society, his criticism of the abuses of sovereignty, his love for liberty and hatred of tyranny in any form, and his faith in the fundamental unity of mankind that recognized no frontiers either racial or otherwise are some of the most important features of his constructive political philosophy.[3] The limitations of Laski's political thought arose from the insufficiency of his political experience which was mostly confined to the political conditions of an insular country like England. Apart from the utopian element, the realistic suggestions of Laskian socialism are specially suited to British conditions. The political grammar of Laski will continue for long as the recognized moral code of the Labour Party and socialist intellectuals in Britain. But this was not a final statement of his opinions which were destined to receive a new shock in the form of the economic crisis which shook the capitalistic world for four years from 1929-1933. It also brought a crisis in Laski's political philosophy. It brought him closer to Marxian political theory.

Impact of Economic Crisis of 1929-33

After the Russian Revolution, the greatest challenge to the capitalistic system came from an internal crisis popularly known as the great depression. This depression started in 1929 from the United States and gradually enveloped the major capitalistic countries of the world. The only country which remained completely immune from the evil consequences of this depression was Soviet Russia. This proved beyond doubt the superiority of the socialistic system over the capitalistic system. The political institutions of bourgeois liberalism gave way to fascist dictatorships or reactionary coalitions ruling with the help of emergency powers. The parties of the working-class were persecuted and suppressed and an atmosphere of civil war was created.

The working-class of Europe was divided in its ranks. This disunity ensured the success of the counter-revolution all over Europe (*126 : 30-66*).

---

2. Laski was forced to revise his earlier view of the League of Nations in his second edition of "A Grammar of Politics" when he admitted his error in regarding the League as a super-state. See the preface to the second edition of "A Grammar of Politics" which appeared in 1930.

3. For a popular summary of Laski's views during the transitional phase, see his "Introduction to Politics" which was first published in 1931.

In England, the minority Labour government was replaced by the o-called national coalition of reactionary elements drawn from all political parties. These events convinced Laski that the parliamentary institutions of bourgeois democracy were inadequate to meet a crisis of such magnitude. It was clear that the ruling class of Europe, when forced to choose between democracy and capitalism, was more likely to renounce democracy and choose capitalism (*126* : *223-63*).

The Crisis of Democracy in Capitalist Society

In his "Democracy in Crisis", Laski displays some scepticism about the efficacy of parliamentary methods as instruments of social change. "The disintegration of parliamentary democracy", he says, "is due to the fact that the leaders of the class who dominate it cannot meet the demands made upon them. The new class which has arisen to political authority, dissatisfied with the results of the present state, seeks to reorganize it in its own interest. The rise of a new class to political power is always, sooner or later, synonymous with a social revolution. and the essential characteristic of a social revolution is always the redistribution of economic power. Here. is may be urged, is the centre of the *malaise* in representative democracy, the root of the crisis it confronts. A new society is struggling to be born within the womb of the old; it finds the forms of that old society resist its effort at emergence. It is, I think, wholly natural that, if those forms should be found too inflexible to permit the easy birth of the new order, an attempt should be made to break them" ([illegible]).

He notices a number of constitutional impediments in the parliamentary system of England which prevent it from becoming an instrument of a radical socialist policy. The social implications of monarchy as the protector of feudal traditions, the influence of a reactionary House of Lords in legislative affairs, the conservative predilections of the army leaders. the prepossessions of the bureaucracy for the *status quo,* the anxiety of the courts to protect the privileges of property, the capitalist control of public opinion through large-scale ownership of the press, the influence of money in corrupting politicians, the vagaries of the electoral process, the indifference of the multitude towards serious political issues, and, finally. the remnants of bourgeois psychology may well make the realization of a socialist experiment completely impossible within the limits placed by the parliamentary system (*126* : *67-146*).

Laski and Fabian Socialism

This distrust of parliamentary institutions distinguishes Laski's socialistic thought from Fabian socialism. The characteristic British socialism before him was Fabian. Its ideology was based more on Mill's ideals than those of Marx. The Fabians argued that revolution as a method of social change was not suitable to England. They were rationalists in their outlook and believed in the realisation of socialism through rational persuasion. They thought it was quite possible to educate the electorate and convince a majority about the case for socialism. A parliamentary victory of the socialist party was sufficient to bring about the desirable changes in the capitalistic system in the direction of socialism. Moreover, they did not think in terms of challenging the fundamental economic postulates of liberal capitalism. The Fabians could hardly understand the inherent crisis of the capitalist system which led to the world depression of 1929 after the First World War and paved the way for the rise of fascism. This implied that the owners of capital sacrificed democracy in order to preserve their privileged positions in the economic system (*132* : *241*).

Criticism of the Fabian Approach

The Fabians did not realize that the political institutions of bourgeois liberalism reflected the economic purposes of a capitalist class which could not permit their use by its class enemies for its own destruction. The socialists could use parliamentary institutions to secure minor concessions in a period of capitalist expansion and within the framework of the capitalistic system. If they tried to use them to undermine the foundations of capitalism, the capitalists replied by suspending the normal constitutional machinery and suppressing the parliamentary institution in favour of a counter-revolutionary dictatorship. "Neither Fabians nor advanced liberals", says Laski, "had seen that the success of parliamentary government was dependent upon two conditions. It required, first, the sense of security that came from the ability to go on making profit, that enabled it, from its surplus wealth, to continue the distribution of amenities of the masses. It required, in the second place, an agreement among parties in politics to all matters of fundamental social constitution in order that each might succeed the other as the government of the day without a sense of outrage. Without the ability to operate these conditions, parliamentary government was powerless to settle differences in terms of reason. The political forms of liberalism, in a word, were dependent upon a conjuncture or economic circumstances the permanence of which could alone guarantee their effective functioning" (*132* : *242*).

The error of the Fabian hypothesis, according to Laski, was its failure to assert that a fundamental change in the economic structure requires a corresponding change in the form of political institution as well. When feudal economy gave way to capitalist economy, the feudal state was replaced by a new liberal state. When socialist economy replaces capitalist economy, the liberal state is bound to undergo a revolutionary metamorphosis (*132* : *243*).

Laski's Theory of State Drifts Closer to Marxism

The theoretical implications of Laski's attack on the political institution of the liberal state were subsequently elaborated by him in "The State in Theory and Practice" which is probably the best of his works on political philosophy. It contains the classic statement of Laski's political theory based upon his own revised version of Marxism. He now accepts a definition of the state which now contradicts some of his old pluralistic assumptions. He says, "By a state I mean a society....which is integrated by possessing a coercive authority legally supreme over any individual or group which is part of the society. An examination of any national society will always reveal within its boundaries not only individuals, but also associations of men grouped together to promote all kinds of objects, religious, economic, cultural, political in which they are interested. Such a society is a state when the way of life to which both individuals and associations must conform is defined by a coercive authority binding upon them all. The French state, for example, is a territorial society, divided into government and subjects, whether individuals or associations of individuals, whose relationships are determined by the exercise of this supreme coercive power. This power is called sovereignty; and it is by the possession of sovereignty that the state is distinguished from all other forms of human association" (*50 : 21*). The exigencies of a collectivist society have led Laski to accept the theoretical validity of a doctrine he had himself once challenged.

Sovereignty as Coercive Power of the Ruling Class

But the sovereignty that he now ascribes to the state is not a legal formality in the traditional Austinian sense. It is rather the logical predecessor of the Marxian conception of the nature of the state which interprets it as a coercive instrument of brute force for the exercise of class tyranny. The history of political societies is a history of permanent dictatorships established successively by the victorious economic classes. The Marxian motive in Laski's definition of sovereignty as organised communal force for economic domination is manifest when he says, "The control of legal relations in a society is in the hands of those men who, as the government, have the formal right to exercise sovereign power. To determine the way in which it shall be used is, accordingly, to determine how the fruits of the productive process shall be distributed; and it is impossible to make this determination save by having the right to exercise sovereignty. Those, therefore, in a society who seek to alter the character of the distributive process in any fundamental way, who want, that is, to alter the productive relations of the system under which they live, must do so by altering the legal foundations of the society. This they can only achieve by possessing themselves, either peacefully or by violence, of the state-power; for that is the instrument through which alone essential legal relations can be changed" (*50 : 111*).

Idealist Theory Ignores Basic Contradictions of Society

The idealist theory of the state is rejected by him on the ground that it ignores the basic contradiction of society. The idealist writers are preoccupied with the harmony of a conceptual state and, therefore, fail to observe the character of states as they have existed in history. They have evolved a theory of political obligation which does not take into account the dominating influence of the property-relation in determining the purposes of the state. Instead of relying on historical induction, they deduce their political norms from *a priori* metaphysics. Their *a priori* reasoning leads them to believe that the real is rational and slavery is freedom. The class struggle of history is transcended in the harmonious unfolding of a moral idea. Legal relations for the idealist become the expressions of a moral drive of the absolute instead of representing the productive relations of a given period. Laski has no use for the idealist theory because it is not grounded in historical experience.

Class Bias in the Functioning of State

To a Marxian mind, the conceptual harmony attributed to state purposes is at best an article of faith of the idealist. Marx argued that state purposes in history have always been biased in favour of the dominant economic class at a particular period and Laski also holds an approximately similar view. He points out that historical evidence conclusively proves the existence of a bias in the functioning of all states. The Greek city-state favoured the slave-owners and was biased against the slaves. The imperial state of Rome helped the patricians in their exploitation of the plebeians. The feudal state guaranteed the oppression of the serfs by the landed aristocracy. After the Industrial Revolution, the state was captured by the owners f capital, who used it to exploit the working-class. So the modern state, till the Russian Revolution, everywhere represented the rule of the bourgeoisie over the proletariat (*50 : 104*).

Political Evolution in Economic Context

It is obvious that the Marxian induction from history is primarily an interpretation of political evolution in its economic context. Laski has brilliantly re-stated in the second chapter of "The State in Theory and Pratice" what Karl Marx succinctly described in his preface to "The Critique of Political Economy" a few decades ago. "In the social production of their life", said Karl Marx, "men enter into definite relations that are indispensable and independent of their will, relations of production which correspond to a definite stage of development of their material productive forces. The sum total of these relations of production constitutes the economic structure of society, the real foundation, on which rises a legal and political superstructure and to which correspond definite forms of social consciousness. The mode of production of material life conditions the social, political and intellectual life process in general."[4]

Material Basis of Social Change

Laski argues in a similar vein, "The basic factor in any given society is the way in which it earns its living......changes in the methods of economic production appear to be the most vital factor in the making of change in all the other social patterns we know. For changes in those methods determine the changes of social relationships; and these in their turn, are subtly interwoven with all the cultural habits of men. We cannot write the history of law without looking at its roots in the methods of

4. Karl Marx and Frederick Engels : "Selected Works", Vol. I, pp. 328-29 (Moscow Ed. 1950).

economic production. We cannot explain the history of religious doctrines without relating them to the social background in which they evolved; and the key to that social background is always to be found in the relationships built upon the methods of production.[5] Our educational systems seek to prepare the child for life; but the kind of life for which it is to be prepared is a function, once more, of the material relations of the productive system which obtains in a given society. Our styles of architecture, the forms of our literature, the character of our science, the basic framework of all that we call civilisation, is, at bottom, determined by these productive relationships......(*50 : 108*). The economic factor, then, is the bedrock upon which the social super-structure is built; and the way in which it mainly operates is through the struggle of economic classes to possess the state power" (*50 : 122*).

Critical Attitude towards Marxism

It should be noted that Laski's adherence to Marxian political philosophy was even at this stage half-hearted. He thought that though Karl Marx did not make any serious misinterpretation of facts yet his theory suffered from its basic simplicity. His differences with the communist interpreters of Karl Marx were profound and of a far-reaching character. It is true that he was a great admirer of the Russian Revolution but at the same time he was also a remorseless critic of some aspects of the Soviet regime and the communist method in general.

In his "Reflections on the Revolution of our Time", Laski has given us a critical estimate of the Russian Revolution. While criticising the presence of dictatorship and absence of the so-called political democracy in the Soviet Union, he concludes that the socio-economic achievements of the Soviet system have a profound significance for the whole world which is, at present, passing through an era of revolutionary transition. In spite of their fallibility and important errors in policy, the Soviet leaders have been successful in building up a revolutionary social order that represents an important advance towards the creation of a progressive world society (*131 : 41-85*).

Uncompromising Opposition to Fascism

His attitude to fascism, as it should be, is that of uncompromising opposition. He has used both Marxian and liberal arguments in discredit-

5. Engels, elucidating the materialist conception of history, said, "Not only for economics, but for all historical sciences (and all sciences which are not natural sciences are historical) a revolutionizing discovery was made with this proposition, that the mode of production of material life conditions the social, political and intellectual life process in general; that all the social and political relations, all religious and legal systems, all the theoretical outlooks which emerge in history, are to be comprehended only when the material conditions of life of the respectively corresponding epochs are understood and the former are derived from these material conditions" (*146 ; Vo.I-334*

ing the totalitarian regimes of Mussolini and Hitler. As a socialist, Laski agrees with Marxists in regarding fascism as the defence mechanism of monopoly capitalism in decay or the last counter-revolutionary effort of the capitalist class to prevent the occurrence of a proletarian revolution. As a liberal, he attacks the fascist ideology for bringing about a ruthless political system that has put an end to the finest traditions of liberal individualism at one stroke. As he was a Jew, Laski was motivated by a strong racial feeling in his criticism of the Nazi system. But the most effective criticism that he brings forward against fascism is Marxian in character. The defeat of the fascist powers in the battlefield would not mean, as Laski said, the end of fascism until it was followed by a social revolution in those countries which is conceived by him in Marxian terms (*131* : *86-127*).

Compromise between the Liberal and Marxian Approaches to Politics

The political philosophy of Laski is essentially based on a compromise between the liberal and Marxian approaches to political philosophy. His brilliant but critical interpretation of the British constitution in his "Parliamentary Government in England" shows his preference for the Parliamentary system to any other conceivable system of political organisation. His only anxiety is to reform it so that it may answer the needs of the impending social revolution (*130* : *13-70*). His scholarly analysis and indictment of the American political system in "The American Democracy" has a clear Marxian basis but the institutional reorganization proposed by Laski is more in conformity with the British system than with any other system including the Soviet (*121* : *72-263*). It may be safely asserted that despite his theoretical adherence to his own version of Marxism, he always remained a practical Liberal.

Democratic Socialist Philosophy

In the twentieth century, Laski may be regarded as the most important spokesman of the democratic socialist philosophy in the English-speaking world.[6] However, he had been a pluralist and an individualist in his early days but changed his views later to propound a theory of the collectivistic state. His ideas of collectivism were partly derived from the English school of Fabian Socialism and partly from the writings of Karl Marx and Engels (*145* : *72-75*). He actively participated in the political activities of the Labour Party in England and ultimately rose to the position of its national chairman. "Harold Joseph Laski", observes George-Catlin, "was also, at first a continuator of the tradition of J. S. Mill in that last phase of *The Principles of Political Economy* which leads on to Fabianism. Laski's work, moreover, was marked by more stress than was placed by the Fabian majority on the individual, even to the point of 'conditional anarchism'. In the

6. Speaking in the Labour Party Conference of 1942 held in London, Laski summed up his faith in democratic socialism in these words, ''The age of competitive capitalism is over. A democracy means nothing less than a society of equals planning full production for community consumption''.

end, however, he identified his position with Marxism far more closely than did this majority. He resigned from the Fabian Executive Committee on the ground of lack of sympathy with them in their traditional positions as exponents of an Anglo-Saxon 'Gradualist' brand of Social Democracy" (*92 : 654*). Inside the Labour Party Laski was the spokesman and sympathiser of its left-wing section and in 1937 he advocated, along with Stafford Cripps, the policy of political association and collaboration with the British Communist Party (*145 : 102-120*).

Three Aspects of Laski's Socialist Theory

Laski's theory of democratic socialism may be conveniently studied by dividing it into three parts. In the first place, it envisages a technique of peaceful change in the present socio-economic structure. He does not agree with the Communist view that a violent revolution is necessary for the overthrow of capitalism. Secondly, his theory involves an assumption that capitalism has outlived its day and the victory of political democracy with its universal adult suffrage has created the conditions of its inevitable decay.

Moreover, the economic institutions of capitalism have become anachronistic and cannot survive in the context of the modern technological advances and development. In other words, the forces of production have become incompatible with the relations of production (*50 : 114-117*). Lastly, his socialistic theory includes a vision of the socialist society based on a rational and equitable distribution of wealth which should replace the existing capitalist system based on glaring disparities of income. But his conception of democratic socialism envisages a happy harmonization of the social control of economic processes with the liberty of the individual in political and intellectual spheres (*145 : 220-252*).

On a superficial view, there appears to be no necessary connection between Laski's pluralistic theory and his subsequent socialistic outlook. Had he remained faithful to his pluralistic past, he would have adopted a guild-socialist theory like G.D.H. Cole or found comfort in the syndicalist views of Sorel or, again, approved anarchist visions of Kropotkin and Tolstoy as sound political sense. But anarchism, syndicalism and guild socialism failed to impress Laski and so he had to repudiate openly his earlier pluralistic position.

Link between Pluralism and Socialism

Even then there is a connecting link between his pluralistic and socialistic theories. Both pluralism and socialism aimed at discrediting the capitalist state and both emphasized the autonomous position of trade unions in the modern society. In defending the freedom of associations against the sovereign state, Laski was by implication also defending the right of workers to organize themselves into trade unions and thus protect them from undue interference of the capitalist state. Even during the pluralistic phase, Laski shows distinctly pro-labour and anti-capitalist tendencies.[7] When he finally adopts socialism as his favourite political doctrine, he still remains opposed to what he describes as totalitarian dictatorship of the Communist type because it makes trade unions the convenient instruments of state policy by completely subordinating them to the Communist state (*134* : *6-12*).

Opposition to Dictatorship

He retains a pluralistic bias even in his most hard-boiled collectivistic phase. He remains up to the end a champion of the autonomy of the group against the tyranny of the state. He is opposed to dictatorship even if it is exercised by the socialists to promote the aims of socialism because it will bring about the coercion of certain sections in the community in a highly undesirable manner. A socialist dictatorship which begins by persecuting the enemies of socialism may end in the persecution of one group of socialists by another. So Laski's theory of democratic socialism has a firm root in his political pluralism which resists the idea of an omnicompetent state in all its forms (*127* : *84-90*).

A Technique of Peaceful Change

Laski thinks that the advent of political democracy in certain major countries of the world has created favourable conditions for a peaceful transition from capitalism to socialism. In a parliamentary system like that of England, all that the English workers have to do is to organize themselves into a Labour Party and work patiently for achieving an electoral victory of this party (*126* : *184-192*). As Laski says, "Once the division between parties is set by acceptance or rejection of the capitalist method of production, the logic of the contest turns upon the clash of these purposes. Nor is it, let me add, a contest in which the evolution can be so gradual as slowly to accustom the owners of economic power to the transformation. The announced programme of the Labour Party itself excludes that possibility. It is committed by its terms to a direct parliamentary attack upon the central citadel of capitalism. Once it is given authority by the electorate to fulfil its programme, it would be psychologically impossible for it to attempt its abandonment. To do otherwise is to commit suicide, for to abandon the attempt at the transformation of capitalism would be to surrender the whole ethos of its being (*130* : *89*). Thus he believes that the success of a socialist party in a national election is a sufficient guarantee of the achievement of socialism because any alternative policy for a victorious socialist party will be tantamount to its own disintegration and annihilation.

As he further points out that a political democracy has certain built-in compulsions which drive it towards economic and social democracy.

---

7. This is evident from Laski's support of the Boston police strike in 1919 which brought fantastic charges against Laski of being a Bolshevik agent in the American press. See Laski's biography by K. Martin, Chapter II, pp. 35-43.

However, the capitalist basis of political democracy prevents this kind of transformation for a long time. The parties of social change, therefore, begin by challenging the economic basis of bourgeois democracy and make it "the central issue in politics". The parties of the *status quo* try to justify capitalistic institutions by "offering a constantly increasing standard of life to the masses". So long as the people remain satisfied with the achievements of capitalism, they vote for the *status quo* parties. When the people realize the drawbacks of the existing social order dramatized by a war or a depression of international magnitude, the radical and socialist parties get their opportunity of being elected to power. They can, then, start the process of transforming the capitalistic foundations of the existing social order without resorting to a violent revolution. Laski is, therefore, convinced that a capitalist democracy can be transformed into a socialist democracy in a constitutional and peaceful manner.

Resemblance to the Fabian Approach

The above formulation of Laski's theory of peaceful transition to socialism is on the whole indistinguishable from the theory of Fabianism. The Fabians also believed in the gradual transformation of the political democracy into an economic and social democracy. Laski shares this belief when he says that the electoral victory of the Labour Party will bring about this transformation. But the old Fabianism was a theory of the era of capitalist expansion and so the dominating characteristic of the Fabian theory was its robust optimism. In sharp contrast to Fabianism, Laski has developed an attitude of scepticism and pessimism towards the political institutions of a capitalist democracy.[8]

Difference with the Fabian Approach

He recognizes the fact that a victorious socialist party may be prevented from translating its socialist programme into practice on account of the opposition of the army, the bureaucracy and the courts. The Fabians and advanced liberals did not realise that the success of parliamentary government was dependent upon two conditions. It required, first, the sense of security that came from the ability of the capitalist class to go on making profit that enabled it, from its surplus wealth, to continue the distribution of progressively higher wages to the workers. It required, in the second place, an agreement among political parties on all matters of fundamental social constitution in order that each might succeed the other as the government of the day without a sense of outrage. Without conforming to these conditions, parliamentary government was powerless to settle political differences peacefully (*132 : 242*).

In this way Laski shows his doubt in the possibility of achieving socialism by the straightforward capture of Parliament by the conversion of an electoral majority in favour of socialism. The experience of the

8. See George Catlin's remarks about Laski's pessimism and scepticism in "The Story of the Political Philosophers" Chapter XX, pp. 663-667.

post-war rule of the Labour Party in England justifies Laski's pessimism and scepticism in this respect.[9]

Contradiction in Laski's Theory of Peaceful Transition

The important contradiction of Laski's theory of peaceful changes is that though he recognizes the inadequacy of the constitutional method, yet he is unable to recommend any alternative strategy. He himself admits that no social class in history has ever surrendered its power and privileges peacefully. Some sections of the ruling class, when faced with the prospect of total defeat, may agree to offer concession to the subject classes. Even for obtaining minor concessions, the exploited and oppressed sections of the community have to take recourse to perpetual struggles. Slavery is now considered an indefensible institution but the Americans learnt this elementary truth after fighting a bloody civil war just a century ago. Religious tolerance is now an accepted principle of civilized political behaviour though religious persecution and riots survive in some form in many countries even now. History shows that this achievement too was based on the realisation of utter futility of religious conflicts and wars that were fought both in Europe and Asia.

The French and Russian Revolutions signify that neither the nobility nor the bourgeoisie was prepared to abdicate without violence. Algeria and Vietnam have demonstrated the cost in suffering and privations for these peoples in their search for national identities. Even minor demands of peoples such as the right of franchise, equality for women, reasonable conditions of work for factory workers and abolition of racial discrimination have been rejected or conceded depending upon the intensity of struggle not precluding violence and pressures of mass movement behind them.

Thus Laski does not completely rule out the necessity of a violent revolution for effecting social change. But the revolutionary means should be employed only when the constitutional means have been tried and found inadmissible or infructuous.

The Danger of Fascism

Moreover, the rise of fascism between the two world wars shattered Laski's faith in peaceful evolution towards a socialist society by the use of parliamentary methods. As he pointed out, "It is not a great discovery to insist that solutions made in terms of rational consent are always to be preferred to those made by violence......My point has been the wholly different one that democratic institutions are judged valid in a capitalist society so long as they do not so function as to destroy the essential implications of capitalism, that is, the class-relations which the private ownership of the means of production involve. I have been arguing that when the political democracy seeks to transfer that ownership to the community

9. See Laski's remarks about the post-war Labour Government in England in "The Dilemma of Our Times", Chapter VI, pp. 109-112, Chapter XIII pp. 242-249.

the capitalist class will, if it can, use the state-power to suppress democratic institutions. I have therefore urged that, at this stage of economic development, the difference between classes can only be settled by force" (*50 : 143*).

The examples of Italy, Germany, Austria and Spain proved that the ruling classes in those countries preferred the establishment of fascist dictatorships on the ruins of parliamentary regimes to the constitutional victory of socialist forces which could have brought about important changes in the socio-economic structure of these countries.

The Experiment of Parliamentary Socialism in England

Laski unfortunately did not live long enough to see the final outcome of the Labour rule in England and certain other countries. A neutral observer can, however, say that the post-war Labour Governments of England have no better record to show than that of the Social Democrats of Germany after the first world war.[10] England still remains a capitalist country after several years of the Labour rule from 1945 to 1951 and from 1964 to 1970. What Laski wrote in the thirties in this connection may still be regarded as valid in the sixties or seventies. "If socialist government in Great Britain or France or the United States", he said, "were peacefully to transform the basis of the property-system from private to public hands the argument that fundamental changes could be accomplished by democratic means would be immensely strengthened. That evidence does not exist, and what there is for consideration, even in the democratic countries, raises doubts the other way" (*50 : 146*).

The Situation in America, France and Italy

While in England even Labour Governments have failed to bring about the socialist transformation of the country, the working-class of the United States is as yet too unorganized and politically unconscious to constitute a serious menace to the existing capitalistic order. In France and Italy, the emergence of powerful Communist groups foreshadows the possibility of a forcible overthrow of the capitalist system on the familiar patterns of Russia, the countries of Eastern Europe and China. But nowhere in the world there appears to be a possibility of achieving the goal of socialism in a constitutional way.

Piecemeal Reforms by Labour Parties

The socialist and labour parties have succeeded in certain countries in achieving piecemeal reforms but they have invariably failed to make any serious inroads upon the central citadel of capitalism. This is as true about England as about Scandinavia or Australia where right-wing socialist governments have governed for a considerable time.

It appears that Laski did not realize the full implications of his

10. Kingsley Martin mentions in his biography of Laski that he was much dissatisfied with the work of the Labour Government just before his death. See Martin's "Harold Laski : A Biographical Memoir", Chapters IX, X and XII.

own conclusion that the political democracy does not provide the technique of peaceful change in the social and economic structure because it would have neessitated a significant revision of the whole theory of democratic socialism propounded by him.

Laski's Pessimism About the Constitutional Method

That he certainly reached this inevitable conclusion may be demonstrated by the following remark of Laski about the liberal state. "It does not provide a technique of peaceful change. For men who have the privileges of ownership seek to maintain them, the more vehemently as they contract; and they are certain to be resisted by those excluded from them as these find their expectation of increasing material welfare disappointed. The only way open to the latter if they wish to avoid this disappointment is to capture the state-power in order to use it for a redefinition of class-relations. Theoretically, no doubt, this can be done peacefully in a constitutional system based on universal suffrage. In fact, historically, whenever an attempt at such redefinition has been made, it has always been resisted by the owners of property who, thereby, have been possessed of the state-power. The result of the incompatibility of the views of the use to which the state-power should be put is revolution *(47 iv)*".

Laski never examined in detail the shape and character of this revolution to come because it was in direct conflict with the basic assumptions of democratic socialism. It must be admitted that this is an important omission in Laski's theory of socialism.

Why Capitalism Cannot Survive?

It is true that Laski shares the general Marxian belief in the inevitable decline of the capitalist system and its replacement by a new socialist order. He regards the twentieth century as an epoch of transition from capitalism to socialism. He has interpreted history as a continuous march towards greater freedom. The arrival of capitalist democracy represented a greater scope for freedom in camparison with the feudal autocracy which it replaced. Similarly, the struggle for socialist democracy is a struggle for a still greater scope for freedom than what people have enjoyed in a capitalist democracy (*127* : *70-80*).

The triumph of capitalist democracy secured genuine freedom only to the capitalist minority and converted the overwhelming majority into mere wage-slaves. The advent of socialist democracy will bring about the universalization of freedom by banishing economic inequalities from society. This means that the overwhelming masses of the world are bound to participate in the global struggle for the achievement of socialist democracy. The final success of the socialist movement is ensured by the fact that it is an international movement for the benefit of the overwhelming majority of mankind. The ultimate collapse of the capitalist system is certain with the increasing realization that it benefits the capitalist class only which constitutes a hopeless minority of every nation.

Lack of Planning in Capitalism

Laski criticizes the capitalist method of production for its wastefulness and lack of planning. As he says, "Production is caried on wastefully and without adequate plan. The commodities and services necessary to the life of the community are never so distributed as to relate to need or to produce a result which maximises their social utility. We build picture places when we need houses. We spend on battleships what is wanted for schools. The rich can spend the weekly wage of a workman on a single dinner, while the workman cannot send his children adequately fed to school. A rich *debutante* will spend on an evening frock more than the annual income of the workers who have made it. We have, in fact, both the wrong commodities produced, and those produced distributed without regard to social urgency. We have a large class maintained in parasitic idleness, whose tastes demand the application of capital and labour to the satisfaction of wants unrelated to human need" (*47 : 175*).

The implications of this situation are obvious. The goods needed for the wantonly luxurious life of the richer classes are produced in abundance. But even the primary needs of the working classes such as food, clothing, shelter and medical aid remain unprovided for in a capitalist society.

Profit Motive in Production

Moreover, the central motive of production in a capitalist society is the securing of profit. The capitalists produce only those goods which are in effective demand in the market and can be sold at great profit. As Laski says, "They produce goods and services, not for use, but to acquire property from their production. They produce not to satisfy useful demands, but demands which can be made to pay. They will ruin natural resources. They will adulterate commodities. They will float dishonest enterprises. They will corrupt legislatures. They will pervert the sources of knowledge. They will artificially combine to increase the cost of their commodities to the public. They will exploit, sometimes with hideous cruelty, the backward races of mankind. They infect with their poison those who work for the wages they offer. They induce sabotage in its varied forms. They compel strikes which result in serious damage to the community. And it is the grim irony of the system that the vaster part of those engaged in its promotion have little or no hope of enduring gain from the process they support. They may possess themselves, as in America, of the educational instruments of the community. They may even pervert religious institutions to the protection of their ideas. They do not, nevertheless, secure a well-ordered State. It remains historically obvious that a community divided into rich and poor is, when the latter are numerous, built upon foundations of sand" (*47 : 175*).

Thus the root cause of the instability of a capitalist regime is that it is built upon the profit motive which penetrates in all spheres of human activity and corrupts them. The private ownership of the means of production and the craze for increasing profit prevents the full use of our natural resources and technological development and deprives the common people from sharing the fruits of such material progress which has come within the realm of technological possibility. The capitalist relations of production now work as fetters on the technological forces of production and so they must be replaced by new socialist relations.

Anxiety of the Ruling Class for Protection of its Privileges

The ruling class always makes a desperate effort to protect its privileges. But Laski thinks that all such attempts of the ruling class to save it from its inevitable downfall are foredoomed to failure As he says, "It may limit the right to a share in political power to those only possessed of a certain property qualification. It may model its constitution so as to limit the power to criticise the existing regime or to prevent the passage of statues which limit the power of property. It may keep the non-possessing classes deliberately ignorant, as William Windham urged, in 1810, that they be kept ignorant. It may, as in Czarist Russia, so fiercely stifle protest that the mass of men is, over a long period, stricken into dumb inertia. It may even confer political power on the masses, and then, by the control of opinion, frustrate the full use of that power to its own needs. It may, as with Napoleon, seek by military adventure to divert attention from domestic concerns. Yet the State remains divided into rich and poor; and men, after a period, refuse to suffer quietly. Then revolution supervenes to alter the balance in the State" (*47 : 716*).

Laski thus concludes that the exploitative and oppressive character of the capitalist society is bound to provoke active resistance on the part of those who are exploited and oppressed by it. This resistance, he thinks, is bound to be successful in the sheer predominance in number of those who will participate in this resistance.

Periodical Crises of Capitalism

Laski agrees with Marx that the capitalist methods of production are bound to lead to periodical crises. The great depression of 1929 was the most severe crisis in the history of world capitalism and the rise of fascism and the Second World War were the inevitable consequences of the crises of capitalism. Laski is convinced that this crisis of capitalism can be solved only by adopting the socialist methods of production in the major capitalist countries. If we postpone the socialist solution of this crisis, the only alternative remains a cycle of imperialist wars.

Fascism as a Symptom of Weakness of Capitalism

The emergence of fascist dictatorships is a symptom of the inherent weakness of the system of world capitalism. When a capitalist democracy embraces fascism, it thereby denies the possibility of peaceful achievement of socialism. But fascism with its natural corollary of an aggressive imperialism cannot be a permanent solution of the crisis of capitalism as has been demostrated by the experiences of Italy, Germany and Japan. The Second

World War resulted in the defeat of fascism both in Asia and in Europe and large parts of Eastern Europe and Eastern Asia were liberated from the yoke of capitalism.

Socialism and Violence

It is true that these countries are not following the road of constitutional socialism that Laski would have liked them to follow. But he had foreseen the necessity of violent overthrow of the capitalist system in certain circumstances as early as 1935 when he wrote, "The transition from feudal to bourgeois society was only accomplished by heavy fighting. There is no reason to suppose, unless we assume that men are now more rational than at any time in the past, that we can transform the foundations of bourgeois society without heavy fighting also and the assumption of greater rationality is an illusion born of special historical circumstances and now fading before our eyes" (*50 : 271*).

If the capitalist class meets the socialist challenge by establishing a fascist dictatorship, the working-class is bound to retaliate by a proletarian dictatorship making revolution and war a necessary element in the transition from capitalism to socialism.

Rearmament and Militarism in America

In the post-war era, the major capitalist countries of the world including the United States are again facing a crisis of a still greater magnitude. The ruling classes of these countries are again trying to meet this crisis by a policy of increasing rearmament and the cold war. The failure of the Labour Government in England in bringing about the necessary socialist transformation of the British society was due to the increasing burdens of rearmament. The American policy of rearmament resulted in complete reversal of the New Deal policy of President Roosevelt. But militarism and rearmament cannot be regarded as a permanent solution of the crisis of capitalism (*121 : 499*). Either capitalism would be obliged to stage a peaceful abdication in a constitutional way or it would inevitably lead to an aggressive war and perish in the course of its militarist adventures.

Preference for the Constitutional Method

Laski prefers the constitutional road towards socialism because he does not want to lose the gains of liberal democracy in the process of achieving socialism. He wants to win socialism by peaceful persuasion rather than by the compulsion of arms. He is quite justified in believing that the zero hour of capitalism has arrived and that it must now give place to a new social system based on socialist principles. It is yet to be seen whether capitalism is capable of making a peaceful abdication from the world stage. If this happens, it will be a vindication of Laski's faith in democratic socialism. If it does not happen, it will reveal another misconception in his theory. It must be admitted that Laski's belief in the peaceful transformation of capitalist democracy into socialist democracy was somewhat shaken after the rise of fascism in Europe.

LASKI AND FABIAN SOCIALISM—A STUDY IN THEORY OF POLITICAL OBLIGATION

1. A Pluralistic Theory of Obedience

Laski's theory of political obligation constitutes an important element of his political philosophy. The problem of the basis of political obedience is one of the fundamental issues of political theory in the history of Western political thought. In every political system, liberal or autocratic as Laski argues, we notice a small minority exercising the functions of legislation and administration over the large majority of the population, which is in a position to obtain habitual obedience from them. Political obligation has two aspects. One of the aspects is the psychological and sociological basis of actual obedience on the part of a people to the rulers and the second aspect is the ethical justification of this obedience. While explaining the second aspect, different answers have been suggested by various political thinkers. It has been said that obedience to authority is ordained by the will of God or by natural law or by the obligations assumed in a social contract. The first aspect has received less attention but one explanation which has been given is that obedience is based either on fear of the punishment which follows an act of disobedience or on recognition of the fact that the security and welfare of an individual depends upon general obedience to political rulers.

According to Laski, "the fundamental problem in politics is not the description or maintenance of the organs of authority but the inquiry into their legitimacy". (*122 : 234*). As a pluralist, Laski's main anxiety is to repudiate the state's title to absolute and unchallenged obedience to its laws and so the question of political obligation for him becomes a very important issue. He depicts contemporary social scene as a battle-field where the state and other associations are involved in a perpetual struggle. As the desires and aspirations of these associations differ, a general will cannot emerge from this conflict and no final reconciliation of the rival interests is possible. Laski has argued that the will of the state is no more than a competitor with the wills of other associations and we cannot conclude in advance which of these wills is likely to emerge supreme in the conflict ultimately. At other occasions, Laski points out that the will of the state is the final product of the competing wills of all other social groups. Law is regarded as the result of a successful attempt to harmonize the conflicting interests of different associations. Yet, he insists that law, as the expression of the state's will, cannot and should not claim any pre-eminence over the expression of the will of any other group. Laski says, "whenever in a state a group of persons large enough to make its presence felt demands the recognition of certain claims, it will not recognize a law which attempts defiance of them; nor will it accept the authority by which that law is enforced." (*122 : 34*)

Law, according to Laski, is a rule of practical convenience, whose usefulness can be determined by its consequences. Right conduct is attended by the best possible results.. Apart from the circularity of this definition, this pragmatic formulation fails to provide an adequate norm for judging between various courses of action that are possible in a given historical situation. In practice, this would equate the ethical with the more powerful and the successful. Laski says that the American rebels were right in 1776 and the French revolutionaries were right in 1789. But can we similarly say that the Germans and other Europeans were wrong in 1848 because their revolutions failed? Thus success or failure does not determine the ethical character of a political act. Yet Laksi presents the same realistic or pragmatic view of the problem of obedience. Social groups, he says, frequently come into clash with each other. The group will that emerges as victorious in this Darwinian struggle for supremacy is also, according to Laski, the moral will as well. In this contest, the Church or the trade union has as much chance of winning as the state in a given historical situation.

At the same time, Laski suggests, not very consistently, a radically individualistic solution of the problem of political obligation. He observes: "The only ground for state–success is where purpose of the state is morally superior to that of its opponent. The only ground upon which the individual can give or be asked his support from the state is from the conviction that what it is aiming at is, in each particular action, good. We deny, that is to say, that the general end of the ideal state colours the policy of a given act of a special state. And that denial involves from each member of the state continuous scrutiny of its purpose and method." (*122 : 45*). Laski conveys the same idea more explicitly at another place: "So I would urge that you must place your individual at the centre of things. You must regard him as linked to a variety of associations to which his personality attracts him. You must on this view admit that the state is only one of the associations to which he happens to belong, and give it exactly that pre-eminence–and no more–to which on the particular occasion of conflict, its possibly superior moral claim will entitle it. In my view it does not attempt to take that pre-eminence by force; it wins it by consent. It proves to its members by what it performs that it possesses a claim inherently greater than, say, their Church or trade union. It is no dry *a priori* justification which compels their allegiance, but the solidity of its moral achievement. So, I shall fight for England because I can genuinely accept the rightness of its cause; not because when the call comes I must unheedingly and, therefore, unintelligently obey it." (*210 : 19*)

Thus every citizen must investigate the purpose of every state action in order to decide whether it is ethically higher than that of any other group, involved in the competition for his loyalty. He should obey the state only when he regards that particular state action as ethically satisfying for himself. Apathy of citizens to acts of governmental injustics and their passive obedience to unjust commands of the sovereign is condemned by Laski, when he says that "the slavery of inertia is a weed that grows everywhere in wanton luxuriance; and we are, above all, concerned to make provision against its instrusion." (*122 : 122*). As Herbert Deane suggests, Laski's theory of political obedience can be described as political Protestantism with a vengeance. It is natural that he quotes the words of Luther, Lamennais and other Protestant rebels against the claims of the Roman Catholic Church for absolute allegiance. If his conscience tells him that a given law does not advance the true end of the state, he must disobey it without fear of penalties. In the last analysis, loyalty is in every case a matter of the private judgement of each thinking citizen. Deane observes: "Laski's ultra-Protestant theory of obedience is, for all its nobility, a doctrine fraught with great danger. Since it gives the state no greater claim to men's allegiance than any other social group, it would tend to produce anarhcy if put into practice in a modern society made up of a variety of competing groups. Furthermore, the theory elevates that state of anarchy to the level of a moral imperative by urging each citizen to disobey a governmental order unless he is convinced that the moral worth of the government's decision is greater than the appeal made to his conscience by the contradictory demand of another group. By isolating the problem of obeying a particular command of the state from the general context of the nature and value of law-abidingness, Laski ignores the fact that in a given case it may be better to obey a command of which one does not approve than to disrupt the entire fabric of allegiance to the state." (*191* : *39*).

Moreover, the individual does not possess the capacity for a limitless and ever-wise exercise of the faculty of ethical evaluation. Even if this was practicable, the result of attempting an exercise of indiscriminate moral judgement by every individual may lead to the paralysis of the moral will of the community. Deane observes: "A Laskian state, kept in constant tension and alarm because of the possibility of individual and group disobedience for trivial as well as grave reasons, would be a state verging on anarchy. The usual consequences of a period of anarchy are widespread demand for security and order, and the emergence of a new political authority that endeavours to reimpose order by strong measures designed to curb the power of the warring factions. Thus our last state is worse than our first; the over-emphasis on individual and group antonomy leads to a reaction in the course of which authority, from being despised, comes to be venerated, while the freedom of men and their groups is sharply curtailed. (*191* : *41*).

Laski justifies resistance to the will of the state apparently in the name of the individual or the group even though he may be actually thinking in terms in the resistance of a social class. He believes that the maintenance of peace and order cannot be regarded as the ultimate purpose of the state. The supreme interest of the state is justice and it is likely that justice and social peace may come into clash with each other. The traditional theory of state sovereignty places the coercive power of the state at the disposal of the capitalist class, which uses it to maintain order at the cost of social justice. Laski's denigration of the value of order like his general attack on the doctrine of sovereignty, should be interpreted in the context of his hostility to be capitalist order, which the existing state upholds, and his desire to create a new socialist order based on his concept of justice. Criticising Laski's theory of political obligation during his pluralistic phase, Deane says : "In place of a frank avowal of the goal of social and political reconstruction and a clear statement and defence of the values in terms of which he regards a labour order as preferable to a capitalist order, he elaborates a confused and complex ideological apparatus to defend the interests of labour against a hostile state—a moralistic theory of obedience, not grounded upon a consistent and examined ethical theory, and difficult to reconcile with his pragmatic view of group conflict. He maintains that order must be sacrificed to the demands of justice, but he attempts no inquiry into the nature of 'justice' or of the means by which it is to be attained." (*191* : *43*).

2. A Fabian Approach to Political Obligation

In *A Grammar of Politics,* Laski's ultra-individualistic thesis about political obligation is qualified by his newly acquired enthusiasm for Fabian socialist ideals. He now begins his analysis of the problem of political obedience by regarding human nature as inherently social. If human beings are obliged to live together, there must be laws to determine their social relations and an authority to enforce these laws. Thus the obligation to obey the orders of a government is derived from the fact that man is essentially a social being. Laski does not regard human beings as fully rational and, therefore, those theories of political obligation which attempt to explain the obedience of the many to the few solely in terms of rational factors, such as utility, consent or fear of penalties, do not satisfy him. He observes : "The State as it was and it finds the roots of allegiance in all the complex facts of human nature; and a theory of obedience would have to weight them differently for each epoch in the history of the state if it were to approximate to the truth." (*47* : *22*).

Laski has not completely discarded his basic individualistic approach to the moral problem of the obligation to obedience, which he had adopted earlier. He points out in explicit terms : "Our obligation to obey the state is, law apart, an obligation dependent upon the degree to which the State achieves its purpose. We are the judges of that achievement. We must obey the State, not because its theoretic purpose is a splendid one, but because of our conviction that it is genuinely seeking to make that purpose valid in events......Our ultimate allegiance is always to the ideal; and to the legal power that seeks to bind us; our loyalty is conditioned by the purpose and substance we can discover in its effort." (*47* : *26*). Force amounts to compulsory subjection of the individual to an experience he would not share voluntarily and so it should be used only when the common sense of society approves its exercise in general interest. If a citizen feels that force is being used, which is not compatible with its purpose, he may opt for his civic duty of resisting the will of the state. However, Laski now recognizes the state's new role as the promoter of men's common interests and, therefore, admits new and greater qualification on this civic duty of resistance.

We find that Laski now formulates his theory of political obligation in terms of his views on human rights. A citizen has a inherent right to whatever is required for the development of his moral personality. Therefore, he judges the state by the manner in which it seeks to secure for him the substance of these rights. Laski says: "Every government is thus built upon a contingent moral obligation. Its actions are right to the degree that they maintain rights. When it is either indifferent about them, or wedded to their limitation, it forfeits its claim to the allegiance of its members." (*47* : *57*). The individual, according to Laski, is quite justified in his disobedience, if he discovers that the state's action infringes upon his rights. But he again qualifies this individualistic theory by adding that this right or resistance "is, of course, reasonably to be exercised only at the margins of political conduct. No community could hope to fulfil its purpose if rebellion become a settled habit of population." (*47* : *62*).

The joining of ultra-individualistic and Fabian socialist points of view in Laski's theory of political obligation creates confusion. At moments, he affirms that the citizen can violate any law which is against his conscience and flatly denies that submission can ever be regarded" a moral obligation unless, as an act, it carries with it the individual conviction of rightness which makes it moral." (*47* : *288*). At other times, he declares that individuals must not disobey the state unless its commands offend their vital beliefs and its policies come into clash with public welfare. As Deane observes: "In this view, disobedience and, a *fortiori*, rebellion are the ultimate reserve weapons against perversion of the state power, to be used only in the marginal situation where the dictates of authority seem to deny all that men hold most certain and most valuable in their experience." (*191* : *102*).

When Laski points out that the actual incidence of state power is mostly a function of the property relations, which exist in a society, he tends to uphold the view that the large majority of citizens, who do not own property and have no access to economic power, have no moral obligation to obey every command of the state. He said: "Every generation contains examples of men who, in the context of ultimate experience, deliberately decide that an anarchy in which they seek to maintain some principle is preferable to an order in which that principle must be surrendered." (*49* : *71*).

The qualifications and limitations that Laski now proposes regarding his individualistic theory of obedience can be explained in terms of certain changes in the English political scene such as the possibility of the Labour Party coming to power. The capitalist minority could, in this siutation, use Laski's theory of political obligation to justify its resistance to the commands of a Labour regime. Herbert Deane observes: "By 1931 Laski shifts the ground of obedience away from the moral adequacy of the state's commands as judged by the individual and makes the obligation to obey a function of the degree to which the state secures to the individual at least a minimum of material well-being......This thesis is obviously a development of Laski's view that the state is entitled to allegiance only if it secures to its citizens those rights that are the conditions of self-realization; the rights now stressed as essential to the development of the individual are economic and material demands. The theory is useful, too, in that it justifies the title to obedience of a government which undertakes measures leading to greater economic equality at the same time that it leaves room for disobedience in the present society, which in his opinion, is becoming ever more sharply divided into the two nations of rich and poor." (*191 : 105*). Laski as a Fabian Socialist, thinks that a socialist regime that promotes the material welfare of the majority has a better title to political obedience than a capitalist regime which promotes the interests of a minority.

3. A Class Perspective on Political Obligation

In 1932 and 1933, when Laski becomes increasingly fascinated by the Marxist approach to politics, his ultra-individualistic theory of political obligation vanishes from his works and the focus of his attention shifts from the individual to the 'proletariat' as a class. He is no longer interested in the individual or a minority group that refuses to obey the government in the name of conscience but in the socio-economic conditions under which the working-class, which constitutes a majority in every advanced capitalist society, is likely to withdraw its collective allegiance from the government that protects the interests of the property-owning minority. So long as capitalism remains an expanding system, the workers receive generous concessions from their employees and the government. Hence, they are inclined to obey the commands of the rulers. However, when capitalism faces contraction the working class becomes conscious of the injustices, inequalities and irrationality of the capitalist system. Thus in a period of economic crisis, the workers become rebellious and follow a policy resisting the will of the state which is indifferent towards their problems or even hostile to their pressing demands.

In this discussion, Laski seems to accept the Marxist argument that capitalism inevitably means increasing privation for an ever-expanding proletariat and that misery forces to revolt against the system. The rest of his analysis is, however, a denial of this basic Marxist tenet. He argues that capitalism, during its period of expansion, was able to make great concessions to the demands of the workers and to offer them a constantly rising standard of living; the masses therefore became accustomed to continuous improvement. The trend in state legislation after 1870 has been to soften by governmental action the harsh contrast which would otherwise obtain between the lives of the rich and the poor. And, on any long view, the ability of the state to win the loyalty of its citizens depends upon its power continuously to soften the contrast. Laski admits that though the workers have been receiving large concessions, they are no longer satisfied with them. Yet he notes that the process of capitalist development has led to the *embourgeoisment* of large sections of industrial workers both in Europe and the United States and so the workers in these countries have failed to develop real proletarian class consciousness. Hence, the proletariat in these countries continues its loyalty to the bourgeois state.

But the onset of the economic depression rudely shakes the confidence of the working-class in the capacity of the capitalist state to solve their demands of employment and economic security. Laski suggests that the sense of allegiance to capitalist democracy has declined because the capitalist system can no longer offer the common people the constantly increasing standard of living. He observes that the ruling class can secure allegiance only by demonstrating "that its power is continuously coincident with an increase of material well-being for the working classes, or that, where sacrifices have to be imposed, their incidence is genuinely equal. The former......is a function of an economic recovery which is dubious; the latter is prohibited by the psychology which our inegalitarian system has created." (*126* : *224*).

According to Deane, Laski's portrait of the development of capitalism during the century preceding the crisis of 1929 contradicts the main assumptions of Marxist theory, though he claims to subscribe to it now. Deane says: "He states that the standard of living of the average worker rose constantly, while Marx held that the condition of the proletariat was growing steadily worse. Laski concedes that the state has increasingly organized for its citizens the material conditions of an adequate life.... while the Marxist theory insists that the state is the coercive instruments by which the capitalist class protects its privileges and profits. Laski admits that the development of capitalism has given a large number of workers a real stake in the present system and he laments the *embourgeoisment*, that has resulted from their material prosperity, while Marx built his system on the postulate that the deterioration of the position of the proletariat and the middle class would inevitably lead to the growth of revolutionary consciousness among the members of an ever-expanding proletariat." (*191* : *174*).

Laski appears to argue that so long as the capitalist mode of production satisfies the rising expectations of the working-class, capitalist democracy retains the loyalty of its working-class population, But as soon as a serious depression occurs, the workers develop an attitude of disobedience and rebellion. The crisis reveals the contradictions of capitalist society but the workers' disobedience is caused by their psychological disillusionment rather than by those economic factors which Marx had mentioned. In effect, Laski is arguing that the basic reason for the workers' disaffection with capitalist democracy is its long record of success—a process suddenly reversed by the depression. Deane thinks that Laski's theory that the masses will no longer give their allegiance to capitalist democracy after their catastrophic experience of the depression era is not convincing. His assumption is that capitalist democracy would adopt a sharply deflationary policy leading to curtailment of social services, decline in wages and salaries and acceleration of the rate of mass unemployment. He formulated this view primarily on the basis of the policies of the Conservative coalition government in England in 1931 and those of the Hoover Administration in the United States at that time. But Laski continued to adhere to this explanation as late as 1938 when President Roosevelt showed that capitalism could resolve the problems of the depression by the opposite technique of inflationary policies advocated by Keynes. The Roosevelt Adiministration "sharply increased payments to the unemployed and the underprivileged, and in the midst of the depression it inaugurated a series of long delayed social reforms. These payments, financed largely by government borrowing, not only restored morale and prevented the drift towards a revolutionary temper, but also revived effective demand and thereby stimulated the private sector of the economy." (*191 : 177*).

Laski thought that the economic crisis of 1929-1933 signified the final collapse of the capitalist system and felt that economic recovery was impossible without a change in the capitalist mode of production. As Deane says: "This thesis, confidently advanced during the depth of the depression, is still maintained in 1937 and 1938 in the face of the general recovery of both the American and British economies. Ignoring the actual increases in production, he continues to assert that the contradiction between the relations and the forces of production makes it impossible for production and consumption to increase......He assumed in 1932 that the final collapse of capitalism had begun....the assumption was unwarranted, and so American capitalism, at least, emerges untouched by his critical assault. (*191 : 178*). Lastly Laski argued that in order to avoid large-scale disobedience and resistance, the bourgeois state must offer the working-class a constantly increasing standard of living. Laski did not think that capitalist democracies as we know them "are inherently capable, granted the class-relations they maintain, of fulfilling demand on the largest possible scale, and that, therefore, they have a moral claim to the obedience of their members on this ground." (*47:V*). The justification for the preservation by the state of "the present system of private property in the instruments of production must be that this results in a greater total satisfaction to all who are affected by its maintenance than would be the case under such an alternative system as socialism." (*50-22*).

By Laski's criteria, American capitalism today has a better title to the allegiance of the ordinary citizen than any other existing socialist system because the standard of living of the average American worker is higher than that of the average worker in any socialized economy. Deane observes: "His adoption of a purely materialistic standard of judgement is a fatal error. Since he bases the state's title to allegiance on the level of material satisfactions that it provides for its citizens; he surrenders the right to criticize capitalism for its ethical and social shortcomings and for its tendency to its system of values on the foundations of the 'cash nexus'.... If American capitalism continues to offer greater economic benefits to the average worker, Laski can hardly complain if the American remains a victim of 'embourgeoisment', unable to see the advantages that socialism will bring to him." (*191 : 179*).

In *Reflections on the Revolution of Our Time,* Laski continued to focus his analysis of the problems of political obligation on the social conditions under which the state can retain the allegiance of the working masses rather than on the issue of the conscientious objections of the individuals protesting against personal injustices. He insists that "every system of consent in modern times has required a faith as its basis that men can accept; and the roots of that faith are its ability, as a going economic concern, to satisfy the wants it encounters." (*131* : *123*). As capitalist democracy is no longer capable of meeting the people's demands for expansion of services, the traditional authority of the state is declining due to protests and rebellions from below as more and more people refuse to give their allegiance to the bourgeois government and its laws. The answer of the ruling elite to this spirit of revolt is the imposition of a fascist dictatorship and the abolition of democracy.

Laski associated this spirit of mass rebellion with the decline in the influence of the religious tradition. Religion, in earlier times, helped to support the state's claims to the obedience of its citizens. This admission, however, is not consistent with his thesis that obedience to the state has invariably been a simple function of the level of material satisfaction. Laski now argues that a decisive change in men's material expectations and the decline of religious beliefs in favour of a secular way of thought and action have created new possibilities of human development through adequate control over the forces of nature. In a period of the general crisis of capitalism, popular dissatisfaction with the performance of the existing economic system leads to the demand for the creation of a socialist society which alone, in Laski's view, can satisfy the rising expectations of the masses for a constantly expanding welfare system. Deane observes: "Laski is here advocating a quantitative and materialistic conception of the good life and of the good society that he condemns in his attacks on an acquisitive capitalist society". (*191* : *252*). Laski's analysis of the conditions under which men will now obey the state is correct in so far as it describes the popular materialistic attitude of Western society and the conviction that the state should guarantee to all citizens at least a minimum of well-being. He errs, however, in believing that this attutude will necessarily lead the worker to demand the replacement of capitalism by socialism. By a Keynesian programme designed to prevent depressions or to cushion their effects and by the measures of the welfare state, a bourgeois government may well be able to satisfy the popular demand for economic security without abandoning the capitalist system.

44—17 149

CHAPTER 33

FASCISM AND NAZISM

1. THE MEANING OF TOTALITARIANISM

In current political literature the term 'totalitarian State' is used in contrast with the term 'the liberal democratic State'. The totalitarian State claims jurisdiction over the whole of man's life. No part of the individual's life is outside its detailed supervision and control. If the Bible teaches that we live, move, and have our being in God, totalitarianism teaches that we 'live, move and have our being in the State'. According to totalitarianism, the individual's life is not his own. It is a trust given to him by the State to be used in the service of the State. In the words of Mussolini, if the nineteenth century was an age of socialism, liberalism, and democracy, the twentieth century is to be a century of authority, collectivism, and the totalitarian State.

According to totalitarianism, the State is all in all. It is omnipotent and infallible. In the words of Mussolini, 'Beyond the State, nothing'. The State is an absolute in comparison with which all individuals and groups are relative. It is an absolute, permanent and supernaturally sanctioned institution. Mussolini's motto to the Italian people is: 'All within the State; none outside the State; none against the State'.

The Foreign Policy Association of America defines the totalitarian State as follows: 'For the pluralism of the modern democratic State, where the Government is only one of several groups which have the individual's allegiance, fascism has substituted the totalitarian State which embraces all the activities of individuals and subordinates them to national ends'. A high Italian official defined the totalitarian State as 'a State of truly sovereign authority which dominates all the forces of the country'.

Ttotalitarianism assiduously cultivates State worship. According to its teaching, the individual is to attain significance only by his service to the State and is to find complete self-fulfilment in this service. Seiburg says that with the coming of Nazism 'there are to be no more human beings in Germany but only Germans' ! Any one who wants to live 'in Germany, with Germany and through Germany is obliged to submit to the nation and to adapt himself to the totalitarian State'. 'Every individual's life belongs not to him but to the State and to the State alone.

The Totalitarian State is thus an unlimited State. It does violence to the richness and variety of voluntary group life. Religion, morals, and education are subordinate to the State. In Italy even sporting, educational, and recreational associations were centralized in Fascist hands. Franz Schanwecher, a Nazi theorist, wrote: 'The Nation enjoys a direct and a very deep unity with God.... Germany is the Kingdom of God'. The aim of totalitarianism is to obliterate the fundamental distinction between the State and society and make the State omnicompetent.

Totalitarianism assumes different forms in different countries. It assumed the form of Fascism in Italy, and Nazism in Germany. Even in the Anglo-Saxon countries where the love of individual liberty has been strongly rooted, State activity is on the increase, and this may lead to a new type of totalitarianism which may be called democratic totalitarianism. It is possible that the United States may evolve a form of 'constitutional dictatorship'.

It is a mistake to assume that the totalitarian theory of the state was a full-fledged theory to start with, in response to which recent totalitarian movements have sprung into existence. What has happened is that the totalitarian theory has been worked our of practical movements and actual life situation. Here is a case where theory has followed facts, instead of it preceding them. This is particularly true as regards Fascism and Nazism, both of which were essentially anti-intellectual movements which could only be understood in the light of the peculiar economic and political conditions of Italy and Germany in the years succeeding World War I.

2. FEATURES OF THE TOTALITARIAN STATE

1. The totalitarian State is a repudiation of reason and a glorification of instincts and impulses. This was particularly true in Fascist Italy and Nazi Germany. The theory of the State developed in those countries was anti-intellectual. Instinct and will were given priority over reason. In the western world as a whole the conception of man as made in the image and likeness of God is declining.

2. The totalitarian State is dictatorial in character. It is opposed to liberalism and to parliamentary government[1]. It vests supreme power in the hands of one individual or in one party. Russian dictatorship is a dictatorship of the left, while Italian and German dictatorships were dictatorships of the right. The former is on the whole the dictatorship of a party, while the latter was the dictatorship of an individual. In both Fascist Italy and Nazi Germany there was unquestioned odebience to the leadership of one man.

Parliamentary democracy is anathema to the totalitarian State. It is criticised as being stupid, corrupt, and slow-moving. Parliaments are looked

1. The Nazi Party slogan ran thus—'*The nation and not the individual is the first concern of Law*'.

'Liberalism is the philosophy of life from which German youth now turns with nausea, with wrath, and with a quite peculiar scorn, for there is none more repugnant, more opposed to its own philosophy. German youth today recognises the Liberal as the enemy'.

(Moeller Von Der Buck, 1934.)

down upon as mere talking shops, incapable of accomplishing results; at times of emergency they are absolutely helpless. According to a Fascist apologist, democracy is a decaying corpse. Totalitarianism believes in the gospel of direct action. Yet it is not autocracy pure and simple. It combines the aristocratic principle of government by a privileged *elite* with a democratic width in the basis of selection

3. The Totalitarian State crushes individual liberty. The periodical purges of its political opponents and army generals are illustrative of this fact. Fascism and Nazism do not believe in the common man at all. They regard the conception of individual liberty as a fetish of the past.

Totalitarianism tolerates no political opposition. It is government by one party. Whatever criticism is allowed is within the party. In criticizing, the aim should be to make the existing machine work better but not to overthrow it under any circumstance. The totalitarian State allows no liberty of thought, speech, and writing. Severe censorship is exercised over the press, publication of books, radio, moving picture industry, theatre, music and art. There is no liberty of meeting or liberty of association.[2] Strikes were forbidden in Fascist Italy.

In Italy and Germany professors and schoolmasters were sifted and resifted. The school was used for political propaganda purposes. State centralization took the place of local life. The civil service, judiciary, army and university were purged of 'anti-national elements'. University Presidents in Germany were appointed by the Kultur Minister. No criticism of the regime was permitted in the press. Leading Italian intellectuals were killed, imprisoned or exiled. The mysterious diisappearance of Matteotti in Italy in 1924 and the execution of Roehm and his group in Germany in 1934 are too well known to require comment.

According to totalitarianism, ideas are more dangerous than actions. The totalitarian state completely swallows up the individual; individual has no right against the State.

Both Fascism and Nazism carried on intense propaganda and used all possible psychological methods to appeal to the mob. They made use of marches, military uniforms, and rhetoric to rouse the people. Germany maintained poisons and concentration camps for her political opponents. Within the first few months of their coming into power, the Nazis put fifty

2. 'There is no freedom of the individual : There is only the freedom of peoples, nations or races; for these are the only material and historical realities, through which the life of the individual exists'.

(Dr. Otto Dietrich—1937).

'The denial of the right of freedom of movement is a pre-requisite for the whole of our future life and must be insisted upon even if millions consider these restrictions on personal liberty as harmful.'

(Rosenberg).

'Equality before law will be conceded to all who assist the nationai cause and do not refuse to support Government.' (Hitler—1933).

to eighty thousand political prisoners into concentration camps. Hitler's teaching was that in propaganda the end justifies the means.

The press in the totalitarian States was required solidly to support the Government. According to Dr. Goebbels, the press was to be developed into a piano upon which the Propaganda Ministry could play any time it liked. There was to be only one public opinion and the nation was to think unitedly. German wireless talks were one series of military and warlike harangues. Preparation for war was the one constant theme. Under war conditions to litsen to enemy propaganda was a crime punishable with death. In Fascist Italy, likewise the government head of the press decided what news was to be published and what suppressed. In these circumstances it was no wonder that people even gave up the habit of reading newspapers.

The individual in the totalitarian State is completely subordinated to the authority of the leader and the hierarchy. The Fascist oath reads : 'In the name of God and Italy I swear to execute without discussion the orders of the Duce and to serve with all my strength and if necessary with my blood the cause of the Fascist revolution'. Authority, discipline, and subordination were the watchwords of the Fascist Party. The motto given by Mussolini to the youth organization of his country was 'To believe, to obey, to fight'.

4. Totalitarianism glorifies the nation and emphasizes the idea of the State as a power system. Narrow nationalism, chauvinism, aggressive warfare, and imperialistic expansion were some of the essential features of Fascism and Nazism.

According to Fascism, international peace is a coward's dream; pacifism is 'an act of cowardice in the face of sacrifice'. The Fascists exploit the nationalistic sentiment. They exaggerate and distort the internationalism of the socialists and communists. The jibe thrown at socialists is that they are the friends of every country but their own. In the words of Ebenstein : "Totalitarian, imperialist fascists look on war as the highest form of national life; communists—while rejecting in theory, war between nations—accept the inevitability of war between classes and the liquidation of the *bourgeoisie* by violent means", (op. cit. pp. 342-43).

Fascist Italian education was chauvinistic to the highest degree. The schools were conducted under a system of drill and discipline, military in its character. Force and violence were extolled. The man of action was praised rather than the thinker.

Both Italy and Germany wanted colonies for expansion for raw materials, and for the sale of their manufactured goods, as well as for the satisfaction of their 'will to power'. Mussolini said : 'Imperialism is the eternal and immutable law of life.... We are forty millions squeezed into our narrow but adorable peninsula'. Italian expansion, said Mussolini, was a matter of life and death. Italy 'must expand or perish'.

Mussolini and Hitler openly preached the necessity of war. It was necessary for the development of manly qualities. Fascism chose an internal policy which involved war as an external consequence. Hitler believed in the power of the victorious sword. He demonstrated the truth of the remark of Lord Birkenhead that the world continues to give its glittering prizes to those who have sharp swords and stout hearts. Roehm said : 'Pacifism is, according to the view of the soldier, cowardice on principle. Cowardice is no philosophy, but a defect in character'. Totalitarian countries are militaristic and spend huge sums of money on armaments, even at the expense of food.

Hitler's ambition was not only to reconquer the territories lost under the Treaty of Versailles but to annex all those lands where there were substantial German minorities. Events after the Munich Agreement (1938) made it clear that Hitler would not be satisfied till he established something like a Monroe Doctrine over Central and Eastern Europe. But the series of military reverses which he suffered at the hands of Russia made such a dream impossible of realization.

5. The totalitarian State is exclusive. It does not believe in liberalism and humanitarianism. Germany built up strong race prejudices and hatreds. It believed that the Nordic race was the best of all, although science gives us no conclusive evidence of racial superiority. While probably only less than half of the German population is Nordic, the evolution of a pure Aryan race was the aim of Nazism. The Nazis strove to safeguard the purity of their language, literature, and race.

The totalitarian State is exclusive, further, in the sense of trying to make itself economically self-sufficient. The economic policy of both Italy and Germany was to make themselves as little dependent as possible upon foreign countries for the supply of materials required for the prosecution of war. In pursuit of this policy Germany produced considerable quantities of synthetic wool, cotton, and rubber. As a State she entered the field of foreign trade and commerce with a view to pushing forward the sale of her finished goods.

6. The totalitarian State became a rival of religion. While Fascism made religion a tool of the totalitarian State, Nazism particularly bade men give unto Caesar that which belongs to God. It was out to establish a narrow, excluisve, and un-Christian Christianity known as Nordic Christianity. Whatever in the Bible, in the teachings of Jesus, and in Christian traditions did not fit into the Nordic ideology was thrown overboard. Hitler was the New Saviour. He was the Messiah, the vicegerent of God upon earth. The totalitarian State was an enemy of the totalitarian religion. J. A. Spender wrote : 'Russia has tried to extirpate religion, Mussolini to sterilise it, Hitler to annex it'[3]. It may be added that Franco exploited it.

3. '*German land, German blood, German soul and German art*—these four must become for Germans the most sacred things on earth. And when every man and woman is penetrated by these four sacred feelings, then they will be ready for that which unites and crowns them all, namely the acceptance of the German Nordic Religion.'

7. Totalitarianism in all the dictatorial States beacme a mass movement. In the absence of a free vote it is difficult to say how far totalitarianism is based on genuine popular support. To start with, totalitarian ideas and dictatorial methods were confined to a few and were even scoffed at by the many. But by grim determination and resolute purpose a handful of well-organised and well-disciplined members of such a group, with a clear idea of their political and national objective, succeeded in placing themselves at the helm of affairs. Not only that, they managed to win the solid support of the masses. In winning this support, especially in Italy and Germany, knowledge of mass psychology and practice of direct action and of terrorism played a notable part. In Germany and Italy the passion of hatred and vengeance, the bogey of Communism, and the wonderful opportunity of conquering far-flung empires, which, it was supposed, would place the people above want and give them plenty of room to expand—all these were used in winning popular support. Appeal was made not to reason but to the baser passions of man, with the result that the masses obeyed the behests of the State in a blind and mechanical manner. They were drilled and disciplined so thoroughly that they rushed to the battlefield and the conquest of other people's territory like a swarm of locusts driven to action by some blind, unreasoning instinct.

3. WHAT TOTALITARIANISM HAS DONE

However much we may disagree with the aims and policies of totalitarianism, we cannot gainsay the fact that Fascism, and Nazism gave to the people of the respective countries 'a faith to live by and a cause to die for'. It unified the people and promoted national solidarity.

Totalitarianism in Nazi Germany and Fascist Italy did some good things for the people, but it was at the expense of their freedom. It meant iron discipline, military might, and war. Whatever prosperity there was short-lived having been based on false premises. Today under democratic regimes West Germany and Italy have made much economic progress, far greater than their progress under dictators.

Although totalitarianism in these countries has been defeated, there is no guarantee that it may not rise again. How an intelligent and intellectual people like the Germans could have given themselves over to totalitarianism and dictatorship will long remain a mystery. What the success of totalitarianism indicates is that there is in man a craving to follow leadership and authority as well as for action. If this desire is to be directed along right channels, it needs to be corrected and limited by the other desire to develop one's own resources of self-help and self-direction as well as of one's own reflection.

4. WHAT OF THE FUTURE?

The good which the totalitarian States have accomplished is nothing when compared with the price that people have had to pay for it. As A. D.

Lindsay says: 'Democracy's fundamental quarrel with such a government is not that it is a dictatorship, but that it is totalitarian, not with how the government comes into being—by elecion or otherwise—but with what the government sets out to do. For the totalitarian government proclaims that the only business of individuals is to serve and exalt the power and might of the State, while the democrat maintains that the only business of the State is to serve and further the free life of society' (*52:7-8*).

Totalitarianism has meant the crushing of individual liberty and the suppression of human personality, violence at home and unshamed aggression abroad, the brutalizing of human nature and the militarization of a whole people. The injustices of the Versailles Treaty, which have been a blessing in disguise to the dictators in their militaristic and aggressive policies, or other injustices of the present cannot last for all time.

Totalitarianism has shown clearly that eternal vigilance is the price we have to pay for liberty. Lip service to individual liberty, equality, fraternity, and humanitarianism is not enough. It should be buttressed by positive action. What the rise and spread of modern dictatorships show is that dictatorship is the outcome of fear and insecurity. Fascism arises when the middle classes become panicky.

Totalitarianism succeeded to a remarkable extent because it exploited to the full the half truth that men are fundamentally irrational. By a careful study and skilful use of man's instincts, feelings, and prejudices, it rose to power. It has shown clearly the urgent need there is for every statesman and administrator to possess a sound knowledge of group psychology and mastery of the technique of propaganda. At a time when society and culture are becoming politicised, totalitarianism calls our attention to the urgency of an intelligent and realistic study of political forces. It further directs attention to the fact that any philosophy is better than no philosophy so long as there are people earnest about it and willing to work and die for it.

One of the fundamental weaknesses of totalitarianism is that while it has a full grasp of the gregarious nature of man, it overlooks the craving there is in every man for solitude, reflection, and self-examination.

If democracy is to succeed there is no use of it simply fighting dictatorship. Instead of being a formal concept, democracy must become a living reality, divesting itself of class domination, economic injustice and imperialistic exploitation. It must invade every sphere of life, holding aloft the apparently conflicting principles of liberty and equality.

FASCISM IN ITALY

Totalitarianism in Italy and Germany is directly traceable to the Versailles Treaty and to the events following it as well as the Communist wave which was spreading over Europe soon after World War I.

The end of the Great War witnessed the ascendancy of liberal democracy for a while at least. Both the victors and vanquished were thoroughly tired of war. There was a genuine enthusiasm for peace, internationalism, and democracy. But the statesmen who gathered together at Versailles to shape the world were not equal to the task. The outworn doctrine of the sovereign nation State in the form of 'the self-determination of nations' was made the basis of future arrangements. This brought into existence a number of small States which could not stand on their own feet. Instead of working out a genuine European federation, the League of Nations was set up, which was used by Great Powers as their interest dictated. Colonies were added to the victors under the guise of the Mandatory System.[4] Huge reparations were inflicted on the vanquished. Germany was told that she was solely responsible for the war, the 'war guilt clause' becoming a sore point with Germany for many long years afterwards. No serious attempt was made, at least in the early years after the war, to tackle the economic problems following the war despite the League loan to Austria and the Dawes loan to Germany. Politics and economics were kept in two different compartments, the financial control of the world being in the hands of the victor powers. Provision was made for collective security, but it practically remained a dead letter, its place being taken by what Crossman calls 'collective pacifism'. 'Victory seemed to have deprived France and Britain of their dynamite; their conservatives ceased to be ardent imperialists, and their socialists lost their revolutionary power'. (Crossman, 256). They still had considerable military strength, but disdained to use it so long as the *status quo* was tolerable. The myth of sanctions was invented, but was hardly used. The only time it was used (during the Abyssinian war of 1935-36) the very powers using it sabotaged it. All this meant the collapse of the democratic morale. On the other side, particularly in the immediate post-war years, there was the bogey of communism threatening to bring about a world revolution. It is against this background of the post-war European situation that Fascism in Italy and Nazism in Germnay have to be understood and interpreted.

1. The Emergence of Fascism in Italy

The term 'fascism' is derived from the word 'fascio' which means a bundle of rods, symbolizing discipline, unity, and strength. During the Great War it meant all those who bound themselves together to live or die 'for the good of Italy'. The first 'fascio' with Mussolini as leader was formed at Milan in 1915 and was reformed in 1919 as a 'Fighting Band' to combat communism. In the parliamentary election of 1919, the Fascists failed to secure even a single seat. Mussolini himself, heavily defeated at Milan, was described as 'a corpse awaiting burial in a ditch'. But the 'corpse' lived and

4. In the words of Crossman : 'The old order of national states was re-established, the colonial empires enlarged, economic imperialism encouraged and Central Europe Balkanised'. (12 : 253).

within three years Fascism became the governmental authority of the country.

A series of events conspired to the meteoric rise of Fascism to power. One of these was the weakness of the post-war liberal governments of Italy. These were blamed for not having fully secured the interests of Italy in the Peace Conference at Paris. Although one of the victors of the War, Italy received no valuable addition to her territory. She was bitterly disappointed at not receiving Smyrna or any of the mandates. To add fuel to the flame, the debt to the Anglo-Saxon countries was mounting up high. A series of strikes broke out, seriously dislocating the economic life of the country. The socialists were planning a revolution. Parliamentary obstructionists were having a free hand. In the face of all this, the government of the day remained inactive, afraid to strike.

At this moment, Mussolini appeared on the scene as the 'champion of the united Italy standing for order, discipline, and a strong government.' During World War I he had shed his earlier revolutionary zeal and faith in international socialism and fought as a soldier for two years. He was now burning with a sense of outraged patriotism and was determined to make Italy a first-rate European power. He claimed that liberal democracy was a luxury which wealthy countries like England, France and America could afford, but not a poor country like Italy. What Italy wanted, he said, was leadership and discipline. The ineffectiveness of democracy in Italy, in the eyes of her people, was coupled with the effectiveness of western democracies against Italy in the Peace Conference and the years following it. This made democracy anathema to the Italians. Along with distrust in democracy there went a deep distrust of the League of Nations and a grim determination to destroy the Anglo-French hegemony. All this surging discontent found an embodiment in Mussolini.

Earlier in his life, Mussolini was strongly influenced by the syndicalist teachings of Sorel. Under his influence he was a firm believer in the general strike and class war. But the post-war Italian situation compelled him to abandon these tenets of Sorel, while not surrendering his faith in the general syndicalist position, particularly in the gospel of direct action. On August 1, 1922, a general strike was declared, and this proved to be a godsend to the Fascists. By taking over the essential services themselves, the Fascists brought the strike to a close within twenty-four hours, thereby earning the gratitude and confidence of large numbers of people.

On October 28, 1922, after the government of the day had further discredited itself, Mussolini and his followers marched on Rome and occupied the public offices, railways, post and telegraph offices, etc. This was on the whole a peaceful event. The government could do nothing but resign. A day later the King sent for Mussolini to form the Ministry, and this he did readily on October 30, 1922. After that day he was the undisputed ruler of Italy till his fall on July 24, 1943.

In the early days of the movement, Mussolini, feeling his way to power, had no fixed programme and he changed his position more than once. He declared that what Italy wanted was 'not a programme, but action'. His early cabinets consisted of persons belonging to various parties, and it was only after 1926 that the government became exclusively Fascist and completely dictatorial. In November of that year, all political parties, except the Fascist, were suppressed and the press was muzzled. By a series of enactments the Ministry was relieved of its responsibility to parliament and Mussolini became the 'Head of the Government', solely responsible to the King and issuing decrees having the full force of law. The ministers became the subordinates of the dictator instead of being his colleagues. He himself was called *'Il Duce'*, which means 'the leader'.

The old Chamber of Deputies was abolished in 1928 and its place was taken by a 'Corporative Parliament'. This Parliament comprised 400 members representing economic interests, instead of territories and population and membership to it was manipulated by the Fascist Party organization called the Grand Council of Fascism, which was also the Grand Council of the National State. The Chamber was given no power of initiative. It could submit only proposals submitted to it by the 'Head' but could not reject them. The Head of the Fascist Party was also the head of the Fascist Government.

The Senate consisted of Princes of the Royal House and an unlimited number of members appointed for life by the King on the advice of the Prime Minister. It could debate, amend, approve or reject bills set up by the lower house. Bills amended or rejected by it were returned to the lower house for reconsideration.

2. The Ideology of Fascism

In spite of the fact that Fascism reigned supreme in Italy for twenty-one years, it did not have a well-worked out theory behind it. It is the practical outcome of Italian conditions immediately after World War I. It preaches a gospel of National Action. Vitalism is its keyword. It is opposed to Individualism, Capitalism, International Socialism, Liberalism, and Parliamentary Democracy. It is particularly opposed to Communism, which is based on the idea of class war and dictatorship of the proletariat. However, unlike Communism, which has a philosophy of its own which is logically worked out in the light of evidence rationally evaluated, though the method adopted may rest upon an intellectual confusion, 'the philosophy of fascism has been largely *ad hoc* and has been patched together from the existing fund of ideas either to justify what had already been done or to meet situations that were immediately in prospect.' It 'is fundamentally irrationalist, offering a myth created by intuition or by instinct and made 'true' by the very act of willing or believing it' (*Sabine*).

Fascism advocates a State with vigorous action. Mussolini wrote: 'Fascism is a religious conception in which man is seen in immanent relation to a higher law, an objective will that transcends the particular individual and raises him to conscious membership of a spiritual society.' This is a modern version of the Hegelian theory of the State. It rejetcs the Marxian interpretation of history as well as democratic individualism. Its basis is the idea of the Nation as the ultimate moral being.

In 1911, Mussolini wrote: '.......against others and against ourselves....we have destroyed every known creed, spat upon every dogma, rejected every paradise, flouted every charlatan—white, black or red—who deals in miraculous drugs for restoring happiness to the human race. We put no faith in any system, nostrum, saint or apostle; still less do we believe in happiness, salvation, or the promised land.... Let us get back to the individual. We stand for everything that exalts and ennobles the individual, gives him more comfort, more liberty, and a wider life. We fight against everything that restricts and harms the individual. Two religions, one black, one red, are fighting today for the mastery of our minds and of the world; two Vaticans are sending forth encyclicals, one in Rome and the other in Moscow. We are the heretics of both these religions' (*12:268*).

Believing as it does in action and national unity and solidarity as against government by discussion and compromise and allegiance to international movements, such as Communism, Fascism distrusts reason. It makes a powerful appeal to sentiments and emotions, making use of such means as militray uniforms, rituals, and rhetoric. It invents a myth which is calculated to rouse the feelings of the people. It assumes that the masses are not interested in politics and do not have the capacity to govern themselves. According to its teaching, what the average man wants is not the control of industry or self-government, but opportunity to earn a decent living and a national leader whom he can follow blindly. It is worthy of note that parliamentary democracy never became deeply rooted in Italian traditions; dictatorship was not an unusual phenomenon.

Based as it is on the national idea in a country where parties and the party system of government have been a source of weakness, Fascism is openly and avowedly government by one party. It allows no opposition. The murder of Matteotti, a member of the Italian Parliament, in 1924, under mysterious circumstances, is not something which can be easily explained, his only fault having been that he spoke his mind freely in parliament. Count Balbo lost his life in Africa in an equally mysterious manner. The Fascist party is considered to be the incarnation of the new spirit. Anyone opposed to it is an enemy of the country. Even trade unions were dissolved in favour of Fascist labour organization. Unlike Nazi Germany, Fascist Italy allowed a certain degree of freedom to the workers' syndicates and to the peasants' co-operatives.

It is a mistake to assume that there was nothing but terrorism in Italy. The chief reason for the success of Fascism for over twenty years was the dynamic leadership of Mussolini. At the time that he came into power, Italy was treated as an inferior nation by western democracies. But in a few years Mussolini succeeded in making Italy the chief Mediterranean power biding his time for domination and Empire in northern Africa. Neither the socialists nor the communists in the early years after the war were able to give Italy the leadership which she required. The socialists were slaves to parliamentary mentality, seeking to win support by argument and persuasion. The communists, on the other hand, were incessantly talking about class-war and world revolution, thus frightening not only the middle classes and financiers, but even the bulk of the labouring classes. In these circumstances it was easy for Mussolini and his party to come into power and claim that they were truly representative of the whole people.

The Fascists were nationalists first and last, but their nationalism was of a narrow and chauvinistic kind, openly advocating aggressive warfare and imperialist expansion. In their teaching and practice, Machiavelli came back to life. Any course of action was justifiable, according to the Fascists, if it redounded to the glory of Italy. During World War II Italy followed a frankly opportunist policy. The moment she found that France was weakening, she threw in her lot with Germany and succeeded in bringing about the collapse of France.

Fascism is an enemy of Internationalism. 'International peace,' it proclaims, 'is a coward's dream'. 'Imperialism', said Mussolini, 'is the eternal and immutable law of life'. Elsewhere he wrote: 'We are forty millions squeezed into our narrow but adorable peninsula.' And in order that the people of this 'adorable peninsula' may have elbow room, Abyssinia was annexed in 1936 under a slight pretext after a most brutal warfare. 'Italian expansion', said Mussolini, 'is a matter of life and death'. Italy 'must expand or perish'. Mussolini further wrote: "War alone brings up to their highest tension all human energies and puts the stamp of nobility upon the peoples who have the courage to meet it."

War was used in Italy to divert peoples' attention from the internal difficulties of government. Fascism deliberately chose an internal policy whose external consequence was war. It believed neither in the possibility nor the utility of world peace.

Writing on the Fascist ideology, Hallowell says that fascism repudiates the concept both of individual liberty and of equality. The individual exists for the sake of the State, which Mussolini described as 'a spiritual and moral factor in itself'.

Fascism acts instinctively, and not rationally. It considers all values as relative. Truth is what the dictator declares is to be and right is what he wills. If Nazism is a myth of race, Fascism is a myth of the nation. At the basis of both lies despair.

Ebenstein on Fascism. Analyzing the ideology of Fascism, Ebenstein claims that fascism is a post-democratic political system which cannot be understood except as a reaction to democracy. It is not possible of development except in countries with some democratic experience. But in countries where democracy has been practised for a number of years, fascism cannot easily take root.

Fascism also calls for some industrial experience. Industrial skills and resources, says Ebenstein, are necessary for the success of fascism. In its early stages it appeals to industrialists and landowners who support it with a view to averting communism or other radical political movements. The lower middle classes also support it because of their aversion to the proletarization of society. "In times of depression, fascism appeals to the unemployed, hopeless, cheerless—the forgotten men of society". (Ebenstein, op. cit. p. 575).

In the realm of ideas fascism believes in racialism and imperialism. It believes in the idea of the *elite* nation. It denies the principle of the basic equality of people. It accepts man's inequality and even raises it to the status of an ideal.

Fascism advocates violence and falsehood and rejects accepted standards of moral conduct. It regards the State as an end in itself and the individual as a means to it. It advocates authority and totalitarian uniformity in all spheres of social activity. It places reliance upon military training and indoctrination.

It is regrettable that fascist tendencies are beginning to appear in some of the political parties of India.

3. Achievements of Fascism

In the early years of their advent to power, Mussolini and his followers undoubtedly did much for their country. National finance was restored. Every aspect of national life was reorganized with a view to efficiency. Agriculture was improved. Industry was established on a firm basis. Marshes were drained and new city was built on what was once the abode of mosquitoes. Means of transportation were improved beyond recognition. Buildings of imposing designs were constructed.

Later years, however, told a different story. The cost of living went up while wages were deliberately reduced. More was done for landlords and peasants than for industrial workers. Unemployment became a serious problem prior to the Abyssinian War, and intensive military preparation was resorted to as a measure of relief to the unemployed. There was a lowering of the standard of living. The unwholesome diet of the Italians became still worse under Fascism. Small businessmen suffered more than big capitalists. Under Fascism, as under capitalism, there were business cycles and recurring periods of depression. As Sabine observes: 'The ideals of self-sacrifice, obedience, and devotion to national welfare are not really preached with a whole-souled acceptance of their moral value. Always the hope is held out that they are means which will lead to future economic gains in the place of present sacrifice and for those upon whom the sacrifice bears most heavily. . . . It is the emotional substitute for a tangible good that honest fanaticism or shrewd self-interest offers to simple-minded idealism'. (*12:774-5*).

The Corporative State. Fascism claims that its most original and distinctive contribution in the economic field is the Corporative State. Its boast is that it is neither capitalism nor socialism, but something new and infinitely superior. In the words of Mussolini : 'Corporatism supersedes Socialism and supersedes liberalism : It creates a new system'. Elsewhere he says that 'of all his actions, the Corporative State is the most courageous, audacious and original, in other words, the most revolutionary'. Although we may not be willing to concede these extravagant claims, we are prepared to believe that in the idea of a corporative society, as against the Corporative State, it is possible to find the basis for the reorganization of the modern State.

In the idea of the Fascist Corporative State, medieval guild and modern syndicalist ideas are blended. As Miss Wilkinson points out, Fascism is not a blank capitalist reaction. It has its socialist elements. The Fascists, as another writer says, are socialists as well as capitalists, because both capitalistic and socialistic tendencies are real.

The Fascist criticism of present-day capitalism is that under it the employees and employers are organized into opposite camps and the common interest of the people is ignored. Fascism tries to bring together the interest of the workers, of the employers, and of the consuming public into a common whole. The guiding principles are national production and promotion of the common interest. Workers, masters, and consumers, it is claimed, all belong to an organic unity and, therefore, their interests are to be correlated.

While all this may be true in theory, the practical question which confronts us is the extent to which the Fascist State accomplished the end in question. Until 1934, Italy was a corporate State without corporations, the Ministry of Corporations having been in existence for many years preceding. Corporations were officially established by the law of February 5, 1934.

The organization of the Italian Corporative State makes it clear that to the State and the Fascist Party is given a dominant part. The reason for this exalted position is the assumption that the State and the Fascist party represent the interests of the consumers—an assumpion which cannot be eaily substantiated. The employers and employees are represented by two parallel sets of institutions, with the State and the Fascist Party acting as the supreme arbiter and connecting link. Government lays down certain conditions for the recognition of Corporations. Associations which do not fulfil these conditions have no legal standing. A corporation includes all the phases of production from the stage of raw materials to that of finished goods. Each Corporation is controlled by a Council which is headed by a member of the cabinet, an Under-Secretary of State or the Secretary of the Fascist Party. According to Ebenstein, the corporative state implies a distrust of the people.

The organization of the Corporative State is exaraordinarily complicated. There is much duplication and overlapping. In 1925, there were 22 Corporations and 9 national confederations (later 13). The latter represent the associations of employers and of workers on the vertical principle, while the former represent them on the horizontal principle.

The powers of the corporate bodies are largely advisory. They undertake the settlement of labour disputes, conclusion of collective labour contracts, educational and social work, and improvement of national production. They also determine wages, hours of labour, production and distribution, and exercise supervision over apprentices.

The Corporative State suggests the idea of planning, based on a collectivist rather than an individualist conception. But in reality it is not so. Production still rests upon private enterprise. Private initiative and private property are retained. According to Mussolini, private property completes human personality. It is a right, and if it be a right it is also a duty. John Strachey, who is an unsympathetic critic of the Corporative State, claims that Fascist planning is planning with the consent of the capitalist. It is planning along the lines of least resistance.

Trade unions and associations of employers were replaced by 'Corporations' wholly dependent upon the State. Workmen and employers had equal representation in the Corporation, but as Sabine says, 'it would be taking a good deal for granted to assume that equal representation means equal power or equal access to the ministry and that influence goes always through the regular channels of the Corporation'. Strikes and lock-outs were forbidden by law. The maximum punishment for striking was imprisonment for seven yeras. Special Labour Tribunals were granted power to punish workers if more than three simultaneously quit work. Labour courts settled all differences arising between the classes in the interest of the whole nation. They did not have to wait till they were called upon to arbitrate but could intervene even before. This, said John Strachey, looked like a reimposition of old Combination Acts. A Charter of Labour was given to the labouring classes guaranteeing to them certain privileges such as holidays with pay, medical aid at nominal cost, compensation of various kinds, old age and death insurance, etc. Joad hailed the Charter as the 'Magna Carta of Labour'.

Not only strikes were forbidden, but also speculative and excessive profits Prices were lowered by government decree in 1930 and 1933. The employer was not allowed to do what he would with his own.

The Corporative State increased production, but did not bring about any great improvement in real wages. After 1926-27, the Italian banks were controlled, the Bank of Italy regulating all credit. No new bank could be opened without government consent. Certain industries such as the iron industry were amalgamated, while others such as shipping were sub,idized.

The motive behind all this planning in both Italy and Germany was imperialistic expansion and war. Industry and even agriculture were under the control of an advanced degree of government regimentation. The whole structure was patterned after the army and 'built around the principle of hierarchy, unity of command, and discipline'. It rested entirely on the

Party, 'which is just as much the mainstay of the economic system as it is the pillar of the political regime'.

Although we do not approve of all that was done in Italy in the name of the Corporative State, the idea of corporative society is one which cannot be slighted. As Rev. P. Carty points out, the common good of society, the rights of the State, and those of individuals should be equally respected and promoted. The trouble with the Corporative State of Italy was that it was organized for war. What we want is a corporative society organized for peace. Instead of the State taking the initiative in creating corporations, corporations should be the result of 'the private initiative of free men organising themselves with the approval of the State'. This is the chief difference between the Corporative State and Corporative Society. Besides, a corporation should be free from the control of a political party, its functions being economic and social and not political. Instead of trade unions and employers' associations being abolished, as in Italy and Germany, they should become part and parcel of the corporative society.

To quote Prof. Carty again, in the corporative society each corporation which represents the permanent interests of a definite community will be approved and controlled by public law. Within the limits allotted to it by the Charter, it will be governed democratically, exercising over its members legislative, executive, and even judicial functions. This does not mean the annihilation of State sovereignty. It only means 'autonomy to a degree compatible with the general public good and limited by the Charter conferred by the state' (*11:154*). Equal representation will be given to employees. After full discussion the corporation will draw up a code which will be 'binding on the whole professional group for a specified time' (*11:155*). Such a code, before becoming effective, will have to receive the approval of the State which will scrutinize it from the point of view of the general common good and integrate the various codes into a human economy.

The code will regulate 'the strictly economic activities of the given professional group; volume, trade, quota and technique of production; prices and marketing; advertising; tariffs; proposed dealings; with allied occupational groups etc.;' (*11:155*). It will also 'regulate social-economic relations within the profession itself; wages, hours and condition of work; compensation; paid holidays; family allowances; profit and management sharing various forms of insurance' (*11:155*).

With such a system of Corporations, the State will be free to devote its time to political and military functions, the corporations looking after the economic and professional interests of its members. It is difficult to say in detail what the ends, methods and powers of each corporation should be. The aim may be 'to maximize production, to maintain remunerative prices, to eliminate competition, to seek the maximum national strength or the maximum social peace.' Whatever the aim may be, which is bound to vary according to time and place, 'the governing consideration should be the promotion of an intelligently and practically human end'.

NAZISM IN GERMANY

1. The Emergence of Nazism

The circumstances under which Nazism arose in Germany were in many respects similar to those under which Fascism had its origin, although there were some striking differences.

Germany was defeated and disillusioned country in 1918. The people had been taught to believe that their army was invincible, and when it went down before the allied troops, it caused great consternation. The Treaty of Versailles, which brought the war to a close, was never popular in Germany. It soon came to be characterized as a dictated peace. Many of the terms were harsh and were calculated to reduce Germany to a second or third rate power in the international world. A heavy disarmament programme was laid down, lowering the military prestige of Germany, For years, a German air force was officially forbidden by the Treaty. Huge reparations were demanded from Germany which, in the very nature of the case, she could not pay. It is true that they were scaled down later, specially by the Dawes Plan and Young Plan, and were finally repudiated altogether. But as long as the demand lasted, it infuriated the people and made the young feel that for many long years to come they were destined to be wage slaves of the allies.[5] The zone to the left of the Rhine was demilitarised and severe restrictions were placed on the possibility of Germany reasserting herself in the military field. When the reparations were not forthcoming, France and Belgium invaded the Ruhr in 1923 and kept their armies of occupation there for some years.

To add to all this, Germany was deprived of her colonies, which, by the astuteness of the allied politicians who were able to pull the wool over the eyes of President Wilson, were parcelled out among the allies in the form of mandated territoreis. A high-sounding scheme known as the Mandatory System was brought into existence, and the claim was made that the primary object of the Mandatory powers was to train their wards to the status of self-government as speedily as possible. What a vast gulf there has been between profession and actual deed is too well known to need comment ! Barring a few exceptions, the victors proceeded to treat the Mandates as their colonial possessions.

Within Germany itself there was economic collapse. The mark was depreciating fast and inflation came about. This meant the virtual wiping out of the professional classes. While the middle classes were reduced to poverty, the new rich who had profiteered during and after the war were making a conspicuous display of their wealth; and among this group there were not a few Jews. Unemployment was mounting up high, the number in

5. Writing in 1932, a young German said : 'We belong to a youth without hope in the future and without happiness in the present.'

1932 reaching the peak figure of 6 millions. German heavy industries were dismembered by the new frontiers which completely altered the map of Central Europe, depriving Germany of part of her territory and distributing some of her nationals over foreign lands.

When Germany was in this precarious condition, communism was making rapid headway and it looked as though Germany might fall a prey to the rapidly spreading communistic ideologies and methods. The only alternative to such a possibility seemed to be to frame a democratic constitution for Germany on the traditional lines of Western democracies. The Weimar Republic was the result of it. But from the beginning it was unpopular with the people. It was a professor's constitution, altogether academic and failing to take into account peculiar German traditions and temperament.

Instead of enthroning autocratic authority which the German adores, he was given a President, a Chancellor, and a Cabinet responsible to Parliament, and a long list of fundamental rights. Besides, those who were responsible for the Weimar constitution were blamed for not securing the best terms possible from the allied victors. The humiliation of national pride deeply affected the old ruling class, the bureaucracy, and the middle classes. The Treaty of Versailles and the German Republic were accepted as necessary evils; and the only ones who had any enthusiasm for them were the industrial workers.

The various governments which came and went under the Weimar constitution had insuperable difficulties to face : discontent and sullenness within the country and attempt to fulfil impossible conditions imposed upon them from without. Between 1919 and 1933 there were 21 cabinets headed by Chancellors. There were innumerable parties working at cross purposes with each other, 38 having participated in the 1932 elections to the Reichstag. The Social Democrats who had a large following could have been the saviours of the country if they had been true to their professions and adopted a far-reaching and constructive programme for the economic rehabilitation of the country. But in their fear of communism, they were afraid to take bold steps, and instead, compromised with the industrialists and the landed aristocracy. The consequence was that so far as the distribution of political power is concerned, Germany under the Republic was not much different from Germany of the pre-war days. According to John Strachey, it was the weak-kneed and compromising policy of the Social Democrats which directly led to rise of the Nazis to political power.

The allied policy was to weaken Germany and to keep the democratic government of the country under their control. In the early years of the Peace, there was a disposition to extract Shylock's 'pound of flesh' from Germany. Nothing but cold reception was accorded to any suggestion for the removing of some of the unjust clauses of the Versailles Treaty. Even some of the most modest requests of the German statesmen were contemptuously rejected. Concessions were made subsequently but they were too late. The

Rhine was evacuated in 1930, five years before the time contemplated. In 1932, the reparations were written off. But for none of these credit was given to either the Republican Government of Germany, which won these diplomatic victories, or to the allies which granted them.

It is against this political and economic background that we have to understand the rise to power of the Nazi movement. When it originated, it was an inconspicuous movement confined to some 28 people. The founder of the movement was a locksmith by the name of Anton Drexler. It had not definite programme to start with, except its refusal to accept the defeat of the German army, claiming that at the moment of success it had been 'stabbed in the back'. Of the 28 original members only six were active. Adolf Hitler was admitted to it as the seventh member. At the time, Hitler was an altogether unknown person. He was an Austrian German and had migrated to Germany in 1912. He fought during the war and was wounded, receiving an Iron Cross in recognition of his services, and having risen to the rank of a corporal. Mussolini, his counterpart in Italy, on the other hand, was a national leader and had played a notable part during the War even before he established the Fascist dictatorship.

A point of difference between the two men was that while Mussolini was a brilliant thinker and had a flair for philosophy and political theorizing, Hitler was an imperfectly educated man, though endowed with great native gifts. He was a bundle of sentiments and emotions, with an overdeveloped sense of his own importance. He had probably never read in their original, the writings of Hegel or Houston Chamberlain, many of whose ideas he incorporated into *Mein Kampf*.

The movement to start with was known as the German Workers' Party. But in 1920, the second year of its existence, it came to be known as the National Socialist German Workers' Party and still later as simply the National Socialist Party. The final change was indeed significant because it served as a party label in bringing together all those who claimed to be nationalists and socialists. The programme of the party, as outlined at the beginning by Gottfried Feder in twenty-five paragraphs, contained several radical demands such as the abolition of unearned incomes, the confiscation of war profits, nationalization of trusts, expropriation of land, etc. Nobody took the movement seriously during its early days, although it was clear that it was a reaction to the national humiliation to which Germany had been subjected by the allies. Members of the lower middle class and of military organization and students were attracted to the movement, but the bulk of the industrialists and the upper middle classes kept away from it. Those who were drawn to the movement were drawn not so much by the radical programme as announced by the party, but by its militant spirit. Hatred and vengeance were the bases upon which the party was founded. It was pledged to fight all the enemies of 'true Germany', particularly the 'Marxist-Liberals', the Communists and the Jews.

Up to 1923, the movement spread gradually. In that year, Hitler participated with General Ludendorf in a *putsch* in Munich, which was a failure. Hitler was arrested, tried and sentenced to imprisonment for a period of five years but was released after eight months. During this period of enforced leisure he wrote his *Mein Kampf,* which became the Bible of Nazism.

From this time on the movement began to increase in numbers and popularity, gaining momentum as it went on. The radical programme of its earlier days was modified in such a manner as not to frighten the propertied classes. 'Expropriation of land without compensation' was, for instance, interpreted in such a manner as to apply only to 'Jewish speculators in land'. Some of the ex-efficers of the Army who had joined the party helped to build up the 'Storm Troopers', who became the military backbone of the party. Military marches, uniforms, party symbols, like the swastika, and fist fights with the police and the communists all these appealed to the romantic and fighting instinct of the German youth. Other factors which played a notable part in winning adherents to the party were the skilful use of progapanda by the Nazi leaders, the passionate oratory of Hitler, and the incessant appeal by leaders to sacrifice and discipline in the name of a greater and unified Germany.

As time went on the industrialists, propertied classes, and bureaucracy became more and more sympathetic towards the Nazi cause. The advocacy of an aggressive nationalism appealed to them especially when they knew that Hitler did not mean to put into operation the radical demands of the party as expressed in its earlier days.

Although there was nothing spectacular in the growth of Nazism in its early years, the tide turned definitely in its favour in 1929, and the world depression and widespread unemployment of this period gave a fillip to the movement. In the 1932 election to the Presidentship, Hitler stood against Hindenburg and secured 11.3 million votes on the first ballot and 13.4 million votes on the second. From this time on, the Nazi party was the strongest party in the legislature, although there were some temporary setbacks later. The Social Democrats had little more than half the number of seats secured by the Nazis. Hindenburg called upon Hitler to form a coalition government in November, 1932, but this he refused. The offer was repeated on January 30, 1933, and this time it was accepted. From that time on, Hitler and his Nazi associates reigned supreme in Germany.

The first Cabinet of Hitler was rather mild and non-revolutionary. But the party had immense sway over the country by its thorough organization and the control it had of the political machine and the police. The Reichstag was dissolved on March 5, 1933, and the mysterious fire which had consumed the Reichstag building a few days earlier was made out to be the signal for a great communist rising. In the confusion which followed, the President suspended several of the fundamental rights of the citizen guaranteed by the constitution. Elections to the Reichstag were held in this tense atmosphere and the Nazis secured 52 per cent of the seats. The 'Enabling Act' over which the election was fought and won gave the

Nazi government practically unlimited power for four years.

From then on, the typical Nazi programme was put into operation. The civil services and the judiciary were purged of 'non-Aryan' elements. A people's court was set up to act as a convenient tool in the hands of the Government. The press, the radio, the theatre, and the cinema were placed under the control of Dr. Goebbels, Minister of Enlightenment and Propaganda. Schools and universities were similarly placed under the guardianship of the Minister of Education. A law was issued making the Nazi Party the only legal party in the country, and the setting up of any other party was declared to be a criminal offence. Trade unions were dissolved and labour was brought under the control of the Nazis. Elections to the Reichstag were held in November, 1933, and the Nazis secured 92 per cent of the total votes cast, not without the use of much direct and indirect pressure. On the 1st December, the party was incorporated into the machinery of the State.

The federal system was abolished and each of the Reich State (now divided into artificial districts) was placed under a personal representative of Hitler, endowed with virtual dictatorial powers. The next step was to abolish the upper house, the Reichsrat, which had hitherto represented the component units. When Hindenburg died in 1934 Hitler combined in his own person the powers of the President and Chancellor, and in his hands were also concentrated supreme executive and legislative powers. He became the Chancellor and Fuehrer and the undisputed ruler of Germany. The Reichstag was summoned occasionally, not to make decisions but to applaud the doings of Hitler.

2. The Ideology of Nazism

It is not easy to state the ideology of Nazism, inasmuch as Nazism is not a well-worked out theory of State or government, but a movement which arose in response to a widely felt emotional need. Its roots, therefore, are founded in the peculiar mental and emotional set-up of post-war Germany, and especially of Hitler. It is true that some of the elements of the Nazi political theory run true to the German type, but many of them can be explained only in terms of conditions in post-war Germany. The personality of Hitler and his peculiar psychological complexes on such questions as rank and the place of women in society have been so inter-twined with the Nazi theory that it may be more accurate to describe Nazism by the appellation "Hitlerism'. The spiritual progenitors of the movement were such great German idealists as Kant, Fichte, and Hegel, Gobineau and H. S. Chamberlain, and the Italian Mussolini.

True to the German tradition, Nazism elevates the State to a dizzy height. But this is done not in a highly philosophical way as was done by Hegel, but in a tremendously practical way in response to the actual needs of Germany. Realizing that national unity is the first requisite of redeeming the national pride of the country the Nazis look upon the State as a superhuman entity. The *Volk* or, Community, is the raw material out of which the State is built; and in order that the *Volk* may be strong, the motto which the Nazi party continuously placed before the country was 'the interests of all before the interests of one'. According to Hitler's philosophy, 'the individual is nothing, *das volk* is everything!' Emphasis is placed on duties rather than on rights.

Contrasting the English tradition of the State, which looks upon the State as a servant, with the Prussian tradition, according to which the State is a master, Spengler writes: 'There we see personal responsibility, self-determination, resolution, initiative; here loyalty, discipline, selfless renunciation, self-training.... The individual does not count; he must sacrifice himself to the whole. Not each for himself but all for all, with that inner freedom in obedience'. This means that the individual is to have no freedom of choice or private initiative. He is to find his meaning and happiness in implicitly obeying the behests of the well-ordered State. Compulsory service of the State constitutes perfect freedom. In this teaching of the Nazis we hear an echo of Hegel's teaching on the Sittlichkeit. The practical outcome of this type of teaching, as a shrewd observer has remarked, was to make Germany great but the Germans small.

The Nazi Party was the connecting link between the Volk and the State. It organized the people into a strong unit and enabled them to work together in union under common leadership. What the State did was to lend the weight of its sovereign authority to the programme and activities of the Party. This meant in practice that the State was the Party and the Party was the State. No other party could be tolerated because it meant the weakening of the State and the frittering away of its energies. According to the Law of July 1933, '(1) the National Socialist German Workers' Party is the only political party in Germany; (2) Whoever undertakes to maintain the organization of another political party, or to form a new political party is to be punished with imprisonment in a penitentiary up to three years'. It was no wonder that Hitler and his associates poured contempt on parliamentary democracy and democratic institutions. What they wanted was national unity and solidarity, and no opposition of any kind.

True to their traditions, the Nazis conceived of the party in terms of leadership and hierarchy. The hierarchy which they advocated was not one which worked from bottom upwards but in the reverse direction. The leadership contemplated by them was not the democratic leadership which was broad-based and was both responsive and responsible to the desires of the people, but a leadership which was taken by the strong arm and was maintained by it. According to the Nazi philosophy, some are born to lead and others to follow. Hitler was the head of the State, of the Government, and of the Army. His word was law. All his associates in the task of government were his nominees and extended to him the most loyal support. The Storm Troopers and the Black Guards who were originally formed to protect the party and maintain public peace and on whose backs the Nazis rose to power, were organized in a military fashion, and their first concern was the safety and welfare of the Leader. There were even suicidal squads in Germany ready to commit suicide if Hitler gave the word on behalf of the State and the Party. The party invaded every sphere of life. The provincial and district officers were all leading members of the Party appointed by Hitler on the recommendation of the Minister of the Interior. In the place of the old trade unions there were Nazi cells in the labour unions carrying on vigorous Nazi propaganda. The Labour Front was a complete Nazi organization. Nazi agents were found everywhere, even in the innermost recesses of the family. It was not unusual for children to give evidence against their parents or vice versa if there was the least suspicion of the slackening of enthusiasm for the Nazi cause on the part of the parents or children. The Hitler Youth, which was an organization of the young people of the country, was a powerful ally of the Nazis.

The ascendancy of the Nazi Party and its spreading itself over the whole life of man meant regimentation of the worst kind, although such regimentation was in accordance with the German temperament and tradition. Prince Bulow was not wrong when he described his countrymen as 'unpolitical' in the sense that they lacked a sense of civic rights and civic courage. However courageous the German may be on the battlefield, he has not got the moral courage to stand up to his rulers. He simply kow-tows before them. This accounts for the startling acquiescence of the German in war and aggression, and for his dubious political morality. It also explains the reason why he readily agrees to strict censorship and imprisonment without trial. According to a well-known German newspaper (1936), 'Concentration camps are no disgrace; on the contrary they are an ornament to Kultur. Here neglected individuals are educated to real life with the firmest kindness!' While listening to enemy broadcast in Germany was a serious crime, the harangues of Lord Haw Haw from Berlin formed a national amusement of Englishmen.

The characteristic feature of the State is, according to the Nazis, Vigour and Force, and not Justice or Morality. Nazism stresses the German doctrine that might is right. In the words of Fichte who wrote in the nineteenth century: 'Between states there is no law save the right of force'. Nazism preaches and practises the gospel of the victorious sword. In the words of Hitler: 'He who would live must fight. He who does not wish to fight in this world has not the right to exist. Such a saying may sound harsh, but that is how the matter stands.' Dr. Krieck, Headmaster of the Mannheim Public Schools, said: 'The task of the universities is not to teach objective science, but the militant, the war-like, the heroic'. General Von Seeckt, a former chief of the Reichswehr, wrote: 'War is the climax of human achievement. War is the natural and last phase of development in the history of mankind. War is the father of all things. War is the most simple affirmation of life. Suppress war, and it would be like trying to suppress the operations of nature. These are also terrible. Every living thing is terrible'.

While they were making vigorous preparations for war, the Nazis made the world believe that they were ardent lovers of peace and that whatever military preparations were being made were in the interest of all. As late as 1935, Hitler said at a party meeting: 'There can be only one yardstick for our conduct, our great, unshakable love for peace.' In accordance with the Nazi creed, pacific professions were made in order to lull the enemy to sleep. But the moment Hitler felt strong enough to exhibit his military strength, he began to annex neighbouring territories under one pretext or another.[6]

The early pretexts for the use of force were the undoing of the injustice of Versailles and the gathering together of all German people under one flag. From being a purely nationalist movement, Nazism soon came to mean a pan-Germanic movement.

German minorities living in foreign lands were instigated to stir up trouble and pretend that they were being mercilessly treated by their foreign masters in order to give the Nazis a chance to annex the territories in question. This happened to Austria, Czechoslovakia, and Poland.

Not content with annexing territories where there were considerable German minorities, Hitler, set on world domination, brought under his heel Norway, Denmark, Belgium, Holland, France, Greece and the Balkan States.

For months before World War II commenced, Hitler made it a matter of deep grievance that the colonial possessions of Germany, taken away by the Versailles Treaty, had not been returned to Germany. His constant plea was for the restoration of the 'stolen property', taking care at the same time not to say anything about the rights of those from whom the original theft took place. He also used such plausible arguments as were contained in phrases like 'living space' and 'encirclement', to cover up his aggressive design and to stir up the emotions of his followers. The Nazi movement thus begun as a purely nationalist movement, soon passing into a pan-Germanic movement, became a ruthless imperialistic movement and a menace to world peace.

Standing as it did for a strong and vigorous German people and a warlike German State endeavouring to assert itself over the whole world, Nazism was intensely racialistic and found in the Jew a convenient scapegoat for the miseries of Germany during the preceding twenty years. The myth of the Aryan race was invented and drastic steps were taken to extirpate the so-called non-Nordic element from the German soil. Blatant lies were uttered in rousing popular indignation against the Jews. In one of his earlier speeches Hitler exclaimed: 'What? You German people, the noblest in the world, you in whose veins runs the Germanic, Nordic, Aryan blood, you are

---

6. Apropos of German militarism, Mirabeau once said about the third Reich, "Prussia is not a state possessing an army, but an army possessing a state." (101 : 697).

reduced to poverty, to misery! You know not whence your bread will come tomorrow, and why? Because your armies were defeated in the war? No. They were never defeated. Never! They were victorious everywhere, but when they were on the eve of final victory they were stabbed in the back by Jewish-Marxist traitors.' A popular Nazi saying was: 'The Jew is our misforture. Hitler is our Saviour'. In the treatment of the Jews and their political opponents, the Nazis practised cruelty and acts of sadism unbelievable in the twentieth century.

The Nazi theory was that the Aryans were the master builders of civilization and that the rest of the world was composed of lesser breeds. Accor-ding to Hermann Gauch, 'The non-Nordic man occupies an intermediate position between the Nordics and the animals, next to the anthropoid ape. He is not a complete man. He is really no man at all in true contradistinction to animals, but a transition, an intermediary stage. Therefore, apt for him is the appellation subhuman.' According to the same high authority: 'It has not been proved that non-Nordics cannot mate with apes.' They cannot profit by education or changed environment.

The scientific belief that there is probably no pure race anywhere in the world did not trouble the Nazis in the least; nor the fact that probably less than half of the German population is 'Nordic', a large part of the remainder being of the Alpine stock. In the name of race purity, mixture of races was totally prohibited and public servants could not retain their posts if they or their forbears as long ago as two or three generations had had Jewish blood in their veins. Even if the wife of a public servant had a trace of Jewish blood in her veins, the husband could not retain his post.

To this extreme racialism were added an intense devotion to German paganism in religion and to the theory that the German woman is valuable only as a breeder of pure Nordic children and the preserver of the Nordic race. Both Catholicism and Protestantism were condemned because of their internationalism and 'slave morality'. Prof. Ernst Bergmann wrote: 'We of the German religion today turn to this ancient Nordic, Indo-Germanic Light-Hero figure and get rid of a false and diseased Christ picture created by the Christian Pope and Church to the hurt of humanity. The high priest of the new German paganism is Hitler himself. He is the real Holy Ghost. Hitler is lonely. So is God. Hitler is like God. Hitler is a new, a greater, and a more powerful Jesus Christ.' The Christian churches of Germany were muzzled and dared not open their mouths for fear of concentration camps.

In the Nazi scheme of things, according to Herr Von Papen. 'Mothers must exhaust themselves in order to give life to children. Fathers must fight on the battlefield in order to secure the future for their sons.' The declaration of the Women's Order of the Red Swastika claimed: "There is no higher or finer privilege for a woman than that of sending her children to war'. According to Hitler, who was a confirmed bachelor until shortly before his death, 'In the education of women emphasis must be laid primarily on physical development. Only afterwards must consideration be given to spiritual values and lastly to mental development. Motherhood is undeniably the aim of feminine education'.

Some Nazi writers openly advocated sex immorality if it would result in the multiplication of thorough-bred Nordic children. Thus Dr. Willibald Hentschel wrote : 'Round up a thousand German girls of the purest stock. Isolate them in a camp. Then let them be joined by a hundred German men equally of purest stock. If a hundred such camps were set up, you would have a hundred thousand thorough-bred children at one stroke.'

The Nazi State encouraged large families by its taxation policy and in a score of other ways. It looked upon birth control as a sin against the nation and it regarded the home as the natural place for women. This latter belief was later relaxed on account of the exigencies of war.

In all of this there is no doubt a high type of 'idealism', but it is directed along wrong channels. There is no humanity or fellow-feeling for outsiders. The Nazi theory of the State, as well as of Society, places great emphasis on leadership, discipline, authority, unity, and even rigid uniformity. Nazism is a sworn enemy of individualism, liberalism, pacifism, internationalism, socialism and communism. It condemns liberalism as too easy-going and characterises it as a luxury which a struggling people like the Germans, can ill afford It frowns upon the Marxist class struggle as being destructive of the spiritual unity of a nation. It looks upon international peace as a coward's dream. In the words of Herr Buch (1937) : 'Whoever wishes to play a leading part in Germany can no longer belong to any group which in any way has internationalities.'

When we turn from the political to the economic theory of the Nazis, we find the same emphasis on national unity and solidarity. General welware is placed above private interests, and a policy of autarchy aiming at the economic self-sufficiency of Germany was systematically followed. Both undiluted capitalism and socialism are rejected because they divide the people into warring camps. The capitalist as well as the labourer is controlled in the name of the State and for the sake of the people, and there was in Germany no separate organization for employers and employees as was in Corporate Italy, because Nazism denies the existence of any conflict of interest between capital and labour. Both employers and employees were induced to join the Labour Front, which was closed to Non-Aryans. Big industries were allowed to continue but were rigidly controlled by the State. No money was allowed to be taken out of the Reich. Fresh capital could be obtained only with the approval of the State. The Reich Chamber of Economics, working under the Minister of Economics, controlled industry, commerce, banks, insurance, public utilities, and handicrafts without disallowing private enterprise. After 1933, the German Government exercised complete control over the banking system of the country. Government permission was to be secured for the import and export of goods. Strikes and lockouts were forbidden. 'Courts of Labour' were set up for trying offences which were considered a breach of 'social honour', *i.e.* against the self-respect of labourers. Wages and prices were fixed.. Hitler believed in giving the small man a chance. The whole economic structure, like the political, was built on the leadership principle and was patterned after the army. The rights of private property and individual initiative were subjected to greater restrictions in Nazi Germany than in Fascist Italy.

In relieving unemployment, the rearmament programme of Germany, coupled with public works programmes including housing, highway construction and land reclamation, played a notable part. Young men under 25 in some cases were replaced by older people. Women were displaced from industries in order to give place to men. Families were encouraged to engage extra domestic servants by granting them a special income-tax allowance.

In order to conserve their food resources for war purposes, many articles of food were severely rationed. 'Guns for butter' was the slogan of the country. Outlining the Nazi policy in 1935 Goering said: 'We had to make up our minds whether we would use our foreign exchange for metals or for other things. We could either buy butter and surrender our freedom or we could seek to win our freedom and give up butter. We have decided in favour of the latter. The German people has demonstrated that it is ready to make great sacrifices for a great purpose'. 'Eat National Socialist'! was a slogan issued by the Nazi Health Bureau in 1936. All of this goes to show that for many years the German people were placed under a 'perpetual war economy'.

In the carrying out of the Nazi programme and the working out of the Nazi theory, the powerful personality of Hitler, ruthless organization and vigorous propaganda played an unusual part. Though a man of action, Hitler was also a dreamer and mystic. He looked upon himself as an instrument of world destiny. In order to keep himself fit for the service of his country he was abstemious in his habits, ate no meat and neither drank nor smoked. The same rigid discipline and single-minded devotion to the State and the people he demanded of his followers. He was the incarnation of an idea. By his savage oratory he exercised mass hypnotism. It was no wonder that the people of Germany elevated him to the level of a deity. In the words of a writer of that time: 'He does not talk—he orates; he does not discuss—he pronounces judgment; he does not walk—he strides'. It is likely that history will consider Hitler the most conspicuous madman of modern times.

The Nazis proved themselves to be powerful organizers and master propagandists. There was no one in Germany who did not feel the influence of the Nazis at every turn. Children, young people, women, industrialists, and labourers were all organized into Nazi propagandists. Men like Goebbels, Goering, and Ley gave the word and, in the twinkling of an eye, it was broadcast through the length and breadth of the country. Hitler, who was a master of the art of propaganda, gave his own prescription for successful propaganda in the pages of *Mein Kampf*. 'Effect on the broad masses, concentration on a few points, unremitting repetition of them, self-assured and self-confident formulation of the text in the form of apodeictic assertions, the greatest perseverance in propagation and patience in awaiting result Hitler laid down the maxim that the lower the intellectual level of propaganda the greater the number of people who will be embraced by it. Paraphrasing it, Goebbels said: 'Propaganda is the art of simplification'. Writing on the gullibility of the Germans, Hitler said: 'The German has no idea how much people must be misled to obtain the support of the masses.' Propaganda, he further said, had nothing to do with abstract truth. He expressed the view that 'a bold life, if big enough, is likely to gain credence by its very bigness.'

The pulpit and school, the stage, cinema and radio, the press, art, science and literature were all made to do service to the Nazi cause. Nazi propaganda was introduced into every subject at school. Arithmetic was made a matter of estimating the size and destructive force of bombs, and religion became worship of the Fuehrer. When the child returned home from school for lunch the parents greeted him with 'Heil Hitler,' a phrase which the German used from 50 to 150 times a day. Every man, woman, and child was required to belong to at least one Nazi organization. A Nazi school text-book which every German child was required to use contained the following precious sentiment:

'Our Leader, Adolf Hitler.
We love you
We pray for you
We like to hear you
We work for you, Heil'

3. Estimate of Nazism

Nazism was the greatest menace of mankind in the thirties and forties of the present century until it was thoroughly defeated in 1945. Though defeated, it is still capable of resuscitation in new forms. It shows how ordinarily intelligent people can be led astray by constant appeal to their baser instincts and emotions.

Nazism has the wit to make the maximum use of the grievances of a war-weary people, to find a scapegoat for all their ills, and to offer them specious remedies. It started as the last bulwark of capitalism. Once in power, it acted independently of capitalists and proceeded to destroy capitalism. It used socialistic methods and socialistic institutions not to establish socialism and social justice but to build up a military state on a totalitarian basis. Economic considerations were subordinated to military expediency. A dictatorship was established on a broad popular base, and the leader came to be regarded as almost God on earth. Liberal traditions were swept aside with a few master strokes and people became hypnotized. Brutality and violence came to be the order of the day. The greatest war of all times was let loose on earth, causing incalculable destruction for almost six years.

The myth of race was so assiduously cultivated that the Jews came to be pictured as the very embodiment of evil. Nazism was in the words of Hallowell 'the political manifestation of spiritual, intellectual, social and political anarchy'.

The lessons to learn from the rapid rise and downfall of Nazism and Fascism are many. Man is still far from being a completely rational creature. Therefore, his blind passions and impulses need to be kept under proper control. If liberalism becomes weak-kneed and is afraid to protect the civic and political rights of its people, it throws the door open to Fascism. Democracy as a political constitution is of no avail unless it can daily be translated into economic and social justice and has behind it an unshakable faith in God and an equally unshakable faith in human beings and their high destiny, not as a mass but as individuals.

Irrationalism and militarism bring their own reaction sooner or later. Thought and reflection are inimical to the fascist mentality which is a denial of reason. Militarism soon brings its own destruction. They that take the sword perish with the sword. Racialism is a barbarism which the world cannot tolerate any longer with safety. Political and economic nationalism are fast becoming outmoded and, therefore, people need to orient themselves to the new concept of a world democracy and world citizenship.

Fascism as an Antithesis of Laski's Political Philosophy

The exact antithesis of Laski's political theory may be found in fascism. The fascist conception of political dictatorship may be contrasted with Laski's faith in paliamentary institutions and constitutional government. Similarly, the refusal of the fascists to alter the class relation of a capitalist society is in direct opposition to Laski's demand for a redefinition of class relations on a socialist basis (*50:130*). Aggressive militarism and imperialism of the fascist nation-state may be regarded as the repudiation of Laski's ideal of world peace and international co-operation through the agency of a world organization like the former League of Nations or the present United Nations Organization. Lastly, the Nazi policy of a systematic suppression and persecution of the Jews had a personal significance for Laski inasmuch as he himself was a Jew. It is not surprising, therefore, that Laski should reserve his bitterest comments he ever made to be hurled against the fascist system (*131:105*).

Incoherence of Fascist Theory

It is not easy to describe the theoretical assumptions of fascism in a coherent way because it has no consistent philosophy of its own. The fascist theory is rather a generalization of the fascist practice. In fact, the fascist movement has preceded the fascist theory. It has been constructed partly as a justification of the strategy and tactics of the fascist movement and partly as a repudiation of the principles and policies of its political rivals.[7]

7. See Mussolini's essay on "The Doctrine of Fascism" quoted by Oakshott in "Social and Political Doctrines", pp. 164-179.

Fascist Movements Born of National Humiliation

Both in Italy and Germany, the fascist movements were born out of national humiliation and frustration. The aggressive nationalism of the fascists was an antidote to this aspect of national psychology. The economic crisis was ruining the middle class in both these countries. The fascist theory of the corporate state based on the cooperation of all classes retaining the privileges of the upper and middle classes and guaranteeing full employment to the working-class created a powerful mass movement with the main support of the middle class but in which all other classes also participated. The fascists also exploited certain myths like the racial myth of the Nazis to consolidate their movement and attempted to put forward a pseudo-scientific explanation of such myths.

Need for Contradicting Rival Political Theories

Besides this rationalization of the strategy and tactics of fascism, the fascist theory included certain assumptions which were accepted for no other reason but to contradict the theoretical assumptions of the political rivals of the fascist movement. In the first place, its theory was built upon the negation of Marxism. Secondly, it was a repudiation of the assumptions of liberalism.

Negation of Marxist Doctrines

As the Marxists were self-proclaimed materialists, the fascists became the believers in a form of ethical and political idealism. Since communists and socialists advanced the theory of class war, the fascists rejected it as harmful for the nation and said that class conflicts are superseded in the corporate state. While the Marxists desired a radical change in the relations of production, the fascists became conservative defenders of the *status quo* in the economic sphere. If the Marxists believed in an international brotherhood of workers, the fascists denied the principle of international solidarity of the working-class by supporting an aggressive nationalism in their own countries.[8]

Repudiation of Liberal Principles

Finally, the fascist theory contained a dogmatic repudiation of the basic principles of liberalism. Fascism believed in the primacy of the state over the individual and did not attach any significance to individual liberty. The freedom of speech and thought has no meaning in the fascist state. The press, the cinema, the arts and sciences, literature and philosophy, and educational institutions are controlled by the state.

No political party but the fascist is tolerated in the state. All political opposition is ruthlessly suppressed. The opponents of the fascist government

8. The opposition of fascism to democracy, liberalism, socialism and internationalism has been clearly emphasized by Mussolini in his essay on "The Doctrine of Fascism."

are either executed or tortured to death in the concentration camps. The Nazis even considered the systematic annihilation of the Jews as a race as necessary for the political safety of their system. Elections and franchise became meaningless in such a totalitarian society. The representative institutions of the liberal state are mutilated and suppressed. All power is concentrated in a small party caucus around the fascist dictator who receives the reverence of a demigod in his country.[9]

The Meaning of Fascism

In the opinion of Laski, fascism is a counter-revolutionary movement of the capitalist class to resolve the contradiction between the political democracy and an economic oligarchy by overthrowing the former in the interest of the latter. In its early phase of expansion, capitalism could work the democratic compromise by extending certain concessions to the working-class which it is unable to do now. "The situation is wholly different", says Laski, "when capitalism is in a phase of contraction. The price of the concessions expected by democracy then appears too high. The assumptions of capitalism then contradict the implications of democracy. If the phase of contradiction is prolonged, it becomes necessary either to abrogate the economic assumptions upon which the society rests" *(50:130)*

Fascism as an Effort to Save Capitalism

The fascist movement is an effort to save capitalism by abrogating the democratic process and instituting a totalitarian dictatorship in its place. In its phase of contraction, the capitalist system leads to continuous decrease in wages, mass unemployment, and a deterioration of the standards of living for the common people. The capitalists clamour for a reduced taxation of their profits and a withdrawal of the welfare activities of the state. This cannot be effectively done in a political democracy based on universal suffrage. Hence, the capitalist class encourages a fascist party to capture the state power on its behalf and carry out its desired programme *(131:27)*.

Alliance with Capitalist Forces

The technique of fascism whether in opposition or in government may best be understood only in the light of its alliance with the capitalist forces of the community. "By the abrogation of democracy, in one form or another", says Laski, "it has entrusted unlimited political power to those who won and control the means of production. Its methods have followed a fairly uniform pattern. All political parties which deny its purposes have been suppressed. The free trade unions have gone, and with them, the right to strike. Wages have been reduced either unilaterally by the employers, or with the approval of the state. The right to free criticism has been suppressed; and the power of the electorate to change its government has been withdrawn" *(50:131)*.

---

9. See Oakeshott's remarks about Nazism in "Some Notes on the Doctrines of *Mein Kampf*", in his "Social and Political Doctrines", pp. 203-205.

Alliance with the Militarists

Moreover, the fascist movement is built up and the fascist authority is consolidated on the basis of an understanding with the army leaders who are interested in the preservation of the vested interests. The fascist party also creates a private armed band of its partisans to terrorize its political rivals into submission and seize power by a demonstration of force. It is only with the cooperation of its armed forces that the fascist government is able to establish a totalitarian society.

Control over the Church, Bureaucracy and the Mass Media

The so-called neutral character of the bureaucracy is entirely destroyed and it becomes completely subservient to the fascist party. The churches are compelled to glorify fascist ideals and remodel their dogmas in the light of the fascist ideology. The press, the wireless, the cinema, the literature, arts and sciences have to identify themselves with the objectives of the fascist party and government *(49:13)*.

Stability of the Fascist Regime

But the stability of the fascist regime and its capacity to preserve the capitalist structure depend solely on its success in maintaining the loyalty of the army generals. It can crush all internal opposition and discontent so long as these generals remain loyal to the fascist leaders. The fascist concern for the popular or national well-being is dismissed by Laski as propaganda which has no substance behind it.

Suppression of Trade Unions and Working Class Parties

Laski says that the policy of fascist state safeguards the right of profit-making for the capitalist class. It is a capitalistic state without the liberal features of a bourgeois democracy. Hence, trade unions and political parties of the working class are suppressed though the fascists justify this on the ground that such class organisations hinder popular or national well-being. Both Hitler and Mussolini pointed out the value of propaganda, however deceitful it might be, in the pursuit of their political objectives and their struggle against ideological adversaries. Neither the individual nor the class could have any claims against the state or nation. But the end of a fascist state was quite compatible with profit-making motive of the capitalist class. This class and the fascist ruling elite determined what constituted the good of the nation.

Capitalistic Nature of Fascist State

When the profit-making motive is the basis of production in the fascist societies, it clearly demonstrates the essentially capitalistic character of the fascist state and government. Neither in Italy nor in Germany the fascist state attempted any alteration in the socio-economic structure of the community. The class relations of the capitalist society were preserved and strengthened by the corporate state. The suppression of trade unions and political parties of the working class deprived it of its capacity of resisting the domination of the capitalist class. This clearly shows the contrast between the social objectives of the Russian Revolution and the fascist counter-revolutions of Italy and Germany.

Contrast with the Dictatorship in Russia

In Russia the class relations were fundamentally altered and the dictatorship was exercised for the suppression of capitalism. The ownership of the means of production was transferred from private individuals to the community as a whole. In fascist regimes the means of production are privately owned and the workers even lose their right of advocating public ownership because of the loss of civil liberties. In a capitalist democracy the working class, at least, enjoys the right of criticizing the principles of distribution and the relations of production and the right of forming trade unions and political parties. Under the iron heel of a fascist dictatorship, the working class loses its right to question the class hierarchy of the corporate state and the unjust distribution of wealth in the community.

Fascism not Neutral Between Labour and Capital

Laski does not agree with the fascist argument that the state acts as an agency of independent arbitration between labour and capital. He says that it is impossible for the fascist state to act as an impartial or neutral body by virtue of its economic assumptions. ([illegible]). "The fascist state", he says, "must obey its fundamental postulates; and these, by the fact that the private ownership of the means of production is maintained, imply subordination of its habits to the motive of private profit. It was the threat to private profit in the first year of his *regime* which compelled Hitler to move to the right and abandon those policies which had a socialist emphasis. It was the threat to private profit, also, which has made the Fascist state in Italy acquiesce continually in the reduction of wages. Once capitalist postulates are assumed, that is to say, the incidence of state action must necessarily be biased in favour of owners of capital. To resort to different principles would be incompatible with the inherent nature of Fascism" *(50:134)*. Thus Laski concludes that the fascist government, like any other government in a capitalist society, remains an executive committee of the class which dominates the system of production.

Professor Gregory's Argument

There are certain writers like Professor Gregory who argue that it is wrong to identify fascism with capitalism in decline because the essence of fascism is its authoritarian character while the basis of capitalism is individual liberty and private enterprise.[10] Professor Gregory also points out

10. Laski criticizes Professor Gregory's interpretation of fascism because his view represents the outlook of all liberal anti-Marxist critics of fascism like Professor Catlin, Professor Maxey and others.

that the twenty-five points of the Nazi programme and the Communist doctrine have many similarities but they have little in common with the theory of capitalist democracy.[11] Moreover, he thinks that the rise of fascism does not indicate the breakdown of capitalism because it succeeded only in those capitalist countries where democracy had not taken firm roots in the local soil. The post-war situation and certain other non-economic factors were more responsible for the growth of fascism than economic difficulties of the capitalist system.

Deceptive Similarity Between Fascism and Communism

Laski, however, strongly disapproves Professor Gregory's interpretation of the rise of fascism. He says that the resemblance between the fascist and communist programmes is deceptive because the socialist part of the fascist programme is never meant to be translated into practice. It is true that the fascist state is authoritarian and it interferes in the economic affairs of the community to a very great extent. "But", as he points out, "the character of the interference, both in Italy and Germany has been interference of capitalists in the interests of capitalist recovery" *(50:153)*.

Business Depression of 1929-33

Moreover, the intensity of the business depression of 1929-33 clearly demonstrated the inadequacy of the capitalist system in the world as a whole and exposed its inherent weakness. Fascism was a temporary but desperate effort of the capitalist class to prevent its final collapse. Laski admits that there are non-economic factors which also played their part in the rise of fascism but these factors in the absence of a world crisis of capitalism could not have produced fascism by themselves *(131:113)*.

Totalitarianism and Aggressive Imperialism

While the economic content of fascism is capitalistic, its political creed is a combination of totalitarian dictatorship inside the country and aggressive imperialism outside. Internally, the fascist party is completely identified with the state and so it controls and regulates all spheres of national life on behalf of the state. It embarks upon a policy of intensive rearmament and militarization of the country. The war efforts of the fascist regime provide employment to the unemployed which solves an important problem created by the capitalist crisis *(131:92)*. The totalitarian control of industry and labour enables the fascist government to exploit the productive potentialities of the industrial machine at a full level although the character of production targets to be achieved is largely military in character.

Fascist Dictator as Machiavelli's Prince

Laski regards the fascist dictator as Machiavelli's *Prince* in action *(50:197)*. "To continue in office", says Laski, "he must destroy the pos-

11. For the twenty-five principles of he Nazi programme see Oakshott's "Social and Political Doctrines", pp. 190-193.

sibility that any constitutional procedure may throw him out of office; hence he must be a despot of unlimited authority and unlimited tenure. But unlimited despotism can only impose itself by fear; hence the rule of law must go, to be replaced by that of terror.... His principles of action, for this end, are essentially two in number. The first is the exploitation of national sentiment; he redresses real grievances, he discovers imaginary ones for which he can demand an accounting. But to do this, once more, he must be armed. To arm himself means at once to dominate the economy of the nation and to minimize the risk attendant upon the redress of grievances which imply a threat to other states" (*131:95*).

Fascism Leads to War

This shows that the aggressive foreign policy of the fascist state is a necessary corollary of the internal rule of terror. It is not surprising, therefore, that the fascist policies are bound ultimately to bring about the catastrophe of an international war. Fascism is a denial of the rule of law in international relations and believes in the principle that might creates rights. This is evident from the policies adopted by Italy, Germany and Japan during the years preceding the Second World War.

Fascism has No Philosophy

Finally, Laski thinks that it is futile to search for a philosophy of fascism which is nothing more than an incoherent jumble of opportunistic generalizations. "Much effort has been expended", he says, "to discover a philosophy of Fascism. It is a waste of effort. Fascism is power built upon terror and organized and maintained by the fear of terror and the hopes to which conquest gives rise. It is the disciplining of society for a state of war in which martial law is permanent because the nation is forced to spend any brief period of peace in the preparation for war. It survives in peace by the intensity of the terror it imposes; it survives in war just to the degree that it is successful in war" (*131:96*).

Use of Violence to Undermine Reason

This clearly implies that fascism is a systematic use of force and violence to undermine the rule of reason in society. "All the fustian of doctrine, its exponents have presented us with", he points out "reveal themselves, on examination, as propaganda expedients which have no meaning except their power to bolster up the particular regime. The doctrine of Nordic superiority works in Germany; the doctrine of the Latin genius works in Italy, Anti-semitism is the historic weapon of every ruler who needs an enemy to exploit and property to distribute; and it is always popular with the illiterate masses in a period of economic strain. The insistence on the "manifest destiny" of the nation, whether Germany or Italy, is, at bottom, simply the search for new sources of wealth to be exploited as a means of maintaining acquiescence in the regime. Conquest means posts, investments, a market to be politically controlled. The attack on the democratic principle necessarily follows from the need of the leader to justify his own exercise of absolute power. If a constitutive principle in Fascism exists at all, it is simply and solely the principle that power is the sole good and that values attach only to those expedients which sustain and enlarge it" (*131:97*).

Denial of the Liberal Faith in Government by Discussion

Thus fascism is a total denial of the liberal faith in the rationality of man and the possibility of government by discussion. As the fascist himself accepts the irrational basis of his ideology, it is not necessary to refute it on rational grounds. Laski's answer to fascism consists in three things. First, he considers those steps which should have been taken to prevent the rise of fascism. Secondly, he urges that the only practical answer to fascism is to overthrow it by force. Thirdly, he considers the probable alternatives to fascism, when it has been overthrown, and their relative efficacy to prevent a re-occurrence of fascism in those countries.

The Alternative to Fascism

Before considering Laski's answer to the fascist challenge, it is necessary to emphasize that he does not regard fascism as an ideological system comparable to the ideologies of liberalism, socialism or communism. As Laski points out, "Fascism, in any of its forms, is at bottom a doctrineless nihilism; the attempt to provide it with a philosophic basis is the usual attempt of scholars to explain, or to provide a pedigree for, something altogether remote from serious influence upon its fortunes" (*131:107*).

The So-called Intellectual Roots of Fascism

There are many writers, who have tried to discover the philosophical basis of fascism in the doctrines of such diverse philosophers as Hegel, Nietzche, Schopenhauer, Bergson and Pareto.[12] Efforts have been made by learned men", Laski sarcastically remarks, "to find the roots of this outlook in the metaphysics of famous philosophers. One tells us that it comes from Kant; another blames its evil upon the fierce nationalism of Fichte; a third tells us that it is Hegel who introduced this servile worship of the state-power; yet another insists that the poison of Nietzsche's superman is, as it were, by inheritance in the veins of every German. Or we are bidden to note the influence of Sorel's confused mixture of Puritanism and Marx upon the mind of Mussolini; there we are told, in the volunminous speculations of Pareto, are the true sources of Italian Fascism. Others explore the philosophy of the German historians; it is Treitschke or Von Sybel, Mommsen with his Caesar-worship, or Droysen, who beget this dread temper."[13]

---

12. See Professor Maxey's remarks about fascism and nazism in his "Political Philosophies", Chapters XXXI and XXXII, pp. 636-661. See also Professor Sabine's analysis of fascism in his "History of Pol. Theory", Chap. XXXIV. pp. 747-775.

13. Laski : "Reflections on the Revolution of Our Time", Chapter III, p.. 107. At another place, Laski says, "Fascism, when closely examined, proves

Thus Laski concludes that fascism has no philosophical background or doctrinal coherence. It is, at best, an opportunistic collection of often conflicting ideas and there is a great divergence between its programme in opposition and its practice as government.

Danger of Fascism Inherent in Capitalist Democracy

Every capitalist society in its period of contraction runs the danger of succumbing to fascism. The rise of fascism can be prevented only by the transformation of the capitalist democracy into socialist democracy. The capitalist parties of the liberal democracy cannot provide any effective resistance to fascism because they are paralysed by their partial sympathy for the movement and its objectives. They even collaborate with the fascists and connive for their success on account of their fear of socialism.

Socialist Parties as Opponents of Fascism

The most serious opponents of fascism are the socialist parties which stand for a redefinition of class relations in a capitalist democracy. The fascists must paralyse and destroy the socialist movement of their country before they can hope to achieve victory. This is done by incorporating a semi-socialist programme as a part of the fascist programme which contains liberal promises of relief and betterment to all classes in society without noting the fact that the interests of one class clash with those of another. In Italy, the fascists before their coming to power agitated for abolition of the monarchy, expropriation of church property and war-profits, nationalization of banks and certain key-industries, and abolition of land-lordism and distribution of land to the tillers.

Semi-Socialist Slogans of Fascists are Deceptive

The twenty-five points of Hitler proposed abolition of incomes unearned by work and emancipation from the slavery of interest charges, nationalization of all business companies, confiscation of war-profits, expropriation of land for communal purposes without compensation, and reorganization of industries on the principle of profit-sharing between labour and capital. Both the Nazi and Fascist parties advanced these semi-socialist slogans with the object of breaking the anti-fascist solidarity of the working-class and winning the support of a section of the workers (*50:194*).

Disunity of Socialist Parties Helps Fascism

The socialist parties could not provide an effective resistance to the fascists on account of two important reasons. Laski says that the most important factor in this respect was division in the ranks of the working-class itself which was created mainly by the emergence of the communist parties as separate and independent organizations outside the socialist front. He

to be nothing more than an all-assorted rag-bag in which all kinds of remnants from the most diverse philosophies seek, as best they may, to find a place". ("The State in Theory and Practice", Chapter II, pp. 193-94).

wants that the communist parties should have functioned as part of a broad coalition of socialist parties and only then they could meet the fascist challenge with success. He thinks that the Communist policy of regarding "Social Democracy' as a moderate wing of fascism was wrong and fatal to the unity and solidarity of the working-class.[14]

Premature Communist Threats of Armed Revolution

The Communists wanted to destroy the influence of the Social Democratic leaders over the working-class and win it over for their revolutionary cause. But a larger section of the workers remained loyal to their socialist leaders and refused to cooperate with the Communists in their programme of revolution. The Communists, he alleges, not only disunited the working-class, they also spread panic in the circle of the ruling class by a premature threat of an armed revolution. This threat of an armed revolution by the communists was largely responsible for the creation of a counter-revolutionary force in the form of a fascist party. Laski, therefore, suggests that the problem of fascism could not have arisen if the Communists had refrained from advancing their premature threat of an insurrection and cooperated with the Social Democrats in achieving the common goal of socialism.

Failure of the Social-Democrats in Power

But as an impartial observer, Laski admits that certain policies of the Social Democrats were also wrong and contributed to the success of fascism. When the Social Democrats came to power in Germany, they refused to transform the socio-economic structure on socialist lines. They did not care to remove disloyal elements from the army and the bureaucracy. They did not nationalize the key-industries and refused to suppress the feudal privileges in land ownership. They allowed the Nazi party to grow and develop its influence to dangerous proportions under a cover of legality. They did not join the Communists even in their anti-fascist resistance and acquiesced in the unconstitutional dismissal of a Social Democratic government of Prussia without any effective protest, which is apparent from rejection of the Communist call for a general strike by the Social Democratic leaders (*131:90*).

"The Russian Revolution", says Laski, "is an example of the full use of favourable circumstances by men who had steeled themselves to the task of grasping their opportunity when it occurred; the German Revolution is the history of a missed opportunity. For while the Social Democrats willed the creation of a socielist state, when the state power fell into their hands they were not prepared to adopt it to socialist purposes. They left the main instruments of political authority in the hands of their opponents; effectively,

14. For the Communist explanation of Social Democracy'' as the moderate wing of fascism, see the remarks of Ralph Fox in his ''Communism and a Changing Civilization'', Chapter VI, pp. 111-124.

the counter-revolution in Germany was in being from the day when the old regime was overthrown" (*50:294*).

United Front of the Working Class Parties Against Fascism

Thus Laski concludes that the success of the Nazi counter-revolution in Germany was ensured by the hesitating and vacillating policies of the Social Democrats who failed to bring about the socialist transformation of the German economy and society. The only effective way to check the rise of fascism is to destroy the class which begets it. It implies the necessity of a united front of the working class parties against fascism and for defending democracy at all cost. If the representatives of the working class are able to seize the power of the state, they must use this opportunity to transform the capitalist system by a rapid introduction of socialist measures. Moreover, a socialist government must not extend its protection to fascist organizations which should be banned and effectively suppressed before they gather strength.

Fascism as a Menance to Civilization

But the contemporary history of Germany and Italy shows that the steps which were necessary to check the rise of fascism in those countries could not be taken. Fascism was victorious in both these countries owing to the weakness and vacillating policies of its opponents. The triumph of fascism was not only a calamity to those nations where it succeeded, but it was, in fact, a menace to human civilization. The destruction of fascism, says Laski, was a question of survival of the human civilization.[15] "For in any civilized community of nations", he says, "the necessity of its destruction is axiomatic. A system which annihilates all values save that of power, and is prepared, without repining, to use war as the natural instrument of national policy, must either be destroyed or enslave mankind. There is no middle term between these alternatives" (*131:97*).

Laski believes that civilized conduct depends upon two things. In the first place, individuals must learn to subordinate themselves to the sovereign power of reason. Secondly, all organised groups in society must conduct themselves within a framework of "settled legal principles". German and Italian fascists denied both the supremacy of reason in the life of individuals as well as the principle of legality in the life of communities and nations. By these denials, fascism automatically became the acknowledged enemy of human civilisation. The triumph of the fascist doctrine sympolized the victory of bestiality in man's nature over its humanist sublimation.

Laski, it is evident, cannot accept any compromise with fascism. As it recognizes no other argument than that of force, it must be destroyed either by an internal revolution or by an armed intervention from outside. The fascist regime, as Laski says, is essentially a government of gangsters and

15. See Laski's remarks in his essay on "The Strategy of Freedom" in which he regards fascism as a negation of civilization.

outlaws, who depend for their survival on a perpetual civil war within and a permanent international conflict outside. The only answer to this war-like ideology is to crush it by its own weapon and overthrow it on the battlefield.

Conservative Parties Sympathetic to Fascism

In capitalist democracies, the conservative sections did not recognize the nature of the fascist menace. At certain occasions, the conservative leaders of these countries openly expressed their sympathy for the aims of fascism while disapproving its methods. This sympathetic attitude was evident from the policy of appeasement, which the capitalist democracies adopted in their diplomacy with the fascist dictators. The Soviet Union was the only country to recognize the true character of the fascist regime and to oppose the policy of appeasement. The Soviet government advocated a policy of collective security and alliance with the capitalist democracies against fascism. This policy was not accepted by the appeasers in capitalist democracies.

Soviet Opposition to Fascism

Laski thinks that the Soviet policy was the only correct answer to the fascist challenge to world peace. The conservative leaders of the capitalist countries were motivated by a greater hatred towards communism and were misled by the anti-communist statements of the fascist leaders. The conclusion of the Nazi-Soviet non-aggression pact was the natural outcome of the policy of appeasement pursued by the capitalist democracies. Ultimately, the fascist powers were defeated on the battlefield by a world coalition of nations in which the Soviet Union also played an important role.

How Resurgence of Fascism to be Checked

When Fascism has been defeated on the battlefield, it is pertinent to ask what steps should be taken to prevent its resurgence in the modern world. The annihilation of this warlike ideology has cost too much both in men and materials and humanity cannot afford a repetition of this colossal effort. Laski is clear on this point when he thinks that a revival of capitalist democracy cannot remove this danger. The relations of production in a capitalist society are no longer in conformity with the forces of production. If the post-war reconstruction is again planned on a capitalist basis, the impending catastrophe would be certain. Laski does not believe that a capitalist federation of Europe or a capitalistic Anglo-American Union is a successful guarantee of world peace.

The U.N.O. Unable to Guarantee World Peace

Even a world organization on the pattern of the League of Nations or the present U.N.O. cannot provide any security for mankind against the recurrence of war and fascism unless the capitalist system of production is replaced by a socialist system. The post-war events both before and after Laski's death have demonstrated the validity of his conclusions. The replacement of the fascist regimes in Italy, West Germany and Japan by the regimes of capitalist democracy has not solved any problem and we again see these peoples drifting towards rearmament and war. As Laski had foreseen, the capitalist government of the United States has assumed the leadership of the counter-revolutionary forces of the world.[16]

Communist System as a Lesser Evil than Fascism

But capitalism has been overthrown from a large part of the world on account of direct intervention of the Soviet Union in the affairs of Eastern Europe and because the Chinese Communists were able to defeat their own reactionaries in a civil war. For Laski the substitution of a Communist dictatorship for a fascist regime is only a replacement of the greater evil by a lesser evil (*127:154-68*). He thought that the Soviet system of government would become democratized after the war and perhaps the cooperation between the socialists and Communists of Western Europe would bring about a peaceful transformation of the capitalist system into a socialist society in those countries.

Failure of the European Socialists to Redefine Class Relations

But the cooperation between the European socialists and Communists was short-lived and the changes expected by Laski in the Soviet regime did not occur (*127:227-233*). The socialists of Europe, after their rupture with the Communists, completely identified themselves with the foreign policy of the United States and joined the Americans in their cold war against Russia. Like the Social Democrats of the pre-war Germany, the European socialists have failed to bring about that redefinition of class relations, which Laski desired and regarded as indispensable for a decisive defeat of the counter-revolution.[17]

It has also changed the entire perspective of the struggle between the European revolution and counter-revolution. The Communists and socialists, instead of cooperating in a common endeavour, are again dissipating their energies in mutual bickerings and thus strengthening the forces of counter-revolution in their countries. The post-war progressive regimes were gradually replaced by reactionary administrations in all capitalist countries and rearmament and neo-fascism again threatened the peace of the

16. Laski : "The American Democracy", Chapter XI, pp. 501-517. As he says, "The Russian way of life, moreover, seeks as clearly to prevent external economic exploitation as the American way of life inherently dirves its business leaders at once to seek for that exploitation and to regard its critics as dangerous stumbling blocks in the way of the fulfilment of America's "manifest destiny". There is, to put it shortly, a grave contradiction between the objective purpose of the United Nations and the impersonal drive of economic forces in America". (p. 516).

17. For Laski's proposals in this respect, see his "Reflections on the Revolution of Our Time", Chapter VII, pp. 278-304.

world.[18] The defeat of fascism on the battlefield did not mean the end of fascism as an ideology, which is bound to recur in one form or the other until the final collapse of the capitalist system is brought about at least in the major capitalist countries.

Marxist Critique of Fascism

The Marxist critique emphasizes that fascism is the ideology of the monopoly capitalist class in decay. It arose in Italy and Germany because the capitalist class was then facing a grave economic crisis and was also threatened by the possibility of a socialist revolution. The socio-economic basis of fascism is frankly capitalistic. It suppresses all working-class organisations such as the trade unions and socialist and communist parties. During the fascist and Nazi rule in Germany and Italy, the state protected the interests of landlords and capitalists in every way, while the real wages of industrial and agricultural workers declined substantially.

The Marxist critique also emphasizes that fascism is an imperialistic and racialist doctrine, which aims at conquest and exploitation of other nations. The doctrine of the superiority of the Nordic race is used to justify acts of aggression against the so-called inferior races. The Nazis adopted a policy of genocide against the Jews and Slavonic nationalities of Eastern Europe. Though the socio-economic basis of liberal democracy and fascism is similar as both of them are based on the capitalistic mode of production, yet the Marxists regard fascism as much worse than capitalist democracy because the latter, at least, allows civil liberties to the working-class parties, while the former suppresses them.

> "It is often said that Fascism is an extreme example of the state's domination of society .... But the formula ..... is misleading.... it obscures the degree to which the Fascist state acted in ways enormously advantageous to the business and possessing classes......... it fails to take into account the fact that 'the state' continued to be manned by people who belonged to the traditional administrative, military and judicial elites.... there were .... more aristocrats in positions of power between 1933 and 1945 than between 1918–1933, and fewer people of working class origin." (*236 : 84*).

18. For Laski's comments about the post-war Anglo-American policy in the Middle East, Greece, Italy, Germany and Japan, see his "Dilemma of Our Times", Chapters I, X and XIV.

CHAPTER 34

THE UNITED NATIONS

When the world was plunged into a colossal war in 1939, primarily as a result of the ambitions of Hitler, Mussolini, and the war lords of Japan, the first thought of the allies who fought them was to win the war.

As the war advanced the allies who were fighting the Axis powers (Germany, Italy, and Japan) came to be called the United Nations. The phrase was a coinage of Roosevelt. It was out of deference to his memory that after his death the organization came to be called the United Nations Organization; and now simply the United Nations.

Without waiting for the war to be over the allied statesmen got busy with the organization of the United Nations when the war was on. There was general disillusionment with regard to the League of Nations. Yet they found that the structure of the League was in the main satisfactory. Therefore, on that structure they began to build the new organization.

The Conference which laid down the framework of the U.N. was held at Dumbarton Oaks, a private mansion in Washington D.C., in October, 1944. The proposals made at this Conference aimed at the creation of a General Asembly, a Security Council of eleven members, an Economic and Social Council, an International Court of Justice, and a permanent Secretariat. The question of an International Police Force also was considered.

A serious gap left by this conference was the voting procedure in the Security Council. This question was solved at the Yalta Conference which was attended by Stalin, Roosevelt, and Churchill. Besides settling this question, they proposed a conference of all the nations fighting the Axis powers to be held in San Francisco in April 1945.

The Conference was attended by fifty nations and these became the original members of the United Nations. On October 24, 1945 when the signatory states ratified the Charter and deposited their notification to this effect with the U.S. State Department the U.N. came into existence. Since then October 24 has been observed as the United Nations Day. The first General Assembly of the U.N. met in the Central Hall, Westminster, London. The League of Nations formally ceased to function thereafter.

The Charter consists of one hundred and eleven short articles. The Preamble to the Charter sets forth the basic aims of the U.N. It starts with the significant words: "We, the Peoples of the United Nations", instead of the words "The High Contracting Parties", used by the Covenant of the League of Nations signifying thereby that the U.N. speaks in the name of the peoples of the world. But too much ought not to be read into the verbal difference inasmuch as the members of the U.N. are still member States, sovereign and independent. The U.N. does not call upon its members to surrender their sovereignty any more than did the League of Nations. The U.N. is "a voluntary co-operation of sovereign states". It is not a super-state.

PURPOSES OF THE U.N.

The four purposes of the United Nations are:

1. to maintain international peace and security;

2. to develop friendly relations among nations based on respect for the equal rights and self-determination of peoples;

3. to co-operate in solving international problems of an economic, social, cultural, or humanitarian character, and in promoting respect for human rights and fundamental freedoms for all; and

4. to be a centre for harmonizing the actions of nations in attaining these common ends.

PRINCIPLES

In fulfilment of these purposes, the United Nations acts in accordance with the following principles:

1. the Organisation is based on the principle of the sovereign equality of all its members;

2. members are to fulfil in good faith the obligations they have assumed under the Charter;

3. they are to settle their international disputes by peaceful means;

4. they are to refrain in their international relations from the threat or use of force in any manner inconsistent with the purposes of the United Nations;

5. they are to give the United Nations every assistance in any action it takes in accordance with the Charter, and to refrain from giving assistance to any state against which the Organization is taking preventive or enforcement action;

6. the United Nations is to ensure that non-members act in accordance with these principles so far as is necessary for maintaining international peace and security;

7. the Organization is not to intervene in matters which are essentially within the domestic jurisdiction of any state. This provision does not apply, however, when enforcement action is taken with respect to threats to peace, breaches of the peace, and acts of aggression.

Membership. The original number of members of the U. N. was fifty-one. Only ten were admitted up to 1955, because the admission of new members became a matter of conflict between the two power blocs. In 1955 as the result of a compromise between the two blocs sixteen new members were admitted all at one time by 'a package deal'. The U.N.O. has 188 members now. Membership is "open to all peace-loving states". Communist China became a member of the U.N.O. in 1971. Members must accept the obligations contained in the present Charter and be able and willing to carry out the obligations of membership. New members are admitted by a two-thirds vote of the General Assembly upon the recommendation of the Security Council where any of the 'Big Five' (China, France, the United Kingdom, the U.S.A. and Russia) can exercise its veto power. During the short life-history of the U.N many vetoes have been exercised by Soviet Russia (a hundred times); and several of these have been exercised in this connection. The power has been so much abused that there is a general feeling that some way must be found of the imphasse.

A member may be expelled for "persistent" violation of Charter principles.

No specific provision is made for the withdrawal of a member, as was the case in the League of Nations. But there is no intention of preventing a member from withdrawing because of exceptional circumstances. So far no member has withdrawn, although France and South Africa have staged walk-outs.

THE ORGANS OF THE UNITED NATIONS

THE GENERAL ASSEMBLY

The General Assembly is the only organ of the U.N. on which all members are represented. Each member is entitled to five representatives exercising one vote among them. The Assembly meets regularly once every year, commencing usually in September. Special session may be convoked at the request of the Security Council or of a majority of the members of the U.N. It is essentially a deliberative body, which can only make recommendations. In the field of peace and security which is assigned almost exclusively to the Security Council, the Assembly cannot even make recommendations when the matter is under consideration by the Security Council. But under the famous 'United Action for Peace' Resolution (or Acheson Resolution) of 1950, if the Security Council fails to take action on any important matter, it may be taken up by the General Asembly for consideration and appropriate recommendation.

One chief difference between the League Assembly and the General Assembly is that the former could make decisions binding on the members, while the latter can only make recommendations; but even these carry considerable moral weight behind them.

Voting procedure in the General Assembly is an advance upon the League procedure. While the League Assembly required a unanimous vote for decisions, i.e., of the members present and voting, decisions of the General Assembly on important questions are made by a two-thirds vote of the members present and voting. These questions include recommendations with respect to the maintenance of international peace and security, the election of members of the Councils, the admission of new members to the U.N., or the suspension and expulsion of members, questions relating to the operation of the Trusteeship system, and budgetary questions. Decisions on other matters are taken by a simple majority vote of the members present and voting. Decisions in the committees of the General Assembly are taken by a majority of the members present and voting.

The General Assembly is given wide powers to initiate studies and make recommendations to promote international co-operation in the political field and to encourage the progressive development of international law and its codification. It also has the power to consider, "principles governing disarmament and the regulation of armaments" and make recommendations. Under Article 14 it is authorized to "recommend measures for the peaceful adjustment of any situation, regardless of origin, which it deems likely to impair the general welfare or friendly relations among nations".

Under its *organizational functions,* the Assembly elects the non-permanent members of the Security Council for two-year periods, the members of the Economic and Social Council and the elective members of the Trusteeship Council as against the *ex-officio* ones. It appoints the Secretary-General of the U.N. upon the recommendation of the Security Council. Voting independently along with the Security Council, it elects the judges of the International Court of Justice.

The General Assembly receives and considers reports from the other oragns. The annual report of the Secretary-General is submitted to it. It considers and approves the budget of the entire organization and apportions the expenses among the members.

Under Articles 15 and 24, the Security Council is to make annual and special reports to the General Assembly. It is not made clear when these reports are to be submitted. The Security Council appears to retain considerable freedom of action.

The Assembly is supposed to act through an Interim or a Little Assembly in between sessions. It is represented by one representative from each member state. It is practically an effete body because of the stern opposition of Russia to it. The General Assembly functions through some very important standing committees such as the First Committee known as the Political and Security Committee and the Second Committee known as the Economic and Financial Committee.

Effectiveness of the General Assembly. Although the priamry purpose of the Assembly is "to consider, discuss, and make recommendations," it is by no means an ineffective body. Its moral authority has been increasing every day.

THE SECURITY COUNCIL

The Security Council deals almost exclusively with matters pertaining to the maintenance of international peace and security. In this sphere its powers are greater and more well-defined than those of the League Council. It has a fixed membership of fifteen (unlike the League Council), five being permanent members representing the "Big Five". Non-permanent members are elected for two-year terms, five members being elected each year. These members are not immediately re-eligible. India has served one term as a non-permanent member and she was elected a second time in 1972. In electing non-permanent members, two considerations are taken into account: (1) the contribution of members of the U.N. to the maintenance of international peace and security and to the other purposes of the organization; (2) equitable geographical distribution. These are only general exhortations which the General Assembly may disregard, and this has really happened in more than one case, even as late as 1955. It has become an item in the two-power conflict. In practice one seat went to one of the states of Latin America and another to one of the states in the former Soviet bloc. In recent years one seat has been given to Asian countries, and one to African countries.

There is provision for occasional members. These may be invited to represent member States which are not represented in the Council or non-member states when it is a matter which concerns them. They take part in the meetings of the Council, but have no vote.

Each member of the Council has one vote. The reason for having permanent members is that they are supposed to be the most important guarantors of security and a stable element in the family of nations. Change in the composition of permanent members can be made only by amending the Charter according to Articles 108 and 109.

The presidency of the Council rotates monthly among the members according to the English alphabetical order of their names. The Council adopts its own rules of procedure and establishes such subsidiary organs as it considers necessary for the performance of its function. The two Standing Committees, made up of representatives of the fifteen members of the Council, are the committee of experts which deals with rules of procedure and the committee on the admission of new members.

The Veto. Each of the permanent members has the right of veto on all substantive questions. Abstinence does not constitute a negative vote: nor does absence. This latter point was decided in 1950 when Mr. Jacob Malik representing Russia absented himself from the Council as a protest against the continued seating of the unrepresentative delegate from Nationalist China. When he later returned to the Security Council and claimed that the action of the Council taken during his absence was invalid, the Council overruled him. A valid decision on all substantive questions requires 10 votes including the votes of the permanent five. On procedural matters the affirmative votes of any 10 members are sufficient. What is substantive and what is procedural is a substantive question.

Pacific Settlement. When the pacific settlement of a dispute (Ch. VI) is under consideration by the Security Council the parties to the dispute must abstain from voting when the Council takes a decision. When preventive or enforcement action is to be taken by the Security Council the parties to the dispute need not refrain from voting.

The Security Council is in permanent session. The interval between meetings is not to exceed fourteen days. The Council is to be ready to meet as soon as there is a situation or dispute which threatens the maintenance of international peace and security.

There are four ways in which attention may be called to any dispute or situation which may threaten international peace: (1) Under the Charter, as under the Covenant, members have the right to bring to the attention of the Security Council or the General Assembly "any dispute or situation which might lead to international friction or give rise to a dispute". (2) The Security Council, on it own initiative, may investigate any situation or dispute in order to determine "whether its continuance is likely to endanger the maintenance of international peace and security" (Art. 34). (3) The General Assembly may call the attention of the Security Council to situations which are likely to endanger international peace and security (Art. 11, para 3). (4) The Secretary-General may bring to the attention of the Security Council any matter which in his opinion may threaten the maintenance of international peace and security. From this last point it will be seen that the Secretary-General is not a mere glorified head clerk. He is endowed with considerable initiative.

Under Article 35 (2) even a state which is not a member of the U.N. may bring any dispute to which it is a party if it accepts in advance, for the purposes of the dispute, the obligations of pacific settlement provided in the present Charter.

The obligation of members to refrain from war is absolute, except in cases of international or collective self-defence (Art. 51). Any threat to the peace, breach of the peace, act of aggression of whatever nature is subject to preventive and enforcement action by the Security Council. The Council may adopt several methods of pacific settlement: (1) Parties to a dispute may settle the matter by themselves through arbitration or judicial settlement, negotiation, enquiry, mediation, conciliation or resort to regional agencies and arrangements. (2) The Security Council may call upon the parties to settle their dispute by such means when the parties fail to act and when the continuance of the dispute is "likely to endanger" peace and security. (3) The Security Council may at any stage of a dispute recommend appropriate procedures or methods of adjustment. But these are not legally binding on the parties, although they may have the greatest political and moral weight. Legal (former "justiciable") disputes, however, are as a rule to be referred to the International Court of Justice. From all of this it is clear that the procedure of pacific settlement is more flexible in the Charter than in the Covenant.

Enforcement Action. (1) The Security Council determines threat to, peace, breach of the peace, act of aggression, etc., according to Article 39. Once it has decided, it can take action immediately. The decision is on behalf of the entire U.N. Therefore, all members are bound to assist the Security Council in any manner that may be called for (Article 48). Decision

47—17 149

is no longer left to the individual members of the organization. (2) The Security Council can call for provisional measures as it deems necessary to prevent deterioration of the situation. (3) Members of the U.N. are bound by the decisions of the Security Council both in the case of military and non-military sanctions. (4) The League of Nations had no armed forces at its disposal. The Charter makes provision or advance planning concerning the application of armed forces. Under Article 45 members are to "hold immediately available national air force contingents for combined international enforcement action". The arrangement has been strengthened by the provision for the Collective Measures Committee contained in the *United Action for Peace Resolution*. The snag is that no military action is binding unless all the Big Five agree. The U.N. can take effective preventive and enforcement action against small powers, if the Big Five agree or at least none of them disagrees.

The Security Council may take two types of enforcement action :—(1) Measures not involving the use of armed forces—economic and diplomatic—complete or partial interruption of economic relations and of rail, sea, air, postal, telegraphic, radio and other means of communication, and the severance of diplomatic relations. (2) Action by air, sea or land forces, including demonstrations, blockades, and other operations by air, sea or land forces of the members of the U.N. The Council decides whether action is to be taken by all members or by some; whether directly or through the appropriate international agencies to which they belong.

Any state, whether a member or not, which finds itself confronted with special economic problems arising from the carrying out of enforcement measures directed by the Security Council, may consult the Council regarding a solution of those problems.

Regional Arrangements. At Sen Francisco the nations of the Western hemisphere insisted on the recognition of the validity of regional arrangements and agencies. The result of it was Article 52 of the Charter which provides for a positive relation between regional agencies and the U.N. These agencies are to assist in the maintenance of international peace and security. The arrangements or agencies and their activities are to be consistent with the purpose and principles of the United Nations.

The major Western powers and their satellites claimed that the NATO, SEATO, and the MEDO came within the purview of regional arrangements. The rest of the world did not believe it. As a matter of fact, these regional alliances which were primarily military and alleged to be defensive were one of the greatest threats to peace. The Soviet-sponsored pact made up of several Communist countries in Europe was known as the Warsaw Pact. It was meant as a counterblast to the alliances sponsored by the Western powers. It became diffferent after the disintegration of the USSR

Domestic Matters. On domestic matters the provision of the Charter is broader than that contained in the League of Nations. According to Article 2, para 7, the U.N. is not 'to intervene in matters which are essentially within the domestic jurisdiction of any State' or to 'require the members to submit such matters of settlement under the Charter.'

Other Functions of the Security Council. To the Security Council belongs the supervision of trust areas classified as 'strategic.' The permanent members of the Security Council are *ipso facto* members of the Trusteeship Council. Voting simultaneously, but independently, the Security Council and the General Assembly elect the judges of the International Court of Justice. The Security Council makes annual and special reports to the General Assembly. It may request the assistance of the Economic and Social Council; also of the Trusteeship Council with regard to strategic areas. It may ask the International Court of Justice for advisory opinion on any legal matter.

Amendments to the Charter (Articles 108 & 109). Amendments can be made by the General Assembly or by a General Conference of members of the United Nations. Amendments adopted by a vote of two-thirds of the members of the General Assembly (not merely of those present and voting) need to be ratified by two-thirds of the member States, including all the permanent members of the Security Council, before they can take effect.

A second way of amending the Charter is through a General Conference decided upon by a two-thirds vote of the General Assembly and a vote of any seven members of the Security Council. If such a conference is not held before the tenth annual session of the General Assembly, the proposal to call such a conference is automatically placed on the agenda of the tenth session of the General Assembly[1]. The Conference is to be held if so decided by a majority vote of the General Assembly and by a vote of any seven members of the Security Council.

THE ECONOMIC AND SOCIAL COUNCIL

If the object of the Security Council is to free the world from fear, the object of this Council is to free it from want. As someone has aptly put it: "It is the silent twin of the talkative Security Council."

Article 55 of the Charter provides that the U.N. shall promote—(a) "higher standards of living, full employment, and conditions of economic and social progress and development;

(b) "solutions of international economic, social, health, and related problems; and international cultural and educational co-operation;

(c) "universal respect for, and observance of, human rights and fundamental freedoms for all without distinction as to race, sex, language, and religion."

The last of these (c), is an innovation, although the League did much to protect the rights of "national minorities" under special "minorities treaties". Most of the League Commissions and Committees were respon-

1. Member States of the UN did not avail themselves of this provision when the first ten-year period was over in 1955.

sible to the Council; whereas the Economic and Social Council operates entirely under the authority of the General Assembly.

On the organizational side, the Economic and Social Council consists of eighteen members elected for three-year terms by the General Assembly. Six are elected every year. Members may be re-elected immediately after their term is over. No provision is made for permanent members as in the Security Council nor for such factors as geographical diversity or the balancing of industrialized against underdeveloped regions, or of imperial powers against those without colonies. Yet in practice the Big Five have always been elected, and have literally become permanent members of the Council. The principle of 'geographical balance of representation' also has found its way in actual practice.

As in the General Assembly, all member nations have an equal position. Each member is allowed one representative and one vote. A simple majority can pass a resolution. It meets at least twice a year normally at the seat of the U.N. It may meet elsewhere if it so decides. It makes its own rules of procedure and elects its President and Vice-President. It can only make recommendations, and has no real "executive" power.

The Council must invite any member state not a member of the Council to participate, but without a vote, in discussion of any matter of particular concern to that member.

It may arrange for representatives of specialized agencies to participate without vote in discussions of the Council and its commissions. It may also be represented at the deliberations of the specialized agencies.

Further, it may arrange for observers from non-governmental organizations having consultative status to attend its meetings.

Some special functions of the Economic and Social Council are:

(1) It makes or initiates studies and reports on all matters within its concern—economic, social, cultural and educational, health and related matters.

(2) It makes recommendations to the General Assembly or to the member governments or to the Specialized Agencies.

(3) It submits draft conventions to the General Assembly which when adopted are sent to the member States for acceptance and implementation.

(4) It sets up Commissions for the performance of its functions.

(5) It calls international conferences on matters within its competence.

Limited Nature of the Work of the Council

The Economic and Social Council does not attempt to deal with much less solve, the most urgent economic problems of the entire world. The limited nature of its work, as that of the U.N. as a whole, is indicated by a statement of an American Secretary of State when he says:

"An international organization could aid in the solution of economic and social problems but could not interfere with the functions and powers of sovereign states. It could not command performance by individual member nations: it should not reach into domestic affairs of members. Its tools and procedures are those of study, discussion, report, and recommendation." Intended originally to function within very narrow limits, the pressing economic and social problems of the world since 1945 have tended to widen the scope of the work of the Council.

THE TRUSTEESHIP COUNCIL

Trust Territories and Non-Self-Governing Areas

Members of the UN administering non-self-governing territories, whether they are placed under the International Trusteeship System or not, agree to administer them in such a way as to promote to the utmost "the well-being of the inhabitants of those territories." To this end they undertake:

(1) To insure the political, economic, social and educational advancement of the inhabitants without in any way undermining their indigenous cultures;

(2) To treat them justly and protect them against abuse;

(3) To develop self-government and to assist the people in the progressive development of their own free political institutions;

(4) To further international peace and security;

(5) To promote constructive measures of development, to enconrage research, and to co-operate with each other and with specialized international bodies so as to achieve the economic, social, and scientific advancement of the territories in question; and

(6) To transmit regularly to the Secretary-General for the purpose of information, subject to such limitation as security and constitutional considerations may require, statistical and other technical information relating to economic, social, and educational conditions in the Non-Self-Governing countries not under the Trusteeship system.

The International Trusteeship System. This applies to territories placed under the system by individual agreements worked out between the U.N. and the state to which a trust territory is entrusted. The areas so administered are known as trust territories. The system does not apply to terriories which have become members of the United Nations.

The System has a fourfold aim:

(1) To further international peace and security;

(2) To promote the political, economic, social and educational advancement of the people and their progressive development towards self-government or independence;

(3) To encourage respect for basic human rights and recognition of the interdependence of the peoples of the world; and

(4) To insure the equal treatment of all member states of the U.N.

and their nationals in social, economic, and commercial matters, and in the administration of justice so long as it is consistent with the attainment of the other objectives of the Trusteeship System.

The Trusteeship Council

is made up of:

(1) Permanent members of the Securitly Council, which do not administer trust territories;

(2) Member states which administer trust territories;

(3) Other member states elected by the General Assembly to maintain equality of members between those which administer territories and those which do not. The Council meets regularly twice a year and in such special sessions as are requested by a majority of its members. Decisions are made by a majority of the members present and voting.

Functions and Powers of the Council

Under the authority of the General Assembly it carries out the functions of the UN with regard to trust territories which are not designated as "strategic". The Security Council exercises the UN functions over the latter, with the assistance of the Trusteeship Council in political, economic, social, and educational matters.

The Trusteeship Council considers reports by the Administering Authority; examines petitions in consultation with the Administering Authority;

Provides for periodic visiting missions to Trust Territories at times agreed upon with the Administering Authority; takes other actions in conformity with the terms of the Trusteeship Agreements;

Formulates a questionnaire on the political, economic, social, and educational advancement of the inhabitants of each Trust Territory, on the basis of which the Administering Authorities submit annual reports on all Trust Territories for consideration by the Trusteeship Council.

SPECIALIZED AGENCIES

Article 57 of the Charter provides that the various specialized agencies, established by inter-governmental agreement and having wide international responsibilities, as defined in their basic instruments, in economic, social, cultural, educational, health, and related fields shall be brought into relationship with the United Nations in accordance with the provisions of Article 63.

The Economic and Social Council, subject to approval by the General Assembly, is the body which negotiates agreements with the agencies, defining the terms under which each of them is to be brought into relationship with the UN. The Council seeks to coordinate the activities of the specialized agencies through consultations with them and through recommedations to the General Assembly and the members of the UN.

The Specialised Agencies are:

1. The International Labour Organization.
2. The Food and Agricultural Organization.
3. The United Nations Educational, Scientific and Cultural Organization.
4. The World Health Organization.
5. The International Monetary Fund.
6. The International Bank for Reconstruction and Development.
7. The International Finance Corporation.
8. The International Civil Aviation Organization.
9. The Universal Postal Union.
10. The International Telecommunications Union.
11. The World Meteorological Organization.
12. The International Maritime Consultative Organization.
13. The International Trade Organization (General Agreement on Tariffs and Trade).

THE INTERNATIONAL COURT OF JUSTICE

In many respects this is a continuation of the Permanent Court of International Justice under the League of Nations. While the Permanent Court was an "autonomous organ" of the League, the present court is a principal organ of the U.N. It functions in accordance with its Statute, which is based upon the Statute of the Permanent Court.

All members of the U.N. have automatic access to the Court. Even non-members may use it on conditions recommended by the Security Council and approved by the General Assembly. Only nations can use the Court.

A state cannot be dragged before the Court because a suit has been filed against it. The defendant state should agree to the trial. The Court has no compulsory jurisdiction over nations. Members of the U.N. are not obliged to take their cases before it. However, it is open to them to pledge beforehand when they sign a treaty that they will use the Court when dispute arises on the interpretation of the treaty.

By signing 'optional clause' nations may pledge themselves to use the Court for certain types of cases. This means all cases concerning:

(a) 'The meaning of treaty clauses.

(b) 'All matters concerned with the field of international law.

(c) 'The existence of any fact which, if established, would constitute a breach of international obligation.

(d) 'The nature or extent of the payment that must be made for breaking an international agreement or obligation.'

Out of a total membership of 64 states only 38 have opted for the compulsory jurisdiction of the Court even within the limited sphere of settlement of non-political disputes.

The jurisdiction of the Court includes all cases which the parties concerned wish to refer to it as well as matters specifically provided for in the

U.N. Charter in treaties or conventions in force. Inasmuch as the statute of the Court is based upon the Statute of the Permanent Court, stipulations in treaties or conventions to refer matters to the Permanent Court now refer to the International Court of Justice. Disputes between members of the U.N. need not always be referred to the International Court. They may be referred to other courts already in existence or to courts to be established in the future.

A peculiar feature of the Court is that it shares with the Security Council the power of making decisions binding upon States. The binding decisions of the Court are nevertheless reviewable, under certain conditions, by the Security Council. Another feature is that the Big Power conflict has to some extent found its way into the composition and working of the Court.

Basis of the Court's Decision

In deciding cases, the Court applies:

(1) International conventions, whether general or particular;

(2) International customs;

(3) The general principles of law recognized by civilized nations;

(4) Judicial decisions and the teachings of the most highly qualified publicists of the various nations.

Where the parties concerned are agreeable, the Court may use the principles of justice and the general welfare of the nations involved.

Decisions of the Court. According to the Charter of the U.N., every member agrees to abide by the decisions of the Court in any case to which it is a party. If one party is willing to carry out its obligations under a judgment delivered by the Court and the other party is unwilling, the former can bring up the matter to the notice of the Security Council which can adopt measures or make recommendations for the execution of the Court judgment. The Court may also indicate what provisional measures need to be undertaken in order to protect the rights of either party. Decisions of the Court bind only the parties concerned in respect of the case decided. The judgment of the Court is final.

Advisory Opinions. When called upon to do so, the Court gives advisory opinion on legal questions. The General Assembly and the Security Council can make the request directly. Other organs of the U.N. and Specialized Agencies require the authorization of the General Assembly in dealing with legal questions which fall within the scope of their activities.

THE SECRETARIAT

The Secretary-General is appointed by the General Assembly on the recommendation of the Security Council and acts in that capacity at all meetings of the General Assembly, the Security Council, the Economic and Social Council, and the Trusteeship Council. He performs various duties in relation to the Security Council, the General Assembly, the summoning of special sessions of the General Assembly, the receiving of reports from countries administering non-self-governing territories, the registration of treaties, and the election of judges to the International Court of Justice. One of his special priveleges is to bring to the notice of the Security Council any matter which in his opinion is a threat to the maintenance of international peace and security. The Charter requires him to submit an annual report to the General Assembly on the work of the organization. The first Secretary-General was appointed for a term of five years. He can be re-elected at the end of the period. Some time ago Russia made the preposterous suggestion that the Secretray-General's work should be divided among three Secretaries, one representing the western powers, one the Soviet bloc, and a third the neutral or non-aligned powers. Fortunately, after the appointment of U Thant as Secretary-General, this suggestion known as Troika has been dropped, at least for the time being.

The Staff

The staff of the Secretariat is appointed by him under regulations established by the General Assembly. In making the appointments, the highest standard of efficiency, competence and integrity are to be considered; also fair geographical distribution is to be taken into account. Neither the Secretary-General nor the staff is to seek or receive instructions from any government or any other authority outside the organization. The members of the U.N. on their side undertake to respect the exclusively international character of the Secretary-General and his staff and not to influence them in their discharge of their responsibilities. This has not always been done in practice. A few years ago when anti-communist feelings were at their height, the U.S.A. used its influence with the U.N. and Secretary-General in removing some of the U.N. employees of U.S. nationality who were suspected of communist proclivities.

REVISION OF THE CHARTER

Although several loopholes have been found in the Charter of the United Nations and the work of the Organization, there was no disposition to revise the Charter because of the veto power which was bound to be used by one or the other of the Big Five so long as the two-power conflict continued. Anyhow, from the academic point of view, certain lines may be indicated along which changes may be made in the future :—

1. Restriction of the power of veto, particularly as regards the admission of new states. It is used much less now.
2. A closer definition of 'Domestic Jurisdiction' so that a country like the Union of South Africa cannot go on flouting the United Nations indefinitely on such a matter as the uncivilized and inhuman way of dealing with people of non-white races. South Africa is now a multi-racial democracy with equal rights for all races.
3. Bringing of the entire colonial world under the Trusteeship System and the liquidating of colonialism according to a given time table.

4. More attention to disarmament and effective steps being taken in the direction of an International Police or Peace Force and the proportionate reduction of national forces as the international force increases.

5. A closer definition of Articles 51 and 52 so that geographically separate states cannot be brought together into a military alliance such as the NATO which dominates the whole world.

6. A closer definition of what constitutes the use of force for defensive purposes.

7. Close restriction of the right of a nation to carry on experiments with the exploding of atomic and hydrogen bombs and other such deadly weapons. It is high time that a convention was established to the effect that no nation had a right to pollute the air or the waters of the seas. It must be regarded as a crime against humanity.

8. Closer attention to the utilization of 'atoms for peace'.

9. An adequate machinery for the enforcement of human rights already provided in the form of a Declaration.

10. The adoption of active steps for the creation of world citizenship and a limited world government.

11. With the disintegration of the USSR, the United Nations has come under the domination of the USA, the remaining super-power. Adequate steps should be taken to reduce this domination through suitable changes in the UN charter.

12. Kofi Annan was imposed as the Secretary-General of the UN against the wishes of 14 members of the Security Council and an overwhelming majority of members in the General Assembly, who wanted to give another term to Boutras-Boutras Ghali. Such abuse of Veto by USA has to be curbed.

13. Today NATO speaks in the name of the UN and international community. This is quite impermissible and against international law.

14. Concerted efforts should be made to democratise the functioning of the UN to prevent it from succumbing to the fate of the League of Nations.

CHAPTER 35

POLITICAL THOUGHT OF MAHATMA GANDHI

Mahatma Gandhi was not primarily a political thinker, not even a political agitator. He was essentially a religious-minded man, a humanist, and a man of action and intuition. He was a curious amalgam of a mystic and a pragmatist. In his own words, he was not a politician masquerading as a religious man, but a religious man who entered politics because of his great concern for his fellow human beings. He rightly placed *Swaraj* in the forefront of his programme, and in attaining it he worked out certain principles which could be woven into political philosophy by others. In his case, it was action which led to a certain amount of theorizing and not *vice versa*. With him, to think was to act. Vinoba Bhave writes that someone had suggested to Mahatma Gandhi that he should set forth his ideas in a systematic and formal treatise. To this Mahatma Gandhi replied : 'For one thing, I have no time; for another I am still experimenting. Hence let the treatise develop slowly of itself; if it does at all.' (*147:217*) 'One step is enough for me. Why should the Lord show me two ?'

Sources of Gandhi's Thought. Mahatma Gandhi had read little in the realm of political thought. But what he read he profoundly assimilated and made his own. His interpretation of some of the original texts such as the *Bhagavat Gita* was novel. Thus he claimed that while on the surface the *Gita* taught the use of violence in the vindication of truth and righteousness, it really taught non-violence because of the qualification contained in it, viz., that even if one took up arms he should do it disinterestedly.

Besides the Gita, Mahatma Gandhi had read Patanjali's *Yogasutra,* the *Ramayana* and the *Mahabharata* as well as some Jaina and Buddhist writings which abound in exhortations to truth and non-violence. From the Upanishads he drew much inspiration for his firm faith in non-possession.

The ancient teachings of Lao-Tse and Confucius also had some influence on Mahatma Gandhi's moral and political philosophy. Lao-Tse had taught the philosophy of non-assertiveness.

From Confucius, Mahatma Gandhi learned the principle of reciprocity, according to which men should not do to others what they would not have done to them.

Among secular writers, Thoreau, and Ruskin influenced Mahatma Gandhi most. From Thoreau he got much of his inspiration for civil disobedience and the non-payment of taxes. Thoureau's political philosophy was 'maximum co-operation with all people and institutions when they lead towards good and non-co-operation when they promote evil.' Through his works 'Unto this Last' and 'Crown of Wild Olives,' Ruskin instilled in

Mahatma Gandhi respect for manual labour which lesson he practised until the end of his days.

Commenting upon these various sources, Mr. Pyarelal, a Secretary and biographer of Mahatma Gandhi, writes: 'Tolstoy moulded Gandhi's whole outlook on life. His views on art, religion, and economics, on the relationship between the sexes, no less than on politics were profoundly influenced by Tolstoy.'[1] 'The kingdom of God is within you' (Tolstoy's masterpiece) contains practically the whole of Mahatma Gandhi's non-violent non-co-operation programme in its essentials.[2]

In spite of his philosophizing on these writings, Mahatma Gandhi was not a system-builder. Comparing Thoreau and Mahatma Gandhi in this respect Pyarelal says that neither of these thinkers was a system-builder; but both were profound thinkers, truth-seekers, and truth-speakers. Both had a passion for truth and both represented a philosophy in action. Both also believed in the ideal of voluntary poverty.

Writing on the lack of a system in Mahatma Gandhi's thought, Humayun Kabir rightly says that Mahatma Gandhi was an objective student of reality and that his method was essentially experimental and scientific. Intuition and action rather than logic and system-building characterized Mahatma Gandhi's life. Jawaharlal Nehru who knew Mahatma Gandhi for many years, more intimately than did many others, says: "We were associated (with him) seldom in logical debate and argument or philosophical discourse; we were associated in action." N. B. Sen, in his *Wit and Wisdom of Gandhi*, writes "Gandhi was an odd kind of pacifist, for he was an activist full of dynamic energy" (p. 14).

Not a Politician

If Mahatma Gandhi was not a systematic political thinker, much less was he a politician. As said above, it was his concern for the welfare of the masses which pushed him into politics. But there were times when in the very thick of it, he abandoned the political struggle for such matters as the eradication of untouchability, the elimination of drink, the popularizing of village industry and the promotion of Hindu-Muslim unity. It is because of all this that Acharya Kripalani regards Mahatma Gandhi as essentially a social reformer. But such a view, in our judgment, is narrow and one-sided and does not do full justice to the many sidedness of Mahatma Gandhi.

Though not a politician in the ordinary sense of the term, Mahatma Gandhi exhibited unusual shrewdness in choosing the time as well as the methods and techniques to be used in launching his non-violent programme. From this point of view we may partially agree with the *Manchester Guardian* when it wrote at the time of his assassination that Mahatma

1. *The Statesman*, February 1, 1957.
2. *Ibid.*

Gandhi was a saint among politicians and a politician among saints. Every time he launched his attack against the British he chose new symbols and new techniques. In 1919-20 it was non-violent non-co-operation calling upon students, lawyers and government servants to give up their respective vocations; in 1930 salt became the symbol of opposition to government; in 1939 it was individual civil disobedience by selected individuals; in 1940 it was defiance of law against the assembly of people; in 1942 it was the drastic "Quit India" programme with its battlecry of "Do or die". All through the struggle for freedom the boycott of British goods and the patronizing of hand-spun and hand-woven goods with the *charkha* (spinning wheel) as symbol played a vital part.

Spiritualization of Politics

A lasting contribution of Mahatma Gandhi to politics and political theroy was his spiritualization of politics. It was his firm conviction that if politics was to be a blessing and not a curse to mankind, it should be undergirded by the highest ethical and spiritual principles. Expediency in the bad sense of the term hardly ever appealed to him. He held that means were just as important as ends. Only right means, he believed, could lead to right ends. In other words, ends and means are the same thing looked at from different points of view. If one takes scrupulous care of means, ends will take care of themselves. Complete honesty of means was one of the essentials in Mahatma Gandhi's thought and practice. Apropos of this, Dr. Alve Myrdal, one of the delegates to the Gandhi seminar in New Delhi in 1953, wrote: Means and ends are inseparable because wrong means cannot lead to the right end.

To quote from Mahatma Gandhi himself: "Politics bereft of religion are a death-trap because they kill the soul". "I have sacrificed no principle to gain a political end". "Politics without morality is a thing to be avoided". (N. B. Sen: *The Wit and Wisdom of Gandhi,* p. 14). "I could not be leading a religious life unless I identified myself with the whole of mankind, and that I could not do unless I took part in politics. The whole gamut of man's activities today constitutes an indivisible whole. You cannot divide social, economic, political and purely religious work into watertight compartments. I do not know any religion apart from human activity".

Philosophical Anarchism

If one wants to find a parallel to Mahatma Gandhi's thought in Western political philosophy, one finds it in philosophical anarchism. This was partly due to the influence of Thoreau. In his introdudction to an unauthorized Indian edition of Thoreau's *Essay on Civil Disobedience*, Mahatma Gandhi (quoted by Pyarelal) writes: I heartily accept the motto, 'That government is best which governs least'.... Carried out, it finally amounts to this, which also I believe, "That Government is best which governs not at all."

Instead of invoking a large measure of state activity, as many in India do today, Mahatma Gandhi firmly believed in self-directed activity. His major emphasis was on voluntary co-operation at the village level. He realized that undue state action kills initiative and leads to jobbery and nepotism. With the philosophical anarchists, Mahatma Gandhi believed that the compulsive nature of the state robbed individual action of its morality. When men act like machines or automatons, there can be no question of morality. Both Mahatma Gandhi and Thoreau looked upon the state as a soulless machine. Therefore the ideal society which Mahatma Gandhi envisaged is stateless democracy. Writing in his *Young India* (July 2, 1931) he says, "In such a state (of enlightened anarchy) everyone is his own ruler. He rules himself in such a manner that he is never a hindrance to his neighbour. In the ideal state, therefore, there is no political power because there is no State." Mahatma Gandhi wanted all reform to come from within. He did not want progress to be imposed by an outside authority.

State Action

Though inclined towards philosophical anarchism Mahatma Gandhi did not dogmatize about it. He was far from being doctrinaire in his thinking and action. He wanted the State to exercise minimum functions, transferring more and more authority to voulntary associations. Every case of state action was to be judged on its own merits; and where state action was likely to advance the welfare of the people, Mahatma Gandhi would welcome it in spite of his distrust of the state. In performing its functions, the object of the State was to serve the masses. But the functions must be performed with the minimum use of coercion. "People", he says, "are the roots, the State is the fruit. If the roots are sweet, the fruits are bound to be sweet".

On the whole Mahatma Gandhi's belief is that the State is rooted in violence, exploits the poor, and by enforcing action restricts the scope for self-rule on the part of the individual. So in a predominantly non-violent society the State will govern the least and use the least amount of force. Consistently with the moral level of the people it will aim at reducing its functions so as to efface itself ultimately and thus lead to self-regulated and ordered anarchy.

The Welfare State

According to Humayun Kabir, Mahatma Gandhi was an inheritor of the liberal tradition (the value of personal liberty and the like), of the tradition of philosophical anarchism, and of the tradition of collectivism found in the socialistic thought that the good things of life ought to be shared. If Mahatma Gandhi were living today, it is likely that he would support the social welfare state ideal, but the interpretation of such a state would be his own. He would support a welfare state because of his great concern for the masses, because of his instinctive sympathy for and understanding of those whom we regard as the uneducated and backward. The socialistic pattern of society and the various five year plans would have appealed to him if they had originated from the people themselves and largely executed them and did not mean the multiplication of government posts, huge wastage of public money, the increase of opportunity for corruption and laziness, undue concentration of heavy industries, and grand multi-purpose river valley schemes whose benefits have not yet trickled down to the poor to any large extent proportionate to the huge amount spent on them. He would have supported such projects as the community welfare projects and made them the spearhead of the welfare state.

Against Misery and Exploitation

Mahatma Gandhi was first and foremost against all misery and every form of exploitation. While condemning caste and regarding untouchability as a sin, Mahatma Gandhi at the same time upheld the Hindu ideal of the *Varnashramadharma,* according to which every person was to perform his allotted task in society in accordance with his capacities and training. Mahatma Gandhi's fervour for the masses did not divide society into 'the haves' and 'the have-nots' or the exploiters and the exploited. It took the form of complete identification with the masses. Mahatma Gandhi was not a Marxist. He called himself 'a weaver and cultivator' by profession and identified himself with the people as regards food, dress, speech and the like.[3] He broke the back of the caste system by such means as temple entry and continuous propaganda against untouchability. He adopted an untouchable girl as his own daughter, coined the word 'Harijans' (children of God) to replace the ugly word untouchables, and gave them an honoured place in the Hindu society. He fasted against separate electorates for these people and gave them more than their share of seats in the legislature through the system of reservation of seats in joint electorates. He had a special concern for women and children and discovered the moral strength of women in his early non-violent campaigns in South Africa. He had an equal concern for the kisans (peasants) and labourers. In his earlier days when he had more time at his disposal, even the most insignificant person could go to him and discuss his personal problems in great detail as though he was his Father confessor. Mahatma Gandhi's new system of education known as the *Nai Talim* had at its bottom the two principles of truth and human dignity. While thinkers before him spoke and wrote eloquently on human dignity, equality, and brotherhood, Mahatma Gandhi practised them; and this may be regarded as his greatest contribution to politics and to life in general. In short, he spiritualized politics.

THE PHILOSOPHY OF NON-VIOLENCE

When everything is said and done, it will be readily admitted that

---

3. Gandhi's well-known words are : "To a people famishing and idle, the only acceptable form in which God can dare appear is work and promise of food as wages."

Mahatma Gandhi's greatest contribution to politics in particular and life in general was his teaching and practice of non-violence. As long ago as 1920, he wrote, "Non-violence is the law of our species as violence is the law of the brute. The spirit lies dormant in the brute and he knows no law but that of physical force. The dignity of man requires obedience to a higher law—the struggle of the spirit.... Non-violence is a perfect state. It is the goal towards which all mankind moves naturally, though unconsciously." (*Young India,* August 14, 1920). He again wrote: "For me non-violence is not a mere philosophical principle. It is the rule and breath of my life.... It is a matter not of the intellect but of the heart." Mahatma Gandhi was by no means the originator of the principle of non-violence and similar principles. But he was the first to apply them on a huge mass scale and in the political field. Writing on Indian freedom, he said, "My interest in India's freedom will cease if she adopts violent means, for their fruit will be not freedom but slavery in disguise".

Non-violence is not Passivity

As taught and practised by Mahatma Gandhi, non-violence does not mean passivity or pacifism or sitting with one's hands folded in the face of danger or evil. It does not mean meek submission to the will of the evil-doer. "It is soul-force or truth force or truth-seeking force. It is in short *satyagraha* which means resistance to evil with all the moral and spiritual force that a person can command. It is the use of moral force or firmness in the vindication of Truth". It is "soul-force or the power of the Godhead within us." It is in accordance with the ancient Hindu law of self-sacrifice. It means conscious suffering. In Mahatma Gandhi's own words, "It does not mean meek submission to the will of the evil-doer." "It is no negative force.... It is a force which is more positive than electricity and more powerful than even ether." "The highest violence can be met by the highest non-violence." Mahatma Gandhi called himself "the keeper of the light house called Satyagraha (or soul-force)". "It is a principle for which I live, for which I desire to live, and for which I believe I am equally prepared to die". (The test contained in the last part of the sentence came true on January 30, 1948).

Others interpreting Mahatma Gandhi's type of non-violence have called it "a bravery of the soul," "a warfare of the ascetic", and "an adventure in love". Far from being negative, it is positive, dynamic, and constructive.

Non-violence Rooted in Ahimsa

Non-violence, as taught and practised by Mahatma Gandhi is rooted in the Indian doctrine of *ahimsa* or non-injury. Negatively, it means refraining from causing pain or the taking of any life. "Ahimsa means avoiding injury to anything on earth in thought, word & deed," (The *Harijan,* Sept. 7, 1935, p. 235). It means the avoidance of harsh words, harsh judgments, ill-will, anger, spite and cruelty. It means in particular that one should not harbour an uncharitable thought even for one's enemy.

On the positive side, ahimsa is coterminous with the Christian principle of love. It is omnipotent, infinite, and synonymous with God Himself. It is an all-pervasive eternal principle applicable to every life situation. In his pioneer work, *The Political Philosophy of Mahatma Gandhi*, Dr. G. N. Dhawan writes, "Ahimsa means an effort to abandon the violence that is inevitable in life. Ahimsa stands for the ultimate deliverance of man from the bondage of the flesh so that he may attain the state in which life is possible without the necessity of a perishable body whose sustenance inevitably involves destruction." (*96:60*) "Ahimsa", says Mahatma Gandhi is "a weapon of matchless potency. It is the *summum bonum* of life". (Sen, op. cit., p. 16).

Weapon of the Strong

Satyagraha is a weapon of those who are physically weak but morally strong. It can also be the weapon of those who are both physically and morally strong, but never of those who are morally weak. Pyarelal, however, writes, "The starting point of Mahatma Gandhi's technique was that non-violence is the strength of the weak."[4] When brought under a strong influence non-violence can be used by women and children and by illiterate men and others whom we generally regard as weak. Non-violence involves opposition to evil, not by another evil but by good. It is the overcoming of evil by good. In Mahatma Gandhi's own words: "The injunction 'love your enemies' is not only the noblest idealism, it is also the most practical politics."

Basic Principle is Truth

Truth is the basic factor of non-violence. According to Mahatma Gandhi it is not enough to say that God is truth, but Truth is God. In Mahatma Gandhi's own words: "For me, truth is the sovereign principle, which includes numerous other principles. This truth is not only truthfulness in word, but truthfulness in thought also, and not only the relative truth of our conception, but the Absolute Truth, the Eternal principle, that is God". (Sen, op. cit., p. 228). "Truth quenches untruth. Love quenches anger, self-suffering quenches violence. This eternal rule is a rule not for saints only, but for all". (Sen, p. 230). According to Niemoller, the famous German Christian pastor and thinker of our day, what Hindus call Truth, Christians call faith in God. Non-violence is a struggle, for truth. In this struggle, if conducted along right lines, both parties are seekers after truth and, therefore, there is no question of one side being the victors and the others the vanquished. There is nothing like 'fight to the finish'. In waging

4. *Gandhian Outlook and Technique* (Government of India publication, p. 168).

a non-violent struggle one should take care to see that the cause for which one is fighting is absolutely true so far as God enables one to see the truth. If at any point in the course of that struggle, a person has a fear that he has departed from truth, he should have no hesitation in confessing his guilt and renouncing whatever gain he may have made, even as Mahatma Gandhi did when he called off one of his non-violent movements (1922) when he was within an ace of success saying that he had committed a "Himalayan blunder". Truth to the Satyagrahi is more precious than victory. The principle of truth, as implied here, means that non-violence cannot be undertaken in a light-hearted spirit. It means that one should live close to God and take his marching orders from Him even as Mahatma Gandhi did.

Appeal to the Moral Sense in a spirit of Love

The Satyagrahi's chief forte is that there is something of God in every man and that appeal can be made to the Divine in man through love and conscious self-suffering. It is the conviction of the Satyagrahi that through the principle of love and self-suffering he can rouse the moral giant which lies in the nature of his opponent. In the words of Pastor Niemoller: "Suffering strengthens those who suffer and weakens those who inflict suffering." If truth is the basic principle, according to Mahatma Gandhi, love is the means by which it is realized. Non-violence, says Mahatma Gandhi, can "melt even the stoniest of hearts." Mahatma Gandhi believed in winning over people by persuasion rather than by compulsion. It was equally his conviction that one could have evil without hating the evil-doer. This he showed clearly, on more than one occasion, in his relation to the British. He trained himself and others to realize that it was possible to hate the British system of government and call it even "Satanic" without entertaining any hatred for the Briton. This is in accordance with Christ's injunction to love one's enemies. In Mahatma Gandhi's own words: "If my love is sincere, I must love the Englishman in spite of my distrust." At another time he said: "I am fighting British imperialism, but I am not fighting the Britisher; I am not fighting the Englishman or anybody. They are my friends, but I will fight British imperialism."

To give some practical examples of this practice of love, Mahatma Gandhi had nothing but unqualified praise for the English judge who performed his *dharma* in convicting him for a six-year imprisonment in 1922; for the doctor who operated on him for appendicitis in 1924; and for successive Viceroys such as Lord Irwin, Lord Linlithgow and Lord Wavell with all of whom he had sharp differences of opinion at times. His immediate response to the war issue in 1937 was most moving when he contemplated the possibility of the aerial destruction of London by Nazi bombing. Mahatma Gandhi repeatedly humiliated himself in relation to Jinnah in trying to work out a solution for the political impasse of the time. Jinnah always made it a point to make Mahatma Gandhi run up to him for negotiations and seldom, if ever reciprocated his visits.

Writing on the importance of love in the practice of non-violence, Mahatma Gandhi writes : "Love never claims. It ever gives. Love ever suffers, never resents, never revenges itself." "Ahimsa, in its positive form, means the largest love, the greatest charity". (Sen, op. cit., p. 163). He further says that in the practice of non-violence truth is the foundation and love the weapon. Writing on self-suffering, Mahatma Gandhi says : "A nation that is capable of limitless sacrifices is capable of rising to limitless heights. The greater the sacrifice, the quicker the progress." Mahatma Gandhi taught and practised self-suffering, sacrifice and self-immolation.

OTHER REQUISITES OF NON-VIOLENCE

1. Inner Purity

In Mahatma Gandhi's view a satyagrahi should not only practise love, but also observe inner purity. If non-violence is to be a warfare of the ascetic, according to Mahatma Gandhi, he should prepare himself for it by self-discipline, civility, and inner purity. "Incivility", he says, "spoils Satyagraha like a drop of arsenic in milk." Elsewhere he writes that a stayagrahi should observe chastity, adopt poverty, follow truth, and cultivate fearlessness. Stressing inner purity Mahatma Gandhi called Satyagraha a movement of national perfection. In his own life, he observed Brahmacharya or continence from his thirty-seventh year in response to a great call, although he did not make it a universal rule for everybody.

2. Fasting

Even fasting Mahatma Gandhi regarded as an important element in the practice of non-violence. It is in accordance with the Indian tradition and practice.

Against the charge that fasting is a form of moral coercion, Mahatma Gandhi vigorously defended himself saying that it was in accordance with an inner voice and that it was "against nobody in particular". "It is particularly against myself."

Mahatma Gandhi advocated both private and public fasts; but neither kind had its value if it was undertaken for a selfish purpose. At times he used fasting against the impurities of his followers. As important as outer fasting he claimed was inner fasting through such means as working for truth, practising love, and abjuring earthly possession and ambition. In extreme cases, according to Mahatma Gandhi, "fasting unto death is an integral part of satyagraha". Fasting, like other good acts, should be undertaken without any expectation of fruits. "He who fasts in the expectation of fruit generally fails." In short, it is wrong to fast for selfish ends.

3. Fearlessness

As important as purity and fasting is fearlessness or *abhaya*. A satyagrahi has to shed even the last vestige of cowardice if he is to practise non-violence successfully. The fearlessness which Mahatma Gandhi practised was fearlessness which arises out of selflessness. In Mahatma Gandhi's own words : "If you want to follow Truth, fearlessness is absolutely necessary. Fearlessness is the first requisite of spirituality. Cowards can never be moral." Apropos of it, Lao-Tse has said : "We have fears because we have a self. When we do not regard that self as self, what have we to fear ?"

4. Non-possession

The kind of fearlessness that Mahatma Gandhi calls for necessitates the cultivation of an attitude of non-attachment i.e., one of detached interest in the material things of life. According to him, one has to be as care-free as the birds of the air or the lilies of the field. Mahatma Gandhi held that so "many of the so-called comforts of life are not only indispensable but positive hindrances to the elevation of mankind". Renunciation is the way to realization. Interpreting Mahatma Gandhi's teachings Pyarelal says that the holding of possessions is incompatible with non-violence and the ideal of identification with the whole world. Non-possession is the ideal and exclusive possession calls for the use of violence. This being so, Mahatma Gandhi calls for a duty-centred economy rather than a right-centred economy.

5. Perseverance

If non-violence is an eternal principle, one should not be in a hurry for results. One should cultivate a divine patience and perseverance, realizing that non-violent methods at times take a much longer time for their fruition than violent methods. It must be borne in mind at the same time that quick results brought about by warfare are never stable and lasting. A non-violent person knows no defeat because of his infinite faith in God.

Mahatma Gandhi did not equate patience and perseverance with lethargy and fatalism, so common in India. At times when the situation warranted it, he had a sense of urgency and would not brook delay. A good example of that is his "Do or die" policy of 1942. In the midst of a deadly conflict (1942) when the fate of India was hanging in the balance, Mahatma Gandhi had the moral courage to call upon the British rulers to quit India, and leave her to God and anarchy.

Gandhiji's Non-violence Graded

Students of Mahatma Gandhi's thought have often wondered whether the non-violence that he taught was absolute and unlimited. While men like Maulana Abul Kalam Azad thought that it was absolute, the general opinion seems to be that it was not absolute. As seen earlier, it was Mahatma Gandhi's conviction that those who did not have faith in absolute non-violence might resort to such force as they had. Even in the conflicts between nations, Mahatma Gandhi did not always teach passive resistance. In the 30's and 40's when Japan was carrying on an aggressive, ruthless, and unprovoked warfare in China, Mahatma Gandhi thought that it was relatively right for China to take up arms against Japan. He held a similar view with regard to Poland when she was brutally attacked by Germany in 1939. Physical resistance in those cases, he regarded as the nearest approach to non-violence. At the same time, he refused to endorse non-violence as a mere expediency and insisted that the satyagrahi should observe non-violence in thought, word, and deed.

Gandhiji's Non-violence Religiously Motivated

As has been said repeatedly, Mahatma Gandhi was essentially a man of religion; and it is his religious convictions that led to his practice of non-violence. To him morality was synonymous with religion. Rites and ceremonies, Dogmas and creeds had little place in his religion. "Morality", he said, "is the basis of things and truth is the substance of morality." Men's spiritual salvation is not divorced from life and the activities of the world. "Salvation is nothing more and nothing less than living well in every way."

Mahatma Gandhi a tower of Strength

What made Mahatma Gandhi a tower of strength to millions of people was his moral and spiritual eminence. In delineating this eminence, we find at least five major elements. Mahatma Gandhi was a tower of strength because of his unswerving faith in God and his continuous practice of the presence of God.

As important as his faith in God was Mahatma Gandhi's unshakable faith in his fellow-men. He had abounding faith in human possibilities. It was his firm conviction that human nature was never beyond redemption. Such conviction is most refreshing in a world which is fast losing its faith in God and man and pins its faith to the machine.

Finally, Mahatma Gandhi was a tower of strength because of his spirit of magnanimity, forgiveness, and reconciliation. He never drove his victory to the breaking point. Humiliation of the opponent was never his aim. There was nothing like a victor and vanquished in the various non-violent campaigns conducted by him. In the midst of a victorious struggle he was willing to negotiate and come to terms so long as honour was not sacrificed. It was the same spirit of magnanimity which made him insist that whatever money India owed to Pakistan at the time of partition should be paid to her despite the atrocities of Pakistan against India and her failure to fulfil her end of the contract. The same magnanimity characterized him when he fell at the mortal gunshot of Godse, his assassin who regarded him as a mad man because he was advising his fellow Hindus to turn the other cheek also to the Muslims. But at that time when almost everybody was going off the deep end in India, Mahatma Gandhi was about the only sane man. Yet as Rousseau says, "To be sane in a world of mad men is itself a form of madness" and Mahatma Gandhi dared to be a mad man of that kind.

Non-violence a total Philosophy of Life

As taught and practised by Mahatma Gandhi, non-violence was a total philosophy of life pervading the whole being of man and not applied merely to isolated acts. It applies to both the private and public spheres of life. In the economic field it means a decentralized village economy opposed to both capitalism and communism, both of which are forms of exploitation. In the political field it means a federation of autonomous village republics. In the field of international relations it means negotiation, arbitration and adjudication necessitating in extreme cases in the formation of an International Peace Force (*Shanti Sena*) placing itself between the contestants and even allowing itself to be annihilated before one side destroys the other. In its relation to other faiths, cultures, and ideologies Mahatma Gandhi's non-violence means the cultivation of a spirit of true tolerance rooted in mutual sympathy, humility and understanding. It is capable of being applied to caste, class and racial conflicts too. Nay, it can be applied to the whole creation.

Non-violence not Dependent on Numbers

Mahatma Gandhi rightly believed that masses are not always necessary for the successful practice of non-violence. According to his teaching, "one man can offer it just as well as millions." "In satyagraha it is never the numbers that count.... Indeed one perfect civil resister is enough to win the battle of Right against Wrong." One man with soul force or moral courage can do the work of a thousand. Because of this conviction, Mahatma Gandhi was never afraid to stand alone. At times even the Indian National Congress which he had built up through the years disowned him and his programme. At other times he disowned it and refused to be even a four-anna member.

Non-violence not Coercion

In spite of the repeated charge that satyagraha was a form of coercion, Mahatma Gandhi held that it was not coercion from any point of view—economic, psychological, political or moral. It was based upon the idea of persuasion. It is calculated to appeal to the moral giant that lies dormant in the bosom of one's opponent. It is not moral coercion. It is appeal to man's reason and his sense of decency and not a threat to his person. It does not humiliate the opponent. It dazzles him and at last compels recognition from him. It shows a tremendous and almost child-like faith in the moral capacity of one's opponent.

Non-violence and Passive Resistance

The four successive stages through which Mahatma Gandhi's philosophy of non-violence has passed are: (1) passive resistance (in South Africa); (2) non-co-operation (1920-21); (3) civil disobedience (1930-31); and (4) *satyagraha* (1940-41).

The last three stages may be roughly grouped together as *satyagraha*. Writers have taken pains to distinguish passive resistance from *satyagraha*. According to them (1) passive resistance is not completely wedded to non-violence. It may use violence, if the circumstances demand it, while *satya-graha* does not recognize the use of force at all. While this may be true in theory, it needs to be remembered that Mahatma Gandhi himself claimed that under certain extreme circumstances, force may be used to resist force. Physical force, he says, is better than moral cowardice. (2) Passive resistance may mean the use of compulsion in the case of the person against whom it is directed, while *satyagraha* believes in the infliction of suffering on one-self. In practice, however, *satyagraha* may mean a subtle form of coercion. (3) More than passive resistance, *satyagraha* aims at the change of heart of the opponent. (4) Passive resistance may be motivated by jealousy, while satyagraha is governed by the principles of love and charity. (5) Passive resis-tance is negative and is the instrument of the weak, whereas *satyagraha* is positive and is a weapon of the strong.

MAHATMA GANDHI'S VIEWS ON ECONOMICS

The Gandhian economy includes aspects of anarchism, individualism, socialism, and idealism. It seeks to apply the principle of non-violence to man's economic life. It sees clearly that large-scale mechanized production leads to materialism of the worst type, to the conquest of the backward coun tries of the world from which raw materials may be imported and to which finished goods may be exported, to war, militarism and imperialism.

Over against capitalism which emphasizes material value, the Gandhian economy emphasizes humanitarian and cultural values. It sets its face re-solutely against all forms of exploitation, whether this exploitation is from within the country itself—of one class by another—or from outside. As against standardized production, it seeks to establish a system in which the initiative and originality of the individual will be given the freest scope in which to operate.

The keywords of Gandhian economy are self-sufficiency, decentralized production, and equitable distribution. Under this system large-scale produc-tion by impersonal agencies will disappear except as regards goods and services which cannot very well be left in the hands of private individuals. The postal and telegraph sytsems, roads and other means of communication will continue to be owned and controlled by the State. Railways, mines, forests, irrigation, and the management of heavy industries will be the mono-poly of the State. But primary commodities such as food, clothing, and shelter will be produced on a decentralized basis, the government providing the necessary means by which goods produced will be properly coordinated and marketed. The middleman's profit of the industrial magnate and of impersonal companies will disappear. The primary producer will receive a reward which will be much more equitable than is possible at present. Goods locally produced will, for the most part, be locally consumed. In certain situations, barter economy may replace money economy. Taxes, for example, may in some cases be paid in kind.

International trade will be on a much reduced scale, except as regards surplus goods. Commodities which are necessary for the health and well-being of the people will not be shipped out of the country as at present. Such restriction will cut the ground under militarism and warfare. Each country and each natural region within the country will become a logical unit by itself. It will not be possible for any country to make itself rich by riding on the backs of others.

The gulf between the rich and the poor will become less and less marked, there being no opportunity for the exploitation of one individual or class by another individual or class.

It is true that this system calls for extended State action. But it is not the same as socialism. For, while socialism believes in a controlled distribution of wealth, the system under consideration advocates an automatic distribution of wealth by carefully decided policies at the source. Besides, while both capitalism and socialism stress material values, this system regards material values as of significance only in relation to human values.

Criticism

When we look at the Gandhian economy critically, we are bound to say that it is not distinctive enough to be regarded as an alternative to capitalism or communism. One of its chief defects is the assumption that men work only out of profit motive—an assumption which becomes all the more difficult to understand when we remember that in the political field the Gandhian philosophy called for rare self-sacrifice and utter devotion to a cause. Both socialism and communism believe that in inducing people to work we can appeal to higher motives than mere profit motive, such as the motive of good citizenship.

While the decentralized programme of Gandhian economy is a step in the right direction, it is possible to overdo it. There are many advantages to be derived from concerted production. Therefore, the system which we require is one which develops centralization and decentralization *pari passu*. With special reference to India, it must be said that a programme of decentralization may accentuate our inherent inability to unite, making us still more individualistic than we are today.

In the interdependent world in which we live and which promises to become more and more of a single economic unit, a programme of decentralization has its obvious dangers. It will make international trade and commerce and international intercourse difficult, if not impossible. What the world requires today is some form of world planning of which national, provincial, and village planning are a part. Over-emphasis on cottage industries is likely to arrest our economic development and keep things at a primitive level. Hand-made goods will consume more time and energy than machine-made goods and are likely to be more expensive.

The Gandhian economy admits that in every system there is bound to be some discipline or coercion. But it is difficult to uphold its contention that under it there will be voluntary discipline, while under other systems the discipline imposed will be involuntary or compulsory. The line between justifiable and unjustifiable coercion is not easy to draw.

Exploitation is not the monopoly of the big capitalist or of an impersonal corporation. It can be carried on even by the small man. What is needed is (a) the reformation of individual character and (b) the reduction of opportunities for exploitation.

In spite of these difficulties, the Gandhian economy offers a valuable programme in the present state of affairs prevalent in India. The part of wisdom is to make decentralized village economy an intrinsic part of a mixed economy which borrows features of value from different systems and adapts them to Indian tradition and genius.

The Machine Age

It is often assumed, particularly by Western writers, that Mahatma Gandhi was antiquated in his views with regard to economic matters and that he was quite out of step with the vast scientific and economic development taking place in the world including India today. The fact is that Mahatma Gandhi was opposed to the machine age, but not to the machine as such. He rightly believed that machine is good when it serves man, but not when it seeks to master him. To certain types of small-scale machinery such as the sewing machine Mahatma Gandhi had no objection. On the other hand, he warmly welcomed it as it served to save the back-breaking work connected with hand stitching. He also made a personal use of railways and automobiles and did not seriously object to their use by others. As far as man-power and mechanical power are concerned, he rightly wanted the immense man-power and cattle power of India to be utilized first before turning to large-scale machinery. Industrialization, he held, might lead to greater production of goods, but not necessarily to greater moral progress.

It is possible to argue that machine civilization and decline in morals are not related to each other as cause and effect. But even in the Western countries where one often finds a high level of personal and social morality, such matters as family solidarity and loyalty to a large family circle have suffered a setback. Neighbourhood associations and an informal community sense tend to become formalized. In spite of it, it must be said that machine is as much a gift of God as hand-labour. Therefore, the part of wisdom is to develop both and not allow the machine to displace human beings or crush personality.[5]

---

5. The author is indebted to Mr. Sen quoted above for the following excerpts from Mahatma Gandhi's writing, bearing on machinery : "Machinery has its place; it has come to stay", "I am aiming not at the eradication of all machinery, but its limitation". "What I object to is the craze for machinery, not to machinery as such". "Today machinery helps a few to ride on the backs of millions".

Revival of Village Economy

Mahatma Gandhi whose thought centred on an essentially village economy devoted much time and thought to the internal development of the village. His first thought was to revive indigenous industries so that people could have enough to eat and keep the wolf off their doors. In his judgment any kind of economy which exploits people and concentrates wealth in a few hands stands self-condemned. His major emphasis was upon hand-spinning and hand-weaving both of which had an economic significance and helped to shake the mighty British Empire from the citadels of power. Attention was also paid to such cottage industries as gurmaking, paddy dehusking, oil-pressing, paper-making, leather work, basket-making, and the like. But it is obvious that such revival alone cannot feed, clothe, and shelter the teeming millions of India. Mahatma Gandhi gave birth to the idea of the uplift of all through the scheme of Sarvodaya which is being expanded and applied against a wide canvas today.

In the matter of economics and politics, Mahatma Gandhi wanted that India should become a network of self-governing and self-sustaining village republics, each village or group of villages having its own industries and each of them living an autonomous existence. Decentralization in both economics and administration was the keyword. Mahatma Gandhi also supported the idea of regional self-sufficiency dovetailed into a national economy. International trade was to be not in food and clothing, but only in surpluses and luxuries. The situation, however, today is that a certain portion of cultivable land which should be made available for food crops is used for raising cash crops in order to earn dollar assets. It may be that as a result of the vast irrigation and power schemes now undertaken, India in the future will not require as much land as she does now for raising an adequate supply of food.

A recent writer says that Mahatma Gandhi's views on economic matters may sometimes sound visionary and unrealistic to the bourgeois class, but he is one who correctly diagnosed the disease that had overtaken the Indian society during years of subjection to foreign rule. His views really are marked by a pronounced realism. "He is no agrarian reactionary when he opposes urbanization, mechanization, large-scale nationalization, and capitalism. He realized that the only way to harness the huge man-power is to strengthen cottage industries".

The Doctrine of Limits

In his attitude to property, Mahatma Gandhi adopted something like a doctrine of limits and the simplification of the standards of living. One should place voluntary limits on his property and practise self-renunciation. Mahatma Gandhi realized that property is worry and that it produces a great many anti-social results. Man becomes entangled in a web of his own creation. Mahatma Gandhi rightly held that so "many of the so-called comforts of life are not only indispensable but positive hindrances to the elevation of mankind".

In continuation of the doctrine of limits, Mahatma Gandhi developed the doctrine of trusteeship. The rich were to regard themselves as trustees for the community. They were to use property in the interest of the community as a whole. In Christian terminology, nobody *owns* wealth; he simply *owes* it as a solemn responsibility to God. In Mahatma Gandhi's own words :"Those who have money are not expected to throw it away, but they are expected to be indifferent about it."

Unfortunately for this point of view, it has not worked very well in history except in rare cases. Man is so attached to property that, in the forcible language of Machiavelli, he much sooner forgets the murder of his father than the loss of his patrimony. Yet the fact that Vinoba Bhave has been able to secure four and a half million acres of land as voluntary gift from land-owners, both big and small, gives some hope for the future. It may be that under a proper moral and spiritual climate, the doctrine of trusteeship will become a reality. At the present level of man's development, however, compulsion of some kind seems necessary, but Mahatma Gandhi would regard it as violence.

Was Mahatma Gandhi a Socialist ?

From what has been said above, it is clear that Mahatma Gandhi was not a socialist in the usually accepted sense of the term. If he was a socialist at all, his type of socialism was village socialism. He was not a doctrinaire socialist believing in the state ownership of the means of production. He believed, however, that one who consumed more than what one actually needed was depriving the poor of their due. In an interview with Louis Fischer, answering the question what he meant by socialism Mahatma Gandhi said, "My socialism means even unto this last. I do not want to rise on the ashes of the blind, the deaf, and the dumb;.... I want freedom for the full expression of my personality.... Under other forms of socialism, there is no individual freedom. You own nothing, not even your body".[6]

Thuogh not a socialist in the usually accepted sense of the term, Mahatma Gandhi was a firm believer in various methods of cooperation. He used to say: "I am a born co-operator." At the same time he recognized elements of value in conservatism and liberalism, in socialism and communism, as well as in anarchism.

Summing up what we have been saying in the above paragraph, Kaka Saheb Kalelkar says that Mahatma Gandhi's solution to India's problems was 'Decentralization of production and regional self-sufficiency; avoidance of the extremes of wealth and poverty; equal reverence for all religions; removal of the sense of high and low in the social scale, acceptance of wealth as a trust for the betterment of the whole of humanity; raising of the moral

6. Quoted by Pyarelal in *Harijan,* 4 Aug., 1946.

standard of life by reducing the material standard of luxurious living; renunciation of all vindictive punishments and reprisals; and reducing the use of physical force to its minimum in the task of maintaining law and order."[7]

Mahatma Gandhi and Marx

Mahatma Gandhi was not a believer in class struggle. His emphasis was on class co-operation, all working together for a common good. Mahatma Gandhi was a philosophical idealist, whereas Marx was a dialectical materialist. Religion meant nothing to Marx whereas to Mahatma Gandhi it was the warp and woof of his life. Social change to Mahatma Gandhi is to be brought about by non-violent methods, while Marx believed in revolution even by armed violence. Yet both Marx and Mahatma Gandhi reacted to western civilization, each in his own way. To Mahatma Gandhi it was a symbol of imperialism, whereas to Marx it was the equivalent of capitalism.

Was Mahatma Gandhi an Internationalist ?

In their own day, the winning of national freedom was the sole passion of patriots in India. Mahatma Gandhi was no exception to it. Yet he was interested in what was happening elsewhere in the world. In a French paper he said, "My nationalism is intense internationalism". According to Dr. Ralph Bunche, one of the participants in the Gandhi seminar in Delhi (1955), though Mahatma Gandhi's efforts were concentrated on India, he was a true internationalist. At one time he wrote, "My mission is not merely the brotherhood of Indian humanity. My mission is not merely the freedom of India, though today it undoubtedly engrosses practically the whole of my life and the whole of my time. But through the realization of the freedom of India I hope to realise and carry on the mission of the brotherhood of man."

Mahatma Gandhi was at the same time a true nationalist in that he wanted every people to make its own contribution to the total community of nations. What he condemned in nationalism was its narrowness, selfishness, and exclusiveness.

Mahatma Gandhi did not approve of trusteeship in the international sphere which meant something of a one-sided boon. What he wanted was mutual respect and mutual promotion of each other's interests.

Mahatma Gandhi was a true internationalist inasmuch as truth, and non-violence, the two great foundation principles of Mahatma Gandhi's life and thought are universal principles. Yet he did not evolve a complete theory of international relations and obligations.

The Religious Ideals of Mahatma Gandhi

The political thought of a writer usually does not include his religious views. But the case is different as regards Mahatma Gandhi. In him religion

7. *Gandhian Outlook and Technique*, pp. 372-73.

and politics were so blended together that it is not out of place to give a brief sketch of his religious views.

The Equality of all Religions

It was Mahatma Gandhi's firm conviction that all religions are true; that all are equally valid; and that all are imperfect. To quote his own words. "Every nation's religion is as good as any other. Certainly India's religions are adequate for her people. We need no converting spiritually". "The need of the moment is not one religion, but mutual respect and tolerance of the devotees of the different religions."

He freely used the prayers and Scriptures of various religions such as the Bhagavat Gita, the Avasta, the Sermon on the Mount, the Granth and the Koran. At the same time he stoutly denied that he was an eclectic who had no moorings in any particular faith.

A Hindu of Hindus

Though broad-minded and tolerant towards all religions, including the primitive, Mahatma Gandhi called himself a "Hindu of Hindus" and a Sanatanist. But he qualified it by saying that he was as much of a Christian or Muslim as he was a Hindu. He was aware of the defects of Hinduism, but tried to reform it from within. He upheld idol worship, although he was no idol worshipper himself. He believed in cow protection, but did not carry it to extreme limits as some politicians and pseudo-religious people do. He waged a relentless warfare against untouchability but at the same time upheld Varnashrama. He regarded the repeated utterance of 'Ramanama' as an infallible remedy for human ills. He had a special reverence for and tender feeling towards Hinduism because of its tolerance. He regarded it as all-inclusive and all-sufficing. He said that it "will live as long as the sun shines because of its tolerance". He also held that people of other religions need have no fear of Hinduism and Hindu rule.

Regard for the Gita

Mahatma Gandhi had a special regard for the Gita. "I regard it", he said, "as the book *par excellence* for the knowledge of truth." In his later years it satisfied him even more than did the Sermon on the Mount.

Opposition to Proselytism

Mahatma Gandhi was opposed to conversion from one religion to another, especially when it took forms of mass conversion and proselytism—conversion primarily for the sake of material ends.

Final Estimate

The world cannot easily forget a many-sided person like Mahatma Gandhi who shunned delight and lived laborious days and who practised truth and non-violence for over forty years of his life. He rightly said about himself, "The law of complete love is the law of my being". Those who did not have the imagination or spiritual insight to understand him, called him "a throw-back" (Herbert Mathews in the *New York Times*). The fact was that he was a "throw-forward", centuries in advance of his day. Bernard Shaw, the most famous cynic of our day, commenting upon Mahatma Gandhi's assassination said, "It is dangerous to be too good". George Marshall as Secretary of State of U.S.A. remarked, "Mahatma Gandhi is the spokesman for the conscience of all mankind". Writing in much the same strain, the late Sir Stafford Cripps, a life-long friend of India, said: "I know of no other man of any time or indeed recent history, who so forcefully and convincignly demonstrated the power of spirit over material things".

During the post-independence period, the Indian socialists grew closer to Gandhism. Jayaprakash renounced materialism as a philosophy and embraced spiritualism as a way of life. The communal frenzy and violence of India's partition days shattered his faith in the economic approach to politics. This change in his thinking led him to review his earlier critical approach to Gandhi's social and political philosophy. "He recognized new virtues in Gandhi's policy of economic and political decentralization. He now accepted the philosophy of *Sarvodaya* which promoted the concept of the common good and harmony between classes." (*238 : 316*).

The influence of Gandhism led Jayaprakash to severe his connection with the Socialist Party. He joined the *Bhoodan* movement led by Vinoba Bhave. Ram Manohar Lohia also accepted the Gandhian concept of economic and political decentralization. Jayaprakash said, "The first aspect of Gandhism that must interest the socialist in its moral or ethical basis, its insistence on values... and when the end is .... personal and group power – there is no limit to which the means will sink to secure the objective..... To the horrors of this unscrupulous, amoral political philosophy, Gandhism offers a corrective." (*263-572*).

CHAPTER 36

POLITICAL PHILOSOPHY OF LASKI

Versatile Genius of Laski

Harold Laski is widely known to the intelligentsia particularly in India and the English-speaking world as a teacher of established repute, as a prolific writer of political literature, as an iconoclast in political philosophy and, finally, as a partisan of the Labour Party politics in England.[1] He was indeed a man of versatile genius, tastes and activity. He is interesting to us not only as a political thinker but also as a man because he always combined his theory with practice. His political thought is vital because it is never divorced from life. It will not be far from truth to observe that Laski lived his principles.[2]

The contemporary generation remembers Laski in a number of ways. In the first place there are not a few fortunate individuals who came into personal contact wth him either as his colleagues or as his pupils. The pupils of Professor Laski can be found in different parts of the world. They have wellnigh developed a Laski legend that pictures him as a professor-saint who taught socialism with a religious passion in the London School of Economics.[3] There is, however, an insignificant minority that indulges in a cult of violent criticism of Laski. Even this minority concedes the great personal qualities of Laski both as a teacher and as a man, His profound sociableness, his innocent egoism, his interest in the youth, his love for the oppressed, his passion for concrete justice and his capacity for hard work even at the cost of his health are qualities to be found in a really great man.[4]

---

1. See the Laski Memorial Issue of the ''Clare Market Review'' (July 1950) for some biographical articles on Laski.
2. Bill Balfour writes about Laski : ''The impact of his personality was great, both on the fledging fresh from school and the ex-serviceman cynical from war. The former saw, perhaps for the first time, a man who linked theory with practice; the latter, after years of obediance and ''turning the blind eye'', saw a man leapt into action at the whiff of injustice.'' (Clare Market Review, July, 1950, p. 31).
3. Bill Balfour says : :''Many people knew Harold Laski as a socialist without knowing that he was a professor. The reverse was never the case. His standpoint was clear from the opening words of one of his addresses to new students; 'I am a socialist and I shall preach socialism, though from time to time I shall prescribe other books as an antidote to my poison.' '' (Ibid).
4. Key Daniels says, ''There was a special essence which made him always young enough to be one of us. He had passion....He was exciting and interesting as a friend and teacher because he was excited and intreseted as a man.'' (''Clare Market Review'', July, 1950; p. 28) K. H. Propper

Laski's Lectures on Political Theory

Lastly, it is as a teacher that Laski's immortality is assured. "The lectures on political theory", says Bill Balfour, "were always packed. Here was no dry as dust theory, but principles relating to real situations and people, so that when he spoke, the great figures of contemporary history leapt into life—Kerensky and Keir Hardie, Lansbury and Lenin, Shaw and Stalin".[5] As Felix Frankfurter writes, "His central significance was that of a teacher. To that calling he gave all he had—his learning, his eloquence, his imagination, his absurd feats of memory, his dialectic powers, above all, what had rightly been called his "quite passionate interest in young people". There can be few countries in the world where there is not some one who will cherish for the rest of his days what Laski meant to him as a teacher. Through his students, apart from his writings and speaking, Laski's thinking about problems of society had made a difference in the thoughts of men....He met the test of Socrates for a great teacher, that of a midwife for the minds and spirits of his students."[6]

Laski as Leader of the Labour Party

Along with his academic duties in the London School of Economics, Laski led another life of a practical sort as a member of the British Labour party. His restless and energetic spirit could not be satisfied with lecturing and writing about socialism. It needed a practical outlet in the form of effective participation in the Socialist movement of his country. The British Labour Party was the symbol of this movement in his country, and he decided to join the ranks of this party quite early in his life. He was elected to the National Executive Committee of the Labour Party in 1936 and rose to the position of its Chairman in 1945. During this historic year the Labour Party was returned to power as a Parliamentary majority for the first time in England's constitutional history though there were two previous instances of minority Labour Governments in 1924 and 1929.[7]

Laski's share in the formulation of the policies and programmes of the Labour Party has been very significant. In August, 1941 it adopted a policy statement entitled, "The Old World and the New Society" which has been described as a landmark in its history. "Laski's prolific mind", says Morgan Phillips, "was the moving spirit behind the production of this statement of policy which laid down the lines of further statements and paved the way for their eventual fulfilment after 1945."[8] The Labour Party found in Laski an honest and outspoken critic, a sincere and scholarly adviser

---

writes. "It was as a teacher that he was a giant amongst men, and it was as a teacher that we loved him". (*Ibid*, p. 29).

5. "Clare Market Review" July, 1950, p. 31.
6. Felix Frankfurter's article in the "Clare Market Review", July, 1950, p. 52.
7. Morgan Phillips : "Harold Laski and the Labour Party", in the "Clare Market Review", July, 1950, p. 42-43.
8. *Ibid*, p. 42.

and above all a great comrade who never failed it. "As a member of the National Executive Committee," says Morgan Phillips, "he was a loved and respected colleague, the more so for his quickness of perception and individuality which at times resulted in a cleavage of opinion. But his generous capacity was limitless. He performed the most prodigious tasks of research and report in a matter of hours. One only had to lift the telephone and the request was granted and fulfilled with amazing rapidity ......He was generous to a fault. No one, however humble, appealed for his counsel in vain, nor was any good cause ignored by him........ He was a great comrade and a tower of strength to the international Socialist Movement."[9]

Laski as a Progressive Journalist

Evidently, Laski lived a busy life both in the committees of the Labour Party and the London School of Economics. Besides, he regularly contributed articles to various magazines and papers[10] which together constitute a political literature of immense value for the contemporary generation. He wrote articles on legal, political and economic topics of the day, which were published in various liberal and progressive magazines and papers in England and America. Most of these articles have been written when he had already adopted a Marxist view of society and politics. They are written in a popular style and are meant mainly for the consumption of the masses and labour intelligentsia. Their theme is usually applied socialism or criticism of the existing social order.

Probably no single writer in England and America has attacked the foundations of the capitalistic system from as many directions as Laski did. He wrote some of his most inspiring essays between 1934 and 1939 when the Socialists and Communists had combined in a mighty united front to oppose the menace of fascism in Europe. This was the era of the Left Book Club and the Popular Front when Laski lived some of the most excited moments of his life. He could not recapture the exultant mood and intellectural opitimism of those years in the rest of his life.[11]

---

9. Ibid, p. 43 : Describing how Laski was loved and regarded by ordinary working folk, Bill Balfour says : ''Far away from the School, his weekly articles in 'Forward' were read by Scottish Socialists. In these circles, where the word ''professor'' is almost a term of reproach, he won, as he had done in so many countries, affection and respect. There was no 'talking down' to these miners and shipworkers, and yet they understood him better than most. One docker, whom I knew very well, whose life had been grinding hard with little time for study and reflection, always read Laski's articles. He remarked to me, 'This man says just what I have been thinking—only he says it so much better.' And if those words had been his epitaph from those workers, I'm sure Harold Laski would have been content.'' ('Clare Market Review', July, 1950, pp. 31-32).

10. Some important journals in which Laski's articles were published are as follows : (1) The Century Magazine, (2) The Yale Review, (3) The Quarterly Review (London), (4) Harper's Magazine.

11. Norman Mackenzie writes : He reached the climax of both his academic and political careers in the years of the Left Book Club and the Popular

A Great Political Thinker of the Twentieth Century

It is possible that Laski's name as a teacher, journalist or practical politician may not survive long. But there is no doubt that his fame rests on a securer foundation for he is also one of the greatest political philosophers that the English-speaking world has produced during the first half of the twentieth century. The idealist writers do not regard him as a political philosopher because he was not a system-builder like the philosophers of the old school. He did not consider political philosophy as a static system consisting of some *a priori* and rationalistic concepts. He regarded political theory as constantly evolving and developing out of political practice. If Laski failed to produce a dogma-ridden conception of political rationalism, he succeeded nevertheless in collecting a large amount of empirical material to explain and interpret 'the crisis in the theory of the state' *(47 : Introductory Ch.)*. In view of his emphasis on the scientific method in politics, he may be more legitimately called a political scientist rather than a political philosopher in the old rationalistic sense.

A Philosopher of the Age of Transition

It has been rightly said that the modern epoch is essentially an epoch of transition in the history of our civilization. The twentieth century represents an important turning-point in the cultural and political history of the human race. The world, which began with the French and American revolutions of the eighteenth century, is drawing to an abrupt close. Political democracy, capitalism and nationalism were the distinguishing features of the old world. A new world is now arising before our very eyes and the Russian and Chinese revolutions are its leading symbols. Economic democracy, socialism and internationalism are the significant watch-words for the new world. Laski is essentially a political philosopher of this age of transition, whose sympathies are unmistakably with the protagonists and builders of the new civilization.

A Comparison with Rousseau

The political theories of Laski and Rousseau may be compared in one significant respect. Both of them contain brilliant polemics of the abuses of the system in which they lived respectively. Both of them are on sure grounds in what they have to deny. But both are equally wavering in what they have to affirm.[12] Rousseau was right in denouncing the corrupt

---

Front, symbols of a sweep of sentiment which he helped substantially to create. The war years and what came after, were both an anticlimax and a political disappointment to him. His social analysis and his political inclinations were best suited to the years when Franco was outside Madrid and Munich was in the making. When he died he was still searching for some way of adjusting them to a world under the shadow of a third war whose general character seemed like the catastrophe he had always foreseen and hoped to avert.'' (''Clare Market Review,'' July, 1950, p. 41).

12. See George Catlin's remarks in this connection in ''The Story of Political Philosophers'', Chapter XX, p. 663. He says, ''Laski is becoming the modern Rousseau, as sensitive as the original.''

monarchy of France but he did not realize that the only remedy was to overthrow it by a revolution and establish a democratic republic in its place. Laski is quite justified in attacking the system of capitalist democracy, which leads to imperialism and war, but he is unable to foresee that its end can only be brought about by a revolutionary overthrow of the existing capitalist regimes in imperialist countries and the triumph of national liberation movements in the colonies.

Peaceful Political and Social Change

Laski, therefore, believes in the peaceful transformation of capitalism into socialism with the help of a parliamentary socialist party and the peaceful abrogation of imperialism by the action of an international organization like the League of Nations (*47 : 228-295* and *589-624*). The course of historical events both before and after Laski's death has falsified his conclusions in both these respects. But this does not minimize the value of his contribution to those aspects of political theory, which deal with the interpretation of the political institutions of the modern state, or try to discover the meaning of the philosophies of the representative political thinkers of the past or present.

The Pluralistic Phase of Laski's Thought

During his first pluralistic phase, Laski's main pre-occupation is with the problem of the status and privileges of particular social groups in the organized political community. His significant contribution to political theory at this stage is a critical review of the varied aspects of the doctrine of sovereignty as developed by many political thinkers from Bodin to Austin. In "The Problem of Sovereignty" Laski has made a strong plea for religious freedom, which can be secured only by allowing autonomous functioning of all religious sects and denominations and by keeping the state aloof from any sectarian connection implying thereby a preferential treatment of a particular sect.[13] Laski has been a consistent critic of the patronage that the state exercizes in relation to the Anglican Church of England.

Sovereignty as a Doctrine of Crisis

In "The Foundations of Sovereignty" he traced the historical evolution of the doctrine of sovereignty and came to a significant conclusion that it was essentially a doctrine of crisis. The feudal and religious conflicts of the sixteenth century had produced it and the subsequent extension of those conflicts to the later centuries further consolidated it (*129 : 232-249*).

Wider Problem of Political Authority

In his "Authority in the Modern State", Laski attempted a discussion of the wider problem of political authority. He examined the political assumptions of certain post-revolutionary French thinkers like de Bonald and Lamennais and concluded that the modern sovereign state was as great a

13.. Laski : "The Problem of Sovereignty", Chapters II, III and IV; pp. 40-54, 88-112, 126-185.

danger to human freedom as the papal authority had been before its power was challenged by the leaders of the Reformation. He developed a federalistic conception of political authority, which implied the diffusion of political power and responsibility on innumerable peripheral points rather than concentrating it on a single centre (*122 : 4-89*).

Suspicion of the Monistic State

It is not generally known but it is a fact that Laski retained his suspicion of the monistic state even during the latest Marxian phase of his political thought. Just before his death in 1949, he wrote, "I confess to a frank fear of what I used to call the "monistic" state; the fashionable phrase of the moment is "monolithic". The consequence is in a high degree evil. By concentrating power in a very few hands it reduces the ordinary **citizen to the position of an instrument serving one end he is decreasingly** permitted to define and increasingly commanded to applaud, with the knowledge, on his part, that if he is silent, or, still more, if he is critical, he will be regarded at best as a person upon whose loyalty no reliance can be placed" (*134 : 42*). Laski's insistent demand for a wide dispersal of political and economic power in the society has been one of his most distinctive contributions to modern political theory.

Laski's Uncompromising Individualism in Thought and Action

Besides being a zealous supporter of the autonomy of social groups, Laski has also been a consistent believer in the dignity of human personality. He was temperamentally an uncompromising individualist in thought and action. His arguments show a subjectivistic bias at every point. In the committees of the Labour Party, he usually remained an isolated intellectual, who often found himself as the lone supporter of his theories (*145 : 98-113, 156-162, 169-174, 184-192* and *206-219*). Even when he accepted the broad details of the Marxian analysis of society, he remained opposed to the Leninist theory of proletarian dictatorship, which would have denied an intellectual like Laski to give free reins to his intelligence. He put a great emphasis on the value of human personality as the creator of a free society (*49:122-160*).

The Dangers of Obedience

In "The Dangers of Obedience", he contended that the individual must consult his conscience before deciding to obey or disobey the particular command of the sovereign. The state, which insists upon an unquestioning obedience to its orders by its citizens, reduces them to the status of moral slaves (*125 : 2-30*).

Rejection of Hegel's Conception of Freedom

In "A Grammar of Politics", he defined liberty as absence of restraints and criticized the Hegelian conception of freedom as a dialectical fraud, which equated slavery with freedom. He suggested certain checks upon the unlimited right of property only because he wanted to universalize the enjoyment of liberty. Even the goal of his socialist reform is to secure better conditions for the cultivation of human personality. He was interested in bringing about that egalitarian society in which the full and free development of every individual constitutes the guiding principle of social policy (*47 : 215-217*).

A Plea for Equality and Liberty

In "The Danger of Being a Gentleman" he criticized the inegalitarian society of the present day precisely because it prevents a great majority of the people securing the material foundations of a spiritually enriched life (*124 : 13-32*). In his "Liberty in the Modern State", Laski revived some of the well-known dogmas, which Mill stated in his essay "On Liberty" and discussed them in the context of an international situation, when the success of fascism was posing a serious danger to the ideal of freedom in all countries. He always remained a consistent champion of human freedom in all its variegated aspects (*49 : 13-47*).

Laski's Monumental Work on Political Theory

While his earlier works were fragmentary in nature and dealt with only some selected aspects of political theory, he made his first monumental effort to interpret the political problems of the modern age in a comprehensive way in his much publicized "A Grammar of Politics", which still remains the most outstanding contribution to political theory of any single author in the twentieth century. He rejected both *laissez faire* individualism and conservative idealism as the basis of politics and regarded the progressive liberalism of Hobhouse and the reformist collectivism of the Fabians as imperfect solutions of the problems of the industrial age (*45:iii-xvii*).

Laski's main contribution to political theory at this stage was his criticism of the theory of the general will, a pragmatic theory of government, a federalistic conception of political authority, and a socialistic approach to industrial problems. He regarded the general will as a fiction existing in the brain of an idealist philosopher and pointed out that society exhibits a multiplicity of wills. He also declared that the doctrinal implications of the general will were dangerous to individual freedom.

A Pragmatic Theory of State and Government

He took a pragmatic view of the state and government and concluded that it is only a set of persons exercising political authority without any *a priori* claim to receive the obedience of its subjects (*45:17-35*). The only way to safeguard the freedom of the common people is to decentralize the bases of political and economic power in the community. Our representative institutions should be so organized as to secure greater participation of the people and affected interests in the administrative and industrial processes. Laski demands greater democracy in the political and industrial fields so that the existing perversion of our political and economic institutions in the interests of the class of property-owners may be effectively checked (*45 : 438-488*).

Interest in Proudhon and Fabian Socialism

Together with Sidney Webb, Bernard Shaw and G. D. H. Cole, Laski was one of the chief exponents of Fabian Socialism in England. He had also taken a keen interest in Proudhonism and the French syndicalist movement at this stage but his political theory was little influenced by the Marxian tradition as represented by the post-revolutionary Russian theoreticians.[14] He regarded Marx as a bad economist and an equally bad philosopher, whose ill-assorted ideas had only a crude propaganda value for the working-class agitators. In his brief Fabian pamphlet, "Karl Marx", Laski declared Marxism as incompatible with democracy.

Laski as a Critic of Marxism

As he wrote, "There is no room in Marx's thought, save perhaps as an ultimate, for any democratic system. Revolution opposes counter-revolution, and a reign of terror is the path to triumph......Once a really vital point is touched by the workers' demands, they are met by armed resistance. That means, of course, that only by conscious violent intervention can communism be realized. The proletariat must seize a propitious moment for the revolution."[15] In "Communism" Laski elaborated the same line of argument, when he declared that communism was a new religion, pointed out that its success in Russia was an outcome of the exceptional circumstances prevailing in that country, and concluded that the insurrectionary tactics of the communists were bound to serve the strategy of fascism (*123 : 223-251*)

Laski's Libertarian Socialism

In his essay entitled "Socialism and Freedom" Laski catgorically stated in a true Fabian fashion that the true socialism is a libertarian, and not an authoritarian, doctrine. He declared that freedom and equality are inseparable from one another and socialism aims to combine these two principles in practice. Laski's ideas are at this stage a curious mixture of ethical individualism, political pluralism and economc collectivism. But this unsteady combination of contradictory ideas could not endure indefinitely. The beginning of the great depression, the Japanese attack on Manchuria, and the rise of Hitlerism in Germany provided new food for thought to Laski, which compelled him to revise some of his earlier views of politics and society (*145 : 83-91*).

Laski on the Crisis in Capitalist Democracy

As a consequence of these developments, Laski had to renounce his Fabianism and adopt a far more conciliatory attitude towards the Marxian doctrine, which he had so vigorously fought against in the past. In his "Democracy in Crisis" he rejected the gradualist thesis of Fabianism and suggested a modification in the working of parliamentary institutions in

---

14. Quoted by George Catlin in his "Story of the Political Philosophers", on page 659.
15. Quoted by George Catlin in his "Story of the Political Philosophers", on page 659.

England. He thought that the attainment of power by a genuine socialist party even in the normal electoral fashion is bound to bring about a radical change in the assumptions of a parliamentary system (*126 : 67-99*).

Socialist Government and Institutional Changes

A socialist government, if it wanted to put its programme into practice, could not accept the existing forms of procedure. It must exercise a wide range of authority and secure rapid socialist legislation by means of ordinances and decrees. It must repudiate the traditional toleration of a formal opposition in the House of Commons. It must abolish the House of Lords as a constitutional anachronism. It must reform the bureaucracy and the judiciary, which at present work as the allies of capitalism. In other words, Laski has now come very close to the vanguard theory of the Marxian dictatorship (*126 : 30-66*). It may be pointed out here that the British Labour Party did not act according to Laski's expectations. The post-war history of its rule amply proves that it has refused to convert itself into an instrument of proletarian dictatorship as a revolutionary vanguard of the working-class of England.

The State No Longer Considered Neutral in Class Conflict

This attempt to analyse the crisis of democracy led Laski to revise his fundamental assumptions about the nature and development of the state. In "The State in Theory and Practice" he reinterpreted the nature and functions of the state on a Marxian basis. He has now finally rejected the classical view of the state as a neutral force in the community and definitely affirms that every state possesses a class bias (*50 : 104*).

The Idealist Thesis of National Unity Denied

In the first place, this view rejects the liberal and idealist thesis about the fundamental purposive unity of the national community. The class, and not the nation, now becomes the centre of his political thought. The key to political understanding lies in the class relations of a particular society. Imperialism, fascism, capitalist democracy and Communism are alike judged on the basis of the underlying class interests that they represent. The state, both in its internal policies and external relations, remains the political instrument of the particular class that owns the means of production in that country (*50 : 139*).

HISTORICAL EVOLUTION OF THE LIBERAL IDEOLOGY

In "The Rise of European Liberalism" he traced the historical evolution of the theory and practice of Liberalism and interpreted this evolution in economic terms. He concluded that the changes in the political theory and practice of Liberalism were conditioned by the economic exigencies of the different phases of capitalism. In this way, he substantiated his thesis about the class character of the modern liberal state by examining its historical background (*132 : 17-29*). Finally, he concluded that the philosophy of liberalism has now entered into a phase of decline on account of the developing crisis and contradictions of the capitalist system. The only philosophy, which can take its place now, is the philosophy of socialism (*132 : 224-236*).

Laski as a Critic of British Parliamentary System

In the realm of constitutional theory, Laski has bequeathed to us two monumental works entitled "Parliamentary Government in England", which is a critical commentary upon the British constitution, and "The American Democracy", which is probably the most comprehensive survey of the American democracy in action ever undertaken by any single writer. In his analysis of the parliamentary system as it works in England, he has reached certain remarkable conclusions. In the first place, he declares that the existence of monarchy even in the present form is inconsistent with the true spirit of democratic equality. Moreover, the influence of the monarch in any constitutional crisis or emergency is bound to be exerted on the side of reaction as typified by the resignation of the MacDonald government in 1931 and an immediate formation of a reactionary national coalition in its place (*130 : 396-417*). Similarly, he proposes abolition of the House of Lords and considers a hereditary second chamber as inconsistent with a genuinely democratic system.

A Plea for Strong Cabinet Government

He is thus visualizing the creation of a strong cabinet effectively controlling the House of Commons bringing about the socialist transformation of the British society through legislative decrees and immediate administrative action. The reactionary checks like the discretion of the monarch in forcing untimely plebiscites and the power of a second chamber to delay legislation should be removed (*130 : 221-280*). Criticising his proposal, George Catlin remarks that this constitutional thesis is only superficially non-monarchical and democratic. In fact, it implies a belief in the government of a veiled socialistic dictatorship, which does not recognize any checks upon its power whether by the constitution, judiciary, a second chamber or an electoral referendum (*92 : 669*).

Laski Opposed to the Theory of Checks and Balances

Laski has made similar observations about the working of the American constitution. In "The American Presidency" he analysed the nature of the working of the Presidential government in the U.S.A. and concluded that the system of checks and balances is not conducive to real efficiency in Government. The fathers of the American constitution had designed it to suit the needs of a social structure based upon the ideals of *laissez faire* but these ideals have now become quite irrelevant in the present context of the worldwide vogue of positive government (*121 : 79-171*).

Laski as a Critic of the American Political System

In "The American Democracy" he examined other political institutions through which the democracy in America operates and also discussed the impact of the social, economic and cultural environment upon its functioning. He declared that the spectacle of the separation of powers was really a spectacle of confusion of powers and the pattern of division of powers between the federal and state governments had become obsolete in the context of modern developments (*121 : 72-137*). The difficulties, which President Roosevelt faced in the realization of his New Deal Programme, showed clearly how the American political system was designed to serve the interests of reaction. He regarded the Supreme Court's veto over legislation as undemocratic and pleaded for the full legislative sovereignty of the Congress on a British pattern. Similarly, he pleaded for a strengthening of the Presidential office and proposed devices for a closer co-operation between the legislative and executive wings of Government.

Laski's Prediction about Developments in America

Laski also assails the party system of America, which he regards as corrupt and antiquated and laments the fact that a socialist party has not yet developed in the United States (*121 : 214-224*). He foresees two alternative lines of development for the capitalist democracy in America. It must either renounce its capitalist character and become a socialist democracy or choose the second alternative of dissolving democracy internally and seek the solution of its economic crisis in aggressive imperialism abroad. The post-war policy of the American government typified by its aggression in Viet Nam shows that it has chosen the second of Laski's alternatives (*121 : 552-563*).[16]

Revolution and Counter-revolution

From the point of view of Laski's contribution to political theory, the significance of his "Reflections on the Revolution of Our Time" cannot be ignored. In this book he has surveyed the whole international scene and critically examined the nature of all political systems struggling for supremacy in the modern world. The most significant point is that he has interpreted the political forces of the world in a dialectical way. It is a description of the world political scene in terms of revolution and counter-revolution (*131 : 252-304*).

A Period of Revolutionary Change

He thinks that our civilization is passing through a period of revolutionary change with an accompanying process of conflict and disintegration. While there are certain elements and forces actively working for the culmination of this revolutionary process, there are at the same time other elements and forces trying their best to delay or prevent the final victory

16. In "The Dilemma of Our Times" on page 109, Laski says, "The Truman doctrine, as soon as it is seriously applied, means the endowment with American strength of all the interests which seek to prevent the working-class from winning its place in the sun. That is why American aid is given to what is, in essence, a middle-class government in France, a middle-class and near-fascist government in Greece".

of the revolutionary ideal. The conflicts between religion and science, between imperialism and the right of national self-determination, between fascism and democracy, or between capitalism and socialism are regarded by Laski as so many aspects of the international struggle between reaction and revolution (*131 : 9-40*).

Contrast between Communism and Fascism

In spite of his criticism of doctrinaire communism and condemnation of some aspects of the Soviet domestic and foreign policies, he regards the Russian Revolution as a progressive force in our epoch and thinks that the Soviet Union definitely stands on the side of revolutionary forces in the world. On the other hand, he regards fascism as an embodiment of the counter-revolutionary idea in every way. Its racial arrogance, its militarist dictatorship, its suppression of democracy, its concentration camps and mass lynchings, its gangster diplomacy, its aggressive imperialism and its misuse of science for destructive purpose make fascism an utterly detestable creed of irrationalism (*131 : 86-127*).

Imperialism and Fascism and Forces of Counter-revolution

But he is careful enough to point out that British imperialism in India or the colonial domination of Africa by the capitalist democracies of Europe should be equally regarded as a counter-revolutionary force like fascism which differs from the former only in degree and not in kind. He emphatically says that the forces of counter-revolution are deeply rooted in the inner structures of capitalist democracies themselves. He thinks that the appeasement policy, which the capitalist democracies of Western Europe pursued in relation to the Nazis, and the subsequent co-operation of the European quislings with Hitler showed the depth of the counter-revolution entrenched in the political life of the capitalist democracies (*131 : 162-204*).

The United Front of Liberals, Socialists and Communists

The revolutionary camp of the world consists of the anti-fascists and anti-imperialists of all countries, which includes liberal democrats, socialists and Communists of different countries. Laski thinks that the defeat of counter-revolution will not be achieved by the defeat of Hitler and his allies in the battlefield. In fact he regards the achievement of democracy and socialism on an international scale as synonymous with the final defeat of the counter-revolution (*131 : 205-251*).[17]

---

17. In his "Faith, Reason and Civilization" Laski warned, "The Axis powers are already on the way to defeat both decisive and overwhelming. But there remains for us a greater issue of seeing to it that in their defeat there is involved also the destruction of the counter-revolution for which they stand. Our victory will be thrown away unless we devote it to great ends." (Chapter I, pp.. 10-11).

LASKI'S DILEMMA AND DISAPPOINTMENT

In "The Dilemma of Our Times", which is a posthumous publication, he revised some of his opinions expressed in his "Reflections on the Revolution of Our Time" because he was disillusioned by the post-war policies of the governments of the Soviet Union as well as of the United States and even the Labour regime in England did not work according to his expectations (*127 : 13-17* and *43-51*). Laski had optimistically believed that the war-time collaboration between the Soviet Union and the capitalist democracies would result in a peace-time alliance between them for the achievement of democracy and socialism on an international scale.

Laski's Hopes about Russia, America and England

Given an atmosphere of external security, the Soviet Union would democratize its political system because Laski did not see any inherent contradiction between Marxian socialism and political democracy. Similarly, he expected the growth of a powerful socialist movement in the United States bringing about the extension of the democratic principle in industrial relations. He also hoped that the post-war left-wing governments in Western Europe would be able to establish a socialistic order in their countries and act as a balancing third force between Communist Russia on the one hand and conservative America on the other (*145 : 182-205*).[18]

In the magnanimous grant of self-government to India by the Labour government, Laski foresaw the possibility of peaceful liquidation of the colonial system but he was disappointed to find that the example of India could not be extended to some other colonies in his life time. All these facts and trends of the world politics led Laski to restate his earlier thesis, which he had developed in an optimistic atmosphere of the war-time cooperation between Russia and the capitalist countries.[19]

No Liberalisation of Soviet Dictatorship

The post-war events refuted most of the optimistic prophecies of Laski and confirmed his pessimistic forebodings. Contrary to Laski's hopes, the Russian leaders did not liberalize their political dictatorship, extended the same system of government to the People's Democracies of Eastern Europe, refused cooperation in a general plan of European recovery, directed the Communist parties of Western Europe to bring about the breakdown of national economies of those countries, and disrupted the war-time unity of the Allies by every sort of diplomatic provocation (*127 : 253-261*).

America's Reactionary Policies

Similarly, the ruling circles in the United States discarded the New Deal liberalism of President Roosevelt, propagated and developed a

18. Kingsley Martin : "Harold Laski : A Biographical Memoir", Chapter IX, pp. 182-205.
19. See R.T. Clark's comment in his Foreword to "The Dilemma of Our Times", who edited this posthumous work of Laski.

morbid fear of Communism, started a very deplorable witch-hunting of liberal and progressive intellectuals in the country, pursued a very reactionary foreign policy in Greece, the Middle East, China and Japan, prevented the left-wing governments of Europe from embarking upon a real socialist programme in their countries, and adopted finally a policy of economic imperialism and military encirclement of the Soviet Union (*127 : 258-266*).

European Socialists Fail to Develop as a Third Force

The Labour Government of England and the socialist parties of the continent similarly failed to act as a balancing third force between Russia and America because they merely supported the American line in foreign policy, which aimed at isolating Russia diplomatically by refusing to make any sincere effort for enlisting Russian co-operation in the reorganization of the post-war world. Laski desired that the socialists of Western Europe should not work as the allies of America in a cold war against Russia but rather evolve an independent policy of their own, acting as a third force for the realization of democracy and socialism (*127 : 43-51*).[20]

Laski as a Critic of the Labour Foreign Policy

He strongly criticized the foreign policy of the Labour Government which he regarded as the continuation of the old Tory policy with all its anti-Soviet bias. He cited as an example the support which the Labour Government extended to a semi-fascist regime in Greece.[21] In this way neither the Russians nor the British and Americans justified Laski's expectations about them in the post-war world. In "The Dilemma of Our Times", he restated his belief in the inseparability of democratic freedom and socialistic equality. He felt that the world was today facing the twin dangers of an atomic war and economic breakdown because the major nations of the world had failed to realize and reconcile the concepts of political liberty and social justice in the institutional patterns adopted by them.

---

20. Laski says, "Despite all his noisy thunder, foreign policy was a realm in which to Mr. Bevin, Mr. Churchill's word was law. The outcome was his choice of a full-blooded alliance with America, the essential plans for which Mr. Churchill drew, and the implementation of which Mr. Churchill really superintended. The Atlantic Security Pact was signed by Mr. Bevin; but Mr. Churchill's was the hand which guided his pen. Despite all Mr. Bevin's claims, the Pact was, in its real roots above all a threat to Russia". "The Dilemma of Our Times", pp. 44-45).

21. With characteristic bitterness, Laski told the Labour Party Conference in 1946, "As a Socialist Party, we must regard it as a tragedy, in which our responsibility is grave, that Spain is still crushed beneath the ugly tyranny **of Franco.... What is true of Spain, is true also of Greece. For us, as Socialists, the return of the King would be a sorry end to the brave struggle** of a nation which first taught the world the significance of freedom." (Quoted by Kingsley Martin in his "Harold Laski : A Biographical Memoir", p. 187).

Laski as a Rhetorical Writer

Laski's political philosophy is at once an interpretation of the existing society and a plea for changing it. He has combined in his approach the functions of a political philosopher and a party agitator. As Kingsley Martin has remarked, "Laski was a rhetorical not a scientific writer. His writing, like his speeches, was effective because it was outspoken, rich in vocabulary and vitality. Sometimes, if he wishes to make a point about, say, the way in which the class structure of society load the constitutional dice against social change, he will pile up illustrations, and repeat, in slightly different form, previous arguments until the reader is too exhausted to formulate any objections. Sometimes one feels......that Laski is the most verbose and redundant of writers and that a quarter of the words could be advantageously deleted. At other times one is impressed by a constant brilliance which is rare in political writing (*145 : 85-86*)."[22]

Evaluation of his Political Philosophy

His rhetorical style in writing and continuous association with the politics of the Labour Party have led some of his critics to underestimate his contribution to political philosophy. These critics have misconceived the functions of the political philosopher by restricting them to a contemplative life, which Laski regards as a sign of cowardly escapism from the world of realities. In "Faith, Reason and Civilization", he said about the role of intellectuals in the society, "It was a failure of the Italian intellectuals......that allowed Mussolini to steal into power. It was the failure of the German intellectuals which permitted Hitler to establish his ugly empire. It was the failure of the French intellectuals, after 1919. which created the conditions out of which France was overthrown in 1940. Let us not deceive ourselves into the belief that the conditions in Britain and the United States are different." [23]

Great Intellectual Impact of Laski's Thought

There is no doubt that Laski's conception of the function of intellectuals was right and he fully applied this conception into his practical life. This explains the secret of his influence over a large group of Europeans, Americans, Asians and Africans who came into personal contact with him in the London School of Economics or understood his philosophy only through his voluminous writings.

As Kingsley Martin says, "when Harold died hundreds of letters of sorrow and gratitude poured in from men and women in positions of influence in England. But more remarkable still was the testimony from every country where young men and women, Asians and Africans as well as Europeans, have been helped by Laski in the struggle for national inde-

22. Kingsley Martin : "Harold Laski : A Biographical Memoir", Chapter IV, pp. 85-86.
23. Quoted by Kingsley Martin in "Harold Laski : A Biographical Memoir", p. 261.

pendence and democratic freedom. In no part of the world did Harold have more influence than India; Krishna Menon, the first High Commissioner in London of free India and one of Harold's most devoted friends and admirers, represents literally hundreds of Indians who as students came under Harold's spell in England. They owed far less to meetings that he eloquently addressed than to the personal talks and tuition with a philosopher who took it for granted that Indians were the equals of Europeans and who also reminded them, when necessary, that they were not necessarily their superiors" (*145* : *263*). This is probably the greatest tribute to the living principles of Laski's political philosophy.

Laski was Chairman of the British Labour party when it took office in 1945. The labour government headed by Prime Minister Attlee did not come up to his expectations. He wanted a quicker process of decolonisation, rapid introduction of socialist reforms, cooperation with Soviet Russia, non-alignment of the British and European socialist parties in the Cold War and also opposition to Franco's dictatorship in Spain. But the Labour leadership of Britain and European Social democrats did just the reverse of this. "Historically, labour and socialist movements have been the main driving force for the extension of democratic features of capitalist societies. But their performance of this role has been very substantially and very negatively affected by the constantly more pronounced ideological and political integration of social democratic into the framework of capitalism. Social democratic parties have long ceased to suggest that they were concerned with the business of bringing about a socialist society." (*236* : *244*).

CHAPTER 37

COMPARATIVE STUDY OF IDEOLOGIES

Liberalism and the Capitalist World

Liberalism is the dominant ideology of advanced capitalist countries today. Evolutionary socialism is no longer an independent ideological trend and has now merged with the mainstream of liberalism. Fascism arose as an influential ideological movement and captured state power in some of the advanced capitalist countries during the inter-war years. Liberalism, evolutionary socialism and fascism equally recognise the need for retaining and strengthening the existing capitalist mode of production. With some marginal differences, they safeguard the privileges of private property and support the principle of a free market.

The typical economy under liberalism, fascism and evolutionary socialism is capitalistic which is based on individual entrepreneurial initiative, with little or limited centralized planning, generally in social welfare or military sectors. There are strong tendencies towards monopolistic control of large corporate wealth and creation of large private power blocs in the economy.

While liberalism and evolutionary socialism accept the principle of consumer sovereignty, fascism emphasizes a tighter control of consumption and production. Evolutionary socialists earlier supported the principle of nationalizing the banks, key industries etc., but this demand has been practically given up now. The fascists believe in a regulated capitalist economy without nationalization. Liberals are generally opposed to the principle of nationalization in any form but usually do not try to denationalize public sector industries already brought under state ownership by labour, socialist or social-democratic parties.

Agriculture forms a very small proportion of the national economy of advanced capitalist countries. Industrial development has reached a high stage but the growth rate has now stabilized. The capitalist economy is subject to periodical crises, recessions and depression due to unplanned production, market fluctuations and labour unrest. Trade unions are strong and highly organised and constitute an important economic force, but only in the sense of maintaining the *status quo*. They are guided by the principle of 'economism' and do not, as yet, represent a challenge to the capitalist system. Under fascism, free labour unions are banned.

Liberalism adopts the principle of parliamentary democracy with minor changes to suit national circumstances. Evolutionary socialists also accept a similar political system. Liberal democracy is based on the rule of law and upon economic law of market. The political system is ideologically conservative or reformist. It accepts the expression of conflicts between social groups within rules of the game. Party rivalry is allowed and there is a tendency to have a few major political parties, with pragmatic rather than ideological differences prevailing between them. Policies are formulated by these parties and interest groups. Range of party activity is narrowly political. The political elite is small and inactive except during elections.

Party organisation as well as government is highly bureaucratized and the members of the upper and upper middle classes dominate party as well as government structures. Elected representatives come from traditional classes and establish an oligarchical control over the political system. They remain sensitive to expressions of public protest and have the capacity to mould public opinion through the control of the mass media. Policy implementation is under the control of a bureaucratic elite functioning in alliance with and nominally under political executives. Judiciary is in principle independent of executive influence but ordinarily judges and administrators follow parallel policies which seldom come into conflict. The military elite is subordinate to civil authority but exercises considerable authority behind the scene.

Under fascism, liberal pluralist democracy is suspended and party rivalry is disallowed. The ruling fascist party controls the government, its armed forces, bureaucracy and judiciary. The ease with which a liberal democratic system is absorbed under fascism during the period of a crisis of capitalism is remarkable. Both Italy and Germany were transformed into fascist states through gradual erosion of liberal constitutionalism. Post-war Italy, West Germany and Spain are the examples of easy conversions of fascist political systems into the pluralist parliamentary democracies. In Japan also, pluralist and fascist political systems have alternated each other with ease. Many Latin American countries are transformed from liberal democracies into fascist dictatorships and *vice-versa* in a week without any qualitative change in the socio-economic basis, which continues to be capitalistic and semi-colonial. Fascism is really the emergency or crisis regime of a capitalist society. The class character of the political, economic and military elites is almost identical in liberal, evolutionary socialist and fascist political systems.

The capitalist world of liberalism, evolutionary socialism and fascism has been expansionist and imperialistic in the past and supports the policy of economic domination and exploitation in relation to the countries of the third world, which are still a part of the international capitalist system. It also exercises considerable ideological influence on the intelligentsia of the third world countries. Liberal societies of the west remain stratified with great differences of incomes between the corporate rich, the professional classes in the middle and industrial and agricultural workers at the bottom. They want to preserve similar stratified societes in the ex-colonies and want to perpetuate their economic underdevelopment. As Andre Gunder Frank says, capitalist development of the Western countries and the underdevelopment of the colonies and ex-colonies is an integrated and inter-connected phenomenon and a part of the same historical process. The same social forces which brought about economic development in Western

Europe and North America are also responsible for the retarded economic development of Asia, Africa and Latin America today.

Marxism and the Socialist World

Marxism, like liberalism, evolutionary socialism and fascism, is also an ideology produced by the western capitalist society but, nevertheless, stands in a dialectical, contradictory relationship with it. It would like to change the socio-economic basis of the existing system by abolishing the capitalist mode of production itself. Neither liberalism, nor evolutionary socialism, nor fascism would like to change the capitalist mode of production based on private property. Marxism wants to destroy the capitalist system, equally supported by liberals, evolutionary soocialists and fascists, through a revolutionary class struggle of the working-class culminating in a proletarian revolution and dictatorship of the proletariat.

Unfortunately for the Marxists, no advanced capitalist country of the west has so far succumbed to a proletarian revolution of Marx's vision. Revolution did occur in a relatively less developed capitalist country. Russia, which had no tradition of liberal democracy. After Russia's victory over Nazi Germany, socialism became the dominant mode of production in some countries of Eastern and Central Europe as well. During the post-war period, the Marxist Parties captured state power in China. North Korea, Vietnam, Laos, Cambodia and Cuba. These countries, though ruled by Marxist parties, are economically underdeveloped and still considered by many as parts of the Third World comprising of Asian, African and Latin American nations. Marxism, as a minority ideological opposition trend, is today represented in almost all major capitalist countries and has become particularly significant in Italy and France. It exercises considerable influence in some sectors of the Third World as well.

Socialist system in the Soviet Union and other allied socialist countries is based on public or state ownership of the means of production as well as a strictly controlled internal and external market. It aims at a comprehensive planning of its resources and centralization of all sectors of the economy. The economy is geared to proletarian aims. Emphasis is on heavy industrial production. The economy is free from slumps and recessions. Trade agreements are largely confined within the socialist bloc but excluding China, which has opted out of the Soviet bloc of socialist nations. Growth rates are generally high and imbalances are controlled by state planning. Agriculture forms a smaller sector of the economy in the Soviet bloc countries but absorbs a relatively large labour force. The state directly controls production and distribution of consumer goods. Labour unions are official state agencies and the workers' councils play a restricted role in decision-making.

The political system of socialist countries is based on democratic centralism and the dictatorship of a single political party or an alliance of parties led by the Communist Party. The Marxist-Leninist ideology as interpreted by the ruling political elite, is the basis of all official policies.

50—17 149

There is absolute suppression and prohibition of political opposition and dissent. Strong one-party system dictates all interest articulation and aggregation. Discipline and centralisation are the guiding principles of administration and industrial management. Though party membership is broad-based, leadership is determined through bureaucratic principles of selection. The governing elite is selected through the Party and is not responsible to any electorate. Party activity is all-encompassing and continuous. There is no separation of powers; bureaucrats function under party executives, judiciary is not independent; and legislation is imposed from above. Army is entirely subordinate to civilian party control. Religion is discouraged and even suppressed. Education and media are controlled by the state or the party, which are indistinguishable.

Marxist and fascist political systems are often compared and declared to be identical. Of course, they have some striking resemblances. They are both one party states. The party is often led by a supreme leader, Mussolini, Hitler, Lenin or Mao Tse-tung. It is generally forgotten that the Marxist Party is revolutionary, derives strength from the oppressed social classes, and changes the capitalist mode of production into a socialist mode through its dictatorial rule. The fascist party is counter-revolutionary, represents the offensive of the capitalist class, suppresses trade unions and the working-class movement, and uses its dictatorial rule to protect and consolidate the capitalist mode of production. Fascist system seldom survives the death of its supreme leader. Marxist systems are not as dependent on the charismatic leaders, who founded them. Russia survived the death of both Lenin and Stalin. China has similarly remained socialist after the death of Mao Tse-tung and the same is true of Vietnam after the demise of Ho Chi Minh. Marxism is essentially the ideology of the working-class, while fascism is the ideology of the capitalists under distress.

Evolutionary socialism arose as a revision of the revolutionary doctrines of Marxism and ended finally in the bosom of liberal capitalism. Today liberalism, in its conservative form, and evolutionary socialism, which is a radical form of liberalism, have some programmatic differences but they share a similar ideology and are equally hostile to Marxism, when it poses a challenge to a national capitalist system within which they may be working. Conservative liberals and socialist liberals often form coalition governments in Italy and France keeping the Marxist Parties, with broad working-class support, permanently in opposition. Some European Communist Parties, which are trying to build alliances with the Socialist parties, have now rejected the Marxist theory of proletarian dictatorship and want to function within the frame-work of a pluralist democracy. So far this strategy has not enabled the Marxists to capture state power in any Western capitalist country.

Marxism aims at setting-up people's democracies in Asian and African countries as a first step in the direction of building socialism in these countries. People's democracy is an anti-imperialist, national state with a mixed economy, ruled by a Marxist Party drawing support from the united front of the workers, peasants, intelligentsia and small capitalists.

China claimed to be a people's democratic state from 1949 to 1956. It is a socialist state now with nearly complete socialization of the means of production, though at a lower level of economic development. The Chinese Marxists today consider China as a truly socialist society, more egalitarian and free than any other socialist country in the West. They criticize the Soviet Union as a social-imperialist country which is trying to restore bourgeois social relations. According to Ralph Miliband, this criticism is more polemical than factual.

Political Ideologies in the Third World

Liberalism, evolutionary socialism, fascism and Marxism are involved in a perpetual clash for the control of people's minds and their political behaviour in large parts of Asia, Africa and Latin America. In a way, all these ideologies appear as foreign transplants on the native political soil of the Third World countries. The typical ideology of the Third World is nationalism, mass democracy and a vague kind of socialism using liberal as well as Marxist rhetoric and occasionally even fascist slogans.

The third world consists of the ex-colonial, non-aligned and formally independent nations of Asia, Africa and Latin America. They have mixed economy, with both private and public sectors. Economy reveals conflict between desire for independent economic development leading to national integration and consolidation and need for foreign aid which is accompanied by neo-colonial pressures and domination. There is conflict between the interest of foreign capital allied to big native capital and landowners on one side and the patriotic bourgeoisie, intelligentsia, peasants and workers on the other side. The typical economy is agrarian and based on the peasant sector. The ruling elite puts emphasis on basic industrial development but the rate of industrialization is very slow.

Liberal democracy exists in India, Sri Lanka and a few other countries of the Third World. The majority of the third world countries are ruled by a military-bureaucratic elite under a regime of dictatorship. Many others are one-party dictatorships, where a party elite governs in alliance with a bureaucracy. Ideology professed by the ruling elite may be radical or conservative but the policies, which are implemented, support the interests of the privileged, wealthier classes. All ruling elites in the Third World countries use a socialist jargon to enhance their popular appeal. The announced ideology is based on the vocabulary of evolutionary socialism, which is supposed to be neutral between liberal capitalism of the west and Marxist communism of the Soviet type. In India both Congress and Janata parties profess the ideology of evolutionary socialism. In reality, the ruling elite in the Third World countries is building a model, which is a mixture of capitalism and state capitalism in the economic field, supported politically by an authoritarian and bureaucratic state structure. This ruling elite also maintains a highly undemocratic, inegalitarian and stratified social structure.

Liberalism in the west was the ideology of a historically progressive capitalist class. In the existing conditions of the Third World countries, the native capitalist class cannot play that progressive role of achieving rapid industrial development and consolidating national independence. The experience of Latin American countries proves this. Evolutionary socialism, again, is relevant in countries which have already achieved their economic development under capitalism. In the absence of the possibilities of rapid economic development under the leadership of capitalists, the ideologies of liberalism and evolutionary socialism become irrelevant in the context of the politics of the majority of the countries in the Third World.

Capitalism, which is itself very retarded and underdeveloped, faces a real threat of mass upsurge against it. But, despite growing mass discontent, the popular-democratic movement is still weak and poorly organised in large parts of Asia, Africa and Latin America. Democratic movement threatens the ruling elite but cannot overthrow it through a revolution. The ruling elite in distress resorts to fascist and semi-fascist measures to retain its authority. The military dictatorships, which thrive in Latin America and some African and Asian countries, are really the third world adaptations of fascism. The social basis of these fascist regimes in the third world is to be found in the native class of landowners, foreign capitalists and indigenous capitalists allied with them. The countries of the Third World, if they want to put an end to this neo-colonial fascism, must organise a patriotic united front of the four oppressed classes—peasants, workers, petty bourgeoisie and patriotic bourgeoisie. National consolidation and socio-economic progress can be achieved only under a regime of socialist democracy after a popular-democratic movement has crushed the state power of the landlords and capitalists.

According to C.B. Macpherson, three concepts of democracy are contending for supermacy in the present day world. He calls them the Liberal, Communist and Underdeveloped variants of democracy. He has observed: "One such fact, to which I have already referred is, that democracy is not properly to be equated with our unique Western liberal democracy, but that the clearly non-liberal systems which prevail in the Soviet countries, and the somewhat different non-liberal systems of most of the underdeveloped countries of Asia and Africa, have a genuine historical claim to the title democracy." (*219 : 3*).

A second fact about liberal democracy is that it is also a system of power. A liberal-democratic government exists to enforce a certain set of social relations based on property rights which are indirectly power relations. A third fact, which some would prefer not to have mentioned, is that liberal-democracy and capitalism go together. In the Western societies democratic franchise was installed after the liberal society, and the liberal states were firmly established.

Democracy, as Macpherson says, came as a top-dressing. It had to accommodate itself to the conditions of a fully developed market economy based on competition and individualist enterprise. The liberal state in its earlier phase had freely competing though not democratic political parties. It was this liberal state which was democratized and in the process democracy was also liberalized and became identified with market society and capitalist enterprise.

In other parts of the world i.e. in the existing socialist societies and newly-liberated countries of Asia and Africa, democracy came as a revolution against the liberal capitalist society and state. The political movements, which came to power there had a self-image of being democratic. For them democracy has had something like its original meaning, government by or for the common people, by or for the hitherto oppressed classes and masses. Democracy originally meant rule by the common people, the plebeians. It was very much a class affair. It meant the sway of the lowest and largest class. That is why it was feared and rejected by the upper classes. Plato and Aristotle, Cromwell and Locke, even J.S. Mill and De Tocqueville rejected democracy which could give power to the labouring class. Marxism in socialist countries and Third World nationalism in Asia and Africa have revived this original meaning of the term democracy.

Marx called the period of proletarian rule as democracy. This seems outrageous to the liberals. Of course, proletarian dictatorship has nothing liberal about it but to call it democracy, as Marx did, was simply to use the word in its original and then normal sense. This was Marx's meaning when he talked of winning the battle of democracy against the capitalists. Democracy was to be a class state; it was to use its power to abolish the legal basis of capitalism and put the productive powers of the whole society, including its accumulated capital, at the service of the entire community. The Marxian idea of democracy started from the age-old notion of democracy as class rule. But it was only the first step in the direction of the humanization of the whole society. The vanguard state of the existing communist countries claims to be democratic in the non-liberal sense i.e. it represents the interests of the majority class.

Macpherson insists that there is also a distinctive third world conception of democracy. The nations of this new world have achieved independence from colonial rule only after a revolutionary struggle. These national revolutions are made by an organised popular movement under leaders who are able to get mass support for their vision of the future. This vision has generally been a vision of democracy. This third world vision of democracy, Macpherson points out, neither corresponds to Western liberal-democracy nor to the proletarian democracy of Marx. It is newer than both of these and yet it recaptures the spirit of the old, pre-industrial notion of democracy. It rejects the basic ideas of liberal-individualism as well as the class analysis of Marxism and is akin to Rousseau's doctrine of the general will and mass democracy.

That their concept of democracy is not liberal-individualist should not surprise us. The competitive market society was not natural to them but an imposition from outside by the colonialists. Their traditional culture was not attuned to competition. Wealth-getting and individual gain were not the predominant motives in their society. The notion of political competition was as foreign to them as the notion of economic competition. Moreover, the colonial state neither encouraged free private enterprise nor free political activity. The community was divided on regional, tribal, ethnic or religious basis. Political competition meant national disunity. The requirements of the anti-colonial struggle necessitated the emergence of dominant single nationalist party. In the post-colonial phase, this meant a system of single party dominance with ineffective minor parties in opposition or just one-party dictatorship where opposition is banned as treasonable activity.

The dominance of a single party is considered necessary not only for the attainment of national independence but also, thereafter, for achieving modernisation and economic development. Modernisation and rapid economic growth require a non-liberal national state administered by a vanguard nationalist party. If the general will of the community has already accepted these goals of the nationalist elite, the people as well as the governing elite see no reason for having competing parties. If there are some sections, which oppose the general will, this opposition is criticised as anti-national and has to be suppressed. These conditions not only militate against a competitive party system but also against the maintenance of civil liberties in any real sense. This pressure for a non-liberal state in underdeveloped countries is likely to last longer as the task of economic development and accumulation of capital for that purpose will require a whole epoch in history. The other factor is the need to create a pervasive loyalty to the nation rather than to the tribe, caste, community or region.

Despite these non-liberal features of the political systems of the underdeveloped countries, these national states can claim to be democratic in a specific sense. This claim rests largely on the proposition that there is in those countries a general will, which can express itself through a single nationalist party committed equally to the goals of consolidation of national independence and rapid socio-economic progress. This also applies to those military dictatorships in the Third World, which pursue the two nationalist goals of modernisation and economic development. The nationalist vanguard party, Macpherson argues, represents the general will of the nation in the sense attributed to the phrase by Rousseau. The anti-colonial modernising nation-state of the Third World is democratic in Rousseauistic sense. Macpherson asserts this conclusion in the following words: "To call it democratic is to put the emphasis on ends, not means. It is to make the criterion of democracy the achievement of ends which the mass of the people share and which they put ahead of separate individual ends. And this of course is the classic, preliberal, notion of democracy. The classic formulator of this democratic doctrine was Rousseau, and there are strong echoes of Rousseau in many of the theoretical statements made by leaders in the underdeveloped countries. Like Rousseau they find the source of their social ills of moral depravity, of dehumanization and loss of human freedom, in the institution of inequality. Like him they believe that men can be restored to full freedom and humanity by, only by, the operation of a general will. Dignity, freedom, and humanity are to be achieved by re-establishing the equality that had been forcibly or fraudulently taken from them. This requires a revolution at once political and moral, an assertion of the will of an undifferentiated people as the only legitimate source of political power. (*219 : 20*).

How does the third world vision compare with the Marxian concept of democracy? The nationalists appreciate Marx's general critical analysis of capitalist society as applied to the imperialist West. Marx also appeals to them when he speaks of the dehumanisation of man by capitalism. His analysis of the alienation of man and his belief that man can shape his own history and overcome his dehumanisation by revolutionary struggle also attract the nationalists' imagination in the third world.

But here the attractiveness of Marxism to the third world bourgeois nationalist mind ends. The bourgeois nationalist thinks that the theme of class struggle and revolution is not relevant to his own country. He also rejects Marx's proposition that the state is necessarily an instrument of class domination. He does not visualize the post-colonial nation-state as representing the class interests of the landowners or the capitalists. He may agree that Marx was probably correct in his analysis of the capitalist class state of Europe but his theory of class struggle and class-dominated state is unsuitable to the third world in general or, at least, to his own country. The nationalists see their revolution against Western capitalism as a national revolution rather than a class revolution. Macpherson observes: "In freeing themselves from capitalism by throwing off imperial domination, they see themselves freed *immediately* from the whole class system of political power......there is no strong capitalist class that needs to be suppressed by a proletarian state. What they find they require, therefore, is not a dictatorship of a proletariat but the dictatorship of general will (or of vanguard in the name of the general will) over an undifferentiated people." (*219 : 31*).

Thus the characteristic political ideology of the Third World nationalists is Rosseaustic vision of democracy, which is distinct both from liberal individualism and Marxian socialism.

The Concept of Underdevelopment

Underdevelopment of the countries of the Third World today does not just mean the lack of development in the quantitative sense. All societies, before their industrial development, in Europe as elsewhere could be called undeveloped but they could not be properly described as underdeveloped in the sense most Afro-Asian or Latin American societies are designated as underdeveloped now. The fact is that underdevelopment, like development is a modern phenomenon. It is a particular type of development which has to be compared to and distinguished from another type of development i.e. the developmental pattern of the developed countries. The two phenomena of underdevelopment of the colonies, semi-colonies or neo-colonies and development of the metropolitan centres of the empire are related, both through the common historical process that they have shared during the past several centuries and through the mutual impact that they have exercised on each other throughout past history and will continue to exercise in the near future as well.

Andre Gunder Frank in his work, *On Capitalist Underdevelopment*, has tried to show that underdevelopment of some countries and development of the now-developed countries are the simultaneous results of a unified historical process of capitalist development over the past several centuries. Paul Baran in his work, *The Political Economy of Growth*, has also argued that this process of ever growing development in the advanced capitalist countries and *growing underdevelopment* in the neo-colonial societies of the Third World is a still continuing trend which has relevance for the present and the future too. Paul Baran points out that underdevelopment is systematically and everywhere associated with and produced by colonisation. The term colonialism was given a somewhat narrow meaning when it came to describe among other things, military conquest and political subjugation along with an exploiter-exploited relationship in the economic sense.

Portugal which was a mercantile colonial power in her own right, became a neo-colonial dependency of Great Britain during the eighteenth century. Portugal produced wine and failed to industrialize while England produced textiles and increased her industrial capacity further. The English not only controlled the entire commerce of Portugal, they also monopolized the commerce of Brazil, which was a political dependency of Portugal. Similarly, Ireland and many southern, central and eastern states of Europe and formally independent states of Latin America remained underdeveloped constituents of the developing and now-developed capitalist world along with large parts of fully colonized African and Asian countries. If Japan in Asia achieved industrial development, this is precisely because, it was never colonized by a capitalist power in the first instance. Japan is thus the unique case of a country where its ruling class decided to develop the country before it might become incorporated into the capitalist-colonialist system in the regular way. The Japansese elite profited from the example of semi-colonial China and semi-colonial Latin America and decided to industrialize the country without foreign 'aid' or investment. The United States, Canada and Australia, which have achieved economic development, were not 'colonial' in the economic sense and, therefore, escaped the fate of underdevelopment. The historical evidence conclusively proves that the economically exploited colonies and semicolonies were the only countries, which remained underdeveloped today.

The concept of economic surplus is crucial for the study of development and underdevelopment. Economic surplus may be defined as the actual or potential excess of a social unit's production over its necessary consumption which may or may not be invested or exploited. Though there are some conceptual and statistical difficulties, as admitted by Paul Baran, yet this concept fairly and correctly sums up the exploitative relation between the imperial power and its colony. For purposes of development and underdevelopment, what is important is not the sacrifice of the loser nation in terms of its actual loss of income or wealth or the absolute gain of the recipient country but the contribution to economic surplus accuring to the imperialist country from the colony. It is the loss of present and potential capital. While the colonies and semi-colonies are denied the developmental possibilities of this capital, the metropolitan country can use it for its own economic development.

However great or small the contribution to metropolitan development may or may not be, the associated sacrifice in terms of underdevelopment for the colony can readily be much larger. While the imperialist gains a pound of flesh, the colony may lose ten times more. It may lose resources, its essential irrigation system, or its civilisation or even its physical existence. Many Indian tribes and nationalities were wiped out in North America through genocide. Thus development and underdevelopment are not the summation only of economic quantities. They are their cumulation and the whole social structure and process which determines that accumulation. It is quite obvious that the existing participation of the now-underdeveloped countries in the international capitalist system keeps them permanently underdeveloped.

In order to understand the significance of the contribution of an underdeveloped country, it is not relevant to examine the gain for the whole of a recipient economic system of an advanced country but only a particular part thereof which plays a critical role in the economy. The drain of wealth from India contributed to the growth of a mercantile or industrial sector in England and is significant in that context only. The same can be said of the African slave trade. Its significance should not be estimated in terms of the total British or European economy. Today, it is not so much the American economic system which does business in Saudi Arabia or Brazil but only a few multi-nationals representing the most monopolized sector of the American economy. The fact that these corporations have excess capacity shows that their foreign investments and earning are quite important to them. Their contribution to general welfare of the American people may be marginal but the foreign empire of American big business supports in a significant way the monopoly structure of the American economy.

The control exercised by the multinationals on strategic sectors plays a critical role in preserving the pattern of underdevelopment. One example is the extraction and distribution of petroleum in underdeveloped countries. Examples may change with time and circumstance. However, it is the principle of metropolitan control over the existence or non-existence of critical or key sectors in underdeveloped countries in general which keep these economic systems perpetually underdeveloped. Probably, the most critical sector for several underdeveloped economies has been that of foreign trade and that is precisely the sector most under imperialist control. Thus the control not over all the population, but only over a section of the bourgeois class and its instruments of power in the neo-colonial state apparatus is sufficient to keep a country underdeveloped indefinitely and to distort and aggravate its underdevelopment in future. The bourgeois classes of a large number of African, Asian and Latin American societies are today highly dependent on the economic power of the multinationals and political power of the governments of advanced capitalist countries.

Thus the ruling elites of the underdeveloped countries have a vested interest in preserving indefinitely the system and pattern of underdevelopment.

Diffusion of Liberalism in the Third World

Through its pressure demonstration effects, the imperial-capitalist country tried to diffuse its several varieties of liberalism down to Latin America and other 'colonial' areas. We can distinguish an economic liberalism, a political liberalism, a cultural liberalism, a social liberalism and even a technological liberalism. In the underdeveloped countries, economic liberalism really meant mercantile monopoly which made native enterprise really quite un-free to start or 'competed' it out of existence where it had already begun. If metropolitan interests, demanded it, imperial capital set up extractive industries in the colonies which were brought up or just simply stolen in the form of mines, plantations, rail-roads and oil fields. Their resources were extracted and diverted towards the metropolis and all this was done in the name of economic liberalism. The entire economic surplus of the colony or the semi-colony was drained out in the name of the economic philosophy of mercantilism as well as liberalism.

Latin America, Asia and Africa also imported from the colonialists the political outlook of liberalism. The contribution of political liberalism to Latin American and Afro-Asian under-development has been quite significant. In his *Economic Theory of Democracy,* Anthony Downs analyses the political process and organisation in the United States as a market place for votes and influence in the same terms that neo-classical economists discuss and analyse the economic market place. Whatever the structure of the market societies in advanced capitalist countries may be, their structure in Asia, Africa or Latin America, the economic as well as the political, continues to be rigidly oligopolistic. It is a convenient fiction to talk about a 'liberal' economic and a separate political structure. There is only one such structure really, and the key positions in it have from its initial stages been captured by the commercial and financial bourgeoisie. The leading section of the Third World bourgeois class today is the export-production bourgeoisie. Even the regional political bosses represent more the commercial than the productive interests of their constituencies, including the landowners of their regions. Despite all talk of the survivals of feudal and semi-feudal relations in the Third World countries, the real power at the national level is concentrated in the top layers of the financial and commercial bourgeoisie. So far 'free elections' have admirably served to keep this bourgeoisie in power. If the political elite fails to protect their interests through elections, the bourgeoisie lends support to the military elite, which instals a fascist or semi-fascist dictatorship, with the whole-hearted approval of the multi-nationals.

The diffusion of social liberalism, which is popularly known as 'open society' and called 'social mobility' by the sociologists, was a consequence of the introduction of economic and political liberalism. Industrialization carries with it greater division of labour. But social mobility in the countries of the third world increases in the absence of any significant industrial development. In their cases, social liberalism is closely associated with the expansion of a primary export sector (often single product), which directly supports a growing service or tertiary sector without the manufacturing sector in between. The dissolution of the pre-capitalist economy or disintegration of its natural self-sufficiency takes place in an underdeveloped country too. Commercial agriculture replaces traditional subsistence farming to a considerable extent and manufactured commodities from the metropolis invade the market of the native artisans and craftsmen.

Technological and cultural liberalism of the third world countries may be regarded as the technological and cultural aspects and consequences of economic, social and political liberalism. The real importance of these different dimensions of liberalism for the third world is to promote and maintain the system of underdevelopment. Andre Gunder Frank has constructed an 'ideal type' to show how these forms of liberalism interact in the political system of a Latin American or Afro-Asian society. The requirements of the world market or one of its monopolized sectors result in the relatively rapid expansion of a primary export product such as petroleum in Saudi Arabia, copper in Chile, coffee in Brazil or some other minerals in the Congo. Though an impression is created that foreign resources are flowing into development of this sector, yet the bulk of them are often national resources, which are canalized by a foreign company. The industry offers privileged positions to members of the local elite. It may give rise to a larger number of other privileged positions in satellite industries, which serve the productive or consumption demands of the elite.

According to Paul Baran and Andre Gunder Frank, liberalism of the parliamentary regime and fascism of a military dictatorship in the context of a third world country are linked with the structure of its underdevelopment. The indigenous elites and the foreign capitalists use the two ideologies to suit their specific requirements of a given situation. Both liberalism and fascism serve the class interests of the native and foreign elites in all neo-colonial societies of Asia, Africa and Latin America.

In most countries of Asia, Africa and Latin America these neo-colonial regimes could have been toppled through social revolutions by now but for the aid and support, military and financial, given to them freely by Western capital and Western governments acting on their behalf. The continued foreign exploitation of underdeveloped countries and their domination by the imperialist powers depends on the preservation of these *comprador* administrations and the feudal-mercantile social order.

Evolutionary Socialism in the Third World

There are some elites ruling some of the third world countries, which proclaim democratic or evolutionary socialism as their official ideology. Paul Baran calls the regimes professing this ideology as the governments with a 'New Deal' orientation. India under Nehru, Indonesia under Soekarno or Egypt under Nasser could be cited as examples of this type. Their governments were brought to power by broad popular movements.

The basic and unifying purpose of these movements was the overthrow of colonial rule and the establishment of a nationalist government. Fighting against imperialism and its domestic allies, the mercentile-monopolist-feudal coalition, these national movements were transformed into a united popular front of the progressive, industrial bourgeoisie, the intelligentsia and some active elements of the oppressed peasantry and the urban proletariat. Some segments of the landowning class or the reactionary bourgeoisie, who joined the national movement, used their positions to divert popular energies from the struggle for social change.

With the achievement of political independence, the basic class conflict of an antagonistic society becomes more intense and clear. While some issues of economic and social development are closely linked with the question of national political emancipation, there are several others which are directly connected with the programme of social and economic emancipation. The exploitation of the peasants by the landowning elite or the strangulation of industrial development by a monopolistic oligarchy are basically *social* questions requiring radical *social* remedies. The socially heterogeneous elements fail to preserve unity during the post-independence period and get polarized. If the worker-peasant alliance becomes strong to threaten a social revolution, the capitalist, bourgeois component of the national movement, swiftly moves backward to enter into an alliance with the former enemies—imperialists and native landowners. The bonds of class are stronger than those of nationality.

In some countries, the pressure for social liberation may not be great at the time of the establishment of the free national state. As a result, the national bourgeoisie may feel more secure and may try to meet a potential threat of social revolution by making an all-out effort to lay the foundations for the evolution of an indigenous industrial capitalism and to create a modern capitalist state. Such a nationalist elite may also create the state-capitalist sector to expedite the rate of economic development and may proclaim evolutionary socialism as its official ideology though the outcome of the state-capitalist planning is bound to be capitalism and not socialism. The experience of Egypt and India confirms the truth of the above generalization.

It is necessary to note the dilemma faced by the evolutionary socialists in underdeveloped countries like India. The social forces impeding capital formation and productive investment in both the urban and rural sectors of the economy are as powerful in India as anywhere in the underdeveloped world. Therefore, in a country like India which suffers from underdevelopment, it is only the state that is in a position to mobilize the surplus which is potentially present in the economic system and to invest it for the expansion of national production. Actually, the petty-bourgeois rulers in India, who prefer the ideology of evolutionary socialism, allow the state to seize a very small proportion of the potential economic surplus. Further, the Indian state fails to use it even this small amount of resources to provide for most rapid and balanced economic growth.

Realism and pragmatism became the permanent feature of India's evolutionary socialist planning during the last three decades of its economic growth. At the present stage of India's underdevelopment, the only adequate policy for accelerating economic growth should be the investment of as large a share of national income as possible in the development programmes. Paul Baran suggests that 15 per cent of national income could be invested without reducing the level of mass consumption. For this purpose, it is necessary to acquire all the potential economic surplus that is currently generated by the Indian economic system. This can be found in the more than thirty per cent of India's national income which the poverty-stricken masses of India place at the disposal of its unproductive classes. It consists of the share of agricultural output appropriated by the landowners in the form of rent and by the money-lenders in the form of usury interest from the productive peasant strata. It also consists of the profits of the business class, a large portion of which is not re-invested into productive enterprise but wasted in conspicuous consumption by the propertied classes.

It is obvious that this mobilization of the potential economic surplus amounting to about fifteen per cent of the national income would be opposed by the Indian landlords and capitalists. It can be accomplished only as a result of a relentless struggle against the privileged classes, which have a vested interest in the preservation of India's underdevelopment.

Thus evolutionary socialism, like liberalism, or fascism, has failed to evolve a successful strategy of economic development, which can provide an underdeveloped country an escape route from the vicious cycle of underdevelopment. In an advanced capitalist society, evolutionary socialists defend the interests of monopoly capital. In the third world, evolutionary socialists protect the privileges of the capitalists and landowners and preserve the underdeveloped character of the nation's economy. In actual practice, the evolutionary socialists are indistinguishable from other liberals and their strategy of development does not provide adequate safeguards from neo-colonial domination and exploitation and from incipient fascism and military dictatorship.

Marxism and the Socialist Path of Development

Marxism has exercised a great impact on the ideology and strategy of development adopted by some underdeveloped countries. However, it is not the classical, ethnocentric writings of Marx and Engels but rather the Marxist ideas mediated through the political thinking of Lenin and Mao Tse-tung that have inspired revolutionary changes in the social and political systems of the Third World. Even Russia was underdeveloped by European and North American standards, when Lenin brought about a socialist revolution there. Soviet Russia included further several other more underdeveloped territories in Asia, which had been colonized by Tsarist imperialism. Socialist planning and the socialist path of development rapidly transformed the Soviet Union, including its excolonial regions and peoples into an advanced industrial society within a few decades. Many underdeveloped countries of Eastern Europe similarly succeeded in transforming themselves into developed industrial nations during the post-war period by adopting the path of socialist development. But the example of a semi-colonial, agrarian society of China, transforming itself into a sufficiently industrialized nation by the thirdworld standards, is quite significant. The example of socialist Cuba is also illuminating.

Andre Gunder Frank observes: "Only the elimination of the capitalist structure, within a certain territory and among a certain people, and its substitution by socialist ones has so far offered any escape either from imperialism or from underdevelopment. The destruction of capitalism and the introduction of socialism may then......be regarded so far as the only possible escape from imperialism and from underdevelopment. Socialism may be regarded, then, as the continuance of the historical process which through capitalist expansion and development has produced development and underdevelopment and which requires the development of mankind into socialism in order to avoid still further underdevelopment. Notable, in this connection is the fact that all the countries which have turned to socialism indeed were part of the captalist exploited underdeveloped periphery before doing so." (*202 : 103*).

The above formulation has serious political implications. It implies that the principal contradiction today is between the developed capitalist countries on the one hand and underdeveloped capitalist countries on the other. As a result, the contradiction between the bourgeoisie and the proletariat within a developed capitalist country has become secondary. Andre Gunder Frank further argues that even the contradiction between the capitalist bloc and the socialist bloc has become less important than the internal contradiction within the capitalist world itself. He, however, regards the present contradiction between the Soviet bloc and socialist China as a reflection of temporary clash of national interests.

Not only did underdevelopment develop as a result of the historical growth of capitalism in the past, but the same process continues in the present as well. There have been several efforts during the contemporary period to escape from neo-colonial domination and underdevelopment through independent national capitalism. All these attempts did not succeed so far. The experience of Latin America conclusively proves that no national bourgeoisie can in the long run, liberate itself from the domination of the imperialist bourgeoisie.

The proper development strategy, which the proletariat, including also the peasantry, should follow, ought to be based on the destruction of capitalism and the overthrow of the bourgeois class in its country and the development of a socialist structure in its place. To take its country out of the world capitalist system, which produces underdevelopment there, the proletariat must eliminate capitalism inside its own country through a revolution. As Frantz Fanon pointed out in his work *The Wretched of the Earth,* the imposition of the capitalist colonial structure on the people of the third world was an act of naked force and violence. Consequently, the oppressed masses of the Third World can destroy this system of 'capitalist underdevelopment' only by using revolutionary force and violence. Since the development strategy of the proletariat, including the peasants, must be the elimination of the bourgeoisie as a class, any alliance between the revolutionary proletariat and any part of the bourgeoisie is dangerous.

Frantz Fanon has argued that the bourgeoisies of the Third World necessarily divert the process of national and social liberation from the system which produces underdevelopment into a prolongation of the colonial system of exploitation through other forms. He notes also that the introduction of the liberal party and parliamentary regime, professing even a radical nationalist ideology and employing a social-democratic jargon, can only serve as an instrument of this continued exploitative and underdevelopment-producing relation. The intelligentsia and the petty-bourgeoisie get further corrupted by participating in the commercial and political institutional apparatus of capitalism and neo-colonialism.

Once the proletariat, which here includes the peasants, has seized political power through a political revolution, the socialist path of economic development overcoming the underdevelopment syndrome becomes feasible. Lenin's famous law of uneven development suggests that the historical process is different in different societies and that the stage reached at any given time differs from country to country. There is thus no general formula which can be applied to all countries of the third world without taking into account the peculiarities of the specific nations.

Paul Baran has noted three kinds of development strategies basing himself on the historical experiences of different socialist nations. Regarding the first of these strategies, he observes: "Consider for instance a country in which there exists a certain nucleus of an industrial economy and where the peasantry, whether exploited by kulaks, or held in servitude by feudal landlords, is intensely land hungry, and longs for nothing but individually owned plots of land. In such a country it may be possible to generate a sizeable amount of economic surplus via the economy's industrial sector. If, in addition, the country is relatively small so that whatever aid it may receive from abroad can materially influence the volume of its capital accumulation, it may well be able to afford to allow its peasants to 'sit it out' for a while, and to learn by observations and experience the advantages of a rational and modern organization of agricultural production. Such has apparently been the broad perspective of some socialist countries in Eastern and Southern Europe." (*174 : 39*).

Drawing lessons from Socialist China's developmental experience, Paul Baran says: "Take, on the other hand, a large country with a small industrial oasis in a vast sea of subsistence farming. Here the industrially generated surplus is of necessity small, and the practically accessible foreign assistance can constitute at best only a drop in the bucket of development requirements. If in such a country, the peasants' craving for *individually* owned plots is for any number of economic or cultural reasons not urgent or even absent, its agricultural economy can be shifted on to new tracks based on cooperative farming or even on a system of state-operated, large-scale, and increasingly productive 'factories in the field.' The gentry, rich peasants, village storekeepers, and moneylenders displaced in the process may either be integrated into the new agricultural economy or find employment in the expanding industrial and distributive sectors. And surplus which they used to appropriate may become available for purposes of economic development. This would seem to be—in a nutshell—the model of the Chinese strategy of economic development." (*174 : 40*).

A third strategy of economic development is typified by the Cuban experience. Paul Baran observes: "And visualize finally a banana or sugar republic—if that flattering designation is considered applicable to the semi-colonial dictatorships involved—where the bulk of agricultural output is produced in plantations, and where the agricultural population consists predominantly or in large part not of peasants but of agricultural workers. In such countries the expropriation of the peasant was so thoroughly completed by the domestic and foreign plantation-owners that even the image of individual land holdings has all but evaporated from the mentality of the rural proletariat. There mass parcelling of land is not on the agenda at all, and the nationalization of the plantations places immediately at the disposal of society as a whole the surplus that was previously appropriated by foreign and domestic corporations. This is not to say that all of the surplus so released can be turned to investment, much of it may have to be used to raise immediately the wretched living conditions of the working population. Also complications and frictions in the process of the reorganization of the economy, difficulties in securing new sources of essential supplies, as well as in finding new markets for customary exports all largely due to the sabotage and obstruction on the part of the former ruling class at home and its allies and protectors abroad——may temporarily reduce aggregate output and accordingly also the volume of available surplus. In such a situation the possibility of overcoming all these hurdles is to such an extent dependent on various economic and political factors at home and abroad that there can hardly be a generalization that would fit the individual case. The obvious example of what I mean is the dramatic experience of Cuba since its great Revolution." (*174 : 41*).

Thus each of the underdeveloped nations of the Third World presents a very broad spectrum of social, economic, political and cultural configurations. It is not possible to prescribe an exactly identical strategy of economic development for every underdeveloped country, which decides to embark upon a socialist path of development after a successful proletarian revolution at the political level. Paul Baran speaks of two principal insights that he has gained from the study of the developmental strategies of the socialist countries. Baran's first insight is that rapid economic development of an underdeveloped nation can be brought about only through a *comprehensive* economic planning. Small and marginal changes can be achieved by a spontaneous process of trial and error. A few per cent increase in a particular product already being produced may be secured by raising its price without any major planning. However, if the increase in a country's aggregate output is desired, say, to the extent of 8 to 10 per cent per annum, it would require a large-scale centralized planning of national resources. Then, the mode of utilization of human and material resources of the country will have to be altered radically replacing less productive economic activities by more productive ones. Paul Baran observes: "While the most conservatively estimated *per capita* rates of economic growth in the socialist countries have been in the order of 10 per cent per annum, in capitalist countries—advanced and underdeveloped alike—they rarely exceed 3 per cent, except for extraordinary circumstances of war booms and post-war reconstruction." (*174* : *42*).

The second insight of Baran is that no worthwhile planning is possible in a society in which the means of production remain under the control of private interests which manage them in order to secure maximum profits for the proprietors. Since the prevailing pattern of the allocation and utilization of resources serves the best interests of the dominant class, it is inevitable that any serious planning effort would come into sharp conflict with the dominant class and its internal and external friends. This conflict can be resolved in three ways. The Planning Commission, if created by a capitalist government, can be taken over by the capitalist class itself. Its activities may become a sham and its existence may create an illusion among the masses that something constructive is being done to remove poverty and accelerate economic growth. The second possibility is that the Planning Commission is established by a reformist government and its members remain impervious to the pressures and bribes of the capitalist class. They set out to introduce farreaching changes in the national economy. In that case, the planning effort meets the tenacious resistance and sabotage on the part of the ruling class, achieves very little if anything and, thereby, discredits the very idea of planning in the eyes of the people. Paul Baran adds: "The third alternative is that planning becomes the battle-cry of a broad popular movement, is fought for relentlessly against the entrenched beneficiaries of the *ancien regime,* and is turned into the basic organizational principle of the economy by a victorious social revolution sweeping aside the former ruling class together with the institution of private property in the means of production on which its very existence rests." (*174* : *43*).

The warning of history is loud and clear. Latin America has failed to achieve economic development during the last 150 years of its independent political existence by following the capitalist path. Cuba has achieved spectacular economic development within a short period of just two decades through socialist planning. Socialist China, similarly, has achieved the status of a developed economic nation within a period of thirty years while capitalist Brazil has been unable to overcome its economic underdevelopment even after a century and a half of its existence as the largest 'free' nation of Latin America.

The planning endeavour in India, the Marxists argue, has run into persistent resistance and sabotage on the part of the capitalist and landowning classes. It has failed to overcome the underdevelopment of its economy inherited from the colonial past and has ended up in a state of frustration and impotence with the fatal byproduct of discrediting the very principle of planning in the eyes of a section of the Indian electorate. The only alternative before the Indian people now is to accept a comprehensive economic planning on a genuinely socialist basis and convert it into a rallying slogan of a broad mass movement that should culminate into a socialist revolution destroying the state apparatus of the ruling elite. The Marxists in South Asia as well as other countries of the Third World have so far failed to develop appropriate strategies for realizing their goal of social and political transformation in accordance with the specific conditions prevailing in different national environments. The dilemmas which the Marxist ruling groups face in countries like Afghanistan and Ethiopia show that even capture of state power is an insufficient guarantee for translating a dogmatic ideological program into successful political practice.

The last decade of the twentieth century has seen the demise of several Marxist regimes in Eastern Europe, the former USSR and even Ethiopia and Afghanistan. Capitalism and the old social order have been restored in these countries in the name of a superficial process of democratisation. In Russia, a mafia-directed capitalism has come into existence which has reduced the GNP by half, created sectors of absolute poverty and converted Russia into a third world society. In Afghanistan, a progressive, forward looking and modernist regime has been replaced by an antediluvian, fundamentalist regime of the socially backward *Taliban* administration. Even in China, the ruling communist party is following a market-oriented policy of economic growth. For the time being, the neo-liberal capitalism has become the ruling ideology and strategy of development in the First, Second and Third Worlds.

CHAPTER 38

BEHAVIOURALISM

Behaviouralistic Approach in Political Science

The publication in 1908 of two significant books on politics marks the beginning of the behaviouralistic approach in contemporary political science. The first book was published in England entitled *Human Nature in Politics* written by Graham Wallas who said, "The study of politics is just now in a curiously unsatisfactory position…nearly all students of politics analyse institutions and avoid the analysis of man." (262 : 7). His sentiments were reciprocated in the United States by Arthur F. Bentley, though for different reasons. He wrote in *The Process of Government* : "It is a formal study of the most external characteristics of governing institutions. It loves to classify governments by incidental attributes…When it is to touch up this barren formalism with a glow of humanity, an injection of metaphysics is used." (262 : 7). Both men criticized the formalism and legalism of traditional political theory.

Behaviouralism arose as a protest movement in contemporary political science during the first half of the twentieth century but by the middle decades of the century, it acquired the characteristics of a dominant tendency and was thoroughly integrated into the main body of the discipline. Behaviouralists turned their attention from the study of governmental institutions, especially legal and constitutional arrangements, to observe the political behaviour of the individuals and social groups. This change of perspective was quite important. In the words of David Apter : "The main emphasis of behaviouralism is on the *relationship between* political knowledge and political action, including how political opinion is formed, how political acumen is acquired, and the ways people learn about political events. Such categories of thought are commonly referred to as ideologies, or belief systems, which create meaningful patterns of behaviour. The behavioural approach takes into account factors of socialization, how we 'internalize' values and prevailing beliefs, and how changes in outlook occur. (172 : 215-16).

The theoretical basis of behaviouralism can be located in the skeptical philosophy of David Hume, the pragmatic world view of William James and Charles S. Pierce and the instrumentalist outlook of John Dewey. All of them stressed empiricism, voluntarism, individual activity and a practical approach to truth based on observation of an objective, pluralistic world. They rejected the speculative, idealist mode of thinking and the rationalistic or logical deductive analysis of the political thinkers belonging to the classical tradition. David Apter says : "Philosophy and history seemed fundamentally at odds with behavioural experimental methods. If they were interested in philosophical questions at all, behaviouralists inclined towards the philosophy of science exemplified in the work of figures like Alfred North Whitehead, Rudolph Carnap, Carl Hawpel, or Karl Popper. The object was to supplant metaphysical perspectives, replacing certainty with probability, rationalism with measures of central tendency, and description with distributions and measures of dispersion. Disparaging generalized and intuitive hypotheses in favour of more rigorously empirical ones based on observation, the behavioural point of view was a-historical and non-revolutionary." (172 : 217).

Thus, behaviouralism was a response to the shortcomings of the institutional political analysis based on a legal, historical and philosophical approach to the study of political phenomena. The behavioural movement favoured a natural science paradigm, sought inspiration from Comte's positivism, emphasized scientific methods and experimentalism, and displayed special interest in the scientific tradition represented by Mach, Poincare, Frege, Wetlgenstein and the social scientists of the 'Vienna Circle', who wanted to develop a unified science of human behaviour linking politics to a theory of the social system. Linking the great theories of logic, language and biology with those of psychology, sociology and political science, the behaviouralists offered a new scientific orientation called *general systems analysis*. David Easton emerged as the main advocate of the systems theory of behaviouralism in political science.

Explaining the nature of the behavioural approaches to politics, David Apter points out : "The political behaviour of the individual person is the central and crucial datum of the behavioural approaches to politics. This does not mean that research is restricted to the individual person as the theoretical focus of investigation. Indeed, most behavioural researchers are not concerned with the individual political actor as such. A small group, an organisation, a community, an elite, a mass movement, or a national society may be the focus of behavioural inquiry and events, structures, functions, processes, or relations may serve as categories of behavioural analysis." (172 : 218).

Behavioural research uses empirical and predominantly inductive methods and also mathematical and statistical techniques such as interviewing and sample survey. It uses indicators that identify regularities in conduct. Instead of emphasizing ideal types dichotomies, it places stress on continuous variables and distributions. They avoid large omnibus categories like power, authority, class or culture. Their techniques for establishing important variables include factor analysis, regression analysis, Guttman scaling, indicator analysis and other statistical measures.

Important Features of the Behavioural Approach

Rather than being a specific field of investigation, the behavioural approach is applicable to all the conventional themes of politics and all the arenas of power. The difference between the traditional and behavioural approaches lies in their different orientations. Yet the emergence of the new approach created a great deal of controversy. Kirkpatrick has noted : "Between World War II and the mid-fifties, the term political behaviour represented both an approach and a challenge, an orientation and a reform movement, a type of research and a rallying cry, a 'hurrah' term and a 'boo' term. Debate about behavioural techniques and methods was often accompanied by vituperation; discussions were often aimed at clarifying issues." (256 : 43).

Eulan, Eldersveld and Janovitz clarified the main features of the behaviouralist approach in the following words : (1) It specifies the behaviour of individuals and social groups rather than events, structures, institutions or ideologies as the unit or object of both empirical and theoretical study; (2) It places political science in a conceptual framework which is common to that of social psychology and cultural anthropology; (3) It emphasizes the independence of theory and research; theoretical questions should be stated in operational terms for conducting empirical research; and in turn, empirical findings should assist in the development of political theory; and (4) It tries to develop rigorous research design and to apply precise methods of analysis to the problems of political behaiviour and organisation. (238 : 83-84).

David Easton identified the major characteristics of behaviouralism as follows : (1) That regularities exist which can be discovered and expressed in generalizations. (2) Such generalizations must be tenable with reference to behaviour. (3) Means for acquiring and interpreting data cannot be taken for granted; they are problematic and should be examined self-consciously. (4) Measurement and qualification are necessary but only where such measurement makes sense in terms of other purposes. (5) Ethical evaluation should be separated from empirical explanation. (6) Research ought to be systematic. Empirical research untutored by theory may prove trivial and theory unsupportable by data, futile. (7) The understanding and explanation of political behaviour should precede application of this knowledge. (8) Knowledge from the various social sciences should be integrated. (238 : 84).

Every behaviouralist did not subscribe to all elements as listed by David Easton. The interdisciplinary approach of the behaviouralists implied that they have borrowed some of the features of the related social sciences in terms of methods and even theories. The sociologists and psychologists compelled the political scientists to pay attention to their work when they investigated phenomena clearly related to politics. The first studies in the area of voting behaviour were conducted by the sociologists. However, some political scientists realized that they were explaining the phenomena of voting in terms of such concepts as socio-economic status, ethnic origin etc., thus ignoring the political factors. Political scientists took up the subject both by using their tools and concepts drawn from their own experience such as party identification. In the absence of formal party membership, the psychological identification an individual feels with a particular political party becomes quite important in explaining decisions to vote for certain parties or candidates. The sociologists had de-emphasized the significance of politics and government in local community decision-making. This prompted the political scientists to study community power structures to assess the validity of the conclusions of the sociologists in this respect. In addition, the behaviouralists showed interest in such subjects as political socialization, the attitudes underlying the decision of judges, public opinion, and factors which explain the activity of legislators, administrators and ministers. For the study of these themes, the students of political behaviour depended on psychology.

Behaviouralists have generally avoided the use of historical and legal materials in their study and research. They ignored history because of its emphasis on the uniqueness of events and felt that historical approach could lead to the vice of historicism. It was an attempt to explain phenomena exclusively in terms of the historical period in which the events occurred and this clashed with the behaviouralist's desire for generalizations which were not bound by time. The behaviouralists have been criticized for concentrating on description of static situations. Recently, some behaviouralists in the field of comparative politics have started studies of political stage, modernization and development. Lasswell has studied what he calls the pathological elements of politics. Walter Lippmann lamented the fact that when he attended college, it was considered unnecessary to discuss the politician. The boss and the district leader, the caucus and the conference, spoils and deals constituted the psychology of politics and the student was required to read only the unperverted political system in which the pathological elements of politics were not permitted to intrude. Political behaviouralists now study these subjects without any feeling of guilt and inhibition. (263 : 76).

Distributive Analysis of Harold Lasswell

According to Harold Lasswell, political science is a study of the distribution of power, influence and values in society. He thus holds a very comprehensive view of the discipline. Politics for him exists throughout the whole matrix of society. Unlike other behaviouralists, he is not satisfied with merely providing the conceptual framework for explaining the systemic relations between various segments of the political system. Lasswell says : "One aspect of the task of the systemic student of politics is to describe political behaviour in these social situations which recur with sufficient frequency to make prediction useful *as a preliminary to control*." (238 : 86). The political scientist is as much concerned with prediction and prescription as with analysis and description.

Lasswell summed up his purposes of political investigation in the phrase: "who gets what, when, how?" This led him to move the focus of interest from concepts of social system, role structures and the interactive processes of politics to a study of the persons who actually perform functions and fulfil the roles. He regards the structures of social and political order as the relatively stable constructs which provide the parameters of political life. His main concern is to explain the motivations, hopes and activities of the actors within the system and the causes of their successes or failures. All human endeavours are aimed at securing certain values which enhance a person's status and prestige in society. Knowledge of the distribution of these values throughout society and the process by which this distribution takes place can give us important insights into the nature of the political system.

At one place, Lasswell mentioned three values of deference, income and safety. Later he expanded his list to eight values : Power, respect, affection, rectitude, well-being, wealth, skill and enlightenment. Success or failure of an individual in seeking any of these values is measured in terms of *indulgences* and *deprivations* and this can be expressed according to an Indulgence-Deprivation ratio. The values may be sought either as ends in themselves or merely as instrumental factors in realizing a more important set of goals. Almost every value is to some extent exchangeable with other values. Power provides a good example of this. Competition for power is found in every political community. Yet it is rarely sought for its own sake. Power enables a person to achieve other values such as respect, wealth, affection and well-being. (263 : 77).

Harold Lasswell has developed a number of conceptual devices, which he subsumes under the title of configurative analysis. Two concepts used in this analysis are called *equilibrium* and *development*. The categories used by him in his equilibrium approach are actions, symbols, demands and practices. *Actions* such as fighting, negotiating, boycotting etc. affect the distribution of values in society. Consequently, some individuals will stop seeking certain values, be deprived of them, or change the goals of their involvement in politics. *Symbols* are either ideologies in the broad sense or value-oriented concepts like class, race, church, nation or state. Symbols create certain habits of social and political behaviour, foster certain stereotyped images in the minds of the people and facilitate the propaganda which is a functional need of an equilibrated political system. *Demands* are the outcome of symbolic activity and may relate to the objectives of peace, security, welfare, abundance etc. and thus affect the conduct of political life as well as the values sought by individuals. *Practices* refer to the corpus of interactive behaviour of the structures of political life. They include the methods by which elites are recruited and trained, the institutional arrangements through which the political system functions as well as the less formal strategies and tactics which elites use in the competitive struggles of political life.

Though *equilibrium analysis* as defined above is an important element in Lasswell's behavioural approach, it should be supplemented by a *develop-*

mental analysis. Equilibrium analysis facilitates an explanation of the interaction of political forces at definite points in time only and not of the changes over a period of time. An assumption of Lasswell's approach is the concept of historical uniformities. According to him, there exist certain political situations in history which recur with great frequency and science can identify these broad patterns of political development. He does not postulate any inevitable goal as the final point of the historical process and thus does not subscribe to the point of view called *historicism.* He uses the concept of 'elite symbol changes' to describe the process of political development. Changes in the structure and recruitment method of elites and shifts in the nature of orienting ideologies lead to a new configuration of the political system over a period of time. In this way it is possible to identify current trends in a polity and the directions of its future development. (263 : 78).

An interesting aspect of Lasswell's behavioural political analysis is his belief in the relevance of psycho-analytical perspective in the study of politics. His analysis of various types of political leaders in terms of psychopathic traits shows how some political agitations and movements are influenced by the irrational and subconscious drives of individuals who participate in them. The interest in the relationships between personality types and political processes is quite legitimate for Lasswell because this knowledge of human motivations in politics provides him a basis for social control or what he describes as the politics of prevention. He believes that all psychological deviations in the character of individuals are politically harmful, and must be controlled if the excesses associated with fanaticism, tyranny, violence and war are to be reduced and ultimately eradicated. The politics of prevention cannot be achieved through the formal political processes such as legislation, institutional reorganisation, or public discussion and participation. It should be based on the *manipulative activity* of the technocrat and the social scientist. The social scientist must develop interest in policy-oriented research. The political scientist must give up his exclusively *contemplative standpoint* which concentrates on describing social processes, determining the interconnection of variables and their causal relationships and, lastly, predicting their development. The *manipulative standpoint* concerns itself with the choice of goals and the rational control of social and political processes on the basis of the explanation of the alternative choices. For Lasswell, political science is one of several policy sciences and its subject-matter is the distribution of power and influence. (238 : 88).

Pluralistic Analysis of Robert Dahl

According to Dahl, the purpose of behaviouralistic political analysis is to locate not only the differences but also the common characteristics of various political systems. In the first place, competition for leadership takes place in all modern political systems. It arises due to conflicting ideals and interests of various groups and the political system is an instrument for resolving these group conflicts. Secondly, political influence is always unevenly distributed among different sections of the people. Some individuals and groups exercise greater influence on the decision-making process than other individuals and groups. Thirdly, the political leaders desire that their decisions should be accepted as authoritative by all citizens. People ought to obey them not because they are just afraid of sanctions but because they feel a sense of moral obligation.

The differences between political systems are stressed for the purpose of classification. Dahl presents a scheme of classification in his *Modern Political Analysis* by combining the criteria of Aristotle and Max Weber with a further yardstick of *autonomy of subsystems* within society. Using this scheme he classified political systems into sixteen conceptual categories. Each category presents a great deal of information about a system and implies much more which can be measured and tested empirically.

Robert Dahl identifies four basic socio-political processes and suggests that actual systems can be classified according to the varying relations between these processes. This approach attempts to incorporate both economic as well as political aspects of the social process. The ideologies around which polemical debates often take place cannot adequately determine political choices. Socialism and capitalism, planning and laissez faire, regulation and free market are not appropriate conceptual frameworks for explaining and analysing the social and political systems which exist today. Rational social action as well as rational comprehension of the social and political reality are possible only through 'painstaking attention to technical details' and the 'countless particular social techniques' which create a system. Dahl's criterion for social action is simply its capacity to attain its goals. Unlike Weber and Lasswell, he freely accepts the essential rationality of much subconscious behaviour. Dahl mentions seven goals toward which rational action can be directed such as democracy, freedom, equality, security, progress, rationality and appropriate inclusion. At another place, he adds a few more goals such as respect, skill, love, affection and enlightenment. But this does not exhaust the list. (263 : 80).

Processes of social control must also be instituted if rational social action is to be meaningful. In certain cases, the two processes may be identical. The market mechanism and the electoral system simultaneously facilitate rational calculation as well as rational social control. Dahl distinguishes four basic processes through which social control is exercised. Firstly, *spontaneous field control* when the activities of one person unintentionally produce new perceptions in others and lead them to behave in a particular way. The second type is *manipulative field control*. This occurs when leaders learn over a period of time that certain actions invariably produce specific responses from the electorate. A third type of control is possible when leaders are sure that they can enforce obedience from their subordinates. This takes the form of the issuing of *commands*. The fourth technique of control is based on *reciprocity.* This exists when two or more people control each other through the techniques of command or manipulation or both. The differences between various societies can be understood in terms of the different ways in which they combine the use of various techniques of social control.

Dahl has suggested models of four socio-political processes which are distinguished by the nature of the relations which would exist under idealized conditions between leaders and non-leaders. They are respectively the *price system* in which there is no central control; *hierarchy* in which leaders exercise a high degree of unilateral control over non-leaders; *polyarchy* in which non-leaders exercise a high degree of control over governmental leaders; and finally *bargaining* in which there is reciprocal control among leaders.

The price system mainly operates in the economic sphere. It is a political system too in the sense that the decision-making power lies with an elite of businessmen. They control the quantity and mechanism of production but their power to manipulate the economy is limitedly by consumer preferences. The consumer's purchases correspond functionally to the acts of voting in a democratic state. Each purchase is a vote for continuing the policy of producing the commodity purchased. The initiative for making policy is in the hands of the elite but the individual has a degree of freedom to determine his pattern of consumption and his occupation. (238 : 90).

Hierarchy is the term employed by Dahl to describe the social process represented by bureaucracy. It establishes relationships of unilateral control. Unlike polyarchal and bargaining systems, hierarchy does not provide for any procedure whereby non-leaders can peacefully displace their leaders or even influence them in the act of decision-making. Hierarchical systems have two basic structural principles. First, the rational goals are prescribed by the top leaders and the institutional structures are adopted in order to realize these goals effectively. Secondly, hierarchy assumes a pyramidal structure. It is marked by a lengthy chain of controllers and subordinates.

Polyarchy is a process commonly observed in a sector of modern democracy. It is a process by which non-leaders exercise a high degree of influence over leaders. Elections conducted in a free atmosphere and based on universal adult franchise signify polyarchal control. In policy matters, polyarchy requires that electorate should give a mandate to its elected leaders and these elected leaders should have the authority and capacity to control non-elected officials.

Bargaining is a form of reciprocal control among leaders. In countries with polyarchal institutions, bargaining is a complementary technique and the culminating point of the decision-making process. Leaders of pressure groups, party leaders, governmental leaders and leaders in other fields constantly engage themselves in the bargaining process at various levels of decision-making before policy choices are finally made. (263 : 82).

All these techniques are used in different proportions and combinations in every social system. The way in which they are combined depends on the ideology, values and interests of various groups as well as the objectives and perceptions of contemporary elites. Robert Dahl has used this model to inquire primarily into the politics and economics of the United States and to some extent his model suffers from ethnocentrism. A critic of Dahl felt that the pluralist model could be likened to the balancing trick of a surf-rider, with a pretty damsel perched on his shoulders, while floating on the surging waves of the Miami beach. A skilful administrator does the same while dealing with the competing pressures of numerous interest groups in a pluralist democracy such as the United States.

General Systems Theory of David Easton

The behavioural theory of Easton is called the *General Systems Analysis* of politics. It is general in two senses. First, he claims that it is capable of explaining the behaviour of national and international political systems and can also be used for comparing different political systems. The same categories could be applied to all the sub-fields of political science. Secondly, an important task of political science is the analysis of the *general problems* common to all political systems. These problems relate primarily to the question of system persistence over a long period of time. While Almond, Coleman and Apter are concerned with the particular kinds of governments and *partial theory*, Easton is concerned with the problem of establishing criteria for identifying the important variables, which can help us in the investigation of all political systems. He is, therefore, concerned with the *general theory* of politics. (238 : 91).

David Easton also rejects the view that political analysis should primarily concern itself with the distribution of power and influence in society. Though he agrees that authoritative allocation of values is the distinguishing characteristic of a political system, yet this description merely asserts the analytically unique quality of the political system in inquiring about its capacity for *survival*. Unlike Almond, Easton is very much concerned with the *conditions* of survival of political systems. He is also critical of the structural-functional approach. He thinks that the concept of function lacks precision and cannot be applied empirically to yield causal relationships. He also criticized the equilibrium model of the functionalists on the ground that they assumed that the empirical system was characterized by a condition of equilibrium. Thus a conceptual device was transformed into a substantive fact. He disagreed with Parsons that political theory could be analyzed in terms of a general theory of social institutions. He emphasized that political life was quite autonomous and asserted the independence of political science as a discipline.

The systems analysis which Easton has developed is not based on the models borrowed from other social sciences such as anthropology, psychology, sociology or economics. His construction of an input-output framework only superficially resembles that of economic analysis. Instead, he has been influenced by the new 'communications services' and, therefore, his model is closer to the 'communications model' or Karl Deutsch. The idea that a political system has feed-back mechanisms which are capable of transmitting information of a positive or negative kind to the system is common to the analysis of David Easton and Karl Deutsch. The feedbacks provide information about the reaction to decisions which have emerged within the system. For Almond, however, changes within the system will finally restore the *original* equilibrium state. For Easton and Deutsch, a particular state of equilibrium can change though the political system still retains its identify as the same political system. Easton claims that his analysis is dynamic rather than static and the concept of system persistence permits gradual structural changes unless they lead to complete disintegration of the rule-making mechanisms.

Easton asserts that there are two types of stresses to which the political system may be subjected and the system is capable of different types of references by which the stresses can be coped with. The stresses mentioned by him are *demand stress* and *support stress*. Demand stress may result from the failure of the existing system to deal effectively with the information feedback from its original output. It may also result from the system's inability to cope with certain demands made upon it. The situation is called 'demand-input-overload'. The overload may be due to the nature or content of the demands or simply due to a large inflow of demands at a particular occasion. Support stress arises when the system suffers an erosion or withdrawal of the support given to it by the members of the system. It may result from internal group conflicts of the system or from some structural failure of the system itself due to its defective institutional arrangements. Support stress may arise when the system does not produce outputs in response to demands made upon it or produces outputs which are regarded unsatisfactory by its members.

According to Easton, the main structures or objects of support of the political systems are : the *authorities*, the *regime* and the *political community*. As he puts it : "Authorities typically come and go, regimes or constitutional orders may change. In both cases, the community may remain quite stable... But political communities are capable of changing. This occurs at moments when the membership undergoes some internal subdivision indicating that whole groups have withdrawn their support from the pre-existing division of political labour." (263 : 84).

It is the authorities who have to process the inputs from the internal and external environment into outputs. They also have to cope with the information in the form of new demands and supports, which is the outcome of original outputs, i.e., decisions and actions. The political system consists of various other sub-systems, such as mediating groups which are involved in the conversion process i.e. in coping with stresses before they reach the authorities. According to David Easton, many conflicting demands over scarce values will be settled among groups and individuals themselves. The subsystems consist of the activities of partial associations in society called by Easton as parapolitical systems like the activities of trade unions, churches, business groups, etc. which relate to the allocation of scarce resources.

Almond's Structural-Functional Analysis

Structural functional theory is a form of *systemic analysis* which looks at political systems as coherent wholes which influence and are influenced by their environments. A political system is held together by the presence of legitimate force throughout the system. It has three characteristics : comprehensiveness, inter-dependence and existence of boundaries. The interactions which take place within a system are not between persons but between the roles which the individuals adopt. Lastly, the political system is an open system and is involved in communication with systems beyond its own boundaries. (238 : 93).

The basic assumptions of this analysis are that the political system consists of certain structures which can be identified and the parts of these structures perform functions which acquire meaning in relation to the working of the system. The constituent parts of the system are interdependent in the functional sense and the system has a tendency towards *equilibrium.* In a general sense, equilibrium exists if within a system no variable changes its position or relation with other variables. It implies a condition of harmony, stability or balance.

According to Almond, there are two basic sets of functions which are being performed in every political system : *input* and *output* functions. The political system is made up of a set of roles, structures and sub-systems. Their interactions are influenced by the psychological motivations of the political actors. The process can be seen as consisting of either inputs from the environment or from within the political process itself, or the conversion of these inputs within the system into outputs to the environment. In course of time the outputs may cause changes in the environment which may give rise to new demands on the system or changes in the system itself. The idea of feedback enables the systems theorist to take account of the dysfunctional factors in the political life which lead to political development and change.

Almond mentions four input functions, which are : (1) political socialization and recruitment, (2) interest articulation, (3) interest aggregation and

(4) political communication. He refers to three output functions which are : (1) rule-making, (2) rule application and (3) rule adjudication. Based on the western experience, input functions are seen as being performed by non-governmental structures of the political system, the society and the general environment : by family, school, interest groups, political parties, mass media and so on. Output functions are predominantly governmental : ministers, civil servants, legislators, judges and so on. Two of the input functions — political socialization and political communication are concerned with political values and constitute the psychological dimension of the political system. Further, the input-output analysis shifts the focus from institutional analysis of traditional political science to the analysis of functions and roles of both governmental and non-governmental structures. (263 : 85).

Political systems can be compared with reference to the degree of specialization of their political structures. In modern political systems, these structures are specialized, political roles are differentiated and functions are specific., This is just an abstract model of modernity. As Almond admits, even developed systems are dual in their political culture which includes both traditional and modern elements. Multifunctional structures and undefined boundaries can also be found in the modern systems which co-exist with specialized structures of interest articulation, interest aggregation and political communication. All political systems exist in societies which are in some degree culturally mixed. Almond's developmental model helps us in distinguishing the extent of the 'mix', indicating the point when a traditional system becomes transitional and the transitional system may be characterized as modern.

Systems operate at different levels of functioning. The theory of the political system consists of a framework which explains the relations among these different levels of functioning such as capabilities, conversion functions, system-maintenance and adaptation functions. The theory of political development deals with those transactions between the political system and its environment which produce changes in general systemic performance. The mechanisms through which demands from various groups are converted into decisions and policies of governmental structures constitute the conversion process. The system's capabilities are measured by the extent to which it can cope with these demands effectively. The socialization and recruitment functions aim at the maintenance of the system. Almond identifies three sources of political change : the elites within the political system itself, social groups in the environment, and other political systems.

Criticizing the abstract nature of the systemic analysis of Easton, Eugene Meehan observes : "Easton does not think of a theory in terms of explanation but in terms of the creation of conceptual frameworks. The result is a highly abstract structure that is logically suspect, conceptually fuzzy and empirically almost useless. Easton's 'political system' turns out to be an abstraction whose relation to empirical politics is virtually impossible to establish." (238 : 95).

This criticism is equally valid as regards the structural-functional model of Almond and other exponents of this model. Highlighting the defects of the general systems theory and the structural-functional analysis, S.P. Verma says : "Like the general systems theory, structural-functionalism is also ill-equipped for the study of the phenomena of power and influence. It provides relatively little scope for the discussion of goals and objectives, and is equally inadequate for policy studies. One has also to admit that structural-functionalism is especially a static system of analysis. One might mention in this connection that it has certain ideological implications. It seems to justify the status quo. It is also somewhat mechanistic in its approach. It is difficult to say whether it is more due to the way in which it has been applied or to the approach itself, but there is no denying the fact that the nature of the approach makes it relatively easy for it to creep into conservative patterns. A conservative bias is an inbuilt feature of functionalism from which the systems analysis has been adapted in political science." (263 : 86-87).

Some critics believe that the functional approach has been cultivated by western social scientists as an alternative to Marxist approach. W.G. Rumiman says : "Functionalism as a theory is not a set of causal laws, but an interpretation which places a great deal of emphasis on the normative elements of social systems just as Marxism places a prior emphasis and value on the essential conflicts that it points in such systems...Functionalism can indeed be interpreted as a conscious alternative to Marxism. Some of its writers have wanted to interpret it as a political ideology conditioned by the structure of American capitalism." (238 : 96).

The ideological elements are equally present in the political analyses of other behavioural writers. Whether it is the distributive analysis of Harold Lasswell or the pluralist-democratic approach of Robert Dahl, its main objective has always been to validate the assumptions of the dominant ideology of a liberal capitalist society. The behaviouralists think otherwise : "In general the political behaviour approach has been catholic and eclectic. Although the ultimate objective of some of its practitioners may be the construction of 'systemic theory', it has remained eminently pragmatic in application. Whether this has been a handicap or not is a matter of individual judgment." (262 : 4). However, the behavioural approach was criticized by some behaviouralists later, like Easton, who then pleaded for a new Post-Behavioural approach.

CHAPTER 39

POST-BEHAVIOURALISM

Basic Assumptions of Behavioural Paradigm

As an academic discipline, political science after the second world war experienced a major methodological and thematic shift in the form of behaviouralism. Robert Dahl calls it a successful protest against the formalism and historicism of traditional political theory. Behaviouralism has been accompanied by an increasingly complex technology of research and a self conscious effort to elevate one component of traditional political theory, the empirical part, to the position of primary importance.

David Easton, the foremost leader of the systemic school, laid the foundations of the behavioural movement in contemporary political science by publishing *The Political System* in 1953. He criticized the historicist writings of Dunning, Sabine and McIlwain because they thought of political ideas as mere consequences of historical conditions. For them, political theory was a mere epiphenomenon with no effects or influence on social or political reality. Their approach was still similar to that of the majority of political theorists who assume that "aside from historical description, their major task in moral matters is to clarify, like extreme semanticists, and not to reconstruct, like imaginative moral architects:". (238 : 127). Easton's objective was to put an end to political theory as a sterile exercise in intellectual theory and history.

Barbara Smith believes that behaviouralism is still considered as mainstream political science. In *Political Research Methods*, she mentions six major tenets of behaviouralism. The first tenet according to her view is that political science can eventually more closely approximate a science capable of prediction and explanation. Thus the goal of political science is the construction of systematic, empirical theory. It assumes that human behaviour is not without a pattern and can be explained in terms of certain regularities. Political scientists should search out these regularities and the variables associated with them. It emphasizes explanation rather than pure description.

The second tenet according to her view is that research in political science should be theory-oriented and there should be a close interplay between theory and empirical data. Narrow empiricism and haphazard collection of datas will not help us in the development of a broad, systematic general theory. We must move beyond merely reporting empirical facts and place them in a larger explanatory context. Theory devoid of empirical substantiation is undesirable and empirical findings not connected with a broader explanatory scheme are likely to be trivial.

Thirdly, Barbara Smith states that questions of fact are kept by the behaviouralists analytically separate from questions of value. She observes :

"The argument underlying this point is that there is no way of scientifically establishing the truth or falsity of statements of value, whereas there are methods of tentatively establishing the truth-value of statements of fact. Understanding cannot be advanced by these different kinds of questions and the modes of explanation appropriate to each." (263 : 89).

The fourth tenet of behaviouralism is that there is an essential unity among the various social sciences and that they could benefit by working together in an interdisciplinary manner. Interdisciplinary work does contribute enormously to political science. Many important problems are basically interdisciplinary in nature and implication. Many current social problems that concern political scientists cannot be divorced from their economic, social and psychological context.

The fifth tenet of behaviouralism according to her is that political scientists should become more self-conscious, precise and sophisticated in their methods. Political scientists should emulate the natural sciences by making use of precise research methodology. To a large extent, methods influence conclusions. As she puts it : "It is important therefore that political scientists make every effort to be aware of and to discount or outline their own value preferences and biases in planning, executing and analysing research. Sophisticated contemporary research methods help social scientists check their biases at various stages of research design. A thorough understanding of methodological problems will result in a more reliable, valid and generalizable results." (238 : 129).

The sixth tenet of behaviouralism according to her view is that analysis should focus on individual and/or group behaviour. Behaviouralists argue that the reduction of individual or group behaviour to institutional prescription results in unrealistic and inadequate explanations. Thus she concludes that the behavioural revolution represents a basic redefinition of political science as a discipline in terms of objectives, methods and scope. Her conclusions regarding behavioural political science can be summarized as follows :

1. *Theory and data* :" More inductive theory. Data are used for testing hypothesis. Theory and data are interdependent.

2. *Generalization and the unique case* : Regularities of behaviour can be found and expressed in generalizations which are probability statements.

3. *Facts and values* : Facts and values should be kept analytically distinct. Scientists must control for personal biases of observer.

4. *Method and data* : Methods are self-conscious, explicit and quantitative. Use of statistical methods is recommended.

5. *Pure and applied research* : Knowledge of behaviour is the main goal. Generalizations are partial, incomplete and tentative. There are dangers of partial understanding.

6. *Political Science and other academic fields* : Influence of psychology, biology, statistics and econometrics is highlighted. (263 : 90).

Earlier Critics of Behaviouralism

Post-behavioural critics of behaviouralism were preceded by some earlier critics who were generally political philosophers desiring inspiration from the classical tradition or institutionalists embedded in the historical-legal tradition of analysis. Bernard Crick in *The American Science of Politics* offered a critique of behaviouralism which in some ways was similar to David Easton's self-criticism when he renounced his own behaviouralist antecedents to initiate the 'post-behavioural revolution' in political science.

Bernarc Crick argued that units of analysis in political science are not identical to those of natural science. Human beings are unique because they possess self-consciousness and capacity for changing and planning their behaviour on the basis of their experiences and expectations. Political behaviour is not amenable to experimental inquiry because it is unique and non-recurring. Hence, the behaviouralist's quest for regularities is fruitless.

As human behaviour is too complex involving too many variables and contingencies, behavioural political science cannot adequately deal with all the complexities and contingencies of individual and group behaviour in politics. It is therefore, impossible to develop a political science which can match the exactness of a natural science.

Charlesworth points out that quantification and rigorous analysis go against the nature of political science. The discipline of political science does not possess precise concepts and required metrics. The problems that can be quantified easily are trivial and the significant ones cannot be quantified. Behaviouralists can use mathematical and statistical tools only in the study of insignificant questions. Eugene Meehan argues that values, emotions and biases cannot be eliminated from social science inquiry because social scientists cannot treat their subject-matter dispassionately and objectively. Behavioural political science also contains biases of the individual writer. Sometimes the biases are implicit and therefore not easily visible to a superficial reader.

Malcolm B. Parsons, however, says that the behaviouralists and their opponents have adopted extreme positions on the nature of the scientific methods : "It is possible to define science and scientific inquiry so narrowly that only a few special areas in the physical sciences could qualify. On the other hand, it is possible to establish such broad meanings that almost any systematic accumulating of information could be so designated. When it is not clear what claims are being made for or against science, there is an artificiality about debate. In recent years philosophers of science have persuasively stated the case for a view of science and scientific methods that falls between the above extremes." (238 : 130)

Lasswell's Advocacy of Policy Science

Harold Lasswell was one of the first to urge the behaviouralist approach in the study of politics and was a pioneer in political psychology. His early arguments regarding the future of political science, which should now go beyond the behavioural stage, were stated by him in *The Policy Sciences : Recent Developments in Scope and Method* as early as 1951. At that time, the behaviouralist movement was in its infancy and so Lasswell's arguments for initiating a post-behavioural phase did not find a receptive audience. Lasswell declared that the battle for the scientific method was won and political science must now turn to investigation of significant problems. He urged political scientists to choose new areas of inquiry and new problems according to their relevance for all and their goal values. This showed Lasswell's insight in pointing towards the coming issues of the post-behavioural period.

As Barbara Smith suggests in her comments, Lasswell was not arguing that personal value preferences and relevances should become substitutes for scientific objectivity. On the contrary, he clearly affirmed : "The place for non-objectivity is in deciding what ultimate goals are to be implemented. Once this choice is made, the scholar proceeds with maximum objectivity and uses all available methods." (263 : 92). Lasswell made no attempt to hide his value preferences. He wanted that American political science should be directed towards providing the knowledge needed to improve the working of its democratic system. He raised the important question : Knowledge for what? The scientific method must demonstrate its utility through its links with the human environment in which it is applied. Recognizing this, Lasswell suggested that political science ought to ask fundamental questions directly relevant to social needs and governmental policies.

Although some political scientists took up Harold Lasswell's challenge by moving towards a more policy-oriented study of politics, the problems indicated by him did not generally become the recognized concerns of the scholars of the discipline until the mid-1960's. Robert Dahl's essay *"The Behavioural Approach to Political Science : Epitaph for a Monument to a Successful Protest"* was published in 1961. Dahl's critical overtones in the essay created a mild stir among the behaviouralists and prepared the intellectual climate for coming post-behavioural orientation in American political science.

The events of the 1960s convinced a number of American political scientists of the urgency of Lasswell's early appeal which was now reinforced by Robert Dahl's 'epitaph' of behaviouralism. Besides, several compelling issues such as the civil rights movement, racial riots in a number of American cities, a series of assassinations of major American political leaders, popular opposition to the American interventionist war in Vietnam and the student revolt in major American university campuses, compelled many scholars of the discipline to raise basic questions about the relevance of their work, the adequacy of their methods and the quality of their scholarship in terms of their general responsibility to the community.

Easton on the Post-Behavioural Revolution

As David Easton admits, American political science had never been united in its acceptance of the theoretical and technical aspects of behaviouralism. Dissatisfaction was always there especially among the traditionalists who would reject the feasibility of ever creating a science of politics. In the 1960s, however, "new and louder rumblings of discontent" began to be heard. The voices of protest did not demand to "turn the clock back to traditional intuition and non-methodology." They saw deficiencies in behaviouralism but wanted to improve the quality of research by building upon the existing behavioural foundations. Easton took note of these criticisms in the Address to the Annual Meeting of the American Political Science Association held in New York in September 1969. He heralded *The New Revolution in Political Science* which became the testament of the post-behavioural critics of behaviouralism.

David Easton observed : "Some may object to characterizing this new movement as a revolution and argue that if anything it is only a shift in emphasis. Whether it in fact penetrates far more deeply than a change in emphasis must be left to history to decide. It does seem to be encouraging profound changes in the character of the discipline, and this is all I would imply in labelling it a revolution. But to avoid arguments about degree, it would be equally acceptable to speak of the *post-behavioural reformation*. The only important point for us to recognise is that as we move into the 1970s new and powerful winds of change are sweeping through our discipline." (195 : xii)

Just as behaviouralism once implied discontent with traditional theorization, so post-behaviouralism is a sign of increasing frustration with the products of behavioural research. While the behaviouralists were deeply concerned with the problematic of method, the post-behaviouralists are turning towards "unsettling questions" about the subject-matter or research and the utility of political knowledge. Easton commented in a mood of disappointment : "There can be little doubt that political science as an enterprise has failed to anticipate the crises that are upon us. One index of this is perhaps that in the decade from 1958 to 1968, *The American Political Science Review* published only three articles on the urban crises; four on racial conflicts, one on poverty, two on civil disobedience; and two on violence in the United States." (238 : 133).

These figures are quite startling and show the bias of the most prestigious journal in the discipline of political science in America. This neglect of very relevant and significant subjects in behavioural research led to the post-behavioural revolution described above. The post-behavioural developments, according to David Easton, are not reactionary but rather future-oriented. It does not seek a return to either classicism or traditionalism and has no intention to undo the positive gains of the behavioural revolution.

Post-behaviouralism is both an intellectual tendency as well as a movement supported by a group of people. As a movement it has some of the chaotic and prickly qualities that the behavioural movement itself possessed initially. As a tendency, it cannot be associated with any particular ideology. Its advocates include some well-known conservative scholars as well as a group of politically active left-wing radicals.

Moreover, post-behaviouralists also lack any firm methodological commitments. Some of them are dedicated classicists but many others are rigorous scientists and empiricists. Neither does post-behaviouralism appeal to any one age group alone. Its adherents include all the generations from young graduate students to older members of the profession. This amazing variety – ideological, methodological, and generational – is motivated by a deep desire to make the discipline more 'relevant' and action-oriented.

Main Assumptions of Post-behaviouralism

Despite its diffuse character, David Boston felt bold enough to identify the main characteristics of the post-behavioural movement. He described them as a Credo of Relevance. The first and foremost tenet of post-behaviouralism is : "Substance must precede technique. If one *must* be sacrificed for the other – and this need not always be so – it is more important to be relevant and meaningful for contemporary urgent social problems than to be sophisticated in the tools of investigation. For the aphorism of science that it is better to be wrong than vague, post-behaviouralism would substitute a new dictum, that it is better to be vague than non-relevantly precise." (195 : 325).

But the most important conclusion of David Easton's address on the post-behavioural revolution was his support to political activism by the academic profession. If the intellectual has the duty to implement his knowledge, as he put it, then "those organizations composed of intellectuals – the professional associations – and the universities themselves, cannot stand apart from the struggles of the day. Politicization of the professions is inescapable as well as desirable." (195 : 327). This was the period when the American youth was in revolt and the humanist writings of young Marx had created a stir in the university campuses and the Black people of America were struggling for their civil and political freedoms.

Other points of Easton's post-behavioural credo are stated as follows : (1) Behavioural science conceals an ideology of empirical conservatism. It unwittingly purveys an ideology of social conservatism tempered by modest incremental changes. (2) Behaviouralism has lost touch with reality. The task of post-behaviouralism is to help political science reach out to the real needs of mankind in a time of crisis. (3) Post-behaviouralism cannot be morally neutral and is aware of the value premises on which it stands and the alternative for which this knowledge could be used. (4) The historical role of intellectuals has been and must be to protect the humane values of civilization. They should abandon their special privileges and engage in social criticism. (5) To know is to bear the responsibility for acting and to act is to engage in reshaping society. We need an action science reflecting the contemporary conflict in society. (195-326).

As David Easton clarified no single post-behaviouralist could be expected to agree with all the assumptions of his post-behavioural testament or the credo of relevance as he called it. It was only "a distillation of the maximal image", or a "Weberian ideal type of the challenge to behaviouralism". The "Credo of Relevance" was also a document representing self-criticism by an ex-behavourialist. (238 : 135). The heart of behaviouralism, Easton said, was abstraction and analysis which concealed the brute realities of politics. The task of post-behaviouralism was to break these barriers of silence that behavioural language and style had created. The task of political scientists now was to facilitate this transformation.

Continuities in Political Analysis

As a matter of fact, many post-behaviouralists are just chastened behaviouralists, who were so overwhelmed by great changes taking place in the social and political environment that there was no escape for them from a limited rejection and modification of the dogmatic empiricism which had circumscribed their political vision and confined their research to small and isolated social milieu. This was necessary for the renewal of their credibility as political theorists. David Easton's address to the American Political Science Association mentioned various tenets put forth by the contemporary critics of behaviouralism. In practice, only the first point was broadly appreciated where Easton had asked for greater emphasis on the content and comparably less stress on the technique.

The last point regarding the politicization of the profession was not acceptable to Easton personally and did not find favour with the American academicians generally. Only a few left-wing intellectuals supported it due to the impact of the New Left resurgence during the late 1960s and forgotten thereafter. The second point regarding the ideological basis of empirical research was not admitted by many who still called themselves post-behaviouralists. The only other point about which some post-behaviouralists were enthusiastic as well as vocal was the re-introduction of 'values' in social science research and treorization.

Thus David Easton's tenets taken together required a substantial revaluation of current images of what political scientists were doing and ought to do, what research priorities should be set, and what aspects should be stressed. They advocated a need for the restructuring of much present inquiry and also new directions in professional competence. They also raised a number of different questions regarding professional morality, the relationship between science and man, freedom of research and the relation between the intellectuals and the rulers.

In practice, there was no visible change in the character and quality of American political science after the so-called post-behavioural revolution. There were far greater continuities than discontinuities between the political analysis of the behaviouralists and that of the post-behaviouralists.

As Barbara Smith correctly points out, the plea of the post-behaviouralists for a shift in scope and objectives of political science need not be taken as a call for change in scientific method in the broad sense. She considers post-behavioural criticism of the limited scope and objectives of behavioural political science as an attack on *de facto* rather than inherent limitations of political inquiry posed by the scientific method. Moreover, such pleas for shift in scope and objectives are not confined to political science.

She observes : "The interdisciplinary nature of the post-behavioural ranks is understandable : many of the most urgent social, economic, ecological, and political problems do not fit neatly into one field of inquiry. For this reason Lasswell, Easton and others suggest the need for broad interdisciplinary work. Easton, in particular, sees systems analysis as an appropriate analytic framework for integrated, interdisciplinary work." (238 : 136). But this emphasis on the inter-disciplinary focus or the analytical scheme of systems does not represent something novel as both Lasswell and Easton had emphasized these points earlier also during the behaviouralist phase.

Like political science, sociology has also been influenced by the post behavioural credo. As Herbest Gams points out : "Judging by all the anthologies on poverty that have been announced, sociologists seem to be mainly concerned with informing their students about the existence and causes of poverty. I see a much more urgent concern " research to eliminate poverty. A particularly great need is policy-oriented research, for example studies that evaluate current anti-poverty efforts and propose or test alternative solutions," (263 :98)

Similarly, a mood of questioning is growing among the psychologists too. In his essay, Psychology Can Now Kick the Science Habit, David Bakan complains that many psychologists fail to see that their discipline is not an autonomous field of inquiry and that they can stultify themselves by adhering to an outdated model of science. He says : "They are often unaware of the social and historical forces that have shaped psychology–unaware specially of the ways in which the development of the university, and the natural science within it, have shaped their attitudes and interests. This lack of awareness has handicapped the field internally, in its emergence as an authentic discipline, and externally, in its usefulness to society. (238 : 137).

David Bakan's explicit conclusion is that social science must commit itself to making a better world. He feels that the major function of social science should be to make man aware of the forces that operate on him. He observes : "We made it to the moon, but did less to improve the earth.....Military research produced defoliants, napalm and poison gases but did not end the conflict in Viet Nam. Indeed, the association between the military and science meant that as the prestige of one fell, so did not that of the other. By early 1970, The reaction against science was considerable." (263 : 99). David Bakan, however, does not suggest that we should abandon 'Science'. He, like many after post-behavioural critics of 'scientism', argues for a more relevant science with a stress on methods most suitable to resolution of current social conflicts and fulfilment of urgent human aspirations.

Barbara Smith feels that two points in the post-behavioural credo deserve detailed scrutiny. The first concerns the demands of scientific method in the context of justification. The second pertains the place of values in scientific research under conditions of limited responsibility for the acquisition and application of knowledge. Easton has suggested that too rigid adherence to the tenets of empirical method explains the failure of behavioural science to meet the need for action oriented, meaningful social inquiry. Empirical research is a time-consuming process showing meagre results in the end. Post-behavioralists argue that time is running out making temporal frames of reserved judgment inadequate and useless. She observes : "if contemporary social scientists continue to retreat into inaction through reference to the scientific canon of reserved judgment, there may be no world to judge in decades ahead, Our problems simply may outrun our ability to deal with them." (238 : 138).

Alvin Toffler in *Future Shock* argued that the meanings of time and space have changed, and research techniques and objectives must consider this if the human race is to survive in a decent environment - indeed, if it is to survive at all. Today, the United States and Russia possess a nuclear arsenal which can destroy the whole of humanity. But social scientists have been blissfully oblivious of this extra-ordinary danger to human civilization and do not consider it a fit subject for their research or theorization.

Post-behaviouralists also affirm that political scientists should learn to recognize and explicate the value preferences which are implicit even in much of the behavioural research. The recognition that values are an immovable part of the research process is not new. Even Max Weber and Karl Mannheim, despite the general impression that they advocated value-free social science, had recognised the relevance of values in social inquiry. Even David Easton in *The Political System*, which he wrote in 1953, had stressed the role of values in social and political studies.

However, The current dichotomy between acquisition of knowledge, which is the responsibility of academics, and its application, which is the task of the political and economic elites, makes the problem of values somewhat complicated. Those who use 'scientific results' of a given piece of research, may fail to comprehend the value preferences of the researcher. For example, Philip Green in his work, *Deadly Logic : The Theory of Nuclear Deterrence*, argues that questionable value judgments characterize the application of game theory to problems of nuclear war and deterrence by the decision-makers in the U.S.A. and other countries which have developed nuclear arsenals. (263 : 100).

The Question of Paradign Displacement

Does the transmission from the behavioural to the post-behavioural phase in social science imply a scientific revolution involving displacement of one paradigm by another ? David Easton, the author of the post-behavioural credo, admitted : "It should be clear that the differences between *The Political System* and *The New Revolution in Political Science* do not lie in basic assumptions either about the utility of scientific method in political research or about the integrity of political science as a discipline. In both these essays I see modern behavioural science and its methodologically commitments as central to the growth of more reliable understanding of political systems." (195 : 376) In other words, the post-behaviouralists were not at all anxious to adopt a new paradigm replacing the older behavioural paradigm.

Thomas Kuhn in *The Structure of Scientific Revolution* had defined the paradigm as a universally recognized scientific achievement that for a time provides model problems and solutions to a community of practitioners. The history of science shows that there is one dominant theory which constitutes the dominant paradigm in each scientific domain. The dominant paradigm dominates for considerable periods providing the answer to the main problems but its assumptions also specify and determine its limitations.

A time comes when the limitations of these assumptions end the further growth of the theory. Theorists do not recognize this limitation and engage in theoretical exercises which are no more than puzzle solving. It is only when an alternative conceptual scheme emerges that the new theory will displace the old one and will become a dominant paradigm in a scientific revolution. A state of crisis demonstrates the inability of the existing paradigm to explain things, which results in its revolutionary overthrow by another paradigm.

This explanation largely fits the situation in the social sciences. However, the social relations of production do not have geographical, cultural or ethnic boundaries and the same is true of the general theory which arises from them. If it can be affirmed that there is a general theory reflecting the ideas of capitalism which legitimizes its existing, it must follow that within capitalism there is a single dominant paradigm. Institutionalism, behaviouralism and post-behaviouralism are conceptual adaptations within a single dominant paradigm which legitmizes the existence of capitalist society in America and other countries recognizing the bourgeois mode of social production. Thus the conceptual shift from behaviouralism to post-behaviouralism cannot be termed as an example of paradigmatic change. David Easton is therefore not justified in calling either behaviouralism or post-behaviouralism as a revolution in political theory.

CHAPTER 40

POLITICS OF THE MILLENNIUM

The Era of Democratization

With the decline and disintegration of Soviet-style socialist states, the world has entered into a new era of democratization. The French Revolution, which ushered into an age of democracy, revisited the countries of eastern and central Europe and like an avalanche swept off the dictatorships from their moorings. 1989 remains a remarkable year that foreshadows the politics of the new millennium. At the beginning of that year, communist parties ruled in eight countries : Poland, Czechoslovakia, East Germany, Hungary, Bulgaria, Romania, Yugoslavia and Albania. By 25th December 1989, when Romanian dictator Nicolae Ceausescu and his wife Elena were executed, communist leaders remained firmly in control of only Albania. With the defeat of the communist candidate in presidential elections in Slovenia in 1989, the various republics of Yugoslavia began to go their separate ways. All of them finally repudiated rule by the Yugoslav League of Communism. The year 1989, therefore, marked a qualitative change in the character of regimes and even reconfiguration in national boundaries.

It was often pointed out that it took Poland ten years of struggle to overthrow the communist regime; it took Hungary just ten months of anti-regime movement to topple it; but it took Czechoslovakia only ten days of agitation to achieve their so called velvet revolution. If Poland had to struggle longer to end communist rule, it was precisely their long-drown struggle, which facilitated the struggles of other East European peoples and they could thus achieve quicker successes. The other revolutions may not have occurred at all, if the Poles had not demonstrated the vulnerability of their regime. Moreover, the Solidarity movement of Catholic trade unions showed how deep-rooted popular discount was against the policies of their communist rulers. It also convinced the Soviet leadership, which controlled the communist parties of Eastern Europe, how alienated these parties had become from their own people. Without Solidarity, there would probably have been no *glasnonst, no perestroika* and no Gorbachev in The Soviet Union. Gorbachev wanted democracy without renouncing the basic principles of socialism but inadvertently brought about the disintegration of the Soviet Union and with it a restoration of capitalism in the Russian federation and other seceding republics of the former U.S.S.R.

Gorbachev in his book *Perestroika* said, " Europe from the Atlantic to the Urals is a cultural-historical entity united by the common heritage of the Renaissance and Enlightenment... Europe's historic chance and its future lie in peaceful cooperation." (pp.190,197). Using the General Secretary's power to the full, Gorbachev succeeded in getting his proposals passed by the Supreme Soviet in 1989 and 1990. Free elections were held for the first time for soviets at the centre and in the regions. All the regimes making up the communist bloc collapsed and gave way to multi-party parliamentary regimes in actually bloodless popular revolutions. Divided Germany was allowed reunite and even to join NATO. The newly elected governments of various republics making up the Soviet state were one by one declaring their sovereignty within the union. All of this provided ample evidence that between 1989 and 1990 Communist Party rule was breaking down throughout the Soviet Union and Eastern Europe. On 25th December, 1999, the USSR ceased to exist and Boris Yeltsin became the President of the new, democratic Russian Federation.

When the elections were held, parties opposed to Yeltsin captured about 40 percent of the seats. At the same time, Yeltsin's draft constitution was approved by the voters. Russia now had a new constitutional structure. The Constitution established a dominant presidency. Yeltsin called it a 'presidential republic'. In its continuation of elements of presidentialism and parliamentarism, it resembles that of the Fifth French Republic. In contrast to most parliamentary systems, in Russia the make-up of the government is not directly determined by the party composition of the parliament . The relationship between the party forces in the Duma and the political balance of the government can be very loose. The president can change his Prime Ministers as often as he likes and impose his choice on an unwilling Duma by threatening its dissolution.

President Yeltsin has not identified himself with any party or created a party organization of his own. This refusal means that pro-reform forces continue to splinter and divide among multiple personal followings. In the Russian Presidential election of 1992, Yeltsin received 35.28 percent votes in the first round and 53.83 per cent votes in the second round. Zyuganov, the Communist party candidate, received 32.03 per cent votes in the first round and 40.31 per cent votes in the second round. This shows that the communists remain a strong force in the Russian federation even after democratization. They also constitute the largest single party in the Duma, the lower house of the Russianm Federation. A similar situation has persisted in most of the former communist regimes in Eastern Europe such as Poland and Hungary, where they have entered into coalition governments with other like-minded parties. However, they have fully accepted the new democratic frame-work alongwith certain market-oriented reforms.

The wave of democratization has also swept large parts of the third world as well. Military regimes used to be the dominant features of Latin America for a long time. Argentina, Brazil and ultimately even Chile succumbed to military dictatorships. The whole of Latin America has now reestablished its institutions of democratic governance. The same can be said about Africa and Asia, where constitutional regimes created by first leaders of national independence were overthrown by military dictators, We find a revival of democracy in many of these countries. The successful experiment in parliamentary democracy in India has convinced many third world elites that they can also practise democracy despite their economic underdevelopment.

Globalization and Liberalization

As we march into the new millennium, democratization in the political sphere is being accompanied by a new policy of globalization and liberalization in the economic sphere. China and India, the two largest countries of Asia and the World, had opted for state-directed and planned economies as well as for maximum self-reliance after their 'communist' and 'nationalist' revolutions respectively. China, despite its ideology, opted for market-oriented reforms and expansion of her trade with capitalist countries under Deng Xiaoping's leadership. India, despite her Nehrurian tradition of Fabion socialism, did the same during the last decade. Today the capitalist model of development had superseded the statist model of nation-building conceived by the nationalist elites a few decades earlier. At that time, the World Bank, The International Monetary Fund and Foreign Aid agencies were regarded as instruments of neo-colonialism.

However, the rise of economic tigers in East and South East Asia like South Korea, Taiwan, Singapore and Hong Kong apparently demonstrated the superiority of the free market model over the traditional, statist model. The fall of command economies in the communist countries themselves discredited the statist, autarchic model of development all over the third world. Taking advantage of financial imbalances, the World Bank and the IMF imposed severe conditions on the third world debtor governments to bring about rapid market-oriented reforms in their economies. Globalization and liberalization became the running theme of their advice which fell on receptive ears of the many third world statesmen and political leaders.

The World Trade Organisation is another important international agency to coordinate the policies of various nations in the direction of closer trade relations which has repercussions for their domestic economic arrangements as well. The W.T.O. insists that its members open up their economies fully for capital investments from outside and carry out market-oriented reforms as quickly as possible. 'Globalize or perish' is the motto of the new generation of economic reformers as well as the finance ministers and prime ministers. Shock therapies are being applied in one country after another to remould the contours of their economy in the capitalistic direction. In Russia it brought the GNP down to mere 53% of what it was before the free market reforms commenced. In China, on the other hand, the Communist Party itself is carrying out market- oriented changes in the economy without loosening its dictatorship though it has achieved one of the fastest rate of economic growth during the last two decades. China today has become the second largest economy from the standpoint of purchasing power parity (PPP) production in the world.

Democracy Against Hegemony

The March 28 issues of the *New York Times Magazine* contains an article on U.S. political strategy. Its content, according to Samir Amin, is summed up by an eloquent image that is spread over a page of the publication : a boxing glove in the colours of the American flag plus the following caption : "what the world needs now–for globalization to work, America can't be afraid to act like the almighty superpower that it is." The reason for this strong threat is stated in these words :

"The hidden hand of the market will never work without a hidden fist. MacDonalds cannot flourish without McDonnell Douglas, the designer of the F-15. And the hidden fist that keeps the world safe for Silicon Valley's technologies is called the US Army, Air Force, Navy and Marine Corps." The writer of these provocative words is Madelline Albright's adviser, Thomas Friedeman.

This is very different from the discourse spouted by mainstream economists on the selfregulating market as a guarantee of peace and prosperity. The American ruling class knows that economic issues are deeply political and that it is relations of power- that economic issues are deeply political and that it is relations of power – military including force that command the market. There will be no 'global market' without an American empire, as these ideologues affirm, because the above mentioned article is just one among the several hundred. The brutal frankness is possible because the government's strategic objective can never be a subject of debate in the selfcensored American media. More curious is the silence of the European powers on the other side of the Atlantic who never question the basic assumptions of Washington's global hegemony in the name of defending democracy and human rights. There can be no question of human rights and self-determination as long as the iron fist of the United States continues to enforce its economic preponderance.

America knows that, without its military hegemony, it cannot force the world to finance its savings deficit, which is the condition for the artificial maintenance of its economic position. The instrument of choice in the imposition of this hegemony is therefore military, as the highest U.S. authorities always insist. The hegemony guarantees that America's allies will obey its commands without raising any basic objections, some mercantile disputes notwithstanding. The weapon against America's global strategy is a process of globalization which should be at once democratic, at least potentially, multipolar and the outcome of free negotiations. The autonomy that this process allows is the only means of correctly resolving fundamental social problems, which differ due to the unequal development of regions. It is by the same token the condition for democracy to take root seriously, since it gives a better chance to demilitarisation, stability and peace. In contrast, American hegemony, as an instrument of neo-liberalisation and enforced globalization, has so far only produced chaos, multiplication of conflicts and large-scale military intervention.

The principal tool in the service of America's chosen strategy for world hegemony in the name of globalization is NATO. Its *raison d'etre*, the Warsaw Pact of the Communist bloc, collapsed a decade earlier but it is not only surviving but even expanding by recruiting new members. Today NATO speaks in the name of the 'international community', thereby showing its contempt for the democratic principle enshrined in the United Nations for the conduct of international relations. In debates conducted in the USA on the global strategy, human rights and democracy are invoked when this is useful for the functioning of that very strategy. This explains the blinding cynicism and systematic use of double standards in American diplomacy.

There is no question of intervening in favour of democracy in Afghanistan or in the Gulf or where dictators have ruled for decades with the consent of the American ruling class. People's rights are sacred in certain cases such as Kosovo and East Timor today, perhaps Kashmir and Tibet tomorrow. They were not sacred in East Pakistan, Palestine, Turkish Kurdistan, Cyprus or Krajina. Even the terrible genocide of Rwanda did not generate America's concern. Earlier, the killings of four million peasants in Indonesia by pro-American dictator, Suharto, and similar killings in East Bengal by pro-American military dictator, Yahya Khan, never received even a few words of protest from Washington. Pinoche's Chile received the same indulgence from the USA and for the same reason. Modern technology has empowered the United States and the NATO to attack other nations like Saddam's Iraq or Milosovic's Yugoslavia without any fear of reprisals by offering pretexts that are easy to exploit.

But the total silence that meets other cases deprives the discourse of democracy and human rights of any credibility. This really renders great disservice to the cause of democracy and human freedom without which no economic process is possible where it is most urgent. The avowed goal of the US search for hegemony is to eliminate the existence of any rival states which resist Washington's orders. Alignment with the strategy of the USA and its subaltern NATO allies has dramatic results. The UN is about to succumb to the fate of the League of Nations. Fortunately, American society is not that of Nazi Germany, but for the rulers of America today like those of Hitler's Germany before them, force has been established as a supreme principle, to the complete detriment of international law. America today claims 'the right of intervention' in other people's affairs, disturbingly reminiscent of 19th century imperialism.

"The struggle for democracy will remain completely ineffective if it is accompanied by submission to American hegemonism. The struggle for democracy is indissociable from the fight against Washington's hegemony." (Samar Amin, *EPW*, May 8-14, 1999).

Fractured Societies and Fractured Histories

The post-colonial class system refers not to the weakening of the state and class relations. It signifies an attempt by the capital to reorganise the economy without the constraints of a nation-state. On the relations between international capital and the nation states, the global capital has created a political situation which resists the diktat of nation-state. While searching for ethnic identity and roots, the ideology of cultural nationalism has connected itself to this changing nature of global capital. The US official multi-culturalism, telecommunication revolution and large presence of Indian migrants in the US academia helped the dissemination of their recoded concepts of ethnic identity, communalism, family values (e.g. patriarchal control over women). The support to cultural nationalism by the Indian diaspora is phenomenal and this gives a new dimension to its linkage with transnational capital.

The upper and middle classes in India stand for globalization and neo-liberalism. The contradiction between the regional capital and pan-Indian, so distinct earlier, is no longer there. Both are equally eager now to collaborate with global capital. The lower classes, workers and dalits, are not permitted to interfere with the neo-liberal policies of the ruling class at the centre. Indian society has become even more fractured today because it denies the realities of its fractured history based on cleavages of caste, class and gender. What is true of India is true of most nations in the world. Third world countries, of course, cannot hide the conspicuous manifestations of class and gender oppression. The second world has reinvented class antagonisms and gender exploitation after abandoning socialism and recreating mafia capitalism. The first world, despite the affluence of the corporate rich has not done away with class inequalities, gender disparities and ethnic exploitation. Capitalism, and its offshoot, imperialism, have created fractured societies and factured histories at national and global levels.

Ralph Milihand says : "It is perfectly true that civil and political liberties in advanced capitalist regimes have been severely circumscribed by the economic, social and political framework in which they have existed; that they have often been infringed in practice and, particularly in times of crisis, even more drastically narrowed; that constitutional guarantees have not prevented the systematic discrimination and oppression of such minorities as the black people in the United States; that the liberties enjoyed by the citizens of metropolitan capitalist countries were more often than not conspicuous by their absence in the territories which succumbed to imperialist occupation;

and that, for all their democratic and liberal rhetoric, these regimes have shown themselves capable of massive crimes in the protection of sordid interests." (236 : 238). Globalization and neo-liberalism advocated by the upper and middle classes all over the world has created a new alignment of social forces at the global level – the alliance of the rich against the poor of all countries. World society at this historical conjuncture stands irretrievably fractured.

From Neo-liberalism to Neo-fascism

The latest shift in the dominant ideology of the countries as diverse as the United States and India is from some kind of new-liberalism to a particular version of neo-fascism. The United States under President Bush has embarked upon a policy of suppression of civil liberties and democratic rights in the name of fighting terrorism through the draconian Patriotic Act. He invaded two countries, namely, Afghanistan and Iraq arguing that he was doing so in order to crush Al-Qaedah terrorism. He falsely declared that Saddam was in possession of nuclear, chemical and biological weapons of mass destruction.

As Arundhati Roy says, the Indian polity is also in a process of basic transformation. Each time there is a socalled 'terrorist strike', the government assigns culpability with little or no investigation. Take the case of Godhra or the earlier December 13th attack on Parliament. The home ministry immediately announced that it was an ISI plot.

In Gujarat after 2002 state-assisted pogrom, 2000 Muslims were killed and 150,000 driven from their homes. 287 persons were arrested under POTA out of which 286 were Muslims and one was a Sikh. POTA courts are not open to public scrutiny.

In Jammu and Kashmir and many North-Eastern states, the Armed Forces Special Powers Act allows even junior army officers to use force or even kill on suspicion of disturbing public order. Recently, a young Manipuri woman, Manorama, was raped and killed by soldiers, inciting a state-wide public rebellion and mass protests. A few years ago, a J.N.U. students union president Chandra Shekhar and Shankar Guha of Chhattisgarh Mukti Morcha were similarly killed. These are only a few examples.

Meanwhile, economists advocating neo-liberalism inform us that the G.D.P. growth is phenomenal, Shops are overflowing with consumer goods, Government stores are also overflowing with food grain. Yet farmers, steeped in debt, are also committing suicide in hundreds in several states. Reports of starvation and mal-nutrition come from all over the country. Yet the Government allowed 63 million tonnes of grain to rot in its granaries, 12 million tonnes were exported at a subsidised price but the poor in India were denied any help.

Utsa Patnaik calculates that food-grain consumption in 1990s dropped in per capita terms from what it was during 1940s including during the Bengal famine when3 million people died. As Professor Amartya Sen rightly says, democracies don't take kindly to starvation deaths. They attract too much adverse publicity from the "free press". 47 per cent of India's children suffer from malnutrition and stunted growth.

The show-pieces of neo-liberalism in urban India–shops, restaurants, railway stations, airports, hospitals etc. advertise election promises–*India Shining, Feeling Good* etc. But you have to close your eyes and ears to the sickening crunch of the policeman's boot on someone's ribs, you have to raise your eyes from the squalor, the slums, the ragged broken people on the streets and seek a friendly TV monitor which will take you to the other beautiful world of privilege and comfort.

According to Arundhati Roy, the neo-liberalism of the rich has started a new kind of secessionist movement. We can call it New Secessionism : "It is an inversion of Old Secessionism... It is the kind of secession in which a small section of people become immensely wealthy by appropriating every thing—land, rivers, water, freedom, security, dignity, fundamental rights including the right to protest–from a large group of people. It is a vertical secession, not a horizontal, terristorial one...that separates India shining from India, India Pvt. Ltd. from India, the Public Enterprise." (*The Hindu*, 25 April, 2004, p.14).

It is the kind of secession, in which public infrastructure, productive public assets are sold to private corporations. This happended on a large scale in Russia and Eastern Europe, in several capitalist countries also and is now taking place in India as well. In India 700 million people live in rural areas. Their survival depends on access to natural resources. To sell them as stork to private companies will result in depriving the poor people from their livelihood and lead to their impoverishment on a barbaric scale. India Pvt. Ltd. is on its way to being owned by a few corportions and multinationals. The chief Executive Officers who run them are more powerful than cabinet ministers.

Today Corporate Globalisation needs an international confederation of corrupt, loyal and authoritarian regimes in poorer countries, to push through neo-liberal, unpopular reforms and to suppress mass protests. This is called "Creating Good Investment Climate". Elections imply a choice between political parties which are, more or less, equally committed to goals of neo-liberal capitalism and are equally prepared to use repressive powers to suppress democratic dissent. This leads to a kind of neo-Fascism.

When ManMohan singh, the then Finance Minister in Narsimha Rao government, was preparing India's markets for neo-liberalism, L.K. Advani was making his first Rath Yatra, fuelling communal passion and preparing us for neo-fascism. In 1992, the Babri Masjid was demolished leading to mass killings in several states. In 1993, the congress government of Maharashtra signed a power purchase agreement with Enron, which proved disastrous in the end. It kickstarted the era of Privatisation in India.

During the BJP rule from 1998 to 2004, the government was conducting an extraordinary, dual orchestra. While one arm was busy selling the nation's assets to capitalists, the other, to divert attention, was raising a mad chorus of cultural naionalism. Economically too the dual orchestra was a good working model. Privatisation generated enormous profits; a part of these was directed to the vast army of Hindutva forces – the RSS, the VHP, the Bajrang Dal and the myriad other trusts and charities which ran schools and hospitals.

Right now in India, we are facing the cross-currents of neo-liberal capitalism and communal neo-fascism. when a government openly supports a pogrom against members of a minority community in which 2000 people are killed, it is neo-fascism. When women of that community are publicy raped and burnt alive, it is again fascism. When 1,50,000 people are rendered homeless, ghettoised, and economically and socially boycotted, it is also fascism. When writers, scholars, painters and filmmakers who protest are abused, threatened and have their work burned, banned and destroyed, it is surely fascism.

Similarly, when mobs attack and burn archives of ancient historical documents, when every minor politician pretends that he is a professional medieval historian and archaelogist, when painstaking scholarship is rubbished using baseless populist assertion, it is also fascism. When murder, rape, arson and mob justice are condoned by the party in power and its pseudo-intellectuals as a proper response to a real or imaginary wrong committed in the past, it is certainly fascism. When the middle and affluent classes see this but seem disinterested and prefer to live thier own lives, this is also fascism. When the Prime Minister, who presided over all of this, was hailed as a statesman and visionary, we were really laying the foundations for full-blown fascism in our country.

The targets of the dual assault of neo-fascism and neo-liberalism are the poor. The space for non-violent civil disobedience has atrophied. we need to look up and urgently discuss strategies of resistance. We must remember that the Dandi March was not just a fine political drama. It was a direct assault on the economic power of British imperialism. We need to re-invent the strategy of civil disobedience.

Perhaps we need an elected shadow Parliament, outside the Lok Sabha which has lost its democratic ethos, as the apex of myriad, social movements of active resistance. We need to redefine the meaning of politics. Fearlessly and nonviolently we must disable the working parts of the machine that is consuming us. Only then, we can fight the twin evils of neo-liberalism and neo-fascism. Let us hope that such a grass-root movement does arise in the near future.

BIBLIOGRAPHY

1. Appadorai, A. *The Substance of Politics.* Madras, Oxford University Press.
2. Barker, Ernest. *Greek Political Theory: Plato and his Predecessors.* London, Methuen.
3. Barker, Ernest. *Political Thought in England: Spencer to Present Day* (*H.U.L.*). London, Oxford University Press.
4. Barnes, Leonard. *Future of Colonies.* London, Hogarth.
5. Bosanquet, B. *The Philosophical Theory of State.* London, Macmillan.
6. Brown, Ivor. *English Political Theory.* London, Methuen.
7. Bryce, Lord. *International Relations.* London, Macmillan.
8. Buell, R.L. *International Relations.* London, Pitman.
9. Burns, C.D. *Democracy* (*H.U.L.*). London, Oxford University Press.
10. Burns, C.D. *Political Ideas.* London, Oxford University Press.
11. Carty, P. *Economics : A Social Science.*
12. Crossman, R.H.S. *Government and the Governed : History of Political Ideas and Political Practice.* London, Christophers.
13. Davidson, W.L. *Political Thought in England: Bentham to Mill* (*H.U.L.*). London, Oxford University Press.
14. Dewey, J. *German Philosophy and Politics.*
15. Dicey, A.V. *Introduction to the Study of the Law of Constitution.* London, Macmillan.
16. [illegible]. *Modern French Legal Philosophy.*
17. Dunning, W.A. *History of Political Theories* (3 Vols.). New York, Macmillan.
18. Eldridge. *The New Citizenship.*
19. Elliot. *Lectures at Harvard.*
20. Finer, H. *Theory and Practice of Modern Government.* London, M thuen.
21. Ford, J. *Social Problems and Social Policy.* London. Ginn.
22. Garner, J.W. *Introduction to Political Science.* London, American Book Supply Co. Ltd.
23. Garner, J.W. *Political Science and Government.*
24. Gettell, R.G. *Political Science.* London, Ginn.
25. Gettell, R.G. *History of Political Thought.* London, Allen & Unwin.
26. Gettell, R.G. *Problems of Political Evolution.*
27. Gierke, O. *Political Theories of the Middle Ages.* (Tr. Maitland). London, Cambridge University Press.
28. Gilchrist, R.N. *Principles of Political Science.* London, Longmans.
29. Green, T.H. *Lectures on the Principles of Political Obligation.* London, Longmans.
30. Harrison, Frederic. *On Jurisprudence and the Conflict of Law.*
31. Hallowell, J.H. *Main Currents in Modern Political Thought.*
32. Hayes, C.J.H. *Essays on Nationalism.* London, Macmillan.
33. Hearnshaw, F.J.C. *Democracy at the Crossways.*
34. Hegel, G.W.F. *Philosophy of History.*
35. Hobbes, Thomas (Ed. Pogson Smith). *Leviathan.* London, Oxford University Press.
36. Hocking, W.E. *The Philosophy of Law and of Rights.* New Haven, Yale University Press.

37. HOCKING, W.E. *Lectures at Harvard.*

38. HOLLAND, T.E. *Elements of Jurisprudence.* London, Oxford University Press.

39. JENKS, EDWARD. *The State and the Nation.*

40. JOAD, C.E.M. *Liberty Today (Thinker's Library).* London, Watts.

41. JOAD, C.E.M. *Modern Political Theory.* London, Oxford University Press.

42. JONES, SIR HENRY. *Idealism as a Practical Creed.*

43. JOSEPH, BERNARD. *Nationality.* London, Allen & Unwin.

44. KRABBE. *Modern Ideal of State.*

45. KRANENBURG, R. *Political Theory.* London, Oxford University Press.

46. LAHIRI & BANERJEE. *An Introduction to the Principles of Civics.*

47. LASKI, H.J. *A Grammar of Politics.* London, Allen & Unwin.

48. LASKI, H.J. *Introduction to Politics.* London, Allen & Unwin.

49. LASKI, H.J. *Liberty in the Modern State.* London, Allen & Unwin.

50. LASKI, H.J. *The State in Theory and Practice.* London, Allen & Unwin.

51. LEACOCK, STEPHEN. *Elements of Political Science.* London, Constable.

52. LINDSAY, A.D. *I Believe in Democracy.*

53. LINDSAY, A.D. *Parliament or Dictatorship*

54. LORD, A.R. *Principles of Politics.* London, Oxford University Press.

55. MACIVER, R.M. *The Modern State.* London, Oxford University Press.

56. MCILWAIN, C.H. *Poltical Science Quarterly.* March, 1933, pages 98-100.

57. MAINE, SIR H. *Early History of Institutions.*

58. MARRIOTT, J.A.R. *Mechanism of the Modern State.* London, Oxford University Press.

59. MAZZINI, GUISSEPPI. *Life and Writings.*

60. MERRIAM, C.E. *History of the Theory of Sovereignty since Rousseau.*

61. MILL, J.S. *On Liberty (Thinker's Library).* London, Watts.

62. MILL, J.S. *Utilitariunism (N. Univ. Series).* London, Routledge.

63. MOON, P.T. *Imperialism in World Politics.* London, Macmillan.

64. RALEIGH, T. *Elementary Politics.* London, Oxford University Press.

65. RAMAIYER. *Politics.*

66. RITCHIE, D.G. *Natural Rights (Philos. Series).* London, Allen & Unwin.

67. ROUSSEAU, J.J. *Social Contract (Everyman's Library Series).* London, Dent.

68. RUTHNASWAMY, M. *Making of the State.* London, Williams & Norgate. Ltd.

69. SASTRI, S. *Rights and Duties of the Indian Citizens.* Calctutta, University Press.

70. SCHUMAN, F.L. *Imperialism and World Politics.*

71. SETH, JAMES. *Study of Ethical Principles.* Edinburgh, William Blackwood & Sons, Limited.

72. SIDGWICK, HENRY. *Elements of Politics.* London, Macmillan.

73. SPECTATOR BOOKLETS. *Parliament or Dictatorship.* London, Methuen.

74. SPENCER, H. *Social Statics.* London, Watts.

75. STEPHEN, SIR, LESLIE, *Science of Ethics.* London, John Murray.

76. TAWNEY, R.H. *Equality.* London, Allen & Unwin.

77. TAYLOR & BROWN. *Human Relations.*

78. TOYNBEE, A.J. *A Study of History.* London, Oxford University Press.

79. VAUGHAN, G.E. *Studies in the History of Political Philosophy Before & After Rousseau.* Manchester, Manchester University Press.

80. WARD, J. *Sovereignty.*

81. WILDE, N. *Ethical Basis of the State.* London, Oxford University Press.

82. WILLOUGHBY, W.W. *Social Justice.*

83. WOOLF, LEONARD. *Imperialism and Civilisation.* London, Hogarth.

84. ZIMMERN, A.E. *The Third British Empire.*

85. THE LEAGUE OF NATIONS. *Aim,s, Methods & Activity.* London, Allen & Unwin.

ADDITIONAL BOOKS CONSULTED

86. BANDOPADHYAYA, J. *Social and Political Thought of Gandhi.* Delhi, Allied Publihsers.

87. BARKER, ERNEST. *Principles of Social and Political Theory.*

88. BHATTACHARYA, B. *Evolution of Political Philosophy of Gandhi.* Calcutta, Calcutta Book House.

89. BUEL. *Contemporary French Poltics.*

90. BURNS, E.M. *Ideas in Conflict.*

91. CARLYLE, A.J. *Political Liberty*

92. CATLIN, G. *Story of the Political Philosophers.*

93. COKER, F.W. *Recent Political Thought.*

94. COLE, G.D.H. *Fabian Socialism.*

95. COLE, G.D.H. *Self-Government in Industry.*

96. DHAWAN, G.N. *The Political Philosophy of Mahatma Gandhi.*

97. DOBB, LEONARD, W. *Public Opinion and Propaganda.*

98. EBENSTEIN, WILLIAM. *Great Political Thinkers.*

99. EBENSTEIN, WILLIAM. *Modern Political Thought.*

100. EBENSTEIN, WILLIAM. *Political Thought in Perspective.* New York, McGraw-Hill.

101. EBENSTEIN, WILLIAM, *Today's Isms.*

102. ELLIOTT, W.Y. *The Pragmatic Revolt in Politics.*

103. FISHER. *The Republican Tradition in Europe.*

104. FOX, RALPH. *Communism and a Changing Civilization.*

105. GABBRIEL, RAPLPH H. *The Course of American Democratic Thought.*

106. GANDHI, M.K. *Speeches.*

107. GASSET, JOSE Y. *The Revolt of the Masses.*

108. GIDDINGS, F.H. *Principles of Sociology.*

109. GINSBERG, MORIS. *The Psychology of Society.*

110. GOODRICH and HAMBRO. *Charter of the nUited Nations. Commentary and Documents.*

111. GRAZIA, ALFRED DE. *The Elements of Political Science* (2 Vols.). New York. Alfred A. Knopf.

112. HEATER, D.R. *Political Ideas in the Modern World.* London, Harrap.

113. HSIAO. *Political Pluralism.*

114. INDIA, GOVERNMENT OF. *Gandhian Outlook and Technique.*

115. JAMES, WILLIAM. *Pragmatism.*

116. JAMESON. *The Constitutional Convention.*

117. KAPUR, A.C. *Principles of Political Science.*

118. KING, C.H. *Political Pluralism : A Study in Contemporary Political Theory.*

119. LAIDLER. *History of Socialistic Thought.*

120. LAIDLER. *Socio-Economic Movement.*

121. LASKI, H.J. *American Democracy.*

122. LASKI, H.J. *Authority in the Modern State.*

123. LASKI, H.J. *Communism.*

124. LASKI, H.J. *The Danger of Being a Gentleman.*

125. LASKI, H.J. *The Dangers of Obedience and Other Essays.*

126. LASKI, H.J. *Democracy in Crisis.*

127. Laski, H.J. *The Dilemma of Our Times.*
128. Laski, H.J. *Faith, Reason and Civilization.*
129. Laski, H.J. *Foundations of Sovereignty.*
130. Laski, H.J. *Parliamentary Government in England.*
131. Laski, H.J. *Reflections on the Revolution of Our Time.*
132. Laski, H.J. *Rise of European Liberalism.*
133. Laski, H.J. *The Social and Political Ideas of Some Representative Thinkers of the Victorian Age.*
134. Laski, H.J. *Trade Unions in the New Society.*
135. Lavalye, E. *Le government deus la democratique.*
136. Lecky. *Democracy and Liberty.*
137. Lenin. *Selected Works.*
138. Lewis, G.C. *Use and Abuse of Political Terms.*
139. Lippmann, Walter. *Public Opinion.*
140. Lipson, L. *Great Issues of Politics.*
141. Mabbott, J.D. *The State and the Citizen.*
142. MacIver, R.M. *The Web of Government.*
143. Maine, Sir H. *Popular Government.*
144. Maritain, J. *Man and the State.*
145. Martin, Kingsley. *Harold Laski: A Biographical Memoir.*
146. Marx and Engels. *Selected Works.*
147. Mashruwala, K.S. *Gandhi and Marx.*
148. Maxey, C.C. *Political Philosophies.*
149. Misra, K.K. *Studies in International Relations*
150. Mukerji, H.N. *Gandhiji : A Study.*
151. Munro, W.B. *The Government of the United States.*
152. Oakshott. *Social and Political Doctrines.*
153. Oppenheim, L. *International Law.*
154. Palmer & Perkins. *International Relations.*
155. Pease. *The Hisotry of Fabian Society.*
156. Plekhanov, G.V. *Anarchism and Socialism.*
157. Rockow. *Contemporary Political Thought in England.*
158. Roll, Erich. *A History of Economic Thought.*
159. Roucker, Joseph S. *Contemporary Political Ideologies,* London, Vision Press.
160. Roucek, Joseph S. (Ed). *Twentieth Century Political Thought.*
161. Russell, Bertrand. *Roads to Freedom.*
162. Sabine, George H. *A History of Political Theory.*
163. Sidgwick, Herny. *Development of European Polity.*
164. Strong, C.F. *Modern Political Constitutions.*
165. Tocqueville. *Recollections.*
166. Treitschke. *Politics.*
167. Wayper, C.L. *Teach Yourself Political Thought.*
168. Webb, Sidney. *A Constitution for the Socialist Commonwealth of Great Britain.*
169. Webb, Sidney. *Soviet Communism : A New Civilization.*
170. Willoughby, W.F. *The Government of the Modern State.*
171. Young Kimball. *Social Psychology.*
172. Apter, David E. *Introduction to Political Analysis.*
173. Avineri, S. *Hegel's Theory of the Modern State.*
174. Baran, Paula. *The Political Economy of Growth.*
175. Barker. *Principles of Social and Political Theory.*

176. BARKER, ERNEST (Ed.). *Politics of Aristotle.*
177. BENN, S.I. & PETER, R.S. *Social Principles and the Democratic State.*
178. BERKI, R.N. *Socialism.*
179. BOTTOMORE, T. (ed.). *Sociology and Social Philosophy of Karl Marx.*
180. BURLATSKY, F. *The Modern State and Politics.*
181. BURNS, E.M. *Ideas in Conflict.*
182. CHAMBLISS, W. (ed.) *Sociological Readings in Conflict Perspective.*
183. CHURCHWARD, L.G. *Contemporary Soviet Government.*
184. CORNFORTH, M. *Dialectical Materialism.*
185. COX, RICHARD (ed.). *Ideology, Politics and Political Theory.*
186. CRESPIGNY & MINOGUE (ed.). *Contemporary Political Philosophies.*
187. CRICK, BERNARD. *In Defence of Politics.*
188. DAHL, ROBERT A. *A Preface to Democratic Theory.*
189. DAHL. ROBERT A. ET AL. *Social Science Research on Business.*
190. DANIELS, NORMAN (ed.). *Reading Rawls,*
191. DEANE, HERBERT. *Political Ideas of Harold J. Laski.*
192. D'ENTREVES, A.P. *The Notion of the State.*
193. DRAPER, HAL. *Karl Marx's Theory of Revolution.*
194. DRUCKER, H.M. *The Political Uses of Ideology.*
195. EASTON, DAVID. *The Political System.*
196. ENGELS, F. *Anti-Duhring.*
197. ENGELS, F. *The Origin of Family, Private Property and the State.*
198. ENGELS, F. *Socialism—Utopian and Scientific.*
199. FINER, H. *Mussolini's Italy.*
200. FINER, S.E. *Comparative Government.*
201. FISCHER, E. *Marx in His Own Words.*
202. FRANK, A.G. *On Capitalist Underdevelopment.*
203. GALBRAITH, J.K. *The New Industrial State.*
204. HEGEL, G.W.F. *The Philosophy of Right.*
205. HOBHOUSE, L.T. *Elements of Social Justice.*
206. HORWITHZ, I.L. *Three Worlds of Development.*
207. HUNT, RICHARD N. *Marxism and Totalitarian Democracy.*
208. KAUFMANN, W. *Hegel's Political Philosophy.*
209. KOLAKOVSKI & HAMPSHIRE. *The Socialist Idea—A Reappraisal.*
210. LASKI, H.J. *The Problem of Sovereignty.*
211. LASKI, H.J. *The State in the New Social Order.*
212. LASKI, H.J. *Where Do We Go From Here.*
213. LASSWELL, H.D. & KAPLAN, A. *Power and Society.*
214. LENIN, V.I. *Selected Works.*
215. LENIN, V.I. *State and Revolution.*
216. LIPSET, S.M. *Political Man—the Social Bases of Politics.*
217. LIPSET, S.M. (ed.). *Politics and the Social Sciences.*
218. MACPHERSON, C.B. *Democratic Theory.*
219. MACPHERSON, C.B. *The Real World of Democracy.*
220. MACPHERSON, C.B. *The Rise and Fall of Economic Justice.*
221. MAO ZEDONG. *Selected Works.*
222. MARCUSE, H. *Reason and Revolution.*
223. MARX, KARL. *Capital.*
224. MARX, KARL. *Grundrisse.*
225. MARX, KARL. *The Civil War in France.*
226. MARX, KARL. *The Communist Manifesto.*

227. MARX, KARL. *Economic and Philosophic Manuscript.*
228. MARX, KARL. *The German Ideology.*
229. MARX, KARL. *The Holy Family.*
230. MARX, KARL. *The Poverty of Philosophy.*
231. MCLELLAN, D. *Karl Marx—Early Texts.*
232. MCLELLAN, D. *The Thought of Karl Marx.*
233. MELOTTI, U. *Marx and the Third World.*
234. MESZAORS, E. *Marx's Theory of Alienation.*
235. MILIBAND, RALPH. *Marxism and Politics.*
236. MILIBAND, RALPH. *The State in Capitalist Society.*
237. MILLS, C. WRIGHT. *The Power Elite.*
238. MISRA, K.K. *Contemporary Political Theory.*
239. MISRA, K.K. *Marxism and Liberalism.*
240. MISRA, K.K. *Political Ideas of Harold J. Laski.*
241. MOSKICHOV. *The End of Ideology—Illusions & Reality.*
242. OLLMAN, B. *Alienation : Marx's Critique of Man in Capitalist Society.*
243. O'ROURKE, JAMES. *The Problem of Freedom in Marxist Theory.*
244. PLAMENATZ, J. *Man and Society.*
245. POPPER, KARL. *The Open Society and its Enemies.*
246. POULANTZAS, N. *Political Power and Social Classes.*
247. POULANTZAS, N. *The State, Power, Socialism.*
248. QUINTON, A. (ed.) *Political Philosophy.*
249. RAWLS, JOHN. *A Theory of Justice.*
250. SARTORI, G. *Democratic Theory.*
251. SCASE, RICHARD (ed.). *The State in Western Europe.*
252. SLADKOVSKY, M.I. *Present Day China's Socio-Economic System.*
253. STALIN, J.V. *Foundations of Leninism.*
254. STALIN, J.V. *Problems of Leninism.*
255. VERENE, D.P. (ed.) *Hegel's Social and Political Thought.*
256. WASBY, S.L. *Political Science—The Discipline and its Dimensions.*
257. WELLS, D. *Marxism and the Modern State.*
258. WOLFE, ALAN. *The Limits of Legitimacy—Political Contradictions of Contemporary Capitalism.*
259. WOLFF, R.P. *Understanding Rawls.*
260. WOLIN, S. *Politics and Vision.*
261. WU, YUAN-LI (ed.). *China—A Handbook.*

262. EULAU, HEINZ *et al.* *Political Behaviour.*
263. MISRA, K.K. *Modern Political Theory.*
264. QUINTON, ANTHONY (ed.) *Political Philosophy.*
265. VERMA, S.P. *Modern Political Theory.*

INDEX

NOTES

NOTES

NOTES

NOTES

NOTES

NOTES

NOTES